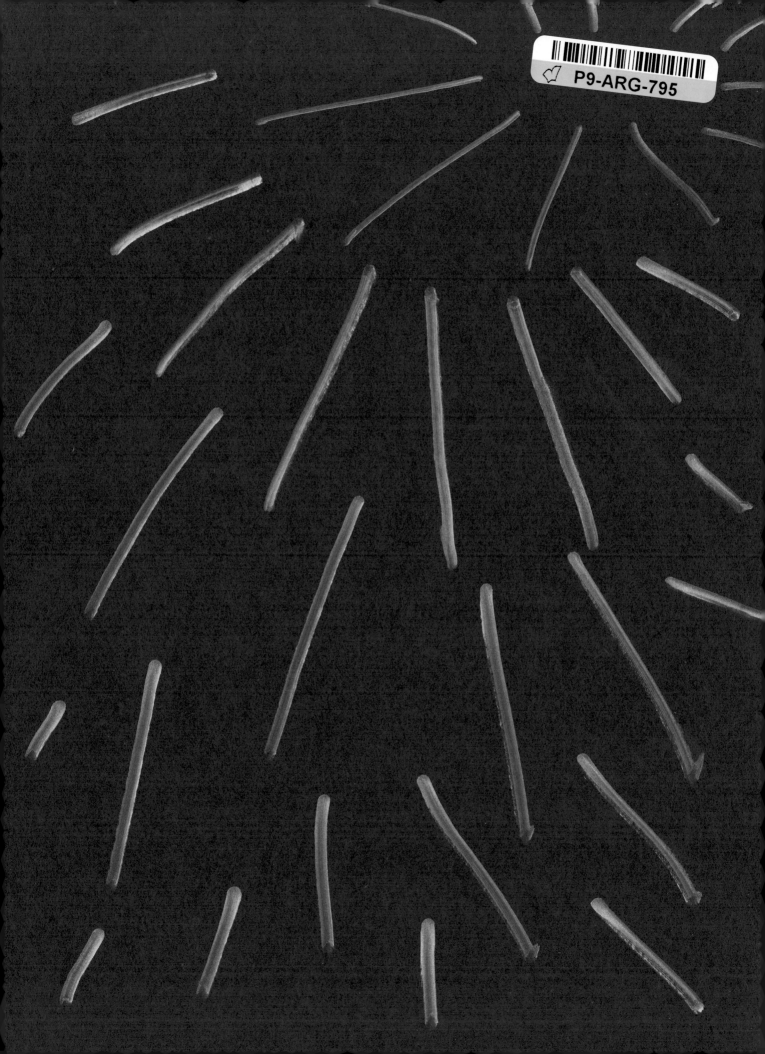

VIOLENCE
IN AMERICA

An Encyclopedia

Editorial Board

VIOLENCE
IN AMERICA
An Encyclopedia

RONALD GOTTESMAN
Editor in Chief

RICHARD MAXWELL BROWN
Consulting Editor

VOLUME 2

Charles Scribner's Sons

An Imprint of The Gale Group
New York

Charles Scribner's Sons
An Imprint of The Gale Group
1633 Broadway
New York, New York 10019

1   3   5   7   9   11   13   15   17   19   20   18   16   14   12   10   8   6   4   2

PRINTED IN THE UNITED STATES OF AMERICA

Library of Congress Cataloging-in-Publication Data

Violence in America : an encyclopedia / Ronald Gottesman, editor ; Richard Maxwell
Brown, Consulting editor . . . [et al.].
    p. cm.
   Includes bibliographical references and index.
   ISBN 0-684-80487-5 (set : alk. paper)—ISBN 0-684-80488-3 (vol. I : alk. paper)
    1. Violence—United States—Encyclopedias. 2. Violent crimes—United
States—Encyclopedias. 3. Violence in popular culture—United States—Encyclopedias.
I. Gottesman, Ronald.

HN90.V5 V5474   1999
303.6'0973'03—dc21   99-052027

ISBN 0-684-80489-1 (vol. 2)   ISBN 0-684-80490-5 (vol. 3)

The paper used in this publication meets the requirements of ANSI/NISO Z39.48-1992
(Permanence of Paper).

G

GACY, JOHN WAYNE
(1942–1994)

Apparent respectability can sometimes conceal the darkest impulses. This may be the most unnerving aspect of the serial murder phenomenon. The solid citizen next door might be living a horrifying secret life, even within the confines of a tidy suburban home. For seven years John Wayne Gacy carried on just such a dual existence, as both a conscientious businessman and a killer of boys and young men.

Gacy grew up in Chicago, the son of an abusive father who berated him for being insufficiently masculine. As an adult, he not only gained a reputation as a successful Chicago building contractor but was also active in Democratic Party politics and periodically performed as a clown named Pogo for the benefit of hospitalized children. At his most visibly legitimate, he posed for a now-famous photograph in which he is seen shaking hands with First Lady Rosalyn Carter. What he had managed to conceal from his neighbors and business associates was a 1968 conviction for sodomy. Living in Iowa at the time, he had sexually assaulted a fifteen-year-old boy and had served eighteen months in prison. During the period when he was establishing a reputation in Chicago for hard work and generosity, he had been on parole. In 1971 the Iowa authorities, under the impression that Gacy had rehabilitated himself, discharged him from parole and from all supervision. Gacy committed his first murder two-and-a-half months later.

He brought his victims to his home in the Chicago suburb of Norwood Park. His targets were usually male employees, runaways, and street hustlers, ranging in age from nine to twenty. Sometimes he posed as a plainclothes policeman to lure them into his trap. When he had them alone, he handcuffed them and subjected them to hours of torture before he finally killed them by strangulation. The victim's death would bring him to sexual climax. For seven years he maintained his ordinary, middle-class facade while corpses decomposed in the crawl space beneath his house.

The police began to suspect Gacy in 1978 when they were investigating the disappearance of a fifteen-year-old boy who had had an appointment for a job interview with him. As they delved into Gacy's background, they uncovered his Iowa sodomy conviction. After they got a glimpse behind Gacy's mask of normalcy, they decided to search his home. Beneath the house, they discovered twenty-nine bodies. They later learned that four more victims had been dumped in a nearby river. Gacy had murdered all of them.

Once in custody, Gacy confessed, but he soon reverted to his habit of inventing a mask to distance himself from his crimes. The persona he conjured up this time he named Jack, one of the multiple personalities that Gacy claimed were responsible for all the bodies concealed beneath his house. This attempt at an insanity plea did not prevent the court from imposing a death sentence. Appeals postponed his execution for fourteen years, in which time Gacy denied everything. He occupied himself on death row by painting pictures

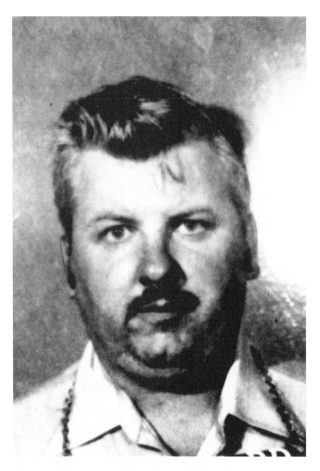

A December 1978 police photo of John Wayne Gacy.
CORBIS-BETTMANN/UPI

of Walt Disney characters and crying clowns and in May 1994 died by lethal injection.

BIBLIOGRAPHY

Cahill, Tim. *Buried Dreams: Inside the Mind of a Serial Killer.* New York: Bantam, 1986.

Newton, Michael. *Hunting Humans.* Port Townsend, Wash.: Loompanics, 1990.

Sullivan, Terry. *Killer Clown.* New York: Grosset and Dunlap, 1983.

DAVID EVERITT

See also **Serial Killers.**

GAMBINO, CARLO
(1902–1976)

Carlo Gambino was one of the most cunning and successful American gangsters of the twentieth century. His success as a racketeer is best measured by the fact that he died peacefully in old age of natural causes, leaving a substantial fortune; most of his contemporaries atop the American Mafia died violently or in prison, with relatively little to show for their notoriety.

Gambino was born in Palermo, Sicily, on 24 August 1902 (or 1900). He reputedly came to the United States in 1921 as a stowaway. He settled in Brooklyn, New York, and worked with the borough's Mafia groups, which specialized in bootlegging, extortion, gambling, and loan sharking. Gambino was part of a Mafia faction, or family, headed by Vincent Mangano that counted hundreds of initiated members, or "made men." When Mangano died in 1951, the new boss, Albert Anastasia, made Gambino the underboss. But Anastasia was shot to death on 25 October 1957, as he sat in a Manhattan hotel barber's chair, his face covered by hot towels. The murder was plotted by Anastasia's Mafia rival, Vito Genovese. The police came to believe that Gambino was behind the shooting, including the disappearance of Anastasia's bodyguards just before the assassins arrived.

Gambino then turned his sights on Genovese and reputedly framed him in a heroin-trafficking case in 1959. Other Gambino rivals met similar fates. Joseph Bonanno, the founder and boss of another of New York City's five Mafia families, was kidnapped in 1964 and forced to retire after a failed grab for power. Joseph Colombo, the boss of another family, was shot and critically wounded at a public rally in 1971. He had reportedly angered the notoriously publicity-shy Gambino by arranging demonstrations to protest what he said was discrimination against Italian Americans by the Federal Bureau of Investigation and the New York Police Department's organized crime unit.

Now Gambino became known as the "capo di tutti capi," boss of all bosses, but he was more of a first among equals. The racketeers in his crime family were independent criminal entrepreneurs who passed tribute payments up to the boss. Gambino provided contacts with corrupt public officials, capital for new ventures, protection from other gangsters, and arbitration in intramob disputes. Although his power rested on violence, Gambino specialized in the more subtle organized crimes that ultimately proved most lucrative, including labor union corruption and bid rigging. The Gambino family dominated the Brooklyn docks and Manhattan's garment district, adding

A police photo of Carlo Gambino. CORBIS/BETTMANN

what police termed a "mob tax" to business transactions.

Gambino dressed simply and unfashionably, lived with his family on the upper floor of a two-family brick house in middle-class Sheepshead Bay, Brooklyn, and was driven around in a Chevrolet or Buick sedan. A government informer, Joseph Cantalupo, described Gambino as "very even-tempered, very polite, very much the gentleman in the presence of others." Although Gambino was frequently called before grand juries investigating organized crime, he typically declined to appear for health reasons; his lawyers were able to produce detailed medical reports substantiating this claim.

Gambino died of heart failure on 15 October 1976. More than two decades later, the crime family that he headed still bore his name and was one of the nation's largest.

BIBLIOGRAPHY

Davis, John H. *Mafia Dynasty: The Rise and Fall of the Gambino Crime Family*. New York: Harper, 1993.

Meskil, Paul. *Don Carlo: Boss of Bosses*. New York: Popular Library, 1973.
Sifakis, Carl. *The Mafia Encyclopedia*. New York: Facts on File, 1982.

RICK HAMPSON

See also **Genovese, Vito; Mafia; Organized Crime.**

GAMBLING

During the early years of the twentieth century, when it was widely believed that the character of individual citizens could be improved by legislating to improve their social environment, laws were passed to restrict or forbid gambling. Some religious denominations, such as Roman Catholics, Episcopalians, and Jews, opposed gambling not in principle but in excess. However, a number of mainline Protestant denominations—Methodists, Baptists, and Presbyterians, as well as the Mormon Church—were militant in their antigambling posture and in their support for legislating reform.

Out of this same wave of moral reform came the Eighteenth Amendment to the U.S. Constitution, passed in 1919, which forbade the manufacture, sale, or transportation of intoxicating liquor. And as laws against gambling became more stringent, the same underworld influences that were active in providing illegal alcohol to eager consumers were equally willing to provide illegal gambling opportunities. Jurisdictional warfare between rival gangs for the same territory often resulted in violence, thereby associating "gambling" with "danger" in the public mind.

The Gambling Mecca

In March 1931 Nevada legalized casino gambling, making it an anomaly among states. The religious traditions that opposed gambling were extremely weak in Nevada, and the way was open for the state, with its meagre population, unviable economy, and impoverishment caused by the Great Depression, to attract tourists and newcomers.

The influence of organized crime not only built up Nevada gambling; it also lent it an air of raciness and netherworld allure. The celebrity racketeer Benjamin "Bugsy" Siegel hit the Las Vegas scene in 1942, determined to build a luxury hotel outside of town on the road to Los Angeles—later to become the famous "Strip." The hotel, financed with mob money and built during a period of wartime shortages, opened during the Christmas season of 1946. Siegel—in trouble with investors who were waiting for a return on their profits and suspected by other crime bosses of skimming money from the hotel's building budget—was soon murdered at his girlfriend's Beverly Hills mansion. The murder of Harry Sherwood at Lake Tahoe and an attack on the Reno gambling figure Lincoln Fitzgerald, formerly of the Detroit mob, both in the late 1940s, made the extent of mob infestation in Nevada gambling all too obvious, and the connection could no longer escape the gaze of the federal government.

The Kefauver Committee and the Kennedy Crackdown

"As a case history of legalized gambling, Nevada speaks eloquently in the negative," reported the U.S. Senate Special Committee to Investigate Organized Crime, headed by Senator Estes Kefauver from Tennessee, which had been formed in 1950 to respond to allegations that organized crime was engaging in interstate gambling and racketeering activities (U.S. Senate 1951, p. 94). In 1951, after several months of hearings that were broadcast on the relatively new medium of television and followed avidly by a nationwide audience, the final report of the Kefauver Committee verified the existence of a nationwide mafia that had interests in offering prostitution, narcotics, alcohol, but, most of all, gambling to an enthusiastic public. Gambling was alleged to be the principal source of income for organized crime, and it was prevalent, in the committee's words, in "every community." The report criticized gambling for preying upon the "weakness and indifference of the average citizen" rather than for any violence it caused. According to the Kefauver Committee, the extent of gambling was shocking, causing $20 billion to change hands every year and leading to extensive corruption of elected officials.

This moralistic attitude against gambling was adopted by Robert F. Kennedy, the U.S. attorney general from 1961 to 1964 (and brother of President John F. Kennedy), who had made a priority of combating the mafia and was convinced that Las Vegas, using laundered money, served as the banker for organized crime. Federal hit teams were organized to harass Nevada gambling out of existence. As he indicated to then Governor Grant Sawyer of Nevada, Kennedy "wanted to show the people of the United States that he was the guy to clean up all sin and corruption, and Nevada was a great place to start" (Sawyer 1993, p. 90).

Gambling as Popular Recreation

Kennedy's efforts notwithstanding, mainstream America's acceptance of gambling waxed rather than waned in the second half of the twentieth century. In 1946, the first year in which systematic records were kept, the gross receipts from gambling (the money the customers lose) amounted to $21 million in Nevada. But by 1955 the total was $94 million, $301 million in 1965, $1.1 billion in 1975, $3.2 billion in 1985, and $9 billion in 1998.

The mushrooming popularity of gambling opened up the American imagination to new forms of recreation. In 1969 corporations were allowed for the first time to operate casinos in Nevada, and this seemed to put the state's chief industry much more in the mainstream of business and provided new opportunities for obtaining desperately needed money for the construction of new

State police raid a gambling establishment in southern Illinois during a statewide campaign initiated in 1950. Racing papers dropped by surprised patrons litter the floor. LIBRARY OF CONGRESS

casinos and ever-larger hotels. Once the state began to regulate gambling with the creation of the Gaming Control Board in 1955, there was more confidence in its ability to control the worst influences, although in fact the state allowed the "grandfathered" licensing of casino owners who had long been in business.

The criticisms mounted against gambling by certain religious organizations also abated during the late twentieth century. In 1976, the State of New Jersey joined Nevada as a destination for those who wished to partake of the pleasures of gambling, when it voted to legalize casino gambling in Atlantic City. After that, gambling spread to other states as well as to Indian reservations (which are not under the jurisdiction of state governing authorities) throughout the United States.

Most religious organizations did not exactly forsake their officially stated antigambling attitudes, but these attitudes lost the attention and involvement of the denominational leadership as other issues, such as abortion and drugs, became a higher priority. Symbolic of the change is that in the early 1980s the Southern Baptists selected Las Vegas as the location for their 1989 national convocation, citing the convenience and excellence of the city's convention facilities, which were capable of handling the fifteen thousand estimated attendees and their families. Although there was considerable controversy within the church over this decision, the delegates duly met in Las Vegas at the stipulated date, although the world was assured by Southern Baptist leaders that the convention delegates did not gamble at the machines or tables.

An even more significant adjustment toward gambling was made by the Mormons; in January 1987 all Mormon casino workers were finally admitted into the temple. Mormons have all along been important in the higher echelons of the gambling industry, and the earliest transfusion of legitimate money to the industry came from the Mormon-led Bank of Las Vegas.

The Legacy of the Mob in Nevada

The domination of organized crime in Nevada gambling actually increased after the Kefauver hearings, as mobsters, chased out of other locales by the authorities, ran for sanctuary to the one state where gambling was in fact legal. In time the Nevada "boys" became model members of the community, dispensing money freely to churches, philanthropies, and other causes. Beginning in the 1950s there seems to have been some sort of implicit agreement, as Robert Laxalt points out in his bicentennial history of Nevada (p. 108), that murders would not occur on Nevada soil, since that might turn local authorities (or more to be feared, federal authorities) against Nevada's "peculiar institution." If someone was designated for execution—for example, Gus Greenbaum (who had managed the Flamingo after Siegel's murder)—he or she would be lured to some other locale, such as Chicago or Phoenix.

In retrospect, the mob's contribution to Nevada was quite salutary. Mafia involvement showed the huge potentialities of Nevada gambling and demonstrated its profitability: organized crime brought the professional expertise necessary to develop Nevada's gambling operations into well-supervised businesses assured of making money. Mob investment provided for the construction of new casinos and hotels in a capital-starved industry. Banks were conservative, and loans for building casinos were considered too shady and risky. Much of this allegedly tainted money was funneled through the Teamsters Union Central States Pension Fund, which poured at least $269 million in the 1950s and 1960s into Nevada casinos—money apparently well invested for its retirees and certainly indispensable for the growth of Las Vegas (although this hand-in-glove relationship provoked fierce criticism from the federal government). Not least, mob connections to show-business personalities brought glamour to Las Vegas, cemented the desert city's relationship with Hollywood, and in so doing lured millions of tourists to Las Vegas at a crucial stage of its development.

After the 1940s, there seemed to be a moratorium on mob violence in Nevada, although the most notorious elements of mob activity were still located in Las Vegas. It was not until after the introduction of corporate gambling, with the more attractive image it gives the state, that mob violence occurred in Las Vegas. In 1982 there was an attempted murder of Frank "Lefty" Rosenthal (his car was bombed while he was in it). Rosenthal was a sometime sports-book bettor, local television host, and hotel executive who had run afoul of the Nevada Gaming Control Board. It was widely believed that his assailant was Anthony "Tony the Ant" Spilotro, himself murdered in an Indiana cornfield in 1986. By that time, the corporate types had taken over; in the words of Nicholas Pileggi, in his revealing work *Casino*, "Today in Las Vegas, the men in fedoras who built the city are gone. The gamblers with no last names and suitcases filled with cash are reluctant to show up in the new Las Vegas, for fear of being turned in to the IRS by a twenty-five-year-old hotel school graduate working casino credit on weekends" (p. 307).

BIBLIOGRAPHY

Farrell, Ronald A., and Carole Case. *The Untold Story of the Control of Nevada's Casinos.* Madison: University of Wisconsin Press, 1995.

Laxalt, Robert. *Nevada: A Bicentennial History.* New York: Norton, 1977.

Pileggi, Nicholas, and Martin Scorsese. *Casino.* New York: Simon and Schuster, 1995.

Reid, Ed, and Ovid Demaris. *The Green Felt Jungle.* New York: Trident, 1963.

Sawyer, Grant. *Hang Tough! Grant Sawyer: An Activist in the Governor's Mansion.* Reno: University of Nevada, Oral History Program, 1993.

Skolnik, Jerome H. *House of Cards: The Legalization and Control of Casino Gambling.* Boston: Little, Brown, 1978.

Turner, Wallace. *Gambler's Money: The New Force in American Life.* Boston: Houghton Mifflin, 1965.

U.S. Senate, Special Committee to Investigate Organized Crime in Interstate Commerce. *Second Interim Report,* 32d Congress, Senate Report No. 141. Washington, D.C.: Government Printing Office.

———. *Third Interim Report Pursuant to S. Res. 202,* 81st Congress, Senate Report No. 307. Washington, D.C.: Government Printing Office, 1951.

JEROME E. EDWARDS

See also **Las Vegas; Organized Crime; Prohibition and Temperance.**

GANGS

Gangs have been in the United States since at least the nineteenth century and were increasingly found all over the world at the end of the twentieth century. Youth gangs have existed in the United States since at least the 1870s. Malcolm Klein (*The American Street Gang*) has documented many cycles of gang activity, which vary by history, type of gang, geographic location, and ethnicity. In the latter part of the nineteenth century, when large numbers of immigrants arrived in cities, which were simultaneously undergoing increased industrial development, organized adolescent groups heavily involved in crime began to emerge in places like New York City, Philadelphia, Boston, Chicago, St. Louis, and Pittsburgh. These gangs tended to be loose aggregations of the children of recent immigrants from Ireland and Italy. They roamed their neighborhood streets, largely as disorganized groups, engaging primarily in petty forms of property crime and directing violence against one another and members of rival gangs. As in late-twentieth-century America, these gangs comprised individuals from the bottom of the socioeconomic scale.

One generation later, during the 1920s, the next gangs emerged in American cities. It is important to distinguish between youth gangs and organized crime. Like their late-nineteenth-century predecessors, most youth gangs of the 1920s were disorganized groups of recent immigrants, but they had symbols of membership and engaged in more crime.

Gangs again emerged during the 1960s. For the first time, significant numbers of racial and ethnic minorities joined gangs. However, the economic and demographic parallels between 1960s gangs and earlier ones point to the underlying causes of gang membership. Blacks and Hispanics were heavily represented in the gangs of the 1960s, and like their earlier counterparts, they generally were at the bottom of the social and economic ladders of American society. The availability of guns and automobiles changed the nature of gangs. These gangs were more extensively involved in criminal activity, especially violence, which in turn led to increased convictions and prison time. As a consequence, the prison became an important site for the growth and perpetuation of gangs.

Gangs are not confined to the United States. They have been reported in many of the nations that emerged from the breakup of the Soviet Union and Soviet bloc nations. Klein (*The American Street Gang*) has documented the growing number of European nations plagued by youth gangs, including Germany, Holland, and France. American popular culture, in particular movies, music, and other forms of media, has had an important impact on these developments.

Defining Gangs and Gang Members

Six elements are typically necessary for a group to be considered a gang: a collection of individuals, the use of symbols, special forms of communication, permanence, a sense of turf, and involvement in crime. Although there is disagreement about the exact definition of a gang, everyone agrees that it must include a group. Some definitions specify the number of members, such as a minimum of two. Since most delinquent acts committed by juveniles are done in groups, distinguishing between groups and gangs is important, and so the definition must be refined.

Most gangs have some symbols of membership, which can take a variety of forms, including clothes, certain ways of wearing clothes, and hand signs such as forming the letters *c* and *k*, which stand for "crip killer." Most symbols have meaning only within the gang, and an effort is generally made to keep their meaning from non–gang members.

Most gangs have developed a series of verbal and nonverbal forms of communication. Some gangs devise particular words, typically through trial and error rather than intentional effort. Nonverbal forms of communication include graffiti and hand signs. Graffiti are used to deliver a variety of messages; for instance, they might announce a death, the presence of a gang or gang turf, or an invitation to violence. The role of graffiti varies across gangs, communities, and ethnic groups.

To be defined as a gang, a group must have a degree of permanence. Most definitions of a gang require that it be in existence for a year or more. Some extant Chicago gangs were formed in the 1960s, while some gangs in Los Angeles have been around since the 1940s. Most gangs in America are considerably newer than that, and many quickly disband shortly after they are formed.

Many gangs stake out turf, or gang-identified territory, which may be the place where the gang began or where most of its members live. This is not a feature of all gangs, however; for example, Asian gangs do not claim turf but otherwise meet all of the other criteria of a gang.

A final element typical of a gang is involvement in crime. A large number of groups might meet the first five criteria but not qualify as gangs. What distinguishes a gang from other groups is its involvement in crime, which is often heavy and recognized as a key feature of membership.

It is easier to define a gang member than to define a gang. The best indicator of gang membership is usually self-identification. In addition, symbols and behavior can be used to distinguish gang members from nonmembers. Many police departments keep detailed records of the names of gang members; however, this source is not the most reliable because it might be based on dated information or misinformation or fail to reflect changes in gang affiliation. Asking gang members and neighborhood residents, especially other youths and teachers, to identify gang-involved people is another way to determine who is in a gang. The company an individual keeps can also be a key to determining gang membership. Members often have tattoos announcing their gang affiliation. They may also have a distinctive way of dressing and carrying themselves. However, due to the influence of popular culture, especially as manifested in clothing style, movies, music videos, and magazines, gang styles enjoy widespread popularity across a broad range of youth, making clothes an unreliable marker of gang membership.

Counting Gangs, Members, and Crimes

Determining the number of gangs, members, and crimes is not easy. Most information about the gang problem on a national level comes from surveys conducted since 1975, when the first survey of the nation's gangs was published by Walter Miller, who concluded that six of twelve major cities had gang problems. Miller estimated that there were 760 to 2,700 gangs and 28,500 to 81,500 gang members in those six cities. Between 1975 and 1995 the Department of Justice funded five more national surveys. Each revealed the nation's gang problems to be more serious and more widespread, with new problems emerging in suburban and even rural jurisdictions. In 1993 conservative estimates based on local law-enforcement records included 8,625 gangs, 378,807 gang members, and 437,066 gang crimes. In 1995 the newly established National Youth Gang Center (NYGC) conducted its first assessment of the problem. A total of 664,906 gang members in 23,388 youth gangs were reported for 1,741 jurisdictions, many of them smaller cities and suburban and rural counties. By linking cities surveyed in 1995 with those surveyed earlier, G. David Curry and Scott H. Decker (1998) showed that there had been an unprecedented increase in the number of cities reporting gang problems between 1993 and 1995.

In 1996 the NYGC National Gang Survey implemented a systematic sampling strategy intended to improve the comparability of the national gang crime problem over time. A comparison between the 1997 and the 1996 National Gang Survey showed for the first time a leveling off of the number of cities reporting gang crime problems. While a number of jurisdictions reported newly emerging problems in 1997, a greater number reported declines. Similarly, more jurisdictions reported declines than increases in the number of gang homicides between 1996 and 1997. Perhaps most significantly, the two urban jurisdictions with the most serious gang problems, Los Angeles and

Los Angeles police search suspected gang members in 1985. CORBIS/
BETTMANN

Chicago, reported declines in gang-related homicides between 1996 and 1997.

Still, there was no question that gang problems had spread across the country over two decades. As of 1999, gangs were documented in every state in the nation and throughout small, medium, and large cities. Two explanations for this spread have been suggested. First, it might be part of a planned effort by more established gangs. According to this perspective, gangs in cities with chronic gang problems such as Chicago and Los Angeles are looking for new territory to expand their membership and acquire new drug turf. Second, the spread of gangs may be due to natural migration patterns as well as the influence of popular culture. Cheryl L. Maxson and Klein (1994) interviewed police officials across the United States to determine the cause of this spread and learned that, by and large, it was due to the movement of gang members' families from one city to another, usually to be close to relatives or to find employment. At the same time, popular culture, through movies, videos, and television shows, was disseminating gang culture nationally, providing symbols of gang membership and displaying aspects of gang life and gang style for adolescents to emulate. According to this second explanation, gang migration can be seen as part of a larger set of processes rather than the intentional movement of gangs into new territory.

The Link Between Gangs and Crime

Gang members participate in a variety of serious delinquent and criminal acts. However, the role of gang membership in such acts is not always clear. That is, many members commit crimes that have nothing to do with the gang.

The distinction between gang-related crimes and crimes committed by gang members is important. Gang-related crimes are committed in support of gang motives such as retaliation. A large number of gang members commit crimes that have nothing to do with their membership in the gang. Gang members are responsible for greater levels of crime and delinquency than non–gang members, as they are more often involved in offenses such as drug sales and gun assaults then their non-gang peers. In addition, gang-related delinquency is more violent than non-gang-related delinquency. Finally, the scope and nature of gang-related crime and delinquency vary considerably across time, communities, and gangs. These three conclusions have emerged from field studies of gang activity, analyses of criminal justice data, and survey studies of gangs.

Frederic Thrasher's 1927 work was the first serious research on gangs. He found that they originate from the spontaneous group activity of adolescents and that patterns of association are strengthened by conflict. In its earliest stage a gang is diffuse, has little leadership, and is potentially short-lived. Some gangs progress to the next stage, where they become solidified. Conflict with other gangs plays a notable role in this process, helping to define group boundaries and strengthen the ties between members, uniting them in the face of threats from rivals. In their final stage gangs become conventionalized, and members assume legitimate roles in society. For those groups that fail to make this transition, delinquent or criminal activity becomes their dominant focus.

Working in Chicago decades later, James F. Short and Fred L. Strodtbeck (1965) emphasized the importance of the gang as a unit of analysis. They described the community context, relationships among members, and the social characteristics of members that influenced the degree to which gangs engaged in conflicts. Two concepts central to their perspective on gangs were threat and status.

Klein's (1971) evaluation of two programs, the Group Guidance Project (1961–1965) and the Ladino Hills Project (1966–1968), formed the basis of his analysis. He found that delinquency increased among gang members who received the most group-oriented services and that their solidarity seemed to increase in proportion to the amount of attention they received from street workers in the program assigned to work with groups. Based on these results, Klein concluded that gang-intervention programs might enhance the attractiveness of gangs as well as their solidarity, thereby promoting violence. He also concluded that most characteristics of a gang were difficult to differentiate from those of adolescent street culture and that gang members shared many features with non-gang adolescents. Equally important, Klein found that criminal offending among gang members was cafeteria-style; that is, they rarely specialized in a particular form of crime and generally committed a variety of offenses including burglary, assault, and car theft.

Joan W. Moore (1978) has conducted the longest ongoing field research into gangs. To explain gang formation and activities among Chicanos, she focuses on Chicano culture and the position of Mexican Americans in the cultural and institutional life of East Los Angeles, in particular their detachment from mainstream society and politics. Moore and her associates isolated three distinctive characteristics of Chicano gangs: (1) they were territorially based; (2) they had a strong age-graded structure resulting in *klikas,* or cohort groups; and (3) they

were preoccupied with fighting. In addition to fighting, drugs played a prominent role in their lives.

James Diego Vigil (1988) spent three years compiling sixty-seven life histories of gang members in Los Angeles. Like Moore, he emphasized the role of Chicano culture in the formation of gangs, pointing to *choloization*, the process by which Chicano youth are marginalized from mainstream society. He described the position of Chicano youth as one of multiple marginality; that is, they are marginalized from several aspects of mainstream cultural and institutional life, such as schools and the job market. The street provides an alternative socialization path for these youths, leading to increased involvement in crime and delinquency. Because gang members share many negative experiences, they find a collective solution to the problem of identity in the gang.

The growth of an urban underclass has been linked to an increase in gangs by Pamela Irving Jackson (1991), who argued that local economic and demographic factors were the most important variables in explaining the emergence and nature of gangs. John M. Hagedorn (1988) found that most gangs in Milwaukee emerged more or less spontaneously from corner groups, young men who hung out together in their neighborhoods. Others emerged from groups of young people who attended dances and reacted to physical threats by fighting, thereby strengthening their alliances and ultimately resulting in gang formation. All of these groups were affected by their membership in an underclass. The lack of available jobs in the legitimate economy led gang members to seek economic solutions in the illegal drug market.

Decker and Barrik Van Winkle conducted a field study of gang crime in St. Louis (1994; 1996). Their work described gang structures and processes, local neighborhood dynamics, and the diffusion of gang culture on a national level. In St. Louis decades-old neighborhood rivalries and contemporary friendship networks were transfigured into a system of conflict structures that took the names and symbols of California's long-standing gangs the Bloods and the Crips, as well as some symbols from Chicago gang culture. Decker and Van Winkle's research underscored the cafeteria-style offending patterns of gang members and emphasized the ever-present violence.

Analyses of local law-enforcement data have also provided information about gang-related

Two teenaged members of the Crips gang in Venice, California, in 1982. CORBIS/KEN O'BRIEN COLLECTION

crime and delinquency. Maxson, Margaret A. Gordon, and Klein (1985) examined Los Angeles Police and Sheriff's Department records to document differences in social characteristics between gang and non-gang homicides. Gang homicides were more likely to involve minority males, automobiles, a greater number of participants, and the use of firearms, and to take place in public. The victims of gang homicides tended to be unknown to the perpetrators, and both parties were significantly younger than those involved in non-gang homicides, though older than the typical youth-gang member.

Curry and Irving A. Spergel (1988) identified characteristics that distinguished gang crimes from non-gang crimes in Chicago. Social variables, particularly ethnicity and poverty, were significantly related to differences in homicide rates across areas and time. Carolyn R. Block and Richard Block (1993) used Chicago Police Department incident data to study patterns of lethal and non-lethal gang-related violence in Chicago. Their work demonstrated that (1) gang violence was more likely to be related to turf than to drugs; (2) patterns of violence of the four largest established street gangs and smaller less established gangs were different; and (3) guns were the lethal

weapons in practically all gang-related homicides between 1987 and 1990.

Surveys of at-risk youth have been another source of information about gangs. Jeffrey Fagan (1989) interviewed high school students and dropouts in Chicago, Los Angeles, and San Diego. The interviewees, both male and female, were predominantly African American and Hispanic. He found that gang members committed more delinquent acts than non–gang members, as well as more serious offenses. Overall, he concluded that gang members, male and female, had more serious delinquent involvement than non–gang members.

Curry and Spergel studied middle-school students in Chicago to determine the nature of gang socialization. They found differences between Latinos and African Americans in the variables that predicted gang involvement. Latino involvement was associated with social and psychological variables and school and peer groups, whereas African American involvement was associated with exposure to gang members. Curry analyzed longitudinal police data on the population with social connections to gangs in Chicago over the five years following the initial survey in 1988 and found that the study population was at extreme risk for involvement in serious gang-related crime. As with other research, the number of offenses attributed to gang delinquents far exceeded those attributed to non–gang delinquents.

Finn-Aage Esbensen and colleagues (1993) used a longitudinal survey of an at-risk youth population in Denver to identify factors that differentiate gang and non-gang youths, the involvement of gang members in delinquent activity, and the relationship between criminal offending and gang membership. They found that gang members do not differ from other youth involved in serious street-level offending on factors such as commitment to delinquent peers and commitment to positive peers. Although gang membership was rare among the Denver respondents, gang members reported two to three times as much delinquency as non–gang members. When gang members were asked what kinds of activities their gang was involved in, fighting with other gangs was most frequently reported. From longitudinal survey results on a representative sample of youth in Rochester, New York, Terence Thornberry and his colleagues (1993) found that gang members were significantly more likely to report involvement in violence and other delinquency. By following youths over time, their analysis revealed a transitional process, with delinquent activity increasing during gang involvement and declining afterward. In their research both Esbensen and Thornberry concluded that crime and delinquency increase while individuals are gang members and are lower before and after membership. These results underscore the role of gang membership in enhancing involvement in crime and delinquency.

Gang membership increases criminal and delinquent behavior. The group context provides support and opportunities for members to engage in more illegal behavior as well as more serious illegal behavior. Esbensen and colleagues (1993) found that gang members do not differ from other street-level offenders on a number of social and psychological measures, yet their level of offending is greater. Thornberry and colleagues (1993) suggest three alternative explanations of gang delinquency: (1) a person model, (2) a social-facilitation (or group) model, and (3) an enhancement (or interaction of person and group) model. They found that gang members are more often delinquent than non–gang members and that the social-facilitation model was the most useful for explaining gang delinquency.

Decker and Van Winkle (1996) suggested that the growth in gangs and gang violence can be de-

scribed by contagion. For contagion to occur, three conditions must be present: (1) a spatial concentration of assaultive violence; (2) a reciprocity to assaultive violence; and (3) an escalation in assaultive violence. The reciprocity of gang violence accounts, in part, for how gangs form initially, as well as how they increase in size and strength of membership. The need to engage in retaliatory violence also helps to explain gang members' need for increasingly sophisticated weapons.

Drugs and Gangs

There are two competing views about the role of gangs and gang members in drug sales. The first argues that street gangs are well-organized purveyors of illegal drugs who reinvest the profits from drug sales into the gang (Jankowski 1991; Taylor 1990; Skolnick 1990). First, an organizational structure must be present. This hierarchy must have leaders, roles, and rules. Second, group goals must be widely shared among members. Third, allegiance to the larger organization must be stronger than that to subgroups within it. Finally, the gang must possess the means to control and discipline its members to produce compliance with group goals.

A second approach rejects this notion. Its proponents (Klein, "Street Gang Cycles"; Hagedorn 1988, 1994; Decker and Van Winkle 1996; Fagan 1989) claim that drug sales by gangs are seldom well organized and that gang members often act independently when selling drugs. According to this approach, gangs are loosely confederated groups that generally lack persistent cohesion and organization, and the link between gangs and drug sales is very casual. Traditional street gangs are not well suited for drug distribution or any other businesslike activity. They are weakly organized, prone to unnecessary and unproductive violence, and full of brash, conspicuous, untrustworthy individuals who draw unwanted police attention. For all these reasons, big drug operators, those who turn to drug dealing as a serious career, typically deemphasize their gang activity or leave the gang altogether.

This second view is supported by field research with gangs in Milwaukee (Hagedorn 1988), San Diego (Sanders 1994), and St. Louis (Decker and Van Winkle 1996), among other places. In Milwaukee gangs were characterized as dynamic, evolving associations of adolescents and men. In general, gangs lacked formal roles and effective organizational structures for achieving consensus about goals or techniques for achieving goals. Hustling (including street drug sales) was seldom well organized because gangs lacked the structure to control their members. In St. Louis virtually all of the gang members reported using the profits from drug sales to buy items for individual consumption, such as clothes or compact discs, not to meet gang objectives. Few gang members reported that they joined a gang to sell drugs; instead, they joined for reasons having to do with prior associations in the neighborhood.

A review of arrest records from five police stations in the Los Angeles area examined the differences in crack sales involving gang and non–gang members (Klein et al. 1991). In Los Angeles gangs appeared to lack an effective organizational structure, permanent membership or roles, and shared goals. Compared with non-gang transactions, gang crack sales were more likely to occur on the street, involve firearms, include younger suspects, and disproportionately involve black suspects. However, most of the differences between the two groups were small.

Female Gang Involvement

From the first national survey of gang problems, Miller (1975) estimated that 10 percent or less of gang members were females. No recent studies of police data on gang members have approached 10 percent. In fact, surveys of police officials have indicated that female gang membership may be as low as 4 percent. These findings were challenged in the 1990s by school-based surveys of students, which indicated that the number of female gang members was growing and that they may make up 40 percent of all gang members (Esbensen et al. 1993; Thornberry et al. 1993). In all likelihood, the discrepancy between these two estimates reflects differences in methodology. Police statistics are more likely to represent serious crimes and include a disproportionate number of males. School surveys, on the other hand, are more likely to capture information on less serious self-reported delinquency and usually include equal numbers of males and females. In addition, Moore (1991) has found that females tend to leave gangs at an earlier age than males.

Gangs and Social Institutions

It is important to remember that all but the most hard-core gang members lead a considerable portion of their lives outside the gang. As is the case for most adolescents, institutions such as family and school play important roles in their lives. The work of Moore and Vigil in Los Angeles has pointed to adolescents' need for order and regulation. Children naturally seek these conditions, and gangs have come to meet them for a growing number of youths. In many instances, the gang functions as an alternative family. Gangs provide social cohesion and status, which are typically provided by a functioning family. As gangs proliferate and last longer, gang members become parents and raise children who are at risk for gang membership.

Decker and Van Winkle (1996) interviewed gang members and their families about life in the gang. They found that while some gang members often characterized the gang as family, few actually viewed it as such and regarded their natal family much more positively. Family members usually were unaware of gang membership, especially at its earliest stages. Few family members approved of gangs, and gang members uniformly denied wanting their children to join gangs.

After the family, school is the most powerful socializing agent for adolescents. Most children attend school every day, where they interact with students from different backgrounds. They influence each other in various ways, both positive and negative. Schools have an important impact on the lives of gang and non–gang members and provide opportunities for non-gang youths to learn about and become involved in gangs.

For a growing number of youths, the criminal justice system plays an increasingly important role. The United States has come to rely on incarceration as a means to solve the crime problem, and as it does so, contacts between gang members and agents of the criminal justice system increase. There is evidence that prison propels many young men who were not gang members toward gang membership. Imprisonment also strengthens the ties between many gang members and their gang, because the gang is one of the few sources of identification open to them.

Responding to Gang-Related Crime and Delinquency

Typically, one of five strategies has been used to respond to gangs: (1) suppression, (2) social intervention, (3) social opportunity, (4) community mobilization, and (5) organizational change (Spergel and Curry 1990). Suppression includes law-enforcement and criminal justice interventions like arrest, prosecution, imprisonment, and surveillance. Most jurisdictions use this as their primary response to gang problems. The second-most-used strategy is social intervention such as crisis intervention, treatment for youths and their families, social service referrals, and counseling. Organizational change is the next most common gang-intervention strategy. This method typically includes the development of task forces to address gang problems. A small number of communities respond to gangs through mobilization. This strategy is designed to create cooperation across agencies and better coordination of existing services. Social opportunity is the primary response for the smallest number of cities and towns across the country. This approach stresses education, job training, and job provision. Cities with chronic gang problems least often employ social opportunity and community mobilization, yet these strategies are considered most effective by individuals who work closely with gangs.

BIBLIOGRAPHY

Block, Carolyn R., and Richard Block. *Street Gang Crime in Chicago.* Washington, D.C.: U.S. Department of Justice, Office of Justice Programs, National Institute of Justice, 1993.

Curry, G. David, and Irving A. Spergel. "Gang Homicide, Delinquency, and Community." *Criminology* 26 (August 1988): 381–405.

Curry, G. David, and Scott H. Decker. *Confronting Gangs: Crime and Community.* Los Angeles: Roxbury, 1998.

Decker, Scott H., and Barrik Van Winkle. *Life in the Gang: Family, Friends, and Violence.* New York: Cambridge University Press, 1996.

———. "'Slinging Dope': The Role of Gangs and Gang Members in Drug Sales." *Justice Quarterly* 11 (December 1994): 583–604.

Esbensen, Finn-Aage, and David Huizinga. "Gangs, Drugs, and Delinquency in a Survey of Urban Youth." *Criminology* 31 (November 1993): 565–589.

Esbensen, Finn-Aage, David Huizinga, and Anne W. Weiher. "Gang and Non-Gang Youth: Differences in Explanatory Factors." *Journal of Contemporary Criminal Justice* 9 (1993): 94–116.

Fagan, Jeffrey. "The Social Organization of Drug Use and Drug Dealing Among Urban Gangs." *Criminology* 27 (November 1989): 633–669.

Hagedorn, John M. "Homeboys, Dope Fiends, Legits, and New Jacks." *Criminology* 32 (May 1994): 197–219.

———. *People and Folks: Gangs, Crime, and the Underclass in a Rustbelt City.* Chicago: Lake View, 1998.

Jackson, Pamela Irving. "Crime, Youth Gangs, and Urban Transition: The Social Dislocations of Postindustrial Economic Development." *Justice Quarterly* 6 (September 1991): 379–397.

Jankowski, Martin Sanchez. *Islands in the Street: Gangs and American Urban Society.* Berkeley: University of California Press, 1991.

Klein, Malcolm W. *The American Street Gang: Its Nature, Prevalence, and Control.* New York: Oxford University Press, 1995.

———. "Street Gang Cycles." In *Crime,* edited by James Q. Wilson and Joan Petersilia. San Francisco: Institute for Contemporary Studies, 1995.

———. *Street Gangs and Street Workers.* Englewood Cliffs, N.J.: Prentice-Hall, 1971.

Klein, Malcolm W., Cheryl L. Maxson, and Lea C. Cunningham. "'Crack,' Street Gangs, and Violence." *Criminology* 29 (November 1991): 623–650.

Maxson, Cheryl L., and Malcolm W. Klein. "The Scope of Street Gang Migration in the U.S." Paper presented at the Gangs Working Group. National Institute of Justice, Washington, D.C., 1994.

Maxson, Cheryl L., Margaret A. Gordon, and Malcolm W. Klein. "Differences Between Gang and Nongang Homicides." *Criminology* 23 (May 1985): 209–222.

Miller, Walter B. *Violence by Youth Gangs and Youth Groups as a Crime Problem in Major American Cities.* Washington, D.C.: U.S. Government Printing Office, 1977.

Moore, Joan W. *Going Down to the Barrio: Homeboys and Homegirls in Change.* Philadelphia: Temple University Press, 1991.

Sanders, William. *Gangbangs and Drive-bys: Grounded Culture and Juvenile Gang Violence.* New York: Aldine de Gruyter, 1994.

Short, James F., Jr., and Fred L. Strodtbeck. *Group Process and Gang Delinquency.* 1965. 2d ed. Chicago: University of Chicago Press, 1974.

Skolnick, Jerome. "The Social Structure of Street Drug Dealing." *American Journal of Police* 9, no. 1(1990): 1–41.

Spergel, Irving A. *The Youth Gang Problem: A Community Approach.* New York: Oxford University Press, 1995.

Spergel, Irving A., and G. David Curry. "Strategies and Perceived Agency Effectiveness in Dealing with the Youth Gang Problem." In *Gangs in America,* edited by C. Ronald Huff. Newbury Park, Calif.: Sage, 1990. Pp. 288–309.

Taylor, Carl S. *Dangerous Society.* East Lansing: Michigan State University Press, 1990.

Thornberry, Terence, Marvin D. Krohn, Alan J. Lizotte, and Deborah Chard-Wierschem. "The Role of Juvenile Gangs in Facilitating Delinquent Behavior." *Journal of Research in Crime and Delinquency* 30 (February 1993): 55–87.

Thrasher, Frederic. *The Gang: A Study of 1,313 Gangs in Chicago.* Chicago: University of Chicago Press, 1927.

Vigil, James Diego. *Barrio Gangs: Street Life and Identity in Southern California.* Austin: University of Texas Press, 1988.

SCOTT H. DECKER
G. DAVID CURRY

See also **Drive-by Shooting; Immigration; Teenagers; Urban Violence.**

GARRETT, PAT
(1850–1908)

Patrick Floyd Garrett was a western lawman best known for killing Billy the Kid. Born 5 June 1850, in Chambers County, Alabama, and raised in Louisiana, Garrett left home in 1869 for a career as a cowboy and buffalo hunter in Texas. In 1876 he killed a young man named Joe Briscoe, who had tagged along on a buffalo hunt and had been taunting the six-foot, five-inch Garrett to fight. Garrett turned himself in, but officials at Fort Griffin declined to prosecute.

In 1879 Garrett moved to Lincoln County, New Mexico, where he was elected sheriff on 2 November 1880, serving as deputy sheriff until he took office on 1 January 1881. Garrett vowed to bring the reign of lawlessness in the region to an end, and on 20 December he and his posse set out to bring in Billy the Kid (William Bonney), who had a $500 reward on his head for murder. They captured the Kid at Stinking Springs, after Garrett mistakenly shot a member of the Kid's gang, who he thought was Billy. In April 1881 the Kid was convicted and turned over to Garrett to be hanged in Lincoln on 13 May, but the Kid escaped after killing his guards. Garrett gave chase and on 14 July found the Kid at Pete Maxwell's ranch, an adobe house converted from the abandoned quarters of Fort Sumner. Garrett waited in Maxwell's darkened bedroom until the Kid entered, recognized the Kid's voice, then shot twice, one bullet hitting the Kid in the heart.

In 1882 Garrett published a wildly inaccurate and exaggerated account of Billy the Kid, *The Authentic Life of Billy the Kid*, which was actually written by his friend Ash Upson, a former reporter. When an anonymous letter criticizing the book was published, Garrett sought out the letter's writer, believing it was a local attorney, W. W. Roberts. Garrett bashed Roberts in the head at least twice with his Colt .45 revolver, leaving Roberts unconscious in the street.

Garrett then became a rancher, was elected sheriff of Doña Ana County (1896–1902), and, having switched from the Democratic to Republican Party, was appointed U.S. collector of customs (1902–1906) in El Paso, Texas, by President Theodore Roosevelt. He returned to New Mexico in 1906 and purchased a horse ranch at San Andres Mountain. The ranch failed, and he became quarrelsome and insulting, often brawling drunkenly in the streets and once threatening to rope-whip a man who objected to the way he drove some stock away from a waterhole.

Mystery and conspiracy theories surround Garrett's death on 29 February 1908, on a road to his ranch. Wayne Brazel, who was leasing Garrett's ranch and whom Garrett wanted to evict, came upon Garrett riding in a buggy with Carl Adamson, a prospective buyer for his ranch. Garrett saw Brazel as the major obstacle to a land deal that would end his financial troubles. Brazel supposedly shot Garrett in the back of the head as he was relieving himself and then shot Garrett in the stomach while he lay on the ground. Brazel pleaded self-defense at his trial and was freed. Other theories have Adamson pulling the trigger or Jim "Killer" Miller, a relative by marriage of Adamson, doing the shooting for $10,000. It was believed that Garrett had unearthed new information about the

Pat Garrett slays Billy the Kid in New Mexico on 14 July 1881. Woodcut from *Beadle's Half Dime Library.* HULTON GETTY/LIAISON AGENCY

disappearance in 1896 of Judge Albert Fountain, a strong supporter of wealthy, big ranchers who had been behind Garrett's installation as sheriff of Doña Ana County.

BIBLIOGRAPHY

Dykes, Jeff C. *Law on a Wild Frontier: Four Sheriffs of Lincoln County.* Washington, D.C.: Potomac Corral, 1969.

Metz, Leon C. *Pat Garrett: The Story of a Western Lawman.* Norman: University of Oklahoma Press, 1973.

Rickards, Colin. *Sheriff Pat Garrett's Last Days.* Santa Fe, N. Mex.: Sunstone, 1986.

Sonnichsen, Charles Leland. *Tularosa: Last of the Frontier West.* New York: Devin-Adair, 1960.

Utley, Robert M. *Billy the Kid: A Short and Violent Life.* Lincoln: University of Nebraska Press. 1991.

LOUISE B. KETZ

See also **Billy the Kid; Frontier; West.**

GATED COMMUNITIES. *See* Private Security: Gated Communities.

GATLING, RICHARD JORDAN
(1818–1903)

Richard Jordan Gatling was an inventor of agricultural and military machinery who created the first successful rapid-fire rifle, the Gatling gun, paving the way for the modern-day machine gun.

Gatling was born in North Carolina, where his father was a slave-owning planter. He cut his teeth helping his father invent agricultural implements and proved a capable student in local schools. While running a small store, he developed a screw propeller, though the device was already patented.

Gatling moved to St. Louis in 1844 to market a rice-sowing implement he had invented, and one year later he devoted himself to promoting his own creations. A bout with smallpox spurred him to attend medical school; he received a medical degree in 1850, though he never practiced medicine. Gatling's farm-machine business grew in the meantime, but the Civil War shifted his concentration to military machinery.

Gatling began to experiment with weapons, inventing a marine steam ram in 1862. But he found his greatest success in developing a rapid-fire rifle. His invention—known as the Gatling gun—consisted of six or more rifle barrels placed around a common axis. The operator turned a hand crank,

Richard Jordan Gatling. LIBRARY OF CONGRESS

rotating the barrels that fired in succession, each barrel firing once per revolution. Ordnance flowed into the breech, and the shells were discarded automatically. Once Gatling perfected this design, it proved to be the first successful machine gun.

While he demonstrated that his weapon could fire 350 shots per minute, Gatling's attempts to market the arm to Union commanders proved a failure, in part because of the army's conservatism and its lack of experience with the new gun. The weapon had little or no effect on the Civil War. Since scholars have linked Gatling to membership in a Confederate sympathy group, his motivation in presenting his invention to Union officers might have had as much to do with profit as with patriotism.

After the war the U.S. Army officially tested the Gatling gun, adopting the weapon in 1866. The gun's size and weight—it was usually mounted to a cart—led many to consider it an artillery piece, to be used primarily for defense. For years the weapon saw only sporadic use as military theorists debated its tactical role. The army did use the Gatling gun sparingly at frontier and coastal outposts. Its largest role in American military action was in the Spanish-American War, in which its offensive prowess aided a successful charge on San Juan Hill, Cuba, in 1898. Gatling also promoted his weapon abroad, and nearly all the Western world's armies had adopted his invention by the late 1800s, including the British, who used it in colonial expeditions in Africa.

The machine gun saw widespread use after its tactical considerations were sorted out in World War I. By that time the Gatling gun was obsolete, the mobile, automatic weapon having superseded the hand-cranked, artillery-style weapon. Late in life Gatling sold the patent rights of his weapon to the Colt Company and moved to New England, where he continued to invent while serving as president of the American Association of Inventors and Manufacturers. He died in 1903.

BIBLIOGRAPHY

Armstrong, David A. *Bullets and Bureaucrats: The Machine Gun and the United States Army, 1861–1916.* Westport, Conn.: Greenwood, 1982.

Ellis, John. *The Social History of the Machine Gun.* London: Croom Helm, 1975.

Wahl, Paul, and David R. Toppel. *The Gatling Gun.* New York: Arco, 1965.

GREGORY L. PARKER

See also **Bowie, James; Colt, Samuel; Deringer, Henry, Jr.; Remington, Eliphalet; Weapons.**

GAY BASHING

The history of violence against lesbians and gay men in the United States is a long and complex one. In the early modern period (about 1500–1700) the term *sodomy* was commonly used to denote the entire range of nonprocreative sexual acts outside marriage. Jonathan Goldberg has analyzed the ferocious punishment of acts "tending to sodomy" in the Massachusetts Bay Colony—ranging from the case of sixteen-year-old Thomas Grainger, who was discovered having sex with a mare and executed for his crime, to that of a woman accused of incest with her brother and that of two men accused of engaging in "lewd" acts with each other (all three accused were publicly whipped for their transgressions). As Goldberg has also shown, the ascription of sodomitical tendencies to the natives of the New World played an important part in the rationalization of violence against them on the part of European colonizers during the early phases of contact. Jonathan Ned Katz provides a useful account of (and an invaluable collection of documentary material bearing on) attitudes toward same-sex relations in the American colonies. As Katz shows, seventeenth-century colonial authorities explicitly prohibited sexual relations between women as well as between men; the New England Puritan leader Reverend John Cotton, for example, proposed the death penalty for acts of "sodomy" between women.

Waves of persecution against large numbers of persons for alleged crimes of heresy and witchcraft as well as "sodomy" in the sixteenth and seventeenth centuries probably provide the broad context for violence, state-sponsored and otherwise, against same-sex relations and other forms of officially forbidden sexuality in the American colonies, although the bulk of historical research on the connections among these sanctioned practices remains to be done. The biblical story of the destruction of Sodom and Gomorrah by fire and brimstone and the lethal injunctions of Leviticus have set the precedent for justifying violence against persons who engage in same-sex sexual relations, exemplified by laws written in medieval times, by Blackstone in his *Commentaries* (1765–1769), and by scripture-citing advocates of gay bashing in the late twentieth century. In England, according to Louis Crompton (1985), the death penalty for sodomy was most rigorously enforced during the early nineteenth century, when convicted "sodomites" were executed by hanging or were sometimes bludgeoned to death before they could be hanged by the mobs who attended their pilloryings.

Violence against persons accused or convicted of such relations was enforced with less spectacular publicity in the nineteenth-century United States, but surviving evidence (much of it anecdotal) suggests that American society witnessed a mounting level of hostility and intimidation toward perpetrators or would-be perpetrators of same-sex relations. The long-standing legend of the young Walt Whitman's having been driven out of a Long Island town where he had been working as an itinerant schoolmaster, supposedly for having shown undue attention to a male pupil, suggests that Americans of the period may have commonly dealt with the threat of unauthorized sexualities by extralegal means. The Reverend Horatio Alger's expulsion from the Unitarian ministry on Cape Cod in 1866, on account of his having had sexual relations with some of the boy members of his congregation, suggests that, at least in some cases, the punishment of elite transgressors could be limited to professional and social disgrace; and escape from that disgrace was possible by moving to the relatively anonymous spaces of a large city and changing professsions (Alger moved to New York City and became a successful author of boys' books).

The expansion of legal and medical attention on behalf of the state to all forms of erotic desire and behavior in the last third of the nineteenth century resulted in what Katz, following the French historian and theorist Michel Foucault, has called "the invention of the homosexual." A host of sexual identities, subjected to substantially increased social regulation, were criminalized and pathologized, with the result that the "homosexual," male or female, became the object of legal and extralegal surveillance and punishment. George Chauncey discusses the dynamics governing relations between "fairies" in turn-of-the-century New York and the Irish and Italian youths with whom they sometimes had sex. Ralph Werther, one such fairy and a student living in the city in the 1890s, in a memoir of his experiences deplores the frequent and brutal beatings and robbings by members of the city's youth gangs of the effeminate men with whom some of them had sex. In his account of the phenomenon, Werther blames the violence on the hatred preached against "perverts" by clergymen and doctors. "Such violence," Chauncey writes, "often served a more instrumental purpose [than simple robbery] in reinforcing the boundaries between fairies and other men. Some men beat or robbed their effeminate male sexual partners after sex as if to emphasize that they felt no connection to them and had simply 'used' them for sexual release" (p. 60). Toward the end of the twentieth century, the most important focus of thinking about the phenomenon of gay bashing has been perhaps the analysis of the social and psychological meaning of such violence for its perpetrators.

Chauncey, following the work of John D'Emilio, also examines how the stereotype of the ridiculously effeminate fairy, popular in the United States in the early decades of the century, "was supplemented by another, more ominous image of the queer as a psychopathic child molester capable of committing the most unspeakable crimes against children" (pp. 359–360). As Chauncey notes, the replacement of the stereotype of the hypervisible fairy with that of the perverted psychopath who could pass for "normal," at least for a while, contributed to a considerable increase in

paranoid hostility toward persons thought to be homosexual. D'Emilio recounts how gay men in the 1930s and 1940s began to unite as they initiated various collective responses to the increasing violence directed at them by individuals and groups ranging from newspaper pundits to street gangs.

Leslie Feinberg's popular novel *Stone Butch Blues* represents a young lesbian's experiences of a range of violence, from verbal harassment to gang rape, as she grows up in a blue-collar town in the 1950s. Elizabeth Lapovsky Kennedy and Madeline D. Davis's history of lesbian communities in Buffalo, New York, from the 1930s to the 1960s provides extensive testimony about the pervasiveness of violence in the bar culture of the period, in which patrons were frequently harassed by hostile men, including policemen who carried out raids and sometimes battered and forced sex on lesbians and gay men.

Since the Rise of Gay Liberation

In late June 1969 a police raid on the Stonewall Inn on Chrisopher Street in New York City's Greenwich Village resulted in a riot against police harassment that inaugurated the international gay and lesbian liberation movement. In the decades that followed, significant increases in the social and political visibility of lesbians and gay men were met from various quarters with a wave of backlash movements, including the singer Anita Bryant's Save Our Children campaign of the 1970s, which equated homosexuals with murderers, and Jerry Falwell's Moral Majority and other rightwing fundamentalist organizations that treat the existence and visibility of gay life as a dire threat to "family values," which they see as the exclusive property of the heterosexual conjugal household. Episodes of gay bashing have sometimes jumped dramatically in number after television broadcasts portraying gays as direct threats to national wellbeing (see Greenberg 1988, pp. 466–467).

Reliable statistics on gay bashing have been difficult to collect. The crime is chronically underreported, owing to a widespread (although somewhat decreasing) sense on the part of many gays and lesbians that local law enforcement personnel are generally indifferent or hostile to victims of gay bashing. The assassination in 1978 of Harvey Milk, an openly gay municipal politician in San Francisco, contributed to gay and other communities' increased awareness of antigay violence in its most extreme forms. Grassroots organizing against antigay violence has been a notable feature of lesbian

Stonewall Riots

On the night of 27 June 1969 in New York City, during what was supposed to be a routine police raid on the most popular gay bar in Greenwich Village (the Stonewall Inn), gay patrons, drag queens, and bystanders began to fight back as the police attempted to load some of them into a paddy wagon. Eight cops swung nightsticks and hurled epithets, and a rapidly formed mob hurled back bottles and more epithets, then squirted lighter fluid through the bar's shattered front window and ignited it. At 3 A.M. two dozen members of riot police were summoned to the scene. Several people were badly beaten, and four police officers sustained minor injuries. Thousands gathered at the site the next evening, chanting gay political slogans and blocking traffic. Violence broke out again, this time on a larger scale. Cars were ambushed, more fights broke out, and the police pulled out at 4 A.M. Another sizable demonstration occurred a few nights later.

The Stonewall rebellion has come to be regarded as the galvanizing event that transformed a tiny homophile network into a mass political movement. The events of late June and early July 1969 came to symbolize, to many gays and lesbians across the United States and beyond it, a newfound collective desire to affirm their rights to exist and to assemble by whatever means necessary, including fighting back.

and gay political activism in the post-Stonewall period, first peaking in the years around 1980. San Francisco's CUAV (Community United Against Violence) and the New York City Gay and Lesbian Anti-violence Project, both founded around 1980, exemplify long-standing initiatives aimed primarily at responding to verbal and physical violence against gays and lesbians.

The early 1980s also witnessed the first waves of the HIV/AIDS pandemic. The emergence of this syndrome among gay men has had the effect on some groups of renewing and intensifying phobic stereotypes of gays and gay sexualities as infectious and lethal and as somehow themselves inherently violent and predatory. As it is commonly understood, gay bashing has its roots in homophobia, an attitude of irrational fear of same-sex sexual relations or of men or women believed to have engaged in such relations. As homophobia

has increased in some quarters in response to the fear of the threat of AIDS, antigay violence has also increased. Eve Kosofsky Sedgwick (1985, 1990) has related the enforcement of antigay attitudes in the modern period to the phenomenon of "male homosexual panic," which Sedgwick defines as "a defense strategy that is commonly used to prevent conviction or to lighten sentencing of gay-bashers." She continues:

> Judicially, a "homosexual panic" defense for a person (typically a man) accused of antigay violence implies that his responsibility for the crime was diminished by a pathological psychological condition, perhaps brought on by an unwanted sexual advance from the man whom he then attacked. (1990, p. 19)

This defense, Sedgwick concludes, rests on the false assumption that hatred of homosexuals "is so private and so atypical a phenomenon in this culture as to be classifiable as an accountability-reducing illness," when "the widespread acceptance of this defense really seems to show, to the contrary, that hatred of homosexuals is even more public, more typical, hence harder to find any leverage against than hatred of other disadvantaged groups."

The effects of homophobia in general and of antigay violence, both verbal and physical, on lesbian and gay youth have in the 1990s become the focus of some preliminary study. The Seattle Public Schools' Teen Health Risk Survey (1995) reported, for example, that about one-third of teenagers surveyed who identified themselves as gay, lesbian, or bisexual reported that they had been verbally or physically abused at school because of their sexual orientation. The survey also showed that gay teenagers were 75 percent more likely than their heterosexual peers to have been threatened or injured with a weapon at school in the past year.

Further study is needed on gay bashing as a widespread component of adolescent male subcultures. Gregory M. Herek and Kevin T. Berrill have focused attention on the cultural and psychological functions of gay bashing for its perpetrators, providing both anecdotal and analytical accounts. Gay bashers, according to the studies they review, "are very largely male, in their late teens or early twenties, strangers to the victim(s), in groups, and not engaged in victimization for profit" (p. 113). In *Licensed to Kill*, a documentary by filmmaker and onetime gay-bashing victim Arthur Dong, Dong interviews six convicted murderers of gay men, several of whom speak of the murders they committed as the more or less accidental outcome of a pattern of robbing and otherwise preying on gay men whom they took to be unlikely to turn to the police. Several of Dong's subjects speak of the "license" to commit violent attacks against gays, including casual murder, which they felt was granted by society's attitudes toward homosexuality—particularly the virulent attitudes of religious fundamentalists. National networks for reporting antigay violence, established since the early 1980s, have made it clear that gay bashing, ranging from verbal harassment to battery to murder, can occur anywhere; incidents are frequently reported from the "gay ghettos" of San Francisco and New York as well as from small towns, isolated rural areas, and college campuses across the country.

Preliminary studies show (unsurprisingly) that lesbians and gay men of color are at increased risk for attack as potential objects of both racist and homophobic violence (Herek and Berrill 1992). Perpetrators of antigay violence often point to the rhetoric of organized hate groups (the Ku Klux Klan, neo-Nazis, and others), who have increasingly targeted gays and lesbians in the 1980s and 1990s, as having contributed significantly to their decisions to act on their violent impulses against homosexuals. Incidents of violence include the firebombing of a gay church in Missouri by members of a neo-Nazi group, the execution-style murders of three gay men in North Carolina by men linked to the White Patriot Party, and the national dissemination of antigay propaganda via computer bulletin boards by affiliates of the Aryan Nation (Berrill, in Herek and Berrill). The lynching-style murders of Matthew Shepard in Wyoming in October 1998 and of Billy Jack Gaither in Alabama in February 1999 have increased pressure on state and federal legislatures to treat incidents of antigay violence as hate crimes.

Further research is urgently needed on the comparative histories of and relations between antigay violence and other kinds of hate crimes; lesbian and gay antiviolence activists and scholars have much to learn, for example, from the history of lynching and of organized resistance to lynching in this country. Antihomophobic scholarship and activism have as yet made little impact on the systemic patterns of violence against gays institutionalized in the U.S. prison system, in which inmates identified as gay are particularly vulnerable to battery and rape. The situation of gays in prison has of course been exacerbated by phobic response to HIV/AIDS among closed populations.

The Buddhist scholar Jeffrey Hopkins, in his article "The Compatibility of Reason and Orgasm in Tibetan Buddhism: Reflections on Sexual Violence

A candlelight vigil for the University of Wyoming student Matthew Shepard, killed by gay bashers in 1998, and other victims of hate crimes. GAMMA/LIAISON AGENCY

and Homophobia," sends the debate on the social origins and contexts of homophobic violence in potentially productive new directions. Hopkins argues that, whereas in Tibetan Buddhism levels of consciousness including conceptual reasoning and orgasmic bliss occupy positions on a single continuum of states of mind, many Westerners tend to think of a state of intense sexual pleasure as "lower" than, and as radically discontinuous from, a "higher," rational state of mind. "This radical division," Hopkins writes, "lays the groundwork for projection of the lower self onto others, especially women and male homosexuals, and . . . [for] brutal attempts at control." This brutality ranges from actual physical violence to suppression of information about sex and sexual orientation.

The legal scholar Kendall Thomas takes a quite different, but no less provocative, tack in exposing the ways in which long-standing laws and legal tradition in the United States support antigay violence. Thomas opposes the widely held view that a right to privacy is the most desirable vehicle for ensuring the safety and security of gay and lesbian Americans. He argues that sodomy laws themselves significantly contribute to a social atmosphere conducive to violence against gays: "the criminalization of homosexual sodomy *legitimizes* homophobic violence" (p. 1486, n. 194). The distance between Hopkins's and Thomas's analyses of the roots of gay bashing and of American homophobia in general suggests something of the range of responses by scholars and activists alike to ongoing antigay violence.

BIBLIOGRAPHY

Bray, Alan. *Homosexuality in Renaissance England.* London: Gay Men's Press, 1982.

Chauncey, George. *Gay New York: Gender, Urban Culture, and the Making of the Gay Male World, 1890–1940.* New York: Basic, 1994.

Crompton, Louis. "Georgian Homophobia." In *Byron and Greek Love: Homophobia in Nineteenth-Century England.* Berkeley: University of California Press, 1985.

———. "The Myth of Lesbian Impunity: Capital Laws from 1270 to 1791." *Journal of Homosexuality* 6 (fall–winter 1980–1981): 11–25.

Dong, Arthur. *Licensed to Kill.* Los Angeles: DeepFocus, 1997. Film.

Duberman, Martin. *Stonewall.* New York: Dutton, 1993.

D'Emilio, John. *Sexual Politics, Sexual Communities: The Making of a Homosexual Minority in the United States, 1940–1970.* Chicago: University of Chicago Press, 1983.

Feinberg, Leslie. *Stone Butch Blues.* Ithaca, N.Y.: Firebrand 1993.

Goldberg, Jonathan. *Sodometries: Renaissance Texts, Modern Sexualities.* Stanford, Calif.: Stanford University Press, 1992.

Greenberg, David F. *The Construction of Homosexuality.* Chicago: University of Chicago Press, 1988.

Herek, Gregory M., and Kevin T. Berrill, eds. *Hate Crimes: Confronting Violence Against Lesbians and Gay Men.* Newbury Park, Calif.: Sage, 1992.

Hopkins, Jeffrey. "The Compatibility of Reason and Orgasm in Tibetan Buddhism: Reflections on Sexual Violence and Homophobia." In *Gay Affirmative Ethics.* Vol. 4, Gay Men's Issues in Religious Studies Series, edited by Michael L. Stemmeler and J. Michael Clark. Las Colinas, Tex.: Monument, 1993. Repr. in *Que(e)rying Religion: A Critical Anthology,* edited by David Comstock and Susan E. Henking. New York: Continuum, 1997.

Katz, Jonathan Ned. "Early Colonial Exploration, Agriculture, and Commerce: The Age of Sodomitical Sin, 1607–1740." In *Gay/Lesbian Almanac: A New Documentary,* edited by Katz. New York: Harper and Row, 1983.

Kennedy, Elizabeth Lapovsky, and Madeline D. Davis. *Boots of Leather, Slippers of Gold: The History of a Lesbian Community.* New York: Routledge, 1993.

Sedgwick, Eve Kosofsky. *Between Men: English Literature and Male Homosocial Desire.* New York: Columbia University Press, 1985.

———. *Epistemology of the Closet.* Berkeley: University of California Press, 1990.

Thomas, Kendall. "Beyond the Privacy Principle." *Columbia Law Review* 92 (1992):1431–1516.

MICHAEL MOON

See also **Hate Crime; San Francisco.**

GEIN, ED
(1906–1984)

The name Ed Gein may not be easily recognized today beyond a tight circle of crime buffs, but this psychotic necrophiliac and murderer is well known throughout the world by his appearance in various fictionalized cinematic guises: Norman Bates in *Psycho* (1960), Leatherface in *The Texas Chainsaw Massacre* (1974), and Buffalo Bill in *Silence of the Lambs* (1991). Through his pop culture incarnations, Gein has become a veritable modern-day ogre and a folkloric monster.

Gein's atrocities came to light at the peak of the Eisenhower era, revealing a depravity that festered beneath America's wholesome 1950s veneer. On 16 November 1957, in the small Wisconsin town of Plainfield, the police were investigating the disappearance of Bernice Worden, the fifty-eight-year-old owner of a local hardware store. The trail led them to the farm of Ed Gein, a reclusive middle-aged handyman, generally considered to be a quirky but harmless oddball. When the police entered the shed behind Gein's house, they found the naked, headless body of Worden, strung up by the heels, gutted like a butchered deer. Inside the farmhouse were many more revelations—a virtual museum of artifacts cobbled out of female corpses.

Women's faces had been stuffed and were mounted on the walls. The tops of human skulls had been fashioned into soup bowls, and human skin transformed into lampshades. Vaginas were found squirreled away in boxes. As for Worden's missing head, it was eventually discovered under Gein's mattress. To prepare this latest trophy, Gein had hammered nails into the ears and skull and connected the nails with twine to allow him to hang the head on a wall.

The source of Gein's madness was apparently a poisonous relationship with his mother, who gave birth to him in La Crosse, Wisconsin. For years she had harangued her son about the evils of sex, singling herself out as his only fit form of female companionship. When his mother died in 1945, Gein found substitutes for her in the graveyard. He dug up the bodies of older women and displayed about

Ed Gein, in police custody in November 1957. CORBIS/ BETTMANN

his home their "customized" remains. At perhaps his most bizarre, he used the skin of dead women to fashion a bodysuit for himself. The violence he directed at corpses was refocused for the first time on living women in 1954, when he murdered a saloonkeeper named Mary Hogan and added her body parts to his collection. Worden was his second and final living victim.

Gein's two murders pale in comparison to the body count of more recent serial murderers, but the memory of his crimes has reverberated throughout our culture. Ever since December 1957, when *Life* magazine published an eight-page exposé entitled "House of Horror Stuns the Nation," Ed Gein and his filmic characterizations have shaped the public's perception of the obsession-driven serial killer. While his fictional counterparts brutalized their victims onscreen, Gein spent his remaining years quietly, lending a hand occasionally with carpentry and masonry tasks around Central State Hospital for the Criminally Insane. He was a model inmate.

BIBLIOGRAPHY

Everitt, David. *Human Monsters*. Chicago, Ill.: Contemporary Books, 1993.
Gollmar, Judge Robert H. *Ed Gein: America's Most Bizarre Murderer*. Delevan, Wis.: Chas. Hallenberg, 1981.
Schechter, Harold. *Deviant: The Shocking True Story of Ed Gein, the Original "Psycho."* New York: Pocket Books, 1989.

DAVID EVERITT

See also **Serial Killers.**

GENDER

The terms *gender* and *sex* are often used interchangeably by the general public. Technically, *gender* refers to socially constructed differences between masculine and feminine identity, behavior, and roles, while *sex* refers to biological differences between males and females. But even among social scientists the two words are often and increasingly used interchangeably, as, for example, in references to "gendercide" for the sex-selective killing of female fetuses.

By whatever name, male-female differences are important for understanding patterns of American violence. Since 1900, 88 percent of those arrested for homicide have been men, as have been more than 98 percent of the inmates on death row. The most spectacular forms of homicide, serial killing and mass murder, have been virtual male monopolies, as has the crime of rape.

Males are more often victims, as well as perpetrators, of lethal violence. Since 1900 American men have outnumbered women as homicide victims by roughly four to one and as suicide victims by between two and three to one. (The higher male suicide rate can be explained partly by the choice of surer means; men most often use firearms, women poison.) Young men have been killed in accidents five times as often as young women, older men twice as often as older women. Male deaths classed as accidental or homicidal often conceal an impulsive, thrill-seeking, or self-destructive tendency, manifest by such behavior as driving recklessly or picking fights. Higher rates of drinking and drug use by men, particularly by young men, also have been linked to their higher rates of traumatic death.

The male propensity to suffer and inflict violence, lethal or otherwise, has been documented for all human societies. In evolutionary terms, male aggression can be explained by the principle of sexual selection. Males who fight hard, mate often, and die young have a greater genetic influence on posterity than do passive males who seldom mate and live to ripe old age. In hormonal terms, male aggression is linked to testosterone, which organizes the fetal nervous system and exerts anabolic and androgenic effects on boys, especially at puberty. The psychologist David Lykken once joked that the surest way to reduce crime would be to put all able-bodied males between the ages of twelve and twenty-eight into cryogenic sleep. In fact, the surest, most radical (and morally dubious) way to reduce crime and violence would be to reverse gendercide against male offspring or to clone only females.

Gender is both socially and hormonally constructed. Testicular grafts in hens produce the comb and wattles of a cock; steroids in female bodybuilders produce bigger muscles, larger clitorises, and greater aggressiveness. Hormones, however, are not the whole story. Though males everywhere statistically are more violent than females, the rates of male violence vary widely from culture to culture, as do the ratios of male-to-female killers. Countries with relatively high homicide rates like the United States are societies with unusually large numbers of young men killing other young men.

The explanation for why young American men are statistically more violent than those of most other countries is social, cultural, and demographic rather than biological. It involves sensitivity about personal honor, racial and class attitudes, drinking practices, religious beliefs, family life (or its absence), poverty, the availability of firearms, illicit-drug markets, exposure to media violence, population structure, and migration patterns.

BIBLIOGRAPHY

Courtwright, David T. *Violent Land: Single Men and Social Disorder from the Frontier to the Inner City.* Cambridge, Mass.: Harvard University Press, 1996.

Daly, Martin, and Margo Wilson. *Homicide.* New York: de Gruyter, 1988.

Wilson, James Q., and Richard Herrnstein. *Crime and Human Nature.* New York: Simon and Schuster, 1985.

DAVID T. COURTWRIGHT

See also **Endocrinology: Testosterone; Machismo; Masculinity; Sex Differences; Sexual Harassment; Women.**

GENETICS

The impact of genes on violence and aggression is examined in three subentries: **Chromosomal Abnormalities; Molecular—Humans;** *and* **Twins, Families, and Adoptions.** *For information on genetics of nonhuman animals, see also* "Animal Studies of Aggression and Violence," *and for a survey of genetic influences on repeated violent offending, see* "Recidivism of Violent Offenders: Genetic Factors."

CHROMOSOMAL ABNORMALITIES

Behavioral genetics and criminology intersected in the 1960s, when isolated cases of XYY males committing heinous acts of violence gained media attention. The notorious mass murderer Richard Speck was one of the first defendants to use the XYY defense. Such a defense was met with skepticism by some scientists and politicans who felt that identifying biological causes of crime might diminish individual responsibility for criminal behavior. Consequently, a debate ensued on whether the presence of the supernumerary Y chromosome was associated with criminal violence. "Normal" males are born with one X and one Y chromosome and the extra Y chromosome was conceptualized as carrying the excess testosterone associated with violent tendencies. The sources of this interpretation were case studies and studies using select samples that examined the link between the extra Y chromosome and aggressive behavior. Despite inconsistent results from these studies, the link remained a popularly held belief by a subgroup of the general public and scientists. However, several important methodological limitations of these studies must be highlighted.

First, the samples used were taken from populations that carried a higher likelihood of containing XYY males such as prison inmates, the mentally ill, and tall men. Second, the imprisoned offenders represented a select, recidivistic group whose members, because of their diminished intellectual capacities, were more likely to be apprehended, as compared to criminals with normal or above normal intelligence. Because males with the XYY chromosomal abnormality may have intellectual deficits, these studies were ill equipped to tease apart whether criminal behavior is an outcome of chromosomal abnormalities or impaired intellectual functioning. Third, many of the studies of XYY males failed to include XY controls. Further, the selection factors did not allow for valid estimates of the prevalence rate of XYY in the general population. Last, a causal association between two traits (an extra Y chromosome and criminal offending) cannot be established simply by demonstrating their coincidence. Criminal behavior is a complex and multidimensional occurrence that may have both genetic and evniornmental causative agents.

In short, what was needed was a study of a large, unselected sample and a comparison of the identified XYY individuals to appropriately matched XY controls. In response to these concerns, a group of investigators led by Herman A. Witkin set out in the 1970s to design a study at the Psykologisk Institul (now called the Institute for Preventative Medicine) in Copenhagen, Denmark. The study was to address the methodological limitations inherent in previous studies. Witkin and his associates sought to answer two key questions. First, are XYY males in the general population more likely to commit crimes than XY controls? Second, if XYY males are found to be more criminal than control subjects, are there any intervening variables that may mediate the relationship between the extra Y chromosome and increased criminality? The investigators also include three variables that might be potential mediators—height, intelligence, and aggressiveness.

The study's sample was drawn from a cohort of 31,455 males born in Denmark between 1944 and 1947. To maximize the chances of obtaining XYY men, chromosomal screenings were conducted on all men in the top 15 percent of the height distribution in the Danish male population. Specifically, Witkin and colleagues established a cutoff height of 184 centimeters, or just over 6 feet. At the time of data collection, men in the group were to be at least twenty-six years old, the age by which Danish men are required to report to their draft boards for a physical examination. Height information was determined from draft board records.

Intellectual measures were obtained from two sources. First, potential army recruits are routinely administered the Borge Priens Prover (BPP) intelligence test, the results of which provided the investigators with a rough indicator of cognitive functioning. The second measure of intellectual functioning was the educational level achieved. In order to measure aggressiveness, conviction data and types of offenses were obtained through the Danish National Police Register in Copenhagen. (The Danish criminal register has been described as probably the most thorough, comprehensive, and accurate in the Western world.) The final sample size was 4,139 men.

Once all the men in the sample underwent the chromosomal screening, twelve XYY males were identified, a prevalence rate of 2.9 per 1000. A search of the Danish criminal register revealed that 41.7 percent of the XYY males (or five of the twelve) had been convicted of one or more criminal offenses, compared to 9.3 percent of the XY controls. Although men with the extra Y chromosome were more likely to evidence criminal behavior than XY men, none of the XYY men had been arrested for violent acts. Put another way, the presence of an extra Y chromosome did not confer risk for serious violent offending. Height was not found to act as an intervening variable. Intellectual dysfunction, however, was found to be an important intervening variable mediating the relationship between the extra Y chromosome and criminal behavior. The XYY males had lower overall scores on the BPP and lower educational levels than the XY controls.

The earlier studies that had heralded a link between the supernumerary Y chromosome and criminal offending were weakened by questionable methodological techniques and sampling bias. On the other hand, Witkin's study of Danish males showed that XYY males were more likely to have a criminal conviction as compared to XY controls. This finding, however, cannot be construed as a causal relationship because of the identification of intelligence as an important mediator. A 1999 study carried out by M. J. Gotz and colleagues in Edinburgh, Scotland, agrees with Witkin's study in that the relationship between XYY males and an elevated rate of criminal convictions was mediated through lowered intelligence.

Further research endeavors in this area, however, must also consider the questionable utility of reviving this debate, particularly in light of the data suggesting that XYY males account for only a fraction of all crimes committed and that their behavior tends not to be violent.

BIBLIOGRAPHY

Gotz, M. J., E. C. Johnstone, and S. G. Ratcliffe. "Criminality and Antisocial Behavior in Unselected Men with Sex Chromosome Abnormalities." *Psychological Medicine* 29 (1999): 953–962.

Owen, D. R. "The 46 XYY Male: A Review." *Psychological Bulletin* 78 (1972): 161–240.

Sarbin, T. R., and J. E. Miller. "Demonism Revisited: The XYY Chromosomal Anomaly." *Issues in Criminolgy* 5 (1970): 195–207.

Shah, S. A. *Report on the XYY Chromsomal Abnormality.* Chevy Chase, Md.: National Institute of Mental Health Center for Studies of Crime and Delinquency, 1970.

Witkin, Herman A., et al. "Criminality in XYY and XXY Men." *Science* 193 (1976): 547–555.

Jasmine A. Tehrani
Sarnoff A. Mednick

MOLECULAR—HUMANS

In humans there is no such thing as a gene for violence. Violence is a complex, multifactorial behavior that is triggered by a specific set of environmental conditions. Under the right set of circumstances anyone can become violent, regardless of that individual's genetic makeup. The genetics of violence refers to the fact that individuals differ in the likelihood that they will resort to violence given the appropriate environmental triggers. Variants of many different genes can act as risk factors, and the more of these variants a person inherits the greater the probability that some form of violent behavior will occur.

The interaction between environmental and genetic factors is illustrated in figure 1, which points to a number of important concepts. First, for some individuals violent behavior is entirely due to environmental factors; for some it is due almost entirely to genetic factors; for most it is a result of an interaction between environmental and genetic

factors. Second, for those with a high genetic risk, violence may be triggered by minimal environmental stress. The less the genetic risk the greater the environmental trigger required to precipitate violence. Third, the widespread view that criminal and violent behavior can be decreased by manipulating environmental factors—improving socioeconomic status, controlling gangs, and increasing education and employment—is valid for the violence that is predominantly attributable to environmental factors. However, because of the major role of biological and genetic factors in some individuals, even in a utopian world where all the negative environmental factors were eliminated, criminal and violent behavior would still exist.

A large number of studies have consistently shown that childhood conduct disorder (CD), characterized by the persistent disregard for the rights of others, is the single most important and reproducible predictor of adult criminal, aggressive, and violent behavior (Comings 1998). The first and classic study of the ability of childhood conduct disorder to predict adult antisocial behavior was by Lee Robins. She obtained the records of a large group of children referred for treatment of delinquent behaviors and reexamined those individuals when they were adults. The study showed that it was not the specific type of behavior but rather the number of aggressive behaviors in childhood that was the greatest predictor of adult antisocial behavior. Other longitudinal studies have shown that childhood attention deficit hyperactivity disorder (ADHD) is also a predictor of adult antisocial behavior. However, 30 to 40 percent of children with ADHD also have conduct disorder, and it is the subgroup with conduct disorder that subsequently have problems with adult antisocial behavior.

Twin studies have shown that 70 to 90 percent of both conduct disorder and ADHD are due to genetic factors (Sherman, McGue, Iacono 1997; Slutske et al. 1997). A number of other disorders are very common in children and adolescents with conduct disorder and ADHD. These include learning disabilities, dyslexia, drug and alcohol abuse, and oppositional defiant disorder, all of which have a strong genetic component and all of which have also been implicated as risk factors for adult antisocial behavior.

These observations indicate that conduct disorder with or without ADHD (CD ± ADHD) is largely genetic, and, when present, it is a strong predictor of adult antisocial behavior. If we can

FIGURE 1.   Diagram of the Relative Importance of Environmental Versus Genetic Factors in Any Behavior, in This Case Violence

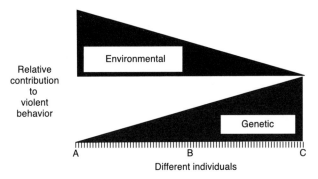

Relative contribution to violent behavior

Different individuals

identify the genetic factors associated with childhood CD ± ADHD we can begin to better understand the causes of aggressive, antisocial, criminal, and violent behavior in adults.

Understanding, treating, and preventing these behaviors depends on identifying *which* genes are involved. Because all behavior is ultimately regulated by the nerve chemicals that allow neurons to communicate with each other, it is reasonable to start by examining the genes that regulate these chemicals. The major neurotransmitters are dopamine, serotonin, norepinephrine, GABA, NMDA/glutamic acid, acetylcholine, and neuropeptides such as endorphins and enkephalins. The genes that relate to these neurochemicals include genes for the receptors (to which the neurotransmitters must bind to initiate their action on neurons), the transporters (which transport the neurotransmitters across cell membranes), and the enzymes (which are responsible for the synthesis and breakdown of the neurotransmitters). (A detailed listing of the specific genes that have been identified can be found in Comings.)

Behavioral disorders are polygenically inherited, which means they result from the additive effect of multiple genes. Individuals are affected when they inherit a sufficient number of variant genes to develop symptoms. In studies of the effect of many different genes on a range of behavioral phenotypes, it was found that each gene accounts for only 0.5 to 7.5 percent of the total picture (variance), with the average contribution being less than 2 percent. Studies examining the additive effect of over twenty different genes involved in neurotransmitter functions on CD + ADHD showed that, when combined, these genes accounted for 10 percent of the symptoms (Com-

ings). These results support the statement that there is no single gene for violence. These studies also showed that other behaviors that are common in children with CD + ADHD and likewise predictive of adult antisocial behavior, such as oppositional defiant disorder, learning disorders, and substance abuse, have these genes in common.

Though still in their infancy, these studies hold promise for understanding the biological basis for a risk of antisocial and violent behavior; they also provide new insights into methods of treating these disorders that are more effective and vastly less expensive than a lifetime of incarceration.

BIBLIOGRAPHY

Comings, David E. "Molecular Genetics of ADHD and Conduct Disorder: Relevance to the Treatment of Recidivistic Antisocial Behavior." In *Science, Treatment, and Prevention of Antisocial Behavior: Application to the Criminal Justice System,* edited by Diana Fishbein. New York: Civic Research Institute, 1998.

Robins, Lee N. *Deviant Children Grown Up: A Sociological and Psychiatric Study of Sociopathic Personality.* Baltimore: Williams and Wilkins, 1966.

Sherman, D. K., M. K. McGue, W. G. Iacono. "Twin Concordance for Attention Deficit Hyperactivity Disorder: A Comparison of Teachers' and Mothers' Reports." *American Journal of Psychiatry* 154 (1997): 532–535.

Slutske, Wendy S., et al. "Modeling Genetic and Environmental Influences in the Etiology of Conduct Disorder: A Study of 2,682 Adult Twin Pairs." *Journal of Abnormal Psychology* 106 (1997): 266–279.

DAVID E. COMINGS

See also **Developmental Factors; Nature vs. Nurture; Neurotransmitters.**

TWINS, FAMILIES, AND ADOPTIONS

Violence runs in families. This fact can reflect shared environment or shared genes; therefore, to determine the effects of genes on a given trait, behavioral geneticists employ adoption and twin studies to tease apart genetic from family environmental influences. Adoption studies allow estimates of the contribution of genetics and shared family environment by comparing the similarity of the adoptee to his or her biological and adoptive parents for a given trait. Such estimates can also be obtained by comparing the resemblance between members of monozygotic (MZ) twin pairs to that between members of dizygotic (DZ) twin pairs. MZ twins, known as identical twins, occur when a single fertilized egg splits and each half develops into a separate individual; MZ twins share 100 percent of their genes. DZ twins, known as fraternal twins, occur when two different eggs are fertilized by different sperm at the same time; DZ twins share about 50 percent of their genes, the same as any pair of non-twin siblings.

In genetically informative studies, the variance of an observed trait, or phenotype, is partitioned into three general sources: heritability (h^2); common, or shared family, environment (c^2); and unique, or nonshared, environment (u^2). Heritability refers to the proportion of the phenotypic (observed) variance attributable to genetic variability. Common environment refers to the proportion of phenotypic variance attributable to all of the environmental factors that members of a family share and that make them similar. Unique environment refers to the proportion of total variance attributable to all the idiosyncratic environmental experiences of an individual that create differences among relatives. Each source of variance can be visualized as a piece in a pie graph; although the size of each piece varies by trait, their sum equals the whole pie (see figure 1).

Data from twin and adoption studies on aggression and general antisocial behavior suggest a moderate heritability for both of these phenotypes, but it is important to be aware of how the behavior is measured. In studies that use psychometric measures of aggressive behavior, genes are estimated to account for anywhere from 20 to 70 percent of the individual differences in aggressive behavior.

FIGURE 1.   The Total Phenotypic Variance of any Given Trait Is Equal to the Sum of the Heritability (h^2), the Common Environment (c^2), and the Unique Environment (u^2)

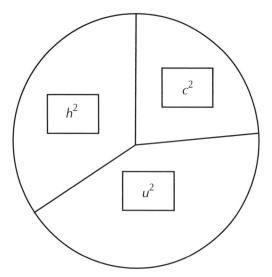

The majority of such studies report intermediate figures in the 40 to 50 percent range. In addition, genetic factors appear to be more influential in males than in females and to be more important in adulthood than in childhood or adolescence. Studies that assess antisocial behavior in other ways, such as through self-reported delinquency checklists, symptom counts, and court convictions, demonstrate a similar pattern of results.

Unlike genetic factors, common environmental influences appear to be more important in childhood than in adulthood for psychometric measures of aggression and for conduct disorder. Little is known, however, about the sources of shared family environmental influences. There is some evidence for sibling imitation effects on aggression and criminal behavior, suggesting a familial influence making siblings more similar than individuals in the general population. Still, in general, the family environment appears to be less important than a person's idiosyncratic environment for producing individual differences in aggression and antisocial behavior.

The influences of the environment may also depend on the genetic makeup (genotype) of an individual. Some studies report a significant interaction between genes and family environment, and others have found a nonsignificant trend in the same direction. That is, in the presence of a specific genetic factor, an adverse home environment may act as a catalyst for the production of antisocial behaviors. Conversely, individuals with a strong genetic predisposition to antisocial behavior may never express it if they are reared in a favorable environment.

A perplexing issue is that the consistent pattern of high heritability and low shared environment found in studies of aggression and antisocial behavior is not found in studies of serious violence (e.g., assault). One problem that plagues this area is the overlap among the definitions of antisocial personality, antisocial behavior, and violence. For example, violence has been defined by the American Psychiatric Association (1997) as "the exertion of any physical force, so as to injure or abuse another person or thing." In the association's *Diagnostic and Statistical Manual*, however, this is one of the diagnostic criteria for antisocial personality disorder, but it alone does not lead to an antisocial personality diagnosis.

The genetics, if any, of serious interpersonal violence may not follow the pattern of more general antisocial behaviors, as discussed earlier. Three large studies focusing on felonious, interpersonal violence failed to report significant heritability and have important internal contradictions among them. One study reported no familial resemblance between Danish adoptees and their biological relatives or between adoptees and their adoptive relatives for crimes against persons, suggesting neither genetic nor shared environmental influences. In a large twin study from Denmark, researchers reported strong familial resemblance in both MZ and DZ twins for crimes against persons, but there was no significant heritability. These two studies clearly contradict each other, because interpersonal violence does not run in families in one study (the adoptees) but does run in families in the other (the twins). The third study, of Swedish adoptees, found no correlation between the adopted children and their biological parents in terms of violent behavior. Given that none of these three large studies found any evidence for the heritability of violent crimes, one can conclude that there is as yet no solid evidence for a genetic contribution to interpersonal violence.

The failure to find significant heritability estimates for violence but consistently positive results for general antisocial behavior may be because of the indirect pathway by which genes may assert their effect on violence. For example, genes may have their primary influence on psychological traits that predispose an individual to general antisocial behavior that, in turn, confers liability toward violence. This view is consistent with the research on repeat offenders, which has found that people who engage in violent acts, but not other forms of criminal behavior, are rare. Most violent offenders have histories of nonviolent crime as well.

A second factor that might lead to low estimates of heritability for violence is an interaction between genotype and unique environment. An important aspect in the expression of violence is an environmental trigger. Like the alcoholic who needs to be exposed to alcohol to exhibit the behavior, an individual who is predisposed to violent behavior needs to be in a situation that provokes him or her to exhibit violence. These situations are likely to be unique, idiosyncratic experiences of the individual, as elaborated by many contextualists in criminology and sociology. In terms of behavioral genetics analysis, this type of interaction between genotype and unique environment reduces the estimate of heritability and increases the estimate of unique environment.

Clearly, the relationship among genes, environment, general antisocial behavior, and interpersonal violence is currently obscure; more empirical data are needed before any firm statements can be made.

Although twin and adoption studies have helped discriminate genetic from shared family environmental influences, the results of these studies must be interpreted with caution. One limitation of twin studies is the potential to underestimate shared environment, c^2. "The equal environments assumption of the twin method assumes that environmental similarity is roughly the same for both types of twins reared in the same family. If the assumption were violated because identical twins experience more similar environments than fraternal twins, this violation would inflate the estimates of genetic influence" (Plomin et al. 1997, p. 73), thereby underestimating common environment. Adoption studies may be limited by the selection of adoptive parents. The high standards to which adoptive parents are held leads to a restriction in the range of adoptive home environments, which in turn prevents (or at least greatly restricts) the study of adverse home environmental conditions.

There are several limitations in generalizing the results of twin and adoption studies to the general population. For example, the majority of large-scale twin and adoption studies have been conducted in Scandinavian countries, which are quite homogeneous in terms of socioeconomic status and ethnicity. Extrapolation of Scandinavian results to more heterogeneous societies, such as the United States, must always be done with caution. Furthermore, women are often not included in studies of violence and antisocial behavior, owing to the difficulties in obtaining adequate sample sizes. The research suggests that heritability may be different for women than for men, but small sample sizes means that it is difficult to discriminate such differential genetic effects. In addition, because most studies of violence have relied on court convictions and hospital records, factors involved in "getting caught," such as socioeconomic status, are confounded with those that influence the actual violent act. Thus standardization of the definition of violence comes at the expense of obtaining a truly random sample of violent individuals. Finally, it is also possible that the genetic and environmental architecture of aggression and violence may change over time. But this is often not assessed, because most studies employ a cross-sectional design. For example, many of the studies in this area are conducted on groups of individuals born before 1960, making it difficult to generalize findings to younger generations, who have experienced different environmental pressures and social norms.

From the 1950s to the 1990s, research found clear evidence supporting a genetic influence on general antisocial behavior, with estimates of heritability increasing over the life span. Research on genetic influences associated with interpersonal violence, however, remains inconclusive. Although much has been learned about aggression and violence, there is clearly a need for more research to focus on serious violence, to include adequate numbers of female subjects, and to follow the same sample of individuals over time to further our understanding of the development of these behaviors.

BIBLIOGRAPHY

Bohman, Michael, et al. "Predisposition to Petty Criminality in Swedish Adoptees: I. Genetic and Environmental Heterogeneity." *Archives of General Psychiatry* 39, no. 11 (November 1982).

Cadoret, Remi J., Colleen Cain, and Raymond Crowe. "Evidence for a Gene Environment Interaction in the Development of Adolescent Antisocial Behavior." *Behavior Genetics* 13, no. 3 (May 1983).

Carey, Gregory. "Genetics and Violence." In *Understanding and Preventing Violence*. Vol. 2, *Biobehavioral Influences on Violence*, edited by A. J. Reiss, Jr., and J. A. Roth. Washington, D.C.: National Academy, 1994.

Cloninger, C. Robert, and Irving Gottesman. "Genetic and Environmental Factors in Antisocial Behavior Disorders." In *The Causes of Crime: New Biological Approaches*, edited by S. A. Mednick, T. E. Moffitt, and S. A. Stack. New York: Cambridge University Press, 1987.

Elliott, Delbert S. "Serious Violent Offenders: Onset, Developmental Course, and Termination—The American Society of Criminology 1993 Presidential Address." *Criminology* 32, no. 1 (February 1994).

Lyons, Michael J., et al. "Differential Heritability of Adult and Juvenile Antisocial Traits." *Archives of General Psychiatry* 52, no. 11 (November 1995).

Mednick, Sarnoff A., William F. Gabrielli, Jr., and Barry Hutchings. "Genetic Influences in Criminal Convictions: Evidence from an Adoption Cohort." *Science* 224, no. 4651 (May 1984).

Miles, Donna R., and Greg Carey. "The Genetic and Environmental Architecture of Aggression." *The Journal of Personality and Social Psychology* 72, no. 1 (January 1997).

Plomin, R., et al. *Behavioral Genetics*. 3d ed. New York: W. H. Freeman, 1997.

Sigvardsson, Sören, et al. "Predisposition to Petty Criminality in Swedish Adoptees: III. Sex Differences and Validation of the Male Typology." *Archives of General Psychiatry* 39, no. 11 (November 1982).

CHAYNA J. DAVIS
CAROL A. VAN HULLE
COLLEEN M. COFFEY
GREGORY CAREY

See also **Developmental Factors; Intergenerational Transmission of Violence.**

GENOCIDE. *See* American Indian Holocaust; Holocaust; Mass Murder: Collective Murder.

GENOVESE, KITTY, MURDER OF

The killing of Catherine "Kitty" Genovese in 1964 is considered one of the most infamous and brutal murders of the twentieth century. It shocked the nation at the time and has continued to trouble people with its symbolism of urban apathy.

On 13 March 1964, at 3:20 A.M., twenty-eight-year-old Kitty Genovese returned home from work as a manager at a bar and parked her car 150 feet from her apartment at 82–70 Austin Street in Queens, New York, a residential borough of New York City. Genovese had walked only a few feet when a man came out of the shadows, stabbed her, and began to assault her sexually. As she screamed, lights blinked on in the apartment houses along Austin Street. For the next twenty-five minutes the attacker assaulted and stabbed Genovese until she eventually died just before 3:50 A.M.

Detectives investigating the murder discovered that no fewer than thirty-eight of Genovese's neighbors had witnessed from their windows at least one of the killer's three attacks on the young woman. Although the thirty-eight witnesses heard her cries for help and watched the assault, the first call to the police did not occur until some minutes after her death—almost half an hour after the attack had begun.

Expressions of outrage immediately came from public officials and private citizens not only in the New York area but across the United States. Days later, while the nation was still shocked over the witnesses' behavior during the crime, the following editorial comment appeared in the *New York Times*:

Seldom has the *Times* published a more horrifying story than its account of how thirty-eight respectable, law-abiding middle-class Queens citizens watched a killer stalk his young woman victim in a parking lot in Kew Gardens over a half-hour period, without one of them making a call to the police department that would have saved her life. They would not have been exposed to any danger themselves: a simple telephone call in the privacy of their own homes was all that was needed. How incredible it is that such motives as "I didn't want to get involved" deterred them from this act of simple humanity. Does residence in a great city destroy all sense of personal responsibility for one's neighbors? Who can explain such shocking indifference on the part of a cross section of our fellow New Yorkers?

Police officials conceded that there was no law that required someone witnessing a crime to report it to the authorities, but they contended that morality should oblige a witness to do so.

Less than a week after the murder, police arrested a suspect, twenty-nine-year-old Winston Moseley, a business-machine operator who lived with his wife and two children in another part of Queens. Although Moseley had no criminal record, he quickly confessed to the murders of Kitty Genovese and two other women. Moseley told police that he had "an uncontrollable urge to kill" and that he prowled the streets looking for victims while his wife was at work. Three months later he went on trial for the murder, pleading not guilty by reason of insanity and testifying in detail about how he had stalked and stabbed Genovese to satisfy this "uncontrollable urge." The jury, however, rejected the insanity defense and rendered a guilty verdict. One month later Judge J. Irwin Shapiro of the New York State Supreme Court sentenced Moseley to die in the electric chair at Ossining Correctional Facility (also known as Sing Sing). As he gave the sentencing order, Judge Shapiro commented: "When I see this monster, I wouldn't hesitate to pull the switch myself."

In 1967, three years after Moseley's conviction, the New York State Court of Appeals reduced his sentence to life imprisonment on grounds that Judge Shapiro had erred in refusing to admit evidence on Moseley's mental condition at a sentencing hearing. The following year, after being taken from prison to a hospital in Buffalo, New York, for minor surgery, Moseley struck a corrections officer, escaped, obtained a gun, and held five people hostage, raping one of them, before agents from the Federal Bureau of Investigation finally recaptured him. As of 1999, Moseley was still incarcerated.

In the decades after the murder of Kitty Genovese, scholars and legal reformers attempted to change the "no duty to aid" rule in both federal and state statutes, which as of 1999 still did not require affirmative aid to strangers in peril. At a 1997 University of Chicago Law School conference titled "The Good Samaritan and the Bad," a range of questions were raised about the scope of the "no duty to aid" rule:

> Is a citizen required, and should he be required, to lend assistance to another who is in danger of severe personal injury or substantial loss of property? Should it make any difference if the potential loss stems from the commission of a crime, or from accident, Act of God or other causes? Must the passer-by intervene only when he can do so at no peril to himself? Only when the peril to himself is less than the harm which the victim will suffer?

The "no duty to aid" rule and the murder of Kitty Genovese were recalled in 1998 during the trial of nineteen-year-old Jeremy Strohmeyer, who was found guilty for sexually assaulting and murdering seven-year-old Sherrice Iverson in a Nevada hotel bathroom. Strohmeyer's close friend David Cash had followed the two into the restroom and had observed the beginnings of the assault. But Cash failed to do anything about the attack or even report it. He just walked away and later stated that it was not his concern. Many felt that Cash should have been charged with complicity in the crime or at least obstruction of justice, but as the Clark County, Nevada, district attorney stated, Cash's inaction "may be a crime in the eyes of God, but not in the eyes of the Nevada legislature."

Despite the continuing debate, legislatures have been reluctant to modify the "no duty to aid" rule. They argue that it would be costly to enforce and would interfere with individual liberty. Only a few states—Vermont, Minnesota, Rhode Island, Colorado, Ohio, Massachusetts, Florida, and Washington—have enacted statutes requiring bystanders to aid someone in peril. Violation of such statutes is generally a petty misdemeanor.

BIBLIOGRAPHY

D'Amato, Anthony. "The Bad Samaritan Paradigm." *Northwestern University Law Review* 70 (1975).

Payne, Kathleen E. "Linking Tort Reform to Fairness and Moral Values." *Detroit College Law Review* (winter 1995).

Prentice, Robert A. "Expanding the Duty to Rescue." *Suffolk University Law Review* 19, no. 4 (1985).

Radcliffe, Elaine. "A Duty to Rescue: The Good, the Bad, and the Indifferent—The Bystander's Dilemma." *Pepperdine Law Review* 13 (1986).

Rosenthal, Abraham M. *Thirty-Eight Witnesses*. New York: McGraw-Hill, 1964.

Staub, Ervin. "The Psychology of Bystanders, Perpetrators, and Heroic Helpers." *International Journal of Intercultural Relations* 17 (1993).

JAMES A. INCIARDI

See also **Bystanders; New York.**

GENOVESE, VITO
(1897–1969)

Vito Genovese was present at the creation of the modern American Mafia. But he unwittingly helped transform this obscure (and thus hugely successful) criminal conspiracy into a primary target of federal law enforcers. He plotted some of the mob's most spectacular assassinations, led its move into narcotics trafficking, and helped plan an infamous gangland conclave that focused national attention on organized crime.

Genovese was born near Naples on 21 November 1897. He came to the United States in 1913, settled on New York City's Lower East Side, and became a small-time gangster, shaking down shopkeepers. In 1917 he met the fellow thief who would become his famous partner in crime, Charles "Lucky" Luciano. The two men moved into more organized crimes: bootlegging, prostitution, and narcotics. Dealing in narcotics had been viewed dimly by Mafia leaders, mostly because it meant more attention from police and stiffer penalties from judges.

In 1930 the pair became involved in a New York City Mafia conflict known as the Castellammarese War. They were part of a faction led by Joseph Masseria but tried to make peace with the rival boss, Salvatore Maranzano. When that effort failed, they decided to kill both men. Genovese and several other gunmen shot Masseria to death in a Brooklyn restaurant while Luciano, Masseria's dining companion, was in the men's room; Maranzano subsequently was killed in his Manhattan office by a squad of hit men whom Luciano and Genovese dressed up as police.

The city's Italian American gangsters arranged themselves into five "families," one headed by Luciano and Genovese, who made hundreds of thousands of dollars each year. But in 1937 Genovese ordered the murder of an underling, Ferdinand Boccia, who dared demand a cut of a card-game swindle; when the killing attracted the attention

Vito Genovese waits to be called before a Mercer County, New Jersey, grand jury, on 3 December 1957.
CORBIS/BETTMANN

of New York's mob-busting prosecutor, Thomas Dewey, Genovese fled to Italy and stayed there through World War II.

After the war he returned, won acquittal on the murder charge, and began to reassert his influence. He had several rivals murdered, including Albert Anastasia, who was shot to death in 1957 as he sat in the barbershop of a Manhattan hotel, his face covered with hot towels. Later that year, Frank Costello, the mobster the newspapers called the "Prime Minister of the Underworld," was ambushed as he walked into the lobby of his apartment house. The gunman fired at point blank range but only grazed Costello's scalp.

Genovese then called for a meeting of more than one hundred mob leaders from around the nation, apparently hoping to ratify his position as the top boss. The meeting was held at a mafioso's farm in Apalachin, New York, on 14 November 1957, but local police raided it. The Mafia, the existence of which the Federal Bureau of Investigation director J. Edgar Hoover had long denied, became an undeniable fact, and Genovese became a prime target of law enforcement.

Like most mob bosses, Genovese was insulated from street-level crimes but in 1959 he was identified as a participant in a heroin-dealing conspiracy. His accuser was a pusher named Nelson Cantellops, who claimed to have talked with Genovese about drugs, testimony that a police expert later called "almost unbelievable." Many have suspected he was framed by his mob rival, Carlo Gambino. Genovese was convicted and sentenced to fifteen years in federal prison. He died in the Leavenworth, Kansas, penitentiary on 14 February 1969, of a heart ailment.

BIBLIOGRAPHY

Abadinsky, Howard. *Organized Crime.* 3d ed. Chicago: Nelson-Hall, 1990.

Gage, Nicholas, ed. *Mafia, U.S.A.* Chicago: Playboy Press, 1972.

Sifakis, Carl. *The Mafia Encyclopedia.* New York: Facts on File, 1987.

RICK HAMPSON

See also **Costello, Frank; Gambino, Carlo; Luciano, "Lucky"; Mafia; Organized Crime.**

GEOGRAPHY OF VIOLENCE

That violence and geography would be linked comes as a surprise to many people. Geography, after all, is remembered by most as a rather tedious subject that was confined to coloring the states and learning state capitals in grade school. What could it possibly have to do with violence? Modern geography, in fact, goes beyond coloring and capitals and is now closely related to other social sciences in its methods and topical coverage. Just as violence can be viewed from the perspectives of history, sociology, and psychology, it can also be seen from a geographic viewpoint. What distinguishes the geographic approach is an emphasis on locations of events, just as an emphasis on time is the underpinning of history. Historians are, of course, concerned with much more than time; they are also concerned with processes. Likewise, geographers work with processes over geographic space, asking why violence varies so greatly from place to place.

Geographers' interest in violence roughly coincides with the realization within all the social sciences that each discipline has something useful to say about almost every imaginable topic having to do with human occupancy of the planet. Since the first two book-length treatments of the geography of crime in 1974 by Keith Harries and Gerald F. Pyle, studies have continued in a steadily increasing stream. Disciplinary distinctions have blurred, with contributions to the geography of violence coming from sociologists, criminologists and law enforcement specialists, social psychologists, epidemiologists, and others. Interest has been spurred by extraordinary increases in violence in the United States in the later decades of the twentieth century, and also by the geographic unevenness of that increase.

How can this geography of violence be best summarized? The approach used here is to examine violence at various geographic scales, starting with an international perspective, then focusing on regional variation within the United States, and finally zooming in to the metropolitan, city, and neighborhood levels. Violence is here taken to mean criminal violence rather narrowly defined to cover certain acts that would be regarded as violent by the typical law of a U.S. state. Thus, acts of terrorism or essentially political violence (violations of federal law) are excluded on the grounds that they are very rare events (particularly in the U.S. context) and as such have no particularly distinctive geographic patterning. The emphasis here is on murder and aggravated assaults. Rape is not emphasized, since its causal mechanisms are somewhat peculiar and geographic analysis is hobbled by the chronic underreporting of rape cases. Also excluded are acts of legal violence, such as a killing carried out by a police officer in the proper course of duty (justifiable homicide), and executions by the state. (The geography of state executions is quite distinctive, with a southern emphasis both historically and in the late twentieth century.) Our understanding of patterns of violence is assisted by the fact that crimes have a tendency to cluster; areas that are chronically afflicted with high crime rates tend to suffer from high rates of all types of crime, whether against property or persons, although some subtle regional variations do exist. Violent crimes are described here in terms of rates, which adjust counts of incidents for population. Clearly, it makes little sense to compare raw numbers of violent acts between countries, states, or cities, since these units vary so greatly in population size. Thus India has about forty thousand murders a year, the United States about twenty thousand. But India has nearly a billion people, the U.S. less than three hundred million, so when we adjust for population we find that India has a murder *rate* less than half that of the U.S.

International Variations in Violence

The rate of violent crime in the United States is among the highest in the world and is certainly the highest among developed nations, at least with respect to homicide, declines in the late 1990s notwithstanding. The United Nations *1992 Demographic Yearbook* cited homicide rates for the years 1990 to 1992 showing the U.S. rate at 10.0 per 100,000 persons, compared with 0.6 for the Republic of Ireland, 0.7 for the United Kingdom, 1.1 for France, and 2.1 for Canada. What factors explain these large variations? No simple answer is adequate. The effects of drug culture and levels of substance abuse in general, gun control laws, attitudes and laws relating to violence and violent offenders, the sociology of the family (particularly in relation to child rearing), economic conditions, and other factors all come into play. Explanation is complicated by the changing interplay of different conditions from one country or locality to another.

It is tempting to conclude that, since the poorest neighborhoods seem to be high-violence environments, poverty must cause violence. Yet when we compare the United States to India, we see an enormously greater number of poor people in India, typically living in conditions far worse than those seen in U.S. inner cities, where at least potable water and some degree of medical attention, education, and nutrition are available. The comparison also holds with respect to social status, since lower-caste Indians experience discrimination not entirely dissimilar to that suffered by certain U.S. minorities. This vast poverty in India would seem on its face to predict high levels of violence there; but

such a conclusion would ignore cultural factors like the virtually complete absence of private gun ownership, lower levels of substance abuse, and the Hindu ideals of tolerance and nonviolence that permeate society. Another complicating factor in examining international variations is that in some cultures political violence, interethnic or interclan vendetta-related violence, and terrorism may be common enough to blur the distinctions that are more easily drawn in societies where these types of violence are rare. Amid the genocide in the former Yugoslavia or Rwanda, for example, "ordinary" violence is for all intents and purposes statistically lost.

Regional Variations in the United States

When regional patterns are considered, a fundamental question centers on how rates of violent crime vary according to whether a place is urban or rural. This question is not quite as straightforward as it may seem, owing to the way in which places are classified. As noted in table 1, one approach to classification is to divide areas into metropolitan areas, other cities, and rural areas. In this approach, "metropolitan" refers to combinations of socially and economically integrated counties centered on at least one city with a population of at least fifty thousand. Such Consolidated Metropolitan Statistical Areas (CMSAs) may be large: Chicago includes the counties of Cook, DeKalb, Du Page, Grundy, Kane, Kendall, Lake, McHenry, and Will. They may also be small, as in the case of the Chico-Paradise CMSA in California, composed of Butte County only. CMSAs may include large rural areas, tending to confuse the metropolitan-rural distinction. However, CMSAs do include all large "central" cities that tend to have high levels of violence. Table 1 shows violent crime rates combined

TABLE 1.   Violent Crime Rates per 100,000 Inhabitants by Offense and Extent of Urbanization, 1994

Area	Violent Crime	Murder and Nonnegligent Manslaughter	Forcible Rape	Robbery	Aggravated Assault
U.S.	716.0	9.0	39.2	237.7	430.2
CMSAs*	812.0	10.0	41.2	288.5	472.4
Other cities	500.3	4.8	39.3	74.6	381.7
Rural	236.6	5.0	26.3	16.8	188.6

*Metropolitan Statistical Area (made up of counties).

SOURCE: Maguire, Kathleen, and Ann L. Pastore, eds. *Sourcebook of Criminal Justice Statistics 1995*. U.S. Department of Justice, Bureau of Justice Statistics. Washington, D.C.: U.S. Government Printing Office, 1996. Table 3.110, p. 325.

(Violent Crime) and also broken down into their component offenses. The highest rates are found in CMSAs, where murder rates, for example, are at least twice those of "other cities" and "rural." "Other cities" (cities with populations under fifty thousand that lie outside CMSAs) generally fall outside the orbit of metropolitan areas and are more likely to lack close urban neighbors and to be embedded in more purely rural contexts. Rural areas have the lowest violence rates, with homicide, rape, and assault rates roughly half those of CMSAs. Robbery is exceptionally low in rural areas, with rates only 6 percent of those in CMSAs, reflecting in part lower levels of robbery opportunity in rural environments.

When city violent crime rates are viewed from the perspective of a more detailed breakdown of city size, quite a strong relationship is found between size class and rate. Almost without exception, larger cities have higher rates of violence than smaller, whether violence is viewed in aggregate terms or broken down into component crimes. Data for eight size classes of cities from 1973 to 1990 revealed almost no cases of smaller size classes with higher rates of violence than larger.

Generalized classification masks regional variations, however. It does not follow that simply because a given area is rural it will necessarily have lower rates of violence than a particular urban place, as illustrated in figure 1 (on p. 34), showing county-level homicide rates per 10,000 persons. A

zone of counties, some metropolitan, some rural, in what could be roughly described as the Piedmont-Coastal region of Georgia, the Carolinas, and Virginia has intermediate homicide rates equivalent to 1.0 to 26 per 100,000. In contrast, counties in northern states tend to have lower rates. Note that large western counties tend to show up more prominently on maps simply because of their size. California's 20,000-square-mile San Bernardino county, for example, is twenty-one times larger than Cook County, Illinois. It should also be pointed out that the data shown in figure 1 represent but a single year.

Historically, the South and West have tended toward higher rates of violent crime, particularly homicide, and this is reflected in figure 1. The map should be reviewed in conjunction with table 2, listing the top twelve states for violent crime rates. If we disregard Washington, D.C., which is more appropriately regarded as a city than a state for the purposes of this discussion, seven of the top eleven homicide states were in the South in 1994, and overall only one southern state (West Virginia) was ranked lower than twenty-fifth. Although no sweeping conclusions about regional patterns can be drawn, it is worth noting that three of the ten notorious public-school-based multiple murders in the 1990s occurred in the South: in Mississippi (three killed, seven wounded), Kentucky (three killed, five wounded), and Arkansas (five killed, ten wounded). The importance of the West was

TABLE 2. Top Twelve States According to Rates of Violent Crime per 100,000 Inhabitants, 1994

		Violent Crime		Murder and Nonnegligent Manslaughter	
Rank	State	Rate		State	Rate
—	U.S.	716.0		U.S.	9.0
1	District of Columbia	2,662.6		District of Columbia	70.0
2	Florida	1,146.8		Louisiana	19.8
3	South Carolina	1,030.5		Mississippi	15.3
4	California	1,013.0		Arkansas	12.0
5	Nevada	1,001.9		Alabama	11.9
6	Louisiana	981.9		California	11.8
7	New York	965.6		Illinois	11.7
8	Illinois	960.9		Nevada	11.7
9	Maryland	948.0		Maryland	11.6
10	New Mexico	889.2		New York	11.1
11	Alaska	766.3		Texas	11.0
12	Michigan	766.1		North Carolina	10.9

SOURCE: Maguire, Kathleen, and Ann L. Pastore, eds. *Sourcebook of Criminal Justice Statistics 1995.* U.S. Department of Justice, Bureau of Justice Statistics. Washington, D.C.: U.S. Government Printing Office, 1996. Table 3.113, p. 336.

FIGURE 1. Homicide Rates per 10,000 Inhabitants, U.S. Counties, 1996

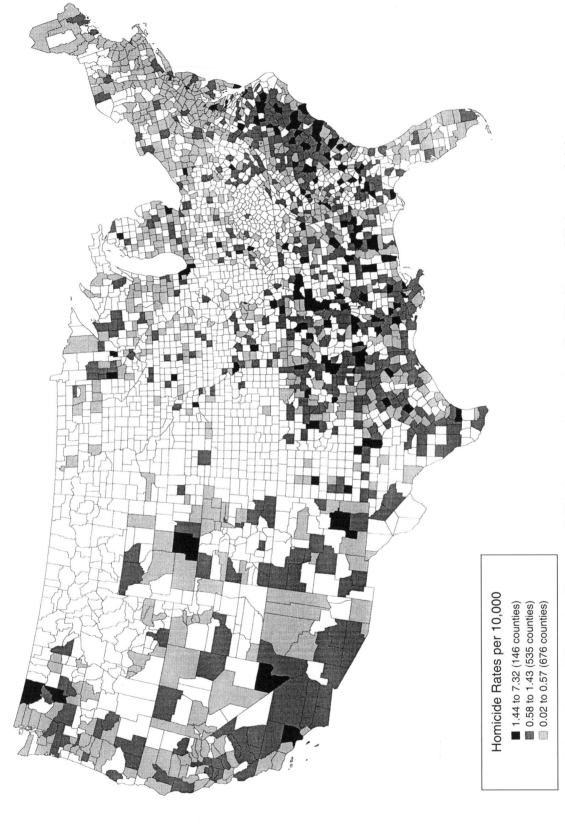

Homicide Rates per 10,000

- 1.44 to 7.32 (146 counties)
- 0.58 to 1.43 (535 counties)
- 0.02 to 0.57 (676 counties)

Rates were calculated only for the 1,357 counties with more than 10,000 inhabitants and at least one homicide in 1996. Hawaii and Alaska were excluded. SOURCE: Department of Justice, Federal Bureau of Investigation. Uniform Crime Reporting Program Data (United States). County Level Detailed Arrest and Offense Data, 1996. Made available through the Inter-university Consortium for Political and Social Research at the University of Michigan.

tragically underscored by the fifteen deaths at Columbine High School in Littleton, Colorado, in April 1999.

The persistence of the southern pattern is sometimes referred to in the literature as the southern violence construct. Why and how is the South different, and why should it seem to be more prone to violence? This question has generated a stream of research, beginning with articles by Stuart Lottier (1938) and Lyle W. Shannon (1954). Debate began in earnest, however, following publication of a historical analysis by Sheldon Hackney (1969). In the resulting research, arguments have tended to fall into two broad categories: cultural and economic. The cultural position, outlined initially by Hackney and elaborated by Raymond D. Gastil and others, suggests that the southern way of life differs markedly from that in the rest of the country, as reflected in child-rearing practices, levels of gun ownership and use, the South's historically rural and military orientation, and a more traditional concept of honor according to which an individual who feels that his honor has been challenged is more likely to react violently. Also relevant is the history of slavery in the South, with its implication that violent means could be used to control an entire class of people. With respect to the firearms issue, southerners tend to report consistently higher levels of gun ownership and of agreement with the proposition that gun ownership is the best defense against criminals.

Those such as Colin Loftin and R. H. Hill adhering to the economic position argue that higher rates of violence in the South are the result of the historically depressed economic position of the region, with its dependence on primary modes of production, such as plantation agriculture. Essentially, there is more violence in the South because poverty has been more prevalent there. The modern inner city is analogous; we should expect to see more violence in the South just as we should expect more in our deprived inner cities. As research has continued, the complexity of the issue has become apparent, and it is now clear that no one factor, such as levels of gun ownership, can provide a satisfactory explanation. For example, research has shown that although gun ownership is higher in the South than in other regions, it is highest in the rural South, where rates of violence are lower than in the urban South.

Our entire conceptualization of the regionalization of violence issue was challenged by a 1995 analysis (Whitt and colleagues suggested that homicide should not be examined in isolation from suicide). The authors' combined measure of violence (mean lethal violence) had high values in both the South and West, implying that a focus on the South may not be entirely appropriate.

Cultural and subcultural interpretations of regional variations in violence have not fared well in the research literature, although they seem plausible in intuitive and anecdotal terms. However, 1990s opinion polls suggest some convergence in attitudes among regions and possible blurring of regional distinctions. Furthermore, from an analytical perspective, economic indicators are more readily available than cultural indicators from census and other sources, and the apparent weakness of cultural models may be attributable in part to measurement difficulties. (For a review of regional interpretations of violence, see Harries 1997 and also Mackellar and Yanagishita 1995.)

Comparing Cities

Comparative rates of violence as expressed by homicide rates for the top twelve large U.S. cities are shown in table 3. The list may be surprising not so much for the cities that are on it as for those that are not, such as Los Angeles (23.8/100,000) and New York (21.3/100,000). The ranking of cities is partly a function of their "real" level of violence, but also of the way that their boundaries are drawn. Cities that are "underbounded" (to exclude suburbs) will tend to show up with higher rates. Cities

TABLE 3. Top Twelve Cities with Populations over 250,000 According to Homicide Rates per 100,000 Inhabitants, 1994

City	Homicide Rate
New Orleans, La.	85.8
District of Columbia	70.0
St. Louis, Mo.	63.5
Detroit, Mich.	52.9
Birmingham, Ala.	49.8
Atlanta, Ga.	46.4
Baltimore, Md.	43.4
Oakland, Calif.	36.9
Newark, N.J.	35.4
Chicago, Ill.	33.1
Kansas City, Mo.	32.3
Miami, Fla.	30.5

SOURCE: Maguire, Kathleen, and Ann L. Pastore, eds. *Sourcebook of Criminal Justice Statistics 1995.* U.S. Department of Justice, Bureau of Justice Statistics. Washington, D.C.: U.S. Government Printing Office, 1996. Table 3.117, p. 340.

like Los Angeles that are highly suburban will see high inner-city violence rates diluted by suburbs when an overall statistical picture is drawn. Western U.S. cities, being newer, are more likely to have generous boundaries including suburbs and are therefore more likely to have apparently lower violence rates. The converse will tend to be true for older eastern cities, like Baltimore. Thus, uncritical comparisons between city rates of violence may not be very meaningful. The central problem is to determine which comparisons are valid.

Urban Violence

Study after study of U.S. cities suggests a link between poverty and other forms of deprivation on the one hand and violent crime on the other. The link is so strong that it is tempting to go to the next level and announce a causal relationship. Here we should recall H. L. Mencken's remark to the effect that for every question there is an answer that is simple, straightforward, and wrong. But for a fuller understanding one must consider multiple complex relationships that include not only poverty but also race relations and the effects of racial discrimination; family structure (including child-rearing practices); the effects of the welfare system; the impact of the media; the role of substance abuse and addiction; unemployment; the quality of public schools, policing, courts, and corrections systems; housing quality; the adequacy of the transportation system; firearms availability; and health care.

All these factors are relevant, all vary geographically, all interact with each other, and none can be pointed to in isolation as the cause of violence. However, several if not all the relevant factors tend to occur in neighborhood clusters and define urban areas that are pathologically blighted. In a study of juvenile shootings in Baltimore, Keith Harries and Andrea Powell (1994) developed an index of urban pathology and found a strong correspondence between high values of the index and the occurrence of shootings. Such findings are typical, as are extraordinary variations in the geographic distribution of violence. Albert J. Reiss and Jeffrey A. Roth (1993), for example, noted that of all Minneapolis addresses, 97.8 percent experienced no robberies in 1986, while eight locations had more than twenty calls apiece, exemplifying spatial gradients in violence commonplace in U.S. cities.

Details of the demographics of violence—concentration among African Americans and young men—can be found elsewhere in this volume. From a geographic perspective it is sufficient to note that salient demographic characteristics vary geographically. Poor, young African American men tend to be concentrated in the central parts of cities and tend to be the most frequent victims and offenders. For the period 1989–1991, the homicide rate for whites in the United States was 5.7 per 100,000; for blacks it was 38.8. Some 55.8 percent of those arrested for homicide in 1994 were African Americans, although blacks constituted only about 12 percent of the total population. Such statistics tend to lead to the conclusion that race is somehow related to violence. Rigorous analysis as well as commonsense observation refute this; when the effects of poverty are removed statistically, race has no significant residual effect. It is *poor* African American neighborhoods that have high rates of violence; middle-class black neighborhoods or middle-class black persons in predominantly white neighborhoods exhibit behaviors that are stereotypically middle-class.

Violence and the Weather

From time to time—particularly during long, hot, humid summers—media attention turns to the role of the weather in the generation of violence. Our folklore is steeped in the sense that hot weather somehow causes violence. Even Shakespeare referred to the "mad blood" being stirred by hot weather. Analysis suggests that heat has an effect that is at best marginal. Much more powerful are influences such as day of the week or hour of the day, with weekend evenings especially troublesome. The fact that aggravated assaults peak in the summer does not necessarily inform us about heat. Summer is a time of greater personal interaction and perhaps of greater alcohol consumption, as more beverages are consumed to counter summer thirst. In this regard heat could be indicted as an indirect cause at best. Although clinical psychological evidence suggests that behavior is degraded by exposure to heat, it is difficult to translate this into a direct connection between hot weather and violence. Indeed, such studies have raised the question of a relationship between cold weather and the potentially violent behavior of people cooped up and suffering from cabin fever.

Conclusion

Violence is a subset of criminal behavior, and as such it is subject to wide geographic variation in response to differences in social and physical environments. The fundamental control is the geography of population. By definition, people must be present for violence in some form to occur. One person is the minimum needed for suicide, two or more for other forms of violence. Thus, the global geography of violence is first and foremost a reflection of where people are located. As we are able to learn more about the geographies of cultural factors, our understanding is then enhanced. Ultimately, people make decisions to commit violent acts in the context of their local, regional, and national ways of life.

BIBLIOGRAPHY

Gastil, Raymond D. *Cultural Regions of the United States.* Seattle: University of Washington Press, 1975.

———. "Homicide and a Regional Culture of Violence." *American Sociological Review* 36 (1971).

Hackney, Sheldon. "Southern Violence." *American Historical Review* 74 (1969).

Harries, Keith. *The Geography of Crime and Justice.* New York: McGraw-Hill, 1974.

———. *Serious Violence: Patterns of Homicide and Assault in America.* 2nd ed. Springfield, Ill.: Charles C. Thomas, 1997.

Harries, Keith, and Derral Cheatwood. *The Geography of Execution: The Capital Punishment Quagmire in America.* Lanham, Md.: Rowman and Littlefield, 1997.

Harries, Keith, and Andrea Powell. "Juvenile Gun Crime and Social Stress: Baltimore, 1980–1990." *Urban Geography* 15 (1994).

Harries, Keith, Stephen Stadler, and R. T. Zdorkowski. "Seasonality and Assault: Explorations in Interneighborhood Variation, Dallas, 1980." *Annals of the Association of American Geographers,* 74 (1984).

Loftin, Collin, and R. H. Hill. "Regional Subculture and Homicide: An Examination of the Gastil-Hackney Thesis." *American Sociological Review* 39 (1974).

Lottier, Stuart. "Distribution of Criminal Offenses in Sectional Regions." *Journal of Criminal Law and Criminology* 29 (1938).

Mackellar, F. Landis, and M. Yanagishita. *Homicide in the United States: Who's at Risk?* Washington, D.C.: Population Reference Bureau, Inc., 1995.

Pyle, Gerald F., et al. *The Spatial Dynamics of Crime.* Chicago: University of Chicago Press, 1974.

Reiss, Albert J., and Jeffrey A. Roth, eds. *Understanding and Preventing Violence.* Washington, D.C.: National Academy Press, 1993.

Shannon, Lyle W. "The Spatial Distribution of Criminal Offenses by States." *Journal of Criminal Law and Criminology* 45 (1954).

Whitt, H. P., J. Corzine, and L. Huff-Corzine. "Where Is the South? A Preliminary Analysis of the Southern Subculture of Violence." In *Trends, Risks, and Interventions in Lethal Violence,* edited by C. Block and R. Block. Washington, D.C.: National Institute of Justice, 1995.

KEITH HARRIES

See also **Rural Violence; South; Suburban Violence; Urban Violence; West.**

GERMAN AMERICANS

The popular reputation of German Americans as a model immigrant group that quickly assimilated into the ranks of "white" America is a relatively recent development. In fact, throughout much of the nineteenth and early twentieth century, many Americans viewed German immigrants as a cultural and political threat. As the largest non-English-speaking immigrant group during this time period, German Americans appeared to many native-born Americans to be taking over many cities. This perception only increased as German Americans successfully sought to preserve their language and culture (albeit within the bounds of loyal American citizenship). For example, thousands of parochial schools flourished in which German was the primary language of instruction. Many cities adopted German-English bilingual education programs in their elementary public schools. Some regions, such as the Mississippi and Ohio River Valleys, began printing ballots in German and passing ordinances requiring cities to publish public announcements in German-language newspapers. It is important to note that German Americans were often sharply divided along regional, religious, and political lines but reunited when their shared cultural heritage came under attack. Divisions among German Americans, however, were often ignored by fearful native-born Americans, who lashed out against what they perceived as an intruding monolithic German influence. German Americans often responded in kind.

With the onset of the Industrial Revolution in Germanic countries during the early nineteenth century, preindustrial trades quickly disappeared and vast numbers of workers were unable to find employment within the adolescent industrial economy. By comparison, the United States had a relative shortage of workers during this period. In the 1840s and 1850s, German immigrants arrived at unprecedented rates (435,000 in 1841–1850; 952,000 in 1851–1860) and soon formed a substantial minority in many urban economies. Driven by a combination of political, economic, and social fears, many native-born Americans flocked to the Know-Nothing Party (American Party). Playing upon these fears, the Know-Nothing Party enjoyed a brief but meteoric rise during the early 1850s by espousing a strong anti-immigrant and anti-Catholic platform. In 1855 voters in Chicago elected Levi Boone, a Know-Nothing candidate, as mayor. Boone soon ordered the Sunday closing of all taverns and raised the price for liquor licenses by 600 percent. To the city's German workers, this was a clear attack upon their traditions. The police selectively enforced this blue law by charging the German saloon keepers but ignoring the most respectable taverns in operation. In addition, the rise in liquor license fees forced many of the taverns catering to working-class Germans to close. When the German taverns continued to operate without licenses, the city moved in to arrest over 200 Germans. The city's Germans protested and clashed with police in a melee, known as the Lager Beer Riots, that ended with the death of one German, the severe injury of one policeman, and an unknown number of other injuries. Upon reflection, the mayor decided to rescind his orders. In the same year, Louisville exploded into brutal riots over perceived undue influence by Germans in the

city's politics. Following attempts to block Germans and other undesirable immigrants from voting, pitched battles between nativists and German Americans left the city smoldering with twenty-two persons killed and hundreds wounded. Though this cycle of violence diminished in the wake of growing sectional tensions that gave rise to the Republican Party and the Civil War, German Americans did not quickly forget these attacks.

During the national rush toward industrial power in the wake of the Civil War, German Americans were at the forefront of the labor movement. Though most German Americans did not embrace the more radical workers' protest movements such as socialism and anarchy, German immigrants were natural scapegoats in the midst of the ensuing labor violence and strikes. This was most readily visible in the Haymarket Square Riots in 1886. During an otherwise peaceful labor rally in Chicago, the police attempted to break up the gathering. In the middle of the confusion, someone tossed a bomb into the crowd, killing one police officer and injuring many others. Desperate to find the culprits, police arrested the leaders of the Chicago anarchist organization, five of whom were German immigrants. They were sentenced to

A pro-Hitler rally of the German-American Bund, 18 May 1934, at Madison Square Garden in New York City. HULTON GETTY/LIAISON AGENCY

death, not on the basis of physical or circumstantial evidence, but because it was supposed that their un-American, radical ideas had incited the violence. Though three of the five convicted Germans were later pardoned, many Americans regarded this episode as confirmation of the subversive and violent influence of Germans and other immigrants within American society.

The last widespread outbreak of violence against German Americans occurred in the aftermath of U.S. entry into World War I. While the United States was neutral, most German Americans endorsed Germany and attempted to influence U.S. policy in favor of their ancestral homeland. After the U.S. declaration of war, however, most German Americans declared their loyalty to the United States. Nevertheless, a vigorous anti-German propaganda campaign by the Committee on Public Information, an executive committee created by Woodrow Wilson and run by presidential appointee George Creel, soon created a public backlash against those who had until recently supported the enemy. Many states began enacting legislation not only outlawing German-language instruction but also limiting the use of German in public settings. Venerable German-language newspapers were forced to close across the nation. Violence against German Americans became commonplace as children coming home from German-language schools were stoned, suspected German sympathizers were tarred and feathered, and German American businesses and homes were vandalized. The most publicized incident occurred in the spring of 1918 when a transient miner with suspected radical labor sentiments was lynched in Collinsville, Illinois. In contrast to previous, more localized outbreaks of violence against them, most German Americans acquiesced in the face of this nationwide hysteria. Only in the more isolated rural settlements did German Americans continue to preach and teach in their mother tongue with relatively minor opposition. Elsewhere, however, this violence hastened the end of most German American cultural and political institutions and sped the group's assimilation into the mainstream of American society.

In the 1930s, however, a minority of German Americans attempted to lash out at their own scapegoats through the German-American Bund, a pro-Nazi group with loose ties to Germany. The organization's violent anti-Semitic rhetoric often sparked minor street violence similar to that surrounding Ku Klux Klan meetings in the late twen-

tieth century. Though German Americans were slow to condemn this movement publicly, the vast majority of the Bund's modest membership were recent German immigrants rather than established German Americans. The organization attracted considerable national attention beyond its numerical size and influence through well-publicized rallies as well as photographs taken with Hitler during the 1936 Berlin Olympics. Scandals within the Bund's leadership discredited the organization even before U.S. entry into World War II led to its dismantling. During this war, however, German Americans were not targeted as scapegoats. Instead, the Japanese Americans had taken their place.

In part, this shift in public attitudes can be attributed to the degree to which German Americans had already permeated all aspects of mainstream American society, from the military to business. German Americans, for better or worse, had completed the journey from scorned interlopers to respected members of the establishment.

BIBLIOGRAPHY

Diamond, Sander. *The Nazi Movement in the United States, 1924–1941.* Ithaca, N.Y.: Cornell University Press, 1974.

Kamphoefner, Walter, et al., eds. *News from the Land of Freedom: German Immigrants Write Home.* Ithaca, N.Y.: Cornell University Press, 1991.

Luebke, Frederick. *Bonds of Loyalty: German-Americans and World War I.* DeKalb: Northern Illinois University Press, 1974.

PAUL R. FESSLER

See also **Immigration.**

GETTYSBURG, BATTLE OF. *See* Civil War.

GHETTO VIOLENCE. *See* Gangs; Urban Violence.

GHOST DANCE. *See* Wounded Knee, 1980; Wovoka.

GIANCANA, SAM
(1908–1975)

Sam Giancana rose swiftly to power in the violent underworld of Chicago, the city where he was born. His Sicilian-born parents settled in the Patch, a poor and predominantly Italian neighborhood. Adolescent street gangs proliferated in Chicago's ethnic neighborhoods, and Salvatore "Sam" Giancana, a dropout in the seventh grade, was engaging in petty theft and other misdemeanors even before puberty.

Giancana demonstrated leadership qualities throughout adolescence. He organized the "42 Gang," many of whose members carried out mob hits for Al Capone and other Chicago organized crime leaders. His skills as a driver of getaway vehicles and his organizational abilities brought him to the attention of the men who ran Chicago's legendary Outfit, the name given to the multiethnic organized crime group whose leaders developed mutually supportive relationships with so many of the elected officials of Chicago and Cook County.

After World War II Giancana and his Chicago associates, like many of their peers across the nation, saw the potential of investing in Nevada. Nearby California's population was booming, and voters in Nevada were increasingly willing to elect reform administrations that aimed to put an end

Sam Giancana. LIBRARY OF CONGRESS

to the cozy relationship between politicians and bookies, thus making gambling more inviting. Both these factors enhanced Nevada's attractiveness as a place for investment. Giancana took the approach of most of the Italian-American organized crime leaders and invested silently in the casinos on the Las Vegas Strip and in Lake Tahoe. His visits to these casinos drew increasing media attention following the revelations of a meeting of Italian-American organized crime figures at Apalachin, New York, in the fall of 1957. While Giancana used aliases and other means of deception to avoid the media spotlight, his long-term affair with entertainer Phyllis McGuire made him even more newsworthy. Surveillance by federal law enforcement agents was even more troublesome for the reputed head of Chicago's underworld.

Giancana and several other organized crime leaders from across the United States sought to "turn down the heat"—to have the constant surveillance called off, or at least reduced—by helping to elect John Kennedy president. In spite of their dislike of Robert Kennedy, they provided his brother with support that proved crucial to his 1960 victory. When Attorney General Robert Kennedy launched a renewed campaign against organized crime, Giancana and his partners felt betrayed and angry. Several of them, probably including Giancana, were also involved with Central Intelligence Agency officials eager to eliminate Fidel Castro; the Kennedy administration's failure to get rid of Castro along with what they saw as a lack of gratitude for their support added to their frustration.

Sam Giancana spent more and more time outside the United States in the years following the 1963 assassination of Kennedy. He traveled to Europe, the Middle East, and the Caribbean. Seeking relief from the prying eyes of law enforcement agents, he moved to Mexico. As increasing numbers of journalists, scholars, and even members of Congress questioned the lone-assassin explanation of the Warren Commission, Giancana's travels lent credence to the suggestion that he was involved in President Kennedy's death. Evidence, however, was circumstantial or based on hearsay.

In 1974 the Mexican government responded to pressure from its powerful neighbor to the north and deported Giancana. In the spring of the following year, he was subpoenaed by the Senate Select Committee on Intelligence to testify regarding his connection to the CIA's plot to assassinate Castro. Sam Giancana was scheduled to testify on 24

June 1975. But on 19 June 1975 he was murdered in typical gangland fashion. A few hours after Giancana had dinner with family members in his suburban Chicago home, an experienced hit man entered the basement area and pumped enough carefully aimed bullets into the skull of the most prominent of the Chicago Outfit's leaders to ensure immediate death. The funeral, too, was predictably gangland style with numerous reporters, Federal Bureau of Investigation agents, and local police rubbing shoulders with organized crime associates and family members.

BIBLIOGRAPHY

Giancana, Antoinette, and Thomas C. Renner. *Mafia Princess: Growing Up in Sam Giancana's Family.* New York: Avon, 1985.
Giancana, Sam, and Chuck Giancana. *Double Cross.* New York: Warner, 1992.
Reid, Ed, and Ovid Demaris. *The Green Felt Jungle.* New York: Pocket, 1964.

ALAN BALBONI

See also **Capone, Al; Chicago; Mafia; Organized Crime.**

GILMORE, GARY
(1940–1977)

Soon after the U.S. Supreme Court upheld the constitutionality of capital punishment in 1976, a Utah firing squad shot Gary Mark Gilmore to death, making him the first person to be executed in the United States in more than ten years, and his case one of the most controversial in the nation's history. An editorial written at the time expressed the hope that given Gilmore's well-publicized desire to be executed, the act would be remembered as a state-assisted suicide. In fact, Gilmore twice attempted suicide while waiting for his death sentence to be carried out. Despite numerous efforts to block the execution by the American Civil Liberties Union and other opponents of the death penalty, Gary Gilmore insisted on being put to death.

Gilmore, the second of four sons, was born in Texas while his parents were en route to California after running from the most recent scam they had committed in Alabama. Gilmore was originally named Faye Robert, but upon exiting Texas his parents ripped up his birth certificate. The family moved often before finally settling in Portland, Oregon, where Gary began his criminal career at

the age of thirteen. He spent a year in reform school.

On 7 October 1976 Gilmore was sentenced for the murder of two young Mormon men in Utah. He robbed a gas-station attendant and then shot him twice in the head. The following day he drove to a motel and ordered the clerk to lie down on the floor. Gilmore shot him in the head and then left with the motel's cashbox. There was a brief trial in which Gilmore was rapidly found guilty, in no small measure because of his menacing looks at the jury and his belligerent testimony.

After the sentence was handed down, Gilmore waived all rights to appeal and requested that his execution be carried out. The Utah Supreme Court, Governor Calvin Rampton of Utah, and the U.S. Supreme Court all issued stays over his objections. However, after the pardons board decided to allow the execution to go forward and after Gilmore's

Gary Gilmore, on 15 December 1976, arriving at the Provo, Utah, courthouse to be told his third date for execution. CORBIS/BETTMANN

mother withdrew her legal opposition at her son's request, the U.S. Supreme Court lifted the stay. A firing squad executed Gilmore at a cannery warehouse behind the state prison on 17 January 1977.

That date marked a turning point in the national consensus on the death penalty. In the decade preceding Gilmore's death, there had been a steep decline in federal and state government executions: from 1965 to 1977, only ten people were put to death, in contrast to 3,859 from 1930 to 1971. The Gilmore case, however, imparted renewed momentum to advocates of capital punishment. In 1977 there were only 123 prisoners on death row; by 1983 the number had risen dramatically to 1,209, and by 1989 it had nearly doubled to 2,250. Very few were actually executed, however: from 1977 to 1989, only 120 prisoners were put to death.

Although the period after Gilmore's death did see a marked rise in the number of executions in the United States, most of the increase was confined to the states that had implemented capital punishment most often before the moratorium of the 1960s and early 1970s that resulted from diminishing support for capital punishment in the United States and other Western countries. For example, Texas, Florida, Georgia, and Louisiana— the country's past leaders in capital punishment— carried out thirty-six of the fifty executions that occurred from 1977 to 1985. This largely regional upswing had national implications, however; at the end of the twentieth century, more than 70 percent of Americans polled favored the death penalty.

In 1979 Norman Mailer published *The Executioner's Song*, a fictionalized account of the Gilmore case.

BIBLIOGRAPHY

Gilmore, Mikal. *Shot in the Heart*. New York: Doubleday, 1994.

DEIRDRE M. BOWEN

See also **Capital Punishment.**

G-MEN

The G-man, or special agent of the Federal Bureau of Investigation—like the FBI itself and like its most famous director, J. Edgar Hoover—was the stuff of fact and myth, a composite persona created by pulp magazines, film, radio, and television. The nature of the G-man's identity, in both popular entertainment and reality, was bound up with a relentless search for truth and lies, for good guys and bad guys. The G-man was an icon of U.S. watchfulness, a symbol of security in the rugged-individual mode, and a focus of paranoid fears of a perceived communist threat.

A New Breed of Hero

The history of G-men is a mundane affair that has little to do with their Hollywood image and is firmly grounded in popular conceptions of crime and criminality in the 1930s. The Great Depression brought grave concerns over the increase in violent crime, among other things, and the daily headlines focused on the violent exploits of rumrunners and petty thugs. The St. Valentine's Day Massacre of 1929 (a violent shoot-out between the gangs of Al Capone and George "Bugs" Moran in Chicago) and the John Dillinger jailbreaks of 1933 and 1934 were big news stories because they epitomized the romantic myth of the daring criminal mastermind. In the same way, figures like "Dutch" Schultz (Arthur Flegenheimer), Capone, and George "Machine Gun" Kelly were all, at various times, labeled "Public Enemy Number One," a catchy tag that raised newspaper circulations as well as domestic fears. Hollywood movies like *Little Caesar* (1931) and *The Public Enemy* (1931) showed Edward G. Robinson and James Cagney as exotic types living the thrill-a-minute life of the gangster.

It fell to Attorney General Homer S. Cummings to counterbalance the growing public love affair with the new breed of criminal, which he did by melodramatically declaring a war on crime and designating the tiny, undermanned FBI as the government's elite strike force. The FBI, created in 1908, was under the purview of the Justice Department and was largely used to hound communists, playing a major part in the 1919–1920 Red Scare raids (also known as the Palmer raids, after Alexander Mitchell Palmer, the U.S. attorney general who initiated them), in which three thousand allegedly subversive foreign-born residents were rounded up for deportation.

Initially, the FBI had 460 field agents, all of whom were under the direct administrative control of Director J. Edgar Hoover. Supposedly divorced from political influence, the G-men were also agents for the attorney general, and were backed up by thirty-seven state-level field offices. G-men were held to rigorous standards: they had to be physically fit, between the ages of 25 and 35, and they had to pass a competitive entrance examination, as well as hold a legal or accounting degree. Each candidate was scrupulously investigated, and if selected, undertook a three-month course in technical criminology and investigation, and multiple weapons proficiency.

J. Edgar Hoover was appointed director of the FBI in 1924, inheriting a badly organized area of the Justice Department. He not only laid down a new code of ethics, training, and mission, but he also managed to improve FBI laboratories and data resources until they became an indispensable national resource. Eventually, Hoover's control of the agency became a virtual dictatorship, and in his later years, FBI resources were used to support his own paranoia.

To match the dynamic exploits of the public enemies, Cummings created the G-man myth with the help of Rex Collier and Ryley Cooper, publicists who had a background in crime reporting. Through pulp magazines, radio shows, and eventually films, the two men generated scenarios designed to represent the gangsters of the day as formula villains, with the G-men set up as the villains' moral antithesis. The G-men were to be dynamic recruits in a tough war against crime, specially trained at the FBI's facilities in crime-fighting tactics, backed up by scientific theories of detection and a readiness to do battle for the public good. In short, they were super police, and the pulp magazines (especially *G-Men Magazine*) actively promoted this image. When G-men managed to trap the likes of Dillinger, Kelly, "Baby Face" Nelson, and "Pretty Boy" Floyd, their mystique and romanticization were enhanced.

Following the imposition of the Motion Picture Production Code in 1934, which banned "glamorized gangster" movies, the Hollywood studios shifted the focus of their formula to the other side of the law. In 1935 Warner Bros. released *G-Men*, which starred Cagney as the embodiment of American goodness and virtue. *G-Men* worked effectively as FBI propaganda, though it was never officially endorsed by Hoover (who had by now muscled Cummings out as the nation's number one crime buster by promoting himself as a more dynamic figure than Cummings). This movie and others like it succeeded in furthering the G-man myth and glorifying the notion of a neutral public-service agency staffed by highly trained technicians with a no-holds-barred strategy. The flurry of G-men movies in 1935, including *Show Them No Mercy* and *Let 'Em Have It*, showed a real determination by Hollywood to make the G-man an icon of American goodness and manliness.

The Postwar Era

With the entrance of the United States into the European war in 1941, the G-man moved from gang busting to spy busting. This transformation broadened his scope from serving the public to serving the national security interest, a shift that would be his ultimate undoing. Documentaries like *The FBI Front* (1942) and radio shows like *The FBI in Peace and War* (1944–1958) used the familiar formula of smart criminology, dedicated teamwork, and a swift uppercut to break up Nazi and Japanese spy rings. With the gangster threat largely forgotten, this cleverness was parlayed into the anticommunist hysteria following the end of the war, when the G-man became a patriotic figure, working on an ideological and psychological level. Dana Andrews in the radio show *I Was a Communist for the FBI* (1951) typified this new G-man focus and exemplified the tricky and subversive nature of the new "criminals." Hoover's message was clear: no one could be trusted, and only the G-man had the ability and wherewithal to save the American way.

By 1965 the character played by Efrem Zimbalist, Jr., on *The FBI* television series (1965–1973) became the new image officially endorsed by Hoover. *The FBI* was a clean, tightly censored television show that turned the G-man into a technician and a rule follower who defended the status quo against all subversive elements. Yet while the G-man's image changed to fit the world, his simplistic notions of crime fighting were largely anachronistic in the complex political context of the United States in the 1960s. The massive shifts in cultural values at home and the acceleration of an unpopular war in Vietnam robbed the G-man of his early focus. It was impossible for the general public to construct Martin Luther King, Jr., civil rights workers, and peace protesters as threats to the American way. Hoover's insistence on the anti-Americanism of such persons failed to consider current political complexities and public sentiments. In the political climate of the 1960s, the G-man's role as defender was virtually robbed of meaning.

By the 1970s the G-man was not only dead as a pop icon but was becoming a positive danger to the civil liberties of many Americans. The Watergate scandal and increasing evidence of illegal procedures by the FBI, as well as a growing barrage of indictments and convictions within the bureau, turned the former hero into his darkest possible antithesis: the secret police. Hoover's death in 1972 marked the demise of the G-man's strongest proponent and put to rest the forty-year fantasy of the G-man.

BIBLIOGRAPHY

Breuer, William B. *J. Edgar Hoover and His G-men.* Westport, Conn.: Praeger, 1995.

Clark, George, and Lou Hanlon. *The G-man on the Crime Trail.* Racine, Wis.: Whitman, 1936.

Powers, Richard Gid. *G-Men: Hoover's FBI in American Popular Culture.* Carbondale: Southern Illinois University Press, 1983.

Shadoian, Jack. *Dream and Dead Ends: The American Gangster/Crime Film.* Cambridge, Mass.: MIT Press, 1977.

Thorwald, Jurgen. *The Century of the Detective.* New York: Harcourt, 1964.

PAUL HANSOM

See also **Federal Bureau of Investigation; Hoover, J. Edgar.**

GOETZ, BERNHARD H.
(1947–)

On a Manhattan subway car on 22 December 1984, an unidentified white man shot four African American youths who had demanded he give them five dollars. The gunman quickly fled the scene, and New York City as well, renting a car and driving to New Hampshire. Nine days later he surrendered himself to New Hampshire police. His name was Bernhard Hugo Goetz, a thirty-seven-year-old self-employed electrical engineer.

Goetz claimed that when the youths approached him, he determined that he was within seconds of becoming a mugging victim and discharged his weapon in self-defense. Three of the four youths did not sustain serious injuries as a result of the shooting, and these three would be subsequently arrested on various criminal charges. At that time, street and subway crime in New York City was seemingly out of control; when it was learned that the youths had criminal records, many urban dwellers, fed up with crime, immediately saw Goetz as a hero. He became known as the "subway vigilante." Although subsequent evidence suggested that Goetz's actions may have been unprovoked, when one of his victims was arrested six months later on rape and robbery charges, Goetz received new support. In a national poll conducted by the Roper organization in September 1985, Goetz ranked sixth (following Chrysler chairman Lee Iacocca and television news personalities Dan Rather, Peter Jennings, Mike Wallace, and Tom Brokaw) among the most admired people in the nation. Moreover, many observers in New York and across the country likened him to actor Charles Bronson's character in the 1974 film *Death Wish*, in which a mild-mannered businessman turns into a gun-toting

Bernhard H. Goetz being escorted out of court in New York City on 3 January 1985. CORBIS/ROBERT MAASS

vigilante after his wife and daughter are savagely attacked by street thugs.

Although Goetz was considered a hero by some, others called him a racist. In the years immediately following the shootings, the Goetz case was seized upon by advocates on both sides of such urban issues as crime, race relations, gun control, and vigilantism. Goetz ultimately went to trial in 1987 on charges of attempted murder, assault, and illegal possession of a firearm, but his only conviction was on the gun charge, for which he served eight months in jail.

One of the youths, Darrell Cabey, was left paralyzed and partially brain damaged by the shootings. He sued Goetz for $25 million in compensatory damages and a similar amount in punitive damages. In April 1996 a civil jury awarded Cabey $43 million, but his attorney stated that Cabey would likely never see any of it. Goetz had a net worth of only $2,000 at the time and immediately filed for bankruptcy. Court officials indicated that Goetz would be required for the next twenty years to pay 10 percent of his income to reimburse the state for Cabey's Medicaid bills. A month later, Goetz left New York City for an undisclosed location in New England, where he had been offered a position in a scientific think tank.

BIBLIOGRAPHY

Fletcher, George P. *A Crime of Self-Defense: Bernhard Goetz and the Law on Trial.* New York: Free Press, 1988.

Rubin, Lillian B. *Quiet Rage: Bernie Goetz in a Time of Madness.* New York: Farrar, Straus and Giroux, 1986.

JAMES A. INCIARDI

See also **Self-Defense and Security; Vigilantism.**

GOTTI, JOHN
(1940–)

In less than five years, John Gotti became the most famous American gangster since Al Capone. But that notoriety—and Gotti's compulsion to talk about his crimes as government agents eavesdropped—earned him a sentence of life in prison and crippled the Mafia crime family that he headed.

Gotti was born in 1940 in the Bronx, New York, one of thirteen children. His father, John Joseph Gotti, was a sporadically employed laborer who liked to gamble. "We never had nothin'," John later

John Gotti, in January 1989 in New York City. CORBIS/ ROBERT MAASS

complained. The family moved to Brooklyn when John was ten, and within a few years he had joined a gang of young would-be mafiosi who stole cars and fenced stolen goods.

Gotti made his mark in the Mafia in 1973 by killing a thug named James McBratney who had kidnapped and murdered the nephew of Carlo Gambino, the boss of one of New York City's five Mafia families. Found guilty, Gotti was sent to prison; after his release in 1977, he was formally inducted into the Gambino crime family. Gotti rose quickly in its ranks, but by 1985 he and members of his crew had fallen out of favor with Gambino's successor, Paul Castellano. Gotti decided to seize power himself by killing Castellano. With another disaffected family member, Salvatore "Sammy Bull" Gravano, Gotti arranged for a group of gunmen to ambush Castellano on his way into Sparks, a popular steakhouse in midtown Manhattan. On 2 December, as Gotti and Gravano waited anxiously in a car nearby, the men shot down Castellano and his driver and disappeared into streets crowded with Christmas shoppers.

The new boss was nothing like the reclusive Castellano. With his designer suits, hand-painted silk ties, and distinctive swagger, Gotti was the "Dapper Don," a celebrity in a city of celebrities. He was quick with a quip for reporters and a smile for photographers and became a sort of folk hero to some New Yorkers. Meanwhile, the Gambino family feasted on the city's construction boom.

Gravano, now Gotti's underboss, used the family's control of labor unions to extort a "mob tax" that helped make Manhattan's building costs the highest in the nation.

But Gotti's reputation was based primarily on his ability to defy prosecutors. In 1987 and again in 1990, Gotti was found not guilty after long, highly publicized racketeering trials. Later, law enforcers would prove that Gotti had tampered with the first jury, but the acquittals earned Gotti his other nickname: the "Teflon Don."

The federal government was now more determined than ever to get Gotti, who had become an unbearable affront. Federal Bureau of Investigation agents planted electronic listening devices in Gotti's Manhattan clubhouse and in the private apartment upstairs where Gotti conferred with underlings. They recorded him confessing to murder and complaining about Gravano's greed. Gotti and Gravano were indicted in 1990, and Gravano discovered how damning the FBI tapes were and learned of Gotti's insulting statements. After several weeks in jail, Gravano decided to cooperate with prosecutors and to testify against Gotti in return for a more lenient sentence.

Because of Gravano's riveting testimony and his own taped admissions, Gotti's trial in 1992 was a rout for the prosecutors. He was convicted of murder and racketeering and sentenced to life in federal prison. A string of appeals were rejected, and Gotti's attempt to leave his son, John, in charge of the Gambino family faltered in 1999, when the younger Gotti pleaded guilty to racketeering and was himself sentenced to prison.

BIBLIOGRAPHY

Capeci, Jerry, and Gene Mustain. *Gotti: Rise and Fall.* New York: Penguin, 1996.
———. *Mob Star.* New York: Franklin Watts, 1988.
Cummings, John, and Ernest Volkman. *Goombata: The Improbable Rise and Fall of John Gotti and His Gang.* New York: Avon, 1992.

RICK HAMPSON

See also **Mafia; Organized Crime.**

GOVERNMENT COMMISSIONS

Large-scale, illegal violence in the twentieth century encouraged U.S. presidents, governors, mayors, and leading citizens to appoint high-profile commissions. Politicians announced that they were appointing government commissions to sort out what actually happened during tumultuous episodes of widespread violence, analyze why the violence happened, and then recommend public policies intended to prevent further outbreaks of violence. Officials usually appointed government commissions to address two types of violence.

The first type of commission-targeted violence was urban racial conflict. Early in the twentieth century, East St. Louis, Chicago, Detroit, and other cities experienced race riots in which marauding bands of angry whites (often tolerated if not assisted by local law-enforcement officials) harassed, injured, and killed African Americans. Occasionally, white violence focused on other minorities, for example, Latinos in East Los Angeles during the Zoot-Suit Riots of the 1940s. Urban America again experienced massive civil disorders in the 1960s when mostly minority men and women in hundreds of U.S. cities destroyed white-owned property and attacked other symbols of white authority.

The second type of commission-targeted violence was associated with public fears of rising crime rates and powerful criminal organizations. Especially in the 1920s, the late 1940s, and the 1960s, millions of Americans expressed grave anxieties about soaring urban crime rates as well as about major underworld crime syndicates involved in gambling, bootlegging, prostitution, illegal drugs, theft, and murder. During each race riot, civil disorder, and crime scare, widespread public anxiety generated significant demand for government action to restore peace and ensure people's safety.

Why did politicians respond to public disorders and public anxieties by creating violence commissions? After all, they could have claimed (and sometimes did claim) that local police, state patrolmen, or National Guardsmen restored order, arrested the perpetrators, and thereby transmitted the message that illegal violence would not be tolerated. They could have employed the state's monopoly of legitimate coercion to enforce peace and considered that sufficient. In addition, politicians who believed that large-scale, illegal violence was symptomatic of deeper social problems such as poverty, unemployment, deteriorating housing, poor schools, and racism could have relied on established government agencies to investigate the causes of violence, develop sophisticated analyses, and recommend measures to reduce future violence. The need for special temporary government commissions was not obvious. Nonetheless, the appointment of these commissions became typical between World War I and the 1970s.

Furthermore, why did national politicians go into the violence-commission business? Historically, responsibility for law enforcement in the United States was fixed at the local level. Indeed, most riot and crime commissions early in the century were appointed by state and city officials or by concerned local citizens. The first national commissions explicitly reaffirmed that primary responsibility for preventing violence still was located in state and city jurisdictions, not in Washington, D.C. Accordingly, the need both for national violence commissions and for national action against violence was not obvious. However, Presidents Lyndon Johnson and Richard Nixon in particular did not hesitate to create national violence commissions calling for national solutions.

Finally, did the national violence commissions serve any useful purposes? Two widely quoted remarks from the 1960s cast doubt on the utility of highly publicized but temporary violence commissions. After having examined many riot-commission reports, Dr. Kenneth B. Clark told the National Advisory Commission on Civil Disorders (the Kerner Commission) in 1967:

I read that report . . . of the 1919 riot in Chicago, and it is as if I were reading the report of the investigating committee on the Harlem riot of '35, the report of the investigating committee on the Harlem riot of '43, the report of the McCone Commission on the Watts riot. I must again in candor say to you members of the Commission—it is a kind of Alice in Wonderland—with the same moving picture reshown over and over again, the same analysis, the same recommendations, and the same inaction.

A few years later, the frustrated federal judge A. Leon Higginbotham, who was vice-chair of the 1968 National Commission on the Causes and Prevention of Violence (the Violence Commission), called for "a national moratorium on any additional temporary study commissions to probe the causes of racism, or poverty, or crime, or the urban crisis." Higginbotham and others felt that it was time to stop studying the problem of violence and start implementing previous commission recommendations. His point was that, regrettably, violence-commission recommendations were usually filed and forgotten.

This article provides a brief history of U.S. violence commissions in the twentieth century and examines the political reasons why U.S. politicians, including federal politicians, have come to rely on them. The article then considers their patterned assumptions and predictable recommendations, and concludes with an analysis of what, if anything, they have accomplished to reduce incidents of large-scale, illegal violence in the United States.

Former Illinois Governor Otto Kerner, who headed the 1968 National Advisory Committee on Civil Disorders, warns in testimony before the Senate Judiciary Subcommittee on 25 May 1971 that unemployment among minority groups could cause future civil unrest. CORBIS/BETTMANN

A Brief History of Violence Commissions

Violence commissions were twentieth-century phenomena. They were created mostly by citizen groups and local politicians in the aftermath of large-scale, illegal violence. Typically, citizens complained of race riots or crime waves, and politicians responded either by legitimizing existing citizen commissions or by appointing their own government commissions. In both cases, their announced goal usually was to gain a better understanding of the causes of the violence and to take appropriate action to ensure that it never happened again.

Riot Commissions. In the early twentieth century, "race riots" referred to incidents in which bands of white people ignored the law and indiscriminately attacked African Americans, usually for several days running. Local law-enforcement officials regularly watched while the attacks took place; white police officers sometimes joined in the racial violence. Almost immediately, however, respectable citizens called for renewed peace, the rioters returned to their homes, and different local interests began to compete to pin the blame for the violence on one group or another. One increasingly popular means to make certain the blame stuck here rather than there was to establish a highly publicized commission to investigate and report on the riot. The 1917 race riot in East St. Louis, for example, produced four competing commissions and reports on the causes of the violence.

The summer of 1919 was punctuated by race riots in twenty-six U.S. cities. The most notable, the Chicago riot, began when four black youths swam into what was designated as a white area on a Lake Michigan beach. White beachgoers attacked the youths with a barrage of rocks, killing one of them. The refusal of police officers to arrest the perpetrators triggered more violence, which spread throughout the city. Soon, roving white mobs attacked any African American in sight. The riot finally ended when the state militia was mobilized and two days of rain dampened tensions. Thirty-eight people died, 537 were injured, and more than a thousand black people lost their homes to arson. After the riot was over, civic leaders created the Chicago Commission on Race Relations to study the causes of the riot and make recommendations to prevent future riots. The commission's report identified gross inequities in recreational facilities, deficiencies in minority schools, and job discrimination against black workers as contributing factors to the explosive racial tensions in the city.

Henceforth, the practice of appointing riot commissions to study, explain, and prevent urban race riots became commonplace among state and local politicians. By the time Michigan's governor appointed his own commission to investigate the causes of the 1943 race riot in Detroit, at least twenty-one commissions had been appointed to investigate incidents of white urban violence against African Americans. The governor's Commission on Detroit Riots ultimately justified both policemen's and politicians' misconduct during the riots. Critics considered the Detroit report a whitewash and generated a competing citizens' commission appointed by the National Association for the Advancement of Colored People (NAACP) and headed by future Supreme Court Justice Thurgood Marshall. The title of the NAACP report captured its main counter-theme: *The Gestapo in Detroit.*

The first riot commission of great note in the post–World War II era was the 1965 Governor's Commission on the Los Angeles Riots, better known as the McCone Commission. In August of that year, the Watts section of south Los Angeles experienced six days of civil disorders. The final tally of the damage to life and property included thirty-four deaths, over one thousand injuries, nearly four thousand arrests, and the destruction of approximately $40 million in property. One week after relative calm was restored, Governor Edmund G. Brown appointed a commission headed by John McCone to investigate the violence. Within months, the McCone Commission issued its report, *Violence in the City—An End or a Beginning?*

Almost immediately, critics ripped into the report. They claimed that the McCone commissioners failed to do their homework. The commissioners had substituted impressions for facts, mischaracterized the rioters as recent migrants, missed most African Americans' sympathy with the rioters, ignored justifiable charges of racial discrimination and police brutality, and wrongly dismissed the possibility that much of the violence was an expression of legitimate political grievances. Overall, the critics were convinced that the McCone Commission gave priority to pleasing civic leaders rather than producing a sound analysis of the disorders or effective policy recommendations to prevent future violence.

Crime Commissions. Riot commissions were generally established to address matters of collective and spontaneous race violence. Crime commissions were appointed primarily to address public perceptions of growing individual violence (for example, crime waves) and organized violence (for example, crime syndicates). In many cities private citizens and civic leaders created unofficial or quasi-official crime commissions in response to public fears that violent crimes such as muggings, armed robbery, and murder were on the rise. They also created crime commissions in response to widespread public perceptions that organized criminals were acting with impunity, in part because they systematically corrupted police personnel and other public officials.

In 1922 the city of Cleveland established a model for the more than forty crime commissions that would be created in the next twenty years. Cleveland officials decided to dispense with traditionally partisan, highly politicized investigations of police and prison problems. They opted instead for objective scientific study, policy analysis, and recommendations. Accordingly, they appointed Roscoe Pound (dean of the Harvard Law School) and Felix Frankfurter (future Supreme Court justice) to direct an investigation and study that eventually recommended measures to ensure better training, higher levels of professionalism, and greater efficiency in the Cleveland criminal justice system.

Public support for crime commissions received a big boost in 1929. In that year President Herbert Hoover responded to perceptions of epidemic crime rates, abuses in law enforcement, and the growth of organized crime by appointing the National Commission on Law Observance and Enforcement (the Wickersham Commission). For the next two years, the Wickersham Commission conducted numerous studies and published a full fourteen reports. However, with the coming of the Great Depression, most of the commission's reports ended up on the political back burner.

The end of the Great Depression (and World War II) invited many Americans to refocus their fears on crime. In the late 1940s, the Truman Administration responded in a fairly traditional manner. It suggested that local governments carried the chief burden of fighting crime. At best, the federal government involved itself in limited but complementary programs. This response was not reassuring to Americans caught up in an emerging postwar hysteria about internal threats (crime) and external threats (communism) to American security. U.S. Senator Estes Kefauver, a Democrat from Tennessee, sought to fill the vacuum in national leadership, first by promoting and then by chairing a congressional subcommittee to investigate how organized crime operated across state lines and corrupted the very fabric of American public life.

In 1950 and 1951 the Kefauver Committee held hearings in major cities across America. It relied mostly on local law-enforcement officers, local crime commission officials, and local politicians to provide investigative work and information, and it called on major underworld figures to give what amounted to celebrity testimony. Kefauver agreed to televise the committee's 1951 New York City hearings in an effort to dramatize the nature and scope of the problem. The three national television networks and several independent stations broadcast the hearings to an estimated audience of twenty to thirty million people. The committee hearings broadcast two main messages to the American people. First, "a national crime syndicate does exist in the United States." Second, local crime mobs were linked together by "a shadowy, international organization known as the Mafia." Having characterized organized crime in terms of an international conspiracy akin to the communism simultaneously being investigated by Joseph McCarthy, Kefauver hoped to legitimize new federal agencies and greater federal involvement in U.S. crime control.

The 1960s. The heyday of U.S. violence commissions was in the latter half of the 1960s. The Civil Rights movement, the student movement, and the anti–Vietnam War movement in tandem with significant growth in urban crime rates, massive urban race disorders, and assassinations of major political figures such as Robert F. Kennedy and Martin Luther King, Jr., generated heightened public anxiety about lawlessness and violence in America. President Lyndon Johnson became known as "the great commissioner," in effect, because he never saw a social problem that did not deserve its own commission. Johnson appointed presidential commissions at an astonishing rate, and President Richard Nixon kept the momentum going into the 1970s. Together, the two presidents created four major violence commissions aimed at assuaging public anxiety about the massive disorders that swept through U.S. cities and college campuses.

The presidential nominee Barry Goldwater made law and order a major issue in the 1964 election. President Johnson appropriated the issue for himself by creating the 1965 President's Commission on Law Enforcement and Administration of

Justice (the Crime Commission or the Katzenbach Commission). When 150 U.S. cities erupted in racial violence during what became known as "the long hot summer" of 1967, Johnson then appointed the National Advisory Commission on Civil Disorders (the Kerner Commission) to investigate what happened, why it happened, and how it could be prevented in the future. In 1968 criminal violence and civil disorders were highlighted by the assassination of presidential candidate Robert F. Kennedy. The assassination prompted Johnson to establish the National Commission on the Causes and Prevention of Violence (the Violence Commission), which eventually reported to President Nixon. Finally, with violence escalating on hundreds of the nation's college campuses, especially after the U.S. invasion of Cambodia and the shooting of students by National Guardsmen and police at Kent State University in Ohio and Jackson State College in Mississippi in 1970, Nixon established the President's Commission on Campus Unrest (the Scranton Commission).

The violence commissions of the 1960s overlapped considerably. They referred to each other, quoted each other, and rehearsed many of the same assumptions, analyses, and recommendations. They also encountered many of the same criticisms and objections. Such a flurry of violence-commission activity has not recurred since then. After the 1960s, violence-commission work tended to become more privatized and routinized as the national turbulence of the civil rights and antiwar years settled into the more localized grassroots politics of the 1970s and the increasingly conservative "get tough" approach to crime in the 1980s. For example, Milton Eisenhower (who chaired the Violence Commission) established the Eisenhower Foundation to carry on the work of his commission under private auspices. When the Reagan Administration addressed criminal violence, it opted to create a more low-key "Task Force on Violent Crime" rather than a high-profile national commission. And when civil disorders tore across Los Angeles in 1992—with a toll of more than fifty dead and hundreds of millions of dollars in property damage—in the wake of the acquittal of four white police officers tried for the beating of an African American, Rodney King, the creation of a new violence commission was no longer the automatic political response.

The Politics of Violence Commissions

There is little reason to doubt that the citizens, mayors, governors, and presidents who estab-

lished their own violence commissions wanted to ascertain the truth: they sought an accurate accounting of the facts of the violence, an insightful analysis of the causes of the violence, and some useful policy recommendations for preventing future incidents of violence. Indeed, the one factor that virtually all violence commissions shared was an explicit belief that peaceful means must be found to resolve the nation's social conflicts and solve the nation's social problems. Nonetheless, politicians who were solely interested in the search for truth in the cause of peace could have and probably should have pursued their goal by means other than appointing high-profile violence commissions.

Violence commissions were temporary institutions with extremely limited resources. Lasting anywhere from a few months (the norm) to a few years, these understaffed institutions had very little time and even less money to investigate or settle disputed facts, hear testimony from all or even most participating and affected parties, sponsor expert studies aimed at separating causes and symptoms, weigh competing analyses, and test the effectiveness of a multiplicity of possible policy options. By contrast, established government agencies with stable staffs and budgets were probably better situated to produce more accurate reporting of the facts, more incisive analysis of the causes of violence, and more effective recommendations for preventing future violence.

Violence commissions were usually high-profile public affairs beset by potent political pressures. Generally, presidents, governors, and mayors appointed well-known public figures to chair violence commissions. Then they chose representatives of powerful interests to sit on the commissions. Finally, they usually selected notable lawyers to head and fill the ranks of commission staffs. Quite often, the politician who created a violence commission held a press conference to announce its formation and introduce its chairman; the press then disseminated news about the commission's activities and covered its public sessions, testimony, and the publication of its final report.

In most instances, the public spotlight proved to be counterproductive to the search for objective truth. Publicity regularly invited individual, social, and political pressures. It often fostered internal conflicts between commission members and their staffs. And it always invited simplistic sound bites, dramatic explanations, and rhetoric-laden recommendations rather than more subtle, nuanced, and complex analyses. Ultimately, a politician who supported subdued academic inquiry was more likely to facilitate the search for truth, probe underlying causes, and provide competent recommendations than was a politician who played the politics of public inquiry.

Indeed, a crucial reason why so many politicians appointed violence commissions was that they had a strong stake in playing the politics of public inquiry. First and foremost, the politician's major advantage in appointing a temporary, highly publicized violence commission was to ease public anxieties and buy time without committing himself to any specific or controversial course of action. In the aftermath of large-scale, racial disorders, for example, a politician who appointed a high-profile violence commission broadcast the appearance of decisive action. He transmitted the symbolic message that he was in control, that the government apparatus was functioning, and that the people's representatives continued to command the capacity to confront violence, defeat it, and restore order to society. The politician thereby reassured masses of worried people that they soon would be able to resume peaceful living.

At the same time, the politician did not have to take a stand on the nature of the violence, its causes, or its preferred remedies. He thereby avoided treading on ideological turf that almost certainly would alienate significant constituencies. In effect, he put decision-making on hold while the commission studied, deliberated, and developed its report. In 1967, for example, Lyndon Johnson was pressured to take strong action against the civil disorders that spread across urban America, but the pressures were varied and contradictory. Key members of Congress wanted Johnson to use massive military force against urban rioters. However, major black civil rights leaders urged him to legislate controversial civil rights measures and massive social programs to alleviate racial injustices associated with ghetto life. Johnson bought time and avoided alienating both groups by going on national television during the height of the Detroit riots to announce the formation of the Kerner Commission. He acted decisively—although he did not commit himself to any particular anti-violence strategy.

Sometimes, buying time by appointing a commission proved to be a sufficient political response to large-scale, illegal violence. By postponing action, a president or governor often created enough breathing room for agitators to tire out, for rioters to return to their everyday lives, for group passions to dissipate, and for mass arousal to give way to mass quiescence. By the time the appointed violence commission actually issued its report or reports, months if not years after the triggering event, most people felt that the violence was sufficiently distant and the commission's analysis sufficiently uninteresting to evoke little response. As a result, politics as usual prevailed for the moment.

The second major political advantage of appointing highly publicized violence commissions was that they tended to deflect public attention away from the government officials responsible for maintaining order by refocusing public attention on the commission process itself. Once a president announced the creation of a violence commission and publicized its mission (the search for truth), the press and the public would shift their focus to the commission chair, its members, its staff, and its proceedings. Who are these people? Whom do they represent? Are they unbiased? Will they give a fair hearing to all sides? What will they report?

Actually, the answers to most of these questions are fairly predictable. Historically, riot commission membership overrepresented upper-middle-class, middle-aged white males who were predominantly professionals and government officials. Commission membership underrepresented the lower-class and working-class young men who typically participated in civil disorders as well as the predominantly minority and low-income men and women who lived in the affected areas. This skewed commission membership usually generated immediate criticism that the commissions were unrepresentative and biased. This criticism, in turn, was usually countered by commission claims to impartiality.

Commission chairs and members virtually always received public instructions to be impartial observers and analysts. In turn, they publicly committed themselves to undertaking an impartial investigation of the violence. They then reinforced their claims to impartiality, for example, by announcing that the commission would hold public hearings in which the people participating in the violence and living in the affected areas would have an opportunity to testify. Also, they usually hired respected social scientists and attorneys to undertake studies and craft recommendations based on objective knowledge rather than ideological prejudice. Most commissions worked hard to establish legitimacy among an otherwise anxious and skeptical public.

The third political advantage for a president, governor, or mayor to appoint a violence commission was that he could be fairly confident that he would receive from the commission a report that was relatively restrained in tone and content, and more or less politically acceptable to him. The people who were appointed to violence commissions tended to be moderate to conservative in their political views. They were highly unlikely to develop or agree to any analyses that suggested that U.S. society was flawed or suffering from structural problems. Conspicuously absent from commission membership lists throughout the century were individuals who were likely to express fundamental discontent.

Indeed, commissioners rarely considered fundamental matters. Historically, crime commissioners preferred to focus on individuals and conspiracies (e.g., the Mafia) rather than dwell on the more complex social inequalities that gave rise to crime. Accordingly, riot commissioners tended to blame "the riffraff" for sparking violence and then noted average people's vulnerability to mob psychology to explain their participation in violence. The commissions did little if anything to identify or analyze racial discrimination, social subordination, and political violence as major causal factors. Even the reputedly liberal Kerner Commission, which named "white racism" as a crucial factor in the civil disorders of 1967, failed to define white racism, analyze it, or recommend antidotes for it.

Most commissioners agreed to serve because they were hopeful that the politician who appointed them would hear and then actually heed their advice. They knew, however, that the politician could accept their recommendations, ignore all of them, reject all of them, choose among them, or even appoint another commission to provide what he considered more appropriate advice. This foreknowledge encouraged commission members to tailor their advice to what they presumed would be politically acceptable to the president or governor or mayor who appointed them. The result was that, quite often, commission members gave politically acceptable advice that actually contradicted their own studies and staff analyses. Violence commissioners regularly ignored testimony given in public hearings and social-scientific investigations conducted by their own staff to make what they anticipated would be acceptable and therefore potentially effective recommendations. Time and time again, the violence commissions' putative search for truth was compromised by commission members' desire to stay within the scope of political acceptability in order to have their recommendations heard and heeded.

Commission Recommendations

The presidential violence commissions of the 1960s were based on shared assumptions that supported a similar pattern of recommendations. The most important shared assumption was that large-scale, illegal violence was irrational and self-destructive. Commissioners believed that such violence was born of frustration, anxiety, and other social-psychological pathologies that were especially widespread among ghetto youth. Ultimately, ghetto violence produced more conflict and chaos, not a better society. Commission critics pointed out that harboring this assumption dissuaded commission members from considering the possibility that large-scale, illegal violence sometimes was a purposive political strategy for correcting injustices rather than a spontaneous emotional explosion. Critics also noted that this assumption prompted commission members to focus almost exclusively on African American ghetto residents while ignoring the pervasive, large-scale, state-authorized violence perpetrated by numerous law-enforcement agencies at home and by the U.S. military in Vietnam, Cambodia, and elsewhere in the world.

Another shared assumption was that crime waves and civil disorders were mostly the product of a few hard-core agitators whose incendiary rhetoric and illegal actions transformed masses of otherwise nonviolent individuals into sympathizers, if not active accomplices, in violence. Commissioners criticized a handful of crime bosses here, a score of ghetto malcontents there, or a small cadre of revolutionary students and professors on college campuses for igniting the mass violence of the late 1960s. Were it not for them, most commissioners felt, the bulk of Americans who participated in, sympathized with, or simply tolerated the violence of the times would have instead upheld law and order. In the final analysis, according to the Kerner Commission, what most participants in riots really wanted was "a place for themselves" in modern America.

These assumptions helped to shape the recommendations of the four major violence commissions of the decade. The Crime Commission (or Katzenbach Commission) adhered to President Johnson's express belief that "effective law enforcement and social justice must be pursued together." On the one hand, the Crime Commission recommended more efficient law-enforcement practices. That meant higher qualifications and better training for police; improved equipment, technology, and management techniques; greater emphasis on community relations; and more federal dollars devoted to underwriting the upgrading of America's war against crime. On the other hand, the Crime Commission also recognized that many Americans were drawn to crime because they suffered from poverty and discrimination, and reacted with feelings of cynicism, despair, anger, and aggression that gave rise to criminal activity. If better policing would control hard-core agitators, a national effort to secure greater racial equality and social justice was also needed to insulate other Americans from the lure of crime.

The Kerner Commission adopted the same two-pronged approach. It called for greater law-enforcement professionalization and especially closer police-community relations. Simultaneously, it recommended a major national effort to improve educational and recreational facilities for blacks, fight unemployment and underemployment in ghettos, provide better housing and welfare benefits for the indigent, and defeat all aspects of racial discrimination. In short, the federal government should give priority to a massive effort to improve its twin capacity to exercise social control and achieve social justice.

President Johnson's Violence Commission, explicitly drawing on the work of the two earlier commissions, took the same basic approach in making its policy recommendations. It called for a "double investment" in the criminal justice system to enhance the efficiency of law-enforcement officials and the equity of the law-enforcement system in the United States. Simultaneously, it recommended a sweeping plan for investing in U.S. cities in ways that would enhance prosperity and improve family and community life, especially in African American ghettos. The key to a more peaceful nation was greater police professionalism and economic opportunity.

The Scranton Commission on campus disorders employed similar reasoning in its recommendations. It called for increased law-enforcement control over the handful of individuals thought to provoke violence on college campuses. It also recommended greater federal control of explosive materials, better training and equipment for police and National Guardsmen, and, especially on predominantly black campuses, improved community relations and mutual tolerance between law-enforcement officers and students. Additionally, the Scranton Commission called for social justice in the form of greater national solidarity. From the president of the United States, through state and local politicians, and finally to campus administrators, faculty, and students, all Americans needed to make a much greater effort to identify the common values that unify Americans rather than dwell on the differences that divide them. Ultimately, the nation's crisis of violence could be resolved only by resolving the nation's crisis of misunderstanding.

In addition to agreeing on two-pronged recommendations for better law enforcement and more social justice, the violence commissions concurred on the need for greater federal government involvement in stopping violence in America. Several factors added impetus to commission efforts to federalize the war against violence. First, the growth of the television industry helped to nationalize the public's sense of violence. Nightly news broadcasts publicized violence across the nation. National television enabled a spark set off in Los Angeles to ignite a fire in Newark, New Jersey. Unlike the relatively isolated urban riots earlier in the century, the civil disorders of the 1960s rapidly spread to hundreds of cities and college campuses. Violence commissions generally saw growing public awareness of violence and recognition of the national scope of violence as an opportunity to transform violence into a federal issue.

Second, improvements in telephone service and transportation (especially airplanes) made it possible for violence commissions to conduct investigations of a national scope as well as to search out and identify patterns of violence that cut across local, state, and regional boundaries. Not surprisingly, as both the problem of violence and the scope of violence investigations assumed national proportions, commission calls for the federal government to assume greater responsibility for understanding violence and eradicating it began to accompany the more traditional recommendations that federal agencies merely complement local efforts.

Thus, despite the mostly conservative credentials of their members, the crime commissions and riot commissions of the 1960s recommended massive federal spending to underwrite new federal agencies and new national programs to control hard-core perpetrators of violence and to eradicate the social causes of violence. The Crime Commission wanted "not only to endorse warmly federal participation in the effort to reduce delinquency and crime but to urge that it be intensified and accelerated." The Kerner Commission called for "a commitment of national action on an unprecedented scale." The Violence Commission recommended a federally funded "domestic Marshall Plan" to revitalize U.S. urban economies. And both the Violence Commission and the Scranton Commission suggested that federal efforts to restore domestic tranquillity were contingent on the federal government's ending the war in Vietnam—to free up federal dollars for desperately needed social programs and to diminish animosities that polarized American campuses.

The Impact of Commission Recommendations

Did the violence-commission reports have a discernible effect on public policy? Were commission findings useful for ameliorating if not eliminating future incidents of violence? The 1929 Wickersham Commission set a sort of precedent. Those of its reports that recommended ameliorating the social conditions that gave rise to crime were ignored. However, its report on the police gave impetus to a new generation of reform-minded police chiefs to professionalize police personnel and enhance the efficiency of the criminal justice system. The historical record suggests that violence commission recommendations that promoted greater law-enforcement effectiveness were often heeded, but those that called for greater social justice were mostly disavowed, ignored, filed, and forgotten.

For example, the Crime Commission recommended both a major federal effort to both improve policing and eradicate the social causes of crime. The first recommendation was translated into the 1968 Omnibus Crime Control and Safe Street Act, which established a new federal agency to improve policing: the Law Enforcement Assistance Administration (LEAA). Over the course of the next two decades, the LEAA served as the central headquarters of the federal war against crime. It disbursed billions of dollars to support research and development, supply new police hardware, provide better command and control systems, improve planning and coordination between local agencies, increase court efficiency, and take other measures that promised to enhance the government's ability to fight crime. However, President Johnson essentially ignored the Crime Commission's second recommendation to mount a national mobilization against the poverty and discrimination that bred crime.

The Kerner Commission, the Violence Commission, and the Scranton Commission recommendations that aimed at improving the efficiency of the criminal justice system helped to legitimize the LEAA and build congressional support for appropriations that would allow massive infusion of funds into it, for example, to underwrite national and local efforts to improve police-community relations in the United States. However, the Kerner Commission's call for unprecedented national action to improve educational and recreational facilities for blacks, fight unemployment and underemployment, provide better housing, improve welfare, and defeat racial discrimination went unheeded. Likewise, the Violence Commission's recommendation to develop a domestic Marshall Plan for U.S. cities and the Scranton Commission's cry for greater social justice in the form of national solidarity were ignored. Ultimately, President Johnson wrote off Kerner Commission recommendations as unrealistic and, some speculated, appointed the Violence Commission to make more modest and acceptable recommendations. President Nixon then deemed the Violence Commission's domestic recommendations too expensive and disavowed the Scranton Commission's report as too liberal.

It is important to recognize that there was no parity in the two-pronged approach to national violence. Throughout the twentieth century, violence commissions were quite successful in building support for improving social-control mechanisms but were consistently unsuccessful in getting politicians to seek greater social justice. Out of the volumes of commission reports and recommendations issued in the 1960s came substantial improvements in police funding, riot-control tactics and weaponry, police intelligence programs, interagency coordination, and so forth. However, there was extremely little evidence of any major shift in national priorities toward eliminating poverty, unemployment, poor housing, bad schools, racial discrimination, and political underrepresentation.

What accounts for the lack of parity? The answer may be that politicians appointed violence commissions to serve two major functions. One function was to buy enough time to placate impassioned citizens without committing themselves to controversial actions, such as mounting massive social programs. The other function was to legitimize federal efforts to put more personnel and money into America's social-control apparatus. By the early 1980s, one suspects, violence commissions had outlived their usefulness. Conservatism in America had become sufficiently strong to legitimize financial support for "get tough" social-control mechanisms and to delegitimize liberal notions that massive social spending was necessary to reduce violence. What need was there for violence commissions when even "liberal" presidents like Bill Clinton prided themselves on increasing police personnel while cutting social spending?

BIBLIOGRAPHY

Chicago Commission on Race Relations. *The Negro in Chicago: A Study of Race Relations and a Race Riot.* New York: Arno, 1968.

Curtis, Lynn A., ed. *American Violence and Public Policy: An Update to the National Commission on the Causes and Prevention of Violence.* New Haven, Conn.: Yale University Press, 1985.

Kefauver, Estes. *Crime in America.* New York: Greenwood, 1968.

Lipsky, Michael, and David J. Olson. *Commission Politics: The Processing of Racial Crisis in America.* New Brunswick, N.J.: Transaction, 1977.

Moore, William Howard. *The Kefauver Committee and the Politics of Crime, 1950–52.* Columbia: University of Missouri Press, 1974.

National Commission on the Causes and Prevention of Violence. *To Establish Justice, to Insure Domestic Tranquillity.* Washington, D.C.: U.S. Government Printing Office, 1969.

Platt, Anthony, ed. *The Politics of Riot Commissions, 1917–1970.* New York: Macmillan, 1971.

Records of the National Commission on Law Observance and Enforcement. 1931. Reprinted as *Records of the Wickersham Commission on Law Observance and Enforcement.* Bethesda, Md.: University Publications of America, 1997.

Report of the National Advisory Commission on Civil Disorders. New York: Bantam, 1968.

Report of the President's Commission on Campus Unrest, Including Special Reports: The Killings at Jackson State, the Kent State Tragedy. New York: Arno, 1970.

Walker, Samuel. *Popular Justice: A History of American Criminal Justice.* 2nd ed. New York: Oxford University Press, 1998.

Winslow, Robert W., ed. *Crime in a Free Society: Selections from the President's Commission on Law Enforcement and Administration of Justice.* Belmont, Calif.: Dickenson, 1968.

MARK E. KANN

See also **Polictics: Government; Riots.**

GOVERNMENT VIOLENCE AGAINST CITIZENS

Government violence against civilians remained a fact of life in the United States from the country's founding through the twentieth century. Amnesty International USA and Human Rights Watch report that government violence against civilians continues to be commonplace in some sectors of U.S. society. (The International Association of Chiefs of Police criticized the 450-page Human Rights Watch study [1998], arguing that reforms backed by the police association were reducing incidents of arbitrary brutality.) State-sponsored brutality has become institutionalized in some police departments and in prisons, according to experts, at least in part because the individual perpetrators of violence *for* the government are all too often protected from punishment *by* the government.

The U.S. Constitution of 1789 codifies legal protection for some forms of government brutality against civilians. The opening sentence of that document states that one of the federal government's most fundamental responsibilities is to "insure domestic Tranquility" throughout the country. Most state constitutions contain similar language. The phrase is usually interpreted to mean that the government has the authority to protect civilians from crime, insurrection, or similar attacks on their lives, rights, or property.

Yet the duty to "insure domestic Tranquility" has long provided the legal rationale for government violence against other civilians viewed as less deserving of protection. Article IV, section 2 of the Constitution legalized slavery in the United States, for example, and required security officials from every state to hunt down escaped slaves and return any captured prisoners to slave owners. (This section was eliminated in 1865 by the Thirteenth Amendment.) "The first American modern-style policing occurred in the 'slave patrols' developed by the white slave owners as a means of dealing with runaways" (Williams and Murphy 1990).

In the late twentieth century, a feature of high-profile, violent showdowns between the government and rebellious civilians has been the government's often highly militarized response, employing advanced weapons and tactics that suggest to some critics that the state is actually at war with its own population, at least at the moment at which such crises reach their peak.

Historical Summary

For many decades the U.S. federal government, state governments, and especially the rowdy local militias of armed men organized under government authority took up the task of catching escapees from the slave system and putting down rebellions. Government-organized militias crushed slave revolts led by Gabriel Prosser (in 1800) and Denmark Vesey (in 1822). Thousands of U.S. soldiers and deputized vigilantes hunted down the rebel slave leader Nat Turner and his followers in 1830–1831. They hanged Turner and executed scores of his sympathizers without a trial.

Throughout the nineteenth century, federal troops and state militias perpetrated what many regard as genocidal crimes against Native Americans. Early in the century regular U.S. army troops enforced the Native American "removals"—better known in the twentieth century as the Trail of Tears—which deported about ninety thousand indigenous people from Florida, Georgia, Illinois, and other states to arid deserts in present-day Oklahoma. Thousands of deportees died of exposure and disease along the way. Government troops perpetrated large-scale massacres against undefended natives such the Sac people of Illinois (1831), the Cheyenne at Sand Creek, Colorado (1864), and the Lakota at Wounded Knee, South Dakota (1890), to name only a few of the more notorious examples. Smaller-scale massacres, bloody confrontations between European settlers and indigenous peoples, and early forms of biological warfare carried out against the natives recurred so frequently that even counting the dead remains impossible.

Some observers contend the Civil War of 1861–1865 can be viewed at least in part as government warfare waged against civilians. That claim is clouded by the fact that most of the fighting took place between troops of rival governments based in Washington, D.C., and Richmond, Virginia. Nevertheless, the scorched-earth warfare—that is, destroying all homes and crops and killing civilians—characteristic of the Union general William T. Sherman's march through Georgia in 1864 was by any measure brutality against civilians.

Industrialization and the arrival of millions of new immigrants in the century following the Civil War brought new forms of government violence against civilians. Police violence, frequently carried out in cooperation with private armies hired by major businesses, focused especially on workers attempting to organize labor unions or exercise First Amendment rights to speak and publish in favor of civil rights for immigrants.

From about 1870 through the 1930s, waves of strikes and riots repeatedly swept through U.S. mills, mines, and factories. "In 1877 . . . the major

rail centers from Baltimore west were struck. Nineteen died, and one hundred were wounded, in a skirmish on July 26, in Chicago, between police, National Guardsmen, and a mob. At the Carnegie Steel plant in Homestead, Pennsylvania, in the early 1890s, strikers fought Pinkerton [company] guards. In Coeur D'Alene, Idaho, in 1892, metal miners attacked the barracks where strikebreakers lived. In the disorders that followed, five miners died, and troops were called out" (Friedman 1985, p. 555). Among many other similar incidents, one particularly horrifying example took place on Easter 1914, when company police and National Guardsmen attacked striking mineworkers at a Colorado Fuel and Iron Company mine near Ludlow, Colorado. After killing five miners in a shooting spree through the strikers' tent camp, the guards set fire to the shelter where strikers' children had taken refuge, killing two women and eleven children. The incident has come to be known as the Ludlow massacre.

These violent collisions between the government's self-proclaimed forces of order, on the one hand, and civilians exercising what most people regard as civil rights or human rights, on the other, bring into focus certain aspects of United States law. Lawrence Friedman writes: "The courts [of the period] could afford to indulge in principles and ideologies" in the midst of violent class conflict. Most judges "were terrified of class struggle, mob rule, the anarchists and their bombs, railroad strikers, and the collapse of the social system as they knew it" (p. 555). They took refuge in legal interpretations of the Constitution that generally favored the property rights of mine and factory owners over the civil liberties that are articulated in the Bill of Rights, which were often claimed by dissidents as legal authority for nonviolent labor organizing and related activities. Contemporary court rulings also provided de facto immunity from prosecution for government agents and even for mercenary armies for crimes such as murder and assault, so long as the offenses took place in the context of enforcing court orders—orders that themselves were often highly prejudicial, at least from the perspective of strikers and union organizers.

American law obviously has evolved quite a bit since the days of the Homestead strike and the Ludlow massacre. Nevertheless many of the laws and regulations that underpin modern structural violence (discussed below) and related government violence against civilians in the United States were first spelled out in legal decisions during these years. Those court decisions were designed at least in part to protect the late nineteenth century's version of social order from the challenges inherent in industrialization, mass immigration, and the emergence of the United States as a global power.

Incidents of Government Violence and Their Impact

Over the years, dramatic, brutal showdowns between U.S. security agencies and civilians have captured national attention. One such incident was the widely televised police beating of Rodney King, which set off the Los Angeles riots in 1992 when the officers were acquitted, and which provoked national debate about racism and the use of excessive force on the part of the police. The April 1993 confrontation between the small Branch Davidian religious sect, which had prophesied a worldwide religious war and armed itself with powerful but apparently legal weapons, and the Federal Bureau of Investigation and Bureau of Alcohol, Tobacco, and Firearms (BATF) resulted in the deaths of eighty people, at least ten of whom were children less than ten years old, within the church compound in Waco, Texas. Four BATF agents had already been killed in a poorly organized raid on the church in February 1993. The government's arsenal included tear gas, five armored fighting vehicles, two tanks, stun grenades, a military helicopter, aircraft equipped with infrared cameras for tracking church members' movements, and night-vision devices and other surveillance equipment.

In the 1992 Ruby Ridge incident, FBI agents and U.S. marshals, intending to capture Randy Weaver, a violent white supremacist and former Green Beret special forces soldier who lived with his family in a remote cabin in northern Idaho, employed the FBI's "rules of engagement" for this particular incident—that is, to shoot to kill anything that moved near Weaver's cabin as they attempted to capture him. When the raid was over, federal marshals had shot and killed Weaver's teenaged son and an FBI sharpshooter had killed Weaver's unarmed wife as she held the couple's infant daughter. One U.S. marshal also died in the incident. The government eventually dropped the weapons charges against Weaver and paid him more than $3 million to settle a civil suit stemming from the death of his family. Weaver has come to be regarded as a celebrity among white supremacists and the extreme right.

On a local level, Philadelphia police attempted in 1985 to evict a radical African American political rights organization named MOVE from a block of rowhouses. After a series of MOVE protests, city police SWAT teams armed with M-16s and Uzi automatic weapons, .50-caliber sharpshooter's rifles and C-4 plastique explosive provided by the FBI, raided the block in early May. Police poured more than ten thousand rounds of ammunition into MOVE homes, but MOVE did not surrender. Later, a SWAT squad in a police helicopter dropped an incendiary bomb on the roof of the apartment block, setting the entire structure ablaze; killing eleven MOVE members, five of them children; and leaving homeless more than 250 people from neighboring houses. No police officer or government official was punished for the MOVE deaths. The earlier MOVE protests and the police killing of MOVE members, in turn, helped set the stage for the highly politicized trial of African American journalist and political activist Mumia Abu Jamal, who was sentenced to death for the murder of a Philadelphia police officer.

The FBI, the BATF, and state and local police departments are rarely viewed as being "at war" with U.S. civilians. Yet these and other high-profile incidents demonstrate that some domestic security agencies have adopted military weapons and psychological warfare tactics—developed during the Vietnam War and in so-called "low intensity warfare" operations against guerrillas—for use against American civilians whom security officials regard as threats to public order. The Branch Davidian, Ruby Ridge, and MOVE incidents are late-twentieth-century examples of violent political confrontations that pit the government against civilians. The problem of how (and whether) to separate inflammatory political, racial, or religious confrontations from ordinary law enforcement against common crime goes back to the beginning of the republic, and some analysts contend that it is inherent in any system of law.

Structural Violence. Some criminologists and sociologists use the term *structural violence* to describe societal conditions or government practices that can have a brutalizing effect on citizens. Forms of structural violence that are built into the day-to-day operation of society and that have persisted even at the height of national prosperity are poverty, especially among children; the enormous U.S. prison population and the execution of some prisoners; homelessness; police brutality (especially when driven by racial prejudice); and layoffs and loss of job security. Other incidents of structural violence include dubious "medical" testing on prisoners, soldiers, and civilians performed without informed consent; police and Central Intelligence Agency complicity in certain aspects of the trade in addictive drugs; and the inaccessibility of basic medical care for millions of people. Paradoxically, the heavy publicity given to some social problems in the United States sometimes permits these forms of violence to become taken for granted; once they are out of the media's spotlight, they continue to operate almost invisibly.

To the extent that civil liberties and civilian protections from government violence have prevailed and grown over the nation's history, almost without exception this progress has been won only at the price of long struggle, sacrifice of lives, and careful political organization. Abolitionist leader Frederick Douglass summed it up shortly before the Civil War: "Power," he wrote, "concedes nothing without a demand."

BIBLIOGRAPHY

Amnesty International Report 1998. London: Amnesty International Publications, 1998. Pp. 349–353.

Brenner, Harvey. "Estimating the Social Costs of National Economic Policy: Implications for Mental and Physical Health, and Criminal Aggression." Paper no. 5. In *Achieving the Goals of the Employment Act of 1946: Thirtieth Anniversary Review, Vol. 1: Employment,* Congress of the United States, Joint Economic Committee. Washington, D.C.: U.S. Government Printing Office, 1976.

Brown, Dee. *Bury My Heart at Wounded Knee.* New York:Bantam, 1972.

Central Intelligence Agency, Office of the Inspector General. *Report of Investigation: Allegations of Connections Between CIA and the Contras in Cocaine Trafficking in the United States, Vol. II: The Contra Story.* 8 October 1998.

Chevigny, Paul. *Edge of the Knife: Police Violence in the Americas.* New York: New Press, 1995.

Collins, Allyson. *Shielded from Justice: Police Brutality and Accountability in the United States.* New York: Human Rights Watch, 1998.

Crutchfield, Robert. "Labor Markets, Employment, and Crime." In *National Institute of Justice Research Preview.* Washington, D.C.: U.S. Department of Justice, Office of Justice Programs, National Institute of Justice, 1997.

Department of Energy, Advisory Committee on Human Radiation Experiments. *Final Report.* Washington, D.C.: U.S. Government Printing Office, 1996.

Department of Justice and Department of Defense Joint Technology Program: Second Anniversary Report. NCJ 164268. Washington, D.C.: U.S. Department of Justice, National Institute of Justice, February 1997.

Friedman, Lawrence M. *A History of American Law.* 2nd ed. New York: Simon and Schuster, 1985.

Sheehan, Bernard W. *Seeds of Extinction: Jeffersonian Philanthropy and the American Indian.* Chapel Hill: University of North Carolina Press, 1973.

Walter, Jess. *Every Knee Shall Bow: The Truth and Tragedy of Ruby Ridge and the Randy Weaver Family.* New York: Regan Books, 1995.

Williams, Hubert, and Patrick V. Murphy. "The Evolving Strategy of Police: A Minority View." In *Perspectives on Policing,* no. 13. Washington, D.C.: U.S. Department of Justice, National Institute of Justice, 1990.

CHRISTOPHER SIMPSON

See also **American Indian Holocaust; Federal Bureau of Investigation; Los Angeles Riots of 1992; Militias, Authorized; Militias, Unauthorized; MOVE Bombing; Ruby Ridge; Structural Violence; Trail of Tears; Waco.**

GRAFFITI

Thought of broadly as the informal marking of public space, graffiti incorporates an endless array of signs, symbols, and visual alterations and captures the long human history of episodic public writing, wall painting, and transitory folk art. In the United States graffiti dates as early as the colonial period and includes such folkloric manifestations as tree carvings by Daniel Boone. In the twentieth century during World War II, "Kilroy" drawings and "Kilroy was here" inscriptions were ubiquitous. In late-twentieth-century usage, however, *graffiti* more specifically denotes illegal or officially unsanctioned public markings, and in this way references both modern arrangements of law, property, and power, and visual violations of these arrangements. Graffiti in the United States can be seen in a remarkable range of forms and styles: it might appear as a declaration of romantic love and remembrance, a scrawled allegiance to a musical group or sports team, an injunction of religious faith, or an exhortation to political activism. Among the many contemporary manifestations of graffiti in the United States, though, two forms in particular incorporate most directly the collective interplay of property, power, and public symbolism and for this reason dominate both everyday perceptions of graffiti and the ongoing debate over graffiti's interconnections with violence.

Gang Graffiti

Street gangs and youth gangs regularly utilize graffiti as a medium for denoting individual and collective identity, for demarcating social property

A hip-hop graffiti mural, or "piece," adorning an abandoned wall in a downtown railyard in Denver, Colorado. As is often the case with hip-hop graffiti pieces, the writer has included a stylized image, here substituting a voodoo doll for the letter "I" in the word *TIME*. COURTESY OF JEFF FERRELL

and cultural space, and for issuing symbolic warnings or threats. The particular uses and meanings of this graffiti vary significantly, however, between different ethnic gangs. Chicano, or Mexican American, gang graffiti in many ways symbolizes the long historical convergence among these gangs and the barrios in which they reside. As a form of "barrio calligraphy," it draws on long-standing styles of public writing and, at times, on the Mexican and Mexican American traditions of public mural painting. In this cultural context Chicano gangs mark barrio walls with their *placas*, stylized gang insignias used for communicating collective gang identity and the status of individuals and cliques (*klikas*) within the gang, defining and enforcing gang and barrio boundaries, and warning off potential intruders.

African American gangs, on the other hand, more often use graffiti to symbolically reinforce internecine divisions, including most famously those between the Bloods and the Crips. They employ graffiti as a medium for elevating gang status, in part by degrading rivals through public threats (for example, Crip graffiti written "B/K" suggests that the Crip writing it is a "Blood Killer") or by crossing out rival graffiti.

The forms of both Chicano and African American gang graffiti thus incorporate a degree of symbolic threat or violence, which can within particular situations invite interpersonal or intergang conflict. Often, though, this seemingly causal relationship between the violent message implicit in gang graffiti and broader patterns of gang violence remains ambiguous, or is altogether reversed. At times the symbolic violence of gang graffiti functions as a secondhand, self-congratulatory substitute for directly violent conflict, thereby displacing or diffusing more dangerous solutions to street-level disagreements. Gang graffiti as often includes memorials to murdered gang members or "roll calls" of those lost to gang and police violence as it does the promise of further violence; in such cases, it serves more as sorrowful warning than as threat.

Further, by organizing cultural space and social property and by setting normative and territorial boundaries, gang graffiti functions in many situations to at least regulate, if not fully obviate, intergang violence. A much clearer link between symbolic violence and interpersonal violence is found in the graffiti of groups often and erroneously omitted from discussions of youth gangs and street

59

gangs: skinheads and neo-Nazis. Written on synagogues, cemeteries, and gay and lesbian gathering places, skinhead and neo-Nazi graffiti communicates terror and threat and supports a broader campaign of direct and aggressive violence against the targeted groups.

Hip-Hop Graffiti

The most widely dispersed and visible form of graffiti in the United States in the late twentieth century, hip-hop graffiti emerged out of the boroughs of New York City during the 1970s as part of a larger, homegrown hip-hop youth subculture built around break dancing and rap music. Like the larger subculture, hip-hop graffiti developed initially as a stylized, street-level alternative to a traditionally gang-oriented or interpersonally violent means of acquiring status or resolving conflict. Hip-hop graffiti "writers" and the "crews" to which they belong thus write or "tag" their subcultural nicknames throughout public places, spray paint two-color "throw-ups," and design and spray paint larger multicolored murals, or "pieces," all as part of a system of highly stylized subcultural communication and status attainment. Ironically, as this subculture of hip-hop graffiti writing spread to large and small cities throughout the United States, and to Europe and beyond, public misperception of hip-hop graffiti as gang graffiti likewise spread. Those who conflate hip-hop and gang graffiti, though, overlook not only the alternative subcultural dynamics underlying hip-hop graffiti but a key experiential dynamic as well: the "adrenaline rush" of illicit artistry and outlaw creativity that hip-hop graffiti writers consistently recount as a key reason for their ongoing involvement.

Developments in the 1990s furthered the saturation of hip-hop graffiti into everyday environments in the United States. Hip-hop graffiti writers continue to invent new forms of tagging, including the etching of tags into glass windows and the mass production of pretagged stickers that are easily affixable. They likewise persist in finding new outlets for their more elaborate design work, such as sign-painting for small businesses and commissioned "rest-in-peace" memorials to victims of street violence. In addition, hip-hop graffiti writers continue to gain subcultural status through various attempts at new territorial expansion and through their risk-taking efforts to achieve these goals. By "tagging the heavens"—that is, by tagging the highest and most inaccessible spots on buildings or freeway signs—and by dispersing their tags throughout various neighborhoods, and thus "going citywide," writers work toward heightened subcultural visibility and legitimacy. In attempting to "go nationwide" by painting hip-hop graffiti on outbound freight trains, writers in turn take this expansive orientation to a certain subcultural and geographic extreme.

Though products of distinctly different dynamics, then, both gang graffiti and hip-hop graffiti stand as markers of subcultural identity and affiliation. As such, both types of graffiti exist as public displays but function as private conversations among those privy to their symbolic and stylistic codes. While both gang graffiti and hip-hop graffiti at times do violence to public and private property, and in some sense to existing assumptions about property and power, this violence results less from intentional vandalism than from the ongoing expansion of subcultural expression. Likewise, with the exception of skinhead or neo-Nazi graffiti, these graffiti forms are designed and utilized primarily to communicate subcultural status, rather than to communicate threat or intimidation to the general public. Their widespread misperception as generalized threat or violence results in some degree from the emergence of high-profile antigraffiti campaigns financed by many millions of dollars in public and private funds and aimed at reducing the damage done by graffiti to public and private property. In their zeal to generate public concern and enlist support, these campaigns have systematically conflated the various types of graffiti, confused subcultural communication with external aggression, equated violence to property with personal violence, and thereby distorted and amplified the meaning of that which they seek to control.

BIBLIOGRAPHY

Ferrell, Jeff. *Crimes of Style: Urban Graffiti and the Politics of Criminality.* Boston: Northeastern University Press, 1996.
———. "Urban Graffiti: Crime, Control, and Resistance." *Youth and Society* 27 (1995).
Sanchez-Tranquilino, Marcos. "Space, Power, and Youth Culture: Mexican American Graffiti and Chicano Murals in East Los Angeles, 1972–1978." In *Looking High and Low: Art and Cultural Identity,* edited by Brenda Jo Bright and Liza Bakewell. Tucson: University of Arizona Press, 1995.
Walsh, Michael. *Graffito.* Berkeley: North Atlantic Books, 1996.

JEFF FERRELL

See also **Gangs; Geography of Violence; Symbolic Violence; Urban Violence; Vandalism and Violence Against Property.**

GUERRILLA WARFARE

Guerrilla warfare is the strategy employed, usually spontaneously, by invaded or colonialized peoples combating an enemy army that they cannot stand up to by conventional means. Operating in irregular bands, often with little reference to formal command structures or governments, guerrillas make use of stealth and hit-and-run tactics rather than frontal assaults, and they rely on the local terrain and population for cover and support. By such means guerrillas can put enormous pressure on invading armies to abandon the restraints of organized warfare. Almost in imitation of their guerrilla opponents, regular armies develop brutal tactics of counterinsurgency, including burning wide areas of land, slaughtering innocent civilians in search of the guerrillas in their midst, depopulating the countryside, and creating concentration camps. Nearly inevitably, such occupation armies adapt racist ideologies to justify their invasions and brutal military measures. Much of American military history has consisted of guerrilla warfare, with European-Americans participating more often as invaders than as the invaded.

Guerrilla war, as a protracted means of resistance to British expansionism, began nearly one thousand years ago in Wales, Scotland, and, most notably, Ireland, where it continued throughout the twentieth century. The English developed both brutal tactics and a racist ideology when they drove Irish Catholics southward in the sixteenth and seventeenth centuries and colonized the northeastern reaches of that island with Protestants from elsewhere in the British Isles. In the eyes of English Protestants, the Irish, both barbarian and heathen, deserved displacement to create living space for a superior people such as themselves.

What they learned in Ireland the English then applied to the native peoples of North America. To many colonists the natives seemed "Irish-like," as at least one New England settler put it when he met them. And so, from the start of their settlement, English and other white European colonizers aggressively sought to drive out or otherwise eliminate aboriginal peoples, whom they contemptuously viewed as godless, lawless savages. The new land was the settlers' land by right, be-

cause God or nature deemed that the higher civilization should replace the lesser. In response, Native Americans sometimes sought to make treaties among themselves and fight an organized war; but more often their political alliances failed and they adapted instead the tactics of guerrilla war that they had long used against one another to attempt to repel the new invaders. These tactics often resulted in the slaughter of women and children as well as of combatants on both sides. Such warfare continued off and on for 270 years, until the last tribes of the Great Plains were conquered and put in reservations, permanent prisoner-of-war camps.

During the American Revolution the English deployed a powerful European army against the Americans—in this conflict the colonized rather than the colonizers. The Americans resisted both with a standing army and, much more widely, with guerrilla squads. Considerable areas, including Westchester County, New York, and the swamps of the Carolinas, became sites of American guerrilla raiding and brutal, retaliatory English occupation. Moreover, the revolutionists often used terror tactics against local Tory populations; these tactics were sufficiently nasty and prolonged to drive large numbers of them off the land, to the West Indies and to what would become Canada.

Guerrilla warfare also was quite widespread in the hills along the ragged border between the North and the South during the American Civil War. In much of Appalachia, the Confederate army in effect occupied their own territory, which was populated by anti-Confederate Unionists who took up guerrilla tactics. Similarly, in the Southern settled, slaveholding Union states of Missouri and Kentucky and also in Confederate territories that were occupied by Union troops during the war, Confederate sympathizers organized guerrilla bands.

In all of these cases wild young men were beyond the reach of military control from the government that they were ostensibly serving; they fought without reference to the limits regular armies attempt to impose on their own soldiers. For example, they almost always shot their prisoners rather than take them into custody, which is something that rarely happened in the formal theaters of war except when black troops surrendered to Confederates.

To take Missouri, the most egregious example, in response to hit-and-run guerrilla tactics used by the South, the Union armies, realizing that the citizenry was sympathetic to their enemies, tried a variety of measures—confiscatory taxes, scorched earth, and search-and-destroy missions from armed camps that doubled as civilian relocation camps—none of which eradicated guerrilla warfare. Compelled to copy guerrilla tactics to engage the enemy and caught with them in a seemingly endless cycle of vengeance, the Northern armies' morale crumbled as, in tandem with their opponents, they looted, burned, and killed without mercy, and often mutilated corpses.

Especially at the war's end, the Confederate leadership chose to forgo guerrilla tactics, preferring to lose rather than to adopt such savage and undisciplined tactics, which might have given poor whites too much independence both in war and in the subsequent peace. Considering the extent of Southern lands and the difficulty of much of its terrain, the armies' dispersal into small bands might well have proven effective; but the Christian gentry in charge of the Confederacy could not countenance the loss of control such war making implies.

After the war, however, responding to what they considered a Union occupation of their land, and shorn of a governmental structure of their own, ex-Confederates opened a second round of armed violence by adopting the very guerrilla tactics they had rejected earlier. The Ku Klux Klan and other guerrilla bands operated against blacks and their few white supporters in a bloody campaign that succeeded in reestablishing white supremacy in the South. In effect these night riders served as the paramilitary branch of the Democratic Party to achieve what they called "redemption" from the American military units in their midst and from the political effort to transform the South in the direction of racial justice. They would continue to impose power over blacks by any means necessary, including lynching and other forms of terror.

While the white South reasserted racial dominance, a last round of counterinsurgency cleared the West of Native American guerrilla warriors. If one could characterize the piecemeal destruction of Native American autonomy as an interior form of colonial warfare against guerrilla bands, in the period from 1899 to 1903, Americans engaged in a brutal episode of an expansionist imperial war of the European variety. After having disposed of the Spanish government in the Philippine Islands the United States imposed its own rule, and the U.S. army went in to destroy stubborn bands of Philippine guerrillas, who fought for independence against Americans as they had against the Spanish. American soldiers tortured enemy soldiers, burned villages, and shot down perhaps as many as two hundred thousand unarmed men, women, and children.

Not coincidentally, this colonial guerrilla war took place at the same time as the Belgians were employing a similar strategy against the Congolese and while the British were taking many of the same measures against the Boers in South Africa. During the last third of the nineteenth century, the English, the Germans, the French, the Portuguese, and others completed their African and Asian empires by violent conquest of guerrilla insurgents. Indeed, in 1900 Americans joined with several other European powers in putting down the Boxer Rebellion, an essentially guerrilla war in which outgunned Chinese nationalists tried unsuccessfully to stop the creeping European domination of their trade and their society. Despite a hesitancy to join the mad rush of European imperialism (and many Americans resisted the Philippines invasion), the United States engaged in forms of military conquest quite similar to those used by European nations.

Guerrillas do not always lose wars against invaders from more technologically advanced lands. The Germans learned this in Yugoslavia during World War II, as did the Japanese in China in World War II, the French in Vietnam in 1946–1954, and finally the Americans in Vietnam in 1965–1975. Yugoslavia's Josip Broz Tito, China's Mao Tse-tung, and Vietnam's Ho Chi Minh were the great modernizers of guerrilla warfare. They were the first military commanders to move political cadres into guerrilla bands as the means to impose systematic discipline on such warriors, thereby broadening the anticolonial potential of such a means of military struggle.

Ho Chi Minh, who could lay claim to being an authentic nationalist anticolonial resistance leader and not merely a communist, had public opinion on his side, as well as a jungle terrain hard to dominate by occupation forces. The tactics he had learned and used against other invaders, Ho could deploy against the Americans. And as was the case for the American colonists in fighting off the English during the Revolution, the Vietnamese needed not to vanquish the Americans but only to resist them until they got sufficiently discouraged to leave. Guerrilla tactics worked more effectively against a democracy than they would have against a totalitarian invader: as the democratic U.S. media revealed the costs—human and economic—of the war (including the killing of fifty-eight thousand Americans and approximately three million Vietnamese), opposition among the American populace and within government escalated, and the guerrillas profited from the political ramifications of their enemy's internal opposition.

American guerrilla wars have contained repeated ideological as well as military themes, most notably assertions of cultural superiority linked to racism. The name Union soldiers gave Missouri guerrillas and their civilian sympathizers, whom they saw as culturally inferior "white trash," was "Pukes." In the Philippines, American soldiers, including black troops, called the local brown-skinned population "niggers" and "Gu Gus," a dehumanizing term like "Gooks," which American soldiers called the Vietnamese population. In all these conflicts, guerrilla resistance and invader counterinsurgency deteriorated into vicious attacks on the part of both sides, with the line between civilian and soldier often erased and the language of destruction merged with that of liberation.

BIBLIOGRAPHY

Canny, Nicholas P. "The Ideology of English Colonization: From Ireland to America." *William and Mary Quarterly* 3, no. 30 (October 1873).

Fellman, Michael. *Inside War: The Guerrilla Conflict in Missouri During the American Civil War.* New York: Oxford University Press, 1989.

Kim, Sung Bok. "The Limits of Politicization in the American Revolution: The Experience of Westchester County, New York." *The Journal of American History* 80 (December 1993).

Miller, Stuart Creighton. *"Benevolent Assimilation": The American Conquest of the Philippines, 1899–1903.* New Haven, Conn.: Yale University Press, 1982.

Michael Fellman

See also **James, Jesse; Quantrill's Raid; Vietnam War.**

GUILT. *See* Emotions.

GULF OF TONKIN RESOLUTION

On 2 August 1964 in the Tonkin Gulf near the coast of North Vietnam, the American destroyers *Maddox* and *Turner Joy* traded fire with North Vietnamese patrol boats, though it was unclear who pro-

voked the attack. Two days later, when the same American ships were supposedly attacked again, President Lyndon B. Johnson, citing North Vietnamese aggression and American self-defense, pushed for a joint congressional resolution allowing him additional military measures in the region. Secretary of Defense Robert S. McNamara played a large role in presenting the resolution, which raced through committee and was passed by a combined vote of 502 to 2 only three days after the Tonkin Gulf incidents.

On 10 August 1964 President Johnson signed the Gulf of Tonkin Resolution, which authorized the commander in chief "to take all necessary measures" and "all necessary steps" to defend "freedom" in Vietnam. Unless repealed by Congress, the resolution expired at the president's discretion. That night, the president addressed the nation to announce the resolution and the bombing of North Vietnamese targets. This was as close as the United States ever came to declaring war on North Vietnam.

The resolution was passed under the assumption that any military action would be limited in scope, and it followed the precedent of similar resolutions passed under the Eisenhower administration. But by 1965 the public and politicians alike began to question whether Johnson had raised American participation in Vietnam to a level beyond "limited." Senator J. William Fulbright, who chaired the Senate Foreign Relations Committee, investigated the intent of the resolution in a television drama that captivated the nation in February 1966. The investigation damaged the Johnson administration by questioning the commander in chief's power to wage war and fostered skepticism about the legitimacy of America's intervention in Vietnam. Fulbright and others did not call for a repeal of the resolution, deeming repeal too harmful for the country.

Further questions and new information surrounding the August 1964 incidents prompted more hearings by the committee in 1968. McNamara defended the resolution in testimony, but the hearings disclosed that the *Maddox* was on a reconnaissance mission that tested North Vietnamese boundary claims, and secret American attacks on North Vietnam before August 2 may have justified retaliation. Most revealing, though, was the possibility that the reports of attacks on 4 August had been mistaken or intentionally faked. Finally, the hearings unearthed Johnson administration plans for escalating the war before the August 1964 incidents. The committee again stopped short of calling for a repeal of the resolution.

While politicians stopped short of accusing the Johnson administration of having staged the incidents, the investigations raised the possibility that McNamara and Johnson had exploited the episode to facilitate the war's escalation. In retrospect, the timing of the resolution was crucial. Passed three months before the 1964 election, the resolution firmly placed Congress behind Johnson's actions in Vietnam and allowed him to escalate the war without appearing as the aggressor to the American electorate.

Congress repealed the resolution in December 1970 in response to Cambodian air raids ordered by President Richard Nixon. This gesture did not deter Nixon from waging war in Southeast Asia since congressional budget appropriations, not the Gulf of Tonkin Resolution, were the real enabling mechanism for military action in the region.

BIBLIOGRAPHY

Austin, Anthony. *The President's War: The Story of the Tonkin Gulf Resolution and How the Nation Was Trapped in Vietnam.* Philadelphia: J. B. Lippincott, 1971.

Moïse, Edwin E. *Tonkin Gulf and the Escalation of the Vietnam War.* Chapel Hill: University of North Carolina Press, 1996.

Siff, Ezra Y. *Why the Senate Slept: The Gulf of Tonkin Resolution and the Beginning of America's Vietnam War.* Westport, Conn.: Praeger, 1999.

GREGORY L. PARKER

See also **Government Commissions; Vietnam War.**

GULF WAR

On 2 August 1990 Iraqi troops invaded and occupied Kuwait, Iraq's rich but weak neighbor. It was an act of brazen aggression that sent shock waves through the region and the world. The pretext for the invasion was an accusation of oil theft and economic warfare, but Iraq's leader, Saddam Hussein, had larger ambitions.

Beyond Kuwait lay the vast oil deposits of Saudi Arabia and the equally oil-rich and militarily even weaker United Arab Emirates. Should Iraq gain control of these vast resources, it would have enormous economic power and, consequently, immense political leverage—not only in the Middle East but worldwide. The regional balance of power would be destroyed, and pro-Western allies like Jordan and Egypt would be neutralized, if not de-

stabilized. Even regional enemies and potential rivals, like Iran, would be forced to accommodate Iraq. Israel would face the prospect of a war with a vastly stronger, larger, and more aggressive regime—a war that would present the West with grim choices.

The two principal leaders of the Western alliance, Britain's prime minister Margaret Thatcher and U.S. president George Bush, realized immediately that the stakes were enormous. Bush heatedly declared that "this aggression will not stand." What could be done to stop Hussein was another matter. Quick deployment of U.S. advance forces, Operation Desert Shield, heightened the risks to Iraq and appeared to contain whatever further territorial ambitions Hussein might harbor. But Kuwait remained occupied, and international opinion was split on the necessity or virtue of dislodging Iraq, especially if a war was required to do it.

Some Arab countries were caught between their awe of Hussein's audacity and their fear of it. Many had little respect or sympathy for what was seen as the arrogance and weakness of the Kuwaiti rulers. And when Hussein refused to back down in the face of U.S. threats, he inflated Arab pride and gained new regional stature, thereby helping to overcome historical feelings of humiliation blamed on the West and its allies. Some Arab leaders might well have reason to fear a triumphant Iraq, but their masses were another story.

Nor was the United States strategically poised to evict Iraq. The Cold War was over. Domestically, the Democrats were focused on how to spend the "peace dividend" they assumed was a by-product of this newly transformed international system. And the tragic loss of life and purpose in Vietnam remained a painful memory of the costs of U.S. involvement.

Internationally, the United States' allies, principally France, but also newer, more ambiguous allies like Russia, sought a peaceful solution. They were joined by many self-appointed and United Nations mediators in a search for formulas that would give Hussein a reason for leaving Kuwait. However laudable in intent, such efforts heightened the paradoxical possibility that he would be rewarded for his invasion, an outcome the United States and Britain steadfastly opposed.

Some argued for an economic boycott, but historical experience, together with Iraq's ability to buy what it needed with its newly acquired oil wealth, offered dim prospects for success. The principal question was whether the coalition as-

U.S. F-15 C fighters fly over a Kuwaiti oilfield that has been torched by retreating Iraqi troops during the Gulf War. HULTON GETTY/LIAISON AGENCY

sembled by the United States could endure the public displays of suffering that were sure to be orchestrated by the Iraqi leader to sap its will.

The Gulf War was unique in involving images as much as soldiers. Each side targeted the publics they sought to sway. The onset of the U.S. bombing of Iraq was televised live on CNN, providing some of the eeriest pictures of this or any other war. After decisive U.S. air and ground victories decimated Iraqi elite troops, pictures of them straggling back toward Baghdad along the "Highway of Death" proved a powerful and negative worldwide image. With the United States caught among humanitarian impulses, longer-term strategic concerns, anguished allies, and outraged foes, formal hostilities ceased.

The Paradoxes of Victory

In a massive display of high-tech sophistication, enormous and focused power, and political determination, the war was "won" in just forty-three days. In the land assault called Operation Desert Storm, begun on 24 February 1991, between two and three hundred thousand Iraqi troops were swept from the field in only a hundred hours, with almost fifty-eight thousand taken prisoner. Yet Saddam Hussein remained in power. His military suppression of Iraqi Kurds and Shiite Muslims and his continued defiance of UN arms inspections led some to say the United States achieved a "triumph without victory."

The Allies' war goals were to expel Iraq from Kuwait, restore the Kuwaiti government, protect U.S. citizens in the Gulf area, and maintain the security and stability of Saudi Arabia and the Persian Gulf. At war's end, only the last remained a question. Was stability achieved by the severe damage to Iraq's military infrastructure and weapons capacity? Was the cause of security advanced by the UN monitoring of Iraqi nuclear, biological, and missile ambitions that followed the war? Is Iraq less of an immediate and direct military threat to other regional countries because of the war? The answer to all appeared to be yes.

Some argued that the decision not to remove Hussein was a mistake—yet, without a strong, effective leader Iraq might have ceased to be an intact country. Had Shiites and Kurds successfully pressed their wish for autonomy, Iraq might have splintered, and with its military capacity severely degraded by the war, become vulnerable to Syria or Iran. Removing Hussein would have required occupying Baghdad and the attendant risk of high U.S. casualties. Few, if any, allies were prepared for that, and certainly the American public was not. General Norman Schwarzkopf, commander of Allied forces, characterized the White House decision to stop the war as humane and courageous. Nonetheless, leaving Hussein in power guaranteed further conflict.

The Legacy of the Gulf War

Almost two years to the day after the beginning of Operation Desert Storm, the United States and its coalition partners again became engaged in military actions against Iraq. These continued intermittently for years thereafter: in 1996, in response to Iraqi moves against Kurdish dissidents in the north; in 1999, in response to Iraqi challenges to Allied "no-fly" zones. Biological arms inspections standoffs were diplomatically "resolved" in 1998, only to collapse totally in 1999.

Continuous "crises" throughout the 1990s also drained Allied resources, heightened response fatigue, and perhaps weakened resolve. Many Gulf War coalition partners publicly doubted the wisdom of continuing military actions against Iraq. Saddam Hussein's full-time concern, on the other hand, was maintaining and expanding his power. The United States and its allies simply could not keep Saddam Hussein and Iraq on the front burner for an extended period of time.

After the war, the United States and its chief allies pursued a policy best described as intrusive containment. They (1) imposed a postwar inspection regime on Iraqi biological and nuclear weapons facilities, (2) maintained their economic embargo (allowing for humanitarian supplies), (3) tried to keep Saddam Hussein from reconsolidating his authority and power (especially in the northern and southern regions of the country), and (4) pressed (but not strongly) the issue of war reparations. Those policies certainly slowed, but did not stop, Iraq's military and economic recovery.

Saddam Hussein was equally consistent, and at least partially successful, in his postwar efforts to rebuild his country's economic and military infrastructure, to evade and frustrate the UN inspection regimes, to secure the lifting of the UN economic embargo, and to solidify his power and authority within Iraq. At the close of the century, he continued to project his presence in the Middle East.

BIBLIOGRAPHY

Bennett, W. Lance, and David L. Paletz, eds. *Taken by Storm: The Media, Public Opinion, and the Gulf War.* Chicago: University of Chicago Press, 1994.

Blair, Arthur H. *At War in the Gulf : A Chronology.* College Station: Texas A & M University Press, 1992.

Freedman, Lawrence, and Efraim Karsh. *The Gulf Conflict 1990–1991: Diplomacy and War in the New World Order.* Princeton, N.J.: Princeton University Press, 1993.

Grossman, Mark, Rolin G. Mainuddin, and Sheikh R. Ali. *Encyclopedia of the Persian Gulf War.* New York: ABC-Clio, 1995.

Nye, Joseph S., Jr., and Roger K. Smith, eds. *After the Storm: Lessons from the Gulf War.* New York: Madison Books, 1993.

Renshon, Stanley A., ed. *The Political Psychology of the Gulf War: Leaders, Publics, and the Process of Conflict.* Pittsburgh: University of Pittsburgh Press, 1993.

U.S. Department of Defense. *Conduct of the Persian Gulf War.* 3 vols. Washington, D.C.: U.S. Government Printing Office, 1992.

U.S. News and World Report. *Triumph Without Victory: The Unreported History of the Gulf War.* New York: Times/Random House, 1992.

Woodward, Robert. *The Commanders.* New York: Simon and Schuster, 1991.

STANLEY A. RENSHON

See also **War: Aftermath of.**

GUN CONTROL

The term *gun control* can be understood to mean either contemporary political efforts to regulate the manufacture, sale, possession, and use of various types of firearms, primarily handguns and semi-automatic rifles and shotguns, or the previous historical record of such legislation.

Federal Firearms Legislation, 1934–1994

The most important document in the modern gun-control debate is the Second Amendment to the Constitution, which reads: "A well regulated Militia, being necessary to the security of a free State, the right of the people to keep and bear Arms, shall not be infringed." However, does the Second Amendment confer an individual or a collective right? That is, does it enshrine an absolute individual right to own firearms, or does it guarantee citizens the right to arm themselves only when banded together for communal defense? Supporters of gun control argue for a collective interpretation in which the term *militia* refers to the "organized" militia (in the contemporary context, the National Guard), while opponents insist that the framers meant the militia of English common law: all adult male citizens, or the "unorganized" militia. Although legal scholars are divided over the question of how much protection the Second Amendment provides for the purely individual right to own firearms, a consensus of legal opinion does support the federal regulation of firearms (requirements for purchase, licensing of dealers, prohibition of certain weapons, and so on). Thus, inasmuch as the U.S. Supreme Court is unlikely to soon issue either a definitive individualist interpretation of the Second Amendment (which would invalidate much existing firearms law) or a definitive collective interpretation (which could permit broader firearms bans and confiscations), the public debate will continue to center on the necessity, effectiveness, and fairness of specific regulatory measures. This regulatory approach would in fact be a continuation of the basic pattern of firearms legislation in the United States since the 1930s: slow, incremental, and bitterly contested change, with advocates of gun control pressing for bans on specific types of "illegitimate" nonsporting weapons, and opponents arguing instead for increased punishments for individuals using firearms to commit crimes. While both types of legislation were passed from the 1930s to the 1990s, the authors of limited bans on the manufacture or importation of concealable handguns, military-style rifles, and high-capacity detachable magazines have achieved substantial success only in 1968 and 1993–1994.

Before the New Deal era, no national consensus existed to invoke the interstate commerce or "escalator" clauses of the Constitution to regulate the manufacture, distribution, or importation of firearms within the United States. Thus, before the 1930s all firearms law was state or local. The foundation of modern federal firearms regulation was laid with the National Firearms Act (NFA) of 1934 (Public Law 73-474). Passed after a failed attempt on the life of President Franklin D. Roosevelt, the NFA was at least in part a reaction to the gangland violence of Prohibition and the social banditry of the early Depression years. It identified three categories of weapons whose manufacture, sale, and subsequent transfer were to be taxed and carefully monitored: Class I, or "sawed-off" rifles and shotguns with barrels under sixteen inches (rifles) or eighteen inches (shotguns) and overall lengths under twenty-six inches; Class II, or destructive devices (antitank weapons and so on) including firearms silencers; and Class III, or weapons capable of fully automatic fire (those that continue to fire as long as the trigger is depressed or until the magazine is emptied, as opposed to semiautomatic or self-loading weapons, which fire and reload themselves only once for each pull of the trigger). The manufacture of all three classes is overseen by the Treasury Department's Bureau of Alcohol, Tobacco, and Firearms (BATF). Individual purchasers of such weapons are photographed, fingerprinted, and given a background check by the Federal Bureau of Investigation and must pay a transfer tax of $200 per weapon owned. The NFA also requires owners of these weapons to obtain the permission of local law-enforcement authorities to bring them into their jurisdictions, which allowed many states to ban the ownership of such weapons. There are thus "Class III states," where automatic weapons can be owned, pursuant to the above restrictions, such as Texas, Arizona, and Nevada, and "non–Class III states," such as New York and California. Some provisions of the NFA have been extremely effective: while over 175,000 classified weapons

have been registered, none is known to have been used in a crime.

The Federal Firearms Act of 1938 (Public Law 75-785) began the federal regulation of firearms manufacturers, dealers, and importers. This created the Federal Firearms License (FFL), required of all individuals trading in firearms. The 1938 act also prohibited sale or delivery of firearms to individuals known to the seller to be criminals.

The omnibus Crime Control and Safe Streets Act of 1968 (Public Law 90-351) and the Gun Control Act of 1968 (Public Law 90-618) were overlapping statutes passed after the assassinations of Martin Luther King, Jr., and Senator Robert F. Kennedy. They expanded the list of individuals barred from buying or possessing firearms to include all felons, fugitives, illegal-drug users, mental patients, dishonorably discharged servicemen, illegal aliens, and minors. They also tightened record keeping by manufacturers, prohibited the mail-order sale of firearms (such as the rifle used by Lee Harvey Oswald to kill President John F. Kennedy and the pistol he used to kill police officer J. D. Tippett); fixed the minimum age for purchasing handguns and rifles at twenty-one and eighteen years, respectively; restricted all purchases of firearms to the buyer's state of residence; and ended the importation of foreign handguns not meeting specific overall size and safety criteria. The omnibus act also prohibited the importation of military surplus handguns, rifles, and shotguns from outside the United States (Oswald's weapons were an Italian military rifle and a U.S.-made revolver supplied to an allied nation during World War II but subsequently reimported).

The Armed Career Criminal Act of 1984 (Public Law 98-473) is an example of the type of firearms legislation supported by opponents of gun control: rather than regulating weapons per se, it punishes firearms-related criminal acts. An amendment to the Gun Control Act of 1968, it imposed a term of not more than two years and a fine of not more than $10,000 on felons, aliens, dishonorable dischargees, and mental incompetents who possess, receive, or transport firearms.

The Firearms Owners Protection Act of 1986 (Public Law 99-308), passed during President Ronald Reagan's administration, represented a sweeping, if perhaps temporary, victory for opponents of gun control. In effect, it loosened many of the specific provisions of the Gun Control Act of 1968 that regulated firearms dealing, while lifting the ban on the importation of most types of surplus military weapons. Other provisions raised prison sentences for specified firearms- and drug-related crimes.

The Law Enforcement Officers Protection Act of 1986 (Public Law 99-408) banned the further manufacture, sale, or importation of armor-piercing handgun ammunition or cartridges with bullets having increased penetrative power based on new technologies or special alloys. These are widely referred to as "cop-killer bullets" because of their ability to penetrate police officers' protective vests.

The Brady Handgun Violence Prevention Act of 1993 (Public Law 103-159) restored parity in the contest between opponents and advocates of gun control by requiring a national five-day waiting period between the purchase of a handgun from the holder of an FFL and its actual transfer to the buyer. It also required that by 30 November 1998 a national "instant criminal background check" be instituted to enable dealers to deny weapons to individuals proscribed under earlier legislation. An additional provision of the act reduced the number of FFL holders from more than two hundred thousand to fewer than one hundred thousand.

The Omnibus Violent Crime Control and Prevention Act of 1994 (Public Law 103-322) was aimed primarily at handguns having a high magazine capacity and at a category of firearms known as assault rifles. Originally that term was used to describe a type of fully automatic or selective fire (either semiautomatic or full automatic) military rifle developed after World War II. These weapons use a detachable magazine holding twenty to thirty intermediate cartridges (or rounds) midway in velocity, bullet diameter, and weight between earlier rifle and machine-gun ammunition and the pistol cartridges fired in submachine guns. In the mid-1970s several foreign and domestic manufacturers began to produce externally similar semiautomatic only models with barrels lengthened where required to conform to the provisions of the NFA. At roughly the same time a number of new semiautomatic pistols began to appear with detachable magazines capable of holding up to eighteen rounds. These firearms enabled a criminal or psychotic to fire a large number of aimed rounds at police or bystanders in a very brief time—which is exactly what happened during several tragic incidents in California and Texas during the 1980s. These episodes led to a poorly designed assault-rifle registration law in California and later the Omnibus Act of 1994. The 1994 act did not precisely define assault weapons, however, nor did it

ban their manufacture. Instead, it prohibited future production of detachable rifle or pistol magazines holding more than ten rounds while imposing a set of essentially cosmetic requirements on the future manufacture and importation of semiautomatic rifles. This weak prohibition permitted the continued production of copycat weapons that were somewhat less military-looking but no less lethal. At the same time handgun manufacturers, in response to the ten-round magazine limit, began to design and manufacture a new category of much smaller automatic pistol not prohibited by any existing federal legislation. This development was especially frustrating to the coalition that had secured passage of the Brady Bill, whose follow-up goal was a broader ban on concealable pistols and revolvers.

Arguments for and Against Gun Control

The contemporary gun-control debate addresses three principal questions. First, does the Constitution permit federal, state, or local regulation of individual firearms ownership? Second, do such laws effectively and materially reduce violent crime? And third, what further regulations are needed? Because an answer to the fundamental constitutional question will probably have to await a major change in the Supreme Court's ideological center of gravity, short-term arguments for and against further firearms regulations will likely be based on the second and third of these questions.

Even the harshest critics of gun control generally concede that the United States is historically a violent country and that firearms, chiefly handguns, are used in a majority (70 percent) of murders and in a large percentages of robberies, rapes, assaults, and incidents of domestic violence. In addition, handgun-related suicides and accidental shootings claim more than twenty thousand lives a year, many of them children. However, gun-control advocates and opponents agree on very little else, drawing fundamentally different conclusions from the voluminous statistics on violence in the United States.

The opponents are two large groups of interlocking organizations that conduct the gun-control debate at the national level. Specific organizations perform legal and statistical research, conduct public opinion polls, lobby Congress, and mobilize individual supporters at the grassroots level. Organizations favoring gun control include the Center to Prevent Handgun Violence; the Educational Fund to End Handgun Violence; Handgun Con-

President Bill Clinton sits with Jim Brady, for whom the Brady gun-control bill was named, at the White House on 6 August 1998. CORBIS/WALLY MCNAMEE

trol, Incorporated; the National Coalition to Ban Handguns; and the National Violence Policy Center. Organizations opposing gun control include the Citizens Committee for the Right to Keep and Bear Arms, the Firearms Coalition, Gun Owners of America, the National Rifle Association, and the Second Amendment Foundation.

While often differing on short-term goals and tactical approaches, these groups usually employ elements of the following two basic arguments: gun-control advocates begin with the basic premise that the fastest and most effective means of reducing the number of handgun-related deaths would be to prohibit the further manufacture of all nonsporting (i.e., nonhunting or target-shooting) handguns and to reduce the number of existing weapons through both positive and negative incentives (buy-back programs, stiff individual licensing and weapons registration fees, taxes on

ammunition). Such legislation would be effective alone or as a component of a comprehensive antiviolence program incorporating both punitive and preventive anticrime measures (increased prison sentences, support for education, more effective antidrug programs). To support their conclusion that handguns are a public-health menace requiring immediate federal action, gun-control supporters cite the far lower rates of firearms-related homicides in other industrialized nations (Japan, the United Kingdom). They argue that reducing the number of handguns in the United States would curtail murders and felony murders carried out by strangers as well as impulsive non-stranger homicides committed by family members, friends, and so on; if fewer handguns were in private homes, fewer murders in hot blood would occur, to say nothing of accidental shootings. Thus, they claim, rates of handgun-related deaths would drop in proportion to falling rates of handgun ownership.

In the absence of a total ban on the manufacture of nonsporting handguns, a remote possibility in the political climate at the end of the twentieth century, gun-control advocates tended to focus on intermediate goals such as the prohibition of assault pistols and Saturday night specials. Both types of handgun are inexpensive to manufacture, often making use of cast polymers and nonferrous alloys, and thus have a low retail price. Assault pistols, usually in 9 mm or .380 caliber, were formerly sold with high-capacity detachable submachine gun–style magazines. Although the 1994 Omnibus Act banned the future manufacture of high-capacity magazines, those made earlier remain legal, and many thousands are in circulation, often sold at higher prices than the guns themselves. Saturday night specials are small, concealable revolvers or automatic pistols firing low-powered yet lethal .32-, .25-, or .22-caliber cartridges. Many crime-scene handguns traced by the BATF at the request of local law-enforcement agencies are either assault pistols or Saturday night specials. Beyond bans on these weapons, a long-term goal of handgun-control advocates is the creation of a point system to end production of weapons most likely to be used in street crimes. In such a system a weapon could be produced only if it earned enough points for such features as steel construction (as opposed to polymers or nonferrous alloys), multiple safety systems, a minimum barrel length of six inches, adjustable sights, and a magazine capacity of eight rounds or less.

In contrast, opponents of gun control avoid discussions of specific categories of weapons, preferring to fall back on their basic principle that any firearm is inherently inert and can only be actuated by the will of its possessor—hence the slogan, "Guns don't kill people, people kill people." Whereas gun-control advocates tend to support the concept of an activist federal government promoting the general welfare through protective legislation, opponents are typically suspicious of the state and are likely to seek individualist solutions to social problems. Thus, the right of an individual citizen to own firearms for any legitimate purpose takes precedence over any collective benefit that might result from limitations on the right to keep and bear arms. Most of those opposed to gun control would also argue that firearms, especially handguns, can be an essential means of legitimate self-defense of the law-abiding citizen against professional criminals, shopkeepers against gangs, women against sexual predators, and so on.

Opponents of gun control deny the legitimacy of distinct categories of sporting and nonsporting firearms, arguing instead that the vast majority of weapons can be used for both recreation and defense. They also reject the value of comparative statistics on firearms-related deaths from national cultures as diverse as the United States and Japan. Criminals will have indefinite access to the millions of handguns in circulation in the United States, they argue, making other citizens more vulnerable to crime if defensive or concealable weapons are banned. Although gun-control opponents concede the tragic nature of nonstranger homicides and domestic murders, they argue that human nature will always lead to spasms of violence and that people are just as likely to kill loved ones with knives as with handguns. Likewise, the answer to accidental shootings, they hold, lies with individual safety instruction and proper gun-handling skills, not with the elimination of any specific category of firearm.

Not content to remain on the defensive, gun-control opponents have begun to propose "concealed carry." A number of states in the South and the Mountain States have passed laws allowing their residents to request permits to carry handguns on their person or in their vehicles after they have passed FBI background checks, firearms safety and qualification courses, and, in some states, psychological examinations. Concealed-carry supporters cite statistics to the effect that few holders of such permits improperly use their weapons and that handgun-related crime immediately falls in states that permit concealed carry. While such laws could, in theory, be used to gradually establish a higher threshold for legal gun ownership, they are nonetheless anathema to advocates of traditional handgun-control measures, who view them as putting more, not fewer, handguns on the street.

As the twentieth century was ending, the gun-control debate seemed to be once again in equilibrium, with little prospect of national firearms legislation beyond the provisions of the 1993 and 1994 acts. Even a rash of public school shootings during 1998 and 1999 failed to convince a majority in the House of Representatives to pass legislation approved by the Senate that would have tightened regulations on firearms at so-called gun shows, where guns are more readily obtained by unqualified and underage purchasers. While up to 70 percent of poll respondents continue to support additional restrictions on handguns, they remain unwilling to discipline their political representatives for blocking such legislation. To break this deadlock, the gun-control movement began to employ civil lawsuits and their attendant damage awards to raise the retail price of handguns, force manufacturers to add additional complex safety devices, and coerce them into changing their distribution practices. The goal of one lawsuit in the late 1990s was to limit the flow of handguns into southern states, where they are purchased in large quantities and then illegally transferred to eastern states in which they are regulated or prohibited. While several municipalities obtained favorable rulings in such suits during 1999, their impact on manufacturers' practices was not readily apparent. Handgun-control advocates are also lobbying the federal government to pass national legislation restricting legal purchases of handguns to one per month per individual, which would eliminate "straw purchasers" who buy multiple handguns and resell them at inflated profits to felons, gang members, and so on.

Civil lawsuits, however, promise only incremental changes. Barring a significant change in the electorate's sense of urgency, the equilibrium between opponents and advocates of gun control will likely extend well into the twenty-first century.

BIBLIOGRAPHY

Edel, Wilbur. *Gun Control: Threat to Liberty or Defense Against Anarchy?* Westport, Conn.: Praeger, 1995.

Kates, Don B., and Gary Kleck. *The Great American Gun Debate: Essays on Firearms and Violence.* San Francisco: Pacific Research Institute for Public Policy, 1997.

Kruschke, Earl R. *Gun Control: A Reference Handbook.* Santa Barbara, Calif.: ABC-CLIO, 1995.

Spitzer, Robert J. *The Politics of Gun Control.* Chatham, N.J.: Chatham House, 1995.

Weir, William. *A Well Regulated Militia: The Battle over Gun Control.* North Haven, Conn.: Archon, 1997.

JOHN SCOTT REED

See also **Gun Violence; Militarism; National Rifle Association; Right to Bear Arms; Weapons: Handguns.**

GUNFIGHTERS AND OUTLAWS, WESTERN

Gunfighters were men skilled in the use of firearms, noted not so much for their fast draw or even for their number of kills as for their cold deliberateness under fire and their willingness to kill. Beyond those characteristics they came in various forms. Some, like Billy Brooks and "Mysterious" Dave Mather in Kansas, "Deacon" Jim Miller in Texas, and Tom Horn in Wyoming, were rogues who walked a thin line between law and outlaw. Others, like Luke Short, John Henry "Doc" Holliday, Ben Thompson, and "Rowdy" Joe Lowe, were professional gamblers. Still others, including Wyatt Earp, Bat Masterson, "Wild Bill" Hickok, Jim Courtwright, Dallas Stoudenmire, and Commodore Perry Owens, were peace officers who often supplemented their income as gamblers or private detectives. Only a few, men like Billy the Kid, John Ringo, Curly Bill Brocious, the Sundance Kid, and John King Fisher, were outlaws in the accepted sense of the term.

And yet in all their variations, the gunfighters were—wittingly or unwittingly—players in what Richard Maxwell Brown has called the "Western Civil War of Incorporation." Even the most casual review of the gunfighter phenomenon reveals the extent to which gunfighters acted as agents for or against the forces of change in the late nineteenth century. In Tombstone, Arizona, Wyatt Earp was clearly allied with the Republican and business elite, and throughout his life, even when not wearing a badge, he worked for Wells Fargo, the Southern Pacific Railroad, the Santa Fe Railroad, and other corporate interests as an enforcer of the new order.

"Mysterious" Dave Mather of Kansas, who walked a thin line between law and outlaw. THE KANSAS STATE HISTORICAL SOCIETY, TOPEKA, KANSAS

The Lincoln County War in New Mexico (1878–1881), the Johnson County War in Wyoming (1892), and the Maxwell Land Grant conflict (1875–1885) in Colfax County, New Mexico, all offer strong evidence to demonstrate the conflict between the capitalist establishment and the small ranchers and workers. The likes of Billy the Kid, Jim Masterson, Frank Canton, Tom Horn, and others who played roles in those sanguinary affairs were partisans for or against modernization as certainly as the labor disputes at Homestead, Pullman, and Haymarket Square.

The values of the period also affected western outlaws. There were, of course, then as now, thieves, thugs, ruffians, and murderers that no one thought of as heroic. The Benders of Kansas, Boone Helm from Virginia City, Montana, and Zip Wyatt of Oklahoma had few admirers. But the western frontier romanticized a class of outlaws who have come down to the present more as Robin Hoods than as common criminals. These men—and a few women—had a surprisingly broad base of support among the respectable elements of the community.

The preferred targets of the day—banks, railroads, stage lines, and the herds of the big cattlemen—were all identified with the exploitation of the common man. Moreover, as Richard White has noted, ordinary folk were drawn to "strong men who defended themselves, righted their own wrongs, and took vengeance on their enemies despite the corruption of the existing order." As a result, outlaws of the period profited from the resentment that ordinary citizens felt against the economic elite, as well as from their acts of daring. The Jesse James gang was the classic manifestation of the "rob the rich and give to the poor" mentality of the public, and Frank and Jesse James took full advantage of it.

What is most surprising is the extent to which romanticization of the western outlaw was a contemporary phenomenon. The James boys consciously exploited it; subsequently outlaw bands like the Daltons and the Doolin gang imitated it; and even peace officers and editors could not hide their admiration for the attributes, if not the acts, of certain outlaws. Billy the Kid was romanticized even before his death in 1881. Butch Cassidy and the Sundance Kid, the entire Hole-in-the-Wall bunch, and even morose killers like John Ringo profited. The "good bad man"—whether a horse thief like Hurricane Bill Martin or a cattle thief like Curly Bill Brocious or gentlemen outlaws like Bill Miner and Black Bart—enjoyed a certain insulation from his crime by virtue of the myth. In an odd way the myth drove the reality.

Curiously, except for Wild Bill Hickok, peace officers were not idolized in the same way until the passing of the frontier was almost complete. Then, near the dawn of the twentieth century, the transformation of these "agents of incorporation" into the solitary law bringers of the western myth was accomplished, elevating men like Wyatt Earp, Bat Masterson, Pat Garrett, Bill Tilghman, and Commodore Perry Owens to hero status. By then the forces of change had won the day, and their role as law bringers recognized as positive.

Origins of the Term *Gunfighter*

The term *gunfighter* first appeared in California in 1874 in connection with a man known as Cemetery Sam, who appropriated the term. But the term did not gain wide usage for almost two de-cades after that. By far the most common appellation was simply *badman*, which meant a "bad man to tangle with" rather than a criminal. Other terms used to describe them included *shootists*, introduced by Clay Allison, the Texas gunfighter, in 1878, *shooters, pistol brigands, pistoleros, man-killers, pistoleers*, or, more elaborately, "the gentleman who has killed his man."

Ironically, not until the era of the gunfighter was passing did the term itself gain widespread usage. In 1889, in the aftermath of the shooting of David Terry by David Neagle, a former Tombstone marshal and bodyguard for Supreme Court Justice Stephen J. Field, the *Chicago Tribune* of 17 August 1889 noted that Neagle, "like many veteran gunfighters," preferred the "old fashioned single action Colt six-shooter." By 1907, when Bat Masterson wrote his series on "Famous Gunfighters of the Western Frontier" for *Human Life* magazine, *gunfighter* was entrenched as the favored descriptive term and few even realized the recent origin of the usage.

Gunfighters, the Civil War, and the Boomtown

The gunfighters and outlaws of the post–Civil War West were products of their time. Unlike the romanticized heroes and villains of earlier frontiers—men like Davy Crockett and Simon Girty—the badmen of the trans-Mississippi West were not solitary figures who lived their lives remote from "civilization." They were the spawn of the clank and clatter of the machine age as surely as robber barons and absentee landlords. Without industrial growth, railroads, and laissez-faire capitalism, they would never have existed at all.

Outlaws and gunfighters alike moved in an environment charged with change. The Civil War was the crucible of change. It stoked the furnace for industrialization. It left a legacy of bitterness and resentment that moved west with burgeoning settlement. It fostered the cynical and callous materialism that made "root hog or die" more than a philosophy for Americans of all classes. It taught an entire generation expertise in firearms. It exaggerated praise for the masculine virtues of courage, self-reliance, and honor. It bred tolerance for violence.

Not surprisingly, then, some of the most notorious outlaws and gunfighters operated in an atmosphere charged by the war. Wartime guerrillas like Jesse James and Cole Younger found it hard to adjust when the war ended and made only the slightest effort to change their ways before launching their careers as outlaws in an era still torn by the animosities of the war. Cullen Baker in Arkansas and John Wesley Hardin and Bill Longley in Texas were man-killers who pursued their murderous careers in areas charged by Reconstruction unrest. The boomtowns of the West were all marked by conflicts that could be traced to sectional loyalties. The Kansas cow towns in particular, such as Abilene and Dodge City, with their mix of Texas cowboys and Kansas marshals, were the scenes of fighting rooted in wartime loyalties.

But while the Civil War helped to create the violent climate of the nation—not just of the West—in the 1860s and 1870s it was industrialization that sustained it. To a surprising degree—in light of the myths of the violent frontier—western violence followed national trends. Industrialism unsettled things. It broke up communities, disrupted comfortable social norms, and undermined traditional values and restraints on behavior.

The clearest manifestation of these effects was the boomtowns. End-of-track towns (such as Bear River City, Wyoming, and Kit Carson, Colorado), mining camps (such as Deadwood, South Dakota, and Virginia City, Montana), and cattle towns were mostly new settlements without the usual social constraints of established communities. In the beginning of their existence, they were marked by large floating populations of young, unattached males and a coterie of gamblers, saloonkeepers, whores, and thugs. In the absence of adequate law enforcement or other social controls, this boom phenomenon produced an exaggerated level of violence. The gunfighter was a product of that world.

Despite some interpretations, notably Robert R. Dykstra's treatise (1968) on the cattle towns, the level of violence in the boomtowns was significantly higher than in other environments. In the first year that Abilene was a cattle town, seventeen men died there. During the first year of Dodge City's existence, before the cattle trade arrived, between twenty-five and thirty-five homicides occurred in this settlement, whose population never exceeded four hundred. Violence in the "hell-on-wheels" towns that accompanied the advance of the Union Pacific railroad between 1867 and 1869 was so great that vigilantism was considered a necessary corrective.

In 1875 the *Wichita Eagle* in Kansas wrote about the "manifest bloodthirstyness of the times" and deplored both the "boastful manipulators of the ready revolver" who "school themselves to do these bloody deeds" and the public that looked "with some of admiration upon the party who has killed his man." Months later the *San Antonio Ex-press* editorialized about the "murder mania" in Texas.

Gunfighter Myths

Most of the gunfights that erupted did not conform to the stereotypical walkdown of motion-picture fame. Often they were simply brawls growing out of the coarse pleasures of saloons and gambling halls. The Newton, Kansas, massacre in August 1871, which left five men dead; the gunfight in Caldwell, Kansas, in which Michael Meagher, a former marshal of Wichita and a former mayor of Caldwell, was killed in December 1881; and the shoot-out at Pat Hanly's Saloon in Hunnewell, Kansas, in August 1884, which took the life of a town marshal and a cowboy, were general melees involving several shooters.

Moreover, many of the gunfights were not evenly matched. The Clantons and McLaurys, though game and with the advantage of numbers, lost to the Earp brothers and John Henry "Doc" Holliday at the so-called O. K. Corral gunfight in Tombstone. The sheriff of Apache County, Arizona, Commodore Perry Owens, while trying to arrest a young horse thief, single-handedly killed three men and wounded a fourth in Holbrook, Arizona, in 1887. The "professionals" on both sides of the law were smart enough to play the odds.

The gunmen's adversaries, recognizing their superior marksmanship, frequently killed them from ambush or in other premeditated ways. Ben Thompson and King Fisher, each noted for his expertise with firearms, were both killed in a setup at a San Antonio vaudeville theater. Dallas Stoudenmire died in a similar fashion in El Paso, Texas. Pat Garrett, John Wesley Hardin, and Morgan Earp were all ambushed.

The classic gunfight, immortalized in Owen Wister's *The Virginian* (1902) and transformed into cliché in hundreds of movies and television episodes, was rare. The prototype of this style of gunfight, the walkdown, was set on 21 July 1865 at Springfield, Missouri, when "Wild Bill" Hickok killed Dave Tutt in a one-on-one encounter. Luke Short settled quarrels in this manner, killing Charles Storms in Tombstone and James Courtwright in Fort Worth. The Frank Loving–Levi Richardson affair in Dodge City also fit this mold.

Actually, as Roger D. McGrath (1984), John Bossenecker (1997), and others have demonstrated, the gunfighters first appeared in the mining camps of California, Nevada, and Montana before and during the Civil War although gunmen are most often associated with the postwar expansion. Men such as Jack Slade, an agent of the Overland Stage Company, and Henry Plummer, the Virginia City sheriff turned outlaw, were early manifestations of the western badman and were both hanged by Montana vigilantes in 1864. By the time that George Ward Nichols wrote his piece on Wild Bill Hickok for *Harper's New Monthly Magazine* in 1867, the image of the gunfighter, if not the label itself, was fixed.

At the turn of the twenty-first century the impact of the western myth continues and profoundly affects Americans' perception of themselves. Richard Slotkin defines the United States as the "gunfighter nation" in the third volume of his trilogy on the myth of the frontier. Movie heroes in the second half of the twentieth century, from Luke Skywalker to Rambo, were variations on the theme, and if Westerns have declined in popularity, the values personified by the gunfighter myth have not. The western badmen and the legends they spawned remain important dimensions of American history and life.

BIBLIOGRAPHY

Bossenecker, John. *Gold Dust and Gunsmoke: Tales of Gold Rush Outlaws, Gunfighters, Lawmen, and Vigilantes.* New York: Wiley, 1997.

Brown, Richard Maxwell. *No Duty to Retreat.* New York: Oxford University Press, 1991.

Dykstra, Robert R. *The Cattle Towns.* New York: Knopf, 1968.

McGrath, Roger D. *Gunfighters, Highwaymen, and Vigilantes: Violence on the Frontier.* Berkeley: University of California Press, 1984.

O'Neal, Bill. *Encyclopedia of Western Gunfighters.* Norman: University of Oklahoma Press, 1979.

Prassel, Frank Richard. *The Great American Outlaw: A Legacy of Fact and Fiction.* Norman: University of Oklahoma Press, 1993.

Roberts, Gary L. "The West's Gunmen." *American West* 8 (January 1972): 10–15, 64; (March 1972): 18–23, 61–62.

Rosa, Joseph G. *The Age of the Gunfighter.* Norman: University of Oklahoma Press, 1996.

———. *The Gunfighter: Man or Myth?* Norman: University of Oklahoma Press, 1969.

Slotkin, Richard. *The Fatal Environment: The Myth of the Frontier in the Age of Industrialization, 1800–1890.* New York: Atheneum, 1985.

———. *Gunfighter Nation: The Myth of the Frontier in Twentieth Century America.* New York: Atheneum, 1992.

Wellman, Paul I. *A Dynasty of Western Outlaws.* Lincoln: University of Nebraska Press, 1986.

White, Richard. "Outlaw Gangs of the Middle Border: American Social Bandits." *Western Historical Quarterly* 12 (October 1981): 387–408.

GARY L. ROBERTS

See also **Dodge City; Frontier; O. K. Corral Gunfight; Walkdown; West; Western Civil War of Incorporation; Women: Outlaws.**

GUN VIOLENCE

*Following the **Overview**, two subentries examine the **Epidemiology of Injuries** and **Gun Culture.***

OVERVIEW

For most of the twentieth century, violence caused by guns was almost strictly associated with high-crime urban areas of the United States. Beginning around the early 1990s, however, gun violence was increasingly prevalent in the suburbs and in rural America as well. An array of statistical perspectives together illuminate the pervasiveness of guns and gun-related violence throughout the United States: In 1995 alone, there were close to forty thousand fatalities caused by gun violence. Gun violence ranks as the second leading cause of death owing to trauma in the United States, and among U.S. mortality rates for all causes of death—including cancer and heart disease—deaths caused by guns have consistently ranked as number seven or number eight: guns are the cause of death in 60 percent of all suicides and 63 percent of all homicides. Most severely affected by the magnitude of America's gun problem are African American males between the ages of fifteen and thirty-four, for whom gun violence is the number-one cause of death. The gun homicide rate in the United States is 175 times greater than in Great Britain.

The number of nonfatal injuries caused by guns is roughly seven times greater than the number of gun-related deaths; in fact, firearms are the leading cause of serious injuries and disability in the United States. Victimizations from gun violence encompass a large number of persons who are seriously injured, sometimes suffering permanent disability as a result of their injuries; the cost of medical care and lost wages as a direct result of injuries caused by firearms was estimated at $20.4 billion in 1990.

Demographics and Gun Violence

The most violent crimes in the United States are criminal homicides (which include murder and nonnegligent manslaughter), armed robbery, forcible rape, and aggravated assault. According to researchers Franklin Zimring and Gordon Hawkins (1997), the crimes (other than homicide) that most often involve lethal violence in the United States are aggravated assault (using guns or knives) followed by armed robbery. Guns are used in about 70 percent of criminal homicides and in the majority of armed robberies. When a firearm is used in the commission of a robbery, it is almost inevitably a handgun. For example, in 1993, 96 percent of guns used in armed robberies were revolvers or other handguns and 4 percent were long rifles (also known as long guns).

The Federal Bureau of Investigation compiles annual statistics for crimes such as these from thousands of police departments throughout the United States, with a focus on arrest rates for seven major offenses, including criminal homicide. Summary data from these yearly reports is released to the press as the FBI Uniform Crime Reports. The FBI also prepares an annual monograph entitled Supplementary Homicide Reports, which breaks down the frequency of criminal homicides by categories—such as crimes in which the assailant and victim had a prior relationship, versus crimes involving an assailant and victim who were strangers—as well as by apparent motive; region; and the age, race, and gender of the perpetrator.

Homicide (from all causes, including guns) is the tenth leading cause of death in the United States. When homicide rates are assessed in terms of age, race, and gender, African American males ages fifteen to twenty-nine have the highest death toll. The homicide rate for young black males is twenty-nine per one thousand population; white females are forty times less likely to be murdered. For the U.S. population in general, the highest-risk category for being murdered is late adolescence and young adulthood. The lowest rates of homicide are among young children, middle-aged individuals, and the elderly.

Regional Variation. Regions of the United States that have a greater availability of firearms have somewhat correspondingly higher rates of firearm-related homicides and suicides. For example, the Southeast and Southwest have the highest levels of gun ownership and also have the highest per capita rates of gun violence. The New England and mid-Atlantic regions, with relatively low rates of gun ownership, have lowest per capita rates of gun violence. The region of the United States with the highest rates of homicide is the South, while the lowest rates are in the Northeast. The easy access to guns in the southern states compared with the much more stringent gun-control policies, including waiting periods, in the Northeast may well be a major contributing factor to the regional variation.

Variation by City. The highest risk of gun-related homicides in the United States is in the nation's twenty most populated cities. Statistically speaking, the aggregate homicide rate nationwide

Gun Violence and the City

According to statistics from the Federal Bureau of Investigation and the U.S. Bureau of Justice, in the urban United States, from Los Angeles to Baltimore, Chicago, Detroit, Miami, New Orleans, and Washington, D.C., the most concentrated rates of gun-related homicide in cities occur in and around inner-city housing projects. In impoverished communities where many residents have witnessed some sort of shooting and the neighborhood is perceived from inside and out as a dangerous place to live, guns abound, and oftentimes children, from toddlers to high-school age, are the victims. But in the late 1990s several horrific acts of gun violence in the suburbs received extensive media attention.

In April 1999 two students at Columbine High School in Littleton, Colorado (outside Denver), went on a shooting rampage and killed twelve students and a teacher before they killed themselves. In August 1999 a gunman entered a Jewish community center in Granada Hills, California (a suburb of Los Angeles), with a Glock semiautomatic revolver, spraying bullets throughout the lobby and wounding five people, including three children. The gunman later murdered a postal worker with a Uzi machine gun. In contrast to these extraordinary manifestations of rage and hate are the episodes of gun violence so common to American life that their regular occurrence relegates them to the inside pages of our nation's metropolitan newspapers. One such story appearing on 13 August 1999 involved a twenty-three-year-old New Brunswick, New Jersey, man who was indicted and charged with attempted murder for a shooting incident that had occurred in May of that year; the gun violence followed an argument that erupted after the alleged perpetrator and the victim played a game of dice.

was 9.7 per 100,000, while nineteen of the twenty biggest cities in the United States had a homicide rate of 27 per 100,000 (Zimring and Hawkins 1997). Gun-related homicides are statistically less prevalent in suburbs, towns, and rural areas, but although homicide rates are generally higher in cities, it is important to note that the risk of gun-related fatalities is not spread uniformly throughout each urban area. The place within the city where one resides has a profound effect on the homicide risks of a resident.

Research in Chicago that examined homicide rates by geographical distribution showed a high concentration of murders occurring in inner-city areas densely populated by blacks. Homicide statistics from New York City in 1998, for example, revealed that while there were areas of the city where the danger of deadly crime was high, residents living on the Upper East Side between 60th and 95th Streets were as safe as the residents of Cedar Falls, Iowa.

Youths and Gun Violence

The incidence of gun-related homicides in which the victims are children has reached alarming proportions, and the number of murders committed by juveniles using guns more than doubled between 1985 and 1992. The use of firearms by juveniles has had a profound impact on the homicide rate. The percentage of homicides in the ten-to-seventeen-year-old age category that were gun-related (as opposed to those homicides by other methods such as by choking or from knives) rose from 57 percent in 1978 to 78 percent in 1992 (for young adults aged twenty to twenty-nine, gun-related homicide figures rose only 5 percent, from 62 percent to 67 percent, for the same period) (Zimring 1996).

Guns at Home. Children in possession of guns all too frequently kill other children, sometimes purposefully and other times by accident. A common tragedy is that in which a child of seven or eight kills his playmate while playing a "game" of cops and robbers with a real gun that was supposedly hidden at home. In the aftermath of such horrible accidents, parents are inevitably quoted as saying that they thought the gun was unloaded or was hidden so well in the top of the closet that they were certain the child would never find it.

Guns at School. In a sample of national surveys of high school seniors, the Institute for Social Research at the University of Michigan found that a large number of students reported being threatened with a weapon. For example, 22 percent of the African American students who participated in a survey between 1979 and 1990 indicated that they had been threatened with a weapon at school and 6 percent had actually been injured (Maguire and Flanagan 1991).

During the period from 1992 to 1994, the number of school-related homicides and suicides more than doubled, and researchers reported that guns were used in three out of four (77 percent) of these cases. The victims and motivations involved in these school-related deaths can be classified as follows: interpersonal disputes (33 percent); gang-related activities (31 percent); bystanders who were not involved in the original dispute (18 percent); suicides (18 percent); and problems in romantic relationships (11 percent) (Kachur et al. 1996).

A young person who wants access to a gun usually finds that one is readily available—a gun may be taken without permission from the youth's own home, or stolen from a stranger. In fact, most juveniles obtain their guns through illegal means, such as theft or the underground market; rarely do they purchase their guns in retail outlets. Thus, as sociologists Joseph Sheley and James Wright (1995) emphasize, gun control that places restrictions on the market of legally owned guns will not significantly reduce the number of guns in the hands of juvenile lawbreakers. Prevention strategies for limiting gun-related violence among juveniles in school, therefore, have been increasingly focusing on the use of metal detectors, ID badges, video surveillance, and implementing zero-tolerance, gun-free policies.

Guns and Drugs. According to the American Psychological Association, youths who have easy access to firearms and a psychological propensity to exhibit violent behavior have increasingly been prone to be involved in deadly shootings (American Psychological Association 1993), a formula that is exacerbated by involvement with drugs as a user or dealer. In the view of Alfred Blumstein, dean of the School of Urban Systems and Public Affairs at Carnegie Mellon University in Pittsburgh, the increase in juvenile gun violence begins with drugs and can largely be explained through a "diffusion hypothesis"—juveniles become immersed in drug dealing; then they illegally obtain guns to use as a show of force and as self-protection in this dangerous enterprise. When disputes occur in connection with their illegal drug activities, the juveniles attempt to win the argument by using guns. Whereas such arguments once would have been settled through a fistfight, in the current environment, both sides resort to using guns, and serious injuries and deaths ensue.

The work of Blumstein (1994), the American Psychological Association Commission on Violence and Youth (1993), and the Office of Juvenile Justice and Delinquency Prevention at the U.S. De-

A gun found in the backpack of a high school student. Gamma/Liaison
Agency

partment of Justice (1996), viewed together, suggests the following set of comprehensive prevention strategies to reduce youth gun violence:

Prevention services: Identify, assess, and refer at-risk children to anger-control, decision-making, and social-skills programs.

Public education: Increase availability of family-life education programs and school-based gun safety programs.

Policies to reduce fear: Teach youths that they do not have to be armed with guns in order to survive; create safe communities; and improve the school environment.

Drug prevention and treatment: Invest in the development of comprehensive substance-abuse treatment programs in order to reduce youth alcohol and drug abuse.

Gun regulation: Ban the foreign importation of handguns and assault weapons to limit access to these firearms, and require background checks that would focus on limiting gun sales to minors.

Gun safety: Improve gun design, make trigger locks foolproof, toughen product liability laws.

Historical Background

The Nineteenth Century. Attempts to ban concealed weapons date to the early 1800s, but enforcement of these laws did not begin in earnest until the period between 1870 and 1934, when mainstream population groups in the United States "felt themselves threatened by a number of forces they associated with the handgun: blacks who wouldn't keep their place; radicals, labor agitators, assassins, robbers, and by a process of further association, the foreign-born" (Kates 1979). Attempts to legislate the use of guns commonly used in crimes dates to the late nineteenth century. Around that time, the wearing of a conspicuous side arm—that is, a weapon such as a revolver holstered at the side (and at the ready)—formerly worn only by military cavalry, was taken up by cowboys, ranchers, lawmen, and outlaws, by men on the western frontier, in eastern mining towns, and throughout the expanding United States, wherever the potential for violence was high and a display of manly preparedness seemed desirable. At the same time, small concealable "hideout" handguns became popular with the general public, and handguns likewise became the preferred weapons in criminal activity (guns used for crime earlier, in the early 1800s, were typically rifles).

Romanticized twentieth-century notions about quick-draw duels are no more accurate in their portrayal of the Wild West than were contemporary portrayals, in the dime novels of the 1800s. "Gunfighters" were commonly hired by respectable members of communities to dissuade unruly behavior, or limit it to certain parts of town, but fights involving side arms were typically spontaneous outbursts, and most participants were not very proficient in their use. Gunfights were seldom elaborate affairs, and generally pistols were simply produced from holsters, pockets, waistbands, sleeves, or boots, and so forth, as quickly as possible, and fired at opponents.

With the taming of the West (1890s–1900s), a man's need to display his ability to protect himself decreased and smaller, less obtrusive handguns became the norm.

The Early Twentieth Century. The development of automatic machine guns for military use during World War I (see Ezell 1983) precipitated the next notable era in civilian gun violence: criminal elements were quick to pick up on the new gun technology following the war. The havoc wreaked by organized crime gangs toting Thompson submachine guns (and sawed-off shotguns) in the 1920s and 1930s led to the passage of the National Firearm Act in 1934 prohibiting anyone except military and law-enforcement personnel from possessing fully automatic weapons without permission of the U.S. Department of Treasury.

Although violence was rampant among crime syndicates, it generally did not directly involve "outsiders." And in general, violent street crime decreased during the late 1930s and 1940s, perhaps because of decreasing poverty rates and a decreased proportion of the population that was juvenile. After World War II, while organized crime continued to play a role in street crime, most urban locales were more concerned with the threat (real or perceived) from a postwar boom in juvenile gang activity. These gangs generally did not use sophisticated weapons, but the public responded to increased rates of post–World War II violence with calls for gun control.

The 1960s and After. Increased juvenile populations in the 1960s and a corresponding increase in homicide rates (beginning in 1961) taxed law-enforcement agencies, leading to lighter penalties for many violent criminal acts. The general sense of civil unrest during the latter half of the 1960s, along with the public's perception that deterrents to crime had eroded (because punishment was less certain and less severe), prompted many citizens to purchase handguns—in particular, the small-caliber, inexpensive handguns known as Saturday night specials.

Technological development in weapons during the Vietnam War soon underwent a predictable trickle-down from military to nonmilitary applications. Although the production of "assault" weapons (typically, weapons of military origin, either automatic or semiautomatic) and pistol-sized semiautomatic handguns with large magazines (capable of being converted to fully automatic weapons) were significant developments, sophisticated bullets and sighting devices also upped the ante in street crime in the United States. The Gun Control Act of 1968 prohibited the importation of surplus military firearms and Saturday night specials, prohibited the interstate retailing of all firearms, and prohibited felons from purchasing guns. The most popular handguns since the 1960s have been in larger calibers with greater likelihood of inflicting fatal wounds. Until the mid-1970s most pistols produced in the United States were .22 or .25 caliber. Beginning in the late 1970s, the handguns most frequently produced were .38 and .357 caliber. In the late twentieth century it became difficult to distinguish handguns from machine guns, as all such weapons generally became more compact and more lethal.

By the 1990s, the emphasis of regulatory efforts, gun-control policies, and prevention strategies had shifted to specific, high-capacity, semiautomatic assault weapons. To some extent, late-twentieth-century developments in gun technology changed the manner in which street-level violence was conducted. The fear circulating among the general public, however, that military-style assault rifles are responsible for a large percentage of violent crime incidents—particularly drug-related crimes and crimes committed by youth gangs—as compared with traditional handguns, is not borne out by the facts. Some researchers have suggested that most gang-related homicides are not committed in face-to-face altercations but instead are the result of guerrilla tactics such as drive-by shootings—in which automatic or semiautomatic handguns are used, but Gary Kleck (1991) persuasively argues that the primary problem related to gun violence continues to be crimes committed with handguns, not assault rifles. Indeed, in 1993, over 83 percent of nonhomicide violent crimes where firearms were used involved handguns, and over 53 percent of all homicides involved handguns (Zawitz 1995). Kleck maintains that drug dealers rarely use machine guns because they are inaccurate, preferring medium-bore handguns and shotguns instead. James Wright and Peter Rossi (1994) also found that most inmates they surveyed prefer handguns—in particular, guns that are easily concealed, of large caliber, and well made. Although assault weapons are extremely deadly, they are also quite difficult to conceal. Whether a gun user's intent is to commit a crime or to defend against possible criminal activity, the gun of choice will probably continue to be the smaller, easily concealable handgun rather than an assault weapon.

The Brady Bill of 1994 required that handgun purchasers wait five business days between applying for handguns and actually purchasing them. In the same year, an omnibus federal crime bill, signed into law on 13 September as the Violent Crime Control and Law Enforcement Act of 1994, increased the penalties for drive-by shootings and included a section banning certain types of weapons from purchase by the general population, including MAC-10s and MAC-11s (automatic handguns). Similar restrictions were placed on handguns with barrel shrouds (devices that diminish the barrel or muzzle flash of a weapon), guns weighing more than fifty ounces, semiautomatic shotguns, and semiautomatic handguns. In November 1998 the National Instant Check System went on-line, affording immediate background checks and eliminating the five-day waiting period required by the Brady Bill.

Despite such laws, in many cases the criminal element carries state-of-the-art weaponry that means it is better armed than the law-enforcement personnel it faces. Improvements in bullet-proof protection, developed for law-enforcement personnel, have, of course, also become available to the criminal element. Armor-piercing bullets (whose misnomer is "cop killer") have been banned since 1987.

Developments in military weaponry during the 1980s and 1990s centered on extending the range at which an infantryman is effective. This includes combining different forms of guns into a single weapon and increasing the long-range effectiveness of rifles. These do not seem congruent with the drive-by nature of shooting commonly conducted by youth gang members because their targets are usually close-range, but they have serious implications for terrorists and snipers, who would benefit from the latest technology in military weaponry. Developments in law-enforcement technology at the end of the twentieth century generally focused on nonlethal weapons capable of subduing criminal suspects.

Conclusion

In 1999 about half of the households in the United States owned at least one gun, a figure that had been stable for over four decades despite increases in population (and corresponding numbers

of households). The average number of guns per household, however, increased from about three in the late 1970s to about four in the 1990s. This suggests that most new guns entering circulation in the United States were being purchased by people who were already gun owners, which perhaps also meant that mandated waiting periods for purchasing a gun from a retail sales outlet (in order to "cool off" the purchaser) would have little effect.

Most privately owned guns were used for sport or recreational purposes. Two-thirds of these were rifles or shotguns. Of handgun owners, roughly 40 percent indicated they owned their gun for sport or recreational purposes, another 40 percent used them for self-protection, and 20 percent used them for their jobs. It is difficult accurately to estimate the effectiveness of handguns for self-protection, in part because one element of "effectiveness" presumably is preventive—knowing a potential victim is armed may deter a perpetrator from engaging in the criminal act in the first place. Even if the security provided is only illusionary, this psychological advantage is worthwhile to many. Given that most violent crime occurs in the most marginal socioeconomic areas of urban America, it should not be a surprise that residents of these areas almost unanimously report the use of guns for self-protection.

While it is difficult to know exactly how the future development of weaponry will translate to street-level violence and crime, it is certain that there will continue to be instances in which sophisticated weapons are used for illegal enterprises. Equally certain is the likelihood that the general public will voice its concern by attempting to restrict the availability of these weapons.

BIBLIOGRAPHY

American Psychological Association, Commission on Violence and Youth. *Violence and Youth: Psychology's Response.* Washington, D.C.: American Psychological Association, 1993.

Baker, Susan P., et al. *The Injury Fact Book.* 2d ed. New York: Oxford University Press, 1992.

Bijlefeld, Marjolijn, ed. *The Gun Control Debate: A Documentary History.* Westport, Conn.: Greenwood, 1997.

Blumstein, Alfred. *Youth Violence, Guns, and the Illicit-Drug Industry.* Pittsburgh, Pa.: Carnegie Mellon University, 1994.

Boylen, M., and R. Little. "Fatal Assaults on United States Law Enforcement Officers." *Police Journal* 63, no. 1 (1990).

Bruce, John M., and Clyde Wilcox, eds. *Changing Politics of Gun Control.* Lanham, Md.: Rowman and Littlefield, 1998.

Bruce-Briggs, B. "The Great American Gun War." *Public Interest* 45 (1976).

Ezell, Edward C. *Small Arms of the World*. Harrisburg, Pa.: Stackpole, 1983.

Kachur, S. P., et al. "School Associated Violent Deaths in the United States, 1992–1994." *Journal of the American Medical Association* 275, no. 22 (1996).

Kaplan, John. Foreword to *Firearms and Violence: Issues of Public Policy*, edited by Don Kates. San Francisco: Pacific Institute for Public Policy Research, 1984.

Kaplan, M. S., and O. Geling. "Firearm Suicides and Homicides in the United States: Regional Variations and Patterns of Gun Ownership." *Social Science in Medicine* 46, no. 9 (1988).

Kates, Don B. "Toward a History of Handgun Prohibition in the United States." In *Restricting Handguns: The Liberal Skeptics Speak Out*, edited by Don Kates. Croton-on-Hudson, N.Y.: North River, 1979.

Kates, Don B., J. K. Lattimer, and J. R. Boen. "Problematic Arguments for Banning Handguns." In *The Great American Gun Debate*, edited by Don B. Kates and Gary Kleck. San Francisco: Pacific Institute for Public Policy Research, 1997.

Kennett, Lee, and James L. Anderson. *The Gun in America: The Origins of a National Dilemma*. Westport, Conn.: Greenwood, 1975.

Kizer, K. W., et al. "Hospitalization Charges, Costs, and Income for Firearm-Related Injuries at a University Trauma Center." *Journal of the American Medical Association* 273, no. 22 (1995).

Kleck, Gary. "Capital Punishment, Gun Ownership, and Homicide." *American Journal of Sociology* 84, no. 6 (1979).

———. *Point Blank: Guns and Violence in America*. New York: Aldine de Gruyter, 1991.

Lott, John R. *More Guns, Less Crime: Understanding Crime and Gun-Control Laws*. Chicago: University of Chicago Press, 1998.

McEwen, T., and F. J. Leahy. *Less Than Lethal Force: Technologies in Law Enforcement and Correctional Agencies*. Washington D.C.: U.S. National Institute of Justice, 1994.

Maguire, Kathleen, and Timothy Flanagan, eds. *Sourcebook of Criminal Justice Statistics: 1990*. Washington, D.C.: U.S. Government Printing Office, 1991.

Max, Wendy, and Dorothy P. Rice. "Shooting in the Dark: Estimating the Cost of Firearm Injuries." *Health Affairs* 12 (1993).

Muraskin, Roslyn, and Albert R. Roberts, eds. *Visions for Change: Crime and Justice in the Twenty-first Century*. 2d ed. Upper Saddle River, N.J.: Prentice-Hall, 1999.

Rice, Dorothy R., and Ellen J. MacKenzie. *Cost of Injury in the United States: A Report to Congress*. San Francisco: University of California Institute for Health and Aging and Johns Hopkins University Injury Prevention Center, 1989.

Sheley, Joseph F., and James Wright. *In the Line of Fire: Youth, Guns, and Violence in Urban America*. New York: Aldine de Gruyter, 1995.

Tonso, William R. *Gun and Society: The Social and Existential Roots of the American Attachment to Firearms*. Washington, D.C.: University Press of America, 1982.

Walker, Samuel. *Sense and Nonsense About Crime and Drugs: A Policy Guide*. 3d ed. Belmont, Calif.: Wadsworth, 1994.

Wright, James D. "Ten Essential Observations of Guns in America." *Society* (March–April 1995).

Wright, James D., and Peter H. Rossi. *Armed and Considered Dangerous: A Survey of Felons and Their Firearms*. New York: Aldine de Gruyter, 1994.

———. *Weapons, Crime, and Violence in America: Executive Summary*. Washington, D.C.: U.S. Department of Justice, National Institute of Justice, 1981.

Zawitz, Marianne W. *A Report on the Use of Guns in Crime Commission*. Washington, D.C.: U.S. Bureau of Justice Statistics, 1995.

Zimring, Franklin E. "Kids, Guns, and Homicide: Policy Notes on an Age-Specific Epidemic." Working paper no. 25. Earl Warren Legal Institute, School of Law, University of California at Berkeley, 1996.

Zimring, Franklin E., and Gordon Hawkins. *Crime Is Not the Problem: Lethal Violence in America*. New York: Oxford University Press, 1997.

ALBERT R. ROBERTS
GORDON MACNEIL

See also **Gun Control; Militarism; National Rifle Association; Right to Bear Arms; Weapons: Handguns.**

EPIDEMIOLOGY OF INJURIES

As the twentieth century came to a close, firearm-related injuries were a frequent, severe, and costly public health problem in the United States. On an average day in 1996, some 93 people died from such injuries and another 219 were treated in hospital emergency departments. This article examines the human and economic toll of this problem.

Impact on Mortality

Firearm-related injuries are an important cause of mortality in the United States. During 1996 firearm-related injuries, if considered as a cause-of-death category, were the eighth leading cause of death in the United States, taking a total of 34,040 lives (Peters, Kochanek, and Murphy 1998). Some 53 percent of these deaths were due to suicide, 42 percent to homicide, 3 percent to unintentional circumstances (accidents), and about 1 percent to circumstances that could not be determined. In the same year firearm-related deaths ranked as the second leading cause of death among children and young adults from ten to twenty-four years of age and the leading cause of death for both African American males and females fifteen to twenty-four years of age.

Overall, according to 1996 statistical data, men were 6.3 times more likely to die from firearm-related injuries than women. Among men, blacks were 2.6 times more likely to die from such injuries as whites. Black men between the ages of fifteen and twenty-nine faced the greatest risk of death from firearm-related injuries of any other group regardless of age, race, or sex. For firearm-related suicide, elderly white males were at highest risk of death. For both firearm-related homicide and unintentional circumstances, adolescent males in general, and young adult black males in particular, were at highest risk of death.

The number of firearm-related deaths increased by 43 percent (from 23,875 to 34,040) between 1968 and 1996. In contrast, over this same time period, the number of motor-vehicle-related fatalities (the leading cause of injury death) declined by 20 percent (from 54,862 to 43,649). (See figure 1.) The 1968–1996 trends projected firearm-related deaths to surpass motor-vehicle-related deaths as the leading cause of injury mortality in the United States in 2003.

Firearms have also played a key role in increasing rates of violent death among youths. Increases in rates of youth homicide and suicide in the decades since the 1950s are almost entirely attributable to increases in homicide and suicide from firearms.

According to comparisons made by Etienne G. Krug, Linda L. Dahlberg, and Kenneth E. Powell, the risk of firearm-related death in the United States in the late twentieth century far exceeded that for countries of comparable economic development. Overall, Americans were about eight times more likely to die from firearm-related injuries than citizens of comparable high-income countries. During the 1990s rates of firearm-related homicide were nineteen times higher than those for comparable countries; rates of firearm-related suicide were five times higher. In addition, the impact of firearm-related mortality was relatively greater on children, adolescents, and young adults in the United States than in other nations.

Impact on Morbidity

Firearm-related injuries also have a significant impact on morbidity in the United States. For every fatal firearm-related injury in 1996, two nonfatal firearm-related injuries were treated in hospital emergency departments according to the Centers for Disease Control and Prevention (1999). Of the estimated 69,554 nonfatal firearm-related injuries treated in 1996, about 53 percent resulted in hospitalization. Of these injuries, 69 percent were due to assaults or legal intervention, 6 percent to suicidal behavior, 15 percent to unintentional circumstances, and 9 percent to undetermined circumstances. Firearm-related injuries cause an unknown number of permanently disabling injuries. Anecdotal reports (e.g., from rehabilitation hospitals) at the end of the twentieth century suggested that permanently disabling spinal-cord injuries were becoming increasingly more frequent as the result of gunshot wounds than in earlier periods.

Lethality

Firearm-related injuries are highly lethal. According to Valerie Beamon and colleagues (1999), overall between 1992 and 1995, about 29 percent of firearm-related injuries that resulted in wounds serious enough to at least require emergency department treatment resulted in death. The lethality of firearm-related injuries depends on the circumstances. Suicide attempts with firearms resulted in death in 75 percent of cases; assaults with firearms were fatal in 20 percent of cases; and unintentional firearm-related injuries were lethal in 7 percent of cases. The lethality of firearm-related injuries exceeded that for all other major causes of injury in the United States, including such categories as motor-vehicle crashes, falls, and burns.

Economic Costs

While the human toll of firearm-related injuries in our society is significant, the economic cost is substantial as well. The lifetime costs of firearm-related injuries that occurred in the United States in 1990 were an estimated $20.4 billion (Max and

FIGURE 1. Observed and Projected Firearm- and Motor-Vehicle-Related Deaths, United States, 1968–1996

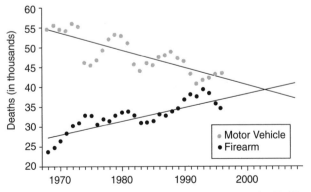

SOURCE: National Vital Statistics System, National Center for Health Statistics

Rice 1993). This figure includes $1.4 billion for direct expenditures for health care, $1.6 billion in lost productivity resulting from nonfatal injury and disability, and $17.4 billion in lost productivity from premature death.

Firearm-related injuries are, on average, more costly than most other types of injury for at least two reasons. First, the indirect cost per firearm-related death is higher because of the relatively young age of the victims; second, nonfatal firearm-related injuries tend to be more severe than other types of injury.

Prevention

The prevention of firearm-related injury may be approached through a broad array of strategies. Unfortunately, few of these strategies have been rigorously evaluated to determine their effectiveness, and even for those that have been evaluated (e.g., restrictive licensing, restriction of gun carrying in public), the scientific consensus on their effectiveness is lacking. Albert J. Reiss and Jeffery A. Roth (1993) offer a comprehensive review of the evidence for the effectiveness of intervention strategies in preventing firearm-related injuries.

The list of strategies presented in table 1 is not comprehensive, but it provides examples that have been suggested by scientists and advocates from all sides of the debate on how to prevent firearm injuries. Greater attention should be given to determining the efficacy and cost-effectiveness of alternative strategies for preventing firearm-related injuries. In addition to the strategies listed in table 1, we must recognize that any strategy that reduces interpersonal violence or suicidal behavior in general has the potential to also reduce firearm-related injury. Efforts to prevent suicide through better identification and treatment of depression, for example, may be an effective strategy for preventing firearm-related injuries as well.

Firearm-related injuries have a substantial impact on the health of Americans. Progress in preventing these injuries depends, in part, on the availability of objective scientific information to

TABLE 1. Strategies for Preventing Firearm-Related Injuries

Strategy	Interventions
Reduce inappropriate access to firearms.	Establish waiting periods. Forbid sales to high-risk purchasers. Disrupt illegal gun markets. Put combination/electronic locks on firearms. Restrict purchases to one per month. Buy back firearms. Increase taxes on firearms. Promote safe storage. Make owners liable for negligent damage by firearms. Develop "safe" or "childproof" firearms. Institute restrictive licensing (e.g., only police, the military, guards).
Change how or where guns are used.	Institute concealed-carrying laws (i.e., laws that permit eligible citizens to carry concealed firearms in public). Restrict gun carrying in public. Require mandatory sentences for firearm use in crimes. Conduct safety education. Use metal detectors. Establish firearm-free school zones.
Reduce lethality of guns.	Reduce magazine size. Ban dangerous ammunition. Require loading indicators on firearms. Require drop safeties on firearms (to prevent discharge when dropped).

SOURCE: Adapted from Reiss and Roth 1993.

document the magnitude and characteristics of the problem, risk and protective factors, and the effectiveness of interventions designed to reduce these injuries. Although progress has been made in our understanding of firearm-related injuries and their prevention, much work remains to be done.

BIBLIOGRAPHY

Beamon, Valerie, Joseph L. Annest, James A. Mercy, Marciejo Kresnow, Daniel A. Pollock. "The Lethality of Firearm Injuries in the United States Population." In *Annals of Emergency Medicine* (1999).

Boyd, Jeffery H., and Eve K. Moscicki. "Firearms and Youth Suicide." *American Journal of Public Health* 76 (1986).

Centers for Disease Control and Prevention. *Firearm Injury Surveillance Study.* Atlanta: Office of Statistics and Planning, National Center for Injury Prevention and Control, 1999.

———. "Homicide Among Fifteen- to Nineteen-Year-Old Males—United States, 1963–1991." *Morbidity and Mortality Weekly Report* 43, no. 40 (1994).

———. "Suicide Among Children, Adolescents, and Young Adults—United States, 1980–1992." *Morbidity and Mortality Weekly Report* 44, no. 15 (1995).

Grahm, P. M., and S. I. Weingarden. "Targeting Teenagers in a Spinal Cord Injury Violence Prevention Program." Paper presented at the Fourteenth Annual Scientific Meeting of the American Spinal Cord Injury Association, San Diego, Calif., 1988.

Krug, Etienne G., Linda L. Dahlberg, and Kenneth E. Powell. "Childhood Homicide, Suicide, and Firearm Deaths: An International Comparison." *World Health Statistics Quarterly* 49 (1996).

Krug, Etienne G., Kenneth E. Powell, and Linda L. Dahlberg. "Firearm-Related Deaths in the United States and Thirty-five Other High- and Upper-Middle-Income Countries." *International Journal of Epidemiology* 27 (1998).

Max, Wendy, and Dorothy P. Rice. "Shooting in the Dark: Estimating the Cost of Firearm Injuries." *Health Affairs* 12, no. 4 (winter 1993).

National Center for Injury Prevention and Control. *Injury Mortality, United States, 1990–1996.* Atlanta: Centers for Disease Control and Prevention, 1998.

Peters, Kimberley D., Kenneth D. Kochanek, and Sherry L. Murphy. *Deaths: Final Data for 1996.* National Vital Statistics Reports, vol. 47, no. 9. Hyattsville, Md.: National Center for Health Statistics, 1998.

Reiss, Albert J., and Jeffery A. Roth, eds. *Understanding and Preventing Violence.* Washington, D.C.: National Academy Press, 1993.

Rice, Dorothy P., et al. *Cost of Injury in the United States: A Report to Congress.* San Francisco: University of California Institute for Health and Aging and the Johns Hopkins University Injury Prevention Center, 1989.

JAMES A. MERCY

See also **Medicine and Violence: Emergency Medicine; Statistics and Epidemiology; Weapons.**

GUN CULTURE

In discussions about violence and crime in America, it has been popularly posited and argued that the United States is a "gun culture." That this is essentially an undefined, generalized, and politically charged polemical statement in no way detracts from its journalistic and intellectual currency or credibility. To truly understand the place of firearms in American life, however, one must focus on the role and evolution of the iconography of firearms in media and popular culture and study the characteristics of the cultural entity "bedrock America" against those of its antithesis, "cosmopolitan America." Such an analysis reveals that it is more meaningful to speak of the American gun culture (and its subcultures) than of the United States as itself a gun culture.

Additionally, it may be that urban gun culture, that is, the culture of violence and gangs usually associated with the inner city, does exist. But guns are a relatively recent addition to the arsenal of such groups and little has been written on their role in the symbolism and socialization in gangs. In any event, this subculture is an outgrowth of certain specific social factors, such as poverty, lack of opportunity, and racism, and has only a tenuous linkage with mainstream American gun culture—that connection being a common experience with pervasive violent imagery and subject matter in the mass media. Anyone reared in the United States, regardless of class background, cannot escape the barrage of violent cartoons, Westerns, police and courtroom dramas, reality-based programs, and, of course, news, that constitute the preferred subject matter of the cinema and television media.

The pervasiveness of firearms in early American history certainly seems unquestionable in both the popular and scholarly imagination. The image of besieged pioneer men fighting off fierce "savages" while the womenfolk reload is part of the national collective consciousness. Citizen-soldiers—minutemen—fighting a well-armed and well-disciplined foreign foe at Lexington and Concord and eventually winning the day at Yorktown (the "world turned upside down") is a deeply cherished part of the American mythos. Ancestors in blue or gray battling over defining principles in the chaos and black-powder smoke of Gettysburg is a vivid image at the center of the American national identity. Accounts of Alvin York's impressive marksmanship during World War I and Audie

Murphy's heedless World War II heroics point to modern mythologizing of the role of the citizen-soldier, again against a foreign foe. The argument that American arms did not ultimately prevail in Korea or Vietnam seems heretical, or certainly beside the point.

Despite this store of rich arms-associated imagery, evidence exists that firearms ownership and competence with arms was not universal in colonial or pre–Civil War America. In fact, research suggests that the gun culture is a relatively recent development in American society. Militia training and quality of armaments was uneven from the colonial period until the Civil War, particularly in the North. In fact, local militias were frequently a source of derision for the press and professional military alike. The citizen-soldier was not well regarded, despite the folklore, patriotic historiography, and popular media imagery to the contrary. Also, individual farmers and frontiersmen were

---

Cultures in Opposition

In the debate over gun ownership, cosmopolitan America, identified with the cities, the media, and academe, is pitted against bedrock America over a range of issues. Bedrock America is rural, conservative, nativistic, and individualistic. Cosmopolitan America is urban, liberal, internationalist, and establishmentarian. The two are almost polar opposites. What one group celebrates, the other derogates. Cosmopolitan America sees the Constitution as evolving and subject to interpretation based on current conditions; bedrock America sees the Constitution as holy writ, again with some degree of selectivity. In the latter view, the Second Amendment is clearly a sacred grant of the right of self-defense and of the right and obligation to fight against oppressive foes both foreign and domestic. Cosmopolitan America, with its faith in evolutionary meliorism and governmental intervention, sees such a view as anachronistic and paranoid. As cosmopolitan America carries the day in an increasingly urbanizing society, the gun culture, as a particularly beset element of bedrock America, will continue on the defensive as its cherished worldview and mythology are disconfirmed, stigmatized, and inevitably criminalized.

---

not particularly well armed, as a number of historical sources attest. Even in the Wild West, aside from localized pockets of extreme violence, it seems that guns and gunplay were much less prevalent than is popularly believed.

Modern firearms-manufacturing pioneers such as Samuel Colt, in conjunction with post–Civil War Unionist shooting enthusiasts, were chiefly responsible for creating a receptive climate for popular gun ownership. Through clever advertising and domination of the "hook and bullet" (fishing and hunting) media of the late 1800s and early twentieth century, New England gun manufacturers were able to create a pervasive consciousness of threat and menace and thereby stimulate a huge new market.

By the time World War I ended, an incipient gun culture was firmly in place, especially in rural America. Gun ownership was given salience through the new medium of popular film and, later, radio and television. Still, interest in firearms remained primarily confined to hunting arms such as simple, low-capacity rifles and shotguns, even though more sophisticated and modern semiautomatic weaponry was legally available. It was only the specter of rising crime, political assassinations, and media-driven gun control efforts in the mid–twentieth century that gave the modern gun culture more cogent organizational focus, a complex ideology, and a raison d'être.

The National Rifle Association (NRA), founded in the 1870s, emerged in the 1960s as the embodiment of "the gun lobby" and as the media's chief exemplar of obscurantism. The organization presented an anachronistic view of American society, firearms, crime, and indeed human nature. It must be noted that in the late twentieth century the NRA and other such interest groups, while purporting to speak for all gun owners, had a relatively small membership and declining influence in both federal and local venues. Despite its visibility in the media, the NRA was no longer central to the American gun culture, being increasingly viewed as too compromising or too immoderate by different factions within that grouping.

Characteristics of the Gun Culture

In a society in which over half of all Americans own guns and in which there are over 235 million firearms in private hands, it is presumptuous to overgeneralize about the characteristics or existence of a monolithic gun culture. There are, after all, subcultures of hunters, gun collectors, target

The original Colt's revolver, patented by Samuel Colt in the United States in 1836.
CORBIS-BETTMANN

shooters, and survivalists, as well as business people who just want to make money in this legal but besieged industry. However, the ideology of these groups overlaps. Certain commonalities have been noted by scholars in the context of focusing on the "cultures of gun owners" and the antitheses of those cultures.

Like other increasingly stigmatized "pariah" groups, gun owners have developed a characteristic ideology and worldview. Perhaps the most fundamental element in this weltanschauung is an anachronistic and paternalistic understanding of reality. That is, gun owners generally look to and revere a mythopoeic heroic American past when men were men—the rulers of the roost, breadwinners, and paterfamilias. Until the late twentieth century the role of women in the gun culture was as auxiliaries, although as in other areas of endeavor, female participation in target events and hunting is growing. Indeed, firearms aimed at the female market are now widely advertised and available. But the gun culture's view of the past is highly (if selectively) patriotic (some would say chauvinistic) and authoritarian. This is seemingly paradoxical given the often bitter antigovernment screeds and jeremiads—as disseminated in magazines, editorials, bumper stickers, and casual conversation—emanating from some quarters within the gun culture. Government enforcement blunders such as Ruby Ridge and Waco are seen as proof positive of sinister, totalitarian designs and methods of the various federal agencies charged with law enforcement, particularly the Bureau of Alcohol, Tobacco, and Firearms. The authoritarian mood of many within the gun culture, then, be-

speaks a loyalty to a previously extant reality: the good old days. One has the impression that had time stopped in the early 1950s (1850s?) many committed gun enthusiasts would have been pleased.

Another theme of the gun culture is totemism: a concern with the gun as a physical representation of the old order, a concrete and spiritual link to a heroic past. In the South this takes the form of "southern Shintoism," where guns carried in "the War" are a very real and highly valued link to one's venerated ancestors. These weapons are often displayed quite attractively and elaborately, often forming the focal point of the family or living room. To paraphrase William Faulkner, to many in the South, the past is not even past, hence the high degree of interest, commitment, and involvement in such expressive activities as Civil War reenactment. Within and outside the South, some guns evoke a certain mystique and hold a special place in the hearts of collectors. Many serious collectors seek only firearms of a certain war, era, caliber, or manufacturer.

That gun owners enjoy the aesthetic aspect of certain guns seems paradoxical to the uninitiated but is a very real phenomenon. The history of certain firearms and the cultural meanings assigned by the gun culture generally determine such associations. The "cult" of the Colt .45 semiautomatic pistol is especially notable in this regard. A boxy, heavy weapon with an unforgiving recoil, it owes its mystique to its use by the U.S. armed forces in colonial conflicts, World War I and World War II, Korea, and Vietnam. Its replacement by the more efficient Beretta 92 .9mm, a weapon with no present cult status, has been bitterly lamented by the gun press and its self-appointed gurus for years.

The firearm enjoys iconic status in popular culture as well. Colt and other revolvers were celebrated in pulp novels of the late 1800s. In gangster films of the 1930s and 1940s the chattering tommy gun is omnipresent. Television Westerns of the 1950s and 1960s often featured the hero's gun in a critical supporting role. Who can forget (and did not eagerly anticipate) Paladin's ("Have gun will travel.") handy derringer used as a last resort? What grade-school boy of this era did not enjoy the opening credits of the television show *The Rifleman,* when the hero's custom-made rapid-cocking Winchester fired like a submachine gun at an unseen foe? In *Colt .45* a descendant of Samuel Colt peddled the eponymous six-guns around the West. It might be argued that in certain films dating from the 1960s and later the featured guns are the stars of the show: the vast firepower employed by Rambo, James Bond's Walther (and Q's other inventions), McQ's Ingram submachine gun, and of course Dirty Harry's .44 Magnum, "the most powerful handgun in the world." In many movie advertisements the firearms are prominently featured, often enjoying equal space with the stars. In the films themselves, the weaponry is often featured in loving close-ups. Some films seem like training films put out by the military or arms manufacturers—the audience sees guns being assembled, loaded, cleaned, and fired in a variety of configurations. The gun has become a central element in dramatic action, evolving from an image used in foreshadowing a story's resolution to an almost sentient being or force (.44 caliber as Excalibur?) accompanying the hero through his mythic labors.

Firearms are also used in the media as a negative icon to denote crime stories on local and national news broadcasts, even when the featured crime, though violent, may not have been committed with a firearm at all. The NRA and its members are similarly stigmatized in media coverage as mindless advocates of senseless violence; contempt in the voices of interviewers and newscasters is commonly undisguised. Another cliché designates the firearm as a phallic symbol. Some gun critics have asserted that gun owners are sexually inadequate and that the gun serves as a sexual substitute. This priapic theory of gun ownership, although thoroughly discredited, enjoys wide currency among the intelligentsia and in pop psychology circles. So the firearm, although used to sell violence by both entertainment and news media, is a symbol that has an oddly ambivalent status.

Gun owners frequently engage in recruitment activity. Hunting and gun magazines often stress the purported character-building attributes of hunting, the discipline of marksmanship, and the appreciation of the outdoors shared by those who enjoy shooting sports. A frequent theme in these

A turn-of-the-twentieth-century woman firing a small-caliber, lever-action rifle. LIBRARY OF CONGRESS

Al Pacino in Brian DePalma's film *Scarface* **(1983).** PHOTOFEST

magazines is the importance of exposing young people to shooting. Gun shows, shooting matches, hunting, and casual plinking are all means by which newcomers, usually young men, are brought into the fold. Typically within a family context, a boy receives a BB gun as a preteen, a .22-caliber rifle as an adolescent, and shotguns and high-powered rifles as a young adult. In increasingly urbanizing modern society, however, many young men never get beyond the .22-caliber stage and really never become more deeply involved in the gun culture—there are fewer isolated places to plink freely. Yet it can be argued that each evolving stage of gun ownership is a rite of passage in which a youth, in a very real though symbolic sense, can say before his family and folk community, "Now I am a man." Attempts by politicians to disarm largely rural youth ignore the critical role of firearms as a signifier of adult status. The notion of locking up the family arsenal to inhibit access by such proven and responsible young adults is seen as bizarre, ludicrous, and insulting to both young person and family alike. The infrequent and tragic abuse of family firearms by ostensibly well-reared boys who have been socialized in the gun culture is seen as incomprehensibly aberrant and pathological—not as indicative of a "gun obsessed" culture, nor as evidence of over-

access to guns. Such legislation is widely resented by those in bedrock America and is seen at best as naïve, and at worst as a kind of cultural genocide.

BIBLIOGRAPHY

Bruce-Briggs, Barry. "The Great American Gun War." *The Public Interest* 36 (fall 1976).

Bellesiles, Michael A. "The Origins of Gun Culture in the United States, 1760–1865." *Journal of American History* 83, no. 2 (September 1996).

Gibson, James William. *Warrior Dreams: Violence and Manhood in Post-Vietnam America.* New York: Hill and Wang, 1994.

Hawley, F. Frederick. "Culture Conflict and the Ideology of Pariah Groups: The *Weltanschauung* of Gun Owners, Southerners, and Cockfighters." In *The Gun Culture and Its Enemies,* edited by William R. Tonso. Bellevue, Wash.: Merril, 1990.

Hawley, Frederick. "Guns." In *The Encyclopedia of Southern Culture,* edited by Charles Reagan Wilson and William Ferris. Chapel Hill: University of North Carolina Press, 1989.

Kleck, Gary. *Targeting Guns: Firearms and Their Control.* New York: Aldine de Gruyter, 1997.

F. FREDERICK HAWLEY

See also **Frontier; Militarism; Right to Bear Arms; Weapons.**

H

HAITI, REBELLION IN

The transformation of Saint Domingue from a wealthy French colony to the first independent black nation in the Americas was marked by almost unparalleled violence. Between the slave uprising of 1791 and the creation of the independent nation of Haiti in 1804, one-third of the population of five hundred thousand died. Conflict raged between white slave owners, free mulattos and blacks, African slaves, and various invading European armies. In the United States the Haitian revolution, with its extreme violence, came to symbolize very different things to disparate groups. White slave owners feared that the revolution would inspire slave revolts and race war in the American South. White abolitionists argued that Haiti illustrated the bitter fruit of slavery itself. African Americans used the rebellion, and the image of its brilliant and sometimes ruthless leader, Toussaint-Louverture, as a source of pride, resistance, and black nationalism.

The origins of the Haitian revolution lay in the country's complex caste and class system. In the 1780s Saint Domingue was the world's largest producer of sugar and coffee. Wealthy white French landowners supervised plantations worked by hundreds of thousand of slaves, the majority of whom were African-born. However, plantation society also possessed a sizable educated and artisan free black and mulatto population that identified with French culture and cared little for the slaves.

The American and French Revolutions inspired the free colored to organize armed resistance to white elites, but it was an unexpected revolt of plantation slaves in 1791 that sparked over ten years of armed conflict between the country's white, mulatto, and black inhabitants, as well as foreign armies. Radical French whites wanted to retain their valuable colony, and free colored forces wanted to retain their relatively privileged social status. Both groups then vacillated between fighting one another and cooperating against the slaves, but all three sides employed mass executions as a battle tactic. Free colored forces jailed and executed whites across Saint Domingue, prompting some ten thousand whites to flee to America. Radical whites from Revolutionary France, in conjunction with free colored forces, finally suppressed the slave revolt in 1793, and slavery in Saint Domingue was soon abolished so that freed slaves could be used as troops in the face of Spanish military threats. Between 1793 and 1798, white radicals and a variety of black and colored military leaders commanded armies composed of former slaves that defeated Spanish and British invasions. Toussaint-Louverture, a charismatic leader and brilliant military strategist, earned the approval of Revolutionary France and emerged as the most powerful figure in Saint Domingue.

Genocide became an all-too-common tactic of warfare after 1798, when Toussaint-Louverture battled the colored strongmen in several different regions of Saint Domingue. During the "War of Knives" in 1798–1799, Toussaint-Louverture and one of his generals, Jean Jacques Dessalines, waged a campaign of extermination against mulattos throughout the country. By 1800 Toussaint-

Louverture had complete control of the island, which he skillfully kept under French jurisdiction; he also reinstated plantation labor via force. However, Napoleon Bonaparte, who was suspicious of Toussaint-Louverture's ambitions, ordered an invasion of Saint Domingue in 1802. Toussaint-Louverture waged a guerrilla campaign against the French, but he eventually surrendered. Rival political figures accused him of planning a rebellion, and French authorities jailed him in France, where he died in prison. When the French attempted to reinstate slavery in Saint Domingue in 1802, Dessalines led a black rebellion that defeated French forces in 1803 and declared independence in 1804. Both sides employed mass killings, but Dessalines's massacre of the country's few remaining whites after independence generated the most infamy. The legacy of the rebellion's brutal carnage, mulatto and black racial tensions, and the former slaves' desire for subsistence agriculture, in combination with international ostracism of Haiti, led to a dramatic decline in the country's standard of living and a pattern of military dictatorship and political violence that persisted well into the late twentieth century.

The impact of the Haitian rebellion reverberated throughout North America, but it had particular resonance in the southern United States. White refugees who settled in Charleston, South Carolina, and New Orleans recounted the horror of the Haitian slave rebellion. Southern slave owners feared that Caribbean slaves tainted by the rebellion in Haiti and imported to the United States would incite slave revolts. Beginning in the mid-1790s, political authorities across the Deep South enacted policies to keep slaves escaping Saint Domingue from entering the United States, strengthened slave codes and plantation discipline, and curtailed the rights of free blacks. Proslavery advocates argued that if the institution of slavery were weakened in any way, white Americans would suffer from brutalities like those in Haiti. Slave owners' fears of Haitian-inspired resistance gained more currency in 1822 when a free black named Denmark Vesey attempted an organized slave revolt in Charleston. Vesey had sent letters to Haitian authorities asking for help, and one of his coconspirators testified that Vesey modeled his plan to massacre whites after the pattern of the Haitian revolution.

Up to the time of the Civil War, Southerners insisted that slavery was the only institution that could prevent race war and that terror was the only result of black freedom. The "lesson" South-erners drew from the Haitian revolution reappeared during the ascendancy of scientific racism in the early twentieth century and continued to shape white southern racist arguments in the 1920s about African Americans' supposed penchant for violence. White abolitionists and African Americans took different lessons from the violence of the Haitian Revolution. Some abolitionists, such as William Lloyd Garrison, disdained the carnage of the Haitian revolution but argued that the brutality was a logical symptom of the institution of slavery. White opponents of racism stressed that the military genius of Toussaint-Louverture proved that people of African descent were just as capable of political, intellectual, and social skills as were whites. Many African Americans regarded Toussaint-Louverture as a black hero. The Haitian revolution inspired black antislavery activists such as David Walker and Henry Highland Garnett to articulate a militant program of resistance. In the early twentieth century, black nationalists saw Haiti as a successful alternative to white-dominated societies. Long after its violent revolution, Haiti continued to have an impact beyond its shores.

BIBLIOGRAPHY

Fick, Carolyn E. *The Making of Haiti: The Saint Domingue Revolution from Below.* Knoxville: University of Tennessee Press, 1990.

Gaspar, David B., and David P. Geggus, eds. *A Turbulent Time: The French Revolution and the Greater Caribbean.* Bloomington: Indiana University Press, 1997.

Hunt, Alfred N. *Haiti's Influence on Antebellum America: Slumbering Volcano in the Caribbean.* Baton Rouge: Louisiana State University Press, 1988.

James, C. L. R. *The Black Jacobins: Toussaint L'Ouverture and the San Domingo Revolution.* 2d rev. ed. New York: Vintage, 1989. Originally published in 1963.

Ott, Thomas O. *The Haitian Revolution, 1789–1804.* Knoxville: University of Tennessee Press, 1973.

MICHAEL JONATHAN PEBWORTH

See also **Slave Rebellions.**

HARDIN, JOHN WESLEY
(1853–1895)

Of all the old-time western gunfighters, John Wesley Hardin of Texas had the greatest claim to the title of "man killer." In a span of nine or ten years, he killed at least twenty, perhaps as many as fifty, men. And yet he was never regarded as a psychopath. Indeed, despite his penchant for homicide, he was a good husband and father, a man of his word, and a Christian. He was not a thief and worked variously as a farmer, cowboy, gambler, saloonkeeper, logger, and schoolteacher. Many Texans saw Hardin as a hero in their struggle against Reconstruction in Texas and amidst the hostility against blacks. Nevertheless, although the violent climate of the times doubtless contributed to his lethal disposition, his killings do not all appear to have been motivated by Reconstruction issues. Many were personal quarrels.

Hardin was born in Bonham, Texas, the son of James Gibson Hardin, a Methodist minister who named him for the founder of Methodism. He was a bright child, but even as a boy he stabbed a classmate in a fight over a girl and threatened a teacher who was about to whip one of his friends. He killed his first man, a former slave, in a personal quarrel when he was fifteen, as well as the three soldiers who came to arrest him. Between those killings and the shooting of Deputy Sheriff Charles Webb at Comanche, Texas, on 26 May 1874, he left a trail of dead men that made him one of the most feared men in Texas. After Webb's murder, Texas placed a $4,000 reward on Hardin's head.

Hardin fled the state in 1875 with his wife, Jane Bowen, and daughter and lived under an assumed name, J. H. Swain, Jr., in Florida and Alabama for two years, where he was party to more killings. He was captured on a train near Pensacola, Florida. Back in Texas, he was convicted in 1877 of second-degree murder in the shooting of Charles Webb

and sentenced to prison. He studied law in prison and was released in 1894. By then his wife had died. He practiced law briefly in Gonzales, where his children lived. Later he married Callie Lewis, a young woman who left him within hours of the wedding.

Eventually Hardin drifted into El Paso and opened a law office. In El Paso, home to a variety of aging gunmen, Hardin drank and grew morose. There, on the night of 19 August 1895, he was shot from behind by John Selman, Sr., an off-duty policeman and former professional gunman; some say the motive was a personal quarrel. Hardin left behind an unfinished autobiography that provides ample evidence of his intellectual gifts—gifts overshadowed and nullified by his homicidal record.

BIBLIOGRAPHY

Hardin, John Wesley. *The Life of John Wesley Hardin as Written by Himself.* Originally published 1896. Norman: University of Oklahoma Press, 1961.

Marohn, Richard C. *The Last Gunfighter: John Wesley Hardin.* College Station, Tex.: Creative Publishing, 1995.

Metz, Leon. *John Wesley Hardin: Dark Angel of Texas.* Norman: University of Oklahoma Press, 1996.

Tatum, Stephen. *Inventing Billy the Kid: Visions of the Outlaw in America, 1881–1981.* Albuquerque: University of New Mexico Press, 1982.

GARY L. ROBERTS

See also **Gunfighters and Outlaws, Western.**

John Wesley Hardin. LIBRARY OF CONGRESS

HARPERS FERRY, RAID ON

In 1794 George Washington chose Harpers Ferry as the site for building a new federal armory, which was completed in 1796. By 1859, the year of John Brown's raid on the Virginia (now West Virginia) town, it had grown into a small industrial center with two arms factories containing thirty-four armory buildings, two arsenals, and several streets of government housing.

In August 1855 John Brown (1800–1859), a radical abolitionist, and five of his sons went from North Elba, New York, to Kansas to oppose the proslavery movement. In 1856, to avenge an attack on Lawrence, Kansas, by proslavery forces, Brown, with four of his sons and two other men, murdered five proslavery farmers. For the next three years he evaded arrest while raising money for a raid he was planning on Harpers Ferry.

Without telling his backers his plan, Brown conspired to strike a blow against slavery by freeing men in bondage and arming them to wage war

"The Last Moments of John Brown," an 1884 painting by Thomas Hovender, showing the abolitionist being led to the gallows in 1859. CORBIS-BETTMANN

against their masters. Although Brown of course wanted to free all slaves, including women and children, his plan was to focus on freeing men; he could not arm the women and children and saw them as a potential burden to his black army as it plunged into the South. Harpers Ferry provided the perfect means to implement his plan: it was located in an important slaveholding state, and it contained an enormous store of muskets. Brown also believed that slaves in the area (who made up approximately 10 percent of the population of the county and surrounding area) could be recruited to fight beside him. Equally important, Harpers Ferry was located at the foot of the Blue Ridge Mountains, where Brown intended to take and sustain his army as it drove deeper into the South.

Posing as Isaac Smith to avoid detection, Brown arrived in Harpers Ferry with two sons and a bodyguard on 3 July 1859. He rented an obscure farmhouse set back from the road in Maryland, across the Potomac River, and began to gather an army together while reconnoitering the town. Because the farmhouse out of which he operated was

in a remote location, and because neighbors and local authorities believed that Brown had come with his sons to mine the hills, his real activities went unnoticed until October. Although he intended to gather a much larger force, Brown's army consisted of only twenty-two men, five of whom were black.

Although out of money, Brown launched his attack on Harpers Ferry on the night of 16 October 1859. He entered the town while its citizens slept and took possession of the armories and arsenals, taking as prisoners armory employees, townsfolk, and various inhabitants of Maryland and the Virginia countryside. During the raid Brown's son Watson accidentally shot a black baggage handler who panicked. News of the raid reached townsfolk when a local physician, Dr. Starry, heard the shot and went to the wager house to investigate. After finding the baggage handler mortally wounded, Starry mounted his horse and raised the militia. After placing guards on both bridges leading into town, Brown set up headquarters in the armory's engine house. At daylight townsfolk took to the streets with arms. By midday militia companies from the surrounding area began arriving and forced the members of Brown's outposts into the engine house. Casualties mounted on both sides, among them Brown's two sons and the town's mayor, Fontaine Beckham.

An urgent call to Washington brought Brevet Colonel Robert E. Lee with a company of marines to Harpers Ferry by train. At daylight on 18 October, Lee ordered the marines to attack the engine house. Moments later Brown fell wounded, and the members of his band were either killed or captured. All of the survivors were transferred to Charles Town, Virginia, for trial. Brown died on the gallows on 2 December 1859; the others followed later.

Abolitionists fueled the Civil War, and John Brown, an ultra-abolitionist, acted with the violence that his contemporaries only threatened. He predicted the Civil War and, in his own way, attempted to start it. After the raid, the town of Harpers Ferry continued to produce rifled muskets. Then, at the outbreak of the Civil War in 1861, the Confederacy accomplished what Brown had failed to do. Colonel Thomas J. Jackson came to town with the Virginia militia, cleaned out the arsenals, packed up all the musket-making machinery, and sent everything south. Harpers Ferry never recovered economically.

BIBLIOGRAPHY

Bushong, Millard K. *Historic Jefferson County.* Boyce, Va.: Carr, 1972.

Hearn, Chester G. *Six Years of Hell: Harpers Ferry During the Civil War.* Baton Rouge: Louisiana State University Press, 1996.

Smith, Merritt Roe. *Harpers Ferry Armory and the New Technology: The Challenge of Change.* Ithaca, N.Y.: Cornell University Press, 1977.

U.S. Senate. Mason Committee. *Inquiry into the Harper's Ferry Invasion.* 36th Cong., 1st sess., 1859. S. Rept. 278.

Villard, Oswald Garrison. *John Brown, 1800–1859: A Biography Fifty Years After.* New York: Knopf, 1910.

Chester G. Hearn

See also **Brown, John; Slavery.**

HATE, POLITICS OF

Hate is a form of belief that seeks safety and self-protection on the one hand, destruction and annihilation on the other. One learns to hate; one is not born knowing hate. The politics of hate constructs borders that are not to be crossed and entities that are not to be blended. Hate creates communities segregated by religion, class status, gender, sexuality, age, and so on. The isolation inherent in such segregation breeds the ignorance and limited experience that nurture further prejudice.

Borders define an inside and an outside, a center and a margin, inclusion and exclusion, sameness and difference. To foster hate, a neutralized standard is privileged, and a notion of difference becomes embedded, stigmatizing those who are said to be different. Difference defined by borders creates otherness, and this otherness is inscribed on bodies; racism uses the physicality of bodies to punish, to expunge, and to isolate the outsider. Physicality is key to constructing and seeing hatreds. The other is a foreigner, an immigrant, or a stranger. Hatred and fear of one outsider beget hatred and fear of another; not neat and separate, hate is multiple and continuous.

Women of all colors and nationalities are a key object of hate. Women and girls have continually been the targets of sexual abuse, sexual harassment, and domestic violence. In times of war, girls and women are subjected to the brutality of rape and murder, as was seen in World Wars I and II and in places like Bosnia, Algeria, and Rwanda.

In the United States a complicated racial politics forms a color hierarchy that places blacks lower than whites. Skin colors other than "white" are demeaned and punished for being different. The racializing of difference has led to the deaths of hundreds of thousands of blacks in the slave trade, the brutal treatment of slaves in the United States, the use of black slave girls as breeders, and lynching as a method of white supremacist political control.

The Western divisions of black versus white and woman versus man impede the full pluralization of diversities—individual, racial, political, religious. This leads to false homogenizations of people around the globe; Arabs are not seen in terms of their specificities—Berber, Palestinians, Kurds, Bedouins, and Yemeni. In the United States, to use the word *black* is to elide the specificities of Jamaican, Trinidadian, Dominican, and other identities.

Falsely homogenizing peoples leads to false notions of purity and identity. Purity of blood almost never exists, so neither does purity of race. The construction of the "other," however, depends on this notion of purity, of separateness. Yet racial purity is a construction of the mind's eye: a fantasy, a fiction. Thus, hate is both fixed and utterly unstable: it defines the other—the color of skin, the shape of a nose, the texture of hair—before an individual is seen, and then that individual is seen only through the context of the mind's eye. Such "seeing" is hate itself.

These hate-filled constructions of identity are encoded in the nationalist struggles that carry over from the twentieth century into the twenty-first. Nations themselves imply borders and boundaries that bespeak both openings and closings. A nation requires an inside and an outside and is defined by its unity. The differences of the globe challenge

---

Symbols of Hate

Hate sometimes operates through symbols. In Nazi Germany green triangles noted criminals, black triangles designated antisocials, red triangles were affixed to political dissidents, yellow stars marked Jews, and pink triangles indicated homosexuals. In colonial New England a scarlet letter *A* worn by a woman marked her as an adulteress; later the white hood and the burning cross were symbols of white supremacy, and the swastika, an emblem of the Nazi Party, was used by those in sympathy with Nazi Germany's aims.

the unity of nations—hence the wars in Chechnya, Bosnia, and the Persian Gulf region.

Although nation-building draws exclusionary boundaries, the people it attempts to contain are complex and diverse. Because the identity of individuals, as well as that of nations, derives from race, gender, sexuality, religion, ethnicity, age, geographic location, and so on, multiple identity and open borders must challenge constructs of hate.

The greatest challenge facing the twenty-first century is to address the many forms of hatred that plague the politics of the globe. Hate fuels the conflicts on the streets of Los Angeles, Detroit, and New York City. In the 1990s the brutal murders of Matthew Shepard, a gay student in Wyoming, and of James Byrd, Jr., a black man dragged to his death behind a truck in Texas, as well as the beatings of Rodney King by white Los Angeles police officers and of Abner Louima, a Haitian immigrant, by white New York City police officers, bespeak a deep body politics of hatred with a long history in the United States. These acts provoked outrage both locally and nationally, and served to remind the nation that the rejection of hate requires a worldview that embraces and encourages the multiplicity of identities and the richness of difference. The tonic for the politics of hate is the nurturance of pluralism: fear must be replaced by curiosity, singularity must be replaced by multiplicity, and exclusion and war must be replaced by tolerance.

BIBLIOGRAPHY

Eisenstein, Zillah. *Hatreds: Racialized and Sexualized Conflicts in the Twenty-first Century.* New York: Routledge, 1996.

Fanon, Frantz. *Black Skin, White Masks.* New York: Grove, 1967.

Gilroy, Paul. *"There Ain't No Black in the Union Jack": The Cultural Politics of Race and Nation.* London: Hutchinson, 1987.

Sartre, Jean Paul. *Anti-Semite and Jew.* New York: Schocken, 1948.

Takaki, Ronald. *Iron Cages: Race and Culture in Nineteenth-Century America.* New York: Knopf, 1979.

ZILLAH EISENSTEIN

See also **Extremism; Foreign Intervention, Fear of; Gay Bashing; Immigration; Militias, Unauthorized; Race and Ethnicity; Terrorism.**

HATE CRIME

Hate crimes are criminal attacks upon a person or property that are motivated by a characteristic such as race, religion, gender, sexual orientation, or ethnicity. Hate crimes obviously are not unique to U.S. society, but they have occurred throughout its history. Lynchings, for example, are as much a part of the nation's past as are ringing proclamations of equal rights. The melting pot of U.S. history at times has boiled over in the ugliness of hate directed at people because of their color, religious beliefs, ancestry, or sexual orientation.

Some studies at the end of the twentieth century indicated that the frequency of hate crimes had been on the increase beginning in the late 1980s (Levin and McDevitt 1993; Walker 1994). Because of what has been called a rising tide of hate crimes in the United States, new laws have been enacted at both the federal and state levels. These laws reflect increasing social awareness and concern. The seriousness of the problem, especially in light of its long history in the United States, should not be underestimated. How successfully hate-crime laws will deter and control hate-motivated crimes has yet to be seen.

Prevalence of Hate Crimes

Because so many hate crimes are never reported, accurate measure of their frequency is impossible. Also, classification is difficult because the category is defined by the subjective motivation of the perpetrator. According to Federal Bureau of Investigation statistics, there were 7,684 reported hate crimes in 1993, including twenty homicides; the number for 1996 went up to 8,734 (although the number of reporting agencies also increased). The statistics from 1996 indicate that 62 percent of all hate crimes involved racial bias; for racial-bias crimes, African Americans were the most frequently targeted group. Sixteen percent of hate crimes were motivated by religion, with Jews being the most common target. Hate crimes directed against gays and lesbians represented 12 percent of the total, and those directed against Asian Americans 8 percent. Thirteen percent of hate crimes were targeted at whites.

Some organizations attempt to monitor and measure hate crimes directed at particular groups. The most systematic collection of data concerning hate crimes is done by the Anti-Defamation League (ADL), which tracks anti-Semitic acts. Since 1979 the ADL has published an annual report of hate activity directed at Jews; in 1997, for example, there were about sixteen hundred reported anti-Semitic incidents, including harassment, vandalism, and assaults. The August 1999 shootings at a Jewish community center in Granada Hills, California, by an avowed racist and anti-Semite, were a tragic example. Similarly, Klanwatch annually reports on the level of racially motivated crimes. Both of these sources report an increase in hate crimes in the United States. Klanwatch, for example, in 1993 reported a "raging hate epidemic" on college campuses. Likewise, studies of violence directed at gays and lesbians find a dramatic increase in such hate crimes (Herek and Berrill 1992). Given the paucity of data from earlier periods and the subjective nature of the reporting of hate crimes, comparisons of their frequency over time are difficult. Yet there is no doubt that there is a serious social problem with hate crimes directed at racial, religious, ethnic, and sexual-orientation minorities.

Hate crimes directed at gays and lesbians have been pervasive. A study of gay men and lesbians in major cities found that 19 percent reported having been punched, hit, kicked, or beaten at least once because of their sexual orientation and that 44 percent had been threatened with some form of physical violence (Herek and Berrill 1992). The October 1998 murder of the University of Wyoming student Matthew Shepard drew national attention. Groups such as the Lambda Legal Defense and Education Fund and the New York City Gay and Lesbian Anti-Violence Project have formed to stem violence against gays and lesbians.

It should be noted that statistical measures of hate crimes generally do not include rape and physical spousal abuse, which are generally treated as a separate category of offenses. Indeed, if such crimes were included in the data, they would be the most frequent types of hate crimes. The Violence Against Women Act of 1994 created the first federal authority over such crimes.

Historical Background

Hate crimes have occurred in the United States since colonial times. Not surprisingly, Native Americans were one of the first and most frequent targets of hate crimes. In fact, the government was actively involved in many ways in the persecution of American Indians. During the 1820s in North Carolina, Georgia, and other southern states, Cherokee Indians were marched by the military, at gunpoint, to Oklahoma. During this three-thousand-mile march, known as the Trail of Tears, hundreds of Cherokees died. During the 1850s and 1860s, the military killed Navajos in a "carefully orchestrated campaign" (Jacobs and Henry 1996, p. 387). In the late 1800s counties in New Mexico and Arizona

Los Angeles Police Department's SWAT members survey the scene at the North Valley Jewish Community Center in the Granada Hills suburb of Los Angeles in August 1999, after an avowed anti-Semite allegedly opened fire and wounded five people, including three boys. CORBIS/REUTERS NEWMEDIA INC.

95

offered bounties for Indian scalps, $500 for males and $250 for women and children. These practices, of course, are simply examples of the systematic persecution of Indians throughout the United States.

Hate crimes against African Americans also have a long history in the United States. Slaves had little or no protection against violence. After the Civil War, the Ku Klux Klan formed and began to terrorize blacks; between 1882 and 1968, it is estimated that almost five thousand people were lynched, the vast majority of them African Americans (Jacobs and Henry 1996). Among countless incidents of violence directed at blacks were shootings and murders.

Hate crimes directed at ethnic minorities increased as their population in the United States rose. In the mid–nineteenth century, the Know-Nothing Party arose, with anti-immigrant and anti–Roman Catholic views as its central theme. The nativist rhetoric spawned hatred and violence in the East, with burnings of Catholic churches and attacks by gangs and mobs against priests and immigrants occurring from Maine to Maryland. Similarly, as Jewish immigration increased, anti-Semitism flourished. Hate crimes such as fire-bombing and desecration of synagogues and individual attacks have been directed against Jews by such groups as the Klan, neo-Nazis, and skinheads.

Historically, hate crimes have increased during wartime, as international tensions exert pressure on relations between various ethnic communities. The identification of any racial or ethnic group as an enemy in wartime is likely to provoke hate crimes against American members of the group. This was especially true during World War II, when Japanese Americans were constant targets of hate-motivated crimes. Earlier, in 1915, hostility against German Americans was intensified by the sinking of the *Lusitania* prior to the United States' entry into World War I; hate crimes directed at German Americans continued throughout the war.

At the end of the twentieth century, U.S. involvement in the Persian Gulf War was accompanied by a dramatic increase in anti-Arab hate crimes. According to newspaper reports in 1991, hate crimes against Muslims and Arabs quadrupled in Los Angeles County in the months after the Iraqi invasion of Kuwait. In fact, it was in response to this increase in hate crimes that Lieutenant Governor Leo McCarthy introduced the California hate-crime statute. The Bosnian conflict in the 1990s produced a number of hate crimes in the United States among the various ethnic groups involved. In one incident, vandals spray-painted Croatian profanities on the wall of a Serbian Orthodox Church in Phoenix, Arizona.

Statutes

Legislatures throughout the country have enacted laws aimed at dealing with the problem of hate crimes. At the federal level, the Federal Hate Crime Statistics Act was signed into law by President George Bush on 23 April 1990. The law directs the U.S. attorney general to collect and report data about crimes motivated by hate based on race, religion, sexual orientation, or ethnicity. The statute's goal is to provide comprehensive data about the problem of hate crimes to inform the public and government officials as to when further action is needed.

By 1999 almost every state had adopted some form of hate-crime legislation, and forty states had laws that provided for penalty enhancements for hate-motivated crimes. In other words, a crime such as battery will receive a greater punishment if it is proven that the crime was motivated by hatred (rather than, for example, the desire to rob). California law provides that a person who commits a felony, or attempts to commit a felony, against a victim because of the victim's race, color, religion, nationality, disability, or sexual orientation will receive an additional term of one to three years in prison. A key issue surrounding such statutes concerns their constitutionality, particularly with regard to free speech. In *Mitchell v. Wisconsin* in 1993, the Supreme Court upheld a state law that imposed greater punishments if it could be proven that a victim was chosen because of his or her race. The Court emphasized that such penalty enhancements are directed at conduct, not at speech. The Court said that greater punishments for hate-motivated crimes was justified because of their harm to society. Chief Justice William H. Rehnquist, writing for a unanimous Court, explained that the law "singles out for enhancement bias-inspired conduct because the conduct is thought to inflict greater individual and societal harm. For example . . . bias-motivated crimes are more likely to provoke retaliatory crimes, inflict distinct emotional harms on their victims, and incite community unrest. The State's desire to redress these perceived harms provides an adequate explanation for its penalty-enhancement provision over and above mere disagreement with offenders' beliefs or biases."

Although the evidence of hate motivation might be speech, it is also true under other civil rights laws that proof of discriminatory intent might include words and other speech activities. For example, proof of discriminatory purpose in the employment discrimination context can be speech expressing racist views. The Supreme Court explained that where the law punishes conduct it may consider racist intentions as a basis for enhancing penalties.

Legislative attention to the problem of hate crimes increased significantly in the 1990s. It is too soon to know if these legislative efforts will make a difference. The Supreme Court's approval of such laws makes their enforcement likely. At the very least, the legislatures have tried to send a strong message condemning hate-motivated crimes.

BIBLIOGRAPHY

Dinnerstein, Leonard. *Anti-Semitism in America.* New York: Oxford University Press, 1995.

Herek, Gregory M., and Kevin T. Berrill, eds. *Hate Crimes: Confronting Violence Against Lesbians and Gay Men.* Newbury Park, Calif.: 1992.

Jacobs, James B., and Jessica S. Henry. "The Social Construction of a Hate Crime Epidemic." *Journal of Criminal Law and Criminology* 86 (1996).

Levin, Jack, and Jack McDevitt. *Hate Crimes: The Rising Tide of Bigotry and Bloodshed.* New York: Plenum, 1993.

Walker, Samuel. *Hate Speech: The History of an American Controversy.* Lincoln: University of Nebraska Press, 1994.

Zangrando, Robert L. *The NAACP Crusade Against Lynching, 1909–1950.* Philadelphia: Temple University Press, 1980.

ERWIN CHEMERINSKY

See also **African Americans; Asians; Class; Gay Bashing; Jews; Language and Verbal Violence; Lynching; Race and Ethnicity; Rape; Religion; Women.**

HATE SPEECH *See* Language and Verbal Violence.

HAYMARKET SQUARE RIOT

What came to be known as the Haymarket Square Riot occurred in Chicago on 4 May 1886 and was one of the most spectacular episodes of violence in nineteenth-century America. The event helped raise the "labor question" to preeminence in public awareness and highlighted the fragility of the country's commitment to freedom of speech and freedom of assembly.

Haymarket originated in the so-called great labor upheaval of the mid-1880s. Confronted with industrial overproduction and cutthroat price competition, employers at the time sought to reduce their costs by cutting wages and replacing skilled workers with machinery and unskilled labor. Up until then, organized skilled workers in Chicago had been able to win strikes with the help of Mayor Carter Harrison's policy of police neutrality. However, under intense business pressure, Harrison in 1885 appointed an antilabor police captain, John Bonfield. No longer able to rely on the police, many skilled unionists embraced more inclusive forms of organization, notably the Knights of Labor. They also gravitated toward more militant and broadly based forms of collective action, such as the boycott and sympathy strike.

In the spring of 1886 tens of thousands of American workers, men and women of all nationalities and races, rallied. Labor leaders hoped to inaugurate the movement on 1 May 1886 along with its plank for the eight-hour workday. In Chicago about eighty-eight thousand workers struck that year, more than thirty thousand of them on 1 May. Following an attack by Bonfield's police on strikers at McCormick's Reaper Plant on 3 May that killed and wounded several workers (the precise number was never established), a group of anarchists called a protest meeting to take place the next evening at Haymarket Square (at Randolph and Halsted Streets). Affiliated with the revolutionary International Working People's Association, most of the city's twenty-eight hundred anarchists were recent émigrés from central Europe. Viewing the wage system as a type of slavery, many anarchist activists subscribed to Johann Most's strategy of "the propaganda of the deed," in which recently invented dynamite bombs were to be used to spark a workers' insurrection. The eight-hour-workday movement seemed a propitious occasion for such action.

The first one hundred copies of the anarchist leaflet advertising the Haymarket meeting contained the words "Workingmen Arm Yourselves and Appear in Full Force," a fact later utilized by the prosecution of the anarchist leaders for conspiracy. Still, the meeting at Haymarket Square was peaceful, as attested by Mayor Harrison, who

Days after the Haymarket Square Riot, *Harper's Weekly* **published this wood engraving in its 15 May 1886 issue.** LIBRARY OF CONGRESS

was briefly in attendance. As the crowd dwindled a phalanx of police suddenly appeared, and Bonfield ordered the assemblage to disperse. At this point someone—no one knows who—threw a dynamite bomb into the ranks of the police. The police responded by firing indiscriminately into the crowd. Eight police officers ultimately perished along with a comparable number of workers. Ironically, most of the policemen who died were killed by gunshot wounds inflicted by bullets from fellow officers.

Called a "riot" by the press, the Haymarket Square event set off a widespread panic, kindling the nation's first Red Scare. The press fed the public fear that a revolutionary conspiracy existed among foreign-born radicals to overthrow the Republic and called for stern action to vindicate law and order. Under pressure from leading businessmen, Mayor Harrison the next day banned public meetings and processions. Meanwhile, Chicago's police ruthlessly suppressed existing strike activities, closed down the anarchist press, and arrested over two hundred anarchist leaders and suspects. On 5 June the state indicted thirty-one anarchists, and eight eventually stood trial for murder and conspiracy: August Spies, Albert Parsons, Samuel Fielden, George Engel, Adolph Fischer, Louis Lingg, Oscar Neebe, and Michael Schwab.

The prosecution had virtually no evidence linking the indicted anarchists to the bomb-throwing. Not only had the state failed to apprehend a sus-

pected bomb thrower, but six of the eight indicted anarchists had not even been present when the bomb exploded. Early in the trial State Attorney Julius S. Grinnell switched the burden of the prosecution to conspiracy, alleging the existence of a bomb-throwing plot planned on 3 May. When it became impossible to demonstrate that the meeting had taken place, Grinnell turned to the theory that all that was necessary to convict the defendants was proof that they had advocated violence against the forces of order, a readily demonstrable proposition. Judge Joseph E. Gary concurred with Grinnell in his instructions to the jury. On 20 August 1886 the jury capped the highly celebrated trial with a verdict of guilty and sentenced all except Neebe to death by hanging.

Over the next year a small but significant clemency movement spread across the nation. Trade unionists, led by Samuel Gompers of the American Federation of Labor and newly formed labor parties in Chicago, New York, and other cities, bitterly rejected the verdict and condemned Bonfield's attack on the Haymarket meeting as a violation of workers' rights. The fact that the anarchists had been convicted for their opinions and not their deeds, the hysterical atmosphere surrounding the trial, and the fear that their execution would generate further class violence prompted some opinion leaders in Chicago, including the reformer Henry Demarest Lloyd, William Salter, leader of the Ethical Cultural Society, and the banker Lyman

Gage, to urge clemency. The nation's most respected man of letters, William Dean Howells, also stood against the tide of public opinion to condemn the miscarriage of justice. But most of the defendants, still protesting their innocence, refused to request mercy from the Illinois governor, Richard Oglesby. On 11 November 1887, Spies, Parsons, Engel, and Fischer were hanged; Lingg had earlier committed suicide in prison, and the others had their sentences commuted.

The Haymarket martyrs received a measure of vindication in 1893 when Governor John Peter Altgeld pardoned the two remaining in prison and issued a message rebuking the prejudiced behavior of the judge and prosecutor and placing much of the responsibility for labor violence on police violation of workers' civil liberties.

The Haymarket Square affair and the public debate it generated proved to be an important moment in the transformation of nineteenth-century liberalism. Within the decade after 1886 leading businessmen, politicians, judges, reformers, and journalists—many of them the same people who had dissented against the Haymarket verdict—would accept the need for collective bargaining and arbitration to resolve labor disputes and advocate measures of progressive reform. Violence and disorder, including the use of dynamite, continued to plague industrial relations after 1886, but insofar as strikers used violent tactics, violence was generally associated with union attempts to deter strikebreakers and not with revolutionary anarchism.

BIBLIOGRAPHY

Avrich, Paul. *The Haymarket Tragedy.* Princeton, N.J.: Princeton University Press, 1984.

Nelson, Bruce C. *Beyond the Martyrs: A Social History of Chicago's Anarchists, 1870–1900.* New Brunswick, N.J.: Rutgers University Press, 1988.

Schneirov, Richard S. *Labor and Urban Politics: Class Conflict and the Origins of Modern Liberalism in Chicago, 1864–1897.* Urbana: University of Illinois Press, 1998.

RICHARD SCHNEIROV

See also **Anarchism; Bombings and Bomb Scares; Chicago; Labor and Unions; Riots.**

HAYWOOD, WILLIAM
(1869–1928)

William Dudley "Big Bill" Haywood, the labor leader and political radical, was born in Salt Lake City, Utah, to William Dudley and Elizabeth Haywood. As a teenager, Haywood became a hardrock miner, and he worked underground until 1901, when he became a full-time union official in the Western Federation of Miners (WFM).

Haywood built a reputation as a solid citizen and responsible union official in Silver City, Idaho, where he became a charter member of the WFM. He rose rapidly within the WFM, first becoming president of his local and then joining the national executive board of the WFM. Haywood edited the *Miner's Magazine* and served as secretary-treasurer of the WFM. As an international union official, he participated in a struggle for union recognition and power between miners and mine owners in Colorado (1903–1905) that produced great violence, including the destruction of mines, the dynamiting of a railroad depot, at least fourteen deaths, and numerous injuries; in response Governor James H. Peabody dispatched the National Guard, imposed martial law, and arrested Haywood and other union leaders. The Colorado labor war radicalized Haywood, making him a socialist and a founder, in 1905, of the Industrial Workers of the World (IWW), an organization dedicated to the destruction of capitalism. Haywood's association with the IWW won him the reputation as the "most dangerous man in America."

In February 1906 investigators from the Pinkerton Detective Agency arrested Haywood for his alleged role in the December 1905 assassination of Frank Steunenberg, a former governor of Idaho who had played a role in suppressing labor unrest. Haywood became the focus of a sensational murder trial in which he was defended by the famed defense attorney Clarence Darrow. The prosecution's primary witness charged Haywood not only with conspiring to assassinate Steunenberg but also with directing a WFM reign of terror that included multiple dynamitings and murders. The jury, however, acquitted Haywood. After the trial Haywood's continued advocacy of violence split the Socialist Party. He publicly condemned "bourgeois" laws and extolled actions considered lawless by other socialists. In 1913 a majority of the party removed Haywood from the national executive committee.

Repudiated by his socialist comrades, Haywood became more active in the IWW. Between 1912 and 1916 he participated in a series of violent strikes, the most notable of which occurred in Lawrence, Massachusetts (1912); Paterson, New Jersey (1913); and Minnesota's Mesabi Iron Range

William Dudley Haywood. LIBRARY OF CONGRESS

(1916). Although he regularly counseled the strikers to act peaceably by keeping their hands in their pockets, Haywood could not shake his association with violence. The links between IWW strikes and violence worsened during World War I, when walkouts by IWW members affected industries vital to the war effort. Haywood, the top official of the IWW, found his organization subjected to private and public repression. In September 1917 U.S. Justice Department agents raided IWW headquarters and arrested Haywood and more than a hundred other IWW officers, charging them with violations of the wartime sedition and espionage acts. In May 1918 a jury found Haywood and his co-defendants guilty, and the judge sentenced them to terms in federal prison.

Released on bail while attorneys appealed his conviction, Haywood became sick, the IWW suffered grave financial, membership, and leadership losses, and his final legal appeal failed. Unable to face a future in prison, Haywood jumped bail, fled to the Soviet Union, and spent the remaining years of his life mostly in Moscow. There he completed his autobiography, *Bill Haywood's Book* (1929), which added to the association between Haywood and labor violence.

BIBLIOGRAPHY

Carlson, Peter. *Roughneck: The Life and Times of Big Bill Haywood*. New York: Norton, 1983.

Dubofsky, Melvyn. *"Big Bill" Haywood*. New York: St. Martin's, 1987.

Haywood, Big Bill. *Bill Haywood's Book: The Autobiography of William D. Haywood*. New York: International Publishers, 1929.

Lukas, J. Anthony. *Big Trouble: A Murder in a Small Western Town Sets Off a Struggle for the Soul of America*. New York: Simon and Schuster, 1997.

MELVYN DUBOFSKY

See also **Industrial Workers of the World; Labor and Unions; Strikes.**

HAZING. *See* Campus Violence.

HEALTH AND MEDICAL FACTORS

*This entry is divided into four parts: **Body Types, Cholesterol, Diet and Nutrition,** and **Lead.** See also "Alcohol and Alcoholism" and "Drugs."*

BODY TYPES

Folk psychology has long been filled with characterizations of the relation between body type and personality: the jolly obese man and the skinny wallflower come to mind as stereotypes. But is there a genuine association between body type and behavior and, more specifically, violence? The technique of somatotyping, or body typing, has been used to investigate the relation between physique and both crime and aggression.

Although Cesare Lombroso (1835–1909) discussed the relation between various physical stigmata (e.g., a receding forehead) and criminality, he did not examine body type per se. Ernst Kretschmer (1888–1964) first formalized somatotyping in the 1920s. He identified three major physiques: asthenic, athletic, and pyknic. Asthenics are tall and thin; athletics are of average height but are muscular and rugged; and pyknics are notable for their width and the pronounced development of fat around the trunk and face. Kretschmer described a fourth minor category, the dysplastic type, which comprised individuals with either an uneven development of features or a combination of features from the other types. Kretschmer reported that manic depressives tended to be pyknic, whereas schizophrenics tended to be asthenic, athletic, or dysplastic.

William H. Sheldon was the first to systematically examine the relation between somatotyping and crime. He derived a tripartite classification scheme: ectomorphy, mesomorphy, and endomorphy, which roughly correspond to Kretschmer's asthenic, athletic, and pyknic types, respectively (see figure 1). Sheldon hypothesized that each body type derived from the dominance of one of three layers of the blastula during development. Ectomorphy ostensibly relates to dominance of the ectodermal layer, from which the skin and nervous system develop; mesomorphy to dominance of the mesodermal layer, from which bones and muscles develop; and endomorphy to dominance of the endodermal layer, from which digestive organs develop. Sheldon developed a system in which each individual's degree of endomorphy, mesomorphy, and ectomorphy is rated on a scale of one to seven. In 1949 William Sheldon and his colleagues classified two hundred male delinquents according to this scheme and found that most had mesomorphic and nonectomorphic physiques. In other words, they had a muscular build with a wide neck and chest. Sheldon and colleagues also found that andromorphy, a physique comprising such features as prominent muscles and a wide chest flaring toward the shoulders, was frequent among delinquents.

Other investigators have replicated Sheldon's findings. In 1950 Sheldon Glueck and Eleanor Glueck classified five hundred delinquents and five hundred matched nondelinquents according to William Sheldon's system and reported that significantly more delinquents than nondelinquents were mesomorphs and nonectomorphs. In a British sample T. C. N. Gibbens found that delinquents exhibited significantly higher rates of mesomorphy than nondelinquents. In a reexamination of Glueck and Glueck's data using path analytic techniques, Robert Sampson and John Laub found a weak but statistically significant association between criminality and mesomorphy after controlling for such social factors as school attachment and supervision. Nevertheless, Sampson and Laub found that childhood somatotype was not predictive of subsequent crime. Adrian Raine and colleagues reported that large body size at age three, but not age eleven, correlated with aggression at age eleven, although they did not utilize Sheldon's somatotyping scheme. In general, mesomorphy appears to be a modest correlate of aggression and crime, although its predictive utility remains to be ascertained.

Research on somatotyping has been attacked on several methodological grounds. Virtually all of this research is based on male samples, rendering its generalizability to females unclear. In addition, Sheldon has been criticized for the fact that in many cases, he was aware of subjects' psychological backgrounds when making somatotype ratings. Moreover, the Gluecks have been criticized for their failure to examine the role of ethnicity. Because their sample included many Italian immigrants (who are predominantly mesomorphic), and because there may have been police bias against Italians at the time, their results are potentially attributable to a confound between body type and ethnicity. This possibility is consistent with findings that the relation between body type and criminality is stronger for official than unofficial crime reports (Sampson and Laub 1997).

The factors underlying the relation between mesomorphy and crime are unknown. Because mesomorphs are stronger than other individuals, their use of physical aggression for instrumental purposes may meet with greater success. Another possibility is that the association between body type and crime is attributable to personality traits. Several investigators have reported that mesomorphy is associated with dominance, extroversion, and activity level, three traits that appear to be associated with criminality. Further examination of other possible mediating factors, such as hormones (e.g., testosterone) and neurotransmitters

FIGURE 1. William H. Sheldon's Body Types: (from left) Endomorphy, Mesomorphy, Ectomorphy.

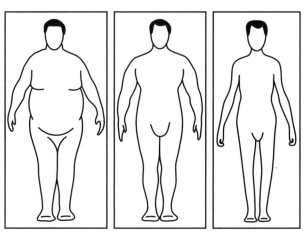

(e.g., serotonin) potentially linked to aggression, is warranted. Finally, it will be important to determine whether body type combines or interacts with learning history or personality variables to increase the risk for violence.

BIBLIOGRAPHY

Gibbens, T. C. N. *Psychiatric Studies of Borstal Lads.* New York: Oxford University Press, 1963.

Glueck, Sheldon, and Eleanor Glueck. *Unraveling Juvenile Delinquency.* New York: Commonwealth Fund, 1953.

Raine, Adrian, et al. "Fearlessness, Stimulation-Seeking, and Large Body Size at Age Three as Early Predispositions to Childhood Aggression at Age Eleven Years." *Archives of General Psychiatry* 55 (August 1998).

Sampson, Robert J., and John H. Laub. "Unraveling the Social Context of Physique and Delinquency." In *Biosocial Bases of Violence,* edited by Adrian Raine et al. New York: Plenum, 1997.

Sheldon, William H., et al. *Varieties of Delinquent Youth.* New York: Harper, 1949.

ALEX B. MORGAN
SCOTT O. LILIENFELD

CHOLESTEROL

Many studies suggest a relationship between low or lowered blood cholesterol levels and violence, and some evidence suggests this relationship may be causal. Cholesterol is a molecule manufactured by the liver that circulates in the blood and is a constituent of cell membranes; it has many functions in the body but is best known for its role in accelerating coronary heart disease. Low cholesterol could induce violent behavior by any of several mechanisms; some support exists for a mechanism involving a connection with low or lowered brain serotonin activity. Serotonin is a chemical that, among other functions, acts in the brain to improve mood and social affiliativeness and to influence one's desire to do harm (it is the brain chemical that is boosted by fluexetine, popularly known as Prozac).

The evidence for a connection between cholesterol and violence appears in a number of documented studies. Several large community studies have shown a higher rate of violent death (as a result of homicide, suicide, or accident) in individuals with low cholesterol, controlling for age and other factors. One study showed that not only the absolute level but also the degree of the drop in cholesterol was predictive of a subsequent risk of suicide. Risk of violent death increased with lower cholesterol in several significant studies. More-

over, studies of psychiatric patients and of criminally violent individuals (in forensic institutions to which they had been admitted) have shown a significant connection between low cholesterol levels and violent-criminal status, suicide attempts, and severity and frequency of violent crime or aggressive behavior. Several randomized controlled trials have noted a significant number of violent deaths among men without established heart disease who had been randomly assigned to cholesterol reduction programs—an effect that has been statistically significant in some pooled analyses. Studies in primates appear to corroborate these findings. Monkeys assigned to cholesterol-lowering diets exhibit more aggression toward other monkeys, and monkeys with natively low cholesterol exhibit excess agonistic behaviors. Many peer-reviewed studies (around twenty as of 1999) show a statistically significant connection between low or lowered cholesterol levels and increased violence. The evidence for a link between cholesterol levels and psychological factors, such as depression and nonbehavioral hostility, is more mixed.

The connection between low cholesterol and violent behavior may be mediated by low levels of the brain-signaling chemical serotonin. A large literature connects natively low or experimentally lowered serotonin levels with violent behavior in humans (including suicides, violent suicides, and homicide-suicides) and in animals. Moreover, low-serotonin monkeys exhibit what might be termed increased "risk-taking" behaviors (that is, they show signs of using poor judgment); thus low serotonin may serve biologically to connect the occurrence of certain accidents with other forms of violence. Finally, several observational studies of humans, along with experimental studies using monkeys, find a significant association between low or lowered cholesterol levels and low serotonin levels in the central nervous system, suggesting that low serotonin may mediate the connection between low cholesterol and violence. It is also possible that cholesterol, rather than being causal, serves as a marker for some other metabolic or biochemical factor associated with violence, but no such factor has been identified.

Further work is needed to define more clearly the effect of low cholesterol on serotonin activity and on violent behavior; to evaluate the role of lipoprotein subfractions, if any; to identify other factors, such as baseline neurochemistry, use of alcohol, psychiatric history, and family or personal history of violence, that may influence which persons are at a higher risk for exhibiting violent behavior associated with low or lowered cholesterol; and to clarify whether violent behavior can be linked with the popular new cholesterol-lowering drugs, known as HMG-CoA reductase inhibitors.

BIBLIOGRAPHY

Golomb, Beatrice A. "Cholesterol and Violence: Is There a Connection?" *Annals of Internal Medicine* 128, no. 6 (1998): 478–487.

———. "Cholesterol and Violence: Is There a Connection?" *Annals of Internal Medicine* 129, no. 8 (1998): 669–670.

Kaplan, J., et al. "Demonstrations of an Association Among Dietary Cholesterol, Central Serotonergic Activity, and Social Behavior in Monkeys." *Psychosomatic Medicine* 56 (1994): 479–484.

Muldoon, M., et al. "Low or Lowered Cholesterol and Risk of Death from Suicide and Trauma." *Metabolism* 42, no. 9, suppl. 1 (1993): 45–56.

Raleigh, M. J., and Michael T. McGuire. "Serotonin, Aggression, and Violence in Vervet Monkeys." In *The Neurotransmitter Revolution,* edited by Roger D. Master and Michael T. McGuire. Carbondale: Southern Illinois University Press, 1994.

Zureik, M., D. Courbon, and P. Ducimetiere. "Serum Cholesterol Concentrations and Death from Suicide in Men: Paris Prospective Study." *British Medical Journal* 313 (1996): 649–650.

BEATRICE A. GOLOMB

DIET AND NUTRITION

The relationship between diet and aggressive behavior has not been clearly established. The possibility that a causal relationship exists, however, has produced considerable interest as well as debate. Generally, diet has not been singled out as a simple or direct cause of aggressiveness. Instead, researchers investigating this association have proposed more complex pathways by which nutrition may be linked to aggressive or antisocial behavior.

Diet has been associated with conditions such as hyperactivity, conduct disorder, attention deficit disorder, learning disabilities, depression, alcoholism, and drug abuse, all of which are considered risk factors for aggressive or antisocial behavior. If aggressiveness stems from these conditions, dietary factors may be seen as an indirect influence. For example, malnutrition in childhood may impact intellectual development. Lower intelligence has been linked to both behavior problems in childhood and juvenile and adult criminal behavior. Improper nutrition may lead to chemical or physiological imbalances in the brain that may subsequently influence a wide range of behavioral

and psychological outcomes, including aggressive or antisocial behavior. Dietary influences on behavior have been examined in relationship to neurotransmitter imbalances, reactive hypoglycemia, marginal malnutrition, and specific food sensitivities and reactions.

Three primary strategies have been employed by researchers to investigate the effects of diet on behavior. A majority of the reported research derives from correlative studies, which are used to generate hypotheses about diet-behavior relationships. Causal relationships between dietary factors and behavior cannot be established from correlative data, however, because of the difficulty in separating the effects of nutrition from other cultural, social, economic, and individual factors that may influence both diet and behavior.

Properly designed and controlled experimental studies are needed to identify causal links between diet and behavior. In dietary replacement studies, the effects of two separate diets are compared. Generally, one diet contains the specific food element of interest and the other does not. Such studies are useful for examining the long-term, cumulative effects of certain dietary components. Alternatively, dietary challenge studies are used to investigate more acute, short-term effects. In these studies, cognitive or behavioral measures are obtained shortly after subjects consume either the food component of interest or a placebo. This type of study allows for greater control over variables, and the effects of various doses can be examined.

Neurotransmitter Imbalances

Neurotransmitters are chemicals in the brain that send signals between neurons, affecting intellectual functioning, emotions, and behavior. Neurotransmitter imbalances have been linked to a wide range of psychiatric disorders. Researchers have attempted to relate aggressive and antisocial behavior to indices of neurotransmitter activity in the brain. The specific neurotransmitters that have been studied in relation to aggressive behavior include norepinephrine (NE), dopamine (DA), and serotonin (5-HT). The production of neurotransmitters is largely dependent on the availability of certain dietary elements such as vitamins, minerals, proteins, carbohydrates, and fats. Some researchers believe that this connection supports the notion of dietary influence on neurotransmitter levels and behavior.

Iron, an essential mineral nutrient, is needed as a cofactor for the enzymes that metabolize dopamine, serotonin, and norepinephrine. Animal research studies indicate that iron deficiencies may cause learning deficits and behavioral impairments by diminishing dopamine transmission in the brain. It has also been suggested that iron deficiencies are associated with aggressive behavior among adolescent males. In one study, researchers found the prevalence of iron deficiency among incarcerated adolescents to be nearly twice that of nonincarcerated adolescents.

Tyrosine and tryptophan are essential amino acids found in protein foods. Depleted levels of these neurotransmitters have been associated with depression and drug abuse, both of which are risk factors for aggressive behavior. Tyrosine is necessary for the production of dopamine and norepinephrine; concentrated forms of tyrosine have been used to increase levels of these neurotransmitters. Tryptophan is the dietary precursor to serotonin. Research indicates that, in some subjects, low levels of serotonin may be associated with aggressive, violent, and impulsive behavior. In addition, tryptophan-rich diets and tryptophan supplements have been used in the treatment of aggression, depression, and alcoholism.

Reactive Hypoglycemia

Hypoglycemia is a physiological state characterized by abnormally low levels of blood glucose. When blood sugar levels decline, counterregulatory hormones such as adrenaline, prolactin, and cortisol are released. The release of these hormones may promote a wide range of behavioral symptoms as well as an increase in dopamine production. Some of the behavioral symptoms that have been associated with hypoglycemic states include faintness, weakness, hunger, irritability, nervousness, anxiety, attention problems, confusion, headaches, and destructive outbursts.

Carbohydrates ingested into the body are converted into glucose and enter the bloodstream. An increase in blood glucose triggers the release of insulin, which transports glucose to cells for energy and storage. Complex carbohydrates are broken down slowly, while refined or simple carbohydrates, such as refined sugar and alcohol, are broken down more readily. Thus, it has been suggested that repeated intake of large quantities of refined carbohydrates may stimulate excessive insulin production, causing blood glucose levels to decline too rapidly. Research has indicated, however, that the differential effects of simple and com-

plex carbohydrates on insulin responses and blood glucose levels are not entirely clear.

Reactive hypoglycemia is most commonly induced by drugs or excessive intake of carbohydrates, including alcohol. Low levels of blood glucose occurring several hours after a meal suggest reactive hypoglycemia. The laboratory technique that is generally used to identify reactive hypoglycemia is the five-hour oral Glucose Tolerance Test (GTT). An official diagnosis also requires the presence of related symptoms and the amelioration of these symptoms once blood glucose levels are restored to normal. Treatment of hypoglycemia involves reducing the amount of refined carbohydrates and increasing the proportion of complex carbohydrates and proteins in the diet.

The results of several research studies suggest that reactive hypoglycemia may be associated with criminal and violent behavior. For example, a series of studies by Matti Virkkunen indicate that lower blood glucose levels and higher insulin levels, as measured in response to the GTT, are found among violent offenders. Adolescent males adjudicated for violent offenses were also found to have lower blood glucose levels following the GTT. Similarly, Harper Gans and others reported significantly lower post-challenge glucose levels and higher insulin levels for a group of male adolescent delinquents, as compared to a control group of age-matched subjects.

Other researchers, however, have been critical of the reported association between reactive hypoglycemia and aggressive behavior. For example, in a review of the literature on hypoglycemia and psychopathology, Stephen Messer and others concluded that there is evidence supporting a relationship between low or rapidly declining blood glucose levels and transient cognitive, affective, and somatic symptoms. However, no clear evidence was found that hypoglycemia contributes to antisocial or aggressive behavior. Similar conclusions were drawn by Robin Kanarek, and both reviews discuss several methodological limitations of the available studies.

One methodological issue addressed is the lack of a clinical diagnosis. The tendency toward reactive hypoglycemia was identified in these studies by measured responses to the oral GTT. No assessment of related symptoms was made, thus preventing an official diagnosis of hypoglycemia. Additionally, the validity of the oral GTT as an assessment tool has been questioned. Responses to the oral GTT may not be indicative of the typical changes in blood glucose levels that occur after meals.

Another problem in many of the reported studies is the relationship between alcohol abuse, antisocial behavior, and hypoglycemia. Criminal behavior is associated with a high incidence of alcoholism and alcohol abuse, and poor dietary habits are prevalent among alcoholics. Thus, to obtain a more meaningful evaluation of the relationship between antisocial or aggressive behavior and hypoglycemia, future research must control for the effects of alcohol abuse.

Marginal Malnutrition

A popular notion is that large amounts of sugar in the diet promote hyperactivity and behavioral problems in children. While positive correlations have been reported between sugar intake and hyperactivity, cause-and-effect relationships cannot be inferred from these data. Experimental studies have not found evidence that sugar intake has any significant effects on cognitive functioning or behavior. Nevertheless, a diet high in refined carbohydrates may often be lacking other beneficial nutrients. Deficiencies in several essential nutrients including niacin, pantothenic acid, thiamine, vitamin B6, vitamin C, iron, magnesium, and tryptophan have been associated with impaired cognitive functioning, depression, and aggressive behaviors.

A series of dietary replacement studies by Stephen Shoenthaler examined the effects of reduced sugar consumption and vitamin and mineral supplementation on the behavior of inmates in juvenile and adult correction facilities. The first group of studies, in the early 1980s, involved reducing overall sugar intake by replacing soft drinks and junk-food snacks with fruit juices and nutritious snacks and eliminating high-sugar desserts and cereals. Schoenthaler reported that following the dietary policy changes, a significant decrease in violent and antisocial behavior among male inmates was observed in twelve separate facilities. Similar behavioral improvements were not observed among female inmates.

Numerous criticisms have been raised in response to the reported findings of these studies (Fishbein and Pease 1994; Kanarak 1993). In all of the studies, there was a failure to demonstrate what specific factors accounted for the improvements in behavior following the dietary interventions. One problem is that none of the studies used standard double-blind procedures. Both the subjects and the institutional officials were aware of the dietary changes, although they were not informed of their purpose. In addition, questions have been raised regarding the changing nature of the subject populations, as well as the statistical methods employed in these studies.

Another problem is that it is impossible to determine whether or not the dietary changes actually reduced overall sugar consumption. In many cases, one type of sugar was simply substituted for another. For example, fruit juices contain considerable amounts of sugar in the form of fructose. Given this fact, Schoenthaler later speculated that improvements in behavior may have stemmed from a greater amount of nutrients in the replacement foods rather than a reduction in sugar consumption. Further studies were then developed to examine the effects of vitamin and mineral supplementation on institutional violence and antisocial behavior. In one such study, residents of a juvenile treatment facility were given either vitamin-mineral supplements or placebos for a period of thirteen weeks. It was reported that the subjects given supplements displayed fewer acts of violent and nonviolent antisocial behavior than those given placebos. Furthermore, proper nutrient concentrations in the blood were found to be the best predictor of good behavior.

A diet high in refined carbohydrates and processed foods may contain higher levels of dietary toxins relative to protective nutrients, contributing to an accumulation of toxins in the body. Toxins are elements such as lead, cadmium, arsenic, aluminum, and mercury. Toxic elements can damage organ systems, impair cognitive functioning and intellectual development, and possibly lead to behavioral problems, including aggression. Certain nutrients such as zinc and calcium help cleanse the body of toxins and protect the brain and other organs from their negative impacts.

Food Allergies and Sensitivities

Clinical reports indicate that some individuals may be highly sensitive, or allergic, to a variety of common foods or food additives. The most commonly identified food allergies include milk, chocolate, corn, eggs, peanuts, tomatoes, citrus fruits, wheat, yeast, and various food additives, such as artificial food coloring. Several case studies have suggested that a few individuals may have extreme reactions, including violent or aggressive behavior, to these common foods. Such cases are unusual, however, and most of the evidence supporting a link between food allergies and aggressive behavior is strictly anecdotal.

In the 1970s Ben Feingold contended that between 30 percent and 60 percent of childhood hyperactivity cases are caused by central nervous system reactions to artificial food additives and natural salicylates. Feingold claimed that hyperactivity problems could be cured with a special diet that excluded these additives. Subsequent experimental research, however, produced conflicting results. A number of dietary challenge studies did not find any evidence to support the food additive–hyperactivity hypothesis. Conversely, a few studies that used higher doses of the additives and younger subjects did report significant behavioral and cognitive effects in hyperactive children (Swanson and Kinsbourne 1980; Weiss et al. 1980). As a whole, the combined research suggests that Feingold's claims were greatly overstated. Nonetheless, a small percentage of young children may exhibit sensitivities to food additives.

Conclusions

The relationship between diet and behavior is a growing field of inquiry. Research has provided many clues, but few definitive answers. Future studies, employing appropriate experimental research designs and more sophisticated controls, will doubtless provide more useful information about the role of dietary factors in aggressive or antisocial behavior.

BIBLIOGRAPHY

Conners, C. Keith. *Food Additives and Hyperactive Children.* New York: Plenum, 1980.

Crapo, Phyllis A. "Simple Versus Complex Carbohydrate Use in the Diabetic Diet." *Annual Review of Nutrition* 5 (1985): 95–114.

Feingold, Ben F. *Why Your Child Is Hyperactive.* New York: Random House, 1975.

Fishbein, D. H., and Pease, S. E. "Diet, Nutrition, and Aggression." *Journal of Offender Rehabilitation* 21 (1994): 117–144.

Gans, Dian, Alfred Harper, Jo-Anne Bachorowski, Joseph Newman, Earl Shrago, and Steve Taylor. "Sucrose and Delinquency: Oral Sucrose Tolerance Test and Nutritional Assessment." *Pediatrics* 86 (1990): 254–262.

Kanarak, Robin B. "Nutrition and Violent Behavior." In *Understanding and Preventing Violence.* Vol 2, edited by Albert J. Reiss and Jeffrey A. Roth. Washington, D.C.: National Academy Press, 1993.

Kaplan, Henry K., Frederick S. Wamboldt, and Mary Barnhart. "Behavioral Effects of Dietary Sucrose in Disturbed Children." *American Journal of Psychiatry* 143 (1986): 944–945.

Linnoila, V. Markkis, and Matti Virkkunen. "Aggression, Suicidality, and Serotonin." *Journal of Clinical Psychiatry* 53, supp. 10 (1992): 46–51.

Matykiewicz, Lynn, Linda La Grange, Peter Vance, Mu Wang, and Edward Reyes. "Adjudicated Adolescent Males: Measures of Urinary 5-Hydroxyindoleacetic Acid and Reactive Hypoglycemia." *Personality and Individual Differences* 22 (1997): 327–332.

Messer, Stephen C., Tracy L. Morris, and Alan M. Gross. "Hypoglycemia and Psychopathology: A Methodological Review." *Clinical Psychology Review* 10 (1990): 631–648.

Milich, Richard, and William E. Pelham. "Effects of Sugar Ingestion on the Classroom and Playgroup Behavior of Attention Deficit Disordered Boys." *Journal of Consulting and Clinical Psychology* 54 (1986): 714–718.

Rapp, Doris. *Allergies and the Hyperactive Child.* New York: Sovereign Books, 1979.

Rosen, G. M., A. S. Deinard, S. Schwartz, et al. "Iron Deficiency Among Incarcerated Juvenile Delinquents." *Journal of Adolescent Health Care* 6 (1985): 419–423.

Schauss, Alexander G. *Diet, Crime, and Delinquency.* Berkeley, Calif.: Parker House, 1980.

Schoenthaler, Stephen J. "Abstracts of Early Papers on the Effects of Vitamin and Mineral Supplementation on I.Q. and Behavior." *Personality and Individual Differences* 12, no. 4 (1991): 335–341.

Swanson, James M., and Marcel Kinsbourne. "Food Dyes Impair Performance of Hyperactive Children on a Laboratory Learning Test." *Science* 207 (1980): 1485–1486.

Virkkunen, Matti. "Insulin Secretion During the Glucose Tolerance Test Among Habitually Violent and Impulsive Offenders." *Aggressive Behavior* 12 (1985): 303–310.

———. "Reactive Hypoglycemic Tendency Among Habitually Violent Offenders." *Neuropsychology* 8 (1982): 35–40.

Weiss, Bernard, J. Hicks Williams, Sheldon Margen, Barbara Abrams, Bette Caan, L. J. Citron, Christopher Cox, Jane McKibben, Dale Ogar, and Stephen Schultz. "Behavioral Response to Artificial Food Colors." *Science* 207 (1980): 1487–1488.

Werbach, M. R. "Nutritional Influences on Aggressive Behavior." *Journal of Orthomolecular Medicine* 7, no. 1 (1995).

Youdim, Moussa B. "Putative Biological Mechanisms of the Effect of Iron Deficiency on Brain Biochemistry and Behavior." *American Journal of Clinical Nutrition* 50 (1989): 607–615.

AMY C. ABRAHAMSON

See also **Neurotransmitters.**

LEAD

Substantial evidence supports a link between abnormal lead levels in children and a range of serious health and behavioral disorders, including aggression and criminality. In light of estimates that one out of nine children is adversely affected by lead, a growing consensus concludes that lead poisoning "is the most common and socially devastating environmental disease of young children."

Children of all socioeconomic classes are vulnerable to the effects of lead, although urban-dwelling black children appear to be most susceptible. Of the many ways children acquire lead toxicity, the key source is lead-based paint, which, although outlawed, remains in older homes. Children ingest the paint by eating paint chips or swallowing the lead-paint dust that settles on walls, windows, and floors. Other lead sources include drinking water, soil, food, gasoline, and industrial pollution.

Research indicates that both high and low lead levels can impair children's physiological development and therefore initiate potentially lifelong debilitation. Impairments can range from reading and learning disabilities, school absenteeism and dropping out, and delayed nervous system development to deficits in vocabulary, fine motor skills, reaction time, and hand-eye coordination. Behaviorally, lead intoxicated children can demonstrate hyperactivity, hypoactivity, distractibility, impulsivity, disorganization, restlessness, and abnormal social and aggressive conduct.

For decades, criminological research has demonstrated that many of these physiological and behavioral conditions are associated with criminality. Not surprisingly, research has also uncovered direct ties between lead poisoning, physiological and behavioral impairment, and criminality.

The first major analysis of the lead poisoning and crime relationship resulted from the Biosocial Study, one of the largest longitudinal studies of biological, sociological, and environmental predictors of crime ever undertaken in the United States. The Biosocial Study was unique because it examined numerous interdisciplinary variables relating to a group of 987 black male and female subjects from their birth through age twenty-two. The subjects and their families were originally part of the Collaborative Perinatal Project in Philadelphia, which was launched in 1957 by the National Institute of Neurological Diseases and Stroke to determine the causes of childhood illnesses and disorders. In 1978 the Sellin Center for Studies in Criminology and Criminal Law at the University of Pennsylvania was awarded a grant by the National Institute of Justice to examine the ten thousand Philadelphia Perinatal Project children. As part of the grant, public school and police record data were collected on all the youths. For eight years thereafter detailed data were organized and analyzed on the subsample of 987 individuals who made up the Biosocial Study. While controlling for many other factors, the Biosocial Study found that lead poisoning among males only was the most significant predictor of school disciplinary problems and among the most significant predictors of juvenile delinquency and adult criminality (see table).

The Biosocial Study's results were confirmed in a 1996 prospective study of 301 males selected from a group of students in the Pittsburgh Youth Study, a prospective longitudinal project examining how delinquency develops. The sample was selected to create a balanced group at high and low risk of delinquency; the research on bone lead and

TABLE 1. Strongest Predictors of School Disciplinary Problems and Number of Juvenile and Adult Offenses in a Study of 487 Males from Birth to Age 22

School Disciplinary Problems	Number of Juvenile Offenses	Number of Adult Offenses
1. *Lead poisoning*	1. School disciplinary problems	1. Number and seriousness of juvenile offenses
2. Anemia	2. Time father unemployed	2. Mother's educational level
3. Number of household moves	3. *Lead poisoning*	3. Father's educational level
4. Left-handedness	4. Low language achievement	4. Low language achievement
5. Lack of foster parents	5. Number of household moves	5. *Lead poisoning*

Lead poisoning is the strongest predictor of school disciplinary problems from age 13 to 14; school disciplinary problems are the strongest predictor of the number of juvenile offenses from age 7 to 17; the number and seriousness of juvenile offenses are the strongest predictors of the number of adult offenses from age 18 to 22. Of all the numerous biosocial variables examined, lead poisoning was the only variable that significantly predicted all three outcome measures: school disciplinary problems, number of juvenile offenses, and number of adult offenses.

The total sample in the Philadelphia Perinatal Project reflects, in part, the characteristics of families who would be interested in receiving inexpensive maternity care provided by a public clinic. The sample's socioeconomic levels were also slightly lower than those of the U.S. population at the time. Therefore, the results of the Biosocial Study are not necessarily generalizable.

SOURCE: Denno, Deborah W. *Biology and Violence: From Birth to Adulthood.* New York: Cambridge University Press, 1990.

psychological measures of this sample was supported by grants from the National Institute of Environmental Health Sciences and the Howard Heinz Endowment. The study found statistically significant relationships between bone lead levels, aggression, and juvenile delinquency, while controlling for social and economic variables. Other researchers have found links between lead and troublesome behavior that is highly predictive of, or equivalent to, juvenile delinquency. Moreover, several correlational studies have reported significantly higher levels of lead or other toxicities in the head hair of violent prison inmates when compared to nonviolent inmates or controls. Finally, ecological approaches to studying crime suggest that county-level reports of alcoholism and environmental pollutants, including lead, can significantly predict rates of criminal violence while controlling for key demographic and socioeconomic variables.

There are a number of explanations for how lead might influence behavior, either directly or indirectly. Lead appears to induce neurochemical alterations in the brain that have been shown to disrupt inhibitory processes that could be expressed behaviorally as impulsivity. In turn, impulsivity and its correlates (such as aggression and academic failure) are strong predictors of delinquency and crime. Other intervening factors enhancing the potential for a lead-crime link include dietary deficiencies, drug or alcohol consumption, and familial stress.

The interaction between lead and certain crime correlates is complex and variable. Yet one element is clear: although the physiological and behavioral consequences of lead poisoning appear to be biologically based, they are actually environmental in origin. Lead is one of the most prevalent environmental enemies of children, yet it is also among the most preventable. Acknowledging the link between lead and crime can be an important step in reducing violence in general.

BIBLIOGRAPHY

Denno, Deborah W. *Biology and Violence: From Birth to Adulthood.* New York: Cambridge University Press, 1990.
———. "Considering Lead Poisoning as a Criminal Defense." *Fordham Urban Law Journal* 22, no. 3 (spring 1993): 377–400.
———. "Gender, Crime, and the Criminal Law Defenses." *Journal of Criminal Law and Criminology* 85, no. 1 (summer 1994): 80–180.
Masters, Roger D., et al. "Environmental Pollution, Neurotoxicity, and Criminal Violence." In *Aspects of Environmental Toxicity,* edited by J. Rose. London: Gordon and Breach, 1998.
Needleman, Herbert L., et al. "Bone Lead Levels and Delinquent Behavior." *Journal of the American Medical Association* 275, no. 5 (1996): 363–369.

I am most grateful to Juan Fernandez and Lydia Bronte for their contributions to the creation of the table.

DEBORAH W. DENNO

See also **Children; Developmental Factors: Childhood.**

HEARST, PATRICIA. *See* Symbionese Liberation Army.

HEARST, WILLIAM RANDOLPH (1863–1951)

Born in 1863 in San Francisco, William Randolph Hearst began his career in journalism as the editor and publisher of his hometown paper, the *Daily Examiner,* which was owned by his multimillionaire father. He hired the best writers by paying them the highest wages. His dual purpose was to entertain his readers as well as to inform them about current events.

In 1895, seeking to reach a wider audience, he moved to New York and bought the *New York Morning Journal.* Soon thereafter, in 1897, the era of yellow journalism began: Hearst and Joseph Pulitzer, of the *New York World,* were the prime initiators as well as the foremost advocates of this form of sensational newspaper reporting. Their all-out competition for newspaper supremacy in the United States centered on a propaganda crusade for "Cuba Libre." So successful was their campaign that the McKinley administration yielded to public demand for war with Spain in 1898.

Apart from the drive to sell newspapers, Hearst truly believed that the Cubans, who had rebelled against Spain in 1895, deserved political and economic freedom from their "cruel" oppressors. He therefore villainized the Spaniards at every opportunity. For example, General Valeriano Weyler, the captain-general of Cuba who was assigned to crush the rebels, was weekly—and at times daily—characterized in the Hearst newspapers as "Butcher" or "Wolf" Weyler, who burned people alive—a "mad dog" who feasted on the flesh of

William Randolph Hearst. LIBRARY OF CONGRESS

his victims, a "destroyer of families," an "outrager of women," a "pitiless exterminator of men."

Hearst also welcomed news with any anti-Spanish slant, seemingly unconcerned about its origin or authenticity. He often accepted stories handed to his reporters from the revolutionary Cuban junta in New York City, whose objectivity was, at best, questionable. To guarantee a steady flow of information Hearst sent *Journal* "special correspondents" to Cuba with instructions to detail the valiant resistance of the rebels against overwhelming odds as well as describe, in lurid detail, their suffering at the hands of the Spaniards. One of his correspondents, the noted western artist Frederic Remington, telegraphed to the *Morning Journal* soon after arrival early in 1897: "Everything is quiet. There is no trouble here. There will be no war. I wish to return." Hearst allegedly replied: "Please remain. You furnish the pictures and I'll furnish the war."

That was exactly what Hearst did. On 9 February 1898 the *Morning Journal* published a letter written by Enrique Dupuy de Lome, the Spanish minister to the United States, severely criticizing President William McKinley, and it promptly caused an international firestorm. Just as this incident was subsiding, the U.S. battleship *Maine* blew up and sank in Havana Harbor on the night of 15 February. Despite a lack of evidence that the Spaniards were responsible, the Hearst papers provided a steady drumbeat of accusatory innuendos, if not fictionalized accounts. On 20 February a front page headline read, "Journal Here Presents, Formally, Proof of a Submarine Mine"; the article stated that *Journal* divers had inspected the hull of the *Maine,* though the Spanish government had prevented any such action. The catchphrase thoughout the nation was "Remember the *Maine,* to hell with Spain." Early in May, after McKinley gave way to the popular will for armed intervention and Congress passed a war resolution, Hearst offered to raise at his own expense a cavalry regiment, but the McKinley administration rejected this proposal. Hearst then donated to the U.S. Navy his 138-foot steam yacht *Buccaneer,* agreeing to equip, arm, and service it, again at his own expense, with the stipulation that he be appointed commander or second-in-command of the vessel. Again the administration rejected him as a volunteer, but it did accept the *Buccaneer* for navy service.

Hearst therefore decided to lead his own expeditionary force, both as admiral of a *Journal* squadron and general of its troops. In 1898 he set sail on a chartered steamship stocked with food and drink and medicine, along with journalists and photographers assigned to cover the upcoming conflict. For a month he became a war correspondent, weekly, and sometimes daily, reporting on-the-spot activities of U.S. fighting forces. After the U.S. Navy destroyed the Spanish fleet near Santiago, Cuba, on 3 July, Hearst helped capture twenty-nine marooned enemy sailors the next day.

Hearst thus considered the Spanish-American War "the grandest adventure of his life." Among his other endeavors was running for president of the United States, governor of New York, and mayor of New York City (all unsuccessfully); in 1902 he did win election to the House of Representatives, though he was roundly criticized for his absenteeism. He married a showgirl in 1903 and had five sons with her. In 1917 he began a liaison with another showgirl that was to last until his death in 1951 at the age of eighty-eight. Over the years he had established an enormously powerful journalistic empire, owning twenty-eight major newspapers and thirteen magazines.

BIBLIOGRAPHY

Procter, Ben. *William Randolph Hearst: The Early Years, 1863–1910.* New York: Oxford University Press, 1998.
Swanberg, W. A. *Citizen Hearst.* New York: Scribners, 1961.

BEN PROCTER

See also **Journalism; Spanish-American War.**

HEAVEN'S GATE

On 27 March 1997 the media reported that thirty-nine members of a religious cult, Heaven's Gate, had committed the largest mass suicide ever on U.S. soil. Their bodies, dressed in black uniforms and covered with purple shrouds, were discovered in their communal home in Rancho Santa Fe, California.

Early History and Beliefs

Heaven's Gate was founded in 1975 by Marshall Herff Applewhite, a former music professor (he taught at the University of Alabama and later at St. Thomas University in Houston, Texas), and Bonnie Nettles, a registered nurse. Applewhite and Nettles claimed they would fulfill the prophecy of Revelation 11 by being assassinated, resurrecting like Jesus, and ascending to heaven in a spaceship. To accompany them, their followers had to give up human attachments such as jobs, family, friends, possessions, and sex. Applewhite and Nettles, known as Bo and Peep or the Two, claimed the only way to enter the "level above human" was in a living physical body.

The cult, then called Human Individual Metamorphosis, first made headlines in 1975 after dozens of people disappeared and joined the cult following public lectures given by the Two. Most came from the hippie counterculture, but a few were middle-aged, middle-class seekers with ties to the New Age movement. At its peak, the cult had approximately two hundred members.

During its first year, the group had little structure. Most members had no contact with the Two, who had secluded themselves in Oklahoma. Members traveled the country in small groups, spreading the "message" in public meetings while sur-

Marshall Applewhite and Bonnie Nettles in 1975.
CORBIS/BETTMANN

viving on donations from mainstream churches. Without their leaders and almost no indoctrination, the cult began to fragment. Members tired of waiting for the spaceships, and by early 1976 at least half had defected.

Revitalizing the Cult

The Two rejoined the group in 1976 and began sweeping changes that cut the dropout rate. The first was to stop recruiting, which reinforced members' belief that they were the only humans eligible to enter the "next kingdom." Next came the announcement that the "liftoff" had been postponed because members were not ready to leave the planet. The Two also expelled nineteen of the least committed.

During the next two years, the group lived in isolated campgrounds in Wyoming, Utah, and Texas. Applewhite and Nettles, now calling themselves Do and Ti, introduced elaborate procedures to teach members how to function as a crew aboard a spacecraft, and members called "eyes" reported infractions. To keep followers from thinking about the past or worrying about the future and focused on the present, Nettles and Applewhite required each member to check in at a central location every twelve minutes throughout the day, and members used tuning forks to stay "in tune" with the vibrations of the "next level." (The note from a tuning fork supposedly was the vibration that connected these members with members of the next kingdom.) They also wore hooded uniforms with cloth-mesh eyes to minimize their personalities.

The 1980s and 1990s

With money from a member's trust fund, the cult began renting luxurious houses. Members also started taking jobs, some as computer programmers. Despite ruses to fabricate credentials and references, they proved to be good renters and skilled workers. To insulate themselves from outsiders, they told neighbors and employers they were monks. Throughout the late 1970s to the early 1990s, the group moved to a different city approximately every six months.

Within each house, called a "craft," routines were prescribed down to the minute. Regular confessions were required, and the slightest departures from procedure were discussed in group meetings. Those who had trouble following the rules were asked to leave. Men and women wore short hair and dressed in baggy unisex clothing to minimize sexual differences, and eight men, including Applewhite, had themselves castrated to eliminate sexual urges.

The suicides occurred in the context of this regimented existence. Most members who died in Rancho Santa Fe had spent much of their adult lives in this encapsulated world, where every procedure was designed to eliminate independent thinking.

Suicide in Rancho Santa Fe

Several developments opened the door to suicide. Most important was Nettles's death from cancer in 1985. Her death forced Applewhite to reevaluate his belief that members had to leave the planet in living bodies. Claiming Nettles had returned to the "next level" in disincarnate form, he explained that Nettles's mind was so powerful that it destroyed its human "container." Even before Nettles died, the cult had been disappointed repeatedly while waiting for the ships. For years

members had taken nightly shifts looking for UFOs, and once the group spent a night waiting in the Texas desert to be picked up. More disappointments followed Nettles's death. Satellite television broadcasts of the cult's message produced few inquiries, and attempts to advertise over the Internet were met with ridicule. In 1994 the group, whose membership was down to twenty-four, again searched for new members, setting up recruitment meetings in over sixty cities in twenty-two states, but few joined and most new recruits dropped out within months. Two years later Applewhite confided that he too was dying of cancer, although official investigation of the suicides showed he was in good health for a man his age, then sixty-six.

Suicide had been discussed at least since 1994, but the precipitating factor was the discovery of the Hale-Bopp comet, predicted to be the most spectacular comet of the twentieth century. Applewhite claimed Nettles was returning for him and his followers, noting that the comet Kohoutek had marked in the 1970s the beginning of his mission with Nettles. Early in 1997 the cult, now calling itself Heaven's Gate, warned the end was near with a flashing "red alert" signal on its Web site, but not until after the suicides did anyone understand its meaning.

The suicides followed a meticulous plan carried out over three days (23–25 March). Death was caused by phenobarbital and vodka, following strict procedures dictating who would die on which days. Shortly before the suicides, the group made two videotapes in which Applewhite and his followers said their good-byes. The police investigation concluded there was no evidence of coercion.

As of 1999 only a handful of believers remained, all former members who believed they had missed their chance to leave the planet because of personal weaknesses. (Two former members, Wayne Cooke and Chuck Humphrey, later committed suicide.) While still loyal to Nettles and Applewhite, they claimed no interest in rejuvenating the cult. Applewhite's "exit," they said, marked the end of Heaven's Gate.

BIBLIOGRAPHY

Balch, Robert W. "Bo and Peep: A Case Study of the Origins of Messianic Leadership." In *Millennialism and Charisma*, edited by Roy Wallis. Belfast, Northern Ireland: The Queen's University, 1982.

———. "Waiting for the Ships: Disillusionment and the Re-vitalization of Faith in Bo and Peep's UFO Cult." In *The Gods Have Landed: New Religions from Other Worlds*, edited by James R. Lewis. Albany: State University of New York Press, 1995.

Bearak, Barry. "Odyssey to Suicide." *New York Times*, 28 April 1997.

ROBERT W. BALCH

See also **Cults; Extremism; Religion.**

HICKOK, JAMES BUTLER "WILD BILL"
(1837–1876)

James Butler Hickok, the man who came to be called the Prince of Pistoleers and the most celebrated of western gunfighters, was born on 27 May 1837 in Homer (later Prairie Grove), Illinois, the son of William Alonzo Hickok, the town's first storekeeper. The boy who was to achieve fame as "Wild Bill" may have derived his fighting genes from his mother, the former Polly Butler, daughter of one of Ethan Allen's famed Revolutionary War "Green Mountain Boys," and an aunt of the noted Civil War general, Ben Butler.

The Hickoks were abolitionists and their home became a station on the Underground Railroad, which helped runaway slaves in their flight to freedom. Drawn to Kansas in 1856 by farming opportunities in the new territory, young Hickok was quickly caught up in the bitter controversy over whether Kansas should be admitted to the Union as a free or slave state. He saw his first military action as a member of James H. Lane's Free State Army during the 1850s, the turbulent years of violence over the slavery question that earned for the new state the title "Bleeding Kansas." He pinned on his first badge in 1858 as a constable in Monticello, Kansas. Later employed at an express station in Rock Creek, Nebraska, he participated in a shooting in which three men were killed on 12 July 1861. A highly exaggerated account of this affair, written by George Ward Nichols and published in the February 1867 issue of *Harper's New Monthly Magazine*, described Hickok as personally killing ten armed ruffians—and a legend was born.

During the Civil War, Hickok served as a civilian scout for the Union army where he had numerous perilous adventures and earned his nom de guerre, Wild Bill. In Springfield, Missouri, on 21 July 1865, he shot and killed Dave Tutt in an

"Wild Bill" Hickok. HULTON GETTY/LIAISON AGENCY

infamous pistol duel. In the late 1860s he served as a deputy U.S. marshal and army scout at Fort Riley, Kansas. He became intimately acquainted with William F. "Buffalo Bill" Cody, Lieutenant Colonel George A. Custer, and other notable frontier figures. Wherever he appeared, Hickok impressed men and women alike. Elizabeth Custer, the colonel's wife, found him "a delight to look upon" and could "not recall anything finer in the way of physical perfection than Wild Bill."

The first of many dime novels describing his purported adventures appeared in July 1867. While serving as interim sheriff of Ellis County, Kansas, in 1869, Hickok shot and killed two men in gunfights in Hays City. In a saloon fight with soldiers in Hays on 17 July 1870, he killed one and wounded another. In April 1871 he became city marshal of the riotous cattle town of Abilene, Kansas, and there encountered the legendary gunfighters Ben Thompson and John Wesley Hardin. In a gunfight on 5 October 1871, he fatally wounded Thompson's gambling partner, Phil Coe, and in the excitement accidentally killed Mike Williams, his own deputy. For several years, he traveled extensively, capitalizing on his celebrity status. He appeared at fairs and various theatrical shows, including productions staged by Ned Buntline that featured Buffalo Bill Cody.

On 5 March 1876 Hickok married the theatrical performer Agnes Lake Thatcher. In the spring of that same year, he started for the Black Hills, a region of Dakota Territory in which an expedition led by General George A. Custer had discovered gold deposits in 1874. In mid-July he arrived in Deadwood, the principal town of the new mining district. Within three weeks he was dead, shot in the back as he sat in a poker game on 2 August 1876 by a ne'er-do-well named Jack McCall. A Deadwood miners' court exonerated Wild Bill's slayer, but in a later trial in Yankton, Dakota Territory, a jury convicted him. Jack McCall was hanged on 1 March 1877. The body of "Wild Bill, the Prince of Pistoleers," rests in Mount Moriah Cemetery in Deadwood.

BIBLIOGRAPHY

Rosa, Joseph G. *They Called Him Wild Bill: The Life and Adventures of James Butler Hickok.* 2nd ed., rev. Norman: University of Oklahoma Press, 1974.
———. *The West of Wild Bill Hickok.* Norman: University of Oklahoma Press, 1982.
———. *Wild Bill Hickok: The Man and His Myth.* Lawrence: University Press of Kansas, 1996.

ROBERT K. DeARMENT

See also **Cody, William "Buffalo Bill"; Custer, George Armstrong; Frontier; Gunfighters and Outlaws, Western; Hardin, John Wesley.**

HIJACKING

Hijacking is not a legal but rather a popular term referring to the forceful seizure of a conveyance or its contents for the purposes of robbery, inciting fear, murder, or terrorism. The conveyances involved are typically automobiles, trucks, ships, and aircraft.

The roots of the word *hijacking* are quite old, dating back more than a century to early American tramp and railroad slang. During the closing decades of the nineteenth century, the generic name for a hobo or tramp was "Jack," and the usual greeting between two members of this wandering fraternity was "Hi, Jack." It was a contraction of "H'are ye, Jack," which, in turn, was a contraction of "How are you, Jack." If one of the jacks was a "yegg" or "jungle buzzard" (a tramp thief or robber), he would produce a gun after the greeting and demand, "Hands up, Jack!" If this command was not quickly obeyed, the next order would be "High Jack!" (meaning raise your hands high over your head). By the second decade of the twentieth century, "high Jack," contracted to "hijack," had entered general American underworld slang, and the "hijacker" was a criminal who robbed other criminals.

During the Prohibition era, hijackers were armed predators who robbed trucks or rumrunners owned by bootleggers and other gangsters, typically after the liquor had been smuggled past revenue officers. Because the hijacking of liquor was both widespread and profitable, bootleggers were forced to take special precautions to protect their product. George Remus, one of the more enterprising bootleggers of the early 1920s, turned his Death Valley operation into a fortified enclave to safeguard against hijackers. There were floodlights and a permanent contingent of armed men. His trucks were armor-plated, and he had a fleet of bulletproof Marmots, Packards, and Cadillacs carrying squads of armed men to accompany the trucks and fend off attackers.

Treacherous Seclusion

Drug shuttles in the 1970s would begin along the Caribbean coast from secluded ports between the Colombian cities of Cartagena, Barranquilla, and Santa Marta. Shipments bound for Florida's Key West and Gulf Coast ports followed a northwesterly bearing, passing to the west of the Cayman Islands and Cuba, and through the Yucatan Channel into the Gulf of Mexico. Those heading toward Atlantic Coast ports went in a more northerly direction, selecting the Windward Passage between Cuba and Haiti and then sailing northwest in a straight line through the Bahamas.

These passages provided relative seclusion combined with relative ease of navigation. Moreover, with some seven hundred islands and no less than two thousand "cays" (from the Spanish *cayo,* meaning a low island or reef) within the Bahama chain alone, there were many isolated locations where drug transactions could take place.

Piracy in the grand manner of Blackbeard and Captain Kidd was an early form of hijacking at sea. The voyages of Columbus had provided Spain with an early start in seeking the treasures of the New World. The ensuing territorial conquests gave that nation an almost total claim on the Americas, as well as the financial strength to construct the most powerful navy in Europe. Trade, often with cargoes in excess of $100 million per ship, found a natural right-of-way through the Caribbean, made highly navigable by the Gulf Stream currents, prevailing winds, and sheltering islands of the West Indies. During the seventeenth and eighteenth centuries, moreover, the West Indies became a depository for transported convicts, social and political refugees from France, Spain, and Great Britain, and vagrant sailors, especially after the Treaty of Utrecht in 1713 brought an end to the War of the Spanish Succession.

The grand era of piracy began in 1714 when Captain Henry Jennings of Jamaica and three hundred seamen descended upon the salvage crew of a grounded Spanish galleon, looting the vessel of some three hundred thousand "pieces of eight" (pesos worth eight *reales*). News of the event proved inspirational to social pariahs and displaced mariners on the Caribbean waterfronts, and ships were seized, manned, and turned pirate. The topography of the Indies made piracy a lucrative pursuit: Located along the heavily traveled Gulf Stream routes, the islands provided landside strongholds close to the illicit maritime ventures. The endless number of coves offered natural op-

portunities for ambush, and with the area's scattered habitation and development, the marine bandits could swiftly retreat to the security and sanctuary of unobserved seclusion.

Factors that spawned piracy in the Caribbean during the 1700s—ease of navigation and access to secluded ports and coves—contributed to its reemergence during the 1970s. Much of the drug smuggling from South and Central America to North America during the 1970s was by sea. The piracy of pleasure craft, or "yachtjacking," as some have called it, began during the early 1970s. Some vessels were pirated and used for transporting drugs. Others were seized because they had come too close to drug-transaction areas or were mistaken for rival drug craft. In all instances, the passengers and crew of the stolen boats were killed, tossed overboard, and likely devoured by sharks and other sea creatures. So prevalent had the problem become that warnings to mariners repeatedly appeared in U.S. Coast Guard bulletins and respected yachting publications. By 1981 the problem peaked, and aircraft then became the more popular form of smuggling transport.

The hijacking of aircraft, more commonly known as air piracy or "skyjacking," first became visible in the United States beginning in the 1960s, with Cuban refugees attempting to return to Cuba. Typically boarding as a passenger on a flight originating in Miami, the hijacker often acted alone, nervously pointing a pistol at anxious airline personnel. With the introduction of airport security measures during the 1970s, piracy of aircraft orig-

A Kuwait Airways jumbo jet arrives at Larnaca airport in Cyprus after being hijacked by terrorists in April 1988. Corbis/Francoise de Mulder

inating in the United States declined sharply, and by the 1990s it was virtually nonexistent. Elsewhere in the world, however, it has tended to persist at low levels, generally as a form of political terrorism. The use of sky marshals has had some impact on the problem. Sky marshals are armed deputies whose sole purpose on board an aircraft is to prevent a hijacker from completing a takeover, either through negotiation or through the capture or death of the hijacker. The Federal Aviation Administration places sky marshals on selected U.S. flights. Israel is the only country using marshals on all of its flights.

Perhaps the most well-known U.S. skyjacker was D. B. Cooper, the man who boarded a Northwest Airlines jet on 24 November 1971 and then hijacked it. After the $200,000 ransom he had demanded from airline officials was delivered to him on board the plane at a designated stop, he parachuted from the plane over Ariel, Washington. The Federal Bureau of Investigation launched a massive manhunt, but Cooper was never found. Almost immediately he became a modern-day folk hero—a twentieth-century Robin Hood. Popular mythology holds that he got away, that he beat the system. Festivities commemorating D. B. Cooper Day are held in Ariel every year on the Saturday after Thanksgiving. Hundreds of people clog the little town's only street to pay tribute to the perpetrator of the only unsolved U.S. skyjacking. Though the cultists believe that Cooper went on to live a discreetly decadent life somewhere on his marked money, it is highly unlikely that, after jumping from an altitude of ten thousand feet from a plane moving two hundred miles per hour, dressed only in a light business suit and raincoat, he survived even long enough to open his parachute.

BIBLIOGRAPHY

Ott, James. "Sky Marshals Reduce Hijacking Threat." *Aviation Week and Space Technology* (16 December 1996).

Ritchie, Robert C. *Captain Kidd and the War Against the Pirates.* Cambridge, Mass.: Harvard University Press, 1986.

Trotter, Robert J. "Psyching the Skyjacker." *Science News* 101 (12 February 1972).

Willard, Josiah Flynt. *Tramping with Tramps: Studies and Sketches of Vagabond Life.* New York: Century, 1899.

JAMES A. INCIARDI

See also **Blackbeard; Carjacking; Crime, Legal Definitions of; Kidd, Captain William; Piracy; Terrorism.**

HINCKLEY, JOHN W., JR.
(1955–)

On 30 March 1981 John W. Hinckley, Jr., fired six shots at President Ronald Reagan as the president walked toward his waiting limousine outside the Washington Hilton Hotel. When the shooting stopped three seconds later, three members of the president's entourage lay seriously wounded on the sidewalk. Hinckley's sixth bullet glanced off the side of the limousine and struck the president in the left armpit, splintering a rib before entering his lung. Without the swift actions of his Secret Service detail and the expertise of emergency room physicians, the president surely would have died.

The president's attacker seemed an unlikely assassin. Hinckley was born on 29 May 1955 in Ardmore, Oklahoma, the youngest of three children dearly loved by a mother and father who took great pride in their devotion to traditional family

John W. Hinckley, Jr., in September 1982. CORBIS/
BETTMANN

values and their children's well-being. There were loving grandparents, family vacations, pets to play with, and new toys to look forward to every Christmas. Hinckley's father, an exceedingly ambitious man, had earned a degree in mechanical engineering and served as a naval officer before working his way to the top as an oil industry executive. In 1965, at the age of forty, he established his own company in Dallas and was soon earning millions, and enjoying a lifestyle to match in the wealthy suburbs, before his namesake entered high school. It was quite an example for any son to follow.

John Hinckley, Jr., was a quiet, timid child. He attended public schools where records show that, in the primary grades, he was an average student with no special talents or obvious problems, except for his timidity, which was indulged by a mother similarly hampered. In junior high school, with his parents' encouragement, he did hesitantly participate in athletics as a team manager, but the pattern of shyness and excessive dependence on his mother had become more evident. In high school he gradually withdrew from virtually all social activities, preferring instead to listen to Beatles records in his room and to have conversations with his mother. At the same time, an emerging estrangement between a disappointed father and his resentful son deepened.

Hinckley graduated from high school in 1973 and enrolled, at his father's insistence, at Texas Tech University in Lubbock. An indifferent, socially isolated student, he never graduated. In 1976 Hinckley was profoundly affected by the film *Taxi Driver* and especially by the actress Jodie Foster, who played an underage prostitute. Three years later, clinical depression accompanied the deteriorating relationship with his parents, his failure to establish a career as a songwriter, and futile, obsessive efforts to meet Foster. At his trial, defense attorneys convinced the jury that these difficulties were symptomatic of a mental disorder that was the cause of his attempt on President Reagan's life. In April 1982, after a trial that included an unprecedented amount of testimony about the defendant's mental state, a jury found Hinckley not guilty by reason of insanity. It was one of the most controversial verdicts ever reached in an American trial. Hinckley was confined as a patient at St. Elizabeth Hospital in Washington, D.C. In January 1999, he won court permission to leave the hospital for brief, supervised visits with his family and a girlfriend.

BIBLIOGRAPHY

Caplan, Lincoln. *The Insanity Defense and the Trial of John W. Hinckley, Jr.* Boston: Godine, 1984.

Clarke, James W. *American Assassins: The Darker Side of Politics.* Princeton, N.J.: Princeton University Press, 1990.

———. *On Being Mad or Merely Angry: John W. Hinckley, Jr., and Other Dangerous People.* Princeton, N.J.: Princeton University Press, 1990.

Hinckley, Jack, and Jo Ann Hinckley. *Breaking Points.* Grand Rapids, Mich.: Chosen Books, 1985.

JAMES W. CLARKE

See also **Assassinations.**

HIROSHIMA AND NAGASAKI

At 8:15 A.M. on 6 August 1945 and then at 11:02 A.M. on 9 August, the cities of Hiroshima and Nagasaki experienced a destructive force that few Japanese (or Americans) knew existed: the atomic bomb. Not only did the bombings dramatically alter the lives of the survivors in these two cities, they changed the way the world looked at warfare and at itself.

Non-Japanese Casualties

Many people mistakenly think that all the victims of the Hiroshima and Nagasaki bombings were Japanese. The Committee for the Compilation of Materials on Damage Caused by the Atomic Bombs in Hiroshima and Nagasaki notes that there were western POWs in Hiroshima, as well as citizens of Germany, the USSR, and many other nations. Nagasaki was also home to many Chinese nationals. The vast majority of non-Japanese victims, however, were Koreans, most of whom had been forcibly brought to Japan while Korea was a Japanese colony. It is estimated that 40,000 Koreans died in the two cities, with as many as 30,000 survivors, but for decades there was no official government response to these victims. Finally, in 1970, a memorial to the Koreans who perished was erected near the peace park in Hiroshima. More important, in a 1978 U.S. Supreme Court decision Korean victims were finally given the same rights as Japanese victims. The bitterness felt by the Korean *hibakusha* has not gone away.

The devastation caused by the atomic bombs is truly beyond comprehension. More than 80 percent of the people within one kilometer (six-tenths of a mile) of the hypocenter were killed, most of them instantly (all numbers from *Hiroshima and Nagasaki* 1981). Estimates of the total loss of life vary, but a 1946 Hiroshima city report estimates that 122,338 of the approximately 245,000 residents died as a result of the atomic bomb; later reports placed that number as high as 165,900. Nagasaki was no less decimated: a 1949 Nagasaki city report estimates that 73,884 of the approximately 195,000 residents were killed (although other reports estimated a number ranging from 25,000 to 40,000). It is estimated that, in Hiroshima, between 80 and 90 percent of all medical workers were killed; thus no medical care was available for those who managed to survive.

Few physical structures remained standing. In Hiroshima more than 90 percent—fifty to seventy thousand structures—of the buildings within three kilometers of the hypocenter were destroyed. In Nagasaki roughly twenty thousand of the forty-nine thousand buildings in the city were destroyed. This resulted in an incredible monetary loss: according to the Committee for the Compilation of Materials on Damage Caused by the Atomic Bombs in Hiroshima and Nagasaki, the total damage would be equivalent in 1977 currency to 258 billion yen and just under 111 billion yen respectively, or roughly one billion U.S. dollars. And this is for Hiroshima and Nagasaki alone; these numbers do not take into account the effect on the tattered Japanese economy.

The damage goes far beyond the loss of people and property. Given the social breakdown that occurred in the aftermath of the atomic bombings, the actual amount of damage may never be known; but then mere numbers fail to capture the devastation wrought on these cities.

Those who survived the atomic bomb, in Japanese the *hibakusha*, continued to suffer physically and mentally long after the bombing. Merely having to recount the terrible days produced psychological, even physical, trauma. Ota Yoko, a prominent writer who survived Hiroshima, stated, "I gaze fixedly at these events I have to call up from memory in order to write, and I become ill; I become nauseated; my stomach starts to throb with pain" (Minear, ed. 1990, p. 124). These traumatic memories would not fade with time.

Moreover, survivors were afraid that they would eventually fall ill from the effects of radiation, or even pass the effects on to their children; these fears, on the part of both the *hibakusha* and other Japanese, made it difficult for survivors to marry or have children or even to gain employment. Worse yet, the Japanese government waited

An Allied correspondent surveys the wreckage of Hiroshima, Japan, in September 1945. UPI/CORBIS-BETTMANN

How Many Were Killed?

Soon after the bombings the grisly task of counting the dead and wounded began. The extreme destruction wrought by the atomic bombs made this count difficult, however, and differing sources and methods of calculation produced estimated death totals that ranged from as low as 32,959 to as high as 165,900. When the count was taken was itself a factor—the longer one waited, the more deaths would be included, as more people succumbed to the effects of their injuries or to radiation poisoning. Some totals are even more controversial; the Register of A-Bomb Victims in Hiroshima continued to add names each year even up to the late 1990s, as those who were present in Hiroshima on 6 August died, whether or not their deaths were related to the bombings. How many people really died in the bombings? No one will ever know for sure.

until 1954—nearly ten years after the bombing—before making an official effort to help the *hibakusha*, efforts that have been widely seen as inadequate, even with subsequent revisions. Thus, the *hibakusha* have had to fight not only to survive their trauma but also to be seen as legitimate victims by their own government.

Were the Bombings Justified?

As the scope of the devastation caused by the two atomic bombs became clear, there began in the United States a debate as to whether their use was justified in the first place. Although none would disagree that the atomic bomb had terrible effects, some feel its use was justified. The main purpose of the bomb, in this view, was to end the war quickly, and the Japanese did indeed surrender within days of the bombings. More important, perhaps, this speedy ending saved countless American (and Japanese) lives that would have been lost in a full-scale invasion of Japan; it was assumed that Japan would never surrender but fight to the last man.

Others have challenged this view, arguing that the Japanese may have been closer to surrender than the United States government had thought, or that the United States could have dropped the bomb on an uninhabited area as a warning. Some see a more insidious motive, arguing that the bombs were used in part to justify their $2 billion price tag or, worse, that the United States was exhibiting its strength to the rest of the world (particularly to the Soviet Union) at the expense of the Japanese. Some see all use of atomic weapons as immoral.

The debate continues, evidenced forcefully by the public battle over the exhibition of the *Enola Gay* in 1995. In 1988 the Smithsonian National Air and Space Museum, in Washington, D.C., began planning an exhibition featuring the *Enola Gay*, the B-29 bomber used to drop the first atomic bomb. The target date of 1995, the fiftieth anniversary of the bombings, was itself bound to spark controversy; moreover, as people became aware of the exhibition's content, some complained that it cast Japan as a victim and was overly critical of the United States. This built into a firestorm of criticism, reigniting a national debate about the bombings, and eventually led to the cancellation of the proposed exhibition. Such passionate debate, even fifty years after the event, shows what a powerful psychological effect the atomic bomb had, not only on Japan but on the United States as well.

Influence on Global Politics

This profound psychological effect produced somewhat contradictory outcomes. On the one hand several nations acquired nuclear weapons (India and Pakistan are the most recent), and the United States and the Soviet Union adopted a doctrine of mutually assured destruction (MAD), by which the production and stockpiling of thousands of nuclear weapons would be used as a deterrent to nuclear war. On the other hand, there have been international attempts to curb the spread of nuclear weapons, the most important being the 1968 Treaty on the Non-Proliferation of Nuclear Weapons. Even adversaries on the issue of the bombings generally agree that, if Hiroshima and Nagasaki had any positive effect, it is that having seen the devastation of atomic warfare, no one ever wants to see it again.

BIBLIOGRAPHY

Alperovitz, Gar. *The Decision to Use the Atomic Bomb.* New York: Knopf, 1995.

Committee for the Compilation of Materials on Damage Caused by the Atomic Bombs in Hiroshima and Nagasaki. *Hiroshima and Nagasaki: The Physical, Medical, and Social Effects of the Atomic Bombing,* translated by Eisei Ishikawa and David L. Swain. New York: Basic, 1981.

Harwitt, Martin. "How Lobbying Changed the History of *Enola Gay*." *Japan Quarterly* 44, no. 3 (July–September 1997).

Lifton, Robert J. *Death in Life: Survivors of Hiroshima*. New York: Random House, 1967.

Minear, Richard H, ed. and trans. *Hiroshima: Three Witnesses*. Princeton, N.J.: Princeton University Press, 1990.

Nobile, Philip, ed. *Judgment at the Smithsonian*. New York: Marlowe, 1995.

Thomas, Evan. "Why We Did It." *Newsweek*, 24 July 1995.

HOWARD E. STINE

See also **Disarmament and Arms Control; Weapons: Nuclear; World War II.**

HISPANIC AMERICANS. *See* Cubans; Immigration; Mexicans; Puerto Ricans.

HOFFA, JIMMY
(1913–1975)

James Riddle Hoffa was born on 14 February 1913 in Brazil, Indiana. In 1931 he was working for the Kroger Grocery and Baking Company in Detroit, Michigan, when, experiencing the hard working conditions and the job insecurities brought on by the Great Depression, he and several friends in his work shift called a work stoppage, which ended in a successful settlement with the management and a charter as Federal Local 19341 of the American Federation of Labor. As an organizer, Hoffa ordered and participated in numerous physical confrontations with management, for which he was arrested several times. Hoffa was responsible for the decision to use muscle to settle many labor disputes. At one union meeting, Hoffa had a protester clubbed on the head with a mallet and removed from the meeting. By 1932 he was active in the affairs of the International Brotherhood of Teamsters, Chauffeurs, Warehousemen and Helpers of America, commonly known as the IBT or Teamsters; he rose through the ranks to become president of the union in 1957.

Organized crime has had a long and significant association with organized labor, from influencing the International Longshoremen's Association shortly after its formation in the 1890s to influencing the Laborers International Union and a succession of IBT presidents. In 1941, needing help to end a labor dispute, Hoffa turned to organized crime figures in Detroit, and thereafter, he made connections with gangsters all over the country. One of his attorneys was related to an organized crime boss on the East Coast and another associate of his was a capo (leader of organized crime) in Chicago who also served as the president of a local chapter of the IBT. Allen Dorfman, stepson of the mobster Paul "Red" Dorfman, who was associated with organized crime in Chicago, was an important figure on the board of the Central States Pension Fund, the overseers for the Teamsters' pension. Another of his attorneys was Frank Ragano, who was also an attorney for Santo Trafficante, a noted crime figure in Florida.

Hoffa was capable of violent rages, which he could direct verbally or physically. According to Ragano, Hoffa once engaged in a physical confrontation with Attorney General Robert F. Kennedy. Hoffa allegedly choked Kennedy and was forced to release his hold. The hatred between Hoffa and Kennedy began during acrimonious exchanges during a Senate hearing and continued throughout their lives, often clouding the professional judgment of both. As the chief counsel of

Jimmy Hoffa at a Senate meeting, 13 October 1961.
CORBIS/BETTMANN

the Rackets Committee, in 1952 Kennedy had set out to uncover corrupt practices in Hoffa's Teamsters Union and became extremely intent on getting Hoffa. Hoffa at one time is said to have suggested a way to assassinate Robert Kennedy.

The Select Committee on Assassinations appointed by the U.S. House of Representatives in 1964 reviewed the evidence that Hoffa had once spoken about a plan to kill Robert Kennedy. The plan he allegedly proposed closely resembled the circumstances surrounding President John F. Kennedy's assassination in 1963. In addition to his connection to organized crime figures who were alleged to have been involved in the assassination of President Kennedy, namely, Santo Trafficante and Carlos Marcello, Hoffa also had a possible connection to Jack Ruby, Lee Harvey Oswald's murderer.

Convicted of fraud, jury tampering, and conspiracy in the disposition of union funds, Hoffa began serving a thirteen-year prison sentence in 1967. While Hoffa was in jail, Frank Fitzsimmons became the president of IBT and negotiated Hoffa's release with the Justice Department. Hoffa, however, distrusted Fitzsimmons and plotted to have him murdered.

One of the terms of his release from prison in 1971 was that he not run for office in the IBT. Hoffa disregarded this provision and began to plan his return to union leadership. Forces supporting Fitzsimmons strongly opposed this initiative. Tony Provenzano, New Jersey Teamster leader and noted organized crime figure, opposed Hoffa's return and came to represent the dissatisfaction of organized crime with Hoffa. On 30 July 1975 Hoffa was to meet with Provenzano and Anthony Giacalone, a Detroit crime figure, to discuss their differences. It is a matter of dispute as to who actually met Hoffa for this meeting or what specifically occurred, but he never returned from the meeting and was never seen again.

BIBLIOGRAPHY

Moldea, Dan E. *The Hoffa Wars.* New York: Paddington, 1978.

Neff, James. *Mobbed Up.* New York: Atlantic Monthly Press, 1989.

Ragano, Frank, and Selwyn Rabb. *Mob Lawyer.* New York: Scribner, 1994.

Sloane, Arthur A. *Hoffa.* Cambridge, Mass.: MIT Press, 1991.

DAVID FABIANIC

See also **Kennedy, Robert F.; Labor and Unions; Strikes.**

HOFFMAN, ABBIE
(1936–1989)

For the generation that came of age during the Vietnam War, Abbie Hoffman became the hero of an iconoclast movement. A master of guerrilla theater, he staged events at the Pentagon, the New York Stock Exchange, and the House Committee on Un-American Activities, attracting the mass media and polarizing public opinion.

Born to a middle-class Jewish family in Worcester, Massachusetts, in 1936, Abbott Howard Hoffman grew up in awe of the American Revolution and in admiration of Samuel Adams and Paul Revere. While many 1960s radicals turned to third-world and Soviet revolutionaries for inspiration, Hoffman placed himself in a tradition of American radicalism and insisted that revolution in the United States would have to spring from native soil.

A college athlete and playboy at Brandeis University, Hoffman did not awaken to radicalism until he became a graduate student at the University of California at Berkeley in 1959. As an opponent of capital punishment, he joined with others to protest the execution at San Quentin of Caryl Chessman, a convicted rapist who had rehabilitated himself and become the focus of worldwide concern. In the mid-1960s Hoffman joined the northern Civil Rights movement and took part in nonviolent sit-ins to integrate the industrial workplace in Worcester, Massachusetts.

In Manhattan's East Village in the mid-1960s, Hoffman enticed hippies into the antiwar movement and persuaded sectors of the Marxist left that cultural revolution, including radical changes in consciousness and lifestyle, constituted a significant component in the movement for social change. In August 1967 he and a small group of activists invaded the New York Stock Exchange, dropped dollar bills from the visitors' gallery, and caused trading to come to a brief standstill. Along with Paul Krassner and Jerry Rubin, in the winter of 1968 Hoffman created Yippie!, a freewheeling anarchist group.

In the summer of 1968, members of Yippie! showed up in Chicago to protest the 1968 Democratic National Convention. During the turbulent convention, which brought him notoriety as an international figure of rebellion, Hoffman pushed freedom of speech to the limit, urging protesters to use any means necessary to change society. Characteristically, he got himself arrested, not for throwing rocks or battling the police, but for writing an obscenity on his forehead. Subsequently, though, he was prosecuted on federal charges of conspiracy and crossing state lines with the intent of rioting. Hoffman and his codefendants, known as "the Chicago Eight," disrupted the courtroom and used this opportunity to ridicule the judicial system. Though they were initially found guilty of rioting, the convictions were overturned on appeal. The National Commission on the Causes and Prevention of Violence, which was appointed by President Lyndon Johnson to investigate the causes of the disturbance, concluded later in 1968 that, while Hoffman and his cohorts engaged in provocative speech and action, the events that shook Chicago could best be described as a "police riot."

Hoffman also achieved recognition as the author of *Revolution for the Hell of It* (1968), *Woodstock Nation* (1969), and *Steal This Book* (1971), which provided information on how to make explosives. In the Reagan era, he opposed drug testing, supported the Sandinistas in Nicaragua, and took part in nonviolent demonstrations to protest nuclear power and to save the environment. Diagnosed with bipolar disorder, he disregarded the advice of his doctors, neglected to take his prescription drugs, and plunged deeper and deeper into despair. Before he committed suicide in April 1989 by taking the equivalent of 150 phenobarbital pills, he made one last valiant effort to reach generation Xers and to awaken the conscience of former 1960s radicals. Speaking on college campuses, he defended the role of political protest during the Vietnam era and urged young people to renew the sprit of rebellion. His own strategy for social protest is perhaps best summarized by his quip, "You don't use a gun on an IBM computer. You pull the plug."

BIBLIOGRAPHY

Raskin, Jonah. *For the Hell of It: The Life and Times of Abbie Hoffman.* Berkeley: University of California Press, 1996.
Simon, Daniel, ed. *The Best of Abbie Hoffman.* New York: Four Walls Eight Windows, 1989.

JONAH RASKIN

See also **Antiwar Protests; Yippie!**

HOFMANN, MARK
(1954–)

In 1987 thirty-two-year-old Mark William Hofmann, a dealer in historical manuscripts, pleaded guilty to fraud, in particular to forging historical documents, and to the pipe-bomb murders of two members of the Church of Jesus Christ of Latter-day Saints (LDS). Prosecutors contended that Hofmann had set out in the early 1980s to defraud the church and other investors by selling forged documents. He committed the murders, prosecutors said, under pressure to close a deal involving a nonexistent manuscript collection intended for the church. Thus, he faced exposure.

Hofmann was born on 7 December 1954 to William Hofmann and Lucille Sears, who was the child of a polygamous Mormon marriage. With the birth of their child, the Hofmanns became newly mainstream, and therefore monogamous, and held high hopes for Mark, who, showing signs of his later skill at forgery and bomb making, delighted early in fooling people with magic tricks, exploding chemicals, and collecting coins (with an unusual number of valuable mint marks). He was also known to torment cats and enjoyed baiting his father with scientific theory. An indication of Hofmann's dislike of his family's religion may be found in his hating the secrecy surrounding his grandparents' marriage, contracted after the Mormons renounced polygamy in 1904. On an LDS mission to England in 1974–1976, he photographed bombing sites credited to the Irish Republican Army and bought old anti-Mormon books.

While in college at Utah State University from 1976 to 1980, Hofmann entertained the idea of poisoning a coin and thereby a currency collector to acquire certain items. Hofmann had paid his own college expenses largely through trading and selling coins, many of which were probably counterfeit. He told his fiancée that he wanted to find documents disproving Mormonism. He then married a different woman, Doralee Olds, in 1979 and involved her in "finding" his first prominent manuscript, the Anthon Transcript, which Hofmann had forged and sealed inside a Bible.

On 16 October 1985 Hofmann was seriously injured when a bomb exploded in his car in downtown Salt Lake City. On the previous day, pipe bombs in boxes had killed a thirty-one-year-old businessman and LDS bishop, Steven F. Christensen, and fifty-year-old Kathleen Sheets. Christensen had been facilitating the sale of Hofmann's "McLellin Collection" that morning, in concert with several LDS church leaders. The bomb that killed Sheets was in a box addressed to her husband, J. Gary Sheets, Christensen's former business partner, who was also an LDS bishop. The blast that injured Hofmann canceled the second scheduled sale of the McLellin Collection, which Hofmann purported to be the papers of a nine-teenth-century renegade apostle of the LDS, but which actually consisted of only a forged papyrus and land deed. Hofmann intended both bombs to divert attention from the McLellin Collection sales, fearing that the collection would be examined and discovered a forgery. Shortly after the 16 October explosion, Hofmann was named a suspect in the previous day's bombings. Investigators believed that Hofmann had inadvertently detonated the bomb that injured him, and that it had been intended for a third Mormon bishop.

Hofmann seemed an unlikely murderer. A clean-cut husband and father, he associated with a high LDS leader, Gordon B. Hinckley (who later became church president), and at the time of the Salt Lake City bombings, he had been on the East Coast, marketing what was purported to be America's first printed document, the Oath of a Free-man, dated 1638 or 1639.

On 6 January 1984 Christensen, a history buff, had paid Hofmann $40,000 for a document known as the "white salamander letter," an 1830 epistle purportedly written by an early Mormon convert, in which the founder of Mormonism, Joseph Smith, is described as having received guidance from a white salamander—rather than from the angel Moroni, as was traditionally believed—in finding the golden plates on which the Book of Mormon was understood to have been written. The letter, which had been authenticated by eastern experts and later passed muster with forensic examiners at the Federal Bureau of Investigation, was extremely controversial because it framed Mormon origins in folk magic rather than divine revelation. By 1985 the letter had become so controversial that Christensen donated it to the LDS Church. The church attempted to suppress it, but news of that letter as well as another forged letter that Hofmann had sold shortly before circulated through the LDS historical community as it prepared for its annual history symposium in May 1985. The church was then forced to admit its possession of both letters. Hofmann had deliberately leaked information about the two letters to force the church to bring them forward. The McLellin Collection also contained materials that contradicted the church's historical teachings. On the morning he died, Christensen had been expecting to authenticate the collection, which had been resold to a party who was going to donate it to the church. Because of

Mark Hofmann at a preliminary hearing in Salt Lake City on 14 April 1986. CORBIS/BETTMANN-UPI

the enormous threat that the apocryphal McLellin Collection posed to the church, Hofmann was able to sell it again and again, convincing his buyers that their purchase would prevent the collection from falling into the hands of anti-Mormons who sought it in order to discredit the Mormon Church.

After the bombings, investigators found that Hofmann's attempts to sell the Oath of a Freeman were partly motivated by a need to retain legitimacy in the face of increasingly chaotic double-dealing. Hofmann grew desperate when the Library of Congress refused to pay the $1 million he had anticipated receiving for the document. He owed a bank $185,000, loaned on an LDS leader's verbal guarantee. In addition, Hofmann had borrowed large amounts of money from other parties, in each case using the McLellin Collection as collateral, and these loans also were in arrears. On behalf of church leaders, Christensen had been pressuring Hofmann to turn over the collection.

Ultimately, forensic experts found that Hofmann had forged his manuscripts, using old paper and chemicals to make the ink appear aged. The Oath of Freeman was forged; Hofmann had at least two copies printed, and his McLellin Collection did not exist except as a few forged documents. In January 1987 Hofmann pleaded guilty to two counts of second-degree murder and to fraud. He was sentenced to life in prison. Arguably the best forger ever caught, Hofmann disrupted the Americana market and brought scandal upon the Mormon Church.

BIBLIOGRAPHY

Lindsey, Robert. *A Gathering of Saints.* New York: Simon and Schuster, 1988.

Nickell, Joe. *Detecting Forgery: Forensic Investigation of Documents.* Lexington: University Press of Kentucky, 1996.

Sillitoe, Linda, and Allen D. Roberts. *Salamander: The Story of the Mormon Forgery Murders.* Salt Lake City, Utah: Signature, 1988.

LINDA SILLITOE

See also **Bombings and Bomb Scares; Mormons.**

HOLLIDAY, JOHN HENRY "DOC"
(1851–1887)

The western gambler and gunfighter John Henry "Doc" Holliday was born into a highly respectable, well-to-do Southern family on 14 August 1851, in Griffin, Georgia. He attended schools in Griffin, Bemiss, and Valdosta. Caught up in the violent racial turmoil of the Civil War and the tumultuous Reconstruction period, he first gained local notoriety as a teenager by firing a shotgun over the heads of several black youths at a river swimming hole. At the age of eighteen he joined a band of young southern firebrands in a plot to blow up the Lowndes County Court House, headquarters of the hated Freedmen's Bureau. Older, wiser heads, however, convinced the conspirators to abandon the plan. Holliday attended the Pennsylvania College of Dental Surgery at Philadelphia and received a dental degree in March 1872. He had a practice for a short time in Atlanta, but in 1873 he developed tuberculosis and doctors recommended a move to a drier climate. In September of that year he headed west, never to return.

After a series of unsuccessful attempts to practice dentistry in several western towns, he took increasingly to the whiskey bottle and the gambling table. On New Year's Day 1875 he engaged in his first gunfight, trading ineffectual shots with a Dallas saloonkeeper. Plying the professional gamblers' circuit, he reportedly killed a soldier or two in Jacksboro, Texas, cut up a rival gambler in Denver, and shot another in Trinidad, Colorado. These tales, however, seem to be the sort of fables that invariably attach themselves to characters like Holliday. In July 1877 he did clash with another gambler in Breckenridge, Texas, and was severely wounded. Although a Dallas newspaper prematurely reported his death, he recovered and moved on to Fort Griffin, where he first met the two people with whom his name would always be associated—Wyatt Earp, a fellow gambler and sometime lawman, and Mary Katherine Harony (1850–1940), an immigrant from Hungary known in the sporting houses she frequented as Big-Nosed Kate. Holliday reportedly stabbed a man to death at Fort Griffin and was rescued from the authorities by Kate, who started a fire as a diversion.

A late-nineteenth-century painting of John Henry "Doc" Holliday. CORBIS/BETTMANN

As a gambler ever in search of new boomtown excitement, Holliday kept on the move. In Dodge City, Kansas, he is said to have saved Wyatt Earp's life by backing him up at a critical moment in a street confrontation between city officer Earp and rampaging cowboys. Holliday traded bullets with a bartender in Las Vegas, New Mexico, in 1880, but he only grazed his adversary in that encounter.

Rejoining Wyatt Earp in Tombstone, Arizona, the consumptive dentist became a staunch fighting supporter of the Earp brothers in their conflict with their political and economic enemies. Several violent altercations led up to the famous O. K. Corral gunfight, when he and the Earps shot and killed three adversaries. Later Holliday was at Wyatt's side in his bloody vendetta against those responsible for the killing of one Earp brother and the maiming of another, and participated in several revenge killings. Fleeing murder warrants in Arizona, Holliday went to Colorado, where, in 1884, he wounded a gambler named William "Billy" Allen in what would be his last gunfight. On 8 November 1887, at the age of thirty-seven, in Glenwood Springs, Colorado, he succumbed to the tuberculosis that had ravaged his body for fourteen years.

BIBLIOGRAPHY

Jahns, Patricia. *The Frontier World of Doc Holliday, Faro Dealer from Dallas to Deadwood.* New York: Hastings House, 1957.

Myers, John. *Doc Holliday.* Boston: Little, Brown, 1955.

Tanner, Karen Holliday. *Doc Holliday: A Family Portrait.* Norman: University of Oklahoma Press, 1998.

ROBERT K. DEARMENT

See also **Clanton Brothers; Earp Brothers; Frontier Violence; Gunfighters and Outlaws, Western; O. K. Corral.**

HOLMES, H. H.
(1860–1896)

The term *serial killer* is usually applied to those multiple murderers who are not driven by such traditional motives as revenge or greed. Instead, this type of criminal tends to be motivated by sexual sadism. For this reason, America's first highly publicized serial killer, H. H. Holmes, seems to be atypical. His many crimes, both lethal and nonlethal, were perpetrated primarily for the sake of profit. Still, an element of sadism courses through his career, spanning nearly ten years between the mid-1880s and 1894.

Clearly a criminal of his time, H. H. Holmes provided a dark, sociopathological reflection of the Gilded Age. During a period when the self-made man was lionized as a role model for all ambitious young Americans, Holmes presented a dapper, professional exterior, while he secretly resorted to any devious means necessary to acquire wealth.

The process of his self-making began in his twenties when he assumed a new name. Born Herman Mudgett in a small New Hampshire town, he began presenting himself as Dr. Henry Howard Holmes sometime between graduating from medical school at the University of Michigan in 1884 and his arrival in Chicago in 1886. Although he took a job as a druggist's assistant, he was not one to be content with this lowly position. Within a few years, the elderly female proprietor of this pharmacy had mysteriously disappeared, and Holmes himself emerged as owner of the establishment.

Other people who came into close contact with Holmes also vanished mysteriously. Some represented an opportunity for profit to Holmes: their skeletons fetched a premium price at medical schools that did not ask questions about the provenance of their anatomical specimens. Others were lovers of Holmes who expected more of a commitment than he was willing to give—he was already a bigamist at the time (the late 1880s). Soon Holmes acquired enough money to build a sprawling house for himself across the street from his pharmacy; presumably the money was acquired through various scams. The home's labyrinthine interior included pipes that could feed poisonous gas into rooms that were rented out to people visiting Chicago's 1893 World's Fair. Chutes that connected upper floors to the basement allowed bodies to be delivered to Holmes's dissection laboratory. Although he also dabbled in relatively innocuous scams, such as the sale of useless patent medicines, Holmes clearly gravitated to swindles that involved cruelty and death. This inclination was illustrated by his final murderous escapade, the only one to be well documented.

Holmes and a partner named Ben Pitezel planned to fake Pitezel's death and collect on the man's life insurance policy. Holmes, however, supplied the insurance company with an authentic corpse after murdering his partner. He then proceeded to kidnap and kill three of Pitezel's children to prevent them from talking about the scam: he asphyxiated two of them in a trunk outfitted with a gas pipe and strangled the third with his bare hands. He was planning on killing Pitezel's wife and remaining two children, when he was finally arrested. The police had tracked him down after receiving information on the insurance scam from a disgruntled accomplice.

Eventually Holmes confessed to twenty-seven murders. In a trial as infamous in its day as the O. J. Simpson murder case one hundred years later, Holmes was condemned to hang. The sentence was carried out on 7 May 1896.

BIBLIOGRAPHY

Boswell, Charles, and Lewis Thompson. *The Girls in Nightmare House.* New York: Fawcett, 1955.

Franke, David. *The Torture Doctor.* New York: Hawthorn, 1972.

Schechter, Harold. *Depraved: The Shocking True Story of America's First Serial Killer.* New York: Pocket Books, 1994.

DAVID EVERITT

See also **Serial Killers.**

HOLOCAUST

The Holocaust is the name generally given to Nazi Germany's racially inspired murder of five to six million Jews and as many as half a million Gypsies before and during World War II. Literally millions of others—among them Poles, Soviet prisoners of war, political dissidents, homosexuals, and Jehovah's Witnesses—were harassed and incarcerated in concentration camps and died at the hands of the Nazis from sickness, starvation, overwork, and execution, although none of these as a group was targeted for extermination. In a narrow sense an event in European history, the Holocaust has had a broad and deep effect on the politics, culture, and psyche of American society as well. Paradoxically, the Holocaust's importance in American consciousness has grown larger even as the actual events have receded into the past. At the turn of the twenty-first century it stands as one of the most potent symbols of evil and of the ultimate violence of genocide, helping to shape the way Americans see and act upon issues foreign and domestic.

The Holocaust's powerful hold on the American psyche began with the liberation of Dachau, Buchenwald, Bergen-Belsen, and other concentration camps by American, British, French, and Canadian troops as they swept through Germany in the spring of 1945. Nazi mass murder of Jews had been

reported during the war, but few could imagine the reality of such stories until they saw the newsreels and photographs of the liberated camps. Piles of emaciated bodies stacked neatly or bulldozed into mass graves, gaunt survivors staring blankly into space, crematoria, and heaps of human ashes —all such images came to summarize the vast Nazi war against humanity and, especially, Jews.

The immediate impact of the liberations and the revelations of the concentration camps was ambiguous. They helped to give final justification to the war and legitimacy to the Nuremberg Trials, which prosecuted Nazi war criminals. In America, the liberations served to delegitimize a virulent strain of anti-Semitism that had persisted throughout the war. Once-common public expressions of anti-Jewish stereotypes dwindled, and public opinion polls indicated a sea change toward acceptance of Jews as Americans like others. The horrors of the camps pointed to the dangers of racism in general, thus bringing greater urgency to the African American pursuit of civil rights. Recognition of Nazi crimes also created strong support among Americans for the founding of a Jewish homeland in Palestine, which became a reality with the creation of the State of Israel in 1948. This began an enduring American-Israeli alliance that soon became a crucial element of American foreign policy.

At the same time, the inclination to forget surfaced as well. The Cold War and an American alliance with the new Federal Republic of Germany (West Germany), formed in 1949 from the American, British, and French zones of occupation, made reminders of Germany's Nazi past an inconvenient embarrassment. More profoundly, like the new reality of the atomic bomb, the memory of the Nazi concentration camps was too close and too terrifying to contemplate directly for very long. For a decade or more after 1945, a kind of amnesia set in when it came to the Nazi mass killings of European Jews. The facts were only partially known and hard to face, yet the reality of the camps continued to haunt historical consciousness.

Presentation of Anne Frank's diary attested to these contradictory impulses to remember or to forget. The enormous appeal of the book, written by a thirteen-year-old Jewish girl who later died in a concentration camp, satisfied the need to remember, yet the limited setting of the diary—the Frank family's hiding place in Amsterdam—and the superimposed upbeat vision of the stage and film dramatizations in the 1950s attested to the limit of the public's ability to face the worst realities.

A large crowd attends the official opening ceremonies at the U.S. Holocaust Memorial Museum in Washington, D.C., in April 1993. CORBIS/IRA NOWINSKI

This method of coming to terms with the Holocaust began to change in the early 1960s. Hollywood's 1961 film *Judgment at Nuremberg* provided Americans with a searing reminder of Nazi crimes. Also in the early 1960s, the Israeli kidnapping of Adolf Eichmann, one of the Nazis' chief architects of genocide, from Argentina and his subsequent trial in Jerusalem recounted Holocaust history in unprecedented detail before television cameras and the world press. This new interest in the Holocaust coincided with a period of major cultural self-scrutiny in which virtually every aspect of American history, culture, and moral self-image came under the microscope of often unfriendly commentators.

The Holocaust emerged in the early and middle 1960s as a universal reference point for ultimate evil against which society might be judged. Allusions to Nazi genocide appeared in such folk revival songs as Tom Paxton's "Last Train to Nuremberg" and Bob Dylan's "With God on Our Side." Sylvia Plath identified herself with the Jews and her father with the Nazis in an angry poem, "Daddy." Civil rights advocates noted parallels between segregation and Nazi race policies. By 1967 and 1968, those protesting the war in Vietnam made frequent allusions to Nazi genocide and accused the United States of war crimes. Antiwar

graffiti summed it up with an ironic new Germanized spelling of America: AMERIKA.

Scholars also began to look critically at America's part in the Holocaust itself. Once Americans had seen themselves simply as liberators of Nazism's victims. Beginning in the late 1960s and culminating in the 1980s, numerous historians held America and its allies accountable for blocking rescue attempts, limiting refugee immigration, and missing opportunities to slow down the killings by threat of revenge and by direct military intervention. Scholars also noted instances of the U.S. Army's less than humane treatment of Jewish displaced persons after the war and the anti-Semitic assumptions of some of those officers, notably General George S. Patton, who were in charge. The historian David Wyman described the basic thrust of this research in his 1984 best-selling book, *The Abandonment of the Jews*.

While most Americans accept the historical reality of the Holocaust, a small minority with an anti-Semitic agenda deny that it ever happened. These so-called revisionists, intimately connected to American and international neo-Nazi and other hate groups, have so far been unable to make much headway in American life. Paradoxically, neo-Nazi organizations such as the National Alliance, Christian Identity, and others embraced the exterminationist mission of the Nazis and in the 1980s and 1990s stepped up isolated but tragic killing and vandalism against Jews and nonwhites. It seems that the Holocaust, a tragedy and warning to most citizens, can be an inspiration to a few.

Raising the question of responsibility had more than academic implications. Beginning with the Carter administration (1976–1980), American presidents have utilized the example of the Holocaust and the past accusations of American inaction to justify U.S. policies—sometimes including direct military intervention—concerned with human rights violations and the prevention of genocide all over the world. The U.S. government in the late 1980s, in cooperation with Holocaust survivors and other private supporters, constructed in Washington, D.C., the U.S. Holocaust Memorial Museum, in which the fate of European Jews under Nazism is presented both in its historical uniqueness and as a universal warning against the dangers of racism and genocide.

Such use of the Holocaust has arisen in tandem with an ever increasing treatment of the subject in popular entertainment, especially in films, among them *Holocaust* (a 1978 television miniseries), *Sophie's Choice* (1982), and *Schindler's List* (1993). In the late twentieth century, new discoveries about individual, corporate, and national complicity with the Nazis began to appear in the headlines. Questions of international responsibility to end outbreaks of genocide (for example, in Bosnia and Rwanda at the end of the twentieth century) are asked and answered in terms derived directly from contemplation of the Holocaust. For better and for worse, in America the Holocaust has become the metaphor and the yardstick for evil in the modern world.

BIBLIOGRAPHY

Abzug, Robert. *Inside the Vicious Heart: Americans and the Liberation of Nazi Concentration Camps.* New York: Oxford University Press, 1985.

Linenthal, Edward. *Preserving Memory: The Struggle to Create America's Holocaust Museum.* New York: Viking, 1995.

Neusner, Jacob. *Stranger at Home: "The Holocaust," Zionism and American Judaism.* Chicago: University of Chicago Press, 1981.

Wyman, David. *The Abandonment of the Jews: America and the Holocaust, 1941–1945.* New York: Pantheon, 1984.

ROBERT H. ABZUG

See also **Eugenics; Euthanasia; Human Rights; Jews; Race and Ethnicity; Religion; War Crimes; World War II.**

HOMELESSNESS

Poverty, an inadequate stock of affordable housing, and mental illness are the principal factors contributing to homelessness, and violence plays a central role in the lives of homeless people. Violence both precedes homelessness and is a condition of life on the streets and in emergency shelters. The association of violence with homelessness has led many municipalities to pass and enforce laws regulating the use of public spaces, in effect criminalizing homelessness.

Domestic Violence as a Cause of Homelessness

At least 25 percent of homeless people are women, and women and children together make up nearly 40 percent of the total homeless population. Domestic violence is a significant cause of homelessness among women. Between 1983 and 1987 the number of people entering shelters for battered women increased 100 percent. In 1988 more than three hundred thousand women and their children in the United States sought admittance to eleven hundred shelters and safe houses.

Because many shelters have limited lengths of stay, women and children fleeing domestic violence often end up among the homeless population. In a 1986 study of the inhabitants of Massachusetts family homeless shelters, Ellen Bassuk found that although domestic violence was not always the immediate cause of their homelessness, 45 percent of the women interviewed reported being the victims of domestic violence (Fantasia and Isserman 1994). A 1992 study of the characteristics, life circumstances, and needs of homeless women and their families found that a significant number had moved as many as six times within the previous five years for various reasons, including domestic violence and interpersonal conflict (Khanna, Singh, and Nemilm 1992).

Victimization and Aggression in Homeless Lives

When coupled with mental illness or substance abuse, homelessness often results in criminal victimization. More than half of those in a family homeless shelter in Detroit in 1986 reported having been victimized within the previous six months. Homeless persons in the inner city of Los Angeles reported a similar rate of victimization. In a systematic study, nine hundred randomly chosen homeless adults in St. Louis described violence in their lives, with themselves as both victims and

A homeless mother and her three children who live in a field along a highway in Tennessee. Photo taken in the 1930s. HULTON GETTY/LIAISON AGENCY

victimizers. Post-traumatic stress disorder was common among the members of this group, and substance abuse and severe mental disorders were often the consequences of a traumatic event. The majority of men and a substantial proportion of women also had a history of physically aggressive behavior, which often began in childhood. Aggressive adult behavior was often the result of substance abuse and clinical depression. The aggressive behavior usually predated homelessness and in about one-half of the cases continued after the individual became homeless (North, Smith, and Spitznagel 1994).

Crime is common among homeless people. In one study more than 60 percent of the homeless acknowledged participating in criminal activity. Certain activities such as trespassing, burglary, and shoplifting may supplement meager economic resources. Some homeless people engage in chronic and serious criminal activity, and approx-

imately 5 percent of released prisoners become homeless. About one-third of the homeless people in inner-city Los Angeles had been picked up by the police in 1985, and a comparable percentage had spent time in jail during that period. Among Chicago's homeless, almost one in five had been in federal or state prisons, two in five had been in jail, and one in four had been sentenced and placed on probation.

Rates of victimization vary among different groups of homeless people. The mentally ill are more likely than other groups to be victimized, which may be attributable to their attention-attracting behavior or to their vulnerability and poor skills in avoiding danger. Women are most at risk of assault. Men are more likely to be robbed.

The relationship between substance abuse and criminal activity is well established. Homeless substance abusers are likely to be victimized and to engage in criminal behavior. Researchers have consistently documented high rates of severe substance abuse among homeless people. Whether substance abuse is viewed as pathological or as a means of adapting to homelessness, it is more common among homeless than among domiciled adults.

Municipal Criminalization of Homelessness

American cities have responded to the specter of violence surrounding homeless people by enacting criminal sanctions to protect public spaces. Such laws prohibit begging, camping, and sleeping in public places, effectively banishing the homeless from such areas. This municipal trend has engendered acrimonious legal controversy among scholars, lawyers, public officials, social service providers, and activists.

Supporters of these laws rationalize them in terms of communal quality of life as well as public safety. They argue that the presence of homeless people contributes to a cycle of deterioration in communities that leads to violence and criminal activity. This argument has been labeled the broken-window theory by Professors James Q. Wilson and George Kelling, who compare one vagrant in a neighborhood to a broken window in a building. The comparison can be articulated as follows: when a window is broken in a building, that building becomes fair game for vandalization. Homeless people, left untended in public places, may indicate that an area is vulnerable to criminal activity. City officials defend the laws as necessary to attract and retain business and revenue. Communitarians support the laws as a way to preserve public safety, civility, and the attractiveness of civic spaces. Cities that rely heavily on tourism are concerned about their image and public order as well.

Advocates for the homeless have challenged these regulations as legally sanctioned persecution of the poor. They contend that most homeless people lack reasonable, safe, and legal alternatives to homelessness and that their offenses are petty and would not be grounds for legal or police action if committed by a member of the non-homeless population. They further note that the criminalization of homelessness is futile and merely shifts the problem from one municipality to another. Finally, advocates for the homeless argue that anti-homeless ordinances are discriminatory and violate constitutional protections of free speech, freedom from search and seizure, freedom to travel, and equal protection.

The occupation of public spaces by the homeless, and the omnipresent threat of violence posed by this occupation, will continue until homelessness is alleviated.

BIBLIOGRAPHY

Baumohl, Jim, ed. *Homelessness in America*. Phoenix, Ariz.: Oryx, 1996.

Fantasia, Rick, and Maurice Isserman. *Homelessness: A Sourcebook*. New York: Facts on File, 1994.

Khanna, Mukti, Nirbhay Singh, and Mary Nemilm. "Homeless Women and Their Families: Characteristics, Life Circumstances, and Needs." *Journal of Child and Family Studies* 1, no. 2 (June 1992).

North, Carol S., Elizabeth M. Smith, and Edward L. Spitznagel. "Violence and the Homeless: An Epidemiological Study of Victimization and Aggression." *Journal of Traumatic Stress* 7, no. 1 (January 1994).

Schutt, Russell K., and Gerald R. Garrett. *Responding to the Homeless: Policy and Practice*. London: Plenum, 1992.

MADELEINE R. STONER

See also **Poverty; Structural Violence.**

HOMICIDE

Homicide is an umbrella term covering diverse situations with the same outcome—a person has died at the hands of another person. Yet homicides do in fact differ so much from each other that homicide is not a single phenomenon: a robbery that ends in death is qualitatively different from fatal child abuse or domestic violence, and these in turn are qualitatively different from fatal street-gang turf battles. These different types of homicide each have their own distinct types of victims and offenders; the ways in which situations escalate to homicide tend to be different; and the types of weapons and decisions about weapon use tend to be different. In addition, various homicides have varying patterns over time and across space. Some types tend to increase and decrease in sharp spurts, whereas others are usually stable over time; some types tend to be scattered across neighborhoods or across rural, suburban, and urban settings, whereas others tend to be clustered in certain areas. Thus, to understand homicide one cannot look only at its lethal outcome; one must also examine the violent and nonviolent events that underlie and lead to homicide.

Definitions

The United States is similar to most other countries in that two official entities, criminal justice and public health, maintain parallel systems for defining and measuring homicide. In criminal justice, the Federal Bureau of Investigation's Uniform Crime Reporting (UCR) program has compiled data from local agencies since 1933. In public health, the National Center for Health Statistics (NCHS) Mortality System has collected vital statistics on deaths since 1850. UCR statistics on homicides are based on police investigation (as opposed to judicial determination); NCHS statistics on homicides are based on death certificates. Although the criminal justice and public health systems usually investigate the same fatal incidents and sometimes collaborate with each other, they report through separate conduits to different national databases and define homicide somewhat differently. Rand summarizes their differences by commenting, "The UCR measures crimes, of which death is one outcome. The Mortality System measures deaths, of which crime is one cause" (Rand 1993, p. 112).

In the criminal justice system homicide is "the killing of one human being by the act, procurement, or omission of another." (Procurement includes paying someone to kill the victim. Omission might be letting someone starve to death.) Homicide is not necessarily a crime; some homicides are the result of justifiable self-defense or legal intervention (e.g., capital punishment). Criminal homicide includes murder, manslaughter, and

A doctor and detectives examine the corpse of a man found floating in the East River, New York City, July 1963. CORBIS/BETTMANN

negligent homicide. The FBI defines murder and nonnegligent manslaughter as "the willful (nonnegligent) killing of one human being by another," which includes any death due to injuries received in a fight or in the commission of a crime. It does not include suicide, accidental deaths, accidental traffic deaths, or fetal deaths.

Key terms in the definition of criminal homicide are *willful* and *negligence*. According to the FBI an incident in which a robbery victim dies of a heart attack does not meet the criteria for criminal homicide, since "a heart attack cannot, in fact, be caused at will by an offender." *Black's Law Dictionary* defines negligent homicide as similar to involuntary manslaughter in that the defendant's negligence without malice "is the direct and proximate cause" of the death, but differing in that the defendant of involuntary manslaughter does not realize "the risk of death involved" in his or her behavior.

Definitions and terms used for criminal homicide differ across states. Murder may be called capital murder or first-degree murder; negligent manslaughter may be called second-degree murder or voluntary manslaughter; nonnegligent manslaughter may be called involuntary manslaughter. Many state statutes (such as in Alaska and in Arizona) define four types of homicide: first-degree murder, second-degree murder, manslaughter, and criminally negligent homicide. Some add additional types to the list, such as capital murder (Arkansas) or vehicular homicide (Col-

orado, Louisiana, and Tennessee). Others make finer distinctions. California law, for example, distinguishes between vehicular homicide with or without "gross negligence." Connecticut law has a separate category for arson murder and for manslaughter in the second degree with a motor vehicle while intoxicated, and distinguishes between manslaughter with and without a firearm. In Delaware promoting suicide is a Class D felony listed with homicides. Despite statutory differences at the state level, however, all state reports to national criminal justice database systems must use standard FBI definitions.

In public health the NCHS has compiled death-certificate data since 1850 and has provided nationwide data since 1933; Eckberg has calculated reliable and comparable national rates from 1900. The NCHS now registers more than 99 percent of the deaths occurring in the country. Homicide definitions follow the International Classification of Diseases (ICD) E (external causes of injury) codes developed by the World Health Organization and are divided into two categories, homicide and legal intervention.

The Department of Health and Human Services defines homicide (ICD codes E960–E969) as "injuries inflicted by another person with the intent to injure, harm, or kill including child battering and rape. Excludes injuries due to legal intervention and war." Like the criminal justice definition of homicide, the public health definition is neutral as to criminal culpability. In general, the single

NCHS homicide category corresponds most closely to criminal homicide plus justifiable homicide; though they are not identical, these NCHS and FBI homicide categories contain the same basic elements: fatal injury caused by another human being, with intent. Negligent manslaughter, on the other hand, corresponds more closely to NCHS codes for accidental death. Legal-intervention homicide (ICD codes E970–E978)—defined by the Department of Health and Human Services as "injuries inflicted by the police or other law enforcing agents, including military on duty, in the course of arresting or attempting to arrest law breakers, suppressing disturbances, maintaining order, and other legal action" or "legal execution"—generally corresponds to homicides "done in the lawful execution of a judicial sentence . . . or as the only possible means of arresting an escaping felon," noted in *Black's Law Dictionary*.

Reporting and Records

Homicide is widely regarded as the most accurately enumerated crime. Assaults, robberies, and rapes are often underreported by victims or witnesses and, therefore, are underrecorded by the criminal justice system. Definitions for such crimes are often subjective, especially for the less serious offenses. Homicide, in contrast, is less subjective and much more likely to be counted, specifically because there is usually a body. Indeed, despite differences of reporting conventions, updating practices, and definitions, research has found that annual homicide counts in the public health and criminal justice systems are close and generally track each other over time. Comparing FBI and NCHS counts from 1976 through 1982, Rokaw, Mercy, and Smith found an overall 9 percent difference. Of the fifty states plus the District of Columbia, the FBI and NCHS figures were within 10 percent of each other in twenty-eight states and within 20 percent in another twelve. The occasional large difference occurred, for example, when a state had not reported to one of the systems in a given year. Riedel also found close agreement between homicide counts in the FBI and NCHS for 1968 through 1978.

Some types of homicide, however, may slip through the official recording net. One of these is death caused by negligence, especially deaths of young children, the elderly, and the sick or disabled. An investigation by a team of child-fatality experts over a four-year period in Missouri, for example, found that only 39 percent of "definite maltreatment fatalities" of children from birth to age four had been recorded in any official record, such as coroner's records or police reports. With the advent of child-death review systems around the country, Finkelhor expects to see an increase in child homicide as an artifact of increased reporting.

Also, Cantor and Cohen warn that the degree to which NCHS and FBI homicide counts track each other depends upon the time period in question. They are not comparable before 1949, when ICD first separated legal intervention from the rest of the homicide category, and they moved in opposite directions from 1960 to 1963. Even if aggregate homicide counts were exactly the same, however, they might still mask case-level inconsistencies. In addition, specific cases may differ though total counts are the same. In a case-by-case attempt to match each of the 1,855 NCHS homicide cases to a UCR case for a specific one-month period (July 1986), Rand found only 1,191 exact matches (64 percent), though the two total counts were within 4 percent of each other.

Historically, there have been other changes in the way in which homicides are defined and records kept. Once separately defined in the early years of the NCHS, infanticide is no longer a category. Vigilante "justice" and lynching, crimes not uncommon up through the 1930s, were not necessarily defined as homicide in official records of the time. The general lesson to be learned is that every measure of homicide is somewhat subjective. Further, no single set of data provides complete and accurate counts of the number of homicides, whatever the definition. Therefore, the most accurate indication of homicide levels will be based on a combination of information from different sources.

Understanding Types of Homicide

When we turn from homicide counts to examine details of specific homicide types, multiple data sources become both more important and more problematic. Criminal-justice data provide certain information (on the offender, on the relationship between offender and victim, and on the weapon) not available in public health data; conversely, public health data are the only source for medical information on the victim, such as blood alcohol levels. For example, the NCHS has separate E-code categories for handgun, shotgun, hunting rifle, military firearms, and "other and unspecified" firearms, though weapon codes have changed with the decennial ICD revisions, and only an aggregate category for "firearms and explosives" was available through 1979. UCR weapon categories are historically more detailed and the information is more complete, since police investigation may uncover through witnesses or physical evidence facts not revealed in an autopsy report.

Homicide syndromes are a classifying tool that can elucidate a homicide by examining the events that lead up to it. Homicide syndromes combine sibling offense with the offender's immediate and primary motive, defined as (1) instrumental versus expressive and (2) rational versus impulsive. A sibling offense is a crime that the homicide is connected to, such as burglary or rape. In instrumental violence the assailant's goal is to acquire property; in expressive violence the assailant's goal is violence itself. Rational violence is planned, whereas impulsive violence is spontaneous. Most actual homicide situations are neither purely instrumental nor purely expressive but fall somewhere on a continuum between the two types. Similarly, most violence is neither completely rational nor completely impulsive, but somewhere between the two extremes. Motives for violence are often complex, but most acts of violence tend toward either the instrumental or the expressive.

Using this perspective, in child-abuse homicides the sibling offense is child abuse and the primary and immediate motive tends to be expressive and impulsive. In contrast, a murder of a young child during a burglary or a street-gang confrontation is another kind of homicide, differing from child-abuse homicide in many ways. In a street-robbery homicide, the sibling offense is street robbery and the motive tends to be instrumental and rational. Street-gang-related homicides may be expressive (turf battles), instrumental (drug-market battles), or a combination, and implications for intervention differ. For example, a violence-reduction program might reduce the risk of gang homicide in a neighborhood that is a hot spot for gang turf violence but be ineffective in a neighborhood that coincides with a gang drug market, and drug programs that work in the latter neighborhood may be useless in the former. Still other intervention strategies may be necessary in neighborhoods where the two kinds of hot spot areas intersect.

Despite the common belief that homicide cannot be prevented, a growing body of research indicates that it is possible to reduce lethal-violence levels, but only by focusing on particular types of homicide—such as the homicide syndromes. Working together, community members, law enforcement and other criminal justice agencies, medical and public health organizations, and other community groups must key prevention strategies for a specific type of homicide to those high-risk places, situations, victims, and potential offenders associated with that type. For example, interventions for expressive homicide in bars or taverns may include changes in the liquor laws and training for tavern owners; the prevention of instrumental street-robbery homicide may include increased surveillance around rapid-transit stops; the reduction of expressive intimate-partner homicide may involve community education and support services for abused women. In general, homicide syndromes are a system for building explanatory models and for developing ways of preventing lethal violence.

BIBLIOGRAPHY

Black, Henry Campbell. *Black's Law Dictionary: Definitions of the Terms and Phrases of American and English Jurisprudence, Ancient and Modern.* 6th ed. Joseph R. Nolan and Jacqueline M. Nolan-Haley, contributing authors. St. Paul, Minn.: West, 1990.

Block, Carolyn Rebecca, and Richard L. Block. *Street Gang Crime in Chicago.* NIJ Research in Brief. NCJ 144782. Washington, D.C.: National Institute of Justice, 1993.

———. "Homicide Syndromes and Vulnerability: Violence in Chicago's Community Areas over Twenty-five Years." *Studies on Crime and Crime Prevention* 1, no. 1 (1992).

Cantor, David, and Lawrence E. Cohen. "Comparing Measures of Homicide Trends: Methodological and Substantive Differences in the Vital Statistics and Uniform Crime Report Times Series (1933–1975)." *Social Science Research* 9 (1980).

Children's Safety Network. *E Codes: The Missing Link in Injury Prevention.* Brochure. Newton, Mass.: National Injury and Violence Prevention Resource Center, 1996.

Department of Health and Human Services. *The International Classification of Diseases, Ninth Revision: Clinical Modification.* 4th ed. Pub. #91–1260; also CD-ROM (017–022–01268–5). Washington, D.C., 1991.

Eckberg, Douglas Lee. "Using Econometric Forecasting to Correct for Missing Data: Homicide and the Early Registration Area." In *Trends, Risks, and Interventions in Lethal Violence,* edited by Carolyn R. Block and Richard L. Block. NCJ-154254. Washington, D.C.: National Institute of Justice, 1995.

Federal Bureau of Investigation. *Crime in the United States, 1996: Uniform Crime Reports.* Washington, D.C.: U.S. Department of Justice, 1997.

———. *Uniform Crime Reporting Handbook: National Incident-Based Reporting System Edition.* Washington, D.C.: U.S. Department of Justice, 1992.

Finkelhor, David. "The Homicides of Children and Youth: A Developmental Perspective." In *Out of the Darkness: Contemporary Perspectives on Family Violence,* edited by G.

Kaufman Kantor and J. Jasinski. Thousand Oaks, Calif.: Sage, 1997.

Hindelang, Michael J. "The Uniform Crime Reports Revisited." *Journal of Criminal Justice* 2 (1974).

Huff-Corzine, Lin, and Jay Corzine. "Datasets for the Study of Lynching." In *Questions and Answers in Lethal and Non-Lethal Violence, 1993: Proceedings of the Second Annual Workshop of the Homicide Research Working Group,* edited by Carolyn R. Block and Richard L. Block. NCJ-147480. Washington, D.C.: National Institute of Justice, 1993.

Logan, Wayne, Lindsay S. Stellwagen, and Patrick A. Langan. *Felony Laws of the Fifty States and the District of Columbia, 1986.* Bureau of Justice Statistics, NCJ-105066. Washington, D.C.: U.S. Department of Justice, 1987.

Rand, Michael R. "The Study of Homicide Caseflow: Creating a Comprehensive Homicide Dataset." In *Questions and Answers in Lethal and Non-Lethal Violence, 1993: Proceedings of the Second Annual Workshop of the Homicide Research Working Group,* edited by Carolyn R. Block and Richard L. Block. NCJ-147480. Washington, D.C.: National Institute of Justice, 1993.

Riedel, Marc. "Nationwide Homicide Data Sets: An Evaluation of the Uniform Crime Reports and the National Center for Health Statistics Data." In *Measuring Crime: Large-Scale, Long-Range Efforts,* edited by D. J. MacKenzie, A. J. Bannock, and R. R. Roberg. Albany, N.Y.: State University of New York Press, 1990.

Rokaw, William M., James A. Mercy, and Jack C. Smith. "Comparing Death Certificate Data with FBI Crime Reporting Statistics on U.S. Homicides." *Public Health Reports* 105, no. 5 (1990).

CAROLYN REBECCA BLOCK

See also **Crime, Legal Definitions of.**

HONOR

Honor, a masculine-dominated ethic, has always functioned to assure the protection of self and family from outside aggression, the defense of local values and moral consensus, the sexual purity of women, the condemnation of effeminacy, and the bonding of men to achieve mutually beneficial results. The age-old ethic has always encompassed many universal virtues—valor, trustworthiness, magnanimity, hospitality, graciousness, and familial as well as patriotic loyalty. For men at war, faith in the ethic helps to reduce a sense of vulnerable isolation and fear of dying alone and unmourned. With all its qualities of discipline and heroic bearing, honor's relationship to violence—not always justified—is undeniable.

In America honor's foundation rested on hierarchies of superiority: male over female, white skin over black, the agile over the ungainly, and the wealthy over the poor and landless. At the heart of the code was a requirement for men to prove their manliness and always dread shame. A woman's obligation was to obey men and also to rear sons valorously dedicated to the protection of dependent family members. Young Sam Houston's mother once handed him a musket and reminded him that she preferred that all her sons "fill one honorable grave, than that one of them should turn his back to save his life" (Wyatt-Brown 1982, p. 51). The ethic to which she referred and patterns of personal and collective violence have been closely associated with the South and the West, into which southerners migrated.

Throughout history the code of honor has revealed a psychological and moral flaw—the choice of immediate gratification of the appetite for honor over long-term gain—willfully defiant of the consequences. Consider a scientifically conducted experiment reported by the philosopher George Ainslie. When given the choice, the subjects chose to receive $100 immediately rather than $120 if they waited a month. But when told they could obtain $120 in a month's time or $100 in a month minus three days, they were most likely to wait those extra days for the larger sum. Shortsightedness is likewise characteristic of the honor code—reckless action for immediate vindication takes precedence over the greater advantages that prudence and calculation provide. Immediate loss of face looms as a greater hazard than the perils to survival itself even in the forseeable future (Ainslie, cited in Offer 1995, p. 224). Under circumstances when a man feels his honor is threatened, he ordinarily rejects self-revelation. Since women are considered unequal in status, they cannot be genuine confidantes. They could place men in dependent positions. The wiser course would be to show a careless "cool" and avoid public shame. Yet the result of repressed emotions can be explosive. James Gilligan points out, "many violent men would rather die than let you know what is distressing them." In their eyes, to "lose face" signifies not only cowardice but also disintegrating self-esteem, respect, and even identity (Gilligan 1996, pp. 111–112). Under the rubric of honor, conformity to strictly defined gender roles permits little individualization. Deviants from the norm have often been the subjects of ridicule, revilement, and even death.

War

Rallying support for armed assault has often required an appeal to glory and honor—a readiness to sacrifice the lives of some for the sake of all. The targets of such drum-and-trumpet rhetoric have generally been juveniles and young men. Whenever that motive is weak, as in the American effort in Vietnam, for instance, low morale will probably ensure defeat. Most American wars, national and civil, have been fought with honor high on the list of the justifications for war making. In the American Revolution, colonial grievances largely concerned the British demand for taxes rather than voluntary subsidies. This and other insults, as they were deemed by the colonials, denied them "the rights of Englishmen." Likewise, the motives for secession in the Lower South upon Abraham Lincoln's election in 1860 cannot be understood without recognizing how outraged Southerners were. The secessionists interpreted Republican victory as a sign of contempt. The sectional issue had earlier reached a climax when in 1856 in the Senate chamber Representative Preston Brooks of South Carolina mercilessly assaulted Charles Sumner, a senator from Massachusetts, with a cane. The antislavery senator had questioned Carolinian bravery in the Revolution and insulted Brooks's kinsman and South Carolina's senior senator, Andrew Pickens Butler. Boasting that the South stood unanimously behind him, Brooks explained that "the fragments of the stick are begged for as *sacred relics*" (Donald 1960, p. 304). The decision to se-

cede was reckless and suicidal, but it represented a vindication of white supremacy and slaveholding. Defense of the latter aim survived the results of the war, which included Union conquest and occupation, slave emancipation, and Confederate defeat.

In the next American war—in 1898—the imperialist actions against Spain deeply involved the revival of a truculent virility, along with a wish for territorial expansion. World War I was likewise closely tied to the dictates of a code of honor. The Serbian "insult" to Austria-Hungary with the assassination at Sarajevo and Kaiser Wilhelm's contempt for "shopkeeping" (that is, unwarlike) countries like England and the United States destroyed a world order with benefit to no participant. The U-boat sinking of U.S. ships indicated the German disdain for the American will to fight and was seen by Americans as a humiliation not to be tolerated. In World War II Americans condemned the Japanese attack on Pearl Harbor as a cowardly strike —to be avenged, at a later point, by nuclear bombs. Lyndon Johnson's dogged persistence in Vietnam stemmed in part from the fear of being called a dishonorable quitter, a stigma no proud Texan could accept. Reckless haste in the name of honor furnished few long-term gains for the causes various war leaders pursued, whether saving

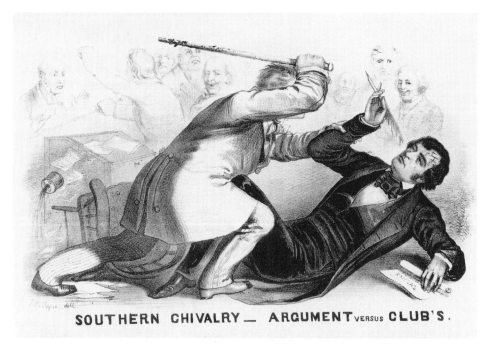

SOUTHERN CHIVALRY — ARGUMENT versus CLUB'S.

A nineteenth-century cartoon shows Congressman Preston Brooks of South Carolina attacking Senator Charles Sumner from Massachusetts after Sumner expressed antislavery sentiments and insulted a kinsman of Brooks's. CORBIS/BETTMANN

slavery, preserving the dying European monarchies, or halting the unification of Vietnam, and in fact consigned millions to death.

Regional Traditions

In the regional life of the United States, honor-related violence has helped to set the South apart from the rest of the country. The code of honor found its most loyal adherents in the region where African slaves were long the subjects of degradation and where whites accorded themselves the absolute right of command. Ebenezer Hazard, a New Englander visiting Georgia in 1778, remarked: "The *Country Gentlemen* are . . . accustomed to tyrannize from their Infancy. . . . If a man has not as many Slaves as they, he is esteemed by them their Inferior, even though he vastly exceeds them in every other Respect" (Shelley 1957, pp. 318–319). That habit of mind continued even after emancipation, when landowners held black tenants under their command.

For much of their history, southerners had to deal with the lack of an urban middle class, rural isolation, and poverty in the lower ranks. Mistrustful of outsiders, they held to clan loyalties. Southern ways included a suppression of unconventional thought and action, a tendency to alcohol, and fatalism about the future. A factor that some scholars say contributed to the South's record of violence was the migration of Scots, Scots-Irish, and Irish, the largest single immigration group of that period, into the southern interior. These seminomadic herdsmen of sheep, cattle, and hogs had long been accustomed to hard living and hard drinking. They first settled along the edge of the Appalachians as far South as Georgia. From there, in the nineteenth century, their descendants migrated westward to the Mississippi and into the trans-Mississippi West. According to the political scientists Richard Nisbett and Dov Cohen, the southern Scots-Irish have always adhered to the North Carolina proverb "Every man should be sheriff on his own hearth," which helped to explain how honor-connected violence could be found in areas of the Mountain South where slavery and its violent propensities had little impact (Nisbett and Cohen 1996, p. 9).

In all parts of the South an allegiance to the cult of the gun has contributed to the persistence of the code of honor. In antebellum days the dueling pistol was the upper-class weapon of choice, instruction in swordplay and the rapier being a rarity.

Duels were rare after the Civil War, which had decimated and impoverished many members of the landholding elite. Yet personal violence of a more informal variety endured throughout the nineteenth century. In the Black Hills divisions growing out of Civil War loyalties pitted honor-conscious families against each other in generational feuds.

Like the duel, mob violence, for which the nineteenth- and early-twentieth-century South was famous, was illegal but covertly sanctioned. In antebellum times defense of community honor meant the persistence of such Old World forms of local punishment as tarring and feathering, riding a victim on a rail, or forcing the offender to leave town. The victims' alleged offenses often were interpreted as violations of community expectations. In the Old South disputes over issues of personal vindication among neighbors and rivals accounted for most killings. Fewer homicides were outgrowths of other crimes such as bank robberies or house break-ins. So embedded in the culture was the acceptance of homicide in honor's name that conviction rates were very low. The Episcopal bishop B. B. Smith of Kentucky complained that between 1835 and 1838, out of thirty-five murder trials, juries had returned only eight convictions. (Wyatt-Brown 1982, p. 368). The pattern continued even after the Civil War.

In the Reconstruction era (1865–1876) politics could not be separated from the issue of family-protected honor. Black Republican leaders and voters fell victim to raging Ku Klux Klansmen and other terrorist groups. Intimidation, murder, and arson were designed to return political rule to the Democratic Party—and to prevent the occurrence of what was called "mongrelization" or the staining of white bloodlines by supposedly licentious black males armed with political power. Lynchings occurred primarily to assert the principle of white domination, particularly when free blacks acted too independently. Of some thirty-three hundred lynch victims between 1885 and 1903, prospering blacks were more often the target of white vengeance than were alleged rapists. Black advancement suggested a loosening of white control. Even local white professionals and authorities sometimes led and often approved such means to degrade the subordinated race.

In the post–World War I era, the Ku Klux Klan revived its ritualized code of honor to enforce white supremacy and repress black advances. Southern whites felt threatened by the changes in

A 1938 lynching in Ruston, Louisiana, of W. C. Williams, a black man who admitted to clubbing a white mill worker, Robert Blair, to death and assaulting Blair's female companion. CORBIS/BETTMANN

social and moral customs that the wartime disruptions engendered. In Muskogee, Oklahoma, for example, a believer in the old order applauded the work of the Klan: "I have not seen a case . . . that all the leading good people of the town had not said, 'It's a good thing, push it along.'" The work of Klansmen, he observed with satisfaction, "moves out the gangster, bootlegger . . . fast and loose females, and the man who abuses and neglects his wife and children" (Wyatt-Brown 1982, pp. 449–450.) In Gainesville, Florida, in 1923 the chief of police and mayor headed a gang in disguise that seized Father John Conoley, the Roman Catholic chaplain at the state's all-male university. Taking him into a neighboring county, they beat and castrated him. The chaplain had boldly started a drama club that was popular among the students (Prescott 1992, pp. 28–40). His tormentors thought the priest was encouraging homosexuality.

Whereas antebellum southerners (dueling planters and politicians excepted) seldom owned or used pistols in their encounters, today the handgun has provided a ready means to vindicate personal and familial honor. Gun ownership is highest and most prevalent in the South. Laws against the ownership of weapons, openly carried or concealed, are more lenient in the South than they are in the Northeast and parts of the Midwest. In addition, gun-control legislation has less support in the South than it does in the rest of the country. Nearly half of all southerners, regardless of color, possess at least one firearm. About a quarter of northeastern homes have a gun; in the rest of the states, 39 to 42 percent of household possess weapons (Kantor 1998, p. A17).

Comparative statistics bear out the South's legacy of honor-related violence. The thoroughly urbanized state of Massachusetts in 1960 retained a century-old rate of 1.3 murders per 100,000 people, whereas Alabama's was 8.1 times higher. According to figures tallied by the Federal Bureau of Investigation and reported by Fox Butterfield, the homicide rate in 1996 in Louisiana was 17.5 per 100,000 people, as compared, for example, with 1.2 murders in South Dakota and 4.8 in Connecticut (per 100,000 people) (Butterfield 1998, pp. 1, 16). American homicide rates at the close of the twentieth century were among the highest in the industrialized world, and southern society has made a disproportionate contribution to that record.

Community and Group Values

It would be wrong, however, to assume that the South stands alone. Late twentieth-century hate groups have promoted the honor of skin color and Anglo-Saxon "purity." The Northwest and Texas have been the chief locales for such militia and paramilitary organizations as "the Order," "Christian Identity," and "Aryan Nations." Various militia, extremist Christian, and white supremacist organizations have indicated a selective but dangerously lively appeal for preserving the primitive code, usually in their hatred for Jews, homosexuals, abortion providers, and African Americans.

American urban subcultures have also adhered to principles of honor. In fact, ethnic groups not fully integrated into the American mainstream—the Irish and Italians in the nineteenth century, Hispanics and Asians in the twentieth—have used the honor codes of their respective heritages to preserve a masculine order, sometimes existing beneath police scrutiny. In a 1983 study of Chicano gangs in Los Angeles, the sociologist Ruth Horowitz found that these groups followed "the expressive code of honor" in their behavior and values. A member's honor was established "by following particular norms and being evaluated by others as having done so successfully" (1983, p. 23). In the absence of meaningful jobs, teenagers and poor young men in the streets bonded for the purposes of mutual protection and for preserving the boundaries of their territory. As Horowitz points out, those who obtain regular employment quickly learn that the world of work differs from that of the community. A construction worker who carried a revolver for personal security on the neighborhood street told her, "I wouldn't ever bring a gun downtown; why should I want one there anyway? There's no one there I got to protect myself against" (p. 171).

The precepts of honor and the avoidance of shame have motivated the inner-city drug wars that have so thinned the ranks of young African American males. Sociologist Orlando Patterson argues that southern blacks who migrated North carried with them some of the distortions of family life that the system of slavery had imposed. He mentions most particularly the abuse of husbands against their wives out of frustration and sense of self-diminishment (1998, pp. 37, 137). In the urban ghettoes that arose from the vast twentieth-century movement of southern blacks to northern cities,

poverty, discrimination, and inner-city crime compelled some but by no means all African American men to apply the code of honor to their conduct in and out of the home. By that means, which included violence if need be, they asserted their masculinity. Male slaves had earlier engaged in violent acts to obtain respect among their fellows. Sometimes infuriated slaves killed masters and overseers particularly when their women were subjected to rape or whippings.

The harsh and dangerous conditions of black ghetto life have led to honor-related incidents of violence. Yet that racial group has been only one of other ethnic minorities prone to this form of behavior. Street gangs have created for those joining a sense of family and belonging, but membership is transitory. On the other hand, the structure of the Italian American mafia, a hierarchical organization led by a capo, has been based on the patriarchal traditions of particular villages in southern Italy and Sicily. As James Gilligan observes, "the mafia calls itself both a 'family' and a 'society of honor'" (Gilligan 1996, p. 262). The clannishness, siege mentality, and stress upon silence about criminal activity appear justifiable to the mafiosi under the rule of "rispetto" (Blok 1974, pp. 62, 146n). By their understanding the ethic of honor offers no place for moderation, gentleness, chivalry, and refinement. These virtues had belonged to the Roman Stoic or Anglo-American Victorian conventions of the code.

To a greater degree than popular and academic opinion have acknowledged, honor has helped to perpetuate the violent traditions of American culture. Mainstream society has found ever less value in the preservation of the male-dominated hierarchies, particularly those hostile to the advancement of women and minorities. Yet, honor should be seen as a factor in the romanticized cult of violence that celebrates in fiction and film heroic villains from Jesse James and other wild West figures to mafia "godfathers" (Lifton 1999, p. 49). With more than two hundred million weapons in the hands of American citizens, it is unlikely that those still influenced by the ancient ethic will submit to government restrictions on their weapons (p. 24). Military challenges will inevitably arise in a chronically unstable world, for principles of honor cannot be extinguished altogether. A nation at war can ill-afford to denigrate themes of glory by which its youth seek heroic, self-sacrificing roles. "Mine honour is my life. . . . Take honour from me and my life is done" says Norfolk in Shakespeare's

Richard II. The language is antique, but for modern-day warriors—male and female—the sentiment still has meaning. The ethic of honor neither can nor should be entirely eliminated in national life, but so truculent and rigidly male a code of conduct exacts a high price in blood and social inequities.

BIBLIOGRAPHY

Ayers, Edward. *Vengeance and Justice: Crime and Punishment in the Nineteenth-Century American South.* New York: Oxford University Press, 1984.

Blok, Anton. *The Mafia of a Sicilian Village, 1860–1890: A Study of Violent Peasant Entrepreneurs.* Oxford: Blackwell, 1974.

Butterfield, Fox. "Why America's Murder Rate Is So High." *New York Times,* 26 July 1998.

Center for Democratic Renewal. "White Supremacy in the 1990s." http://www.webcom.com/pinknoiz/right/cdr1.html.

Donald, David. *Charles Sumner and the Coming of the Civil War.* New York: Knopf, 1960.

Fischer, David Hackett. *Albion's Seed: Four British Folkways in America.* New York: Oxford University Press, 1989.

Gilligan, James. *Violence: Reflections on a National Epidemic.* New York: Random House, 1996.

Horowitz, Ruth. *Honor and the American Dream: Culture and Identity in a Chicano Community.* New Brunswick, N.J.: Rutgers University Press, 1983.

Kantor, Irving. *New York Times,* 28 July 1998, A17.

Lifton, Robert Jay. *Newsweek,* 23 August 1999.

Nisbett, Richard E., and Dov Cohen. *Culture of Honor: The Psychology of Violence in the South.* New York: Westview, 1996.

Offer, Avner. "Going to War in 1914: A Matter of Honor?" *Politics and Society* 23 (June 1995).

Patterson, Orlando. *Rituals of Blood: Consequences of Slavery in Two American Centuries.* Washington, D.C.: Civitas/Counterpoint, 1998.

Peristiany, John G., and Julian Pitt-Rivers, eds. *Honor and Grace in Anthropology.* Cambridge: Cambridge University Press, 1992.

Presscott, Stephen R. "White Robes and Crosses: Father John Conoley, the Ku Klux Klan, and the University of Florida." *Florida Historical Quarterly* 71, no. 1 (July 1992).

Shelley, Fred, ed. "The Journal of Ebenezer Hazard in Georgia, 1778." *Georgia Historical Quarterly* 41 (September 1957).

Wyatt-Brown, Bertram. "Honour and American Republicanism: A Neglected Corollary." In *Ideology and the Historians,* edited by Ciaran Brady. Dublin, Ireland: Lilliput, 1991.

———. *Southern Honor: Ethics and Behavior in the Old South.* New York: Oxford University Press, 1982.

BERTRAM WYATT-BROWN

See also **Dueling; Gangs; South; Urban Violence.**

HOOVER, J. EDGAR
(1895–1972)

John Edgar Hoover was born on 1 January 1895, the youngest of four children, in Washington, D.C., where his father was a government clerk. He graduated from George Washington University with a master's degree in law in 1917. He grew up very close to his mother, and although he was an achiever in school, socially he was a loner. Hoover was special assistant to the attorney general of the United States from 1919 to 1924, when he became acting director and then director (1925) of the federal Division of Investigation, renamed the Federal Bureau of Investigation in 1935, an agency he headed until his death.

Throughout Hoover's career as director of the FBI, he molded and shaped its structure to be responsive to his personal interests and concerns. Within a few years after his becoming director, there was no doubt within the bureau that Hoover was in complete control, with virtually all departments reporting to him. He insisted on personal loyalty, and members of the bureau were expected to reflect his personal traits of fastidiousness and diligence.

Although his term as director had many noteworthy achievements, Hoover personalized his directorship and increasingly used the bureau's resources to pursue political, social, and economic goals, as well as to secure and protect his position as director. One of his main objectives during much of his tenure was to ferret out of U.S. institutions subversives and communists, whom he believed had infiltrated many groups and organizations. Of particular concern to Hoover was the problem of internal subversion, that is, initiatives designed to undermine the U.S. government. To counteract this perceived threat, he approved the illegal tapping and bugging of residences and organizations in an attempt to gather information and evidence supporting his suspicions. However, in time, the term *subversive* was applied to any person or organization Hoover wished to examine for whatever purpose. Consequently, illegal tapping and bugging by FBI agents became frequent practices under Hoover. These practices were used on people who aggressively advocated social, political, or economic change in the United States and who challenged existing social, political, or economic institutions. Among the early activities of dubious or illegal nature carried out under Hoover's direction or with his approval were the

J. Edgar Hoover in 1957. LIBRARY OF CONGRESS

tapping and bugging of labor union offices in order to obtain information incriminating these groups and certain individuals belonging to them that Hoover thought detrimental to the national interest.

Under Hoover the Counter Intelligence Program (COINTELPRO) was implemented in 1956. This program utilized FBI personnel and resources to undermine organizations that Hoover considered a threat to the United States, including groups that advocated racial integration, opposed the Vietnam War, and disagreed with the invasion of Cambodia by the United States during the administration of Richard Nixon. Among other things, COINTELPRO attempted to disrupt the operations of these organizations.

Hoover also undermined the interests of groups and individuals by providing detrimental information on them to others who would use it to suit Hoover's purposes, such as newspaper columnists who shared his interests. Similarly, he leaked information to the administrations of both Lyndon Johnson and Nixon if the purpose for which the information was intended was consistent with his perspective. The FBI also cooperated with the House Un-American Activities Committee by providing information to committee members that was gathered illegally and concerned legitimate, but in Hoover's eyes suspicious, behavior. Similarly, Hoover provided information for Senator Joseph McCarthy when he chaired the infamous Investigations Subcommittee in 1953.

Hoover established policy for the FBI, including the focus of its investigative efforts. But what he decided not to pursue was just as important as those issues and people he inappropriately and illegally followed. He opposed racial integration, and Martin Luther King, Jr., charged that many of the FBI agents in the South were natives of that region who were sympathetic to the cause of segregation during the time of the civil rights protests, demonstrations, and consequent violence. As a result, with the exception of scrutinizing the Ku Klux Klan, the FBI was dormant during the early years of the Civil Rights movement and only became aggressively active after the violence had escalated against civil rights workers from the North. The FBI's reluctance to investigate civil rights abuses could have been interpreted as a sign of government indifference by those opposing integration, resulting in the advocacy and use of violence in the South.

Similarly, the FBI under Hoover did not recognize the existence of organized crime as a federal problem for decades. For reasons of interagency governmental politics, and perhaps because he felt that the FBI could not succeed against organized crime, Hoover adamantly refused to admit that organized crime existed; when he began to recognize its existence, he insisted it was not an FBI matter. His passive approach to this problem contributed to the ability of organized crime groups to gain a strong foothold in several large cities and to conduct business without much regard for the prospect of federal intervention. This situation continued until after the Apalachin meeting in 1957, during which a number of high-level figures in organized crime were arrested, forcing Hoover to acknowledge the problem.

The principle instrument of Hoover's power was a large collection of files containing information obtained both legally and illegally. These files included embarrassing or incriminating information on individuals that Hoover used to secure and maintain his position in the bureau and to further his vision of the United States by threatening to release it or selectively leaking it where it would do him the greatest good. One notable instance of this form of intrusion involved the National Association for the Advancement of Colored People (NAACP) and Martin Luther King, Jr. Hoover had both the headquarters of the NAACP and the private life of King bugged and tapped with the objective of discrediting them as subversive and communist-inspired.

Immediately after Hoover's death in 1972, most of the files containing incriminating or embarrassing information on government officials, celebrities, and public personalities, obtained illegally or inappropriately, were purged, moved, or disappeared.

BIBLIOGRAPHY

Gentry, Curt. *J. Edgar Hoover: The Man and the Secrets.* New York: Norton, 1991.
Powers, Richard Gid. *Secrecy and Power: The Life of J. Edgar Hoover.* New York: Free Press, 1987.
Theoharis, Athan G., and John Stuart Cox. *The Boss: J. Edgar Hoover and the Great American Inquisition.* Philadelphia: Temple University Press, 1988.

DAVID FABIANIC

See also **Dillinger, John; Federal Bureau of Investigation; G-men.**

HORMONES. *See* Endocrinology.

HOUSE COMMITTEE ON UN-AMERICAN ACTIVITIES. *See* McCarthy, Joseph; Red Scare.

HOUSTON

Since World War II Houston has consistently ranked as the most violent city in the South, which in turn is the nation's most violent region. Every year Houston rates as one of the top ten American cities in number of homicides, according to the Federal Bureau of Investigation's annual Uniform Crime Reports, while the homicide rate per one hundred thousand residents often exceeds that of larger cities such as New York. These high murder rates persist despite Houston's position as the nation's leader in number of convicted murderers executed. One-third of all executions in the United States takes place in Texas. Harris County, home of Houston, accounted for 30 percent of the state's death row population in 1997. Even if the rest of Texas ceased executions, Houston alone could maintain Texas's place as the leading state in executions.

Henry P. Lundsgaarde's study of Houston violence (1977) suggests that the civic culture is shaped by a frontier ethos that sanctions violence as a means of resolving personal conflicts, defending property, and preserving honor. Among the factors contributing to the high homicide rate are relaxed gun laws, racial discrimination, state criminal codes permitting lethal force in defense of property, and jury leniency in cases of domestic violence. Lundsgaarde's study demonstrates that Houston juries more lightly punish homicides provoked by personal insults than property crime. This study matches the findings of the social psychologists Richard E. Nisbett and Dov Cohen (1996), who suggest that southern violence represents a regional "culture of honor." Nisbett and Cohen assert that southern culture approves of violence as a way of restoring social status in the face of theft, adultery, and verbal insult.

Antagonism between whites and African Americans and Latinos may also contribute to Houston violence. FBI crime statistics confirm that most homicides in Houston occur within racial groups and disproportionately within poor and minority neighborhoods. Racial discrimination is thought to contribute to the high homicide rate because African Americans are denied equal access to jobs and living wages, thus increasing the poverty in black neighborhoods, which in turn is a factor in criminal activity and violence. According to some writers discrimination also plays a role in the number of black defendants sent to death row in Harris County because prosecutors are more likely to seek the death penalty against black defendants and juries are more likely to convict and send them to death row. Lundsgaarde notes that the city's homicide rate provokes relatively little alarm among the city's middle class because it primarily affects the poor and powerless.

A long history of alienation between the Houston police and minority communities undoubtedly hampers the effectiveness of homicide investigations within minority communities. Houston has the largest black population of major Texas cities, with African Americans constituting between 20 to 40 percent of the population from 1850 to 1990. Elites have often characterized Houston as the southern city most hospitable to African Americans. In 1929 Jesse O. Thomas of the National Urban League concurred, claiming that in Houston "there is a freedom from the tension and the intensity that characterizes the behavior of [blacks and whites] in a larger measure than is true in the average Southern community."

The comments came, however, just twelve years after African Americans blamed police excesses for the worst riot in the city's history, the 1917 skirmish between the Houston police and black soldiers stationed at Camp Logan, just west of downtown. African American soldiers resented the insulting behavior of streetcar conductors who, when the segregated section of the cars overflowed, insisted that black soldiers stand in the aisles rather than take empty seats reserved for whites. Many black soldiers occupied those seats anyway. When a soldier ripped a "colored only" sign from the wall in a segregated restaurant, ordering the proprietor not to display it again, a policeman, aided by a white mob, raided the restaurant and attacked the soldiers.

Camp Logan soldiers were predisposed to believe rumors, later proved false, that a Houston police officer had killed a black soldier. On the night of 23 August a hundred members of the Third Battalion marched toward the city's downtown area. In the ensuing mayhem, fifteen whites and four blacks died, while at least another twelve whites were seriously wounded. Following subsequent courts-martial, the military authorities executed eighteen black soldiers. Although local blacks were not involved in the riot, the Houston police continued official harassment of African Americans, conducting door-to-door searches and seizing all firearms owned by local blacks.

Police beatings of blacks continued throughout the 1930s. The *Informer*, a black newspaper, regularly reported police abuses, characterizing local law enforcement as made up of "ex-convicts, discarded police officers from other towns [and] roughnecks." In 1940 the *Informer* complained that "policemen are beating [blacks] at will, and the authorities are refusing to do anything about it."

Although racial tensions in Houston in the 1960s did not reach the intensity seen in cities like Birmingham, Alabama, confrontations between police and students at Texas Southern University, a black institution, resulted in bloodshed. The most serious instance was a May 1967 riot on campus in which gunfire was exchanged, leading to the death of a police officer and the arrest of 488 students. The university again became a battleground in 1970, when police claimed they were fired upon from a campus building and fatally shot the twenty-one-year-old black nationalist leader Carl Hampton.

Houston's business leadership, its self-interest actuated by the public-relations disaster of the city's violent image, has moved with swiftness and unity to counter racial tensions. A broad coalition backed the 1997 mayoral campaign of Lee Brown,

On the campus of Texas Southern University, a police officer guards some of the five hundred students arrested after an on-campus rally against racial discrimination turned violent in May 1967. CORBIS/BETTMANN

a former New York City police commissioner. A moderate African American Democrat presenting himself as a law-and-order candidate, Brown became the city's first black chief executive by winning the support of white conservatives like the outgoing mayor, Bob Lanier. The victory of the consensus-building Brown struck some analysts as less a signal of policy change than as an attempt to make over the city's violent, redneck image. Brown's victory allowed city officials and business leaders to depict Houston as a "metropolitan, cosmopolitan . . . open city," according to Texas Southern University political scientist Franklin Jones, as reported in the *Houston Chronicle*.

Many doubted Brown's ability to solve problems such as segregated housing that contribute to Houston's high crime rate. Few doubted the power of Houston's business community to douse racial tensions when it served their financial interests. "Almost in every instance in which acts of violence and brutality against blacks have been stopped, the business community has been responsible," the black nationalist publication *Voice of Hope* observed in 1970. "Not that members of the business community are so liberal or sympathetic to the Black struggle. . . . They are, however, extremely concerned about eliminating . . . conditions . . . not conducive to making a profit."

BIBLIOGRAPHY

Beeth, Howard, and Cary D. Wintz, eds. *Black Dixie: Afro-Texan History and Culture in Houston.* College Station: Texas A&M Press, 1992.

Lundsgaarde, Henry P. *Murder in Space City: A Cultural Analysis of Houston Homicide Patterns.* New York: Oxford University Press, 1977.

McComb, David G. *Houston: The Bayou City.* Austin: University of Texas Press, 1969.

Rodriguez, Lori. "Brown Makes History in Victory: Mayoral Win Sends Message About Houston." *Houston Chronicle,* 7 December 1997.

MICHAEL PHILLIPS

See also **Urban Violence.**

HOWARD BEACH INCIDENT

On 20 December 1986 a group of white adolescents attacked three black men in the Howard Beach section of the borough of Queens of New York City. With the trial of Bernhard Goetz—a white man who had shot four African American youths on a Manhattan subway car—a month away, mounting racial tension fueled the legal dispute over what happened at Howard Beach that night. The ensuing marches, boycotts, and protests, punctuated by racial attacks throughout the city, were a constant reminder of this explosive controversy over justice and politics.

On the evening in question, three young black men—Michael Griffith, Cedric Sandiford, and Timothy Grimes (ages twenty-three, thirty-six, and twenty, respectively)—hiked from their broken-down vehicle to a Howard Beach pizza parlor in search of assistance. A white gang armed with baseball bats confronted the three men as they left the restaurant. The men fled, but the young horde chased them on foot and by automobile through the streets before cornering them. Although Sandiford and Grimes managed to escape, Griffith ran onto a nearby highway, where he was struck and killed by a motorist, Dominick Blum.

The controversy began when Sandiford's lawyer, Alton Maddox, Jr., claimed that the investigation was a racially motivated police cover-up. He argued that Blum, a police officer's son, had participated in the attack and intentionally killed Griffith. Maddox also alleged that Sandiford told the investigators of Blum's involvement in the attack but that the detectives had ignored him. Consequently, Sandiford was advised not to cooperate with the district attorney's investigation until Blum was arrested and a new prosecutor was assigned to the case.

According to District Attorney John Santucci, a full investigation revealed that Blum was not involved in the assault. Santucci suggested that Maddox was jeopardizing the case with his demands and was less concerned with promoting justice than with fanning political discontent. When Santucci attempted to indict three of the assailants on charges of murder, manslaughter, and assault, both Sandiford and Grimes refused to testify (on Maddox's advice), and the charges were dismissed.

While the white community was outraged by what they viewed as obstruction of justice by racial politics, much of the black community publicly endorsed Maddox. Although Blum was never arrested, Governor Mario Cuomo eventually appointed a special prosecutor, Charles J. Hynes, to handle the case. In 1988 a second trial found Jon Lester, Scott Kern, and Jason Ladone guilty of second-degree manslaughter and first-degree assault. In 1990 an appeals court upheld the decision

Demonstrators march through the suburb of Howard Beach in Queens, New York City, on 27 December 1986 to protest the beating of a black man by three white adolescents a week before. CORBIS/BETTMANN

and sentenced the youths to prison terms ranging from five to thirty years.

Perceived by some members of the white community as particularly harsh, the court's decision seemed to reflect the political fervor surrounding the incident. The public questioned the authorities' intentions in the case: Had they focused on achieving justice or sending a political message? This question yields no clear answers. The disparate perceptions of the local white and black communities were an outgrowth of their markedly different experiences with the justice system. Whether justice or racial politics prevailed in this case remains a matter of controversy and a persistent issue in the racially charged atmosphere of America's largest cities.

BIBLIOGRAPHY

Breindel, Eric. "The Legal Circus: Injustice for All." *New Republic,* 9 February 1987.

Rieder, Jonathan. "Inside Howard Beach: Fear and Racism in White New York." *New Republic,* 9 February 1987.

Smith, J. Clay, Jr. "The 'Lynching' at Howard Beach: An Annotated Bibliographic Index." *National Black Law Journal* 12, no. 1 (spring 1990): 29–60.

MAUREEN A. LAGASSÉ

See also **Hate Crime.**

HUDDLESTON, NED
(c. 1849–1900)

Little is known about the origins of the western outlaw Ned Huddleston. Family records of slaves in the old South are scant indeed, and Ned was a black man, born the slave of a man named Huddleston somewhere in the Arkansas Ozarks. The year of his birth is even in dispute; speculations range from 1849 to 1855.

After the Civil War many former slaves in the Southwest became cowboys—the number during the trail-driving period has been estimated as high as five thousand—but very few turned to outlawry. Huddleston began his career as an outlaw by stealing horses along the Mexican border with another bandit remembered only as Terresa. In 1875 Huddleston and his Mexican associate turned up in Brown's Park, an area where Colorado, Wyoming, and Utah meet. There they joined the gang of Tip Gault, a rustler known as the "bad man from Bitter Creek." (Gault's origins are unknown, but he was recognized as a veteran frontiersman who spoke several Indian languages and who was familiar with every inch of Brown's Park and the surrounding country.) At the outlaw hideout, Huddleston befriended a Shoshone woman named Tickup and her young daughter, Mincy,

143

and it cost him a thrashing and a maimed ear. In a fight over the woman and her child, a Ute Indian named Pony-Beater trounced him badly. Shortly after this incident, Tickup left with a Shoshone brave. Huddleston followed, fought the brave, and was about to kill him when a blow from a stone axe in the hands of Tickup severed all but the lobe of Huddleston's left ear. Shortly thereafter, Tip Gault's gang met disaster. A horse kicked one member, killing him, and angry ranchers found the rustler camp and killed Gault, Terresa, and another outlaw. Huddleston alone escaped. He trudged some twenty miles on foot before an opportunity to steal a horse presented itself. As he was riding off, the horse's owner put a rifle bullet through Huddleston's thigh. The injured Huddleston got away, but he finally fell to the road unconscious. A friend found him, took him home, and nursed him back to health.

Having narrowly escaped death several times, Huddleston decided to give up the life of an outlaw. He returned to Texas, took the name Isom Dart, and became an honest, hardworking cowboy. Around the year 1883 he helped drive a herd of longhorns to the Middlesex cattle range in Brown's Park. Both he and the trail boss, Matt Rash, remained in the country and took jobs with other Brown's Park ranchers. They began building little herds of their own, a process that was furthered, some said, by the alteration of brands. Dart was twice arrested, charged with rustling and burning down his accuser's barn. The evidence against him, however, was sparse, and he was never convicted.

Despite his shady past and his occasional use of a running iron (a straight tool without a registered brand symbol formed on the end, which enabled a rustler to alter brands by drawing the hot iron over a previously marked cow), Isom Dart was popular and welcomed in most Brown's Park homes. The big ranchers continued to lose stock, however, and in 1900 they took decisive action to halt the rustling. They sent Tom Horn, a notorious assassin-for-hire, into the country with orders to eliminate the problem. On 8 July 1900 Horn ambushed and assassinated Matt Rash. Three months later, on 3 October, he shot and killed Ned Huddleston, alias Isom Dart. The man who had started his life as a slave and became an outlaw and, finally, a well-liked settler was buried where he fell.

BIBLIOGRAPHY

Burroughs, John Rolfe. *Where the Old West Stayed Young.* New York: William Morrow, 1962.

McClure, Grace. *The Bassett Women.* Athens, Ohio: Swallow Press/Ohio University Press, 1985.

Wilson, Sandy. "Personality." *Wild West,* February 1995.

ROBERT K. DeARMENT

See also **Gunfighters and Outlaws, Western.**

HUMAN RIGHTS

Almost four thousand years ago King Hammurabi decreed that none of his Babylonian subjects could be tortured or enslaved. Hammurabi's Code was one of the earliest expressions of the notion that human beings may claim rights and set limits to the ways in which others may treat them. Over the centuries the notion of human rights has been incorporated in such documents as the American Declaration of Independence (1776), the French Declaration of the Rights of Man and Citizen (1789), and the U.S. Constitution's Bill of Rights (1791).

Just as Hammurabi's Code applied only to his own people, the Babylonians, and said nothing about the rights of their archenemies, the Assyrians, so the Bill of Rights guarantees only the rights of U.S. citizens. It was not until 1948, in the wake of the Holocaust, that the world community, acting through the United Nations, adopted the Universal Declaration of Human Rights (UDHR), a statement of both civil and political rights (such as the right to a fair trial) as well as social and economic (such as the right to housing) that all people may claim simply by virtue of their being human.

The UDHR is now regarded as a statement of "customary law" and has served as the basis for a whole series of additional covenants, treaties, and conventions, from the International Covenant on Civil and Political Rights to the Convention on the Elimination of All Forms of Discrimination Against Women, that, taken as a whole, constitute statements of world consensus about internationally guaranteed human rights. The United Nations Human Rights Commission meets every year to review and sometimes condemn rights-violating states around the world.

Some international courts, such as the European Court of Human Rights, attempt to apply international human rights law to concrete cases. Yet in the absence of consistent enforcement mechanisms, these rights have often remained aspirations. The establishment of International Criminal Tribunals for the former Yugoslavia (1993) and Rwanda (1994) to prosecute cases of war crimes and crimes against humanity arising from conflicts in those places, as well as the continuing efforts to create a permanent International Criminal Court, constitute important steps toward the development of an international system of accountability for human rights crimes.

Nongovernmental human rights groups also play a critical role in addressing violations of human rights by exposing abuses and pressuring governments to take action. The largest of these international groups is Amnesty International, established in 1961 to help free prisoners of conscience imprisoned for their nonviolent beliefs and to stop such violations as unfair trials, torture, disappearances, and executions. Indigenous human rights groups exist in almost every country, even some of the most repressive.

Human Rights in the United States

In the United States the major organizations dealing with international human rights violations, in addition to Amnesty, include Human Rights Watch (1978), the Lawyers Committee for Human Rights (1978), and Physicians for Human Rights (1987). All these organizations frequently join domestic rights organizations in advocating for enforcement of the whole range of human rights in the United States. Antecedents to what became known in the late-twentieth-century United States as human rights movements include efforts to end slavery and lynching; to secure labor rights; to free the accused killers Nicola Sacco and Bartolomeo Vanzetti, who were executed in 1927 despite protests; to win women the right to vote; and to obtain civil rights for all citizens.

Since the passage of the UDHR, the United States has often been an outspoken advocate of human rights around the world, having been particularly critical of the Soviet Union, Cuba, and other communist countries during the Cold War for their treatment of political prisoners. At the same time the United States has itself been party to serious human rights violations in its foreign relations, ranging from its support from the 1960s to 1980s of authoritarian regimes in such places as South Korea, Cambodia, Chile, and South Africa, to its more direct involvement during those years with torture and murder in Central American countries, especially Guatemala and El Salvador. The Vietnam War was also the occasion for war crimes committed by some U.S. troops.

In more recent years human rights organizations have focused their attention on a variety of human rights violations within the United States.

These include police brutality, prison conditions, the treatment of juvenile offenders and women in prison, the use of electroshock equipment, hate crimes against gays and lesbians, incarceration of political-asylum seekers, and the growing use of the death penalty, among others. Many of these violations take place disproportionately against people of color.

Although it is difficult to secure definitive statistics on the incidence of police brutality in the United States, it is clear that municipalities spend tens of millions of dollars each year to settle liability claims brought by victims of police misconduct. Traffic stops based on racial profiling, beating of suspects to obtain confessions, and unprovoked shootings are police practices that have been documented in many U.S. communities.

U.S. prisons, while more sanitary and secure than those in many countries, are still rife with violence, frequently inmate against inmate and sometimes guard against inmate. Women prisoners, many incarcerated for nonviolent offenses, have been subjected to voyeurism, harassment, and sexual violence by male guards or by male inmates with the connivance of guards. In several states young people under the age of eighteen are imprisoned in adult facilities with hardened criminals. Stun guns and stun belts are being used in more and more police stations, prisons, and courtrooms. Crimes committed against people because of their sexual orientation have received growing publicity. Political-asylum seekers who come to the United States out of fear of persecution in their home countries are regularly detained in county jails with the criminal population, sometimes for months on end, while their cases are adjudicated.

The death penalty, no matter what the crime, is considered a human rights violation by human rights organizations. Since its reintroduction in 1977, more than five hundred people were executed in the thirty-eight states in which, as of 1999, the death penalty was legal. At least seventy people convicted of capital crimes and sentenced to death, on the other hand, were released from 1970 to 1999 when they were found to have been wrongfully convicted. Critics charge that racial bias in the application of the death penalty is evidenced by the fact that those who kill whites are far more likely to receive death sentences than those who kill African Americans. Lethal injection, as opposed to electrocution or hanging, became the most common means of execution in the United States, which, along with Japan, remains the last major industrialized country to retain the practice of state-sponsored killing.

BIBLIOGRAPHY

Amnesty International. *United States of America: Rights for All.* New York: Amnesty International USA, 1998.

Human Rights Watch/American Civil Liberties Union. *Human Rights Violations in the United States: A Report on U.S. Compliance with the International Covenant on Civil and Political Rights.* New York: Human Rights Watch/American Civil Liberties Union, 1993.

Lauren, Paul Gordon. *The Evolution of International Human Rights: Visions Seen.* Philadelphia: University of Pennsylvania Press, 1998.

WILLIAM F. SCHULZ

See also **Amnesty International; Capital Punishment; Holocaust; Nonviolence; War Crimes.**

HUMOR

Humor's peculiarity lies in its polar elasticity: it can operate for or against; it can affirm or reject, liberate or oppress. It is a socially binding phenomenon but also offers up pejorative and divisive images. It is a coping mechanism yet a denigrating one. It facilitates the inversion of stereotypes while utilizing them for the sake of a laugh. Just as humor has been a device of subversion and protest, so too has it been an extraordinary weapon of insult and persecution.

All these contradictory interactions have found their niche in the complex passageways of American cultural history. From the early settlements onward, humor has played a pivotal role as a finely turned form of societal communication. Constance Rourke, in her seminal *American Humor: A Study of National Character* (1931), shrewdly insisted that "humor has been a fashioning instrument in America, cleaving its way through the national life, holding tenaciously to the spread elements of that life" (p. 297). Consequently humor encompasses every nook and facet of American cultural activity and profoundly affects attitudes and behavior. The ongoing dynamics of its presence led the essayist E. B. White to savvily pinpoint an exclusive American trait: "Whatever else an American believes or disbelieves about himself, he is absolutely sure he has a sense of humor."

While humor has been a binding force, it has also often obscured an unyielding penchant toward injustice, and at its worst it has contributed to a climate of violence. Its underlying thrusts have involved vicious racial, ethnic, gender, and sexual stereotyping, and it has become a complex social instrument for maintaining the status quo by both demeaning outsiders and immigrants and completing their assimilation.

Racial and Other Stereotypes

Stereotypes are cultural prisms, shaped over time and reinforced through repetition, that bend the light of truth to predetermine thought and experience. Although they originate from a semblance of social reality, stereotypes are embellished and extended to include other notable features. As Gordon Allport observed in *The Nature of Prejudice* (1958), "some stereotypes are totally unsupported by facts; other develop from a sharpening and overgeneralization of facts." Once implanted in popular lore, moreover, such images penetrate the psyche and assume a circular structure within which all behaviors conform to the conceptualized message.

The contumacious tenacity of stereotyping deepens its pejorative impact. "There is nothing so obdurate to education or criticism," noted Walter Lippmann in *Public Opinion* (1922), "as a stereotype." Analyzing its relationship to folklore, Alan Dundes noted that regardless of geographic context, individuals receive their images not from intimate connection or contact but rather from the ongoing sayings, proverbs, songs, and jokes people hear about all their lives.

As historian H. R. Trevor-Roper observed of the witch craze furies of the sixteenth century, "once established, the stereotype creates as it were, its own folklore, which becomes in itself a centralizing force." In this way, a crystallized image can be reproduced and extended as disparate individuals over time lend credence to it. Thus people are made into cultural commodities. From their comedic straitjacket, the group maligned can dislodge its image only after a protracted series of assaults.

Stereotypes often entail ridicule, and ridicule, as every society has always understood, is the ultimate weapon in the psychological storehouse of power. "I have only ever made one prayer to God, a very short one:" wrote Voltaire, " 'O Lord, make my enemies ridiculous.' And God granted it."

Ridicule insinuates inferiority. The aim of such humor is to foster a sense of unworthiness, cutting to the quick one's basic sense of potential value. For this reason, Thomas Hobbes offered that humor must be construed in relation to power. In his naturalistic account of the origins and purposes of humor, Hobbes maintained that the passion of laughter arises from "some eminency in ourselves by comparison with the infirmity of others"—or with our own former position. More blunt was Charles Baudelaire: "Laughing comes from the idea of one's *own* superiority. A Satanic idea, if ever there was one!"

Both Sigmund Freud and Konrad Lorenz expounded on the aggressive ends that ridicule serves. In Freud's analysis, humor gives pleasure by permitting the gratification of a forbidden desire. "Humor is not resigned," he observed of its energy, "it is rebellious." Hostility takes the form of "tendentious laughter," a veiled attack satisfying belligerent intent. Since society seeks to control the aggressive drives of its members, it permits humor to be utilized as an outlet for frustrations and anger. Humor thus has among its properties "a liberating element." Accordingly, derogation—assault by joking—can become a socially acceptable form of hostility designed to release inner tensions.

Lorenz also conceived of humor as a primal expression and motivation of aggressive behavior. His observations on the conduct of geese in *On Aggression* (1958) led Lorenz to conclude, "laughter resembles militant enthusiasm." Lorenz drew comparisons with human activities. When directed against outsiders, as in scornful mocking, laughter becomes "a very cruel weapon, causing injury if it strikes a defenseless human being undeservedly."

From the earliest colonization in Virginia and Massachusetts, minorities have been the objects of intensive, aggressive humor. American pluralism is a unique social amalgam that has produced an extraordinary diversity, and at the same time, a history of comedic pillorying of its newcomers. A powerful pattern of aggressive humor developed with ridicule as its primary wrap, a type of joking folklorists have labeled "numskull" or "idiot."

America's outsiders—African Americans, Jews, women, Latinos, gays, and lesbians—have all been victimized by stereotyping that has pushed them to the margins of the American Dream. Over time, assaultive joking has resulted in hackneyed formulaic conundrums. Such joking pinpoints the connection between humor and aggression. Fill in the blank spaces of an ethnic humor test. Choose from among the following groups: blacks, Italians, Poles, Puerto Ricans, Slavs.

Why do flies have wings?
To beat the _____ to the garbage dump.

Why do the _____ wear pointed shoes?
To get at the cockroaches in the corners.
Why don't they let the _____ swim in the harbor?
They would leave a ring around it.
Who is the bridegroom at a _____ wedding?
He's the one with the clean [T-shirt] [bowling shirt].
Why does it take three _____ to screw in a lightbulb?
You need one to hold the bulb and two to turn the ladder.
Why does it take one hundred and one _____ to paint a house?
You need one to hold the brush and one hundred to turn the house.
Why did the _____ lose his new job as an elevator operator?
He couldn't learn the route.
Why are the mothers of _____ so strong?
From raising dumbbells.
Why can't a _____ commit suicide?
It's hard to jump out of a basement window.

Significantly, the process of comedic ridicule coincided with the development of democratic forms of government early in the seventeenth century. Africans were the initial group to be demeaned. Once the system of denial and humiliation was prescribed, the psychological connection between pejorative image and public policy was direct and unswerving.

This connection was immediately evident in the wholesale renaming of captive Africans, a deliberate move undertaken by Spanish and English plantation masters. Often the names given to adult black men and women were derisively and amusingly juvenile or trivial: Caesar, Cupid, Lies, Vanilla, Bituminous, Pompey, Sambo, Mammy, Uncle, Aunty, and the ubiquitous "boy." Instructively, warrior names were purposefully shunned. "Who steals my history?" wrote the poet Dylan Thomas in words that symbolically call attention to comic ridiculing.

Tales of childlike behavior, of ineptitude and laziness, infused a comic image of the black throughout the colonies; it was an image that reinforced in the majority the notion of a natural jester within their midst. Blacks as both butt and purveyor of jokes became commonplace. By the nineteenth century, the good-natured but feckless black entertainer had become an integral part of the cultural landscape. A sunny, smiling, dancing, and frolicking figure adorned the vernacular culture on sheet music and popular magazine covers; kitchen utensils, plates, and tablecloths; food cartons and jar labels; children's games and books; lithographs and commercial advertisements; playing cards and comic strips; postage stamps and posters.

The stage counterpart in the popular culture was minstrelsy, as white performers applied blackface grease and offered their interpretation of the style and nature of the comical black. Strutting and dancing, mouthing malapropisms, the minstrel players distorted the perception of blacks in white society.

Minstrelsy made its way into the theater and the electronic media of the twentieth century. The joining of blackface and comicality was common in schools, religious groups, circus performances, and fraternal organizations. Instructively, the highest paid African American comic in the early film industry was Stepin Fetchit, the epitome of the slow-drawling, feet-shuffling, bug-eyed, grammatically inept figure. The most popular daily radio show in the 1930s and 1940s was *Amos 'n' Andy*, played by two white men in blackface. The show, with black actors, continued through the 1950s in a television version. Other minority groups, largely poor, endured similar stereotyping. In the first half of the nineteenth century, no sooner had Irish immigrants arrived in substantial numbers than they were saddled with numskull jokes. The figure in a derby hat with clay pipe, a sentimental if not melodic songster, possessing a belligerent attitude and an equal love for the bottle, a quizzical expression in his eyes, was the caricature that pervaded popular lore. An array of "Pat and Mike" jokes demeaned Irish intelligence: "Why is the wheelbarrow the greatest invention ever made? It taught a few Irishmen to walk on their hind legs."

The Irish of the comics lived in poor shanties, the chimney a joined stovepipe that leaned crazily and the front door reached only by ladder. The typical male had numerous children and a hotheaded wife who took in washing. She bore the brunt of many quips: "Houlihan dreamed that he died and was admitted directly to heaven. St. Peter admitted to him that the time spent with his wife was purgatory enough." Despite their social mobility and construction skills, the Irish were constantly portrayed in magazines and newspapers as ludicrous if not outright buffoonish laborers. The complexity of machines eluded them, they toppled from girders and ladders, they were blasted skyward by dynamite, and they reeled from drink.

This numskull theme attached as well to other powerless groups extending into the first half of the twentieth century in vaudeville routines and jokes. Paralleling the "Uncle Rastus and John" jokes directed at African Americans were "Hans and Fritz" tales attached to German newcomers; the "big, dumb Swede" jokes; and the idiot anecdotes foisted on Italians, Slavs, and Puerto Ricans. Interwoven within the jokes and riddles were the kind of epithets attached to all outsiders: *darky, spic, honkey, dago, Polack, hymie,* and so forth. Simplemindedness, in fact, has been a cornerstone of comic stereotyping. Throughout history those lowest on the social scale have been portrayed as mentally incompetent, underscoring Hobbes's theory that laughter arises from the notion of eminency over others. Economic competition and social mobility are factors as well. Whenever any given minority group has ascended the social ladder—and at the same time stretched its political awareness—the increased insecurity of the majority has likewise exacerbated its numskull joking.

Concomitant with the notion of mental deficiency has been the fundamental assumption of intrinsic mirth. Every denigrated group, save Jews, has been viewed as possessing the supposed cheerful haplessness of the mentally deficient. Linguistic befuddlement has been taken as proof of stupidity: "they speak so funny!" For this reason, distorted rhetoric in dialect routines was common from the early decades of the nineteenth century until changes in thinking inspired by the Civil Rights movement began to take hold in the 1970s.

No other group in American culture has been stigmatized for so long as women. "Her expression," wrote Germaine Greer in *The Female Eunuch* (1971), "must betray no hint of humor, curiosity or intelligence." This rigid formula was couched in a single derogatory male phrase: "Chicks ain't funny."

The belief that women were devoid of a sense of humor made them particularly vulnerable to ridicule yet also posed a curious paradox. Inasmuch as women were especially required to complement a man's comic sense, there was a hidden irony: how could they possibly know when to laugh if they lacked comic facility?

Stereotypical humor has been applied to the elderly as well. Many presentations of "senior citizens" reveal a consistent pattern of degradation. Themes of senility, sexually impotency, deteriorating responsibility and doddering foolishness have cluttered the media and circulated in private joking. Invectives against gays and lesbians further inform the complexity of hardened stereotyping. A stream of subterranean jokes and public offerings, their virulence increasing in the latter half of the twentieth century, has portrayed homosexuality in various foppish forms. Its stage and media representations were the male *dandy* and female *dyke*—both subject to such mocking terms as *faggot*, *fruit*, *queer*, *fairy*, and *pansy*.

The sole exception to the numskull comedic idiom, yet one equally ensnared in societal derision, was the Jews. Regarded as possessing superior intellect, Jews were rather mocked for their materialistic propensity and attending values—stinginess, grasping, manipulating—plus certain distinctive physical traits. Traversing the Atlantic to the New World was the unsettling comic figure of Shylock, the sinister moneylending villain of Shakespeare's *Merchant of Venice*.

Opposition

Not without protest or counteraction, however, did the savagery of stereotyping proceed. Minorities devised a variety of tactics to defuse, circumvent, oppose, or totally eradicate the ongoing parody of ridicule. Antidefamation organizations sprang up, stand-up comics assailed ethnic, racial and sexual confinement, and minorities portrayed their oppressors in an equally ludicrous light. Building over the decades, a stockpile of minority humor beneath the cultural surface gradually seeped into the national consciousness.

The first public breakthrough occurred when Lenny Bruce began performing his stand-up comedy routines during the 1950s. In unearthing taboos and social myths, Bruce exploited them for their absurdity and hypocrisy. Less than two decades later, producer Norman Lear introduced the controversial CBS television comedy series *All in the Family* (1971–1983), which explored a range of ethnic stereotypes and their associative epithets. The series paved the way for Mel Brooks's *Blazing Saddles* (1974), a film that spoofed racial stereotypes and iconic images of the western frontier. A new generation of comic performers—Elaine May and Mike Nichols, Mort Sahl, Dick Gregory, Richard Pryor, Lily Tomlin, Jackie Mason, and Robin Williams—enlivened the entertainment industry, demolishing conventional ideas.The dam burst in the 1980s and 1990s, when a new generation of multicultural comedians focused on cultural in-congruities and contradictions to substantially undercut pejorative ethnic, racist, and sexist images. Their social commentary represented a maturation of comedy as a means of confronting sensitive and forbidden topics in American life. By defining and realizing their own comedic identities, moreover, minority performers achieved a degree of empowerment through rejoicing and credentialing laughter.

Joke cycles added further impetus to the comic zeitgeist. From the late 1970s to the 1990s, the "lightbulb" motif reflected the degree to which ridicule had been imprinted on American lore by the pivotal role it played in the joke wars that erupted between minorities and their detractors. A spin-off from a mid-century quip, "How many Poles does it take to screw in a lightbulb?"spared no group, not even the joke-tellers themselves:

How many Puerto Ricans does it take to change a lightbulb?
Three. One to do the work and two to hold the boom box.
How many WASPs does it take to change a lightbulb?
Three. One to mix the martinis, the others to call an electrician.
How many real men does it take to change a lightbulb?
None. Real men aren't afraid of the dark.
How many feminists does it take to change a lightbulb?
That's not funny!
How many psychiatrists does it take to change a lightbulb?
One. But the bulb must want *to change.*
How many doctors does it take to change a lightbulb?
It depends on how much health insurance the bulb has.

The intertwining of humor and violence has been profound. From the minority perspective, such derisive comedy connotes psychological theft, the subversion of individual dignity and creative potential. To demean is to deny the fullness and complexity of humanity. Additionally, the message of inadequacy is too often imbibed subconsciously. It is instructive that until the latter decades of the twentieth century a main characteristic of minority comedy on public stages was self-abasement. An examination of the connection between ridicule and societal behavior indicates that oppressive joking often legitimizes an environment within which physical assault can occur.

In the final analysis, the polar properties of humor continue to instruct. Contained within its subverting forms are its uplifting possibilities. Pinpointing the intricacies of humiliation, Miguel de Unamuno in *The Tragic Sense of Life* (1921) keenly proffered an antidote: "The greatest height of heroism to which an individual, like a people, can attain is to know how to face ridicule; better still, to know how to make oneself ridiculous and not shrink from the ridicule."

BIBLIOGRAPHY

Apte, Mahadev L. *Humor and Laughter: An Anthropological Approach.* Ithaca, N.Y.: Cornell University Press, 1985.

Barreca, Regina. *They Used to Call Me Snow White, but I Drifted: Women's Strategic Use of Humor.* New York: Viking, 1991.

Bergson, Henri. *Laughter: An Essay on the Meaning of the Comic,* translated by Cloudesley Brereton and Fred Rothwell. New York: Macmillan, 1911.

Boskin, Joseph. *Rebellious Laughter: People's Humor in American Culture.* Syracuse, N.Y.: Syracuse University Press, 1997.

————. *Sambo: The Rise and Demise of an American Jester.* New York: Oxford University Press, 1986.

Davies, Christie. *Ethnic Humor Around the World: A Comparative Analysis.* Bloomington: Indiana University Press, 1990.

Delaria, Vine, Jr. *Custer Died for Your Sins: An Indian Manifesto.* New York: Macmillan, 1969.

Grotjahn, Martin. *Beyond Laughter: Humor and the Subconscious.* New York: McGraw-Hill, 1966.

Walker, Nancy A. *A Very Serious Thing: Women's Humor and American Culture.* Minneapolis: University of Minnesota Press, 1988.

Watkins, Mel. *On the Real Side.* New York: Simon and Schuster, 1994.

JOSEPH BOSKIN

See also **Film; Folk Culture; Hate Crime; Language and Verbal Violence; Representation of Violence; Television; Theater.**

HUNT, JOE
(1960–)

Born Joseph Henry Gamsky in 1960 in Chicago, Illinois, Joe Hunt later moved with his family to Los Angeles, California. As a child he was noted for his intelligence. Both he and his brother tested high enough to be able to earn scholarships to an expensive prep school, the Harvard School in Los Angeles. Outcast because of his unfashionable clothes and haircut and general lack of money, Hunt aspired to belong to the higher social standing of his classmates.

In 1980 the twenty-year-old Hunt met two of his former classmates, Dean Karny and Ben Dosti, in a chance encounter outside the Village Theatre in Los Angeles. Karny and Dosti quickly included Hunt in their friendship, and the young men began to plan to go into business together. The business was to be a commodities trading company, of which Hunt would be the leader. By 1982 Karny and Dosti had started using their connections to recruit investors, and the business had acquired a name. It was to be called BBC after Hunt's favorite bar while working in Chicago, the Bombay Bicycle Club, but it would go down in the annals of crime history as the Billionaire Boys Club.

The success of the business was erratic at best. Although excellent at using connections and charisma, Hunt was not as fruitful at actual trading. Several times he lost all of an investor's money. Each time, however, Hunt was able to use his fast-talking to convince the investor that the money would be recovered. The strength of the organization came from the dedication of its members. Practically a cult leader, Hunt exercised a strange power over the group, which numbered close to

Joe Hunt in Superior Court in Santa Monica, California, on 6 April 1987. ROGER VARGO/*LOS ANGELES DAILY NEWS*

thirty members, and heavily influenced many of their decisions.

Hunt met Ronald Levin through a member of the BBC corporation, and, despite warnings of Levin's background as a con man and the uncertain stability of his funds, Hunt pursued Levin as a potential source of income. Levin eventually agreed to invest $5 million with the company. Unfortunately for everyone involved, this too was merely another of Levin's scams. In reality, there was no money. Levin had convinced an investment firm to have Hunt "invest" the nonexistent money in what the company believed to be a promotional deal. Levin's investment seemed to be the most successful of all of Hunt's endeavors, and BBC turned a profit of $8 million. Half of this money was to be returned to Levin, while the other $4 million would go to BBC.

Furious upon learning of the deception, Hunt bided his time and formulated a plan to enact revenge upon Levin. On 6 June 1984 Hunt forced Levin at gunpoint to write a check for $1.5 million to BBC. According to later testimony by Karny, Hunt admitted that he then shot Levin in the back of the head. Hunt and his accomplice, Jim Pittman, transported the body to Soledad Canyon, where they destroyed the identity of the body by shooting the corpse several times. The body was never found.

After the bank refused to pay Levin's check, BBC became desperate. Hunt and four of the central BBC members kidnapped Hedayat Eslaminia, the father of one of the members, with the plan to force him to sign all of his wealth over to his son. They would then murder the father. The plan failed when their victim died in the trunk of a U-Haul following the kidnapping. They disposed of the body, but the body and their plot were discovered.

Jim Graham and Dean Karny both confessed to their deeds. The BBC dissolved, its members fading into obscurity. In 1987 Joe Hunt was sentenced to life imprisonment for the murder of Ron Levin. Hunt's trial for the murder of Eslaminia ended in a hung jury, and the charges against him were dropped. As of 1999, Hunt continued to deny all allegations and was fighting his conviction for the murder of Ron Levin.

BIBLIOGRAPHY

Horton, Sue. *The Billionaire Boys Club.* New York: St. Martin's, 1989.

Sullivan, Randall. *The Price of Experience: Money, Power, Image, and Murder in Los Angeles.* New York: Atlantic Monthly Press, 1996.

TRACY W. PETERS

HUNTING

If violence can be defined as the intentional ending of a life which would otherwise continue, then humans hunting other living things for sport can be construed as intentional violence.

The intentional attempt to capture and consume a wild animal or fish by choice, not necessity, is deemed hunting for sport. Hunting for sport in the United States is violence permitted by the national community. It is opposed by animal rights ethicists and activists and practiced by declining numbers of citizens, owing to shrinking public access to hunting habitats and increased urbanization.

The typical American hunter is a male, middle-aged, nonurban dweller, educated beyond high school, and employed in upper-working-class or middle-class occupations. This typical American hunter earns slightly above the national median income, hunts white-tailed deer in his home state in excess of one week per year, and spends in the low four figures every year on hunting licenses, literature, equipment, and trips. The number of American hunters peaked after World War II at roughly 19 million license purchasers. That number represented about 12 to 13 percent of all Americans, or 25 percent of all males. In the late 1990s licenses sold for all forms of hunting numbered 14 to 16 million per year, representing nearly 6 percent of Americans, or 12 percent of American males, most commonly residing in the less populous states of the Midwest and South. Roughly ten million American hunters pursue the white-tailed deer, America's most popular big game, whose populations have grown to levels capable of sustained harvest. Pennsylvania, Michigan, and Texas are among the leading deer-hunting states, often closing public schools on the opening day of deer season. Elk, mule deer, and antelope are popular hunted species in western states, while hunters of waterfowl congregate in the states constituting the waterfowl migration areas.

The prohunting lobbying groups have their arguments and claims constantly articulated in monthly outdoor magazines known as the "hook and bullet" press. These publications aggressively promote sport hunting in all forms, even introducing and explaining new approaches,

Hunters skinning deer at the turn of the twentieth century. LIBRARY OF CONGRESS

such as the use of the primitive weapons of the pioneers, Native American weapons such as the *atylatl* (a spear-launching device), or handguns. The billions of dollars spent every year on sport hunting significantly nourish the economies of service providers located near or on hunting grounds, in addition to bolstering the profits of national sporting goods manufacturers. License fees make up important portions of the budgets of state wildlife management agencies and finance habitat acquisition and protection.

However, conscientious objectors to "blood sports" condemn the profits of the hunting industry as blood money. They find the profit as morally repugnant as the revenues from the eighteenth-century slave trade, which bankrolled the emerging Industrial Revolution in Western Europe.

The state permits sport hunting under strict regulation. Forty-five states in the 1990s extended protection of this legal violence by enacting laws that restrain objectors from disrupting hunting behaviors in the game fields. The states' monopoly over the means of violence is engaged in protecting the legal violence of the sport hunter. The anti-hunting movement seeks to convince the national community that hunting constitutes unethical violence against life forms, a violation of natural rights. Since all ethical systems are socially constructed and enforced, the debate over animal rights and human wrongs rages interminably in the political arena.

History of Sport Hunting

Europeans who settled North America found what seemed to them a limitless supply of wildlife waiting to be harvested. Wild meat provided crucial food stock for immigrant agriculturists until they cleared land and planted domestic crops. What little time and energies could be spared from crop production they dedicated to supplementing the family food supply with wild game. Hunting produced food, not fun. Few colonists brought sporting traditions from Europe, where only landed gentry and the political elite had access to hunting rights.

In the 1830s a displaced English gentleman, William Henry Herbert, arrived in America. Herbert set out to live the life of a sporting squire and wrote copiously about his reenactment of English sporting traditions in his American homeland. He counseled Americans to appreciate nature, study their sporting prey, use their weapons skillfully, and kill sparingly those animals they stalked by "fair chase" methods. Under his pen name, Frank Forester, he effectively educated the American gentry—mostly southern planters and urban bourgeoisie who ventured afield to game lands—to adopt a program of sustainable harvest.

Most Americans, however, continued to treat wildlife as a resource of the commons to be harvested pragmatically for family and local market exchange. After the 1850s, railroad expansion provided market hunters with ready game markets at a distance. The game stocks rapidly succumbed to the insatiable demand for prairie birds and mammals killed in the Midwest and shipped by rail to New York.

The pace of the wild game harvest motivated several outdoor magazines founded in the 1870s to commence a crusade on their editorial pages to save wildlife. These magazines demonized the "game hog" who killed excessively and wastefully. They demanded establishment and enforcement of limited hunting seasons and condemned methods of unfair chase. Teddy Roosevelt and several of his fellow sportsmen friends from the eastern upper crust established the Boone and Crockett Club in 1887. The club intensified efforts to end market hunting, to establish rational hunting seasons that promoted a sustainable yield of game animals for sporting posterity, and to create a professional wildlife management and law-enforcement service in every state as well as at the national level. Roosevelt, as U.S. president, led the campaign to establish national parks, forests, and wildlife preserves. The capstone of this initial period in the birth of sport hunting was the Lacey Act, passed in Congress in 1900, which effectively ended market hunting in America. This national commitment came just in time—the wildlife stocks in 1900 were at a low ebb.

The next four decades piled protection upon protection of American game species. In 1929 the Migratory Bird Conservation Act authorized the purchase of land for federal waterfowl refuges, albeit with no funding. In 1934 the Migrating Bird Stamp Act generated revenues dedicated to the purchase of refuges. The crowning federal action, which sport hunters enthusiastically supported, was the 1937 Pittman-Robertson Act, which levied an 11 percent excise tax on sporting arms and ammunition. This act funded grants to states, on a 75-to-25 match basis, to conduct ongoing wildlife research, management, and development programs. A later 10 percent excise tax on the sale of handguns further increased funding. Multiple billions of dollars from sportspersons' pockets have flowed into America's wildlife recovery and protection programs. The hunting community believes its house is in order: it pays for a sustainable harvest of wildlife, which benefits nongame species as well, obeys an intricate web of government regulations in order to harvest game, and strongly condemns those who violate hunting laws.

Pros and Cons of Hunting

Opponents of hunting charge that hunter support of wildlife is self-serving—a means of insuring abundant targets for hunters' violence. Opposition to hunting is a common theme in the policy objectives of many of the hundreds of animal rights groups consisting of millions of members. American public opinion seems to oppose hunters. While 80 percent of Americans still approve of hunting for meat, only 40 percent approve of hunting for sport, and close to one-third endorse banning hunting altogether (statistics from the Forty-third North American Wildlife and Natural Resources Conference in 1978). Of less comfort to foes of hunting, on the other hand, is the fact that a majority of states have enacted laws to prevent harassment of legal hunting activities.

To some, hunting is inhumane, sadistic, violent, and brutal, manifesting little or no sensitivity to nature's beauties or the sacredness of all life. Hunters are routinely pilloried as intoxicated slobs who discharge their weapons with abandon, who wound and maim more animals than they kill, and who show little interest in retrieving the wounded victims who escape to die agonizing deaths. Hunters are indicted as contributors to species extinction and the overpopulation of game species. In addition, hunters are accused of heightening risks to society resulting from an eagerness to use deadly weapons. According to the International Hunter Education Association's statistics, in 1997 there were 979 hunting accidents in the United States, 93 of them fatal.

On the other hand, hunters view themselves as an exceptionally peaceful group. Those who oppose hunting would do well to spend some time in the world of a hunter, advocates for hunting rights argue. Attend their fund-raising functions for habitat purchases. Slog through fields and marshes with them as they devote abundant hours to habitat protection and restoration. Visit field research projects on wildlife biology and population dynamics, which are funded by hunters' license fees. Read their literature, which ceaselessly celebrates the ethical consciousness of all consumptive wildlife interactions between humans and animals. An abiding theme in hunting literature is the healing, calming, insight-generating effects of hunter sojourns in natural settings. The hunter ideal is not violent abandon but calm reflection of the holistic circumstances of the irreversible decision to harvest the life of a game animal.

Hunters at their best exemplify ethical, thoughtful citizenship in the natural community, dedicated to sustainable withdrawals from nature's interest-bearing accounts. Hunters at their worst are "bank robbers," and the entire community of hunters and nonhunters justifiably raises the hue and cry in hot pursuit of their capture and censure.

Hunters on Film and in Literature

The most often pictured part of a hunt in American film is the proud hunter with the dead game and perhaps a jump cut to a shot of the trophy mounted in a paneled den. These visuals feed antihunting criticism of hunters as unfeeling show-offs who love to kill and who immortalize their kills with trophy mounts for all to see. The hunting community recognizes the public relations deficit it runs up with such displays and counsels more dignified portrayals.

Movies catering to American audiences, whether from Hollywood or abroad, commonly insert hunting themes as activities pursued by the least attractive personalities in the story line. American films that feature hunters as sociopaths include *The Most Dangerous Game* (1932), *Bambi* (1942), *Track of the Cat* (1954), *The Last Hunt* (1956), *Bless the Beasts and Children* (1972), *The Bear* (1989), and *White Hunter, Black Heart* (1990). In a related vein, movies of the "manhunt" genre, such as *Deliverance* (1972) and *Island of Dr. Moreau* (1977 and 1996), clearly suggest that the hunting urge can metamorphize into sociopathology.

On the other hand, hunters as admirable characters and hunting as a socially respectable pursuit have flickered to celluloid life a number of times: *Life of a Bengal Lancer* (1935), *The Charge of the Light Brigade* (1936), *The Macomber Affair* (1947), *Snows of Kilimanjaro* (1952), *Harry Black and the Tiger* (1958), *Tom Jones* (1963), *Out of Africa* (1985), *The Shooting Party* (1984), *In the Blood* (1989), and *A River Runs Through It* (1992). These titles celebrate, or at least

tolerate, hunters as something other than social pariahs.

The interior mental life of the hunter is described vividly on the pages of several works of classic literature, including Ernest Hemingway's *Green Hills of Africa* (1935), William Faulkner's "The Bear" (1942), and Robert Ruark's collections of stories *Old Man and the Boy* (1957) and *The Old Man's Boy Grows Older* (1961).

Conclusion

To prohunting advocates, hunting is a hallowed American tradition that produces nutritious food and healthy outdoor recreation while contributing billions of consumer dollars to the national economy. The recovery and growth of most game populations, these advocates argue, evidences the sustainability of heavily regulated hunting activities. Hunting does not threaten wildlife species as much as does urbanization, loss of wetlands, and general economic development.

Hunting opponents dismiss hunting traditions, economic impacts, and dietary enhancements. Animals have rights, they say, and the most fundamental right is life without deadly harassment by hunters. Because the contending premises are moral and not empirical, no compromise has yet emerged. Both sides oppose poaching and wildlife law violations; both support habitat protection and restoration. But the intended ends of these common goals remain irreconcilable.

BIBLIOGRAPHY

Fromm, Eric. *The Anatomy of Human Destructiveness*. Greenwich, Conn.: Holt, Rinehart, and Winston, 1973.
Hummel, Richard L. *Hunting and Fishing for Sport: Commerce, Controversy, Popular Culture*. Bowling Green, Ohio: Bowling Green State University Popular Press, 1994.
Morris, Desmond. *Manwatching*. New York: Abrams, 1977.
Reiger, John F. *American Sportsmen and the Origins of Conservation*. Rev. ed. Norman: University of Oklahoma, 1986.
Rohr, Janelle. *Animal Rights: Opposing Viewpoints*. San Diego, Calif.: Greenhaven, 1989.
Swan, James A. *In Defense of Hunting*. New York: HarperCollins, 1995.

RICHARD L. HUMMEL

See also **Animals, Violence Against; Sports.**

I

IATROGENIC VIOLENCE. *See* Medicine and Violence.

IMMIGRATION

During the Civil Rights era (roughly the late 1950s through the 1970s) Americans began paying increased attention to the nature of violence and its historical roots in the United States. In the 1960s the historian Richard Hofstadter, for example, noted that in this country "violence has been frequent, voluminous, almost commonplace." During that same decade the black activist H. Rap Brown proclaimed that "violence is American as cherry pie." And in 1974 the historian W. Eugene Hollon acknowledged that "gentlemen of property and standing" usually led mobs against people of a variety of ethnic backgrounds—Chinese, African, Irish, Mexican, Jew, Italian, Indian—or "any minority group they disliked or distrusted." Violence against immigrants has indeed been frequent and commonplace, persisting because individuals of status and power did little to restrain it.

When the Civil Rights Act was passed in 1964, the federal and state governments started active campaigns to protect individuals from racial, ethnic, or religious violence, countering a long-entrenched cultural tradition that upheld the supremacy of white, Anglo-Saxon Protestants and that fostered the victimization and scapegoating of immigrants and minorities, especially during times of social, economic, and political turmoil.

From the colonial era to the present, immigrant minorities, regardless of their place of origin, have been condemned and victimized by those who had arrived earlier. Immigrants brought their own cultures, and established groups showed little tolerance for diversity. Newcomers were expected to shed their backgrounds instantaneously and Americanize quickly. If they did not do this—and few people could relinquish their heritage as soon as they stepped off the boat—other Americans often disparaged and abused them. Immigrants have always served as scapegoats for social problems.

In colonial America the largest non-English immigrant groups—numbering roughly 450,000—were from Ireland (Scottish Presbyterians—known simply as the Irish in the colonies—whose ancestors had gone to Ireland generations earlier for economic reasons and to escape religious persecution by the Church of England, but who chose to leave for the colonies during hard times) and the German states in Europe. There were also smaller numbers of other peoples whom the British colonists accepted reluctantly: some fifteen thousand French Protestants (Huguenots), Scots (more than twenty-five thousand during the colonial period), and smatterings of Dutch and Swedes.

Roman Catholics from any place in Europe were seen merely as "Catholics" and not as nationals of any particular nation. Protestants despised Catholics and restricted their economic and political opportunities. For example, Protestants who served as indentured servants received more clothes, tools, and land after their indentures than did Catholics. In addition, colonial laws often prohibited Catholics from voting or holding governmental offices, even though they were Christians. In all of British North America the right to vote was restricted to those who believed in the divinity of Jesus Christ, but that criterion did not extend to Catholics. On the other hand, at some times, when bans were not enforced, Jews did vote in New York, South Carolina, Rhode Island, and perhaps in other places as well.

For most of the seventeenth and eighteenth centuries, white colonists from Europe came as indentured servants, having sold themselves into servitude for four to seven years to whoever paid the passage for their ocean voyage. Families who came together were often separated and paid for by different individuals. Some parents even had to sell their children as if they were cattle; if one or both parents died on the journey, the children had to serve time to pay for their passages as well. Unaccompanied children served until their twenty-first birthday. During the time of indenture, people were treated like slaves; their masters controlled their time and their movements. Sometimes there were cordial relations within the household; at other times servants were beaten and brutalized. Treatment of indentured servants usually had less to do with their ethnic backgrounds than with the character and temperament of their masters.

Violence grew out of the stereotypes that the British colonists applied to their neighbors whose religion or national origin differed from their own. In July 1729 a mob of Bostonians prevented a boatload of Scots-Irish from landing; five years later Yankee mobs tore down a newly built Scots-Irish Presbyterian church in Worcester, Massachusetts. In South Carolina a Huguenot church was burned down because of the group's different mode of worship. Germans were looked down upon in Pennsylvania because they were allied with the Quakers, and the English feared that Germans would not adapt to English ways, while the Scots-Irish on the frontier were regarded with scorn because of their supposed irascibility. There were many clashes among these groups; some scholars even contend that the Regulators movement in the Carolinas and the Paxton Boys revolt in Pennsylvania before the American Revolution had as much to do with ethnic rivalries as resentment over taxes. In the Carolinas and Pennsylvania, eastern patricians scorned Scots-Irish and German

farmers in the interior. When the Paxton Boys slaughtered twenty peaceful Indians and then marched east to the capital in Philadelphia, Benjamin Franklin dismissed them as "Christian White Savages." By the time of the American Revolution, however, many of these ethnic rivalries had subsided somewhat, and popular divisions mostly concerned geographical or religious issues.

In the half century between the end of the American Revolution and the eve of mass migration from Europe in the 1830s, fewer than half a million immigrants arrived in the United States. Nonetheless, fear and loathing of foreigners and Catholics persisted. During the 1790s Federalist rioters attacked Irish opponents of the Alien and Sedition Acts, which required newcomers to wait fourteen years to obtain citizenship and allowed the president to expel undesirable aliens from the country. Thenceforth Jews in the United States were often referred to as "Shylocks" and "Christ-killers," terms that remained common, along with sporadic physical attacks on Jews, until well into the twentieth century.

1830s–1890s

During the 1830s immigration began to surge. The Industrial and Agricultural Revolutions in Europe resulted in expulsions of many people from the lands that they had tilled and forced them to seek opportunities elsewhere. Many moved to cities in Europe and then went to America. One of the greatest incentives to move to the United States was what would come to be known as the "American letters," in which newcomers wrote back to friends and relatives in the old country stating how wonderful things were in the New World. Motivated by these glowing words, immigrants streamed out of Europe to the United States, expecting golden opportunities. Unfortunately, the first major wave of Europeans, the Irish, who left their homes because of expulsion from the land and famine, arrived without skills and little money. For most of them, opportunities were meager indeed.

From the 1830s until the Civil War in 1861, the nation witnessed the worst urban violence in its history. Anti-Catholic riots predominated, and as immigration increased, the number and intensity of the riots increased as well. They occurred in major cities like Baltimore, Boston, Cincinnati, Louisville, New Orleans, New York, Philadelphia, and St. Louis. During this era almost two million Irish Catholic immigrants fled Ireland and descended upon the urban Northeast. Until 1854 the Irish dominated the lists of new arrivals but thereafter individuals from the German states in Europe predominated. Once the German influx began, it overshadowed all others for almost forty years. Between 1854 and 1892, Germans led the list of immigrants every year except three, when the Irish totals exceeded theirs. In all, more than five million Germans and four million Irish entered the United States during the nineteenth century. While both groups suffered from bigotry, the Irish bore the brunt of the attacks. Wherever Irish Catholics went they were despised as Catholics and as competitors in job markets. The worst characteristics were ascribed to them. They were thought to engage in crime and vice much more frequently than others, and they also had reputations for being slovenly and ignorant. Moreover, as the historian Eugene Hollon noted, "drinking was interwoven with spontaneous and ritualized aggression in Irish culture."

No group of free immigrants was more severely thrashed than the Irish Catholics. Mobs continually attacked them. The burning of a convent in Charlestown, Massachusetts, in 1834 was only the most notorious of the events that occurred in the Boston area in the 1820s and 1830s; waves of shootings, hangings, and other assaults regularly punctuated community activities. Violence against the Irish, as well as tales about imprisonment and tortures in Catholic institutions, often dominated the local news in cities throughout the Northeast. In the 1850s violence against Catholic institutions was so prevalent that insurance companies rarely issued policies to them.

Perhaps the most notorious of the attacks occurred in the Kensington section of Philadelphia in 1844, where Catholic clergymen requested that their Bible be used for Catholic children in the public schools instead of the King James version that Protestants preferred. This request led to three days of rioting in May by Protestant mobs enraged over Catholic "popery." The violence was so severe that more than three thousand troops were needed to quell the demonstrations. When the attacks ended, more than thirty buildings had been burned, including two Catholic churches and a Catholic school; fifty people were injured and many killed. One historian later wrote that "by any measure the period from 1835 to 1850 was the most violent in Philadelphia's history."

Although the Germans of various religious persuasions bore their share of animosity, their reception was less traumatic than that of the Irish. Two-thirds of the Germans were Protestant and, unlike the Irish, had a reputation as hardworking, thrifty, and sober. But the Germans were not immune to assaults, especially in Louisville, Hoboken (New Jersey), and on several occasions New York City, where Irish and Germans also battled one another. Irish policemen clubbed striking German laborers frequently. Perhaps the worst incident, a police attack on a German labor rally in Tompkins Square in 1874, has been described as an "orgy of brutality."

The Irish were viewed as the most violent of the nineteenth-century immigrant groups. In 1850 about five hundred of them, responding to rumors that some Jews had killed a gentile girl, raided a New York City synagogue on the holiest day of the Jewish calendar, beat and robbed the worshipers, and then went on to ransack apartments in a Jewish tenement. The Irish battled, in different times and places, with members of many other ethnic groups, including Czechs, French Canadians, Greeks, Poles, Italians, and Jews. The historian James Richardson wrote that for the Irish, "beating up newcomers was a kind of sport."

During this era of ethnic turmoil in the East, the discovery of gold in California triggered a worldwide migration to the "golden state" in the late 1840s and thereafter. At first the new arrivals, including Chinese immigrants, were welcomed because their labor was needed, but within a few years they were disdained. "No variety of anti-European sentiment," the historian John Higham wrote, "has ever approached the violent extremes to which anti-Chinese agitation went in the 1870s and 1880s." Some white people even regarded the Asians, in the words of one contemporary, as "more slavish and brutish than the beasts that roam the fields. They are groveling worms." Throughout the West the Chinese suffered boycotts, lynchings, and mass expulsions; their shops and laundries were burned, they were attacked on the streets and upon exiting the mines, and they were victims of riots in Seattle, Tacoma, Denver, and Rock Springs, Wyoming. During one riot in Denver they were jailed for their own protection. In the 1870s Irish workingmen in California supported labor agitator Denis Kearney, who proclaimed that "the Chinese must GO!" A Chinese immigrant recalled, "It was the jealousy of laboring men of other nationalities—especially the Irish—that raised all the outcry against the Chinese." In 1882 the U.S. Congress suspended all

In this political cartoon, circa 1880, Americans of various ethnicities hang a Chinese man. CORBIS/BETTMANN

immigration from China for ten years and then extended that ban in 1892. The legislation, however, did not protect the Chinese already in the United States. During an 1898 Independence Day celebration in a Butte, Montana, mining camp, one man "hanged the Chinaman to a cottonwood tree just for the devilment and in the hopes it might bring good luck."

The last third of the nineteenth century witnessed violence against immigrants in all sections of the country. There was a prolonged depression in the nation after the panic of 1873 through 1897, with only a few good years interspersed. Workers and farmers felt aggrieved because they toiled so hard and earned so little. As was usual in times of crisis, people not only protested but also took the law into their own hands. Often, without any proof to bear out their suspicions, authorities arrested members of immigrant groups, which became the scapegoats for societal ills. After a strike in 1875 in the coal regions of Pennsylvania, for example,

twenty-four of the former strikers, all of Irish ancestry, were arrested and charged with having perpetrated savageries in the region for years as members of the Molly Maguires, an Irish group supposedly responsible for the crimes. No one denies that the Molly Maguires engaged in brutal activities and assassinated their enemies. And many of them were involved in the 1875 coal miners' strike. Nonetheless, the trials of 1876–1878 struck many observers as a travesty of justice. Those accused of the crimes had certainly engaged in criminal activities as members of the Molly Maguires; they were not blameless victims. Yet the prosecutors of most of these men failed in court to provide specific evidence linking the individual defendants to the specific crimes for which they were charged. Thus the amorphous evidence should at least have resulted in the jurors having a reasonable doubt about the individuals' culpability, but it did not. All of the defendants were found guilty; ten of them were hanged, and the rest were jailed.

Attacks on immigrants, however, did not depend on whether they had or had not engaged in criminal activity. In the last decades of the nineteenth century, popular frustrations resulted in the attack and ousting of several Greek store owners from Omaha, Nebraska; the killing of nineteen Slavic coal miners in Pennsylvania; the assassination of six Italian laborers in the coal-mining areas of Colorado; and the lynching of five Sicilian shopkeepers in one southern town for working alongside African Americans and treating them well in shops. Moreover, two hundred Italians were driven out of Altoona, Pennsylvania, in 1894; and in 1899 "white American citizens" vandalized an Italian agricultural colony in Arkansas and burned down its schoolhouse. Almost every one of these attacks occurred in areas of economic desperation.

In 1891 a horrifying incident occurred in New Orleans, where eleven Italians were arrested after a police superintendent was killed. They were indicted, but the jury refused to convict all of them for lack of sufficient evidence. A number of "good citizens" then stormed the jail, kidnapped the prisoners, and lynched them. The event created international tensions as the government of Italy demanded payments to the victims' families and punishment for members of the lynch mob. Neither demand was granted, and after a few months the Italian government no longer pursued the issue. Despite the international attention the incident received, treatment of European newcomers barely changed. "From the outset," the historian John Higham has written, "the Slavic and Italian immigrants ran a gamut of indignities and ostracisms. They were abused in public and isolated in private, cuffed in the works and pelted in the streets, fined and imprisoned on the smallest pretext, cheated of their wages, and crowded by the score into converted barns and tumble-down shanties that served as boarding houses."

Eastern European Jews, who also started arriving in the United States in the late nineteenth century, were attacked as alien, non-Christian "Christ-killers." In New York, Cleveland, Boston, and other major cities, Jews suffered an array of indignities: youths pulled old men's beards, children were beaten by the offspring of other immigrants, and in 1902 Irish workers at a New York City factory pelted a Jewish funeral cortege with a variety of wood and metal objects. The police were called and when they arrived, instead of arresting the perpetrators, they wielded their clubs at the Jewish mourners. One of the victims later told a reporter:

"It was a thing that even a Russian, with all of his dislike of our people, would have been ashamed of." Both a police committee and a citizens committee investigated the riot at the funeral; the police were found to have behaved unprofessionally, and a new police commissioner was appointed. However, no significant change in police behavior toward Jews or other minorities resulted.

In urban areas labor unrest sparked much of the violence directed toward ethnic groups. Hard-pressed laborers often turned on immigrants who were lower in the pecking order, especially since employers preferred hiring the recent arrivals for a variety of unskilled tasks, viewing them—often accurately—as more docile, amenable to discipline, and ignorant of American ways. And, in fact, most of the new immigrants fit into those categories. However, the exploitation of workers led to horrendous working conditions, and law-enforcement officials, generally supportive of management, treated discontented workers ruthlessly. It took many decades, into the 1930s for some groups, for workers to realize that their problems could be better solved by working with one another rather than beating and berating people who were different.

Throughout the country, but especially in the South, peonage existed. Greed, rather than any specific hostility toward any one group, probably spurred entrepreneurs to use and exploit convict laborers, African Americans, and immigrants. The state "rented" the convicts, but the employers practically imprisoned the others. Immigrants would be hired off the boat wherever they landed and taken to farms in the Cotton Belt from the Carolinas to Texas; to the turpentine areas of Georgia, Alabama, and Florida; and to the railroad construction camps, mines, and sawmills wherever they were needed. At many sites armed guards controlled the workers' behavior. Those who performed their tasks slowly or questioned authority were flogged or beaten with iron bars, gun butts, or heavy wooden paddles. At night they were locked in stockades, some of which were converted barns and chicken coops. In Georgia, when one Hungarian worker tried to escape, his bosses followed with trained dogs. After they captured him, he was horsewhipped and then tied to a buggy and dragged back to the camp. Eventually these establishments were disbanded, and workers went on to seek other labor, but peonage, which had its heyday before World War I, continued well into the twentieth century. Incidents of peonage were reported even as late as the 1960s.

The Twentieth Century

During the Progressive Era, from about 1903 to 1917, concerned citizens in practically every state tried to improve the quality of people's lives. Progressives may have wanted to make government more honest and society more moral but somehow largely bypassed the needs of urban laborers, most of who were immigrants. In fact, aside from those who ran settlement houses, like Jane Addams in Chicago and Lillian Wald in New York City, many Progressives were condescending and hostile to immigrants and rarely intervened in conflicts between employers and employees, an attitude that left immigrants more vulnerable in the face of violent reprisals for strikes. In Ludlow, Colorado; Lawrence, Massachusetts; and the steel mills in western Pennsylvania the police were often violent in their treatment of strikers and unrestrained in their use of fists, feet, and clubs. In cities like Chicago and New York mounted Irish policemen plunged through the crowds, pummeled ethnic strikers, and called them "kikes," "dagos," and "Polacks."

Progressives turned somewhat from domestic concerns after the United States entered World War I in 1917, when patriotic fervor stimulated Americans in their common goal to win the war. Although many Americans of Irish and German background found it difficult to support a war against Germany (just as most of the Irish could not stomach being on the side of England), once the United States entered the conflagration they reacted as Americans, not as hyphenated Americans. Many Americans of non-German background, however, attacked German Americans in the United States. Mobs of "superpatriots" beat Germans on the street, looted their stores, burned their books, and even tarred and feathered them. Boy Scouts in Cleveland overturned delivery carts of German-language newspapers, and the governor of Iowa issued a proclamation stating that while freedom of speech existed for everyone who spoke English in public, the same was not true for those who expressed themselves in other languages. "Freedom of speech is guaranteed," he proclaimed, "but this guarantee does not protect [individuals] in the use of a foreign language . . . when to do so tends, in time of national peril, to create discord among neighbors and citizens, or to disturb the peace and quiet of the community."

Moreover, throughout the nation, a uniformity of opinion was demanded, and many American citizens and foreigners were beaten or jailed or both for criticizing policies of the U.S. government. When the war ended, the U.S. attorney general, A. Mitchell Palmer, ordered the roundup of many eastern European nationals suspected of being socialists or communists. Over six thousand people were incarcerated without a hearing, denied bail, and held for deportation. Many of those arrested during the infamous Palmer Raids were Americans with no record of subversion; one-third of those confined were subsequently released. However, in Detroit, eight hundred of those detained were housed in a windowless area, forced to sleep on stone floors, and provided with only one toilet and drinking fountain.

Although Progressive ideals persisted through the 1920s, that decade witnessed a burgeoning hedonism, a turning away from international concerns, and a general but unspoken demand that the United States should be for Americans. As a result, a reborn Ku Klux Klan not only promoted the supremacy of Protestant Americans but also vilified Catholics and Jews and tormented immigrants who did not conform to their religious, moral, or national standards. According to Klan doctrine, the only real Americans were white Protestants whose moral values derived from the Bible; therefore these values should guide the behavior of all the people living in the United States. Catholics were thought to be subversive agents of a foreign power, and African Americans were expected to "know their place." There was no national pattern of systematic violence by the Klan, but there were sporadic outbreaks against various groups. In the West, for example, Asians and Jews were subjected to intense verbal abuse and occasional physical assaults.

One did not have to be a member of the Klan to abuse foreigners, however. Perhaps the worst case of ethnic violence during that decade occurred in a court of law. In 1921 two men of Italian birth, Nicola Sacco and Bartolomeo Vanzetti, were arrested and charged with robbery and murder in South Braintree, Massachusetts. After a trial dominated by controversial and circumstantial evidence, the jury found the defendants—who were also self-proclaimed anarchists—guilty. The judge, Webster Thayer, sentenced them to death. Because of the nature of the evidence and the tendentious conduct of the trial, almost everyone recognized that the judge wanted a guilty verdict. The governor of Massachusetts appointed an investigative committee that concluded that the presiding judge had been guilty of a "grave breach of official decorum" but recommended that the judicial decision stand. The obvious injustice led to worldwide protests, but the governor of Massachusetts in 1927 allowed the electrocution of the two convicts. Millions of people, however, believed that Sacco and Vanzetti were "murdered" because of their ethnicity and their political views.

Ethnicity also determined the treatment of immigrants and minorities in the West. Two major immigration restriction laws were written by Congress during the decade, in the years 1921 and 1924, the second being the Johnson-Reed Act, which excluded most Asians from the country. Nonetheless, Asians had already come to the United States, and a half million more managed to reach American shores during the 1920s. Throughout the 1920s and 1930s Koreans, Chinese, Japanese, and Filipinos clashed with whites in California. An anti-Filipino riot in an agricultural area in Exeter, California, in 1929 resulted in the burning of a Filipino camp. The following year, in Watsonville, California, there was another series of riots against Filipinos. That same year about four hundred white vigilantes attacked people in the Northern Monterey Filipino Club.

Mexicans, often overlooked by historians and the media until the 1960s, have lived in the Southwest since the United States acquired the territory from Mexico in the middle of the nineteenth century (although most of the Mexicans in the West arrived after the Mexican Revolution of 1910–1920). Mexicans were ranked with the Chinese, Japanese, Filipinos, and other Asians as the most exploited and disparaged groups in society. Some Americans of European heritage considered them an inferior, degenerate, and alien race and stole their lands. One chronicler of California noted that in the 1850s "it would be impossible . . . to catalogue the number of hangings, brandings, whippings, ear croppings, and banishments of Latins." In Texas, where Mexicans were slaughtered by the hundreds in the late nineteenth and early twentieth centuries, part of the state police terrorized them. They were employed in the most menial occupations and then disparaged as lazy and worthless people with criminal tendencies.

From 1929 to 1941 the United States underwent the worst economic depression in its history. In every section of the country, citizens and immigrants alike suffered. But for Mexican Americans there was an additional penalty. Whether born in the United States or south of the border, many of the poorer ones were rounded up and forced to return to Mexico. East of the Mississippi River, however, and especially in the Northeast, eastern European Jews suffered to a greater extent from prejudice and violence than other white immigrants. Attacks on Jewish schoolchildren by Christian pupils were not uncommon, but during the Great Depression of the 1930s, the animosity spilled over into violence against all Jews. Before 1933 there had been perhaps five organized groups hostile to Jews; by the beginning of World War II there were over a hundred, with names like the Silver Shirts and the Christian Front, which relished having a human scapegoat for their woes. They were encouraged by their religious leaders, by the propagation (especially during the 1920s) of the fraudulent but inflammatory "Protocols of the Elders of Zion," and by the anti-Semitic propaganda emanating from Germany.

Spurred on by the anti-Semitic radio broadcasts of the Catholic priest Father Charles Coughlin, Catholic youths assaulted Jews in large cities, including New York, Boston, and Philadelphia. After one incident in Boston in 1942, police arrested the victim and then pummeled him in jail. An investigation ordered by the governor of Massachusetts led to the removal of the police commissioner for having tolerated such inappropriate behavior from the officers; the Boston police were reprimanded as well.

Even the massive undertaking of U.S. involvement in World War II did not entirely drain the energies of ethnic hatred on the home front. During the summer of 1942 between ten and twenty Mexican American teenagers were arrested and tried for murder in Los Angeles. The only "evidence" the police had was that the youths were the last people to have seen the dead man alive. A week before the trial the prosecutor instructed the sheriff to prevent the defendants from bathing, shaving, or changing their clothes so that they would appear menacing and disheveled in court. The jury listened to the "evidence" and convicted the young men, who were then sent to San Quentin. Two years later, following an investigation of the trial that concluded that the Mexican Americans were convicted "without a shred of evidence," they were released. The other major episode of anti-Mexican violence during World War II also occurred in the Los Angeles area and is now referred to as the Zoot-Suit Riots. One night in 1943 U.S.

sailors on leave from their ships walked through a Mexican neighborhood and were attacked by persons who were never found. During the next few nights these sailors and others rampaged through Mexican American neighborhoods beating up every Mexican they saw. The police followed the sailors but arrested the Mexican victims. The riots ended only after the Mexican government contacted the U.S. secretary of state and demanded a cessation of the riots. The secretary of the navy canceled all shore leave, sailors returned to their ships, and the ships sailed out to sea.

The worst case of prejudice during World War II resulted from an executive order issued by President Franklin D. Roosevelt and enforced by American troops. Although lacking any evidence, the commanding general on the West Coast feared that Japanese Americans might plot or engage in subversive activities. Wartime hysteria about the Japanese on the West Coast combined with residues of "yellow peril" fears dating back to the turn of the century, and the result was a recommendation to the president that all Japanese Americans, even native-born citizens, be removed from their homes and put into internment camps in the rural interiors of states like California, Wyoming, Arizona, Idaho, and Arkansas. Some were even put to work picking sugar beets in Colorado. Without any justification for this move, approximately 120,000 American residents and citizens were rounded up on the West Coast and removed to what one historian has dubbed "concentration camps, USA," where they remained for almost three years. Although the U.S. Supreme Court upheld the measure, subsequent reevaluations concluded that the removal of Japanese Americans was a dastardly deed and should never have happened. In the 1970s the federal government provided monetary compensation to the survivors of this injustice. (In Hawaii, because the entire territory was under martial law during World War II, few Japanese were interned.)

After World War II Americans became more tolerant. Some historians attribute this change to wartime propaganda fostering the belief that all citizens were Americans and of an America fighting for values like freedom of religion and speech and freedom from want or fear. (Even Japanese Americans over the age of eighteen were allowed to join the army; their division served in Europe.)

World War II slogans obviously nurtured patriotic feelings, but whether they also contributed to changed attitudes afterward is more difficult to say. Prosperity returned after the war, and most veterans wanted to obtain an education, start a career and a family, and get on with their lives. After the horrors that occurred in Europe and Asia during the war as a result of prejudice, many Americans began to reevaluate their treatment of immigrants and minorities. For the first time in American history, the president appointed commissions to examine college and university educational opportunities for all and treatment of minorities specifically. The commissioners appointed to investigate these matters discovered that prejudice prevented many Americans from obtaining equal opportunities in society. President Harry S. Truman then proposed legislation promoting civil rights and equal opportunities—a proposal that Congress ignored but which alerted the rest of the nation to some severe problems that needed handling. Supreme Court decisions—notably *Brown v. Board of Education*, which struck down the "separate-but-equal" rationalization for segregated public schools—also led to the reevaluation of American policies toward minority groups. The Court also overturned California laws preventing land ownership by Asians, along with restrictive covenants in housing that prevented selected ethnic groups from purchasing homes in some of the more desirable residential areas. Of course, not every law was observed, nor were policies changed immediately, but there were signs that greater tolerance was being fostered by federal, state, and local governments. Various ethnic lobbying organizations, including those of Jews, African Americans, and Asians, also campaigned for the end of discriminatory legislation in housing, education, and employment. The combined efforts of both private and public groups certainly led to a decline in, but not an elimination of, violence toward immigrants and minorities.

Most of the ethnically motivated violence in the United States since the end of World War II has been directed against African Americans, Asians, and Latino refugees; but the attacks do not approach those of prewar America in severity or frequency. Perhaps the worst attacks in the late twentieth century against immigrants occurred during the 1992 riots in Los Angeles, when groups of African Americans, resentful of Koreans' alleged prosperity, attacked Koreans in their neighborhoods.

It would be untrue, at the close of the twentieth century, to say that violence no longer occurred against members of immigrant groups. But it would be absolutely true to say that violence against these people was no longer sanctioned by law or by community mores.

BIBLIOGRAPHY

Daniels, Roger. *Prisoners Without Trial: Japanese Americans in World War II.* New York: Hill and Wang, 1993.

Dinnerstein, Leonard, and David M. Reimers. *Ethnic Americans.* 4th ed. New York: Columbia University Press, 1999.

Gambino, Richard. *Vendetta: A True Story of the Worst Lynching in America, the Mass Murder of Italian-Americans in New Orleans in 1891, the Vicious Motivations Behind It, and the Tragic Repercussions that Linger to This Day.* Garden City, N.Y.: Doubleday, 1977.

Gyory, Andrew. *Closing the Gate: Race, Politics, and the Chinese Exclusion Act.* Chapel Hill: University of North Carolina Press, 1998.

Higham, John. *Strangers in the Land.* Westport, Conn.: Greenwood, 1981.

Hollon, W. Eugene. *Frontier Violence: Another Look.* New York: Oxford University Press, 1974.

Kenny, Kevin. *Making Sense of the Molly Maguires.* New York: Oxford University Press, 1998.

McWilliams, Carey. *North from Mexico.* New York: Greenwood, 1990.

Mazon, Mauricio. *The Zoot-Suit Riots: The Psychology of Symbolic Annihilation.* Austin: University of Texas Press, 1984.

Novak, Michael. *The Guns of Lattimer.* New York: Basic, 1978.

Richards, Leonard L. *"Gentlemen of Property and Standing": Anti-Abolition Mobs in Jacksonian America.* New York: Oxford University Press, 1977.

Saxton, Alexander. *The Indispensable Enemy: Labor and the Anti-Chinese Movement in California.* Berkeley: University of California Press, 1971.

Storti, Craig. *Incident at Bitter Creek: The Story of the Rock Spring Chinese Massacre.* Ames: Iowa State University, 1991.

LEONARD DINNERSTEIN

See also **Alien and Sedition Acts; Asians; Chinese Americans; Chinese Exclusion Act; Cuban Americans; Extremism; Gangs; German Americans; Irish Americans; Italian Americans; Japanese Americans; Korean Americans; Mexican Americans; Molly Maguires; Nativism; Polish Americans; Puerto Ricans; Religion; Vietnamese Americans; Zoot-Suit Riot.**

INCEST

Incest has been forbidden throughout human history in almost all cultures and societies. The taboo on sexual relations, cohabitation, or marriage between related individuals served two primary purposes: it prevented inbreeding and it averted conflicted relations and rivalries within families by establishing sexual boundaries. Societal prohibitions against incest have been so strong that occurrences have been thought to be exceedingly rare and aberrant, usually the result of considerable pathology. As recently as 1955, published statistics estimated that incest occurred in only one or two cases per million people per year. These statistics were corroborated in major psychiatry and psychology textbooks written in the 1960s. In contrast, research conducted in the last quarter of the twentieth century documented that incest is anything but rare and occurs routinely at quite a high rate of frequency, especially cases involving sexual contact between adults and minor children. Evidence suggested that incest has been embedded in and covertly allowed in most cultures, while being overtly and publicly decried and denied. This finding has led some researchers to comment that the taboo on incest seems to refer more to its acknowledgment rather than to its occurrence.

Incest as Child Abuse

Incest between adults and minor children is considered to be child abuse in North America. In fact, if a broad definition of incest is used, incest is possibly the most common form of child sexual abuse. The following definition of incest as child sexual abuse is noteworthy for its inclusiveness:

> [Incest] refers to sexual contact with a person who would be considered an ineligible partner because of his blood and/or social ties (i.e., kin) to the subject and her family. The term encompasses, then, several categories of partners, including father, stepfather, grandfather, uncles, siblings, cousins, in-laws, and what we call "quasi-family." The last category includes parental and family friends (i.e., mother's sexual partner). Our feeling is that the incest taboo applies in a weakened form to all these categories in that the "partner" represents someone from whom the female child should rightfully expect warmth or protection and sexual distance. Sexual behavior recorded as positive incest ranged from intercourse with consent; intercourse by force; attempted intercourse or seduction; molestation, primarily fondling of breasts and genitals; and exposure. We included other sexual behaviors as intercourse, namely, all penetration, anal, oral, and vaginal, both passive and active. Cunnilingus and fellatio were not uncommon activities, nor was sodomy.
>
> (Benward and Densen-Gerber 1975, p. 326)

As this definition implies, incest involves a wide range of behaviors alone or in combination and occurs within different kinds of familial relationships. Such a broad definition is useful for research purposes and for understanding incest and its psychological dimensions and consequences but may not meet the legal criteria of what constitutes incest. In the United States, incestuous contact is defined differently by each state, making it necessary to research state law when a legal definition is required. In general, incest laws forbid marriage, cohabitation, and sexual relations (usually defined as sexual intercourse) between individuals who are closely related by blood (consanguineously) and by marriage or adoption (affinely or contractually). It should be noted that the occurrence of incest is not always abusive even though it may not be legal. In cases of consensual sex between related adults and mutual exploratory sex play between peers of the same age (such as cousins and siblings), it may be nonabusive.

As of 1999 research suggested that the rate of child sexual abuse in the form of incest in the United States was 10 to 30 percent among girls and 2 to 9 percent among boys. In her *Incest: The Secret Trauma* (1986), a report of a large random-sample study of incest among girls and women, Diana Russell found evidence that incest is underreported even at these rates and that its prevalence has increased in the last several decades. Other research suggests that this finding is equally applicable to boys, who are even more reluctant than girls to admit to incestuous contact. According to Russell's analysis of her findings, the increased prevalence appears to be due in large measure to the following factors: untreated sexually abused children and an intergenerational cycle of abuse in many incestuous families; a male backlash against sexual equality for women; availability of child pornography and its increasing emphasis on the sexualization of children; and the societal increase in cohabitation, divorce, and remarriage, which results in an increase in blended families. Data are now available to suggest a much higher rate of abuse when a stepfather or other male authority figure acting as a father is in the home.

Causes and Patterns of Incest

A variety of family and individual dynamics have been found to account for the occurrence of incest. Most perpetrators (and their partners when incest occurs in the nuclear family) have themselves been exposed to sexual abuse and other forms of family violence as children—their abuse of others is believed to represent a reenactment of some sort and an attempt to master their own victimization. Incest has been found to occur across all demographic groups and in all cultures. Some studies suggest that poverty may be implicated in family violence and child abuse, including incest, but other studies suggest that incest may take place more frequently in higher-income families.

Other significant findings about the occurrence of incest are the following: It appears that males are the most frequent perpetrators of incestuous abuse, whether the victims are males or females, and engage in more traumatic and physically intrusive abuse than do females. Same-sex abuse occurs but at lower rates than opposite-sex abuse and is more likely to involve male-to-male contact. Most perpetrators are older and often considerably older than their victims. Parent-child incest is by far the most damaging of all types and cross-generational abuse tends to be more serious than abuse by peers (although some brother-sister sibling abuse is documented as being very severe). The occurrence of incest varies greatly from incident to incident: it can range from a one-time occurrence to literally hundreds of occurrences spanning decades. It may occur only occasionally or quite frequently in a compulsive or addictive fashion. The average duration of childhood incest when no intervention occurs is approximately four years. When an extended time period is involved, the sexual behavior usually escalates in seriousness and physical intrusiveness. Some incest, however, begins with intrusive sexual contact.

Many studies indicate that most incestuous abuse between adults and children does not involve physical violence, although, as with other characteristics, a wide range of force and violence is evident. Most commonly, incest occurs through coercion of some sort and by "grooming" the child to the activity. Often, the child is coerced to remain silent through verbal and implied threats. Over time, the child who does not tell often feels culpable for the continuance of the activity and remains silent owing to shame and a fear of being blamed by others if the behavior is exposed. Thus, many abused children are trapped in a cycle of ongoing and progressively serious abuse, nondisclosure, and resultant nonintervention.

Consequences of Incest

Incest constitutes a major physical and mental health risk to the individual and the family. A host of initial and long-term aftereffects have been correlated with a history of incestuous abuse. Children's reactions are often manifested as behavioral symptoms that vary according to the child's level of physical and psychosexual maturity. The infant, toddler, and young child show signs of acute anxiety as a result of being assaulted or overstimulated. These symptoms are nonspecific to the sexual trauma and include withdrawal, fretfulness, crying, clinging behavior, movement impairment, conduct disturbances, sleep problems, feeding disturbances, speech disturbance, and a general failure to thrive. Trauma-specific symptoms may emerge in early childhood on a transient basis or may be relatively persistent. These include compulsive and inappropriate sex play; sexually aggressive behavior with peers, adults, and objects; and knowledge of sexual activity that is inappropriate for the child's age. Other symptoms include those associated with depression (nightmares, concentration problems, poor sleep patterns, suicidal feelings, suicide attempts, and attempts at self-injury), fears and phobias, dissociation, eating disorders, attachment and relationship disturbances, delinquent behavior, pseudomature or regressed behavior, and psychotic or borderline states. School and social functioning may or may not be affected.

In adolescence, acute anxiety and rage may be acted out in angry, rebellious, delinquent behavior (including sexual promiscuity and substance abuse) or may result in a depressive state characterized by social withdrawal or overly compliant behavior. Psychosomatic complaints may continue on a transient or relatively stable basis. Attempts to develop peer group identification may be impeded by strong feelings of stigma, shame, embarrassment, and being "out of sync" with peers. An early pregnancy or series of pregnancies or abortions, early marriage, or runaway behavior may be indicative of a history of abuse.

Adults who report traumatic incest histories have been found to exhibit a number of posttraumatic reactions (mistrustfulness, hypervigilance, sleep disturbances, startle responses, dissociation, hyperarousal, fear of revictimization, and perceptual disturbances); emotional reactions (depression, anxiety, self-blame, guilt, and suicidal tendencies); an inability to identify and modulate emotional states; identity difficulties (negative self-image, feelings of shame, low self-worth, and stigmatization); physical and sexual difficulties (various physical symptoms and ailments, somatization, addictions, and difficulties with sexual development, sexual identity, and sexual functioning); and dysfunctional interpersonal relationships (discord with family members, disturbed relationships, difficulty with trust and intimacy, and disturbances in parenting).

Despite this host of serious mental health consequences, incest has had a long history of going unrecognized by mental health professionals, owing largely to the effect of Freud's repudiation of his seduction theory, in which he postulated incest as the root of hysterical symptoms. He replaced the seduction theory with the oedipal theory, which posited incest as a wish or fantasy on the part of the child. Freud's oedipal theory profoundly affected the medical and psychiatric profession and the way in which it responded to accusations of incest. Freud's reformulation of the causes and consequences of incest virtually ensured that such complaints were treated as childhood fantasy and not as a reality. It had the additional effect of exonerating the involved adult while allowing for both the continuation of the incest and society's denial of it.

As data have accumulated about the prevalence of incest and the patterns of serious aftereffects, mental health professionals have responded by developing treatment protocols and programs, and child welfare and criminal justice professionals have developed assessment and intervention methods. Individual and group treatment is now available for child and adolescent victims, for perpetrators, and for individual family members and entire families as well. Safety and the cessation of abuse are at the root of all treatment approaches. While some perpetrators are successfully rehabilitated and reunited with their families, others are not. A posttraumatic model of treatment has also been developed for adults who were formerly abused. Because of the range of aftereffects that are often involved, treatment is carefully sequenced and involves a number of healing tasks addressed in a somewhat hierarchical fashion. The issue of incest is discussed only after the individual has developed sufficient defenses and skills for coping so that such reexposure results in resolution and not retraumatization. Treatment models are continuing to develop as more outcome research becomes available.

BIBLIOGRAPHY

Benward, J., and J. Densen-Gerber. "Incest as a Causative Factor in Anti-social Behavior: An Exploratory Study." *Contemporary Drug Problems* 4, no. 3 (1975).

Courtois, Christine A. *Healing the Incest Wound: Adult Survivors in Therapy.* New York: Norton, 1988.

Finkelhor, D. "Current Information on the Scope and Nature of Child Sexual Abuse." *The Future of Children* 4 (1994): 31–53. Special issue on the sexual abuse of children.

Freyd, Jennifer. *Betrayal Trauma: The Logic of Forgetting Childhood Abuse.* Cambridge, Mass.: Harvard University Press, 1996.

Herman, Judith Lewis. *Father-Daughter Incest.* Cambridge, Mass.: Harvard University Press, 1981.

Meiselman, Karin C. *Incest: A Psychological Study of Cause and Effects with Treatment Recommendations.* San Francisco: Jossey-Bass, 1978.

Russell, Diana E. H. *The Secret Trauma: Incest in the Lives of Girls and Women.* New York: Basic, 1986.

CHRISTINE A. COURTOIS

See also **Child Abuse; Domestic Violence; Rape; Sex Offenders; Sibling Abuse.**

INCIDENCE OF VIOLENCE

Acts of interpersonal and collective violence have permeated U.S. society at nearly every stage of its development, characterizing U.S. history as one of continuous and often intense violence. While the violent crime rate in the United States declined in the 1990s, it was still relatively high in comparison with other industrialized nations.

The validity and adequacy of statistics about crime in general and violent crime in particular are always questionable because of inevitable inaccuracies in the collection of crime statistics. Nonetheless, the measurement of crime is important in providing an understanding of the social forces that contribute to crime. There are three primary sources of crime statistics: the Uniform Crime Reports based on police data gathered by the Federal Bureau of Investigation, victim surveys, and self-report studies of criminal behavior. While all three sources provide data on criminals and victims, this essay focuses on the official crime measurement, the Uniform Crime Reports.

Crime Statistics

The most widely publicized source of crime statistics in the United States is the FBI's Uniform Crime Reports (UCR). The FBI receives and compiles records from more than sixteen thousand city, county, and state law enforcement agencies serving most of the United States.

The UCR are divided into two major categories: Part I (index crimes) and Part II (nonindex crimes). Part I crimes, the most serious, include murder and nonnegligent manslaughter, forcible rape, aggravated assault, robbery, burglary, motor vehicle theft, larceny, and arson. Part II covers twenty-one less serious offenses and those committed by juveniles.

Despite the refinements and improvements in the UCR since their inception in 1930, the data have limitations and should be interpreted with caution. Perhaps the most prominent drawback of the UCR is their restriction to reported crime. Much crime goes undetected and is therefore not reflected in the official statistics. Likewise, there are crimes that for various reasons are not reported to the police. These crimes are also excluded from the officially recorded crime statistics. An elaborate discussion of the limitations of the UCR is provided elsewhere (Hagen 1990, Hindelang 1974, Savitz 1978, Siegel 1995, and Skogan 1974).

It is well documented that the United States has the highest violent crime rate of any industrialized nation. The annual U.S. homicide incidence of 7.9 per 1,000 citizens has prompted government officials to declare interpersonal violence a national health emergency. The high violent crime rate is also a concern for the American public, with eight out of ten Americans reporting that they are concerned about the consequences of violence. Although the UCR have identified eight violent and serious offenses, this essay examines the incidence of violent crime in the United States by focusing on four of the most violent and serious offenses—murder, rape, robbery, and assault—plus domestic violence and the act of stalking.

Murder: Prevalence and Incidence. According to the UCR, homicide is classified as murder and nonnegligent manslaughter. Murder and nonnegligent manslaughter are defined as the willful (nonnegligent) killing of one human being by another (which excludes deaths caused by negligence, suicide, or accident). Homicide, as all other violent crimes, includes force or threat of force.

Since 1980 the U.S. homicide rate has fluctuated. Following a peak in 1980, the homicide rate reached 7.9 per 100,000 population in 1985. In 1991 the homicide rate increased 24 percent, reflecting a peak of 9.8. However, since 1991 the homicide rate has steadily declined, falling to 7.4 per 100,000 in 1996. The 1997 homicide rate fell below 7 per 100,000, lower than any annual rate since 1967. By the first half of 1997, murder had declined by

9 percent. There were 19,645 murders in the United States in 1996, in comparison to the 21,606 that occurred in 1995.

The number of persons murdered in the United States in 1997 was estimated at 18,209, representing a 7 percent decline from the 1996 estimate of 19,645. When compared to the 1996 figures, the 1997 murder volumes in the nation's cities dropped 9 percent. In comparison with the 1995 murder rate (21,606), murder volumes reported in 1997 dropped 10 percent in the nation's cities, 9 percent in the suburban counties, and 6 percent in rural counties.

The southern states had the nation's highest homicide rates (43 percent of the 1997 murders). The western states accounted for 22 percent of the murders; the midwestern states, 21 percent; and the northeastern states, 13 percent. While the percentage of murders varies by region, all areas experienced declines in the number of murders reported from 1996 to 1997. The greatest decreases in murder for 1997 were in the Northeast (12 percent) and West (11 percent), with the smallest decreases recorded in the South (6 percent) and Midwest (3 percent). The South averaged 8 murders per 100,000 inhabitants; the West, 7; the Midwest, 6; and the Northeast, 5. Compared to 1996 rates, murder rates in 1997 declined in all four geographic areas.

Supplemental data for 15,848 of the 19,645 murders that occurred in 1996 and 15,289 of the estimated 18,209 murders that occurred in 1997 reveal that the victim data were stable between 1996 and 1997. In 1997, 77 percent of the murder victims were male, 88 percent were eighteen years old or older, and 45 percent were twenty through thirty-four. The percentage of black and white victims was evenly distributed at 49 percent each. Of murder offenders (data were reported on a total of 18,108 male offenders), 90 percent were males, 87 percent were persons eighteen or older, 52 percent were black, and 45 percent were white. The 1996 and 1997 data support the intraracial research on homicide. Ninety-four percent of black murder victims were killed by black offenders, and 85 percent of the white murder victims were killed by white offenders. Similarly, males were most likely to be slain by other males (89 percent) while females were more likely to be slain by males (nine out of every ten females were slain by males).

Consistent with the data from previous years, firearms were the weapons of choice in seven out of every ten murders that took place in 1997.

Handguns accounted for 53 percent of the total murders for which weapon data were available. Nonfirearm weapons included knives or cutting instruments (13 percent of the murders); personal weapons such as hands, feet, and fists (6 percent of murders); blunt objects such as hammers and clubs (5 percent of murders); and other dangerous weapons (poisons, explosives) accounted for the remaining murders.

Rape: Prevalence and Incidence. Forcible rape is defined by the UCR as the carnal knowledge of a female forcibly and against her will. Included in the definition of forcible rape are attempts to commit rape by force or by threat of force. Statutory rape (without force), same-sex rape, and other sex offenses are excluded.

The 1997 UCR data reveal that 96,122 rapes were reported to law enforcement officials, representing the fifth consecutive annual decline and the lowest total since 1989. The forcible rape total for 1997 was nearly unchanged from the estimated forcible rape total in 1996 (96,252). The 1997 forcible rape total was 9 percent below the 1993 level but was higher than the 1988 count by 4 percent. The South (as with murder, robbery, and assault) reported the highest percentage (40 percent) of the forcible rape total, followed by the Midwest (25 percent), the West (23 percent), and the Northeast (13 percent). While the rape totals for 1997 in the South and West have remained relatively stable since 1996, there was, however, a 2 percent decline in rape in the Midwest and a 1 percent decline in the Northeast.

By UCR definition, rape victims are females. Of the 96,122 rapes that were reported in 1997, approximately 71 of every 100,000 females were rape victims. Compared to the 1996 rape rate, the rape rate for 1997 declined by 1 percent. Four-year trends revealed that the 1997 rate for forcible rape had declined by 13 percent. Rape by force was the largest category (87 percent) of the total number of reported rapes. Rape declined by 4 percent from 1995 to 1996.

In an attempt to understand the prevalence, incidence, and consequences of violence against women, the National Institute of Justice and the Centers for Disease Control and Prevention conducted the National Violence Against Women Survey (NVAW), which focused on violence against women from November 1995 to May 1996 and was based on data collected from a representative sample of eight thousand women and eight thousand men. The NVAW provided data on women's and

TABLE 1. Violent Crime Total, 1994–1997

Year	Number of Offenses*	Change vs. Previous Year, %	Rate per 100,000 Inhabitants	Change vs. Previous Year, %
1994	1,857,670		713.6	
1995	1,798,792	–3.1	684.6	–4.1
1996	1,688,540	–6.1	636.5	–7.0
1997	1,634,773	–3.1	610.8	–4.0

*Violent crimes consisting of murder and nonnegligent manslaughter, forcible rape, robbery, and aggravated assault.

men's experiences with rape, physical assault, and stalking. The NVAW found that one of every six U.S. women and one of every thirty-three U.S. men have experienced an attempted or completed rape as a child or adult or both. This estimate reveals that approximately 302,100 women and 92,700 men are forcibly raped each year in the United States. Because some women experience multiple rapes, the incidence of rape exceeds the prevalence of rape. During one year preceding the NVAW, approximately 876,100 rapes were perpetrated against women and approximately 111,300 rapes were perpetrated against men.

Robbery. Robbery is the taking or attempting to take anything of value from the care, custody, or control of a person or persons by force or threat of force or violence or by putting the victim in fear. The estimated total volume for robbery in the United States during 1997 was 497,950, a 7 percent decrease from 1996 (535,594). The 1997 robbery total was the lowest since 1985. The robbery volume dropped in all locales except rural counties: there was a 10 percent decrease in cities with one million or more inhabitants and a 6 percent drop in suburban counties. Rural counties experienced an increase of 11 percent in the robbery volume. The South accounted for the highest percentage of reported robberies in 1997, accounting for 36 percent of all reported robberies; the West, 23 percent; the Northeast, 21 percent; and the Midwest, 20 percent. All regions experienced a decrease in the robbery volume for 1997, 11 percent in the Northeast, 10 percent in the West, 5 percent in the South, and 2 percent in the Midwest.

In 1997 the national robbery rate was 186 per 100,000 people, 8 percent lower than in 1996. The 1997 robbery rate was 223 per 100,000 people in metropolitan areas, 72 in cities outside metropolitan areas, and 18 in rural areas. Robbery rates per 100,000 people decreased in all regions from 1996 to 1997.

While the types of robbery weapons vary, firearms were the weapons used in 40 percent of all robberies in 1997; strong-arm criminal tactics were used in 38 percent; knives or cutting instruments in 9 percent, and other dangerous weapons in the remaining 13 percent. From 1996 to 1997 robbery totals by weapons used declined for knives and other cutting instruments (9 percent), strong-arm tactics (8 percent), firearms (7 percent), and other dangerous weapons (6 percent).

In 1997, 88 percent of all robbery clearances (i.e., cases resolved through arrest) involved individuals under eighteen years of age. Eighteen-year-olds accounted for 17 percent of the suburban county clearances, 18 percent of those in the nation's cities, and 12 percent of those in rural county agencies. From 1996 to 1997, arrests for males for robbery were down 12 percent; arrests for females were up 2 percent; the robbery arrest rate for those eighteen or older decreased 17 percent; and juvenile robbery arrests increased 7 percent. In 1997, 65 percent of those arrested for robbery were under the age of twenty-five, and 90 percent were males; 57 percent of those arrested were African Americans, 41 percent were white, and the rest were of other races.

Physical Assault: Prevalence and Incidence. Physical assault includes a wide range of acts, including slapping or hitting to using a knife or gun. Research shows that physical assault is widespread and that the national incidence of physical assaults is underestimated. Approximately 1.9 million women and 3.2 million men are physically assaulted annually in the United States. Female victims averaged 3.1 assaults and male victims averaged 2.5 assaults per year, a rate that translates to approximately 5.9 million physical assaults perpetrated against women from November 1995 to May 1996.

Domestic Violence. Violence against women perpetrated by intimate partners gained national attention as a social problem during the 1970s. The NVAW revealed that women are significantly more likely than men to be victimized by intimate partners. The survey also found that approximately 1.5 million women and 834,700 men are raped or physically assaulted or both by an intimate partner annually in the United States.

In 1996 more than 50 percent of all murder victims knew their assailants, 13 percent were related, and 38 percent were acquainted. Fifteen percent of the victims were murdered by strangers, while the relationships among victims and offenders were unknown for 35 percent of the murders. Among all female murder victims in 1996, 30 percent were slain by their husbands or boyfriends, while only 3 percent of the male victims were killed by wives or girlfriends.

In their landmark study of 8,145 families, Murray Straus and Richard Gelles (1990) estimated that just over 16 percent of American couples experienced an incident of physical assault during 1985, which means that approximately 8.7 million couples were involved in spousal abuse. Victims, especially women who are physically assaulted, raped, or both, are likely be injured and to require medical attention. The NVAW found that in approximately one-third of all rapes and physical assaults perpetrated against women, the victim was injured. Of the estimated 6.8 million rapes and physical assaults perpetrated against women in the United States annually, 2.6 million will result in an injury to the victim, and 792,200 will result in the victim receiving some form of medical care. At least 20 percent of women seek emergency treatment as a consequence of battering.

Stalking. Stalking refers to a pattern of willful, malicious behavior. Stalking can include, but is not limited to, the following acts: lying in wait, surveillance, harassing phone calls, nonconsensual communication, and vandalism. While the definition of stalking varies from state to state, most states require that evidence show the stalking is not an isolated incident and that it occurred on at least two different occasions. Interest in stalking in the 1990s led to a number of prevention and intervention measures: passage of antistalking laws in all fifty states and the District of Columbia, and the development of a model antistalking code. Although the media have highlighted accounts of stalking involving celebrities and laws have been developed to deal with the problem, the data in this area are quite limited. According to the NVAW, approximately one million women and 371,000 men are stalked annually in the United States. Approximately 12.1 million women and 3.7 million men are stalked at some time in their lives.

Unofficial Measurements of Crime

Modern crime statistics are useful, but they do not provide the whole picture of the prevalence and incidence of crime. Academicians, criminal justice practitioners, and students of criminal justice must continually employ crime measurements that fall outside of official data. There are two primary sources of unofficial measurements of crime: victimization studies and self-report studies. The National Crime Victimization Surveys (NCVS) were designed in the mid-1960s to gather data about victims and to provide a comparative tool for gauging the accuracy of the Uniform Crime Reports. Victimization data are collected annually by the Bureau of Justice Statistics. Published as *Crime Victimization in the United States*, the NCVS use interview data assessing whether respondents have been victims of any of the FBI's index crimes (except murder and arson) and other crimes during the past six months, and their victimization experiences. The total sample size is roughly 66,000 households, containing 110,000 individuals over twelve years of age.

A major shortcoming of official data is that such statistics fail to account for undiscovered and unreported crimes (the dark figure of crime). The NCVS reveal that the official crime statistics reported in the UCR underestimate the total amount of crime to which individuals have been victims. The NCVS reports some 40 to 50 percent more crimes than are recorded in the UCR.

A second unofficial crime measurement is self-report surveys. The National Youth Survey began in 1976 to measure the extent to which people self-report criminal behavior and the types of crimes people are most likely to self-report. Most self-report studies have focused on youth crime and have been administered to schoolchildren in order to measure drinking behavior, illicit drug use, and smoking. Unlike official measurements, self-report data do not depend on the apprehension of the offender as a condition for measurement. Self-report studies reveal that much crime is hidden and that youth from all classes commit delinquent acts. In fact, self-report studies have revealed that more than 90 percent of all Americans have committed crimes for which they could have been imprisoned.

BIBLIOGRAPHY

Bohm, Robert, and Keith Haley. *Introduction to Criminal Justice.* New York: Glencoe, 1996.

Federal Bureau of Investigation. *Crime in the United States.* Washington, D.C.: U.S. Government Printing Office, 1995, 1996, 1997.

Hagen, Frank. *Introduction to Criminology.* Chicago: Nelson Hall, 1990.

Novello A. "A Medical Response to Violence." *Journal of America Medical Association* 267 (1992).

Reiss, Albert, and J. Roth. *Understanding and Preventing Violence.* Washington, D.C.: National Academy Press, 1993.

Savitz, Leonard. "Official Police Statistics and Their Limitations." In *Crime and Society,* edited by Leonard Savitz and Norma Johnston. New York: Wiley, 1978.

Siegel, Larry. *Criminology.* St. Paul, Minn.: West Publishing, 1995.

Skogan, Wesley. "Fear of Crime and Neighborhood Change." In *Communities and Crime,* edited by Albert Reiss and Michael Tonry. Chicago: University of Chicago Press, 1974.

Straus, Murray, and Richard Gelles. *Physical Violence in American Families.* New Brunswick, N.J.: Transaction Publishers, 1990.

Tjaden, Patricia, and Nancy Thoenne. "Prevalence, Incidence, and Consequences of Violence Against Women: Findings from the National Violence Against Women Survey." Washington, D.C.: National Institute of Justice and the Centers for Disease Control and Prevention, 1998.

IDA M. JOHNSON

See also **Methodologies of Violence Research; Statistics and Epidemiology; Uniform Crime Reports.**

INDEX CRIMES. *See* Legal Definitions of Crimes; Uniform Crime Reports.

INDIAN REMOVAL. *See* Trail of Tears.

INDIANS, AMERICAN. *See* American Indians.

INDUSTRIAL WORKERS OF THE WORLD

Founded in l905 by William "Big Bill" Haywood, Daniel De Leon, and Eugene Debs, the Industrial Workers of the World (IWW) was a radical union with the motto "an injury to one is an injury to all." The IWW was an international organization, with the goal of organizing unskilled and foreign-born workers in mass-production industries. The "Wobblies," as they were derisively called by Otis Chandler, publisher of the *Los Angeles Times*, were the target of enormous violence by corporate interests. During the early part of the twentieth century, members were tarred and feathered, beaten, jailed illegally, and burned out of their meeting halls.

The Wobblies flourished between 1905 and 1917. Although they were defamed in the press as promoting violence, their actual participation in violent attacks on employers was minimal and vastly exaggerated. However, some Wobbly literature advocated, without the permission of the union leadership, acts of workplace sabotage. Such advocacy encouraged isolated incidents involving damage to machinery and slowdowns in production. The Wobblies fought for free speech, which represented the right to organize, and members were often jailed as punishment for speaking out. What made the IWW truly threatening was not sabotage but its members' strong belief in the antagonism inherent in the relationship between employers and the working classes and their refusal to cooperate with capitalism.

An IWW leader, Elizabeth Gurley Flynn, organized textile workers in Paterson, New Jersey, in 1913. The IWW successfully organized loggers in 1917 and won the eight-hour day by blowing the whistle themselves after eight hours. After World War I began, the Wobblies were swept up in the Palmer raids (named for President Woodrow Wilson's attorney general Alexander Mitchell Palmer), which began in 1919 against immigrants and continued, against foreign born and native born, until the middle of 1920. The raids aimed to deport, jail, and harass all radical activists. After the government raids ended, vigilante action against radicals continued.

The attacks on the IWW in Centralia, Washington, were characteristic of the violence directed at the organization. In 1918 the IWW hall was raided, its records burned, its furniture stolen. Wobblies were beaten and arrested by government officials, the National Guard, and the American Legion. In 1919, on Armistice Day, the rebuilt IWW hall was again invaded, but this time shots were fired from inside the hall. Two of the invaders were killed by the IWW member Wesley Everest. Everest escaped through the rear entrance and was chased by the mob; he killed another attacker as they closed in on him. Everest was then kicked and beaten and dragged senseless to jail. During the night he was taken out, allegedly castrated, and lynched. Other Wobblies were tortured into false confessions; the torture drove the IWW member Lorens Robert into insanity. Seven Wobblies were sentenced to twenty-five to forty years in jail. Not one member of the mob that raided the hall, murdered Everest, or persecuted Roberts was ever punished. Years later, six jurors gave affidavits stating that their verdict had been the result of intimidation by soldiers who camped on the lawn of the courthouse; the jurors asserted that, had they known the full story, they would have voted for acquittal of the Wobbly defendants.

Although persecution of the Wobblies led to the virtual disintegration of the union by 1924, their militancy left a lasting impression on trade unionists who founded the Congress of Industrial Organizations a decade later. At the close of the twentieth century, the IWW continued as a small organization reaching out to workers in industries that had not previously been unionized. Other former Wobblies continued to work for social justice through a variety of political and social organizations. The IWW continued to organize the organized, in the United States, the British Isles, and Canada.

BIBLIOGRAPHY

Chaplin, Ralph. *Wobbly: The Rough and Tumble Story of an American Radical.* Chicago: University of Chicago Press, 1948.

Dubofsky, Melvyn. *We Shall Be All: A History of the Industrial Workers of the World.* Chicago: Quadrangle, 1969.

Renshaw, Patrick. *The Wobblies: The Story of Syndicalism in the United States.* Garden City, N.Y.: Doubleday, 1967.

LAUREN HELENE COODLEY

See also **Anarchism; Haywood, William; Labor and Unions; Red Scare; San Diego.**

INFANTICIDE AND NEONATICIDE

Few crimes evoke as much horror as the murder of an infant. Despite this horror, child murder has existed for centuries in many cultural contexts. Motives for child murder include illegitimacy, population control, superstition, inability to care for the child, greed, congenital defects in the child, and ritual sacrifice. The ancient Egyptians entombed live children to keep their parents company. Romans and Greeks sacrificed their children to the gods. In ancient Rome the child was viewed as property of the father, and *patria potestas* referred to the father's right to kill an unwanted offspring. In some instances parents left children with birth defects on dung heaps to be devoured by wild animals.

In the Middle Ages, children in Europe were purportedly buried alive in the foundations of buildings to bring luck. Children with birth defects were viewed as the product of consorting with Satan and were allowed to die. In Australian aboriginal culture, the maternal grandmother killed one of the twins to allow the mother to fully care for the surviving baby. Female children have been at particular risk of being killed simply for being unwanted. In China, where families have been limited to one child, female children have been drowned to allow the family to have a boy to pass on family lineage and to avoid paying for a dowry. In Japan the practice of killing newborns is called *mabaki,* which loosely translates to "thinning vegetable sprouts."

Infant Murder in the United States

Homicide is the fifth-leading cause of pediatric mortality in the United States. Children under one year old are at particular risk. It is this age group to which the term *infanticide* applies; *neonaticide* is the murder of a child under twenty-four hours old. In 1994, 290 children under one year old were murdered. A majority of these murders were filicides, defined as murder of a child by its parent. Mothers kill children under one year of age more frequently than do fathers.

According to the Federal Bureau of Investigation's Uniform Crime Reports (UCR), the reported rate of murder of children under one year old remained relatively stable in the 1980s and 1990s. The rate of neonaticide is 1.3 per 100,000 live births, the rate of infanticide 4.3 per 100,000 live births. Caution must be exercised in interpreting these data because of the possibility of unreported murders. Some researchers believe that a subgroup of babies reported to have died of Sudden Infant Death Syndrome (SIDS) is likely to have been deliberately smothered without detection.

The data about the relationship of neonaticide and abortion are inconclusive. The hypothesis that neonaticide is linked to the availability of abortion is supported by the decreased incidence overall of neonaticide since the 1973 *Roe v. Wade* decision legalizing abortion; it is also supported by the higher incidence of neonaticide in rural areas where abortion is unavailable. On the other hand, neonaticide is highest in the Northeast and the South; that the Northeast has easy access to abortion argues against the hypothesis.

Crime Characteristics

Neonaticide. According to the UCR, babies killed within their first twenty-four hours of life most often die at the hands of their mothers, who tend to be young, single, first-time parents. They rarely have a history of legal problems, psychiatric problems, or substance abuse. In most instances the child is not planned. The young mothers conceal their pregnancy from their families and may deny being pregnant to themselves. Usually giving birth alone, they betray few signs of difficulty until after killing the baby. The most common methods of killing newborns include drowning, particularly in toilets, smothering, strangling, and neglect (leaving the baby to die of exposure). More unusual methods include beating, poisoning, and burning. The killing is often denied after it is carried out. The mothers most often act alone, and in most instances the father of the baby is unaware of the neonaticide. The lower incidence of paternal neonaticide is related to the father's lack of motive or opportunity to participate. A notable exception is the 1996 case of Amy Grossberg and her high school sweetheart, Brian Peterson. The couple, both college freshmen and children of affluent suburban parents, went to a motel in Newark, Delaware, where Grossberg gave birth to a baby boy, who was placed in a dumpster by Peterson. The infant's body, with evidence of multiple blows to the head, was discovered after Grossberg sought medical attention for complications following her pregnancy. The couple pleaded guilty to manslaughter and were sentenced in July 1996; Grossberg was sentenced to two-and-a-half years in prison and Peterson to two.

Mothers who kill their newborn babies offer a variety of explanations for their crime once they are caught. They often express fear of the stigma and shame attached to having an illegitimate child. This fear prevents them from seeking help. For some women, neonaticide functions as a substitute for abortion or birth control. Some young women are so eager to please their parents that they fear rejection if they reveal their secret. Mothers who commit neonaticide are often passive, immature women capable of massive denial when confronted with an unwanted pregnancy. Some deny knowing of the pregnancy until the time of the baby's birth. They may view their fetus as a foreign body passing through them and never develop the usual maternal bonding. Absence of preparation for the birth often goes along with denial of pregnancy. Mothers who kill neonates may be detected when they come to emergency rooms with birth-related complications such as heavy bleeding, cramping, and undelivered placenta. Once confronted, the young mother usually admits to giving birth but shows little immediate emotion about her dead baby.

An example of alleged neonaticide that captured national attention is the case of Melissa Drexler, an eighteen-year-old senior at Lacey High School in New Jersey who gave birth to her baby while in the bathroom at her high school prom on 6 June 1997. Known as the "Prom Mom," Drexler was reported to have placed the infant in a plastic garbage bag, thrown the bag in the trash, and returned to the dance floor. Drexler was tried in October 1998 and sentenced to fifteen years in prison.

Infanticide. Children are at particular risk to be killed during their first year of life. The perpetrators of infanticide are most frequently mothers, with fathers second. The risk of a father killing his child rises significantly after the child attains the age of three. Young, unmarried women are at higher risk of killing their infant. Financial stress and emotional immaturity often play a role in infanticide, which is usually carried out in the home. Murdering parents most commonly act alone, although instances of couples murdering infants have been reported. The most common methods of infanticide are battering, smothering, strangling, and drowning. Although substance abuse is common among men who murder infants, women who kill their infants usually are not abusing substances at the time. Mental illness is more common in women who kill infants than in those who kill neonates. The incidence of maternal mental illness rises with the age of the child killed.

Women who kill infants may have psychotic or nonpsychotic motives. In the nineteenth century, British physicians spoke of "puerperal psychosis" or "lactational insanity" to explain motives of young mothers who murdered infants. A woman with psychotic depression may believe she must kill her baby to save it from suffering after her planned suicide. But there is little evidence to support a hormonal basis for such mental illness. Mothers with psychotic motives are more likely to confess, more likely to attempt suicide at the time of the crime, and more likely to have sought help or given warnings before the crime.

A young mother who beats her six-month-old to death because she is exasperated by the child's screaming is driven by a nonpsychotic motive. Nonpsychotic women who kill infants—often young, vulnerable, overwhelmed, and unsupported—may do so out of frustration or anger at their babies.

Munchausen Disease by Proxy, a syndrome wherein a caregiver causes illness in a child so as to gain attention, accounts for some cases of infanticide. For example, a young mother who brought her six-month-old to the hospital after multiple episodes of alleged respiratory distress was later detected, by means of a video camera secretly installed in the infant's hospital room, smothering her child on purpose. These "near death" episodes can go too far, resulting in a child's actual, if unintended, demise. SIDS has also been linked to infanticide. In one New York family, five babies were believed to have died of SIDS before the mother confessed to smothering her infants. Some researchers believe that infanticide is underreported and that many cases of SIDS deaths may actually be nonaccidental.

Legal Issues. In England the Infanticide Act of 1939 formally mandated that women charged with the death of their own children under one year be charged with manslaughter rather than murder. The act protected mothers, who were perceived as emotionally fragile and recovering from pregnancy. The United States has no comparable law. Yet, although women may be charged with murder in the deaths of infants, they are more often convicted of lesser offenses (negligent homicide, child abuse, child neglect). Less than a quarter of women who kill infants receive prison sentences. Men who kill infants receive longer sentences and offer fewer insanity defenses than their female counterparts.

Compared to perpetrators of other types of homicide, women who kill infants tend to get lighter sentences. In many instances they are released on bail prior to trial. Their families and communities are often empathetic and supportive during the judicial process. There is a low incidence of psychiatric hospitalization following neonaticide because, in fact, the majority of neonaticidal women do not have serious mental illness.

Women who kill their infants also tend to receive light sentences in comparison to other murderers and fathers perpetrating the same crime. The exception comes in rare instances when the victim is not the woman's natural offspring. In these cases, penalties are typically lengthy prison sentences. When mothers kill their own infants, society tends to view the mother with sympathy and often believes she has suffered enough for her actions. About a third of women who commit infanticide are mentally ill at the time of their offense; their rates of insanity pleas and subsequent psychiatric hospitalization are predictably higher than the rates for women who kill their newborn babies.

A variety of challenges confront prosecutors investigating homicide of children under one year old. In neonaticide the crime is often concealed, there are few witnesses, the body is disposed of, and the mother usually denies what occurred. In some instances mothers claim that a baby was stillborn or died during birth. In order to convict for murder, prosecutors must show that the baby was alive at birth and the mother killed it with an intentional, specific act. Forensic tests, such as examining lungs to see if the baby took a breath, are critical but not infallible in determining the baby's viability. The last difficulty arises from the fact that there is not an aggrieved party. The newborn is dead, its mother relieved, and the family focused on rebuilding their lives. According to Philip J. Resnick (1970), women who kill a newborn are not likely to repeat the offense unless their first offense is undetected and unpunished.

Cases of infanticide pose similar difficulties. Mothers may claim to have tripped when carrying the infant, to have found the baby dead, or to have discovered the child choking. Communities may be supportive of young mothers facing charges for killing their newborn or infant. The women do not "look like" murderers and are often not seen as a threat to society. A common belief that women who kill their own infants "must be crazy" helps to explain lenient sentences.

Prevention

Neonaticide, which usually occurs without warning and with no sign of mental illness, is particularly difficult to prevent. The absence of substance abuse or legal difficulties among perpetrators makes detection by the criminal justice system unlikely. Many teenage mothers who kill their newborns are described as "perfect daughters." Access to birth control, sex education, and a safe environment to discuss sexual issues may help to decrease neonaticide.

An increased focus on psychiatric symptoms during the postpartum period may help prevent women at risk of harming their babies from actually doing so. Women who batter their infants to death sometimes have prior contact with Child Protective Services or the criminal justice system. Increased attention on minimizing danger in the home (substance abuse, domestic violence) and developing programs to support young mothers would decrease rates of infanticide by battering. These steps are also likely to reduce infant abuse and neglect, which are far more common than infant murder.

BIBLIOGRAPHY

d'Orban, P. T. "Women Who Kill Their Children." *British Journal of Psychiatry* 134 (1979).

Jason, Janine, et al. "Homicide as a Cause of Pediatric Mortality in the United States." *Pediatrics* 72, no. 2 (August 1983).

Lewis, Catherine F., Madelon V. Baranoski, Josephine A. Buchanan, Elissa P. Benedek. "Factors Associated with Weapon Use in Maternal Filicide." *Journal of Forensic Sciences* 43, no. 3 (May 1998).

Resnick, Phillip J. "Child Murder by Parents: A Psychiatric Review of Filicide." *American Journal of Psychiatry* 126, no. 3 (September 1969).

———. "Murder of the Newborn: A Psychiatric Review of Neonaticide." *American Journal of Psychiatry* 126, no. 10 (April 1970).

Scott, P. D. "Parents Who Kill Their Children." *Medicine, Science and the Law* 13, no. 2 (April 1973).

Silverman, Robert A., and Leslie W. Kennedy. "Women Who Kill Their Children." *Violence and Victims* 3, no. 2 (1988).

CATHERINE F. LEWIS
PHILLIP J. RESNICK

See also **Abortion; Child Abuse; Women: Women Who Kill.**

INTERGENERATIONAL TRANSMISSION OF VIOLENCE

Harsh punishments, child abuse, and paternal criminality presage serious criminal behavior, according to relationships demonstrated in studies (in Scandinavia, Great Britain, the United States, and Australia) of children as they grow to maturity. Studies of delinquency are peppered with reports that crime tends to run in families. Abused children frequently become abusing parents. Children who witness their parents being violent to each other often become partners in violent relationships. Longitudinal studies (involving the repeated observation or examination of a set of subjects over time with respect to one or more variables) tie childhood aggressiveness to similar behavior of parents and then find comparable behavior in the subjects' offspring up to twenty-two years later. Aggressiveness and criminality among the parents of delinquents have been reported in Canada, the United States, Great Britain, Sweden, and Finland. In short, having a family history of violence is among the most reliable predictors that offspring will become violent.

Nature and Nurture

Although there is widespread agreement that similarities exist between generations with regard to violence, no such agreement has been reached regarding the sources of that connection. Until recently, genetic and environmental factors for transmission were typically treated as providing alternative and conflicting explanations for violence. That view is beginning to change as social scientists increasingly recognize that biological processes do not operate in environmental vacuums, that social and physical processes alter when associated with different types of organisms (for example, alcohol affects alcoholics and nonalcoholics differently, and loud noises affect hyperactive and nonhyperactive children differently), and that environmental conditions influence biological processes. Before turning to a discussion of the possible interacting processes that contribute to violence, it will be useful to consider some of the evidence adduced to show a genetic component to the transmission of violence.

Heritability

Adoption Studies. In the closing quarter of the twentieth century, studies of adopted children and of twins have been used to investigate the role of genetic factors in the transmission of behaviors related to crime. The adoption studies typically compare the aggressive or criminal behavior of sons with the behavior of an adoptive and a biological father in what has become known as a cross-fostering technique. Many of these studies have been carried out using a sample from Denmark, where adoption and criminal records have been carefully kept over many years but where there is little social variation. These studies show greater concordance in criminality between sons and their biological fathers than between sons and their adoptive fathers, but the concordance in violent behavior was almost the same for biological and adoptive fathers. Nevertheless, genetic contributions to intergenerational similarities regarding violence have been proposed by C. R. Cloninger, Sarnoff A. Mednick, and Adrian Raine (and their colleagues), among others. These explanations have been based on the possible heritability of hyperactivity, sinistrality (e.g., left-handedness), slow resting heart rate, and dampened autonomic (involuntary) reactivity.

Twin Studies. Studies of twins by C. Edelbrock and his colleagues (among others) have been used to tease out a genetic effect by comparing the similarity of behavior in monozygotic (single egg) twins with the similarity of behavior in dizygotic (two eggs) twins. Yet the comparisons rely on phenotypes (that is, properties produced by the individual's genetic constitution and the environment and their interaction), not genes, and causal inferences are specific to the population under study at the time they are studied. The technique has resulted in identifying heritability for hyperactivity, whether hyperactivity is rated by fathers, mothers, or teachers. Several studies also report heritability for such related concepts as activity level, impulsivity, and desire for excitement. Additional suggestions regarding heritable sources of violence have rested on empirical relationships between aggression and hormones, criminality and low autonomic arousal, and difficulties in learning found among hyperactive and conduct-disordered children.

Behavioral Genetics. The development of a field called behavioral genetics (after World War II) has produced research that attempts to answer the question "How much of a trait is inherited?" Answers to this quantitative question will differ in relation to the populations being studied, the measures used, and the variation to be explained. Behavioral geneticists parse sources of various classes of behavior into genetic and environmental components. The most commonly used measure of heritability, h2, was devised by D. S. Falconer. The formula for calculating h2 assumes that heritability can be ascertained by doubling the difference obtained after subtracting similarities in some characteristic measured for dizygotic twin pairs from similarities for the same characteristic measured for monozygotic twin pairs.

The heritability formula rests on several assumptions. One is that dizygotic twins share 50 percent of their genes; this assumption ignores the tendency of people to mate with others who are similar in terms of religion, ethnicity, and social status. Assortative mating (nonrandom mating) results in greater genetic similarity for siblings than would be expected by the distribution of genes at random. The heritability formula also assumes that the similarity of environments for twins who look alike is no greater than the similarity of environments for twins who do not look alike. Yet two people who are difficult to distinguish are more likely to be treated similarly than are two people who can be easily distinguished. Among other conditions, differential attractiveness influences interactions. Dizygotic twins will be differently attractive in larger measure than monozygotic twins; therefore, dizygotic twins are likely to be exposed to greater variation in environment.

The heritability formula also assumes that the effects of genetic and environmental conditions are additive; that is, this formula does not account for the possibility of interaction between these two types of conditions. This assumption, too, is dubious. Experimental studies based on children behaving according to a predesignated script indicate that parents respond differently to apparently bright and apparently dull children. Therefore, environments and their effects differ in response to differences in possibly genetically determined intelligence. Similar interaction effects can be seen in relation to childhood hyperactivity, aggressiveness, and impulsivity. That is, genetic effects on behavior influence environmental responses even as environmental responses have an impact on subsequent behavior.

Calculations using the heritability formula make the assumption that variations around an average value for a characteristic are constant throughout the range of that characteristic. For example, the calculations assume that compliant infants are treated in the same way as aggressive ones, that differences in maternal behavior are unaffected by biological deformities, and that responses to infants who cry a lot are similar to those to infants who do not. Some evidence shows, however, that genetically disadvantaged infants are exposed to greater variability of environments than are their normal peers. One interpretation of this fact is that caretakers differ considerably in their responses to infants who are premature, deformed, or emotionally unstable, whereas they tend to have common responses to unexceptional infants.

Differences that depend on genes would be constant across environments. Yet the value given heritability using the Falconer formula varies in relation to environmental conditions. In a homogeneous environment, other things being equal, heritability's influence will be large.

The behavioral genetic approach essentially assigns to environment what is left over after identifying genetic impact. Few behavior geneticists actually measure relevant environmental features. They ignore the fact that genetically determined characteristics require certain environments for realization. For example, the azalea will not grow without sufficient shade, warmth, and moisture. In an environment where these factors are present, differences among plants will appear to be entirely genetic. On the other hand, where there are variations in shade, warmth, and moisture, genetically identical plants will develop differently.

Mostly working with nonhuman animals, researchers have identified the organic compound serotonin (which is responsible for transmitting impulses between nerve cells and regulating cyclic body processes) as a probable locus for genes involved in the transmission of a propensity for violence. Serotonin inhibits aggression and impulsivity. Although serotonin function in humans is difficult to study, preliminary analyses suggest that it plays a role in the transmission of violence.

Neuropsychologists have identified two types of deficits related to violence. First, violent people tend to have problems with what neuropsychologists call the executive function. This function is carried out in the frontal lobes, an area of the brain responsible for self-control and judgment. Second, violent people tend to show deficits in verbal intelligence. The cumulative effects of these deficits can result in academic failure, attachment failure (inadequate interpersonal commitments), and associations with peers likely to encourage violence. The neuropsychological deficits may be inherited or may be a consequence of the ways violent children have been reared.

Social and Physical Environments

Some combination of environmental and genetic conditions most likely accounts for the transmission of violence within families. Thus, for example, the fact that most parents treat boys and girls differently may be responsible for some of the sex differences in rates of violent behavior. Unfortunately, efforts to understand how the environment interacts with various biological factors in the production of violence have seldom received more than lip service. The Pittsburgh Youth Study is among the rare exceptions. That study indicates that good neighborhoods reduce the risks of antisocial behavior among boys who are neurologically healthy but not among those who are neurologically impaired.

A variety of social conditions should be considered as possible explanations for the high degree of concordance between parental and offspring violence. These social conditions involve disciplinary practices, modeling of interpersonal behavior, choice of mates, and selection of environments conducive to violence.

Disciplinary Practices. Criminal violence tends to be promoted by harsh physical punishments. A variety of studies have shown that the types of discipline a parent uses in attempting to bring about desired behavior in a child is strongly influenced by the discipline that the parent experienced as a child. If parents who are violent have experienced harsh discipline and use similar types of discipline in rearing their own children, then this continuity in child-rearing techniques would provide a basis for reproducing violence in the children of such parents. Teaching parents to use consistent, nonphysical punishments has reduced the amount of physical aggression in offspring, though the degree to which such changes in child-rearing techniques affect the intergenerational transmission of violence has not been assessed.

Modeling of Interpersonal Behavior. Using laboratory techniques, psychologists have repeatedly shown the powerful effects of behavioral modeling. Many of the studies (summarized in A. Bandura 1986) have adults perform bizarre aggressive actions (such as hitting a large inflated doll) and then watch to see the conditions under which children imitate the actions. Children learn to imitate behavior even when they do not immediately practice what they see. They learn about behavior through verbal descriptions as well as visual cues, so imitation can occur even if they do not actually witness violent events. Violent adults are likely to expose their children to parental conflict, which in a general sense conveys the information that it is normal for people to inflict pain on each other. More specifically, parents who are abusive to each other teach their children a style of interaction that the children may adopt when they become adults. Exposure to parental domestic violence figures heavily in the backgrounds of both victims and perpetrators of domestic violence, who may have learned marital roles through observation.

Abused children also have heightened risks for becoming violent. Several factors may account for this. First, abused children realize that their feelings do not influence their abusers. Second, abused children tend to be insensitive to their own pain; they are unlikely, therefore, to learn from punishments. Third, abused children lack empathy with others who are injured. They seem to learn to ignore pain and become violent through a lack of caring about how their actions affect themselves or others.

Choice of Mate. Violent men tend to marry aggressive women. Aggressive women tend to use harsh punishments and to be erratic in their discipline. Children of such parents receive the type of discipline most conducive to violence. In this way, the choice of mate contributes to the continuity of violence through generations.

Selection of Environments. Violent adults tend to have difficulties keeping jobs and marriages. Thus, they are likely to live in low-status communities, and their children are likely to be reared in single-parent homes. Low-status communities have bars where fights tend to be common. Children reared of single-parent homes frequently go unsupervised when not in school. Both conditions contribute to a heightened likelihood of violence for the offspring of violent adults.

Conclusion

Although violence in one generation tends to be repeated in subsequent generations, attempts to demonstrate a genetic link for this continuity have been, at best, only marginally successful. Nevertheless, it seems likely that biological deficits contribute to the transmission of violence. Perhaps more important, the transmission of violence between generations seems also to rest on concomitant circumstances that may, in fact, be altered to help end the continuity of violence from one generation to another.

BIBLIOGRAPHY

Bandura, Albert. *Social Foundations of Thought and Action: A Social Cognitive Theory.* Englewood Cliffs, N.J.: Prentice-Hall, 1986.

Cicchetti, Dante, and Vicki Carlson, eds. *Child Maltreatment: Theory and Research on the Causes and Consequences of Child Abuse and Neglect.* New York: Cambridge University Press, 1989.

Cloninger, C. R., and I. I. Gottesman. "Genetic and Environmental Factors in Antisocial Behavior Disorders." In *The Causes of Crime: New Biological Approaches,* edited by Sarnoff A. Mednick, Terrie E. Mofitt, and Susan A. Stack. New York: Cambridge University Press, 1987.

Crowell, David H., Ian M. Evans, and Clifford R. O'Donnell, eds. *Childhood Aggression and Violence: Sources of Influence, Prevention, and Control.* New York: Plenum, 1987.

Edelbrock, C., R. Rende, R. Plomin, and L. A. Thompson. "A Twin Study of Confidence and Problem Behavior in Childhood and Early Adolescence." *Journal of Child Psychology and Psychiatry and Allied Disciplines* 36, no. 5 (1995): 775–785.

Ferris, Craig F., and Thomas Grisso, eds. *Understanding Aggressive Behavior in Children.* New York: New York Academy of Sciences, 1996.

Mednick, Sarnoff A., Terrie E. Moffitt, and Susan A. Stack, eds. *The Causes of Crime: New Biological Approaches.* New York: Cambridge University Press, 1987.

Mednick, Sarnoff A., W. F. Gabrielli, and B. Hutchings. "Genetic Factors in the Etiology of Certain Behavior." In *The Causes of Crime: New Biological Approaches,* edited by Sarnoff A. Mednick, Terrie E. Moffitt, and Susan A. Stack. New York: Cambridge University Press, 1987.

Plomin, Robert, and Gerald E. McClearn, eds. *Nature, Nurture, and Psychology.* Washington, D.C.: American Psychological Association, 1958.

Raine, Adrian, Patricia A. Brennan, David P. Farrington, and Sarnoff A. Mednick, eds. *Biosocial Bases of Violence.* New York: Plenum, 1997.

Stattin, H., H. Janson, I. Klackenberg-Larsson, and D. Magnusson. "Corporal Punishment in Everyday Life: An Intergenerational Perspective." In *Coercion and Punishment in Long-Term Perspectives,* edited by Joan McCord. New York: Cambridge University Press, 1995.

Stoff, David M., and Robert B. Cairns, eds. *Aggression and Violence: Genetic, Neurobiological, and Biosocial Perspectives.* Mahwah, N.J.: Lawrence Erlbaum, 1996.

Straus, M. A. "Discipline and Deviance: Physical Punishment of Children and Violence and Other Crime in Adulthood." *Social Problems* 38, no. 2 (May 1991): 133–154.

JOAN McCORD

See also **Bosket Family; Developmental Factors; Genetics; Nature vs. Nurture; Sociobiology.**

INTERNET

The Internet is a powerful medium. One can have instant access to world-class art collections, great books, and various methods of instant communication. With its reach extending across the globe, the Internet allows anyone with the proper setup to tap into a plethora of information on virtually any topic, from those provided by academic institutions and government agencies to those supplied by unnamed individuals. With almost instantaneous speed the Internet, especially the World Wide Web (a segment of the Internet that offers a "hypertext" multimedia environment), also contains a plenitude of content considered offensive or harmful, including pornography. Cybersex and its sometime cousin, cyberviolence, seem all too real to many people, but violence on the Internet can roughly be classified into the representational and the real. Although representational violence seems the most common on the Internet, real violence does occur, especially in the form of cyberterrorism. In fact, the representational can cross over to the real quickly and easily as demonstrated by the Nuremberg Files, a Web site that implicitly encourages the violence against abortion providers.

Representational Cyberviolence

Representational violence on the Internet refers to words and images that are abusive and that violate the standards of civil behavior. It principally takes the forms of sexual and prejudicial expression. As in the real world, cybersex and cyberhate invariably bring up issues of constitutional free

---

The Nuremberg Files

The Nuremberg Files, an antiabortion Web site, first appeared on the Internet in 1994. It featured personal information about abortion providers all over the United States, including the doctors' names, home addresses, photos, and sometimes even the names and ages of the doctors' children. In addition to images of mangled fetuses and dripping blood, the site boasted a handy checklist of what its authors called "baby butchers." The healthy doctors were listed in black. Those who had been wounded were listed in gray, and the murdered ones were crossed out. In 1995, Planned Parenthood and several targeted doctors sued the site's backers, charging that it illegally incited violence. In February 1999 a Portland, Oregon, jury agreed with the plaintiffs and handed them a $107 million verdict. The pro-choice movement hailed the verdict as a new weapon in the fight against those who oppose abortion with violence. As of March 1999 the Nuremberg Files was still looking for a home on the Internet, since its host pulled the plug on it after the Portland judgment.

---

speech and the government's legal obligation to protect children and minorities. The already vexing issue of whether a communications medium such as the Internet actually causes physical violence is further complicated on the Internet by a number of additional factors. The sheer volume of information makes control virtually impossible. Estimates from the 1990s suggest that twelve tetrabytes of accessible data were available on the Internet—roughly equivalent to twenty thousand copies of the complete *Oxford English Dictionary*—and this figure is growing exponentially. There is also the issue of ownership. Even though copyrighted information exists on the Internet from authorized individuals, academic institutions, government agencies and commercial entities, most of the information that is freely exchanged on the Internet in discussion groups and personal Web sites is in fact anonymous or from individuals assuming different identities. With that much information available and most of it having no discernible ownership, there cannot be any real control. The volume of information available and the uncertainty of ownership complicate the problem of jurisdiction. Because the Internet is open to all, and because it is decentralized and worldwide, one government's action to regulate the potential for violence on the Internet will clash with another country's sovereignty. Many founders and promoters of the Internet have argued that its very nature resists control or censorship. The denizens of cyberspace have resisted government restrictions. They argue that because the Internet differs from traditional media, a wide spectrum of contents and viewpoints should be tolerated and even encouraged on-line, especially on the freewheeling, anarchistic Usenet. Since the Internet opens the historic opportunity for almost anyone to express his or her views to a mass audience at a low cost, the strong libertarian bent of the Internet culture vows to fight state control in the workings of the Internet from objectionable content to the encryption of sensitive data.

Cybersex. The passage of the Communications Decency Act (CDA) by both houses of the Congress in 1995—and the Supreme Court's ruling on its unconstitutionality in 1996—raised public consciousness of on-line obscenity. How pervasive is pornography on-line? *Interactive Week,* an industry publication, projected in March 1996 that the Internet had about ten thousand adult sites that generate one billion dollars a year in sales (Hayes 1997). In response to potential governmental regulations, the on-line adult industry began taking measures to protect children and other unsuspecting adults from entering their sites inadvertently by enforcing a strict registration scheme with a required credit card number. The on-line adult industry is probably not the worst offender in the link between sex and violence, especially sexual violence against children. The real on-line predators are the individuals posting pictures of nude children on their Web sites, swapping stories or fantasies of having sex with children in newsgroups, and discussing their unlawful acts in chat rooms (a part of the Internet that allows live conversation with multiple users). Yet there is also an unholy alliance between those individuals and the on-line adult industry. "A good 40 percent of the messages sent to Internet newsgroups established for software downloads are 'spam' messages touting adult Web sites," according to one estimate by an Internet services provider (Hayes 1997). (*Spam* refers to unsolicited advertisements on the Internet, usually sent to many e-mail addresses or newsgroups at once.) Even though the number of children being victimized by means of Internet chat rooms is small—only twenty-three incidents involving chat rooms were reported between 1994 and 1996, according to the National Center for Missing and Exploited Children—the danger of potential violence to children cannot be underestimated. While the CDA may be too broad in its attempt to curb indecency on the Internet, the voluntary actions taken by the on-line community as a whole to rate the content of the Internet could be a viable step toward taming the wild world of the Internet.

One such rating system, the Platform for Internet Content Selection (PICS), has been developed. PICS can act as a kind of peer-review system and can be used to guide users toward useful sites and aid in parental advisory of children. The World Wide Web Consortium first released the PICS specification in December 1995, and some Internet-filtering tools implemented it three years later. PICS is being adopted as a very open-ended standard, offering flexibility but creating an environment in which site developers can rate themselves using any of several competing systems. Rating systems from the Recreational Software Advisory Council and SafeSurf are designed primarily to restrict access to undesirable sites, but ratings may also measure the usefulness of specific sites and pages to help users become more productive on the Web.

The home page of a white supremacist Internet site.
GAMMA/LIAISON AGENCY

Cyberhate. Although child pornography on the Internet is unlawful and information related to it can be unambiguously denied, cyberhate is an entirely different situation. While there is no accurate data as to the number of hate Web sites, an informal poll by the author revealed thousands of Web pages set up by numerous groups promoting bigotry and violence against racial and sexual minorities. The presence of hate on the Internet is becoming increasingly bothersome to many users. One such hate group, the Carolinian Lords of the Caucasus, whose Web site features a burning cross and boasts of being on the forefront of the Aryan domination of the Internet, regularly invades innocuous newsgroups with race-baiting messages, harassing over half a dozen groups including alt.fan.barry-manilow, the newsgroup for fans of the popular singer. Virulently anti-Semitic passages such as "Americans, don't let the Jews enter America.... You have to get rid of the Jews.... If the Jews remain in America a hundred years, they will be dominating the economy.... They spoil public life, they spoil your morals...." appeared on the Internet and were purported to be the words of Benjamin Franklin in an address to the Constitutional Convention, when in fact they were delivered by one Rajib Najib in 1990 at the annual convention of the Muslim Arab Youth Association in Kansas City. The Internet has become the newest purveyor of prejudice in America; its misuse has opened a free and universal platform for ignorance and hatred. The Simon Wiesenthal Center, one of the world's largest Jewish human rights organizations, for example, has asked Internet providers to refuse messages that "promote racism, anti-Semitism, mayhem, and violence" (Lopez 1997). The center sent out hundreds of letters to Internet providers to help draft a code of ethics that would help curb cyberhate.

Besides child pornography and cyberhate, the Internet is host to countless other images and messages that are objectionable and violent. From pictures of serial killers to videos of postmortem violence to newsgroups dedicated to mayhem, the Internet serves as a new outlet for popular culture's propensity for violent content. Moreover, the Internet can also be at the forefront of championing violent popular culture. The violent television cartoon show *South Park*, for example, evolved from several short movies that were circulated on the Internet.

Real Cyberviolence

Not all cyberviolence is purely representational, even though representational violence can cause real-world damage to people and property. As commercial activity is expanded on the Internet, it will become a greater target for terrorists. In this new age of cyberspace, the traditional terrorist method of assassinating a nation's leader or bombing significant buildings will become less and less attractive. A single attack on electronic switching can produce far more dramatic, long-lasting, and cruel results. In all electronic networks, a "bottleneck" area usually exists through which all transactions must pass. Imagine one such electronic switch to be the Federal Reserve's electronic network in Culpepper, Virginia, which handles all federal funds and transactions. Manipulation or destruction of this system by terrorists could bring about financial chaos in the United States as well as around the world. The Internet, in connecting all types of electronic systems and being open, makes all of us vulnerable to this new brand of terrorism, whose focus on information warfare could be as destructive as biological and chemical weapons.

Cyberspace can be a wonderful tool of democracy and commerce, but there is the potential danger that the ease of access will spread violence and hatred and undermine the more noble objectives of this global communications network.

BIBLIOGRAPHY

Hayes, David. "Pornography's Presence on the Internet Is Unlikely to Be Unfettered." *Kansas City Star,* 23 June 1997.

Lopez, Claude-Anne. "Prophet and Loss: Benjamin Franklin, the Jews, and Cyber-bigotry." *New Republic,* 27 January 1997.

Lopez, Claude-Anne, and Eamonn Sullivan. "Web Ratings Invite as Well as Deter." *PC Week,* 8 July 1996.

Trebilcock, Bob. "Child Molesters on the Internet: Are They in Your Home?" *Redbook,* April 1997.

W. CHERRY LI

See also **Bombings and Bomb Scares; Photography; Pornography; Television.**

IRISH AMERICANS

The history of ethnic violence in America has long included attacks on and by Irish Americans. As early as 1798 and as recently as the school busing controversy in South Boston in the late 1970s, there have been examples of collective violence in America involving the Irish.

The causes of this violence can be traced to two sources. First, Irish immigrants brought with them a strong strain of antiauthoritarianism and a faith in violence born out of the sectarian controversies that had marred their homeland for centuries. Second, the Irish, especially the Catholic Irish, ran into prejudice and discrimination that often relegated them to poverty and substandard housing. The result was that the Irish were frequently cast into conflict with themselves and with other ethnic and racial groups.

Holidays offered one arena of conflict. During the 1790s Protestant Americans began parading on St. Patrick's Day with effigies they called "stuffed paddies" to insult Irish pride. In 1799 local Irish residents attacked one such procession in New York City. One person died in the ensuing melee. A similar conflict erupted in 1806 in New York City when a Protestant gang called the Highbinders decided to harass a Christmas Eve service at a Catholic church. Although there was no major confrontation that night, rumors spread the next day that the Highbinders planned to enter the predominantly Irish Five Points neighborhood to harass the Catholics. In an effort to avoid an Irish battle with nativists, some eighteen watchmen went to Augustus Street in the heart of that neighborhood on Christmas night. When one watchman attempted to disarm an Irishman, who apparently thought he was defending his home from Protestants, a riot broke out in which a watchman was killed. In the 1820s and 1830s Protestant and Catholic Irish clashed with each other several times over the celebration of the Battle of the Boyne on 12 July (this holiday commemorates William of Orange's 1690 victory over the Catholic Irish). In 1870 three people were killed and seventeen wounded in an Irish Catholic attack on an Orange Protestant procession. The next year the governor of New York, who was not a Catholic sympathizer, decided to ensure the protection of a similar Orange parade by providing a militia escort consisting of twelve regiments. The Irish Catholics were not intimidated. Someone fired at a soldier. In the ensuing street battle two policemen and two soldiers died. A third soldier died later from injuries incurred at the riot. The military, however, had greater firepower. Fifty-seven civilians died in the riot. Twenty-eight had been born in Ireland. The ethnicity of most of the remaining fatalities remains unclear, but they were probably Catholic Irish Americans or Catholic sympathizers.

Political issues offered another arena for ethnic conflict. Starting in the 1820s and 1830s the Irish often became associated with Democratic Party machines. In some instances, as in the 1834 election in New York City, this meant that the Irish engaged in fisticuffs with their political opponents. In other instances, however, the degree of violence could be more serious. In Philadelphia in 1844, for example, political debates over the use of a Protestant Bible in the public schools created a furor. The American Republicans, a nativist political group, organized several rallies in support of the Protestant Bible. On 6 May they convened a meeting in a schoolyard in the predominately Irish Kensington district. A riot broke out when Protestants sought cover in a rainstorm at Nanny Goat Market in the very center of an Irish neighborhood. One member of the nativist crowd was killed. Fueled by resentment over that death, a larger riot erupted in July when nativists decided to attack a Catholic church. The militia was called out to protect Catholic property, and in the ensuing street battles at least twelve were killed.

During the 1850s the American, or Know-Nothing, Party often focused its attacks on election day on the Irish. In Baltimore several gangs allied themselves with the nativists, including the Blood Tubs, who obtained their name for capturing a would-be Irish voter, tossing him in a tub of cow blood (obtained from butchers), and chasing him through the streets with blood-drenched knives. Nativist gangs engaged in street battles with Irish Democrats that occasionally resulted in fatalities. Similar nativist sentiments underpinned the vigilante movement in San Francisco, which purged Irish politicians from the city administration in 1856.

Labor was another important area of conflict. The Irish were often recruited to dig the canals,

A woodcut depicting the Irish Orange Riots in New York, 1871. CORBIS/BETTMANN

construct the roads, and build the railroads that became so essential to American economic development in the nineteenth century. But these endeavors were also marked by an exploitation that led to resentment and violent conflicts. Canal contractors, for example, would delay paying their workers, and then they would bring in other laborers, recruited from another part of Ireland or from another ethnic group, and watch the two groups erupt into fighting. The new and old groups of workers recognized the threat to employment that each represented to the other. Fisticuffs might then lead to rioting. At that point the contractor would dismiss all the workers and use the violence as an excuse not to pay them. The Irish also took a lead in labor radicalism after the Civil War. The secret organization known as the Molly Maguires created a reign of terror intended to bring justice and fair wages to the Pennsylvania minefields from the mid-1860s until 1877, when Pinkerton detectives broke the organization, and with it the nascent labor movement in the state.

The Irish often found themselves competing for jobs and housing with African Americans. This competition resulted in violent confrontations ranging from minor clashes to larger disturbances. The Irish played a central role in the New York City draft riot of 1863, which began as a working-class protest against an unfair draft law that allowed the rich to buy their way out of being drafted. Many Irish feared that a Union victory would lead to a wholesale exodus of freedmen from the South to the North. Such a migration would threaten the job security of Irish laborers who remained trapped on the bottom rung of the occupational ladder. The riots began with attacks on the draft headquarters, spread to attacks on the homes of the rich and on Republican newspapers, and ultimately included an assault on the city's black population and its institutions. The army had to be brought in to restore order. Although several blacks were murdered, at least one hundred rioters, many of whom were Irish, were killed. More recently, Irish and African American animosity underpinned the tension in the busing controversy in South Boston in the 1970s. The Irish of South Boston objected to the threat to their neighborhood identity posed by a plan to integrate public schools through busing. Fights between black and Irish youths broke out at schools, and white and black mobs attacked one another in the streets.

Through the twentieth century Irish Americans became more integrated into the mainstream of American society. As such, they were less often the targets of and actors in outbreaks of collective violence. The problems in South Boston were more the exception than the rule.

BIBLIOGRAPHY

Gilje, Paul A. *Rioting in America*. Bloomington: University of Indiana Press. 1996.

Gordon, Michael. *The Orange Riots: Irish Political Violence in New York City, 1870 and 1871*. Ithaca, N.Y.: Cornell University Press, 1993.

Knobel, Dale T. *Paddy and the Republic*. Middletown, Conn.: Wesleyan University Press, 1986.

Wakin, Edward. *Enter the Irish American*. New York: Crowell, 1976.

PAUL A. GILJE

See also **Catholics; Draft Riots; Immigration.**

ITALIAN AMERICANS

The Italians' reputation for violence antedated their mass migration to the United States. Anglo-American writings on Italy historically had been replete with bloodthirsty and treacherous characters. In the nineteenth century, travel accounts and novels featured picturesque *banditti* with stilettos, such as in W. J. C. Moens's *English Travelers and Italian Brigands: A Narrative of Capture and Captivity*. American commentaries on the Risorgimento (the movement for the unification of Italy, 1830–1870) emphasized the brutal, vengeful behavior of Italian mobs. The Italian penchant for violence was thus a central theme of traditional Anglo-American "Italophobia."

Reports about the criminal Camorra and Mafia preceded the arrival of large numbers of Italian immigrants in the United States. However, the alleged assassination by mafiosi of the police chief of New Orleans, David Hennessy, in 1890 and the subsequent lynching of eleven Italians (six of whom had been acquitted, three of whom had mistrials declared because of hung juries, and two of whom had not been brought to trial) focused national attention on this reputed Sicilian criminal association. From that date on, Italians were suspected of sinister, conspiratorial activity. From the cartoons of the 1890s to the films of the 1990s, the Italian mobster has been a stock ethnic stereotype of American popular culture.

More than any other European immigrant group, Italians were victims of mob violence. In

Strikers from Lawrence, Massachusetts, many of whom were Italian immigrants, paraded through the streets of New York City to protest a 1912 wage reduction for workers from one of the largest textile mills in the United States. CORBIS

addition to the New Orleans incident, other lynchings occurred in Louisiana, Mississippi, Colorado, Florida, and Illinois. In some cases, Italian merchants had earned the enmity of whites because they served a black clientele. The in-between status of Italians, their ambiguous place in the race hierarchy, made them particularly vulnerable to such attacks.

Labor Violence

Recruited into the industrial proletariat, often as strikebreakers, Italian workers suffered aggression from Irish and other labor competitors. They were also forcibly kept in a condition of peonage on isolated work sites. When Italians organized, they in turn vented their wrath on scabs of other ethnicities. Armed clashes between Italian strikers and public and private police were a recurring feature of the labor history of the early twentieth century. Anna Lo Pizzo, killed during the Lawrence, Massachusetts, strike of 1912, was but one of many casualties of the industrial wars. In a 1914 strike in Ludlow, Colorado, forty-five Italians, including two women and ten children, were killed when National Guardsmen fired with machine guns on

the strikers' tent colony. Numerous Italians also met violent ends in industrial disasters, such as the 1909 Cherry, Illinois, mine explosion and the 1911 fire at the Triangle Shirtwaist Company's factory in New York City.

Among the Italian immigrants were radicals opposed to the capitalist system. Some, such as the followers of Luigi Galleani (known as Galleanisti), embraced direct action. Several heads of European states were killed by Italian anarchists in the 1890s: the French president Sadi Carnot, 29 June 1894, by Sante Caserio; the Spanish prime minister Antonio Cánovas, 8 August 1897, by Michelle Angiolillo; and Empress Elizabeth of Austria, 10 September 1898, by Luigi Luccheni. In 1900 Gaetano Bresci, a silk worker and anarchist, returned to Italy from Paterson, New Jersey, to assassinate King Umberto I. Thereafter, American journalists repeatedly depicted coveys of Italian anarchists conspiring to commit terrorist acts.

During World War I, the U.S. government's campaign against foreign radicals intensified with mass arrests, imprisonments, and deportations. In response, the Galleanisti launched a series of bombings, which culminated in the Wall Street bombing on 16 September 1920 in which thirty-three persons were killed. Among those caught in the antiradical repression were Nicola Sacco and Bartolomeo Vanzetti. Although their guilt for the particular crime (a robbery and murder) of which they were convicted and finally executed on 23 August 1927 is still debated, they were Galleanisti and involved in the terrorist campaign. The drawn-out Sacco-Vanzetti case, an international cause célèbre, embedded the image of the sanguinary Italian anarchist in the minds of many.

Organized Crime

A criminal element that accompanied the immigrants to the United States were the padrones (labor bosses) who flourished in the Little Italys. Using strong-arm methods, they preyed on their hapless countrymen. A notorious form of extortion, the Black Hand (threatening letters were signed with a *mano nera*), terrorized Italian neighborhoods. When Lieutenant Giuseppe Petrosino, a detective with the Italian squad of the New York City Police Department who had gone to Sicily to trace the criminal antecedents of certain suspects, was killed 12 March 1909 in front of the courthouse in Palermo, Italy, sensational reports on the Black Hand appeared on the front pages of newspapers in Italy and the United States. Emulating the Irish and the Jews who had dominated organized crime, more enterprising Italian gangsters moved into racketeering and trafficking in gambling, prostitution, and drugs by the 1920s. Prohibition proved a bonanza for people such as Al Capone, "Lucky" Luciano, and Frank Costello. With increasing numbers born in the United States, many individuals of Italian descent were nurtured in lives of crime not by a Mafia heritage but by the mean streets in which they grew up. Gang wars for control of illicit markets took a heavy toll in the number of young men killed. However, this brutal reality was glamorized by Hollywood in films such as *Little Caesar* (1930) and *Scarface* (1932). In the 1930s Italian American mobsters rivaled and eventually replaced western outlaws as icons of macho violence in popular culture.

Between the world wars, politics generated violent conflicts among Italian Americans as well as with others. Blackshirt groups, inspired by fascism in Italy, clashed with antifascists in the Little Italys, resulting in several killings. The Italian American labor movement, particularly in the garment unions, was also racked by internal struggles pitting communists against the established leadership, with both sides enlisting criminals as enforcers. Labor racketeering, with its violent methods, came to dominate sectors of longshoring, the teamsters, and construction, occupations in which Italian Americans were concentrated. Progressive labor leaders such as Giovanni Pippan and Peter Panto were killed by gangsters.

Representations of Italian Americans

Whether Italian American life has been characterized by greater violence than that of other ethnic groups is debatable. However, there is no doubt that beginning in the 1950s government bodies and the mass media have credited Italian Americans with primacy in criminal activity. Congressional hearings such as those of the Kefauver Committee competed with television series such as *The Untouchables* (1959–1963; made into a film in 1987) in lurid depictions of Italian hoodlums. Sensational revelations, such as the testimony of Joseph Valachi about the inner structure of the Mafia, became fodder for books and films. In the minds of many, the distinction between government investigations of the Mafia and fictional depictions became blurred. Highly placed public officials and academic criminologists gave credibility to the myth that a criminal cartel known as La Cosa Nostra, originating in Italy and controlled by Italians, dominated organized crime in the United States.

While some Italian Americans were distressed by this stereotype, others embraced it as their ethnic identity, and still others profited from it. A major cultural event in shaping the Mafia mystique was the publication of Mario Puzo's *The Godfather* (1969) and the subsequent *Godfather* films. The saga of the Corleone family ennobled violence by placing it in the service of an ancient code of honor. Italian American filmmakers, such as Francis Ford Coppola and Martin Scorsese, have reprised this theme.

Films that focus on the brutality of prizefighting, such as Scorsese's *Raging Bull* (1980) and John G. Avildsen's *Rocky* (1976), also have exploited the Italian American association with violence. Boxers like *Raging Bull*'s Jake La Motta exemplified the raw brute force of the ghetto survivor, which in the last decades of the twentieth century was embodied by African Americans. Since World War II, Italian Americans and African Americans have engaged in often violent struggles over turf. The 1989 killing of Yusuf Hawkins, an African American teenager, in Bensonhurst, New York; Spike Lee's *Do the Right Thing* (1989); and Robert De Niro's *A Bronx Tale* (1993) have as their common theme the deadly encounter between these two ethnic groups. Yet the affinity between African Americans and Italian Americans may lie in part in their shared heritage of violence.

As a marginal group, Italian immigrants for much of their history were subject to various forms of violence: racial, economic, and state. Some of them, as anarchists or outlaws, resorted to counterviolence for revenge, self-preservation, and profit. As they became Americanized, others, drawing on old-country values and new-country street smarts, learned to use violence as a time-honored way of gaining power, money, and status. Ironically, in the public imagination (which is both fascinated and repelled by violence) this criminal minority has come to represent the Italian American persona.

BIBLIOGRAPHY

Avrich, Paul. *Sacco and Vanzetti: The Anarchist Background.* Princeton, N.J.: Princeton University Press, 1991.

Harney, Robert F. "Italophobia: An English-Speaking Malady." In *From the Shores of Hardship: Italians in Canada*, edited by Nicholas De Maria Harney. Welland, Ontario, Canada: Soleil, 1993.

LaGumina, Salvatore J., ed. *WOP! A Documentary History of Anti-Italian Discrimination in the United States.* San Francisco: Straight Arrow, 1973.

Smith, Dwight. *The Mafia Mystique.* New York: Basic, 1975.

RUDOLPH J. VECOLI

See also **Black Hand; Capone, Al; Costello, Frank; Immigration; Luciano, "Lucky"; Organized Crime; Sacco-Vanzetti Case; Valachi, Joseph.**

J

JACKSON STATE

The killing of four students at Kent State University on 4 May 1970 punctuated the most contentious chapter in the history of American higher education. May 1970 was marked by campus demonstrations and confrontations, burnings and bombings, student strikes and administrative shutdowns. At Jackson State College (now Jackson State University) in Jackson, Mississippi, antiwar animosity was aggravated by racial tensions that erupted into lethal violence on 14 May, when white state troopers and city police opened fire on a crowd of black students, killing two and wounding twelve.

The predominantly African American student body of Jackson State was not known for antiwar activism. But on 7 May some five hundred students did assemble to criticize the draft, Mississippi's all-white draft boards, the U.S. war in Vietnam and Cambodia, and racial discrimination in America. Two days later, only a dozen or so Jackson State students showed up at a downtown rally held to protest the Kent State killings. Virtually no one imagined that what had happened at Kent State would recur at Jackson State.

On the evening of 13 May, some local "cornerboys" (neighborhood youths who were not students) and Jackson State students engaged in what had become an annual spring ritual: they tossed rocks at white motorists driving down Lynch Street, a thoroughfare adjacent to the campus. The situation became more tense than usual when a rumor began to circulate among the group that someone was going to torch the Reserve Officers' Training Corps (ROTC) barracks on campus. Some youths continued to throw rocks at cars, others chanted antiwar slogans, and a few called for burning down the ROTC building. Later that night, three youths ignited a small fire at the ROTC building, but campus security quickly doused it.

Jackson's Mayor Russell Davis mobilized city police to clear the area. The police contingent was led by a white lieutenant who sent his children to private Citizens' Council schools to avoid racial integration. The police ranks were filled with white officers who had a history of enforcing an "instant arrest" policy aimed at civil rights activists. City forces were assisted by a symbolically charged armored vehicle that had been used six years earlier against Freedom Summer activists seeking to register black voters. Simultaneously, the governor of Mississippi, John Bell Williams, dispatched the all-white state highway patrol, which Charles Evers, the state's most influential black leader, had depicted as "a bunch of redneck murderers" that included avowed racists and members of the Ku Klux Klan. When patrolmen had last been called to Jackson State, in 1967, they opened fire on a crowd of black youths, killing one.

A direct confrontation between students and authorities was averted that night. After a few hours, the cornerboys and students went home, and the authorities remained at their staging areas. The next morning the president of Jackson State,

John Peoples, met with student leaders, listened to complaints, addressed grievances, extracted a promise of campus calm, and later reported to the faculty that the student mood was quiet and conciliatory.

The calm of 14 May was shattered at 9:30 P.M., when some cornerboys resumed rock throwing on Lynch Street, while some Jackson State students cheered them on. A false rumor began to circulate that black leader Charles Evers, like his brother Medgar, had been assassinated. A few cornerboys reacted by driving a construction truck into the street and setting it on fire. By 11:30 P.M. white police and state patrolmen (soon followed by National Guardsmen) had moved into the campus area, where they encountered verbal insults as well as more rock and bottle throwing. Amid considerable confusion, the authorities began to talk about possible sniper fire coming from dormitory windows.

Near midnight, state patrolmen and city police marched down Lynch Street and took up a position directly across from a crowd of students in front of Alexander Hall, a women's dormitory. The crowd was made up of mostly male students who were saying good night to their girlfriends, who had a midnight curfew. The students started shouting curses at the newly arrived cops. Someone in the crowd threw a bottle that crashed at the officers' feet. Suddenly, patrolmen and police opened fire. In a twenty-eight-second barrage of gunfire, Alexander Hall was hit by four hundred bullets and buckshot that extended from ground level to the fifth floor. Two students on the ground were killed. Twelve more students—inside and outside the dorm—were wounded.

In the days and months following the shootings, federal, state, and local officials squabbled over jurisdiction, conducted multiple investigations, held grand jury hearings, and issued official and unofficial reports. Police and patrolmen claimed that their action was in response to sniper fire coming from several directions, including Alexander Hall. Their claim was accepted by a local grand jury and a federal grand jury, but it was rejected by a biracial mayoral commission as well as by President Richard Nixon's Commission on Campus Unrest.

For a few weeks the violence at Jackson State College was national news. Pictures of students staring through the broken windows of Alexander Hall became a part of the visual legacy of the 1960s, a decade of civil rights activism and antiwar protest. Students across the United States organized memorial services, candlelight marches, and demonstrations. Some campuses that had not closed down after the Kent State killings shut their doors after those at Jackson State.

Many African Americans felt that the national reaction to the murders of black students at Jackson State was noticeably mild compared with the national outrage that followed the killing of white students at Kent State. Could the perceived difference in response be attributed to the fact that many students were already home for the summer or studying for final exams or numbed and exhausted by the events of May 1970? Or could it be that white America was so obsessed with the war in Asia that it remained blind to the ongoing racism that was destroying young black lives at home?

BIBLIOGRAPHY

O'Neil, Robert M., John P. Morris, and Raymond Mack. *No Heroes, No Villains: New Perspectives on Kent State and Jackson State.* San Francisco: Jossey-Bass, 1972.

Rhodes, Lelia Gaston. *Jackson State University: The First Hundred Years, 1877–1977.* Jackson: University Press of Mississippi, 1979.

Spofford, Tim. *Lynch Street: The May 1970 Slayings at Jackson State College.* Kent, Ohio: Kent State University Press, 1988.

MARK E. KANN

See also **Antiwar Protests; Campus Violence; Kent State.**

JAMES, JESSE
(1847–1882)

Jesse James, born 10 January 1847, was the second son of Zerelda and Robert James, well-bred Kentuckians who had settled in Clay County in western Missouri. Robert, who farmed 275 acres with the help of seven slaves and preached at the New Hope Baptist Church, took off for the gold rush in California, where he died in 1850. He left behind three young children, including Jesse's older brother, Frank, born in 1843, and Susan, born in 1849. Zerelda remarried twice, her 1855 union with Reuben Samuel producing four more children. When the Civil War came, first Frank and later Jesse were swept up into Confederate guerrilla bands, where they learned the ruthless outlaw trade, including wholesale murder and bank robbery.

After the Civil War, Jesse and Frank James and a changing gang of Missouri toughs, including the Younger brothers, Cole, Jim, John, and Bob, were among the most successful and long-lived gangsters in U.S. history. Starting off as bank robbers after the Civil War, the James gang kept up with developing technology and became innovators in the field of train robbery. Jesse James was also a cold-blooded killer; however, he has been mythologized into a noble outlaw, a social bandit. In life and even more in death, he became the American Robin Hood, a figure who robbed from the oppressor—bankers and railroad moguls—and supposedly gave money to the poor for sixteen years, before being shot down on 3 April 1882 by Robert Ford, a traitor who killed him for political blood money offered by the oppressor state of Missouri.

Jesse James was well aware of the grandeur and protection offered him by the Robin Hood myth. After the occurrence of a robbery for which he was the chief suspect and most likely the perpetrator, he would often write to the newspapers and deny the deed, all the while hinting that he could understand why some brave outlaw might undertake such an action against the corrupt establishment. While James defended himself in this way, the newspaperman Major John Newman Edwards of the *Kansas City Times* served as his unofficial press agent, defender, and promoter, writing floridly of the latest bandit exploits and always linking James to Robin Hood, thereby giving a socially acceptable dimension to the armed robbery.

To some extent, such propaganda was just sensational journalism, but in a larger sense, construing the James gang exploits this way helped to create the illusion that they were resistance fighters defending rural Missourians against the forces of invasive outside capitalists: here were real men who got even with bankers and railroad industrialists, serving themselves and avenging the people at the same time. Many rural, as well as newly urban, Missourians and millions of readers across the United States gained vicarious pleasure from the violent and lucrative attacks of the renowned rebels, though they might at the same time believe that the James brothers deserved punishment. If not redemptive, such violence did reclaim an element of disabused, premodern honor from the capitalist forces that were transforming the countryside and constructing massive, alienating cities.

The James brothers learned to wrap themselves in the flag, to place their gangsterism in larger

A young Jesse James, in 1864. LIBRARY OF CONGRESS

political contexts. Jesse and Frank had been pro-Confederate guerrillas during the Civil War, riding with William Clarke Quantrill, George Todd, and Bloody Bill Anderson. In addition to killing unarmed Union soldiers and civilians during the war, these gangs also robbed banks. Their image as socially conscious bandits after the war was useful to former Confederate sympathizers in the postwar Missouri Democratic Party, who sought a return to power. Such forces opposed the modernizing Republicans of Reconstruction Missouri, who sought to eliminate bandits in order to improve the business climate. These business-oriented Republican politicians, deeply embarrassed by their inability to catch the increasingly popular James gang, brought in the detective agency of Allan Pinkerton, the first such agency in the United States, to eliminate this threat. The Pinkertons firebombed the James home in Kearney, Missouri, in 1875, killing Jesse and Frank's dim-witted nine-year-old half brother, Archie, and maiming their mother, Zerelda. In revulsion, the Missouri legislature nearly passed, by a two-thirds vote, amnesty for the James gang—something of a triumph for reactionary Democrats, who were on the brink of regaining power. But after they turned out the radical Republicans, Jesse James became an obstacle to Democrats too, as they sought to attract northern capital to their more conservative development projects. It was a Democratic governor, Thomas T. Crittenden, who put the bounty on Jesse's head that Robert Ford collected.

After Jesse was killed and following protracted negotiations conducted by John Newman Edwards, Frank James surrendered to Governor Crittenden on 5 October 1882 and was indicted, but a jury of his peers refused to convict him. Going straight, he spent the rest of his life, sometimes accompanied by Cole Younger, as a glorified carny, making his living off his former notoriety when not living quietly on a Missouri farm.

Historians and biographers have found it difficult to write about Jesse James without being taken in by the myth he did so much to cultivate. All writers except William A. Settle, Jr., have succumbed, generally unconsciously, to the story James himself probably believed. Settle leaves out the power of the mythicized James story. In the end, it was James the emblematic hero and not the fugitive robber and killer who counted: he is remembered as a politicized, anarchic, but superhuman figure.

Jesse James was made for Hollywood, which has often renewed his legend of the noble outlaw at odds with the modernizing world. He is a far more satisfying figure than Bonnie and Clyde or John Dillinger, whom some might consider his figurative offspring in crime, because he is more credible as a selfless romantic figure while they seem like self-serving bandits. And because we live in cynical times, we will never allow storytellers to turn the likes of Patty Hearst and the Symbionese Liberation Army into the modern descendants of the safely departed, horse-powered James gang, who attacked industrial capitalism in its formative, not its decadent, stages. As the embodiment of socially conscious banditry, Jesse James is every bit the legend in the United States now that he was during his own lifetime.

BIBLIOGRAPHY

Brant, Marley. *Jesse James: The Man and the Myth.* New York: Berkley, 1998.

Fellman, Michael. *Inside War: The Guerrilla Conflict in Missouri During the American Civil War.* New York: Oxford University Press, 1989. Pp. 247–263.

Love, Robertus. *The Rise and Fall of Jesse James.* 1926. Reprint, Lincoln: University of Nebraska Press, 1990.

Settle, William A., Jr. *Jesse James Was His Name; or, Fact and Fiction Concerning the Careers of the Notorious James Brothers of Missouri.* Columbia: University of Missouri Press, 1966.

Steckmesser, Kent Ladd. *The Western Hero in History and Legend.* Norman: University of Oklahoma Press, 1965.

Thelen, David. *Paths of Resistance: Tradition and Democracy in Industrializing Missouri.* New York: Oxford University Press, 1986.

White, Richard. "Outlaw Groups of the Middle Border: American Social Bandits." *Western Historical Quarterly* 12 (October 1981): 387–408.

MICHAEL FELLMAN

See also **Gunfighters and Outlaws, Western; Quantrill's Raid.**

JAPANESE AMERICANS

The Japanese, like other peoples of color, have endured racist violence since they first arrived in large numbers in North America in the mid-nineteenth century. Although the Japanese population in the United States in the late nineteenth and early twentieth centuries was roughly equal to that of the Chinese, the latter were the targets of more frequent and more serious violence. Until World War II racist violence against the Japanese in the United States and Canada was largely nonlethal. (The only known deaths in North America were five Japanese slain, perhaps mistakenly, by revolutionary soldiers in Torreon, Mexico, in a 1911 massacre that killed 303 Chinese.)

The earliest organized violence against the Japanese in the United States occurred early in 1890 in San Francisco, where members of the shoemakers union—the same union that had pioneered organized violence against Chinese in Massachusetts in 1869—attacked a group of Japanese shoemakers working for less than union wages. Two years later, Fresno, California, police rousted and arrested Japanese farm laborers for vagrancy even though they were employed. There followed a flurry of anti-Japanese agitation in 1892–1893, but the relatively small number of Japanese in the country—fewer than twenty-five thousand in the census of 1900—inhibited the development of a full-fledged anti-Japanese movement.

Such a movement did develop along the entire Pacific Coast in the following century and was accompanied by violence in both town and country. San Francisco was the epicenter of the movement, but the gravest outbreak of violence occurred in Vancouver, British Columbia. The first anti-Japanese mass meeting was held in San Francisco in May 1900. Later that year the national Populist Party added an anti-Japanese plank to its platform, and the American Federation of Labor urged Congress to extend the bar against Chinese laborers to include Japanese. In February 1905, in the midst of the Russo-Japanese War, the most prestigious newspaper in California, the *San Francisco Chronicle,* launched a journalistic crusade against Japanese immigrants. The state legislature quickly followed with a resolution asking Congress to stop Japanese immigration, and in May delegates from sixty-seven organizations, mostly associated with labor unions, formed the Asiatic Exclusion League. The organized anti-Japanese movement soon spread to other western states and endured until after World War II. By 1906 casual street violence against Japanese was occurring frequently in San Francisco and sporadically elsewhere. Japanese restaurants and other businesses were boycotted, picketed, and vandalized. By late summer and early fall of 1906, unprovoked assaults against Japanese pedestrians in San Francisco were frequent and clearly motivated by, in the words of a federal investigator, "racial hostility." If any white persons were ever arrested for any of the San Francisco assaults, which were well publicized, no newspaper reported it, although a number of Japanese were arrested—and some fined—for what seems to have been self-defense.

The worst incident of this era north of Mexico occurred in Vancouver, British Columbia, at a time of heightened racial tension in the Pacific Northwest. On 4 September 1907 a riot directed against immigrants from India drove some 250 people out of the mill town of Bellingham, Washington, just south of the Canadian border, where they had been employed. On 7 September, a Saturday night, a large anti-Japanese mass meeting in Vancouver developed into a full-fledged riot. A mob of at least a thousand persons invaded and looted Chinatown and then turned to Nihonmachi, the Japanese quarter centered on Powell Street. Here it met serious resistance from Japanese, who used fists, sticks, rocks, and knives in a successful defense. No firearms were involved, and the injuries on each side were slight. Eventually, the Canadian government paid $9,000 to the Japanese claimants and $26,000 to the Chinese claimants because there was greater damage in Chinatown. These outbreaks of violence and Japan's growing power and prestige led the U.S. and Canadian governments to negotiate executive agreements with Japan that limited immigration and temporarily calmed anti-Japanese feelings.

Subsequent anti-Japanese violence in the United States centered mostly on rural districts and small towns. The best-known incident was an expulsion of Japanese laborers from the San Joaquin Valley town of Turlock, California, in 1921. This violent activity punctuated an era of steadily increasing state and federal restrictions against Japanese immigrants. The most important restrictive measures were the federal laws that denied the right of naturalization to Japanese and other Asians and steadily narrowed the window of eligibility through which they could immigrate. There were also state statutes that impeded the purchase and transfer of agricultural land to "aliens ineligible to citizenship," barred them from a number of professions and trades, and criminalized interracial marriages. In 1924 U.S. legislation barred further Japanese immigration, and four years later an executive agreement between Canada and Japan cut immigration to 150 Japanese annually.

Violence During World War II

The Japanese attack on Pearl Harbor ushered in an entirely different era of anti-Japanese violence in the United States, culminating in the greatest single mass incarceration of American citizens in history. In the days and weeks after 7 December 1941, increasingly repressive federal and state actions against both Japanese nationals and American citizens of Japanese ancestry were punctuated by individual instances of violence, some of it fatal, directed against persons who were—or in some instances looked—Japanese. U.S. Attorney General Francis Biddle reported thirty-six instances of violence directed against Japanese between 8 December 1941 and 31 March 1942. Federal agents, sometimes accompanied by local and state police, instituted warrantless searches of Japanese homes and businesses, and several thousand Japanese nationals were arrested and interned. Persons of Japanese birth or ancestry, regardless of citizenship, were prohibited from crossing national borders.

Executive Order 9066, issued by President Franklin D. Roosevelt on 19 February 1942, set the stage for the mass expulsion of more than 110,000 Japanese Americans from their homes in California, the western portions of Washington and Oregon, and a small part of Arizona. More than two-thirds of them were native-born American citizens. They were confined in a number of concentration camps, which the government euphemistically called assembly centers and relocation centers. The U.S. Army was responsible for rounding up the Japanese and providing temporary facilities; by the fall of 1942 all had been turned over to a civilian agency, the War Relocation Authority, although army military police detachments provided security and manned the guard towers around the concentration camps.

Canada followed suit with a mass confinement of most West Coast Japanese Canadians. Prime Minister William Lyon Mackenzie King's Order in Council P.C. 1486, issued just five days after Roosevelt's executive order, banished most Japanese Canadians to work camps or "interior housing centres" in the mountain fastness of British Columbia. The Canadian government was somewhat less racist in its definition of who had to be incarcerated—persons in Japanese-Caucasian marriages and their offspring were exiled in the United States but not in Canada. Although the Canadian government did not kill any of its Japanese internees, it expelled a much larger percentage of its ethnic Japanese population after the war and was much slower to allow Japanese persons back to their former homes in maritime British Columbia, which was kept "Japanese-free" until 1 April 1949.

Further violence, some of it incited by various California politicians, greeted some Japanese Americans returning to California. The district attorney of Los Angeles, Fred N. Howser, had called the decision to allow Japanese Americans to return to California "a second Pearl Harbor"; a Democratic congressman from Tulare, in California's Central Valley, had insisted that "the only good Jap is a dead Jap" and predicted death for "every one of them that is sent back." Happily, no returnees were killed, but there was a brief reign of terror in much of rural California, some of it conducted by deputy sheriffs. One count tabulated seventy instances of terrorism—much of it arson—and nineteen shootings into homes and farm buildings in the first six months of 1945.

The Postwar Period

Since the immediate postwar period, specifically anti-Japanese violence in the United States has been minimal, although general anti-Asian violence, most of it directed against new immigrants, is a persistent problem, according to the U.S. Civil

Rights Commission. The most notorious case of anti-Asian violence—the 1982 baseball-bat killing of the American-born Chinese Vincent Chin in Detroit—was a case of mistaken identity: his autoworker slayers thought that he was Japanese.

BIBLIOGRAPHY

Daniels, Roger. *Concentration Camps, North America: Japanese in the United States and Canada During World War II.* Malabar, Fla.: Krieger, 1989.

———. *The Politics of Prejudice: The Anti-Japanese Movement in California and the Struggle for Japanese Exclusion.* Berkeley: University of California Press, 1999.

Hata, Donald T. *"Undesirables": Early Immigrants and the Anti-Japanese Movement in San Francisco, 1892–1898.* New York: Arno, 1978.

Girdner, Audrie, and Anne Loftis. *The Great Betrayal: The Evacuation of Japanese Americans During World War II.* New York: Macmillan, 1969.

"Racial Violence Against Asian Americans." *Harvard Law Review* 106 (1993): 1926–1943.

Sugimoto, Howard H. *Japanese Immigration, the Vancouver Riots, and Canadian Diplomacy.* New York: Arno, 1978.

Sunahara, Ann G. *The Politics of Racism: The Uprooting of Japanese Canadians During the Second World War.* Toronto: Lorimer, 1981.

U.S. Commission on Civil Rights. *Civil Rights Issues Facing Asian Americans in the 1990s.* Washington, D.C.: Government Printing Office, 1992.

Ward, W. Peter. *White Canada Forever: Popular Attitudes and Public Policy Toward Orientals in British Columbia.* Montreal: McGill University Press, 1978.

ROGER DANIELS

See also **Asians; Foreign Intervention, Fear of; Immigration.**

JAPANESE AMERICANS, INCARCERATION OF

The incarceration of 120,000 Japanese Americans by the United States government during World War II was not an aberration or a mistake. It was, rather, the unfortunate but logical outgrowth of a long established pattern of racist discrimination against Asian immigrants and their descendants. For Japanese immigrants, this included discrimination in admission to the United States, total exclusion from immigration after 1924, denial of the right of naturalization and all that this implied, special immigration detention at Angel Island and other facilities, alien land acts in California and ten other western states aimed at "aliens ineligible to citizenship," and many Jim Crow–like measures, such as segregated seating in movie theaters and not being allowed to use public swimming pools.

Despite these acts of hostility, by the time of the Japanese attack on Pearl Harbor on 7 December 1941 there were some 270,000 Japanese Americans: 126,000 on the mainland—all but a few thousand of them in California and the other two West Coast states, Oregon and Washington—and 150,000 in Hawaii. About two-thirds of each group were American-born, and thus citizens by birthright. Each group was economically viable. Many of the Issei (first generation of immigrants) had become farmers and small-scale entrepreneurs, and their children, the Nisei (second generation), were beginning to attend colleges and universities.

The state of war between the United States and Japan transformed the entire Japanese immigrant generation into the status of enemy aliens, and a sizable minority, about eight thousand persons, were interned by internal security forces and placed in camps run by the Immigration and Naturalization Service. Those interned included most community leaders. All of the assets of enemy aliens, including bank accounts, were immediately frozen. Japanese aliens were treated more severely than the more numerous German and Italian aliens, even though most of the Europeans were aliens by choice rather than necessity, unlike the Japanese, who were, with other Asians, ineligible for naturalization. (Some 2,000 of more than 300,000 German aliens were interned in camps run by the Immigration and Naturalization Service, as were a couple of hundred of the nearly 700,000 Italian aliens. No American citizens of German or Italian birth were interned or incarcerated.) Although there was occasional brutality and at least two government-inflicted homicides, the internment of Japanese nationals followed the forms of both national and international law.

What eventually happened to most of the Japanese citizens, especially those who lived on the West Coast, was simply lawless. In effect, their citizenship was revoked for most of the war. By executive fiat in December 1941, Nisei were forbidden to cross American borders, their draft status was changed to that of enemy aliens, and the protection of the Fourth Amendment "against unreasonable searches and seizures" was denied to them. After President Franklin D. Roosevelt issued Executive Order 9066 on 19 February 1942—the only presidential action for which the government has officially apologized—more of their rights and eventually their liberties were taken away from them.

During these post–Pearl Harbor months terrorist violence was visited on many Japanese American families, particularly those who lived in rural areas. Japanese Americans on the mainland were subjected to verbal abuse, denied normal services, and the like, so much so that Chinese Americans began wearing identifying buttons and badges lest they be mistaken for Japanese. The press and radio contributed to the hysteria about the dangers posed by having Japanese Americans at liberty, reflecting the national anger and chagrin over the disaster at Pearl Harbor and the string of Japanese military victories.

Military orders affecting Japanese living on the West Coast flowed from the authority granted by Executive Order 9066. German and Italian aliens and all Japanese Americans were subject to a dusk-to-dawn curfew and travel restrictions. Only at the end of March 1942, nearly four months after Pearl Harbor, during which time not one act of sabotage or espionage had taken place, did the mass incarceration of those Japanese living on the West Coast begin. Eventually all Japanese Americans living in California and the western halves of Oregon and Washington, regardless of their citizenship, gender, age, or even prior service in American armed forces, were rounded up by soldiers and shipped off to makeshift concentration camps (also known as assembly centers), usually near their homes. Then they were transferred to the custody of a civilian agency, the War Relocation Authority (WRA), which ran ten newly constructed concentration camps (relocation centers). These were in desolate areas of the states of California, Arizona, Idaho, Utah, Wyoming, Colorado, and Arkansas. While some Japanese Americans were released from these camps as early as the summer of 1942, others were imprisoned without trial until March 1946.

The WRA camps were not death camps; they were humanely administered by civilians, many of whom sympathized with the inmates' plight. In addition, the process of rounding up and imprisoning Japanese Americans on the West Coast was nonviolent and orderly. The strains and bitterness of incarceration, however, produced intraethnic violence, and conflicts between the armed soldiery and the unarmed prisoners resulted in homicide on three separate occasions. The intraethnic violence occurred during disputes among prisoners about the proper way to respond to oppression.

Japanese Americans being evacuated in Los Angeles in April 1942. LIBRARY OF CONGRESS

Some of the inmates were or became vocal supporters of the Japanese government; thousands of others, while still imprisoned, volunteered or, after 1943, were drafted, to serve in the U.S. Army.

The first significant incident of violence occurred in the temporary camp at Santa Anita racetrack outside Los Angeles on 4 August 1942. A series of minor incidents and evacuee grievances— some of which a U.S. Army report admitted were on "solid ground[s]"—resulted in the formation and dispersion of what the offical report called "two mobs and one crowd of women." The only reported casualty was one inmate—accused by his fellows of being an *inu* (literally "dog," actually

"informer")—who was "set upon and severely beaten by other Japanese." Many of those attacked were identified with the Japanese American Citizens' League (JACL), which advocated cooperation with the federal authorities; many of the attackers were Kibei, American-born Japanese who had been sent by their parents to Japan for some of their education.

The first killings in the camps were in the Manzanar riot of 6 December 1942. The beating— serious enough to cause hospitalization—of the JACL leader Fred Tayama on 5 December by unknown assailants caused the authorities to arrest the "usual suspects," all Kibei. Demonstrations against the arrests and other grievances were led by Joe Kurihara, one of the few Nisei who had been a veteran of the U.S. Army in World War I. A series of heated protest meetings and shouted death threats against Tayama and other *inu* resulted in a call for the military police, who entered the camp and dispersed a crowd of several hundred men and boys with tear gas. The crowd then reassembled, and the soldiers, apparently without orders, opened fire on the unarmed protesters with submachine guns, shotguns, and rifles. Two young men were killed, and ten other inmates were wounded, as was one soldier, apparently by a ricocheting army bullet. In the aftermath, sixteen accused agitators were sent to isolation camps, while sixty-five prominent JACL leaders and their families were removed for their own safety.

A more calculated killing occured in the WRA camp called Topaz in southern Utah. Shortly before sunset on 11 April 1943, James Hatsuki Wakasa was shot and killed near an isolated guard tower at the camp's perimeter. There were apparently no witnesses except for the guard, who testified that Wakasa was trying to crawl through the fence. Although the army quickly removed the corpse, a WRA investigation showed that Wakasa had been found well within the fence, and an autopsy showed that Wakasa had been facing the man who shot him. The army hastily court-martialed and acquitted the sentry.

The most sustained in-camp violence was at the concentration camp at Tule Lake in northern California. Tule Lake had originlly been a "normal" concentration camp, but after a mishandled loyalty investigation connected with the recruitment and eventual conscripting of concentration camp inmates for military service, some six thousand dissidents were segregated at the Tule Lake camp. There was much intimidation and violence among the inmates, including one unsolved murder, and for a time the army took control of the camp from the WRA. During that time one evacuee was shot and killed by a soldier.

Not all Japanese Americans were interned or incarcerated. On the mainland those few thousand who lived east of the forbidden zone created by military orders lived in nervous liberty throughout the war. In Hawaii, where martial law had been declared, the very large Japanese American population—about a third of the nonmilitary population—was not deprived of its liberty. Although a couple of thousand were interned, many of them remained in camps for only a relatively short period of time.

All the evidence indicates that the vast majority of Americans approved what was done to Japanese Americans; many urged even worse treatment. Congress sanctioned military incarceration without significant debate or a dissenting vote. Many legal authorities, including some who helped to execute the program of ethnic incarceration, believed that the Supreme Court would eventually strike down the whole program. For that reason the government delayed the few test cases that challenged its authority. Its fears were unfounded. In the so-called Japanese American Cases of 1943 and 1944, the Supreme Court, in effect, approved the mass incarceration of American citizens by executive fiat. In December 1944, two years and eight months after the incarceration program began, the Court granted a writ of habeas corpus to Mitsuye Endo, a twenty-four-year-old female citizen of unchallenged loyalty to the United States. This enabled her and other citizens in similar circumstances not only to leave camp but to return to their West Coast homes. The first returning Japanese Americans met renewed terrorist violence and much hostility from the public. Many, particularly of the older generation, were never able to pick up where they had left off, and several thousand of that generation of Japanese citizens were disillusioned enough to formally renounce their American citizenship.

Almost forty-seven years after the attack on Pearl Harbor, the Civil Liberties Act of 1988 authorized a formal apology to Japanese Americans for what was done to them and legislated a one-time $20,000 payment to each survivor of wartime incarceration. The act could not, of course, undo the damage and the shame of what had been done, and it came too late for nearly half of those incarcerated, who were dead by the time the bill was passed.

BIBLIOGRAPHY

Commission on Wartime Relocation and Internment of Civilians. *Personal Justice Denied.* 2d ed. Seattle: University of Washington Press, 1997.

Daniels, Roger. *Concentration Camps, USA: Japanese Americans and World War II.* New York: Holt, 1971.

———. *Prisoners Without Trial: Japanese Americans in World War II.* New York: Hill and Wang, 1993.

———, ed. *American Concentration Camps: A Documentary History of the Relocation and Incarceration of Japanese Americans, 1941–1945.* 9 vols. New York: Garland, 1989.

Hansen, Arthur A., ed. *Japanese American World War II Evacuation History Project.* 5 vols. Westport, Conn.: Greenwood, 1990–1992.

Irons, Peter. *Justice at War.* New York: Oxford University Press, 1983.

Tateishi, John. *And Justice for All: An Oral History of the Japanese American Detention Camps.* 2d ed. Seattle: University of Washington Press, 1999.

U.S. War Department. *Final Report. Japanese Evacuation from the West Coast, 1942.* Washington, D.C.: Government Printing Office, 1943.

ROGER DANIELS

See also **Foreign Intervention, Fear of; Hate Crimes; Immigration; Nativism; World War II.**

JEHOVAH'S WITNESSES

The Jehovah's Witnesses are an evangelical Christian sect that grew out of an 1870s-era Bible study group in Allegheny, Pennsylvania. The study group was led by Charles Taze Russell, whose exploration of religion brought him into contact with the teachings of William Miller. Miller was a widely influential millennialist who claimed that the return of Jesus Christ was imminent. Seeking to reconcile these and other biblical interpretations he had encountered, he formed the study group with the goal of resolving doctrinal issues through a close, literal reading of the Bible.

In 1879 Russell sold his business interests and used the proceeds to fund his new religious organization. He began publishing a newspaper entitled *Zion's Watch Tower and Herald of Christ's Presence* and wrote a number of tracts outlining the group's beliefs. From the very beginning, the group sought new converts through the door-to-door distribution of their literature. This practice has continued and is one of the most recognizable characteristics of the Jehovah's Witnesses. Thanks to the group's aggressive proselytizing, it enjoyed rapid growth. As of 1997, the Watchtower Bible and Tract Society (the official name of the Jehovah's Witnesses' governing body) placed the number of Witnesses at 5,559,931 worldwide, of whom 974,719 reside in the United States, making up approximately 0.35 percent of the U.S. population.

A considerable source of controversy for the Jehovah's Witnesses, particularly during World War II, was their doctrine on military service and saluting the flag. The justification for not saluting the flag grew out of their interpretation of Exodus 20:3–5, which contains the commandments against having other gods and making graven images. The Witnesses did not recognize governments as secular institutions but instead saw them as sinful and under the sway of Satan. Thus, the flag was viewed as a graven image, and saluting it was seen as a religious, rather than a political or nationalistic, act. The Jehovah's Witnesses had no official policy on military service in a combat role, and the question was left up to the individual. However, there was widespread opposition to fighting a war on behalf of the worldly, sinful government, and many Witnesses sought conscientious-objector status.

In fact, the rhetoric of the Witnesses with regard to the flag issue was quite mild: they often asserted that they recognized the flag of the United States as worthy of respect, and that the failure to salute it was a purely religious act that was not meant to be disrespectful. This mild tone was not sufficient to protect the Witnesses from a Supreme Court decision followed by a popular backlash. In 1940 the U.S. Supreme Court heard the case of *Gobitis v. Minersville School District*, ruling that schools could legally expel students for refusing to salute the flag. This ruling led numerous states and municipalities to pass laws criminalizing refusal to salute the flag. In Mississippi a statute was enacted making it illegal even to teach an anti-flag-saluting doctrine.

Publicity from the Supreme Court decision, along with public anxiety about the ominous situation in Europe, led to an outburst of mob violence against Jehovah's Witnesses. In 1940 there were 3,035 instances of anti-Witness violence nationwide, with 1,488 people attacked. Almost all the reported incidents occurred in small towns; only a handful were reported in towns with a population above five thousand. Of the forty-five states in which incidents occurred, Texas and other southwestern states had the majority of cases.

Accounts of the mob violence given by the victims of these attacks are consistent in their details. By virtue of their door-to-door proselytizing and distribution of literature, Witnesses tended to be easily recognizable targets. They were set upon by groups of men who admonished them to salute a flag. When the Witnesses refused, they were beaten by the mob. In many cases they were accused of being Nazi spies, communists, or agents of other hostile foreign powers. Usually the incidents ended when local law enforcement appeared and arrested the Witnesses, though in many cases the police participated in or did nothing to stop the violence.

During the war more than eighteen hundred Witnesses were imprisoned for refusing all military service, asserting that they should be recognized as "ministers." (Because the Jehovah's Witnesses reject the conventional structure of traditional organized Christianity, every member could reasonably claim that designation.) Witnesses who were engaged in alternative service as conscientious objectors were also the targets of mob violence.

Violent incidents against Witnesses peaked in the summer of 1940. Then, as a result of a vigorous legal campaign waged by lawyers for the Jehovah's Witnesses, in 1943 the Supreme Court handed down a decision in *West Virginia State Board of Education v. Barnette* that expressly overruled the *Gobitis* decision and prohibited school-mandated flag-saluting. Although anti-Witness ordinances continued to appear on the local level until as late as 1953, this decision marked the end of high-level government persecution of the Jehovah's Witnesses. It also marked, more or less, the end of anti-Witness mob violence.

BIBLIOGRAPHY

American Civil Liberties Union. *Jehovah's Witnesses and the War.* New York, 1943.
———. *The Persecution of Jehovah's Witnesses.* New York, 1941.
Manwaring, David R. *Render Unto Caesar: The Flag Salute Controversy.* Chicago: University of Chicago Press, 1962.
Penton, M. James. *Apocalypse Delayed: The Story of Jehovah's Witnesses.* Toronto: University of Toronto Press, 1985.
Thomas, Stan. *Jehovah's Witnesses and What They Believe.* Grand Rapids, Mich.: Zondervan, 1967.
White, Timothy. *A People for His Name: A History of Jehovah's Witnesses and an Evaluation.* New York: Vantage, 1967.

NANCY GRIER HOGAN

See also **Religion.**

JEWS

Jews in the United States, unlike those in Islamic and other Christian countries, have rarely been subject to violent attacks. No pogroms have occurred in the United States, although there have been many instances of individual brutality, including killings. For the most part, Jews in the United States suffered from bigotry and discrimination in housing, employment, education, and access to resorts and private clubs, not from physical assaults. Overt hostility toward Jews has most often taken the form of verbal abuse; this has not been the case, however, with Jewish children. Incidents of Jewish children being attacked by other youths in and outside of school date back to the nineteenth century.

The view of many non-Jews was that Jews had killed Jesus and had never accepted the truthfulness of Christian teachings. For these "sins" Jews were perpetually subjected to verbal assaults in Christian countries, including the United States. In parts of the United States there were—and still are—people who had never actually seen a Jew, their impressions having been garnered from misguided religious teachings and from economic misperceptions. Although many non-Jews thought of Jews as dishonest and unscrupulous "Shylocks" whose business activities were highly suspect, this view did not necessarily lead to violence.

In colonial America, Jews were often subject to restrictions. In the Old World they were not sought as colonists, and those that arrived in the colonies found economic and political activities circumscribed. In some colonies they could be neither lawyers nor physicians, and governmental service and voting opportunities were restricted to Christians. During the first several decades after the American Revolution, these stipulations were gradually lifted, and by 1877, after New Hampshire changed its voting requirements, Jewish men could vote in all of the states.

There were, of course, cases of individual violence, but most of them occurred in the late nineteenth century and in the twentieth century. In 1842 some students at the University of Virginia beat up a Jewish professor primarily because of his irascible temper and his strongly proclaimed antislavery views. The man left the state by the end of the academic year. In 1850 a group of about five hundred men in New York City, mostly of Irish descent and including members of the police force, ransacked a synagogue on Yom Kippur, the holiest day of the Jewish year. During the Civil War the residents of two small towns in Georgia, Talbotton and Thomasville, believed that Jews were subverting the Southern cause and therefore expelled them from their communities.

The most noteworthy episodes of violence, however, usually resulted in the victimization of children. From the nineteenth century until well into the twentieth century, Jewish youngsters and adolescents were periodically assaulted by their peers. The Easter season, when students were reminded that Jews were responsible for the death of Jesus, could be especially troublesome; other times, Christian children beat up Jews for sport. This was especially true in urban non-Jewish neighborhoods with close proximity to Jewish neighborhoods. Throughout the twentieth century there were repeated cases of assaults that were brought to the attention of the authorities.

Perhaps the most notorious cases occurred from the late 1930s through World War II, when followers of Father Charles Coughlin regularly attacked children in New York and Boston. These episodes

Picketers outside a Philadelphia radio station protest the station's refusal to broadcast anti-Semitic speeches by Father Charles Coughlin. CORBIS/BETTMANN

were so violent, and so often had the support of the police, that public officials had to intervene. In Massachusetts in 1943, the governor condemned these activities and forced the ouster of Boston's chief of police. In New York one twelve-year-old youth brutalized a four-year-old child, and when confronted with what he had done, said that one of the nuns at his school had indicated that it was not a sin to beat up Jews.

Of course, children were not the only Jews attacked. Random episodes of violence against Jewish people occurred in every section of the United States. Populists in Mississippi and Louisiana in the 1890s destroyed property of Jewish storekeepers, who they thought were holding them in economic bondage. In many urban areas, in that same decade and later, neighborhood children often pulled the whiskers of Jewish peddlers while overturning their carts. The author and playwright Edna Ferber, writing about her early years (the 1890s) in Ottumwa, Iowa, recalled Jews being victimized by the "brutality and ignorance" of the town's Christian folk.

The twentieth century has seen further incidents of violence against Jews. In 1902 in New York City, the funeral cortege of a venerated rabbi passed by gentile workers in a factory; the workers suddenly began pelting the mourners with bricks, pieces of iron and wood, and other objects found on the factory floor. When the police arrived, they began clubbing the Jewish mourners, whom they despised simply because they were Jewish. Leo Frank, a Jew unjustly convicted of murdering a thirteen-year-old girl, was lynched outside of Atlanta in 1915; but the circumstances surrounding the event were far too complex to isolate the anti-Semitic aspect as the prime cause. Members of the Ku Klux Klan in the 1920s vented their wrath more against Catholics and African Americans than against Jews, but in the West, especially in Denver, rowdy Klan members (men and women) drove or marched through Jewish neighborhoods shouting obscenities. In 1916 and again in 1927, interns at Kings County Hospital in Brooklyn, New York, physically assaulted Jewish peers. In the former case they bound and gagged one young man, took him to Grand Central Station, put him on a train, and warned him never to return to the hospital. In the latter episode, about twenty rowdy Christians dragged three Jewish interns from their beds, bound and gagged them, and dunked them in a bathtub of ice water. Several other individual in-

cidents of aggression include the murder of an Orthodox Jew during a riot in Brooklyn in 1992.

For the most part the experiences of American Jews differed considerably from those of other ethnic minorities, who were subjected more regularly to cruel and physical violence.

BIBLIOGRAPHY

Dinnerstein, Leonard. *Antisemitism in America*. New York: Oxford University Press, 1984.

———. *The Leo Frank Case*. New York: Columbia University Press, 1968. Reprint, Athens: University of Georgia Press, 1987.

Higham, John. *Strangers in the Land*. New Brunswick, N.J.: Rutgers University Press, 1955.

LEONARD DINNERSTEIN

See also **Crown Heights Riot; Holocaust; Religion.**

JONESTOWN

Jim Jones, the founder and leader of the People's Temple cult, established Jonestown in Guyana in 1977, after he leased approximately 3,800 acres of jungle territory from the South American country's Marxist government. The community was billed as a utopia by Jones, who espoused communal living and racial equality. But reports of abuses had apeared throughout his career as a cult leader in the United States; in fact, the relocation of the People's Temple to Guyana seems to have been motivated primarily by Jones's desire to escape the scrutiny of the American press.

On 14 November 1978 Leo J. Ryan, a Democratic congressman from California, arrived at Jonestown to investigate reports of authoritarian control wielded by Jones at the compound. As Ryan's party attempted to leave Guyana on 18 November with sixteen cult defectors, Ryan, three journalists, and one of the defectors were gunned down, on Jones's orders, on the airstrip at Port Kaituma. Later that day, Jones directed his followers to ingest a mixture of grape drink and cyanide. Armed guards stood by to ensure that the directive was carried out and then drank the mixture themselves. In all, 914 members of the People's Temple, including 278 children and Jones himself, died in what is commonly—and erroneously—referred to as a mass suicide at Jonestown (Jones and two of his associates died from gunshot wounds to the head); another cult member and her three children died in Georgetown, Guyana.

The corpses of the followers of Jim Jones at Jonestown, in November 1978.
CORBIS/BETTMANN

James Warren Jones, born 13 May 1931, was the only child of a poor family in Lynn, Indiana. In 1950, although not an ordained minister, he became a pastor at Somerset Methodist Church in a predominantly poor white area of Indianapolis. He began to label himself biracial, claiming that his mother was a Cherokee Indian, a claim not supported by any of her family. By 1956 he had opened his own church, the People's Temple, the first biracial church in Indianapolis. He and his wife adopted six children, black, white, and Asian.

Jones used a three-part recruiting appeal—religious, political, and racial. By 1978, 80 percent of his followers were black and poor. The remainder were primarily middle class, educated Caucasians and a few Asians. From the very beginning, Jones's personality was central—his political, religious, and social beliefs dominated the group. It was purportedly a Christian sect, but the history of the People's Temple indicates it was always centered around Jones, a master manipulator, who saw to it that only his ideas were obeyed. The primary thrust of the cult was political, with Jones at its head proclaiming that he was Father.

In 1956 Jones organized a cadre of male armed enforcers, known as the interrogation committee, to keep followers in line. They policed the congregation, administering beatings to any member of the People's Temple who dared to question Jones's

ideas, or even to those who were caught in minor transgressions. Jones later called these men angels and apostolic guards.

Reports of terroristic practices at the People's Temple surfaced early on, but many officials dismissed these accounts because Jones was a superb propagandist and could order his followers to do whatever was necessary to ingratiate himself with politicians and community leaders.

In February 1961 the mayor of Indianapolis appointed Jones to the Human Rights Commission at a salary of $7,000 a year. A local newspaper investigating the appointment revealed alleged beatings and interrogations of People's Temple members, and exposed fraudulent faith healings in which Jones claimed that chicken entrails were cancers that he had mentally removed from the bodies of the elderly.

In 1963, after reading a semisatirical article in the January 1962 issue of *Esquire* magazine on the "safest places to live in the event of a nuclear attack," Jones announced his "personal vision" that a nuclear holocaust was imminent. In 1965, to escape mounting journalistic exposure in Indiana, Jones used his apocalyptic vision about a nuclear holocaust as a pretext for moving 165 members of the People's Temple by bus from Indianapolis to the Redwood Valley near Ukiah, California, which had been designated in the *Esquire* article as a "safe place." By 1973 followers were calling Jones "Father" and using the phrase "Father is God."

By 1975 People's Temple assets were at least $10 million, with $65,000 coming in monthly from the social security checks elderly members turned over to Jones. He also had members take in foster children, whose monthly allotments for care from the state of California went into his coffers.

As circumstances changed over the years, so did Jones's predictions of what would cause the end of the world. By 1975 Jones dropped the threat of a nuclear holocaust and stated that fascist despots would kill the members of the People's Temple. He began to talk about "revolutionary suicide" and Temple members meeting "on the other side." He used the threat of external danger to justify the move to Guyana. Upon arriving in Guyana he circulated the belief that the Guyanese Defense Forces were planning on storming the compound to kill the group. He cultivated a siege mentality among his followers to keep them fearful and dependent on him.

The actual threat Jones had fled from, however, was public exposure. During the time that Jones's group was in California, the San Francisco press, including religious writers, had begun to publish reports of brutality and corruption in the People's Temple, relayed by those who had escaped Jones's group. Journalists were learning what was actually going on inside the cult—financial chicanery, brutal beatings, sexual abuse of congregants, and intimidation. One report told of how members were forced to sign false confessions to heinous crimes, which they were told would be used against them in the event of their leaving the cult. Jones broke up families, threatened the lives of defectors, and was himself addicted to amphetamines.

Over the years Jones led his followers to believe that Jonestown was the promised land. Once there, he vowed, all their tribulations would be over. There would be no discipline or hunger or work when they got away from the capitalistic society of America. All the children would have college educations, and death would be vanquished. As Mel White observes, "One of the most powerful tools that Jones used to get people to the church and keep them there, especially the black, older people, was that they would never die as long as they were with him. He promised to bring them back from death" (p. 156). Jones promised nirvana and produced instead an anti-utopia.

BIBLIOGRAPHY

Kilduff, Marshall, and Ron Javers. *The Suicide Cult: The Inside Story of the People's Temple Sect and the Massacre in Guyana.* New York: Bantam, 1978.

Mills, Jeannie. *Six Years with God: Life Inside Reverend Jim Jones's People's Temple.* New York: A and W, 1979.

Reiterman, Tim, with John Jacobs. *Raven: The Untold Story of the Rev. Jim Jones and His People.* New York: Dutton, 1982.

Singer, Margaret. "On the Image of 2000 in Contemporary Cults." In *The Year 2000: Essays on the End,* edited by Charles B. Strozier and Michael Flynn. New York: New York University Press, 1997.

Singer, Margaret T., and Janja Lalich. *Cults in Our Midst.* San Francisco: Jossey-Bass, 1995.

U.S. House of Representatives. Committee on Foreign Affairs. *The Assassination of Representative Leo J. Ryan and the Jonestown, Guyana, Tragedy.* Washington, D.C.: U. S. Government Printing Office, 1979.

White, Mel. *Deceived.* Old Tappan, N.J.: Spire, 1979.

Wooden, Kenneth. *The Children of Jonestown.* New York: McGraw-Hill, 1981.

MARGARET THALER SINGER

See also **Cults; Extremism; Religion.**

JOSEPH, CHIEF. *See* Chief Joseph.

JOURNALISM

Early Print Media

Just as violence has played a role in every era of U.S. history, it has featured prominently in the history of journalism as well. Central to the developing press in the American colonies were reports on relations between the colonists and native peoples, who were described as "noble savages" if they were cooperative with colonists and "hostile savages" if they were not. Violence, in these early news accounts, was almost universally attributed to the "savage Indians." Thus began a long-standing tradition of news accounts infused with white racism and racist fears.

The earliest significant news about violent crime was contained in weekly newspapers known as broadsheets or broadsides, first published in the late 1600s. The crime news in broadsheets provided the few literate citizens with an entertaining blend of details and moralizing about crime and justice, derived from the records of court personnel. The primary mainstream newspapers prior to the 1830s, though, were the party press. These papers were vehicles for political editorializing by the major political parties and contained little that resembled later crime news stories.

The first mass-distribution newspapers in the United States were sold on street corners in cities of the industrial Northeast beginning in the 1830s. Producers of these inexpensive daily newspapers, known as the penny press, discovered early on that news about crime and violence boosted circulation. The penny press received considerable criticism for crime reporting, both from those concerned about the corrupting influences of crime news on youth and from the legal community, which was concerned about pretrial publicity compromising defendants' rights to a fair trial. Notwithstanding such criticism, the crime-and-violence formula proved so successful that it spread to magazines such as the *National Police Gazette.* Feeding the public appetite for the violent and lurid, this weekly publication surrounded scandalous pictures of scantily dressed women with regular reporting on crime, corruption, and the illegal world of bare-knuckled prizefighting.

The white European invasion of the western frontier provided a plethora of violent content both for the developing newspapers of the American West and for papers back East, in which violent conflicts between western pioneers and "hostile redskins" were typically presented as "battles" if whites were victorious and "massacres" if they were not. Perhaps such bigotry should not be surprising, since major publishers, such as William Randolph Hearst, built their publishing empires with gold stolen from Native lands. As in the colonial period, news accounts of violence on the western frontier set an important precedent for future images of violence in the news: the portrayal of victimized groups as violent predators preying on the innocent and law-abiding. Countervailing accounts did not appear until much later. For example, the army surgeon general's "Indian crania study," and the transfer of thousands of Indian skulls to the Smithsonian Institution at the turn of the century went unreported until the 1980s.

After the Civil War the invention of a usable typesetting machine and the development of wood-pulp paper made it possible to print thousands of copies of newspapers. This technology formed a bridge from the era of the penny press to the next period of pervasive sensationalism in the news media, the outbreak of "yellow journalism" during the 1890s. "Yellow journalism" was a highbrow term for what some considered to be a lowbrow popular press that pandered shamelessly to the baser interests of the masses with blaring headlines on scandal, disaster, and violence. (A cartoon character known, because of his garish garment, as the "Yellow Kid" was a popular feature in the highly sensationalistic *New York World,* owned by the publishing magnate Joseph Pulitzer.)

When Hearst purchased the *New York Journal* in 1895, New York City's publishing wars began in earnest. From the first, Pulitzer was seriously outgunned by the resources available to Hearst from his father's mining interests. Between 1895 and 1898, Spanish atrocities in Cuba provided robust ammunition for an all-out circulation war between the two papers. Daily stories on Spanish troops beating prisoners to death or even feeding them to sharks were early examples of an adage of modern journalism: "If it bleeds, it leads." With their dueling headlines, the newspapers helped to foster widespread popular support for the Spanish-American War by fueling the righteous indignation of the American public; Cuba was described as a place with "blood on the roadsides, blood in the fields, blood on the doorsteps, blood, blood, blood!" When the U.S.S. *Maine* mysteriously exploded and sank in the port of Havana, boldly emblazoned headlines blaming Spain and calling for war whipped the American public into a martial fever.

By the onset of the twentieth century, there were two distinct classes of newspapers in the United States. Some, like the highly successful *Kansas City Star,* were marketed as informational papers, targeting the upwardly mobile, the upper class, and the intellectual elite. Newspapers such as the *World* and the *Journal* targeted middle- and working-class people, and were marketed as entertaining newspapers. The tabloid *New York Daily News* was launched in 1919 and within five years had the highest daily circulation in the United States. While the entertaining newspapers made more extensive use of sensationalized crime and violence than the informational papers, both exemplified routines and standards of reporting and production that deemed violence inherently newsworthy. Nevertheless, the informational papers achieved success without resorting to blatant sensationalism.

The development of the specialized police or crime beat initiated a format that continued essentially unchanged for the next hundred years

A 1906 evening edition of the *New York World*. The trial of Harry K. Thaw for the murder of the architect Stanford White in New York City's Madison Square Garden is the headlining article. CORBIS/BETTMANN

and made criminality a staple of the daily American press. Amid the massive immigration, industrialization, and urbanization of the early 1900s, mainstream crime reporting tended to shore up the political and social status quo by portraying crime and violence as acts of individual pathology rather than as indicators of fundamental socioeconomic flaws. This pattern continued to characterize journalistic accounts of crime and violence throughout the twentieth century. Even the vogue for investigative journalism in the 1960s did not substantially alter the standard popular crime reporting style, which focuses on individual acts of violence while providing little social or political context.

Radio and Television

The advent of radio and newsreels in the 1920s and 1930s enhanced not only the capacity for live, up-to-the-minute reporting but also the ability to milk crime and violence for melodrama. Both the emotion of the human voice on the radio and the visual impact of weekly newsreels helped to create the more emotive style of news coverage that later flourished in television news reporting. These decades were also notable for Prohibition and associated organized crime and violence. With five

hundred gangland murders in Chicago alone between 1920 and 1930, there was an abundance of raw material for reporters to exploit in the interest of mass titillation.

Television was first introduced to the public in the United States at the New York World's Fair in 1939, and by the following year there were twenty-three television stations across the nation. Because the development of this new medium was interrupted by World War II, it was not until the late 1940s that television exerted a widespread influence on news and entertainment. The intimacy and immediacy of the medium lent unparalleled impact to a succession of historic events as seen in postwar American living rooms: the 1963 assassination and funeral of President John F. Kennedy and the on-screen murder of Kennedy's assassin; the Vietnam War; the radical student movements of the 1960s, with their mass demonstrations, violent protests, and equally violent police reactions; the peaceful civil rights protests and the violent police and vigilante reactions of the 1960s and 1970s; the violent black urban uprisings of the late 1960s; the 1968 assassinations of Martin Luther King, Jr., and Senator Robert F. Kennedy; the 1979 takeover of the American embassy in Iran; the 1986 explosion of the space shuttle *Challenger*; the Gulf

War; the 1991 videotaped police beating of Rodney King; the 1992 urban rebellion in Los Angeles; the O. J. Simpson murder trial of 1994–1995; and the tragic late-1990s episodes of school violence in Arkansas and Colorado. Beginning with the expansion of nightly local and network news programs to thirty minutes each, the amount of broadcast news available for public consumption increased dramatically in the late twentieth century. In 1980 Cable News Network launched the first twenty-four-hour news channel, and by 1999 there was intense competition among three nationwide round-the-clock cable news networks (CNN, MSNBC, and the Fox News Channel). Today journalistic accounts of violent events are available around the clock.

The drive for ratings and profits directly shapes the form and content of television news, which seeks to grab the viewer's attention early and often, tilting coverage toward the short and snappy at the expense of the thoughtful and thorough. Hence television news is mostly a series of thirty- to sixty-second spots within established news categories, with television news reporters striving for maximum visual impact. News reports in the electronic media, and on television in particular, utilize ten- to fifteen-second "sound bites," which are long on visceral impact, if short on information, to pique the interest of potential viewers and listeners. Again, the maxim "if it bleeds it leads" inspires television news producers take full advantage of the attention-grabbing qualities of visual images of violence to draw viewers to their news programs. A tradition of hour-long news documentary presentations, such as *CBS Reports,* emerged in the 1950s, but by the end of the century such programming had virtually disappeared in favor of short-segment "newsmagazines." While some of the latter, such as *60 Minutes,* had high aspirations, the format also degenerated into a good deal of tabloid exploitation. At the end of the twentieth century, the profit-making potential of violent visual images had inspired the medium to reach new heights (or depths) in the proliferation of "reality crime programs," in which the entertainment value of news about crime and violence is fully exploited. Whether the violent interactions of reality crime programs consist of actual footage (as in *Cops*) or reenactments (as in *America's Most Wanted*), the formula of drawing the viewer into the world of crime and violence has been an enormous success. (See the following section for further discussion of reality crime programming.)

Violence and the Content of Crime News

Media research shows that crime is a significant component of news: crime news is among the top five categories in newspapers; on television 10 to 13 percent of national television news and around 20 percent of local news is about crime. Studies also indicate that reading and watching news about crime is a popular daily ritual in the United States. For instance, among newspaper subscribers retention of crime news surpasses that of any other category of news. To this extent, at least, the culture of crime helps to establish and reinforce the moral boundaries of social life in the United States. Other studies suggest that crime news serves an important ideological function that explains its pervasiveness. News about crime and justice is said to serve the interests of the dominant economic class in U.S. society by continually suggesting to the vast middle class that crime is the work of the poor, thereby stigmatizing the underclass as the source of social problems (including crime) and a threat to civic order, and deflecting attention from their victimization.

Most crime news focuses on violent interpersonal crimes such as murder, rape, robbery, and assault, to the exclusion of the more common nonviolent crimes of burglary and theft. Indeed, to grasp the journalistic establishment's attitude toward violence, understanding what the news media ignore may be just as important as evaluating what they do report. Three points are particularly important in this regard. First, this disproportionate focus on violent crimes distorts reality: violent interpersonal crimes, in fact, constitute only a small portion of crimes known to the police. Second, whereas violent interpersonal crimes are typically depicted as occurring between strangers, the reality is that interpersonal violence occurs mainly between family members, friends, or acquaintances. Finally, the media focus on violent interpersonal crimes gives the impression that most violence in U.S. society is interpersonal as opposed to institutional or organizational. The documented reality, however, is that corporate crimes against health and safety are responsible for a far greater degree of physical injury, illness, and death than individual acts of violent street crime. Thus, the image of violence in American crime news is often distorted, even inverted.

The images of violence in crime news also reveal a good deal about U.S. society's view of the control of violent crime and the protection of citizens from harm. The criminal justice system and its three primary components—police, courts, and corrections—are rarely the explicit subjects of news reporting. Although brutality and corruption make news from time to time, there is very little investigative reporting on the extent of such problems. When some aspect of the criminal justice system does appear in the news media, it is typically as the background setting for a crime story. The courts are the most visible component of the criminal justice system in the news; however, courts most often appear as settings for individual criminal cases in the news rather than as the subject of systematic scrutiny. Occasionally, law-enforcement personnel will appear in the news media. Most often this is in situations in which television news reporters appear live, on-the-scene in the immediate aftermath of a disaster or the discovery of a violent crime. In these situations, as in instances in which the courts appear in the news media, the police are not typically the focus of the news report, but rather are simply viewed as an authoritative source of information. News depicting the correctional system is particularly rare and—except for the occasional violent riot—serves mainly as a backdrop, particularly on television, when no other images are available.

News media images of violent crime that depict the police as the "thin blue line" protecting law-abiding citizens from violent predators, the courts as places in which effective punishments are meted out, and corrections as the end of the line for dangerous criminals are gross distortions of crime and criminal justice in the United States. Not only do such images convey false impressions concerning the most likely sources of physical danger, they also fail to provide information concerning where citizens can turn for protection from the likeliest sources of harm—such as family members, unsafe working conditions, and even the environment itself. Indeed, most of the things that people do to protect themselves from violence, such as installing security locks and burglar alarms and staying at home, offer no protection from the violence they are most likely to experience, either at the hands of a family member or as a result of corporate crimes against health and safety.

The popularity of reality crime programs, such as *Cops* or *America's Most Wanted*, provides numerous insights into the social significance of crime and violence in the news media. These programs are the epitome of the alliance between the news and entertainment media. Reality crime television programs entertain their audiences by presenting actual criminal cases within an authentic-seeming format. Through a variety of production techniques, including reenactments, dramatized stories, or a documentary format, often featuring hand-held cameras with real-time countdown graphics, these programs impart a "live" feel to the sequences. However, despite their aura of realism, these programs typically use a number of dramatic techniques, including entertainment-style plots, complete with the crime, the chase, and the capture. The content of reality-based law-enforcement programs is particularly violent, and audiences commonly perceive these telecasts as raw, unedited crime and violence, with police putting their lives on the line to bring it under control. As in most crime news, the focus is on individual acts of stranger-on-stranger violence, and the programs do little to locate the violence within a broader social and political context.

True-crime stories are not limited to television. The print media have their version of real crimes packaged for purposes of entertainment as well. True-crime books on some of the most horrific acts of interpersonal violence in human history (e.g., serial murder, cannibalism, mass murder, rape, violent satanic rituals, and bizarre sex crimes) have long had a large market in the United States. Like the reality crime programs, true-crime books give the public all of the gruesome details about crime and violence ripped from the headlines of their daily newspaper. In many respects, both true-crime books and reality crime programs hearken back to the "dime novels" of the Old West, which told highly embellished and sensational tales of the violent exploits of gunslingers, bandits, and Indian fighters on the western frontier. Though the dime novels laid less claim to being factual accounts than today's true-crime books and reality crime programs do, much of their popular appeal was due to the fact that they were exciting, albeit embellished, stories of real gunfighters.

Reasons for the Media Preoccupation

It is not enough to recognize the amount of violence in the news media. This is something that most of us know without the help of the social sciences. But in addition to researching news content, media scholars have examined the processes of news production as well and provided us with three alternative models of the news production process. Central to each of these models is the concept of newsworthiness, the criteria by which journalists choose which events are to be presented to the public. The "market model" maintains that the interests of the public determine newsworthiness. In this model journalists are depicted as news collectors and disseminators who objectively report factual events about which the public expresses a desire to know. According to this model, the surfeit of violence in the media is simply a matter of news producers giving the public what it wants.

The "manipulative model" offers a different explanation of what drives the process of news production. Within this model, the selection of news items is driven not by the interests of the public but rather by the interests of those who own the news agencies. Owners of news agencies are said to be actively engaged in the determination of what will and will not be reported in the news based on their own particular class interests as members of the power elite in our society. The manipulative model does not assume that journalistic accounts are generally factual and objective. Rather news is viewed as inherently biased in favor of the rich and powerful because of the direct involvement of corporate owners in their news organizations. According to this model, violence in the news media in some ways reflects the interests of corporate owners.

The "organizational model" of the news production process is the most widely accepted hypothesis. In this model, newsworthiness is said to be determined by an array of organizational realities and relationships within which journalists work. The organizational model does not depict journalists as objectively funneling discovered facts to the public, as suggested by the market model. Rather, it describes news production as necessarily subjective because journalists, after all, are human actors who bring to their work their own backgrounds, experiences, and interests. Furthermore, unlike the manipulative model's picture of journalists as spear carriers for the power elite, the organizational model describes newsworkers as doing their work within a complex web of structurally defined relationships which, though it includes corporate owners, does not always or even usually result in the reproduction of their point of view. The organizational model, then, encompasses a number of factors, including the market and manipulation by media owners.

Perhaps the important question of why there is so much violence in the media is better addressed through thinking about the *type* of violence that characterizes news accounts, rather than just the *amount* of violence in the news. In fact, it is possible that having a clear view of the type of violence that is most common in news accounts will help us to answer the question of why there is so much violence in the news.

Whether the news media transmit violence in general and violent crime in particular according to the market model, the manipulative model, or the organizational model of news production, it is certain that media images of violence are socially significant. They distort the issue of harm from violence by depicting violent crime primarily as "violent street crime." But the random stranger-on-stranger violence of street criminals so prevalent in the news media is rare in real life when compared to both institutional violence and the violence in our homes. Perhaps the violence does not originate with "them" after all.

BIBLIOGRAPHY

Cohen, Stanley, and Jock Young, eds. *The Manufacture of News: Deviance, Social Problems, and the Mass Media.* Beverly Hills, Calif.: Sage, 1973.

Harjo, Suzan Shown. "Redskins, Savages, and Other Indian Enemies: An Historical Overview of American Media Coverage of Native Peoples." In *Images of Color, Images of Crime*, edited by C. R. Mann and M. S. Zatz. Los Angeles: Roxbury, 1998.

Graff, Henry F., ed. *The Life History of the United States.* New York: Time-Life Books, 1974.

Lerner, Eric J. "Television." In *Compton's Interactive Encyclopedia.* 1995.

Surette, Ray. *Media, Crime, and Criminal Justice: Images and Realities.* Belmont, Calif.: West/Wadsworth, 1998.

MELISSA HICKMAN BARLOW

See also **Crime and Violence, Popular Misconceptions of; Hearst, William Randolph; Literature: Nonfiction Prose; Muckrakers; Photography; Radio; Representation of Violence; Television.**

K

KANSAS CITY

A city of more than 400,000 people and the heart of a metropolitan area of 1.7 million inhabitants in the 1990s, Kansas City, Missouri, was an old frontier camp shaped by murder, plunder, and war. Located at the confluence of the Kansas and Missouri Rivers, Kansas City began as a frontier camp on the old middle border, the boundary between the United States proper and what the federal government designated as Indian country. After the 1838 ax murder of Gabriel Prudhomme, the owner of a valuable Missouri River landing, lawyers handling his estate defrauded his widow and children out of the landing and laid out a town incorporated in 1850 as Kansas City. In the 1850s proslavery border ruffians, who were responsible for encouraging sectional strife during the border wars in neighboring "Bleeding Kansas" (a name associated with the violent confrontation between proslavery and antislavery forces in the Kansas Territory following the passage of the Kansas-Nebraska Act of 1854), operated from the small settlement, causing so much street violence that even hardened prostitutes stayed away. During the Civil War, Union soldiers occupied Kansas City; meanwhile, despite harsh antiguerrilla measures, Confederate bushwhackers (including the infamous marauder William Clarke Quantrill) controlled the surrounding countryside.

Following the war, Kansas City was a rapidly growing agribusiness and transportation center. The notorious West Bottoms area of the city featured dozens of saloons, gambling dens, and brothels, and every year arrests in the Bottoms for assault, battery, disorderly conduct, and drunkenness numbered in the thousands. Desperadoes, including Jesse and Frank James, roamed freely in the streets. With a population of 55,775 in 1880, Kansas City was the second largest city in the nation west of the Mississippi River, a bigger and even more violent version of the famous Kansas cattle towns Dodge City and Abilene.

Kansas City's large meatpacking plants and stockyards employed a volatile mix of workers of different colors and nationalities. During the 1890s rioting erupted between members of the nativist American Protective Association and Irish immigrants. Drunken fights and brawls happened almost every night in the honky-tonks of West Bottoms, giving Kansas City a reputation as an untamed place that reflected the more undesirable features of its frontier heritage. Attempts by town leaders to promote a more refined image suffered a serious setback in 1910, when the civic leader Thomas Swope was murdered by arsenic poisoning, possibly by a close relative.

Unruly political behavior was commonplace. At the polls rival factions employed election enforcers, who fought each other and intimidated voters. Casimir Welch, a representative political leader, was a ward boss and justice of the peace. Uneducated in the law, Welch decided cases according to his own rights, acted as his own bailiff, and on occasion slugged lawyers and defendants. A gun battle in his court during Prohibition claimed the life of one of his henchmen. An inordinate number of Welch's men met violent deaths, including Jimmy Howard, the first man in Kansas City killed by submachine-gun fire.

During Prohibition and the Great Depression, Kansas City, dominated by the notorious Thomas J. Pendergast and his Democratic political machine, was a classic "wide-open" town, receptive to corruption in all its forms. The Pendergast machine engaged in massive fraudulent voting and had fairly open ties to the underworld. Hundreds of illegal gambling establishments and houses of prostitution paid millions of dollars in tribute to machine collectors. The underworld crime boss John Lazia enjoyed considerable influence in the police department, vetting officers and openly hiring former convicts to careers in law enforcement. For a price, criminals on the run could stay in Kansas City under police protection. Extortion rings linked to Lazia bombed dozens of businesses. Depredations reached such a point that in 1934 the U.S. attorney general Homer S. Cummings called Kansas City a "hot spot" of crime. Because of the open

collusion between the police and criminal elements, there were no reliable crime statistics.

Sensational acts of violence occurred. In broad daylight on 17 June 1933, in the Union Station Massacre, three perpetrators commonly identified as Charles "Pretty Boy" Floyd, Adam "Machine Gun" Richetti, and Vernon C. Miller failed in an attempt to free a criminal colleague, Frank Nash. During a wild gun battle in the station parking lot, Nash and four lawmen died. Less than a year later, on 27 March 1934, four people died and dozens of others were injured at the polls in a city election, bloody even by Kansas City standards.

Unknown parties murdered Lazia on 10 July 1934, and the federal government moved against the Pendergast machine. In 1937 and 1938, 259 Pendergast machine officials were convicted for vote fraud. In 1939 Pendergast went to jail for tax evasion, and his machine collapsed. The state of Missouri assumed jurisdiction over the police department, and vice became less visible. An attempt by the career criminal Charles Binaggio to restore Kansas City as a wide-open town by entering politics and taking over the remnants of the old

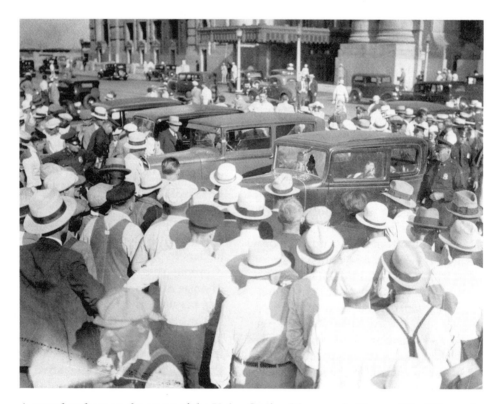

A crowd gathers on the scene of the Union Station Massacre in Kansas City, Missouri, on 17 June 1933. Gangsters killed four police officers and Frank Nash, the man the gangsters were supposed to rescue. CORBIS/BETTMANN

Pendergast organization ended with his 1950 gangland-style murder.

Two spectacular kidnappings were the signature crimes of the generally placid 1950s. In 1953 Carl Hall and Bonnie Heady pleaded guilty and died in a gas chamber for the cold-blooded, premeditated kidnapping and murder of Robert Greenlease, the six-year-old son of wealthy parents. Then, on 4 August 1955, the well-groomed Ross Brown, a thirty-year-old psychopath, at random and in broad daylight took a stylishly dressed woman from an upscale-shopping-district parking lot and brutally raped and killed her. When apprehended, he pleaded guilty, received the death penalty, and was executed on 24 February 1956.

In April 1968 a massive inner-city civil disorder following the murder of Martin Luther King, Jr., in Memphis, Tennessee, resulted in six deaths and dozens of injuries, plus hundreds of arrests and considerable property damage. In the 1970s a dispute inside the Kansas City underworld over the River Cay entertainment district led to several gangland murders and the spectacular detonation of an entire city block. In 1988 five firemen perished in an explosion at a construction site; although several people were convicted in federal court, the motive was never made clear—possible motives include a labor dispute, attempted robbery, and vandalism. One serial killer, Robert Berbella, dismembered victims and disposed of them in the garbage; in another unsolved case, as of the late 1990s, the killer threw the bodies of women victims into the Missouri River. Of countless street crimes, an especially heinous one involved a thief's cutting off an elderly woman's finger to steal her wedding ring.

In the 1990s the annual number of murders in Kansas City hovered around the one hundred mark (per 100,000 inhabitants). Many homicides happened in the inner city, outgrowths of domestic disputes, and drug deals gone sour. It was small consolation that the level of violence in Kansas City was similar to that elsewhere in the urban United States, something that could not have been said of the violent frontier and Pendergast eras.

BIBLIOGRAPHY

Brown, A. Theodore, and Lyle W. Dorsett. *Kansas City: A History of Kansas City, Missouri.* Boulder, Colo.: Pruett, 1978.

Dorsett, Lyle W. *The Pendergast Machine.* 1968. Lincoln: University of Nebraska Press, 1980.

Larsen, Lawrence H. *Federal Justice in Western Missouri: The Judges, the Cases, the Times.* Columbia: University of Missouri Press, 1994.

Larsen, Lawrence H., and Nancy J. Hulston. *Pendergast!* Columbia: University of Missouri Press, 1997.

Reddig, William M. *Tom's Town: Kansas City and the Pendergast Legend.* 1947. Columbia: University of Missouri Press, 1986.

Unger, Robert. *The Union Station Massacre: The Original Sin of J. Edgar Hoover's F.B.I.* Kansas City, Mo.: Andrews McMeel, 1997.

LAWRENCE H. LARSEN

See also **Floyd, Charles Arthur "Pretty Boy"; Frontier; James, Jesse; Prohibition and Temperance; Urban Violence.**

KELLY, GEORGE "MACHINE GUN" (1895–1954)

The violent reputation of notorious outlaw "Machine Gun" Kelly is based more in myth than reality. In the early 1930s—an era during which the Federal Bureau of Investigation came into the media spotlight as it waged war against the "pervading menace" of ruthless criminals—J. Edgar Hoover labeled Kelly a "public enemy" of the nation. The public, equally fascinated by the exploits and actions of these outlaws, followed the developments with unusual interest. When Kelly was finally convicted of kidnapping, he joined Al Capone on the first train to Alcatraz (the prison of last resort), further ensuring his long-lived notoriety for ruthlessness and violence.

"Machine Gun" Kelly was born George Kelly Barnes in Memphis, Tennessee, in 1895. As a small-time bootlegger during the Prohibition era, he disliked violence immensely. Perhaps Kelly's biggest mistake was pairing up with Kathryn Thorne—a devious and domineering woman who eventually became his wife. Thorne chose Kelly as her "subject" and was determined to mold him into one of the most feared and revered criminals of all time—an outlaw bank robber and kidnapper who would provide Thorne with the wealth she longed for.

Thorne bought Kelly his first machine gun, taught him how to use it, and then fabricated stories about his legendary prowess with the weapon. The stories portrayed Kelly as a desperate criminal wanted in several states for murder, robbery, and kidnapping. Likewise, Thorne was responsible for inventing the "Machine Gun" moniker. (Kelly had already dropped his family name, Barnes, to spare

George "Machine Gun" Kelly inside a Memphis, Tennessee, prison in September 1933. CORBIS/BETTMANN

his relatives the association with his bad reputation.) Even the FBI bought into her ruse, describing Kelly on a 1933 wanted poster as an "expert machine gunner."

While practicing and becoming proficient with his new machine gun, Kelly remained a mere bootlegger at heart. In 1930 he was caught selling liquor on an Indian reservation, convicted, and sent to Leavenworth Penitentiary. It was there that Kelly came in contact with some of the most infamous bank robbers of the day. Not content to idle his days away, Kelly eventually masterminded a prison escape, enabling two of his newfound "associates" to walk right through the front gates of Leavenworth with passes Kelly had forged while working in the prison records room. Those who escaped did not forget their debt and began including "Machine Gun" in their bank heists shortly after his release in 1931.

Thorne was soon frustrated with the insignificant amounts Kelly made from bank robberies and persuaded him to try something more lucrative—kidnapping. Kelly's first two kidnapping attempts failed, but then Thorne plotted for him to abduct a millionaire oil man named Charles Urschel. That kidnapping, in Oklahoma City in 1933, went as planned, and Kelly and his accomplices obtained a ransom of $200,000. Thorne thought Urschel should be killed, but Kelly, supposedly the ruthless criminal, would have nothing to do with it. Instead, Kelly and his accomplices returned Urschel to his family—unharmed—after receiving the ransom.

Urschel was able to give the FBI enough information to identify his kidnappers. Within weeks, Thorne and Kelly were arrested, convicted, and sentenced to life in prison. Kelly was first sent to Alcatraz and later moved to Leavenworth in 1954, where he died that year of a heart attack. Thorne was sent to a workhouse and paroled in 1958. She was last seen in the mid-1970s.

BIBLIOGRAPHY

Messick, Hank, and Burt Goldblatt. *Kidnapping: The Illustrated History.* New York: Dial, 1974.

Turner, William W. *Hoover's FBI.* Los Angeles: Sherbourne, 1970.

Whitehead, Don. *The FBI Story.* New York: Random House, 1956.

JARRETT PASCHEL

See also **Kidnapping; Robbery.**

KENNEDY, JOHN F.
(1917–1963)

Born in Brookline, Massachusetts, on 29 May 1917, to a wealthy Irish Catholic family, John Fitzgerald Kennedy received a B.A. from Harvard in 1940 and, after military service, went on to become a congressman and senator from Massachusetts and the thirty-fifth president of the United States. His mother, Rose, was the daughter of John F. ("Honey Fitz") Fitzgerald, mayor of Boston; his father, Joseph Patrick, served as President Franklin D. Roosevelt's ambassador to Great Britain from 1937 to 1941.

Fearing for his country, his financial security, and his family, Joseph Kennedy opposed U.S. entry into World War II and favored accommodating Germany's Adolf Hitler: he had privately stated, "I have four boys and I don't want them to be killed in a foreign war" (Michael Beschloss, *Kennedy and Roosevelt,* 1980, p. 162). Roosevelt was forced to ask for his resignation. Although his father had an enormous impact on his public life,

John Kennedy, then at Harvard, privately rejected his father's isolationism. He and his older brother, Joseph, Jr., served in the armed forces in World War II. Joseph, a navy pilot, died in a plane explosion in August 1944 after volunteering for a dangerous mission. John first experienced violence while serving as a PT boat commander, when a Japanese destroyer severed his boat in the Solomon Islands on 2 August 1943. He and his shipmates showed great courage and fortitude in rescuing drowning crewmen.

For the rest of his life Kennedy remained identified with the heroics of war, thanks in part to the Hollywood movie *PT-109*, released in 1963. Though deprecating his own courage, Kennedy took great pride in being a veteran. As president he often asked whether a prospective appointee had served in the military. Moreover, like other future leaders who emerged from World War II, he understood that war's "lesson"—avoid accommodating totalitarian regimes.

Ironically, Kennedy the war hero was plagued by physical infirmities that should have disqualified him from induction. Born with back problems, he aggravated the condition during his service in the South Pacific and eventually underwent several surgeries. He also suffered from an irritable gastrointestinal tract, resulting in a duodenal ulcer and chronic colitis (the reason for his military discharge in 1944), and from Addisons' disease, a life-threatening failure of the adrenal glands that probably emerged in childhood. Cortisone, available in oral form by 1951, enabled him to live in near normal fashion but could never reverse the condition. These serious health problems probably reinforced Kennedy's detachment and fatalism and perhaps, in turn, affected the way he faced crises. Of course, at the time Americans focused on his youth and apparent vigor and knew little about his illnesses.

Kennedy sought the presidency in a turbulent time. The Cold War had taken a dangerous turn, with the United States and Soviet Union at loggerheads over Berlin and with Communist insurgencies threatening the Third World. Nuclear holocaust seemed possible following the failure to reach an arms control agreement in the late 1950s. At home, racial confrontations were beginning in places like Greensboro, North Carolina, as the Civil Rights movement entered a new phase.

In 1960 Kennedy promised Americans a dynamic presidency, one that would reverse the somnolence and tired leadership of the Eisenhower era. He vowed to overcome the supposed missile gap and to adopt a tougher stance against the Soviet Union. His eloquent inaugural address reaffirmed the globalistic American foreign policy, in proclaiming that "we shall pay any price, bear any burden, meet any hardship, support any friend, oppose any foe to assure the survival and the success of liberty. This much we pledge—and more" (Giglio 1991, p. 28). Kennedy soon increased national defense expenditures, giving the United States a more flexible containment force that was prepared for any eventuality, from counterinsurgency operations in the Third World to a nuclear showdown with the Soviets. Kennedy's hard-line approach did not preclude negotiating Cold War differences, which he thought more possible if the United States strengthened itself militarily. The "arms to parley" mantra fitted well the political considerations of the time. He accommodated hardliners in his own party as well as Republicans who accused Democrats of being soft on communism. He also won the approbation of Democratic liberals who wished to diffuse Cold War issues.

Bay of Pigs

Kennedy's first major challenge came in April 1961 when he implemented a Central Intelligence Agency plan from the Eisenhower presidency to use U.S.-trained Cuban exiles against Cuba. Kennedy saw Fidel Castro's Soviet-backed regime as a threat and concluded that his own criticisms of Eisenhower's failure to subdue the Cuban dictator left him with few choices. After little open discussion and the tepid endorsement of the Joint Chiefs of Staff, Kennedy sponsored the landing of some fourteen hundred anti-Castro rebels at the Bay of Pigs in what turned out to be a tactical and political disaster. Not only did the administration underestimate Castro's strength and fail to provide sufficient air cover, it also mistakenly believed that the invaders could steal away to the Cuban mountains. Moreover, it invited criticism that the United States had violated long-standing agreements precluding unilateral intervention in Latin America. In short, it placed the United States on the side of reaction. In the end Castro captured the surviving twelve hundred Cuban rebels. The Bay of Pigs disaster could have been worse, for at a crucial moment the CIA director Allen Dulles had pleaded with Kennedy to intervene directly with American military forces to save the operation. Kennedy refused to risk more U.S. resources and prestige in such a questionable endeavor.

The failed Bay of Pigs invasion represented the nadir of the Kennedy presidency, eroding much of the administration's luster. Temporarily shaken, Kennedy privately vowed to expand the decision-making process, pay less attention to so-called experts, and tame the CIA. Yet ultimately he emerged with an even greater determination to subdue Castro. The Special Group (Augmented), created by the president, led by his brother Robert, and involving the CIA, initiated Operation Mongoose, sponsoring sabotage operations in Cuba. The CIA also employed Mafia figures to attempt to assassinate Castro, probably with the president's knowledge. The Kennedys' Cuban obsession caused Castro and Soviet premier Nikita Khrushchev to believe that American military action remained imminent.

Vienna Conference

Following the Bay of Pigs fiasco, Kennedy agreed to meet with Khrushchev in Vienna, Austria, in June 1961 to discuss festering Cold War differences, including the nuclear arms race, the civil war in Laos, and the situation in Berlin. (In late 1958 Khrushchev had issued an ultimatum demanding that the Western allies relinquish West Berlin, creating an unresolved crisis.) The summit came at a terrible time for Kennedy, for the recent Cuban crisis made him appear indecisive and inexperienced—a view that Khrushchev shared. Over two emotionally draining days, Khrushchev sought to bully Kennedy over the Western presence in Berlin. Seeking an end to the German problem, he also demanded a long-delayed peace treaty to normalize boundaries in Central and Eastern Europe. Kennedy, viewing the conflict as a test of wills, refused to make any concession over Berlin that called into question Western contractual rights; Khrushchev then threatened a separate agreement with East Germany. If America wanted war, he warned, the Soviet Union could do nothing about it. Kennedy responded that "it will be a cold winter" (Schlesinger 1965, p. 374).

Stunned by the encounter, Kennedy returned home subdued. He took seriously the Soviet threat to West Berlin and immediately strengthened the U.S. military. He also proposed a civil defense program to include fallout shelters stocked with food, water, and other necessities for survival, all of which alarmed Americans, who expected the worst. Yet this military preparedness, including the calling up of reservists, made its point with Khrushchev as well. In mid-August, to end the exodus of East Germans into West Berlin as well as to isolate West Berlin from the East, Khrushchev began the construction of a massive wall to divide the city, an acknowledgment that he could not end Western control in West Berlin. Despite remaining tensions and the Berlin Wall's tragic consequences for Germans, the worst part of the crisis had ended.

Cuban Missile Crisis

Even more serious than the East-West contention over Berlin, the Cuban missile crisis of October 1962 represents the world's closest brush with nuclear war in the Cold War era. Khrushchev saw the Bay of Pigs invasion and Operation Mongoose as pointing to the United States' willingness to use force against Castro. Khrushchev also remained concerned about the Soviet deficiency in intercontinental ballistic missiles. By placing medium- and intermediate-range ground-to-ground missiles in Cuba, capable of hitting American cities, he aimed to reduce the U.S. nuclear advantage.

Scholars acknowledge that Kennedy contributed mightily to the missile crisis, yet he responded to it prudently, measuredly, and courageously. In the end he rejected the advice of hard-liners to impose an air strike against the missile sites followed by a ground invasion. Such action could have invited disaster had the Soviets succeeded in firing even one missile at an American city. Moreover, Soviet forces had tactical nuclear weaponry in Cuba, which might have been used against an invading force. After first taking the country to the brink in his confrontational speech on 22 October, Kennedy—much influenced by Barbara Wertheim Tuchman's *Guns of August* (1962), which traced the spiraling events leading to World War I—refused to permit the missiles of October from overtaking this country in similar fashion. In the end both he and Khrushchev acted responsibly: Kennedy by imposing a naval blockade and Khrushchev by refusing to challenge it. Instead, Khrushchev agreed to remove all offensive weapons from Cuba while Kennedy promised not to attack that country and secretly consented to withdrawing Jupiter missiles from Turkey. The missile crisis had shocked the two superpower leaders into an emerging detente, leading to the installation of a hotline to prevent accidental war and to the signing of the Nuclear Test Ban Treaty of September 1963, which terminated atmospheric testing and which Kennedy hoped would be a prelude to more restrictions on nuclear weaponry.

Civil Rights

Violence accompanied the Civil Rights movement during the Kennedy presidency. In 1961 the Kennedy Justice Department sent federal marshals to Montgomery, Alabama, when local law enforcement proved inadequate to quell violence between southern extremists and civil rights activists from the North. The following year at the University of Mississippi, locals virtually warred against the university over its admission of a black student, and the Kennedy administration again sent in federal marshals and troops—the integration of Ole Miss cost the lives of two bystanders and inflicted injuries on one-third of the marshals. Countless other incidents occurred throughout the rural South as civil rights activists faced retribution from local thugs for voter registration activities. The conflict culminated in Birmingham, Alabama, in the spring of 1963, when in response to the direct-action activities of civil rights leader Martin Luther King, Jr., a reactionary police commissioner used attack dogs and high-pressure fire hoses to subdue protesters. Viewing this on the evening news, Americans were shocked. The Kennedy administration played a significant role in mediating a settlement on behalf of local blacks. By that summer no other president had embraced the cause of black civil rights to the extent that Kennedy did, and his support paved the way for the Civil Rights Act of 1964.

Vietnam

In 1963 Vietnam remained Kennedy's most serious challenge. His emphasis on counterinsurgency had increased American military advisers to sixteen thousand, and his support of the overthrow of Ngo Dinh Diem's regime, resulting in the assassination of Diem and his brother, had committed the United States even more to that war. Moreover, American aircraft in South Vietnam were assisting South Vietnamese military operations, with Kennedy approving the limited use of defoliants and napalm. To what extent the president would have further escalated American involvement, had he lived, will never be known. One thing seems certain: Kennedy would not have unilaterally withdrawn American forces by 1965.

The motorcade carrying President John F. Kennedy moments before his assassination on 22 November 1963. CORBIS/BETTMANN

Assassination

Kennedy's own death—he was gunned down as he rode in a motorcade through the city of Dallas on 22 November 1963—followed Diem's assassination by a scant three weeks. Most scholars agree that Lee Harvey Oswald was a willing and active participant in Kennedy's assassination, but some uncertainty remains as to Oswald's motives and whether he represented a conspiracy involving organized crime, the Castro government, or anti-Castro Cubans, all of whom had the means and motives to kill the president. Kennedy was only forty-seven years old at his death, leaving behind his wife and two young children. The assassinations of King, Malcolm X, and Robert Kennedy soon followed, underscoring the political violence that dominated the decade of the 1960s.

BIBLIOGRAPHY

Giglio, James N. *The Presidency of John F. Kennedy.* Lawrence: University Press of Kansas, 1991.

Reeves, Richard. *President Kennedy: Profile of Power.* New York: Simon and Schuster, 1993.

Schlesinger, Arthur M., Jr. *A Thousand Days: John F. Kennedy in the White House.* Boston: Houghton Mifflin, 1965.

Sorensen, Theodore C. *Kennedy.* New York: Harper and Row, 1965.

JAMES N. GIGLIO

See also **Assassinations; Cold War; Cuban Missile Crisis; Oswald, Lee Harvey.**

KENNEDY, ROBERT F.
(1925–1968)

Born in Brookline, Massachusetts, on 20 November 1925, to a distinguished Boston-area family—the smallest, shiest, and most inarticulate of the Kennedy sons—Bobby Kennedy was faced with high and often contradictory expectations. In reaction, he emerged as a combative, tenacious, and sometimes acerbic personality, an overachiever zealously and energetically dedicated to his chosen causes.

Kennedy graduated from Harvard in 1948 and from the University of Virginia Law School in 1951. His brother John was president of the United States from 1961 until his assassination on 22 November 1963. Bobby Kennedy served as U.S. attorney general in his brother's administration and then represented New York in the U.S. Senate from 1965 until his death on 6 June 1968.

Organized Crime

From 1957 to 1960 Robert Kennedy served as chief counsel of the United States Senate Rackets Committee, which investigated the infiltration of trade unions by organized crime. Kennedy, appalled by the violence and corruption associated with this Mafia-related activity, relentlessly fought a virtual war against that criminal element, focusing on corrupt Teamster Union presidents David Beck and Jimmy Hoffa. Beck went to prison while the brash Hoffa continued to battle Kennedy in the committee room, the courts, and the media until his own conviction in 1964 (he began his sentence in 1967). Kennedy wrote in his 1960 book, *The Enemy Within*, "If we do not on a national scale attack organized criminals with weapons and techniques as effective as their own, they will destroy us" (p. 265).

As attorney general, Kennedy adopted the rationale that the ends justify the means. He increased the size of the Justice Department's Organized Crime and Racketeering Section. He brought in aggressive, tough-minded people willing to use all legal options to the fullest. Under his direction, the department compiled a list of twelve hundred suspected racketeers and then investigated them for criminal violations, including tax fraud. That his department often went after people rather than investigating specific crimes bothered civil libertarians, as did the fact that Kennedy had no moral qualms about wiretapping racketeers. Such authorizations increased during his tenure, despite a long-standing ruling that approval could be granted only when national security was at stake. Bugging operations, involving surreptitious entry, also increased under Kennedy's Federal Bureau of Investigation director, J. Edgar Hoover. Such activities brought results: the number of convictions rose tremendously. It has been argued, but with inadequate evidence, that President Kennedy's assassination involved mobsters—such as New Orleans's Carlos Marcello and Chicago's Sam Giancana—seeking revenge and an end to the campaign against organized crime.

Civil Rights

As head of the Justice Department, Robert Kennedy also found himself serving as the administration's point man on civil rights. When activists known as the Freedom Riders challenged the segregation practices of interstate bus services in the South, Kennedy authorized the employment of

Robert F. Kennedy, middle, with brother John on the Senate Labor Committee. LIBRARY OF CONGRESS

federal marshals to protect them from beatings by white racists—but only after a mob that arrived to thrash Freedom Riders as they unloaded from a desegregated bus in Montgomery had also beaten up Kennedy's administrative assistant, John Seigenthaler, sent there to investigate the crisis. Kennedy initially responded equivocally to the civil rights struggle, and then often found himself caught in the middle of its opposing factions. Damned by racists in the southern leadership for interfering in state-related matters, he also faced the condemnation of civil rights activists for failing to intervene on their behalf in rural Mississippi and Georgia as they engaged in voter registration drives, which were met with the retaliation of local thugs. Rights leaders, including Martin Luther King, Jr., viewed Kennedy as a mediator at best in the face of racial crises in places like Albany, Georgia, and Birmingham, Alabama. He played an instrumental role, however, in the successful handling of the violent confrontation in Oxford, Mississippi, in the fall of 1962, leading to the desegregation of the University of Mississippi. The following year he also contributed to the desegregation of the University of Alabama. By the summer of 1963 Kennedy had become a leading spokesman for civil rights in the Kennedy administration.

Cuba

Kennedy advised the president on all major policy matters, including foreign policy. Although he was not involved in the April 1961 Bay of Pigs fiasco, he soon became obsessed with efforts to overthrow Fidel Castro, contributing to the Soviet decision to place ground-to-ground missiles in Cuba. In the missile crisis of October 1962, however, as nuclear holocaust loomed on the horizon, he abandoned his original position of favoring an air strike against the missile sites in favor of a blockade and a diplomatic settlement. He became a key player in back-channel negotiations with the Soviets, leading to the removal of Soviet missiles from Cuba and U.S. Jupiter missiles from Turkey.

Assassinations

Nothing affected Robert Kennedy more than the assassination of his brother. Devastated by the loss and distraught over the possibility that his actions might have caused his brother's death, he went into a deep depression before reemerging from his dysfunctional state months later. He now displayed a more humanistic and introspective side, identifying with the disadvantaged and the underdog. He entered the U.S. Senate in 1965 and sought the Democratic presidential nomination in

1968 as a critic of Lyndon Johnson's Vietnam policy, which was eroding the Great Society initiatives. Kennedy also became much more sensitive toward the violence-ridden culture of his times. In his visit to the black ghetto of Indianapolis in April, he somberly announced King's assassination. Two months later he also became a victim of violence at the Ambassador Hotel in Los Angeles, where Sirhan Bishara Sirhan, a young Jordanian immigrant probably upset at Kennedy's support for Israel, shot him dead.

BIBLIOGRAPHY

Guthman, Edwin O., and Jeffrey Shulman, eds. *Robert Kennedy in His Own Words: The Unpublished Recollection of the Kennedy Years.* New York: Bantam, 1988.

Hilty, James W. *Robert Kennedy: Brother Protector.* Philadelphia: Temple University Press, 1997.

Kennedy, Robert F. *The Enemy Within.* New York: Harper and Row, 1960.

Schlesinger, Arthur M., Jr. *Robert Kennedy and His Times.* Boston: Houghton Mifflin, 1978.

JAMES N. GIGLIO

See also **Assassinations; Freedom Rides; Giancana, Sam; Hoffa, Jimmy; Politics; Sirhan Sirhan.**

KENT STATE

On 30 April 1970 President Richard Nixon announced that he had ordered U.S. troops into Cambodia to assault guerrilla positions there. Student antiwar activists reacted immediately. Students at sixty colleges throughout the United States went on strike, and activists at three dozen institutions mounted militant protests against the "widening" of the Vietnam War. At Kent State University in northeastern Ohio, campus protests began with a peaceful rally on 1 May and culminated with the death of four students and wounding of nine students by National Guard gunfire on 4 May. "Kent State" quickly became a national landmark for student idealism cut down by state violence.

How and why the killings occurred was disputed by participant and eyewitness accounts; by local police, prosecutors, and a grand jury; by students, faculty, and campus investigations; by press interviews and analyses; by a Federal Bureau of Investigation probe and U.S. Justice Department report; by criminal and civil lawsuits; and by the President's Commission on Campus Unrest. The events leading up to the killings and their national impact, however, are discernible.

On Friday, 1 May, a group of Kent State students formed World Historians Opposed to Racism and Exploitation (WHORE) and organized a peaceful noon rally. Student protesters accused President Nixon of "murdering the Constitution" by illegally invading Cambodia. They held a mock funeral during which they buried a copy of the Constitution. That evening students and nonstudents (including members of a motorcycle gang) emerged from downtown bars and started a street bonfire and broke storefront windows. Whether the vandalism was a product of political protest or youthful rites of spring was unknown. Mayor Leroy Satrom declared a state of civil emergency, ordered the closing of liquor stores and taverns, instituted a dusk-to-dawn curfew, and requested that Ohio's governor deploy National Guard troops to Kent.

The next day students held a large demonstration on campus. During the demonstration the Kent State Reserve Officers' Training Corps (ROTC) building was set afire. Some observers conjectured that the building was ignited by "outside" agitators; others thought the arson was the act of government "agent provocateurs." Most agreed, however, that Kent State students did resist firefighter efforts to douse the blaze. The result was that the ROTC building—the campus symbol of U.S. militarism—was destroyed. Amid this tumult the first National Guard troops arrived and took up positions on campus and in town.

On Sunday, 3 May, Governor James Rhodes came to Kent and held a press conference in which he described student agitators as being worse than "the brownshirts and the communist elements." National Guard General Sylvester Del Corso then pledged that his troops would "use any force that is necessary even to the point of shooting." Student protesters reacted to the incendiary language and National Guard presence by assembling on campus that evening, only to be teargassed and dispersed. That was how they learned that the state of civil emergency included a ban on all student rallies.

On Monday, 4 May, students scheduled a campus rally for noon. The National Guard was committed to stopping it. Approximately two thousand students gathered on campus, and 113 National Guardsmen took up positions with their weapons "locked and loaded." Efforts to disperse demonstrators by use of bullhorns failed. Tear-gas canisters were launched by guardsmen only to be thrown back at them, along with some rocks. At 12:25 P.M. the guardsmen marched in a skirmish

A Kent State student reacts to the sight of a slain fellow student, on 4 May 1970. CORBIS/BETTMANN

line up to the crest of a hill, turned around, and fired their weapons into a group of students one hundred yards away. It took thirteen seconds and sixty-one rounds of ammunition for four students to be shot dead and nine to be wounded. Of those killed, two students had been participants in the rally, one was an ROTC student, and the fourth had been walking to class.

Why the guardsmen fired is still unclear. Were they ordered to fire? Did they feel their lives were jeopardized? Were they reacting to a sniper? Did they overreact? Were they properly trained? A few months later President Nixon's Commission on Campus Unrest would conclude that the National Guardsmen's use of lethal violence and the resulting student casualties were "unnecessary, unwarranted, and inexcusable."

Kent State University closed down for the rest of the spring quarter. Local residents tended to blame the university for creating a permissive atmosphere that invited student vandalism and violence. Some suggested that the guardsmen should have shot more students. Nationwide, the Kent State killings catalyzed student protest and violence. From 5 May to 8 May more than one hundred major student demonstrations per day took place; violence occurred on at least seventy-three campuses; students went on strike at more than 350 institutions; and 536 schools were shut down, fifty-one for the balance of the academic year. During the month, bombing and arson incidents hit

ninety-five college campuses, and dozens of ROTC buildings were damaged, burned, or bombed. On 14 May the Kent State tragedy was repeated, with a racial twist, at Jackson State College (now Jackson State University) in Mississippi when white policemen and state patrolmen opened fire into a crowd of black students. Two students were killed and twelve were wounded.

Kent State became a national landmark for three reasons. First, it revealed the limits of campus freedom. Government officials had demonstrated their willingness to use deadly force against middle-class, white students. They also proved that they would not take action against the uniformed men who committed the violence. U.S. attorneys had ample evidence that Ohio National Guardsmen had committed unprovoked murder and then conspired to lie about it to police and FBI investigators. Nonetheless, the Justice Department refused to convene a federal grand jury. Instead, the Nixon administration increased federal expenditures for local law enforcement and National Guard units. The message was clear. More students would die if they continued to resist public authority.

Second, Kent State represented the polarization of the American people after a decade of protest politics. Students' initial devotion to nonviolence lessened and their militant attachment to confrontational politics increased. Campus cops who once chatted cordially with student demonstrators were replaced by riot squads and armed regiments

217

committed to stopping protest with force. Simultaneously, the traditional split between "gown and town" became a chasm in college towns such as Kent, Ohio. College administrators and faculty tended to recognize, and even tolerate, students' protest politics even if they opposed them, whereas local residents were likely to side with political authority and encourage state violence against protesters. The president's commission characterized this polarization as "a crisis of understanding" that fostered "a crisis of violence."

Finally, Kent State signaled the beginning of the end of the New Left student movement. Years of student idealism manifested in activism for civil rights, student power, and international peace symbolically ended in a thirteen-second shooting spree. Antiwar activists had wanted to "bring the war home." The war did indeed come home on 4 May 1970, when the sons and daughters of middle America were gunned down. To many veterans of the 1960s and new recruits of the 1970s, it was time to pack up their politics and go home for the decade.

BIBLIOGRAPHY

Bills, Scott L., ed. *Kent State / May 4: Echoes Through a Decade.* Kent, Ohio: Kent State University Press, 1982.

The Report of the President's Commission on Campus Unrest. New York: Arno, 1970.

Stone, I. F. *The Killings at Kent State: How Murder Went Unpunished.* New York: New York Review Books, 1971.

MARK E. KANN

See also **Antiwar Protests; Campus Violence; Jackson State; New Left.**

Captain William Kidd at Gardiners Island off Long Island, New York. An illustration from *Harper's New Monthly Magazine,* **November 1894.** LIBRARY OF CONGRESS

KIDD, CAPTAIN WILLIAM
(c. 1645–1701)

The seventeenth-century privateer Captain William Kidd, hanged for murder and piracy, has been celebrated in literature as a colorful outlaw. He was born about 1645 in Greenock, Renfrew, Scotland, and it is believed that he went to sea as a youth. In 1689 he became a privateer for the British against French ships in the West Indies and off the coast of North America. By the following year he was a prosperous captain and shipowner in New York City.

In London in 1695, with the intercession of the colonial governor of New York, Richard Coote, Earl of Bellomont, Kidd received two royal commissions—to apprehend pirates against the East India Company and to cruise as a privateer against the French. Bellomont raised four-fifths of the necessary investment, the profits to be similarly divided. Kidd sailed from England on the *Adventure Galley* with eighty men and thirty-four guns in February 1696 and arrived in New York City on 4 July to engage more crew. He sailed from New York, bound for Africa, in September, but he avoided known pirate haunts and did not take any prizes. In February 1697, off East Africa, because privateers were not paid unless ships were taken, Kidd decided to turn to piracy.

In August 1697 Kidd unsuccessfully attacked the Mocha Fleet from Yemen but then took several small ships. In October, fearing he would be outgunned, Kidd refused to take a Dutch ship, the

Loyal Captain, which led to a near mutiny by his crew. About two weeks later he smashed the skull of his gunner, William Moore, with a wooden bucket. Moore, who died the next day, had argued with Kidd about not plundering the ship.

Kidd's most valuable prize was the *Quedagh Merchant*, taken in January 1698. He divided the booty among his crew, scuttled his own ship, and sailed off on the *Quedagh Merchant*. In April 1699 he arrived in Anguilla, West Indies, where he learned that he had been denounced as a pirate and that a warrant had been issued for his arrest. He bought a new ship, the *Antonio* (possibly scuttling the *Quedagh Merchant* and its booty on Hispaniola), and sailed to New York. Bellomont, unhappy with the loss of his investment, lured Kidd ashore with the promise of a pardon, listened to his appeal of innocence, then sent him to England in 1700 for trial. Kidd was found guilty and in May 1701 was sentenced to hang for the murder of Moore and five counts of piracy.

Evidence concerning two of the piracy charges (for the taking of the *Quedagh Merchant* and the *Rouparelle*, each flying the French flag) was suppressed at trial by the prosecution, and observers questioned the guilty verdict. Kidd was hanged on 23 May 1701 at London's Newgate Prison. (The first attempt failed when the rope and scaffolding broke, and Kidd had to be hanged again from a nearby tree.) Proceeds from the sale of his effects and goods on the *Antonio* were donated to charity. Some of his treasure was recovered from Gardiners Island off Long Island, New York.

Kidd became the romanticized stereotype of the swashbuckling pirate in fiction. Stories concerning his buried treasure include Edgar Allan Poe's "The Gold Bug" (1843) and Robert Louis Stevenson's *Treasure Island* (1883). In reality, he was not the terrible pirate of folklore and fiction.

BIBLIOGRAPHY

Brooks, Graham, ed. *Trial of Captain Kidd*. Holmes Birch, Fla.: Gaunt and Sons, 1995.

Hinrichs, Dunbar Maury. *The Fateful Voyage of Captain Kidd*. New York: Bookman, 1955.

Porter, Winston Alexander. *No Man Knows My Grave: Sir Henry Morgan, Captain William Kidd, Captain Woodes Rogers in the Great Age of Privateers and Pirates, 1665–1715*. Boston: Houghton Mifflin, 1969.

Ritchie, Robert C. *Captain Kidd and the War Against the Pirates*. Cambridge, Mass.: Harvard University Press, 1986.

LOUISE B. KETZ

See also **Piracy; Privateers.**

KIDNAPPING

The term *kidnapping* (from *kid*, a child or small animal, and *nap* or *nab*, to steal) began appearing in English case law at the end of the seventeenth century and applied to the taking of a person, often a child, who was then held for ransom. This crime was punishable by death, particularly if harm came to the victim. The term was also used in colonial America to describe the conscription of slaves and indentured servants. This offense, defined as the forced abduction or stealing of a man, woman, or child and sending him or her to another country, was classified as a misdemeanor.

The original kidnapping statutes that emerged with the slave trade in the United States focused on the harm the victims endured while being carried from one country to another. It was not uncommon for men to be forced onto ships or women to be sold as domestics or prostitutes. But because the slave trade was a flourishing business, kidnappers received slight punishment, if any. Kidnapping was widely practiced by the Western world until it was banned by laws in the nineteenth and twentieth centuries. The element of transport from one country to another soon lost its relevance, and the focus shifted to the involuntary confinement of the victim. Current laws in the United States are designed to secure the liberty of U.S. citizens and assist them in their release from unlawful restraint within the United States or in another country.

Statutes defining the elements of the crime vary from state to state. In most states the intent or motive of the kidnapper is irrelevant, but in some jurisdictions it must be established. In those jurisdictions a clearly established motive constitutes the crime, even when the act is not carried out. An essential element of kidnapping is the use of physical or mental force or fraud to induce the victim to accompany the kidnapper. The victim may initially come willingly, but if she is later restrained against her will, kidnapping is established. Detention is generally another key element of the crime; for example, in California removing an individual from an automobile and holding him for more than twelve hours is considered kidnapping. But some statutes hold that the victim must be taken, led, or carried away from his or her residence, or any place in which the victim has a right to be, and that restraint alone is not enough to establish kidnapping.

Some jurisdictions classify the crime by degrees of seriousness. Generally, first-degree kidnapping

WANTED

INFORMATION AS TO THE WHEREABOUTS OF

CHAS. A. LINDBERGH, JR.

OF HOPEWELL, N. J.

SON OF COL. CHAS. A. LINDBERGH

World-Famous Aviator

This child was kidnaped from his home in Hopewell, N. J., between 8 and 10 p. m. on Tuesday, March 1, 1932.

DESCRIPTION:

Age, 20 months	Hair, blond, curly
Weight, 27 to 30 lbs.	Eyes, dark blue
Height, 29 inches	Complexion, light

Deep dimple in center of chin
Dressed in one-piece coverall night suit

ADDRESS ALL COMMUNICATIONS TO
COL. H. N. SCHWARZKOPF, TRENTON, N. J., or
COL. CHAS. A. LINDBERGH, HOPEWELL, N. J.

ALL COMMUNICATIONS WILL BE TREATED IN CONFIDENCE

March 11, 1932

COL. H. NORMAN SCHWARZKOPF
Supt. New Jersey State Police, Trenton, N. J.

A poster appealing for information regarding the missing son of Charles Lindbergh. UPI/CORBIS-BETTMANN

includes an element in addition to the abduction itself; the victim may have been seriously injured, sexually assaulted, or released by the kidnapper in an unsafe place. In New York, first-degree kidnapping is found when the perpetrator demands that ransom be paid for the victim; when the victim dies while being held; or when the victim is held for longer than twelve hours. Second-degree kidnapping is found when the abduction does not involve ransom or death or when the victim is released within twelve hours. In one case, holding a woman against her will so as to prevent her from attending her wedding was found to be kidnapping in the second degree.

Other jurisdictions classify kidnapping by type: aggravated or simple. Aggravated kidnapping is established when the victim suffers bodily injury while in captivity. A third type of kidnapping, known as abduction, is generally considered a separate and less severe offense. In some states it is a crime to conceal a child or interfere with the lawful custody of a minor, usually under the age of fourteen, in violation of a court order. U.S. courts deal most frequently with this type of kidnapping. Such cases are usually the result of a custody dispute and are typically resolved through mediation, but occasionally the courts impose a fine or prison sentence on the child's abductor.

Kidnapping is ranked as a felony and is punishable with life imprisonment on the federal level. The Mann Act of 1910 prohibited the interstate transport of women for immoral purposes, but this hardly dealt with the issue of kidnapping. The crime first drew serious attention in the United States in March 1932, when the twenty-month-old son of the aviator Charles Lindbergh was kidnapped, held for ransom, and murdered. In response, Congress enacted the Federal Kidnapping Act, also known as the Lindbergh law. Kidnapping was classified as a federal crime if the victim was taken across state lines, thus giving the Federal Bureau of Investigation authority to get involved. An additional law was also passed that created severe penalties for kidnapping during the course of committing a robbery at a national bank. National concern arose again in the 1970s, when U.S. citizens fell victim to a series of airline hijackings and hostage takings in the Middle East.

Famous Cases

The United States' first modern ransom kidnapping occurred in Germantown, Pennsylvania, on 2 July 1874, when six-year-old Charles Ross and his older brother were induced to enter a carriage and driven away by two men. The older boy was released. The Rosses received a ransom note demanding $20,000 for the return of their son. The alleged kidnappers were shot and killed during the course of a robbery attempt. Just before dying, one of them admitted to abducting Charlie Ross, but did not reveal his whereabouts. The boy was never found.

Another sensational case involved the kidnapping of a wealthy victim by wealthy offenders. On 21 May 1924 Robert Franks, the fourteen-year-old son of a Chicago millionaire, was lured into a car by eighteen-year-old Richard Loeb and nineteen-year-old Nathan Leopold, Jr., both sons of wealthy Chicago families. They placed a ransom phone call to the Franks, threatening Robert's death—but in fact they had already killed him. His body was found in a culvert before the Franks received ransom delivery instructions. Loeb and Leopold were caught and received life sentences.

Despite a fairly regular incidence of one kidnapping per year after the Lindbergh case, kidnapping did not again reach national attention until December 1968. Barbara Mackle, whose extremely wealthy family were President Richard Nixon's Florida neighbors, was a student at Emory University. She was staying in an Atlanta motel with her mother during final exams when a man and a woman forced their way into the room. They bound and gagged the mother and kidnapped Barbara. She was taken to a wooded area and buried in a coffin with a life-support system. The kidnappers demanded a $500,000 ransom and fifteen hours later gave instructions for delivering the money and locating Barbara. After spending eighty hours entombed, Barbara Mackle was rescued. The kidnappers were found and convicted.

In the 1960s and 1970s several countries were dealing with kidnapping as a form of terrorism to further political agendas. The United States had had limited experience with this type of crime before 4 February 1974, when Patricia Hearst, the granddaughter of the newspaper publisher William Randolph Hearst and heiress to the family fortune, was abducted in Berkeley, California. This kidnapping drew national attention not only because of the Hearst name but because of its unprecedented political motives. The Symbionese Liberation Army (SLA) confirmed that they were the kidnappers on a Berkeley radio station. They initially warned that Patty Hearst would be executed if a rescue was attempted. The SLA's first ransom letter demanded that her father, Randolph A. Hearst, finance a multimillion-dollar food distribution to the poor people of California. Hearst offered $2 million but received no response from the SLA. On 13 April the SLA released a tape in which Hearst stated that she had voluntarily joined the SLA after the group had offered to set her free. On 16 April a security camera captured an image of Patty Hearst participating in a bank robbery. Hearst's status in the public mind changed from victim to terrorist fugitive. On 18 September 1975 Hearst and six other members of the SLA were arrested in a house in suburban San Francisco after an SLA member unwittingly led the FBI to the SLA's headquarters. In 1976 Hearst was tried for assisting the SLA in the armed rob-

Missionaries in Colombia

Three missionaries, Mark Rich, Dave Mankins, and Rick Tenenoff, were kidnapped on 13 January 1993 by a Marxist guerrilla organization known as the Revolutionary Armed Forces of Colombia (FARC). The men were asleep in their homes when groups of men simultaneously broke into their homes and ordered them to lie face down on the ground. The FARC abductors did not identify themselves or their motives; they instructed the missionaries' wives to pack their husbands' belongings and told them to have faith and that it would end soon. FARC contacted the men's Protestant mission, New Tribes Mission in Florida, and demanded $5 million. FARC and the mission remained in radio contact for almost a year, but the mission refused to pay the ransom and on 4 January 1994 FARC abruptly severed all communication. In December of 1998, mid-level officials at the U.S. State Department reversed their policy and held secret talks with FARC in Colombia. The goal of the talks was to press FARC to account for the three missionaries and to inform FARC of the United States' full endorsement of the antinarcotic measures undertaken in Colombia. FARC is considered a terrorist organization that acquires most of its funds through kidnapping, extortion, and protecting major players in Colombia's notorious drug trafficking rings. As the unresolved case continued in 1999, the missionaries were believed to be the longest-held hostages in U.S. history.

bery of over $10,000 from the Hybernia Bank in San Francisco. At the trial Hearst insisted she had been brainwashed by the organization as well as mentally, physically, and emotionally raped. Hearst was convicted of the robbery and sentenced to seven years in prison. President Jimmy Carter later commuted her sentence.

In the 1990s two cases of kidnapping garnered national attention. On the morning of 4 August 1993, Harvey Weinstein, a sixty-eight-year-old millionaire executive, was forced into a car with a knife to his throat while on his way to work in New York City. Weinstein spent twelve days in a hole eight feet deep and four feet wide covered with a 125-pound steel plate. The kidnappers telephoned Weinstein's formal-wear company and demanded $3 million in ransom. The ransom was delivered, but the kidnappers, sewing-machine operators at the company, were quickly apprehended, and Weinstein was found. As more sophisticated surveillance techniques have become available to police, ransom kidnappings have become more rarely successful.

In October 1993 twelve-year-old Polly Klaas was kidnapped from her bedroom in Petaluma, California, while two friends watched. A massive publicity campaign and police search ensued. She was found murdered with evidence of sexual assault, and the kidnapper was caught and convicted. The wide media attention that the Polly Klaas case received led to a number of child safety measures, largely owing to Klaas's father and the Polly Klaas Foundation. The number of states requiring sex offenders to register with the police upon release from prison doubled, and laws requiring notification to a community when a sex offender moves into the area tripled to thirty-six states. The FBI changed its policy to take on an active partnership with local police departments immediately when a kidnapping case arises. Local FBI agencies created their own Crimes Against Children Task Forces, and even private industry responded by offering space on some consumer products to display the faces of missing children. The results of these reforms are evident in the 15 percent increase in cases solved at the Center for Missing Children since these measures were enacted.

Changing Patterns and Practices

The practice of kidnapping in the United States has changed over time. Historically, kidnapping for money has not been a primary motive: between 1874 and 1974, only 14 percent of kidnappings were for ransom. Having begun as the practice of forcing men into labor or women into prostitution, by the end of the Civil War era, kidnapping predominantly took the form of child stealing. Until the 1920s most kidnap victims were children, and most ransom kidnappings involved wealthy white children located on the East Coast. Children of poorer families from various ethnic groups were sometimes held for ransom—usually sums less than $5,000—in kidnappings that were primarily intended to intimidate immigrant business owners.

In the late 1920s large urban areas across the country experienced a new trend of gangsters kidnapping other gangsters for huge ransoms, with the rivals negotiating the amounts. Wealthy businessmen, largely in the Midwest, also became targets. The shift in the age of the victim was quite dramatic. In 1930, 90 percent of kidnapping victims were white, upper-class men over the age of eighteen. By the mid-1930s kidnapping had reached epidemic proportions, peaking in 1933 with ninety-four general kidnappings, twenty-seven ransom kidnappings, and six occurring within one five-week period during the summer.

In the 1930s swift police reaction and legislation making kidnapping a capital crime punishable by death led to a three-decade period of dormancy. Then, in the late 1960s members of organized crime began kidnapping each other, their motives primarily intimidation or revenge. By 1974 kidnapping peaked once again, reaching its highest level since 1933, with fifty-four cases reported. The Hearst kidnapping, not only because it involved both financial and political issues but also because of the media attention it received, was seen as having contributed to the new trend of kidnapping for money or political attention.

A resurgence in child stealing developed in the 1970s. Reflecting increases in divorce and attendant custody disputes, most of these cases involved parental kidnapping. Wider access to air travel also made it easier for noncustodial parents to snatch their children. (A few cases involved abductions by strangers in which children were taken and sexually assaulted.) As the phenomenon of parental kidnapping crossed all economic classes—that is, once "ordinary" middle-class people were involved—an epidemic was declared.

In the latter decades of the twentieth century, kidnapping became strongly associated with political terrorists, particularly left-wing extremists. During the 1970s terrorists used kidnapping as an effective yet low-risk tool. Diplomats and businessmen became favorite targets. In 1977 three thousand Islamic fundamentalists overran the U.S. embassy in Tehran, Iran. Fifty hostages, mostly diplomatic personnel, were held there for 444 days, with foreign-policy repercussions continuing through the turn of the century. Such dramatic and high-visibility kidnappings allow terrorists to attract the attention of an international audience to their cause. Political kidnappings have also been used to obtain the release of prisoners, broadcast manifestos, extort political concessions, render laws unworkable, erode a nation's economy, and obtain money.

BIBLIOGRAPHY

Alix, Ernest Kahlar. *Ransom Kidnapping in America: The Creation of a Capital Crime, 1874–1974.* Carbondale: Southern Illinois University Press, 1978.

Clutterbuck, Richard. *Kidnap, Hijack, and Extortion: The Response*. London: Macmillan, 1987.

———. *Kidnap and Ransom: The Response*. Boston: Faber and Faber, 1978.

Fass, Paula S. *Kidnapped: Child Abduction in America*. New York: Oxford University Press, 1997.

Gill, John E. *Stolen Children*. New York: Seaview, 1981.

Greif, Geoffrey L., and Rebecca L. Hegar. *When Parents Kidnap: The Families Behind the Headlines*. New York: Maxwell Macmillan, 1993.

DEIRDRE M. BOWEN

See also **Crime, Legal Definitions of; Lindbergh Kidnapping Case; Loeb, Richard, and Nathan Leopold; Symbionese Liberation Army.**

KING, MARTIN LUTHER, JR.
(1929–1968)

Martin Luther King, Jr., pastor and civil rights leader, is arguably one of the most influential Americans of the twentieth century. He was named *Time* magazine's Man of the Year in 1963 and awarded the Nobel Peace Prize in 1964. He is the only American to be celebrated with a national holiday in his name alone.

Martin Luther King is best known as the preeminent advocate of nonviolence. From the time of the yearlong, triumphant bus boycott in Montgomery, Alabama (1955–1956), to his assassination in Memphis, Tennessee, in 1968, King embraced nonviolence absolutely. According to King nonviolence was not only an effective strategy of social change, it was also his religious philosophy of life. There was no limit to his advocacy of nonviolence in conflictive situations. He contended that nonviolence was the most potent weapon both for blacks in the U.S. Civil Rights movement and for other oppressed peoples struggling for justice throughout the world. Nonviolence was not only the best tool for solving conflicts within nations, it could also resolve differences between nations. For King, the acquisition of nuclear weapons by several nations created the situation in which "the choice is no longer between nonviolence and violence. It is either between nonviolence or nonexistence."

Early Influences

The roots of King's journey to nonviolence lie in Atlanta, Georgia, where he was born on 15 January 1929. As the son of the Reverend Martin Luther King, Sr., pastor of the prestigious Ebenezer Baptist Church, young Martin was nurtured in the black Baptist tradition of the Christian faith. He followed his father into the ordained ministry in his late teens. The Christian idea of love, as expressed in Jesus' Sermon on the Mount and his death on the cross, was the hallmark of the religious experience that shaped King's perspective. He combined Christian love with the accommodative and protest philosophies of Booker T. Washington and the National Association for the Advancement of Colored People. Together, these ideas provided the religious and political resources for King to develop a militant, nonviolent philosophy of social change in the context of the black struggle for racial justice in America.

The development of Martin Luther King's philosophy of nonviolence was a gradual process. His unpleasant childhood experiences with segregation had a profoundly negative effect on his initial attitude towards whites. He was introduced to racial prejudice at the early age of five when the father of one of his white friends told young Martin that his son could no longer play with him because he was "colored." This and other encounters with prejudice impressed King deeply, and made it difficult for him to love whites as he was taught to do at home and at church. At one point during his early years, in fact, King was determined to hate all whites.

Martin Luther King's negative attitude toward whites started to change during his time in an intercollegiate organization and later at Crozer Theological Seminary in Chester, Pennsylvania, and Boston University School of Theology. At Morehouse College he read Henry David Thoreau's essay "Civil Disobedience" and was introduced to a wide range of political and religious philosophies that supported the integration of African Americans into the mainstream of American society. In graduate school King met liberal white teachers and fellow students and encountered progressive theological and philosophical ideas that deepened his beliefs about justice and love, integration, and the beloved community. He read Mahatma Gandhi at Crozer and, at Boston University, acquired a knowledge of personalism, a philosophy that accented the infinite value of the human. King read widely in the disciplines of theology and philosophy and concluded his formal education with his doctoral dissertation, "A Comparison of the Conceptions of God in the Thinking of Paul Tillich and Henry Nelson Wieman" (1955).

Beginnings of a Philosophy

In 1954 Martin Luther King became the pastor of the middle-class Dexter Avenue Baptist Church

Martin Luther King, Jr., his wife, and thousands of civil rights demonstrators arrive in Montgomery, Alabama, in March 1965, completing the last leg of a fifty-mile hike from Selma to Montgomery. UPI/CORBIS-BETTMANN

in Montgomery, Alabama. When Rosa Parks was arrested on 1 December 1955 because she refused to give up her bus seat to a white man, the black community was enraged. In protest, blacks initiated a boycott of the city buses on 5 December and asked King, who was not yet committed to nonviolence, to be their leader. After this boycott began, violence and aggression became increasingly focused on King personally through police harassment, the bombing of his house, volumes of hate mail, and frequent telephone threats of harm to his family. After King's application for a gun permit was turned down, armed blacks took turns guarding his home, and his father urged him to leave Montgomery.

The most important factors that influenced Martin Luther King to adopt methods of nonviolence were his grounding in Christian faith and his frequent revisiting of the teachings of Gandhi. In the midst of the bus boycott, King, at the age of twenty-six, faced the possibility of his own imminent death. The experience was overwhelming. As the leader of fifty thousand blacks, he had to be strong, so that the black community would not falter in their struggle. King turned to the God that his parents had taught him about for strength and courage. Through meditation and prayer, the God of Jesus became a powerful existential presence that enabled him to embrace love courageously.

It was one thing for King to love individual whites personally but quite another to use love as an instrument of social change. Gandhi provided him with the insight of nonviolent, direct action. With a deeper knowledge of Gandhi, King became a firm believer and astute defender of nonviolence. Jesus Christ defined the center of King's religious understanding of love, and Gandhi showed him how to use love as an instrument to transform society. King's commitment to nonviolence was also deepened by his knowledge of liberal Protestant theology and the philosophy of personalism. Martin Luther King not only preached nonviolence during the Montgomery bus boycott; in February 1958 he also founded the Southern Christian Leadership Conference, a national organization dedicated to nonviolence and to achieving justice for blacks in every segment of American life. The officers were mostly ministers, and its motto was "to redeem the soul of America."

For King, love was the most powerful force in the world, and nonviolence was love expressed politically. Because nonviolence was widely thought of as "doing nothing," King repeatedly emphasized the active dimensions of nonviolence. It is only passive in the sense of refusing to inflict physical harm on others. Nonviolence, therefore, is not a method for cowards—people afraid to suffer for the cause of justice. Nonviolence resists evil and also refuses to commit evil. The nonviolent activist does not insult or seek to destroy the opponent but rather seeks to make the enemy a friend. Even if nonviolence fails to convert the enemy to a friend, it eliminates hate from the hearts of those who are committed to it. Nonviolence bestows courage and self-respect to oppressed people who were once consumed by fear and low self-esteem.

King viewed nonviolence as the best practical and moral method for achieving justice. Only moral means can achieve moral ends, thus "the end is preexistent in the means." Violence, therefore, was "both impractical and immoral." Even though most blacks were not morally committed to nonviolence, King persuaded them that, as only 10 percent of the population, they had little chance of achieving their goals by violent means and that their best strategy for achieving justice was a nonviolent one.

These practical arguments for nonviolence were presented to those who could not accept the moral arguments. From the first Montgomery bus boycott (1955) to the Selma March (1965), Martin Luther King inspired African Americans to hold firmly to nonviolence in their struggle for justice. The success of the student sit-ins (1960), the Freedom Rides (1961), the Birmingham demonstrations (1963), and the March on Washington (1963) provided King with the opportunity to demonstrate the power of nonviolence in destroying segregation in American life. The triumphant march from Selma to Montgomery was the climax of the first phase of the Civil Rights movement. The Civil Rights Act (1964) and the Voting Rights Bill (1965) were its major political achievements.

Critics of Nonviolence

In the early 1960s Malcolm X was the most effective critic of King and nonviolence. But, isolated in a black separatist religious sect called the Nation of Islam, he was a marginal figure during the first phrase of the Civil Rights movement. After the 1965 Watts riots in Los Angeles and the rise of the Black Power movement in 1966, King's views on nonviolence were seriously challenged by young activists who, disillusioned with the relevance of nonviolence for eliminating poverty in the North, turned to Malcolm X's self-defense philosophy as an alternative to King's teachings.

King was forced to defend nonviolence among critics who romanticized Malcolm X's self-defense philosophy. King met his critics in the Black Power movement head-on and challenged them to prove him wrong. Though many black militants ultimately rejected King's views on nonviolence and integration, they respected him because he embodied the truth about which he spoke.

Martin Luther King's stature in the white community continued to increase as long as he persuaded blacks to hold firmly to nonviolence. But they rejected him when he applied his views to America as a nation. King's opposition to the war in Vietnam won him few friends in government and the society at large. Most whites acknowledged that King was an expert on civil rights. They urged King to stick to civil rights and leave peace issues between nations to the elected politicians and their advisers. The idea that a black preacher's views on America's foreign policy should be taken seriously was ludicrous to most whites, especially to President Lyndon B. Johnson, who saw himself as the Negro's best friend in government. What right did King have to criticize America and its president when they had done so much for the Negro?

Between 1966 and 1968, King struggled against an American public who resisted further advances in civil rights and resented his claim that America was "the greatest purveyor of violence in the world today." King's political optimism in the early phase of the Civil Rights movement was transformed into a tough, religious hope, derived from his deep belief that "unearned suffering is redemptive."

King's faith in nonviolence was first and foremost an unshakable religious commitment. Although he preached the strategic value of nonviolence, the essence of King's belief was his acceptance of it as a way of life, "because of the sheer morality of its claim." Thus, even in defeat, nonviolence still wins. This is so because the universe is moving toward justice. No person or nation can prevent its ultimate realization. This faith sustained the later King in his struggle to achieve economic justice for garbage workers in Memphis as he was preparing for the Poor People's Campaign to pressure the federal government to withdraw from the war in Vietnam and to intensify instead the war on poverty. An assassin's bullet ended King's life on 4 April 1968 while he was standing on the balcony of the Lorraine Motel in Memphis. His hope, however, lives on in those who today still fight for justice.

BIBLIOGRAPHY

Branch, Taylor. *Parting the Waters: America in the King Years, 1954–1963.* New York: Simon and Schuster, 1988.
———. *Pillar of Fire: America in the King Years: 1963–1965.* New York: Simon and Schuster, 1998.
Cone, James H. *Martin and Malcolm and America: A Dream or a Nightmare.* Maryknoll, New York: Orbis, 1991.
Garrow, David J. *Bearing the Cross: Martin Luther King, Jr., and the Southern Christian Leadership Conference.* New York: Morrow, 1986.
King, Martin Luther, Jr. *A Testament of Hope: The Essential Writings of Martin Luther King, Jr.,* edited by James M. Washington. New York: Harper, 1986.

JAMES H. CONE

See also **African Americans; Assassinations; Civil Disobedience; Civil Rights Movements; Montgomery Bus Boycott; Nonviolence; Ray, James Earl.**

KING, RODNEY, BEATING OF. *See* Los Angeles Riots of 1992.

KOREAN AMERICANS

On 2 May 1992 approximately thirty thousand Korean Americans gathered at Ardmore Park in the Koreatown neighborhood of Los Angeles to protest the violence experienced during the riots of 1992. Many Korean immigrants felt they had been victimized and scapegoated for larger societal failures. The riots, or Sa-ee-gu (29 April), as they are known in the Korean American community, brought disproportionately high financial damages and psychological pain to the largely immigrant population. Approximately 2,280 Korean-owned businesses were destroyed, and the cost of physical destruction exceeded four hundred million dollars. Never before had Korean immigrants and second-generation Korean Americans been compelled to speak out to protest their status in America. This "Peace March," believed to be the largest gathering of any Asian American group in the 150-year history of Asian presence in the United States, became an important element in the renewal and development of Korean American identity.

Prior to the Los Angeles riots of 1992, public consciousness of Korea and Korean Americans was for the most part defined by the Korean War and character portrayals in television series such as *M*A*S*H*. The riots further contributed to Korean Americans' status as one of the most misunderstood ethnic groups in the nation. The American public and the world were shocked by images of Korean American merchants on the rooftops defending their stores with guns. The gun-toting vigilante image distorted the community's history and experiences. Once a silent and invisible Asian group indistinguishable from Chinese or Japanese Americans, Korean Americans have come forth as arguably the most visible segment of the Asian American community. They have undertaken the responsibility of battling the negative and stereotypical images of Korean Americans and of representing the Asian American community in general.

On 13 January 1903 Korean immigration to the United States officially began with the arrival of 101 laborers in Honolulu. Between 1903 and 1905, approximately 7,600 Korean immigrants were recruited as cheap contract laborers (prohibited by law at the time) by the Hawaiian Sugar Plantation Association. They endured semislavery conditions, labor exploitation, physical abuses by *luna* (foremen), and low wages. Yet despite these harsh conditions, immigrants continued to seek the promise of opportunities in America. The National Origins Act of 1924 prohibited further immigration of "aliens ineligible for naturalized citizenship" and halted Korean and other Asian immigration to the United States. By 1910 Korea had become a Japanese colony and remained under Japanese oppression until 1945. Under Japanese rule Koreans lost their freedom and suffered severe economic exploitation and attacks on their culture; indeed, Japanese colonial policy attempted to wipe out Korean race and culture. Throughout its history Korea has had to withstand attack, invasion, incursion, and encroachment from its neighboring countries. Yet Korea and Koreans have maintained a homogeneity whose unity is deeply rooted in a common language, culture, tradition, identity, and history. Divided at the thirty-eighth parallel into two zones of occupation at the end of World War II, Korea suffered further devastation as a result of the Korean War. On 25 June 1950 the communist North Korean military attacked South Korea, triggering the war; almost 1.9 million South Koreans lost their lives before the armistice in 1953. In the aftermath of the war, millions of families were separated by the opposing regimes of South and North Korea; as many as ten million Koreans had not been reunited with their families as of the late 1990s.

The passage of the Immigration Act of 1965 opened the door for South Korean immigration to resume. Fleeing political turmoil, memories of a tragic war, and economic devastation of their country, these immigrants came to seek a better life in America. In this new land, Korean immigrants were confronted with problems of race relations and forced to play the role of minority middleman between the dominant white and subordinate black and Latino populations. Faced with language and cultural barriers, racial discrimination in the labor market, and the lack of transferable skills, Korean immigrants were obliged to become self-employed. Indeed, Korean Americans ranked the highest in self-employment rates in 1990.

Signs in Koreatown, Los Angeles, 1997. CORBIS/NIK WHEELER

neighborhoods were murdered during the 1980s and 1990s; four Korean merchants were shot to death in the single month of April 1986 in South Central Los Angeles. These incidents led to the formation in Los Angeles of the Black-Korean Alliance, which aimed to improve relations between the groups.

In retrospect, the 1992 riots were not only a turning point but also a wake-up call for Korean Americans. Korean immigrants believed they could achieve the American dream with industriousness and perseverance. Yet despite the long years of hard work, the merchants could only watch helplessly as their stores burned to ashes. The victims sought assistance from the Federal Emergency Management Agency, but they were confronted with a bureaucracy that was not designed to meet the needs of limited-English or non-English speakers. Faced with these obstacles, Korean Americans began to lose faith in the American dream and their identity as Americans. The Los Angeles riots marked the beginning of a new era for Korean Americans in mainstream America: in the aftermath, the Korean American community searched for a new vision that would return a sense of dignity and hope to those who lost so much in April 1992.

BIBLIOGRAPHY

Cannon, Lou. *Official Negligence: How Rodney King and the Riots Changed Los Angeles and the LAPD.* New York: Times Books, 1997.

Chang, Edward T. "America's First Multiethnic Riots." In *The State of Asian America: Activism and Resistance in the 1990s,* edited by Karin Aguilar-San Juan. Boston: South End Press, 1994.

Chang, Edward T., and Russell C. Leong, eds. *Los Angeles —Struggles Toward Multiethnic Community: Asian American, African American, and Latino Perspectives.* Seattle: University of Washington Press, 1994.

Choy, Bong Youn. *Koreans in America.* Chicago: Nelson Hall, 1979.

Kang, K. Connie. *Home Was the Land of Morning Calm: A Saga of a Korean-American Family.* New York: Addison-Wesley, 1995.

Kim, Illsoo. *New Urban Immigrants: The Korean Community in New York.* Princeton, N.J.: Princeton University Press, 1981.

Lee, Ki-Baek. *A New History of Korea.* Translated by Edward W. Wagner, with Edward J. Shultz. Boston: Harvard University Press, 1984.

Patterson, Wayne. *The Korean Frontier in America: Immigration to Hawaii, 1860–1910.* Honolulu: University of Hawaii Press, 1988.

EDWARD TAEHAN CHANG

During the 1980s and 1990s, the proliferation of successful Korean-owned businesses in African American urban neighborhoods heightened racial tensions between Korean immigrant merchants and poor African American customers. In fact, many observers likened Korean–African American relations to a keg of dynamite ready to explode. Highly publicized boycotts of Korean stores by African Americans in Los Angeles, New York, and other cities further exacerbated tensions between the two minority groups. One such boycott, in the Flatbush section of Brooklyn, New York, known as the Red Apple boycott, lasted fifteen months— from January 1990 to May 1991. The fatal shooting, on 16 March 1991, of Latasha Harlins, a fifteen-year-old African American girl, by Soon Ja Du in South Central Los Angeles also heightened tensions between the two ethnic groups. Many Korean American merchants in African American

See also **Asians; Immigration; Los Angeles Riots of 1992.**

KOREAN WAR

Less than five years after achieving an overwhelming victory in World War II, the United States again found itself engaged in a violent conflict, this time in a remote Asian location that U.S. leaders had not considered strategically vital to the national interest. The United States was so unprepared for war that President Harry S. Truman referred to U.S. intervention in Korea as a "police action." U.S. officials hoped that U.S. military power, backed by the authority of the United Nations, would quickly reestablish peace; they did not foresee that the Korean War would last more than three years (from

South Korean women and children flee from advancing communists in August 1950 while U.S. soldiers march toward the enemy, into the Naktong River area. UPI/CORBIS-BETTMANN

25 June 1950 to 27 July 1953) and conclude in an unsatisfying stalemate.

The independence of Korea, which Japan had annexed in 1910, became a publicly proclaimed Allied aim during World War II. On Japan's surrender in August 1945, the United States and the Union of Soviet Socialist Republics used the thirty-eighth parallel, which roughly bisected the Korean peninsula, to separate their occupation zones. Although the United States considered the parallel a temporary expedient, it became a fixed boundary in the context of the intensifying Cold War between the Soviets and the Americans. Both the U.S.-backed Republic of Korea in the south and the Soviet-sponsored communist People's Democratic Republic of Korea in the north proclaimed their independence in 1948 and continued to exchange threats after U.S. and Soviet troops withdrew from the peninsula.

In 1950 the United States regarded global communism as a monolithic movement directed by the Soviet Union, with the ultimate goal of controlling the world. American concerns about the expansion of communism, which had been heightened by the recent communist victory in China, appeared confirmed on 25 June 1950, when powerful North Korean forces crossed the thirty-eighth parallel and moved rapidly into South Korea. As the United Nations called on its members to repel the aggression, the United States sent first air and naval forces and then ground combat troops to Korea, drawing mainly from the U.S. occupation force stationed in nearby Japan under the command of General of the Army Douglas MacArthur. On 7 July the United Nations created a unified military force under the direction of the United States, which contributed the largest sea and air forces, as well as substantial ground units. Truman appointed MacArthur to head the new United Nations Command.

Initially, North Korea appeared invincible as U.S. and Republic of Korea troops retreated to the southeastern corner of the peninsula, where they established defensive positions along the Naktong River and the coastal port of Pusan. On 15 September U.S. forces made a surprise amphibious assault behind enemy lines at Inchon, the port for Seoul, while the soldiers in the Naktong perimeter took the offensive and moved north to join them. As the dynamics of the conflict shifted, the remnants of the North Korean army retreated across the thirty-

American troops land at Inchon, South Korea, in September 1950. Photographed by Bert Hardy. HULTON GETTY/LIAISON AGENCY

eighth parallel, with Republic of Korea troops in pursuit.

At this point, the United Nations had basically achieved its goal of restoring the prewar status of Korea, but emboldened by the enormous success of the Inchon landing, it changed the war's aim on 7 October to the unification of the peninsula under a single, freely elected government. UN troops entered North Korea in force. On 24 November MacArthur's "end the war" offensive abruptly halted when massive numbers of communist Chinese soldiers, who had secretly crossed the Yalu River into North Korea, suddenly attacked the UN troops and pushed them back across the border and farther south. Not until early 1951 did the United Nations halt its retreat and begin offensive action. By that summer, the battle lines stood fairly close to the thirty-eighth parallel.

On 10 July 1951, shortly after the first anniversary of the war's start, delegates from the United States (representing the United Nations), North Korea, and China began truce negotiations at Kaesong and later at Panmunjom. For the next two years the bitter, acrimonious talks dragged on, while the ferocious fighting continued and casualties mounted. In contrast to the sweeping movements of the first year, relatively little territory changed hands during the negotiations, as each side fortified its defenses and launched intense artillery barrages. Although the war was fought primarily with World War II weapons, its battle-

fields came to resemble the static front of World War I.

In spite of the growing unpopularity in the United States of the costly, indecisive conflict, no significant antiwar movement challenged U.S. participation. The public demonstrated its immense frustration with the war's course in the uproar that followed Truman's firing of MacArthur in April 1951 for publicly disagreeing with the administration. The congressional hearings on the dismissal addressed specifically Truman's decision to wage limited rather than total war in Korea.

Actually, both sides took steps to limit the extent of violence in the Korean War. Even before the entry of China forced the United States to abandon the prospect of liberating North Korea, the Truman administration had sought to contain the conflict to the Korean peninsula. Breaking from its tradition of waging unlimited war, the United States confined its campaign to Korean territory, avoiding incursions across the nearby Soviet border and denying proposals to attack Manchurian supply bases and airfields. Because the government considered western Europe the primary communist target, the United States assigned substantial ground forces there that could have reinforced the troops in Korea. The communist belligerents also limited the war, declining to meet the United Nations in battle on or under the seas. Their aircraft did not seriously challenge U.S. supremacy of the skies. They refrained from using sea or air power to attack vital ports and logistical lines between Korea and Japan. Neither side employed nuclear weapons.

The limits on the war did not alleviate the brutality experienced by the forces on the ground. Caught in a conflict that combined a civil war with the Cold War, U.S. troops and prisoners of war encountered savagery. The harshness of the Korean landscape—mountainous, barren, and subject to extreme temperatures in both winter and summer—was matched by the violence of its warfare. To the U.S. soldiers, the ferocity and determination of their opponents resembled that of the Japanese fighting in the Pacific, made even more complex by the difficulty of distinguishing between ally and enemy. Advancing U.S. troops found evidence of torture and the murdering of prisoners, as well as other atrocities. In captivity, U.S. prisoners were treated harshly and used as tools of communist propaganda. In all, the United States forces incurred 142,091 casualties, including 33,629 battle deaths. Four hundred thousand South Korean troops became casualties, with at least 60,000 dying. The communist forces suffered an estimated 1.5 million casualties, of which 900,000 were Chinese. In addition, perhaps millions of Korean civilians on both sides of the parallel lost their lives.

Three years after it began, the Korean War came to a negotiated close. In January 1953 President Dwight D. Eisenhower's new administration had intensified the urgency of the peace process, which was also affected to some extent by the death of the Soviet premier Joseph Stalin. In the summer the negotiators finally agreed to a military armistice. Although the belligerents signed no peace treaty and the border remained heavily guarded, combat officially stopped on 27 July 1953, bringing a restrained and inconclusive end to a violent but limited war.

BIBLIOGRAPHY

Blair, Clay. *The Forgotten War: America in Korea, 1950–1953.* New York: Times Books, 1987.

Cumings, Bruce. *The Origins of the Korean War.* 2 vols. Princeton, N.J.: Princeton University Press, 1982–1990.

Fehrenbach, T. R. *This Kind of War: A Study in Unpreparedness.* New York: Macmillan, 1963.

Kaufman, Burton I. *The Korean War: Challenges in Crisis, Credibility, and Command.* New York: Knopf, 1986.

ANNE SHARP WELLS

See also **War.**

KORESH, DAVID
(1959–1993)

David Koresh, the leader of the millennialist Branch Davidian sect at the time of its 1993 standoff with U. S. government forces, was born Vernon Wayne Howell on 17 August 1959 in Houston, Texas, to Bonnie Clark, a young unmarried teenager. Originally cared for by his maternal grandparents, at age five Howell moved to the Dallas suburbs to live with his mother and his stepfather, Roy Haldeman. Howell consistently displayed more interest in the outdoors and his guitar than he did in his schoolwork in remedial classes. He eventually dropped out of high school in the eleventh grade. As a teenager, however, Howell developed an intense interest in religion, especially the Adventism to which his grandmother had introduced him. He focused on understanding the Bible and committed large portions of it to memory. Howell first moved to the Mount Carmel Center some ten miles outside Waco in 1981, a tall, thin, bespectacled, and troubled twenty-two-year-old carpenter struggling with his first girlfriend's unplanned pregnancy. After being run out of her life by the woman's father, Howell turned again to the Bible.

In August 1990, Howell legally changed his name to David Koresh, signaling a profound transformative experience that had occurred in Israel in January 1985. His new first name was borrowed from the Israelite king and his surname from a form of the name of the Persian emperor Cyrus, who was hailed in Isaiah 45:1 as an "anointed one" of Yahweh for his victory over the Babylonians. Although Koresh was reticent about the details of his experience in Israel, it gave him a sense of messianic purpose. He came to identify himself as a Christ, or anointed one, and as the only one privileged to open the scroll sealed with seven seals in Revelation 5. The message of the seven seals became the focal point of Koresh's prolonged Bible studies, which were the center of communal life at Mount Carmel. He taught that it was his responsibility not only to interpret the Bible's description of the events of the end-time but also to bring them about in his lifetime, most likely in Israel. Koresh, however, did not anticipate an active role either for himself or for his followers in administering God's judgment.

Koresh worked in obscurity from the mid-1980s through the early 1990s and the Branch Davidian community remained small. In 1988, after pro-

David Koresh. Gamma/Liaison Agency

longed infighting with George Roden, whose mother had led the community, he assumed the leadership of the Branch Davidians. In 1989 Koresh proclaimed his controversial "New Light" revelation in which he imposed celibacy on the community but claimed a personal sexual monopoly on all female members.

The roots of the Branch Davidians in the area went back to 1935 and the group had generally led a peaceful existence. That changed on 28 February 1993, when the Bureau of Alcohol, Tobacco, and Firearms (BATF), in search of illegal weapons, conducted a thoroughly botched "dynamic entry" at Mount Carmel in which six Davidians and four BATF agents died. A fifty-one day standoff ensued, punctuated by negotiations with the Federal Bureau of Investigation in which Koresh asserted that the Davidians acted in self-defense, denied any violent intentions toward the government, and contended that the weapons at Mount Carmel were being stored for later sale at gun shows. Throughout the negotiations, Koresh consistently rejected the idea that the Davidians would commit suicide and the survivors vehemently deny that the Davidians set the fire on 19 April 1993 in which Koresh and seventy-four men, women, and children died.

Opponents of cults, shortly after the incident occurred, blamed the violent outcome at Mount Carmel squarely on Koresh, whom they saw as a manipulative false messiah interested only in personal power and gratification. Various conspiracy theorists, on the other hand, blamed the government and its clandestine war against personal liberties. More compelling and complicated reasons are to be found, however, in the complex interactions of Koresh, the deeply committed Branch Davidian community, and the FBI negotiators, tactical forces, and commanders on the scene.

BIBLIOGRAPHY

Moore, Carol. *The Davidian Massacre: Disturbing Questions About Waco Which Must Be Answered.* Franklin, Tenn.: Legacy Communications, 1995.
Reavis, Dick J. *The Ashes of Waco: An Investigation.* Syracuse, N.Y.: Syracuse University Press, 1988.
Tabor, James D., and Eugene V. Gallagher. *Why Waco? Cults and the Battle for Religious Freedom in America.* Berkeley: University of California Press, 1995.
Wright, Stuart A., ed. *Armageddon in Waco: Critical Perspectives on the Branch Davidian Conflict.* Chicago: University of Chicago Press, 1995.

EUGENE V. GALLAGHER

See also **Cults; Waco.**

KU KLUX KLAN

The First Klan

In the decade following the Civil War in communities throughout the South, white terrorist groups waged a gruesome battle to undermine the social, economic, and political reforms of Reconstruction. The most famous of these groups, the Ku Klux Klan, was founded in Pulaski, Tennessee, in winter 1865–1866 by six Confederate veterans. The group began as a social organization (the name was taken from the Greek word for circle, *kuklos*), but soon became a vehicle in Tennessee and elsewhere for vigilante violence against anyone who appeared to threaten the institutions of white supremacy. While there was no formal organizational structure to unite and coordinate individual Klan groups, the common goals, tactics, and infamous hooded disguises of Klan night riders made them seem like one vast underground army determined to use whatever means necessary to halt racial reform.

African Americans, of course, were the main targets of Klan violence and intimidation. One of the primary purposes of Klan terror was to enforce racial social codes threatened by postwar disorder and the end of slavery. Klan groups patrolled roads to control the movement of black individuals and families, particularly at night. They punished blacks who were insolent or defiant of white authority. They threatened, flogged, and murdered blacks and whites suspected of violating interracial sexual taboos. They singled out and threatened schoolteachers, ministers, and anyone else who might be in a position to encourage former slaves to rise above their station. Klan violence was also used for economic gains, and black workers were forced into compliance. Disputes over wages, debts, or land ownership were resolved with flogging, beatings, and executions. Some of the violence was also directed against whites as a means of settling personal scores, of punishing individuals who had remained loyal to the Union during the war, and of discouraging sympathies for either the freed slaves or federal reforms.

Social and economic violence also served political ends; ultimately, the Klan's main purpose was to uphold Democratic Party rule through the assassination of Republican leaders, both black and white, and through the intimidation of black voters. The federal election of 1868 ignited horrendous racial violence in many states. White men rushed to head off Republican political victories by joining the Klan, "vigilance committees," or similar organizations, particularly in black-belt regions of states such as South Carolina, Georgia, and Alabama. In key, predominantly African American counties, terror tactics kept almost all black voters away from the polls. In Louisiana, Klan groups murdered between eight hundred and one thousand people in 1868, primarily during the elections in the spring and fall. By the time of the November election, those Republican leaders still alive advised supporters in many parishes that it was too dangerous to go to the polls. The Republican vote in Louisiana was sliced in half between the spring primary and the general election in November. In nine of the most heavily impacted parishes that had provided more than ten thousand votes for Republican presidential candidate Ulysses S. Grant in the spring of 1868, a total of only ten votes was cast for Grant in the fall.

Similar waves of political terror washed across different states at different times, reflecting the localized nature of Klan activities. Racial violence declined in Georgia after the 1868 election, for example, only to rise to an even higher level by the next election in 1870. For various reasons, concerns about the black vote had not been particularly high

in Mississippi and North Carolina in 1868. As political circumstances changed in the next few years, however, both states saw huge increases in the level of Klan terror.

Two critical factors helped account for the Klan's ability to function basically as a military arm of the Democratic Party. First, Klan groups drew their members from a wide cross section of white society, and the terror they unleashed was received either enthusiastically or as a necessary evil by most white citizens. Second, before 1871 federal troops did almost nothing to stop the political and racial violence. Reconstruction governments in some states did pass anti-Klan laws, but without federal help they were unable to enforce them. A ferocious escalation of Klan violence in South Carolina in 1870–1871 eventually moved the federal government to investigate the Klan and pass anti-Klan legislation (the Enforcement Acts and the Ku Klux Klan Act of 1870–1871). Subsequent concerted law enforcement efforts by federal troops finally threw the Reconstruction-era Klan into decline.

In the decades that followed, the Klan's powerful legacy would profoundly influence both the nature of racial violence in the postslavery South and the way that many Americans would come to interpret the Civil War era. The Klan had established a grim precedent. White supremacy could be enforced through terrible, grassroots, vigilante violence. That fact, combined with subsequent laws that disfranchised almost all blacks (as well as many poor whites) and created a uniform system of racial segregation, would undermine respect for the rule of law and for human rights in the South—and the nation—for the next century. Less than a generation after Reconstruction, romantic images of the Klan helped shape an apologetic interpretation of slavery, the Confederacy, and postwar violence. In this view, articulated by leading historians, novelists, and, later, filmmakers, slavery came to be seen as a benign institution, the war as a tragic mistake, and the Klan as an understandable, even necessary, response to the chaos brought by misguided, even vengeful, Reconstruction policies. D. W. Griffith's immensely popular 1915 film *The Birth of a Nation* both reflected and helped perpetuate this racist vision. Based on Thomas Dixon's best-selling novel, *The Clansman*, and in technical terms a masterwork, the film characterized the Klan as an organization of heroic citizens that had saved white society and American civilization from ruin.

A midnight meeting of the Ku Klux Klan in 1922. HULTON GETTY/LIAISON AGENCY

The Second Klan

The Birth of a Nation was so popular it eventually became the inspiration (and recruiting tool) for a new Klan movement. When the film appeared in Atlanta in 1915, a struggling itinerant preacher and fraternal organizer, William Joseph Simmons, took advantage of the surrounding publicity—and the remaining ferment from the recent episode involving the lynching of Leo Frank, a Jewish businessman accused of sexually assaulting and murdering a young, white female employee—to found the Knights of the Ku Klux Klan. From 1915 to 1920, Simmons scratched out a living by attracting several thousand dues-paying members, primarily from Georgia and Alabama, into his new fraternity. The new Klan drew on traditional bigotries and the Klan mystique of populist vigilance, presenting itself as a guardian of white supremacy, Protestant Christianity, Americanism, and traditional moral values. It used the opportunity provided by the World War to make appearances in patriotic parades, to threaten blacks, strikers, and draft dodgers, and to punish immoral behavior. Under Simmons's inept leadership this new Klan probably would not have survived the passing of wartime passions. In 1920, however, Simmons turned to two Atlanta public relations experts, who hired

a small army of paid recruiters and transformed the Klan from a regional curiosity into a massive, nationwide, mainstream social movement. Between 1920 and 1925 this new Klan movement—which eventually included a separate organization for women, Women of the Ku Klux Klan—attracted at least two million and perhaps as many as six million members to local chapters in every state and became a powerful force in politics at every level.

The second Klan was significantly different from the first. It had a national headquarters (Atlanta), a formal organizational structure, standardized rituals, and national and regional newspapers. Its members were expected to pay a large initiation fee ($10, at a time when a well-paid worker was lucky to make $40 per week) but also to tender monthly dues and purchase official Klan robes, booklets, trinkets, and even life insurance from the national headquarters (the quest to control the millions of dollars that flowed from individual members became one of the great sources of conflict among Klan leaders). The new movement was also a truly national phenomenon rather than a narrowly Southern one. Its highest levels of membership and greatest political influence came in the Midwestern states of Indiana, Ohio, Illinois, and Michigan. It was extraordinarily successful as well across the West and Southwest in Colorado, Oklahoma, Oregon, and parts of California. Active chapters existed in the Northeast and in major cities throughout the nation. Perhaps most significant of all, the new Klan's popularity could no longer be seen narrowly as a response to social and political challenges to white supremacy in the South (indeed, no such serious challenge existed during the 1920s). Instead, the 1920s Klan was driven by a related but much broader set of ethno-nationalist concerns about the continued dominance of white Protestants and their cultural values in American life.

Those values included racism, anti-Catholicism, anti-Semitism, and anti-immigrant attitudes. Klan recruiters bombarded potential members with wild stories of how the nation was being undermined by Jewish bankers, "black spiders," papist conspirators, and other evil forces. The message varied from place to place, but most often anti-Catholicism was the leading theme. These traditional bigotries were combined with wide range of additional and, on the surface, somewhat surprising concerns: Prohibition enforcement, gambling and other crimes, political corruption, sexual immorality, Victorian family values and gender roles, and declining support for religion. Violence still occurred, particularly in the South, but at nowhere near the level that occurred during Reconstruction, and most often it was directed against white Protestants thought to be violating Prohibition or traditional moral values.

The main political power of the second Klan came not through murdering political leaders or terrorizing black voters but from organizing supporters into a mainstream political movement that influenced political party operations and put candidates up for public office. Klan political influence hopelessly divided the Democratic National Convention in 1924. In the same year the Klan elected senators and congressmen from both parties throughout the nation. In Indiana, Colorado, Oregon, Oklahoma, and Alabama, the Klan gained control of state government from the governor on down and was only narrowly defeated in similar efforts in many other states. In countless communities throughout the nation, the Klan won control of local government.

The Klan's political power served many interests. In some locations, not surprisingly, the Klan focused on the perceived threat from Catholics, particularly Catholic schools. Prohibition enforce-ment, however, appeared to be the single greatest political concern, and much of the Klan's success came from its ability to convince voters that Klan-endorsed judges, district attorneys, governors, and congressmen would enforce the laws that others had not. Confrontations with established political leaders over Prohibition enforcement often took the shape of a "populist" insurgency against political control by the economic elite and influenced the Klan's involvement with a wide range of other issues, including the enforcement of other vice laws, taxes, economic development, schools, and other public services.

The second Klan's mainstream defense of "white Protestant America" was powerful for a time and enlisted a true crosssection of the nation's white Protestants from all economic classes and all Protestant denominations, from rural areas, small towns, and large cities alike. Its success as a populist, ethno-nationalist political movement also established an important precedent. From this point forward, right-wing political movements in the United States (both extreme and mainstream) would be profoundly shaped by the belief that white Protestant values and traditions had been displaced from their rightful place of dominance in American life.

At the same time, however, the Klan had fundamental difficulties maintaining itself as a successful mainstream movement. Catholic, Jewish, African American, and immigrant organizations fought tirelessly against it. Many white Protestant leaders and organizations who admitted that they agreed wholeheartedly with the Klan's ideals were alienated by its association with lawlessness, violence, and secrecy. The Klan's most well-known leaders also showed themselves to be driven by greed, corruption, and other unsavory forces, leading to long jail terms in a number of well-publicized cases. Perhaps most significantly, the Klan's political victories did little to change the conditions in American society that had ignited the second Klan in the first place. This was especially true with Prohibition. By the mid-1920s it became apparent that Prohibition enforcement was a hopeless cause and the second Klan rapidly declined.

Small groups of Klan members remained active through the 1930s, particularly in the South. Klan regalia and rituals continued to be associated with (but were certainly not a prerequisite for) the racial violence that accompanied life in the Jim Crow era. Post–World War II social changes in the South rekindled some interest in the Klan in the late 1940s and early 1950s. The Civil Rights movement of the late 1950s and early 1960s brought it back with a vengeance. While not nearly as large or as powerful as the Reconstruction-era Klan, a variety of independent Klan groups appeared during these years with the same basic mission and tactics of the first Klan: halting racial reforms through terror and violence. Perhaps the most notorious of these groups was Robert Shelton's Alabama Klan, which was responsible for numerous bombings and murders, including one particularly outrageous 1963 bombing that killed four black schoolgirls as they attended service in a Birmingham church that had been the hub of recently successful protest activities. Other Klan groups committed similar atrocities throughout the period, resulting in the deaths of dozens—perhaps even hundreds —of people.

Changing racial attitudes and the successes of the Civil Rights movement after the mid-1960s permanently discredited the Klan and its history. A variety of independent, sometimes rival Klan groups have continued to attract members since the 1970s. These groups are best understood as part of a generally small but militant right-wing extremist subculture representing an array of racist, anti-Semitic, antigovernment, and doomsday beliefs. These extremist groups, including Klan members, have occasionally been quite violent. Periodic Klan marches of fifty or a hundred participants pathetically hoping to reclaim the kind of mainstream status represented by the 1920s Klan consistently have met much larger crowds of hostile protesters. Some Klan leaders and former leaders, most notably, David Duke of Louisiana, had some success as political candidates in the 1980s. Even Duke, however, was forced to renounce his Klan roots in favor of a more acceptable right-wing program in order to gain a seat in the Louisiana legislature and campaign for statewide office. Bigotry remained, but the tradition of Klan member as popular hero had passed.

BIBLIOGRAPHY

Branch, Taylor. *Parting the Waters: America in the King Years, 1954–1963.* New York: Simon and Schuster, 1988.

Chalmers, David Mark. *Hooded Americanism: The History of the Ku Klux Klan,* 3d ed. Durham, N.C.: Duke University Press, 1987.

Goldberg, Robert Alan. *Hooded Empire: The Ku Klux Klan in Colorado.* Urbana: University of Illinois Press, 1981.

Jackson, Kenneth T. *The Ku Klux Klan in the City, 1915–1930.* New York: Oxford University Press, 1967.

Moore, Leonard J. *Citizen Klansmen: The Ku Klux Klan in Indiana, 1921–1928.* Chapel Hill: University of North Carolina Press, 1991.

Trelease, Allen W. *White Terror: The Ku Klux Klan Conspiracy and Southern Reconstruction.* New York: Harper and Row, 1971.

LEONARD J. MOORE

See also **Extremism; Hate Crimes; Lynching; Militias, Unauthorized; Neo-Nazis; Race and Ethnicity; Reconstruction; Skinheads.**

L

LABOR AND UNIONS

The labor movement was sparked into life by the wage-labor market that emerged at the launching of the young American republic. The formation of the Federal Society of Journeyman Cordwainers in Philadelphia in 1794 marks the beginning of sustained trade-union organization. From then on, local craft unions proliferated in cities, publishing lists of wage "prices," protecting the trades from inferior workmanship, and demanding shorter hours for their workers. The early labor movement also harbored a conception of a just society, celebrating equal rights, honest labor, and virtuous citizenship. In defense of this republican vision, workingmen's parties sprang up in the 1830s, followed by wave on wave of like-minded reform movements that challenged industrial capitalism and the ravages it inflicted on wage workers. Contemporaries saw no contradiction between trade unionism and labor reform: the first tended to workers' immediate needs, the second to their higher hopes. Both were held to be strands in a single movement, rooted in a common working-class constituency and, to some degree, even sharing a common leadership. But over time, and ever more insistently, contradictions did emerge. Across the Atlantic, very similar reform currents evolved into the class politics that engaged all the European labor movements by the early twentieth century. But in America the originating reform impulse was mostly expunged and the political bent, though by no means absent, was far overshadowed by economic unionism. It is this job-consciousness that renders violence so persistent a theme in the history of the American labor movement.

Job-conscious unionism depends on economic power, which, in turn, is a function of labor's solidarity: unity gives workers the collective means to extract from the employer "fair" conditions of work—hence the nearly universal rule, grasped by even the earliest journeymen societies, that none but members be permitted to work on union jobs (in later parlance, that rule became the "closed shop"). Because job-conscious unionism staked so much on the maintenance of solidarity, implicit in this rule was the possible use of force as the final sanction against recalcitrant workers. And if employers resorted to the use of strikebreakers in industrial disputes, violence became more than an implicit possibility. Thus, as early as 1800, we have the spectacle of striking New York sailors marching to the docks "with drums and fife, and colours flying" and engaging in a bloody battle with a gang posted there to protect the "rats." The epithets that came into common usage—rat, blackleg, fink, scab—testify to the fury with which striking workers regarded those who broke ranks or sought to take their jobs.

Under certain conditions, employers more or less willingly "recognized" trade unions—as, for example, when they supplied the most competent workers or stabilized competitive markets or, more generally, made resistance costlier than recognition. But to a remarkable degree American employers set themselves against collective bargaining, for reasons embedded in the culture of American industrial capitalism: a legal dogma that sanctified property rights and liberty of contract, notions of managerial prerogative evident long in advance of Taylorism (a term that refers to the practice of scientific management), and a definition of labor as a factor of production with no claim on the profits of the firm. If unions had a stake in building solidarity, so equally did employers in tearing it down. Thus, when it came to the closed shop, the line was drawn not so much between workers as between unions and employers: the closed-shop issue tested the union's standing with the employer. And so, more explosively, did the resort to strikebreakers, which, when it succeeded, dealt a fatal blow to the striking union. Violence in industrial disputes was a two-sided affair, in which employers generally gave as good as they got—hence, to go back to the New York dock dispute of 1800, the gang deployed in wait of the striking sailors.

The Advances of Industrialization

If violence lurked in American labor relations from the outset, it became a prominent feature only as industrialism advanced and class lines hardened. The earliest recorded strike fatalities were two New York tailors who died at the hands of police in 1850. They were the first in a death toll that mounted into the many hundreds—in excess, certainly, of seven hundred—over the next century.

Among early industrial workers, the New England shoemakers showed the greatest militancy because, as outworkers in a rapidly modernizing industry, they were peculiarly exposed to the "slaving conditions" of market-driven enterprise. In 1860 they staged the nation's biggest strike to date, demanding higher wages and union recognition. In Lynn, Massachusetts, where the strike began, the Mechanics Association appointed a committee of a hundred to prevent the shipment of shoes for finishing elsewhere and to visit the city's shops and post the names of scabs, and a vigilance committee was charged with "preserving order" and assisting the police in stamping out drunkenness and arresting "disturbers." The dilemma of every strike leader was how to maintain rank-and-file discipline while knowing, as William Sylvis of the Iron Molders said, that "the results will depend on who can pound the hardest."

No union had to pound harder than the Workingmen's Benevolent Association (WBA), which represented the anthracite miners of eastern Pennsylvania after the Civil War. Anthracite was a boom industry of the postbellum economy and fiercely competitive. The visceral animus against collective bargaining among the mine operators was only partially defused by the stabilizing benefits of the WBA's sliding-scale contract. Maintaining the agreement called for repeated strikes, which were never peaceful despite the pleas of leaders for "strict adherence to social law and order." In fact, terrorism haunted the coalfields, leaving a trail of "coffin" notices and a mounting death toll.

In late 1874, with the country in severe depression, the industry finally broke with the union, and there ensued what became known in labor annals as the Long Strike. The industry's mastermind, Franklin B. Gowen of the Philadelphia and Reading Railroad, brought in his Coal and Iron Police to guard the collieries and kept himself privy to strike plans by hiring at least four Pinkerton spies, who operated within the union and reported to him. It was a fifth detective, however, who gave Gowen his money's worth. This was James McParlan, who had been assigned not to the union but to the Ancient Order of Hibernians, where he infiltrated a murderous inner circle known as the Molly Maguires.

The crimes that McParlan pinned on the Molly Maguires actually did not stem primarily from the strike, but the overlap was sufficient to establish the fact that labor violence could not be separated from its ethnocultural context. In the Long Strike it mattered quite as much that the miners were Irish-American as that they were engaged in a desperate struggle against the Philadelphia and Reading Railroad. The dimension of gender, equally indelible, also stands forth in the Long Strike, as, for example, in this mine inspector's report of an attack on scabs at the Greenback colliery at Shamokin: "Forty union women from the patch met them and commenced stoning them, making it generally unpleasant for them to attempt starting work—the husbands of the women were in the woods enjoying the scene." No single strike was likely to capture all the social forces shaping industrial violence in America. The anthracite fields in 1875, for example, were spared the fierce racial tensions that the introduction of black strikebreakers always inspired. But the Long Strike did demonstrate all too clearly that industrial conflict never occurred in a social vacuum and that the forms it took were molded by the American working-class experience—not least, by poverty and joblessness.

Hard times dangerously magnified industrial conflict. In the wake of the Panic of 1873 the unemployed, often encouraged by exiled German socialists, staged demonstrations and demanded relief. At one such meeting in Tompkins Square on 13 January 1874, New York police suddenly rode into the crowd, swinging their clubs, causing general mayhem, and serving notice that in dangerous times any challenge to public order could end with bloody heads. The explosive moment came in the last stages of the depression when, in June 1877, the railroads imposed another round of wage cuts on their impoverished employees. On 16 July, Baltimore and Ohio workers began to walk off the job. At Martinsburg, West Virginia, they seized the depot and halted the freight trains. When his state militia proved wanting, the governor appealed to Washington, initiating the first use of federal troops against strikers in peacetime. After a week of intermittent battles, the Baltimore and Ohio strikers gave up and trains began to run again. The trouble, however, had already spread to other lines. In some places the show of military force restored order, but elsewhere it backfired and events spun out of control. This was the case in Pittsburgh, for example, where state militiamen retreated into the Pennsylvania Railroad's roundhouse after firing indiscriminately into a crowd and then, when the roundhouse went up in flames, abandoned the city to rioters. Millions of dollars worth of property, including Pittsburgh's important rail facilities, were laid waste before federal troops arrived. In the hysteria of the moment, editorialists spoke of "an insurrection, a revolution, an attempt of communists and vagabonds to coerce society." There was, in fact, an element of truth in these ravings. What the events of 1877 revealed was the social dynamite at the core of relations between capital and labor in America.

From this grim fact employers drew hard conclusions. The state militias, not very effective at maintaining order even where they had not openly fraternized with the strikers, gave way to a reorganized, professionally led National Guard, which, in industrial states like Pennsylvania, became a highly proficient force. Designed as strongholds against mob violence, the great urban armories date from this period. The courts also began to crack down hard on strikers at this time. Employers made their own preparations, emulating Franklin Gowen's reliance on private guards

and labor spies. The Pinkerton National Detective Agency began to flourish. This was a flourishing time, too, for blacklists and "iron-clad" employment contracts. It did not matter that the 1877 strikes had erupted spontaneously among mostly unorganized workers. Nor did it matter that repression of trade unionism itself provoked labor violence. In the name of public order, the propertied classes armed for battle and thereby transformed every industrial dispute into a potential battleground.

In their own fashion, trade unionists were just as aghast at the specter of industrial upheaval. Samuel Gompers had experienced the Tompkins Square riot firsthand, barely avoiding a broken head by leaping into a cellar. It was a formative event for this prominent labor leader, providing "guideposts for my understanding of the labor movement for years to come." As if to confirm Gompers's fears, a robust anarchist movement emerging from the wreckage of the Great Depression developed a considerable following among the trade unions, whose members were drawn by the appeal to workers to meet fire with fire. Thus, the incendiary circular "Revenge! Workingmen, to Arms!!!" was issued after Chicago police shot down McCormick workers striking for the eight-hour day on 3 May 1886. At a protest meeting at Haymarket Square the next night, an unidentified person flung a bomb at the police, who responded with a wild burst of gunfire (causing most of the casualties, including those in their own ranks). The Haymarket Affair called down the nation's wrath not only on the anarchists—four paid for it on the gallows—but on the entire labor movement. Gompers saw all too well "how professions of radicalism and sensationalism concentrated all the forces of organized society against a labor movement and nullified in advance normal, necessary activity."

If trumpeting class war was foolhardy, however, so was the denial of class struggle altogether. This was the utopian stance of the Knights of Labor, the last and in some ways mightiest expression of the American labor-reform tradition. The Knights espoused the cooperative commonwealth to marvelous effect during the early 1880s, but when their members tired of education and cooperative experiments, the Knights got out of their depth, lacking as they did either the skills or the stomach for the great industrial battles that took place in their name. "The Knights, who denounce strikes, have the largest strikes and the biggest failures," remarked Gompers, neatly summarizing the fate of the Knights after its meteoric rise. In the aftermath, Gompers put the finishing touches on what he dubbed "pure-and-simple" unionism, a doctrine always implicit in the job-conscious bent of the labor movement, but only now, in the 1880s, given formal expression and, equally important, institutional embodiment in the newly formed American Federation of Labor (1886).

Doctrine and Structure

Pure-and-simple unionism accepted the inevitability of economic struggle. "No matter how just," intoned Gompers, "unless the cause is backed up with power to enforce it, it is going to be crushed and annihilated." In these unflinching words, of course, there was the shadow of labor violence that had stalked job-conscious unionists from the outset. But the pure-and-simple formulation armed them against that temptation. It did this at the doctrinal level by insulating the labor movement from the big ideas that justified violence by shouting out the evils of the system. Gompers was not embracing capitalism—that only came later—so much as repudiating its theorizing critics. "The ills of our social and economic system cannot be cured by patent medicine," Gompers wrote. "Every step that workers make or take, every vantage point gained, is a solution in itself." And every solution added its bit to the rising edifice of the labor movement. "The unions are organizations that have not been agitated into existence," said Gompers. "They are the outgrowth of our system" and "are the natural organizations of working people." The characteristics that came forth—the national-union structure, occupational restrictions on membership, well-articulated internal rules, and a career leadership drawn from the ranks (and barring outside "intellectuals")—all bespoke a movement bent on disciplined action and, insofar as doctrine and structure could make it so, bent on conducting the struggle against capital by peaceful means.

That was an enduring principle. Practicing it, however, was another matter, as the great Homestead Lockout soon revealed. In 1892, after many years of contractual relations, the Carnegie Steel Company broke off with the union at its Homestead, Pennsylvania, works and declared an open shop. The workers responded by arming themselves, seizing control of the works, and in a bloody battle repelling the Pinkertons sent in to assert Carnegie's property rights. In a few days the National Guard arrived, the union leaders went to

jail, scabs reopened the plant under military guard, and the strike was broken. It was a disastrous defeat from which steel unionism would not recover for half a century. Yet at the time few fellow unionists faulted the Homestead strikers. They were not wild-eyed radicals but skilled workers, members of an exemplary AFL craft union, defending their jobs and community against a powerful corporate employer. Their only recourse, other than surrender, was to keep the plant closed to replacements. Had the Pinkerton guards not been introduced, no bloodshed would have occurred. So the blame lay not with the strikers, argued Gompers, but in "the overweening greed of the corporate and capitalist class." Gompers was making a crucial concession, albeit cloaked in the republican language of liberty and manhood: violence could not be excluded from labor's struggles (any more than it could have been against the crown in 1776). The best he could hope for was that as labor got the upper hand "the conflict in its bitterest form can be avoided" because "the more firmly we are cemented in the bonds of fraternity the more completely will we demonstrate to the employer class that it is to the advantage of all when fair conditions prevail."

Not all unionists shared Gompers's optimism. In the Coeur d'Alene district of Idaho in 1892, hard-rock miners were waging an equally bitter strike against corporate operators. The equivalent of the Homestead gun battle—and partly inspired by it—was the miners' attempt to dynamite the Frisco mine and expel the scabs and mine guards, with equivalent results: the governor declared martial law, federal troops came in, the strikers were herded into "bull pens," and the mines were reopened. Unlike at Homestead, however, defeat did not crush the strikers but, on the contrary, inspired them and other locally organized miners to form the Western Federation of Miners (WFM). The WFM affiliated briefly with the AFL, then broke off on the grounds that pure-and-simple unionism was too tame for the hard-rock miners, and they embraced socialism. In this they were like many others radicalized by the class warfare of the 1890s—the most famous example, of course, being Eugene V. Debs after the suppression of the great Pullman boycott. But the miners always laced socialism with a streak of direct action. The WFM president Ed Boyce, a veteran of the bull pens, called on all union miners to arm themselves with rifles, and his rhetoric had a hard edge. He regarded the wage system as "slavery in its worst form," and the American state "a vicious form of government." In 1905 the WFM sponsored a new radical movement, the Industrial Workers of the World (IWW), also known as the Wobblies. Linked initially to the socialist parties, the IWW soon repudiated politics and settled on a syndicalist course. Through action at the point of production and unremitting struggle against employers—ultimately by means of a general strike—the IWW believed that the workers themselves could bring about a revolution. A workers' society would emerge, run directly by the workers through their industrial unions.

The WFM did not stay around for long. By 1911 it was back in the AFL, locating itself on the left wing, to be sure, but submitting to the hard logic of pure-and-simple unionism. If a union's first duty was to its members, then the WFM had no choice but to do as other trade unions did: organize its jurisdiction and try to "meet the employer halfway." The IWW, however, did not fold up. In the East it acted briefly as a shock force, leading spontaneous strikes in McKees Rocks, Pennsylvania (1909), Lawrence, Massachusetts (1912), Paterson, New Jersey (1913), and Akron, Ohio (1913), but leaving behind no permanent organization. The IWW found its true calling in the West, where it built a loyal following in the lumber camps, construction sites, and wheat fields. Through free-speech fights, missionary delegates, and a vibrant Wobbly culture, the IWW mobilized these rootless workers of the West and gave them dignity and hope. In its final incarnation, before World War I, the IWW might have been described as a kind of trade unionism for the dispossessed, gaining for them some portion of the bargaining power that better-situated workers got by labor-market control and political muscle. Although other variants flourished in Europe in these years, the syndicalism of the IWW was truly homegrown, arising not from the theories of the French syndicalist Georges Sorel but from the unmediated experience of America's brutal industrial life.

Conservative trade unions were, for their part, not left unmarked by the struggle. Consider the AFL's International Association of Bridge and Structural Iron Workers. In 1905 the union fell out with the National Erectors' Association (NEA) over a quintessentially job-conscious issue—the diversion of work to cheaper nonunion contractors—and responded in a quintessentially job-conscious way: it threatened a secondary boycott of the steel suppliers of these sites. At that point the NEA broke off relations, declared an industry-wide open shop, expelled the union workers, and transformed itself into the most belligerent of employer associations. The ironworkers' union answered with dynamite. In four years its operatives bombed some seventy nonunion sites, always one step ahead of NEA detectives. Then, in a ghastly misstep, on 1 October 1910 they planted a bomb that demolished the *Los Angeles Times* building and killed twenty night-shift workers. In a celebrated manhunt, the Burns Detective Agency tracked down the two perpetrators, one of whom implicated the union's national secretary, John J. McNamara. The entire labor movement, having rallied to McNamara and his brother James (the second bomber), was dumbfounded when they confessed and cut short the trial. A shaken Gompers declared it "an awful commentary upon existing conditions when men think they can obtain justice for labor only through violence, outrage and murder."

In fact, other unionists did think that way, but all too commonly without the McNamaras' saving interest in "justice." For some, the culture of violence only bred venality. Corruption would in any case have dogged a movement so instrumentalist in its ethics and so accepting of what the sociologist Seymour Martin Lipset has called the "achievement-equalitarian syndrome" in American life. It was no shame for labor leaders to advance their careers from within the union, nor was it uncommon for them to harvest the extra opportunities that came their way. In many cities, moreover, unions functioned in a world of graft-ridden politics, dog-eat-dog enterprise, and ghetto dislocation. It was not to be wondered at that in the early 1890s the Chicago Trades and Labor Assembly fell into the hands of grafters working the same side of the street as the machine politicians or that the business agents who ran the Chicago Building Trades Council made a handsome living shaking down contractors for "strike insurance." What magnified these tendencies into a serious crisis, however, was the violence of the industrial struggle itself. Employers commonly hired sluggers to break up picket lines and intimidate strikers; unions responded in kind, recruiting strong-arm men from their own ranks or, if need be, from outside. This was true even in the garment trades, where the organizing drives before World War I were social movements partaking of the progessive ethos of that era. Once in, the criminals stayed, allying with corrupt (or corruptible) unionists and making intimidation a condition of life in the afflicted branches of the movement. In the 1920s, with organized crime flourishing under Prohibition, the problem became much worse; even big shots like Arnold Rothstein, "Little Augie" Orgen, and "Legs" Diamond found labor racketeering a profitable sideline.

The legitimate movement was hard put to respond. Trade autonomy, a fundamental principle, meant that the AFL had no right to interfere in the internal affairs of its affiliated unions. In theory, these national unions policed their local bodies, but in practice, especially in local-market industries, they operated on a decentralized basis, and national leaders mostly turned a blind eye on evildoings in well-entrenched locals. It did happen that the crooks were sometimes routed, as, for example, by John Fitzpatrick from the Chicago central labor body in 1905 (not, however, from the Chicago building trades, which remained notoriously graft-ridden until a major state investigation in 1921). The most heroic struggle took place in the New York men's clothing industry, where at real personal risk Sidney Hillman, the president of the Amalgamated Clothing Workers, mobilized his forces and expelled the gangsters and grafters in the early 1930s. Hillman sits in the pantheon of great American labor leaders. Yet in his 1991 biography of Hillman, Steven Fraser acknowledges that Hillman had tolerated racketeering until it became too overreaching and, in the throes of the depression, threatened his union's survival. But gangsters were still around. They held on to the trucking business, and Hillman, bent on reorganizing the industry, made a deal and paid for the strategic support he needed to win that battle.

Paving the Way for Collective Bargaining

At that moment in 1932, public policy was on the brink of a revolution. The furious liberty of American labor relations was a condition ultimately of the nation's laissez-faire stance toward collective bargaining. There was, in fact, no statutory law (except for the Railway Labor Act of 1926) regulating collective bargaining, only a profusion of judge-made law policing the battleground, and this law, originating in criminal conspiracy and enforced by wholesale court injunction, worked so one-sidedly and so oppressively that, in the view of many observers, the law itself contributed to labor violence. Thus, it could be argued, the McNamaras resorted to dynamite not in lieu of but for lack of lawful alternatives: plenty of judges

stood ready to enjoin any effective picketing or boycotting by the ironworkers' union. The U.S. Commission on Industrial Relations, inquiring into the underlying sources of the McNamara outrage, reported that "no testimony . . . has left a deeper impression than the evidence that there exists among the workers an almost universal conviction that they, both as individuals and as a class, are denied justice." The commission's work proceeded amidst one of the most turbulent periods in American labor history, culminating in the Colorado mine war of 1913–1914. The country was treated to the awful spectacle of the tent city at Ludlow (the miners having been evicted from their homes) laid waste by a mob of Colorado national guardsmen. In the rubble lay the bodies of two women and eleven children. Enraged miners took up arms, and anarchy reigned in Colorado until regiments of federal troops arrived.

The commission concluded that it was time to change the rules of the game, so that collective bargaining would be not a prize of industrial war but a right that workers enjoyed by law. It took another two decades, but in 1935 the New Deal finally acted on that proposition. The Wagner Act declared it unlawful for employers to interfere with workers' rights to organize, put into place formal procedures for determining representation, and created a National Labor Relations Board (NLRB) substantially empowered to administer and enforce the law. With the Wagner Act, it was no longer the union's power but the certification it got from the NLRB that provided the foundation for collective bargaining. This was the essence of the New Deal's labor-relations revolution: the state undertook to replace equations of power with a rule of law.

Revolutions are driven by social crisis. This was most certainly the case with the Wagner Act. Industrial strife nearly overwhelmed the early New Deal—1.5 million workers went on strike during its first year—and in Toledo, Ohio (autoworkers), San Francisco (longshoremen), and Minneapolis (teamsters), labor disputes escalated into street warfare and paralyzing general strikes. It was this turmoil that set the stage for the Wagner Act. Indeed, the constitutional argument for enacting a law was that protection of collective-bargaining rights would eliminate industrial disputes that burdened interstate commerce and threatened economic recovery. Not at once, however. After the passage of the Wagner Act, organized labor split apart, setting free a rival to the AFL—the CIO—and inaugurating a titanic battle for industrial unionism in the mass-production sector. General Motors was brought to a halt by the great sit-down strike of 1936–1937 in Flint, Michigan; on the Ford overpass, company thugs viciously beat union organizers; in the Little Steel strike of 1937, Chicago police shot down demonstrators in the Memorial Day massacre. Violence also sprang from the birth pangs of the new industrial-union movement. Rival AFL and CIO unions battled among themselves, wildcat strikes erupted in many newly organized plants, and picket lines were thrown up against nonunion workers.

In the midst of this turmoil, however, the new collective-bargaining regime took hold. One early byproduct, fueled mainly by NLRB staffers idled by massive legal challenges to the Wagner Act, was the La Follette Civil Liberties Investigating Committee, which exposed the widespread use by employers of labor spies, the extraordinary stockpiling of weapons and tear gas (Republic Steel was the nation's biggest purchaser), and the sophisticated campaigns of organized terrorism against union drives. The chastening effect was immense, accounting in part for U.S. Steel's early acceptance of collective bargaining. After the Supreme Court declared the Wagner Act constitutional, corporate employers more generally began to accept the in-

evitable, abandoning their company unions, tolerating CIO activists, and negotiating with unions certified by the NLRB as bargaining agents for their employees. The representation election had a transformative effect; labor organizing began to resemble a political canvass more than a mass mobilization. And there now existed formal machinery, through both the NLRB and contractually based grievance procedures, for channeling discontent and providing a measure of due process to aggrieved workers.

After World War II, the sea change was unmistakable. A strike wave of the first magnitude hit the country, but it was unaccompanied by the usual violence. This was because the postwar strikes involved only contractual issues—bitterly contested, to be sure, but not threatening the standing of the unions themselves. One could already see emerging the new strike etiquette of the Cold War era of "mature" collective bargaining—picketing as a ritual activity, with no resorting to scabs. It was true, of course, that the new labor law did not reach all sectors with equal speed or impact, and in some—over-the-road trucking, for example—organizing muscle mattered more than representation elections. Yet by the 1950s the old order had largely passed and with it, to a remarkable degree, the violence endemic to American industrial conflict.

May Day Parade, New York City, around 1946. CORBIS-BETTMANN

This was not so with the harvest of gangsterism, which in some corners of the economy was replenished by the brass-knuckle battles of the 1930s, most notoriously in trucking. The Teamsters had always harbored gang-infested locals, but only after World War II, under the resourceful leadership of Jimmy Hoffa, did it become the country's most feared union, and also the richest, with a huge pension fund ripe for the plundering. In the 1950s, as the magnitude of the problem emerged, the country finally moved toward a solution, which it found not within the labor movement—the reunited AFL-CIO, despite an admirable code of ethics, was ultimately helpless against the Teamsters—but in the powers of the state.

Until the 1930s, there was no law specifically targeting labor corruption, and not much interest by law enforcement agencies in pursuing what was conceived to be the private business of voluntary unions. But with the Wagner Act, it slowly dawned on the federal government that it had also assumed a responsibility for how state-sanctioned unions conducted their affairs. In 1953 in an unprecedented move, Congress established the New York Waterfront Commission, giving it extraordinary powers to decasualize hiring practices and drive the gangsters out of the International Longshoremen's Association. In 1959, following the revelations of the McClellan Senate hearings, with Hoffa as star witness, Congress passed the far-reaching Landrum-Griffin Act, which, among other things, imposed tight reporting and performance standards on union officials. A second law, much amended in 1962, dealt with the management of pension and welfare funds. Laws were one thing, however, and enforcement another. After several close calls, Hoffa was finally brought down in 1967 by a jury-tampering conviction. When he left prison, Hoffa was evidently bent on reclaiming the Teamster presidency without the mobster allies who had greased his first rise to power. If so, his good intentions proved his undoing, because on 30 July 1975 Hoffa disappeared, the victim, almost certainly, of a gangland slaying. Two of Hoffa's successors followed him to prison, but in 1989, after a massive prosecution under federal racketeering law, the Teamsters agreed to a court-appointed monitor, and the incubus finally lifted from this last refuge of systemic labor corruption.

America, however, may not have seen the last of its heritage of industrial violence. In the modern age of global competition, the rules of the game have begun to revert to form, most tellingly in the rising use of striker replacements, which the law permits in economic strikes but which, in the hands of determined employers, can destroy unions. The incidence of strikes had fallen to historic lows in the last two decades of the twentieth century, but the strikes that did occur were, in their intensity, equal to the bitterest recognition strikes of the pre–New Deal era. They were not accompanied by equal levels of physical violence—evidence, perhaps, of the lingering effects of half a century of the industrial accord. But the labor movement, taking a page from civil rights history (and from one of its own, César Chavez of the Farm Workers), also became more adept at directing the fury of industrial struggle into nonviolent forms of mass action. This was the strategy, for example, by which the miners prevailed in the bitter Pittston, Pennsylvania, strike of 1989–1990. In the service sector, workers with little bargaining power, such as janitors, resorted to civil-disobedience tactics with great effect. It may be that the culture of labor violence is truly finished. What is certain, at any rate, is that the antiunion impulses that fostered it are not finished and, indeed, were as vibrant at the close of the twentieth century as they were at its opening.

BIBLIOGRAPHY

Adams, Graham. *Age of Industrial Violence, 1910–1915.* New York: Columbia University Press, 1966. Covers the era that set the stage for New Deal reform.

Bruce, Robert V. *1877: Year of Violence.* Indianapolis: Bobbs-Merrill, 1959.

Dulles, Foster R., and Melvyn Dubofsky. *Labor in America: A History.* 4th ed. Arlington Heights, Ill.: Harlan Davidson, 1993. The best introduction to the history of labor violence.

Fine, Sidney. *Sitdown: The General Motors Strike of 1936–1937.* Ann Arbor: University of Michigan Press, 1969.

Hutchinson, John. *The Imperfect Union: A History of Corruption in American Trade Unions.* New York: E. P. Dutton, 1970. The standard work on labor criminality.

Jensen, Vernon H. *Heritage of Conflict: Labor Relations in the Nonferrous Industry up to 1930.* Ithaca, N.Y.: Cornell University Press, 1950. The most straightforward account of the hard-rock miners.

Krause, Paul. *The Battle for Homestead, 1880–1892.* Pittsburgh: University of Pittsburgh Press, 1995.

DAVID BRODY

See also **Anarchism; Class; Depressions, Economic; Haywood, William; Hoffa, Jimmy; Industrial Workers of the World; Los Angeles Times Building, Bombing of; Molly Maguires; Mussel Slough Conflict; Riots; Strikes; Wall Street, Bombing of; West.**

LANGUAGE AND VERBAL VIOLENCE

*Following the **Overview** is a subentry on the **Legal Status** of assaultive speech.*

OVERVIEW

In the 1960s H. Rap Brown, a prominent black activist, claimed that "violence is as American as apple pie." Regardless of whether or not this claim is true, its metaphorical form forecasts the topic of this essay: linguistic aspects of violence. Three decades later, U.S. Attorney General Janet Reno referred to "the mysteries of violence" in response to a mass murder involving students at an Arkansas middle school; this phrase serves as an indirect and obfuscating replacement for the direct expression, "We don't understand what happened here." By contrast, a member of the U.S. Congress at one point chose to be direct, as well as aggressive, when he referred to President Bill Clinton as a "scumbag." Words can create hostility, and, on the other hand, they can obscure the causes and results of hostility. In both cases language and violence are related to each other in important ways. Because these relationships are universal, much of this discussion has implications that go beyond American boundaries.

Conceptualizing Language and Violence

Language is a hierarchical, rule-governed system used for the interdependent purposes of thought and communication. At the base of all languages are sounds that are combined according to morphophonemic rules to form higher-order structures (morphemes or words), which in turn are combined via syntactic rules to form still higher-order structures (clauses or sentences); thus, language is structured at the levels of phonology, semantics, and syntax. At the highest level of the hierarchy, the pragmatic level, people use language to get things done and to affect the recipients of their messages.

Violence, on the other hand, is a murkier concept, less easily discussed in terms of structure. Its technical meaning has been widely debated, particularly in mass-communication research on the effects of violent films and television programs. Its everyday meaning is something like "the intentional infliction of harm on someone or something." Clear cases of violence include physical assault, rape, a fistfight, and lynching; less clear are instances of burglary, purse-snatching, and tackling in football.

It may be useful to think of two intersecting continua when describing violent acts: strong-weak and physical-verbal. The intersection yields four quadrants: strong-physical, weak-physical, strong-verbal, and weak-verbal. Perhaps for most people, strong-physical acts of violence are prototypical, whereas weak-verbal acts are peripheral. Many variables (for instance, the number of victims or the severity of consequences) can contribute to how we assess the strength of violence. Often, verbal and physical violence occur in conjunction, with one or the other mode dominating. It should be noted that recurrent weak acts of verbal violence can create a climate conducive to stronger violence, as when a label for a social group ("blacks") is repeatedly associated with a connotatively negative term ("lazy"). When violence and language are linked, the result is verbal aggression in its many forms: insults, obscenity, some types of pornographic discourse, hate speech, and so forth.

Linguistic Antecedents of Violence

With regard to both physical and verbal violence, an important relationship between language and violence is contained in the claim that language triggers violence. Given various psychological predispositions and situational factors, recipients of a message can be induced by communicators to perform violent acts. It should be emphasized that language is not an all-powerful instrument that supremely skillful orators can use to whip anyone at any time into a violent frenzy. Much depends on the psychological states and traits of message recipients, on their prior learning, and on the context of the communication. For example, it is clear that well-learned (high-habit-strength) behaviors are energized by social stimuli that produce high physiological arousal, a process labeled social facilitation. Thus, if a hearer who has had frequent recourse to violence is aroused by a speaker who urges violent action, there is an increased probability that the hearer will behave violently. Relatively high arousal in hearers can be produced by a speaker's use of high-intensity language, which is language that signals strong emotion and a departure from attitudinal neutrality. Sex and death metaphors, for example (as in, "rhetoric is the harlot of the arts"), can increase the intensity of messages as assessed by hearers. Many adjectives exhibit intensity gradations that are understood by native speakers ("terrible" is more intense than "bad").

In some cases, the context of communication carries much of the weight in coercing violence, and language serves merely as a weak catalyst. Thus, when all around us are engaging in mayhem, little needs to be said to push us in this direction. Imitative modeling can be a powerful mechanism, especially where norms for appropriate behavior are unclear. A lack of normative clarity may have been largely responsible for the outcome of the famous studies of "behavioral obedience" conducted by Stanley Milgram in the 1960s. Seemingly average persons complied when an experimenter requested that they deliver ostensibly painful, even dangerous, electric shocks to other persons in another room. (Shocks were not actually received by the "victims"; the important thing is that the experimental subjects believed that they were delivering shocks.) No attempt was made to persuade subjects to harm others; when subjects hesitated to deliver shocks, the experimenter merely said, "The experiment requires that you continue." The subjects' surprisingly compliant behavior was probably produced by several factors, including the experimenter's authority and subjects' lack of knowledge about norms for appropriate behavior in a research facility. Arguably any request made by the experimenter functioned much as would an order given by a superior officer in a military setting. In contexts where authority is clear and legitimate, it can have enormous force, especially where other contextual features are ambiguous. In these contexts, language functions as a relatively simple vehicle for conveying intentions.

Language is a more subtle instrument of violence in situations demanding persuasion, in which legitimate authority is not a factor. According to social-scientific research, there are many language variables that often enhance persuasive effectiveness. For example, the use of a "powerful" language style is relatively persuasive, at least in public-communications contexts. High-power language has been defined as language that avoids some features, such as tag questions ("he deserves our hatred, doesn't he?") and hedges ("he is sort of stupid") while including others, such as a diverse vocabulary and standard (as opposed to nonstandard) dialect and accent. The latter features are usually apparent in the discourse of national newscasters, for example. Also, in some violence-tinged situations communicators may achieve their violent purposes through the strategy of victimization. Essentially, this involves pu-

rifying the image of one's own social group (and that of one's hearers) by scapegoating another group, blaming them for a multitude of societal problems. As a part of this process, communicators typically use various forms of derogation including epithets that draw upon cultural, ethnic, and racial stereotypes. The paradigm case of this kind of communication is the infamous rhetoric of Adolf Hitler, but anti-Semitic and anti–African American comments by contemporary radio "shock jocks" are also pertinent.

As suggested above, before people can be persuaded to perform overtly violent acts, they must be violently predisposed. Typically, would-be persuaders can do little more than direct these predispositions. But it is important to note that these predispositions can be cultivated by communicators, particularly the mass media—newspapers, radio, and television. Totalitarian regimes have always tried to control their countries' agencies of mass communication for the purpose of creating explicitly negative images of dissident groups. More subtle processes of group derogation are apparent in the mass media of democratic, ostensibly open societies. For example, simple association of a group label ("foreigner") with a negative term ("crime") can gradually create negative attitudes toward the group, even when the association occurs in statements that explicitly deny the legitimacy of the association—for example, "Foreigners are not responsible for crime in our country." Verbal contiguity repeatedly occurring in discourse consumed by the public may create the belief that the association has a basis in reality. Repetition of a different sort is responsible for the "cultivation effect" originally hypothesized by George Gerbner. Essentially, this hypothesis indicates that specific background assumptions that recur in television programs can establish beliefs in viewers and that the beliefs will become more deeply established as time spent viewing increases. So, if the world is depicted as a violent place in many programs, frequent viewers, especially, will come to believe that the world is in fact violent—more so than objective statistics would indicate. Or if African Americans are depicted frequently as the agents of violence, viewers will come to believe that members of this group are, in fact, violent.

Referring to Violent Acts and Events

Another important relationship between language and violence is indicated by the claim that language describes violence. Reference to violence—in mass-media discourse and in everyday conversations—can have many important consequences. It can call attention to atrocities and warn about dangers; on the other hand, it can cover up, minimize, or obscure illegitimate aggression. A basic question here is, What kinds of actions or events are referenced as violent? One approach suggests that for both journalists and people engaging in mundane conversations, the "violence" label is used when certain attributes are seen as meeting the criteria for defining that term: violent acts are intentional, injurious, unwelcome, unfriendly, disturbing, arousing, and so on. That a complete list of defining attributes is probably impossible to offer is one problem with criterial theories of meaning. An alternative approach suggests that violence can be viewed as a "fuzzy set," with some acts at the very center of the set (prototypes) and others on the set's periphery. Thus, punching someone in the face for no apparent reason probably would be considered prototypically violent by most people (also prototypically crazy); slapping someone on the back in a congratulatory situation probably would be viewed as peripherally violent. There is often a high level of agreement on prototypical referents of common words within a culture.

When talking about some violent event, a communicator may choose to use direct and unequivocal language, or, on the other hand, to use language that is indirect. There is some evidence that a speaker's use of a directive ("kill him"), a reference to quantity ("there are twelve bodies on the floor"), and a judgmental adjective ("he is a vicious man") will produce an impression of directness, whereas use of questions, hedges, negations ("he is not fit to live"), and "uncertainty verbs" ("I hesitate to describe the carnage") will produce the opposite effect. More generally, indirectness takes many forms. For example, highly familiar or stale metaphors will often go unnoticed, functioning as transparent vehicles of expression ("the victim bit the dust"). By contrast, novel metaphors call attention to themselves and their referents; they are vivid and stimulate thought ("the victim fell like petals from a flower"). Communicators may also use euphemisms (e.g., referring to civilian casualties as "collateral damage").

One context that is particularly important when considering verbal references to violence is that of in-group and out-group communication, particularly within-group communication among members of a given social group about members of

---

Distancing from Violence

Communicators may distance themselves from violence—as a way of indicating their low involvement or low commitment—by using forms of discourse that are low in "verbal immediacy," a language variable that has been the subject of much research.

Low immediacy results from the use of "that" instead of "the," past instead of present tense, later instead of earlier occurrence of reference in a sequence, low implied voluntarism ("must" versus "want"), low mutuality ("you and I" versus "we"), and low probability ("may" versus "will"). An example of a lower-immediacy utterance is "That killing you and I had to do may have been an accident waiting to happen."

---

another group (outsiders) versus within-group communication about members of one's own group (insiders). To give a concrete and extreme example, imagine a situation in which members of a white-separatist group are discussing a possibly violent act performed by another white separatist, and then imagine the same white separatists discussing a similar act, but this time performed by an African American. The discussions would differ in some predictable ways. There is a widespread tendency to present members of one's own group in a favorable light and to downgrade members of other groups, especially when group competition or conflict exists. One manifestation of the in-group bias can be seen when group members use negative "state" verbs when describing transgressive acts performed by members of an out-group, because state verbs imply an enduring tendency ("they hate everyone"), as do adjectives ("those people are violent"). On the other hand, according to Gunn Semin and Klaus Fiedler, descriptive action verbs imply situationally bound, potentially isolated events and are likely to be used when describing transgressive acts performed by members of one's own group ("John hit him").

Extending this kind of linguistic logic, Tim Cole and Laura Leets suggest that nominalization, where verb phrases are transformed to noun phrases ("I will hit you" versus "hitting will occur"), obscures the agent of an action through abstraction, as does generalization, where specific referents are subsumed by general terms ("John is sometimes violent" versus "people are sometimes violent"). Sik Hung Ng and James J. Bradac call these forms of language "masking devices," a category that can also include permutation and truncation. Through the use of permutation, more responsibility for action will be assigned to individuals placed first in an utterance: "John punched Sam" versus "Sam was punched by John." John appears less responsible for the action in the latter case. Through the use of truncation, agents can be deleted when actions are described: "John hurt Sam" versus "Sam was hurt." Thus, particular language choices can mask the people responsible for actions, which may be advantageous to those in positions of power and those describing the violent behaviors of members of their in-group.

Language as an Index of Violent Intentions

A third important relationship between language and violence is expressed in the claim that language produces attributions of violent intent. The corollary is, of course, that language sometimes produces attributions of nonviolent intent. The point is that language, in a role usually labeled the attributional function of language, allows hearers and readers to make inferences about a wide variety of communicator intentions, characteristics, tendencies, and states. In first-impression situations, variations in phonology, word choice, and syntax can stimulate inferences about, for example, a speaker's emotional state. Attributions of violent or nonviolent intent, as opposed to other kinds of attributions, are likely to occur in contexts where violence is a salient possibility.

Especially relevant here are inferences that pertain to a communicator's willingness or desire to behave violently and to the ability to carry out violent intentions. Complex arrays of verbal and nonverbal behaviors are associated with, and to some extent comprise, ethnic and racial stereotypes that in particular cases include the attribute of a violent disposition, which embodies both willingness and desire. A speaker's use of nonstandard dialect may trigger such stereotypes in the minds of hearers. It is important to emphasize that stereotypical beliefs, though they may have no basis in reality, nevertheless may lead to biased notions and to actions based on these notions; an innocent gesture may be seen as threatening, and preemptive steps may be taken to eliminate the threat. Apart from dialects and stereotypes, other forms of language may stimulate inferences about the likelihood of violence. A high level of language intensity may indicate that a speaker is highly emotional, and a hearer's inference of high emotionality may trigger a correlated inference of a high likelihood of violence in a violence-tinged situation. In fact, language intensity has been used as a gauge of the likelihood of violence in crisis-negotiation situations. A high level of repetition (low lexical diversity) can indicate high anxiety in speakers, which may signal instability and propensity toward violence where violence is a possible outcome.

Given an inference of speaker willingness or desire to behave violently, a hearer's inferences about violence capability become important. A person may be seen as intending to create mayhem but also as weak and ineffectual and, accordingly, incapable of fulfilling this intention. High levels of verbal hedging and hesitation (e.g., pauses filled with weak interjections such as "uh") are likely to reduce the hearer's sense that the speaker is capable of violence, as are low levels of verbal immediacy. Use of any form of language that leads to hearer attributions of high uncertainty in speakers is likely to decrease the credibility of a threat. Of course, in addition to information carried by language, many nonverbal factors will be important (e.g., physical size in the case of a physical threat). Knowledge of a person's past success or failure in fulfilling violent intentions may be especially likely to affect assessments of capability in the present. Various external constraints also affect perceptions of capability: a person bound, gagged, and held at gunpoint necessarily will be rendered nonviolent, despite silent fury; less dramatically, a person closely monitored by authorities will be psychologically constrained.

Forms of Verbal Aggression

Perhaps the clearest indicator of a violent intention is verbal aggression, which may be a good predictor of physical violence. Verbal aggression is more than an indicator of the specific intention to engage in verbal (as opposed to physical) violence—it is a manifestation of this intention. Generally, verbal violence occurs when a communicator uses language designed to cause psychological injury to a person to whom a message is directed or to a third party referenced in the message. It is useful to distinguish between the violent intent underlying a message, which often will be clear to both intended message recipients and third parties, and the violent effect of a message. There is a gap between intentions and effects such that an effect that a speaker intends to produce may not occur for any number of reasons: hearer distraction, speaker ineffectiveness, mutual misunderstanding, and so on. Thus, a threat may not have the effect of making its recipient feel threatened. The converse is possible also: a friendly remark may be taken as threatening (by a person with paranoia, for example).

Some forms of verbal violence are highly codified within (and sometimes across) cultures, and communicators learn rules for their construction. Take the formula "if you do/do not do X, I will punish you." A speaker might say, "If you continue to stare, I will make you sorry," or, "If you do not write the check now, I will ruin your credit record." Often threats are expressed implicitly, with the punishment that is contingent upon noncompliance being indicated by context: "Don't stare" or "Write the check." Threats are similar to promises, which substitute a contingent reward for a punishment: "If you work overtime, I will give you a raise." Rewards may also be expressed implicitly.

Insults are another form of verbal violence, which probably represent the concept of "fighting words" as well as or better than any other type of language. The use of "fighting words" is not protected by the First Amendment to the U.S. Constitution, although this concept has been interpreted narrowly to include only speech that is likely to provoke a rational person to respond violently. Clearly, insults are widely used, so in many situations their use is not highly provocative. In fact, insults are used in jokes and comic routines; in these cases, though, the intent of speakers usually is not to inflict psychological damage, so the ostensibly humorous speech acts may be insults in form only. The model underlying insults is a simple one: a targeted person or group is linked with a negative trait ("you are stupid"). Arguably, the utterance linking the target and the negative trait must be perceived as reflecting a malicious intent as opposed to an intention merely to describe the way things are; yet perhaps it is reasonable to claim that there are unintended insults. Metaphors, intense language, and other forms of embellishment are often added to the basic model in the process of speech production: "You are incredibly stupid, slightly less intelligent than a small moth."

A third form of language that is pertinent here is obscenity, although, unlike threats and insults, obscenity is not formulated on a simple linguistic model, which may be related to the notorious problem of specifying its meaning in court cases. Obscenity is not protected by the First Amendment, but demonstrating that an utterance (or a film or a book) is indeed obscene depends on a wide variety of complex contextual factors and how these relate to the utterance (or other artifact) at issue. In some sense, obscene language refers to a domain of objects or actions, often sexual, excretory, or religious, that are mentionable without special permission only in a narrow range of personal contexts. But more than this, the form or style of the language must be vulgar or coarse, because even taboo referents may be acceptable in public contexts if the style used to render them is, for example, "clinical." Obscenity is often used as nothing more than a banal form of interjection. It becomes a form of verbal violence when it is used with the intention of harming the message recipient or a third party.

Verbal aggression often combines threats, insults, obscenity, and other linguistic forms. The term *hate speech* emerged in the 1990s in reference to verbal aggression that is directed at social groups, often minorities, as opposed to individuals. Its use has been prohibited by "speech codes" established on some college campuses, but these codes are being challenged as violating First Amendment protections. At issue is whether hate speech constitutes "fighting words," for example, or instead represents ideas, however ill-formed these may be. Little social-scientific research has been conducted on the effects of hate speech on the attitudes or behaviors of hearers, but one study by Laura Leets and Howard Giles has shown that messages exhibiting hate speech that are addressed to the objects of enmity are evaluated more negatively than are messages exhibiting hate speech that are overheard—presumably a consequence of how the recipient assesses the communicator's intentions. Perhaps surprisingly, this study also demonstrated that in-group members who read the messages, that is, individuals representing the ethnic group attacked, were more negative toward indirect expressions of animosity, whereas out-group members were more negative toward direct expressions. In this study, differences in directness were produced by differences in the form of the communicator's speech acts.

Although much of the research that has been done on the effects of violent messages pertains to physical violence, a pertinent psychological process that may also apply to verbal violence is that of "desensitization." If message recipients are exposed repeatedly to depictions of physical violence, in films or television programs, for example, they will gradually habituate to violent stimuli. This means that high levels of physical arousal produced by initial exposure to violence will decrease with subsequent exposure. In everyday language, violence loses its capacity to shock; it comes to seem normal. By extension, repeated exposure to threats, insults, and obscenity may cause these forms to become familiar and expected. The question of effects is a basic one; equally basic is the question of the antecedents or causes of verbal aggression. Clearly, many factors contribute to the production of a particular act of verbal violence, but at a general level especially important are personality, knowledge, arousal, and evaluation. Some people are relatively aggressive across situations; when this personal tendency is coupled with a lack of knowledge about how to engage in rational argument, verbal aggression is a likely consequence in a situation that elicits arousal and negative evaluation of the source of arousal. Of course, verbally aggressive individuals must also know how to threaten and insult targets and how to use obscene language. This knowledge can be gained by exposure to verbally aggressive models.

Conclusion

Language is deeply implicated in violent behavior; it can trigger violence in both public and personal contexts, as when speakers urge violent action. Language is used to refer to violent occurrences, and this reference can dramatize or obscure the fact of violence and its causes. Language can reveal information about a communicator's violent intention both indirectly—through cues that trigger intention-related attributions—and directly—through verbal forms that express (or even constitute) this intention. Words can hide injuries and mask injurers. Contrary to a familiar aphorism, words *can* hurt.

BIBLIOGRAPHY

Bradac, James J., John Waite Bowers, and John A. Courtright. "Three Language Variables in Communication Research: Intensity, Immediacy, and Diversity." *Human Communication Research* 5, no. 3 (1979).
Burke, Kenneth. *Language as Symbolic Action.* Berkeley: University of California Press, 1966.
Center for Communication and Social Policy, University of California, Santa Barbara, ed. *National Television Violence Study 3.* Thousand Oaks, Calif.: Sage, 1998.
Cole, Tim, and Laura Leets. "Linguistic Masking Devices and Intergroup Behavior: Further Evidence of an Intergroup Linguistic Bias." *Journal of Language and Social Psychology* 17, no. 3 (1998).
Galliker, Mark, Jan Herman, Kurt Imminger, and Daniel Weimer. "The Investigation of Contiguity: Co-occurrence Analysis of Print Media Using CD-ROMs as a New Data Source, Illustrated by a Discussion on Migrant Delinquency in a Daily Newspaper." *Journal of Language and Social Psychology* 17, no. 2 (1998).
Infante, Dominic A., Teresa A. Chandler, and Jill E. Rudd. "Test of an Argumentative Skill Deficiency Model of Interspousal Violence." *Communication Monographs* 56, no. 2 (1989).
Leets, Laura, and Howard Giles. "Words as Weapons—When Do They Wound?: Investigations of Harmful Speech." *Human Communication Research* 24, no. 4 (1997).
Milgram, Stanley. *Obedience to Authority: An Experimental View.* New York: Harper and Row, 1974.
Mulac, Anthony, James J. Bradac, and Pamela Gibbons. "Empirical Support for the Gender-as-Culture Hypothesis: An Intercultural Investigation of Male/Female Language Differences." Paper presented at the meeting of the International Communication Association, Jerusalem (July 1998).
Ng, Sik Hung, and James J. Bradac. *Power in Language: Verbal Communication and Social Influence.* Thousand Oaks, Calif.: Sage, 1993.
Potter, W. James. "Cultivation Theory and Research: A Conceptual Critique." *Human Communication Research* 19, no. 4 (1993).
Rogan, Randall G., and Mitchell R. Hammer. "Assessing Message Affect in Crisis Negotiations: An Exploratory Study." *Human Communication Research* 21, no. 4 (1995).
Semin, Gunn, and Klaus Fiedler. "The Cognitive Functions of Linguistic Categories in Describing Persons: Social Cognition and Language." *Journal of Personality and Social Psychology* 54, no. 4 (1988).
Wiener, Morton, and Albert Mehrabian. *Language Within Language: Immediacy, a Channel in Verbal Communication.* New York: Appleton-Century-Crofts, 1968.

JAMES J. BRADAC

See also **Humor; Symbolic Violence.**

LEGAL STATUS

When they think of crime, most Americans tend to envision violence. Contrary to this popular conception, however, most criminal offenses—and indeed most criminals—are nonviolent. According to a 1997 study conducted by Franklin E. Zimring and Gordon Hawkins, only 26 percent of index crimes committed in Los Angeles in 1992 involved the use or threat of personal violence. (Index crimes are the eight classes of offenses annually reported by the Federal Bureau of Investigation: murder, sexual assault, aggravated assault, robbery, burglary, larceny, motor vehicle theft, and arson.) The proportion of crimes involving violence declines to about 15 percent when nonindex offenses such as drug sales and possession are added. Moreover, under normal conditions, the American legal system is capable of successfully identifying and prosecuting this minority of violent offenders relatively efficiently. But what happens when we shift our attention from the clearly articulated realm of index and nonindex offenses and examine the way in which the legal system addresses the more problematic issue of assaultive speech?

Assaultive speech, defined as words and images that wound, is itself capable of significant, demonstrable violence. The victims of assaultive speech "are daily silenced, intimidated, and subjected to severe psychological and physical trauma by . . . assailants who employ words and symbols as part of an integrated arsenal of weapons of oppression and subordination" (Matsuda et al. 1993, p. 7). Such attacks, when efficacious, are described by Charles R. Lawrence III, an editor of *Words That Wound*, as "immediate," "instantaneous," and "like receiving a slap in the face." Yet despite the violence of assaultive speech, its status in relation to the legal system is less clearly defined. "In the current U.S. political climate, the law that decides the question of hate speech tends to be applied inconsistently in order to further reactionary political aims," according to Judith Butler (1997). For example, in those instances in which the representation of sexuality is at issue, speech is considered unequivocally to be a sort of action or an expression of the intention to act, and the First Amendment suffers correspondingly. The controversial "don't ask, don't tell" policy adopted by the military in the early 1990s regarding gay and lesbian self-declaration provides one pointed example of this tactical inconsistency: that is, the declaration of a homosexual inclination itself becomes tantamount to a homosexual action. However, in instances of racist speech, the courts have considered the relation between speech and action to be equivocal, if not undecidable.

A well-known example is seen in the case of *R.A.V. v. St. Paul* (1992), in which the Supreme Court of the United States found that a burning cross on the lawn of a black family's house is a nonprosecutable "viewpoint" that constitutes a form of "protected speech" in the "free market-

place of ideas." In such cases, the First Amendment, designed to protect freedom of speech, seems to be in direct conflict with the Fourteenth Amendment, protecting the rights of all citizens to fair and equal treatment under the law. Lawrence associates this type of assault with that effected by "fighting words," defined as words "likely to provoke the average person to retaliation, and thereby cause a breach of the peace" (from *Chaplinsky v. New Hampshire*, a 1942 landmark decision). He contends that "racial insults are undeserving of First Amendment protection because the perpetrator's intention is not to discover truth or initiate dialogue, but to injure the victim." As long as burning crosses are construed as speech rather than action, as viewpoints rather than threats, the First Amendment will continue to trump the Fourteenth.

Critical race theorists assert that an uncritical adherence to the First Amendment concerning assaultive speech "arms both conscious and unconscious racists—Nazis and liberals alike—with a constitutional right to be racist." These self-proclaimed champions of civil liberties contend that active juridical regulation is necessary, even mandatory, to ensure that all American citizens enjoy the privileges and benefits of full citizenship. Yet it comes as no surprise that this constituency in favor of regulation is composed primarily of those historically marginalized groups most vulnerable to assaultive speech: women, homosexuals, and persons of color. Catharine A. MacKinnon, Andrea Dworkin, and Rae Langton have forwarded an essentially analogous argument in their campaign against the disempowering effects of pornographic representations of women.

Conversely, advocates of unlimited free speech call proponents of any limitations to those rights "First Amendment revisionists," "thought police," and worse. But rather than denying the potential violence of certain kinds of speech, they contend, often persuasively, that the criminalization of even the most violent speech based on either its content or the subjects it addresses "puts the state in the censorship business." This additional limitation was a second feature of the Supreme Court's decision in the *R.A.V.* case: although the vehicle of expression may be legally proscribable, its content never is. The editors of *Words That Wound* concede that this is perhaps the most compelling argument against juridical censorship; paradoxically, "admitting one exception will lead to another, and yet another, until those in power are free to stifle opposition in the name of protecting democratic ideals. Yet there is no serviceable alternative to this kind of censorial intervention. Richard Delgado, one of the *Words That Wound* editors, established that there exists no tort action for this sort of violence, and, as the *R.A.V.* case proves, there is no room for individualized local legislation in these matters either. (A tort is a private wrong—civil as opposed to criminal—that includes both intentional and inadvertent damages for which the victim may seek monetary compensation.) Ultimately, there is no contemporary legal means of countering the violence of assaultive speech save the equal-protection clause of the Fourteenth Amendment. The force of the equal-protection clause, however, is circumscribed by the "state action doctrine," which is part of the equal protection clause of the Fourteenth Amendment and establishes that only the government and its representatives, not private citizens, are accountable for the effects of such debilitating, segregating speech.

The first question central to an analysis of assaultive speech and the legal system therefore becomes one of sovereignty, a public-private distinction. "To argue that citizens can effectively deprive each other of such rights and liberties through words that wound," Butler contends, "requires overcoming the restrictions imposed by the state action doctrine." And until these restrictions are overcome, recourse to the equal-protection clause will remain severely qualified. Presuming that the state-action doctrine is superseded, however, a second question immediately arises, involving the uneasy (or perhaps too-easy) distinction between speech and action. For if the formerly sacrosanct "content" of speech is not always distinguishable from action or from the intention to act, then the role of the legal system must be reevaluated. As soon as speech stops being "just speech" and functions instead as a species of action, it becomes actionable under the legal system. But how should it be so? Proposals to regulate assaultive speech cite such speech extensively, and, in so doing, they restage the moment of violence repeatedly, in increasingly formal and official contexts. Furthermore, as Butler demonstrates, state-sanctioned legal decisions regarding language and violence will always engage the nexus of language and violence, and "the adjudication of what will and will not count as protected speech will itself be a kind of speech, one which implicates the state in the very problem of discursive power with which it is invested to regulate, sanction, and restrict such speech."

But others equate silence with endorsement and claim that the problem of implication cannot be avoided merely through the avoidance of adjudication. "State silence," Mari Matsuda claims, "is public action." From this position critical race theorists argue that the state's silence may constitute a graver violence than a private citizen's assault. The private challenge to the victim's humanity is compounded by a public challenge to his or her citizenship. Yet Butler, who consistently asserts her adherence to some principle of accountability in addressing assaultive speech—and her sympathy to Matsuda's analysis—concludes that hateful speech cannot effectively be countered by means of censorship. Instead of a legal intervention, she, like Stanley Fish, argues for a nonjuridical approach to the problem of language and verbal violence. Fish concludes that

> First Amendment jurisprudence is inevitably self-defeating and subversive of its own aspirations. That's the bad news. The good news is that precisely *because* speech is never 'free' in the two senses required—free from consequences and free from state pressure—speech always matters, is always doing work; because everything we say impinges on the world in ways indistinguishable from the effects of physical action, we must take responsibility for our verbal performances—*all* of them—and not assume that they are being taken [care] of by the clause in the Constitution.

BIBLIOGRAPHY

Butler, Judith. *Excitable Speech: A Politics of the Performative.* New York: Routledge, 1997.

Fish, Stanley. *There's No Such Thing as Free Speech and It's a Good Thing Too.* New York: Oxford University Press, 1994.

MacKinnon, Catharine A. *Only Words.* Cambridge, Mass: Harvard University Press, 1993.

Matsuda, Mari, et al., eds. *Words That Wound: Critical Race Theory, Assaultive Speech, and the First Amendment.* Boulder, Colo.: Westview, 1993.

Zimring, Franklin E., and Gordon Hawkins. *Crime Is Not the Problem: Lethal Violence in America.* New York: Oxford University Press, 1997.

MATTHEW R. HOFER

See also **Hate, Politics of; Hate Crime; Representation of Violence.**

LANSKY, MEYER
(1902–1983)

Meyer Lansky was said to be the "thinking man's gangster." Where others used their fists, Lansky used his financial acumen or "Midas touch," as the *New York Times* put it, to become a major underworld figure whose forty-year career included bootlegging and the building of casinos. Lansky first became a famous name (even garnering a profile in the *Wall Street Journal*) when he testified on national television before the Kefauver Committee, the Senate subcommittee that investigated organized crime in the United States in 1950 and 1951. For much of his life, though, he successfully avoided the limelight.

Lansky was born in Grodno, Belarus, then a part of the Russian czarist empire, in 1902 and was brought to the United States by his parents in 1911. Lansky grew up in a neighborhood populated by many other Russian Jewish immigrants, on the Lower East Side of New York City, where he not only excelled in his studies but developed a lifelong love of books. Police surveillance reports confirm his abiding interest, detailing how Lansky would visit Brentano's and Barnes and Noble bookstores when in New York.

By the time he was a teenager, Lansky had fallen in with Benjamin "Bugsy" Siegel and other budding troublemakers like "Lucky" Luciano, forging close and enduring ties with both. It was Prohibition, however, that made him into a bona fide criminal. In the early 1920s, financed by the underworld figure Arnold Rothstein, a wealthy and well-connected professional gambler whom he reportedly met at a bar mitzvah, the young Lansky went into business for himself. In addition to operating a car- and truck-rental business on the Lower East Side, he supplied the neighborhood with liquor and floating crap games, all the while keeping violence to a minimum.

Following the repeal of Prohibition in 1933, Lansky applied his business acumen to the world of gambling, owning and operating fancy casinos, "carpet joints," and roadhouses all along the East Coast, from Saratoga, in upstate New York, to Hollywood, Florida. Later, he expanded his U.S. gambling empire to include gaming establishments in the Caribbean, including a lavish, multimillion-dollar hotel, the Riviera, in Havana, Cuba. Through it all, Lansky was careful to avoid potential legal entanglements of any sort, even going so far as to list himself as the director of the Riviera's kitchens rather than its owner.

Having sunk millions of his own money into the Riviera and other Cuban casinos, Lansky lost everything after the rise to power in 1959 of Fidel Castro, when property owned by American inves-

Meyer Lansky. LIBRARY OF CONGRESS

tors was seized and nationalized. By then in his sixties, plagued with heart trouble, Lansky essentially retired. For the next twenty years, until his death in 1983, he lived quietly in Florida, except for a year in Israel, to which he had fled to escape prosecution for tax evasion.

Rumor had it that Lansky was worth over $300 million at the time of his death, but his modest lifestyle as well as the equally modest size of his estate suggested otherwise. A reflection of America's growing fascination with the underworld, the Lansky legend was ultimately greater than the reality of Lansky's life.

BIBLIOGRAPHY

Cohen, Richard. *Tough Jews.* New York: Simon and Schuster, 1998.
Eisenberg, Dennis, Uri Dan, and Eli Landau. *Meyer Lansky: Mogul of the Mob.* New York: Paddington, 1979.
Lacey, Robert. *Little Man: Meyer Lansky and the Gangster Life.* Boston: Little, Brown, 1991.

JENNA WEISSMAN JOSELIT

See also **Costello, Frank; Luciano, "Lucky"; Murder, Inc.; Organized Crime; Siegel, Benjamin "Bugsy."**

LAS VEGAS

Crime and violence have become significant problems in Las Vegas only since the mid-1970s. After Las Vegas was founded in 1905 as a railroad town, its population remained under ten thousand through 1940, when southern Nevada's open spaces brought thousands of Army Air Corps personnel to the area to learn combat skills. Gamblers and gangsters began their migration shortly after World War II. The population of the metropolitan area rose to almost fifty thousand in 1950, and then to 127,000 in 1960. Yet even with the arrival of hundreds, perhaps thousands, of men for whom violence or the threat of violence had been a means to economic advancement, few Las Vegans worried about crime and violence.

The men and women who settled near the railway station before 1920 were not especially law-abiding. A review of local newspapers in the first quarter of the twentieth century reveals coverage of occasional fistfights and larger brawls involving railroad workers of differing nationalities, disputes between spouses and between former business partners, and, as one would expect in a community owing its livelihood to the railroad, incidents of theft and recovery of goods stolen from freight cars. Yet several factors—a stable and slowly expanding economy, available land at low cost, and a relatively homogenous population—kept violence to a minimum.

Las Vegans adapted to Prohibition and the Great Depression without resorting to violence. Bootleggers and moonshiners abounded, particularly because thirsty railroad travelers constituted a steady market. Virtually everyone in Las Vegas knew who was making or selling liquor, and the local police generally took action only to show the federal authorities that the small Mojave Desert city was not an enclave of lawlessness. When Prohibition ended in 1933, many of the more enterprising bootleggers opened bars and liquor stores to serve travelers who welcomed Nevada's decisions in 1931 to legalize gambling again and to make divorces easy to obtain. During the depression the economy remained strong as construction of the nearby Boulder Dam strengthened Las Vegas's role as a transshipment point, which in turn lured construction workers and then visitors to the dam and to the casinos, restaurants, and bars of Las Vegas.

For decades—even into the 1940s and 1950s—Las Vegans coped with the warm nights that followed the blisteringly hot summer days by wrapping themselves in wet sheets and sleeping beneath the moonlight or by sleeping with their windows open, without fear of rapists or thieves.

Increase in Law Enforcement

As the populations of Las Vegas and Clark County increased substantially during World War II, city and county officials provided funds for over a fourfold increase in the number of law enforcement officers. Training, however, remained almost nonexistent until the late 1950s. Officers were neither more nor less violent in carrying out their duties than their counterparts in other cities, and elected officials applauded the periodic loading of vagrants on trains bound for Los Angeles. In time, city fathers began to perceive that the city's reputation for beating suspects and its general penchant for confrontational behavior interfered with

A neon cowgirl perched at the top of the Glitter Gulch casino in Las Vegas. CORBIS/MICHAEL T. SEDAM

Las Vegas's image as a modern metropolis, and by 1960 area leaders were gradually pushing law enforcement agencies toward greater professionalism.

The great majority of residents and visitors continued to feel safe even as scores of gangsters relocated to Las Vegas in the late 1940s and 1950s. They perceived that the men representing the organized crime groups of New York, Chicago, Cleveland, Miami, and Kansas City did not want adverse publicity about violent crime to scare away gamblers and thus break what was through the late 1960s their "golden egg." Each of the major casinos on the Strip had an extensive private security force to guard against robbery and cheating. These forces frequently used violence to encourage the cheaters and other undesirables to leave town immediately.

The struggle of African Americans in Las Vegas for equality was accompanied by limited outbreaks of violence in the late 1960s. No major riots developed, although police were called to high schools when fighting broke out among students and curfews were imposed on the Westside, Las Vegas's black ghetto. Segregation in public facilities ended in 1960, and by the end of the decade, the casino owners understood that African Americans could no longer be relegated only to the menial jobs.

Decline of Organized Crime

After Atlantic City's emergence as a center of casino gambling in the late 1970s, organized crime leaders agreed that Chicago's underworld would play the paramount role in Las Vegas, while its New York counterparts would be dominant in Atlantic City. As men with direct ties to organized crime sold their casinos to corporate interests in the 1960s and 1970s, paramount role meant having control of lucrative money skimming from casino and auxiliary operations. Some of the corporate casino executives actively cooperated with skims initiated by organized crime. Disagreements among those involved with skimming resulted in a few episodes of well-publicized violence. By the late 1980s Justice Department prosecutions and aggressive action by Nevada gaming regulators against casino executives who cooperated with organized crime interests ended the practice of skimming. Traditional organized crime no longer plays a significant role in any aspect of Las Vegas gaming.

Violent crime rates in the Las Vegas metropolitan area have been significantly higher than na-

tional rates since the late 1970s. These figures are somewhat misleading, however, because much of the crime is committed by visitors, whose numbers reached more than 30 million annually by the late 1990s. At the end of the twentieth century, Las Vegas appeared a rather typical American city to anyone reviewing its two daily newspapers. Brief stories of domestic violence, drug-related gang slayings, burglary, and rape were interspersed with longer investigative pieces dealing with police violence. Experienced police officers suggested that domestic violence occurred at a higher rate in Las Vegas because of the lack of family and community ties among much of the population and the frustrations associated with gambling losses.

BIBLIOGRAPHY

Balboni, Alan. *Beyond the Mafia: Italian Americans and the Development of Las Vegas.* Reno and Las Vegas: University of Nevada Press, 1996.

Farrell, Ronald A., and Carole Case. *The Black Book and the Mob.* Madison: University of Wisconsin Press, 1995.

Moehring, Eugene. *Resort City in the Sunbelt: Las Vegas, 1930–1970.* Reno and Las Vegas: University of Nevada Press, 1989.

ALAN BALBONI

See also **Gambling; Siegel, Benjamin "Bugsy"; Urban Violence.**

LENNON, JOHN, MURDER OF

The murder of John Lennon, the world-famous English singer-songwriter—whose band, the Beatles, changed the course of rock music in the 1960s—by Mark David Chapman on 8 December 1980 was a uniquely twentieth-century tragedy. Unlike other infamous assassins, Chapman killed neither out of political motives nor for material gain but simply for fame itself. Also unlike other killers, he made no effort either to escape the murder scene or to avoid punishment for his crime. Against the advice of his lawyers, he admitted in court that he shot Lennon in the back at close range with a .38-caliber pistol.

Contrary to media accounts after the murder, Chapman was not a deranged Beatles fan. A fanatic Christian, Chapman for a decade before the murder had despised and publicly reviled Lennon for his proclamation that the Beatles were "more popular than Jesus" and for the lyrics to his song "Imagine"—"Imagine there's no heaven"—which

Lennon wrote and performed after leaving the Beatles. At the time of his death Lennon's reputation as a musical artist and worldwide antiwar activist had made him enormously popular. This popularity was the primary reason that Chapman, who traveled from his home in Honolulu, Hawaii, to New York City and stalked Lennon for several weeks, selected him as a target.

A narcissist of overpowering ambition but modest talent, Chapman at age twenty-five was a product of American popular culture who craved the sort of recognition and adulation that Lennon received. A self-described nobody who borrowed personality traits from people around him and from fictional characters, Chapman became enraged when he saw photographs published in early 1980 of Lennon living sumptuously in the elegant Dakota apartment building on Central Park West in New York City. At the same time, he had been immersing himself in J. D. Salinger's novel *The Catcher in the Rye* (1951). He took the novel's emotional message about a troubled adolescent's painful search for identity in a world of "phonies" and distorted it to justify his plan to

John Lennon. LIBRARY OF CONGRESS

achieve notoriety. Though he used Salinger's novel to explain the crime, Chapman said during interviews that the main reason he killed Lennon was "to stop being a nobody. The only way I could do that was by killing the biggest somebody in the world."

Following the murder, many entertainment celebrities hired security consultants. The killing provoked at least two copycat attacks. John Hinckley, Jr., who shot President Ronald Reagan on 30 March 1981, and Robert John Bardo, who killed the actress Rebecca Shaeffer on 18 July 1989, were both carrying copies of *The Catcher in the Rye* at the time of their crimes and told police they had modeled their actions on Chapman's.

BIBLIOGRAPHY

Clarke, James. *On Being Mad or Merely Angry: John W. Hinckley and Other Dangerous People.* Princeton, N.J.: Princeton University Press, 1990.

Fawcett, Anthony. *John Lennon: One Day at a Time.* New York: Grove, 1976.

Jones, Jack. *Let Me Take You Down: Inside the Mind of Mark David Chapman, the Man Who Killed John Lennon.* New York: Villard, 1992.

Martin, Jay. *Who Am I This Time?: Uncovering the Fictive Personality.* New York: Norton, 1988.

JACK JONES

See also **Hinckley, John W., Jr.**

LEPKE, LOUIS
(1897–1944)

At the time of his death by electrocution on 4 March 1944, Louis "Lepke" Buchalter was believed to have been the mastermind behind Murder, Inc., a vast gangster operation unparalleled in its ruthlessness. Wielding bludgeons, blackjacks, knives, guns, and corrosive acids, Lepke and his minions, some 250 strong, not only held New York's garment industry in thrall during the 1930s, they also killed an estimated eighty men in the course of their murderous reign.

Born Louis Buchalter to a Russian Jewish family in New York City in 1897, one of eleven children, Lepke was a quiet and rather ordinary child. ("Lepke" was an affectionate nickname bestowed by his family that became the future racketeer's most well-known alias.) When he was thirteen his father, the owner of a modest hardware store, died suddenly; after the ensuing breakup of the family,

Louis Lepke. CORBIS/BETTMANN

he left school and took to the streets, eventually becoming a *shtarke,* or thug, whose stock-in-trade was "settling" industrial disputes within New York's burgeoning garment trades. Throughout the 1920s both labor and management made use of his talents. Sometimes Lepke and his men would enforce a strike, and at other times they would break one.

Before long, though, Lepke went from being a hired gun to becoming a major power within the industry: in addition to exacting tribute from intimidated bosses and workers alike, he acquired a controlling interest in a significant number of clothing concerns as well as a stranglehold over the trucking industry, the key strategic link in the entire business.

In the words of the distinguished crime reporter Meyer Berger (1944), Lepke worked "efficiently and unobtrusively" behind the scenes, creating a "climate of fear." An insider in an insider's business, he effectively exploited its weaknesses. The racketeer also made a point of avoiding the limelight. Unlike the "splashy mobsters of the period, Lepke went his quiet way," observed Berger; "in

due time, he became more powerful" than any of them.

Eventually, though, Lepke's notoriety caught up with him, and in 1937 the New York special prosecutor Thomas E. Dewey, then at the height of his fame as the country's leading racket-buster, indicted the racketeer on charges of violating the antitrust laws. Lepke then went into hiding for nearly two years, moving from a hideout on the Brooklyn waterfront to the back room of a Coney Island dance hall. While on the lam, the increasingly anxious Lepke ordered the murders of dozens of former associates who, he feared, might testify against him. "Whoever was suspect of falling into Mr. Dewey's net—and there were many—was marked for killing," wrote Berger, describing how former Lepke aides and gunmen "made corpses on Catskill, Brooklyn and Bronx landscapes."

In 1941, with the growing realization that the "sands were shifting under his feet," Lepke allowed the columnist Walter Winchell to arrange a meeting with the Federal Bureau of Investigation director, J. Edgar Hoover, and finally surrendered to the authorities. He then stood trial for—and was convicted of—the murder of Joseph Rosen, a former trucker who had shared his knowledge of Lepke's operations with the authorities. By the time he was sentenced to the electric chair, the "soft-spoken, liquid-eyed,"quietly dressed racketeer had come to be identified as America's Public Enemy Number One.

BIBLIOGRAPHY

Berger, Meyer. "Lepke's Reign of Crime Lasted over Twelve Murder-Strewn Years." *New York Times,* 5 March 1944, p. 30.

Fried, Albert. *The Rise and Fall of the Jewish Gangster in America.* Rev. ed. New York: Columbia University Press, 1993.

Joselit, Jenna Weissman. *Our Gang: Jewish Crime and the New York Jewish Community, 1900–1940.* Bloomington: Indiana University Press, 1983.

JENNA WEISSMAN JOSELIT

See also **Murder, Inc.; Organized Crime.**

LETTER BOMBS

Most mail bombs use a mechanical detonation system. In the case of the letter bomb, a detonator and mechanical assembly is often placed between two sheets of cardboard, and plastic explosives are packed around it. The pressure of the envelope around the device keeps it from detonating. But once the pressure is removed, as when someone pulls the contents out of an envelope, the device explodes. Musical greeting cards make particularly lethal mail bombs. These devices, which play musical messages, contain a power source, speaker, and activating mechanism and are designed to operate when opened. They can be easily modified to contain an improvised explosive device by replacing the speaker with a blasting cap.

Letter bombs do not normally contain timing devices because the mail is too unpredictable. Package bombs, including book bombs, are often triggered by electrical systems.

Letter bombs and package bombs must be able to endure the rough handling of the normal shipping process without detonating. Typically, the victim sets off the device by opening it. The most popular ways to deliver these bombs is through a standard delivery service or by personal carrier. The latter is usually the bomber or a paid messenger. Sometimes the bomber will place the bomb in a location frequented by the intended target, as was often the case with the Unabomber, Theodore John Kaczynski. On 25 May 1978 Kaczynski placed his first package bomb in a parking lot of the University of Illinois, Chicago. The package was then sent back to the return address at Northwestern University in Evanston, Illinois, where it injured a security guard, Terry Marker. During his seventeen-year reign of terror the Unabomber placed or sent sixteen bombs, killing three people and wounding twenty-three others.

Mail bombs are usually aimed at specific victims and targets. They have been disguised as greeting cards, books, and packages from the recipients' friends. The mail bomb that killed Robert S. Vance, an appellate judge in Birmingham, Alabama, on 16 December 1989 carried the return address of a fellow federal judge in Atlanta who shared Vance's interest in horses. As Judge Vance broke the package's seal, he detonated a pipe bomb that was packed with nails. Vance was killed instantly and his spouse was seriously injured. Two days later and four hundred miles away, in Savannah, Georgia, the civil rights attorney and community leader Robert E. Robinson opened a piece of mail, a box that he doubtless took to be a gift; the bomb inside exploded with such force that his hands were blown off. Robinson died hours later. Over the next few days, other mail bombs

arrived at the office of the National Association for the Advancement of Colored People in Jacksonville, Florida, and a federal courthouse in Atlanta. These bombs were detected and detonated. Walter Leroy Moody, an embittered, racist felon whose 1972 conviction for possessing an explosive device barred him from pursuing the career in law that he aspired to, was later convicted of the murders.

The incidence of mail bombs is very rare and tends to occur in clusters. Such was the case during a period from December 1996 through January 1997, when sixteen letter bombs disguised as musical Christmas or holiday greeting cards were delivered through the mail to recipients in the United States and the United Kingdom. All the letter bombs bore an Alexandria, Egypt, postmark of 21 December 1996 and contained no return address. Thirteen of these letter bombs, in white envelopes with computer-generated addresses, were received at the offices of the Arabic newspaper *Al Hayat* in New York City, Washington D.C., and London. Three other cards were discovered at the federal penitentiary in Leavenworth, Kansas, which housed members of the World Trade Center conspiracy. One bomb exploded in London, seriously injuring two people. The bomber or bombers in this case was never caught.

While mail bombs tend to be the domain of terrorists, they are also used by individuals seeking retribution. For example, in the 1950s, the Mad Bomber, George Metesky, threatened New York City with bombs sent through the mail. Metesky, apprehended in 1957, said that he launched his attacks to get even with Consolidated Edison, the New York City gas and electric utility, which had discontinued sick pay he had been receiving due to a boiler accident, after doctors failed to find anything wrong with him. But his targets included a movie theater, a bus terminal, and libraries. Many of his explosive devices, simple by technical standards, failed to function, but those that detonated injured many people.

Many government agencies are successful in preventing letter and package bombs from reaching their intended target(s). Since mail bombs as well as package bombs contain metal components, a variety of different metal detectors are employed to identify suspicious letters and packages. Once identified, X-ray equipment is used to determine whether the suspect item is a bomb. Bomb-sniffing dogs and technology similar to medical CAT scans are also used to detect questionable letters and packages.

Typical Characteristics of Letter and Package Bombs

Mail originated from foreign country or is marked priority, air mail, or special delivery.

Package carries restrictive endorsements, such as "confidential," "personal," "to be opened by addressee only."

Box contains other visual distractions, such as "fragile," "handle with care," "do not bend," "rush."

Letter or package contains excessive or inadequate postage.

Package carries a fictitious return address or no return address.

Addresses are handwritten or poorly typed.

Title of recipient is incorrect.

Title of person rather than name is used in address.

Common words in address are misspelled.

Package contains oily stains or discolorations.

Package has a suspicious pungent or almond-like odor.

There is an uneven weight distribution or package seems to be heavy for its size.

Package contains excessive binding materials: masking, electrical, or strapping tape, string, and twine.

Envelope or package appears to have been disassembled and resealed.

Envelope is rigid, lopsided, or uneven.

There are protruding wires, screws, or other metal parts.

Mail is postmarked from an area different from that of the return address.

Letter or package bombs are effective tools of both terrorists and those seeking retribution. Although these devices cannot inflict massive loss of life, they can maim or kill the unfortunate person(s) handling them. In this way, these deadly devices serve the terrorist in creating an atmosphere of fear and enable the individual desirous of retribution to hit a seemingly isolated target.

BIBLIOGRAPHY

Brodie, Thomas G. *Bombs and Bombings: A Handbook to Detection, Disposal, and Investigation for Police and Fire Departments*. 2d ed. Springfield, Ill.: Thomas, 1996.

Graysmith, Robert. *Unabomber: A Desire to Kill*. Washington, D.C.: Regnery, 1997.

Jenkins, Ray. *Blind Vengeance: The Roy Moody Mail Bomb Murders*. Athens, Ga.: University of Georgia Press, 1997.

HARVEY W. KUSHNER

See also **Bombings and Bomb Scares; Terrorism; Unabomber.**

LINCOLN, ABRAHAM
(1809–1865)

Abraham Lincoln, who was shot by John Wilkes Booth on 14 April 1865 and died the next day, was no stranger to violence throughout his fifty-six years.

When he arrived in the village of New Salem, Illinois, in 1831, Lincoln was challenged by Jack Armstrong, the leader of the Clary's Grove boys, to what became a famous wrestling match. While accounts vary as to who won the fight and what occurred in the aftermath, Armstrong and Lincoln became fast friends, a more benign ending than that of many frontier wrestling contests, in which the combatants often were disfigured or died as a result of their injuries.

Lincoln was also familiar with another form of frontier violence: dueling. His practice of writing satirical, anonymous letters to newspapers led to a challenge from the state auditor, James Shields, in 1842, after Lincoln had written a letter to the *Sangomo Journal* calling Shields among other things a "conceity dunce." Since dueling was illegal in Illinois, the parties had to meet across the Mississippi River in Missouri. Before the event could take place, however, Shields was persuaded to withdraw his challenge to Lincoln, and Lincoln denied having had any intention to injure the auditor's public character. Shields, a short man, was probably relieved that he did not have to fight his six-foot-four opponent, who had selected cavalry broadswords (large heavy swords with broad blades used for cutting) as the weapons for the duel. For his part, Lincoln was embarrassed by the episode and thereafter abandoned his practice of writing anonymous letters.

Lincoln had a fleeting acquaintance with warfare, having served in the Black Hawk War in 1832. In 1848 during a speech as a congressman in the House of Representatives, referring to that war, he joked about his lack of combat experience and his bloody encounters with mosquitoes, but he also said that his election as a captain in the militia (he served thirty days) was the most satisfying of his political career. (Lincoln enrolled three more times as an enlisted man, serving an additional fifty-one days.) During the Mexican War while serving as a

An 1865 photograph of Abraham Lincoln, taken days before his assassination. HULTON GETTY/LIAISON AGENCY

congressman, Lincoln made himself unpopular with his Spot Resolutions, which challenged President James Polk to name the exact spot of ground where the conflict began. The Americans and the Mexicans had been in disagreement over the Texas boundary, and Polk had ordered troops into the disputed area apparently in hopes of bringing on a conflict. Polk was a Democrat, and Lincoln and the other Whigs saw this war as a war of aggression and referred to it as "Mr. Polk's War."

As a lawyer, Lincoln defended and prosecuted both the victims and perpetrators of violence. One of his most celebrated murder cases involved the defense in 1858 of Duff Armstrong, the son of Jack Armstrong, his former wrestling partner. During the trial, Lincoln used an almanac to prove that the moon had not been full on the night of the murder, thereby casting doubt on the testimony of a witness who claimed that the moonlight was sufficient for him to identify Armstrong as the killer.

Political squabbles also led to violence in the nineteenth century. In November 1837 an Alton, Illinois, mob killed the abolitionist editor Elijah Lovejoy. Although Lincoln never directly spoke about the killing of Lovejoy, he clearly deplored mob violence. Nonetheless, he had doubts about the sometimes provocative tactics employed by the abolitionists. The attempt to make Kansas a slave-owning state, with its accompanying violence, including the caning of Senator Charles Sumner of Massachusetts by Congressman Preston S. Brooks of South Carolina, brought Lincoln back into the political arena in the 1850s.

In 1860 Lincoln's election to the presidency and the firing on Fort Sumter in South Carolina precipitated the secession of eleven states and a civil war that killed more than 620,000 soldiers and injured countless others. The Civil War was the most violent and traumatic event in American history. Both sides committed battlefield atrocities, the most notable being Confederate general Nathan Bedford Forrest's massacre of black and white Union soldiers at Fort Pillow, Tennessee, on 12 April 1864. There was occasionally talk of war-crimes trials when the war ended, but they were never held.

In the midst of the carnage, Lincoln did not flinch from vigorously prosecuting the war. Despite his reputation for being tenderhearted, he would agree to no compromise to end the bloodshed and supported the Union strategy to fight a war of attrition. Lincoln also was very interested in the weapons of war, sometimes asking weapons makers to demonstrate their wares in the apparent belief that more-lethal weapons would bring the war to a speedier conclusion.

Americans sometimes act as if U.S. history, with respect to violence, is unique in comparison with that of other nations, but Lincoln's life calls that notion into question. In fact, the historian William Tidwell has argued that Lincoln's assassination was hardly the act of a madman, but the result of a calculated political plot. According to Tidwell, there is evidence that Lincoln launched a cavalry raid against Richmond, Virginia, with the intention of killing or capturing Jefferson Davis, who had been elected president of the Confederacy by a provisional Congress on 18 February 1861. In retaliation, Davis recruited John Wilkes Booth to capture Lincoln, whom he would then use as a bargaining chip for the exchange of Southern prisoners. Ultimately, at war's end, Thomas Harney, a member of the Confederate Torpedo Bureau, was dispatched to blow up the White House. When this plan was thwarted because Harney was captured, Booth simply tried to carry out his end of the original plot.

Although Tidwell's thesis is controversial, Booth was clearly not insane but rather a Southern patriot who believed that the president was a tyrant. Lincoln's fatalistic belief that he could not always be adequately protected resulted in lax security surrounding him, making the president an easy target for someone wishing to harm him. In a sense, Lincoln was one of the last casualties of the Civil War. His death capped several decades of violence in which he had played the roles of spectator, participant, and, ultimately, victim.

BIBLIOGRAPHY

Donald, David. *Lincoln*. New York: Simon and Schuster, 1995.

Tidwell, William A., with James O. Hall and David W. Gaddy. *Come Retribution: The Confederate Secret Service and the Assassination of Lincoln*. Jackson: University of Mississippi Press, 1988.

Wilson, Douglas L. *Honor's Voice: The Transformation of Abraham Lincoln*. New York: Knopf, 1998.

THOMAS R. TURNER

See also **Abolition; Assassinations; Booth, John Wilkes; Slavery.**

LINDBERGH KIDNAPPING CASE

In 1927 Charles Lindbergh became the first person to fly an airplane across the Atlantic Ocean alone. Five years later, on Tuesday, 1 March 1932, his only son, Charles Lindbergh, Jr., twenty months old, was kidnapped from their home in Hopewell, New Jersey. Almost immediately news of the crime spread across the nation.

The child had been taken between 8 and 10 P.M. The kidnapper or kidnappers knew exactly which bedroom belonged to the child and had constructed a collapsible ladder to reach the window. Somehow, they also knew that the Lindberghs would stay the night at that residence, despite the fact that the Lindberghs normally spent only their weekends there. This may have indicated that an insider was involved, and the construction of the ladder, with its rungs spread far apart, suggests that there were at least two kidnappers.

A ransom note left on the windowsill of the baby's room instructed the Lindberghs to notify no one, to prepare $50,000, and to await further instruction. The Lindberghs called the police, and by the next morning the police and press had arrived en masse. Horrified, the entire country waited for news, yet there were very few clues. The kidnappers, angry at the press coverage, demanded an extra $20,000 in ransom. A date was set for an

Reporters gather outside the Hopewell, New Jersey, home of Charles Lindbergh, whose son was kidnapped on 1 March 1932. CORBIS/BETTMANN

exchange of the money for information about where the baby could be found.

On 2 April, John Condon, an intermediary chosen by the kidnappers on the basis of a letter about the kidnapping that Condon had placed in a Bronx paper, met with the kidnappers, and after telling them that the Lindberghs had been able to raise only $50,000 (this was not true but was an attempt by Condon to save the Lindberghs money), Condon handed over the ransom money. The kidnappers gave him a note claiming that the baby was on a boat called *Nelly* with two other innocent people on board. No such boat was ever found.

Despite the kidnappers' assurances in ransom notes and in their meetings with Condon that the baby was alive and healthy, his body was found in a state of advanced decomposition on 12 May 1932, only a few miles from where he had been kidnapped. The autopsy report stated that the baby had died of severe head wounds two or three months earlier. The public was outraged at the death, and the wide press coverage put considerable pressure on the police to find the murderer. Violet Sharpe, who was working as a maid for the Lindberghs, was so harassed by the police investigators that she committed suicide.

There is considerable debate that Bruno Richard Hauptmann, a German-born carpenter with no connection to the Lindberghs but found in possession of a portion of the ransom money, may have been wrongly convicted and executed for the crime. Hauptmann, a married man with a young son, maintained his innocence despite deals offering a life sentence in exchange for a confession. Today the identity of the murderer is still intensely debated. Some Lindbergh biographers argue that Hauptmann was innocent and that others were responsible for the crimes. The Lindbergh kidnapping spurred on legislation providing for increased penalties for kidnappers. The nature of the Lindbergh case and other such kidnappings remains a terrifying reminder to many wealthy parents.

BIBLIOGRAPHY

Behn, Noel. *Lindbergh: The Crime.* New York: Atlantic Monthly Press, 1994.

Berg, A. Scott. *Lindbergh.* New York: Putnam, 1998.

Kennedy, Ludovic. *The Airman and the Carpenter.* New York: Viking, 1985.

TRACY W. PETERS

See also **Kidnapping.**

LITERATURE

The first five subentries focus on fiction: **Fiction, Popular Fiction, Pulp Fiction, Nuclear War Fiction,** *and* **Children's and Young Adult Literature.** *The last two subentries discuss violence in nonfiction writings:* **Nonfiction Prose** *and* **Poetry.**

FICTION

In Herman Melville's short story "Benito Cereno" (1855), everything on the slave ship *San Dominick* appears to be ordinary, but beneath the surface the reader is made to feel that despite the apparent calm, "might not the *San Dominick*, like a slumbering volcano, suddenly let loose energies now hid?" The democratic ideals of the Declaration of Independence, the vision of America as the City upon a Hill, a beacon to the nations, the promise of material prosperity that is central to the American dream, the reputed common sense and moderation of middle-class Americans—all have contributed to the creation of the myth of America, and all generate contradictions between promise and performance, between the way things should be and the way they in reality are. This inconsistency provides the narrative tension for much American fiction, a tension that often erupts in violence.

In the traditional American narrative, violence is envisioned as both a moral imperative and a right of passage. Many American writers have challenged this view, implicating the American myth itself in the causes of violence, both physical and psychological. Others have focused on the transformative effects of violence. Still others have concerned themselves with its repression or depersonalization.

Violence and the American Myth

American fiction has rendered the impact of violence on the range, in the forest, and on the battlefield, from James Fenimore Cooper's Leatherstocking novels (1823–1841) to the latest Western to American war narratives. From stories of men in the saddle or detectives in the dark forest of the city, a distinctly American narrative or myth has developed. In this narrative, violence is informed by traditional views of manhood and the Puritan divisions of the world into good and evil, elect and nonelect, "us" and "them." To the extent that violence preserves or restores a valued way of life, it is celebrated and glorified.

In the American narrative, the hero is challenged by a dark foe or nemesis and emerges victorious. This vanquishing of evil invariably occurs through violent means: especially in the Western and its urban analogue, the detective novel, the defining symbols are the gun and the fist. To twentieth-century Americans whose lives have become routine, Westerns and detective fiction offer the experience of vicarious adventure and the sanctioned release of violence.

In his best-selling Westerns written from the 1950s to the 1990s, Louis L'Amour's men ride and mend fences, they have physical prowess that men admire and women can rely on, they do not take advantage, and when savages threaten the vulnerable ranch, they know how to shoot, to wield a knife, to stalk, and to kill. They have mastered the arts of their Indian antagonists and they respect them even as they destroy them, outnumbered as the lone cowboy or hunter always is.

In this narrative Americans are almost always provoked; they are never the aggressors. From the Western novel to the most recent report of American action abroad, the story is structured to put the "good guys"—us—in the best light. In the received or official version of the narrative, Americans invariably act with noble motives, which are contrasted with the evil motives of their enemies. With notable exceptions—Dashiell Hammett's Continental Op stories and *The Maltese Falcon* (1930) among them—ambiguity does not exist in the standard narrative of American violence. The enemy is portrayed as typically evil and dehumanized, made into a despised Other who can be shot and killed with impunity. Another feature of the narrative is that Americans are almost always outnumbered; they are the underdogs fighting against the odds, even when their superior technology gives them the advantage. The enemy against whom the virtuous American unleashes his violence is usually dark-skinned—Indians in the Western; the latest totalitarian dictator in the narrative of the evening news. Americans often project their own fears and despised qualities onto the enemy and then mercilessly punish this representative evil.

The orthodox version of American manhood emerged in Owen Wister's *The Virginian* (1902), the novel that set the conventions for the twentieth-century Western. To preserve his honor, his name,

and his sense of self-worth, the protagonist of this novel must engage in a culminating shoot-out with the novel's antagonist, Trampas. The view that a recourse to violence is the inevitable way to resolve conflicts receives classic expression in Wister's version of the American myth of manhood, wherein the southern code of the duel is transmuted into the code of the West.

The American Myth Under Pressure: War Narratives

In works like Stephen Crane's *The Red Badge of Courage* (1895), Ernest Hemingway's *In Our Time* (1925) and *A Farewell to Arms* (1929), Norman Mailer's *The Naked and the Dead* (1948), Joseph Heller's *Catch-22* (1961), Kurt Vonnegut's *Slaughterhouse-Five* (1969), and Michael Herr's novelistic *Dispatches* (1977), war narratives testify to the compelling role violence plays in the rituals testing American manhood, rituals the writers reinforce even as they view them with varying degrees of irony, horror, and compassion.

Hemingway gives these rituals the authority of his taut prose style and ironic vision in stories like "The Short Happy Life of Francis Macomber." The violence of World War I casts a shadow over much of Hemingway's work. Especially in the interchapters of *In Our Time* (1925), using understatement and irony to heighten dramatic impact, Hemingway returns again and again to show that the immense pressure of war challenges the courage, manhood, and sanity of all those involved. Unlike Stephen Crane, who tests Henry Fleming's courage and goes deep into the psychology of fear and rage on the battlefield in *The Red Badge of Courage* (1895), Hemingway often achieves his best effects by showing the aftereffects of battle, as in "A Way You'll Never Be," where the precisely observed corpses silently tell the tale, as does the gradually revealed breakdown of the narrator.

Using the techniques of fiction, in his reportage, *Dispatches* (1977), Michael Herr deals close up with the violence of the Vietnam War, a violence that for him ranges from the defoliated moonscape of the jungle to the terror that turns ordinary soldiers into deranged killers. Herr renders with tactile immediacy the severed arms and legs, screams, drugs, heat, fatigue, and fear, the bravery of the grunts and the distorted perceptions of the high command. The assumptions of the Western and of American manhood are placed under extreme pressure in Herr's unsparing, sympathetic narrative.

In some contemporary fiction, the dark energies of the battlefield are reenvisioned for the domestic landscape. In the tradition of the female gothic novel, Diane Johnson in *The Shadow Knows* (1974) responds to late-twentieth-century realities and probes the fear of stalking that increasingly terrifies a young, divorced, well-educated woman forced to patch out a living through part-time teaching. As her mutilated door indicates, she has reason to believe someone is threatening her. Johnson, however, sustains a revealing ambiguity that does justice to the terror, the lurking violence women are exposed to, and the possibility that it is imagined, internal, a response to the narrator's newly gained freedom and accompanying vulnerabilities. In this novel, written at the close of the war in Vietnam, Johnson not only opens up a woman's world but also creates a powerful metaphor for the violence Americans unleashed on Vietnam and then exported home.

The Legacy of Slavery

Slavery persisted longer in the United States than in any other European or South American nation and the inequities Americans institutionalized under slavery and after abolition under the sharecropper system—and the racial views these systems fostered—all have contributed to an ongoing strain of violence in American culture and in significant literary responses to that culture. Not surprisingly, then, as much as the Western novel or detective fiction, the slave narrative—from Frederick Douglass's *Narrative of the Life of Frederick Douglass* (1845) and Harriet Jacobs's *Incidents in the Life of a Slave Girl* (1861) to Toni Morrison's *Beloved* (1987) and Charles Johnson's *Middle Passage* (1990)—is an important, continuing genre focused on American violence.

Jacobs organizes her narrative around the implacable attempt of a slave owner, Mr. Flint, to sexually dominate Linda Brant, threatening the core of her being. Linda, however, shows her underlying strength and her sacrificial love of the children she bears her white "protector." By turning the tables on the white people who have constructed the images, Douglass, Jacobs, Morrison, and Johnson are among those who engage and refute the persistent white characterization of black men as rapists, black women as sexually promiscuous, rape as the justification for lynching, and blacks as either helpless victims or violent predators. These demeaning constructions constitute a pervasive form of violence directed at the integrity and hu-

manity of African Americans, and underlie the overt acts of physical violence they are used to justify. Thomas Dixon's *The Leopard's Spots* (1902) and *The Clansman* (1903) give the antiblack version in full, revealing detail. In his *Narrative* Douglass affirms his humanity in two contrasting episodes. In one, he defies both the law and the dictates of his owner and learns to read and write, in the Western world the signatures of humanity and civilization. In the other Douglass shows how, having been beaten, bloodied, and reduced from a man to a brute, he reclaims his manhood by fighting back and drawing blood. Douglass does not, significantly, turn the other cheek but rather argues "that he only can understand the deep satisfaction which I experienced, who has himself repelled by force the bloody arm of slavery."

Beyond the immediate, controversial impetus to overthrow slavery by force, Douglass enters eloquently into the American discourse on manhood. A dominant note in this discourse is that men who have been physically or psychologically infringed on must restore their integrity through acts of violence. The result, as Douglass shows, can be a tremendous sense of personal growth and renewal. "My long-crushed spirit rose, cowardice departed, bold defiance took its place; and I now resolved that, however long I might remain a slave in form, the day had passed when I could be a slave in fact" (*The Narrative of the Life of Frederick Douglass*, New York: Signet, 1968, p. 83).

From Charles Chesnutt's *The Marrow of Tradition* (1902) and W. E. B. Du Bois's "The Coming of John" (1903) to Richard Wright's *Native Son* (1940), from Owen Wister's *The Virginian* (1902) to Ken Kesey's *One Flew Over the Cuckoo's Nest* (1962), American writers have explored the creative and destructive consequences of the discourse Douglass animates. Particularly because of the inequities of American society, African American men have repeatedly been placed in situations that challenge them to claim their manhood through acts of violence.

In an early scene in *Native Son*, Bigger Thomas attacks his friends to conceal his fear: Bigger is terrified of robbing a white man's store and turns on his friends as a distraction. In a narrative that combines realistic detail and dreamlike intensification, Wright shows the outer pressures and inner dynamics that lead to Bigger's murder first of a white woman and later of his black girlfriend and the outpouring of white rage against him and the black community. In the dominant culture and in writers as different as Jacobs, Du Bois, Dixon, Morrison, and Wright, at the center of the American racial narrative, the relationship between blacks and whites leads inexorably to a violent confrontation focused on interracial sex. In the context of and going beyond this feature of American racial mythology, Wright has Bigger achieve his manhood and self-realization in a world of social and psychological violence that exposes the contradictions between American racial realities and democratic ideals.

The Underside of the American Dream

The expectation of worldly success, of making it on one's own, is central to the American narrative. In a memorable group of stories, *The Piazza Tales* (1855), Herman Melville undertakes an intense exploration of the underside of American urban and industrial capitalism. In the first of these stories, "Bartleby, the Scrivener: A Tale of Wall Street" (1853), Melville reveals the violent energies seething under the surface of a Wall Street law office as the clerks abuse alcohol or gnash their teeth in response to deadening, routine work and the patronizing authority of their employer. For Melville, the structures of authority and the values of Wall Street capitalism divide people internally, turn them against one another, and separate them from the renewing religious transcendence Bartleby craves. Like Bartleby, everything in Melville's narrative is "quiet" but charged with a violence that permeates the personality and has powerful social and political implications.

Melville in "The Paradise of Bachelors and the Tartarus of Maids" (1855) and Rebecca Harding Davis in "Life in the Iron Mills" (1861) are among a minority of American writers who deal directly with the physical and psychological violence of industrial capitalism, including its deep impact on women. The most famous achievement is Upton Sinclair's *The Jungle* (1906), a sustained rendering of the maiming, demoralization, and death inflicted on the immigrant laborers of the Chicago stockyards. Sinclair's is a detailed, unforgettable account that uses the killing and processing of the cows as a metaphor for the systematic grinding up of the workers. As with the slave narratives and reform novels of Frederick Douglass, Harriet Jacobs, and Harriet Beecher Stowe, Upton Sinclair selects and emphasizes these scenes not to give a statistically accurate portrait but to heighten the sense of underlying reality and to move the reader to action.

Even in narratives like F. Scott Fitzgerald's *The Great Gatsby* (1925), where the prevailing tone is one of civilized moderation, American writers structure their works around moments of deadly violence. In *Gatsby*, Tom Buchanan in a fit of rage breaks the nose of his mistress, Myrtle. In a crucial scene, his wife, Daisy, later kills Myrtle in a hit-and-run automobile accident. At the end, in a quietly rendered scene, Gatsby himself is shot in his swimming pool. Parties begin with festivity and end with drunken car crashes and wheels "amputated" from their vehicles. The narrative's recurring violence is intensified by contrast with the urbanity of the narrative style. In Fitzgerald's novel, both women and lower-class people are the objects of a violence that for Fitzgerald comments on the underside of Jazz Age prosperity and the failure of American society to realize in practice the promise of the American dream, that "last and greatest dream" he connects with Gatsby and "the fresh green breast of the New World."

The Transforming Power of Violence

As obscure as Hemingway and Fitzgerald are famous, Meridel Le Sueur provides equally telling insights into American violence in the lyric prose of *Salute to Spring* (1940) and *The Girl* (1978). Only the violent release of a religious revival or of a lover's murder and suicide, Le Sueur stresses, can bring together the isolated individuals of the early-twentieth-century Iowa corn village that is the setting for the opening of *Salute to Spring*. At the end of the collection, in "I Was Marching," Le Sueur evokes the unifying power of political violence. Drawing on the imagery of the 1930s Left, for whom the militant actions of the strike and protest march forecast a revolutionary new society, in response to the violence of the employers and the police and from the depths of her commitment to community, Le Sueur celebrates leaving "the disruption, chaos, and disintegration" she has belonged to—she applies to conventional society the words usually turned against revolutionaries—and she joins the strikers, "drawing . . . into a close and glowing cohesion like a powerful conflagration in the midst of the city." At the end of "I Was Marching," the threat of revolutionary violence is qualified by the cohesive rhythm of thousands marching, a sound not of destruction but of affirmation.

Writing from a nondoctrinaire feminist and politically radical perspective, in other pieces in *Salute to Spring* (e.g., "Annunciation" and "Tonight

Is Part of the Struggle") Le Sueur connects the violence of childbirth with the revolutionary violence that for her can and should lead to a renewed America. Le Sueur is one of the few American writers who focuses positively on revolutionary violence. Equally important, she is perhaps the only American writer who acknowledges the violence of childbirth and places that violence at the center of key narratives, including her belatedly published 1930s novel, *The Girl*.

"Progress" and Technology

Deeply grounded as he is in American culture, Mark Twain, in *A Connecticut Yankee in King Arthur's Court* (1889), creates the character of Hank Morgan, who, as a superintendent at the Colt arms factory, fights a subordinate, suffers a blow on the head, and ends up in Camelot. Having the best of intentions, Hank wants to bring nineteenth-century technology and the civilization of the stock exchange to the natives, the "white Indians" whose Catholic religion he condescendingly sees as superstition, whose bathing habits he looks down on, and the cream of whose knighthood he exterminates in a final volcanic eruption of the technology he so reveres. Hank, who repressed the dark side of technology, ultimately unleashes it against his enemies—and himself.

Hank is outnumbered; in his own eyes he is virtuous; he is fighting what he sees as the evil of a rival religion against his own religion of technology, capitalism, democracy, and Protestantism, of soap and sewing machines; and from his point of view he has been attacked and is provoked to defend the nineteenth-century civilization he has created. Hank's identity is intimately related to the values, artifacts, and outlook of this civilization. Also justifying and fueling the cataclysmic outpouring of dynamite bombs, Gatling guns, and electrocutions are threats to Hank's identity and sense of self-worth, his violent response to challenges to his view of himself as a benevolent bringer of light to a dark land. Hank Morgan, with his self-justification and unexamined assumptions, plays a central role in Twain's revealing version of the American narrative, a narrative that in *A Connecticut Yankee* is resonant with insights into American cultural and economic imperialism and a prophetic concern with the incendiary power of war technology.

Rendered through the resources of his eloquence and comic imagination, Don DeLillo presents technology and capitalism as closely related to American violence. The menacing toxic cloud and the satire of consumerism in *White Noise* (1985) reappear in *Underworld* (1997) as the giant waste disposal site, the repository of the world's garbage, and the preoccupation of the characters with atomic technology and corporate profits in the post–Cold War era. For DeLillo this era is symbolized by a cataclysmic underground atomic explosion in the frozen tundra of farthest Russia, no longer the feared enemy but a partner in high-stakes, technology-driven gangster capitalism. The explosion is a worthy successor to the electrocutions and dynamite bombs that a century earlier had ended Mark Twain's *Connecticut Yankee*, as the old century looked ahead to the new.

BIBLIOGRAPHY

Denning, Michael. *The Cultural Front: The Laboring of American Culture in the Twentieth Century.* London: Verso, 1998.

Greven, Philip. *The Protestant Temperament: Patterns of Child-Rearing, Religious Experience, and the Self in Early America.* New York: Knopf, 1977.

Kaplan, Amy, and Donald E. Pease, eds. *Cultures of United States Imperialism.* Durham, N.C.: Duke University Press, 1993.

Shulman, Robert. "Introduction." In *The Virginian,* by Owen Wister (1902), edited by Robert Shulman. New York: Oxford World's Classics, 1998.

———. *Social Criticism and Nineteenth-Century American Fictions.* Columbia: University of Missouri Press, 1987.

Slotkin, Richard. *The Fatal Environment: The Myth of the Frontier in the Age of Industrialization, 1800–1890.* New York: Atheneum, 1985.

———. *Gunfighter Nation: The Myth of the Frontier in Twentieth-Century America.* New York: Atheneum, 1992.

———. *Regeneration Through Violence: The Mythology of the American Frontier, 1600–1860.* Middletown, Conn.: Wesleyan University Press, 1973.

Sundquist, Eric. *To Wake the Nations: Race in the Making of American Literature.* Cambridge, Mass.: Harvard University Press, 1993.

ROBERT SHULMAN

See also **Representation of Violence.**

POPULAR FICTION

According to the literary historian and crime writer Julian Symons, "sensational literature" (including crime fiction), along with romance, was the most avidly consumed genre of fiction in the Western world in the twentieth century. Historians and critics of popular fiction may disagree about the defining features of crime fiction (and the extent to which espionage, action, thriller, legal, and even detective dramas count in that category), but there is general agreement about the appeal of popular fictions of violence, suspense, and adventure, and their tenacity as a form.

Early Sensational Fiction

Many critics and historians marked Edgar Allan Poe's "The Murders in the Rue Morgue" (1841) as the first detective story. But while Poe's tale of C. Auguste Dupin's ratiocinative mastery over the murderous Orang-Utan made a splash with continental readers, it (and most of Poe's work) would not find a popular audience at home in the United States until well into the twentieth century. The detective himself was a relatively unfamiliar figure in early-nineteenth-century literature—English, continental European, and American. Instead, it was the figure of the villain, outlaw, or "cad" popularized by the European picaresque tradition that held sway. In the popular tales of vagabond heroes who uneasily straddle the divide between settled "civilization" and its wild surrounds, one can trace the shadow of the picaro, that "rogue hero who charmed and thieved" his way through adventures and journeys.

The enormous popular success of James Fenimore Cooper's Leatherstocking Tales (1823–1841) effectively laid the foundations for an idiosyncratically American tradition of "sensational" fiction. This was a literature devoted not only to the thrilling trials and heady victories of various picaresque figures, such as the title characters in Mark Twain's *Huckleberry Finn* (1884) and *The Adventures of Tom Sawyer* (1876) but also to a restaging of the dramatic wilderness-versus-civilization confrontation. The setting for this confrontation was as central to the character of the hero as it was to the fiction's scene. The wildness at play in American literatures of sensation is at the same time the wilderness of the heart and the wilds of the land (and, later, the city) with which its hero or heroine must contend.

Jack London is one of America's most read writers of adventure stories. While his most famous works—*The Son of the Wolf* (1900), *The Call of the Wild* (1903), and *The Sea Wolf* (1904)—treat different subjects, their themes are similar. Whether writing about life in the Klondike, the vicissitudes of the dog Buck in the Alaskan wilderness, or a young Yankee gentleman's struggle to survive the morally and materially murderous culture of a sealing vessel, London describes a violence that is absolute—the very ground and condition of life, whether "civilized" or not. When the unfortunate protagonist of the short story "To Build a Fire" (1904) ventures out toward "the old claim," accompanied only by a dog in a temperature of fifty degrees below zero, he is quickly reduced to nothing by what he (cosseted by the vanities of civilization) believes is nothing: the cold that he supposes is a manageable threat. London's description of his protagonist's slow death by freezing is one of the most vivid descriptions in Western literature of desperation, loneliness, and the frailty of the flesh.

London's treatment of violence centers both on the violence of nature and the bestial nature of humanity. Though works like *The Call of the Wild* and *White Fang* (1906) are at least partly anthropomorphic, those featuring human protagonists effect a kind of reverse movement—naturalizing human violence without denuding it of its particular context (male culture, frontier life, colonial power, and so on). London's thematic treatment of violence marked a transition from a time when evil, including violence, was represented "not as what humans do, but as what we suffer" to a more modern conception of evil (and violence) as being inextricably linked to human action.

Pulp Fiction

Westerns. The period of London's popularity also marked the transition from the dime novel to the pulp magazine. From the Beadle dime novels of the 1860s onward, successive generations of authors labored pseudonymously to produce formula adventure stories that sold—in cheaply bound editions printed on low-quality paper (the "pulps")—to a voracious readership. As mass publishing came of age in the United States, so too did a fiction of sensation dedicated to the celebration of a figure that combined features of the knight, the picaro, and the detective—the wild man of the West. According to one proponent of the frontier myth, this wild man "was no new type, no product of the frontier, but just the original kernel of the nut with the shell broken." The new man of the hour was the cowboy (appearing as gunslinger and outlaw), and the reign of the Western over popular fiction until at least the 1940s demonstrated the appeal to the reading public of that "kernel" of essential American Anglo-Saxon masculinity.

Between the wars, Frederick Faust produced some of the most widely read formula Westerns. Faust wrote under the name Max Brand (as well as nineteen other pseudonyms) and, although despising his pulp output—he was a classical scholar—secured a small fortune for himself from the sale of his 196 novels, 226 novellas, and 162 stories. Brand's Westerns, like many pulps, are notable for their relative lack of graphic violence and for their stylized scenes of violent exchange (the ambush, the "walkdown," the brawl, and the fist-fight). But the elegiac quality of Brand's work has a great deal to say about the violence at the heart of an enduring mythos of the frontier, a violence also at the heart of the figure of the mythical cowboy so frequently forced into outlawry. In Brand's *Destry Rides Again* (1930), Harry Destry—framed for a crime he didn't commit—finds himself at the mercy of a jury of twelve of his peers, all of whom he has thrashed, at one time or another, in contests of strength or sharpshooting. The action in the novel surrounds Destry's return from prison and the revenge he exacts, but the theme is a critique of the reflex to violence of the competitive, hell-raising young men celebrated and redeemed by the pulps. Like Sheldon in London's *Adventure*, who realizes during a duel that "never had he felt so great a disgust for the thing called 'adventure,'" Destry has an epiphany about his own hell-raising life. After shooting one of the last jurors, he recalls the dying man as a boy: "Hank Cleeves, treading water and throwing back his long hair from his eyes with both hands—a bold, strong, fearless, reckless leader among boys, until Destry adroitly had pushed him to one side. For that very reason ... Cleeves now lay dying in the attic of the shanty." Shame and envy are the basis of violence.

Hard-boiled Detective Tales. The world of the pulps did not belong solely to the cowboy. From the 1930s through the 1950s, the hard-boiled fiction of Dashiell Hammett, Raymond Chandler, Ross Macdonald, and Mickey Spillane reflected a changed popular consciousness of crime. Crime writers dominating the pulps (and their more expensive counterpart, the "slicks") portrayed the growth of organized crime in America as well as the graft and corruption undermining local municipalities and their police forces. In the ideological universe of the urban wilderness, "right" and "justice" belong not to constituted authority but to the good conscience of a hard-living private detective, the man who had "seen it all." In this way, the hard-boiled detective gave homage to the pulp tradition of the Western. Those "streets dark with something more than night," as Raymond Chandler put it, revisited the West of rival outlaw bands, demonstrating that the violence of the just and the damned both work, often untouched by law.

This new literature of sensation dedicated itself to verisimilitude (in the sense of both lifelikeness and an attachment to the morbid and the visceral). As Raymond Chandler famously observed in *The Simple Art of Murder*, Hammett and other hard-boilers "gave murder back to the kind of people that commit it for reasons." The corrupt, the crazy, the greedy, and the jealous killers in Chandler, Hammett, and Macdonald's fiction put in sharp focus the violence-engendering world in which murder occurs. The detective figure is "a sort of rational strong point from which they [the writers] can observe and report on a violent no-man's-land." But in the fiction of Chandler and Hammett, that "rational strong point" is frequently at the point of being overrun. In the hard-boiled fiction of these two masters of the genre, the detectives Phillip Marlowe (Chandler) and Sam Spade (Hammett) are making a difference where they can, the limits of their action (and the effectiveness of their morality) determined by the degree of the corruption around them. The hard-boiled hero is never wholly heroic, and the violence around him never wholly healed. While Spade might have "the virtues" and "follow the code" of a "frontier male," the ideological universe of the newer urban crime literature made the context of that code less clearly divisible into good and bad; its violence was endemic, rather than an instrumental remedy.

Not all popular crime fiction reflected the same moral uncertainty as that of Chandler and Hammett. Mickey Spillane's first hero, Mike Hammer, renders sense out of his world with what seems like his fists and his gun alone. His later protagonist, Tiger Mann, takes on the dimensions of the "Commie-fighting" comic-book superhero. Although Mike Hammer goes through some fairly terrifying trials, adversity itself is rendered one-dimensional, like much of the violence in the novels. Spillane's later works were accused of being anachronistic; his later heroes use the same street patois as Hammer, and few of the technologies (of crime or detection) seem to have changed. But this characteristic of uniformity and timelessness in Spillane's "mean streets" is an attempt to rationalize violence as being dignified not so much by its cause but by its user—the a priori hero. This kind of representation of the hard-boiled hero as a law unto himself mirrors the ascendancy of American power worldwide. Gone is the ambivalence of Marlowe and Sam Spade, replaced by the can-do aggression of Mike Hammer. The commercial success of pulp crime fiction in the late 1940s and early

The Not-So-Simple Art of Murder

Scenes of murder in sensational literature range from the heavily stylized to the grittily realistic. Many writers seem to take their cues from the stage, where a killing is often signaled by certain kinds of stock gestures familiar to audiences from vaudeville, pantomime, and the genres of tragedy and farce in "serious" theater. In Max Brand's *Destry Rides Again* (1930), one of the scenes of murder occurs framed within a brightly lit window. The witness standing in the dark garden sees the following:

> Bent leaned and actually grasped Clifton by the hair of the head and jerked the head far back. Willie saw the hands of the man stiffen as they clutched at the air, saw his mouth drawn open, and yet did not scream. Then Bent struck. Straight through the base of the throat he drove the long knife, and left it sticking in the wound, then stepped back with blood running down his right hand. Clifton fell on the floor, writhed his legs together, then turned on his back and lay motionless.

The scene is highly stylized—full of exaggerated gestures but lacking in visceral fact (such a small amount of blood from an arterial wound). Raymond Chandler's description of the death of Canino in *The Big Sleep* (1939) is similarly stylized, but—if anything—even more like pantomime:

> I shot him four times, the Colt straining against my ribs. The gun jumped out of his hand as if it had been kicked. He reached both his hands for his stomach, I could hear them smack hard against his body. He fell like that, straight forward, holding himself together with his broad hands. He fell face down on the wet gravel. After that there wasn't a sound from him.

Compare these to Jack London's naturalistic rendering of violence from *The Sea Wolf* (1904). Here the ship's cook attempts to terrify the young protagonist with a tale from his brutal past:

> "Should 'a seen 'im. Knife just like this. I stuck it in, like into soft butter, an' the w'y 'e squealed was better'n a tu-penny gaff. . . . 'I didn't mean it Tommy,' 'e was snifflin'; 'so 'elp me Gawd, I didn't mean it!' 'I'll fix yer bloody well right,' I sez, an' kept right after 'im. I cut 'im in ribbons, that's wot I did, an' 'e a-squealin' all the time. Once 'e got 'is 'and on the knife an' tried to 'old it. 'Ad 'is fingers around it, but I pulled it through, cuttin' to the bone. O, 'e was a sight, I can tell yer."

Many years later, Mickey Spillane would combine the brutality of London with the typically stylized violence of the pulps. The effect isn't nearly as chilling as London's. Spillane's sadistic voyeurism was nevertheless an influential departure for pulp depictions of violence. The following scene is from his short story "The Gold Fever Tapes" (1973):

> He didn't get a second chance with the blade because this was my kind of fight and my boot caught his elbow and the steel clattered against the concrete walkway. I had a fistful of hair, yanking his face into the dirt beside me, one fist driving into his ribs and he tried to let out a yell but the ground muffled it all. For ten seconds he turned tiger, then I flipped him over, got my knee against his spine, my forearm under his chin and arched him like a bow until there was a sudden crack from inside him and he went death-limp in my hands.

In Chester Himes's satirical *Blind Man with a Pistol* (1969), the real heart of the description of the scene of violence is in the reactions of the bystanders:

> The blast shattered windows, eardrums, reason and reflexes. . . . the .45 caliber bullet, as sightless as its shooter, had gone the way the pistol had been aimed, through the pages of the *New York Times* and into the heart of the fat yellow preacher. "Uh!" his reverence grunted and turned in his bible. The moment of silence was appropriate but unintentional. It was just that all the passengers had died for a moment following the impact of the blast.

Himes's fiction opens out the scene of the killing beyond the select pairing of the killer and his victim to include its often chaotic surrounds.

The novelist Raymond Chandler. CORBIS/BETTMANN

1950s (when Spillane's 1947 novel, *I, the Jury*, sold up to six million copies) was a literal by-product of America's mobilization for war—the pulp paperback, small enough to fit in a soldier's kit or pocket, was run off in hundreds of thousands. And the distractions provided by the masculinist drama of the hard-nosed private eye were morale-building—good both for business and the war effort. The mythical and formularized violence of the pulps bled into the real, chaotic violence of a world at war and, later, an America at unsettled peace.

Late-Twentieth-Century Sensational Fiction. Central to the late-twentieth-century popular fictions of sensation—crime fiction and also the espionage genre and the thriller more widely—is the idea that chaos underlies security, that violence underlies settled life. In *The World of the Thriller* (1974), Ralph Harper notes that uncertainty is the place from which violence arises, for "the meaning of chaos . . . is [that] in it you no longer know where you are, who you are, and who anybody else is."

By implication, the hero is vulnerable; force is only partly effective, and threat itself never totally defused. Chaos is the ground of many modern popular fictions of sensation; in these the violence becomes self-sustaining. As Harper put it, if "violence is an answer to chaos it is not because it negates it, but because it is suggested by it" (p. 68). Chester Himes's *Blind Man with a Pistol* (1969) is a fittingly satiric realization of that violence-engendering chaos. Himes gives Harper's general dictum an edge—not only do "you no longer know where you are, who you are, and who anybody else is"—but someone has a gun, and that person is using it.

BIBLIOGRAPHY

Alford, Fred C. *What Evil Means to Us.* Ithaca, N.Y.: Cornell University Press, 1997.

Cawelti, John G. *Adventure, Mystery, and Romance: Formula Stories as Art and Popular Culture.* Chicago: University of Chicago Press, 1977.

Godwin Phelps, Teresa. "The Criminal as Hero." *Wisconsin Law Review* (1983): 1427.

Harper, Ralph. *The World of the Thriller.* Baltimore: Johns Hopkins University Press, 1974.

Macdonald, Ross. *On Crime Writing.* Santa Barbara, Calif.: Capra Press, 1973.

Mandel, Ernest. *Delightful Murder: A Social History of the Crime Story.* Minneapolis: University of Minnesota Press, 1984.

Roth, Marty. *Foul and Fair Play: Reading Genre in Classic Detective Fiction.* Athens: University of Georgia Press, 1995.

Slotkin, Richard. *Gunfighter Nation: The Myth of the Frontier in Twentieth Century America.* New York: Atheneum, 1992.

Symons, Julian. *Mortal Consequences: A History from the Detective Story to the Crime Novel.* New York: Schocken, 1977.

Wister, Owen. *Selling the Wild West: Popular Western Fiction, 1860–1960,* edited by Christine Bold. Bloomington: Indiana University Press, 1987.

SARA LOUISE KNOX

See also **Film; Popular Culture; Representation of Violence.**

PULP FICTION

Sensational violence has always been a prominent feature of American popular literature. In the colonial period, writings about the Indian wars helped the settlers define themselves as Americans, both more Christian and civilized than the natives and stronger and more independent than the Europeans. Stories of settlers captured by Indians often juxtaposed graphic accounts of bloodshed with biblical references, portraying their protagonists' sufferings as spiritual quests for conversion and salvation. These captivity narratives, beginning with Mary Rowlandson's *Captivity and Restoration* (1682), formed an important genre and became increasingly fictionalized in later works like Abraham Panther's *Captivity* (1787) and James Seaver's *Narrative of the Life of Mrs. Mary Jemison* (1824). They also influenced nineteenth-century slave autobiographies and novels like Harriet Beecher Stowe's *Uncle Tom's Cabin* (1852), which present their characters as Christians whose faith sustains them through the torments of slavery.

As the settlements expanded westward, frontiersmen who were able to negotiate successfully between the wilderness and civilization became popular literary figures. One of the first and most famous of these figures was Daniel Boone, the settler and Indian fighter who was first immortalized in John Filson's *Discovery, Settlement, and Present State of Kentucke* (1784) and later mythologized in works like John McClung's *Sketches of Western Adventure* (1832) and Timothy Flint's *Biographical Memoir of Daniel Boone* (1833). Davy Crockett, the soldier and politician who appeared in print for the first time in his autobiographical *Narrative of the Life of Colonel David Crockett* (1834), became another well-known character in the nation's humor and folklore.

Meanwhile, a variety of crime narratives focused on violence within the settlements. While many of these texts claimed to view crime in moral and religious terms, many also revealed ethnic and class conflicts within the European American community, as well as varying degrees of tolerance for criminal behavior. Seventeenth-century execution sermons were joined in the eighteenth century by criminal-conversion accounts, last speeches, confessions, and biographies, many of which were ghost-written and fictionalized. In the early nineteenth century, murder trial reports and pamphlets sold especially well, and many of them were collected into crime anthologies like Joseph Martin's *Select Tales* (1833) and the *Pirates' Own Book* (1837).

Murder and Indian warfare were central to the first generation of American novels, including Gothic writer Charles Brockden Brown's *Wieland* (1798) and *Edgar Huntly* (1799), as well as James Fenimore Cooper's much-beloved and widely copied Leather-Stocking Tales, a series of novels, including *The Pioneers* (1823), *The Last of the Mohicans* (1826), and *The Deerslayer* (1841), that followed the career of scout and hunter Natty Bumppo.

Reform Literature and Cheap Fiction

In the nineteenth century, many social reform movements produced literature that, although ostensibly based on fact, dwelled imaginatively on the terrible results of the vices (such as prostitution or drunkenness) against which it claimed to campaign. Maria Monk's best-selling *Awful Disclosures* (1836), a trumped-up account of rape, prostitution, torture, and murder at a convent, was one particularly sensational example of this type of writing. At the same time, many reformers deplored the sex and violence in the cheap fiction of the period. Written for a predominantly white, working-class audience, this fiction appeared in three major formats made possible by printing innovations of the late 1830s: (1) story papers such as *Brother Jonathan, New World*, the *New York Ledger*, and *Fireside Companion*, eight-page weeklies available by subscription that carried mostly serials; (2) dime novels, which dominated the market especially after New York publisher Erastus Beadle's four-by-six-inch, one-hundred-page dime novels became popular with Civil War soldiers and then inspired competitors; and (3) cheap libraries, series of eight-by-eleven-inch nickel and dime novels introduced in 1875 and distributed by mail. Readership, publishers, and stories were continuous among these formats: the same text might be published first in story papers, then as a dime novel, and finally reissued in a cheap library edition.

One particularly lurid genre of fiction that appeared in these formats was that of the city mysteries. Inspired in part by Eugène Sue's *Mysteries of Paris*, this genre was introduced by George Lippard in his controversial best-seller *The Quaker City* (1845), which claimed to reveal the murderous and lecherous evil hidden behind the facade of respectable Philadelphia society. In Lippard's works and in other urban exposé novels like Ned Buntline's *The Mysteries and Miseries of New Orleans* (1851), Caroline Hargrave's *The Mysteries of Salem!* (1845), and George Thompson's *City Crimes* and *Venus in Boston* (both 1849), shocking accounts of murder, torture, rape, and prostitution were linked to attacks on America's class structure. The criminals in these works are typically either rich hypocrites who revel in cruelty while enjoying the good opinion of the world, or working-class characters who exact bloody revenge on society for the wrongs done to them.

Excerpts from Pulp Fiction

An excerpt from George Lippard's *The Quaker City; or, The Monks of Monk Hall: A Romance of Philadelphia Life, Mystery, and Crime* (1845):

His teeth were firmly compressed, as with one desperate effort he unloosed the arms of the old woman from his throat, and grasped her firmly by the middle of the body. He fixed his eye upon a massive knob surmounting one of the brass andirons before the fire, and, as a blacksmith raises a hammer in his arms, he swung the body of the old woman suddenly on high. She uttered a loud and piercing shriek—it was her last! As the blacksmith with his muscular arms, braced for the blow, brings the hammer, whirling down upon the anvil, so Devil-Bug, with his hideous face, all a-flame with rage, swung the body of the old woman wildly over his shoulder, and with the every impulse of his strength, gathered for the effort, struck her head—her long grey hairs streaming wildly all the time—full against the knob of the brass andiron.

He raised her body in the air again to repeat the blow, but the effort was needless. The brains of the old woman lay scattered over the hearth, and the body which Devil-Bug raised in the air, was a headless trunk, with the bleeding fragments of a face and skull, clinging to the quivering neck.

* * *

The opening paragraph from *The Narrative of the Captivity and Restoration of Mrs. Mary Rowlandson* (1682):

On the 10th of February, 1675, came the Indians with great numbers upon Lancaster: their first coming was about sun-rising; hearing the noise of some guns, we looked out; several houses were burning, and the smoke ascending to heaven. There were five persons taken in one house, the father and mother, and a sucking child they knocked on the head, the other two they took and carried away alive. There were two others, who being out of their garrison upon occasion, were set upon; one was knocked on the head, the other escaped: another there was who running along was shot and wounded, and fell down; he begged of them his life, promising them money (as they told me) but they would not hearken to him, but knocked him on the head, stript him naked, and split open his bowels. Another seeing many of the Indians about his barn, ventured and went out, but was quickly shot down. There were three others belonging to the same garrison who were killed; the Indians getting up upon the roof of the barn, had advantage to shoot down upon them over their fortification. Thus these murtherous wretches went on burning and destroying all before them.

Throughout the nineteenth century, violence was also integral to Western novels, which detailed the adventures of frontiersmen, Indian fighters, and sympathetic outlaw figures like Deadwood Dick, the stagecoach robber hero created by Edward L. Wheeler in 1877. Violence also played a key role in stories like Laura Jean Libbey's *Leonie Locke; or, The Romance of a Beautiful New York Working Girl* (1884), in which working girls typically survived assault, abduction, and attempted rape, emerging victorious and virtuous at the end of the book, as well as in stories about strikes and other labor conflicts.

In the last decade of the nineteenth century, these formats began to succumb to competition from Sunday newspapers and from a crop of new and inexpensive magazines.

Pulp Magazines, Paperbacks, and Comics

For the history of violence in popular fiction, the most significant of these new publications were the pulps, magazines printed on rough wood-pulp paper instead of coated stock, which typically contained more than a hundred pages of stories and serials. The first pulps of the 1890s, like Frank Munsey's *Argosy*, were general fiction magazines, but in their period of greatest popularity, from the early 1920s to the mid-1940s, several hundred pulps catered to a variety of special interests. Some of the most successful included Smith and Street's

Detective Stories, H. L. Mencken and George J. Nathan's detective pulp *Black Mask,* the Western pulps *Wild West Weekly* and *Western Story,* and the horror and fantasy pulp *Weird Tales.*

Beginning in the late 1930s, pulps saw competition from paperback novels, rack-sized paperbound books usually priced at twenty-five cents, which were sold in drugstores, bus stations, and (later) airports. At first, these were reprints of books that had appeared in hardcover, but soon publishers began commissioning works directly for the softcover market. Reaching their peak of popularity in the decade after World War II, paperback novels appealed mainly to middle- and working-class men, many of them former soldiers. They were generally simply written and contained a great deal of realistic sex and violence. Paperbacks were as diverse as pulp magazines and included Westerns and detective stories, as well as books that focused on juvenile crime, homosexuality, drug addiction, horror, and exotic adventure.

The 1930s also witnessed the invention of comic books, which portrayed violence in both words and pictures. In the late 1930s and early 1940s, the most widely read comics starred superheroes like Batman, Captain America, and Black Hood; but after the war, crime comics like *Detective Picture Stories, Detective Comics,* and *Crime Does Not Pay* became the industry's best-sellers. Horror comics like *Adventures into the Unknown* and EC Comics' *Tales from the Crypt, The Vault of Horror,* and *The Haunt of Fear* prospered in the late 1940s and early 1950s. Many writers wrote for both pulp magazines and paperback novels, and stories from both formats were also reworked in crime comics and in Hollywood films.

One of the twentieth-century genres in which violence was most prominent was that of hard-boiled detective fiction, which introduced realistic violence and colloquial language to the American detective story. *Black Mask* first published many of the founding works of this school, including Carroll John Daly's "The False Burton Combs" (1922), "It's All In the Game" (1923), "Three Gun Terry Mack" (1923), and *The Snarl of the Beast* (1927), and Dashiell Hammett's *Red Harvest* (1929). In these works and those of the many writers inspired by them, tough, independent detectives explore irredeemably corrupt worlds full of murder, deception, and beautiful but treacherous women. Among the many popular works in this genre in the following decade were James Cain's *The Postman Always Rings Twice* (1934) and *Double Indem-*

The cover of one issue of *Weird Tales* magazine.
CORBIS/BETTMANN

nity (1936) and Raymond Chandler's *The Big Sleep* (1939). In the late 1940s and early 1950s, Mickey Spillane took the genre to new extremes of graphic violence and misogyny with his monumentally successful Mike Hammer series, which included *Kiss Me Deadly; I, the Jury;* and *Vengeance Is Mine!* Other crime writers of this period included Jim Thompson, famous for his portrayals of psychopathic killers, especially *The Killer Inside Me* (1952), a first-person narrative by an insane murderer; Chester Himes, an African American writer whose works focused on racial inequity; and others such as Harry Whittington, David Goodis, Vin Packer (the pseudonym of Marijane Meaker), Ed Lacy, and David Rabe.

The sex and violence in the paperbacks' texts, as well as on their colorful covers, were considered pornographic by some observers. Sales of the books declined after Congress's 1952 Gathings Committee investigation into pornography, which led many local groups and police to pressure merchants to stop carrying pulps. Comics, which had already been banned or restricted in many communities in the late 1940s, received further negative publicity from two early 1950s congressional investigations and the publication of Frederic Wertham's anticomics tract *Seduction of the Innocent* (1954). The industry then established a Comics Code, which virtually eliminated violence.

Developments Since the 1950s

Although it is always difficult to assess the relative importance of literary developments closer to one's own time, it is clear that hard-boiled detective fiction remained popular through the last decades of the twentieth century, with James Ellroy and Lawrence Block among its most successful practitioners. One interesting change in the genre —especially given that the hard-boiled fiction of 1920–1955 has frequently been interpreted as an expression of white male anxiety at the increase in women's power in society—has been the participation of more women and minority writers. In the 1980s and 1990s these writers included Sue Grafton, author of the Kinsey Millhone series begun in 1982 with *A Is for Alibi*; Sara Paretsky, author of the V. I. Warshawski mysteries; and Walter Mosley, whose African American private eye, Easy Rawlins, appears in a series of mysteries that includes *Devil in a Blue Dress* (1990).

Crime and horror comics experienced a renaissance beginning in the early 1970s, when the Comics Code was relaxed, and continuing through the 1980s, when the growth of specialty comic-book stores created a new market for them. Horror fiction has also prospered, in large measure owing to the influence of the prolific Stephen King, whose *Carrie* (1974), *Salem's Lot* (1975), and *The Shining* (1977) brought horror to unprecedented levels of mainstream success.

At the intersection of horror and crime are a subgroup of books about serial killers, of which Thomas Harris's *Red Dragon* (1981) and its sequel, *The Silence of the Lambs* (1988), are paradigmatic examples. Readers fascinated by the details of killers' lives and actions can also choose from many books of true crime, a genre established by Truman Capote with his groundbreaking book *In Cold Blood* (1966), which combined journalism and imaginative writing in an account of the murder of a Kansas family. In addition, male-action novels, which began with Donald Eugene Pendleton's *The Executioner: War Against the Mafia* (1969), have become

a genre of their own; espionage novels such as Robert Ludlum's were widely read until the end of the Cold War; and the late 1980s and early 1990s saw a vogue for legal thrillers such as John Grisham's *A Time to Kill* (1989) and *The Firm* (1991).

BIBLIOGRAPHY

Cohen, Daniel A. *Pillars of Salt, Monuments of Grace: New England Crime Literature and the Origins of American Popular Culture, 1674–1860.* New York: Oxford University Press, 1993.

Denning, Michael. *Mechanic Accents: Dime Novels and Working-Class Culture in America.* London and New York: Verso, 1987.

Panek, LeRoy Lad. *Probable Cause: Crime Fiction in America.* Bowling Green, Ohio: Bowling Green State University Popular Press, 1990.

Reynolds, David S. *Beneath the American Renaissance: The Subversive Imagination in the Age of Emerson and Melville.* Cambridge, Mass.: Harvard University Press, 1988.

Server, Lee. *Over My Dead Body: The Sensational Age of the American Paperback.* San Francisco: Chronicle, 1994.

Slotkin, Richard. *Regeneration Through Violence: The Mythology of the American Frontier, 1600–1860.* New York: Harper Perennial, 1996.

KIMBERLY R. GLADMAN

See also **Comics; Spillane, Mickey; Serial Killers, Representations of.**

NUCLEAR WAR FICTION

American literature about nuclear war is intertwined with the history of nuclear weapons in the United States, the first nation to manufacture them and the only nation to have ever used them.

The first appearance in any literature of a nuclear weapon of war was in Hollis Godfrey's 1908 novel *The Man Who Ended War*. Like earlier American conceptions of the ultimate weapon, this invention—a radioactive beam that disintegrates the atoms of metals—immediately makes war obsolete. Another American scientific wizard invents an atomic beam weapon that causes colossal explosions and radiation sickness in *The Man Who Rocked the Earth*, by Arthur Train and Robert Wood, serialized in 1914–1915 by the *Saturday Evening Post*; once again all nations disarm and form a world government, guaranteeing perpetual peace.

In the wake of World War I, American fiction was less enthusiastic about nuclear weapons. Pierrepont Noyes's *The Pallid Giant* (1927) tells how atomic weapons developed by prehistoric civilizations almost wiped out the human species;

supposed to deter attack, these weapons instead induced preemptive first strikes.

In 1938 the uranium atom was split in Nazi Germany. By early 1940 dozens of American newspapers and magazines had excited the public with visions of atomic energy and atomic bombs. Fred Allhoff's *Lightning in the Night*, a novel serialized in 1940 and read by millions, developed the doctrine of U.S. global supremacy through nuclear weapons.

In the summer of 1940 the U.S. government ordered newspapers, magazines, and radio networks not to mention atomic power, cyclotrons, fission, or uranium. For five years the only Americans exposed to public thoughts about atomic weapons would be readers of science fiction. In Robert A. Heinlein's "Solution Unsatisfactory" (1941), the United States manufactures radioactive dust, an ultimate weapon whose very existence nullifies democracy. Cleve Cartmill's "Deadline" (1944) suggested that the antifascist Allies would never use atomic bombs because such weapons could eventually threaten the existence of the human race.

Sixty-nine of the scientists actually building the first atomic bombs echoed this belief in a petition to President Harry S. Truman drafted by Leo Szilard, the man most responsible for the development of the atomic bomb and later a writer of antibomb fiction. Debate still rages about the motives for dropping atomic bombs on the Japanese cities of Hiroshima and Nagasaki in World War II, as well as the bombings' effects on the war and the postwar world. Judging by statements made by Truman and his advisers, one motive seems to have been a belief that the atom bomb was the ultimate peacemaking weapon predicted in American fiction.

Although the United States maintained a monopoly on nuclear weapons from 1945 until 1949, many works published in those years anticipated nuclear confrontations and global holocausts. Foreshadowing the 1970s Cold War doctrine of "mutual assured destruction," *The Murder of the U.S.A.* (1946), by Will Jenkins, argued that, because there is no defense against atomic weapons, the only possible deterrent is the certainty of an annihilating retaliation. But Theodore Sturgeon's "Thunder and Roses" (1947) countered that such retaliation would serve no purpose and could lead to human extinction. Until 1947 almost every work of fiction picturing the United States in a nuclear war refrained from identifying the enemy. Cold War literature had no such shyness, as evident in Leonard Engel and Emanuel Piller's *World Aflame: The Russian-American War of 1950* (1947).

Nuclear literature was a male preserve until 1948. Judith Merril authored the first published short story—"That Only a Mother" (1948)—and first novel—*Shadow on the Hearth* (1950)—about atomic weapons by a woman; both are written from a mother's perspective and oppose the male nuclear obsession.

During the 1950s tales such as Alfred Bester's "Disappearing Act" (1953) and Fritz Leiber's "A Bad Day for Sales" (1953) portrayed nuclearism as a symptom of a nation that was becoming dehumanized. Ray Bradbury's "There Will Come Soft Rains" (1950) encapsulates this vision in the last house left standing amid radioactive ruins, an automated futuristic home where the only remaining shapes of humans are silhouettes etched by a bomb.

The postholocaust world, however, has also provided a terrain for survivalist fantasies to run amok, as in Stuart Cloete's 1947 novella *The Blast* and Jerry Ahern's extremely popular *Survivalist* series of the 1980s. An early response to such fantasies came in two classic stories by Ward Moore, "Lot" (1953) and "Lot's Daughter" (1954), which dramatize survivalism as fundamental to the nuclear devastation it may precipitate.

From the late 1950s through the mid-1960s, as the potential global catastrophe foreseen by earlier fiction became a threat hanging over everyday life, American novels about nuclear war, such as Pat Frank's *Alas, Babylon* (1959), Alfred Coppel's *Dark December* (1960), and Eugene Burdick and Harvey Wheeler's *Fail-Safe* (1962), reached a wider audience. *A Canticle for Leibowitz* (1959), by Walter M. Miller, Jr., focuses on the cultural processes that make nuclear annihilation possible. Helen Clarkson's *The Last Day* (1959) witnesses nuclear disaster through the eyes of a woman devoted to family and nurturing.

In Philip K. Dick's *The Penultimate Truth* (1964), the masses live underground, slaving their miserable lives away to defend their nations amid the nuclear war they watch devastating the planet's surface on their cable TV screens. But in fact the war ended long ago, and the earth has been divided up by its new rulers, who control the information that defines reality.

During the Vietnam War the dark vision of "New Wave" science fiction produced such literary masterpieces as Harlan Ellison's "I Have No

---

"The Big Flash"

In "The Big Flash," Norman Spinrad's 1969 "New Wave" science fiction masterpiece, a 1960s demonic rock group called the Four Horsemen seems to offer the perfect solution to those who thought they could win the Vietnam War with tactical nuclear weapons if they were not hamstrung by public opinion. Since the band's whole repertoire consists of orgiastic numbers that mesmerize their audience into lust for the "big flash," the government, the Pentagon, and aerospace companies plan to use the band to remold public opinion into a clamor for nuclear weapons. The campaign succeeds, though far beyond the wishes of the sponsors. Possessed by the Four Horsemen's overpowering beat and command to "Do it!," the missilemen in silos and submarines launch strategic rockets, thus initiating the annihilation of the human species.

Mouth, and I Must Scream" (1967) and *A Boy and His Dog* (1969) and Norman Spinrad's "The Big Flash" (1969).

Roger Zelazny's *Damnation Alley* (1969; film 1977) inaugurated a new round of postholocaust nightmares, which were given an inventive twist in David Brin's *The Postman* (1985; film 1997). In the 1970s and 1980s, this terrain provided locales for important feminist novels, including Suzy McKee Charnas's *Walk to the End of the World* (1974), Vonda McIntyre's *Dreamsnake* (1978), and Sheri Tepper's *The Gate to Women's Country* (1988).

After the end of the Cold War in 1989, writers still found rich veins in nuclearism. John Updike's *Toward the End of Time* (1997) uses a Sino-American nuclear war as a backdrop for a spiritually dying world, while Don DeLillo's *Underworld* (1997) portrays an entire epoch deranged by living under the threat of nuclear weapons.

BIBLIOGRAPHY

Bartter, Martha A. *The Way to Ground Zero: The Atomic Bomb in American Science Fiction.* New York: Greenwood, 1988.

Brians, Paul. *Nuclear Holocausts: Atomic War in Fiction, 1895–1984.* Kent, Ohio: Kent State University Press, 1987.

Franklin, H. Bruce. *War Stars: The Superweapon and the American Imagination.* New York: Oxford University Press, 1988.

H. BRUCE FRANKLIN

See also **Cold War; Hiroshima and Nagasaki; Weapons: Nuclear.**

CHILDREN'S AND YOUNG ADULT LITERATURE

Violence has always been a component of literature, and, for the most part, this is true of both traditional and contemporary stories written for children and teenagers. However, the degree and shape of the violence portrayed in books for young people is determined by society's attitudes toward the perceived function and appropriateness of that violence for different age levels and genders.

Attitudes Toward Violence in Literature for Young Readers

In the United States these attitudes have taken four conflicting forms, leading to much confusion and controversy. First, some critics argue that violent impulses are inborn and it is beneficial for these pressures to be released through the catharsis of viewing or reading about violence, an idea that originated with Sigmund Freud but has been repudiated by James Gilligan (*Violence: Our Deadly Epidemic and Its Causes*, 1996) and others in the late twentieth century. Second, many older and more traditional child advocates feel that children are vulnerable and should be shielded from knowledge of the violence in the world around them until they are older. Opponents of this protective attitude warn that honesty is at stake here. As the children's author and editor James Cross Giblin said: "The smooth, unfelt, superficially pleasant, and happy picture book may actually do more violence in an indirect way to the . . . child's own intuitive, probably inarticulate sense of reality by in effect denying it" (1995). Third, and directly opposed to the protectionists, are those who insist that children's books have an obligation to tell the truth about the pervasiveness of violence in America and to help young readers learn to cope with it; proponents of this position tend to be younger and more liberal librarians and teachers. Fourth, there are those who maintain that vicarious violence is harmless fun—an argument usually raised in defense of horror paperbacks and other popular series fiction by fans of fantasy and genre reading. While each position has its adherents, the confusing factor is that most child advocates will switch back and forth between these four attitudes, depending on the age of the child and the type of literature in question.

While people may have strong feelings about literary violence, there is no empirical data about whether reading it is bad or good for children and teenagers. There have been thousands of studies of the effects of viewing violent images on television and in films but virtually none on the effects on children of reading about violence. We can extrapolate from the studies of television and film—which almost universally show that viewing violence raises the level of aggressive behavior—but the active experience of reading is in many ways quite different from the passive experience of television viewing, and so the effects, too, may be quite different.

Perhaps the most crucial difference is in the responsible way violence is portrayed in realistic children's books as contrasted with the gratuitous mayhem on television. In juvenile fiction the violent act is seen as a bad, abnormal action, and the emphasis is on the consequences and strategies for survival and healing. The protagonist is nearly always the victim, not the perpetrator, of the violence. The quality of the experience is also richer in reading: Giblin has stated that "the authors of books have an opportunity to fill a needed gap in the reader's knowledge and give him a textured, many-leveled experience he cannot get elsewhere."

In the past, the protectionist attitude has prevailed. There are as yet relatively few books for prepubescent children that deal realistically with violent acts, although Eliza Dresang (1997, 1999) sees more such books, of a new type, beginning to emerge as part of the changes of the electronic age that move the Internet generation toward wider access and connectivity to and interactivity with literature. Examples of violence in books for middle-grade readers are *What Jamie Saw* by Carolyn Coman (1995), in which a young boy and his mother flee the abusive stepfather who threw the baby against the wall; *Adam's War* by Sonia Levitin (1994), in which Adam and his friends start a war with rivals over a clubhouse; and *Making Up Megaboy* by Virginia Walter (1998), in which an assortment of witnesses, parents, and bystanders try to make sense of a boy's sudden murder of a liquor store owner. A few extraordinary picture books have dealt with political violence effectively and have sometimes been controversial as a result: *Smoky Night* by Eve Bunting (1994), *Hiroshima No Pika* by Toshiko Maruki (1982), *We Are All in the Dumps with Jack and Guy* by Maurice Sendak (1993), and the magnificent *The Middle Passage* by Tom Feelings (1995).

In fairy tales, however, the oldest form of children's literature, violence is presented in a different way and has been held to have a different function. In these stories, especially those collected by the Brothers Grimm, spectacular cruelties abound and the villains suffer imaginative mutilations and deaths. Bruno Bettelheim, in his landmark book *The Uses of Enchantment* (1976), argues from the Freudian point of view. Because fairy tales have been handed down through the oral tradition for hundreds of years, he writes, they have come to be symbolic renderings of unconscious feelings and crucial life experiences. Therefore, the violent images in fairy tales are beneficial and useful to children, because they represent the child's own chaotic, anxious, and angry fantasies about "sibling rivalry, ambivalence toward parents, separation anxiety, and self-actualization," and thus help the child accept and control these otherwise destructive impulses. Nevertheless, more literal-minded adults continue to object to the many gruesome incidents in fairy tales. As a response, in 1994 the publisher of Golden Books "sanitized" the Three Little Pigs and several other classic tales, to ridicule by critics. However, the general trend is toward softening only the grisly endings: In modern renditions the wolf is never boiled alive, and Cinderella's stepsisters do not cut off their toes to fit into the glass slipper.

The death of animals has often been used in traditional children's literature to provoke tears and sadness, for example, the demise of Charlotte the spider, of Bambi's mother, and of Black Beauty's friend Ginger. Sometimes the violent death of an animal is the means of the protagonist's coming-of-age, as in *The Yearling* by Marjorie Kinnan Rawlings (1938) and *A Day No Pigs Would Die* by Robert Newton Peck (1972). Threatened harm to dogs or cats is frequently used to build suspense; *Shiloh* by Phyllis Reynolds Naylor (1991) is a memorable example. In young adult literature this tendency has grown to include such episodes as the battering death of a cat in *Chinese Handcuffs* by Chris Crutcher (1989).

Young Adult Literature

Young adult (YA) literature is a form that welcomes violence by its very nature. The genre originated in the 1960s with the publication of *The Outsiders* by S. E. Hinton (1967), a story of gang warfare, and soon became known as the "new realism" for its fictional portrayals of gritty social and personal problems. By the end of the twentieth century there was almost no kind of violence that had not been portrayed or examined in YA novels but always in the mode of giving teenagers the information and psychic strength they need to cope with a violent world. The violent action, which often takes place offstage, functions in the plot as the motivating force for the young protagonist to gain maturity by overcoming its consequences.

Violence within the family occurs in many YA novels, usually in the form of an abusive parent— *Staying Fat for Sarah Byrnes* by Chris Crutcher (1993)—or sibling—*When She Was Good* by Norma Fox Mazer (1997). The effects of sexual abuse of a young person by a parent or stepparent abound in the works of Chris Crutcher, a child and family therapist, most notably in *Chinese Handcuffs*. The subject has also been explored in many other YA novels: *Abby, My Love* by Hadley Irwin (1985), *I Hadn't Meant to Tell You This* by Jacqueline Woodson (1994), and *When She Hollers* by Cynthia Voigt (1994). Suicide, which is the third leading cause of death among high school students, appears frequently in YA novels and is the subject of *Remembering the Good Times* by Richard Peck (1985), *About David* by Susan Beth Pfeffer (1980), and *How Far Would You Have Gotten If I Hadn't Called You Back?* by Valerie Hobbs (1995). The aftermath of the sudden violent death of a parent is sensitively portrayed in *Dead Birds Singing* by Marc Talbert (1985), *Walk Two Moons* by Sharon Creech (1994), *Shizuko's Daughter* by Kyoko Mori (1993), and *Tiger Eyes* by Judy Blume (1981).

Plots involving the grieving and healing process for survivors of murder or assault or the violent accidental death of friends are essential learning tools for many teens for whom homicide is a daily reality. In *Calling Home* by Michael Cadnum (1991) a young boy accidentally kills his best friend but hides the crime and his guilt. In *Edge* by the same author (1997) a boy must give up his desire for revenge against the thief who shot and paralyzed his father. A girl mourns her boyfriend, who is killed in a fall in *Sex Education* by Jenny Davis (1988), and a boy mourns his girlfriend, who is killed in a car crash in *Running Loose* by Chris Crutcher (1983). Lois Duncan explores the guilt of a group of teens who accidentally kill their English teacher in *Killing Mr. Griffin* (1976), but in most of Duncan's books murder functions in a more tra-

ditional way as the center of a thriller, as in *I Know What You Did Last Summer* (1973).

Sports as a venue for acting out violent impulses is a frequent theme in YA literature, often centering around the figure of a brutal coach or a frustrated father as provocateur. Some sports that have formed the basis for such stories are hockey in *Iceman* by Chris Lynch (1994), boxing in *Shadow Boxer* by Lynch (1993) and *The Contender* by Robert Lipsyte (1968), football in *Imitate the Tiger* by Jan Cheripko (1996), wrestling in *Vision Quest* by Terry Davis (1979) and *Wrestling Sturbridge* by Rich Wallace (1996) and in many of the short stories in *Athlete Shorts* by Chris Crutcher (1991), swimming in *Stotan!* by Crutcher (1986), and girls' softball in *Bat 6* by Virginia Ever Wolff (1998).

Social violence resulting from the pressures of poverty or racial discrimination or other societal dysfunction appears on a different level. In these YA novels the blame is more diffuse and the solution must compromise with the existing state of the society. Chris Lynch has savaged his own violent Irish American upbringing in the *Blue-Eyed Son* trilogy (1996) and *Whitechurch* (1999); Victor Martinez draws on his roots with a story set in the housing projects of a central California agricultural town, *Parrot in the Oven: Mi Vida* (1996); Jesse Mowry anatomizes a black street gang in *Way Past Cool* (1992) and *Babylon Boyz* (1997); Gary Soto portrays the violence-soaked culture of the barrio in *Buried Onions* (1997); and Richard Peck satirizes the smugness of suburbia in *The Last Safe Place on Earth* (1995). Violence is inherent in each of these settings. Marc Talbert re-creates another violent society, that of the ancient Mayans, in *Heart of a Jaguar* (1995). Violence turns inward on itself in *Crosses* by Shelley Stoehr (1991), in which girls cut themselves to express their anger at their world.

Sexual assault is an especially ugly symptom of social unrest, and it has appeared in YA literature as rape in *Are You in the House Alone?* by Richard Peck (1976), *Fair Game* by Erika Tamar (1993), and *Out of Control* by Norma Fox Mazer (1993). The physical violence of "gay bashing" is vividly pictured in *The Drowning of Stephan Jones* by Bette Greene (1991) and in less overt form, as harassment and insult, in many YA novels, from *Sticks and Stones* by Lynn Hall (1972) to *My Father's Scar* by Michael Cart (1997).

Guns are both fascinating and frightening to teens, with good reason, because one out of every four teenage deaths is caused by a gun. Several YA authors have explored this fatal attraction in compelling novels: *Scorpions* by Walter Dean Myers (1988), *Swallowing Stones* by Joyce McDonald (1997), *AK* by Peter Dickinson (1990), *Edge* by Michael Cadnum (1997), *The Rifle* by Gary Paulsen (1995), and the anthology *Twelve Shots*, edited by Harry Mazer (1997).

Political violence is even further removed from the victim's control, and YA literature has not shrunk from exploring some of the worst violent injustices of the past, such as the Salem witchcraft trials in *Beyond the Burning Time* by Kathryn Lasky (1994). More recent political violence forms the background of *Children of the River* by Linda Crewe (1989), *A Taste of Salt* by Frances Temple (1992), *The Honorable Prison* by Lyle Becerra de Jenkins (1989), and *Among the Volcanoes* by Omar Castaneda (1991). Most visible has been social injustice against African Americans, a subject that has inspired many YA novels, among them the classic *Roll of Thunder, Hear My Cry* by Mildred Taylor (1976) and the more contemporary *The Watsons Go to Birmingham, 1963* by Christopher Paul Curtis (1995).

War, of course, is the ultimate political violence. Because it is men in their late teens who fight wars, the subject should be of vital importance to young adults. Interestingly, there is no glory in YA novels about battle. "War books are likely to center on physical and psychological suffering," observed Alleen Pace Nilsen and Kenneth Donelson in *Literature for Today's Young Adults* (2d ed., 1985). "A romanticized picture of war today would seem dishonest and offensive to most readers." Three of the best realistic portrayals of war are *Soldier's Heart* by Gary Paulsen (1998), *The Last Mission* by Harry Mazer (1979), and *Fallen Angels* by Walter Dean Myers (1988). The Holocaust of World War II, of course, is violence gone mad. A number of fine memoirs exist, beginning with the well-known *Diary of Anne Frank* (1952), and there are many fictional treatments of various aspects of the subject—*Gentlehands* by M. E. Kerr (1978) and *The Devil's Arithmetic* by Jane Yolen (1988) being two of the best.

Violence has been perceived very differently in fantastic literature, a favorite with many young people. The pattern of classic heroic fantasy is inherently violent, as the protagonists journey on their quest toward the ultimate battle between good and evil. (The final volume of C. S. Lewis's seminal Chronicles of Narnia is even entitled *The Last Battle*.) There are myriad violent encounters and skirmishes on the way, and the violence is often colorful and inventive (see, for example, the Redwall series by Brian Jacques or the Shannara series by Terry Brooks). But this has been acceptable to the self-appointed adult guardians of children's literature, because the situations are by definition

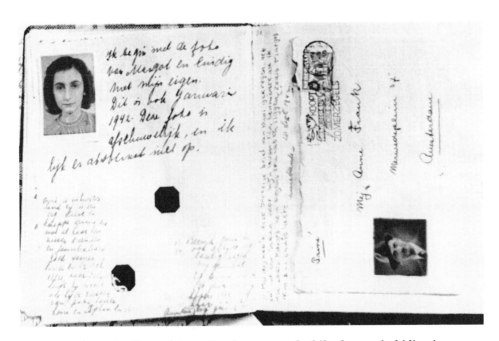

Two pages from the diary of Anne Frank, composed while she was in hiding in Amsterdam from the Nazis during World War II. CORBIS/BETTMANN

unreal, and the violence is thus seen as part of the fun and excitement of the story.

The limit of tolerance of violence began to be reached in the mid-1990s, when the phenomenon of the horror paperback series began to show enormous popularity with teens and then—with the advent of R. L. Stine's Goosebumps books—even with small children. These books, with their flimsy plots and cardboard characters, were certainly not literature, but young people devoured them voraciously. Stine topped the charts for months with the Goosebumps books and his Fear Street series for teens. Called the most popular children's author of all time, Stine and his publishers claimed 140 million copies of his books in print by 1995, while his nearest competitors, Christopher Pike and Diane Hoh, sold hundreds of thousands. Some adults were alarmed by the plethora of horrifically bloody and nauseating scenes in these books, but others were willing to overlook the violence because "at least they're reading." Hostilities broke out in the form of articles in magazines and newspapers, television news coverage, and censorship attempts in schools and libraries. All four of the possible attitudes toward violence in children's literature were invoked, sometimes by the same person, and feelings ran high, while young people continued to demand more and more grisly horror. By late 1997, however, bookstores began to report a drop in sales for Goosebumps books, and it was apparent that the fad had run its course. Patrick Jones defended popular horror paperbacks in *What's So Scary About R. L. Stine?* (1998), while Perry Nodelman deplored the underlying message of the genre in an article in an issue of *Children's Literature Association Quarterly* (October 1997) that was devoted entirely to the theme of violence in books for young people.

BIBLIOGRAPHY

Bettelheim, Bruno. *The Uses of Enchantment: The Meaning and Importance of Fairy Tales.* New York: Knopf, 1976.
Dresang, Eliza T. *Radical Change: Books for Youth in a Digital Age.* New York: H. W. Wilson, 1999.
——. "The Resilient Child in Contemporary Children's Literature: Surviving Personal Violence." *Children's Literature Association Quarterly* (October 1997).
Giblin, James Cross. "Violence, Children, and Children's Books." *School Library Journal* (November 1995).
Jones, Patrick. *What's So Scary About R. L. Stine?* Lanham, Md.: Scarecrow, 1998.
Nodelman, Perry. "Ordinary Monstrosity: The World of Goosebumps." *Children's Literature Association Quarterly* (October 1997).
West, Diana. "The Horror of R. L. Stine." *Weekly Standard,* 25 September 1995.

PATRICIA J. CAMPBELL

See also **Comics; Television: Children's Television.**

NONFICTION PROSE

Nonfictional representations of violence are a feature of American literature from the colonial period onward. They occur in memoirs, personal narratives, and biographies as well as history, political science, sociology, psychology, and law. Accounts of violence also exist in primary documents, including legal, medical, military, and political records.

Nonfiction descriptions of violence fall into four subcategories: (1) personal accounts by victims or perpetrators; (2) third-person accounts by witnesses or other interested parties; (3) theoretical or analytical literature; and (4) documents generated by officers of the state or other social institutions.

First-person testimonial literature is well established within the American tradition and familiar to the average person. Personal accounts of violence date from the earliest days of settlement: they can be found in captivity narratives (describing the kidnapping of whites by Indians) and in accounts of life in the Jamestown and Plymouth settlements, where conflict with the native inhabitants was constant and often fierce. The number of first-person narratives of violence increases throughout the Colonial and Revolutionary periods, encompassing narratives of witch trials, indentured servitude and slavery, political repression, and the earliest first-person accounts of crime victims. During the antebellum period personal narratives were written by some slaves; as the abolition movement grew in strength, slave narratives were widely distributed, presenting images of violence that are still familiar, notably *The Narrative of the Life of Frederick Douglass* (1845). In the period of westward expansion, narratives of frontier violence became a staple of the new "dime novel" publishing industry, though quite a few of those "true stories" were fictionalized representations attributed to such frontier heroes as Buffalo Bill Cody, Billy the Kid, and Calamity Jane. The Revolutionary War, the Indian wars, the Mexican War, the Civil War, and other conflicts also produced their share of memoirs describing conflict and battle.

In the twentieth century, first-person accounts of the frontier were replaced by the "true crime" story in which the new era's hero—the detective or police officer—describes tracking and capturing violent criminals. The true-crime genre has its antithesis in the accounts of police and government repression penned by American political radicals. There are notable accounts in the first half of the century from members of the American Communist and Socialist Parties and labor organizers; in the second half there are writings by participants in the Civil Rights and labor movements, as well as identity movements (Black Panthers, American Indian Movement, Puerto Rican *independentistas*, Sanctuary workers, etc.). In the 1970s published narratives by sexual abuse survivors became common, and later many bookstores devoted entire sections to them. Accounts by the perpetrators of crimes have also gained popularity, and one can find memoirs by violent criminals of various types, ranging from armed robbers to serial killers. In the late 1980s narratives written by African American and Hispanic gang members started to appear on bookstore shelves, and they comprise a small but growing subgenre. At the end of the twentieth century, the most popular forms of first-person narratives were true-crime and war narratives.

Third-person accounts mirror closely the patterns described above. The chief difference between the first- and third-person accounts is the level of authority accorded an "objective" third-person narrator, who is presumably not as emotionally involved in the subject matter as the victim or perpetrator. These accounts include biographies, journalism, polemics, and "as-told-to" narratives. Claims to objectivity vary—some accounts are by intimates or family members with clear interests in the story; others are by persons with distinct political agendas. Like first-person narratives, these accounts must be read in context, and each one must be understood to be the product of a particular set of political, economic, and social pressures.

Theoretical and analytical literature exceeds first-person narratives in both volume and scope, but it is so varied and diffuse as to be difficult to describe either quickly or neatly. It deals with the same subject areas covered in first-person accounts but is less concerned with describing particular incidents of violence than with providing a methodological framework for understanding violence. Social sciences literature on violence is extensive, particularly in psychology and sociology. Psychological literature tends to focus on the violent impulses of individuals, describing motivations and effects. Sociology focuses on the social patterns and institutions in which violence takes place. Philosophical and theological writing on violence deals with the intersection between the individual and society. Historians' descriptions of violence tend toward narrative or a chain of cause and effect. In the 1980s and 1990s a great deal of interdisciplinary work on violence was generated, particularly in the areas of feminist theory and cultural studies. These works combine various disciplinary perspectives to generate new insights on violence, representation, and society, and they have resulted in a new understanding of previously misunderstood phenomena such as posttraumatic stress disorder, the Stockholm Syndrome (the tendency of a prisoner or hostage to identify with his captors), and other responses to violence.

Among documents generated by officers of the state or other social institutions, the most numerous are confessions. The taking of confessions is a practice that predates the formation of the republic, and the public record contains many thousands of confessions of convicted criminals, ranging from "witches" to murderers. Trial records also contain verbatim transcripts of the descriptions of violence told within the framework of the justice system, both military and civilian. Though usually protected by privacy law, there also exist hundreds of thousands of case histories compiled by psychotherapists and other mental health practitioners in the course of their duties, as well as reports by medical doctors documenting that their patients were the victims of violent assault.

BIBLIOGRAPHY

Armstrong, Nancy, and Leonard Tennenhouse. *The Violence of Representation: Literature and the History of Violence.* New York: Routledge and Kegan Paul, 1989.

Brass, Paul R. *Theft of an Idol: Text and Context in the Representation of Collective Violence.* Princeton, N.J.: Princeton University Press, 1997.

Tal, Kalí. *Worlds of Hurt: Reading the Literatures of Trauma.* New York: Cambridge University Press, 1996.

KALÍ TAL

See also **Journalism.**

POETRY

American poets have been no more infatuated with violence than poets of other nations. In fact, only one major American poet, Robert Lowell, has made of violence a primary theme, and several of our best poets have had almost nothing to say on the subject. Ralph Waldo Emerson (1803–1882) was long thought to have no grasp of radical evil or of the violence that men do when they are in the grip of evil, although it was clear that he could celebrate heroic violence, as in the service of revolution and freedom ("That memory may their deed redeem"). Walt Whitman (1819–1892) studied scenes of violence the way he studied everything: as someone eager to celebrate resilience, valor, and ordinary fortitude, and as a witness sympathetic and tender but without an appetite for retribution or for ostensibly final solutions ("The war [that war so bloody and grim, the war I will henceforth / forget] was you and me"). Herman Melville (1819–1891) regarded violence as deeply ingrained in our nature ("In Bacchic glee they file toward Fate"), but often blamed large eruptions of violence on "the champions and enthusiasts of the state" or on the credulous "boys" who fight our wars. Emily Dickinson (1830–1886) alluded more than occasionally to violence, but her taste for metaphysics, deprivation, and obliquity distracted her from any sustained engagement with physical brutality or collective struggle. Although her imagination ran to thoughts of suffering and conflict, violence for her was an abstract, deftly personified ("Death / Who drills his welcome in") and her references to "saw" and "scimitar," "rack" and "torture" are typically in the service of her concern with "soul" and efforts to "gain the sky." Of the most notable nineteenth-century American poets, only Melville may be said to have demonstrated a genuine feeling for the violence associated with the will to vengeance ("Beware the People weeping / When they bare the iron hand"), but that feeling was balanced by his attraction to the softer sentiments, including "clemency and calm," pity and "kindness."

Of course the works of the great American poets together provide some record of response to the violence they witnessed in American society and to the violence they found—often or occasionally—in their own hearts. Both Melville and Whitman were profoundly affected by the Civil War and wrote memorably about it. Others were moved to reflect on the violence associated with slavery, the brutalization of workers in factories or sweatshops. But actual, observable, unmistakable violence did not become a compelling subject for American poets until the early years of the twentieth century, and it has remained so, although *violence* is not the first word that comes to mind when one thinks of the poetry of Wallace Stevens (1879–1955) or Marianne Moore (1887–1972) or any number of other poets we most admire.

Does the violence evoked by American poets of the twentieth century fall into identifiable categories? To be sure, there are poems about abuse, incest, and unjust wars. But the relevant poems of the best poets are not reducible to such categories. They are not protest poems, and they are not narrowly topical or polemical. Typically they engage violence as an aspect of larger issues: the strange admixture of love and hate in personal relationships; the effort to sustain virtue in the face of deep-seated contradictory imperatives rooted in the blood or in cultural beliefs; the relationship between free will and historical determinism. To discuss Sylvia Plath's (1932–1963) "Daddy" as a poem about incest or abuse is to discount much of what is most important about it. To describe Elizabeth Bishop's (1911–1979) "Brazil, January 1, 1502" simply as a poem about imperialist violence is to ignore its status as a poem about the artistic imagination. Robert Lowell's (1917–1977) "Waking Early Sunday Morning" laments U.S. involvement in Vietnam and hears "the blind / swipe of the pruner and his knife / busy about the tree of life," but it has more to do with deformations of faith and conviction in late-twentieth-century America than with imperalist violence.

Although the poetry of Robert Frost (1874–1963) is frequently saturated with intimations of violence, with what he once called "assorted characters of death and blight," it is anything but a programmatic poetry of topics and position takings. "The Subverted Flower" is a poem that a reader obsessed with ideas of abuse and power and gender might well scan with an eye for grievances. In it a young woman confronts an inept young man who wishes to court her and is moved to observe in him "The demon of pursuit / That slumbers in a brute," a creature of menace "Obeying bestial laws"—or so she imagines. But the violence is entirely imagined by the impressionable young woman, and the only overt expression of violence in the poem comes from her: "And oh, for one so young / The bitter words she spit." The poem, it turns out, uses the suggestion of violence and of animal desire in order to get at its true subject, which is fear, a fear created by an exacerbated puritan ethos that has corrupted relations between people who might otherwise see in one another something "Other than base and fetid."

The violence is anything but imaginary in William Carlos Williams's (1883–1963) poem "The

Yachts." Almost from the opening we are confronted with "an ungoverned ocean which when it chooses / tortures the biggest hulls . . . / . . . and sinks them pitilessly." But this violence of the elements is more than matched by the pitiless yachts and their ruthless captains, who cannot be bothered to look after "bodies thrown recklessly in the way," who are unmoved by "a sea of faces about them in agony," those who are "beaten, desolate" and "cry out, failing, failing." Williams does not explain in his poem how these beaten creatures got into the water, but he leaves no doubt that he is evoking "the horror of the race," which is, in effect, the ordinary fallen world of injustice. In this world those who are "in the way are cut aside" and "the skillful yachts pass over." Is the poem a protest against violence or against those who are skillful and determined? It is too delighted with the sheer "feckless" abandon of the yachts to be a protest poem. Its pleasure is in bringing to life the easy ruthlessness of the powerful, so that whatever our desire to find in the poem a sympathy for the desolate and weak, we cannot but feel the surge of vitality and confidence that attends the violence.

There is no ambivalence about violence at all in Ezra Pound's (1885–1972) "Sestina: Altaforte," where the speaker declares that "I have no life save when the swords clash" and that, when "the broad fields . . . turn crimson, / Then howl I my heart nigh mad with rejoicing." Of course the speaker seems to us more than a little mad, and the extravagance of the poem—its theatrical trappings, repetitions, and hyperbolical ejaculations—prevents us from concluding that the poet himself is to be associated with the attitudes so baldly expressed. But in no other American poem is the taste for violence so naked, the celebration of "the blood's crimson" and the detestation of "womanish peace" and "frail music" so powerfully evoked.

By contrast, the violence expressed in the poems of Robinson Jeffers (1887–1962) is more austere, even principled. There is little appetite for color or spectacle, although there is a heightened theatricality in Jeffers's settings, where "Nature" and "Man" are pitted against one another in the most reductive terms. "I'd sooner, except the penalties," Jeffers declares in a characteristic poem like "Hurt Hawks," "kill a man than a hawk." After all, as he says in "Shine, Perishing Republic," we live in a time when "the cities lie at the monster's feet," and the monster is man, who pollutes and corrupts everything he touches. Jeffers prefers the cleansing, uncomplicated violence of the hawk, who is "strong," "intemperate and savage," gifted with

"implacable arrogance." His is the violence that belongs truly to instinct, that asks and needs no forgiveness. Confronted by the "fierce rush" of such a being, we can feel that violence belongs to life and is inseparable from what is most valuable in it. "Civilization," which teaches us to loathe and fear violence, is to be regarded—as in "New Mexican Mountain"—as "a transient sickness."

Jeffers's hymns to cleansing violence can often seem bloodless, abstract, and even laughable. But violence in the poetry of mid- and late-twentieth-century America is typically anything but principled, bloodless, or abstract. When, in "My Papa's Waltz," Theodore Roethke (1908–1963) writes of his drunken father dancing him off to bed, the lines "You beat time on my head / With a palm caked hard by dirt" convey an unmistakably real encounter with a brutishness that was never very far removed from violence. The same father who in other poems could be looked up to for his "manly" attributes and, sometimes, for his mystical affinities with nature was also a fearful figure.

Just so, even when violence is not openly expressed in a characteristic poem by Louise Glück (1943–), it is apt to be intimated, sensed, or feared. Preparations for lovemaking call to mind the fact that there is "so much pain in the world": a Glück "Epithalamium" evokes "a stream of cries," and a husband-to-be whose ostensibly reassuring *Here is my hand that will not harm you* is a promise of imagined or acutal impending violence. In "The Dream of Mourning" there are ever-present "thin ridges of panic," and each day brings a morning "demanding prey." Within the terms of this disposition, anything that does not look or feel like violence is apt to be illusory. The need for release from fear is very great, the sense that nothing will suffice is pervasive. Although the speaker wants to be held, loved, she cannot rid herself of the sense of violence. "Someone fucked me awake," she recalls, aware that her own sick dreams—"the sickness you control"—cannot finally be dispelled by the signs of love or lovemaking. The violence here, although it is a part of the poet's imaginative landscape, never seems abstract or made up. The poet's voice is genuine, grieving, coiled with anger and hurt. The violence she fears is undoubtedly within all of us, not always clear or palpable, but in no sense merely a figment of the poet's fevered imagination.

Violence is also a shared propensity in the work of Randall Jarrell (1914–1965), who wrote some of the most affecting war poems of any American poet in the twentieth century. Unlike many other poets who wrote of war, Jarrell saw clearly the relation between war making and ordinary peace-time life, and he used his World War II poems to study what he took to be characteristic expressions of human nature. In "Eighth Air Force," for example, he is tempted to the conclusion that man is "a wolf to man." Soldiers are casually referred to as "murderers," although they "troop in yawning" and play "like puppies with their puppy" before going out on their killing missions. The poem is saturated in pity and ambivalence. Even the italicized exclamation *"O murderers!"* has a complex ring. We feel that the speaker does not quite mean it as a final summation, that he is trying it on, letting himself discover what it feels like to address his fellow creatures in this way. It may be true, as the poet says, that "Men wash their hands, in blood, as best they can," but the combination of flat, unambiguous indictment and utterly conditional musing—"If, in an odd angle of the hutment . . .", or, "But what is lying?"—complicates the perspective of the poem and makes violence itself problematic. No doubt the poet is appalled at the violence that men do to one another, but he is far from certain about the root causes in circumstance or human nature. The man who murders is also, in the poem's final line, the one of whom the poet can say, "I find no fault in this just man." To come away from this and other poems by Jarrell is to feel the difficulty of knowing to what degree violence was for Jarrell a symptom of other forces or, in fact, the name of our desire and the source of our mortal failings.

American poetry has had one supreme poet of violence—Robert Lowell (1917–1977). From his early books on through his final works, Lowell developed a view of America as a nation built on violence, corruption, and hypocrisy. The promise of America, with its generous frontiers and its commitment to democratic practices, was at once betrayed by the Puritans' commercial zeal and religious intolerance. "Our fathers," Lowell wrote in "Children of Light," came into the new world and "fenced their gardens with the redman's bones." Fired by a spiritual arrogance, those Puritan fathers "planted here the Serpent's seeds" by using their power tyrannically and showing no modesty at all in plundering the environment—land and sea—for purposes of commercial gain. Lowell invokes the figure of Cain in examining the American heritage, and he is relentless in drawing a line that connects the Puritans to their successors in twentieth-century America, who build "riotous glass houses" and allow candles to "gutter by an empty altar." The piety of Americans who pretend to innocence and good works is a sham, according to this vision. Violence is the truth of America, and to refuse to say as much is to deny what we know.

No reader of Lowell's work can doubt that he understood violence and the intoxication associated with the reckless exercise of power. But equally evident is Lowell's sense of violence as corrupting and degrading, his inclination to a moral critique of violence—both as overt practice and as institutional norm, where it is often masked as law or custom. Even Lowell's explicitly religious poems, such as "Colloquy in Black Rock," are wracked by violent images. His Christ is "our Saviour who was hanged till death." St. Stephen is the "martyre" who "was stoned to death." Everywhere Lowell leaves emblems of violent dissolution. His own beating heart demands "more blood-gangs for your nigger-brass percussions." The devotee of Christ is himself a man possessed, in the grip of violent emotion, his head stocked with violent images that hold him in their grip.

In "The Quaker Graveyard in Nantucket," perhaps Lowell's most famous early poem, "the sea was still breaking violently," and the sailors on their whale hunt are relentless in their killing. Although penitence and quiet are built into Lowell's vision, they seem almost inconsequential beside the ghastly evocation of the hunt, itself unmistakably an emblem of American energy and blind murderousness. Knowing the answer to the question he poses, namely, "Will your sword / Whistle and fall and sink into the fat?" Lowell gives us the white whale torn and besieged:

The fat flukes arch and whack about its ears,
The death-lance churns into the sanctuary, tears
The gun-blue swingle, heaving like a flail,
And hacks the coiling life out: it works and drags
And rips the sperm-whale's midriff into rags,
Gobbets of blubber spill to wind and weather,
Sailor, and gulls go round the stoven timbers. . . .

It is impossible not to be moved by the rage and blood lust built into these lines. The momentum achieved by the sequence like "works and drags / And rips" is palpable here, and the communicated sense of transgressiveness—"churns into the sanctuary"—is miraculously of a piece with the equally impressive sensation of being caught up in something unstoppable. The sacred is clearly manifest in the figure of the whale—"Hide, / Our steel, Jonas Messias, in thy side,"—and the violence that is everywhere obvious in the founding and establishment of the American continent is clearly hideous and shameful.

The propensity to violence is also dramatized in Lowell's "Mr. Edwards and the Spider," where a Puritan preacher speaks in images full of menace and bloodlust. "It's well," Lowell's preacher intones, "If God who holds you to the pit of hell, / Much as one holds a spider, will destroy, / Baffle and dissipate your soul." The "Great God" is content to see the souls of sinners "cast / Into a brick-kiln where the blast / Fans your quick vitals to a coal—." Such poetry sharply captures the susceptibility of the American imagination to the lurid and violent and convincingly portrays the threat of a cleansing and retributive violence derived from the American sense of hard-won virtue and beleaguered innocence.

Lowell extended his portrait of things American into other precincts, evoking in less immediate terms responsibility for Hiroshima, the murder of black schoolchildren in bombed southern churches, and the ruinous investment in the Vietnam War. Without going in for blanket indictments of particular groups or policies and without lending his work to specific partisan uses, Lowell made himself a public poet who could get at what was best in the American grain—the gift for spontaneity, a continuing fascination for the pastoral and edenic, and the capacity, now and then, for forgiveness—while forcing us to come to terms with a history steeped in violence. In Lowell's later poems the violence rarely takes center stage and is rarely evoked with the visceral excitement of his early poems. But it is clear that, whatever Lowell's focus—political or historical, personal or religious, sexual or literary—violence was never far from the poet's sense of Americans' common identity.

Other American poets of the late twentieth century were now and then effective in bringing to life the propensity to violence and its sometimes intimate relation to love, awe, or the will to change. In "The Bear," Galway Kinnell (1927–) sets a trap and pursues a wounded, dying creature until, starving and exhausted, the poet picks up "a turd sopped in blood," gnashes it down, and continues on. Later, "I hack / a ravine in his thigh, and eat and drink, / and tear him down his whole length / and open him and climb in" until, in the end, to the end of his days, he wonders "what, anyway, / was that sticky infusion, that rank flavor of blood, that / poetry by which I lived?" What emerges here is a strange, compelling sense that the tame lives we contrive to lead generally distract us from what is most true about ourselves and what therefore most permits us to rise, occasionally, to the eloquence and bewilderment of poetry.

But neither Kinnell, nor the Sylva Plath who fantasizes about joining with the "villagers" to place a stake in the "fat black heart" of her persecuting, scapegoated "Daddy," nor the Ben Belitt who in "Graffiti" strikes in a frenzy of vengeance at the windows and walls of the subway bearing him to undeserved literary oblivion, develops a coherent, comprehensive vision of violence as an essential, inescapable component of American life. In the five lines of "The Death of the Ball Turret Gunner," Randall Jarrell confronts "black flak and the nightmare fighters," but the poem is not an engagement with what Jarrell takes to be a central aspect of our collective experience. We are powerfully affected by the poem's final line—"When I died they washed me out of the turret with a hose"—but the poem as a whole is highly tendentious in its underlying sense of things and does not at all elaborate or evoke the conditions of generalized violence to which it implicitly refers.

For the most part, American poets have not followed Lowell in seeing violence as the central element joining the public experience of Americans and their personal experience as men and women contending with instincts they only half understand and rarely hope to contain. In general, American novelists have been much more absorbed than poets with the task of charting the origin, allure, and consequence of violence.

BIBLIOGRAPHY

Boyers, Robert, ed. *Contemporary Poetry in America*. New York: Schocken, 1974.
Jones, Richard, ed. *Poetry and Politics*. New York: Quill, 1985.
Winters, Yvor. *In Defense of Reason*. New York: Morrow, 1947.

ROBERT BOYERS

LITTLETON SHOOTINGS. *See* Schools.

LOBOTOMY, PREFRONTAL. *See* Medicine and Violence.

LOEB, RICHARD, AND NATHAN LEOPOLD
Loeb (1905–1936); Leopold (1904–1971)

On 21 May 1924 Richard "Dickie" Loeb and Nathan "Babe" Leopold, Jr., kidnapped fourteen-year-old Bobby Franks on his way home from school. The two teenagers lured Franks into their

Nathan Leopold, Jr., left, and Richard Loeb, in July 1924. Hulton Getty/Liaison Agency

rented car, killed him with a chisel, and drove his body to a deserted marshland near the Indiana state line. The body was left naked in a culvert and covered with acid. Leopold's glasses, made with a unique hinge and traceable to a single optometrist in Chicago, were found near the dead boy's body and provided the key piece of physical evidence that foiled the pair's plan to commit the perfect crime. The investigations of the *Chicago Daily News* led to the initial connection between the unidentified body (initially believed to have been drowned) and the kidnapping.

Loeb and Leopold were sons of prominent Jewish families, neighbors of the Franks, and residents of the affluent Hyde Park-Kenwood area, home of the University of Chicago. At the time of the crime, both were attending the university: Loeb, then only eighteen, was doing graduate work in history, and the nineteen-year-old Leopold was a law student. Loeb's charisma and daring found theoretical inspiration and grounding in Leopold's obsession with Nietzsche's concept of the "superman."

The sensationalism surrounding the trial was fed by the brutality of the crime, the youth of the criminals and their obsession with each other, and undercurrents of anti-Semitism. The twelve-hour defense summation by the noted attorney Clarence Darrow was a passionate argument against the death penalty. In September of 1924 the teenagers were found guilty of murder and kidnapping and sentenced to life in prison plus ninety-nine years.

In 1936 Loeb was stabbed to death by another inmate, who claimed that Loeb had made sexual advances toward him; Leopold was released in 1958 and moved to Puerto Rico. He died in 1971.

The irrational motivations and the sexual innuendoes surrounding the 1924 case have inspired numerous literary, stage, and screen interpretations. Hitchcock's *Rope* (1948), composed of eight-minute-long takes edited together to produce the nearly perfect illusion of a single shot, imagined the murderers as the troubled products of New York City high society. Influenced by the Nietzschean theories of their boarding school mentor, Rupert Cadell (James Stewart), Brandon Shaw and Philip Morgan strangle an intellectually inferior associate, hide his body in a chest in their living room, and hold a dinner party, impudently serving dinner on the chest. Their guest list includes the murdered man's father and fiancée. Meyer Levin's best-selling novel *Compulsion* (1956) fictionalized the case history and was later adapted for the stage and screen; the 1959 film version of Levin's novel, featuring Orson Welles as the defense attorney, focuses on the psychological unraveling of the murderers in the interval between the crime and the trial. The film only delicately alludes to their homosexuality, a subject more directly scrutinized in Tom Kalin's low-budget, black-and-white film *Swoon* (1992), a highly stylized and unconventional treatment. John Logan's stage version, *Never the Sinner*, opened in London in 1990 and was produced in the Maryland-Northern Virginia area by the Signature and Rep Stage companies in 1997.

BIBLIOGRAPHY

Fass, Paula S. "Making and Remaking an Event: The Leopold and Loeb Case in American Culture." *Journal of American History* (December 1993).
Higdon, Hal. *The Crime of the Century: The Leopold and Loeb Case.* New York: Putnam, 1975.
Linder, Douglas O. "The Leopold and Loeb Trial: A Brief Account." URL:http://www.law.umkc.edu/faculty/projects/ftrials/leoploeb/LEOPOLD.HTM.
Weiler, A. H. "Compulsion." *New York Times*, 2 April 1959.

TEMBY CAPRIO

See also **Teenagers; Thrill Crime.**

LONG, HUEY
(1893–1935)

"I'm a cinch to get shot," the Louisiana populist Huey Pierce Long once admitted during his only term as governor. Long surrounded himself with a colorful bevy of bodyguards, mainly ex-prize-fighters and hangers-on, one of whom used to carry a sawed-off shotgun in a paper bag with a hole punched in it for his trigger finger. Long himself went armed with a small revolver whenever venturing into a crowd. Despite the armament, Long was gunned down in the skyscraper state capitol he had erected to monumentalize his own power.

Dough-faced pudgy, with a fondness for loud clothes and a knack for grabbing headlines, Long liked to call himself the "Kingfish," after a character in the popular radio program *Amos 'n' Andy*. The sobriquet hinted at Long's boundless ambition, and indeed he amassed a degree of political power unprecedented in American history.

Long's political rise was meteoric: an elected seat on a state regulatory body by age twenty-five; the governorship ten years later; election to the U.S. Senate two years after that (although he postponed assuming his seat for nearly another two years). During the early years of the New Deal, Long launched a nationwide mass movement called "Share Our Wealth" that likely would have materialized into a serious third-party presidential run had an assassin's bullet not intervened.

There is disagreement about whether Long was a physical coward. But no one disputes that his stormy style landed him in one brawl after another, starting in the schoolyards of the small farming community of Winnfield where he grew up and continuing on the streets of Shreveport where he once practiced law. The assaults stepped up after he entered politics. In 1927 he got into a fistfight with a corpulent former governor in the lobby and elevator of a posh New Orleans hotel. On the floor of the U.S. Senate a septuagenarian lawmaker from Virginia had to be physically restrained from attacking Long. Huey's arsenal of barnyard epithets had a way of getting under opponents' skins.

It was the Louisiana ruling class whom Long most provoked. They hated him as much for what he did as for what he said. Unlike other southern demagogues, Huey delivered real social goods to the underlying population and raised taxes on corporations (mainly oil and gas companies like Standard Oil) and upper income groups. As his program took hold, Huey Long drew the growing wrath of Louisiana's ruling groups. By 1934 threats of violence had become commonplace. That May, armed anti-Longites descended on Baton Rouge in an abortive coup attempt. The following month, at a mass rally in the capital that drew thousands, the mayor of Shreveport invoked the ancient methods of Reconstruction: "If it is necessary for us to teach them fairness and justice at the end of the hempen rope, I, for one, am ready to swing that rope."

All too aware of elite predilections toward violence, Long surpassed his enemies in his readiness to deploy force. (The only former Louisiana governor whom Long respected was the carpetbagger Henry Clay Warmoth, another practitioner of power politics.) In August 1934, for example, without court authorization or the declaration of martial law, Long ordered his puppet governor to have the state militia seize the New Orleans registration books, so as to ensure the election of a Long candidate to the state supreme court.

Long was shot on 8 September 1935, during a whirlwind trip to Baton Rouge to oversee a special legislative session that had been called to augment his already formidable power. Long's assailant was a prominent Baton Rouge physician named Carl Weiss, who was married to the daughter of an anti-Long judge. Weiss died on the spot after Long's bodyguards riddled him with bullets. Long died of his wounds on 10 September.

A portrait of Huey P. Long. LIBRARY OF CONGRESS

287

Political Violence in Louisiana at the Turn of the Twentieth Century

In no other state had an oligarchy of big agrarian and big urban property, working in tandem with the conservative political machine in New Orleans, the state capital, pressed down so hard as in Louisiana. What is more, the elite were long habituated to employing political violence to defend their interests. During Reconstruction they resorted to racial terrorism to liquidate biracial government. During the Populist insurgency of the 1890s, they used intimidation and ballot box fraud to turn back that agrarian challenge.

Among the New Orleans upper crust a tradition of silk-stocking vigilantism had held sway since the 1874 Battle of Canal Street (later rechristened the Battle of Liberty Place), which momentarily toppled the Reconstruction state government. Every four years thereafter, young white gentlemen often formed rifle clubs and marched on the polling places to defend the sanctity of the ballot box. In 1891 a mob of gentlemen lynched eleven Sicilian immigrants after a local court acquitted them of involvement in the alleged Mafia slaying of the city police chief.

BIBLIOGRAPHY

Brinkley, Alan. *Voices of Protest: Huey Long, Father Coughlin, and the Great Depression.* New York: Knopf, 1982.

Hair, William Ivy. *The Kingfish and His Realm: The Life and Times of Huey P. Long.* Baton Rouge and London: Louisiana State University Press, 1991.

Williams, T. Harry. *Huey Long.* New York: Knopf, 1969.

LAWRENCE N. POWELL

See also **New Orleans; Politics.**

LONG WALK OF THE NAVAJO

After suffering defeat at the hands of U.S. troops in 1864, the Navajo tribe in the New Mexico Territory was forced to endure a torturous, three-hundred-mile walk from its ancestral homeland at Canyon de Chelly to a small reservation at Bosque Redondo. This Long Walk has been remembered as an especially notorious example of American cruelty to the Indians.

In 1846 the United States and the Navajo signed their first treaty, which called for lasting peace. In 1851 government troops built Fort Defiance in the heart of Navajo country in an effort to end the persistent slave raids and retaliatory strikes between the Navajo and the Mexicans, now considered U.S. citizens. (Mexicans raided Navajo villages for slave children, and Navajos retaliated.) Far from curtailing the violence, however, the troops became a fresh source of conflict. The presence of the fort quickly led to territorial disputes and skirmishes between the Navajo and the soldiers. These clashes culminated in an 1860 attack by the Navajo, who nearly overwhelmed the troops at Fort Defiance. The attack was led by Manuelito, a Navajo who had been appointed "official chief" by the governor of New Mexico five years earlier but who had gained the respect of his tribe through his defiance of U.S. officials.

When General James Henry Carleton assumed command of the New Mexico Territory in 1862, he sought to address Navajo resistance by forcing them to relocate, insisting that he would never negotiate with the Indians. Colonel Christopher "Kit" Carson and the First New Mexico Volunteers moved into Fort Defiance and commenced a "scorched earth" policy, forcing the Navajos into submission by destroying their villages, wells, crops, and livestock. Having crushed the rebellion by early 1864, Carson began the eastward transfer of the Navajo despite minimal supplies, lack of clothing, and continual kidnappings by Mexican slave raiders.

The historian Dee Brown has estimated from officers' reports that of the nearly five thousand Navajo who made the Long Walk in March 1864, one in ten died from blizzard conditions, starvation, disease, and harsh treatment by the soldiers. During the ensuing summer many more Navajo followed; all together, nine thousand Navajo made the forced march to an ill-provisioned, forty-square-mile reservation at Bosque Redondo, where their suffering continued unabated. Many escaped and returned to Canyon de Chelly, joining others who had avoided the Long Walk and had eluded the soldiers' pursuit. Manuelito was one such holdout, though he finally surrendered in 1866. Carson's troops attempted to curb this flight by threatening to kill any Navajo found outside the reservation.

By 1868 the policies at Bosque Redondo had received such widespread criticism from New Mexican civilians and government reviews that a peace commission, which included Lieutenant General William Tecumseh Sherman, negotiated a treaty

Manuelito and his wife, Juanita, in 1882. PHOTO BY BEN WITTICK. COURTESY MUSEUM OF NEW MEXICO, NEG. NO. 16332

that sought to end the frontier violence with Manuelito and the Navajo. The Navajo returned to Canyon de Chelly, though they regained only a tenth of the land they had once inhabited. There are tragic parallels between the Long Walk of the Navajo and the Trail of Tears, the forced removal of five southeastern Indian tribes (Cherokee, Chickasaw, Choctaw, Creek, and Seminole) to Oklahoma during the 1830s.

BIBLIOGRAPHY

Bailey, L. R. *The Long Walk*. Los Angeles: Westernlore, 1964.

Brown, Dee. *Bury My Heart at Wounded Knee: An Indian History of the American West*. New York: Holt, Rinehart and Winston, 1970.

Trafzer, Clifford E. *The Kit Carson Campaign: The Last Great Navajo War*. Norman: University of Oklahoma Press, 1982.

CAROLYN EASTMAN

See also **American Indians; Trail of Tears.**

LOS ANGELES

The California metropolis of Los Angeles, encompassing the city proper (1990 population, 3.6 million) and Los Angeles County (1990 population, 9.1 million), has many associations with violence, but (as urban areas go) it is not distinctively violent as a local setting, except in the fact that it is the most prolific global producer of discursive violence. A look at violence in Los Angeles broken down by type—interpersonal violence, collective violence, and discursive violence—helps demonstrate this reality.

Interpersonal Violence

Interpersonal violence includes all forms of physical violence committed by and between individuals through relatively isolated motivations of malice, passion, or criminal gain. The two most serious forms of interpersonal violence are murder and aggravated assault, and an analysis of Los Angeles County statistics compared to other urban counties in the United States bears out the popular prejudice about Los Angeles as a violent place—but only on average. In 1995 the nation's twenty largest counties (with populations ranging from 1.4 million to 9.1 million) had an average murder rate (per 100,000 population) of 12.3, and Los Angeles County, the most populous county in the United States, ranked seventh among them, with a murder rate of 14 per 100,000 population. In the same year, Los Angeles County ranked third among the twenty largest U.S. counties in terms of its aggravated assault rate (403.1). In order to understand these figures in context, however, it is necessary to understand that large urban centers are by no means the most violent places in the United States. The fifty counties with the highest murder rates had a median population of only 16,865, and the murder rate for Los Angeles County ranked 368 among the 3,145 counties in 1995.

Collective Violence

Collective violence is committed by multiple individuals as members of groups, motivated by reasons directly associated with perceptions of justice or power regarding those groups. Possibly the most distinctive form of urban violence is the riot. American cities experienced mainly class-charged riots during the Revolutionary War period and during the depressions of the 1840s, 1870s, and 1890s, but beginning in the Civil War era riots in

U.S. cities came to hinge on race as often as on class, and after 1900, most U.S. urban riots pitted groups against each other on the issue of race alone.

The city of Los Angeles experienced a major race riot in 1871, when white residents, acting on rumor of an alleged crime perpetrated by a Chinese immigrant, rampaged in the Chinatown section and indiscriminately lynched nineteen Chinese. That Los Angeles riot was essentially typical of a wider wave of collective anti-Asian violence on the West Coast. No further major riots took place in Los Angeles until the notorious Zoot-Suit Riot of 1943. Off-duty U.S. sailors and servicemen, angered by the symbolic rebellion of Latino youths dressed in zoot-suits, accosted, beat, and stripped alleged "pachucos" (gang members) for several days while the police either refused to interfere or abetted the attacks. This incident was sparked by similar wartime tensions that characterized outbreaks in Detroit and Harlem: mainly overheated patriotic fervor that spilled over into domestic race tensions. The war had mobilized large migrations of minorities, and both whites and nonwhites experienced perceived injustices during the process.

The riot that took place in the predominantly African American Watts section of South Central Los Angeles from 11 to 17 August 1965 represented the largest of hundreds of such riots that shook the foundations of social order in the United States in the 1960s. The Watts riot was set off by reports of a police beating of a community member during an arrest. Thirty-four people died (twenty-eight of them African American), and perhaps as many as fifty thousand people participated in some fashion in the week-long fury of looting and burning directed against white-owned businesses and the Los Angeles police. The violence in this riot was highly lopsided: the rioters mainly attacked property (with damage estimated at $40 million), while the police counter-attacked the rioters. Thus, officially sanctioned violence was responsible for the large number of deaths.

The scale of the Watts riots was unsurpassed until 1992, when rioting in Los Angeles was sparked by the news that four white police officers had been acquitted in their criminal trial for the 1991 videotaped beating of the black motorist Rodney King. The upheaval lasted from 29 April to 5 May, and fifty-five people died and twenty-three hundred were injured before it was quelled. The violence of the "Rodney King riots" spread far beyond the relatively poor South Central district to the wealthy Westside and Hollywood districts. More than ten thousand people were arrested, 51 percent of them Latino and 36 percent black. The majority of the victims, however, were Latino and Asian.

In its pattern of violence—primarily black on Latino and black on Korean—the 1992 Los Angeles rioting marked both a continuation of and a departure from the national pattern of "ghetto riots" of the 1960s, 1970s, and 1980s. Although the riots were sparked by anger that an all-white group of policemen was acquitted by an all-white jury in a mostly white suburban jurisdiction, that anger ultimately was vented on Latinos, who were perceived as displacing blacks in employment opportunities, and Korean shopkeepers, who allegedly refused to hire blacks and mistreated black customers. This seeming revival of what might be termed ecological riots occurred on a smaller scale in cities such as Miami and New York throughout the 1980s and 1990s; thus the violence in Los Angeles again appeared symptomatic of a more national stress—in this case, interethnic stress likely traceable to the massive surge in immigration that followed the loosening of immigration laws in 1965.

Also indirectly related to immigration is the gang-related violence that rapidly increased in the 1980s and 1990s, attracting national attention to Los Angeles as a possible leader and even exporter of this kind of violence. Law-enforcement agencies estimated about four hundred gangs with forty-five hundred members in Los Angeles County in 1985 and as many as nine hundred gangs with one hundred thousand members by 1991. Estimates also indicated about 650 gang-related homicides in 1990 and an average of 350 per year from 1987 to 1997 for Los Angeles County. Gang-related homicide rates add significantly to the overall murder rates for Los Angeles.

Youth gangs, with or without illegal drug trade, have been a typical feature of working-class immigrant neighborhood development since the early nineteenth century. Given the role of Los Angeles in the late twentieth century as the leading immigrant metropolis, it naturally has a very high number of youth gangs along the edges of its many hundreds of working-class ethnic enclaves. The violence associated with these gangs increased sharply in the 1990s; the most direct explanation for this escalation is that it was fueled by global circuits of illegal narcotics (especially crack cocaine) in the late 1980s and early 1990s. Propelled by the financial incentives of the traffic in drugs, relatively harmless youth gangs were transformed into small territorial combat units armed with military-issue automatic weapons.

Los Angeles gangs are loosely organized into one of two dominant federations: the most numerous "Crips" (who wear blue markers) and the far smaller "Bloods" (who wear red markers). The basic gang unit is a "clique" or "set" composed of only a few score young men who defend territories averaging only twenty or so city blocks. The ubiquity of gang graffiti in the urban landscape, coupled with the nearly constant coverage of gang violence in print and on television, gives gang violence an importance far beyond its actual rate of occurrence. New York City experienced similar patterns during these same decades.

Discursive Violence

Discursive violence describes all representations of violence circulated in the media of public discourse. The vast majority of discursive violence is produced in the media industry of Los Angeles. Reliable studies during the 1990s estimated that by age eighteen the average American child has watched two hundred thousand acts of violence and forty thousand murders on television and at the movies. Children's television programming alone contains over thirty violent acts per hour. While nearly all of these violent acts and murders are of course fictional, the numbers are staggering and the implications are appalling. Although the relationship between discursive violence and physical violence is not well understood, the National Institute of Mental Health has stated that violence on television leads to aggressive behavior by children and teenagers who watch violent television programs.

The vast majority of discursive violence is produced in the media industry centered in Los Angeles. What can be said about the role of Los Angeles, as an urban place, in the creation of this discursive violence? The Los Angeles–based producers and authors of mass media are primarily well-educated white males born and raised in all regions of the United States (although a significant number come from Great Britain). While these creators of discursive violence undoubtedly draw much of their "material" from the surrounding environment of Los Angeles, it is clear that they draw

more generally on the experience and culture of the United States at large. Since we have seen that the levels of interpersonal and collective violence of Los Angeles is mostly typical of large U.S. urban places, the discursive violence cannot be seen as a unique emanation and export from the physical environment of Los Angeles. Instead, Los Angeles plays the role of a magnifying glass for a violent nation. Violence is here converted artistically and scientifically into a discursive commodity (perhaps the industry's most valuable). Los Angeles is unique only in that it distills representationally the violent content of the society at large and distributes it worldwide.

BIBLIOGRAPHY

Jankowski, Martín Sánchez. *Islands in the Street: Gangs and American Urban Society.* Berkeley: University of California Press, 1991.

Mazón, Mauricio. *The Zoot-Suit Riots: The Psychology of Symbolic Annihilation.* Austin: University of Texas Press, 1984.

Pitt, Leonard, and Dale Pitt. *Los Angeles A to Z: An Encyclopedia of the City and County.* Berkeley: University of California Press, 1997.

PHILIP J. ETHINGTON

See also **Los Angeles Times Building, Bombing of; Police: Police Brutality; Race and Ethnicity; Riots; Simpson, O. J., Murder Trials; Urban Violence; Zoot-Suit Riot.**

LOS ANGELES RIOTS OF 1992

On 29 April 1992 a jury in the Los Angeles suburb of Simi Valley acquitted four white Los Angeles police officers of ten of eleven felony charges stemming from the notorious videotaped beating of Rodney King, an African American. In South Central Los Angeles the verdicts ignited disorders that became the nation's deadliest riots of the twentieth century. During the next five days fifty-four people died in riot-related incidents in Los Angeles County and another 2,328 were injured—the highest toll in a U.S. riot since the Draft Riots of 1863 in New York City and far greater than in the 1965 Watts Riot where thirty-four people died. Property losses in the 1992 riots exceeded $900 million, with 862 structures destroyed by fire. By the time police and the National Guard had restored order, poor neighborhoods throughout South Central, Koreatown, the mid-Wilshire area, and Long Beach were devastated—left without even grocery stores or drugstores.

Racial tensions that had been building for years in Los Angeles were sharply aggravated by the King incident. King, intoxicated and recently released from prison, had ignored police sirens and led the California Highway Patrol on a 7.8-mile chase on freeways and city streets. He said later he did not pull over because he feared being returned to prison for violating his parole. King was finally stopped on a roadside in the early morning hours of 3 March 1991. Sergeant Stacey Koon from the Los Angeles Police Department (LAPD) took charge and at first tried to arrest him peaceably. But King threw four officers who tried to handcuff him off his back and twice rose to his feet after being hit with two volleys of electronic darts that Koon fired from a stun gun. When King rose the second time, he charged toward Officer Laurence Powell, who wildly swung his metal baton and struck King in the head. As King writhed and rolled on the ground, Powell and his rookie partner repeatedly hit him with their batons, more than fifty blows in all, and kicked him until he submitted.

The beating was videotaped by amateur cameraman George Holliday from the balcony of his apartment across the street. Holliday's eighty-one-second videotape began with the frame in which King lunged at Powell, but KTLA, the Los Angeles television station to which Holliday took his video, deleted the first thirteen seconds, ostensibly to remove blurry footage. The edited tape, which magnified the impact of the brutal incident, was played repeatedly on local and national television. It caused a reaction, as a federal prosecutor subsequently put it, of "horror and outrage . . . from Paris to Tokyo."

The incident occurred in an explosive context. The LAPD's critics had long accused it of using force too readily, and civil lawsuits against the department had been multiplying. LAPD Chief Daryl Gates said the police used batons and guns because the city's political leaders had banned the chokehold and refused to provide the department with various nonlethal weapons. Mayor Tom Bradley blamed Gates. On 9 July 1991 the mayor appointed a commission headed by the influential Los Angeles attorney Warren Christopher (later, U.S. secretary of state), which found that Gates insufficiently disciplined officers who repeatedly engaged in excessive force or racism and called for the chief's retirement.

The Christopher Commission report added new fuel to the fire in a city suffering its worst economic downturn since the Great Depression. As ethnic tensions increased, Korean grocers were frequent targets of violence. In a convenience store in South Central thirteen days after the King beating, a fifteen-year-old African American named Latasha

Los Angeles police officers halt a man found looting in South Central Los Angeles during the 1992 riots. REUTERS/LEE CELANO/ARCHIVE PHOTOS

Harlins was shot in the back of the head and killed by a Korean grocer, Soon Ja Du, who mistakenly thought she was shoplifting. The incident was videotaped on an in-store camera, and Du was convicted of voluntary manslaughter by a jury. The presiding judge gave the grocer probation. This light sentence incensed African Americans and was a contributing factor to the tensions that led to the riots, in which many Korean-owned stores were targeted.

The judiciary also contributed to the tensions. An appeals court ignored precedents and directed that the officers involved in the King case be tried outside Los Angeles and its media market. Judge Stanley Weisberg kept the trial in the same media market by moving it to neighboring Ventura County. With no blacks on the jury, prosecutors were at a disadvantage that was enhanced when the unedited videotape was played repeatedly. Jurors accepted the defense's contention that the officers had followed LAPD policy and that King was to blame for what had happened.

Gates and Bradley had anticipated convictions, and the verdicts caught them napping. The LAPD leadership had ignored warnings from its own ranks to prepare for riots, and the department's elite Metro unit was scattered. Gates abandoned his post to attend a political event, and Bradley denounced the verdicts in an inflammatory speech. Outnumbered LAPD officers retreated from the riot flashpoint at Florence and Normandie Avenues, and television soon showed horrific scenes of white, Latino, and Asian drivers and passengers being pulled from cars and beaten by African Americans. Although many victims were subsequently rescued by other African Americans, few of these scenes were televised.

The riots were a series of disorders. The first hours were a cry of black rage. When the LAPD reacted slowly, persons of all races and ethnic groups joined in looting unguarded stores. Although long-established Latino neighborhoods in East Los Angeles remained quiet, recent immigrants from Central America participated heavily in the looting.

Afterward, an outside commission headed by former Federal Bureau of Investigation director William Webster and the former Newark police chief Hubert Williams concluded that the riots could have been quickly contained by prompt police action. An internal LAPD study, never released, reached a similar conclusion. The Webster-Williams study also faulted Bradley for not using his emergency powers.

As a result of the riots, the four officers involved in the King incident were tried again, this time on federal civil rights charges. Koon and Powell were convicted and served prison terms. This verdict was also clouded because some jurors acknowledged they were fearful of another riot if no convictions were returned. Soon after the riots, Los Angeles voters approved a city charter amendment limiting the terms of police chiefs and giving the civilian Board of Police Commissioners greater authority over the LAPD.

BIBLIOGRAPHY

Cannon, Lou. *Official Negligence: How Rodney King and the Riots Changed Los Angeles and the LAPD.* New York: Times Books, 1997.

Independent Commission on the Los Angeles Police Department (the Christopher Commission). 9 July 1991.

Webster, William H., and Hubert Williams. "The City in Crisis: A Report by the Special Advisor to the Board of Police Commissioners on the Civil Disorder in Los Angeles." 21 October 1992.

Whitman, David. "The Untold Story of the LA Riot." *U.S. News and World Report.* 31 May 1993.

LOU CANNON

See also **Civil Disorder; Draft Riots; Los Angeles; Police Brutality; Riots; Watts Riot.**

LOS ANGELES TIMES BUILDING, BOMBING OF

At six minutes past one on the morning of 1 October 1910, a powerful explosion rocked the *Los Angeles Times* building in downtown Los Angeles. The explosion blasted the building apart, and ink stored in an adjacent alley shot through the stairwells like napalm. Within minutes, the entire building was aflame, as terrified newspaper workers leaped from windows to the streets below amid cries of "Nets! Get nets! Nets!" Firemen and bystanders saved some, others either never had a chance or died on the ground. Twenty-one people died in the inferno.

Within hours, the *Los Angeles Times* published a special issue, utilizing auxiliary presses nearby. The paper's owners left little doubt as to their interpretation of the explosion. "Unionist Bombs Wreck the *Times*," screamed the bold headline. "Many lives were jeopardized and half a million dollars' worth of property was sacrificed on the altar of hatred of the labor unions at 1 o'clock this morning, when the plant of the Los Angeles *Times* was blown up and burned, following numerous threats by laborites."

Others countered that the *Times* building had been leaking gas for weeks, that the explosion had been the tragic result of the building's poor condition, and that the paper's owners were at fault. But that interpretation lost force once two unexploded bombs—"infernal machines," the *Times* called them—were discovered at the homes of Harrison Gray Otis, owner and publisher of the *Times*, and Felix Zeehanderlaar, secretary of the city's powerful Merchants and Manufacturers Association. Meanwhile, Los Angeles residents milled around the smoking ruins of the *Times* building as firemen brought victims out in wicker caskets. Within days, the event had been termed the Crime of the Century, and the hunt was on for the perpetrators.

While the *Times* bombing could not have been predicted, it is clear that labor relations in Los Angeles were anything but peaceful. Ironically, on the very day that the *Times* building blew up, the Los Angeles Chamber of Commerce had issued one of its innumerable booster pamphlets about the city.

Titled *Los Angeles Today*, the small booklet extolled the city's beauty and its business potential: "Unparalleled in growth and energy. . . one of the most enterprising business cities in the world." Under the heading "A Few Things We Want You to Know," the pamphlet added, "Los Angeles is not dominated by labor unions."

But between the lines lay a story of desperate struggle between the forces of big capital and big labor. The *Times*, in partnership with the Merchants and Manufacturers Association (M and M), had waged war against organized labor for years. Otis of the *Times*, along with his son-in-law and heir apparent, Harry Chandler, were among the most powerful supporters of the open shop in the West, if not the nation. Recent transit strikes in the city had provoked more trouble as labor unions and officials squared off against the *Times* and other business forces. An antipicketing ordinance had been passed by the city council in the summer of 1910, which served to harden antagonisms further.

Los Angeles officials and the owners of the *Times* mounted an extraordinary and expensive manhunt. William J. Burns, the nation's best-known detective, was hired to search for clues and perpetrators. A year's worth of work resulted in

After the bombing of the *Los Angeles Times* Building on 1 October 1910. THIS ITEM IS REPRODUCED BY PERMISSION OF THE HUNTINGTON LIBRARY, SAN MARINO, CALIFORNIA.

the capture of three alleged conspirators. One, Ortie McManigal, turned state's evidence in exchange for leniency. The others, brothers from the Midwest, pled not guilty to the charge of planning and executing the destruction of the *Times* building. John Joseph McNamara, treasurer of the Bridge and Structural Iron Workers Union, was a respected labor leader. His brother, James Barnabus McNamara, was an itinerant printer.

Across the nation, labor leaders sponsored a huge campaign in support of the McNamaras and their innocence. A legal defense fund paid Clarence Darrow to defend the McNamaras. Darrow's team included Job Harriman, who was running a tight race for mayor of Los Angeles on a Socialist ticket. Just as the trial was to get underway, Darrow stunned the country when he rose in court to change the brothers' plea to guilty. James McNamara admitted to placing a suitcase filled with sixteen sticks of dynamite and a detonation device in the alley behind the *Times* building. The brothers received long prison sentences in exchange for their plea. Harriman lost the race for mayor, perhaps in part because of his association with the guilty conspirators.

Much about the *Times* bombing remains obscure, particularly the intrigue surrounding the trial and the changed plea. Darrow allegedly countenanced the bribery of a juror in the case; he was acquitted of the charge in his own celebrated trial. Lincoln Steffens, the muckraking journalist, played some role in the McNamara trial, apparently trying to broker a peace between labor and capital. It seems clear that there were plenty of closed-door meetings surrounding the change in plea, but actual evidence of exactly what transpired is murky. James McNamara probably saved his life by pleading guilty; his brother, who had superintended a number of sabotage efforts across the Midwest for years, might have done the same. Just exactly what role other labor leaders, particularly from San Francisco, played in the drama remains uncertain.

BIBLIOGRAPHY

Cowan, Geoffrey. *The People v. Clarence Darrow: The Bribery Trial of America's Greatest Lawyer.* New York: Times Books, 1993.

Gottlieb, Bob, and Irene Wolt. *Thinking Big: The Story of the Los Angeles Times, Its Publishers, and Their Influence on Southern California.* New York: Putnam, 1977.

WILLIAM DEVERELL

See also **Bombings and Bomb Scares; Labor and Unions.**

LUCAS, HENRY LEE
(1932–)

From an early age, violence was woven into the life of Henry Lee Lucas. Threaded through his existence as well was a penchant for lying. For years law enforcement experts have debated the truthfulness of many of Lucas's confessions. There is no doubt that Lucas is a murderer, but the number of his victims is open to question, depending on which of his wildly divergent accounts one chooses to believe.

Cruelty and abuse were not uncommon in Lucas's impoverished Blacksburg, Virginia, childhood. His mother, a prostitute, had sex with her clients in front of Lucas and his siblings. She also dressed Lucas in girls' clothing and curled his hair into ringlets on his first day of school. When her son became attached to a pet mule, she killed the animal with a shotgun. When Lucas made the mistake of not fetching firewood fast enough, his mother punished him with a beating that rendered him semiconscious for three days.

In his teens Lucas had sex with his half brother as well as with animals, sometimes slitting the animals' throats during the act. He may have committed his first murder at the age of fifteen while attempting to rape a seventeen-year-old girl. His first clearly documented murder occurred nine years later when, in January 1960, he stabbed his mother to death.

For this crime, Lucas served ten years of a forty-year sentence. He was released in 1970 as part of an attempt to ease overcrowding in the prison. He apparently committed most of his murders in the subsequent thirteen years, although the details of these crimes are sometimes difficult to reconstruct. What we do know is that after an arrest for gun possession in June 1983, Lucas told a jailer, "I've done some bad things," and then he began a series of confessions. When he was done, he had admitted to over three hundred murders, many of them committed with the help of Ottis Toole, his sometime lover. Together, they found their victims as they traveled along highways across the southern states. Their murders were usually accompanied by rape and, in Toole's case, by cannibalism.

Some of Lucas's confessions included details that confirmed his accounts. In other cases he was clearly lying, such as the time he confessed to murdering someone who later turned out to be alive. At his most fanciful, he told a tale about supplying the poison for the 1978 Jonestown, Guyana, massacre. Sifting through this mixed bag of confirmed, probable, and clearly spurious stories, police officials have arrived at various counts of total killings by Lucas, ranging from 69 to 199.

The most compelling evidence led to Lucas's conviction on ten murder charges, for one of which he was sentenced to die by lethal injection. His death sentence was commuted in June 1998 by Governor George Bush because the evidence left some room for doubt. Stirring up controversy even further, Lucas then recanted the vast majority of his confessions, eventually claiming that he was guilty of killing only his mother.

In 1990 film writer and director John McNaughton did his own research into Lucas's unreliable statements and conjured up a harrowing fictionalized version of the case entitled *Henry: Portrait of a Serial Killer.*

BIBLIOGRAPHY

Cox, Mike. *The Confessions of Henry Lee Lucas.* New York: Ivy, 1991.
Newton, Michael. *Hunting Humans.* Port Townsend, Wash.: Loompanics, 1990.
Norris, Joel. *Henry Lee Lucas.* New York: Zebra, 1991.

DAVID EVERITT

See also **Serial Killers.**

LUCIANO, "LUCKY"
(1897–1962)

Charles "Lucky" Luciano was one of the most important gangsters in the history of organized crime in the United States. In 1931 Luciano eliminated the remaining leaders of the Sicilian-style Mafia and created what historians refer to as the American Mafia. Also at that time Luciano, along with the Jewish mobster Meyer Lansky, is credited with founding the American Mafia's "parent" organization, the national crime syndicate, a network of multiethnic criminal gangs that ruled organized crime for more than half a century.

Luciano was born Salvatore Luciana near the Sicilian city of Palermo and immigrated to New York City with his parents in 1906. Luciano soon started his first racket. For a penny or two a day, he reportedly offered younger and smaller youths his personal protection against beatings on the way to school; if they did not pay, he provided the beating himself. A chronic truant, Luciano quit school at fourteen and began peddling narcotics

for the violent Five Points gang. While a member of this group, Luciano reportedly became an expert with an ice pick, a bat, and a gun. Although he was named as a prime suspect in several murders, he was never convicted.

After he left the Five Points gang, Luciano caught the attention of the leaders of New York's underworld. In the late 1920s he became the chief aide to Giuseppe "Joe the Boss" Masseria, who controlled the largest Italian Mafia family in New York City. But Luciano had nothing but contempt for Masseria's devotion to the Old World Mafia ways—respect and honor for the boss and distrust and hatred of all non-Sicilians. Luciano thought that such prejudices created an unnecessary obstacle to making profits.

Luciano arranged for the murder of Masseria in 1928, but the actual murder was committed in 1931, along with the murder of Masseria's successor, Salvatore Maranzano. Maranzano's death essentially finished the "old Mafia" in the United States. Its remnants were incorporated into the new national crime syndicate by Luciano and Meyer Lansky. Luciano's syndicate quickly took control of the bootlegging, prostitution, narcotics, gambling, loan-sharking, and labor rackets.

"Lucky" Luciano, in 1936. CORBIS/BETTMANN

As the leader of this new crime syndicate, Luciano was known as a fancy dresser and habitué of Broadway. A menacing scar—the result of a 1929 kidnapping attempt in which his knife-wielding abductors severed the muscles in his right cheek, leaving him with a profile-length gash and an infamous droop in his right eye—added to Luciano's mystique. Although Luciano had originally been nicknamed Lucky for his success in craps, it was surviving that attack that made the moniker stick.

In 1936 Luciano was convicted of running a prostitution ring in New York and sentenced to thirty to fifty years in prison. He continued to run the syndicate from behind bars and from Italy, to which he was deported in 1946. With the assassination of Albert Anastasia in 1957 and the forced retirement of Frank Costello, both partners in the syndicate, Luciano's influence began to wane. He died of a heart attack at the Naples airport in 1962.

BIBLIOGRAPHY

Feder, Sid, and Joachim Joesten. *The Luciano Story.* New York: McKay, 1954.

Fox, Stephen P. *Blood and Power: Organized Crime in Twentieth-Century America.* New York: Morrow, 1989.

Humbert, Nelli S. *The Business of Crime: Italians and Syndicate Crime in the United States.* New York: Oxford University Press, 1976.

Peterson, Virgil W. *The Mob: 200 Years of Organized Crime in New York.* Ottawa, Ill.: Green Hill, 1983.

NANCY A. BANKS

See also **Lansky, Meyer; Mafia; Organized Crime.**

LYNCHING

Lynching is a term applied to various forms of summary punishment inflicted by self-appointed groups without regard to established legal procedures. Because the word *lynching* has been applied to nonlethal punishments, such as whipping, as well as to brutal executions, its definition has been neither precise nor stable. Lynching is not uniquely American; examples of summary justice include the murder of alleged witches in early modern Europe, pogroms in czarist Russia, and vigilante violence in contemporary Brazil. Lynching, however, has been conspicuous throughout American history and figures prominently in the regional identities of the American South and West. So commonplace were lynchings that Mark Twain, with his characteristic sarcasm, renamed the country the "United States of Lyncherdom." Sociologist James Cutler agreed in 1905, observing that "our country's national crime is lynching."

The origin of the word remains obscure. It has been traced to seventeenth-century Ireland, colonial South Carolina, and revolutionary Virginia. While the practice of communal punishment almost certainly may be dated back centuries, the term *lynching* probably entered the American lexicon during the Revolutionary War. During that conflict Charles Lynch (1736–1796), a justice of the peace in Bedford County, Virginia, and his followers whipped and occasionally hanged suspected local Loyalists. Apparently Lynch's vigilantism was sufficiently notorious that "Lynch's law" became an American colloquial expression for vigilante violence.

In subsequent decades, popular tribunals throughout the nation periodically inflicted "Lynch's law" on transgressors of community standards. In the North, urban public disorder often included mob violence against abolitionists, Mormons, Catholics, immigrants, and blacks. With the discovery of gold in California, vigilante justice invaded western mining camps and boomtowns, reaching a climax in the San Francisco vigilance committees of the 1850s. As lynching spread across the nation during the nineteenth century, two ominous trends emerged. Increasingly, mobs ignored existing legal institutions and meted out extralegal punishment. Also, lynch mobs discarded many of the older forms of discipline, such as whipping and tarring and feathering, and resorted to lethal punishments. By roughly 1830 lynching had become synonymous with death at the hands of a mob.

Patterns of Lynching

Distinctive regional patterns in the phenomenon emerged after about 1830. In the North, extralegal violence declined. Economic development and urban growth there promoted the permanent and dependable exercise of state authority. Courts and law-enforcement agencies, including new police forces, defended the social order by suppressing violent crowds. Collective violence in the form of race and ethnic riots erupted sporadically, but lynchings became rarities. In the West, lynchings occurred more frequently. They were condoned as a lamentable but necessary form of spontaneous communal justice that persisted until formal institutions were established. In fact, western mobs often ignored existing legal institutions and persecuted Hispanic Americans and other vulnerable minorities.

In the South before the Civil War little institutional opposition discouraged mob violence. As of the late 1990s no reliable count of lynchings in the antebellum South had been made. Even so, the practice almost certainly was not uncommon because the institution of slavery required the coercion of slaves and the intimidation of nonslaveholders by white slave owners. The southern code of honor, which in part glorified white feminine virtue, encouraged white men to respond to challenges to their honor, especially to perceived offenses by black men against white women, by acting outside the law. Consequently, antislavery agitators and slaves charged with insurrection became frequent targets of increasingly deadly southern mobs.

With the outbreak of the Civil War, lynching became intertwined with the far more deadly violence of the war itself. Throughout the conflict, southern communities where whites feared imminent slave insurrections experienced spasms of mob violence. Large numbers of slaves were executed in gruesome spectacles aimed at intimidating the slave community into submission and loyalty. In the mountain regions of the South and the border states between the North and South, where allegiances often were divided between the Union and the Confederacy, partisans on many occasions summarily executed their opponents in a manner that cannot easily be distinguished from lynching.

Following the Civil War, lynching became a pervasive feature of southern life and emerged as a chronic threat to life and social peace. The emancipation of African American slaves threatened to deprive white southerners of their traditional prerogative of disciplining blacks as they chose. Southern planters responded to insufficient displays of deference and disputes with former slaves over crop settlements, wages, and labor contracts by hanging, beating, and whipping to death hundreds of blacks. Whites also engaged in systematic political terrorism. The Ku Klux Klan and various informal paramilitary groups resorted to lynching to defend the interests of the Democratic Party, the avowed party of white supremacy in the South.

Lynch mobs in the South continued to execute alleged wrongdoers long after lynching had become a rarity elsewhere in the nation. In the Northeast, where lynchings occurred rarely, mobs killed only two whites and seven blacks between 1880 and 1930. In the Midwest, 181 white and 79 black victims died at the hands of mobs. And in the Far West, where vigilantism persisted throughout the late nineteenth century, mobs lynched 447 whites and 38 blacks. The toll of mob violence outside the South was overshadowed by the estimated 723 whites and 3,220 blacks lynched in the South be-

A California mob chases after lynching victims, in an 1848 painting by Stanley Berkeley. LIBRARY OF CONGRESS

tween 1880 and 1930. The proportion of lynchings that occurred in the South rose during each decade after the Civil War, increasing from 82 percent of all lynchings in the nation during the 1880s to more than 95 percent during the 1920s.

The blatant connection between lynching and racism in the South became glaring over time. Outside the South and border states, 83 percent of mob victims were white. In the South and the border states, in contrast, 85 percent of lynching victims were black. Between 1880 and 1930, the proportion of lynching victims in the South who were white decreased from 32 percent to 9 percent. Lynching had deep roots throughout the nation, and its victims included whites, Native Americans, Chicanos, and Asians, but by the late nineteenth century it had become primarily a southern and racial phenomenon.

The distribution of lynchings in the South was complex. The largest numbers of lynchings occurred in the Deep South, especially Georgia, Mississippi, and Texas. The smallest numbers of lynchings occurred in the border South, in particular North Carolina and Virginia. But the concentration of lynching in the Deep South becomes less clear when the size of the African American population in the various southern states is taken into account. African Americans in Florida and Tennessee as well as Mississippi and Georgia faced the highest per capita threat of lynching. One pattern in the distribution of lynchings, however, is clear: the lynchings of African Americans were most prevalent in southern counties dominated by plantation agriculture. There the concentration of economic and political power in the hands of white landowners went hand in hand with highly exploitative and violent labor relations. Lynch mobs also were comparatively common in newly settled areas of the South, such as the Piney Woods of Mississippi, Georgia, and eastern Texas, where white settlers struggled to establish their authority in the face of the competing aspirations of itinerant black laborers, such as lumbermen, and land-hungry black settlers.

So completely did racial and ethnic stereotypes of criminality shape accounts of most lynchings that no entirely satisfactory portrait of lynching victims is possible. Because lynchings were in part rituals of degradation, they grew from and sustained notions of blacks and other lynching victims as criminally-disposed savages. In both the South and the West news accounts of lynchings and the crimes that preceded them often warped the life

Two victims of lynching in the South, 1932. LIBRARY OF CONGRESS

histories of mob victims to fit conventional portrayals of criminals. Even so, the historical record does allow for some generalizations about them. Mob victims were overwhelmingly male, and in the South, lynching victims often were young black men, especially rootless laborers referred to as "floaters." Southern whites alleged that "floaters," freed from the supervision of whites and the traditional controls of the black community, posed a continual threat to law and order. Lynch mobs in the West also appear to have targeted young itinerant men who were perceived as threatening outsiders.

Lynching mobs only infrequently executed women. Southern lynchers after 1880 murdered at least seventy-four black and five white women. These female mob victims, with few exceptions, were accused of murder or complicity in other violent crimes and were lynched along with the men charged with committing the crime. In the West, no reliable count of women lynching victims exists. But the extant evidence suggests that in the West very few women were lynched after the 1880s.

An objective assessment of the transgressions that provoked lynchings also is difficult because contemporary sources are rife with prevailing racial, ethnic, and class prejudices. The alleged causes of lynching reported in news accounts, however, reveal clear patterns. In the South between 1880 and 1930, the largest number of lynchings, roughly one-half, were prompted by murders and violent assaults. A violent attack by a black against a white, whether an act of self-defense or without premeditation, could prompt the retaliation of a white mob. The murder of a prominent white law officer or planter often provoked especially brutal and indiscriminate lynchings. Roughly one-third of black lynching victims in the South were alleged to have committed sexual assaults. Given the very elastic definition of sexual assaults when black men and white women were involved, everything from willing interracial sexual liaisons to rude, drunken behavior by a black man could serve as the pretext for a lynching. The remaining 20 percent of lynchings in the South were punishment for alleged offenses including arson, theft, conjuring, killing livestock, trying to vote, using obscene language, and a litany of seemingly minor offenses. As this list suggests, black men who routinely flaunted southern racial etiquette by advocating social justice for blacks, by demanding better working conditions, or simply by displaying insufficient deference to whites ran the risk of white violence.

In the West, alleged murders precipitated the largest number of lynchings. Purported theft, especially of livestock, triggered most of the remaining lynchings there. Although extralegal executions of labor activists and radicals account for only a small percentage of Western lynchings, they underscore the point that, as in the South, labor disputes and overt dissent often escalated into deadly violence, sometimes culminating in lynchings.

Types of Lynch Mobs

Lynch mobs, reflecting the disparate alleged offenses that provoked them, assumed a variety of forms in both the West and the South. Terrorist mobs, typically referred to as "whitecappers" or "regulators," operated with great secrecy and sometimes were distinguished by enduring, even elaborate, organization. With a broad range of motives ranging from defense of traditional codes of morality to campaigns to intimidate black farmers or western desperadoes, terrorist mobs often came

closest to conventional notions of vigilante justice. Such violence, which followed in the traditions of rural moral regulation, typically faced opposition only when it seemed to threaten anarchy or when it directly challenged the economic interests of the local elite. Then, officials and the elite predictably suppressed it.

In both the West and the South, small, secretive, and ephemeral mobs were responsible for a significant number of lynchings. The small mobs that carried out these clandestine lynchings may have believed that they were acting in accordance with contemporary justifications for mob violence, but their deeds hardly represented the expressed sentiment of the local white community. More likely, private mobs resorted to an improvised lynching in order to give their private grievances a veneer of legitimacy that would have been absent had they simply murdered their victims in their jail cells or homes.

In contrast, the bloody work of posses in the West and the South came far closer to public events that had the power to mobilize entire communities. The widespread participation in and glorification of posses in the South and West demonstrates how few reservations westerners and southerners had about the violence of posses. The alleged purpose of posses was to capture rather than to lynch criminals, but in hundreds of recorded instances posses in the South and West completed their pursuit by murdering suspects. Sometimes legally deputized groups, but most often spontaneous gatherings composed of neighbors, relatives, or witnesses to a purported crime, posses straddled a very thin line between being a legal and an extralegal arm of the law. They crossed that line when they murdered unarmed suspects or when they made no attempt to negotiate with armed suspects before resorting to violence.

Finally, lynch mobs, especially in the South, sometimes assumed huge dimensions, often numbering in the hundreds, sometimes even thousands. These mass mobs, acting with obvious and widespread local approval, could intimidate all but the most resolute law officers and could force their way into most jails. They wreaked vengeance for alleged crimes that often had attracted widespread local and, in many instances, regional attention. Ritualized violence and degradation, such as torture and elaborate executions, assumed a far greater significance in the lynchings by the largest mobs than in those of any other type of mob.

Lynching by mass mobs, and the massive retaliation it represented, cast a shadow over all other forms of mob violence. They helped to create a climate in which other lynchings, even when unaccompanied by ritual, could seem legitimate to participants.

Explanations for Lynching

The variety of lynching mobs testifies to the range of motivations and the complex shadings of popular support for mob violence. In the South, diverse acts of perceived or real insubordination by blacks—some of which may be cataloged under the heading of minor offenses, ranging from offensive talk to public drunkenness—called for violent sanctions. But the specific form of those sanctions varied. Offenses might be punished by whipping, beating, or lynching. But typically only whites immediately offended by such behavior were likely to resort to extralegal violence. The culminating act of white terror, the ritualized violence of the largest mobs, was reserved for offenses that most threatened the moral and social order. The lynching of blacks accused of attacking white women and lawmen, which were perceived as attacks on the respective moral repositories and defenders of the southern racial hierarchy, represented the most strenuous efforts of the white community to draw a final line of defense against the subversion of white supremacy and community honor. Thus, despite the apparent brutal capriciousness of mobs in the South and West, lynching represented an incremental form of terror.

Various explanations have been offered for the prevalence of lynching in American history. Many contemporaries contended that lynchings occurred where courts and law officers were distant and civil society weak or nonexistent. Little evidence substantiates this justification, however; lynchings routinely occurred in communities where courts operated and law officers were present. Mobs in both the West and the South often wrested their victims from the custody of law officers. For instance, in 1915 a small mob carried out the notorious lynching of Leo Frank, a white Jewish industrialist in Atlanta accused of the rape and murder of a young white female operative, even though Frank had been convicted of the crime and imprisoned. White southerners defended lynchings as their justifiable response to black criminality, especially alleged assaults on white women. But, as noted earlier, alleged assaults on white women comprised only a third of the alleged crimes punished by southern mobs. In some southern states, noncapital offenses provoked nearly an equal percentage of lynchings as did purported sexual assaults.

A more convincing explanation for lynching is that it in part became a forum for the expression and reaffirmation of white masculine authority. While women sometimes participated in lynchings and more often appear to have endorsed them, lynch mobs in the South and West alike were overwhelmingly composed of men. In the late nineteenth and early twentieth centuries, white men in the South and West looked upon lynching as a defensible response of men to threats to their economic privileges (e.g., in the form of labor unrest or theft) and their authority over women (e.g., in the form of perceived sexual transgressions). In the South in particular, the contentious struggle to establish a fixed hierarchy of race, class, and gender in the late nineteenth century provoked white men to deploy extralegal violence as a weapon in the arsenal of white male privilege.

Lynching also almost certainly endured because lynchers seldom risked legal punishment for their extralegal actions. Only a small number of thousands of lynchings between 1880 and 1940 were followed by attempts to prosecute the lynchers, and only a small number of these cases concluded with the convictions of mob members. The weak response of the federal and state governments to lynching reflected the grip of localism, suspicion of government, and contempt for legal procedures throughout American society. Local police forces routinely tolerated or even participated in lynchings. State police forces were not common until the early twentieth century and even then could not be relied upon to prevent lynchings. State officials in the West who were tireless in using state militia to suppress labor violence were less conscientious about using the same power to stifle lynch mobs. In the South, the use of state militia did prevent many lynchings, especially after 1900, but the pervasiveness of extralegal violence there far exceeded either the resolve or capacities of ill-equipped and poorly trained militias. Until the 1940s, federal authorities deferred to state and local officials in matters relating to lynchings. Only in rare instances when lynch mobs attacked federal property or federal employees did the Department of Justice intervene. But even then the clear intention was to punish specific criminal behavior by the lynchers, not to establish a precedent for federal jurisdiction over lynchings.

Opposition to Lynching

As long as local, state, and federal officials either ignored or endorsed lynching, voluntary reform organizations comprised the only consistent opposition to the practice. For African Americans, lynching was one of the most intolerable manifestations of their oppression. African Americans devised a variety of informal responses to lynchings, ranging from flight from lynching-prone areas to outright protest, including even armed resistance to white mobs. But ongoing, organized opposition by southern blacks was always exceedingly difficult and dangerous. Even so, from the 1880s until the 1950s Frederick Douglass, Ida Wells, Walter White, and a succession of black leaders denounced lynchings and their corrosive influence upon the American system of justice. During the 1890s Wells systematically studied white newspaper reports of lynchings and then used her findings to expose the shibboleths that whites used to justify their violence. During speaking tours in the United States and Great Britain, she turned southern justifications for lynchings on their heads by insisting that southern white mobs, not their black victims, represented the gravest threat to civilization. Black newspaper editors, such as Robert S. Abbott of the *Chicago Defender*, hammered away at the barbarism of white lynchers and the craven complicity of law officers and public officials charged with preserving order and protecting life. After the founding of the National Association for the Advancement of Colored People (NAACP) in 1909, W. E. B. Du Bois used its journal, the *Crisis*, to insist that the struggle for black equality could not be separated from the campaign to end lynching.

The ranks of antilynching advocates included some white reformers but very few southerners until the 1920s. After World War I, a small but influential group of white southern moderates organized the Commission on Interracial Cooperation (CIC) to improve race relations in the South. The CIC for the first time brought steady pressure from well-placed southern whites to bear on local and state officials to prevent lynchings. Intent on dismissing white justifications for lynchings, the CIC conducted research, eventually published as the highly influential *The Tragedy of Lynching* (1933). From the ranks of the organization emerged the Association of Southern Women for the Prevention of Lynching (ASWPL), which worked through women's church and civic groups to educate public opinion against lynching. Yet, consistent with the moderate principles that guided them, neither the CIC nor the ASWPL supported legislation to make lynching a federal crime.

A federal antilynching statute remained a major goal of African American activists for decades. Throughout the 1920s and 1930s the NAACP lobbied tirelessly for an antilynching bill. But, beginning in April 1918 with the proposed Dyer antilynching bill (named after its author, Republican representative Leonidas Dyer of Missouri), each antilynching statute went down to defeat because of either southern Democratic opposition or fitful Republican commitment. Antilynching activists were no more successful in prodding President Franklin D. Roosevelt's administration to support antilynching legislation. But while no antilynching law was forthcoming, the Justice Department did finally take tentative steps to punish lynchers during World War II. Prompted by concerns about the effects of lynching on the commitment of African Americans to the war effort, the Justice Department took an active interest in several outbreaks of antiblack violence and lynchings. After the war, the department increasingly interpreted the "equal protection" clause of the Fourteenth Amendment as grounds for federal intervention in racially motivated violence. As a result, the Federal Bureau of Investigation began to investigate lynchings and, for the first time, the threat of the federal prosecution of lynchers loomed as a possibility. That possibility turned to certainty after the passage of the Civil Rights Act of 1964, which finally empowered the federal government to prosecute participants in lynchings.

Increasing federal opposition, relentless African American activism, and the weakening of traditional forms of racial domination in the South during the twentieth century most likely explain the decline in lynching. A gradual decline in lynching in the South during the 1920s was followed by a more marked decline after 1930. Lynching virtually ceased as a regular occurrence during the 1950s, although the murders of various civil rights activists by white supremacists during the 1960s displayed some of the hallmarks of lynchings. In 1981 Ku Klux Klan members in Mobile, Alabama, lynched a black youth named Michael Donald. The lynchers were prosecuted and convicted.

Lynching occupies a prominent place in the history of American institutions and race relations. Extralegal executions symbolized Americans' impatience with the routine operation of the law, prompting many lawyers and judges to endorse reforms intended to speed justice. Such attitudes contributed to frequent "legal lynchings" when the trials of alleged criminals took place in a mob-like atmosphere and without regard for legal procedures.

Lynching in Film and Literature

Lynchings also came to symbolize southern distinctiveness and the region's culture of violence. The horrors of southern lynching figure prominently in the writings of Theodore Dreiser, William Faulkner, Richard Wright, and James Baldwin, and in the poetry of Langston Hughes. The canvases of Romare Bearden and cartoons of Jerry Doyle depicted gruesome images of the savagery of southern mobs. Likewise, southern lynchings inspired the searing lyrics of "Strange Fruit" written in 1939 by Billie Holliday and, more recently, the 1980 song "Burden of Shame" by UB40. Finally, lynchings have figured prominently in film depictions of the South, ranging from Oscar Micheaux's *Within Our Gates* (1919) to Martin Ritt's *The Long, Hot Summer* (1958) and John Singleton's *Rosewood* (1997). Few images of the travail of white-black relations in the South seemingly are more enduring than those of baying hounds and armed whites chasing black men across moonlit swamps, of frenzied mobs torturing and mutilating their victims, and of festive crowds gathering to gawk at the dangling or charred bodies of lynching victims.

Vigilantism similarly entered the mythology of the frontier. Few Hollywood westerns were complete without a scene depicting a mob of stern frontiersmen administering their ruthless but honest brand of backcountry justice upon desperadoes and other deserving criminals. Likewise, lynch mobs loom large in frontier fiction from Owen Wister's *The Virginian: A Horseman of the Plains* (1902) to Peter Mathiessen's *Killing Mister Watson* (1994). But efforts in the 1980s and 1990s to revise the historical memory of western lynching, as evidenced by a contentious 1991 campaign to mark the site of the 1919 lynching of an Industrial Workers of the World activist in Centralia, Washington, have been met with opposition and denial. Thus, although lynchings occupy a prominent place in the historical memory of the American South and West, Americans have yet to acknowledge or understand fully the legacy of centuries of extralegal mob violence.

BIBLIOGRAPHY

Ayers, Edward L. *Vengeance and Justice: Crime and Punishment in the Nineteenth Century South.* New York: Oxford University Press, 1984.

Brundage, W. Fitzhugh. *Lynching in the New South: Georgia and Virginia, 1880–1930.* Urbana: University of Illinois Press, 1993.

———. *Under Sentence of Death: Essays on Lynching in the South.* Chapel Hill: University of North Carolina Press, 1997.

Dinnerstein, Leonard. *The Leo Frank Case.* New York: Columbia University Press, 1968.

Harris, Trudier. *Exorcising Blackness: Historical and Literary Lynching and Burning Rituals.* Bloomington: Indiana University Press, 1984.

Moses, Norton H., ed. *Lynching and Vigilantism in the United States: An Annotated Bibliography.* Westport, Conn.: Greenwood, 1997.

National Association for the Advancement of Colored People. *Thirty Years of Lynching in the United States, 1889–1918.* Reprint. New York: Arno, 1969.

Raper, Arthur F. *The Tragedy of Lynching.* Chapel Hill: University of North Carolina Press, 1933.

Shapiro, Herbert. *White Violence and Black Response: From Reconstruction to Montgomery.* Amherst: University of Massachusetts Press, 1988.

Smead, Howard. *Blood Justice: The Lynching of Mack Charles Parker.* New York: Oxford University Press, 1986.

Tolnay, Stewart E., and E. M. Beck. *A Festival of Violence: An Analysis of Southern Lynchings, 1882–1930.* Urbana: University of Illinois Press, 1995.

Wright, George C. *Racial Violence in Kentucky, 1865–1940: Lynchings, Mob Rule, and Legal Lynchings.* Baton Rouge: Louisiana State University Press, 1990.

Zangrando, Robert L. *The NAACP Crusade Against Lynching, 1909–1950.* Philadelphia: Temple University Press, 1980.

W. FITZHUGH BRUNDAGE

See also **African Americans; Civil Disorder; Civil Rights Movements; Frank, Leo; Hate Crime; Honor; Ku Klux Klan; Race and Ethnicity; Reconstruction; Riots; Slavery; South; Vigilantism.**

M

McCARTHY, JOSEPH R.
(1908–1957)

Joseph R. McCarthy, a Republican senator from Wisconsin from 1947 until his death, is remembered for his role at the height of the Cold War in the early 1950s in intensifying the fear of communism generally and of the violent overthrow of the U.S. government specifically. *McCarthyism* has entered the language not only as a term for the extreme opposition to communism he propagated but for the tactic of attacking individuals by means of public, unsubstantiated allegations.

Playing on the public's concern about the spread of communism following the Korean War (1950–1953), Senator McCarthy attempted to invoke citizens' sense of patriotism and loyalty and encouraged them to come forth with information regarding the "communist tendencies" of their friends and neighbors. As chair of the Senate's permanent investigations subcommittee (the Committee on Government Operations) beginning in 1953, McCarthy used his political power to wage a crusade against communist subversion, which he alleged had infiltrated the U.S. government up to its highest echelons. The anticommunist hysteria became so widespread that mere suspicion of communist leanings could cost one a job or even lead to being blacklisted from an entire profession, such as Hollywood screenwriters and directors.

McCarthy's investigations relied on nontraditional—most argue irresponsible—interrogative practices. His accusations of subversiveness often included the now infamous question, "Are you now, or have you ever been, a member of the Communist Party?" His penchant for taking on the highest-ranking government officials with no substantial evidence only added to the spectacle of McCarthy's witch-hunts. At the same time, investigations of a similarly capricious nature were taking place at lower levels across the nation, often carried out by McCarthy supporters.

In 1954, during a thirty-six-day televised hearing in which McCarthy questioned top officials of the U.S. Army about alleged espionage ties, his facade began to crumble. He increasingly came across to the American people as a man who was ruthless, manipulative, and obsessed, who was taking advantage of his political position to terrorize and persecute citizens on groundless charges. Finally, as McCarthy was interrogating a colleague of Joseph Welch, the chief attorney for the U.S. Army, Welch interrupted: "Until this moment, Senator, I think I never really gauged your cruelty or your recklessness. Let us not assassinate this lad further, Senator. You have done enough. Have you no sense of decency, sir, at long last?"

As a direct result of this hearing, in 1954 the U.S. Senate officially censured McCarthy for his tactics of political innuendo and slander and general abuse of power. The Supreme Court in turn repealed many of the acts that had gone into effect during the height of McCarthy's tenure, arguing that many of these bills blatantly contradicted the Fifth Amendment protection against self-incrimination. Despite his best efforts, McCarthy was

Roy Cohn, left, and Senator Joseph R. McCarthy, 1954.
CORBIS/BETTMANN

never able to obtain a single conviction on the charge of "being a communist." McCarthy remained in his Senate seat until his death from complications related to alcoholism in 1957.

BIBLIOGRAPHY

Anderson, Jack, and Ronald W. May. *McCarthy: The Man, the Senator, the "Ism."* Boston: Beacon, 1952.

Ewald, William Bragg, Jr. *Who Killed Joe McCarthy?* New York: Simon and Schuster, 1984.

Griffith, Robert. *The Politics of Fear: Joseph R. McCarthy and the Senate.* Amherst: University of Massachusetts Press, 1970.

Landis, Mark. *Joseph McCarthy: The Politics of Chaos.* Cranbury, N.J.: Susquehanna University Press, 1987.

JARRETT PASCHEL

See also **Foreign Intervention, Fear of; Nativism; Red Scare.**

MACHISMO

Machismo (from the Latin *masculus*) is a Spanish word that literally means "the quality of male animals"; the adjective form is *machista*. The term denotes characteristics of men who manifest excessively dominant tendencies in interpersonal and political relationships. Positive connotations are a willingness to take risks, defy odds, win in competitive situations, and protect others. The term, used frequently in a derogatory or accusatory manner, became popular in the second half of the

twentieth century. Defenders of male superiority, in defense of machismo, cite anthropological and biological theories that associate it with atavistic remnants of hunting, gathering, and presiding over the needs of the group. In contemporary politics machismo is associated with *caudillismo,* a Spanish word signifying "the ability to lead the pack by acting ruthlessly." Military dictators in Latin America have often described the duties imposed by their position of leadership in terms of machismo, equating their position with the responsibilities of a father to his children and thereby justifying the violence unleashed on their own countrymen. Authoritarian governments often excuse their own use of discipline, suspension of individual rights, and persecution of those believed to constitute a national threat by utilizing the rhetoric of machismo; such questionable methods are described as obligations that result from the leading male's selfless devotion to higher goals. Throughout the Western Hemisphere being a husband and a father and having a wife in a subservient position is an integral part of machismo as it appears in politics and home life. Battering of women and children in order to maintain and assert dominance and justifying such violence in the name of punishment or discipline is a common manifestation of machismo in the domestic domain.

Getting due respect is part of the machismo mentality. Its most salient social manifestations are to be found in street gangs. Some gangs are organized along ethnic lines; others are territorial and cover whole neighborhoods or an area of a few blocks, generally recognizable by the painting of distinctive graffiti. National and ethnic pride are combined with a constant vigilance of established geographic and behavioral borders. Although individual gangs perform different functions, the exaltation of the power of violence is a common characteristic. The link among gang members is portrayed as a blind and unshakable allegiance to the group to be defended at any cost. Painful induction ceremonies are generally associated with proving the endurance of a prospective gang member. Posturing by wearing certain items of clothing, hairstyles, body piercing, and tattoos is part of the staging of male dominance and self-definition as a member of a fighting group. Although in certain areas such as California young women have organized themselves in gangs as well, copying in their internal structure the dominance through violence seen in male street gangs, the subsidiary role of young women as aids in hiding weapons and assisting males is a more common pattern among gangs in the United States.

The challenges of tough army training, the putting down of the weak, the sacrifices of sport practice, boxing, and wrestling, the endurance of pain and bruising, and the search for thrills in nature (as found, for example, in the writings of Robert Bly, James Dickey, and Norman Mailer) are muted forms of machismo that become, instead, a search for manliness when they do not assume an exaggerated form. Machista humor targets women and homosexuals through parodies of their mannerisms and physical characteristics. The fearful, weak, well-dressed gay man and the overly talkative, ignorant but beautiful blonde are but two of the exaggerated stereotypes of this derogatory humor.

Rap music, one of the most accepted forms of machismo in American popular culture, often combines in its lyrics praise of violent and irrational behavior by a supposedly aggrieved individual and a readiness to put down and insult women. Its acceptance by suburbanites domesticates its roughest edges through ironic displacement at the same time that it perpetuates the arrogance and posturing of machismo in attire, tone, and body language. The pornography industry, through videos, literature, and props, stages fantasies of male domination that circulate worldwide.

ALICIA BORINSKY

See also **Gender; Masculinity; Sex Differences; Sexual Harassment.**

McVEIGH, TIMOTHY

On 2 June 1997, twenty-nine-year-old Timothy McVeigh was found guilty of eleven counts of murder and conspiracy related to the 1995 bombing of the Alfred P. Murrah Federal Building in Oklahoma City—the worst act of terrorism in American history—and sentenced to death.

Early Life

Timothy James McVeigh was born on 23 April 1968, the second of three children, in Lockport, New York, a typically middle-American, almost exclusively white community. His father worked at a local auto plant. Neighbors remember McVeigh, who made above-average grades in school, as a "very active and friendly" child who "learned to play by the rules." When he was nine years old, McVeigh's grandfather introduced him to firearms and the rural custom of survivalism. Then, in the winter of 1977, Lockport was hit with a severe blizzard, downing power lines and leaving homes buried for days under mountains of snow. When it was over, Tim began storing water, food, and twenty-gallon plastic storage barrels in the event of another catastrophe. In 1978 his mother filed for divorce, leaving Tim behind with his emotionally devastated father in a new tract home in nearby Pendleton.

In high school McVeigh manifested two cross-currents of behavior that would ultimately merge into his criminal profile. On the one hand, he continued to play by the rules—he saved money from part-time jobs, did not miss a day of classes, and did not drink, use drugs, or fight. He easily made friends, was elected to the student council, ran track, and was considered bright. On the other hand, his interests in guns and survivalism grew into obsessions. He began reading a variety of survivalist magazines and continued stockpiling food, camping gear, and weapons "in case of a nuclear attack." Classmates recall that McVeigh never mentioned his mother.

Following graduation, McVeigh took two computer courses at a local business college but soon quit. In early 1987 he was hired as a guard with a security firm, which gave him the legal right to carry a concealed weapon. He soon began to bring numerous high-powered guns to work, including an AK-47 assault rifle. His behavior became increasingly erratic.

Success as a Soldier

McVeigh enlisted in the U.S. Army on 24 May 1988. Terry Nichols and Michael Fortier, with whom McVeigh would conspire to bomb the Oklahoma City federal building, joined the army on the same day, and the three became friends during their thirteen weeks of military training at Fort Benning, Georgia. McVeigh and Nichols were "hard into guns" and shared a belief voiced in gun magazines that the government would soon take away their weapons. By 1990 McVeigh, Nichols, and Fortier had been transferred to Fort Riley, Kansas, where they joined the army's First Infantry Division. McVeigh advanced in rank faster than any other infantryman at Fort Riley; he was promptly promoted to sergeant and placed in charge of a thirty-five-man unit. An army evaluation rated him as "among the best" in leadership potential

Timothy McVeigh escorted by police and FBI agents, 1995. Justin Sutcliffe/SIPA Press

as part of a security detail assigned to guard General Norman Schwarzkopf during negotiations with the Iraqis. Despite his success, McVeigh grew disillusioned with the army after he failed a physical exam for entry into the Green Berets. He quit the army in 1991 and went home.

Alienation and Drift

McVeigh was deeply angered by the postwar military downsizing and what he saw as a growing intrusiveness of the federal government into the right to keep and bear firearms. He spent most of 1992 and 1993 wandering the gun-show circuit, dressed in camouflage and combat boots, peddling weapons, and absorbing the apocalyptic thinking of the nascent American militia movement. At one point he joined an Arkansas faction of the Ku Klux Klan. From his reading of right-wing literature he acquired what historian Richard Hofstadter has identified as the "paranoid political style."

Shortly after the Bureau of Alcohol, Tobacco, and Firearms raided the Branch Davidians in February 1993, McVeigh traveled to Waco, Texas, where he joined a militia-organized protest against the government. He then went to the home of Terry and James Nichols in Decker, Michigan. After watching televised images of the Federal Bureau of Investigation raid and the ensuing chemical blaze that killed David Koresh and his followers, he immediately returned to Waco to walk through the charred remains. From there he joined Michael Fortier in Kingman, Arizona, and began regularly using crystal methamphetamine —a powerful central-nervous-system stimulant that causes extreme euphoria, paranoia, and, often, assaultive behavior.

The antigovernment bombing conspiracy took root in Decker during late 1993. By November 1994, with his meth-induced paranoia and antigovernment fever, McVeigh had assembled money and composite materials for the bomb (two tons of ammonium nitrate fertilizer, racing fuel, blasting caps, detonator cord, and twenty-gallon plastic barrels) and had selected the Oklahoma City federal building as his target, believing that it housed FBI agents responsible for the Waco tragedy. Like many on the far right, McVeigh had also become fascinated by the significance of 19 April, the date of both Waco and the Battle of Lexington and Concord in 1775.

Reproducing scenes—their timing, means, and motives—almost literally from *The Turner Diaries*, on the morning of 19 April 1995, two years to the

and an "inspiration to young soldiers." McVeigh used this authority, however, to advance his extremist views. He assigned latrine duty to black specialists under his command, made derogatory remarks about blacks, and proselytized for other soldiers to read a futuristic novel called *The Turner Diaries*, a well-known terrorism "guide" depicting an antiblack, anti-Semitic, and antigovernment revolution waged by survivalists. Such conduct was a blatant violation of army regulations, but the army did nothing to stop it.

Instead, McVeigh went on to become a hero of the Persian Gulf War as a Bradley gunner at the Kuwaiti border, winning a Bronze Star and the coveted Combat Infantry Badge. He even served

Bringing Home the War

Since the end of World War II, researchers have consistently documented the importance of decompressing soldiers upon their return from war. Failure to control and reshape the aggressive, primitive urges expressed in the destruction and killing of combat often results in unrestrained patterns of belligerency and violence. Yet the military has consistently failed to rehabilitate its returning combat soldiers; and today, Vietnam and Gulf War veterans are overrepresented in U.S. prison populations.

During his trial, McVeigh's defense team alluded to the fact that McVeigh was following the rules of war. In the tradition of America's Founding Fathers, McVeigh was driven by an ideology of individual liberty. According to defense documents, McVeigh stated that a "high body count" in Oklahoma City was intended to get a point across to the federal government. In response, the prosecution argued that there was no ideological significance to McVeigh's crime; he was an isolated monster driven by his own inexplicable hatred of the government.

The evidence nonetheless indicates that McVeigh *was* motivated by an ideology—the same ideology that drives the militias, the skinheads, and other neo-Nazi groups. To one degree or another, they all share a desire for a campaign of violence against the federal government. This is not an ideology of individualism, but an ideology that demands the sacrifice of the individual for the sake of a collective goal. McVeigh's horrific act of violence was premised on the assumption that the importance of individual lives is subordinated to the importance of a dangerous social movement operating on the margins of American society.

day after Waco, McVeigh detonated his truck bomb in front of the Alfred P. Murrah Federal Building, killing 168 defenseless people and seriously injuring another five hundred in revenge for the government's attack on the Branch Davidians.

BIBLIOGRAPHY

Hamm, Mark S. *American Skinheads: The Criminology and Control of Hate Crime.* Westport, Conn., and London: Praeger, 1993.

———. *Apocalypse in Oklahoma: Waco and Ruby Ridge Revenged.* Boston: Northeastern University Press, 1997.

Hofstadter, Richard. *The Paranoid Style in American Politics.* New York: Knopf, 1965.

Kaplan, Jeffrey. "Right-Wing Violence in North America." *Terrorism and Political Violence* 7, no. 1 (spring 1995): 44–95.

Russakoff, Dale, and Serge F. Kovaleski. "An Ordinary Boy's Extraordinary Rage." *Washington Post,* 2 July 1995.

Stickney, Brandon M. *"All-American Monster": The Unauthorized Biography of Timothy McVeigh.* Amherst, N.Y.: Prometheus, 1996.

MARK S. HAMM

See also **Extremism; Oklahoma City Bombing; Waco.**

MAFIA

The term *Mafia* conjures up dramatic images created by movies, newspapers, and magazine articles intertwining fact and fiction. Scholarly writings on the topic demonstrate that the popular conception of the Mafia is based on media distortion of historical fact and contradictory data produced by two U.S. government commissions.

Journalists, primarily American journalists writing in the twentieth century, helped generate the popularly held view of the Mafia by disseminating the belief that the term *Mafia* was an acronym for a motto employed during Sicily's revolution in 1282—*Morte Alla Francia Italia Anela* (Death to the French Is Italy's Cry). It is doubtful that Sicilians ever adopted this phrase, since they have never conceived of themselves as Italians. A more likely derivation of the word is an 1862 play by Giuseppe Rizzotto, *I Mafiusi di la Vicaria* (later shortened to *I Mafiusi*). The word *mafiusi* was coined by Rizzotto to refer to the criminal practices of prisoners, which consisted of gambling, prostitution, and confidence games, in Palermo's largest prison. The term eventually came to be used as a synonym for organized crime and its participants. Popular writers contributed to the prevailing understanding by using the term *Mafia* to represent one secret criminal organization. Rather, Mafia is a method of criminal procedure best understood as syndicated crime.

As a method, Mafia, or syndicated crime, has three features: the use of violence; the provision of illicit goods and services; and the obtaining of immunity from the law for its participants, such immunity being obtained by contributing funds to a

Two members of the Capone syndicate appear before the Senate Crime Committee in Washington, D.C., 1950. CORBIS/BETTMANN

political candidate's election campaign or by direct payoffs to the police. As a method, Mafia can exist anywhere. Secrecy is a necessary element in its operation; however, its function of delivering goods and services necessitates contact with the customer. Since syndicate operations are illegal, neither the customer nor the criminal has recourse to the legal system. Hence, violence becomes necessary to maintain conformity among participants and gain control over enterprises, as well as to discourage competition.

The word *Mafia* has erroneously been used to refer exclusively to criminals of Sicilian or Italian heritage. This misuse resulted in part from the findings of two U.S. government commissions. In 1950 the Kefauver Commission presented the Mafia as a secret society transported to America from Sicily. Sociologists and historians have criticized the committee for its unscientific and biased method of investigation, and have suggested that the Truman administration used the investigation as a smoke screen to divert attention from its problems.

In 1963 the McClellan Committee, using informant Joseph Valachi's testimony, discovered a new organization that had been created in the 1930s by Charles "Lucky" Luciano. The organization was called Cosa Nostra and consisted of several crime "families" ruled by a "commission." Sociologists have shown the committee findings to be riddled with contradictions, including its assumption that the old Mafia and the new Cosa Nostra were the same organization. The committee also misrepresented Italian organized criminals as a major threat to the nation, when at the time they constituted only 16 percent of those convicted of such crimes. It also neglected to take into account American criminal history prior to 1930; syndicated crime existed in the United States in the early American colonies and during the Civil War, long before the migration of Italians.

The most serious criticism of the McClellan Committee targeted its conclusion that the Mafia was transported from Sicily to the United States. A review of Italian history would have shown that in Italy the Mafia was never viewed as a secret society and that its origins lie in the *feudo*, or landed estate, created after the abolition of feudalism in 1812. The baron of each estate allotted use of the land to sharecroppers (called *gabellotti*) who employed peasants to work the land. When the baron moved to Palermo to enjoy its new cultural life, these gabellotti employed outlaws to steal the livestock and land of other gabellotti. By 1860, the more skilled gabellotti had developed two elements of syndicated crime—the use of violence and the transport and sale of stolen merchandise. Many gabellotti threatened their barons into selling them their estates. With universal suffrage in 1867, the gabellotto became a vote-broker; he could procure votes for political candidates who in turn granted him political immunity. By 1870, following from Rizzotto's play, the gabellotto came to be known as a *mafioso*, whose power was assured by *omerta*, the code that bound Sicilian males from turning to the law for help or divulging information to the police. Omerta developed from Sicilians' distrust of the many governments that had conquered and ravaged their land. This incarnation of Mafia is embedded in Sicily's history and social structure; as such, it cannot be transported.

The reality of syndicated crime in America is that every major ethnic and racial group in the United States, in a process called "ethnic succession," has taken and continues to take a turn operating syndicated crime organizations; these groups include the Irish, Jews, Germans, Africans, Mexicans, Chinese, Puerto Ricans, Cubans, Jamaicans, Japanese, and most recently, Russians. This process bloodies the streets of America as syndicate criminals provide various sectors of the public with the illicit goods and services they request.

As for the existence of a large national criminal organization, research shows that such a structure would require a large number of employees, complex hierarchies, and training and monitoring of street-level performance. These are practices that would seriously endanger the existence of such a large-scale operation. So, too, the successful prosecution of its leaders would, in this conception, lead to its demise. The fact that syndicated crime continues to exist indicates that its structure consists of small groups with short hierarchies, little specialization, and training based upon gradual, unwritten, and informal socialization.

Syndicated crime in America is not an import. It is a product of American society.

BIBLIOGRAPHY

Albini, Joseph L. *The American Mafia: Genesis of a Legend.* New York: Appleton-Century-Crofts, 1971.

Ryan, Patrick J., and George E. Rush, eds. *Understanding Organized Crime in Global Perspective.* Thousand Oaks, Calif.: Sage, 1997.

Southerland, Mitti D., and Gary W. Potter. "Applying Organization Theory to Organized Crime." *Journal of Contemporary Criminal Justice* 9, no. 3 (August 1993).

JOSEPH L. ALBINI

See also **Black Hand; Luciano, "Lucky"; Organized Crime.**

MALCOLM X
(1925–1965)

Malcolm X, Muslim minister and Black Nationalist leader, was the most formidable critic of white supremacy in American history. More effectively than anyone else, he exposed the racist hypocrisy of American democracy and the ethical contradictions of white Christianity. He is best understood in the social and political context of the black nationalist tradition of Marcus Garvey and Elijah Muhammad and the Civil Rights movement of the 1960s. His unrelenting critique of America and Christianity was bold and devastating. Few people could listen to him and not be impressed by the cogency of his analysis.

Malcolm X focused his criticism on the failure of white people to treat black people as human beings. Whites had enslaved blacks for 244 years, segregated them for another 100 years, and lynched them to demonstrate their absolute power over blacks. How could American whites exclude blacks and other people of color from the political process and yet say that this nation is the land of the free? How could white Christians treat blacks as brutes and still claim love as their central religious principle? With rage and humor, Malcolm had a field day exposing these contradictions.

Malcolm X's articulation of the gap between the American creed and the American deed angered many whites because he spoke forcefully and bluntly, refusing to sugarcoat the truth about the crimes whites committed against blacks. He spoke out passionately not only against the brutality and cowardice of the Ku Klux Klan but also against the structural and hidden violence of the American government. "Stop talking about Mississippi," he railed. "America is Mississippi!" To understand Malcolm's perspective on violence, it is necessary to view it within the social and political context of nearly four centuries of racist violence against blacks in America and the white Christian justification and tolerance of that violence.

Born in Omaha, Nebraska, 19 May 1925, Malcolm lived during years when America was defined by overt racist violence. Segregation was the law of the land; the Klan was marching; lynching was commonplace; and the government, educational institutions, and the churches regarded blacks as inferior—mentally and physically. No black could escape the physical and psychological violence of white supremacy.

Malcolm X, in 1963. UPI/CORBIS-BETTMANN

Malcolm's father, Earl Little, a Baptist preacher and follower of the Black Nationalist Marcus Garvey, was a special target of white hate groups. While Malcolm was still in his mother's womb, the Klan terrorized the Little family at their home and forced them to move to Lansing, Michigan, where at the age of four Malcolm witnessed the burning down of their home by a white hate group called the Black Legionnaires. Malcolm called the event "the nightmare night in 1929." Two years later, Malcolm claimed that the same group killed his father (the official statement reported his father's death as accidental), leaving the family fatherless and soon penniless. Unable to cope, Malcolm's mother, Louise Little, had a mental breakdown and was hospitalized in Kalamazoo, Michigan.

The Little children were placed in foster homes. After Malcolm's eighth-grade teacher told him that becoming a lawyer was "no realistic goal for a nigger," he dropped out of school and went to Boston and then to New York, where he became involved in dealing in drugs, prostitution, numbers running, and con games. He described himself as "a predatory animal" who "deliberately invited death." Before he reached his twenty-first birthday,

Malcolm was arrested for armed robbery and sentenced to eight to ten years at a Massachusetts prison in February 1946.

While in prison, Malcolm had two profound conversions: intellectual and spiritual. Through the example of an inmate, he discovered the power of the intellect. He became a voracious reader, disciplined thinker, and skilled debater. In 1948, under the influence of his family, Malcolm became a member of Elijah Muhammad's Nation of Islam (NOI) and its most effective recruiter and articulate defender. The NOI reversed the value system of white America by making everything black good and everything white evil. It substituted black supremacy for white supremacy. While Malcolm accepted the theology of the NOI, it was its black nationalist philosophy, emphasizing black self-respect and self-defense, that inspired his intellectual imagination and fueled his religious commitment.

Malcolm was released from prison in August 1952 and quickly became the most influential minister in the NOI—second only to the Messenger, the Honorable Elijah Muhammad, as Malcolm and other followers called him. Malcolm was appointed to head the prestigious Temple Number 7 in New York and became the NOI's national spokesperson. He distinguished himself as the most feared, controversial, and articulate race critic in America. Since the overt racist violence of the southern conservatives was obvious and effectively exposed in the media by Martin Luther King, Jr., and the Civil Rights movement, Malcolm X focused his critique on the covert racist violence of northern white liberals.

Malcolm's attack on white liberals was persistent and brutal. He exposed their link to the creation of the black ghetto—to drugs, poverty, crime, unemployment, and bad housing. While King praised white liberals for their support of the southern-based Civil Rights movement, Malcolm castigated them for their hypocrisy—professing to support integration while creating de facto segregation in schools, housing, and other segments of American life.

No issue angered Malcolm X more than what whites said about violence and nonviolence in the Civil Rights movement. Whites urged blacks to follow King—embrace nonviolence and reject violence in any form. Malcolm could hardly contain his rage as he pointed out the contradictions between what whites advised blacks to do to get their freedom and what they did to attain their own.

Patrick Henry did not practice the virtues of non-violence. Neither did George Washington. When whites feel that their rights have been violated, they do not advocate turning the other cheek. Because whites did not apply to themselves that same moral logic that they urged upon blacks, Malcolm regarded whites as "the worst hypocrites on the planet."

Malcolm X did not advocate violence; he preached self-defense. He believed that the right of self-defense is an essential element in the definition of humanity. Whites have always recognized this principle for themselves but not for blacks. This kind of racist thinking infuriated Malcolm. If whites have the right to defend themselves against their enemies, why not blacks against their enemies? Malcolm used provocative language to express his rage: "by any means necessary," "reciprocal bleeding," and "we need a Mau Mau"—referring to African freedom fighters. "If you want to know what I'll do, figure out what you'll do. I'll do the same thing—only more of it" (*Malcolm X Speaks*, pp. 197–198). He did not regard such language as violent. He called it intelligent. "A black man has the right to do whatever is necessary to get his freedom that other human beings have done to get their freedom" (*Malcolm X Speaks*, p. 113). No people, he contended, could affirm their humanity without defending themselves against others who refuse to treat them as human beings.

In contrast to the picture of Martin Luther King as a promoter of love and nonviolence, the media portrayed Malcolm X as a preacher of hate and violence. They, along with the Federal Bureau of Investigation, were also effective in creating dissension within the NOI, especially between Malcolm and Elijah Muhammad. In December 1963 Muhammad suspended Malcolm purportedly for saying that the assassination of President John Kennedy (22 November 1963) was a case of the "chickens coming home to roost."

Three months later, Malcolm bolted from the NOI and created two organizations—one religious (Muslim Mosque, Inc.) and the other political (Organization of Afro-American Unity). He made a pilgrimage to Mecca, became a Sunni Muslim, adopted the name El-Hajj Malik El-Shabazz, and rejected the racist ideology of the NOI.

Malcolm also went to Africa to connect the black freedom movement in the United States with liberation movements around the world. "It is incorrect to classify the revolt of the Negro as simply a racial conflict of black against white, or as a purely American problem," he said at Barnard College. "Rather we are today seeking a global rebellion of the oppressed against the oppressor, the exploited against the exploiter" (*Malcolm X Speaks*, p. 217). He appealed to African heads of state to bring the U.S. government before the United Nations and charge it with the violation of the human rights of African Americans.

The animosity between Malcolm and the NOI deepened. The NOI firebombed Malcolm's house one week before a team of assassins murdered him as he was about to speak at the Audubon Ballroom in New York City on 21 February 1965. Three people were convicted of Malcolm's murder, of which two were innocent. The man who confessed to the murder named four accomplices, but they were never put on trial.

It was widely said that Malcolm X died by the violence he fomented. But it is more accurate to say that he died fighting against white violence and for the freedom of African Americans and other oppressed peoples throughout the world.

BIBLIOGRAPHY

Breitman, George, ed. *Malcolm X Speaks*. New York: Grove, 1965.

Cone, James H. Martin. *Malcolm and America: A Dream or a Nightmare*. Maryknoll, N.Y.: Orbis, 1991.

Goldman, Peter. *The Death and Life of Malcolm X*. 2d ed. Urbana: University of Illinois Press, 1979.

Malcolm X, with Alex Haley. *The Autobiography of Malcolm X*. New York: Grove, 1965.

JAMES H. CONE

See also **Assassinations; Civil Rights Movements; King, Martin Luther, Jr.; Muslims.**

MANN ACT (1910). *See* Prostitution; White Slavery

MANSON, CHARLES
(1934–)

The quintessential American murderer of the twentieth century, Charles M. Manson killed not for the customary, personal motives of gain, revenge, or pleasure; rather, it was Manson's uncanny consonance with the zeitgeist that both drove his crimes and made him a figure of fascination and horror. Youth rebellion, Eastern mysticism, rock music, celebrity society, media culture, antimaterialism, sexual freedom, psychedelic drugs—Manson assimilated all these trends in the cauldron of the 1960s and created an apocalyptic vision that led to mass murder. In so doing—and in his masterful manipulation of the news media during his trial—Manson came to symbolize the dark side of the counterculture, if not evil itself, with his gruesome achievement spurring a backlash against one of America's great moments of social ferment.

Manson was convicted of instigating the 1969 murders of the Hollywood starlet Sharon Tate and four of her houseguests; of the grocery owner Leno LaBianca and his wife, Rosemary; and of two acquaintances who crossed Manson. But Manson did not personally kill any of the Tate or LaBianca victims; the murders were committed by his young followers, members of the "Manson Family," who had come to see Manson as a prophet or even messiah and their own actions less as choices than the inevitable unfolding of a Passion play. The brutality of the murders, the prominence of the victims, and the apparently arbitrary origin of the crimes guaranteed that they would be noticed. That they were committed by seemingly privileged children of the baby boom—especially women—who were rejecting a prosperous suburban birthright for some cryptic brand of revolutionary spiritualism made the Manson murders a reference point in U.S. culture.

Born in Cincinnati to hardscrabble beginnings, Manson was sent to live with relatives in West Virginia when his mother—unmarried and age sixteen at Manson's birth—was jailed for armed robbery. Manson grew into a life of petty, largely nonviolent crime, including burglary, auto theft, and, thanks to an easy way with women, pimping. During his frequent stretches in reformatories and jails, the five-foot-two Manson suffered abuse at the hands of larger inmates—and learned to manipulate them as well as the authorities charged with his rehabilitation. A forgery conviction brought Manson to federal prison in 1959, where he honed his skill on the guitar and dabbled in Scientology and assorted mystical beliefs. Released in 1967 in Los Angeles, Manson immediately acclimated to the California counterculture, his former convict identity cementing his antiestablishment credentials.

Manson's goal was a recording contract, and he had enough connections to get interviews and auditions. While waiting for his career to take flight, he began to assemble a following of young outcasts, particularly women, who traveled with him in a search for experiences. The odyssey took Manson throughout underground California, from San Francisco in the Summer of Love across the bay to radical Berkeley; from verdant Topanga Canyon near Malibu to the redwood forests of Mendocino County on the North Coast. Playing his music, spouting obscure views of spirituality, interpreting the day's tumultuous events, and decoding pop lyrics, Manson was an elder brother, a father, and a lover to the dozens of disaffected youths who came his way. LSD helped them overcome middle-class inhibitions, as did group sex. In another era such behavior would have been suppressed, or at least marginalized, but the Manson Family's adventures played out against a chaotic social backdrop that suggested limitless possibilities.

The Manson Family's journeys always led back to Los Angeles, where Manson had gained a toehold in the freewheeling pop culture. He wrote a song recorded by the Beach Boys and consulted with Universal Studios writers developing a movie about the return of Jesus as a black man to 1960s America. The Manson Family, meanwhile, settled at the dilapidated Spahn Movie Ranch northwest of Los Angeles, the site of countless Westerns. The commune acquired some stability there, becoming a destination for runaways as Manson managed affairs through transactions involving drugs, cars, and gifts brought by new recruits.

A researcher who visited at this time described Manson as "an extroverted, persuasive individual who served as absolute ruler of this group marriage commune," having sex with all the females who, in turn, served the male members. Manson, occasionally calling himself "God" or "God and the Devil," espoused "a mystical philosophy placing great emphasis on the belief that people did not die and that infant consciousness was the ultimate state" (Smith and Rose 1970).

The events of 1968—among them urban riots, escalation of the Vietnam War, and the assassinations of Martin Luther King, Jr., and Robert Kennedy—soured not only the national mood but also that of Manson, whose own entertainment career had stalled. His raps grew increasingly pessimistic, and he soon moved the commune to property in Death Valley owned by a follower's relatives. Against this bleak landscape, Manson began to foretell an apocalyptic end to a United States engulfed in race wars—and a special role for his "family" when the dust settled. He drew peculiar inspiration from the Beatles' self-titled

White Album, finding clues in such songs as "Happiness Is a Warm Gun," "Piggies," and, especially, the blaring "Helter Skelter."

In 1969 the Manson Family returned to Spahn Movie Ranch, but a sequence of misfortunes further set back Manson's plans. Drug deals went awry, and several followers were arrested—in the most serious case, for the murder of an amphetamine supplier. On 9 August 1969 Manson dispatched Charles "Tex" Watson, Susan Atkins, Patricia Krenwinkel, and Linda Kasabian to a Bel Air house where a Beach Boys producer once lived. The current occupants were Sharon Tate and her guests, who were shot and stabbed by Watson and the women (except Kasabian, who later testified for prosecutors). The killers made a horrific tableau of the crime scene, mutilating the victims and painting words in their blood—including a misspelled HEALTER SKELTER.

The ghastly killings were splayed across the next day's headlines; the following night, Manson himself selected the LaBianca house and directed the same killing crew, joined by the follower Leslie Van Houten, to complete the murders. They did so, leaving a similarly brutal puzzle for investigators to decipher.

The killing spree then stopped, and it was not until months later that authorities stumbled upon the suspects. In the theory offered by the prosecutor, Vincent Bugliosi, Manson had staged the murders to launch an apocalypse called Helter Skelter; the crimes were designed to implicate black militants, thereby provoking a white reaction and leading to a race war that would end with the Manson Family as rulers of the earth. Manson, Bugliosi argued, was "a vicious, diabolical murderer" who ruled over "a tribe of bootlicking slaves."

The behavior of Manson and his followers seemed to confirm Bugliosi's extraordinary scenario. They did everything possible to disrupt the proceedings, from filing endless motions to a series of shocking theatrical gestures. They shaved their heads, burned Xs into their foreheads, sang songs, and turned their backs to the judge. Outside the court, Lynette "Squeaky" Fromme—who in 1975 would be convicted of attempting to assassinate President Gerald Ford in an effort to draw attention to Manson's plight—and other followers maintained a vigil for their "Christ on the cross." All these efforts were for naught; the Manson de-

Charles Manson, in California in 1969. CORBIS/
BETTMANN

fendants, including Manson himself, were convicted and sentenced to death in 1971. The following year, in an unrelated case, the California Supreme Court found the death penalty unconstitutional. All condemned inmates were therefore resentenced to life imprisonment. Manson is serving a life sentence in a California state prison.

Manson remains unrepentant and denies culpability for the acts of his followers; his few remaining loyalists have argued that the murders were necessary to shock society into recognizing the wrongs it was committing in Vietnam and against the environment. But while his inarticulable cause has gone nowhere, Manson remains an icon for mayhem in the media age. From the Oliver Stone picture *Natural Born Killers* (1994) to the 1990s shock-rocker who performs under the name

Marilyn Manson, Charles Manson remains a standard by which senseless violence is measured.

BIBLIOGRAPHY

Bravin, Jess. *Squeaky: The Life and Times of Lynette Alice Fromme*. New York: St. Martin's, 1997.

Bugliosi, Vincent, with Curt Gentry. *Helter Skelter: The True Story of the Manson Murders*. New York: Norton, 1974.

Schreck, Nikolas. *The Manson File*. New York: Amok, 1988.

Smith, David E., and Al Rose. "The Group Marriage Commune: A Case Study." *Journal of Psychedelic Drugs* (September 1970).

JESS BRAVIN

See also **Cults; Serial Killers.**

MARINES. *See* Military.

MARTIAL ARTS

Although martial arts history and traditions date back several centuries, the art of the empty hand was virtually nonexistent in the United States prior to the mid-1950s. Since its introduction on the West Coast, martial arts practice has attracted literally millions of adherents to this once typically Asian activity. So varied were the martial arts styles brought to this country that American practitioners were able literally to pick and choose from among the traditional arts most commensurate with the individuals' personal goals.

In classical martial arts practice, individuals engage in challenging programs in which they are asked to submit to the requirements of symbolically dangerous activities. In completing the exercises, students acquire self-defense skills, and in the process of learning the potentially destructive techniques, they come to recognize a sense of inner peace and the knowledge that they must refrain from using learned skills in all but the most threatening situations.

The first karate instructors appeared in the United States as early as 1946, when Robert Trias, a U.S. serviceman who studied karate in Asia, gave private instruction to friends in his Arizona community. It was not until 1956 that Edward Parker, a native of Hawaii, opened the first commercially successful karate school in California. In later years many Americans, including Asian Americans who maintained strong affiliations with their home countries, spread martial arts instruction in karate, kung fu, tae kwon do, and other arts throughout the United States.

Perhaps the first national exposure given to the martial arts in the United States can be attributed to Mas Oyama, who in 1952 visited a number of U.S. Air Force bases, demonstrating the ability of highly trained karate personnel. Oyama, who attempted to attract interest in the arts by using his callused fists to break wood, bricks, and stones, inadvertently introduced the grossly popularized image of the Oriental superhero. It was this image of karate as a violent and mystical art form that would later be exploited by karate instructors attempting to attract students. It would seem that American enthusiasts who had grown up with the fast-gun heroes of movie fame were both willing and able to accept the possibility of developing a lethal force through martial arts instruction.

Martial arts in the United States have been patterned after Asian systems, but in many cases have evolved into uniquely American interpretations. The mixing of styles and philosophies and the introduction of distinctive methods and practices by Americans may best be understood by examining the development of martial arts in the United States over the course of five interrelated eras.

Periods of U.S. Development

The years 1954 through 1964 are referred to as the traditional era, which emphasized re-creating the pageantry and ritual of traditional martial arts. The Japanese and Okinawan arts of karate and the Korean art of tae kwon do were introduced by U.S. military men returning from service in Asia and by Korean and Japanese nationals who insisted that the practice of the arts be re-created as closely as possible to the Asian models.

By the mid-1960s karate tournaments had become popular. As American martial artists came together to compete, they were afforded opportunities to mix styles—a previously forbidden practice and the emphasis of the progressive sports era in American martial arts, which lasted from 1965 until 1972. Fighters included national champion Chuck Norris, who mixed Korean *tang soo do* kicks with Japanese *shotokan* punches to develop an unbeatable style.

In 1973 tae kwon do master Jhoon Rhee invented safety gear that encouraged American fighters to make contact in competition. As fighters tested their skills, they discovered that many traditional techniques were invalid in actual combat and began to develop more contemporary fighting

Bruce Lee on the set of *The Chinese Connection*, 1973. CORBIS/BETMANN

methods. Bruce Lee and world champion Joe Lewis led the movement to abandon traditional training and create personal styles of self-defense. The years 1973 through 1982 were the contact era. The technological advances contributed by Rhee and the ideological changes endorsed by Lee and Lewis resulted in a majority of American martial artists advancing traditional martial arts theory to accommodate realistic combat training. Although originally created by Lewis in 1970, the art of American kickboxing was developed during the contact era.

By the early 1980s, American kickboxing had failed to catch the attention of sports promoters even though its most famous champion, Bill "Superfoot" Wallace, continued to attract fans. During the years 1984 through 1992, an emphasis on multicultural adaptations of martial arts became popular. Stephen Hayes introduced *ninjutsu* and Dan Inosanto helped introduce Indonesian, Filipino, and Thai arts to the American martial arts community. Identified as the matrix era, this was a time in which many American martial artists abandoned the single-style and single-range practice of traditional arts and gained proficiency in long (kickboxing), medium (trapboxing), and ground fighting (grappling) ranges.

As numerous arts gained notoriety in the United States, a movement to test the superiority and function of each art became popular. In 1993 Brazilian jujitsu expert Rorian Gracie introduced the concept of no-holds-barred (NHB) fighting to cable television audiences and ushered in what may be referred to as the contemporary era in American martial arts. In NHB fighting events, promoters and fighters emphasized the physical violence of the martial arts and in so doing abandoned the pageantry and traditions of nonviolence once associated with classical martial arts training.

Asian countries are credited with originating a sophisticated use of the unencumbered hands and feet as devastating weapons of defense. As a result of multicultural influences, Americans have organized new systems of fighting reminiscent of the ancient tactics but significantly different both in performance and purpose. Clearly, there are groups who prefer the physical violence of the NHB arts. Yet the inner peace attained through the personal discipline and symbolic violence associated with classical martial arts continues to remain popular.

BIBLIOGRAPHY

Beasley, Jerry. *American Karate: The Master Text.* Dubuque, Iowa: Kendall/Hunt, 1987.
Lawler, Jennifer. *The Martial Arts Encyclopedia.* Chicago: NTC, 1996.

JERRY L. BEASLEY

See also **Self-Defense and Security; Sports; Ultimate Fighting.**

MASCULINITY

There has been no shortage of explanations for male violence. Some theorists rely on biological differences between women and men, suggesting, for example, that androgens, or male hormones, especially testosterone, are the driving forces behind male aggression. It is true that testosterone is highly correlated with aggressive behavior; increased testosterone levels typically result in increased aggression.

Other scholars have used more evolutionary explanations, such as homosocial competition, which envisions male violence as the result of the evolutionary necessity for men to compete with one another for sexual access to females. Men fight with each other to create dominance hierarchies; the winners of those fights have their choice of females.

Unfortunately, the biological evidence is unconvincing. While it may be true that testosterone is associated with aggression, it does not cause the aggression but rather facilitates an aggressive tendency already present. (It does not affect the behavior of nonaggressive males, for example.) Nor does the causal arrow always point from hormone to behavior. Winners in athletic competitions experience increased testosterone levels after they win. Violence causes increased testosterone levels as much as hormonal increases cause violence. Nor does testosterone lead to violence against those who are significantly higher on the dominance ladder. Increased testosterone will cause a midlevel male baboon, for example, to increase his aggression against the male just below him, but it will not embolden him to challenge the hierarchical order.

Nor is there much evidence for the evolutionary theory of homosocial competition. In some cultures, males are not at all violent or competitive with each other. If "boys will be boys," these boys often behave differently in different cultures. And in some societies, including ours, males exhibit especially violent behavior against females—the very group for which they are supposedly competing.

Following the theories of Sigmund Freud, some psychoanalysts have explained male violence in the context of the Oedipal drama: the young boy must prove, to himself and to others, that he has successfully separated from his mother and transferred his identity to his father—that is, that he has become masculine. Male violence is a way to prove successful achievement of masculinity.

While not necessarily a cultural universal, this psychological model does help to explain the particular association of masculinity with violence, especially among younger males. (There are, of course, many societies in which masculinity is not associated with violence; examples include the Arapesh of Papua New Guinea as well as the Navajo, Hopi, and other Native American cultures.) Psychological explanations, however, often assume universal generalizations and do not account for cross-cultural differences or for the historical shifts in any one cultural group over time.

Age and Violence

If we are to understand the association of masculinity and violence, we have, therefore, to be specific. First, we must look at different groups of men. Violent behavior is not evenly distributed among all groups of men, but varies by class, race, age, region, ethnicity, and sexuality. Second, we must explore the historical fluctuations of that association and compare the contemporary United States with other industrial countries. When we do that, an astonishing picture emerges.

Young American men at the end of the twentieth century were the most violent group of people in the industrialized world. The homicide rate in the United States was five to twenty times higher than that of any other industrial democracy, even though we imprisoned five to twenty times more people than any other country on earth except Russia. In 1992 young men between the ages of fifteen and twenty-four had a homicide rate of 37.2 per 100,000. This figure was about ten times higher than that of the next closest industrialized country, Italy, and more than sixty times greater than that of the same age group in England.

Between 1985 and 1994 homicides by fourteen- to seventeen-year-old males more than tripled, as had the numbers of men in prison. In 1996 six states, including California, were spending more on prisons than on their state colleges and universities. Statistics at the end of the twentieth century also showed that one out of every three African American men in their twenties was either in prison, in jail, on probation, or on parole. Nine out of ten of those arrested for drunk driving were men; 84 percent of those jailed for fatal accidents resulting from drunk driving were men; and 86 percent of arson crimes were committed by men.

The criminologist Marvin Wolfgang notes that violent crime rises any time there is an unusually high proportion of young men between the ages of fifteen and twenty-four in the population. The psychiatrist James Gilligan observes that the only two innate biological variables that are predictors of violence are youth and maleness.

Defining Masculinity

Americans have long associated masculinity with violence. Some of our most venerated cultural heroes were soldiers; the actors who portrayed those soldiers in movies even became our heroes. Andrew Jackson's mother told her son—arguably the most mean-tempered and violent president in our nation's history—that "the law affords no remedy that can satisfy the feelings of a true man." The American frontier—perhaps a very large collection of younger males in the history of the industrialized world—provided a legacy of violence to American life.

In the aftermath of the Civil War, after the South had suffered a humiliating and emasculating defeat, young boys took to placing chips of wood on their shoulders, daring other boys to knock it off so they could legitimately have a fight with them. Only in America is "having a chip on one's shoulder" a badge of honor to some young boys.

Violence has long been understood as the best way to ensure that others publicly recognize one's manhood. Fighting was culturally prescribed for boys, who needed to demonstrate gender identity. In one of the best-selling advice manuals of the first part of this century, *The Boy and His Gang,* parents read the following:

> There are times when every boy must defend his own rights if he is not to become a coward and lose the road to independence and true manhood. ... The strong-willed boy needs no inspiration to combat, but often a good deal of guidance and restraint. If he fights more than, let us say, a half dozen times a week,—except, of course, during his first week at a new school—he is probably over-quarrelsome and needs to curb. The sensitive, retiring boy, on the other hand, needs encouragement to stand his ground and fight. (Puffer 1912, p. 81)

In this best-seller, boys were encouraged to fight once a day, except during the first week at a new school, when, presumably, fighting would occur even more often.

Lurking beneath such advice was the fear that boys who were not capable of violent behavior were not men at all. The specter of the "sissy"—the fear of emasculation, humiliation, and effeminacy that American men carry with them—is often responsible for a "masculine" response of violence. Violent behavior is a way to prove masculinity; one is a "real" man because one is not afraid to be violent. The psychiatrist James Gilligan speaks of "the patriarchal code of honor and shame which generates and obligates male violence"—a code that sees violence as the chief line of demarcation between women and men.

For many in the contemporary United States, masculinity is equated with the capacity for violence. From the locker room to the chat room, men of all ages learn violence is a socially sanctioned, credited form of expression. Male socialization is a socialization to the legitimacy of violence—from infantile circumcision (the United States is the only industrial nation to routinely practice male circumcision for nonreligious reasons) to being hit by parents and siblings; to routine fights with other boys; to the socially approved forms of violence in the military, in sports, and in prison (the United States is the only industrialized country that still employs capital punishment); to epigrams that remind us not to get mad but rather to get even, that the working world is the Hobbesian war of each against all, a jungle where dogs eat dogs.

Often, biological explanations are invoked as evasive strategies. "Boys will be boys," we say, throwing up our hands in helpless resignation. Whether a predisposition for violence is programmed biologically by testosterone or genetically by evolutionary reproductive success, the epidemic of male violence in America still begs the question, Are we going to allow our society to turn its back on this propensity for violence, or can we organize and find ways to minimize it? These are political questions and they demand political answers—answers that impel us to find alternative, nonviolent routes for men to express themselves as men.

"All violent feelings," wrote the great British writer John Ruskin, "produce in us a falseness in all our impressions of external things." Until we

---

Men and Crime

Men constitute 99 percent of all persons arrested for rape, 88 percent for murder, 92 percent for robbery, 87 percent for aggravated assault, 85 percent for other assaults, 83 percent for incidents of family violence, and 82 percent for disorderly conduct. Men are overwhelmingly more violent than women.

Men and Partner Abuse

Men learn that violence is an accepted form of communication between men and between women and men. The United States has been among the nations with the highest rates of rape, domestic violence, and spousal murder in the industrial world. Nearly 40 percent of all women who were murdered were murdered by a husband or boyfriend. At the end of the twentieth century the records showed that every six minutes a woman in the United States was raped, every eighteen seconds a woman was beaten, and every day four women were killed by their batterers.

transform the meaning of masculinity, we will continue to produce that falseness—with continually tragic consequences.

BIBLIOGRAPHY

Gilligan, James. *Violence: Our Deadly Epidemic and Its Causes.* New York: Putnam, 1996.

Kaufman, Michael. *Cracking the Armour: Power, Pain, and the Lives of Men.* Toronto: Viking, 1993.

Kimmel, Michael. *Manhood in America: A Cultural History.* New York: Free Press, 1996.

Puffer, J. Adams. *The Boy and His Gang.* Boston: Houghton, Mifflin, 1912.

MICHAEL S. KIMMEL

See also **Endocrinology: Testosterone; Gender; Machismo; Spousal and Partner Abuse; Women.**

MASOCHISM. *See* Sadism and Masochism.

MASS MURDER

*This entry is divided into two parts: **Collective Murder** and **Individual Perpetrators.***

COLLECTIVE MURDER

The United Nations Genocide Convention, passed on 9 December 1948, defines *genocide* as "acts committed with intent to destroy in whole or in part, a national, ethnical, racial or religious group." These acts can range from outright killing to creating conditions calculated to bring about a group's physical destruction. While political groups were not included in the definition (because a number of nations objected), extensive, genocide-like killings can be, and in the twentieth century frequently were, directed at political groups. Such killings have sometimes been called politicide.

A useful definition of *mass killing* is the killing of a large number of people, either at once or over time, who are usually somehow associated as members of a group. How group membership is defined may be imprecise. While usually there is no initial intention to eliminate the whole group, mass killing can be a way station in the movement toward genocide. In this article the term *mass murder* is used to refer to both genocide and mass killing.

Although wars between nations will not be the focus here, mass killing of civilians is frequent in war. The conditions that lead to genocide can also precipitate war, and genocide has repeatedly been perpetrated during war, as in the case of the Holocaust, when about six million Jews were killed by Nazi Germany and its allies during World War II, and the genocide of the Armenians in Turkey during World War I.

The Origins of Mass Murder

Historical Precedents. Mass killing has a long history. In ancient wars it was not uncommon for the inhabitants of entire cities to be massacred. Religious wars throughout history have been extremely brutal and often involved mass killing. Human sacrifice has been a widespread phenomenon in both the Old and the New World; in Aztec Mexico, as a political ritual, human sacrifices often totaled as many as twenty thousand people in one year.

The twentieth century witnessed numerous instances of mass killing, among them the Holocaust, the genocide of the Armenians, the autogenocide in Cambodia with Khmer killing Khmer between 1975 and 1979 (as well as minority groups), and the disappearances in Argentina, primarily between 1976 and 1979. Notable examples in the 1990s included the mass murder in Bosnia and the genocide in Rwanda. As the discussion of mass murders in which the United States was involved as either bystander or perpetrator will demonstrate, with appropriate consideration of the specific circumstances, this conception is broadly applicable.

Instigators of Violence. Difficult life conditions in a society can instigate mass murder. Intense economic problems, great political upheavals, and rapid social change profoundly affect people. They frustrate fundamental human needs, such as security, control over one's life, a positive identity, and connectedness with others. Societal upheaval also makes it difficult to understand the world and one's place in it. Certain cultural characteristics make it more likely that the members of a society will react to life problems and the attendant frustrations in ways that turn them against a group of people and may ultimately result in mass murder.

At times of societal upheaval individuals often turn to an ethnic, religious, racial, national, or political group for a sense of identity. Closely identifying with a group can fulfill basic needs, such as security and connectedness. Problems arise, however, when members elevate their own group by devaluing others or taking action against them. Often such groups scapegoat, or blame, a minority within the society for life problems that result from societal upheaval. Groups often create or adopt ideologies, such as communism or nationalism, that offer them a positive vision in difficult times. An ideology becomes destructive, however, when it is founded on identifying another group as an enemy who stands in the way of its fulfillment.

Intense conflict between groups can also instigate mass murder. Such conflict may involve vital interests, such as territory needed for living space, as in the case of the Israelis and Palestinians. Less vital self-interest is another instigator of mass murder. Wanting an area occupied by a minority for living space or for economic development was one reason for the mass killing of Native Americans in the United States.

Intense conflict may also involve tensions between a superordinate group and a subordinate group with limited power, rights, and access to resources, the most frequent cause of mass killing in the second half of the twentieth century. Economic and political demands, acts of protest, or rebellion by the subordinate group can lead to their mass murder by the superordinate group. Occasionally, as in the case of the Khmer Rouge in Cambodia, following successful rebellion a formerly subordinate group engages in mass murder. Conflict between a subordinate group and a superordinate group is more likely to intensify in difficult times. Life problems, which have a greater impact on groups that are already less well-off, intensify feelings of injustice, a powerful motivator for demands for greater rights and improved well-being.

Conditions Under Which Violence Escalates. As a group begins to harm a scapegoated group or an ideological enemy, discrimination and limited violence tend to give rise to greater harm and more intense violence if there are no countervailing forces to prevent this from happening. As a result of their actions, individuals who inflict harm on others change in ways that make it possible for them to do greater harm: they devalue their victims even more, seeing them as morally bad, as an enemy bent on their destruction. The standards of acceptable behavior in society change. Institutions are changed, or new ones are established to harm victims. According to Ervin Staub (1989), with "steps along the continuum of destruction," violence escalates.

Bystanders, be they individuals, groups, or nations, play a crucial role as witnesses to mass murder. Members of a group who are not themselves perpetrators and outside groups and nations have great potential to influence the course of events. Some bystanders remain passive; others, such as nations that do business with or provide aid to a perpetrator country, are complicit. In either case, they affirm the perpetrators and make increasing violence probable.

A number of social and cultural characteristics, such as prejudice toward or devaluation of a social group, make it more likely that instigating conditions will give rise to mass murder. The following forms of devaluation make this increasingly probable: the other is less intelligent, less likable, lazy; the other is morally bad; or the other is a danger, intent on harming or destroying us. An "ideology of antagonism," which usually results from a history of mutual violence in which each group sees the other as enemy and itself as the enemy of the other, has especially great instigating power, according to Staub.

Another predisposing characteristic is a monolithic, as opposed to a pluralistic, society. In a pluralistic society there are varied values and points of view. The public dialogue among groups in such a society makes scapegoating, the widespread adoption of destructive ideologies, and progression along a continuum of destruction less likely. One scholar concluded that democracies do not tend to engage in genocide. This seems true primarily of "mature" democracies, which are highly pluralistic. Mass murder has taken place in societies where democracy is less deeply rooted, for example in South American countries. Democracy is to varying degrees incomplete in most places. Less privileged groups, the poor and minorities, are frequently excluded from participation in it.

Strong respect for authority is another predisposing cultural characteristic. For example, long before Adolf Hitler came to power, Germans were regarded as especially respectful of and obedient to authority. There is evidence as well of strong respect for authority in Serbia and Rwanda. In such societies people are more easily directed by leaders to turn against certain groups and less likely to speak out against violent policies and actions. In Rwanda, for example, out of a total population of seven to eight million, with a 14 percent Tutsi minority, about eight hundred thousand people were killed between April and June 1994, primarily Tutsis, but also about fifty thousand Hutus who were seen as politically unreliable or for other reasons were regarded as enemies by the Hutu perpetrators. An extremist Hutu leadership used propaganda against the Tutsis, created paramilitary groups, used part of the army, and incited the population.

Unhealed group trauma, especially when it is due to past persecution and violence inflicted on a group, makes it likely that the group will feel endangered in the world and will respond to conflict or threat with violence. Healing by a group makes a continuing cycle of violence less likely.

The United States as Perpetrator

Mass Killing of Native Americans. Native Americans, profoundly different in appearance and ways of life from the whites arriving from Europe, were seen as primitive, uncivilized, and lacking culture. Over time, they also came to be seen as violent and dangerous. Devaluation, fear and self-interest, and desire for the land on which Native Americans lived—all affected government policies toward the Indians, creating an evolution of increasing violence that ultimately led to mass murder.

At first, the intention of U.S. policy was to civilize Native Americans, presumably to lessen their difference from other Americans and to enable them to function in white American society. Trade, religious missions and conversion, and white schooling for Indian children were all to serve this purpose. Whites saw these acts as altruistic. Native Americans were changing in response to their con-

tact with whites but not to a sufficient degree in the eyes of the European invaders. In general, Indians continued to live tribally and to occupy huge areas of land.

This policy of civilizing Native Americans was changed, and the new policy was to relocate them to the West instead. This new policy would both remove them from the vicinity of other Americans and make more land available for white settlement. Many tribes resisted relocation, and Indian battles with the U.S. Army ensued, especially after 1829, when Andrew Jackson became president. Some tribes fought until few of their members remained alive. The policies and practices toward Native Americans became increasingly harsh. While there seemed to be no overall plan, and probably no implicit intention of extermination, these practices constituted mass murder.

Several factors were thus in place for the instigation and escalation of violence by the new American nation against the country's native peoples. Whites viewed Native Americans as profoundly inferior. Implicitly supported by the ideology of manifest destiny, which affirmed the right of Americans to expand westward, the U.S. government policy toward the Indians was also supported by the participation of many Americans who accepted land taken from Native Americans—which the government made available to U.S. citizens at low cost or even free—and by the passivity of the rest of the population.

The policy of relocation and the increasing violence against Native Americans were also justified by the violent response of those under attack, who were reacting to the tremendous upheavals in their lives and to their treatment by Europeans in America. Members of certain tribes, like the Apache, came to be seen as intent on destroying whites; these tribes became the object of especially intense violence by the U.S. Army.

Lynchings of African Americans. Between 1865 and 1955 more than five thousand black people were killed by lynch mobs in the United States, mostly in the South. When taken together, these lynchings represent a form of mass murder. They took place in the context of deep-seated devaluation and hostility. Black people, when they were originally brought to America, were devalued because they were different in appearance, language, ways of life, and culture. In addition, whites had to justify taking these people violently from their homes and making them into and keeping them as slaves. To facilitate such justification blacks had to be seen as less than human, especially in a country founded on the basic principles of the dignity, rights, and equality of human beings. Laws and social customs after emancipation, such as Jim Crow laws and segregation, continued to reinforce the devaluation.

Some evidence indicates that lynchings occurred more often during difficult economic times, when cotton prices were lower in the South. In a climate of devaluation and persecution of blacks, some lynchings were initiated by a white person who out of self-interest could simply start a rumor about a provocative or criminal act committed by a black business competitor. Sometimes lynchings occurred relatively spontaneously; at other times they were planned, especially by the Ku Klux Klan.

An implicit pattern emerges from late-nineteenth- and early-twentieth-century newspaper accounts of lynchings in the South. A black person was accused of a crime, such as the murder of a white person or the rape of a white woman. The community responded with outrage. A mob formed, usually of men and boys (who were thereby socialized into mob conduct and lynching). The mob captured the accused or, if he (occasionally she) had already been arrested, overran the jail where he was being held. The victim was carried to a place of execution and frequently underwent horrendous torture. By this time women and children were often present as spectators. The victim was then hung or burned. Not infrequently, the victim was later found to be not the perpetrator of the crime and another black person, again assumed to be the perpetrator, was found and lynched.

Mass Killing of Civilians During the Vietnam War. In war, enemy images are usually created that evoke fear, hostility, and anger. They make it easier for soldiers to fight and kill and for civilians to accept the hardship of war and support it. There is usually also an ideology, such as nationalism, anticommunism (as in the case of Vietnam), and the defense of liberty. The immediate danger to their lives and the anger generated when friends are killed create additional hostility in soldiers. In Vietnam the belief that civilians aided and abetted the enemy contributed to feelings of distrust and hatred of Vietnamese people in general.

In war, the engagement by soldiers in violence and the orientation toward the enemy that is partly created, partly developed, make the escalation of violence probable. Without strong restraint imposed by authorities, brutality in fighting and violence against civilians become likely. In Vietnam the policy of keeping body counts, of judging success by how many enemies were killed, probably contributed to events such as the rampage in which U.S. soldiers murdered more than five hundred unarmed civilians on 16 March 1968 in the South Vietnamese hamlet of My Lai.

In one postwar study of Vietnam veterans, 20 percent of the men acknowledged having witnessed atrocities such as rape and murder of civilians; in another study 9 percent admitted having committed atrocities. The military and civilian authorities were passive bystanders to this activity; they were in a position to know about harmful, violent behavior but either ignored or did not take in relevant information that was available, thereby allowing atrocities to happen. The media in the United States did not report rumors of atrocities. Nothing was done to counteract the forces that make such behavior possible and even probable.

Mass Killing of Civilians at Dresden and Hiroshima. During World War II the Allied forces' carpet bombing of Dresden, Germany, on 13–15 February 1945 killed much of the population of that city. The devaluation of enemies increases as war goes on and is aided by the creation of intense enemy images. But there were also special sources of hostility toward Germany. Germany initiated the war, it engaged in tremendous atrocities, and it was working on the development of an atomic bomb. Its victory would have been a great threat to the United States. All these factors caused not only the Nazi rulers but to some extent all Germans to be seen as evil. The bombing of Dresden was intended to bring Germany to its knees.

In the case of Japan, also, there were special sources of hostility, such as the country's surprise attack on Pearl Harbor on 7 December 1941, its atrocities in China and other places, the suicidal missions of its kamikaze pilots, and the unnerving determination of its ruling regime and its soldiers generally. The belief that if the United States did not demonstrate its devastating power Japan would never give up fighting was the motivation and justification for the decision to drop an atomic bomb on Hiroshima on 6 August 1945 and on Nagasaki on 9 August 1945. Use of this bomb also may have been intended to communicate a message to the rest of the world, especially the Soviet Union, about U.S. power. There also may have

Dead bodies in the streets of Dresden, Germany, after a February 1944 bombing. CORBIS/HULTON-DEUTSCH COLLECTION

been a strong desire to see how the bomb would operate. The atomic bomb was used in a context of heavy conventional bombing of other Japanese cities, particularly Tokyo, where more than eighty thousand civilians had already been killed.

Both the carpet bombing of Dresden and the use of the atomic bomb in Japan were outcomes of increasing violence during World War II. A system of destruction existed, the enemy in each case was seen as evil and intent on destroying the United States, and the distinction between soldiers and civilians broke down.

The United States as Contributor

Genocide in Cambodia. The United States has a history of contributing to conditions that have led to mass murder in various countries around the world. For example, it can be argued that the United States created a situation that led to genocide in Cambodia in which about a million people were killed. The United States involved Cambodia in the Vietnam War by pursuing Vietnamese

troops into the country. It destabilized Cambodia by supporting the overthrow of its ruler Norodom Sihanouk. It extensively bombed heavily populated areas because they were in the hands of the communist Khmer Rouge. Confusion over who was responsible for the bombing turned the peasants against their own government, radicalized them, and made it easier for Pol Pot, the leader of the dominant Khmer Rouge group, to gain their support. The United States accidentally helped Pol Pot's group, as other Khmer Rouge factions competing with it for power were decimated by heavy bombing in the course of a major offensive in 1973.

Deaths in Central and South America. The United States also contributed to conditions for mass killing in Central and South America, particularly in Guatemala. In 1954 the democratically elected president of Guatemala, Jacobo Arbenz Guzmán, whom the U.S. government denounced as a leftist, was overthrown in an invasion sponsored by the United States that left roughly one hundred casualties on both sides. His overthrow was motivated by a combination of anticommunist ideology, a policy of containing communism, and a desire to protect U.S. economic interests in Guatemala. (The same motivations subsequently led to the support of violent regimes in other Central and South American countries, such as El Salvador and Chile.)

Decades of military rule followed in Guatemala. In the course of fighting guerrillas (that is, subordinate groups rising up against the dominant group) and during anti-insurgency campaigns, many civilians were killed, especially among the native Indian population. In 1990 it was estimated that a hundred thousand people had died in conflict since the 1954 coup. Villages and their inhabitants were destroyed; individuals were "disappeared" (that is, they were abducted and killed by government agents). The United States all along supported the governments that committed these atrocities; indeed, some members of the military that participated in killings were at times on the payroll of the Central Intelligence Agency.

The School of the Americas trained Central and South American military personnel in counterinsurgency techniques. Some of them later participated in severe human-rights violations: the disappearances in Argentina and the abduction, torture, and killing of people in other South American countries. In 1964 Defense Secretary Robert McNamara told the U.S. Congress, "The primary objective in Latin America is to aid, whenever necessary, the continual growth of the military and paramilitary forces, so that together with the police and other security forces, they may provide the necessary internal security." However, the United States continued to provide financial, political, and at times, military support (in the form of arms and advisers) while these forces, including those members who had been trained in the United States, engaged in gross human-rights violations, including torture and the murder of people who were peacefully working for political change or trying to improve the lives of poor people.

In practical terms, contributing to conditions that lead to mass killing is likely to encourage perpetrators even more than being a passive bystander to violence. This was probably the case when the United States increased its aid to El Salvador in 1984, even though about forty thousand people were killed there between 1979 and 1983, a large percentage of them as a result of extrajudicial executions by so-called security forces.

The United States as Passive Bystander

Germany. Being a passive bystander may take the form of continuing to carry on normal relations with a country that is known to be committing atrocities against some of its people. In 1936 the nations of the world, including the United States, affirmed Nazi Germany by holding the Olympic Games in Berlin. U.S. corporations conducted business in Germany during the 1930s despite the German state's increasing persecution of Jews and other forms of aggression. During the 1930s and early 1940s the United States accepted only 10 percent of the Jewish refugees that existing immigration quotas would have allowed into the country. Most of the people denied entry into the United States and elsewhere later faced death in extermination and labor camps.

Iraq. In the 1980s, after Iraq attacked Iran and even after Iraq was known to be using chemical weapons against its Kurdish citizens, the United States and other countries were providing military equipment and economic aid to Iraq. The United States saw Iraq as a counterweight to a fundamentalist, hostile Iran. Since violence tends to escalate rather than abate when bystanders implicitly support perpetrators, it is not surprising that Iraq proceeded to invade Kuwait in August 1990.

Rwanda. The United States and the international community were also passive bystanders to the genocide in Rwanda in 1994, when an estimated five hundred thousand to eight hundred thousand people were killed and two million refugees fled to neighboring countries. Warnings of impending violence and even of plans for genocide from, for example, Human Rights Watch and the commander of the UN peacekeeping force in Rwanda, in the years preceding the genocide as well as immediately before it started, were ignored. Once the killing started, the term *genocide* was avoided. Using the term would have activated the UN Genocide Convention and would have put great pressure on nations to respond. The size of the UN force was greatly reduced after the killing started. Attempts to build it up again were slowed by the resistance of a number of nations including the United States. The United States and the United Nations spent a long time negotiating the price the United Nations was going to pay for leasing equipment to be used by UN peacekeepers in Rwanda while very large numbers of people were being killed.

Domestic Impact of U.S. Action Abroad

In the 1960s and later the United States experienced social changes of many kinds that created social upheaval. Before the great improvement of the U.S. economy in the 1980s, there had been a decline in U.S. economic strength, primarily from the late 1960s through the 1970s. The Civil Rights movement and inner-city riots, the anti–Vietnam War movement, and the assassination of leaders, such as President John F. Kennedy in 1963 and Martin Luther King, Jr., and Robert Kennedy in 1968, brought political turmoil. The feminist movement transformed many aspects of U.S. culture. Family structures changed greatly. Accompanying all of this was a kind of social malaise in the country, a self-doubt, a confusion about the identity of the United States and its people.

This malaise was also partly the result of the psychological and social impact of U.S. behavior in the international realm. U.S. citizens have had a conception of the United States as a moral country. Many people came to see the Vietnam War, the intense destruction the United States perpetrated on a faraway people, as disconfirming this conception. Being involved elsewhere in the world in the creation of murderous systems, supporting such systems, or remaining passive in the face of violence against innocent people raised doubts in the minds of many U.S. citizens about their country as

Refugee corpses at Goma, Zaire, after tribal warfare in Rwanda, 1995. HULTON GETTY/
LIAISON AGENCY

one that uses its power to promote goodness and enhance human welfare.

The confused morality of U.S. actions in the international realm has contributed to the American people's unwillingness to risk American lives for humanitarian causes, as in Rwanda.

Bringing a Halt to Mass Killing

International Responses to Violence. Nations, including the United States, conduct their foreign policy to serve their national interest, which is usually defined in terms of power, wealth, and influence in the world. Nations have not traditionally seen themselves as moral agents responsible for protecting the lives and basic rights of citizens of other countries. The world, however, increasingly has been developing international laws and institutions to protect human rights; the Center for Human Rights and the High Commission for Human Rights are two important examples. In the late 1990s plans were under way for an International Court to punish perpetrators. The creation of these and other institutions has been a slow process, and the translation of these laws and institutions into action even slower, as shown by the failure of the international community to intervene in Rwanda.

An international climate must be created in which governments and the United Nations are expected to act to prevent mass murder and to halt it when it has already begun. Such a climate would require citizens to demand action by their governments and the creation of institutions that make fast action possible. It would also require an expansion of the definition of *national interest* to include the affirmation of basic human rights and moral values and the protection of human welfare. At the end of the twentieth century the international system resisted intervention in the internal affairs of nations, in part because intervention had often been misused. But it is essential that the principle of intervention for the protection of human rights be established and the processes developed by which it is activated.

Institutions must be created for gathering information that would provide early warning and, even more important, for using this information to activate responses by the international community. There are institutions that gather such information, such as Human Rights Watch, Amnesty International, foreign embassies, and UN personnel, but early warning and the analysis required for the information are not their central tasks. Moreover, there are no effective institutions for activating response. Offices within the United Nations that are part of national governments and are connected to each other are needed.

Responses could start with a private warning to offending governments and groups and the offer of mediation, conflict resolution, and help for leaders to find constructive solutions to conditions that instigate violence. If the private warning is unsuccessful, it could be followed by public condemnation, then, if necessary, aid could be withheld, the foreign assets of the country and its leaders seized, and boycotts and sanctions imposed. Early and resolute reactions make it less likely that violence will escalate. However, when necessary, military force ought to be used to halt mass murder. One way to increase the likelihood of action is to develop standards for when actions are required, what actions are required, and who is to take action.

U.S. Intervention to End Violence. The international boycott of South Africa, in which the United States, passing the first major antiapartheid act in 1986, had a significant role, was important to overthrowing the system of apartheid there in 1991. After years of hesitation the limited bombing by the North Atlantic Treaty Organization, led by the United States, stopped the fighting in Bosnia, which was at war from 1992 until 14 December 1995, when the Dayton Peace Agreement was signed.

In other parts of the world as well, the United States has played a constructive role. In Israel its participation in events, as a promoter of peace and a partner in working for a settlement of conflict at various times, substantially reduced the degree of violence by both Israelis and Palestinians. In Northern Ireland the United States was one of the parties that helped to move Protestants and Roman Catholics to negotiation, which led to an agreement in 1998 that offered hope for ending the centuries-old feud there.

Preventive Steps

Healing. Many actors, including nongovernmental civic organizations, can be involved in preventing mass murder. One of their goals must be to help previously victimized groups heal. Healing may be furthered in a number of ways: by the rest of the world acknowledging the group's suffering, offering empathy and support; by members of the group talking about their experiences and receiving empathy and support from each other; by facilitating grieving and mourning through memorials and ceremonies; and by helping victims rebuild shattered communities.

International truth commissions and tribunals are important in establishing what has happened. Knowing the truth has some healing power, as does seeing the rest of the world recognize what has happened. Extensive research with traumatized individuals has shown this. Various observations (for example, the intense distress of the Armenian community and its preoccupation with the world not having acknowledged that they were victims of genocide) suggest that this also applies to groups. The punishment of perpetrators, especially leaders, generates a sense of justice and communicates to potential victimizers that the international community does not condone such acts.

Members of the perpetrator group likewise need to heal. Usually, perpetrators also feel like victims, owing to earlier victimization or to violent responses to their violent acts. Often there is mutual violence. At the very least, their violent actions are wounding to perpetrators, as is the shame, often unacknowledged, that nonparticipating members of the perpetrator group feel. Some healing by both groups is a precondition for reconciliation, which is necessary to break what otherwise may be a continuing cycle of violence.

The Serbs, for example, had been ruled by Turks for centuries, until the second half of the nineteenth century. During World War II hundreds of thousands of these Serbs were killed by a Croat Republic allied to Nazi Germany. The collapse of communism, and then of Yugoslavia, was also extremely threatening to Serbs. The Serbs felt victimized again when, even after they initiated violence—by attacking Croatia when it declared its independence—Croatia ethnically cleansed about two hundred thousand Serbs from its territory. This past history, and the Serbs' vision of themselves as victims, probably contributed to Serb violence in Bosnia and Kosovo.

Unfortunately, there are no clear examples showing that healing has contributed to reconciliation on the group and national level. The world community does not usually try to help groups of people from past victimization. Perhaps Germany provides an example, although it is an example of healing by a perpetrator nation. As a first step, the Nuremberg trials, with their many thousands of pages of documents, most of them gathered by the Nazis themselves, combined with testimonies, provided powerful evidence of the horrors that Germany perpetrated. This made it difficult for Germans to consider themselves victims, especially since only some of the perpetrators were punished, not the population as a whole. The West, rather than isolating the country, reached out to Germany and provided economic aid, political support and guidance, and extensive contact.

Contact and Shared Goals. While superficial contact between antagonistic groups does little, significant contact and engagement with each other can help overcome past antagonisms. Identifying shared goals and working to fulfill them are especially important. This can happen in small groups where members engage with each other to deal with their history or to resolve conflict and work out practical matters of coexistence. It can happen in projects that benefit both groups, whether rebuilding houses or creating joint enterprises. The more such connections can be extended to the community level, the more the attitudes in the group that create the potential for violence will change.

Democratization and Other Culture Changes. Cultural and social systems can be developed that make mass killing unlikely. Economic development to reduce poverty and improve well-being is a primary focus of the UN vision to reduce violence. But it is a long-term strategy and other approaches are also needed. Social justice, which ensures that subgroups in societies are not deprived of rights and opportunities, reduces conflict between dominant and subordinate groups. It might also reduce the desire for ethnic groups to create their own nations, one of the frequent sources of conflict at the end of the twentieth century.

In a pluralistic, democratic society, unquestioning respect for authorities does not exist, and the devaluation of groups and discrimination against them is minimized. While democratization is an important avenue to cultural change, it has to be thorough in order to be effective. In the United States, Native Americans and African Americans were not initially included in pluralism and democracy and were denied access to the public domain. This made continued devaluation of and discrimination and violence against them easier and more likely. Equal civil, political, and economic rights and opportunities, deep contact between groups, and education that empowers all groups can improve group relations and make mass murder unlikely.

Ideology and Group Self-Concept. An abstract ideological vision, whether it be anticommunism, capitalism, freedom, or anything else, can lead to a destructive disregard for the well-being of individuals. Human beings need positive visions, which provide hope and purpose, especially in difficult times. Rather than focusing on identifying enemies, such visions must have as their central concern the well-being of all persons.

The way leaders and members of a society see themselves is also important. A powerful country like the United States has the obligation to provide positive world leadership, which hinges on the people's view of the nation as well as that of the leaders. Seeing oneself as special and superior can lead to a belief in the correctness of one's views and the specialness of one's rights and interests, which in turn can lead to a disregard of the rights of others and inappropriate interference in the affairs of others.

Inclusive Caring by Children and Adults. Mass murder arises out of groups and systems: culture, social conditions, the political system, relationships between groups, and the organization of the international community. But systems are created and maintained by individuals. Children must be raised to care about the welfare of other people and to have the moral courage to act on their caring. Their concern must be inclusive, extending beyond their own group to all human beings.

For this to happen, children require love, affection, and guidance. Adults can set rules and communicate values that imbue children with respect for other people and their needs. They can involve children in actions that benefit people, so that they learn by doing. The example of caring, helpful people is also important. But such caring must embrace people beyond one's own group. In Nazi Europe, people who took risks and in some instances lost their lives to help save persecuted Jews were often people whose parents had set an example by simply having social relationships with or not expressing prejudice toward people historically devalued in their group.

The Individual as Actor. The role of individuals in all this is crucial. As individuals join together, they can create a climate in which nations feel the obligation to be actively engaged in preventing violence. They can create social and political conditions and raise children in ways that make mass murder unlikely. This will happen when individuals develop the values and moral courage that lead them to speak out against policies and practices that harm people in their own group and against the passivity of their nations when this happens in other groups.

BIBLIOGRAPHY

Argentina/Comisión Nacional Sobre la Desaparición de Personas. *Nunca Más: The Report of the Argentine National Commission on the Disappeared.* New York: Farrar, Straus, Giroux, 1986.

Carnegie Commission on Preventing Deadly Conflict. *Preventing Deadly Conflict: Final Report.* New York: Carnegie Corporation of New York, 1997.

Comas-Diaz, L., M. B. Lykes, and R. D. Alarcon. "Ethnic Conflict and the Psychology of Liberation in Guatemala, Peru, and Puerto Rico." *American Psychologist* 53 (1998): 778–792.

Eisenberg, Nancy. *The Caring Child.* Cambridge, Mass.: Harvard University Press, 1992.

Etcheson, Craig. *The Rise and Demise of Democratic Kampuchea.* Boulder, Colo.: Westview, 1984.

Ezekiel, Raphael S. *The Racist Mind: Portraits of American Neo-Nazis and Klansmen.* New York: Penguin, 1995.

Fein, Helen. *Accounting for Genocide: Victims and Survivors of the Holocaust.* New York: Free Press, 1979.

———. "Accounting for Genocide After 1945: Theories and Some Findings." *International Journal on Group Rights* 1 (1993): 79–106.

Ginzburg, Ralph. *One Hundred Years of Lynchings.* Baltimore, Md.: Black Classic Press, 1988.

Herman, Judith. *Trauma and Recovery.* New York: Basic, 1992.

Hovland, C. I., and R. R. Sears. "Minor Studies of Aggression: Correlation of Lynchings with Economic Indices." *Journal of Psychology* 9 (1940): 301–310.

Kressel, Neil Jeffrey. *Mass Hate: The Global Rise of Genocide and Terror.* New York: Plenum, 1996.

Latane, Bibb, and John Darley. *The Unresponsive Bystander: Why Doesn't He Help?* New York: Appleton-Century Crofts, 1970.

Oliner, Samuel P., and Pearl Oliner. *The Altruistic Personality: Rescuers of Jews in Nazi Europe.* New York: Free Press, 1988.

Peck, Morgan Scott. *People of the Lie: The Hope of Healing Human Evil.* New York: Simon and Schuster, 1983.

Rummel, R. J. "Democide in Totalitarian States: Mortacracies and Megamurderers in *Widening Circle of Genocide.*" In *Genocide: A Critical Bibliographic Review 3.* Edited by Israel W. Charny. New Brunswick, N.J.: Transaction, 1994.

Sheehan, Bernard. *Seeds of Extinction.* Chapel Hill: University of North Carolina Press, 1973.

Staub, Ervin. "Altruism and Aggression in Children and Youth: Origins and Cures." In *The Psychology of Adversity,* edited by Robert S. Feldman. Amherst: University of Massachusetts Press, 1996.

———. "Cultural-Societal Roots of Violence: The Examples of Genocidal Violence and of Contemporary Youth Violence in the United States." *American Psychologist* 51 (1996): 117–132.

———. "The Origins and Prevention of Genocide, Mass Killing, and Other Collective Violence." *Peace and Conflict: Journal of Peace Psychology* 2 (December 1999).

———. *The Roots of Evil: The Origins of Genocide and Other Group Violence.* New York: Cambridge University Press, 1989.

Tebbel, John. *The Compact History of the Indian Wars.* New York: Hawthorne, 1966.

Wyman, David S. *The Abandonment of Jews: America and the Holocaust, 1941–1945.* New York: Pantheon, 1984.

ERVIN STAUB

See also **American Indians; Foreign Police, U.S. Training of; Hate Crime; Hiroshima and Nagasaki; Holocaust; Lynching; My Lai Massacre; Oklahoma City Bombing; War Crimes.**

INDIVIDUAL PERPETRATORS

The Federal Bureau of Investigation's *Crime Classification Manual* defines mass murder as "any single event, single location homicide involving four or more victims." The classification is subdivided into "classic" and "family" mass murder, with the former group of crimes excluding victims related to the killer by blood or marriage. A third category, "spree murder," is defined as the murder of multiple victims in "a single event with two or more locations"—in other words, simply mass murder in motion. The distinction does not contribute toward an understanding of the crimes.

The modern explosion of mass murder in the United States dates clearly from 1966, when Richard Speck and Charles Whitman, striking three weeks apart, left a total of twenty-six victims dead and thirty wounded. But a rundown of mass murders in the United States begins a hundred years earlier: In 1866 a Philadelphia resident, Anton Probst, hammered seven members of his employer's family to death. Six years later, in Connecticut, William Beadle beheaded his wife and five children, then shot himself with two pistols (one in each ear). An unknown home invader terrorized black families in Texas and Louisiana between January 1911 and August 1912, claiming forty-nine victims in eleven attacks. From September 1911 through June 1912, white families fell prey to an ax-wielding stalker in Colorado, Kansas, Iowa, and Illinois, with twenty-three slaughtered in five incidents. (A suspect, Henry Lee Moore, was identified but never prosecuted in those cases.) In 1928 Owen Oberst torched his family home in Kansas, killing his parents and five siblings. Howard Unruh—a "spree" killer, in FBI parlance—fatally shot thirteen of his New Jersey

Selected American Mass Murderers of the Twentieth Century

Name	Date	Venue	Approximate Number Killed	Method	Motive
Andrew Kehoe	1927	Mich.	39 + self	explosives	revenge
Robert Segee	1944	Conn.	168	arson	insane
Howard Unruh	1949	N.J.	13	firearm	insane
John Graham	1955	Colo.	44	explosives	profit
Francisco Gonzales	1964	Calif.	43 + self	gun/aircraft	insane
Charles Whitman	1966	Texas	18	knife/guns	insane
Mark Essex	1973	La.	10	firearm	racism
James Ruppert	1975	Ohio	11	firearm	family
Andrew Zimmer	1977	Tenn.	42	arson	jail protest
Humberto de la Torre	1982	Calif.	25	arson	revenge
George Banks	1983	Penn.	13	firearm	family
James Huberty	1984	Calif.	21	firearm	insane
Patrick Sherrill	1986	Okla.	14 + self	firearm	job/revenge
David Burke	1987	Calif.	43 + self	gun/aircraft	job/revenge
Ronald Simmons	1987	Ark.	16	varied	family
Julio Gonzalez	1990	N.Y.	87	arson	revenge
James Pough	1990	Fla.	10 + self	firearm	insane
George Hennard	1991	Texas	23 + self	firearm	insane

neighbors in 1949, in the course of a twelve-minute stroll around the block. A year later, in New Jersey, Ernest Ingenito wounded his wife and killed seven in-laws. In 1963 Frank Harris murdered an Arkansas couple and five of their seven children while robbing their home. The following year Francisco Gonzales shot the pilots of Pacific Airlines flight 773 flying over northern California; none of the forty-four persons aboard survived the crash.

Both the Speck and Whitman murders in 1966 were "classic" mass murders in FBI terms, though Whitman killed his mother and wife before climbing a university tower in Texas and shooting passersby at random. Since 1966 mass murders have recurred in the United States with numbing regularity. In fact, the United States, with barely 6 percent of the world's total population, produced two-thirds of all identified mass murderers in the twentieth century. At least 153 individual mass murderers were found in the United States; Europe (including Russia west of the Urals) produced thirty-two and Asia (including the Middle East) thirteen; only six cases were recorded for Africa and Latin America combined. Australia and New Zealand reported sixteen cases of mass murder and Canada (where social critics often complain of U.S. violence corrupting Canadian society) another ten.

Who Kills? How? And Why?

From American homes emerges the most mayhem, with family mass murders representing 44 percent of those recorded in the United States in the twentieth century. Ronald Gene Simmons is the most lethal family murderer to date: of the sixteen persons he shot and bludgeoned to death around Russellville, Arkansas, over four days in December 1987, fourteen were relatives. James Ruppert fatally shot eleven family members who gathered at his Hamilton, Ohio, home for Easter dinner in March 1975. Lorne Acquin, a pedophile living in Prospect, Connecticut, sought to cover his tracks by bludgeoning his sister-in-law, her seven children, and a six-year-old niece in July 1977. Ronald DeFeo's November 1974 massacre of his parents and four siblings is remarkable primarily for the series of books and movies inspired by "the Amityville horror," alleging demonic infestation of the family home on Long Island, New York.

Whereas most family slaughters occur in the home, classic mass murder may erupt anytime, anywhere. Alvin King invaded a Dangerfield, Texas, church in June 1980, shouting, "This is war!" and shooting fifteen persons, five of them fatally, before he was disarmed. (On 19 January 1982 he hanged himself in jail.) Gian Ferri, incensed by the progress of a lawsuit, raided a San Francisco legal firm in July 1993, killing eight and wounding six more, then turned the gun on himself. Even dining out becomes hazardous in the age of mass murder. Restaurants were selected as killing grounds by two of America's deadliest gunmen: James Oliver Huberty informed his wife that he was "going hunting; hunting humans," before he opened fire on diners at a McDonald's fast food restaurant in San Ysidro, California, in July 1984. Huberty killed twenty-one victims and wounded nineteen more before a police sniper cut him down. Seven years later, in October 1991, George Hennard drove his truck through the window of a Texas cafeteria and opened fire on patrons, killing twenty-three and wounding twenty-five, then shot himself.

Mass murders in the workplace in the United States account for 13 percent of the twentieth-century total. A 1993 report from the National Institute of Occupational Safety and Health listed murder as the third leading cause of occupational-injury death, with an average of 750 slayings per year. David Burke holds the record for workplace mayhem in America. Despondent over his dismissal from Pacific Southwest Airline, he smuggled a pistol aboard a flight going from Los Angeles to San Francisco in December 1987 and shot up the plane, killing himself and forty-three others in the resultant crash.

Homicides at public schools always elicit shock. Before the late 1990s schoolyard rampages of armed teenagers, most perpetrators of mass murder on campuses and in schools were men. Andrew Kehoe, a Michigan farmer enraged by a hike in his property tax, bombed a local school in May 1927, killing himself and thirty-nine others and wounding forty-three. Another suicide bomber, Paul Orgeron, killed himself, his son, and four others and wounded another nineteen on a Houston playground in September 1959. Edward Allaway, a custodian, shot nine coworkers, killing seven, at the California State University at Fullerton library in July 1976. Patrick Purdy, a drifter, raided a Stockton, California, elementary school in January 1989, killing five students and wounding twenty-nine others and one teacher before he committed suicide. Gang Lu, a doctoral candidate at the University of Iowa, reacted to the loss of a $1,000 prize for best dissertation in physics by killing four staff members and the student who outclassed him, then shooting himself, in November 1991.

Only one "classic" mass murderer in U.S. history was female. Priscilla Ford, a former teacher and a mental patient at the time of the incident, claimed to be obeying divine commands when she drove her car along a Reno, Nevada, sidewalk in 1980, killing six persons and injuring twenty-three. Sylvia Seegrist, dubbed Ms. Rambo (after the 1985 violent action movie *Rambo*), came close in 1985, killing three of ten victims she shot at a Pennsylvania shopping mall; but numbers technically exclude her from the list. In the category of family slayings, female perpetrators are more common and more lethal. Between 1926 and 1983 eighteen American housewives claimed eighty-two victims (sixty-six of them children), with eleven of the killers committing suicide. Lethal gas was the chosen weapon for seven of these "gentle" killers; five used firearms, and the remainder killed by arson, drowning, strangulation, stabbing, or defenestration.

Surprisingly, given the United States' racial history, only four mass murders in the twentieth century have been prompted by racism, three of those crimes committed by African Americans. In January 1973 Mark Essex killed ten whites and wounded seventeen before he was shot by New Orleans police. Twenty years later, Roland Smith, a black activist, killed himself and seven others when he torched a white-owned clothing store in Harlem. That same month, December 1993, a

Priscilla Ford, a "classic" mass murderer, sentenced in 1982 in Reno, Nevada, to the gas chamber. CORBIS/ BETTMANN-UPI

deranged black gunman named Colin Ferguson targeted whites and Asians on a Long Island Railroad passenger car, killing five and wounding eighteen. (A jury rejected his "black rage" defense and sentenced him to life imprisonment.) The only white racist mass killer of the twentieth century, Fred Cowan, a neo-Nazi, killed five minority coworkers and a policeman in New Rochelle, New York, then shot himself, in February 1977.

Other African American mass murderers, like their white counterparts, acted out of motives having nothing to do with race. In 1983 a Pennsylvania prison guard named George Banks, presumably under some kind of stress, went berserk and shot thirteen persons, beginning with his wife and five children. James Pough had already served time for one homicide, plea-bargained down to aggravated assault, when he ran amok in Jacksonville, Florida, in June 1990. Pough killed ten strangers and wounded five before shooting himself. In Ridgewood, New Jersey, a mail clerk named Joseph Harris donned a ninja costume prior to killing his supervisor and three others in October 1991.

Violent crime among minors increased exponentially in the second half of the twentieth century, but young mass murderers are rare. Eleven-year-old Ray DeFord, the youngest (and most prolific) solitary mass murderer as of the late 1990s, killed eight victims when he burned a Portland, Oregon, apartment house in July 1996. Five months earlier, in San Diego, fifteen-year-old Josh Jenkins used an ax and hammer to murder five family members. Kipland Kinkel, also fifteen, combined family and classic mass murder in May 1998, first killing his parents, then shooting nine others, two fatally, at his high school in Springfield, Oregon; a majority of the fifteen students injured were hurt trying to escape. The last in a rash of schoolyard shootings that year, Kinkel's rampage inspired psychologists to coin a new term—"intermittent explosive disorder"—as an explanation of sorts for impulsive youth violence.

Although mention of mass murder typically evokes the image of a wild-eyed gunman, the most destructive mass killers have been arsonists and bombers. Robert Segee, a pyromaniac, confessed to setting a Connecticut circus-tent fire that killed 168 persons and injured 174 in July 1944, but he escaped prosecution for murder and was jailed instead on unrelated arson charges. John Gilbert Graham planned to kill his mother for insurance when he bombed a United Airlines flight in November 1955; forty-four others also died in the blast. Andrew Zimmer set fire to a Tennessee jailhouse in June 1977, killing forty-two fellow inmates. In 1982 a family argument drove Humberto de la Torre to burn the Los Angeles apartment house managed by his uncle, incinerating twenty-five residents. In March 1990 ejection from New York's Happy Land social club prompted Julio Gonzalez to torch the building, at a cost of eighty-seven dead. (The Ohio State Penitentiary fire that killed 332 inmates in 1930 is omitted here, along with the Oklahoma City bombing of April 1995, which left 168 dead, because at least two perpetrators were involved in each event.)

Outcomes

Unlike serial killers who cover their tracks and may remain at large for years, traveling widely in search of victims, mass murderers seldom escape their crime scenes; they frequently commit suicide or battle with police. Their violence, whether directed at family members, coworkers, or total strangers, is typically a desperate reaction to some stressful situation in their lives which they attempt to solve with blood and thunder, culminating in their own destruction or imprisonment. The crimes may be elaborately planned, but escape rarely figures into the scenario. Instead, mass murder is more often calculated as a farewell "lesson"—to a loved one, to an enemy, or to the world. The act of murder thus becomes, in effect, a grisly suicide note. (One clear exception to the rule, John List, remained at large for eighteen years after the 1971 murders of five family members in Westfield, New Jersey. Following an account of his case on the *America's Most Wanted* television program, List was traced to Virginia, where he was living under a pseudonym, and apprehended.)

Murder "Teams"

Mass murder, when not committed by some extremist or criminal group, is normally a solitary enterprise. There are, however, rare occasions when two killers operate together. Unlike serial murder, wherein "team" killers are frequently male-female couples, those who commit mass murder in tandem seem to be invariably male. In America's most notorious cases, one of the massacres was apparently committed to disguise a rape; four sprang from greed, robbery degenerating into slaughter; and two present apparent cases of *folie à deux,* with two youths sharing fantasies of violence against perceived enemies.

1905: Mark Gibson and Felix Powell, two farmhands working on the Conditt farm, near Edna, Texas, ran amok after their employer's twelve-year-old daughter rejected Powell's advances on 28 September. After raping and killing the girl, they slaughtered her mother and three siblings with a knife and ax. Powell and Gibson blamed the crime on unidentified blacks, but their own bloody clothing betrayed them. Tried and condemned separately, both were later hanged.

1959: Ex-convicts Richard Hickock and Perry Smith planned to rob Kansas farmer Herbert Clutter of $10,000 allegedly kept in a safe, at his home near Holcomb. Invading the home on 15 November 1959, they bound four members of the family before searching in vain for the mythical safe. Infuriated, the robbers proceeded to kill their prisoners with a shotgun and knife. Upon capture, both men confessed and were sentenced to die. Hanged in April 1965, the murderers were made famous by Truman Capote's "nonfiction novel," *In Cold Blood* (1966).

1973: Drifters Douglas Edward Gretzler and William Luther Steelman present a rare case of serial killers who "graduated" to mass murder. Together, they robbed and killed eight victims in Arizona, during October and November 1973. On 6 November, in Lodi, California, they invaded a private home, binding and gagging nine hostages, afterward shooting their victims a total of twenty-five times. Captured two days later, both men were convicted and sentenced to life imprisonment in California, before extradition to Arizona for additional trials. There, both were condemned. Steelman died in 1987, with his case still on appeal. Gretzler was executed by lethal injection in June 1998.

1983: Gunmen Kwan Fai Mak and Benjamin Ng robbed a gambling club in Seattle's Chinatown on 19 February, shooting thirteen employees and patrons before they fled. Twelve victims died, the survivor identifying his assailants from police mug shots. Ng (also suspected of a double murder in 1982) was sentenced to life imprisonment, while Mak was condemned (his sentence later commuted to life).

1991: Teenage robbers Johnathan Doody and Allesandro Garcia invaded a Buddhist temple near Phoenix, Arizona, on 9 August, stealing cash and electronic gear after executing six monks, an elderly nun, and two male disciples of the sect. Garcia later pleaded guilty, while Doody was convicted at trial. Both received life sentences.

1998: Obsessed with guns and violence, preteen killers Andrew Golden and Mitchell Johnson stole weapons from a relative and staked out the Westside Middle School, in Jonesboro, Arkansas, on 24 March. Setting off a fire alarm to rout staff and students from the building, they shot fifteen persons, killing a teacher and four female classmates. Johnson pleaded guilty and Golden was convicted in juvenile court, each receiving the maximum allowed sentence: confinement to age twenty-one.

1999: Allegedly embittered by harassment from their peers, self-styled Trenchcoat Mafia members Eric Harris and Dylan Klebold were armed with four guns and numerous homemade bombs when they invaded Columbine High School in Littleton, Colorado, on 20 April. Hoping to kill hundreds, they murdered a teacher and twelve classmates before committing suicide. Speculation that they deliberately targeted athletes, Christians, or minorities appears to be unfounded.

The Profile

The profile of an "average" American mass murderer reveals a white male, approaching middle age, who may fairly be described (even if married, with children) as a loner. He is typically preoccupied with "macho" sports and symbolism: martial arts and bodybuilding, military garb and gear, all manner of firearms, explosives, and knives. He is depressed or moody, prone to blaming scapegoats for his private failures, cultivating fantasies of retribution and revenge. Unfortunately, in the high-stress modern world, such individuals are not rare. Most simmer quietly throughout their lives; a few explode. As not everyone who harbors a grudge against a relative or neighbor, an employer or society at large, can be tracked, let alone professionally helped, prevention of sporadic mayhem is essentially impossible.

BIBLIOGRAPHY

Douglas, John E., et al. *Crime Classification Manual*. San Francisco: Jossey-Bass, 1992.

Fox, James Alan, and Jack Levin. *Overkill*. New York: Plenum, 1994.

Frasier, David. *Murder Cases of the Twentieth Century*. Jefferson, N.C.: McFarland, 1996.

Lane, Brian, and Wilfred Gregg. *The Encyclopedia of Mass Murder*. London: Headline, 1994.

Newton, Michael. *Mass Murder: An Annotated Bibliography*. New York: Garland, 1988.

Segrave, Kerry. *Women Serial and Mass Murderers*. Jefferson, N.C.: McFarland, 1992.

MICHAEL NEWTON

See also **Serial Killers; Schools; Speck, Richard; Unruh, Howard; Whitman, Charles.**

MASTERSON, WILLIAM "BAT"
(1853–1921)

Bat Masterson might best be described as a rounder, a likable if quick-tempered peace officer and gambler who gained a reputation as a gunfighter. He was born Bartholomew Masterson in Quebec, Canada, in 1853, but for most of his life he used the name William Barclay Masterson. When and why he changed his name is as mysterious as speculations about his nickname, Bat, but there is no denying that Masterson made his mark on the boomtown West.

Masterson's parents settled in Sedgwick County near Wichita, Kansas, in 1871. In 1872 Bat and his older brother, Ed, hired on as graders for the Santa Fe Railroad and made their first trip to Dodge City. Dodge was the lusty, brawling headquarters for buffalo hunters; between seventeen and thirty men were killed there in 1871–1872, the first year of its existence. The Masterson boys used it as base for their own forays onto the range. Entrepreneurs from Dodge set up the trading post at Adobe Walls on Indian land in 1874, and Bat was there when the Comanche and Kiowa attacked. He enlisted as an army scout for the duration of the Red River War against the southern Plains tribes.

In January 1876, at Cantonment Sweetwater (later Mobeetie), Texas, Masterson killed a soldier, Corporal Melvin A. King. Masterson was wounded in that fight but recovered and was hired as a policeman in Dodge City the summer of 1876. The next year he invested in a saloon, was arrested for interfering with a policeman, and served as undersheriff for Ford County, all before being elected sheriff of Ford County that fall at the age of twenty-four. Masterson proved to be a capable officer, managing a huge county with obvious success. He was effective as a peace officer, but reformers helped defeat him in his bid for reelection two years later. He left Dodge for Colorado, where he worked as a gambler.

In 1881 he followed Wyatt Earp to Tombstone, Arizona, but in April he was called back to Dodge to help his brother James, who was having trouble with his business partner. When he got off the train, a gunfight ensued in which one of the partner's associates was wounded. Bat was fined $8 and costs. Later he became marshal of Trinidad, Colorado, where he helped prevent the extradition of John Henry "Doc" Holliday back to Arizona on murder charges in the aftermath of the O. K. Corral gunfight between the Earp brothers and the Clantons.

Masterson returned to Dodge City in 1883 to assist his friend Luke Short, who had been driven out of town by rivals posing as reformers. With the aid of other gunmen, including Wyatt Earp, Short was reinstated, and the ironically named Dodge City Peace Commission became a staple of the town's legend. In 1884 Masterson tried newspaper publishing, printing one issue of *Vox Populi* before shutting down the presses. After that he briefly took up the cause of prohibition and, as a special officer, closed down Dodge City's saloons.

Masterson's reform zeal waned quickly. He quit Dodge for good, was in Fort Worth, Texas, when Luke Short killed Jim Courtwright (a well-known gunman), but ultimately settled in Denver, where he gambled and enjoyed his reputation as a frontier personality. Occasionally he served as a peace officer, but the sporting life became his vocation. He founded an athletic club and became embroiled in a bitter rivalry with another club. Masterson eventually sold out and, in 1902, following a drunken spree with a gun in his hand, was asked to leave Denver.

Masterson spent the rest of his life in New York City. In 1905 President Theodore Roosevelt appointed him a deputy U.S. marshal for the Southern District of New York, but this position was largely honorary. He became a sportswriter and editor for the *New York Morning Telegraph* and something of a local celebrity. In 1907 he published a series of articles, "Famous Gunfighters of the Western Frontier," in *Human Life Magazine*, but he was never nostalgic for the old frontier days. He died at his desk in October 1921.

BIBLIOGRAPHY

DeArment, Robert K. *Bat Masterson: The Man and the Legend.* Norman: University of Oklahoma Press, 1979.

GARY L. ROBERTS

See also **Dodge City; Earp Brothers; Frontier; Gunfighters and Outlaws, Western; Holliday, John Henry "Doc"; O. K. Corral Gunfight.**

MATERNAL PRENATAL VIOLENCE

Maternal prenatal violence assumes two distinct yet interrelated forms. The first involves some aspect of maternal behavior that is seen as damaging to the fetus. Prenatal maternal conduct has been subject to legal scrutiny since the late nineteenth century. Whereas most early prosecutions stemmed from charges of wrongful death and negligence resulting from physical injury, substance abuse among pregnant women has become the focus of legal sanctions to combat prenatal violence. The second form of maternal violence involves acts perpetrated against pregnant women, usually by intimate partners.

Pregnancy and Drug Use

The use of drugs during pregnancy is relatively common. The National Institute on Drug Abuse estimates that approximately 19–20 percent of women use alcohol or tobacco while pregnant and that 5.5 percent use at least one illicit drug. However, it was the emergence of cocaine, specifically crack cocaine, that generated the states' interest in the prosecution of pregnant drug users. By the end of the 1980s, women suspected of illegal drug use during pregnancy, and those who gave birth to drug-exposed infants, were subject to a variety of criminal and civil actions—for neglect, delivery of drugs to a minor, child abuse and endangerment, and sometimes manslaughter.

The campaign to combat prenatal drug use in the United States has focused on punitive, rather than rehabilitative, intervention, and public policy

battle has occurred under the auspices of the criminal justice system rather than social welfare programs. Jurisdictions have pursued both criminal and civil actions against mothers, and in many cases a combination of the two. Although few of these actions taken by the states have survived legal challenge, the courts have been hesitant to dismantle the states' apparent interest in protecting the fetus and holding the mother accountable for potentially harmful prenatal conduct. Instead, most appellate courts have overturned convictions of women accused of endangering their fetuses on the basis that state action violated the initial intent of the legislature. (The scope of legislation for neglect, delivery of drugs to a minor, child abuse, and endangerment was originally intended to include only children—this protection was not extended to the unborn.)

One of the most striking aspects of public concern over the issue of prenatal substance abuse was the speed with which states sought to make prenatal drug ingestion a criminal, as opposed to a public health or social welfare, issue. Since there were no statutes that specifically criminalized drug use during pregnancy (nor were there any that established criminal liability for maternal conduct resulting in prenatal injuries), prosecutors were forced to use existing laws in creative and often unprecedented ways. Popular prosecutorial strategies included filing criminal charges for child abuse and neglect, involuntary manslaughter and homicide, and use of controlled substances. The American Civil Liberties Union estimated that from the late 1970s to the mid-1990s, two to three hundred women were prosecuted, generally under abuse and neglect statutes. Prosecutors in thirty states have tried to use existing criminal statutes to bring charges against pregnant women. In general, these types of prosecutions have not withstood appellate review, largely because of the ambiguous legal status of the fetus and the departure of such prosecutions from the original intent of state legislatures. In 1987 a South Carolina court ruled, however, that women could be prosecuted under such statutes because the viable fetus is considered a person.

State actions via civil legal remedies have been more pervasive and considerably more successful than attempts at criminal prosecution because the courts give states greater leeway in their justifications for intervention on civil grounds. Civil remedies have broadly included the use of child neglect statutes, involuntary civil commitment, and tort actions. In response to the barrage of "crack baby" stories that appeared in the media throughout the late 1980s and early 1990s, several states tried to adapt existing criminal child neglect and abuse legislation to include the unborn, thus allowing for the prosecution of the mothers. Several prosecutions were unsuccessful when the courts concluded that a fetus did not constitute a "child" within the child-endangerment statutes. The courts further emphasized that it was the responsibility of the legislature to "criminalize the ingestion of cocaine during pregnancy when such ingestion results in harm to the subsequently born child"(*People v. Morabito* 1992). So far, no state has created legislation to impose additional criminal penalties on pregnant drug users.

Violence Against Pregnant Women

Because of the breadth of publicity garnered by the adverse effects of maternal drug use on pregnancy outcomes, the impact of other factors has not been widely assessed. Notably absent from the social science literature is research on violence suffered by pregnant women and its relationship to drug use and pregnancy outcomes. Interpersonal violence during pregnancy is a frequent and increasingly common cause of maternal and fetal injury. Prevalence studies from the 1990s indicate that between 4 and 20 percent of pregnant women are beaten, typically by intimate partners. The wide range of figures indicates the paucity of solid research on the problem.

Many researchers have tried to disentangle the cause-and-effect relationship between the use of alcohol and other drugs and the experience of violence. Studies of violent incidents among pregnant women indicate that victims of violence are more likely to use drugs both before and during pregnancy than nonvictims. Abused women consistently report higher consumption of alcohol and tobacco in pregnancy compared to nonabused women. Furthermore, an intimate partner's drug use has also been associated with an increased risk of being a victim of violence during pregnancy. Although no single pregnancy outcome has been associated with the experience of intimate partner violence, according to a study by Kimberly Theidon in 1992, the percentage of battered women who gave birth to low-birth-weight infants was nearly double that of nonbattered women. Women who experience physical violence during pregnancy are more likely to delay seeking prenatal care, which further confounds and obscures the interactions between victimization and substance abuse during pregnancy.

Thus, maternal prenatal violence is both an act of physical battering perpetrated against a pregnant woman and, as the U.S. justice system defines it, an act attributed to women who use drugs during pregnancy. Although there is evidence of a relationship between these two forms of violence, the extent and direction of this association is unclear. Many women may initiate or increase drug use in response to physical abuse, and the drug use of their intimate partners may perpetuate the cycle of violence. Clearly, prenatal drug use does not occur in isolation, and the pursuit of punitive actions as a response to a serious public health issue must be reevaluated.

BIBLIOGRAPHY

Inciardi, James, et al. *Cocaine-Exposed Infants: Social, Legal, and Public Health Issues.* Thousand Oaks, Calif.: Sage, 1997.

Lieb, J. L., and C. Sterk-Elifson. "Crack in the Cradle: Social Policy and Reproductive Rights Among Crack-Using Females." *Contemporary Drug Problems* 22 (winter 1995).

Mathias, Robert. "NIDA Survey Provides First National Data on Drug Use During Pregnancy." *NIDA Notes* (January/February 1995).

Peak, K., and F. S. Del Papa. "Criminal Justice Enters the Womb: Enforcing the 'Right' to Be Born Drug-Free." *Journal of Criminal Justice* 21 (1993).

Theidon, Kimberly. "Taking a Hit: Pregnant Drug Users and Violence." *Contemporary Drug Problems* 22 (winter 1995).

HILARY L. SURRATT

See also **Alcohol and Alcoholism; Developmental Factors: Prenatal Factors; Drugs.**

MEDIA. *See composite entries on* Television *and* Film. *In addition, the following articles cover media violence:* Advertising; Internet; Journalism; Pornography; Representation of Violence; Serial Killers, Representations of; Sports.

MEDICINE AND VIOLENCE

Following the **Overview** *are two subentries:* **Emergency Medicine** *and* **Medical Experimentation on the Mentally Ill.**

OVERVIEW

In 1991 the Harvard Medical Practice Study concluded that complications caused by physicians, nurses, and other health care providers affect more than 1.3 million patients in American hospitals every year. The occurrence of iatrogenic (literally, caused by a physician) injury or illness is not new. The result of negligence, misdiagnosis, system failure, and abuse, medical harms have been recognized as a growing problem since the 1950s and 1960s, following the dramatic expansion of pharmacological therapies after World War II.

Origins

The concept of iatrogenic injury or illness may be nearly as old as medicine. The Code of Hammurabi, which regulated the practice of Babylonian physicians and surgeons circa 1700 B.C.E., specified punishments for physicians whose patients died under their care. Reflecting the importance of the patient's social status, the penalty for the death of an aristocrat was amputation of the physician's hand or fingers; if a slave died under a physician's care, the doctor was required to pay half the slave's worth in silver. More than twelve centuries later, the Hippocratic tradition established the duty to avoid harm (reflected in the admonition "above all, do no harm," a statement not contained in the Hippocratic Oath, as many mistakenly believe) as the cardinal responsibility of the physician.

Harm is a complex concept. It is useful to distinguish between different kinds of medical harms, between such bad outcomes as death and injury that occur in spite of a caregiver's prudent and diligent treatment and the bad outcomes that arise from intentionally reckless, uninformed, and negligent behavior on the part of doctors, nurses, technicians, and researchers. Historically, medical malpractice suits have been one avenue for patients to pursue in the face of bad outcomes. Large empirical studies of medical injury and malpractice cases, however, suggest that although many medical injuries are indeed caused by negligence, few injuries resulting from negligence (less than 5 percent) actually give rise to litigation. Not only do the instances of medical injury far outnumber claims against physicians for medical injuries, but in many cases malpractice claims arise when there is no medical harm or injury. While malpractice suits and law may shed some light on issues of medical harm and violence, they are an imperfect tool for understanding the rates of medical injury and medical harm in a given time and place.

Evolution of Surgical Science

In the United States, medical malpractice rarely intruded on the lives of physicians and patients before 1840, when a "contagion" of lawsuits startled members of the medical profession. As the his-

torian James Mohr notes, malpractice cases, which soared 950 percent in American state appellate courts in the decades between 1830 and 1860, demonstrated one irony of medical and surgical advancement. Whereas only two decades earlier patients with compound fractures would have undergone amputation of a limb, improved orthopedic techniques made it possible to save the affected arm or leg, although the results were not always perfect. Physicians who attempted to salvage limbs in difficult cases met with inflated public expectations and were sued by patients dissatisfied with a shortened, deformed, or misshapen arm or leg.

Surgery as a discipline experienced rapid growth in the second half of the nineteenth century. Transformed by the introduction of ether and chloroform in the 1840s and the developments in antisepsis introduced in the 1860s by Joseph Lister, surgeons radically extended their explorations of the head and trunk. These advances produced rising public expectations about the capacity of surgeons to intervene effectively in the disease process.

Patient Rights and Informed Consent

At the same time that advances were being made in medical science, the expanding surgical repertoire fostered suspicion that unconscious patients, especially women, would be sexually exploited by physicians. In addition to fears about "anesthetic rape," such critics as the pioneering woman physician Elizabeth Blackwell warned about the large-scale "mutilation" of women by gynecological surgeons intent on removing healthy female sexual organs as treatment for both menstrual problems and a broad range of mental illnesses. Following their investigation of the State Hospital for the Insane in Norristown, Pennsylvania, where a separate annex ward was created for women scheduled to undergo surgery for removal of both ovaries, the Committee on Lunacy of the Pennsylvania State Board of Public Charities in 1893 pronounced the operation not only illegal and experimental in nature, but also "brutal and inhumane." By 1906, when enthusiasm for some varieties of sexual surgery was waning, one physician estimated that some 150,000 women had undergone these operations.

Beginning in the 1890s, accusations by patients about involuntary surgery increasingly clogged American courts, where surgeons found themselves charged not only with malpractice but battery, the unauthorized touching of the body. Four

Medical Experimentation on Slaves

Unlike those Americans in the 1840s–1860s who sued physicians for injuries resulting from medical or surgical treatment, African American slaves had no legal recourse. In a time of considerable uncertainty about effective therapies, some slave owners allowed their sick or injured slaves to become "material" for physicians to test new remedies or procedures. In one of the most notorious examples, the South Carolina physician James Marion Sims, known as the father of American gynecology, acquired seven female slaves who had developed vesico-vaginal fistulas, a debilitating condition in which urine leaks into the vagina, often the result of injury during childbirth. In exchange for feeding and housing these women at his own expense, Sims was permitted, beginning in 1845, to perform experimental surgical procedures on his captive subjects, in an effort to develop an effective surgical treatment for their condition. Several of his subjects underwent as many as thirty procedures; none of the women received the anesthetic agents newly introduced into medical practice. Once Sims perfected the surgical technique for repair of the fistula in 1849, he began performing the surgery on white women.

legal cases involving battery between 1905 and 1914 have been recognized as formulating the basis for informed consent in American law. In the most famous and most frequently cited case, *Schloendorff v. Society of New York Hospitals* (1914), Mary E. Schloendorff consented to an abdominal examination but insisted that "no operation" be performed. After the surgeon removed a fibroid tumor while the patient was anesthetized, Schloendorff sued the hospital where the surgery was performed. In rendering a decision in the case, Justice Benjamin Cardozo of the New York State Court of Appeals offered a classic statement about a patient's right to self-determination and the limits of surgical prerogative: "Every human being of adult years and sound mind has a right to determine what shall be done with his body, and a surgeon who performs an operation without his patient's consent commits an assault, for which he is liable in damages." In light of this ruling and other case findings, surgical journals and hospital administration manuals in the 1910s and 1920s advised surgeons to obtain written permission from patients prior to performing any surgical procedure.

Coercive Sterilization

In virtually the same decades that Cardozo articulated the fundamental importance of individual autonomy in medical care, state legislatures across the nation embarked on an ambitious program to apply surgical solutions to intractable social problems through the passage of compulsory sterilization laws for criminals, the mentally ill, and the mentally retarded. An important part of the eugenics movement, the powerful social and intellectual program to improve human heredity in the early twentieth century, the passage of coercive sterilization laws depended for its success on physicians and surgeons who campaigned for laws to restrict the reproductive freedom of the genetically "unfit." In the late 1890s new surgical techniques for vasectomy (cutting the vas deferens) in men offered an attractive and less mutilating alternative to castration, the removal of the genitals, as a means of preventing reproduction.

In 1899 Dr. Harry Sharp began systematically sterilizing boys at the Indiana State Reformatory using the new technique of vasectomy, but he did so without legal authorization. At Sharp's urging, Indiana in 1907 became the first state to implement legislation authorizing sterilization of convicted criminals, the mentally ill, and the mentally incompetent. Two years later, in 1909, Connecticut, Washington, and California followed Indiana's example in enacting laws that offered institutional physicians broad power to sterilize prisoners, the feeble-minded, and the insane. California emerged as a leader in coercive sterilization; in the years between 1909 and 1921 more than twenty-five hundred people in the state—the majority in institutions for the mentally ill—were legally sterilized without their consent. In addition to vasectomy in males, surgeons performed tubal ligation (cutting the fallopian tubes) to prevent reproduction in women, and experimented with both X rays and radium as nonsurgical methods to achieve sterility in both women and men.

Coercive sterilization laws survived a major constitutional challenge when, in 1927, the U.S. Supreme Court upheld the constitutionality of the Virginia sterilization statute. In *Buck v. Bell* the Court applied the precedent from a 1905 ruling upholding the state's interest in compelling vaccination against smallpox to make the case that the collective interests of society could override the interests of the "manifestly unfit" whose existence posed a threat to societal well-being. In the wake of the *Buck* decision, other state legislatures passed laws enabling similar restrictions on reproductive freedom. By 1932, thirty-two states had laws on the books. Between 1907 and 1970 more than sixty thousand Americans underwent forcible sexual sterilization procedures.

Human Medical Experimentation

The laws that supported coercive sterilization reflected assumptions about the larger social benefits that would accrue from the sacrifice of the few. In the medical research community, a similar ethos apparently worked to normalize the participation of the sick poor, orphans, and the mentally ill in medical experiments with or without the consent of these individuals or their guardians. Although such leading American researchers as the Harvard physiologist Walter Bradford Cannon acknowledged the importance of consent in experimentation, most researchers failed to meet this standard in conducting research, especially in research that seemed to pose little threat to the participants. Historians have only begun to document the extent to which large numbers of institutionalized children participated in clinical trials of vaccines and diagnostic tools for measles, scarlet fever, polio, syphilis, chicken pox, tuberculosis, and other diseases in the first half of the twentieth century. In addition to children, prisoners, the mentally compromised, and the socially vulnerable were pressed into service as research subjects as the scope of scientific medicine expanded.

The most notorious example of human experimentation performed without the knowledge or consent of the participants was a forty-year study of untreated syphilis in more than four hundred black men living in rural Alabama. Conducted by the Venereal Disease Division of the U.S. Public Health Service, the Tuskegee Syphilis Study began in 1932 and ended in 1972, after national outrage at the treatment the men had received at the hands of government scientists. In order to achieve compliance with the study, white researchers deliberately deceived the men they had recruited with promises of therapy for their "bad blood," including advertising a wholly diagnostic procedure like lumbar puncture (which entailed inserting a needle into the spinal canal for removal of fluid) as a "special treatment." In addition, study doctors

took steps to insure that men participating in the study did not receive penicillin or other antibiotics from physicians outside the study.

The Tuskegee Syphilis Study, a powerful and evocative symbol of the exploitation of African Americans by the white medical establishment, may be the longest nontherapeutic study in the annals of medical history. The exploitation of black Americans by the research establishment, however, was hardly unique. Race, like social class, helped to render some Americans especially vulnerable to researchers intent on establishing scientific or medical facts and oblivious to the rights of their research subjects. During World War II, many more Americans became unwitting participants in medical research identified as important for the war effort and for the Cold War that followed.

As a 1995 report from a presidentially appointed committee makes clear, the Atomic Energy Commission and its successor agency, the Department of Energy, and the Department of Defense sponsored research programs that exposed large numbers of Americans to various kinds of ionizing radiation. The Advisory Committee on Human Radiation Experiments estimated that some four thousand experiments involving human exposures to radiation took place in the years between 1944 and 1974. As part of a larger project to establish safety guidelines for occupational exposures to plutonium, eighteen people received injections of the radioactive metal in the 1940s. In 1945 the first patient, a fifty-three-year-old "colored male" named Ebb Cade received an experimental plutonium injection when he was hospitalized in Oak Ridge Army Hospital (in Oak Ridge, Tennessee) following an automobile accident. Similar injections were undertaken at the University of California, the University of Chicago, and the University of Rochester, where cancer patients, because of their shortened life expectancy, were specifically selected to receive the experimental injections.

Although some of these patients may have been informed about their participation, most of the patients, according to their surviving family members, were not aware that they had participated in these injections. The human radiation experiments, in addition to the plutonium injections, included studies at the Fernald School for the Retarded in Massachusetts in which boys were fed oatmeal containing radioactive isotopes, experiments in "whole-body" radiation involving indigent, mostly African American, cancer patients at the University of Cincinnati, the irradiation of testicles of prison inmates in Oregon and Washington, and experiments at Vanderbilt University in which approximately 820 poor, pregnant women were administered tracer doses of radioactive iron as part of a study of iron metabolism. In the 1990s, some of these patients or their surviving family members received financial compensation for their unwitting participation in these research projects.

Psychosurgery and Social Control

In the wake of public disclosure about the Tuskegee Syphilis Study, together with revelations that mentally handicapped children at the Willowbrook State School (in Staten Island, New York) had been purposely infected with hepatitis virus and elderly patients at the Jewish Chronic Disease Hospital (in Brooklyn, New York) had been subjected to cancer injections, the Massachusetts senator Edward M. Kennedy conducted hearings on human experimentation in 1973. At these Senate hearings, the "unlimited freedom of action which physicians have in the treatment of their patients" came under fire.

In addition to experimentation, the practice of psychosurgery, especially prefrontal lobotomy, attracted harsh criticism. Introduced in 1936, lobot-

omy, a surgical procedure involving cutting into the frontal lobe of the brain, became a popular, if controversial, treatment for serious mental illness. Before the decline in popularity of lobotomy in the mid-1950s, more than twenty thousand Americans had undergone the procedure. In 1970 controversy over psychosurgery swelled over proposals advocating lobotomy as a means of controlling violent behavior. In the political and social context of the race riots and urban unrest that rocked Americans in the late 1960s, the specter of forcible surgical control of violent offenders, dramatized in the film version of Ken Kesey's *One Flew over the Cuckoo's Nest* (1975), made lobotomy a highly charged issue.

In addition to an investigation of psychosurgery by the President's Commission for the Protection of Human Subjects of Biomedical and Behavioral Research, which actually endorsed careful, controlled use of the surgery, a coalition of civil rights groups and minority and antipsychiatry groups successfully campaigned in Oregon (1973) and California (1976) for legislation to regulate the practice of psychosurgery. In both states, this legislation, which included provisions for obtaining informed consent from patients and their families, was followed by stricter restrictions on the perfor-

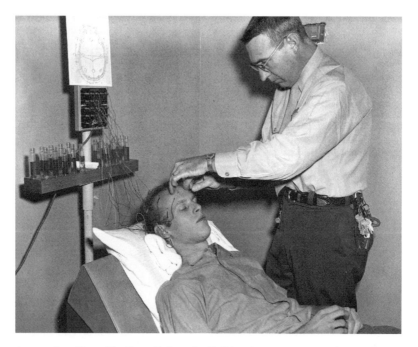

A guard at Vacaville State Prison in California prepares a prisoner for a lobotomy in 1961. The Vacaville warden, William Keating, was a psychiatrist who believed that "criminality" was lodged in certain areas of the brain. CORBIS/TED STRESHINSKY

mance of psychosurgery on incarcerated individuals. These regulations, the controversy surrounding psychosurgery, and the malpractice "crisis" of the 1970s further reduced the number of psychosurgical procedures performed in the United States. In 1982 the Oregon legislature enacted a law prohibiting psychosurgery; by this time, the number of procedures in American hospitals had declined to less than two hundred operations a year.

For many people, the history of lobotomy is an object lesson in medical arrogance and misjudgment, a story of surgeons willing to mutilate patients' brains in the name of therapy and social utility. Such a version of events neglects the complex interactions between surgeons, medical science, and society, and fails to take into account the acute distress that patients and their families experienced in the face of serious, intractable, and seemingly untreatable illness. Such distress led some patients not only to consent to such procedures, but to seek them out, to persuade physicians to undertake desperate remedies, and to thank doctors for offering the promise of relief from suffering.

Efforts Toward Prevention

Since the 1970s medical harm has received increasing scrutiny in an effort to understand both the extent of the problem and the strategies that may be used to limit the damage it inflicts in the lives of patients and their families. In the field of anesthesia, for example, concerted attention to preventable mistakes in the administration of anesthetics identified a number of factors contributing to poor patient outcomes, including nonstandardization of monitoring equipment, poor communication between physicians and nurses, haste, lack of attention, and fatigue. The redesign of machines and the development of new monitoring equipment, shorter hours for anesthesia residents, and the routinization of protocols for evaluating a patient's progress while under anesthesia have each contributed to a decline in anesthesia deaths.

In the field of surgery, similar attempts to reduce such predictable human errors as operating on the wrong body part have been undertaken. In 1998 the American Academy of Orthopedic Surgeons adopted the practice of having the surgeon initial with a marker the body part to be cut before the surgery is performed.

Taking a cue from the aviation industry, physicians and surgeons have looked to computer-driven patient simulators that enable both residents and experienced physicians to confront life-threatening conditions without risking the lives of actual patients. These technologies offer promise for averting preventable error in health care. They do not address, of course, harms that arise from medical ignorance, from the fact that medical science has yet to recognize a particular malady, treatment, or side effect. Nor do such technologies affect the social biases and professional norms that contributed to such profound failures as the Tuskegee Syphilis Study and the coercive sterilization of thousands of Americans identified as "socially inadequate."

BIBLIOGRAPHY

Dally, Ann. *Women Under the Knife: A History of Surgery.* New York: Routledge, 1991.

DeVille, Kenneth A. *Medical Malpractice in Nineteenth-Century America.* New York: New York University Press, 1990.

———. "Medical Malpractice in Twentieth Century United States: The Interaction of Technology, Law, and Culture." *International Journal of Technology Assessment* 14, no. 2 (spring 1998).

Faden, Ruth, and Tom L. Beauchamp. *A History and Theory of Informed Consent.* New York: Oxford University Press, 1986.

Lederer, Susan E. *Subjected to Science: Human Experimentation in America Before the Second World War.* Baltimore: Johns Hopkins University Press, 1995.

Mohr, James C. *Doctors and the Law: Medical Jurisprudence in Nineteenth-Century America.* New York: Oxford University Press, 1993.

Pressman, Jack D. *Last Resort: Psychosurgery and the Limits of Medicine.* Cambridge, U.K.: Cambridge University Press, 1998.

Rothman, David J. *Strangers at the Bedside: A History of How Law and Bioethics Transformed Medical Decision Making.* New York: Basic, 1991.

Sharpe, Virginia A., and Alan I. Faden. *Medical Harm: Historical, Conceptual, and Ethical Dimensions of Iatrogenic Illness.* Cambridge, U.K.: Cambridge University Press, 1998.

SUSAN E. LEDERER

See also **Assisted Suicide and Euthanasia; Euthanasia; Sterilization, Involuntary; Tuskegee Syphilis Study.**

EMERGENCY MEDICINE

Along with coroners and homicide detectives, emergency physicians stand vigil over the consequences of our violent society. There are almost one hundred million emergency department visits in the nation annually, and while the exact number attributable to violence is unknown, it likely exceeds ten million. It has been said that the principal users of U.S. emergency departments are those "too sick, too poor, or too crazy" to receive care anywhere else. For this reason, emergency departments provide a unique window into the unrecognized injustices of American society and the covert and insidious ways in which class, race, age, and gender biases enact their toll on the victims of discrimination.

A Brief History

Up to the time of the Korean War, soldiers accounted for the majority of patients in need of emergency treatment for injuries resulting from violent acts. Five physicians signed the Declaration of Independence, yet Revolutionary War soldiers were responsible for their own health care. It took a letter from General George Washington to prompt Congress to establish the first military hospital.

The heavy, slow, three-quarter-inch musket balls used in the Revolutionary and Civil Wars left victims with a wide swath of injured tissue that typically contained bone fragments, clothing, dirt, and germs carried in from the surfaces of victims' bodies. Cleaning musket ball injuries was difficult for the physician and extremely painful for the patient. The saying "bite the bullet" has a historical origin; bullets with tooth marks have been found at battle sites. The only anesthetic during the Revolution was whiskey. Amputation, a dangerous and costly procedure in terms of human life, was the only definitive treatment for wound infection.

The outbreak of the Civil War in 1861 slightly predated the development of sterile technique and widespread acceptance of the germ theory. Not surprisingly, far more Civil War soldiers died from infections (wound infections and contagious diseases such as dysentery) than directly from injuries suffered on the battlefield. Chloroform and opium provided some comfort to injured Civil War soldiers, but amputation remained the principal treatment for wound infection.

During this war, assistant surgeon and medical director of the Army of the Potomac Jonathan Letterman created what is considered the first ambulance service, a system that provided field aid and transportation to field hospitals for Civil War soldiers. Field hospitals were often unsanitary, located near polluted areas, on damp ground, or near unburied bodies. These hospitals were also often undersupplied and subject to long periods of inactivity interrupted by influxes of overwhelming numbers of patients during battles.

Medical care during the two World Wars was markedly more effective than during the Civil War. For the first time, fewer men died from disease than in battle. Advances in medicine lowered the mortality rate of mobilized men in World War I to 2.5 percent, compared with16.5 percent in the Civil War (Union troops only). In World War II the availability of penicillin and blood plasma helped physicians save patients who would have perished in previous wars.

While improved methods of triage and transport in World War II expedited the administration of definitive medical care, it was the introduction of helicopters in the Korean War that made it possible to deliver patients to MASH (mobile army surgical hospital) units within hours of their injuries. These units, staffed by anesthesiologists and surgeons, were designed to get surgical candidates to the operating room as quickly as possible. The *mobile* in their name was not a public relations ploy—these units relocated as often as every two weeks to maintain a safe distance from the battlefield.

In the Vietnam War, MASH units were replaced with permanent facilities built farther from the front. This strategy was enabled by the introduction of Huey helicopters that could travel longer distances at higher speeds, thereby delivering patients to better hospitals in equivalent or shorter times than in the Korean War. The introduction of medical evacuation planes made it possible for a wounded soldier to go from the battlefield to a California hospital in nineteen hours.

The improvements in medical care and transportation that enhanced the care of soldiers injured overseas did not immediately translate into better emergency care at home. Prior to 1960, most patients could identify a personal physician who they would call if sick or injured, and since the physician's office typically had the same equipment as the emergency room, there was little reason for patients to utilize emergency care. Emergency rooms were typically staffed by nonspecialized moonlighters: resident trainees and itinerant physicians seeking to supplement their incomes. These physicians were not specifically trained in the treatment of trauma.

In the 1960s, as a result of advances in trauma care derived from Korean and Vietnam War experiences and the development of the defibrillator—the first specialized treatment for life-threatening cardiac-rhythm disturbances—the emergency department could provide care that was not available in the physician's office. The development of these methods and technologies created the need for physicians who were specifically trained to execute these techniques and provide general emergency care.

In 1968 the American College of Emergency Physicians was formed, with the goal of fostering the development of emergency medicine, and in 1979 emergency medicine was formally recognized as a legitimate medical specialty with its own certifying board, the American Board of Emergency Medicine (ABEM). The number of residency programs dedicated to training emergency medicine specialists increased from 23 in 1975 to 120 in 1999, and over half of the estimated full-time jobs in emergency departments are now filled by the 20,000 physicians who have achieved ABEM certification. Visits to the emergency department increased from 73 million in 1975 to nearly 100 million in 1997. Reasons for this include: an increasingly mobile society in which patients often move away from their doctor and do not find another; changes in medical practice that diminish the round-the-clock availability of family physicians; the perceived convenience of emergency care for episodic illness; and an ever increasing number of uninsured and underinsured patients who have nowhere else to go.

Penetrating and Blunt Trauma

Although there are many ways to classify trauma, the most widely used conceptual framework distinguishes between blunt trauma and penetrating trauma. This taxonomy has gained favor because strategies for diagnosis and treatment of the two entities are generally distinct. Of course, these categories sometimes overlap. Bombs and other explosives can produce a combination of penetrating injuries (shrapnel), blunt injuries (from sound waves), as well as thermal injuries (burns).

Penetrating trauma typically involves projectiles (bullets, shrapnel, arrows) or sharp objects (knives) that puncture the skin's surface. Penetration occurs when a sharp object or one with high momentum is applied to a relatively small surface area, creating sufficient pressure to exceed the skin's protective strength. This form of trauma is almost always the result of an intentionally violent act, although projectiles can be the accidental by-product of industrial processes. In contrast to the

---

Gun Violence

Between June 1992 and May 1993, there were 100,000 nonfatal gunshot wounds treated in U.S. emergency departments of which 57,500 were due to violent acts. The nation's failure to recognize the importance of firearm violence (and provide meaningful legislation to address the problem) may in part be because the victims are predominantly young black males, a disenfranchised segment of society. In the late 1990s a series of seemingly random acts of gun violence in our nation's schools demonstrated that no group was immune to gun violence and focused the public's interest on gun control legislation. It is unclear, however, whether public concern will be translated into effective legislation. Perhaps more emphasis would be placed on the problem if citizens and public officials recognized that the average cost of medical care for a gunshot victim is $357,000, 80 percent of which is paid through public funds. While many gun owners intend for their weapons to be used as a means of self-defense against robbers, their enthusiasm for this protection might be tempered by the knowledge that guns purchased with this intention are eighteen times more likely to kill a family member than a predator.

---

musket balls used in the eighteenth and nineteenth centuries, modern steel-tipped bullets, traveling at great speed, cut through clothing rather than dragging it into the wound, and are often so hot that they are sterile when they pierce the skin. Any body structure can be damaged, and the degree of injury is highly dependent on the path that the object takes through the body. Millimeters can mean the difference between life and death. A gunshot wound to the chest can bounce off a rib, producing minor injury, or go between the ribs, creating fatal cardiac wounds.

Blunt trauma can result from objects colliding with humans, humans colliding with objects, and from differential deceleration of parts of the human body as a result of these events. Injuries may be limited to the superficial structures and skeleton (bruises, broken bones) or may involve damage to solid organs (liver, spleen, brain, spinal cord) or hollow organs (heart, lungs, digestive tract). Whereas the existence of penetrating trauma is typically obvious (one can see the hole), internal injuries from blunt trauma may be occult (not apparent from superficial examination of the body). Trauma from blunt blows to the body may result from violent acts (the use of fists, crowbars, hockey sticks) or nonviolent industrial processes or household accidents. Trauma in which the human—not the object—is the projectile typically occurs during transportation, when a vehicle undergoes rapid deceleration and passengers are thrown against restraints (seat belts, shoulder belts, airbags), strike objects within the vehicle, or are ejected and collide with objects outside the vehicle.

Vehicular accidents represent the preponderance of blunt trauma and are usually violent. The body is violated and the appearance of injured patients and mangled autos may produce severe emotional reactions, especially among the uninitiated. However, the extent to which these violent acts can be considered *acts of violence* varies from case to case. A driver who intentionally strikes down a pedestrian has committed an act of violence, but what if the incident was accidental and the driver was speeding or intoxicated? Is poor judgment an act of violence when it results in trauma to oneself or another? If so, is poor judgment an act of violence when it does *not* result in trauma? Is excessive speeding a violent act in itself?

Vehicular violence has two prevalent forms: aggressive driving (mainly speeding) and driving under the influence of alcohol. Not surprisingly, these often coincide. In 1995, 41,786 people were killed in motor vehicle accidents at an estimated cost of $11 billion. From 1987 to 1995, 23 percent of the fatal accidents involved both alcohol and excessive speed, 16 percent involved alcohol alone, and 16 percent involved speeding alone. These numbers underscore the importance of public education and legislative efforts to promote sobriety and safe vehicle operation.

Emergency physicians and surgeons work together to care for trauma patients. Experience has shown that there is a window of time (called the "golden hour") during which the medical staff has the best chance of intervening and preventing life- and limb-threatening damage. This means that within sixty minutes of an accident, 911 is called and help dispatched to the scene, emergency medical technicians and paramedics initiate treatment and transport the patient to the emergency department, and the trauma team performs its assessment and initiates critical treatment. Because

the stabilization of critically ill patients may require the intensive application of resources not immediately available at all hospitals at all times, many locales have organized trauma systems that steer patients who have major injuries or are at risk for such injuries to specialized centers. These centers have teams of emergency physicians and nurses, radiology technicians, respiratory therapists, pharmacists, surgeons, and anesthesiologists who work in a rapid, coordinated manner to identify and treat traumatic injuries. These teams often also have social workers and counselors who help families deal with their loved ones' injuries, and help patients deal with the psychological, economic, and social aspects of their predicaments.

The division between blunt and penetrating trauma not only serves a medical purpose, but is also a marker for the demographic and socioeconomic status of the victims. Because they possess the economic resources to own a car, persons of higher socioeconomic status are overrepresented in the population of victims of major automotive trauma. These persons are likely to have medical insurance, and the emergency departments that care for them are likely to operate at a profit. In contrast, persons from minority populations and of lower socioeconomic status are far more likely to be victims of penetrating trauma and are unlikely to have health insurance. For example, a twenty-five-year-old black man is nine times more likely to be stabbed or shot than his white counterpart, but the automotive death rate for that man is only 75 percent of that of the white male. Uninsured trauma patients place tremendous economic strain on the facilities that care for them. As a consequence of the United States' failure to provide basic health care for all Americans, many trauma centers and emergency departments have closed because of lack of funds in the areas where they are needed most. A further irony is that, lacking war-related victims to tend to, the U.S. military has paid inner-city trauma centers for the right to place personnel in these hospitals so that they can gain experience treating victims of penetrating trauma.

Abuse and Neglect

The medical community distinguishes among four types of abuse: child abuse, sexual abuse, domestic violence, and elder abuse or neglect. These labels are mere constructs—patients can be victims of several types of violence at once or suffer abuse that does not fit into a particular category.

The terms are, however, useful in identifying social issues that warrant the attention of public agencies and in grouping patients who require similar intervention.

Initial efforts in the development of emergency medicine were directed at treating acute injuries. Over time, however, it was recognized that there were many patients who came to emergency departments for care, but did not acknowledge that their injuries or conditions were the result of violence or neglect. A child's broken leg may have resulted from a playground accident, or it might represent child abuse. A woman's bruised eye might be attributable to a fall, or it might be the warning sign of domestic violence or sexual abuse. A malnourished elderly patient with bedsores may not have the resources to care for himself, but evaluation of the home situation to exclude the possibility of elder abuse or neglect is warranted. In each of these cases, there is the potential for missing the violence underlying the physical complaint, and thereby missing the opportunity to correct the fundamental problem. These considerations are not solely theoretical. One study found that 54 percent of physicians, nurses, and social services workers do not screen routinely for domestic violence.

Many forces contribute to the underdiagnosis of a violent etiology for trauma in the emergency department. First, in virtually all emergency department encounters, the physician is unlikely to know the patient and may be unable to detect subtle changes in personality or physical condition. Second, the patient, his or her caretaker, or his or her domestic partner may intentionally avoid revealing the truth for fear of reprisal, legal consequences, or social stigma. Third, emergency physicians may be resistant to considering these diagnoses because they: (1) have not been trained to engage in the emotionally uncomfortable task of confronting the patient or his or her family; (2) feel that they are too busy treating emergencies to open a potential "can of worms"; or (3) do not wish to be involved in a process that may result in their having to use private time to testify in court. Moreover, society's tacit acceptance of sexism and ageism, as illustrated by historically poor support provided to victims of domestic violence and elder abuse and the failure to punish and rehabilitate assailants, has made physicians question whether an intervention will produce a better outcome for the patient. To increase the detection of occult violence in trauma cases, training in the identification and handling of these matters has been incorporated into the curricula of medical schools and residency training programs, and screening techniques have been developed to identify each type of abuse. Various state legislatures have augmented existing child abuse and sexual assault reporting laws, which mandate the reporting of all suspected domestic violence and elder abuse and indemnify physicians from countersuit should they, in good faith, mistakenly report an innocent party.

Child Abuse. In 1995 one million children were reported to be abused and one thousand of them died from their injuries. Child abuse can take the form of physical abuse, sexual abuse, and neglect. While some injuries and patterns of injury (including immersion burns, multiple bruises, bruises with finger demarcations, and certain fractures) virtually assure that abuse has occurred, many injuries are insufficient to establish a diagnosis of child abuse. For these cases, attention must be focused on whether the story is consistent with the child's age and the type of injury. For example, it is unusual for nonwalking infants to incur injuries to the long bones of their legs. The child's and parents' behavior also must be carefully assessed. Children beyond infancy may be overly affectionate toward the medical staff or unusually tolerant of painful procedures. Older children, in contrast, may behave in ways that assist the parents in covering up the abuse. Parents of abused children may refuse laboratory or radiological tests for their child, argue with their spouses, or fail to comfort the child during the physical examination or procedures.

The treatment of child abuse begins with the treatment of acute injuries, a full physical examination for the purpose of seeking signs of old or chronic injuries and establishing legal evidence, the completion of standardized child abuse reporting forms, and the notification of police and social services. In small children, total body X rays may be helpful in looking for signs of healing fractures. The differentiation of normal from abnormal genitalia in children with suspected sexual abuse is difficult and is best done by those with special training. Many urban and suburban areas have developed multidisciplinary SCAN (Suspected Child Abuse and Neglect) teams that provide comprehensive care and evaluation of suspected abuse. If the child is medically well enough to go home, the crucial decision concerns whether the home environment poses further risk to the child. If there is any doubt regarding the safety of the child, the child is usually placed in protective custody until the situation can be evaluated.

Sexual Abuse. Adult sexual assault is epidemic in some segments of American society; a study conducted in 1993 found that one in eight women report having experienced some form of sexual assault (Resnick et al). Victims of sexual assault require specialized emergency department care to prevent pregnancy and transmission of sexually transmitted diseases and HIV, provide emotional support and counseling, and collect evidence for legal proceedings. In most states, all suspected and documented abuse must be reported to authorities; however, in most cases the decision to press charges is based on the victim's wishes.

Residency programs in emergency medicine include training in the legal (for example, evidence collection), medical, and emotional aspects of caring for victims of sexual abuse. As with child abuse, however, many populated areas now have specialized teams that provide comprehensive care for rape victims. Some teams are mobile (meaning that they will travel to any local emergency department) and others are based at sites designated as "rape trauma centers." Law enforcement officers preferentially direct victims to these hospitals. The team often includes past victims who use their experiences with the emotional consequences of rape to aid new victims. The examination of a victim of sexual abuse includes combing of pubic hair for particulate evidence, obtaining bacterial cultures of all penetrated orifices, and gathering samples to check for semen. DNA fingerprinting helps confirm the identity of the person who allegedly produced the semen.

Domestic Violence. A visit to the emergency room is commonly a cry for help for many of the two to four million women who suffer from domestic abuse each year. Approximately 90 to 95 percent of the reported cases of domestic violence involve women as the victim (Bureau of Justice Statistics 1993). It is clear that domestic violence is rampant in our society. However, studies vary widely in their prevalence estimates, concluding that as few as 11 percent or as many as 35 percent of women visiting emergency departments have been abused. Emergency physicians who have not trained themselves to question the possibility of domestic violence every time they see an injured patient will seldom make a diagnosis of domestic violence. Certain injuries may suggest domestic vi-

olence, such as injuries to the head and neck, defensive injuries (such as bruising of the forearms from defending one's head and upper body from blows), burns, bites, fingernail scratches, wounds in various stages of healing (suggesting multiple episodes of abuse), or old wounds (suggesting an unnecessary delay in obtaining care). However, there are few injuries that prove that domestic violence has occurred, and victims of such violence seldom volunteer the causes of their injuries to a doctor. To establish a diagnosis of domestic violence, the physician must isolate the patient from the assailant-partner (this can be difficult, since the partner will attempt to control the medical interview and prevent the victim from speaking candidly), and establish sufficient rapport that the patient trusts that the doctor can provide protection from further abuse. Direct questioning regarding the existence of abuse has proven to be the best strategy. Women who are not abused are typically not offended by the question, and victims are more likely to disclose in response to direct questions; subtle allusions tend to provide more opportunity for denial. Unfortunately, abusive relationships are complex, and many victims will not admit to abuse, even if approached in an optimal way. Fear, embarrassment, economic or psychological dependency on the abuser, belief that they deserve the abuse, or belief that society will punish them instead of the abuser, all contribute to victims' unwillingness to disclose the situation.

Regardless of the patient's willingness to admit to the etiology of the injuries, each complaint should be addressed and a full physical examination conducted. Careful documentation of injuries (ideally with photographs) is important, as the patient may decide to take legal recourse at a later date. If the physician suspects abuse despite the patient's denial, he or she should at least remind the patient that such treatment is not deserved. The treatment and prevention of domestic violence extends far beyond the scope of emergency department care. Nevertheless, the emergency department can play an important role in the detection and treatment of victims.

Elder Abuse or Neglect. Up to 10 percent of the elderly fall victim to abuse or neglect. Victims are typically disabled, cognitively impaired, or mentally ill, and are most frequently abused by their caretaker. Neglect, as evidenced by cachexia (low body weight), poor hygiene, pressure ulcers, and disorders of the skin due to exposure to urine or feces, is generally easily recognized. The emergency physician must then engage family mem-

FIGURE 1. Citations on Violence in *Annals of Emergency Medicine, JAMA,* and *New England Journal of Medicine, 1975–1997*

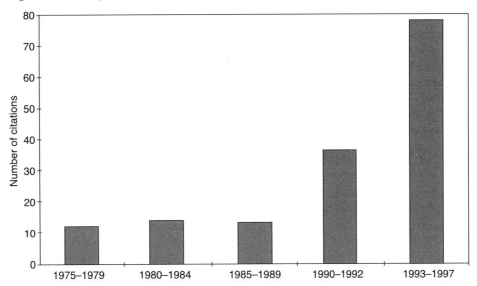

bers and legal authorities to determine who is responsible for the patient's care and whether the neglect is due to insufficient resources (which suggests that the patient requires institutionalization) or willful neglect (which requires prosecution of the perpetrators). Scenarios in which the so-called caretaker is keeping the patient hostage and appropriating his or her finances are common.

As with domestic violence, detection of physical elder abuse can be more difficult than detection of neglect, as there are few injuries that distinctly characterize elder abuse. The elderly are more prone to falls and have skin that is thinner and more easily torn or bruised than that of younger persons. Nevertheless, bruises, especially those on the forearms (from being grabbed or shaken), wrists and ankles (from restraints), or inner surfaces (such as the inner thighs, which are not usually injured in a fall), should not be explained away as part of old age. These findings mandate an investigation into the possibility of abuse, including notification of legal authorities and social services and execution of the appropriate paperwork. Once again, the best way for a physician to address abuse is to ask the patient directly if he or she is neglected or physically abused.

Emergency Physicians and the Prevention of Violence

Though the treatment of injuries resulting from violent acts has been glamorized by the media and popular television, emergency physicians report that the sense of professional achievement derived from expertly repairing injured individuals is quickly replaced by despair or cynicism—a realization that emergency care for violent trauma is merely a finger in the dike of a troubled society. This discovery has led many emergency physicians to take active roles in violence prevention research and policy making. Emergency physicians are now heavily involved in gun control efforts and were seminal in founding Physicians for a Violence-free Society.

Traditionally, trauma has not been considered a legitimate topic for medical research, but since 1990 there has been an explosion of research and publication in this area (see figure 1). Through these efforts emergency physicians hope to decrease the impact of violence on society by preventing the acts in addition to treating the resulting injuries.

The Emergency Department as a Site for Violence

In fantasy, hospitals are sterile, quiet places where people go to get well; places that are inherently immune to violence. In reality, hospitals have the same exposure to violence as every other institution in American society, and emergency departments are the site of 53 percent of in-hospital violence. In 1991 nine emergency department personnel died from violent acts in the department,

Physicians for a Violence-free Society

Physicians for a Violence-free Society (PVS) is a nonprofit organization established in 1993 by Patricia R. Salber and Ellen H. Taliaferro. Confronted on a daily basis with the effects of violence, these emergency physicians decided to take direct action to deal with this public health crisis. PVS trains medical personnel to incorporate violence prevention and intervention into their own medical practices, and acts as an advocate of measures that will lead to violence prevention. There are currently more than one thousand members, and annual meetings are attended by two hundred physicians and allied health professionals. Recent projects include:

- The development and distribution of scripted presentations on family violence. Members can easily teach others in their institutions and communities. Almost three hundred presentations have been made to an estimated audience of ten thousand. Examples of these presentations include programs on teen pregnancy and spousal assault.
- In collaboration with Polaroid Corporation, the development and presentation of a course on documenting injuries that result from family violence.
- The distribution of *Action Notes*, a bimonthly educational newsletter with a readership of more than six thousand.
- The collaboration on violence prevention initiatives with other organizations, including the Trauma Foundation, Annenberg Center, March of Dimes, and Family Violence Prevention Fund.
- The raising of public awareness of violence-related issues through national media coverage via Fox, NBC, ABC, and CNN news centers; the *New York Times, San Francisco Chronicle,* and *Dallas Morning News*; and the *Journal of the American Medical Association.*
- The distribution of ten thousand copies of *The Physician's Guide to Domestic Violence* to physicians and allied health-care providers.

and there have been several multiple casualty events since. Violence can occur when gang members follow an injured victim into the department to "finish the job," when dissatisfied patients seek revenge on staff, or when psychiatric patients arrive in the department in a condition that presents a threat to themselves or others. Police or security officers are present in most large emergency departments, and metal detectors are not uncommon. In some states, legislation requires that staff be protected behind bulletproof glass at the point of first contact. While this might make the staff more comfortable, it decreases the potential for human contact and personal care.

Police often transport to the emergency room persons who, because of psychiatric disorders or substance abuse, exhibit uncontrolled or aggressive behavior that places themselves, other patients, and staff at risk. Emergency physicians use a combination of physical restraints (typically leather handcuffs and footcuffs) and chemical restraints (sedative and antipsychotic medications) to ensure that these patients can be managed safely. The process of securing the physical restraints or injecting the medications is often violent and can result in injuries to patients and staff.

Emergency Medicine as a Form of Violence

Physicians routinely violate the human body, almost always with the informed consent of the patient, and always with the intention of improving the patient's, or—when a live organ donation is involved—a loved one's well-being. A discussion of violence and emergency medicine would be incomplete, however, without some consideration of how the practice of emergency medicine might, when viewed from a certain perspective, be itself considered an act of violence. Not all emergency medical interventions are welcomed, and emergency physicians must act judiciously when treating two types of patients, those who are violent or potentially violent and those who cannot, because of confusion or unconsciousness, convey their desires regarding the care that they receive. With violent or combative patients, physicians must use the minimal amount of force or chemical restraint necessary to establish a safe environment for the patient, other patients, and staff. In some states, laws have been enacted that mandate that physicians specifically define the reason for restraints and write frequent progress notes documenting the patient's condition and the need for continued restraint. These laws are designed to prevent patients from becoming victims of violence themselves.

For patients who are unable to convey their wishes—especially regarding their desires for invasive procedures—physicians should attempt to contact family or caretakers if time permits to determine if the patient has a living will, power of attorney, or other documents that establish how they wish to be cared for. This procedure minimizes the instances in which the physician's well-intentioned delivery of care is perceived by the patient as an unwelcome violent act on their person.

Relevant Web Sites

Further information regarding emergency medicine and violence can be found on the World Wide Web. The Centers for Disease Control and Prevention site (www.cdc.gov) contains many statistics and articles about firearm deaths, domestic violence, and child abuse. Motor vehicle accident statistics may be found at the National Highway and Traffic Safety Association Web site (www.nhtsa.dot.gov). Information regarding emergency medicine in general and legislation regarding violence prevention may be found at the Web site of the American College of Emergency Physicians (www.acep.org), and information on Physicians for a Violence-free Society can be found at the group's official site (www.pvs.org).

BIBLIOGRAPHY

Abbot, Jean, Robin Johnson, Jane Koziol-McLain, and Stephen Lowenstein. "Domestic Violence Against Women: Incidence and Prevalence in an Emergency Department Population." *Journal of the American Medical Association* 273 (1995): 1763–1767.

Bureau of Justice Statistics. *Report to the Nation of Crime and Justice.* Washington, D.C.: Office of Justice Programs, U.S. Department of Justice, October 1993.

———. *Violence Between Intimates.* Washington, D.C.: Office of Justice Programs, U.S. Department of Justice Programs, U.S. Department of Justice, November 1994.

Engle, Eloise. *Medic.* New York: John Day, 1967.

Historical Statistics of the United States: Colonial Times to 1970. Part 2, Bicentennial edition. Washington, D.C.: U.S. Department of Commerce, Bureau of the Census, 1975.

MMWR: Morbid Mortal Weekly Report 39 (1990).

Resnick, H. S., D. G. Kilpatrick, B. S. Dansky, B. E. Saunders, and C. L. Best. "Prevalence of Civilian Trauma and PTSD in a Representative Sample of Women." *Journal of Consulting and Clinical Psychology* 61 (1993).

U.S. Department of Transportation. National Highway Traffic Safety Administration. *Traffic Safety Facts.* Washington, D.C., 1995.

Zwerling, Craig, and McMillian, Daniel. *Firearm Injuries: A Public Health Approach.* Supplement to *American Journal of Preventative Medicine* 3, no. 19 (1993).

DAVID L. SCHRIGER
PATRICK GIBBONS

See also **Child Abuse; Domestic Violence; Elder Abuse; Rape: Incidence and Legal and Historical Aspects; War.**

MEDICAL EXPERIMENTATION ON THE MENTALLY ILL

Experimentation on human subjects without their consent occurred in many different contexts throughout the twentieth century. Noteworthy examples of atrocities committed under the broad rubric of "medical science" include the infamous Tuskegee Syphilis Study, conducted by U.S. Public Health Service physicians from 1932 to 1972, in which African American men with syphilis were deliberately not treated so that doctors could study the "natural history" of this disease; the Jewish Chronic Disease Hospital experiments of 1963, in which live cancer cells were injected into twenty-two chronically ill patients in Brooklyn, New York; the Japanese Army's "Unit 731," which killed and tortured thousands of Chinese by dropping "plague bombs" on villages in order to perform germ-warfare experiments; and the Nazi concentration camp experiments, discovery of which led directly to the realization that the principles of consent and informed consent, autonomy and self-determination, are central to any ethical forum in which experimentation is performed.

The question of informed consent becomes much more complex, however, when the subject of an experiment is mentally handicapped or mentally ill. In such cases, how can we be sure that patients understand their own situation well enough to ensure that their consent is truly informed? Being among the weakest and most vulnerable members of society, the mentally ill have often been denied self-determination, falling prey to rationalizations that their exploitation is in the best interest of a particular research project or of society as a whole. In being denied the right to make decisions about their own bodies and medical treatment, the mentally ill are victims of state-sponsored violence, where the "assault" is carried out by the medical establishment with government support.

Human Experimentation and the Nuremberg Code

The regulation of risks to human subjects from experimentation was initially developed as a reaction against the atrocities of Nazi doctors during World War II. These doctors, in an alleged attempt to advance scientific understanding, performed medical experiments in which there was little or no concern for the safety of the experimental subjects. Subjects were exposed to diseases such as malaria, jaundice, and typhus; injected with poisons; forced to breathe mustard gas; and exposed to extreme high and low temperatures and atmospheric pressures. The mortality rate of the experimental subjects was extremely high. The justification for these "medical acts" arose out of an atmosphere of strong support for both utilitarianism and social Darwinism. Social Darwinism, the belief that nations and races are subject to evolutionary pressures of natural selection similar to those experienced by plants and animals in nature, was both influential and widely accepted in the late nineteenth and early twentieth centuries. Implicit in this belief is the notion that humanity is stratified into the strong and the weak and that the natural order is an ongoing struggle where the strong prey on the weak. Thus, for the strong to subject the weak to dangerous medical research is nothing more than the "survival of the fittest" doctrine applied to experimental science.

At the end of the war, many of the doctors involved in these experiments were arrested as war criminals. Of twenty physicians subsequently tried for "wrongful experimentation" at the 1946–1947 Doctor's Trial in Nuremberg, Germany, fifteen were convicted—fourteen for that offense, one for SS membership. The American judges who conducted these trials drew up a set of ten principles, which they used as the basis for determining the conditions under which medical experimentation is ethically permissible. These ten principles came to be known as the Nuremberg Code.

Perhaps the most memorable edict of this code held that "the voluntary consent of the human subject is absolutely essential." In fact, in many respects the Nuremberg Code has come to represent the instantiation of the principle of "informed consent." The consent principle contained in the code eclipsed other principles of equal, if not greater, ethical importance.

The allowable circumstances for human experimentation were further defined by the 1964 Declaration of Helsinki, which was adopted at the Eighteenth World Medical Assembly by the World Medical Association and then endorsed by the 1966 House of Delegates of the American Medical Association. Although this declaration generally adhered to the Nuremberg Code's principles, it did propose slightly weaker restrictions on human experimentation. In particular, it opened the door to allow human experimentation on the mentally ill or mentally impaired by allowing a parent or guardian to give consent to experimentation on be-

---

Nuremberg Code

In addition to the principle of informed consent, the Nuremberg Code also states:

The experiment should be such as to yield fruitful results for the good of society, unprocurable by other methods or means of study, and not random and unnecessary in nature (principle 2).

The experiment should be conducted as to avoid all unnecessary physical and mental suffering and injury (principle 4).

The experiment should be conducted only by scientifically qualified persons (principle 8).

During the course of the experiment the human subject should be at liberty to bring the experiment to an end if he has reached the physical or mental state where continuation of the experiment seems to him to be impossible (principle 9).

---

half of a subject who is legally incompetent to make such decisions independently.

Not until the passage of the 1974 National Research Act were serious attempts made by U.S. legislators to establish ethical guidelines to protect human subjects. This act established the National Commission for the Protection of Human Subjects of Biomedical and Behavioral Research. In 1978 this commission issued a document known as the Belmont Report, which recommended guidelines for human trials. The Belmont Report stated that the principle of respect for persons necessitated that individuals should be treated as autonomous agents and that persons with diminished autonomy should be entitled to protection equivalent to that given to individuals with full capacity.

Like the Declaration of Helsinki, the Belmont Report did not fully adopt the recommendations of the Nuremberg Code and extended the circumstances under which experimentation may be justifiably performed on vulnerable groups, such as the mentally ill or impaired. Implicit in the Nuremberg Code was the suggestion that experiments should be potentially beneficial to the subject. This condition required any experiment to serve two purposes: helping to advance medical knowledge, and helping the experiment's subjects. The Belmont Report, however, explicitly stated that the only requirement was that the experiment have some potential benefit to society as a whole, thereby substantially weakening the constraints on experiment subject selection. Based on this single requirement of benefit to society, the report further stated that research in vulnerable populations such as children (and, by analogy, the mentally disabled) may be justified. The report concluded with three principles mandated for human experimentation—informed consent, risk-and-benefit assessment, and the appropriate selection of research subjects.

These principles have formed the backbone of peer review legislation such as the Institutional Review Board (IRB). Although legally IRBs are required only for research protocols receiving federal funds, many universities and research hospitals have adopted the broad goals of IRB review, which include a statement of the ethical procedures governing a given institution's policies toward research subjects, a diversified membership of the IRB board, and a written procedure for reporting protocol violations to the government.

The regulations governing IRBs require that the following information be provided to each potential research subject: a research statement that includes the duration of the study and a description of standard experimental procedures; a description of risks and potential discomfort associated with the experimentation; a description of expected benefits; disclosure of alternative procedures; a description of the extent to which confidentiality of records will be maintained; a description of compensation for procedures involving greater than minimum risk; the name of the appropriate person to contact with questions about the study; and a statement that participation is voluntary and that the research subject may end participation at any point in the study.

Federal regulations also state that "additional protections" should be included if "vulnerable populations" are involved. Possible vulnerable populations include mentally disabled persons, pregnant women, children, prisoners, and economically or educationally disadvantaged persons.

Informed Consent and the Mentally Ill

The process of obtaining informed consent is considerably more involved when the subject is a mentally ill person. Federal regulations leave a gap when it comes to procedure guidelines specifically designated for mentally handicapped or mentally ill persons. Currently, a researcher may obtain informed consent via either a long form, which may include a litany of complicated medical terms, or a short form, which may omit crucial aspects of the procedure. The mentally ill patient may be particularly vulnerable to abusive experimentation because his or her "consent" might be more easily obtained through manipulation or deception. The possibility for a research protocol to overlook the concerns of the mentally ill patient is heightened if the peer review process does not place the patient's autonomy at the center of its protocol.

Although the Nuremberg Code has served as the foundational document for all of this subsequent legislation, its complete set of principles has never been fully adopted. Some commentators have been skeptical of the overall impact of the code and the subsequent regulations, claiming that neither the Nuremberg trial nor its codified principles of ethical action have significantly affected the normative research procedures of the U.S. medical community. The 1966 seminal article by Dr. Henry Beecher supported the notion that breaches of medical ethical conduct continued in the United States. Beecher's critique of clinical research procedures outlined over twenty published examples of post–World War II medical studies in which serious violations of ethical conduct had occurred. Although these twenty cases clearly represent only a very small percentage of all medical research studies undertaken in the twenty years following the first formalization of the code, nevertheless his finding is troubling.

Other examples of improper experimentation came to light from 1993 to 1995. A series of highly publicized reports by the Advisory Committee on Human Radiation Experiments of the Department of Energy (DOE) revealed previously suppressed details of Cold War–era human radiation experiments that clearly violated both the letter and spirit of the Nuremberg Code. Of the hundreds of cases made public by the DOE, two of the most infamous studies used subjects from the Fernald State School, a state-run boarding school for the mentally retarded located in Waverly, Massachusetts. From the late 1940s until 1953, researchers from the Massachusetts Institute of Technology conducted periodic studies in which breakfast cereal (such as wheat and barley) containing radioactive calcium and iron was fed to groups of Fernald students. The purpose of these experiments (in which the radioisotopes were "tracers" that would follow nutrient absorption) was to determine whether a diet rich in cereal grains could interfere with absorption of other nutrients and therefore potentially result in malnutrition.

Although consent was sought from the parents of the Fernald students at the time of the experiments, the letters sent to the parents were extremely misleading, suggesting that the research was a nutritional study that would simply involve feeding the children breakfasts that were "rich" in calcium or iron. In particular, no mention was made of the use of any radioisotopes, and there was no discussion of any possible risks. Furthermore, the researchers' communications with the parents falsely suggested that the goal of the experiments was to benefit the children through improved nutrition, which was clearly not the case. Although the levels of radiation involved were very low and these experiments did not pose a significant level of risk to the children, the procedure for obtaining consent was clearly deceptive. No attempt was made to give the participants or their parents an accurate view of what the experiment involved.

The noted medical ethicist and legal scholar Jay Katz offers a paradigmatic example of the way in which unethical experimentation on the mentally ill may continue in spite of legislative inclusion of safeguards such as IRBs. Katz (1993) describes a research study conducted by the Neuropsychiatric Institute of the University of California, Los Angeles, from the 1980s until the mid-1990s. This study required that schizophrenic patients who stopped exhibiting symptoms of their illness have their medication withdrawn. The methods of this study intentionally produced relapse in subjects with the goal of better identifying which patients could effectively function without medication. The study was broadly justified on the grounds that antipsychotic medication can cause tardive dyskinesia, a syndrome consisting of involuntary and potentially irreversible movements for which no known treatment exists. The study's consent form, however, merely informed prospective subjects that "the purpose of this study is to take people like me off medication in a way that will give the most information about the medication, its effects on me, on others and on the way the brain works." Katz emphasizes that "the expectation of relapse was an integral aspect of the research design; it was not an unfortunate consequence of treatment but one which the investigators deliberately induced. This is particularly problematic because of the continuing controversy in psychiatric circles as to whether relapse leads to additional, at times irreversible, injury" (p. 44).

Because of growing awareness of the complex issues that surround obtaining consent from the mentally ill, there is cause for optimism that regulations that promote higher ethical standards will be introduced and enforced. In a landmark 1996 case, the Appellate Division of the State of New York's Supreme Court upheld a lower court ruling that found the state's rules governing psychiatric experiments on children and the mentally ill to be unconstitutional. The rules that were struck down were deemed to have contained an overly broad definition of who was allowed to give consent for a child or mental patient: in particular, the person giving consent was not required to be the subject's legal guardian. At the time, this decision forced the cancellation of between ten and fifteen state-funded psychiatric studies.

The principle that human experimentation must take place in an environment of strict oversight, with careful attention to ethical issues, is today broadly accepted in the United States. With luck, the continued vigilance of the courts and advocates of the mentally ill will be sufficient to protect this vulnerable group from the many abuses they have suffered in the past.

BIBLIOGRAPHY

Annas, George J. *Standard of Care: The Law of American Bioethics.* New York: Oxford University Press, 1993.

Annas, George J., and Michael A. Grodin, eds. *The Nazi Doctors and the Nuremberg Code: Human Rights in Human Experimentation.* New York: Oxford University Press, 1992.

Beals, Walter B. *The First German War Crimes Trial: Chief Judge Walter B. Beals' Desk Notebook of the Doctors' Trial, Held in Nuernberg, Germany, December 1945 to August 1947.* Chapel Hill, N.C.: Documentary Publications, 1985.

Beecher, Henry K. "Ethics and Clinical Research." *New England Journal of Medicine* 274 (1966).

Denno, Deborah W. "Sexuality, Rape, and Mental Retardation." *University of Illinois Law Review* 2, no. 315 (1997).

Department of Energy. *Final Report of the Advisory Committee on Human Radiation Experiments.* Washington, D.C.: U.S. Government Printing Office, 1995. See esp. chap. 7.

Derrickson, Dorothy. "Informed Consent to Human Subject Research: Improving the Process of Obtaining Informed Consent from Mentally Ill Persons." *Fordham Urban Law Journal* 25, no. 1 (1997).

Friedlander, Henry. *The Origins of Nazi Genocide: From Euthanasia to the Final Solution.* Chapel Hill: University of North Carolina Press, 1995.

Gerdtz, John. "Introduction: Historical Summary." In *A Guide to Mental Retardation: A Comprehensive Resource for Parents, Teachers, and Helpers Who Know, Love, and Care for People with Mental Retardation at All Stages in Their Lives,* edited by Mark McGarrity. New York: Crossroad, 1993.

Goddard, Henry H. *Feeble-mindedness: Its Causes and Consequences.* New York: Macmillan, 1914.

———. *The Kallikak Family: A Study in the Heredity of Feeble-mindedness.* New York: Macmillan, 1912.

Grodin, Michael A., and Leonard H. Glantz, eds. *Children as Research Subjects: Science, Ethics, and Law.* New York: Oxford University Press, 1994.

Katz, Jay. "Human Experimentation and Human Rights." *Saint Louis University Law Journal* 38, no. 1 (1993).

National Commission for the Protection of Human Subjects of Biomedical and Behavioral Research. *The Belmont Report: Ethical Principles and Guidelines for the Protection of Human Subjects of Research.* Washington, D.C.: U.S. Government Printing Office, 1978.

Rothman, David J. *Strangers at the Bedside: A History of How Law and Bioethics Transformed Medical Decision Making.* New York: Basic, 1991.

NANCY GRIER HOGAN

See also **Forensic Psychiatry; Tuskegee Syphilis Study; War Crimes.**

MEMORIALS

Events of violence are sometimes commemorated with memorials. These may range from small, sometimes temporary markers such as wooden crosses, signs, and plaques to large, permanent monuments, statuary, and shrines. Some of the largest, such as those erected at battlefields and to honor America's wartime dead, may encompass one or more buildings housing museums and libraries as well as large tracts of land. Memorials are typically erected on or near the site of an event of violence or at the gravesites of its victims. Sometimes memorials appear in other locations, such as a public square or park, or in places associated with events leading up to a battle, riot, or other episode of violence. Memorials may be erected immediately after an event but appear more commonly after several years or decades of preparation. Memorials of all types, not just those associated with violence, are erected to honor leaders, heroes, martyrs; pay tribute to sacrifices made by individuals for their community and nation; make note of important historical events; or convey a lesson, message, or warning to future generations. They are funded by individuals, families and friends of victims, survivors, veterans and veterans' organizations, as well as by local, state, and federal government agencies including the military. Memorials are in this sense an expression of private and public memory and reflect those events and individuals that society wishes to celebrate and remember.

Relatively few events and individuals attain this distinction and usually only after much

Veteran at the public unveiling of the Vietnam Veterans Memorial in 1982. UPI/CORBIS-BETTMANN

353

A memorial at Kent State University commemorates the dead and injured. A major memorial was dedicated nearby on the twentieth anniversary of the 1970 shootings. PHOTO BY KENNETH E. FOOTE

discussion—sometimes controversy—both public and private. Indeed, it is useful to view memorialization not as a single event but as a process through which the meaning of violence is debated and assessed. The outcomes of that process range greatly but fall into four general categories: commemoration, designation, rectification, and obliteration. Each reflects a different interpretation of violence and results in different types of memorials. Commemoration occurs when violence is seen to hold some lasting positive meaning that people wish to remember—a lesson in heroism or a sacrifice for community. The result is a public monument, statue, garden, park, museum, or other sort of building that becomes the focus for continuing ceremonial tribute on anniversaries and national holidays. Designation, or the marking of a violent event with a simple sign or plaque, records that something notable has happened but without assigning an encompassing moral lesson. Rectification, the most common outcome, involves removing the signs of violence and returning a site to everyday use, implying no lasting positive or negative meaning. Rectified sites are often hard to locate because little visible evidence is left behind, apart from an occasional wreath or cross. Obliteration results from events like mass murder that carry particularly shameful connotations that people would prefer to ignore or forget. Attempts are made to efface all evidence of violence, but usually without complete success.

Commemoration

Commemoration results in the most highly visible and best-known memorials, but it is also quite rare and occurs commonly in only three situations. The first is in the aftermath of the violent death of a president, national leader, hero, or martyr. Perhaps the best examples are the memorials raised to the United States' four assassinated presidents. The sites of the assassinations of Abraham Lincoln, William McKinley, and John F. Kennedy are marked; the fourth, James Garfield's, was marked for about twenty-five years after his death. Prominent monuments and museums have been erected in the cities where they were slain and elsewhere around the country. Impressive memorials can be found on the death sites of other slain political leaders like Huey Long (Baton Rouge), Martin Luther King, Jr. (Memphis), and Malcolm X (New York City). Wartime leaders, particularly officers and soldiers who die in combat, are also commemorated on battlefields and elsewhere. Even killings of celebrities are occasionally commemorated, as in the small garden created in New York's Central Park across the street from the site of John Lennon's murder.

A second situation that leads to commemoration are the wars, battles, and heroic struggles most closely associated with nation building. Revolutionary and Civil War battlefields are the most thoroughly commemorated of those on American soil, but other wars are also memorialized here and abroad. Among the best examples are the Bunker Hill and Yorktown battlefields of the Revolutionary War, the Gettysburg battlefield of the Civil War, the USS *Arizona* Memorial in Pearl Harbor, and the Vietnam Veterans Memorial in Washington, D.C. The violence of territorial and frontier expansion is also amply commemorated on battlefields and other sites throughout the United States, such as the San Jacinto and Alamo shrines to the Texas Revolution and the many memorials that mark the path of destruction of Native American cultures.

Efforts are also made to build memorials that illustrate encompassing ethical and moral lessons. These efforts extend to commemorating sites associated with the violent struggles of the labor movement, the Civil Rights movement, and the anti–Vietnam War movement of the 1960s and 1970s. Examples include the Haymarket martyrs memorial near Chicago, the Lattimer Mines massacre monument in Pennsylvania, the memorial to the Ludlow massacre in Colorado, the Civil Rights memorial in Montgomery, Alabama, and memorials to the shootings at Kent State and Jackson State Universities.

The third, though relatively rare, situation is when communities are struck by tragedies that induce a sense of shared loss. Memorials both honor the victims and offer the community a means of expressing bereavement. Examples include the memorial being built in Oklahoma City to the victims of the 1995 bombing of the Alfred P. Murrah Federal Building and the garden in San Ysidro, California, dedicated to the victims of the mass murder at a McDonald's restaurant in 1984. The most important factor in this kind of memorial is whether the tragedy touches a relatively homogenous, self-identified community, one that views the tragedy as a common, public loss. Members of such communities share a sense of identity based on ethnicity, religion, or occupation that encourages them to view the disaster as a loss to the group as a whole, rather than to isolated families.

Designation

Designation is related to commemoration—a site is marked with a sign or plaque—but without great ceremony and rarely with continuing annual celebrations. Designation arises from events that are viewed as important but lacking the heroic or sacrificial qualities associated with commemorated places. Designation is often a transitional phase that leads eventually to commemoration, rectification, or obliteration. It is often the fate of sites of controversial events whose meaning is still in debate or of causes not yet accepted by a large constituency. The Lorraine Motel in Memphis where Martin Luther King, Jr., was assassinated is now established as a major civil rights museum and educational center, but this took twenty years to accomplish. The effort began with a simple plaque erected by the motel's owner. Designated sites can serve as rallying points for causes

Personal memorials at the site of the Alfred P. Murrah Federal Building in Oklahoma City, two years after the 1995 bombing. The groundbreaking for a major memorial site was held in 1998. PHOTO BY KENNETH E. FOOTE

important to minority groups. The location of the Wounded Knee massacre of 1890, which became the focal point of the Sioux Uprising of 1973, is slated to become the site of a new memorial. The Stonewall Inn in New York City has served as a rallying point for the gay rights movement, just as Japanese American relocation centers of World War II became rallying points for redress legislation of the 1980s.

Rectification

Rectification is by far the most common outcome for places associated with events of violence. The sites gain only temporary notoriety before being put back in use. Associations with the violence fade, and the site is reintegrated into the activities of everyday life. No sense of deeper meaning remains attached to the site. Small personal tributes and remembrances are sometimes left at the site, but these are rarely permanent. The sites of almost all homicides are rectified, as are those of other interpersonal violence. The implication is that these events do not achieve the sense of significance that inspires commemoration or designation. They are interpreted as "accidents" or acts of senseless, meaningless violence.

Obliteration

Obliteration occurs in instances of particularly shocking, shameful, or preventable acts of violence from which individuals and communities wish to distance themselves morally. Obliterated sites are associated with notorious and disreputable characters—mobsters, gangsters, organized crime, assassins, and mass murderers—where the sense of shame stems from a community's producing or harboring such individuals or from failing to prevent their crimes. Indeed, large-scale mass murder is one of the events most prone to obliteration, but so too are violent acts of racial, ethnic, and religious bigotry. The site of the Salem witchcraft executions is perhaps one of the earliest and best examples. Though a 1992 memorial pays tribute to the victims, the site itself was ignored for three hundred years as the locus of a shameful outburst of religious factionalism. Obliteration is almost the opposite of commemoration, in that places of violence are scoured of evidence and public memorials are entirely out of the question. But once stigmatized, these sites can be as visually distinctive as commemorated places. They may be isolated from their surroundings as vacant lots and fenced yards that attract vandalism and graffiti. Since there is no easy way for this sense of stigma to be

removed, sites of particularly shameful events of violence can remain scarred for long periods. The Branch Davidian compound outside Waco, Texas, that burned to the ground in 1993 was still in ruins in 1999. Though open to visitors and home to several small memorials raised by different groups, the site also was attractive to vandals. The disposition of sites like these will often remain contested for years as different groups vie for ownership and control of the land and the memorials.

Time and Memory

These four types of memorial are neither predetermined nor necessarily permanent. Discussion and debate over whether to commemorate an event and in what fashion can take years, decades, or even centuries. President Lincoln died in 1865, but his memorial in Washington, D.C., was not completed until 1922, and the restored Ford's Theater was not opened as a national shrine until 1968. Although he is seen now as a hero, contemporaneous opinion about Lincoln was far less posi-

Virtual Memorials

Virtual memorials began to appear in cyberspace as pages in the World Wide Web at the end of the twentieth century. These pages, often authored by anonymous individuals, posted news about events such as the Heaven's Gate cult mass suicide in Rancho Santa Fe, California, in 1997; the Columbine High School shootings in Littleton, Colorado, in 1999; or the deaths of popular political figures. Often these pages allowed visitors to post their own tributes, comments, and questions as well as to hold discussions using electronic mail, discussion boards, and chatrooms. It is an open question whether these virtual memorials represent a development that may supplant physical memorials or whether they are temporary phenomena more akin to leaving flowers and mementos at a grave or sending condolence cards by mail. Ephemeral tokens of grief and bereavement like flowers and crosses are often, however, the first step toward permanent memorials. As virtual memorials proliferate, some may also attain the permanence of physical memorials or evolve into new types of memorials altogether. These virtual memorials already allow people to gather online in unprecedented numbers to share their feelings in real time over great distances.

The cemetery at Wounded Knee, South Dakota. Buried here are the warriors killed in the 1890 massacre as well as two men killed in 1973. A new public memorial has been authorized for the town. PHOTO BY KENNETH E. FOOTE

tive; time was needed to assess his particular accomplishments. Some of the largest memorials to the Revolutionary and Civil Wars did not appear until fifty, seventy-five, and even a hundred years after the battles. Commemoration takes even longer if consensus requires balancing interpretations among a variety of constituencies. The notorious Andersonville prison camp in Georgia, where almost thirteen thousand Union soldiers died during the Civil War, was not opened as a national park until 1971 because it was so difficult to interpret in a positive light. As of 1971, after the site was transferred from the War Department to the National Park Service, the camp was dedicated as a memorial honoring the sacrifice of all Americans ever held as prisoners of war.

Although most memorial sites change very little, others are altered greatly to reflect shifting political sentiments as well as changing social, economic, and cultural values. Commemorated sites may be abandoned or effaced and obliterated sites may become shrines. The site of President Garfield's shooting has been unmarked since 1907, and his memorial statue to the west of the U.S. Capitol was almost removed in the 1950s, perhaps reflecting waning interest in his political legacy. Grant's Tomb, the New York City burial site of President Ulysses S. Grant, was in such poor repair by the 1990s that his family sought to have his body returned to Illinois. The tomb was refurbished in the late 1990s.

In the 1990s the Korean War Veterans Memorial and the United States Holocaust Memorial Museum in Washington were dedicated, and discussion began concerning the creation of national memorials for World Wars I and II. Many key sites of the Civil Rights movement, long ignored, were memorialized as they reached their thirtieth anniversaries in the 1990s. Legislation was passed to create new memorials at both the Little Bighorn battlefield in Montana and at the site of the 1890 Wounded Knee massacre in South Dakota. Both would attempt to provide a more balanced appraisal of these controversial events. Other sites in the process of being commemorated include some of the formative strikes, riots, and massacres of the American labor movement. The meaning of other contemporary events of violence remains unresolved, such as those relating to abortion rights, domestic violence against women and children, antigay violence, and events like the Branch Davidian tragedy of 1993. It remains an open question as to how these events will be memorialized, if at all, in coming years.

BIBLIOGRAPHY

Bodnar, John. *Remaking America: Public Memory, Commemoration, and Patriotism in the Twentieth Century.* Princeton, N.J.: Princeton University Press, 1992.

Foote, Kenneth E. *Shadowed Ground: America's Landscapes of Tragedy and Violence.* Austin: University of Texas Press, 1997.

Linenthal, Edward T. *Preserving Memory: The Struggle to Create America's Holocaust Museum.* New York: Viking, 1995.

———. *Sacred Ground: Americans and Their Battlefields.* Urbana: University of Illinois Press, 1991.

Mayo, James M. *War Memorials as Political Landscape.* New York: Praeger, 1988.

Piehler, G. Kurt. *Remembering War the American Way.* Washington, D.C.: Smithsonian Institution, 1995.

Senie, Harriet F., and Sally Webster, eds. *Critical Issues in Public Art: Content, Context, and Controversy.* New York: HarperCollins, 1992.

KENNETH E. FOOTE

See also **Representation of Violence.**

MENENDEZ, ERIK AND LYLE
Erik (1970–); Lyle (1968–)

The best-known U.S. parricide in the late twentieth century is the shotgun slaying of Jose and Kitty Menendez by their sons, Erik Galen and Joseph Lyle, in the den of their Beverly Hills, California, home on the night of 20 August 1989. The sons discharged at least ten shots into their parents' bodies from 12-gauge weapons that Erik and Lyle purchased just two days earlier. Shortly after the murders, eighteen-year-old Erik and twenty-one-year-old Lyle drove away, disposed of the weapons, and returned home, where Lyle called the police to report the discovery of the victims. The brothers appeared extremely distraught and were not suspected of the crime.

On 31 October, however, Erik confessed to his therapist, L. Jerome Oziel. At Oziel's request, Lyle came to a session, at which time, according to Oziel's tape-recorded notes, Lyle became enraged and threatened Erik, saying, "We've got to kill him and anyone associated to him." Oziel disclosed the threat to his wife and friend Judalon Smyth and taped subsequent notes and actual conversations. On 5 March 1990 Smyth informed police of the tapes. (The California Supreme Court ruled that two of the tapes were exempt from therapist-patient privilege and were admissible evidence, elaborating on decisions that allow disclosure of threats to third parties.)

When the brothers were brought to trial in July 1993, there was no doubt who had committed the murders. They argued, however, that they were guilty only of "imperfect self-defense," which allows a verdict of not guilty for killing done "in the honest but unreasonable belief that it was neces-

Lyle and Eric Menedez in Los Angeles, 1990. CORBIS/BETTMANN-UPI

sary to defend against imminent peril to life or great bodily injury." They contended that they had endured such severe and continuing abuse, including sexual molestation, that they feared for their lives after a domineering father threatened to kill them during a violent family argument earlier in the week. Erik testified that Jose had molested him since the age of six but that he was too terrified to reveal it. Relatives, teachers, and coaches confirmed observing physical abuse and hostile, demeaning verbal criticism. Psychiatric witnesses contended that the brothers exhibited classic symptoms of abuse and were victims of trauma and uncontrollable panic. The prosecution contended that the brothers exaggerated the abuse, that the murder was premeditated, and that the motives were fabricated by two cunning, duplicitous, and spoiled young men whose true motive was to inherit a $14 million fortune, which Jose Menendez had mostly accumulated as chief executive of an entertainment company in Los Angeles.

The brothers were tried separately in the same courtroom with two juries and were represented by different attorneys—Leslie Abramson for Erik and Charles A. Gessler for Lyle. In January 1994 both trials resulted in hung juries. The brothers were tried together the second time, found guilty of first-degree murder, and sentenced to life imprisonment. In the second trial Judge Stanley Weisberg barred the testimony of a number of defense witnesses and all but one of the defense's psychiatric witnesses. He also instructed the jury to discount child abuse and disallowed the imperfect-self-defense argument. The defense was further damaged by disclosures that Lyle had written two letters requesting people to lie on the witness stand.

The case attracted immense attention both because the first trial was televised nationally and because it involved accounts of incest, child abuse, and controversial questions about the right of victims of abuse to react violently. The fact that the violence erupted in a wealthy and ostensibly normal family added to the drama.

BIBLIOGRAPHY

Novelli, Norma, and Mike Walker. *The Private Diary of Lyle Menendez: In His Own Words.* Beverly Hills, Calif.: Dove, 1995.

Thornton, Hazel. *Hung Jury: The Diary of a Menendez Juror.* Philadelphia: Temple University Press, 1995.

ROBERT SCHILDGEN

See also **Borden, Lizzie; Parricide.**

MENTAL ILLNESS. *See* Medicine and Violence: Medical Experimentation of the Mentally Ill; Psychopathy, Biology of.

METHODOLOGIES OF VIOLENCE RESEARCH

H. Rap Brown's dictum from the 1960s—"Violence is as American as cherry pie"—seems to echo prophetically from each day's headlines and newscasts, an unremitting blare of smart bombs, student massacres, hate crimes, domestic and gender assaults, and road rage. No longer merely the preoccupation of social-science professionals, the concern with understanding the pandemic of American violence has spilled over onto the nation's op-ed pages and into television and radio talk shows, workplaces, and living rooms. Yet the proliferation of concern and analysis has not yielded a firm consensual understanding; as in the analysis of many other aspects of human conduct, the terms of the discussion are invariably skewed by conflicting agendas—theoretical, religious, philosophical, and political.

The professional analysts are only slightly closer to a definitive grasp of human violence than their mass-media counterparts. Fragmented into a variety of institutional and disciplinary bailiwicks, the academic study of violence employs diverse and often seemingly incompatible theoretical and methodological criteria that have resulted in a scholarly *dialogue des sourds*.

Microviolence and Macroviolence

The widest theoretical chasm in academic studies of violence is that which separates the micro and macro approaches, the former focusing on violence as a product of individual psychology and the latter seeking answers in various levels of group and social interaction. Given the bureaucratic divides that dictate the terms of discussion in the academy, there have been few systematic efforts to understand the linkages between the various levels of violence: interpersonal, collective, national, and global. At one extreme of this divide is the viewpoint articulated in this remark from one social scientist: "There is no relationship between warfare and wife beating." The opposite view—the indivisibility of the personal and social—holds that it is impossible to divorce individual motivation from group or social influence, that the collective and personal dimensions of thought and action dialectically reveal and determine each other, each providing a kind of reverse-angle lens with which to examine the patterns of the other.

Each academic discipline has its built-in methodological predisposition toward a micro or macro view of violence: psychologists usually focus on individual, or micro, factors, whereas sociologists or anthropologists, whose disciplines by definition study group interaction, are more likely to dwell on the macro level.

Biological and Physiological Theories

One family of theories posits a biological foundation for violence, that is, it is instinctual or genetic or both. Such theories are most prevalent among sociobiologists and behavioral psychologists, much of whose work is an attempt to map the brain for biochemical and neurological correlates of various modes of human behavior. They investigate the relationship between violence and brain lesions, brain dysfunction, endocrinology, premenstrual syndrome, hypoglycemia, genetic composition, and so on but have yet to produce a unified, experimentally verifiable theory that pegs violent behavior to specific biological factors. The practical correlate of such research is that the solution to violent behavior might lie in somatic interventions such as drugs or surgery. This theoretical school straddles the micro-macro divide, because a biological explanation would account for each individual case of sociopathic violence but would also encompass the potential for violence in the human species as a whole. Drive or instinct theory is also at the core of the work of many physical anthropologists such as Robert Ardrey and Konrad Lorenz, who have argued that evolution has favored humans with naturally aggressive, territorial instincts. Other theorists in this field, however, have countered that the hard scientific evidence for such a predominant aggressive drive is sparse, that such behavior can be culturally influenced, and that aggression need not always take violent forms. The biological framework seems to enjoy the widest acceptance among policy makers, because its definitions of pathological violence tend to focus on individual deviancy to the exclusion of large-scale, official modes of collective violence such as policing and the military—in other words, the bias of such research tends more toward interventions against individual or small-scale antisocial violence to the exclusion of officially sanctioned bloodshed, which is deemed necessary and normal. It is thus petty street criminals rather than big-time war criminals that would be the most likely candidates for sociobiologically determined drug therapies. This institutional conservatism of the biological approach arises in part from its physiological reductionism, which precludes the critical and theoretical discriminations that are possible in theories that assign more autonomy and thus causative impact to the mental and cultural life of humans. Bereft of such tools, biological research is necessarily indifferent and blind to judgments about the social and political causes and uses of violent action. Uncritically captive to prevailing social categories, its preoccupation with microviolent deviancy tends to mirror that of official governing interests, thus obscuring rather than clarifying the problem of intra- and intergovernmental macroviolence.

Psychology

Psychology has one foot in the micro level of analysis and one in the macro; its perspective varies with the many theoretical schools that comprise the discipline. There is a broad spectrum of psychological theorizing, ranging from the micro determinism of academic behaviorism to the interpersonal psychology of Erich Fromm to the humanist schools of Abraham Maslow. Freudian psychology dwells simultaneously in the micro and macro, because Sigmund Freud's theories encompass both individual and group psychology. In Freud's basic theory the primal, instinctual impulses of humans—encompassing both the sex drive and the destructive impulses that lead to violence—reside in the id, where a quest for immediate, animal gratification of desires is constrained by the superego, the system of cultural values that is introduced through parental and social influence. The conflicting aims of the id and superego are mediated by the ego, the rational faculty that fosters an integrated, stable personality, imprisoned neither by the repressive constraints of the culture nor the atavisms of the id. A tendency to violence, then, would likely result from an overdeveloped id or underdeveloped superego. Resisting easy categorization as biologically or culturally determinist, Freud's theories of violence provided one bridge from biology to culture, from the individual to the social, from the micro to the macro.

This step toward the social is taken most explicitly in social psychological research, which has focused on the ways in which society and culture influence violent behavior. Stanley Milgram's experiment (1974) in which participants played either the role of prisoner or the role of a prison guard seems to indicate that usually reasonable, ethical persons with well-integrated personalities are willing to inflict violence on others if commanded to do so in a atmosphere of official authority in which the victim is a depersonalized "subject." Other key studies in this field show that when subjects assume roles that confer authority over others and promote the use of violence as a means of control, they are more likely to behave violently. Behavioral social psychologists theorize that violent behavior is learned; some studies have shown, for example, that children thrust into a laboratory environment are more likely to emulate violent behavior patterns. According to this social learning theory, violence observed on television, film, and video games can engender imitative acts of violence in young people.

Social Sciences

The social scientific approach to violence, by definition concerned with group interaction, tilts inherently toward a macro perspective. The work of social scientists thus predictably calls attention to social and cultural causation of violence; despite some efforts to examine macro and micro links (especially as regards the social organization of conflict), there has been a paucity of sociological or anthropological studies attempting systematic linkages of violence across the individual and group levels. Trained to discern specifically cultural and social influences on human behavior, sociologists and anthropologists have understandably tended to challenge the largely instinctivist outlook of Lorenz and Ardrey; several key studies in this vein suggest that levels of violence are not uniform across various cultures and that violence is not invariably gender specific. Whereas some anthropologists and sociologists have attempted to correlate rising contemporary violence with declining social networks and frayed family relationships, conflict sociologists and cultural anthropologists often emphasize social cleavages or categories, such as the tribe or clan in preindustrial societies and race, class, ethnicity, and gender in industrial societies—in this view social inequality is itself a source of violence, which is seen as a last resort of defending privilege by the power elite or of challenging it by the oppressed.

Sociologists from the symbolic-interactionist school point to situational variations in social norms governing the use of violence. For example, violence among civilians might be permissible in self-defense but is otherwise prohibited. Such contextual definitions of socially legitimate uses of violence can render a specific action—say, a lethal shooting—as either moral or immoral, legal or illegal, depending on the social status of the victim and the perpetrator and the professed motivation for the act. Other scholars have sought to understand socially constructed notions of violence through culturally received rhetorical strategies or narratives about the nature of good and evil that either stigmatizes or legitimates various kinds of violence.

Specialists in organizational sociology have noted the increasingly bureaucratic and institutional character of contemporary violence, even among agencies of social control ostensibly charged with countering violence. They analyze the growth in technologically advanced, bureaucratic modes of violence evidenced by, for example, the Pentagon's gloating over the efficient lethality of "smart" bombs during the Gulf War of 1991. They also examine the media's juxtaposition of graphic, celebratory images of the Western military prowess, much of it inflicted on civilians, during the NATO bombing campaign against Serbia in 1998, with solemn horror at the youthful fascination with guns and bloodshed that contributed to the massacre at Columbine High School in Littleton, Colorado, in 1999.

Studies of violence emerging from political science have tended to correlate levels of violence with the character of the prevailing political system. For example, Jeane Kirkpatrick, a former U.S. ambassador to the United Nations, has argued that authoritarian regimes are more likely than liberal democratic polities to rely on violence (or the threat of violence) as a means of maintaining social control. In this view totalitarian regimes are the most violent; even when they are not inflicting actual violence on the populace, they rely on the constant and overt display of weaponry and police to maintain order.

As the key to the origins and frequency of violence, governmental authority is also the answer to controlling it, according to many political scientists, who typically stress the importance of the criminal justice system as the front line of defense, bolstered, if necessary, by increased funding for police departments and other enforcement agencies. This outlook has produced little in the way of linkages between the macro and micro levels of violence.

Although many sociologists and anthropologists have argued that war is unrelated to other forms of violence, contemporary feminist scholars have sought to establish links between the two. Although military and peace studies have yet to attain mainstream status among professional sociologists, scholars in these fields have made real progress toward an interdisciplinary understanding of violence.

Interdisciplinary Approaches

Because of the bureaucratic compartmentalization of academic disciplines, the study of violence has remained a splintered undertaking, with little attempt to forge links between the macro and micro levels of analysis. Yet an interdisciplinary approach to violence studies has begun to flourish on the margins of the academy and has even made modest inroads into the mainstream. The most fruitful and well-funded projects have emerged from criminologists, who have compiled a significant database about illegal violence in North America, Australia, and Western Europe— "illegal violence" meaning the crimes deemed most serious by law-enforcement officials: sexual assault, robbery, aggravated assault, and especially homicide.

Mainstream criminology has contributed a wealth of data and interpretive studies pertaining to crime rates and the impact of crime on victims and the larger society. Comparative studies of empirical data, along with interpretive work on differing definitions of criminality in various cultures, has enlarged the understanding of the causes and nature of criminal violence, linking crime rates to social hierarchies, demographics, and criminal subcultures of both the underclass and white-collar varieties.

One of the more promising trends in this field has been the rise of critical criminology, which seeks to establish links between social macrostructures and violent crime, expanding the definition of crime beyond those acts officially proscribed by the state to include acts committed by establishment organizations and individuals that normally go uninvestigated or unpunished. These studies strive to overcome a purely technical approach to crime research by incorporating notions of social justice and the social context of criminality, whether of the official or unofficial variety. This more encompassing framework thus moves easily between the micro level of individual motivation and the macro level of social influence, thus establishing the linkages so often lacking in traditional academic crime studies. Another significant outgrowth of emerging interdisciplinary approaches is the study of war and the allied discussion of developing alternatives to war as a means of settling international conflict. These peace studies programs often involve scholars from other fields, offering them an opportunity to pursue an interdisciplinary approach to the study of human conflict. Emphasizing what Johan Galtung calls "structural violence," such research seeks to establish the violence, covert or overt, that attends social injustice. Feminist scholars have also found this approach useful in discussing the violence of unequal social relationships, which, they claim, can be just as harmful for being psychological rather than physical. Other peace scholars have sought constructive insights into the nature and history of peace movements and into the possibilities of nonviolent conflict resolution.

Conclusion

The academic study of violence, for all its past compartmentalization, is slowly coming to terms with the need for an integrated approach that no longer divorces the individual and the social, the biological and the cultural, the micro and the macro. Some of the most fruitful possibilities have arisen not from the mainstream disciplines but from the relatively novel, maverick fields of peace studies and feminist studies. Further progress in transgressing artificially imposed disciplinary boundaries will no doubt hinge on rendering more explicit the methodological assumptions about human nature that undergird much of this research: Is the "rational animal" we call "human" more rational, more governed by a measured sense of decency and justice, or more animal, closer to the biological realm of the imperious drives of brute survival at whatever the cost? Adherents of the former thesis seem to presuppose something like a Lockean "tabula rasa" or a Rosseauist "noble savage" upon which society and culture work their insidious and corrupting ways, thus fostering antisocial aggression and violence. Adherents of the latter, on the other hand, smuggle into their studies an instinct-driven mammal who differs in degree but not in essence from other sensate creatures, unlikely—indeed, perhaps unable—to transcend its predatory provenance. This is a grim picture, from which reconciliation, harmony, and redemption seem banished to the dreamlife of an eternally embattled species. The contrasting notion, that we are primal innocents corrupted by some "social beast" lurking somewhere "out there," is subject to the charge of reifying the realm of the social, turning it into a kind of explanatory deus ex machina on which we pile blame for all human follies, all the while wondering what that social beast really might be, if not the collective projection of our inner drives, dreams, and best-laid plans. Perhaps the most decisive steps forward in a theory of violence, then, require a change in the definition of the very subject of scrutiny—humanity itself.

BIBLIOGRAPHY

Adams, David, et al. "The Seville Statement on Violence." *Peace Review* 4, no. 3 (1992): 20–22.

Archer, Dane, and Rosemary Gartner. *Violence and Crime in Cross-National Perspective.* New Haven, Conn.: Yale University Press, 1984.

Ardrey, Robert. *African Genesis: A Personal Investigation into the Animal Origins and Nature of Man.* New York: Dell, 1961.

Barash, David P. *Introduction to Peace Studies.* Belmont, Calif.: Wadsworth, 1991.

Boulding, Elise, et al. "Teaching the Sociology of World Conflicts: A Review of the State of the Field." *American Sociologist* 9 (1974): 187–193.

Cancian, Francesca M., and James William Gibson. *Making War/Making Peace: The Social Foundations of Violent Conflict.* Belmont, Calif.: Wadsworth, 1990.

Chambliss. William, and Milton Mankoff. *Whose Law? Whose Order?* New York: Wiley, 1976.

Coser, Lewis A. *Continuities in the Study of Social Conflict.* New York: Free Press, 1967.

Elias, Robert. *Victims Still: The Political Manipulation of Crime Victims.* Newbury Park, Calif: Sage, 1993.

Elias, Robert, and Jennifer Turpin, eds. *Rethinking Peace.* Boulder, Colo.: Lynne Rienner, 1994.

Etzioni, Amitai. *The Spirit of Community: The Reinvention of American Society.* New York: Crown, 1993.

Galtung, Johan. *Peace: Research, Education, Action.* Vol. 1 of *Essays in Peace Research.* Copenhagen: Christian Ejiers, 1975.

Janis, Irving. *Groupthink: Psychological Studies of Policy Decisions and Fiascoes.* 2d ed. Boston: Houghton Mifflin, 1982.

Kriesberg, Louis. *International Conflict Resolution.* New Haven, Conn.: Yale University Press, 1992.

Lorenz, Konrad. *On Aggression.* New York: Harcourt, Brace, and World, 1966.

Milgram, Stanley. *Obedience to Authority.* New York: Harper and Row, 1974.

Moyer, K. E. *The Psychology of Aggression.* New York: Harper and Row, 1976.

Paige, Glenn D. *To Nonviolent Political Science: From Seasons of Violence.* Honolulu: Center for Global Nonviolence Planning Project, Matsunaga Institute for Peace, University of Hawaii, 1993.

Reardon, Betty A. *Sexism and the War System.* New York: Teacher's College Press, 1985.

Turpin, Jennifer, and Lester R. Kurtz, eds. *The Web of Violence: From Interpersonal to Global.* Urbana: University of Illinois Press, 1997.

Wilson, James Q. *Thinking About Crime.* New York: Vintage, 1975.

Wilson. James Q., and Richard Hernnstein. *Crime and Human Nature.* Cambridge, Mass.: Harvard University Press, 1985.

JENNIFER TURPIN
LESTER R. KURTZ

See also **Incidence of Violence; National Crime Victimization Survey; Statistics and Epidemiology; Uniform Crime Reports.**

MEXICAN AMERICANS

The first Mexican Americans were created at the conclusion of the U.S.-Mexican War (1846–1848), when the United States acquired more than five hundred thousand square miles of Mexican territory. The population of Mexican heritage in the United States has since been augmented by immigration from Mexico. For more than 150 years Mexican American history has been shaped by racial and cultural violence.

In 1848 the Treaty of Guadalupe Hidalgo ending the Mexican War contained provisions to protect the life and property of Mexicans in the conquered territories, but within a short time their status as a "foreign" people was confirmed by law and custom. In gold rush California, Mexicans and other non-Anglo-Americans were forced from the gold fields after the passage of the Foreign Miner's Tax Law in April 1850. In 1855 California's state legislature passed the "Greaser Laws," aimed at controlling the cultural activities and employment of the Mexican population. The first female lynched in the Southwest was a Mexican woman named Josefa in 1851 in Downieville, California. Vigilante lynchings and shootings of Mexican outlaws in California continued up until the 1870s.

The Texas Rangers, formed in the 1830s, had as their mission the subjugation of the Texas-Mexican (Tejano) population through terror. Numerous lynchings and killings of Mexicans punctuated the history of central and south Texas. In 1857 the so-called Cart War erupted between Anglo-Americans and Tejano teamsters and several Mexicanos were killed and scores of wagons confiscated. Local American newspapers talked of "sweeping the Mexicans from the face of the earth."

Perhaps the most notable resistance to Mexican oppression was led by Juan N. Cortina from Brownsville, Texas. In 1859 Cortina led a small army of Tejanos to fight against the Texas Rangers and then the National Guard. For the next twenty years he fought against the Texan forces until he was forced into retirement by the Mexican president Porfirio Díaz, who was anxious to gain U.S. diplomatic recognition for his regime. Another instance of resistance was the El Paso Salt War in 1877, when local Mexican residents fought against the Anglos who had stolen the salt beds from their community. In the late nineteenth century violence along the U.S.-Mexican border was endemic as smugglers, bandits of both nationalities, and filibusters fought with U.S. and Mexican officials.

In New Mexico violence toward Mexican Americans stemmed from the corrupt land grab that took place in the years after 1848, when American land speculators and lawyers conspired to manipulate courts and federal officials to take over Hispano village lands using bribery, fraud, and intimidation. The Hispanos fought back by forming the Gorras Blancas and La Mano Negra, secret societies of night riders who cut fences and burned barns in order to frighten settlers off Hispano lands. Land wars erupted between Hispanos and Anglos in Maxwell, Colfax, and Lincoln counties, and in the struggles scores of Hispanos were killed in ambushes and skirmishes as local political feuds exacerbated territorial disputes.

In 1910 the Mexican Revolution erupted and brought about many changes. Some American officials feared the organization of Mexican revolutionaries in the United States as a prelude to a possible general uprising. In 1916 a group of Tejanos considered staging a revolt against American authorities and issued El Plan de San Diego (Texas). This idealistic plan inaugurated a bloody war of retaliation by Anglos against Tejanos who were suspected of harboring ideas of independence. The same year troops led by the Mexican military leader Pancho Villa crossed the international border and attacked Columbus, New Mexico, and General John J. Pershing organized an expeditionary force to invade Mexico and hunt down Villa. As a result of the revolutionary violence in Mexico,

thousands of Mexicans crossed the border into the United States; more than one million Mexican immigrants had entered the country by 1929.

When the Great Depression began in the 1930s, the federal government orchestrated a repatriation campaign to force Mexican immigrants to return to Mexico. Repatriation was seen as a way of creating jobs for U.S. citizens. Police and immigration officials raided the Mexican colonias and barrios throughout the Southwest. Families were separated, children traumatized, and the civil rights of U.S. citizens of Mexican descent were routinely violated. Probably about one million people went back to Mexico during the 1930s.

When World War II began, hundreds of thousands of Mexicans and Mexican Americans joined the armed services and fought against the Axis forces. On the home front discrimination continued. In 1943 an anti-Mexican riot erupted in Los Angeles between U.S. armed forces personnel on leave and young Mexican American youth called pachucos or zoot-suiters. For about a week the army, navy, and marines rampaged through the downtown area beating up Mexican youth until the U.S. government, urged by the Mexican ambassador, declared Los Angeles off limits to American servicemen.

After World War II Mexican immigration continued under the Bracero Program. But in 1954, due to anticommunist hysteria, the attorney general, Herbert Brownell, Jr., ordered a massive deportation of Mexican immigrants, dubbed "Operation Wetback." Under this program, which utilized the military as well as police, more than one million Mexican immigrants were forced to return to Mexico in the next year. In the process, the civil rights of many people were violated; threats of violence against Mexicans caused many to leave "voluntarily."

During the 1960s the war in Vietnam polarized American society and the Civil Rights movement provoked violent backlashes. The Chicano civil rights movement began in the early 1960s with the founding of *La Alianza*, an organization of land grant activists in New Mexico that sought to reclaim territory stolen from Hispanic villages in the previous century. *Alianza* partisans took over a county courthouse in New Mexico and shots were exchanged. National Guard troops were called out to hunt down the movement's leader, Reies López Tijerina, and his associates. Later the *Alianza* took over a national park. Activists were expelled from the park by force and the federal government tried and convicted Tijerina on charges stemming from this uprising.

Another Chicano civil rights leader, César Chavez, led Mexican American farmworkers on a strike against powerful agribusiness corporations in California's San Joaquin Valley. Chavez espoused nonviolence and followed the teachings of Mohandas Gandhi. Nevertheless, the growers hired goons who beat and terrorized strikers, and several members of the United Farm Workers were killed during the next few years of organizing activities. Chavez himself was the target of death threats and numerous violent attacks.

In 1970 Chicano youth were fighting and dying in Vietnam in an unpopular war. To protest this war and the disproportionate numbers of Mexican American casualties, Chicano activists organized a Chicano Moratorium rally to take place in Los Angeles on 29 August 1970. A peripheral incident erupted into a police attack on the assembly. In the riot that ensued, three people were killed by the police, among them Rubén Salazar, a reporter for the *Los Angeles Times* who had been critical of the police mistreatment of Chicano youth.

In the 1980s and 1990s violence was a fact of life for undocumented Mexican immigrants who entered the United States. Deaths, injuries, rapes, and robberies continued to increase along the U.S.-Mexican border. In the San Diego–Tijuana region alone in 1998, more than 145 immigrants died when attempting to cross the border, many of them violently and some at the hand of the U.S. border patrol. According to the American Friends Service Committee incidents of violence involving Mexicans and officials of the U.S. Immigration and Naturalization Service and customs, as well as local law enforcement officers, are common along the U.S.-Mexican border. In spite of their growing population and increased civil rights and political power, Mexicans continued to be targets for violence. In July 1999 the National Council for La Raza issued a report documenting the increase in hate crimes against Mexicans and Latinos in the United States. Many of these crimes had gone unnoticed by the national media. Discriminatory violence remains a major social problem.

BIBLIOGRAPHY

Acuña, Rudolfo. *Occupied America: A History of Chicanos.* 3d ed. New York: Prentice Hall, 1987.
Balderrama, Francisco E., and Raymond Rodriguez. *Decade of Betrayal: Mexican Repatriation in the 1930s.* Albuquerque: University of New Mexico, 1995.
Garcia, Mario T., ed. *Memories of Chicano History: The Life and Narrative of Bert Corona.* Berkeley and Los Angeles: University of California Press, 1994.
Rosenbaum, Robert J. *Mexicano Resistance in the Southwest: "The Sacred Right of Self-Preservation."* Austin: University of Texas Press, 1981.

RICHARD GRISWOLD DEL CASTILLO

See also **Chicano Moratorium; Immigration; Zoot-Suit Riot.**

MEXICAN WAR

The War with Mexico was one of the deadliest conflicts in U.S. history in terms of deaths per thousands of men who served. Of more than 100,000 soldiers, sailors, and marines, about 1,500 were killed in action, and another 11,000 died from diseases and wounds. The major result of the war was the addition of 500,000 square miles to U.S. territory, which was expanded to the Pacific Ocean.

The immediate cause of the war was the annexation of the former Mexican province of Texas by the United States on 1 March 1845, which was perceived by Mexico as a declaration of war; boundary disputes and U.S. citizens' claims against Mexico for injuries and property losses during the Mexican revolutions since the 1820s also played a role. After a failed attempt to negotiate with Mexico, President James K. Polk ordered General Zachary Taylor to the Rio Grande to repel Mexican efforts to invade Texas. Taylor arrived on 23 March 1846 with four thousand men. On 23 April, Mexico declared a war against the United States, and on 25 April a detachment of dragoons was attacked by General Mariano Arista and sixteen hundred cavalry, who had crossed the Rio Grande. War was under way even before its formal declaration by Congress on 12 May.

Despite Arista's nearly three-to-one numerical advantage, General Taylor and his men twice triumphed over the Mexicans in early May, first at Palo Alto, Texas, and then in hand-to-hand combat at Resaca de la Palma. There, after Taylor's infantry captured the Mexican artillery on 9 May, the panicked Mexicans fled to the Rio Grande, and many of them drowned trying to cross the river.

The U.S. declaration of war authorized a call-up of 50,000 volunteers and more than doubled the strength of the regular army from 7,200 to 15,540. The undisciplined volunteers were the most troublesome for officers; young men who had never been away from home and less savory recruits murdered, robbed, and raped throughout the war in Mexico and were called the "vandals vomited from Hell." War plans, which called for one army to seize New Mexico and California and another to invade Mexico and capture Mexico City, were opposed by such prominent political leaders as Henry Clay, John C. Calhoun, and Daniel Webster and by such intellectuals as Ralph Waldo Emerson and Henry David Thoreau. Ulysses S. Grant, only one of many junior officers during the Mexican War who would win fame and the rank of general during the Civil War, later wrote, "I was bitterly opposed . . . and to this day regard the war . . . as one of the most unjust ever waged by a stronger nation against a weaker nation."

New Mexico and California

On 3 June 1846 Colonel Stephen W. Kearny received orders to take Santa Fe and occupy New Mexico. After arriving unopposed in Santa Fe, he sent Colonel Alexander W. Doniphan and his Missouri Volunteers south, where they defeated Mexican forces at El Brazito on 25 December and occupied El Paso two days later. On 28 February 1847 Doniphan defeated three thousand Mexican troops and one thousand ranchers armed with lances and machetes and superior artillery in the Battle of the Sacramento. Within weeks, however, one-third of the Missouri Volunteers were sick with venereal disease, yellow fever (*vomito*), and other illnesses.

On 25 September Kearny and three hundred dragoons began their march to California, where the Pacific Squadron, under Commodore John D. Sloat, had seized Monterey and San Francisco in July and then other key ports, guaranteeing U.S. possession of California. Kearny learned of this conquest on 6 October from scout Kit Carson and sent two hundred of his men back to Santa Fe. The reduced party was attacked on 6 December by a large, lance-wielding Mexican force at San Pasqual, thirty-five miles northeast of San Diego, but a relief expedition from San Diego enabled Kearny to break out. Kearny and forces from the Pacific Squadron entered Los Angeles on 10 January 1847, the day after California insurgents under John Charles Frémont defeated Mexican army troops.

Back in New Mexico, acting governor Charles Bent and Colonel Sterling Price and his troops faced rebels and insurgents, many of them Taos Pueblo Indians. Bent and five others were scalped and killed there in January 1847, and Price, after three engagements and fourteen more murders, brought the fifteen hundred rebels under control in mid-February.

Taylor and Scott in Mexico

General Taylor's expedition into Mexico began on 18 May 1846 with an army of six thousand. General Arista fled south, leaving behind supplies and his wounded and littering his southward path with exhausted soldiers and dead animals. When Taylor stopped at Camargo in early August, fifteen hundred of his troops had died from heat, poor sanitation, and disease, but on 19 August he continued toward Monterrey, which was defended by ten thousand Mexicans. Fighting began on 21 September, followed by an American assault on the fortified hills and bloody street-to-street fighting; the Mexicans sued for an armistice on 24 September. Eight hundred Americans were killed or wounded before the fighting ended.

On 22 February 1847 Taylor and 4,800 men encountered a Mexican force of 20,000 under General Antonio López de Santa Anna near the hacienda of Buena Vista. Although Americans lost ground the first day against Santa Anna's San Patricio Battalion, a group of American deserters fighting for Mexico, U.S. troops began advancing by nightfall of the second day. With 673 killed and wounded that day, Taylor thought of retreat, but he continued to fight after reinforcements arrived. Daylight on 24 February revealed that Santa Anna had departed, leaving behind his wounded. Mexican losses were close to 2,000.

Command of the Mexico City expedition was given to General Winfield Scott. Since the summer of 1846, the navy's Home Squadron had been blockading Mexican ports on the Gulf, including Veracruz. In the first major amphibious landing in U.S. history, at sunrise on 9 March, Scott began to put ashore about 12,000 men plus horses, cannon, and supplies three miles southeast of Veracruz. After five days of shelling by Scott's artillery and the Home Squadron, the Mexicans surrendered the fortress on 29 March. Only nineteen Americans were killed.

On 18 April, Scott stormed the summit at the mountain pass Cerro Gordo, driving off Santa Anna's 11,000 troops with bayonets and by using pistols and muskets as clubs. Meanwhile, Mexican irregulars were committing atrocities on any American stragglers, usually dragging them naked and bound through cactus and then leaving them to die. Texas Rangers under Captain John Coffee

The Battle of Buena Vista, 1847. Contemporary lithograph by J. Bailie. LIBRARY OF CONGRESS

Hays, called *los Tejanos sangrietes* ("those bloody Texans"), were equally ferocious.

Scott next attacked the Mexican army at the Contreras heights and the fortified convent at Churubusco simultaneously on 19–20 August, suffering 431 casualties as against more than 4,000 Mexicans killed or wounded. The fleeing Mexicans retreated to Mexico City, but American deserters from the San Patricio Battalion were captured and hanged.

On the diplomatic front, Nicholas P. Trist arrived to arrange an armistice through Scott. The Mexicans rejected the terms on 7 September, and on 8 September, reacting to misinformation that there was a cannon foundry at El Molino del Rey, Scott and the Americans stormed the building; the Mexicans put up a bloody fight, and no cannon were found.

On 12 September Scott began bombarding Chapultepec, a citadel set atop two-hundred-foot-high cliffs, while a division of Americans mounted the walls with scaling ladders. When other divisions stormed the gates, the city surrendered; 1,800 Mexicans were dead, wounded, or captured, and American losses were 138 killed and 673 wounded. Scott proceeded immediately to Mexico City, reaching the western gates at dusk on 13 September. Santa Anna and his troops left the city during the night, and the citadel surrendered at dawn on

14 September. Santa Anna tried one more attack, at Puebla, but he was defeated on 9 October and departed Mexico with an escort of U.S. soldiers to protect him from Texans.

The Treaty of Guadalupe Hidalgo was signed by Mexico on 2 February 1848. Under its terms, the United States acquired New Mexico and California for $15 million, and the U.S.-Mexico boundary was established in the middle of the Rio Grande.

BIBLIOGRAPHY

Bauer, Karl Jack. *The Mexican War.* New York: Macmillan, 1974.

Chidsey, Donald Burr. *The War with Mexico.* New York: Crown, 1968.

Connor, Seymour V., and Odie B. Faulk. *North America Divided: The Mexican War, 1846–1848.* New York: Oxford University Press, 1971.

Eisenhower, John S. D. *So Far from God: The U.S. War with Mexico.* New York: Random House, 1989.

Frazier, Donald, ed. *The United States and Mexico at War.* New York: Simon and Schuster, 1997.

Miller, Robert R. *Shamrock and Sword: The St. Patrick's Battalion in the U.S.-Mexican War.* Norman: University of Oklahoma Press, 1989.

Nevin, David. *The Mexican War.* Alexandria, Va.: Time-Life Books, 1978.

Singletary, Otis A. *The Mexican War.* Chicago: University of Chicago Press, 1960.

LOUISE B. KETZ

See also **Frémont, John Charles; Frontier; Texas Rangers; War.**

MIAMI

Miami, the seat of Dade County, is a resort and Atlantic port on Biscayne Bay in southeastern Florida. Miami was a frontier town of about fifteen hundred residents when it was incorporated in 1896 after the arrival of the railroad. One hundred years later, Greater Miami comprised all of Dade County, had a population of 2,076,175, and was the largest urban concentration in Florida. Violence in Miami has been promoted by racism, poverty, and periods of rapid growth. Moreover, Miami has faced unique problems because of its large Hispanic population and proximity to the Caribbean.

Miami Before World War II

Dade County's "bloodiest period" was in 1895, when there was said to be a "murder a mile" among construction workers as the railroad was built south from Fort Pierce. In 1917 the county (population 35,000) had a homicide rate of 19.8 (19.8 murders for every 100,000 members of the populace), similar to that for the entire state. By 1925–1926, however, the rate had surged to all-time peaks (102.6 and 110.1), largely because of instability accompanying the boom of the mid-1920s and Prohibition. The rate quickly declined in the postboom years, dropping into the thirties and twenties during the 1930s.

When frenzied land speculation brought 170,000 mostly transitory treasure-seekers to Miami between 1920 and 1925, crime became rampant. Moreover, Prohibition led to a bootlegging bonanza in 1919 as Miami smugglers distributed Caribbean alcohol to the East Coast. The Coast Guard failed to stop the flow of alcohol, but Duncan Shannon, the "king of the Florida smugglers," was killed by gunfire from a Coast Guard vessel in 1926. The next year, a bootlegger named Horace Alderman killed three law officers after his rum-runner had been intercepted; he was executed in 1929.

Miami's most famous execution, however, was that of Italian-born Giuseppe Zangara. On 15 February 1933 Zangara, for unclear reasons, attempted to assassinate president-elect Franklin D. Roosevelt after Roosevelt's speech in Bayfront Park but instead shot to death the mayor of Chicago, Anton J. Cermak, and wounded five others. Despite Zangara's obvious mental instability, he was sentenced to death in a lynch-mob atmosphere after a trial in which the judge stipulated that court-appointed psychiatrists were not to determine his mental competence.

The Mafia was well established before Prohibition ended. Al Capone, who owned an estate in Dade County, as well as Frank Nitti, Meyer Lansky, and other gangsters, moved in on local casinos and racetracks beginning in 1927. The underworld's investment in the city—and control of the local police force—made Miami the "Las Vegas of the 1930s." Because the Mafia has historically considered Miami neutral ground, gangsters such as Nicodemo Scarfo and Carlos Trafficante established homes there.

Racial Violence

Most of the local Seminoles were forcibly removed to Indian Territory by the U.S. Army in 1842, enabling Miami to avoid serious Anglo-Indian conflict. However, patterns of officially sanctioned segregation and racial violence began early. Colored Town (now Overtown), outside of which blacks were prohibited from living or operating businesses, was established in 1896. A black district later known as Liberty City was built surrounded by a wall in 1937. Until the 1930s, the all-white police force typically ignored the frequent house bombings and beatings of blacks by the Ku Klux Klan or other whites. Likewise, police beatings and killings of blacks were never officially punished before 1928.

After World War II, mass inward migrations of retirees made Dade County a premier retirement community. Likewise, the settling of several hundred thousand mostly well-educated Cuban refugees helped make the county a Hispanic enclave. By 1951, Greater Miami (population 500,000), with almost 100,000 blacks, 55,000 Jews (100,000 in 1955), and over 20,000 Hispanics (100,000 in 1960), was becoming a racially tense multiethnic metropolis.

In 1951 Carver Village, a complex in a heretofore exclusively white area, had been opened to blacks. In response, the Florida Klan executed eleven acts of racial or religious violence between June and December: Carver Village was bombed three times, another black-owned home destroyed, and two synagogues and a Catholic church bombed; three other synagogues were saved when bombs failed to detonate. No one was arrested.

An injured rioter is escorted away by Miami police during riots in August 1968.
CORBIS/BETTMANN

There were at least twenty-one minor or major riots involving Miami blacks between 1968 and 1989. All but two of these incidents followed the arrest, beating, or killing of a black person by the police. Riots in 1980 and 1984 were sparked by trials in which police were acquitted of wrongfully killing black men.

When the Republican National Convention was held in Miami in August 1968, Liberty City was economically depressed and politically impotent. A recent displacement (as a result of highway construction) of eighteen thousand blacks from Overtown to Liberty City had created slum conditions in the latter area. Moreover, a 1967 police crackdown on crime had caused escalating violence toward blacks. Miami's police chief, Walter Headley, was quoted as saying, "We don't mind being accused of police brutality."

On 7 August of that year a crowd in Liberty City gathered to hear a political speech. People grew restless when the speaker did not arrive, and a passing truck with a bumper sticker promoting the racist politician George Wallace prompted the crowd to erupt. During three nights of rioting 3 blacks were killed, 48 injured, and 222 arrested; property damage totaled $250,000.

In 1980 the black community remained politically ineffective and excluded from the economic mainstream, largely because of a massive inward Hispanic migration. While blacks steadily constituted about 17 percent of the Dade population from 1950 to the late 1980s, the Hispanic community grew by nine hundred thousand people to almost 50 percent of the population. The Hispanic community's economic and political successes, which were impressive, had the effect of exerting a limiting or even downward pressure on the black community.

The 1980 riot followed a series of police abuses, including the killing of a black man and the molestation of a black girl, in which offending officers were lightly reprimanded. On 17 May an all-white jury acquitted white Dade police officers of beating to death Arthur McDuffie, a black man. Liberty City erupted in violence. In three days of rioting, 17 people were killed, 371 injured, and property damage totaled $80 million. Although precipitated by the acquittal, the riot occurred because the black community felt powerless to change economic and judicial systems that it perceived as unjust.

The Murder Capital of the United States

After four decades with homicide rates in the teens and twenties, a "mini-peak" in 1980–1981 (35.2 and 36.1) was highly publicized in the national media ("Paradise Lost," was the title of a cover story about Miami in *Time* magazine, 23 November 1981, and the TV show *Miami Vice* enjoyed huge success), leading to the perception of Miami as America's "murder capital." The peak was largely due to racial tension and the growing drug trade. From 1979 to 1981 Colombian "cocaine cowboys" fought among themselves and with Cubans to control cocaine traffic in Miami, which was a valuable distribution center because of its location and large Hispanic population. Drug-related murders, including machine-gun killings on the highway and in shopping centers, mounted.

The crisis ended in 1982, in part because less violent dealers prevailed. Miami's homicide rate declined sharply after 1981 and dipped to 16.0 in 1997, at which point it dropped out of the top twenty of over 250 metropolitan areas ranked by homicides per annum. Moreover, there were no major riots in the 1990s, making the title "murder capital" no longer appropriate for Miami at the end of the twentieth century.

BIBLIOGRAPHY

Lenox, Teresa. "The Carver Village Controversy." *Tequesta* 50 (1990).

Mohl, Raymond A. "On the Edge: Blacks and Hispanics in Metropolitan Miami Since 1959." *Florida Historical Quarterly* 69 (1990).

Porter, Bruce, and Marvin Dunn. *The Miami Riot of 1980: Crossing the Bounds.* Lexington, Mass.: Lexington Books, 1984.

U.S. Department of Justice. *Uniform Crime Reports* (for years 1958–1996). Washington, D.C.: U.S. Government Printing Office. Homicide statistics from Office of Dade County Medical Examiner, 1956–1997.

Wilbanks, William L., and Alan R. Headly. *Forgotten Heroes: Police Officers Killed in Coral Gables and South Miami, Florida, 1895–1995.* South Miami, Fla.: Coral Gables, 1994.

———. *Murder in Miami: An Analysis of Homicide Patterns and Trends in Dade County (Miami) Florida, 1917–1983.* Lanham, Md.: University Press of America, 1984.

WILLIAM WILBANKS
NICHOLAS E. OKRENT

See also **Cuban Americans; Cunanan, Andrew; Riots; Urban Violence.**

MILITARISM

Beginning with the conquest of the native peoples and extending through revolution, civil war, and a continuous history of expansion, the American colonies and nation-state have anchored their raison d'être in a logic of warfare. This national chronicle of war and military intervention has produced little of the classic militarism in which soldiers impose their interests to organize society beyond military needs; but it has produced a relentless climate of civilian militarism, emanating from political leadership, civilian interests, and mass opinion, that reduces social, economic, political, and other issues to military solutions.

Roots in Colonial Culture

Two sources of this easy resort to military solutions are an expansionist ideology and military features of U.S. society that date from the period of British expansion. Early colonial culture brought a revolutionary and expansionist individualism intent on breaking free from medieval strictures. Grounded to varying degrees in Protestant individualism, the early entrepreneurial capitalism of the joint-stock company, and traditions of local self-government, it was a culture reinforced by eighteenth-century Enlightenment principles of liberal democracy.

The instrument of early civilian militarism was the militia, an institution founded in ideology. More than any other colonial offshoot of England, the American colonies were built on the historical battle between a local community and a standing army, with the local community fighting for and winning the right to bear arms to defend itself against the royal authority. In a founding culture built on interdependent social roles, the militia assumed a central place, because near-constant war against the native peoples melded political, economic, religious, and military culture around military motives and means. The role of the military leader in this culture is symbolized by the frequency with which citizens entrusted the leadership of the nation to its most recent military heroes—from George Washington to Andrew Jackson, William Henry Harrison, Zachary Taylor, and Theodore Roosevelt. The military hero as president made the transition from the militia tradition to the professional soldier in the persons of Ulysses Grant and Dwight Eisenhower, but a latent uneasiness about the decline of the citizen in arms is reflected in such late-twentieth-century groundswells as pressure to give the National Guard a seat on the Joint Chiefs of Staff, the emergence of underground militias declaring war on centralized governmental institutions, and the ideological battle to preserve the unrestricted right to bear arms.

While General Washington's Continental army moved the raison d'être of a community founded in war from the colony to the nation, militia-based partisans asserted American independence against loyalist partisans and their native allies. Both the Continental army and the Revolutionary militias produced heroes in the imagery of American freedom founded in war. And the precedent of elevating successful war leaders to lead the nation quickly extended from George Washington to Andrew Jackson and William Henry Harrison, heroes of the War of 1812 and the ongoing war against the native peoples.

The Nineteenth Century

With the founding of West Point in the early nineteenth century, the professional soldier and the citizen militiaman were merged, a process that began in a sense during the American Revolution, when the Prussian officer Friedrich von Steuben successfully reorganized and drilled the Continental army. Accompanying concerns about Prussian-style militarism infecting American military culture had deep roots in British history; they also reflected a fear of local loss of prestige and political and economic power entailed in control over a militia army. The war with Mexico from 1846 to 1848 made citizen soldiers and West Point officers alike heroes. Pushed by the economics and politics of westward expansion, enthusiasm for the war derived from the recent ideological impetus of Jacksonian democracy, the concept of manifest destiny, and the appeal of a war against popery and dictatorship. The first appearance of the penny press and the war correspondent in the 1830s and 1840s intensified public involvement. A vein of realistic and critical reporting was buried beneath the heroic transformation of Generals Zachary Taylor and Winfield Scott into American Napoleons and successors of Washington, imagery that carried Taylor to the presidency in the elections of 1848 and gathered a presidential nomination for Scott.

The coming of the Civil War heightened the predisposition of southern society to grant the soldier and warrior a special place. With roots in the warrior culture of the Irish clan and reinforced by a landholding class that emulated the British aristocracy in recognizing a bond among land, military, God, and country, this military ethos elevated the status of the combined professional soldier and militiaman and was reflected in the disproportionate number of West Point graduates from southern states and in the importance of military academies in the South's educational system. On the road to war southern society developed a full-blown cavalier myth of the South as a warrior culture. This myth was reinforced by boxcars bearing images from Sir Walter Scott's romantic novel of chivalric knighthood, *Ivanhoe*, rolling into the South. More grim, much of the South, under real and imagined northern threats to its society and culture, became a closed society, its leadership arguably transforming itself into a military caste, with militia roles assuming increased importance. The realities of an economy dependent on slavery reinforced the military ethos by transforming the South into a white garrison society ultimately dependent on its militias to enforce repressive slave codes and to guard against rebellions. Events of the nineteenth century intensified this garrison mentality as the northern states abolished slavery at the turn of the century and the British Empire followed in the 1830s at a time when the South was increasingly dependent on an expanding slave economy and "king cotton." Slave rebellions at home and abroad further increased the tension, as did the rising cry of northern abolitionists and the political and economic threat of a northern freehold and industrial economy in growing conflict with an expanding slave economy. By the 1850s the South was withdrawing behind its barricades. It was to a West Point graduate and hero of the Mexican War, Jefferson Davis, that the South turned to lead the Confederacy in war.

The public rhetoric that ushered in the Civil War—which cast the public as the leaders rather than the followers of politicians and generals—invites a psychohistorical analysis of the emotional push of civilian militancy to modern total war. The language of aggressive social pathology, with its themes of humiliation, vengeance, annihilation, and vindication, is overwhelming in the North and in the South. In the wake of work by psychoanalysts Melanie Klein, Alice Miller, and others who have explored the links between aggression and war, such an analysis would help explain the push and pull of modern civilian militarism in citizen armies, where generals and politicians are expected to follow as well as lead. During the Civil War fears were first realized about the modern militarization of politics that the Prussian military theorist Carl von Clausewitz expressed in the early nineteenth century: fear that public opinion behind citizen armies would encourage politicians to look to generals for military solutions to satisfy public craving for military action and fear that this new militarism, armed with the destructive potential of industrial warfare, would shift the balance of historical forces from limiting to totalizing war.

The culture of aggression helped bind together varying loyalties to state, county, family, and God. In the South the early war utterances and achievements of General Thomas J. "Stonewall" Jackson became a focus for these themes. In the North similar themes were present for a while; they subsided from late 1862 through 1863, as the public retrenched in the face of early military defeat, the suspension of civil liberties, and emancipation, and revived with General William T. Sherman's taking of Atlanta and with the inspiration of his accompanying rhetoric of annihilation, vengeance, and vindication. The northern media and Abraham Lincoln's skilled political propagandists seized on this upswell of northern militaristic patriotism to harness democratic nationalism and Christianity in support of the brutality and sacrifice of a total war to the finish.

The victors entrusted the military reconstruction of the South to military governors who were expected to implement the total war aims of destroying the slave economy and its political leadership and to integrate former slaves into southern society and politics. The South honed its military ethos in defeat by seeking military heroes and scapegoats in the "lost cause" debate over how the South could have won the war and who was responsible for defeat. The North, meanwhile, in 1868 elected Ulysses Grant president, while Sherman, who succeeded Grant in army command, led a Civil War–hardened army in the final conquest of the native peoples. His western theater commander was the Civil War general Philip Sheridan, who was remembered for his total devastation of the Shenandoah Valley. Sherman saw the fate of native people as part of an evolutionary logic; the regular army and militias, in waging a total war of annihilation, were, he believed, merely acting as agents of the inevitable advance of civilization across the American frontier.

At the same time the cowboy culture that emerged briefly after the Civil War and focused around trail drives to westward-moving railroads meshed with the world of frontier Civil War guerrilla bands, outlaws, sheriffs, and Texas Rangers to create new imagery of the vigilante living on the edge of the land and the law, fighting to preserve frontier freedoms. It was a radical revision of the citizen in arms, setting him apart from militia and

even from community, instead casting him in an anarchical version, that of a lone ranger drifting across the land. This tradition bred the distinctive vigilante imagery of the twentieth-century movie Western and its heroes, blurring fact and fiction in the characters played by an array of cinematic icons from Tom Mix to John Wayne and Clint Eastwood.

The Birth of U.S. Imperialism

With the settlement of the American frontier, President Roosevelt and his public, like Turner, saw expansion to foreign frontiers as necessary for an American democracy grounded in "free land" to survive and grow. Building on the logic and language of militaristic imperialists like Brooks Adams, Alfred Thayer Mahan, and Homer Lea, Roosevelt as president would exploit his image as the carrier of the imperial flag up Cuba's San Juan Hill in 1898 and as commander in chief of the great white fleet.

The Spanish-American War of 1898 marked the first time that the decision to go to war was made behind the closed doors of the executive office, excluding Congress and the public. President William McKinley consulted a closed group of Republican expansionist interests from business and politics motivated by a mix of economic and political interests and ideology. The result was a policy of military expansion in response to the push of western agricultural interests for markets and the fears of urban entrepreneurial and financial interests that they might be left out of the next round of frontier expansion. The 1898 decision to purchase the Philippines from Spain was made by the president in consultation with a small group of economic, political, and intellectual insiders; military intervention to end the Boxer Rebellion in China in 1900 was initiated by executive order. While the president led, the newspapers of William Randolph Hearst and Joseph Pulitzer supported every expansionist use of force; politicians and lastly the public followed, stirring the traditional imagery of the covenant with God, land, and democracy into a militaristic stew that was buttressed by social Darwinism and the extension of manifest destiny to offshore frontiers.

On succeeding McKinley after he was assassinated in 1901, Roosevelt built on these myths and interests and on McKinley's centralization of power. Motivated by his wish to enhance America's place in great-power politics, Roosevelt used the presidency to lead rather than be led by entrepreneurial and finance capitalists. Though intended as a diplomatic strategy to avoid war, the open-door policy developed under McKinley and Roosevelt to acquire U.S. access to world markets contained contradictions that inevitably brought military conflict with intended beneficiaries who did not share the American vision; in Latin America alone the United States made twenty-one military interventions between 1898 and 1924. President Woodrow Wilson's Central American intervention was a prelude to U.S. entry in World War I against Germany, a major threat to U.S. economic and ideological expansion.

Wilson expanded Roosevelt's political Progressivism, with its belief in the need for an enlightened elite to extend the benefits of the U.S. definition of capitalism, democracy, and Christianity abroad. So motivated, Wilson sent an expedition to fight against the Bolshevik revolution without congressional authority and devised the League of Nations as an instrument to open the world to U.S. capitalism and accompanying values—by military force if necessary.

The Cold War

The National Security State. Herbert Hoover was the intellectual architect of the U.S. corporate state, with international politics organized around rational scientific principles of cooperation to meliorate conflict. But it was the vision of President Franklin Roosevelt and the politics of his successor, Harry Truman, that after World War II transformed the corporate state into the militaristic national security state. Truman inherited Roosevelt's vision of a Pax Americana that would use U.S. hegemony to provide the postwar world with a package of military security, U.S.-style democracy, and economic betterment under U.S.-style capitalism. Such a package would be delivered through the alliance of big government, big business, and big military that emerged from World War II. But with the growing threat of war with the Soviet Union, the New Deal economic and political agenda faded before issues of national security. The concept of the national security state moved beyond policy into an ideology of military power for the Cold War. That the national security state was built on a nuclear strategy based on speed of delivery suggests the validity of the political theorist Paul Virilio's analysis that relates modern political power to speed of movement in military strategy, extending Clausewitz's early-nineteenth-century anticipation that the need to mobilize society to meet the technological and consequent strategic demands of industrial warfare would lead to the militarization of society to meet security needs.

The Cold War stirred unprecedented debate over the nature of U.S. militarism. The debate revolved around whether the Cold War led to a suspension of congressional authority and public participation in military decision-making; the emergence of an alliance of big military and corporate business that captured decision-making power and used it to expand conflict and the arms business; or the loss of control by the executive office of the dangerous area between the formulation of strategy and strategic missions, on the one hand, and operational plans, on the other.

The post–World War II decision-making process extended the centralized and closed decision-making that began with McKinley into peacetime. Asserting presidential leadership and the ideology of the national security state, Truman balanced political, military, and business interests. He used fear of war with the Soviet Union to continue the World War II practice of closed executive decision-making, informing a few chosen congressional leaders just before he put a policy in place. He disciplined politicians, bureaucrats, and the public alike by skillfully reducing any critique of defense policy to a fundamental challenge to American values, a technique that included imposing a loyalty oath on public employees.

Truman took the United States to war in Korea without public discussion, evading the Constitution by calling the war a police action in support of the United Nations, an agency established under U.S. leadership to enhance an American ordering of the post–World War II world. Korea would set the precedent for late-twentieth-century interventions in the developing world arrived at behind closed doors. Truman's foreign policy of Cold War containment based on nuclear deterrence, covert destabilization, and, with Korea, limited conventional war reduced foreign policy to military policy. In implementing a militarily driven foreign policy, Truman, like Roosevelt, appreciated the value of generals and admirals, as long as they respected his place at the head of the bureaucratic table. Truman entrusted both the State and Defense Departments to George Marshall, the World War II army chief of staff and the soldier whose advice Roosevelt most respected. At the same time, like Roosevelt, Truman was wary of the threat of military authority, perhaps remembering his predecessor's warning as early as 1932 that the army chief of staff Douglas MacArthur was as dangerous as the charismatic populist Huey Long.

The postwar reorganization of military decision-making in the new Defense Department, together with the new Joint Chiefs of Staff system with a chairman, consolidated the militarization of foreign policy in the executive office. The newly constituted National Security Council (NSC) served as an instrument for presidential manipulation of military policy. The reduction of the NSC to a covert planning and operational center in support of the contra rebels in Nicaragua in the 1980s under President Ronald Reagan and Vice President George Bush, a former director of the Central Intelligence Agency, was the most extreme but not the only abuse of this council. During this covert interlude the NSC was chaired by military officers who used their staffs to carry out the operation, along with the assistance of a retired air force general and former CIA operative, John G. Singlaub, who had acquired wealth and a network in the business community. The incident was an example not of the military capturing the political process but of a militaristic executive office leading an alliance of the executive branch, the armed services, the CIA, and business in an aggressive policy of counterinsurgency. Bush as president confirmed his militaristic approach to foreign policy by attacking Panama in 1989 and in 1991 pushing a wary military leadership into a war in the Persian Gulf. President Bill Clinton and his powerful secretary of state Madeleine K. Albright continued this quick resort to military force in foreign relations with the ongoing bombing of Iraq and with their leadership on the NATO bombing campaign against Yugoslavia. With the end of the Cold War, which had begun during the presidency of Richard Nixon and culminated in 1991 in the collapse of the Soviet Union (removing a powerful military and ideological threat), the militaristic ethos shifted. Traditional ideological and political arguments behind post–World War II covert counterinsurgency and overt military actions gave way to a rationale more openly grounded in the logic of power politics in pursuit of America's self-appointed mission to lead a new world order that guaranteed U.S. political and economic interests.

The Military-Industrial Complex. Expressions of concern about an alliance of big military and big business capturing military policy first went public when the World War II Allied commander in Europe Dwight Eisenhower ushered out his presidency by warning against the military-industrial complex. Eisenhower and the liberal wing of the Republican Party that he represented did not accept the most important new development to emerge in postwar bureaucratic politics: the rise of big military as a permanent player in the peacetime bureaucracy. Nor did they accept the economic dominance of that sector of the economy grounded in the armaments industry.

Eisenhower's warning was also a legitimate reaction to lobbying and armed-services behavior that challenged executive authority. Eisenhower, like Truman before him and Presidents John Kennedy and Lyndon Johnson after, was concerned about a challenge to containment policy from an alliance of conservative nationalists who advocated rolling back communism with military force. The military participants in this alliance came from the World War II Pacific command and included MacArthur, members of the naval command, and leaders of the strategic-bombing command. The political base of power was in the Asia First conservative-nationalist wing of the Republican Party and in the broad network of the China lobby that supported a military challenge to the communist regime of Mao Zedong. This rollback network included the most powerful and ideologically driven print-media empire in the United States, Henry Luce's *Time* magazine.

Some scholars compellingly argue that the challenge from this network was not resolved but accommodated. As nuclear containment was complemented by containment with conventional weapons, in the wake of Korea and the adoption of General Maxwell Taylor's and Kennedy's strategy of "flexible response," the old Pacific interests got a share of the full-blown counterinsurgency strategy put in place in Vietnam and elsewhere. Kennedy and his high-powered defenders of executive authority in military policy, like those of Johnson after him, accommodated and perhaps, like President Richard Nixon, encouraged rollback forces, allowing them to engage in limited anticommunist militarism in developing countries that did not threaten conflict with China or the Soviet Union in return for supporting containment, including arms-limitations talks, with the Soviet Union.

Conflicts with Military Command. During the Cold War's intense political and bureaucratic com-

American soldiers loading a howitzer during the Korean War. LIBRARY OF
CONGRESS

petition for initiative in military policy and strategy, there were at least two instances of military command exceeding its authority. The first was MacArthur's response to his dismissal by Truman during the Korean War. The second was the insubordination of the air force commander General Curtis LeMay under Eisenhower. Neither event was an aberration, both occurring at the edge of historical tensions over the limits of military authority.

MacArthur considered his dismissal as being based on "a new and heretofore unknown and dangerous concept that the members of our armed forces owe primary allegiance or loyalty to those who temporarily exercise authority of the Executive Branch of the Government rather than to the country and its Constitution which they are sworn to defend. No proposition could be more dangerous." MacArthur was a nineteenth-century soldier: he was born in 1880, was a general in World War I, and held a nineteenth-century worldview, complete with a Victorian rhetorical form. He came from a military culture that was struggling with whether it should restrict itself to a narrow professionalism or continue the citizen-soldier tradition of playing political roles, even while in uniform. Between the World Wars a narrower professional ethos prevented the military leadership from taking an open political role but not from lobbying

allies in Congress, business, science, and the media. Lobbying by the armed services continued after World War II and was the usual balance between excessive interest in politics and legitimate concerns about preparedness.

Within this gray historical area MacArthur's dangerous militaristic stretch of the Constitution nonetheless stepped over the line. Playing on his public image as the greatest military hero since Washington, an image he assiduously cultivated, and letting his presidential ambitions be known, MacArthur in his military actions, public utterances, and playing to political and bureaucratic allies during the Korean War overstepped his authority as a rollback general trapped in a limited war of containment.

The strategic-bombing enthusiasts in the leadership of the U.S. Air Force also overstepped their authority, when air force and related industry interests knowingly distorted the Soviet missile buildup and when Strategic Air Command leadership attempted to conceal from Eisenhower the details of operational plans for nuclear load and targeting against the Soviet Union. Air force chief of staff General Curtis LeMay made Eisenhower as nervous as MacArthur did Truman. The World War II commander of the Army Air Force's strategic-bombing command in the Pacific and the first head of the Strategic Air Command in the independent U.S. Air Force, LeMay was a formidable enthusiast for strategic bombing. A skilled bureaucratic player and advocate of rollback, like MacArthur, he was a conservative nationalist with political ambitions fueled by contempt for the military policy of a liberal presidency.

Both of these military challenges to executive authority occurred in the context of Truman's having won an early battle for presidential control of nuclear strategy, by having nuclear weapons placed under civilian control in the Atomic Energy Commission and subject to military use only with presidential approval. With the loss of the atomic bomb as "just another weapon," rollback military leaders of the early Cold War (who saw the war against communism as just an extension of the total war against fascism begun in World War II) were deprived of a tantalizing means of abruptly extending a limited war into general war. And MacArthur and LeMay represented a spectrum of armed-services opinion, shaped by the total-war strategy of World War II (with roots dating from the Civil War), which had difficulty living with the politically driven military strategy of limited war that Korea introduced into the Cold War.

Militarism and Popular Culture

The nuclear brinkmanship of the Truman, Eisenhower, and Kennedy eras induced two satiric classics of black war humor: the Stanley Kubrick film *Dr. Strangelove; or, How I Learned to Stop Worrying and Love the Bomb* (1964) and the novel *Catch-22* (1961), by Joseph Heller. *Dr. Strangelove* explores the dark vision of paranoia and war-lover pathology taking over the political and military leadership as well as the military rank and file. The central character, Dr. Strangelove, evokes nuclear-intellectual personalities including the real-life scientific force behind nuclear policy, Dr. Edward Teller, and the military insider Dr. Herman Kahn, a RAND think-tank guru whose 1960 book titled *On Thermonuclear War* argued the likelihood of U.S. nuclear survival with tolerable losses. Heller wove the equally unforgettable characters of *Catch-22* through the logic of corporate war ultimately leading to the bombing of oneself.

A still darker vision emerged in post–Vietnam War science fiction, much of it written by combat veterans of that war. Such representative works as Joe Haldeman's *The Forever War* (1975) and Orson Scott Card's *Ender's Game* (1985) create a totally militarized society reduced to the logic of a cybernetic war game in the never-ending war of to-morrow. Their vision exists in the context of a growing body of literary and social scientific theory that reconstructs human nature, culture, and society around issues of the mind, body, and cybernetic technology, a field of technological endeavor drawing much of its impetus from military-related activity. Is it a paranoid vision, or is it related to the telecast of war fans celebrating the Gulf War victory in Buffalo, New York's Rich Stadium—reveling over "our win" in a way indistinguishable from Buffalo football fans. Did the Gulf War and its live television coverage, as a high-tech amusement, fuse with the American fascination with electronic war games and with the genre of war films that reduces the complexities of international relations to high-tech militaristic scenarios?

Nuclear satire in Stanley Kubrick's *Dr. Strangelove; or, How I Learned to Stop Worrying and Love the Bomb* (1964). PHOTOFEST

BIBLIOGRAPHY

Forster, Stig, and Jorg Nagler, eds. *On the Road to Total War.* New York: Cambridge University Press, 1997.

Franklin, John Hope. *The Militant South, 1800–1961.* Cambridge, Mass.: Harvard University Press, 1950.

Hagerman, Edward. *The American Civil War and the Origins of Modern Warfare.* Bloomington: Indiana University Press, 1988.

Huntington, Samuel P. *The Soldier and the State.* Cambridge, Mass.: Harvard University Press, 1957.

Johannsen, Robert W. *To the Halls of the Montezumas.* New York: Oxford University Press, 1985.

McNeill, William. *The Pursuit of Power.* Chicago: University of Chicago Press, 1982.

Melman, Seymour. *Pentagon Capitalism.* New York: McGraw-Hill, 1970.

Mills, C. Wright. *The Power Elite.* New York: Oxford University Press, 1956.

Royster, Charles. *The Destructive War.* New York: Knopf, 1991.

Schurmann, Franz. *The Logic of World Power.* New York: Pantheon, 1974.

Sherry, Michael S. *In the Shadow of War.* New Haven, Conn.: Yale University Press, 1995.

———. *The Rise of American Air Power.* New Haven, Conn.: Yale University Press, 1987.

Taylor, William R. *Cavalier and Yankee.* 1961. Rev. ed. New York: Oxford University Press, 1993.

Vagts, Alfred. *A History of Militarism.* 1937. Rev. ed. 1959. Westport, Conn.: Greenwood, 1981.

Williams, William A. *The Tragedy of American Diplomacy.* 1957. Rev. ed. New York: Dell, 1972.

Yarmolinsky, Adam. *The Military Establishment.* New York: Harper Colophon, 1971.

EDWARD HAGERMAN

See also **Cold War; Gun Violence: Gun Culture; Military Interventions; Militias, Unauthorized; No Duty to Retreat; Toys and Games; Weapons.**

MILITARY CULTURE

The U.S. military is designed to inflict state-sanctioned violence on the state's enemies. It is not surprising, then, that in a country that won its independence through violent means and whose society ranks among the world's most violent, the armed forces, which defend national interests, have themselves endured incidents of internal violence. Some of this violence, such as that authorized by military statute, is defined as legal. Unfortunately, racial and gender jealousies have also sparked violence within the military, as they have in civilian society. Interservice conflicts, training abuses and accidents, and cases in which Americans have accidentally fired upon other Americans

in battle make up a final broad category of violence within the armed forces of the United States.

Violence and Early Military Justice

Like American society as a whole, the military has often used violent means to punish those who break established codes or traditions. The Articles of War, first passed in 1775 and substantially revised in 1806, long served as the basis of the army's justice system, with naval codes passed in 1775, 1797, and 1862. These systems were designed to maintain discipline rather than protect individual rights. Indeed, the close-order tactics of the day, in which soldiers fought in tight linear formations and sailors manned wooden ships, relied upon iron discipline to be effective.

The U.S. Navy had essentially two means of enforcing discipline, modeled after the British naval justice system: nonjudicial punishment by the commanding officer or a general court-martial. In the absence of alternative punishments or petty courts, officers often favored the lash as a quick and public means of enforcing discipline. One hapless sailor, for instance, was given 320 lashes, 64 on each of his squadron's five ships.

Although the army authorized more options, in practice it operated in a similar fashion. With its forces scattered in small garrisons across a rapidly expanding nation, much depended upon the whim of the senior officer on the scene. Privately administered beatings were frequent. Soldiers might be flogged, branded, have an ear cropped, be ducked in water, or be tied up or chained in various contortions and afforded only bread and water. Some seemed to become inured to this brutality; an informal "Damnation Club" was formed at Fort Defiance during the 1790s, admitting only those who were willing to receive one hundred lashes in order to obtain a pint of whiskey. At least one woman civilian, having been drummed out of military camps three times for misconduct, was sentenced to twenty lashes at West Point. The navy finally abolished flogging in 1850; the army followed suit eleven years later.

Reforms came gradually, often reflecting broader societal attitudes. Critics pointed to vast inconsistencies in sentencing. Hoping to attract higher-quality recruits, nineteenth-century reformers within the services often attacked the use of corporal punishment, especially for minor offenses. Congress's decision to ban flogging in the navy was undoubtedly hastened by the negative publicity surrounding the *Somers* incident of 1842.

The ship's captain, Commander Alexander Slidell Mackenzie, came from a wealthy, almost aristocratic family and relied heavily on the whip to enforce strict discipline. One of his midshipmen was Philip Spencer, the son of Secretary of War John C. Spencer. The younger Spencer fantasized about seizing the vessel and becoming a pirate. He and two of his associates were found guilty of mutiny and hanged after a trial during which the accused were not allowed to examine witnesses. Families of the executed men demanded further investigation, but a general court-martial acquitted Mackenzie of murder. Still, the accompanying publicity revealed the navy's widespread dependence upon flogging, a punishment that seemed to contradict society's emphasis on due process and the rights of the common man.

The Civil War saw an enormous expansion of the armed forces with accompanying changes in military justice codes and a huge expansion of provost guards (military police). General Order No. 100, issued 24 April 1863 and drafted by Francis Lieber, represented the North's attempt to codify the "laws and usages of war." A German-born immigrant who had two sons fight for the Union and another for the Confederacy, Lieber sought to instill a basic system of moral values in the army's policies for dealing with enemy civilians, guerrillas, and partisans. European nations soon adopted similar codes, which would continue to influence U.S. policies in occupied territories for the next century and a half.

With regular courts-martial in the North and the South overwhelmed by the sheer volume of cases, many officers took matters into their own hands. Violent punishments, believed many, might have a deterrent effect. Initially, executions were fairly rare, with the letter "D" (deserter) or "C" (coward) branded upon the suspected offender's hand, hip, cheek, or forehead. But as the war wore on, both sides resorted to capital punishment more frequently and expanded the types of offenses subject to such penalties to include rape, murder, and espionage. Eventually, 267 Union soldiers were executed by orders of courts-martial, about half of whom were deserters. A comparable number of Confederate soldiers were probably dealt with in a similar fashion.

Racial Violence and Changes in the Justice System

The post–Civil War period saw a marked increase in racially inspired violence within the armed forces. Blacks had fought in the Revolutionary War and the War of 1812 and constituted between 5 and 10 percent of the navy but were prohibited from official army service until 1862. In the Civil War's most famous incident of racial violence, Confederates massacred several dozen black Union soldiers at Fort Pillow in 1864. After the Civil War, Congress reserved six regiments (army-wide reductions cut this to four in 1869) for black enlisted men. Late in the nineteenth century there were several violent incidents between black and white regulars as well as between black troops and white civilians. In one case in Texas in 1867, a drunken Edward M. Heyl, a white lieutenant, ordered three black enlisted men tied up and suspended by their wrists. Heyl then fired a shot at one of the men, who was attempting to gain his footing on a nearby stump. He then threatened to shoot a black sergeant who complained. The enlisted men rioted, resulting in the death of the sergeant and a white officer who had come to Heyl's defense. Two of the nine soldiers tried for the incident were sentenced to death but had their sentences remitted by the secretary of war because of Heyl's habitual mistreatment of his men. Heyl, however, was not tried and went on to a long military career.

Another highly publicized incident occurred at the United States Military Academy. On the morning of 6 April 1880, Johnson C. Whittaker, the third black cadet to attend West Point, was found lying unconscious in his own room, tied to his bed and covered with blood from several cuts to his ears, left hand, and one of his little toes. Whittaker asserted that three masked assailants had done the deed. To the astonishment of many outsiders, a court of inquiry concluded that the wounds had been self-inflicted. The young cadet demanded a court-martial in hopes of clearing his name, only to have that body find him guilty of staging the incident to win public sympathy and of lying under oath. Although President Chester Arthur threw out the verdict, the case certainly raised doubts about the army's ability to police its own affairs. Whittaker was restored to the academy but was later dismissed for academic failures.

Another incident took place at Brownsville, Texas, in August 1906. Several companies of the Twenty-fifth Infantry Regiment, composed entirely of black enlisted men, were stationed at Fort Brown, where they clashed frequently with civilians at nearby Brownsville. The soldiers, most of whom were veterans of recent fighting in the Philippines, resented the abusive treatment they were receiving from local businessmen. On the night of 13–14 August, a brief shooting spree erupted, resulting in the death of a bartender and the wounding of a Brownsville policeman. Civilians claimed the soldiers had done it, but the enlisted men denied any involvement and refused to cooperate with the investigations. A local grand jury failed to return any indictments, but the army's inspector-general charged that the soldiers' conspiracy had blocked efforts to ferret out the truth. President Theodore Roosevelt dishonorably discharged all 167 of the garrison's enlisted men. A Senate investigation concurred with Roosevelt's decision, but in 1910 a court of military inquiry allowed fourteen of those discharged to reenlist. Sixty-two years after the government's evidence had been discredited as contrived and racially biased, the remaining men were awarded honorable discharges.

Another much publicized case occurred in 1917 at Houston, Texas. The all-black enlisted personnel of the Third Battalion, Twenty-fourth Infantry Regiment, deeply resented the city's segregated streetcars and the strong-arm tactics of the Houston police force. On 23 August trouble started when the police beat up two infantrymen. Not satisfied by the battalion commander's assurances that the offenders would be suspended, between seventy-five and one hundred soldiers determined to exact their revenge against the city's police. Excited by rumors that a white mob was coming to get them, the soldiers seized arms and ammunition and moved into the city, killing four policemen, nine civilians, and two National Guardsmen.

Several men in the regiment cooperated with authorities in return for clemency, and military justice was swift. Nineteen of those soldiers involved were hanged, and sixty-three others were given life sentences. No white civilians were brought to trial.

The lack of an appeals system for those found guilty of serious crimes, along with continued perceptions of command abuse in the military justice system, troubled many Americans. Amendments to the Articles of War in 1920 prescribed a general review process for all cases involving capital punishment, dismissals, and dishonorable discharge. They also required that defense counsel represent all defendants. To provide a more professional internal enforcement body, the army established a permanent Military Police Corps in 1941.

Some two million citizen-soldiers were court-martialed during World War II. One particularly notably case arose at the navy's ammunition base at Port Chicago, California. In July 1944 an explosion killed 320 sailors and blew up two cargo ships. Two hundred fifty-eight black sailors, few of whom had any special training in handling dangerous ordnance, refused to return to work, citing what they regarded to be unsafe conditions. The navy, however, deemed it a mutiny. Fifty of the men were convicted of mutiny; the remainder were either fined or dishonorably discharged. Widespread reports of abuses and injustices in the military justice system eventually led Congress to push through the Uniform Code of Military Justice in 1950. The new system severely restricted the powers of summary and special courts-martial, long

The Texas court martial of sixty-four black soldiers of the Twenty-fourth Infantry for murder and mutiny, August 1917. CORBIS

believed to be a major source of abuse. The civilian Court of Military Appeals was also established.

Despite these changes, racial tensions continued to plague the services after World War II. Eleven black soldiers were charged with mutiny after a riot at MacDill Airfield, Florida, in October 1946. The following year seven men were killed or injured in a fight between black and white prisoners at Fort Leavenworth, Kansas. In 1948 President Harry S. Truman's Executive Order 9981 officially desegregated the armed forces, but this act did not entirely remove the stain of racism within the military. Racially motivated violence was widely reported during the war in Vietnam, especially among support troops and in rear areas.

Gender-Related Violence

Although women have fought and died in all of our nation's wars, traditionally their official roles have been limited to those of laundress, nurse, and as support personnel. Eight military nurses, for example, died in Vietnam. As military opportunities for women have expanded, increasing attention has been focused upon violence against women in the armed forces. One major case was the 1991 annual meeting of the Tailhook Association, a private group of navy and marine pilots named after the arresting hook on the rear of carrier aircraft. That September the Tailhook group held its annual meeting at the Hilton Hotel in Las Vegas. Despite rumors about incidents of drunkenness and lewd behavior at the group's previous conventions, most military officials encouraged attendance.

Lieutenant Paula Coughlin, a navy helicopter pilot and admiral's aide, told her superiors that she had been physically assaulted by some of her male counterparts during the Tailhook convention. Others eventually came forward, claiming that they had been fondled, groped, and forced to run through a hallway filled with drunken male pilots. With internal investigations seemingly stalled, in July 1992 the Military Personnel and Compensation Subcommittee of the House Armed Services Committee began to study allegations of sexual harassment within the armed forces. Navy Secretary H. Lawrence Garrett III, who had attended the convention, was allowed to resign amidst charges that he had failed to respond aggressively to such charges. Chief of Naval Operations Frank B. Kelso II, who also had been present, retired two months early in the face of claims that he had tried to manipulate the investigation. Eventually, the Defense Department listed eighty-three women and seven

men as having been assaulted, and more than 140 officers faced disciplinary action.

The Tailhook incident led to heightened scrutiny of sexually related violence in the armed forces, which revealed just how serious the problem had become. A related case occurred at the Citadel, a state-supported military school in South Carolina. The first four women cadets in the institution's history were admitted in 1996; within the year two of the women had quit, asserting they had undergone sexual harassment and illegal hazing at the hands of their male counterparts. Ten cadets were eventually disciplined. In May 1997 Sergeant Major of the Army Gene C. McKinney, the army's highest ranking enlisted man, was charged with several counts of sexual misconduct by four female subordinates. A court-martial cleared McKinney of the sex charges but found him guilty of obstructing justice. He received a one-rank demotion and an official reprimand.

A landmark case came in 1996, when the army announced that more than fifty women soldiers at Aberdeen Proving Ground, Maryland, had filed official complaints of sexual abuse. Most of the charges were against drill sergeants. A dozen men at Aberdeen were disciplined, and a flurry of similar incidents were reported at military installations around the globe. The case sparked a ten-month investigation, which concluded that sexual harassment in the army was common across racial, gender, and rank lines. Its survey revealed that 47 percent of women soldiers had been the target of unwanted sexual attention, 15 percent had suffered sexual coercion, and 7 percent had endured sexual assault. Males reported rates of 30, 8, and 6 percent, respectively. The army outlined 128 ways to improve internal gender relations, ranging from greater accountability for commanding officers to new screening procedures for those dealing with recruits.

Homosexuals were officially excluded from military service in 1917 as part of that year's revisions of the Articles of War. Sodomy was proscribed three years later. Since such behavior has been defined as illegal, the military has not kept statistics relating to incidents of violence against homosexual military personnel. Anecdotal evidence, however, demonstrates that gays and lesbians have often faced the threat of violence. In 1919, for example, there were reports that navy recruits at Newport, Rhode Island, had been used to "bait" fellow sailors and civilians suspected of homosexuality. Two 1993 incidents highlighted the often-hidden problem of violent acts against homosexuals in the military. A homosexual sailor, Allen R. Schindler, was beaten to death by other sailors while he was stationed in Japan. The same year marine Colonel Fred Peck testified before a Senate committee that although he loved his homosexual son, policy prevented him from entering the Marine Corps and that even if his son could join, he would fear for his son's safety.

Training Accidents and Abuses

During the nineteenth century military training consisted largely of drill, with few attempts to duplicate the sights and sounds of the battlefield. Even target practice was rare. Modern training practices, however, have emphasized the need for realistic simulations of what one might expect in battle. Live-fire exercises became common during World War II, with sometimes tragic results. The premature explosion of an artillery shell at Fort Gordon in 1943, for example, killed three advancing infantrymen. Inevitably, public outrage over such training accidents set limits on the lengths to which instructors might go in their attempts to expose recruits to combat situations.

Greater concern for human life and individual rights has probably reduced the number of sadistic training incidents in recent times, but the line between realism and safety in military training is not always clearly defined. Pilots must practice flying at low altitudes, soldiers and sailors need experience firing live rounds, and military personnel must be disciplined and in good physical condition to perform well in combat. But accidents occur. In 1956 six marine boot camp recruits drowned during a night disciplinary march into the swamps outside Parris Island, South Carolina, forcing the Marine Corps to answer public charges of sadism and brutality during basic training. In 1977 two soldiers died of hypothermia while undergoing the army's notoriously difficult Ranger training exercises. To prevent any recurrences of such deaths, the army declared that such training was permissible only when the water temperature was at least fifty degrees. In February 1995 four Rangers (three officers and one noncommissioned officer) died of similar circumstances in the swamps near Eglin Air Force Base, Florida. The water temperature was fifty-two degrees.

Friendly Fire

Friendly fire, or amicicide, has plagued all military forces since the invention of projected weapons. In some cases troops actually open fire on their own troops by accident. During the American Revolution the Continental Army's failure to win the Battle of Germantown (1777) was at least partially explained by one unit's accidentally having

Contemporary engraving of a friendly-fire incident during the Civil War.
CORBIS

opened fire on another. Potentially just as dangerous, however, are cases in which troops withhold their fire by mistake, thus allowing enemy forces to exploit the situation. At the First Battle of Bull Run (1861), two Union artillery batteries were effectively blasting Confederate lines until a blue-clad regiment emerged from the woods to their right. Assuming the advancing infantry to be friendly, the Union guns fell silent, only to be overwhelmed when the troops, who turned out to be the Thirty-third Virginia Regiment, opened fire and charged. Buoyed by a fierce counterattack, the Confederates swept to victory.

A friendly-fire incident claimed the life of Thomas J. ("Stonewall") Jackson. After a long day's march during the Battle of Chancellorsville (1863), Jackson's Confederate troops had rolled up the Union's right flank, their attack slowed only by the onset of darkness. Desperate to complete his victory, Jackson and his staff rode out ahead to reconnoiter enemy positions in preparation for a night assault. As the collection of horsemen returned to friendly lines, nervous Confederate skirmishers opened fire. Jackson's horse bolted and he was thrown to the ground, his arm shattered by two bullets. The arm was amputated, but pneumonia set in and claimed Jackson's life eight days later.

The problem became even more serious during the twentieth century. During World War I, shifting winds sometimes blew poisonous gases intended for the enemy back into friendly lines. Increased range and technological improvements now meant that artillery could fire upon enemy positions from well behind friendly lines. But mistakes inevitably occurred. Shells exploded prematurely, human error resulted in miscalculations, and poor communications between forward observers and artillery units stationed well in the rear sometimes caused fire to rain down upon friendly units.

On the battlefields of Europe and North Africa during World War II, superior mobility and increased reliance on air power increased the potential for amicicide. Human error, limited visibility, poor communication, the inability to distinguish friendly from enemy units, inadequate training, and technological failures seemed the most common culprits. In Sicily an Allied airborne assault was decimated as the transport aircraft were fired upon by the antiaircraft guns of their own invasion forces. Most casualties probably occurred when artillery rounds fell into friendly positions, but U.S. soldiers in Europe attributed enough of their losses to mistaken attacks by the U.S. Ninth Air Force to dub them the "American Luftwaffe." The most publicized cases occurred during Operation Cobra, the army's July 1944 breakout from Normandy. On two successive days, Allied bombers accidentally released their bombs over American lines, killing or wounding over seven hundred men. Among the dead was Lesley J. McNair, the first U.S. Army three-star general to die in combat.

The Pacific theater claimed its share of friendly fire incidents. Complications resulted from the combined presence of army, navy, and marine units. Several incidents of misplaced artillery fire from the units of one service branch on another branch, for example, plagued army and marine personnel as they moved inland into Saipan in June 1944. Trigger-happy antiaircraft gunners frequently opened up on anything that flew overhead, and the failure (or inability) of pilots to distinguish friendly from enemy units on the ground or at sea sometimes had tragic results as well.

About 2 percent of American casualties suffered during the Korean War were attributed to friendly fire, but the issue came under even closer scrutiny during the war in Vietnam. Much of the public's attention to this problem resulted from the publication of C. D. B. Bryan's *Friendly Fire,* an account (later followed by a television drama) that focused on the efforts of the parents of Corporal Michael E. Mullen to discover the facts relating to their son's death from friendly fire in February 1970.

The increasingly advanced weapons systems in Vietnam exaggerated the single most common cause for friendly fire incidents: human error. In the Mullen case, for example, elements of the Americal Division were occupying a wooded hilltop near Tu Chanh, South Vietnam. Four howitzers provided supporting fire from another site. Unfortunately, fire-control observers miscalculated the height of the trees on the target hill. One incoming round hit a tree and exploded directly over the American position, killing three and wounding six others. Numerous other incidents occurred when one unit fired into another unit's area without first ensuring that no friendly troops were present. In another disaster in 1967, one gun crew loaded the wrong charge, causing their fire to land in a U.S. base camp. Not aware that the strike had come from friendly guns, units at the latter camp immediately initiated tragically accurate counterbattery fire against the offenders. In all, the mistaken barrages cost ninety friendly casualties.

The demand for close air support during conditions of poor visibility also contributed to the problem in Vietnam. At times situations became so desperate that bombing runs were called in almost on top of friendly troops. One such incident occurred south of Hue in 1968. Two marine companies called in strikes against enemy positions so close to their own that friendly casualties seemed almost inevitable. Two marine jets successfully dropped bombs on each of their first three passes over the area. On their fourth run the jets again hit their target, but fragments from the correctly placed bombs also killed four marines and wounded six others.

Faster aircraft and longer-range weapons have continued to confound efforts to minimize friendly fire accidents. The lethality of modern weapons calls for split-second decisions against constantly moving targets. Poor visibility, mistaken identification, poor coordination, and the lack of easily identifiable terrain in the desert proved the biggest culprits during the Gulf War of 1991. In one classic example, a Saudi plane mistakenly identified by radar controllers as being an enemy narrowly averted being shot down because an American pilot, Captain Getnar Drummond, waited to identify the aircraft visually before opening fire. Drummond received the Distinguished Flying Cross for his good judgment, but other victims were not so lucky. Of the 613 American casualties suffered from military action during the operations against Iraq, 107 (35 killed and 72 wounded) fell to friendly fire. Remarkably, 77 percent of all U.S. combat vehicles lost in action (seven of ten tanks and twenty of twenty-five infantry fighting vehicles) resulted from amicicide.

The military has tried many devices to prevent such accidents. In the eighteenth and nineteenth centuries, easily distinguishable uniforms and battle flags were at least partly designed to help units identify one another. With the widespread introduction of indirect fire, special terrain features such as roads, buildings, or rivers were often used to guide aircraft or forward artillery observers. Nervous units near the target area often add huge markers of their own making. Targets are frequently marked with colored smoke or rockets, a system that works well unless the markers hit the wrong place or if winds are too strong. And rather than having friendly aircraft approach an enemy position directly over their own lines, ground commanders often encourage pilots to approach the enemy laterally along the front in hopes of preventing disaster if the bombs fall short. Of course, airmen point out that such tactics expose them to more enemy antiaircraft fire.

Strenuous efforts have been made to improve communications between forward observers and distant artillery or aircraft. Elaborate fire-control systems can also reduce casualties stemming from friendly fire but sometimes prevent effective artillery or air support. An overly complex system of checks slows response time, risking lives while every conceivable unit is contacted to ensure that it is free of the area. And controllers risk missing their targets if they allow too much of a safety zone between friendly and enemy units, because bombs or artillery fire can fall harmlessly behind enemy positions. Some charged that the elaborate safety checks and complex rules of engagement, for example, unnecessarily constrained American firepower in Vietnam.

Modern-day planners have pinned their hopes on more sophisticated technology and better training. IFF (Identification, Friend or Foe) devices are placed in aircraft, but the technical challenges of designing jam-resistant, durable, precise, and long-range systems are daunting indeed. The widespread introduction of global positioning systems, remarkably accurate to within a few yards, also offers much promise. More emphasis on unit identification and more realistic training, during which "friendly" robotic tanks or vehicles are interspersed in firing ranges, may also reduce incidents of amicicide. Still, some degree of human error remains inevitable.

Fragging

Soldiers in all armies have undoubtedly resorted to violence in hopes of ridding themselves of incompetent leaders, but this practice received the widest notice during the Vietnam War. Now called *fragging,* the term refers to the use of fragmentation grenades against superior officers. Among rear-echelon units, the practice was often related to drugs or race. In combat zones, however, such episodes, which became more common in the later years of American involvement, seem to have been closely correlated to a desire to rid a unit of an officer or NCO believed to be either ineffective or unmindful of the risk of casualties. In 1969 the army reported 126 incidents of fragging (0.35 per 1,000 soldiers), which resulted in thirty-seven deaths. By 1971 there were 333 cases (1.75 per 1,000 soldiers) and twelve deaths.

Interservice Rivalries

Rivalries between branches of the armed services can also have disastrous results. During the War of 1812, the failure of the New York state militia to cross the border into Canada in support of other U.S. units contributed mightily to defeat in the Battle of Queenston. Interservice rivalries also influenced the American command structure in the Pacific during World War II. Rather than following normal procedure and placing the entire theater under a single commander, the Americans divided their attacks along two separate axes—Admiral Chester Nimitz oversaw operations in the Central Pacific, and General Douglas MacArthur commanded the drive through the Southwest Pacific. Some historians have argued that the two-front approach divided Allied forces, exposing American military personnel to needless danger in the Bougainville–Empress Augusta Bay operation in 1943 and the Biak campaign a year later.

Interservice rivalries played a role in the abortive attempt to rescue American hostages in Iran in 1980. The previous November, Iranian militants had seized the U.S. embassy in Teheran and taken sixty-six Americans hostage. Diplomatic efforts having proved fruitless, President Jimmy Carter authorized a rescue attempt. The operation entailed setting up two secret bases deep inside Iran, inserting enough troops into a city of three million persons to rescue the hostages while avoiding civilian casualties, and then safely extracting both rescuer and rescued. This dauntingly complex undertaking was doomed by mechanical failures, poor contingency planning, and inadequate training. The insistence by all the services that they be involved—the raid included air force and marine pilots and crews, navy helicopters, army Rangers, and Delta Force special operations troops—further complicated the issue. In the end, the raid was aborted but resulted in the wounding of five Americans and the deaths of eight others.

This humiliating failure prompted more systematic efforts to promote interservice cooperation. Experiences in joint operations against much smaller enemy forces in Grenada (1983), Libya (1986), and Panama (1989) suggested gradual improvements in this area, even if problems remained evident to careful observers. The military did much better during the Gulf War. Operating under a single theater commander and as part of a carefully crafted international alliance, all services contributed mightily to the six-week aerial bombardment and one-hundred-hour ground campaign. Amicicide remained a problem, but interservice rivalries had been minimized.

BIBLIOGRAPHY

MILITARY JUSTICE

Byrne, Edward M. "Military Law." In *Encyclopedia of the American Military: Studies of the History, Traditions, Policies, Institutions, and Roles of the Armed Forces in War and Peace,* edited by John E. Jessup. New York: Scribners, 1994.

Coffman, Edward M. *The Old Army: A Portrait of the American Army in Peacetime, 1784–1898.* New York: Oxford University Press, 1986.

Harrod, Frederick S. *Manning the New Navy: The Development of a Modern Naval Enlisted Force, 1899–1940.* New York: Greenwood, 1978.

Mackey, Thomas C. "The Judiciary and the Military." In *Encyclopedia of the American Military: Studies of the History, Traditions, Policies, Institutions, and Roles of the Armed Forces in War and Peace,* edited by John E. Jessup. New York: Scribners, 1994.

RACIAL VIOLENCE

Allen, Robert L. *The Port Chicago Mutiny.* New York: Warner, 1989; reprint, New York: Amistad, 1993.

Christian, Garna L. *Black Soldiers in Jim Crow Texas, 1899–1917.* College Station: Texas A&M University Press, 1995.

MacGregor, Morris J. *Integration of the Armed Forces, 1940–1965.* Washington, D.C.: Center of Military History, 1981.

Marszalek, John F., Jr. *Court Martial: A Black Man in America.* New York: Scribners, 1972.

GENDER-RELATED VIOLENCE

Holm, Jeanne M. "Women in the Armed Forces." In *Encyclopedia of the American Military: Studies of the History, Traditions, Policies, Institutions, and Roles of the Armed Forces in War and Peace,* edited by John E. Jessup. New York: Scribners, 1994.

Shilts, Randy. *Conduct Unbecoming: Gays and Lesbians in the U.S. Military, Vietnam to the Persian Gulf.* New York: St. Martin's, 1993.

Stiehm, Judith H. "Sexual Orientation and the Military." In *Encyclopedia of the American Military: Studies of the History, Traditions, Policies, Institutions, and Roles of the Armed Forces in War and Peace,* edited by John E. Jessup. New York: Scribners, 1994.

TRAINING ACCIDENTS AND ABUSES

Fleming, Keith. *The U.S. Marine Corps in Crisis: Ribbon Creek and Recruit Training.* Columbia: University of South Carolina Press, 1990.

Kennett, Lee. *G.I.: The American Soldier in World War II.* Norman: University of Oklahoma Press, 1997.

FRIENDLY FIRE AND FRAGGING

Savage, Paul L., and Richard A. Gabriel. "Cohesion and Disintegration in the American Army in Vietnam." *Armed Forces and Society* 2 (May 1976).

Shrader, Charles R. *Amicicide: The Problem of Friendly Fire in Modern War.* Fort Leavenworth, Kans.: U.S. Army Command and General Staff College, 1982.

———. "Friendly Fire: The Inevitable Price." *Parameters: U.S. Army War College Quarterly* 22 (fall 1992).

Summers, Harry G. *Vietnam War Almanac.* New York: Facts on File, 1995.

INTERSERVICE RIVALRIES

Cooling, B. Franklin. "Interoperability." In *Encyclopedia of the American Military: Studies of the History, Traditions, Policies, Institutions, and Roles of the Armed Forces in War and Peace,* edited by John E. Jessup. New York: Scribners, 1994.

Morris, James R. *America's Armed Forces.* 2d ed. Upper Saddle River, N.J.: Simon and Schuster, 1996.

Spector, Ronald H. *Eagle Against the Sun: The American War with Japan.* New York: Free Press, 1984.

ROBERT WOOSTER

See also **Militarism; Military Interventions.**

MILITARY INTERVENTIONS

*Following the **Overview** is a subentry on **Peacekeeping Missions.***

OVERVIEW

This essay addresses the use of armed force in both foreign and domestic situations in U.S. history. The emphasis will not be on the declared (and undeclared) wars of the United States against other nations but on military intervention—the dispatch of U.S. troops onto foreign soil and into domestic situations.

Two of the cherished myths in United States history hold that the government avoids military intervention on foreign soil unless the nation's security is at peril and that it uses soldiers in confronting domestic discord only when there is no alternative. Though the American people are antimilitaristic, they are not hostile to the use of military force—at home or abroad—as a means of preserving the republican form of government, promoting the national interest, protecting the "American way of life," and ensuring order.

The Formative Years, 1780s to 1840s

The early leaders of the United States would have sympathized with General Wesley Clark, commander of U.S. peacekeeping forces in Bosnia in 1997, who responded to random attacks on U.S. soldiers with a defiant challenge: "We will not be deterred by mob violence." His remark is a fundamental acknowledgment that U.S. presidents have generally viewed the sending of troops into unsettled situations as a matter of peacekeeping. President George Washington waged war against Indians; he also dispatched a 13,000-man army in 1794 to intimidate white farmers in western Pennsylvania rebelling against the federal liquor tax. Like President Bill Clinton two centuries later, Washington considered it appropriate that the United States act as a policeman in chaotic situations.

From the onset of Thomas Jefferson's presidency (1801) until the beginning of the Mexican War (1846), a succession of U.S. presidents employed regular troops and militia in a variety of ways. Jefferson may have steadfastly opposed conflict on the high seas to avoid a shooting war with the British (and French), but he pursued a more aggressive approach in advancing the U.S. claim to the Floridas. Madison's reasons in calling for war against the British in June 1812 were more complicated than a single-minded defensive reaction to British violations of neutral rights on the high seas. The president was in a desperate political situation. In addition, the War of 1812 provided an opportunity to fulfill Jefferson's ambitions of acquiring the Floridas. In 1817–1818, as the Spanish-American revolutions (1810–1824) reached their most violent and precarious stage, U.S. policy toward the Floridas became increasingly militant. In the spring of 1818, Andrew Jackson, acting, he later argued, on orders from Secretary of War John C. Calhoun, led an invasion of Spanish Florida. The purpose of the campaign was to retaliate against Indian tribes accused of raiding American settlements. There was an outcry in both London and Madrid, but Secretary of State John Quincy Adams (who was Jackson's political enemy) skillfully exploited Jackson's raid as evidence that the Spanish could not police the Floridas—that is, that they could not control their Indian subjects.

In these formative years the United States experienced an often complex relationship between the national government and the military. Unlike the new republics of Latin America (most of which became independent in the 1820s) and Haiti (which won its independence in 1804), the United States did not suffer from militarism and the parallel intrusion of the military in government. A succession of U.S. presidents, however, used the military to advance the country's continental ambitions and to shield the Louisiana Purchase (1803) from intruders. In the 1820s and 1830s the military became more active in the West through reconnoitering expeditions and the building of forts. In brief, the military played a critical role in the settling of the continent.

From the Mexican War to the War with Spain, 1840s to 1890s

Most Americans remember the Mexican War as either a defensive war, fulfilling the need to "civilize" the vast West and expand from "sea to shining sea," or, conversely, as an unnecessary conflict brought about by President James K. Polk (1845–1849), who arrogantly hounded the Mexican government into a war. President Polk did send U.S. troops under Zachary Taylor into disputed territory south of Texas's Nueces River, and he dispatched an army expeditionary force under the command of John C. Frémont to the California boundary to make sure that defiant *Californios* would not have the opportunity to create a separate republic.

In the Mexican War the United States, not Mexico, was the more aggressive country. Even if one dismisses the question of which side fired the first shot, the manner in which Polk conducted the war and the debate over the conflict within the country and in the U.S. Congress belied Polk's professions of a war waged for defensive purposes. When the northern Mexico campaign of General Zachary Taylor failed to provide a quick victory, Polk sent another army under General Winfield Scott to strike a blow at the Mexican capital and compel a surrender. The "All Mexico" movement, a coalition of proslavery expansionists and Protestant zealots bent on redeeming a "heathen" Catholic neighbor, was invigorated. And, more important, Polk (like President Lyndon Johnson in the 1960s) was able to put an increasingly hostile Congress in the uncomfortable position of having to decide whether or not to provide funds for the campaign. In the end, Polk accepted and the Senate approved the Treaty of Guadalupe Hidalgo negotiated by U.S. emissary Nicholas Trist, in violation of his instructions, with a cabal of Mexican politicians lacking proper authority. Largely because of the Wilmot Proviso (a proposal by a Democratic congressman in 1846 to prohibit slavery in any of the territories acquired in the war) and the social and political divisions of the 1850s, most U.S. historians identify the Mexican War not only as the fulfillment of continentalism but also as a determining event in the coming of the Civil War.

The occupation of Mexico City was the U.S. Army's first "policing" role in a Latin American country. Though the U.S. military presence doubtless provided the only reliable maintenance of civil order, the Americans had not come as liberators but as conquerors. What many Mexicans remembered from this occupation was the behavior of the occupiers, their casual indifference to local customs and unprovoked violent outbursts, and the willingness of some of their own putative leaders to collaborate with the invaders. What the soldiers often bitterly recalled was a sullen and presumably ungrateful populace with an unwarranted loyalty to those Mexicans who had plunged the country into war and an inexplicable hostility to the liberators who had ended it.

The Mexican War reinforced arguments of those who advocated a more aggressive foreign policy, but it also militarized society to a degree unimagined by earlier generations. Public sentiment in the South for the Narciso López expeditions against Spanish Cuba and for William Walker's filibuster invasion of Nicaragua in the mid-1850s paralleled the government's forceful role, especially in the circum-Caribbean. The proslavery foreign policy of Democratic presidents Franklin Pierce and James Buchanan bespoke a different purpose. Throughout Latin America, the U.S. triumph over Mexico persuaded a generation of hemispheric leaders that the U.S. government and especially American filibusters were a threat to hemispheric independence. At the Continental Congress held in Santiago, Chile, in 1856, Latin American emissaries from Chile, Ecuador, and Peru adopted a treaty of mutual assistance in the (unlikely) event of an attack by the United States. In 1856, acting under the authority of an 1846 treaty with New Granada (Colombia) to safeguard the isthmian transit route, the U.S. Navy landed 160 troops to quell riots and stop the destruction of Panama railroad property by mostly black Panamanians outraged over abusive treatment by foreign residents. The intervention was but the first of thirteen U.S. military intrusions on the isthmus between the Mexican War and the November 1903 intervention in the Panamanian revolution.

These interventions were of short duration, but they demonstrated certain lasting features about the U.S. role in the world. First, they showed that the U.S. government would make a show of force to expand markets for its exports or to maintain "law and order" on important transit routes. Second, these incidents made clear that the United States considered the use of military intervention to be an integral part of its "civilizing mission," especially in nearby regions such as Mexico and

William Walker's Invasion of Nicaragua

William Walker (1824–1860) was at twenty-four years of age a doctor, lawyer, and journalist. Just after the Mexican War ended in 1848, he set out for San Francisco. In 1853–1854 he led an unsuccessful filibuster campaign into Lower California. In 1855 he went to Nicaragua to fight with the Liberals in the civil war then raging in that country. In 1856, after the capture of Grenada, Walker turned against his liberal allies and proclaimed himself president of Nicaragua. The U.S. minister recognized his government. Although the State Department repudiated the action, Walker quickly gained fame among proslavery groups because he promised to restore slavery in the country. His arrogance united formerly divided Central Americans against him, and in 1856–1857, they waged a war of national liberation against the Walker regime. Walker also made an enemy of Cornelius Vanderbilt by siding with Vanderbilt's business partners, who were trying to seize control of the Accessory Transit Company, which controlled shipping to Nicaragua. Walker lost out in this war but managed to escape Nicaragua by surrendering to the U.S. Navy in 1857. In 1860 he led another invasion force to Nicaragua, but this expedition never got farther than Honduras. Facing defeat, Walker surrendered to a patrolling British warship, but the captain of the vessel arrested him and turned him over to the Honduran army. After a court martial and conviction, he was shot by a firing squad.

William Walker. CORBIS/BETTMANN

---

the circum-Caribbean. The use of force was seen as unfortunate but often necessary for development and modernization. Such views were common to nineteenth-century Americans' way of looking at things. The use of force offered reassurance that history could not be "reversed"—not by Indians nor by striking industrial workers who stood in the way of progress.

From 1845 to 1860, the United States expanded rapidly, often through military interventions and at the expense of other hemispheric nations and peoples, particularly Mexico. Some prominent Americans of this generation (Abraham Lincoln, for example) were troubled about the use of force to acquire territory (as in the case of Mexico) and sharply critical of the federal government for its aggressive efforts to acquire Spanish Cuba. Yet, during the secession crisis of 1860–1861, many of these same Americans were supportive of the use of force against a defiant South and—after the fighting commenced—demanded that the Union Army become a liberating force to eradicate slavery.

Too often the second half of nineteenth-century U.S. history is seen as being framed by the Civil War and the Spanish-American War. The first was a bloody closure to the divisive issues of secession and chattel slavery, and the second marked a more certain role for the nation in world affairs. The crucial preparatory experience for that imperial role was the "pacification" of the U.S. West and the limited but significant use of the military in the suppression of industrial strikes in the late nineteenth century. Between 1850 and 1865 the army took part in more than thirty conflicts with Indians. From the end of the Civil War until the disastrous Battle of Little Bighorn and Custer's defeat in June 1876, the federal government vacillated

The Geronimo Chase

Geronimo (c. 1829–1909), a Chiricahua Apache, was one of the most famous adversaries of the U.S. Army in its post–Civil War campaigns to "pacify" the West. His war against the whites began in 1876 when the government moved the Chiricahuas from Arizona to a reservation at San Carlos, New Mexico. Geronimo escaped and led a band of Chiricahuas into Mexico. He was captured and returned to San Carlos, where he farmed for several years, until 1881, when he took up raiding in Arizona and New Mexico. Two years later, he was captured and put back on the reservation, but in 1885 he fled. Late in the following year, after a relentless chase by General Nelson A. Miles, Geronimo surrendered his band, most of whom were sent to Florida and then to Alabama. In 1894 Geronimo was sent to Fort Sill, Oklahoma. There, Geronimo finally settled down. He converted to Christianity and became a prosperous farmer, but he never fully went over to "white man's ways." Instead he became a showman. In 1904 he participated in the St. Louis World's Fair and in the following year rode in the inauguration parade of President Theodore Roosevelt. He died in 1909 and was buried in the Apache cemetery at Fort Sill.

An 1887 photograph of Geronimo. CORBIS/
BETTMANN

between accommodation and confrontation. From 1876 until the massacre at Wounded Knee in 1890, when army artillery and sharpshooters cut down Indian men, women, and children in the frozen South Dakota countryside, the role of the military in the West was to subdue the last defiant bands of Indians—the pursuit of Geronimo was the best-known example—and to exercise a policing role.

At critical outbreaks of industrial strife, presidents dispatched troops to maintain order. Federal troops intervened in the 1877 railroad strikes in the East, probably the most destructive in the nation's history, and in similar strikes in 1886 and 1894. The industrialization of the United States was a wrenching and often violent experience. Between 1877 and 1892 authorities called out the National Guard more than one hundred times to deal with a variety of domestic situations, a third of which were classified as "labor troubles."

These internal military interventions paralleled landings of troops on foreign soil. Most of the missions were scarcely noticed by the American public but nonetheless were important for understanding the character of U.S. military interventions. In 1885, 2,200 marines and sailors disembarked at Panama to protect U.S. property and "safeguard the transit route" during the Pedro Prestán rebellion. In 1893 an impetuous U.S. consul in Hawaii called on U.S. Marines to maintain order during a rebellion against the Hawaiian monarchy spearheaded by U.S. growers who feared a resurgence of Hawaiian nationalism. Though President Grover Cleveland ultimately repudiated what the growers had done, the incident was a portent of a more aggressive U.S. policy.

Viewed in the context of these dynamic and often violent changes within the nation after the Civil War, the decision for war with Spain in 1898 was neither an aberration in policy nor a fundamental departure from the way Americans looked at the world. But the circumstances prompting the massive intervention in Spanish Cuba and Puerto Rico are far more complicated than single-minded theories have often suggested. Economic and political issues—a devastating economic depression that fueled industrial strife and political upheaval—were central to understanding the decision for war, certainly, but it is erroneous to suggest that Spaniards, Cubans, Puerto Ricans, and Filipinos were simply victims of an aggressive U.S. government resolved to carve out markets for its exports or to impose its own brand of imperial rule in the Caribbean. Those who chose or acquiesced in a military solution may have acted from multiple motives (strategic, economic, political, and humanitarian), but they shared a fear of the chaos of the times in the workplace, society, politics, and the economy. Federal, state, and local officials, industrialists and manufacturers, and occasionally even prominent civic leaders acknowledged and sometimes even welcomed the use of force against those who threatened the system: Indians who made war against encroaching whites or would not remain on the reservation; unionized strikers who destroyed property; Populists who revived the tradition of grassroots movements, which they transformed into strong regional alliances; and Cuban revolutionaries determined to demolish the sugar-plantation economy and the hierarchical society it sustained. Indians, and some strikers, could be characterized as "savages," Populists and Cuban revolutionaries as economic ignoramuses. Such threats required a less ambiguous response than political reforms or humanitarian gestures.

The Imperial Years, 1900 to World War II

Just as the empire carved out from the U.S. West represented a logical fulfillment of manifest destiny, American leaders arrogantly presumed that their victory over Spain in 1898 was an entitlement to territorial spoils and a more important extracontinental mission, especially in the Caribbean and the western Pacific.

By 1900 the United States had joined the imperial club. In the three decades after the war with Spain, all of the military interventions of the United States—the decision to enter the European war in April 1917 and President Woodrow Wilson's dispatch of troops to Siberia in 1918 are notable exceptions—were linked, directly or indirectly, to the political, economic, and strategic issues surrounding that war. A listing of the major interventions and occupations shows the extent of U.S. military involvement: Cuba (1899–1902; 1906–1909); China (1900; 1928); Philippines (1899–1902); Panama (1902; 1903); Nicaragua (1909–1912; 1926–1934); Mexico (1914; 1916–1917); Haiti (1915–1934); the Dominican Republic (1916–1924); western Europe (1917–1919); and Siberia (1918–1920).

Were these interventions prompted by strategic concerns, economic opportunism, a crusading spirit and determination to make the world over into America's image by spreading the American dream, or a fusion of all these dynamics? National leaders had always expressed the nation's international purpose in universalistic terms, but their actions bespoke a keen awareness of the importance of place. As the country's best-known naval strategist at the turn of the century, Alfred Thayer Mahan, had advised, the United States must dominate the Western Hemisphere, cooperate in Asia, and abstain from involvement in European affairs.

His strictures explain why strategic and economic factors help account for U.S. military interventions in the imperial years. In the Caribbean and the western Pacific, European powers and interests were obstacles to U.S. designs. In the western Pacific the United States was militarily incapable of domination because of the refusal of Congress to provide funding for adequate defense of the Philippines, thus increasing its vulnerability, and because of the decline of western European power and a parallel rise of Japanese power in the region. In the Western Hemisphere and especially in the circum-Caribbean, a melange of strategic and economic concerns—revolution, political disorder, the heightened military ambitions of Germany, the construction of the Panama Canal, and the rapid growth of American entrepreneurs and companies in the region—reinforced arguments for the use of military force.

Strategic and economic imperatives cannot explain why civilian rather than military leaders were the strongest advocates for the use of force. Soldiers and sailors recognized the implications of both Theodore Roosevelt's belief that the United States must be the "policeman" of the hemisphere and Woodrow Wilson's injunction about teaching Latin Americans "to elect good men." Often sharp differences between Roosevelt and Wilson over the motives for U.S. involvement abroad belied a general agreement about the use of force as a critical determinant in foreign policy. Their views about the U.S. role in the world were shaped by the experiences of the late nineteenth century, particularly by the fashioning of continental empire and the parallel containment of the often chaotic forces in the U.S. West. Like Alexander Hamilton and Thomas Jefferson in the formative years of the republic, they were bitter political adversaries, but they shared strong beliefs that the American revolutionary principle of self-determination did not apply universally to all peoples—not to those who were ill-prepared for self-governance and, to use a common phrase of the times, who threatened civilization and progress.

This conviction was a nineteenth-century imperative, and it provides a fuller and more satisfactory explanation than the narrowly construed and separately applied economic, political, or strategic considerations often cited as the causes for the military interventions of the U.S. imperial era. Indeed, in a nation whose people had experienced a violent and turbulent coming of age in the late nineteenth century, the use of military power to police turbulent and chaotic places in the twentieth century seemed preordained. The Boxer Rebellion (1900) and Philippine insurrection (1899–1902) were dual challenges—the first to European and American pretensions in China, the second more directly to the U.S. self-appointed mission of pacifying the defiant Filipino insurrectionists in much the same way that it had subdued the Indians of the West. When Roosevelt dispatched U.S. troops to Cuba in 1906, he called the occupying soldiers an "army of pacification" and staffed it with officers who had had experience in the Philippines. His successor, William Howard Taft, ordered an invasion of Nicaragua, whose successive governments had defied U.S. intrusion in Nicaraguan (and Central American) internal affairs. As it had done in Cuba, the United States transformed Nicaragua into a protectorate.

Republican and Democratic leaders sometimes quarreled over the degree of U.S. involvement in the internal affairs of Caribbean and Central American countries, but they rarely differed over the use of military force if U.S. interests or hegemony was challenged. Theodore Roosevelt seemed more reluctant than Woodrow Wilson to establish military occupations (as contrasted with military interventions) because the American people were uncomfortable with the notion of military rule but quite willing to accept the use of military people who were in the "revolutionary frame of mind." Had Roosevelt been elected in 1912, rather than Wilson, he might have seriously considered a full-scale invasion of Mexico, as some were urging, rather than content himself, as did Wilson, with containing the Mexican Revolution.

In both cases the United States confronted dual challenges. The first, a defiant reaction of political elites, could be confronted with minimal shows of diplomatic and political pressures, as the British had demonstrated in the nineteenth century. The second challenge was the anti-American guerrilla campaigns that erupted in both countries. These challenges served to remind the U.S. military of the Philippine insurrection in the years after the Spanish-American War and to explain why the U.S. government chose a solution—the creation of client governments more beholden to U.S. interests

than to the well-being of their own people—that modern historians and several contemporary commentators have argued was the fundamental mistake of U.S. policy in the circum-Caribbean in the early twentieth century. That choice, it is often contended, made inevitable the post–World War II revolutionary strife in Guatemala, Cuba, and Nicaragua and largely accounted for its strident anti-American character.

What is often forgotten in this critique is another reality—the revolutionary tradition in these countries was not so easily accommodated. Cuban revolutionaries in the late nineteenth century, Haitian and Dominican guerrillas from 1915 to 1919, and Nicaraguans who joined Augusto C. Sandino in 1927 did not really threaten U.S. security interests in the Caribbean nor the sanctity of private ownership of property. Theirs was a defiance of the intruder and a parallel hatred of the countrymen who served the intruder. They, not those collaborators whose governments could be sustained only with American military support, were the true nationalists.

Guerrilla opposition was an alternative vision requiring a fundamental alteration of local politics and economic agendas, however, and U.S. leaders supported only revolutions they were able to control. The challenges of these movements to the country's political and economic hegemony in the circum-Caribbean required a military solution. In threatening the political and social order, these revolutions imperiled progress and civilization as U.S. leaders defined those terms. Such arguments had been used to justify the use of military force against Indians and striking industrial workers in the United States, and in confronting public criticism of the military in its campaigns against Philippine insurrectionists from 1899 to 1902. Persistent and often hostile inquiries about the character of the U.S. military intervention in Haiti and the Dominican Republic after Germany's defeat in 1918 should have reminded U.S. leaders that public support for these interventions had weakened. In the 1920s the interventions in China and especially in Nicaragua prompted sharp criticism throughout the country, particularly in Congress, and among delegates to the sixth regular Pan American conference at Havana in 1928. In a vigorous defense of U.S. policy, Secretary of State Charles Evans Hughes characterized the Sandino rebellion as a threat to order throughout the hemisphere, but in his speech he called the military intervention in Nicaragua an "interposition."

For the moment it quelled the hemispheric criticism of U.S. policy, but the difficulties of fighting a guerrilla war meant that the U.S. government would ultimately find another way to exercise its will. Prolonged interventions too often meant a counterguerrilla campaign in the countryside with no decisive battles and with money and lives spent with too little to show for the effort. Thus, the United States chose client governments, middlemen like Rafael Trujillo in the Dominican Republic, Fulgencio Batista in Cuba, and Anastasio Somoza García in Nicaragua—the notorious trio of Caribbean dictators—whose American-trained national guards could police the countryside. Secretary of State Henry Stimson alerted the country to the subtle but unmistakable shift in U.S. policy when he declared in 1931 that U.S. property owners in Nicaragua must look to Managua, not Washington, for protection. Further, this approach resonated well among Depression-era congresses concerned about the costs of these interventions.

The legacy of military intervention in the imperial era is, however, ambivalent. A generation of young military officers acquired a limited knowledge of guerrilla war, which proved useful in the Pacific island campaigns in the Solomon Islands in World War II. U.S. leaders acknowledged the principle that no government had the right to intervene in the domestic affairs of another hemispheric country. In the process, it is sometimes argued, the Monroe Doctrine was "Pan-Americanized," which proved vital in World War II as the United States became heavily dependent on Latin America for defense sites, natural resources, and labor. But the United States did not repudiate intervention nor the Monroe Doctrine. Its arrogance about its relationship with smaller Caribbean and Central American nations diminished only because of the economic and military restrictions imposed by the Great Depression. More disturbing, the military interventions of the imperial years had undeniable racial overtones that commenced with racist remarks from American soldiers about Cuban guerrillas and permeated public (and sometimes official) commentary about Caribbean peoples (especially Haitians) for three decades.

The Era of Cold War, 1940s to 1980s

U.S. leaders carried this arrogance into the Cold War era. They subsumed their self-assigned role as policemen of the Western Hemisphere in a larger and presumably even more critical role as the principal architects and players in the modern world order fashioned by the victors at the end of World War II. The older categories of strategic priorities and interests once linked largely to geographic proximity—for example, political instability or revolution in Mexico or Cuba was more important than similar conditions in Bolivia or central Africa—were unavoidably intertwined with compelling global concerns and interests. In an era of global confrontation between two superpowers with conflicting ideologies and competing economic and political systems, there was no such thing as a purely "local" economic or political choice. Civil wars could have profound international implications.

But it was neither possible nor desirable to confront every such menace with force of arms. Disorder and violence everywhere could not be eliminated. The old colonial empires were collapsing, and newly independent states were taking their place in the international community. In many cases leaders of these new states had achieved power not by a democratic or peaceful transition but by revolution or guerrilla war. Retention of power required legitimacy, a reliable military to defend the state, and the political and economic savvy to benefit from economic aid and especially from technical assistance from powerful international benefactors; it also required an ability to stave off criticism from powerful interests within the country.

In retrospect it is easy to understand why this logic had such repercussions, how, for example, the militarization of the nation's postwar policies in Europe and the western Pacific led inexorably to Truman's call for a military response in Korea in June 1950 and President Dwight D. Eisenhower's dispatch of marines to Lebanon in 1958; how U.S. antagonism to the Cuban Revolution culminated in the Bay of Pigs in April 1961 and the 1965 military intervention in Santo Domingo; and how the counterinsurgency program of the 1960s metamorphosed into "low-intensity warfare" in Central America in the 1980s. When in 1983 President Ronald Reagan ordered the diversion of a naval task force originally bound for the volatile eastern Mediterranean to Grenada on the specious grounds of "rescuing" a "captive group" of U.S. medical students in a small eastern Caribbean country that had been taken over by "leftist thugs," the justification sounded disturbingly similar to that which Theodore Roosevelt had used three-quarters of a century earlier.

Historians sometimes cite fundamental differences between the military interventions of the early twentieth century and those undertaken during the Cold War years. For example, presidents of the imperial era, especially Theodore Roosevelt, recognized the limits of U.S. military power and did not try to fight "on every front." They did not have an exaggerated faith in the ability of U.S. military technology or mobility, and they did not have to contend with serious disaffection and protest at home when they chose to use armed force on foreign soil.

Actually, these distinctions are too sharply drawn. Criticism of U.S. military interventions abroad was widespread throughout society as well as in Congress during the imperial years. Despite its overwhelming superiority in firepower and technology, the U.S. military in the age of Theodore Roosevelt and Woodrow Wilson was often frustrated in its campaigns in the Caribbean and Central America. Presidents of the era often had to deal with leaders of small, weak countries who were dependent on U.S. support but who also were defiant and obstreperous.

Throughout the imperial era presidents could take some reassurance that military intervention would momentarily distract attention from social and political divisiveness at home. Theodore Roosevelt and Woodrow Wilson could safely invoke such credos as "policing" the turbulent Caribbean or "teaching them to elect good men" with the assurance that the only advocates of guerrilla war or violence at home would be Wobblies or "anarchists." The middle class might become disturbed about stories of atrocities in the Philippine war or in Haiti but it would never identify with such groups. Reform, not revolution, would address social and political injustices in the United States.

The Cold War experience changed such thinking among middle-class Americans even though they were the beneficiaries of the nation's post–World War II economic development, which, they were told, depended on the use of armed force at home and abroad. This alteration of views about military intervention had little to do with the cost of these armed excursions or even the questionable contention that money spent on them could have been diverted to addressing social inequities at home. It was one matter to dispatch troops into Santo Domingo in 1965 on the specious argument that their purpose was to protect American lives and property and to ensure that there would not be "another Cuba" in the Caribbean or to maintain order in the aftermath of riots in the nation's cities. It was quite another to dispatch airborne troops to desegregate the University of Mississippi in 1962 or to send the National Guard or federal troops to antiwar demonstrations. The containment of revolution abroad carried a high price. So too did the preservation of order at home: between 1945 and 1967 the National Guard was used an unprecedented seventy-two times in twenty-eight states. In 1968 state authorities called out the guard more than one hundred times to deal with racial incidents. In May 1970 guardsmen entered twenty-one university and college campuses on seventy-four occasions. One such university was Kent State, which in May 1970 became a metaphor for the "Vietnamization of America" when guardsmen opened fire into a milling crowd, killing four students and wounding nine others.

President Jimmy Carter won the admiration of Cold War critics when he declared that the United States "would not use measures abroad that we would not use at home." Though the comment referred specifically to covert activities and plots to assassinate foreign leaders, his words were a reminder of the militarization of American society during the Cold War. He applauded human rights abroad as well as at home, condemned foreign governments that used the military to attack, not defend, their own people, and brokered a peace between Israel and Egypt. Yet he could not repudiate the military option when vital U.S. interests were at stake, as he clearly demonstrated by his policies in the Persian Gulf and Korea, and in El Salvador he acquiesced in the arguments of those Salvadoran leaders who called for a military solution to the civil war.

The Post–Cold War Era

The ambiguity in Carter's use of armed force to resolve foreign policy issues is yet another indicator that the reasons for U.S. military intervention during the Cold War were complex, and that the end of the Cold War did not necessarily signal the abandonment of the military solution in U.S. foreign policy. Throughout the Cold War presidents knew that appeals to traditional public sentiments were effective in mobilizing support for action. Ronald Reagan, for example, was often more timid than Jimmy Carter in dealing with "flash points" in the world—the Persian Gulf is but one example—yet Reagan did not suffer public slurs for being weak or ineffectual. As did one of his presidential heroes, Theodore Roosevelt, Reagan

A U.S. soldier surveys the damage in Panama City after the U.S. invasion in 1989.
CORBIS/BILL GENTILE

effectively used the rhetoric of bombast and threat—calling the Soviet Union an "evil empire" and Libya an "outlaw nation"—but was selective in using military force. He dispatched twelve hundred U.S. Marines to Beirut in 1982 as part of a multilateral peacekeeping force and then withdrew them in 1984 after a terrorist attack on the marine barracks resulted in more than two hundred American deaths.

President George Bush did not possess Reagan's skills as a communicator, but he made effective use of the "United States as policeman" metaphor and, like his predecessor, was selective in his use of military force. Bush abandoned the military solution in El Salvador but not in Panama, where in December 1989 he dispatched 22,500 troops to arrest General Manuel Noriega (Operation Just Cause) and "bring him to justice" for, among other crimes, drug trafficking. In the early 1980s Noriega had proved useful to the United States, and especially the Central Intelligence Agency, as a source of information in its antidrug and counterinsurgency activities, but in the last years of the Reagan presidency the relationship deteriorated rapidly as Noriega became more defiant. The U.S. government used economic pressures—the most severe was the decision to put Panama Canal payments into escrow—but Noriega would not relinquish his grip. The Christmas Invasion marked the end

of a year of crises—harassment of voters and candidates in a presidential election that Noriega subsequently declared void, installation of a pro-Noriega puppet in the Panamanian presidency, and a failed military coup. Given the widespread hatred of Noriega, many Panamanians welcomed the U.S. invasion despite the four days of fighting and looting that ensued. In the early hours of the invasion Noriega managed to elude his pursuers and took refuge in the Vatican embassy. After ten days of frantic negotiations, Noriega surrendered to U.S. authorities and was flown to Miami. The death toll and physical devastation in the Christmas Invasion soon became a hotly debated issue, as outspoken critics questioned why such destruction was necessary to capture one man. The Pentagon's figures showed that 23 U.S. soldiers, 314 Panamanian military, and 202 Panamanian civilians had died in the fighting. Several independent human rights groups, meanwhile, estimated that the Panamanian military death toll was about 50 and Panamanian civilian deaths around 300.

In some respects the invasion of Panama was a tragic postlude to the Reagan administration's support of the contra war against the Nicaraguan government and the Bush administration's strategy of "cleaning up" the Panamanian mess as a means of demonstrating U.S. capability and purpose. Operation Just Cause removed a petty dictator who had defied the United States and it "restored" legitimate government in Panama. In the aftermath the Bush administration asked Congress for a $1 billion aid package for Panama. It restored to power the ideological kindred spirits of the social class installed in power in November 1903.

Such resolve and philanthropy, it could be argued, offered tangible evidence of a nobler purpose to U.S. military interventions: in Somalia (1992–1994), where more than 28,000 U.S. soldiers protected famine relief supplies from "warlords"; in Haiti (1994), where U.S. armed forces were dispatched to restore the government of Jean-Bertrand Aristide, who had been driven into exile by the Haitian military; and in Bosnia (1995), where 20,000 U.S. soldiers arrived to reinforce a peace accord hammered out between representatives of warring ethnic factions. In a spirited address to the UN General Assembly in 1993, President Bill Clinton invoked Wilsonian credos when he spoke about promoting democracy and economic development throughout the world.

Critics scoffed that such a course was unrealistic and naive, either because we were paying too much attention to places that were only marginally important to our national defense or because the funding was woefully inadequate. In the end it was clear that the critics were correct, but not for these reasons. Military intervention served an immediate, not a long-range, purpose in U.S. foreign policy—the use of force was a reminder to "outlaw governments" or dictators that the powerful are not only willing but capable of punishing or even removing them from power. Military compulsion or retaliation addresses symptoms, not causes; it is a form of damage control in a chaotic world that is both united and fragmented, where leaders of powerful nations preach democracy, self-determination, and individual rights yet insist on defining what these terms mean and, if defied, on enforcing them.

One does not require a postmodern deconstructionist mentality to discern the likely outcome of military intervention. The British statesman Edmund Burke identified the gravamen more than two centuries ago when he declared in Parliament in 1775, "The use of force alone is but *temporary*. It may subdue for a moment; but it does not remove the necessity of subduing again; and a nation is not governed, which is perpetually to be conquered."

BIBLIOGRAPHY

Barnet, Richard J. *Roots of War: The Men and Institutions Behind U.S. Foreign Policy.* New York: Atheneum, 1972.

Blasier, Cole. *The Hovering Giant: United States Responses to Revolutionary Change in Latin America.* Pittsburgh: University of Pittsburgh Press, 1976.

Blechman, Barry M., and Stephen S. Kaplan, eds. *Force Without War: U.S. Armed Forces as a Political Instrument.* Washington, D.C.: Brookings Institution, 1978.

Drinnon, Richard. *Facing West: The Metaphysics of Indian-Hating and Empire-Building.* Minneapolis: University of Minnesota Press, 1980.

Gates, John M. *Schoolbooks and Krags: The United States Army in the Philippines, 1898–1902.* Westport, Conn.: Greenwood, 1973.

Herring, George C. *America's Longest War: The United States and Vietnam, 1950–1975.* New York: Wiley, 1975.

Huntington, Samuel P. *The Soldier and the State: The Theory and Politics of Civil-Military Relations.* Cambridge: Harvard University Press, 1957.

Kane, William E. *Civil Strife in Latin America: A Legal History of U.S. Involvement.* Baltimore: Johns Hopkins University Press, 1972.

LaFeber, Walter. *The American Age: United States Foreign Policy at Home and Abroad Since 1750.* New York: Norton, 1989.

Langley, Lester D. *The Banana Wars: United States Intervention in the Caribbean, 1898–1934.* Lexington: University Press of Kentucky, 1983.

Millis, Walter. *Arms and Men: A Study of American Military History.* New York: Putnam, 1956.

Perret, Geoffrey. *A Country Made by War: From the Revolution to Vietnam, the Story of America's Rise to Power.* New York: Random House, 1989.

Schelling, Thomas C. *Arms and Influence.* New Haven: Yale University Press, 1966.

Utley, Robert M. *Frontier Regulars: The United States Army and the Indian, 1866–1891.* New York: Macmillan, 1973.

———. *Frontiersmen in Blue: The United States Army and the Indian, 1848–1865.* New York: Macmillan, 1967.

Weigley, Russell F. *The American Way of War: A History of United States Military Strategy and Policy.* New York: Macmillan, 1973.

Wolff, Leon. *Little Brown Brother.* Garden City, N.Y.: Doubleday, 1961.

LESTER D. LANGLEY

See also **Foreign Intervention, Fear of; Militarism; Military Culture; Nativism; War.**

PEACEKEEPING MISSIONS

Almost from its inception the United States has conducted military operations that can be classified as peacekeeping missions. During the first 150 years of the nation's history, U.S. troops were used to separate warring Native American tribes or to prevent encroachment of Native Americans and settlers on each other's territory. For example, the 1876 Sioux War, in which Colonel George A. Custer's Seventh Cavalry was defeated at the Battle of Little Bighorn, began as an operation to return the Sioux to their reservations and to separate encroaching settlers from Sioux tribal lands. U.S. interventions in Latin America in the early twentieth century closely resembled modern peacekeeping missions, with their emphasis on restoration of law and order and the separation of opposing factions. Peacekeeping, in its simplest terms, is the use of military force to separate warring factions in order to facilitate a return to the status quo antebellum or to establish a stable and peaceful political environment. From frontier cavalry troopers separating Native American tribes from encroaching pioneers in the nineteenth century, to United Nations–sponsored "blue helmet" missions to Bosnia and Somalia in the late twentieth century, the United States has a long history of military peacekeeping operations.

Types of Missions

The UN and the U.S. military define six military-political missions that may require military forces for resolution. These are preventive diplomacy (prewar); diplomatic peacemaking, military peace enforcement, peacemaking (during war); and peacekeeping and peace building (postwar). Military peace enforcement, peacemaking, and peacekeeping missions are often confused with one another by the average citizen; however, they are distinctly different military missions. Peace enforcement involves the use of military forces to halt a conflict between two warring powers with or without the acquiescence of either side. Military peace-enforcement operations are extremely dangerous, since the external military force enters a conflict ready to fight either party. The UN has yet to formally approve a peace-enforcement operation, although the UNPROFOR (United Nations Protection Force in Yugoslavia), which began in March 1992 and lasted until December 1995; UNOSOM (United Nations Operations in Somalia) I and II; and the UNITAF (United Nations International Task Force in Somalia) were peacekeeping operations that became de facto peace-enforcement operations.

Unlike peace-enforcement missions, peacemaking operations take military action against the attacking power in a conflict already in process. The most notable examples include the 1950–1953 Korean War and the 1991 Persian Gulf War, both of which were formal peacemaking operations led by the United States under the auspices of the UN. Peacemaking often involves the heavy commitment of military forces of the UN-sponsored powers and is the most dangerous and violent of the UN military peace operations.

Finally, peacekeeping operations are aimed at separating warring sides after the end of a conflict. Examples include the UNIFIL (United Nations Interim Forces in Lebanon), which began in 1978; the 1973–1979 UNEF II (United Nations Emergency Force), which acted as a buffer between the Egyptians and Israelis following the 1973 Yom Kippur War; and the UNIKOM (UN Iraq-Kuwait

Two U.S. soldiers help a wounded colleague in Somalia in 1993. CORBIS/BACI

Observation Mission), which began in 1991 following the Gulf War. By their nature peacekeeping operations are hazardous, frustrating, and politically sensitive. Consequently, the United States traditionally avoided large-scale UN-sponsored peacekeeping operations prior to 1991.

History of U.S. Involvement

In the post–World War II world, the United States conducted few large-scale peacekeeping operations under UN auspices. A tacit agreement between the permanent members of the Security Council (the United States, the Soviet Union, China, the United Kingdom, and France) precluded the deployment of large numbers of their soldiers for UN-mandated operations. The permanent members instead would send individual military personnel with specific skills, such as technical expertise or language proficiency, to assist UN peacekeeping operations. This ensured that the Security Council had the ability to monitor peacekeeping operations without the mission becoming a Cold War battleground.

The United States, limited during the Cold War to a supporting role in formalized UN peacekeeping operations, instead conducted numerous unilateral (United States only) or multilateral (with allies) peacekeeping operations. The 1958 deployment of marines to Lebanon, the 1982–1983 multinational force in Beirut (during which 245 U.S. Marines were killed by a terrorist attack in October 1983), and the continuing deployment of a U.S. infantry battalion to the Sinai Peninsula are perfect examples of these operations. With the collapse of the Soviet Union in 1991 and the concordant reduction of international tension, the United States took a much more activist approach to UN-sponsored peacekeeping operations. As the world's sole remaining superpower, the United States possessed the logistical assets, such as transport aircraft and large support ships, and the available military strength to enable it to become involved in peacekeeping missions worldwide.

Following the end of the 1991 Gulf War, the United States became more involved in UN-sponsored peacekeeping operations. The first test for the United States came during the 1992–1993 humanitarian relief operation in Somalia. Initially, the UN operation was welcomed by the war-torn nation. However, the warring factions within Somalia seized relief supplies in order to intimidate and control the populace. In turn, the UN requested the deployment of combat troops, including U.S. troops from the Tenth Mountain Division, U.S. Army Rangers, and U.S. Marines, to guard the shipments from Mogadishu to the outlying communities. By June 1993 the mission in Somalia had changed from supply escort to peace enforcement. After the ambush of a Pakistani column, which resulted in the death of twenty-five peacekeepers, the UN ordered the arrest of Mohammed Farah Aideed, whose troops were responsible for the attack. Retributive attacks on suspected Aideed strongholds ultimately led to direct confrontation. In October, eighteen U.S. servicemen were killed and seventy-eight wounded, and an unknown number of Somalis (estimated by some at over four hundred) were killed during one such raid. Televised images of the American dead being dragged through the streets of Mogadishu by angry crowds soon turned public opinion against the operation. By March 1994 the last U.S. forces left Somalia without having successfully completed the humanitarian relief mission begun two years before.

The experience in Somalia heightened public attention to the dangers of peacekeeping operations and led to a reduction of military assistance to UN operations. Consequently, the genocide conducted by warring tribes in Rwanda was allowed by the United States to take place owing in part to the fear of "another Somalia." Ethnic cleansing (the attempt by a large ethnic group to drive out or eliminate a minority population) in Bosnia-Herzegovina and Kosovo, in the former Yugoslavia, was allowed to continue until U.S. and European public opinion demanded action, again reflecting the long-term impact of the failure in Somalia. By the late 1990s, the United States had troops in both Bosnia and Kosovo conducting peace-enforcement missions, albeit with little input from the UN. In effect, the United States reverted to its pre-1991 policy of multilateral peace operations with its traditional allies, under a unified allied command and without formal UN sanction.

U.S. peace operations depend on the support of the American people and the elected political leadership. The U.S. military, after its experiences in Somalia and Bosnia, has integrated peace operations into the scenarios of its major training facilities, and combat units are evaluated on their ability to conduct these types of missions on an equal basis with their traditional combat roles. The role of the United States in future peace operations, despite a long history, is uncertain. Operations in the Balkans and elsewhere, and the ever-changing face of international politics, guarantee that American military forces will be at the forefront of major peace operations for some time to come.

BIBLIOGRAPHY

Durch, William J. *The United Nations and Collective Security in the Twenty-first Century.* Carlisle Barracks, Pa.: Strategic Studies Institute, U.S. Army War College, 1993. Pamphlet.

Hill, Stephen M., and Shanin P. Malik. *Peacekeeping and the United Nations.* Brookfield, Vt.: Dartmouth Publishing, 1996.

Johnson, Douglas V., ed. *Warriors in Peace Operations.* Carlisle Barracks, Pa.: Strategic Studies Institute, U.S. Army War College, 1999. Pamphlet.

Quinn, Dennis J., ed. *Peace Support Operations and the U.S. Military.* Washington, D.C.: National Defense University Press, 1994. Pamphlet.

Snow, Donald M. *Peacekeeping, Peacemaking and Peace-Enforcement: The U.S. Role in the New International Order.* Carlisle Barracks, Pa.: Strategic Studies Institute, U.S. Army War College, 1993.

ROBERT R. MACKEY

See also **Peacemaking.**

MILITIAS, AUTHORIZED

Throughout much of U.S. history, two images of the soldier predominate. One is that of the militiaman: the full-time citizen and part-time soldier who appears in arms at the call of the authorities in order to defend the community against enemies foreign and domestic, as well as against natural disasters, and who returns immediately afterward to private life. The other is that of the regular soldier whose profession is military service and who forms part of a standing army commanded by the central authorities. Because of early U.S. hostility to European-style standing armies and a preference for temporary, voluntary military service under local command, authorized militias played an indispensable role in the United States until war on Germany was declared in 1917. Not only were they used for purposes of local peacekeeping, but the militia system was the primary basis for recruitment of soldiers for America's wars.

The first American militia was a true *posse comitatus.* The employees of the London-based Virginia Trading Company formed a militia of all available able-bodied men to fight the Powhatan Native Americans. The militia seldom inflicted decisive losses on the natives, and the conflict sputtered on from 1607 until the Powhatans were decisively defeated in 1644. During this time Virginia (like other colonies) ceased to be a trading outpost and became a colonial society, enjoying rapid economic growth. Because volunteer military service held little interest and less profit to the growing populace, a law passed in 1624 established the legal obligation of available men to serve under arms as required by the governor of the colony.

The obligation to render military service on command was declared a citizen's duty by virtually all the colonial governments. This corresponded to an ideology of citizenship dating back to the Italian Renaissance political philosopher Niccolò Machiavelli and revived in the eighteenth century by England's radical Whigs, which based the defense of local freedoms on the existence of an armed, politically active citizenry. In practice, however, the principle was generally undermined by government underfunding and popular hostility to compulsory military service. Thus, while militias became part of the state and county administrative structure, they tended to be staffed by volunteers who were expected to arm and train themselves and who often insisted upon electing their own officers. Ordinarily commanded by the colonial or state governor, they were shaped to satisfy local needs. Overall the militia became an "all-purpose military institution, an expeditionary force, an army of conquest, main line of defense, home guard, and reserve of last resort all in one" (Shea 1982, p. 18).

In the colonies' revolutionary struggle against Britain, patriot leaders portrayed the British army of regular soldiers as an oppressor and called upon the colonial militias to arm themselves, resist, and, ultimately, fight for independence. Although the militias were "poorly trained, equipped, and led in most instances," leaving the Continental Army to carry the brunt of the Revolutionary War's battles, they played a key role in preventing pro-British forces from gaining control of state and local governments (Cooper 1993, p. 52). Following the American victory, Massachusetts militiamen were mobilized to defend the courts (and property-owners' rights) against the populist rebellion organized by Captain Daniel Shays.

Meanwhile debate raged between the advocates of the existing system of confederation—with its weak central government, absence of a standing army, and reliance on locally controlled militias—and the apostles of a strong federal government and regular army. In 1787–1789 the nationalists were successful in securing adoption of the U.S. Constitution, but among the restrictions on federal power contained in the Bill of Rights was the Second Amendment, which provided that, "A well regulated Militia, being necessary to the security of a free State, the right of the people to keep and bear Arms, shall not be infringed." Beginning in the twentieth century the meaning of this language has generated new debate in light of legislation proposing to limit the individual possession of firearms (see, e.g., Shalhope 1982 and Cress 1984). But whether the framers intended to guarantee the right to "keep and bear Arms" outside the militia structure, it is clear that they viewed the militia as a necessary defender of local security and liberty.

In an attempt to put the federal government in control of the system, the Federalists procured passage of the Uniform Militia Act of 1792, which provided for compulsory military service, but enforcement was left to the states, which generally declined to implement it. As a result, the central government came to rely on a volunteer standing army to perform services deemed essential, like periodic campaigns against Native Americans. The law also provided, however, that only the militia could be used to enforce federal statutes. In 1794 President George Washington took command of the militia in order to suppress the Whiskey Rebellion fomented by Pennsylvania farmers protesting a federal excise tax on distilled spirits, and in 1799 the militia was again "federalized" to suppress the Fries Rebellion, an armed stand of resistance by Pennsylvania farmers against a misunderstood tax.

After the War of 1812 the regular army was successfully reorganized. For several decades, state militias atrophied as Americans devoted themselves to economic self-advancement, and by the 1840s compulsory militia service and regular militia training had generally been abandoned, although some states still required payment of a commutation tax by men who did not wish to serve. Nevertheless, the system did not die. The states came to depend upon volunteer units, most of them composed of middle-class and well-to-do citizens, to perform order-keeping duties, including participating in slave patrols in the southern states, suppressing strikes and urban disorders in the North, and responding to natural disasters and other emergencies. These "uniformed militias" also performed the functions of social clubs, and for many men they were a method of acquiring political influence. They depended upon volunteers who could afford to arm, uniform, and train themselves, and they did not enjoy a high reputation for military discipline or effectiveness.

During the Civil War the federal government asserted the right to draft militiamen if necessary to meet manpower requirements. In 1863 Congress passed the Enrollment Act providing for direct conscription of men into the Union army, and the Confederacy resorted to similar measures. These laws contained major qualifications and loopholes, such as provisions granting bounties to enlistees and permitting drafted men to hire substitutes. The Enrollment Act demonstrated the federal government's supremacy over the states in military matters, but its overall effect was to inspire men to volunteer for military service. Once again, the job of recruitment was, in practice, left to the states.

The heyday of the militia movement was the period after the Civil War, particularly after militias were called out to suppress rioting workers in connection with the great railroad strike of 1877. As industrialization spread, and with it labor-management conflict, state and federal funds were used to support volunteer forces that almost always took management's side in suppressing disorders accompanying hard-fought strikes. The main burden of dealing with labor problems was placed on the militia by the Posse Comitatus Act of 1877, which forbade the policing of civilians by the regular troops. The militias also intervened, although less frequently, to suppress election riots, attacks on immigrants by anti-immigrant mobs, and attempted lynchings of African Americans. For the first time substantial state funds were devoted to equipping and training these forces, and their recruitment base was broadened to include more working-class volunteers.

National Guard

States formed select units that they called the National Guard, and "the National Guard of the late nineteenth century took on a permanency never seen in militia affairs. It became a select militia which military reformers had advocated since 1783, albeit a volunteer force funded and controlled by the state not the federal government" (Cooper 1993, p. 84). Especially in the industrial states, guard units often worked in consort with company officials and privately hired security forces to overwhelm workers' organizations and punish their leaders. The guard was very effective in this "union-busting" role, but state officials learned that the public did not soon forget the use of force, especially where deaths resulted, as they did following the railroad strike of 1877; the bloody riots in Cincinnati, Ohio (1884); and Milwaukee, Wisconsin (1886); the strike against Carnegie Steel at Homestead, Pennsylvania (1892); and the Pullman Strike in Chicago (1894).

As the years passed there was little movement to unify the disparate guard units or adopt the regular army command structures and mobilization plans. When deteriorating relationships with Spain led to the declaration of war in April 1898, a nationwide and predictably chaotic mobilization followed Congress's decision to use the National Guard as the primary source of volunteers. The results were in many respects disastrous. Recruiting a sufficient number of men was no problem; a surprisingly large number of volunteers flooded the states' mobilization offices. But the poorly trained, equipped, and led guardsmen did not perform well on the field, and logistical foul-ups increased the devastating effect of epidemic diseases among the troops.

At the war's end President William McKinley initiated military reforms, most of which were carried out under his successor, Theodore Roosevelt. Secretary of War Elihu Root and Ohio Representative Charles W. Dick, chair of the Militia Affairs Committee, shepherded the Militia Act of 1903 through Congress. The act repealed the Militia Act of 1792, for the first time putting state militias

under direct federal supervision. (Following the amendments of 1908 they could also be used outside the territorial United States.) The legislation recognized the National Guard as the nation's organized reserve. It was to be armed and equipped by the War Department, with its members paying for summer camp-training and other duties out of federal funds granted to the states. The other category of citizen-soldiers, called the Organized Militia, also received federal aid in exchange for increased federal control.

The militia movement's supporters, including the powerful National Guard Association, thus gained a great deal of what they had long lobbied for: increased financial support, improved training, and recognition as the nation's primary reserve force. But relations between the guard and the regular army remained stormy, with the former seeking to defend the states' traditional prerogatives and the latter demanding both federal supervision and a separate reserve force raised and supervised by the central government. U.S. mobilization for World War I tilted the balance further toward the regular army. The National Defense Act of 1916 continued the guard as a first-line reserve and granted its members drill pay, but it also created an enlisted reserve corps and increased federal regulation of the National Guard. When mobilized for duty along the Mexican border in 1916, guard units did not distinguish

National Guard troops confront rioters in Chicago, July 1966. CORBIS/
BETTMANN

themselves in their performances, and conscription replaced volunteering when the United States entered World War I.

These trends accelerated greatly after World War I. The National Guard was used extensively in the 1920s and 1930s to suppress labor unrest. During World War II, state units were absorbed into the army, and no attempt was made to preserve their organizational integrity. Later, the Army National Guard was joined by an Air National Guard, both massively funded by the federal government and subjected increasingly to federal control. Guard units in Arkansas were federalized by President Dwight Eisenhower in 1957 in order to protect African American schoolchildren seeking to attend Little Rock's public schools. In the 1960s Presidents John Kennedy and Lyndon Johnson used the guard to protect civil rights demonstrators, suppress urban race riots, and deal with disorders connected with protests against the Vietnam War. Following that war, when the military authorities were compelled to rely on volunteers alone, federal policy mandated that both guard and reserve units be organized and trained for immediate mobilization in wartime. During the Persian Gulf War of 1991, both forces were mobilized, but guard units were found unprepared for combat, and only the reserves were deployed to the Persian Gulf in Operation Desert Storm.

In the form of the National Guard, U.S. authorized militia thus survived the twentieth century as a reserve fighting force supplementary to the regular military reserves. At the state level the guard continued to assist in dealing with local disasters and, at times, in suppressing civil disorders. At the federal level it remained a recognized reserve, although its future role in foreign combat operations was still to be determined. That state military forces survived at all in an age of increasing centralization of power is remarkable. But the price of that survival was increasing subjection to the authority of the national government.

BIBLIOGRAPHY

Cooper, Jerry. *The Militia and the National Guard in America Since Colonial Times: A Research Guide.* Westport, Conn.: Greenwood, 1993.

———. *The Rise of the National Guard: The Evolution of the American Militia, 1865–1920.* Lincoln: University of Nebraska Press, 1997.

Cress, Laurence Delbert. "An Armed Community: The Origins and Meaning of the Right to Bear Arms." *Journal of American History* 71, no. 1 (June 1984): 22–42.

Cress, Laurence Delbert, and Robert E. Shalhope. "The Second Amendment and the Right to Bear Arms: An Exchange." *Journal of American History* 71, no. 3 (December 1984): 587–593.

Shalhope, Robert E. "The Ideological Origins of the Second Amendment." *Journal of American History* 69, no. 3 (December 1982): 599–614.

Shea, William L. "The First American Militia." *Military Affairs* 46, no. 1 (February 1982): 15–18.

RICHARD E. RUBENSTEIN

See also **Government Violence Against Citizens; Military Culture; Right to Bear Arms.**

MILITIAS, UNAUTHORIZED

Until 19 April 1995 most Americans associated the word *militia* with American Revolutionary War units mustering at the colonial town square with musket in hand, ready to fight the redcoats. When the Alfred P. Murrah Federal Building in Oklahoma was blown up that spring day, killing 168 people, including babies at a day-care center, the word *militia* took on a new meaning: paramilitary units targeting government and government employees for violence.

The militia movement has had a long history. America has always had far-right paramilitary groups. The Ku Klux Klan of the 1860s and 1960s, the Minutemen of the 1960s, and the Covenant, the Sword, and the Arm of the Lord in the 1980s are just a few of the better-known formations. Militias in the 1990s fed on that history, as well as on the ideologies developed by other racist groups like the Posse Comitatus and the Aryan Nations.

On the other hand, militias are a new phenomenon—a social movement initially based on four (now five) ideological cornerstones that came together as a matter of coincidence: the collapse of the Soviet Union, Ruby Ridge, Waco, the Brady Bill, and the Oklahoma City bombing.

When the Soviet Union fell apart at the end of 1991, the "evil empire" and its communist ideology were no longer available as a target for many Americans. With the Cold War over, most Americans adjusted to a world in which the United States was the lone superpower. Others, whose disdain for the Soviet system went beyond the rational, saw something sinister in this "new world order." Very quickly many of the old-time anticommunist conspiracy theories made fashionable by groups like the John Birch Society in the 1960s were recycled with a new target. The U.S. federal government became the new "evil empire."

The second ideological cornerstone was an event known as Ruby Ridge. Randy Weaver was a white supremacist who lived at Ruby Ridge, a remote section of northern Idaho. Weaver had connections to the Aryan Nations and was arrested for dealing in illegal firearms. Rather than face trial, he became a fugitive. In summer 1992 federal marshals were scouting his mountaintop hideout when a shoot-out began, leaving Weaver's teenage son and a marshal dead. Weaver's wife was later killed by an errant shot from a Federal Bureau of Investigation sharpshooter. After Weaver's surrender, over 150 key figures on the far right met in Estes Park, Colorado. This October 1992 gathering was convened by Pete Peters, a leader of Christian Identity, a racist and anti-Semitic religion built around distortions of biblical texts to assert that minorities are not even human and that Jews are the literal offspring of the devil. The assembly also marked a major strategic shift for the racist far right: it would attempt to start militia groups, rather than try to draw people into the existing formations, such as the Ku Klux Klan. And these militias would be formed in accordance with the strategy called "leaderless resistance"—creation of small cells to make infiltration by law enforcement difficult.

The third cornerstone was Waco. A religious group known as the Branch Davidians had its compound in Waco, Texas. The Davidians had been under investigation for possessing illegal firearms and committing child abuse. A botched attempt to arrest David Koresh, the Davidians' leader, produced a fifty-one-day standoff. It ended on 19 April 1993, when the compound burned to the ground, killing seventy-four people, including twenty-five children. This tragedy and the government's errors in handling the crisis were distorted by conspiracy theorists on the far right. Waco became an important organizing cry for many militias, signaling the opening shots of what they believed was a war by the U.S. government against its citizens.

The fourth was the passage of the Brady Bill in 1993 and the assault-rifle ban in 1994. The Brady Bill imposed a five-day waiting period for the purchase of handguns, but to many who believed the popular misconception that the Second Amendment gave Americans a personal, inviolate right to bear arms, the bill became a symbol of government repression. In their view gun control was "people control."

The Brady Bill gave John Trochmann an opportunity. Trochmann, known to many in Idaho for his associations with the Aryan Nations, Christian Identity, and Christian Patriotism, formed the Militia of Montana in February 1994. Based in Noxon, Montana, the group organized meetings all around the state, drawing hundreds of people to hear about gun rights and conspiracy theories. The Militia of Montana also had a brisk mail-order business. They sent out militia-formation packets, information about how to make bombs, and details of conspiracy theories, some of which included claims of secret plots involving black helicopters and charges that the government was manipulating the weather to harass loyal Americans.

Two months later, the Michigan Militia was formed by Ray Southwell (a real estate agent) and Norm Olson (a minister). It soon claimed units all over Michigan. The convicted Oklahoma City bombers Timothy McVeigh and Terry Nichols reportedly attended a meeting of this group. The Michigan Militia quickly drew attention for its military training, its conspiracy theories, and its leaders' opinion that America might need a second revolution.

By the end of 1994 there were militia groups active in at least twenty states. Although all were independent and the degree of overt racists' involvement varied, they shared a conspiratorial fear of the "new world order" and of the federal government as its instrument. Although it drew little press attention at the time, one of the few women in the movement—Linda Thompson—created a fierce debate during the summer of 1994. Best known for her videotaped accusations of government conspiracy at Waco, Thompson, having proclaimed herself the "acting adjutant general" of the Unorganized Militia of the United States, proposed that the militias march on Washington, D.C., on 19 September 1994. Once there, they would use guns to arrest Congress, try members for treason, and impose sentence. (The sentence for treason is death.) "We are at war right now," Thompson said. "Make no mistake about it." The militia movement was divided on what she called her "ultimatum." Some thought it a good idea; others questioned whether she was an agent provocateur. Eventually the plan was canceled.

By March 1995 thirty-six states had militia groups, and the paranoia was increasing. Sam Sherwood, the leader of the Idaho-based United

Swearing-in ceremony for the unauthorized Michigan Militia. CORBIS/AGENCE FRANCE
PRESSE

States Militia Association, advised people to "go up and look legislators in the face, because someday you may be forced to blow it off." John Trochmann and others were arrested in a confrontation at a courthouse in Montana, and on the Internet, rumors were running wild, including reports that all leaves of federal law-enforcement officials had been canceled so that on 25 March 1995 a massive arrest of militia members would occur. Part of the conspiracy lore of the movement included a belief that the government had created concentration camps for "loyal Americans" and were using black helicopters for nefarious purposes. Many believed that they would be taken by these secret helicopters to the concentration camps on 25 March 1995. Wild, anxious messages were sent on the Internet leading up to that day, and a member of Congress even inquired of the government whether the rumors were true.

No such event took place, of course, but people who watched the militia movement were concerned about the anniversary of the fiery end of the Waco siege, which was rapidly approaching. In early April, the American Jewish Committee sent out a notice warning of possible attacks on the government by people associated with the militia movement on 19 April 1995.

That morning the Alfred P. Murrah building was demolished, killing 168 people. The weapon was a truck bomb reportedly made of ammonium nitrate fertilizer, the time was shortly after nine, the target was a government building. This was a virtual re-creation of a scene in *The Turner Diaries* (1978), a book written by the neo-Nazi William Pierce of the National Alliance under the pseudonym Andrew MacDonald. The book describes a fictional far-right race war in America, in which minorities are killed, ending in an Armageddon. It was the blueprint for a 1980s terrorist group called the Order, which robbed banks and armored trucks and in 1984 killed the Denver-based talk-radio host Alan Berg. The book was also a favorite of Timothy McVeigh, who brought its pages to life in the worst terrorist attack in U.S. history.

Since the bombing, the militia movement has continued to grow, as have the conspiracy theories about the Oklahoma City bombing itself. Immediately after the bombing, militia groups blamed the government for a "Reichstag fire" type of attack (alluding to the Nazis' scapegoating of German communists). Since then they have taken reasonable questions about who else besides McVeigh and Nichols might have been involved and spun them into an intricate web of fanciful theories designed to demonize government and empower America's "private armies." The bombing became the fifth ideological prong upon which the militias are being built.

Although most people associated with the militias probably would not physically attack people or property, many would—and the movement is designed to encourage such attacks. In the words of Ken Toole of the Montana Human Rights Network, the militias are like a "funnel moving through space." At the wide end are people drawn into the groups by the "mainstream" issues of gun control, the environment, and so forth. In the middle of the funnel are people animated by the various conspiracy theories, including the racist and anti-Semitic ones. And at the short end of the funnel are the people who are ready to make war against America.

Although there have been no scientific studies on the demographics of the movement, it is clear that the majority of members are white males, and that the leadership is trying to attract members from the armed forces and police. There is even an organization known as Police Against the New World Order that promotes the militias.

BIBLIOGRAPHY

Lamy, Philip. *Millennium Rage: Survivalists, White Supremacists, and the Doomsday Prophecy.* New York: Plenum, 1996.

Stern, Kenneth S. *A Force upon the Plain: The American Militia Movement and the Politics of Hate.* New York: Simon and Schuster, 1997.

KENNETH S. STERN

See also **Civil Disorder; Cults; Extremism; Gun Culture; Militarism; Nativism; Oklahoma City Bombing; Right to Bear Arms; Ruby Ridge; Waco.**

MOB VIOLENCE. *See* Civil Disorder; Lynching; Riots; Vigilantism.

MOLLY MAGUIRES

The Molly Maguires of the anthracite coal mining region of northeastern Pennsylvania derived their name from a violent secret society active in Ireland in the 1840s. A response by immigrant workers, mainly young men, to the harsh and often bewildering conditions of industrial capitalism, including low or missing wages and long hours in the mines, the Molly Maguires were the product of U.S. as much as Irish soil. In Ireland its members had disguised themselves in women's clothing (wearing white smocks and using white powder or burned cork on their faces) and pledged allegiance to Molly Maguire, a mythical woman who symbolized their struggle against injustice.

Most of the Molly Maguires in the United States emigrated from north-central and northwestern Ireland, where the Irish Mollys had been active. But direct links in personnel between the Irish and U.S. Molly Maguires have never been discovered. Some continuity with the Irish secret-society tradition was provided by the Ancient Order of Hibernians (AOH), founded in New York City in 1836, which was the institutional cover for the Molly Maguires in Pennsylvania. A peaceful, benevolent organization elsewhere in the United States, the AOH was used in the Pennsylvania coal-mining region for violent as well as fraternal purposes. The violence in the United States began only in the 1860s and peaked in the 1870s, a generation after the activities in Ireland had ended.

There were two distinct waves of Molly Maguire activity in Pennsylvania. The first included six assassinations, committed during and after the Civil War, of which nobody was convicted until the famous Molly Maguire trials of the mid-1870s. At the heart of this first wave of violence was a combination of resistance to conscription and rudimentary labor organizing. The violence subsided in the late 1860s, only to break out with renewed intensity in 1875. The relative tranquillity between the two waves of violence was due mainly to a powerful new trade-union movement, which unequivocally rejected violence. The rise and fall of this union holds the key to understanding the second wave of Molly Maguire activities.

Founded by skilled English workers in 1868, the Workingmen's Benevolent Association (WBA) eventually enrolled forty thousand men, becoming the largest trade union in the nation by the early 1870s. The labor movement in the Pennsylvania coal-mining region now had two distinct but overlapping forms: this powerful trade union, open to all workers and with many Irishmen among its leaders, that united the labor force; and the Molly Maguires, an exclusively Irish organization that favored violent tactics, which the union condemned as self-destructive. This bifurcated labor movement met its nemesis in Franklin B. Gowen, the president of the Philadelphia and Reading Railroad Company, who was determined to destroy all obstacles to his control over the economy of the lower coal-mining region. Gowen hired the foremost private detective in the United States, Allan

Molly Maguires meet during coal strike. Woodcut from *Harper's Weekly*, **31 January 1874.** LIBRARY OF CONGRESS

Pinkerton, who sent several undercover agents to work in the region.

The final confrontation between Gowen and the union took the form of a bitter six-month strike in 1875, culminating in the defeat and collapse of the union. During the strike, union leaders gradually lost control over elements of the rank and file. As the dispute grew more violent, Gowen insisted that there was no difference between the Molly Maguires and the WBA. The Mollys, he claimed, were the violent wing of the trade union, and the trade unionists were therefore terrorists themselves. This ideological strategy helped ensure the destruction of the union by June 1875, but the essential difference between trade unionism and the Molly Maguires was starkly revealed in the violent summer that followed.

With the union in disarray, the Molly Maguires stepped into the vacuum left by its defeat, temporarily assuming unofficial leadership of the labor movement. Between mid-June and early September 1875, the Mollys assassinated two law-enforcement officers, a miner, two foremen, and a superintendent. (All the victims were shot, except one who was beaten to death.) The violence of the Molly Maguires in the United States strikingly resembled that of their prototype in Ireland: for example, tavern keepers played a prominent role in both countries—they were the alleged ringleaders and the assassinations were allegedly planned in their taverns—and assassins were brought in from neighboring or distant AOH lodges to do the killing under cover of anonymity.

In 1876 and 1877 the Molly Maguires were brought to trial. Twenty were convicted of capital murder, and twenty more were sent to prison. The trials were conducted in the midst of enormously hostile publicity. The defendants were arrested by private policemen and convicted on the evidence of informers and a detective, who was accused by the defense attorney at the trials of being an agent provocateur. Irish Roman Catholics were excluded from the juries. Most of the prosecuting attorneys worked for railroads and mining companies. The star prosecutor was none other than Franklin B. Gowen. Twenty Molly Maguires were executed, ten of them on 21 June 1877, which became known in the Pennsylvania coal-mining region as Black Thursday. At the end of the twentieth century the day was still remembered in certain circles.

BIBLIOGRAPHY

Broehl, Wayne G., Jr. *The Molly Maguires.* Cambridge, Mass.: Harvard University Press, 1964.

Coleman, James Walter. *The Molly Maguire Riots: Industrial Conflict in the Pennsylvania Coal Region.* Richmond, Va.: Garrett and Massie, 1936.

Kenny, Kevin. *Making Sense of the Molly Maguires.* New York: Oxford University Press, 1998.

KEVIN KENNY

See also **Immigration; Irish Americans; Labor and Unions.**

MONTGOMERY BUS BOYCOTT

The Montgomery bus boycott began on 5 December 1955 to protest the trial on that day of Rosa McCauley Parks, the secretary of the Montgomery, Alabama, branch of the National Association for the Advancement of Colored People (NAACP), who had been arrested on 1 December for violation of the Montgomery city ordinance requiring racially segregated seating on buses. The boycott, initially planned only for the single day of Parks's trial, proved so effective that black leaders decided on the afternoon of 5 December to continue it until the city commission and the bus company would agree to meet blacks' demand that the form of seating segregation on the buses be altered. The Baptist minister Martin Luther King, Jr., was chosen to head the Montgomery Improvement Association (MIA), the organization formed to administer this extended boycott.

The MIA wanted the bus company to use the same pattern of segregation in Montgomery as the one it used in Mobile. In Mobile the racial designation of seats was not changed until passengers reached their destination and disembarked; but in Montgomery bus drivers were required to unseat passengers as the bus proceeded along its route in order to adjust the racial division of seats to accord with the changing composition of the ridership. Black leaders had pressed Montgomery authorities to adopt the Mobile seating plan at meetings in October 1952, December 1953, and March 1954. The question had become an issue in the municipal election of March 1955, in which an aggressively segregationist candidate had defeated the incumbent racial liberal for commissioner of public safety. In the midst of that campaign (and nine months before the arrest of Rosa Parks), a black teenager, Claudette Colvin, had been convicted of violating the seating-segregation ordinance and declared a juvenile delinquent. The general frustration of black leaders at the city's persistent refusal to consider altering the pattern of bus segregation underlay both Parks's decision not to vacate her seat when bus driver J. Fred Blake ordered her to do so, and the willingness of other prominent blacks immediately to rally to her support.

From the outset King emphasized to MIA members the biblical injunctions against violence. But the early weeks of the boycott were marked by sniper shootings into passing buses and the use of physical coercion to prevent blacks from using the bus system. However, this violence quickly disappeared, both because the MIA succeeded in organizing an efficient carpool operation to get blacks to and from work and because the negotiations with municipal authorities initially seemed to promise a speedy settlement. By January, however, the negotiations had reached a stalemate, and tensions mounted rapidly. At the end of the month, the MIA, at the urging of its attorney Fred D. Gray, abandoned its proposal of the Mobile seating plan and instead filed suit in federal court to have all forms of seating segregation declared unconstitutional. At the same time extreme segregationists bombed the homes of King and black leader E. D. Nixon. The bombs did only minor damage, but an angry black crowd gathered in front of the King house. Speaking from his front porch, King calmed the assemblage, averting what observers thought was an imminent riot.

In February radical segregationists were mollified when authorities indicted the MIA's leadership for violation of a state statute of 1921 that made it an offense to conspire to boycott a lawful business. Thereafter, with the black cause committed to the federal courts and the segregationists

Rosa Parks in December 1956, after the Supreme Court ruling banning segregation on public city vehicles took effect. CORBIS/BETTMANN

Calming the Waters

We believe in law and order. Don't get panicky. Don't do anything panicky at all. Don't get your weapons. He who lives by the sword will perish by the sword. Remember that is what God said. We are not advocating violence. We want to love our enemies. I want you to love our enemies. Be good to them. Love them and let them know you love them. I did not start this boycott. I was asked by you to serve as your spokesman. I want it to be known the length and breadth of this land that if I am stopped this movement will not stop. If I am stopped our work will not stop. For what we are doing is right. What we are doing is just. And God is with us.

Martin Luther King's remarks from the front porch of his bombed home, as reported in the *Montgomery Advertiser,* 31 January 1956

now depending on the state court proceedings, tensions eased somewhat. At the same time black pacifist Bayard Rustin of the War Resisters League and white pacifist Glenn Smiley of the Fellowship of Reconciliation each came to Montgomery to meet with King. In conversations with them, King began to develop a more comprehensive commitment to nonviolence as both a moral necessity and the strategic key to black liberation. The weekly MIA mass meetings thereafter increasingly stressed the significance of nonviolence, and King publicly apologized for his unsuccessful earlier attempt to obtain a permit to carry a pistol. In March, King was convicted of violating the state antiboycott statute and fined $500, but Montgomery's black community took the development calmly. The trials of the other black leaders were postponed while King appealed the judgment.

In June a three-judge federal court voted two to one to declare laws requiring segregated seating on buses a violation of the Constitution's Fourteenth Amendment. The city appealed the decision to the U.S. Supreme Court. In August segregationists bombed the home of the only white member of the MIA's executive board, Robert Graetz, a Lutheran pastor of an all-black congregation. But with this single exception, Montgomery avoided further significant violence until the Supreme Court's decision on the appeal of the bus segregation suit.

On 13 November 1956 the Supreme Court unanimously affirmed the three-judge court's declaration that bus segregation was unconstitutional. On 20 December the federal court order integrating the city's buses became final, and the boycott came to an end. Immediately segregationist violence began to escalate. Sniper shootings into buses culminated on 28 December in an assault that shattered the leg of a pregnant black passenger, Rosa Jordan. Authorities were compelled to suspend evening—and eventually all—bus service. On 10 January 1957 four black churches and the homes of two boycott leaders were bombed and heavily damaged, and on 27 January a new round of bombings completely destroyed a home near King's. On 30 January, Montgomery police arrested seven Ku Klux Klansmen and charged them with these offenses. The first two of the seven to be brought to trial were acquitted in May, despite their confessions and the irrefutable evidence against them; nevertheless, the arrests succeeded in halting the violence. In March bus service had been restored on an integrated basis. In November, Circuit Solicitor William Thetford dropped both the remaining antiboycott prosecutions and the other indictments of the bombers in return for King's agreement to withdraw his state court appeal and pay his fine.

The federal court order, rather than the boycott, brought integration to Montgomery's buses. Yet the boycott established the power of nonviolent direct action so clearly that it would characterize civil rights protests throughout the coming decade. In strategic terms, it served to depict black demonstrators as simply peacefully insisting, in the face of violent and illegal segregationist resistance, on rights that in justice should be theirs. Thus, in the public mind the boycott stripped white supremacist officials, who saw themselves as enforcers of existing statutes and public order, of their legitimacy. And in moral terms it permitted its adherents to hold onto the hope that, by returning love for hatred and contempt, they would eventually be able to transform the white supremacists' hearts, and thus to create a genuinely nonracial democracy. In the long term, events would begin to erode this faith, but not before the faith had itself played a crucial role in destroying legal segregation.

BIBLIOGRAPHY

Burns, Stewart, ed. *Daybreak of Freedom: The Montgomery Bus Boycott.* Chapel Hill: University of North Carolina Press, 1997.

King, Martin Luther, Jr. *Stride Toward Freedom: The Montgomery Story.* New York: Harper, 1958.

Thornton, J. Mills, III. "Challenge and Response in the Montgomery Bus Boycott of 1955–1956." *Alabama Review* 33 (July 1980): 163–235.

J. MILLS THORNTON III

See also **Civil Disobedience; Civil Rights Movements; King, Martin Luther, Jr.; Nonviolence.**

MORAN, GEORGE "BUGS"
(1892–1957)

George "Bugs" Moran is now treated as a footnote to one of the more notorious gangland rubouts: the 1929 St. Valentine's Day Massacre in Chicago, engineered by the far more notorious Al Capone. Moran was a dangerous and powerful thug in his own right. Burglar, bootlegger, bank robber, and killer, Moran earned his nickname from a volatile temper that helped him to bully his way into competition with Capone for dominance of the violent bootlegging business during Prohibition in Chicago.

Moran was born in Minnesota in 1892. As a young boy he moved to Chicago with his parents and was active in marauding North Side Irish gangs in his teenage years, quickly establishing the kind of record that conferred stature in those circles. In 1910 he received his first conviction for robbery and spent nearly two years in Joliet Prison. More arrests and incarcerations followed in 1913 and 1917; his gang chieftain Dion "Deanie" O'Bannion paid bribe money to have the 1917 offense expunged. A 1918 conviction cost Moran the better part of five years in prison. When Moran was released in 1923, he joined O'Bannion, Vincent Drucci, and Earl Weiss in the North Side gang, which he helped organize in 1914. They and their minions controlled the lucrative bootleg liquor and gambling trade in Chicago's Gold Coast, but the near monopoly they held there was not enough for them; Moran took on the South Side mob by hijacking shipments of illegal beer from Capone's trucks.

The violence inevitably escalated. O'Bannion was shot to death, and Moran, Drucci, and Weiss retaliated by gunning down and nearly killing Capone's gangland sponsor, Johnny Torrio, early in 1925. Other murders and attempted murders ensued that year, including one that wounded Moran and Drucci. In September 1926, backed by cars full of heavily armed men, Moran, with his sidekicks Drucci and Weiss, staged a daring daylight attack on Capone's headquarters at the Hawthorne Hotel in Cicero, Illinois, peppering the building with machine-gun fire, nearly hitting Capone, wounding his bodyguard, and injuring an innocent woman bystander.

The Moran-Capone war reached its climax in 1929, when Moran allied himself with mobster Joe Aiello, who had put out a $50,000 contract on Capone. Then, presumably, Moran and Aiello murdered a Capone ally, Pasquilino Lolardo, boss of the Unione Siciliane. At that point Capone allegedly approved the St. Valentine's Day Massacre to murder Moran and as many of his gang as could be lured (by promise of a shipment of illegal Canadian liquor) to Moran's headquarters at the S. M. C. Cartage Company garage on North Clark Street. Moran was late to the meeting, but, although he escaped this attempt on his life, he was never again able to mount a real threat to Capone (although he is believed to have been complicit in the murder of Jack McGurn, one of the St. Valentine's Day hit men, on the seventh anniversary of the event).

Moran was reduced to committing robberies, first in southern Illinois and then in Ohio. He was

George "Bugs" Moran. LIBRARY OF CONGRESS

caught and spent from 1946 to 1956 in prison. On his release he was sent to Leavenworth Penitentiary for a previous robbery. There he died in 1957 of lung cancer, believing that his refusal to include prostitution among his criminal enterprises made him Al Capone's moral superior.

BIBLIOGRAPHY

Allsop, Kenneth. *The Bootleggers: The Story of Chicago's Prohibition Era.* New Rochelle, N.Y.: Arlington House, 1968.

Demaris, Ovid. *Captive City: Chicago in Chains.* New York: Pocket Books, 1970.

Nash, Jay Robert. *Bloodletters and Badmen: A Narrative of American Criminals from the Pilgrims to the Present.* New York: M. Evans, 1973.

ALAN SHUCARD

See also **Capone, Al; Organized Crime; St. Valentine's Day Massacre.**

MORMONS

Members of the Church of Jesus Christ of Latter-day Saints, called Mormons after their central book of faith, have the dubious honor of belonging to one of the most persecuted—and violent—religious sects in American history. Mormonism is founded upon the Book of Mormon, a work believers contend was transcribed by Joseph Smith, the founder of the religion, in 1830 from sacred golden tablets presented to him by the angel Moroni. These writings maintained that Native American tribes were in fact the lost tribe of Israel and had been visited by Jesus Christ following the Resurrection. Smith and the later Mormon leader Brigham Young refined the theology, adding the institution of polygamy and formulating a staunch theocratic religious and political organization. From its early beginning in the "burnt-over" district of western New York, famous for its religious fervor, Mormonism spread quickly, numbering nearly thirty thousand followers by 1844.

As Smith spread his vision, resistance emerged from non-Mormon "gentiles" throughout the Northwest and the Ohio River valley. Mormons were ridiculed, reviled, and attacked for their beliefs, often with the tacit approval of local authorities. This treatment solidified the beliefs of the Mormons and was later used as an argument in defense of their own violent actions against non-Mormon settlers in Utah in the 1850s. When Smith declared the revelation of polygamy in July 1843,

latent animosity turned to violence. Until then, Mormons were treated, on the whole, as a splinter group of mainstream Protestantism, albeit with their own peculiar beliefs. When polygamy was introduced, Mormon communities were attacked and driven out of the more developed lands of the Midwest. Within the community itself, a schism developed with respect to the practice of polygamy. Smith had not wanted the polygamy revelation to become known to the gentiles. When a dissentient newspaper in the Mormon community of Nauvoo, Illinois, published Smith's revelation in 1844, Smith, fearing reprisals and in hopes of placating the neighboring gentile communities, ran the dissenters out of town and ordered the printing press destroyed. He was arrested, and while he was imprisoned in Carthage, Illinois, an anti-Mormon mob stormed the building and lynched him. The Mormons in Nauvoo, now led by Brigham Young, departed for the West, searching for a land of their own outside of gentile influence.

The Territory of Deseret: Utah and the Crisis of 1857

Under Young's leadership, the Mormons established the thriving community of Deseret around the Great Salt Lake in what would become, in 1850, the Utah Territory. Isolated and free, for the most part, from federal influence, Mormons practiced their religion while driving out hostile Native American tribes and allying themselves with friendly tribes. Even after territorial status was granted to Deseret, Young persisted in his leadership of the community, naming Mormons to key political and judicial positions. President Millard Fillmore's appointment of political cronies to other positions led to ongoing conflicts and difficulties between federal and local (i.e., Mormon) officials before 1857. After the territorial secretary, a federal judge, and the agent for Indian affairs fled Utah in the summer of 1851, fearing for their lives, they wrote scathing editorials that accused the Mormons of godlessness and immorality; these writings greatly shaped popular opinion in the East. Federal officials throughout the 1850s, from army survey teams to federal judges, found the Mormons to be less than cooperative, often actively hindering federal officials. In December 1856 prominent Mormon lawyers threatened a federal judge named George P. Stiles with physical harm. Later, Stiles's office was attacked by a mob and his records destroyed. In response, federal officials in

Joseph Smith. LIBRARY OF CONGRESS

the territory appealed to the newly elected president, James Buchanan, for the restoration of federal control in the state. The resulting action, known as the Utah Expedition of 1857–1858, or the Mormon War, was launched under the leadership of Brigadier General William Harney, ostensibly to establish a fort near Salt Lake City. In reality, the expeditionary force marched in to reestablish federal law in the territory.

When the federal expedition arrived in Utah in the winter of 1857, Brigham Young informed Harney that the Mormons would not supply his troops, and he ordered the army to leave the territory. Harney refused, and Young ordered active resistance, perceiving the presence of federal troops as the continuing persecution of his people. Mormon irregulars raided the federal supply trains, burning three hundred thousand pounds of goods and placing the army in a precarious position. Federal troops, lacking logistical support, established Fort Bridger halfway between the Utah border and Salt Lake City to wait out the winter of 1857, while reinforcements and supplies arrived

from the East. Additionally, President Buchanan named a new territorial governor, Alfred Cummings, who promptly wrote to Young and demanded that the Mormon militia return to their homes and cease resisting federal authority. Young refused, and in June 1858 Buchanan, describing the territory as being "in rebellion against the Government," instructed the army to begin calling up troops in the East and to prepare for a full-scale invasion. In the meantime, however, federal officials in Utah had reached a peaceful settlement of the crisis when Young, who had been appointed territorial governor in 1850, agreed to step down, thus guaranteeing the nonresistance of the Mormon population, provided the federals did nothing to interfere in the religious rights of the territory. The crisis began to wind down as federal authorities reestablished control over civic institutions.

The first test of federal authority came in the summer of 1859, with the trial that resulted from the so-called Mountain Meadows Massacre. When federal authorities investigated the massacre of an entire wagon train of settlers heading to Oregon in 1857, they found numerous indications of Mormon as well as Native American involvement. A mixed force of Native Americans and Mormons, led by John D. Lee, was eventually accused of executing 120 men, women, and children, who had surrendered to the group. While Young did not condone the massacre, he and other high-ranking Mormons attempted to obfuscate the involvement of Lee and others. Ultimately, Young kept his word and allowed the trial to progress without hindrance. Lee and his companions were executed by federal troops later that year, a recognition of the dominance of federal authority and the key role played by the Mormon hierarchy in the territory.

Mormons have proven highly resilient in the face of religious persecution. From New York to Utah, Mormons were driven out of their communities by their neighbors and came to inhabit one of the most inhospitable regions of the United States. When faced with the destruction of their community by the federal government, Mormon leaders acted with deliberation and accommodation, as did U.S. military and civil leaders in Utah. Since 1859 the Mormons have become one of the most patriotic groups in the United States, vibrant and productive members of American society despite their history of persecution and violence. In the latter half of the twentieth century, Mormon authorities discouraged conscientious objections to war based on religious beliefs (but not individual conscience); in fact, the doctrine of the Latter-day Saints expressly defines military service as both a duty and a responsibility of church members. During World War II Mormon leaders exhorted their young men to volunteer for service, and this pattern continued in all the conflicts of the latter half of the twentieth century.

Mormonism in the latter half of the twentieth century, while becoming very much a mainstream religion, dealt with several scandals involving early church history. The most notable of these scandals was the Mark Hofmann case in the mid-1980s. Hofmann, who claimed to have original documents implicating Joseph Smith, Brigham Young, and other founders of the church as masterminds of a gigantic fraud, fueled the attacks of anti-Mormon groups. Hofmann's "discoveries," however, were later proven to be forged documents. Hofmann, meanwhile, was convicted of the murder of two Salt Lake City residents to whom he had promised additional evidence. Despite the fraudulent basis of Hofmann's accusations, Mormons still find themselves defending their faith against intolerance and bigotry fueled by anti-Mormon groups (who use Hofmann's forgeries as evidence) more reflective of the 1830s than the twenty-first century.

BIBLIOGRAPHY

Brooks, Juanita. *The Mountain Meadows Massacre.* Norman: University of Oklahoma Press, 1962. Reprint, 1985.

Coakley, Robert W. *The Role of Federal Military Forces in Domestic Disorders, 1789–1878.* Washington, D.C.: Government Printing Office, 1987.

Furniss, Norman F. *The Mormon Conflict, 1850–1859.* New Haven, Conn.: Yale University Press, 1960.

Hansen, Klaus J. *Mormonism and the American Experience.* Chicago: University of Chicago Press, 1981.

Ludlow, Daniel H., ed. *Encyclopedia of Mormonism.* 4 vols. New York: Macmillan, 1992.

West, Roy B. *Kingdom of the Saints: The Story of Brigham Young and the Mormons.* New York: Viking, 1957.

Whitaker, David J. *The Study of Mormon History: A Guide to the Published Sources.* Provo, Utah: Brigham Young University Studies, 1995.

ROBERT R. MACKEY

See also **Hofmann, Mark; Religion.**

MOUNTAIN MEADOWS MASSACRE.

See Mormons.

MOVE BOMBING

At 5:27 P.M. on 13 May 1985, Philadelphia police lieutenant Frank Powell leaned out of the helicopter in which he was riding and dropped a canvas satchel containing a powerful explosive—five pounds of C-4 and Tovex—on top of a row house at 6221 Osage Avenue. A fire was ignited and allowed to burn. Before the flames were extinguished, eleven people in the house were dead, five of them children. Sixty-one homes were destroyed, and a gaping hole was left in a densely populated, predominantly black, middle-class neighborhood in the City of Brotherly Love. Although Philadelphia had been the site of one of the more important chapters of the Black Panther Party and its chapter of the National Association for the Advancement of Colored People had been noted for its militancy during the 1960s, by the time of the 1985 bombing that militancy was a distant memory.

In the broadest sense, Lieutenant Powell was acting in response to complaints from neighbors in this area about MOVE, a radical anarchist organization with elements of black nationalism notorious for its antitechnology views and its penchant for broadcasting its philosophy—liberally peppered with profanity—at odd hours through powerful loudspeakers. MOVE was formed in the early 1970s by Vincent Leaphard, who later took the name John Africa. Originally he called his organization the American Christian Movement for Life or, simply, the Christian Life Movement. Eventually the name was shortened to MOVE. When asked what the name meant, MOVE members would simply shrug their shoulders and say, "Means MOVE." Although MOVE did not espouse violence and criminality, on the other hand, it did not espouse passive resistance and nonviolence. Initially the group settled at 309 North Thirty-third Street, adjacent to the campus of the University of Pennsylvania.

MOVE's philosophy involved "getting back to nature" as a way of opposing the "system," that is, the political, economic, and social structure of the United States. Bathing with soap was forbidden, and members sported dreadlocks, thickly matted braids favored by the Rastafarians of the West Indies. They habitually chewed garlic for medicinal purposes, and at their various homes provided a haven for unwanted animals, particularly unvaccinated dogs, as well as rats, roaches, termites, and various insects. Birth control was not permitted, and natural childbirth was favored. In keeping

Police in the West Philadelphia neighborhood destroyed by the 1985 bombing of the radical African American organization MOVE. CORBIS/BETTMANN

with the group's overall philosophy, MOVE children often went naked, even in the coldest weather.

Such practices brought repeated complaints from neighbors and resulted in frequent confrontations between MOVE and the Philadelphia police. One of the most publicized of these encounters took place on 8 August 1978 when twenty-one MOVE members were arrested as they resisted police efforts to inspect their premises. A battle resulted that ended with one officer dead and seven other police officers and firefighters wounded.

On 13 May 1985 the police were seeking to serve MOVE with warrants for offenses ranging from disorderly conduct to possession of explosives. It is unclear if MOVE members were firing at the officers as these warrants were being served, though that was alleged subsequently. The escalating confrontation between the police and MOVE led to the decision to drop explosives on a rooftop bunker in order to punch a hole to be used as a conduit for tear gas, which the police expected would compel the inhabitants to flee the house.

The only persons to receive a criminal conviction for these events were Ramona Africa of MOVE, the only adult survivor of the bombing, who served a seven-year sentence for riot and conspiracy, and a contractor convicted of stealing $137,000 intended for rebuilding destroyed homes.

A commission of inquiry concluded in 1986 that top city officials, including the mayor and the police and fire chiefs, had been "grossly negligent." The city was forced to pay approximately $10 million in order to rebuild homes that had been destroyed. Michael Ward, once known as Birdie Africa, who was a child at the time of the bombing, received $840,000 plus lifetime monthly payments as the result of a lawsuit.

By the end of the twentieth century, MOVE members had dwindled to a few hundred at most, a disproportionate percentage of whom were children.

BIBLIOGRAPHY

Anderson, John, and Hilary Hevenor Norton. *Burning Down the House: MOVE and the Tragedy of Philadelphia*. New York: Norton, 1987.

Harry, Margot. *"Attention, MOVE! This Is America!"* Chicago: Banner, 1987.

Wagner-Pacifici, Robin Erica. *Discourse and Destruction: The City of Philadelphia Versus MOVE*. Chicago: University of Chicago Press, 1987.

GERALD HORNE

See also **Government Violence Against Citizens; Philadelphia.**

MOVIES. *See* Film.

MUCKRAKERS

After a speech given in 1906 by President Theodore Roosevelt, *muckraking* entered the American vocabulary as a term for investigative reporting. Roosevelt, borrowing from John Bunyan's *Pilgrim's Progress* (1678) the word *muckrake*, which refers literally to a rake for dung and, in Bunyan's usage, suggests a preoccupation with filthy or lowly things, advised, "The men with the muckrakes are often indispensable to the well-being of society; but only if they know when to stop raking the muck." Throughout the twentieth century, for people in power the term carried the connotation of negative, bordering on unfair, coverage; but it also signaled the pride of many journalists who felt that such coverage was helping the underdog. Nearly all muckrakers believed that their stories would lead to peaceful changes, not violent uprisings. At the same time, these journalists chronicled hidden violence in the form of dangerous working conditions, destructive business practices, and unsafe consumer products. Thus muckrakers played a key role in the extension of the definition of the word *violence* beyond that of physical acts of brutality.

Stories denouncing arbitrary power appeared in the press as early as colonial times. The rise of industrial capitalism at the end of the nineteenth century renewed this concern with corruption. During the Gilded Age (1865–1890), Henry and Charles Adams wrote scathingly about high finance in the *North American Review.* The cartoonist Thomas Nast of *Harper's Weekly* drew some of the harshest pictures of politicians ever seen in the U.S. press; for a dozen years after the Civil War he showed northerners how freed slaves in the South were being stripped of their rights. By the end of the nineteenth century, socialist and populist papers circulated widely. Commercial newspaper publishers such as Joseph Pulitzer, Edwin W. Scripps, and William Randolph Hearst reached millions of working-class readers with critiques of big business. But none of this was muckraking in the arresting form it was to take at the turn of the twentieth century.

In contrast to the costly and specialized publications that had carried these earlier investigations, muckraking came in inexpensive, mass-circulation magazines. Local scandals, which newspapers had long covered, were now put in a national context. Most muckraking claimed to be outside party politics and tried to create a new

Ida Tarbell, in 1904. LIBRARY OF CONGRESS

kind of public opinion. The goal was a kinship with reform-minded citizens across the land as part of the Progressive movement (c. 1890–1920).

Nearly two thousand articles, appearing in more than a dozen national magazines, engaged in muckraking at the beginning of the twentieth century. Writers were given months and even years to investigate their subjects and then issue after issue of a magazine to build an audience. The new practice of photojournalism gave the stories documentary authority. At a time when systematic research in the social sciences was just beginning, muckraking rivaled the most serious studies of U.S. society.

Muckrakers stressed that public-policy questions, and the politicians who addressed them, affected all Americans. Thus Samuel Hopkins Adams showed in *Collier's* magazine that the patent-medicine industry threatened everyone's health, and, in the single greatest literary success of muckraking, Upton Sinclair showed that no dinner table was safe from contaminated meat. Although Sinclair's novel *The Jungle* (1906) began as stories about a Packingtown strike in Chicago for the socialist *Appeal to Reason*, the socialist movement played only a minor role in investigative journalism. Self-styled progressives among middle-class

The Great Muckrakers

The voices and points of view of the great muckrakers were compelling. Ida B. Tarbell, whose father was ruined in the oil business, wrote judiciously about the family nemesis, John D. Rockefeller, in her 1902–1905 series on the Standard Oil Company for *McClure's Magazine*. Another *McClure's* author, the elegant and cosmopolitan Lincoln Steffens, won the confidence of crooks (many of whom he liked) to write *The Shame of the Cities* (1904). If readers tired of the moral complexities that Steffens loved, they could find politicians flayed in "The Treason of the Senate," a 1906 series for *Cosmopolitan* by the popular novelist David Graham Phillips. From 1907 to 1908 Ray Stannard Baker brought race back into focus as a white man writing "Following the Color Line" for *American Magazine*.

Republicans and Democrats were the sustaining audience for muckraking. What Roosevelt saw as "reckless" coverage, a modern reader might well find cautious; muckraking journalists seldom used stunts or concealment. (Even Sinclair told no lies to gain access to the slaughterhouses, though he did use mild deception.)

Injustices alone do not explain the timing of the muckraking crusade; thus historians have debated the relative effects of psychological factors and business pressures in setting its course. Most of the social problems muckrakers wrote about had been worse a generation earlier. Fear of bloody class struggle had haunted the industrial United States; with the improved economy, it was easier to face social problems. Suddenly, stories of injustice sold magazines. The muckrakers had been reared in a Protestant faith that they had come to question. Like other middle-class Americans from small towns, they watched new wealth emerge and worried over their status; at the same time, new forms of poverty were spreading through rapidly growing cities. Thus stories about how the United States might save itself from corruption had therapeutic appeal.

A Change of Course

Advertisers grew uncomfortable with critiques of corporate America and pressured some magazines for a different editorial line. But the most powerful limit on muckraking was probably the taste for novelty that affects most trends in popular culture. After a dozen years of success, muckraking seemed stale. The coming of World War I put men and women trained as muckrakers to work on a new, exciting story. Appropriately, President Woodrow Wilson's top aide for public opinion, George Creel, was a veteran muckraker who shifted his talents to selling the war.

The first muckrakers often shared in the work of putting out a magazine. In the years between the World Wars, this tradition was kept alive by independent spirits such as Sinclair and George Seldes, who were often self-published. Nationally syndicated columnists such as Drew Pearson (succeeded by Jack Anderson) carried on the muckraking tradition. Similarly, during the Cold War, I. F. Stone wore the label of muckraker proudly as he skewered U.S. foreign policy. By the 1950s *muckraker* had become a synonym for lone wolf.

A revival of muckraking started in general-interest magazines early in the 1960s. Ben Bagdikian found millions of readers for stories about race and poverty in the *Saturday Evening Post*; these stories were published in a collection in 1964. The socialist Michael Harrington earned national attention for his 1962 work, *The Other America: Poverty in the United States,* by way of Dwight Macdonald's sympathetic review in the *New Yorker.* That magazine opened up a fresh area for reform with a series on the environment by Rachel Carson that was later published as *Silent Spring* (1962). For the first time since the beginning of the century, a reader could find stories about the social failures of the United States in mainstream media, next to ads for the latest luxuries. Social movements of the 1960s—civil rights, antiwar, feminist, environmental—sustained this editorial focus. Many newspapers set up investigative units. In book publishing, celebrity status could be gained through a single exposé, as with Jessica Mitford's writing on the funeral industry, *The American Way of Death* (1963), and Ralph Nader's critique of the automobile industry, *Unsafe at Any Speed* (1965). Television made many of these stories known to a much larger public. The most successful news show in U.S. broadcasting, *60 Minutes,* which began in 1968 on CBS, has been sustained by the same type of investigations that worried Theodore Roosevelt.

In an age of splintering audiences, muckraking became more difficult. Investigative reporters have

Upton Sinclair. LIBRARY OF CONGRESS

been animated by the hope that the injustices they find will become common knowledge. But daily papers, network television, and national magazines reach smaller shares of the public than they once did. A magazine such as *Mother Jones* (1975–) had no realistic hope of matching the circulation of early muckraking. The popularity of economic deregulation in the last third of the twentieth century was also discouraging. Muckraking assumed that there were government solutions to injustice. But muckrakers need not despair. Investigative reporting is likely to thrive again with more inclusive communications networks and the redesign of government. The exposure of arbitrary power remains one of the soundest tools of journalism.

BIBLIOGRAPHY

Fitzpatrick, Ellen F. ed. *Muckraking: Three Landmark Articles.* Boston: Bedford, 1994.

Leonard, Thomas C. *The Power of the Press: The Birth of American Political Reporting.* New York: Oxford University Press, 1986.

Steffens, Lincoln. *The Autobiography of Lincoln Steffens.* 1931. New York: Harcourt Brace, 1958.

THOMAS C. LEONARD

See also **Journalism.**

MUDGETT, HERMAN. *See* Holmes, H. H.

MUGGING. *See* Robbery.

MURDER. *See* Homicide.

MURDER, INC.

Murder, Inc., a 1930s New York City gang, composed of Italians and Jews from the Brownsville–East New York section of the borough of Brooklyn, was notorious for having "shot its way to the top." Known for much of its early history as the Combination, it was christened Murder, Inc., in 1940 by the reporter Harry Feeny in the *New York World Telegraph.*

From its modest headquarters in Midnight Rose's candy store at the intersection of Livonia and Saratoga Avenues, the ethnically diverse criminal outfit engaged in a variety of illicit activities, from loan sharking and strong-arming ("We break heads and strikes") to controlling the supply of pinball machines to neighborhood pool halls and candy stores. Labor racketeering also generated a great deal of income for the gang's members. As Abe Reles, their flamboyant leader, boastfully told the authorities, the Combination had the fruit market, the van movers, the luncheonette workers, and the painters and plumbers unions. From time to time, Reles also worked in tandem with the labor racketeer Louis Lepke, supplying him with the manpower—the *shtarkes* ("strong men," in Yiddish)—to intimidate recalcitrant manufacturers and union leaders.

Later still, when Lepke was sought by the special prosecutor Thomas Dewey and Federal Bureau of Investigation director J. Edgar Hoover, Reles not only supplied Lepke with hiding places but also served as the racketeer's "contact person," or conduit, with the outside world. As Lepke's chances of evading capture eroded, the increasingly desperate racketeer had Reles and his men ruthlessly murder his putative enemies. Using guns obtained from leading Brooklyn mobster Albert Anastasia and following carefully orchestrated plans, the Combination murdered an estimated eighty men at Lepke's behest, thus earning for itself the new name Murder, Inc. Anything but haphazard or spontaneous, this was "wholesale murder by contract." As Reles liked to put it, he was in the "murder business."

Lepke's association with the swaggering Brooklyn gang leader proved to be his undoing. Following Reles's arrest in 1940 for the murder years earlier of a small-time Brooklyn hoodlum named Red Alpert, Reles turned state's witness. His testimony, which filled twenty-five stenographic notebooks, linked both Anastasia and Lepke to the Brownsville gang and detailed its murderous ways. It also helped to convict Lepke of the murder of a former garment trucker, Joseph Rosen, an offense for which the racketeer was electrocuted in 1944. Reles also came to a sorry end. In November 1941, while in police custody in the Half Moon Hotel on the Coney Island boardwalk, he was found dead on a ledge outside his room. The circumstances surrounding his death were never determined.

BIBLIOGRAPHY

Cohen, Rich. *Tough Jews*. New York: Simon and Schuster, 1998.

Joselit, Jenna Weissman. *Our Gang: Jewish Crime and the New York Jewish Community, 1900–1940*. Bloomington: Indiana University Press, 1983.

Turkus, Burton B., and Sid Feder. *Murder, Inc.* New York: Farrar, Straus, 1951.

JENNA WEISSMAN JOSELIT

See also **Lansky, Meyer; Lepke, Louis; Organized Crime; Siegel, Benjamin "Bugsy".**

MUSIC

This entry is divided into three parts: Classical, Musicals, and Popular.

CLASSICAL

Classical music refers here to music derived from existing European traditions and intended for performance in a formal public venue such as (for most of the twentieth century) a concert hall, theater, or opera house. Except for opera, such performances were rare in the United States until well into the nineteenth century. The separation of "classical" music, that is, concert music and opera, from various "popular" musics began in the 1840s and was well established by the late nineteenth century for concert music, somewhat later for opera. The distinction's development paralleled the emergence and growth of Progressive Era social and economic hierarchies. Although the formal institutions of classical music (symphony orchestras, opera companies, chamber music organizations) remained largely in place at the end of the twentieth century, the cultural distinctions associated with those institutions were breaking down and re-forming, this time in response rather than resistance to increasing societal diversity. In addition, classical music in America has represented violence in numerous ways, some of which will be described here.

Overview

The classical-versus-popular dichotomy is artificial because it does not reflect the array of music always present in American life; moreover, the boundaries have never been entirely clear. Early European explorers and settlers used music in their various religious practices, formal military observances, and for dancing. Musicians regularly took part in theatrical productions of all kinds from the late eighteenth century on. A large amount of music composed for home and community use was marginalized by the growth of mass media in the twentieth century. The music of Native Americans and African Americans began to be integrated into concert music only late in the nineteenth century; such integration remained controversial until the late 1900s because it tended to blur the classical-popular polarity.

Opera, now thought of as a type of classical music, had a wide popular audience throughout the nineteenth century and into the twentieth. Obstructed sight lines and limited space in the gallery of the new Astor Place Opera House in New York City excluded workers from this venue for opera and Shakespeare. This was an underlying factor in the famous Astor Place riots of 1849. Large popular audiences continued to attend elsewhere, however. In 1850–1851, P. T. Barnum promoted a concert tour by Jenny Lind, the "Swedish Nightingale," who made her reputation in opera and sang before enormous audiences. Her success, along with a carefully cultivated image of feminine virtue, made it easier and safer for later women to appear in public as performers. Theodore Thomas, who conducted orchestras and toured with them from the 1860s until his death in 1905, greatly influenced the development and repertoire of American orchestras. He worked tirelessly to persuade his audiences to sit quietly and attentively through his performances, a behavior pattern that, once established, has continued to keep audience reactions at formal concerts relatively restrained. Performances by singers and instrumentalists that the audience (relatively homogeneous and generally older in the late twentieth century) considers substandard may draw murmurs of protest, but applause and cheering commonly reward virtuosic singing.

Through experiments with sounds and forms, generations of composers in the twentieth century sought to expand the repertoire and expressive range of formal concert music or to call attention to increasing societal violence by attacking what some saw as the social and political irrelevance of concert life. Starting in the 1920s, the result was the growth of a much smaller audience for the specifically "new." In the 1960s and 1970s, Fluxus, a loose coalition of visual artists, poets, and musicians organized "happenings" that attempted to break down the boundaries between the arts. These events, which often abandoned conventional music notation, sometimes involved violence. Music paper with bullet holes and assaults on performers, audiences, and instruments were occasionally prescribed. Annea Lockwood's literally titled "Burning Piano" (1970, one of a series of *Piano Transplants*) is a spectacular example. Hostile responses to modern or avant-garde music are often reflected in critical reporting, and audiences have responded by leaving (sometimes noisily) or not attending in the first place. The violence or experimentalism of late twentieth-century American music never found a large audience on its own, but the effects created by avant-garde American composers found a very large audience in film and television scores, where audiences came to expect novel effects that heighten tension or support various modes of violence.

Expressions of Violence in Concert Music

Theoretically, music is no more than sound organized over time and is incapable of much in the way of representation. Yet the power of music to suggest or influence emotions and psychological states has been recognized since the time of Plato. In fact, music always exists in cultural contexts that are loaded with signs and symbols. The principles of repetition, variation, and contrast, common to a very wide range of musical styles, can easily suggest conflict and even violence. Thus a great deal of music may be understood as projecting or even inciting psychological and physical violence. Suggestive titles may reinforce such interpretations.

The Battle of Trenton (James Hewitt, 1804–1805) for piano is an example of music about war that is literally programmatic. In a late-eighteenth-century tonal idiom reminiscent of Haydn, it changes melody, tempo, and rhythmic patterns across some twenty-one short sections to fit a narrative indicated by captions in the music. Some of the captions are: "Washington's March," "ardor of the Americans at landing," "trumpets sound the charge," "attack," "cannons," "bombs" (occasional low-pitched notes below a fast-moving accompanying figure), "the Hessians surrender themselves prisoners of war," "grief of the Americans for the loss of their comrades killed in the engagement" (in the minor mode), and "general rejoicing." Other narrative battle pieces followed in a similar style.

Nineteenth-century romantic "tone poems" (most often for orchestra or piano solo) with suggestive titles often reach one or more tumultuous climaxes near their middle or end. Although much less literal, these are sometimes given titles suggesting battles. Anthony Philip Heinrich's *The Ornithological Combat of Kings; or, The Condor of the Andes and the Eagle of the Cordilleras* (first version, 1847) is a work for a large orchestra in which the movements are entitled successively "Conflict," "Repose," "Combat" and "Victory of the Condor." Its rhetoric is that of an inventive four-movement, romantic symphony, but little beyond its romantic rhetoric suggests the violence implicit in its extravagant title. Albert C. Sweet's *Battle of San Juan Hill* (1909), which memorialized the famous cavalry charge, was frequently performed by the Ringling Brothers Circus Band.

Martial elements sometimes remain (consider the trumpet calls of the cavalry coming to the rescue in the 1939 film *Stagecoach*), but much twentieth-century music about war emphasizes destruction, chaos, and loss of life. Charles Ives's song "In Flanders Fields" (1917) reflects on both the patriotism and suffering of World War I. Muffled dissonant low-pitched chords frame the setting with a funerary drumbeat. The piano runs together fragments of the "Marseillaise," "My Country 'Tis of Thee," "God Save the King," and "Columbia, the Gem of the Ocean" to illustrate the collective idealism of France, Britain, and the United States. The dissonant accompaniment and the voice, which sometimes sings scraps of the patriotic tunes but more often declaims the text with its own intense melody, makes the human cost of war very clear indeed. The same composer's "They Are There" gives another, more excited, vicarious view of the conflict. The vocabulary of war widened further for World War II and beyond. Bernard Herrmann, better known for his scores to Alfred Hitchcock's movie thrillers, composed *For the Fallen* (1943) for the New York Philharmonic. Marc Blitzstein's *Airborne Symphony* (1946) for orchestra, male chorus, and narrator celebrates the power and pathos of the war with lines such as "the planes, the planes, you cannot see the sky for planes" and "I take my pen in hand, Emily," the latter in the style of a popular ballad of the day. Leonard Bernstein's *Kaddish* Symphony (1963), really an oratorio, employs instrumental and vocal forces in settings of Hebrew texts in memory of Holocaust victims. R. Murray Schafer's *Threnody* (1966), a memorial to the legacy of nuclear war, begins with electronic sounds so loud that audience members must wear earplugs to avoid physical damage to their hearing.

Works for concert band depicting the violence of war go particularly far afield from the marches and fanfares of military bands in their expressive range. Karel Husa's *Music for Prague* (1968) depicts the Soviet invasion of Prague; his *Apotheosis of This Earth* (1970) depicts "man's brutal possession and misuse of nature's beauty." At the climax of the second movement ("Tragedy of Destruction"), the percussion falls into quiescence as the rest of the ensemble takes over its bursts of staccato sixteenth notes in overlapping cacophonous patterns.

Composers have often chosen myths and legends from various cultures that depict violence, sometimes suggested only by their titles: Samuel Barber's ballet *The Serpent Heart* yielded an orchestral suite entitled *Medea* (1947), and Diamanda Galás composed *Medea tarantula* for solo voice (1977). Ruth Schonthal's opera *Jocasta* (1998) tells the myth of Oedipus from the point of view of the hero's mother/wife. The biblical story of Judith and Holofernes is told in an oratorio/lyric drama by George Whitefield Chadwick (1901) and in *Judith, Choreographic Poem for Orchestra* (1950) by William Schuman. Aaron Copland's ballet setting of American folk hero Billy the Kid's story (1938) contains violent music as well as violent gestures by

the dancers. Chou Wen-chung's *And the Fallen Petals* (1955) is based on an eighth-century Chinese poem that depicts a furious storm with metaphysical overtones. Manmade mechanical violence, seemingly inappropriate for musical settings, is celebrated in Ives's *Over the Pavements* (1906–1917), which suggests the sound of carriage wheels on cobblestones, and the instrumental fireworks of *The Fourth of July* (1913) as well as in Frederick Shepherd Converse's *Flivver Ten Million* (1926) for orchestra, honoring the ten millionth Model-T Ford, and George Antheil's *Ballet mécanique* (1926, initially intended for a silent film), for eight pianos, player piano, two airplane propellers, and percussion. Nancy Van de Vate's *Chernobyl* (1987) for orchestra dramatically memorializes the peacetime nuclear disaster.

Expressions of Violence in Opera

Physical violence, often in the form of murder, is a staple plot element in opera, where the job of the composer is to heighten the impact of the story through music. Violence-laden operas by European composers (*Lucia de Lammermoor, Carmen, Il Trovatore,* and so on) were very widely performed, often in heavily cut or adapted English-language versions, in nineteenth-century America. In their original languages and more elaborate productions, they soon became staples of the elite American musical scene. Operas by American composers are similarly violent. In Victor Herbert's *Natoma* (1911) the villain is conveniently murdered by a Native American woman, herself abandoned by the white male hero. Mary Carr Moore's *Narcissa* (1912) ends with the multiple murders of missionaries in the Pacific Northwest. But Herbert's opera never had the success of his numerous, frothy operettas, and Moore's opera was seen by very few. Later twentieth-century American operas were more successful. In George Gershwin's *Porgy and Bess* (1935), a knifing sets the plot in motion. William Grant Still's *Troubled Island* (libretto by Langston Hughes; produced in 1949) is set in early nineteenth-century revolutionary Haiti; its hero is assassinated at the end. Leonard Bernstein's *West Side Story* (libretto by Stephen Sondheim; 1957) retells Shakespeare's *Romeo and Juliet* in a New York City setting with competing Puerto Rican and white gangs. Carlisle Floyd's *Of Mice and Men* (1970) intensifies the tragic anomalies of Steinbeck's novel. In *X: The Life and Times of Malcolm X* (libretto by Thulani Davis; 1986), Anthony Davis recounts Malcolm X's career. John Adams's *The*

Scene from *The Death of Klinghoffer*. LARRY MERKLE FOR SAN FRANCISCO OPERA

Death of Klinghoffer (libretto by Alice Goodman; 1991) is based on the 1985 hijacking of a tourist ship by Palestinian terrorists in which a wheelchair-bound American Jewish tourist is murdered offstage in the course of a fearsome orchestral storm.

BIBLIOGRAPHY

Davies, Stephen. *Musical Meaning and Expression.* Ithaca, N.Y.: Cornell University Press, 1994.

Hall, Charles J. *A Chronicle of American Music, 1700–1995.* New York: Schirmer Books, 1996.

Hitchcock, H. Wiley. *Music in the United States: A Historical Introduction.* 3d ed. Englewood Cliffs, N.J.: Prentice-Hall, 1986.

Hitchcock, H. Wiley, and Stanley Sadie, eds. *The New Grove Dictionary of American Music.* 4 vols. London: Macmillan, 1986.

Levine, Lawrence W. *Highbrow/Lowbrow: The Emergence of Cultural Hierarchy in America.* Cambridge, Mass.: Harvard University Press, 1988.

Sadie, Stanley, ed. *The New Grove Dictionary of Opera.* 4 vols. London: Macmillan, 1992.

Slonimsky, Nicolas. *Music Since 1900.* 4th ed. New York: Scribners, 1971.

CATHERINE PARSONS SMITH

See also **Dance; Theater.**

MUSICALS

The American musical evolved as a distinct theatrical genre in the early twentieth century. A vehicle for light entertainment in its early years (e.g., *Babes in Toyland,* 1903), the musical soon began to treat complex, serious themes and increasingly became a source for intellectual stimulation and moral reflection. A dramatic genre, the musical necessarily contains conflict. In romantic, comedic musicals, conflict is usually limited to social obstacles confronting its lover-protagonists. More substantive musicals, beginning with *Showboat* (1927), however, address issues of aggression and social injustice and require the staging of explicit violence.

In *Showboat* the primary pair of lovers is finally reunited with help from their friend, Julie, a mulatto woman married to a white man and attempting to "pass" as white in the world of the musical theater. The implicit violence of anti-miscegenation law leaves Julie no choice but to leave the boat when her secret is revealed. In *South Pacific* (1949) Lieutenant Cable's song explains how racial prejudice develops:

> You've got to be taught
> Before it's too late
> . . . .
> To hate all the people
> Your relatives hate . . . .

The song provides a revealing commentary on Cable's unwillingness to marry the Polynesian girl he loves and on Nurse Nellie's initial rejection of the widower de Becque when she learns of his half-native children. In *The King and I* (1951) racial violence is portrayed in the stylized production of *The Small House of Uncle Thomas*, written by the King's most recent harem acquisition, Tuptim, and based on Harriet Beecher Stowe's novel of social injustice *Uncle Tom's Cabin*. More direct violence, however, occurs when the King starts to whip Tuptim after she attempts escape from his harem. He is restrained from carrying out the whipping, however, by his increasing awareness of social injustice, gained through his relationship with the British governess Anna.

In the untamed West of *Oklahoma!* (1943), the female characters Aunt Eller and Laurey are strong and assertive but nonetheless subject to violence, as shown in Laurey's dream of being coerced into prostitution. More overtly violent is the competitive behavior of Laurey's two suitors, Curly and Jud. They discharge their guns in Jud's cabin in a display of daring rivalry, and Jud, jealous over losing Laurey to her husband-to-be, fires the haystacks on the evening of Laurey's wedding. Significantly, Jud's death while fighting with Curly is accidental; Curly, the hero, remains identifiably aligned with moral principles.

The hero of *Destry Rides Again* (1959), another Western musical, refuses to carry a gun even though his father died from a gunshot wound. As newly appointed sheriff of Bottleneck, Destry intends to "clean up the town" unarmed.

Both *Destry* and *Oklahoma!* contain compelling portrayals of violence through dance. The pacifistic Destry arrestingly disarms Bottleneck's whip-wielding villains in the "whip ballet," and a threatening tornado is the background to the bordello scene portrayed in Agnes de Mille's choreography of Laurey's dream sequence. *West Side Story* (1957), too, contains danced violence—the rumble between the Jets and the Sharks and the suggested near-rape of Anita by the Jets when she attempts to deliver Maria's urgent message to Tony. Even Andrew Lloyd Webber's *Cats* (1981), a family musical with engaging feline personalities, contains vivid violence danced by the evil Macavity, the "Napoleon of crime." According to some adherents of René Girard's mimetic theory, the origins of both music and dance may be located in the spontaneous, first dance around the first scapegoated victim of group murder. It should come as no surprise, then, that the use of dance to portray violence in the musical seems particularly appropriate and even "natural."

War—violence on its largest scale—provides the context of many musicals, including *Johnny Johnson* (1936), *South Pacific* (1941), *The Sound of Music* (1959), *Cabaret* (1966), and *Miss Saigon* (1989). Kurt Weill's *Johnny Johnson* is a Chaplinesque satire of World War I in which at one point Johnny, having discovered that the Allied generals have ordered an offensive, douses them with

James Stewart and Marlene Dietrich in *Destry Rides Again* (1939).

laughing gas. Under the influence of the gas, the "laughing generals" countermand the order and call off the attack. Although some scholars criticized *Miss Saigon* for its derivative music and reliance on spectacle, the show explores the violent repercussions of the Vietnam War on the lives of the American soldier, Chris; his wife; and his former lover, Kim, left behind, pregnant, at the fall of Saigon. Kim's desperation in the years after the war leads her to kill her Vietnamese fiancé to prevent him from murdering Chris's son. She later commits suicide in the hope that Chris and his wife will take the child to America.

Finally, Stephen Sondheim's *Sweeney Todd* (1979) and *Assassins* (1991) are dark productions whose entire raison d'être seems to be the exploration of violence and its motives. Todd, the throat-slitting barber, enveloped in a score that often assaults the ear with unpleasantly loud dissonances, enacts private revenge for the violent wrongs inflicted on him and his family. He goes too far, however, unknowingly killing his wife, whose supposed death he had been trying to avenge. *Assassins,* an antimusical about antiheroes, comprises a study of assassins and would-be assassins of American presidents interacting with each other through darkly satirical dialogue that, according to Stephen Banfield, "questions the constructs of history" and "stresses the relativity of viewpoints." The songs of the disaffected assassins force us, says Banfield, "to confront popular music as the opium of the dispossessed, . . . sustaining countless illusions, countless 'lives of quiet desperation' " (pp. 56, 58).

But for all its dark probing, *Assassins,* like its predecessors, is a work of truthfulness and integrity, opposed to violence, although contaminated by the very thing it seeks to overcome or understand. Musicals are, in the words of John Gardner, "moral fiction." They may entertain and delight, but musicals also portray conflict and violence in a moral context, seeking ever more difficult truths throughout the history of the genre.

BIBLIOGRAPHY

Banfield, Stephen. *Sondheim's Broadway Musicals.* Ann Arbor, Mich.: University of Michigan Press, 1993.

Behr, Edward. *The Story of Miss Saigon.* London: Jonathan Cape; New York: Arcade, 1991.

Bordman, Gerald Martin. *American Musical Theatre: A Chronicle.* 2d ed. New York: Oxford University Press, 1992.

Flinn, Denny Martin. *Musical: A Grand Tour: The Rise, Glory, and Fall of an American Institution.* New York: Schirmer; London: Prentice Hall International, 1997.

Gardner, John. *On Moral Fiction.* New York: Basic Books, 1978.

Girard, René. *Violence and the Sacred.* Translated by Patrick Gregory. Baltimore: Johns Hopkins University Press, 1977.

Green, Stanley. *Broadway Musicals, Show by Show.* 4th ed. Revised and updated by Kay Green. Milwaukee, Wis.: H. Leonard, 1993.

Swain, Joseph Peter. *The Broadway Musical: A Critical and Musical Survey.* New York: Oxford University Press, 1990.

JULIA W. SHINNICK

See also **Performance Art; Theater.**

POPULAR

Since its beginnings in the mid-1950s, rock and roll has been associated with violence. Rock musicians have been both victims and perpetrators of violence, and this has been reflected in the lyrics of numerous songs. Moreover, the violent content of many songs, coupled with the spirited moods of live performances, has often precipitated violent behavior in stadiums and concert halls around the world. The music also has been linked to teenage suicide, gang activity, and intimidation by music-industry executives. All of these factors have contributed to the perception that rock and roll and popular music are violent by nature.

Violence by Musicians

Some of the more ruthless forms of violence were already part of the fabric of popular music by the early 1930s. Robert Johnson (1911–1938), for example, one of the first and most important of the Mississippi Delta bluesmen, played haunting songs about desperation, loneliness, and the anguish of a drifter's existence. He wrote many important blues standards, including "Crossroads" and "Love in Vain," and his music is credited with having profoundly influenced the work of Eric Clapton, Muddy Waters, and the Rolling Stones. But Johnson made scores of enemies during his lifetime, and he became the target of many envious musicians and jealous husbands. On 13 August 1938, against the advice of a fellow musician, Johnson drank from an open whiskey bottle and died three days later. The whiskey had been laced with strychnine.

A number of early popular musicians were the perpetrators of violence, and their songs often depicted the violent worlds in which they lived. For example, Leadbelly (c. 1885–1949), known as the king of the twelve-string guitar, led the kind of troubled life that was not uncommon among his peers. As a child, he stopped arguments between his parents by threatening them with a shotgun. In 1918, at the age of thirty-three, he received a thirty-year prison sentence for killing a man. A few years later, however, after writing a song pleading the Texas governor Pat Neff for a pardon, he was released from prison. Leadbelly's hollering vocal delivery echoed his time behind bars, but eventually he was back in prison for attempted murder. An updated version of the song he had first written for Governor Neff earned him a second pardon.

Violence was not uncommon among some musicians later in the twentieth century, either, even while performing onstage. In 1965, for example, Mick Avory, the drummer for the British rock band the Kinks, assaulted the band's guitarist Dave Davies with a microphone stand. In 1973 the Everly Brothers had a falling-out on the stage of the John Wayne Theater at Knott's Berry Farm in Buena Park, California. Phil Everly smashed his guitar and walked off the stage, leaving his brother, Don, to announce the duo's breakup.

Musicians have even attacked members of the audience. In 1978, for example, Sid Vicious of the British punk band the Sex Pistols assaulted a spectator with his bass guitar during a show in San Antonio, Texas. Similarly, during a Rolling Stones tour in 1982, a member of the audience jumped onto the stage and headed toward Keith Richards during his guitar solo. Not knowing the fan's intentions, Richards slammed his guitar over the man's head and then quickly resumed his solo. Such incidents suggest that the energy of the music may ignite emotions on the stage.

Audience Violence

Audience violence also has a long and prominent history. Brawls in roadhouses and juke joints (small, inexpensive establishments where people could eat and listen to music) were commonplace during the 1930s and 1940s, and similar kinds of violence were evident at rock-and-roll concerts in the 1950s and 1960s. Much of the violence grew out of arguments, heavy drinking, or overcrowding—not unlike the fights that were commonplace at sporting events at the end of the twentieth century. The most tragic incident occurred at a concert in Cincinnati, Ohio, by the British rock band the Who on 3 December 1979, when eleven fans were trampled to death after a stampede to claim unreserved seats.

During the peak of England's punk-rock movement in the mid-1970s, audience violence took a new direction. Fans began to dance wildly in the audience. Punk rock's fast, abrasive songs led to a dance called the *pogo*, in which a person jumped up and down repeatedly. Pogoers often bumped into other fans, which led to the slam-dancing craze, in which revelers deliberately crashed into one another. Slam dancing often caused injuries and fights.

Although the pogo and slam dance were largely of British origin, they were adopted and reinvented by audiences in the United States. In the late 1980s and the 1990s rock-music fans at concerts in the United States participated in moshing. Probably a mispronunciation of the British slang word *mashing*, moshing included not only frenzied dancing but also stage diving, with the musicians and fans diving from the stage into the audience, and crowd surfing, in which, lying flat, a person is lifted up to ride across the crowd's raised hands. Bloody noses and broken ankles became commonplace among moshers, and female fans complained about being groped as they floated above the crowd. In 1996 one young woman was killed at a Smashing Pumpkins concert in Dublin, Ireland, when she was crushed by a surging mosh pit. Several deaths have also been reported in the United States. Members of rock bands have differing opinions about moshing. Billy Corgan, the lead singer of Smashing Pumpkins, repeatedly condemned it, whereas Eddie Vedder, the lead singer of Pearl Jam, participated in stage diving.

Altamont

The Woodstock rock festival, which took place near Woodstock, New York, on 15–17 August 1969, was organized to celebrate peace and came to represent the close of the 1960s era of cultural change. The counterpoint to Woodstock occurred on 6 December 1969 at San Francisco's Altamont Motor Speedway, a festival remembered by music and social historians alike as a dark and ugly event that symbolized the end of a violent decade in which John F. Kennedy, Martin Luther King, Jr., and Robert F. Kennedy were murdered. The Rolling Stones had decided to cap their highly successful 1969 tour with a free concert at Altamont. On the advice of the San Francisco–based rock group the Grateful Dead, the Stones hired the Hell's Angels motorcycle club to provide security. The Hell's Angels,

Hell's Angels clash with concertgoers at Altamont, as captured in the 1970 documentary *Gimme Shelter.* PHOTOFEST

reportedly under the influence of amphetamines and alcohol, became a menacing presence, provoking fights and taunting the crowd.

From the outset, the event was fraught with violence. Marty Balin, a singer for Jefferson Airplane, was knocked unconscious by a member of the Hell's Angels while the band performed a warm-up set. And even before the Rolling Stones went onstage, their singer Mick Jagger was attacked by a fan who shouted, "I hate you, I want to kill you." Violence continued throughout the show. The band stopped playing several times but could calm neither the Hell's Angels nor the audience. As the band played, a young black man, who may have been wielding a pistol, was stabbed to death by a Hell's Angel. The murder was filmed by a camera crew making a rock-music documentary, which was released two years later as *Gimme Shelter.*

Violence in Lyrics

Violence is not confined to concert halls and stadiums. Song lyrics have been blamed for the deaths of several rock fans. The heavy-metal star Ozzy Osbourne has been sued by three sets of parents, claiming that their children committed suicide after listening to his song "Suicide Solution." Released in 1980 on his album *Blizzard of Oz,* the song mourns the death of AC/DC singer Bon

Scott, who died after a night of binge drinking. Because "Suicide Solution" has clear antisuicide, anti-substance-abuse messages, Osbourne was exonerated in all three lawsuits. However, many song lyrics are explicitly and intentionally violent.

Rap, a dance-based form of music in which a rapper talks in both rhyme and rhythm, began in New York City's South Bronx during the mid-1970s. Early rap lyrics have no violent content. In fact, the first rap songs are about partying and having a good time. But as the music evolved, it was influenced by the disillusion and violence in U.S. inner cities. Gangster rap, a subgenre, is characterized by violent lyrical content: loud, angry vocals and an inner-city backdrop of recorded police sirens and gunshots. Other themes include misogyny and gay bashing. References to gang activity are pervasive, the result of many rappers' being closely tied to gangs and gang members.

Although popularized by the Los Angeles rap group N.W.A. (Niggaz with Attitude), gangster rap was started by Schooly D on his 1986 song "PSK—What Does It Mean?" (PSK refers to Parkside Killers, a gang in Philadelphia.) In 1988 N.W.A. released its landmark album *Straight Outta Compton,* which went multiplatinum and brought gangster rap into the mainstream. The record included such songs as "F**k tha Police" and "Gangsta Gangsta," which gave the listener a heavy dose of the gang violence and rage that were rampant on the streets of South Central Los Angeles.

The violence depicted in rap lyrics became most evident in the lives (and deaths) of well-known rappers. The East Coast rapper Biggie Smalls was shot and killed in his car on a Los Angeles street on 9 March 1997, just six months after West Coast rap star Tupac Shakur was gunned down. The press reported that the shootings resulted from a feud between West Coast and East Coast rappers.

Death Row Records, a West Coast rap record label that earned more than $325 million in just four years, was repeatedly accused of using violence and intimidation in the course of conducting business. One record promoter, for example, claimed that several Death Row executives strapped him to a chair, assaulted him with broken bottles, and forced him to drink a jar of urine.

Opinion is divided as to how the music industry should deal with violent and misogynist song lyrics. C. DeLores Tucker, the chairperson of the National Political Congress of Black Women, told a 1994 congressional panel investigating the effects of gangster rap that "the record industry is out of control. If it has to be regulated, so be it." Although parental advisory warning labels are placed on records with explicit lyrics, many record executives believed that ratings and labels were not the solution. In the mid-1990s Senate majority leader Robert Dole led a congressional attack against the record companies that were releasing gangster rap. He and former education secretary William Bennett put pressure on Time Warner Inc., which decided to divest its stake in Interscope Records, a company that released numerous gangster-rap albums. Some public-school systems banned students from wearing gangster-style fashions as a way to discourage violence.

BIBLIOGRAPHY

Decurtis, Henke, and George Warren, eds. *The Rolling Stone Illustrated History of Rock and Roll.* New York: Random House, 1992.

Foege, Alec. "Rap at the Crossroads: Why Rap Music Is Surviving Gang Violence." *Playboy,* January 1998.

Guralnick, Peter. *Searching for Robert Johnson.* New York: Dutton, 1989.

Palmer, Robert. *The Rolling Stones.* Garden City, N.Y.: Doubleday, 1983.

Ro, Ronin. *Have Gun Will Travel: The Spectacular Rise and Violent Fall of Death Row Records.* Garden City, N.Y.: Doubleday, 1998.

CRAIG J. INCIARDI

See also **Dance; Popular Culture; Television: Historical Overview.**

MUSLIMS

The history of the world has been marked by violent episodes that have religion as a common theme. Despite being a secular society, the United States has been no less a stage for such incidents. While violence between Muslims and non-Muslim Americans spans the globe, this article deals specifically with acts of violence that occurred on U.S. soil. It would be unfair, however, to characterize the following episodes as the norm. Most Americans harbor no animosity toward Muslims, nor do most Muslims toward non-Muslim Americans. In fact, the root of the word *Islam* means "peace."

The Council on American-Islamic Relations estimates that there are between six and eight million Muslims in America, most of whom are U.S. citizens and 43 percent of whom are African Americans. While every major religion is marked by important divisions, for the sake of simplicity the following discussion will distinguish only between Black and non-Black Muslims in the United States, making no further distinction among these diverse groups, such as Shiite and Sunni.

Black Muslims

The term *Black Muslims* signifies members of the African American religious movement known as the American Muslim Mission, founded by W. D. Fard in Detroit in the early 1930s. The movement, which eventually became known as the Nation of Islam (NOI), called for the separation of blacks and whites and the establishment of an all-black state. The NOI gained significant notoriety during the 1960s Civil Rights movement under the leadership of Elijah Muhammad. While there were scattered violent confrontations between Black Muslims and police since the inception of the movement in the 1930s, the most violence occurred during and after the 1960s. Violence involving Black Muslims consisted predominantly of clashes with police, struggles among factions within the NOI, and conflicts between splinter groups and the NOI.

The passive, nonviolent opposition to racism preached in the 1960s by Martin Luther King, Jr., contrasted with the voices of militant black leaders

Elijah Muhammad addresses Black Muslims in Chicago, 1966. CORBIS/BETTMANN

associated with the NOI, especially that of its spokesperson, Malcolm X. One evening in April 1957 Malcolm led a vigil outside a Harlem police station after a Muslim named Hinton Johnson had been brutalized by police officers. The incident led to the galvanization of the movement in New York City and its rapid spread across the country. As the movement grew, incidents of violence became more frequent. On 27 April 1962 one Muslim was killed and fourteen people were injured (including eight policemen) after the police harassment of two Black Muslims near a mosque in Los Angeles.

On 8 March 1964 Malcolm formally announced his departure from the NOI, and on 21 February 1965 he was assassinated. All persons convicted of his murder were followers of Elijah Muhammad, but many believed that the Federal Bureau of Investigation played a role in instigating the murder. Two days after Malcolm's assassination, an NOI mosque in Harlem was bombed, and the following day another NOI mosque in San Francisco was set on fire.

In 1971 violence again rocked the NOI owing to internal tensions between Raymond Sharieff, Elijah Muhammad's son-in-law, and a small splinter group in Chicago. Two members of the splinter group were killed. In 1972 gunfire erupted during a Black Muslim rally in Baton Rouge, Louisiana, and five people were killed, including two sheriff's

deputies. Of the thirty-one people wounded, fifteen were policemen, four were bystanders, and one was a television newscaster. In 1973, in response to a clash with the NOI, twelve Black-Muslim gunmen took 134 persons hostage in three buildings in Washington, D.C., including the City Hall. After negotiations, which included representatives from Islamic nations, the hostages were released.

In what became known as the Zebra case, twenty-three random attacks resulting in at least eighty deaths were committed in 1973–1974 by a Black Muslim splinter group known as the Death Angels. In order to "earn their wings," prospective members were required to kill a specified number of whites. Violence committed by and among Black Muslims tailed off later in the 1970s, but police brutality against Black Muslims continued.

Non-Black Muslims

From the 1970s through the 1990s, U.S. foreign policy was the bane of Islamic fundamentalists worldwide, making Americans abroad the targets of terrorist attacks. A tense mistrust of Muslims developed among many Americans, and some in the American media were quick to point, mistakenly, to Islamic fundamentalists for the 1995 Oklahoma City bombing and the 1996 explosion of TWA flight 800. Such media coverage was not without consequences; it was blamed for the resulting 227 hate crimes directed against Muslims during 1997. Anti-Arab hate crimes in particular increase during times of national crisis, such as after the U.S. bombing of Libya during the 1980s as well as during the Persian Gulf War. In the late 1990s it remained difficult to document hate crimes against Muslim Arab Americans because the federal government did not recognize Arab Americans as a distinct ethnic group.

In the early 1990s America was rocked by two attacks perpetrated by Islamic fundamentalists. In 1990 Egyptian-born El Sayyid Nosair murdered the militant Jewish leader Rabbi Meir Kahane in New York, and on 26 February 1993 the World Trade Center in New York City was bombed. While unsuccessful in toppling the towers, the bombing resulted in six deaths and injured one thousand people. Perhaps most important, it shattered the myth that the United States was immune to terrorism.

Following the World Trade Center bombing, the FBI increased its surveillance of the activities of several groups in order to prevent terrorist attacks. In 1995 Melvin Edward Mays, a member of the Chicago El Rukns street gang, was arrested for allegedly conspiring to conduct terrorist activities on behalf of Libya as a mercenary. Also in 1995, the FBI apprehended Ramzi Ahmed Yousef in Islamabad, Pakistan, for his alleged involvement in the World Trade Center bombing. He was found guilty in 1997 of masterminding the World Trade Center bombing and was indicted for conspiracy to bomb U.S. jetliners. In 1996 the Egyptian sheikh Omar Abdel Rahman was convicted of seditious conspiracy and other crimes in a June 1993 plot to bomb major landmarks in New York City (including the World Trade Center) and assassinate politicians and foreign leaders.

BIBLIOGRAPHY

American-Arab Anti-Discrimination Committee. *Report on Anti-Arab Hate Crimes and Discrimination Against Arab-Americans.* Washington, D.C.: American-Arab Anti-Discrimination Committee, 1995 and 1997.

Barboza, Steven. *American Jihad: Islam After Malcolm X.* New York: Doubleday, 1993.

Clegg, Claude Andrew, III. *An Original Man: The Life and Times of Elijah Muhammad.* New York: St. Martin's, 1997.

Council on American-Islamic Relations. *The Status of Muslim Civil Rights in the United States, 1998.* Washington, D.C.: Council on American-Islamic Relations, 1998.

Lawrence, Bruce B. *Shattering the Myth: Islam Beyond Violence.* Princeton, N.J.: Princeton University Press, 1998.

Marsh, Clifton E. *From Black Muslims to Muslims: The Resurrection, Transformation, and Change of the Lost-Found Nation of Islam in America, 1930–1995.* 2d ed. Lanham, Md: Scarecrow, 1996.

TODD BELT

See also **Malcolm X; Religion; World Trade Center Bombing.**

MUSSEL SLOUGH CONFLICT

The Mussel Slough conflict in California during the 1870s and 1880s was concerned with the hotly disputed ownership of some twenty-five thousand acres of prime farmland in the Mussel Slough district, about thirty miles south of Fresno. The Southern Pacific, a railroad company, claimed this acreage as part of a federal land grant to subsidize construction of the railroad. The small farmers living on the land strongly opposed the railroad, contending that the Southern Pacific had violated the terms of the land grant. The farmers demanded that the grant to the railroad be canceled and the land opened for settlement in small tracts under the federal preemption law. While the ownership of the land was in dispute for years, the settlers made what had been a sagebrush desert bloom by digging a large, complex system of irrigation canals and branches that tapped the waters of the Kings River, of which Mussel Slough was an arm.

Meanwhile, the Southern Pacific assured the settlers that if its claim was upheld in the courts it would sell most of the land to them for from $2.50 to $5 per acre. When the Southern Pacific's claim was upheld by a federal judge who had close personal ties to the three major owners of the Southern Pacific—Leland Stanford, Collis P. Huntington, and Charles Crocker—the railroad reneged on its promise and put the land on the open market at $20 to $30 per acre. Determined to defend their occupancy of the land, the farmers organized the Settlers' League for daytime political pressure and legal tactics, while after dark they gathered for night-riding intimidation and violence against the local minority of well-heeled people who supported the Southern Pacific and were willing to pay the price of buying this now-productive land. The leaders of the Settlers' League were Major Thomas J. McQuiddy and John J. Doyle. The railroad company generally had an enlightened land policy that favored bona fide settlers over speculators, but in the Mussel Slough district the Southern Pacific ultimately took a hard line in order to repel a direct threat to its land grant and to defeat the Settlers' League's attempt to undermine the railroad's freedom to set its own prices for its property.

On 11 May 1880 a railroad official, escorted by the federal marshal and accompanied by two violence-prone supporters, moved into the Mussel Slough district to dispossess certain settlers from their homes. A confrontation with settlers quickly turned into a blaze of gunfire that left five settlers and two railroad supporters dead or dying. News of the incident was greeted nationwide as a tragedy, with popular sympathy heavily on the side of the settlers, seven of whom spent eight months in jail for conspiring to resist the federal marshal. Eventually rebuffed in the appeal of their land case to the U.S. Supreme Court, the settlers had no choice but to meet the Southern Pacific's terms or vacate their farms and homes, to which they had devoted, as they stated in a fruitless petition to President Rutherford B. Hayes, "the best years of our lives." In 1892 a local atlas revealed, tract-by-tract, the replacement of most of the original settlers by new occupants. Although the settlers lost their long-term conflict, they were winners in the court of public opinion. By far the best of the at least five novels based on the Mussel Slough conflict is *The Octopus: A Story of California* (1901) by Frank Norris. The two sides in the Mussel Slough conflict created an ideological standoff of the sort that made compromise almost impossible and led to disastrous miscalculation and mistrust in both camps. The settlers' idealistic version was that of a cooperatively built community of thriving small landholders united by allegiance to the homestead ethic. The Southern Pacific and its supporters had a no less idealistic dream of success to be gained by individual enterprise in a market economy.

BIBLIOGRAPHY

Bederman, David J. "The Imagery of Injustice at Mussel Slough: Railroad Land Grants, Corporation Law, and the Great 'Conglomerate West.'" *Western Legal History* 1 (summer/fall 1988).

Brown, James L. *The Mussel Slough Tragedy.* Fresno, Calif.: Lavender, 1958.

Brown, Richard Maxwell. *No Duty to Retreat: Violence and Values in American History and Society*, chapter 3. New York: Oxford University Press, 1991.

Lavender, David. *The Great Persuader.* New York: Doubleday, 1970. A biography of Collis P. Huntington.

Orsi, Richard J. "The Big Four: Villains or Heroes?" and "The Confrontation at Mussel Slough." In Richard B.

Rice, William A. Bullough, and Richard J. Orsi, *The Elusive Eden: A New History of California.* New York: Knopf, 1988.

RICHARD MAXWELL BROWN

See also **Frontier; Labor and Unions; West.**

MUTILATION OF THE BODY

Mutilation refers to the deliberate, direct alteration or destruction of body tissue without conscious suicidal intent. A person may self-mutilate, as is the case in mental illness, or allow others to mutilate his or her body, as is the case in many cultural rituals. The behavior is a direct method of affecting body tissue, as opposed to indirect methods such as self-starvation, self-poisoning, or heavy cigarette smoking. It also must be distinguished from suicidal behavior where the goal is to end life. In its simplest forms the body may be mutilated relatively nonviolently for the purposes of aesthetics (earlobe piercing for jewelry) and creating personal marks of identification (tattoos). More complex forms of body mutilation, however, tend to be violent—for example, enucleation of eyeballs and sewing shut of the vagina—and generally serve to correct or to prevent what are thought to be destabilizing conditions that threaten a community or an individual or both. A classification of body mutilation is presented in figure 1.

Culturally Sanctioned Rituals and Practices

Although the distinctions between rituals and practices are sometimes hazy, generally ritual activities are more expressive of basic elements of social life; are repeated consistently over at least several generations; reflect communal beliefs, traditions, and symbols; and may affect not only in-

FIGURE 1.   A Classification of Body Mutilation

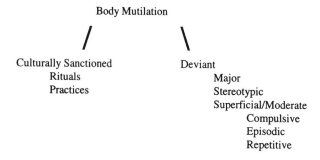

dividual participants but also an entire society. Mutilative rituals serve to perpetuate social order, to preserve and enhance healing, and to appease and curry favor with the spirit world. It should be noted that anthropologists prefer the less emotional term "body modification" to describe rituals and practices, even those that may involve fairly extensive destruction or alteration of body tissue.

Social Order. The Chinook, or Flathead, Indians of the Northwest coast strapped newborn children on a board; a flat piece of wood was placed on their foreheads and tied tightly to the board for an entire year. The process flattened the frontal part of the skull to produce a unique head shape that was readily distinguishable from the round, natural head shape of slaves—thereby preserving social order.

A more severe method of preserving social order is the infibulation of young girls in many African countries, including Egypt, Sudan, Somalia, Kenya, and Nigeria. The practice, commonly called female circumcision, involves cutting off the clitoris, scraping away the labia, and sewing shut the vagina except for a small opening to allow the passage of urine and menstrual blood. An infibulated female is thought to be guaranteed a virgin at the time of her marriage and to be free of powerful sexual desires. Morbidity associated with infibulation includes early hemorrhage, infection, urinary retention, and injury to the urethra and anus, while later complications include chronic urinary and pelvic infections, implantation dermoid cysts and abscesses, painful intercourse, and severe perineal lacerations during childbirth.

A thousand-year Chinese tradition (ended in the 1930s), of controlling female behavior involved binding the feet of young girls with tight bandages in order to break many of the foot bones, to bend the toes into the sole of the foot, and to juxtapose the sole and the heel as closely as possible. These practices assured Chinese men that their wives and mistresses could not "run around."

Healing. The members of many aboriginal tribes in Papua, New Guinea, consider themselves to be contaminated by menstrual blood during fetal development; men envy the natural self-purification of women's menstrual cycles. In order to maintain their health and to treat illness supposedly caused by residues of womb blood, men periodically induce artificial menstruation by gashing their penises with knives and arrows and by pounding sharp leaves into their nostrils to produce copious nasal bleeding.

Shamans are men and women who have, from the earliest days of humankind, devoted themselves to healing the illnesses and reversing the misfortunes of the members of their community through contact with the spirit world. In order to become healers they must overcome an initiating sickness by voluntarily participating, in dreams and vision, in their own body mutilation. During the process their bodies are dismembered, flesh is scraped away to reveal their skeletal bones, their viscera are substituted, and their blood is renewed. The skulls of would-be Dyak (Borneo) shamans are cut open and their brains are washed and returned to their heads in order to achieve insight into healing. Gold dust is inserted into their eyes so they may better see any souls that might wander off. Their hearts are pierced with arrows in order to enhance their capacity to sympathize with the sick and the suffering. Although the suffering and mutilation occur in dreams and visions, in the shamanic world these intense experiences are perceived as real and dangerous. When the mutilated body has been reconstructed, the shaman emerges as a wiser and healthier person with the capacity to heal himself or herself and others.

Pleasing the Spirits. Body mutilation in many cultures is seen as pleasing to spirits and, according to some mystics, useful for the acquisition of insight and the experience of ecstasy. As signs of devotion and penitence, the Olmec, Aztec, and Mayan Indians anointed sacred idols with blood from their penises. Two of the most profound and well-known religious symbols in the world are the Christian cross, where Jesus voluntarily accepted mutilation and death, and lingam stones, which represent the self-castrated phallus of the Hindu god Siva. Some zealous Christian saints and mystics grossly mortified their bodies in emulation of Christ's passion. The medieval German mystic Heinrich Suso, for example, flagellated himself with a spiked scourge that tore into his flesh and left his naked body covered with blood. Among North American Plains Indians the Sun Dance was the index ritual of the entire culture. At its climax incisions were made on the backs and chests of warrior-dancers. Wooden skewers were inserted under the cut muscles and attached by long leather thongs to the top of a pole. While gazing directly at the sun the participants were then hoisted into the air. They struggled until the skewers ripped

Mutilation in the Bible

Both the Old and New Testaments contain references to body mutilation. In some ancient religions that competed with Judaism, especially those in which the Great Mother Goddess known as Ishtar, Astarte, and Cybele was worshiped, priests castrated themselves. Thus, Deuteronomy 23:1 warns that "He whose testicles are crushed or whose male member is cut off shall not enter the assembly of the Lord." Jews considered eunuchs to be impure, imperfect men and not fit to participate in communal life and religious rituals. During the exile, however, many Jews became eunuchs in the palace of the king of Babylon. Isaiah 39:7 foretells this; chapter 56 states that eunuchs who keep the Sabbath and hold fast to the covenants will be welcomed in the house of the Lord.

An important rule of Christian comportment is found in Mark 9:47–48: "If your eye is your downfall, tear it out! Better for you to enter the kingdom of God with one eye than to be thrown with two into Gehenna, where the worm dies not and the fire is never extinguished." Although there are many stories from disparate cultures about self-enucleation—for example, Oedipus—clinical cases have been reported only in Christian culture areas.

In Genesis 15–17 circumcision was made a sign of the covenant between Abraham and God. Circumcision was a divisive practice in the early days of Christianity. Jewish converts insisted that all Christians must be circumcised, but Gentile converts refused. Paul was so angry with the agitators who were turning Christians against each other over this issue that he wished they would castrate themselves (Gal. 5:12).

Mark 5 describes the visit of Jesus to the land of the Gadarenes. He met a troubled man who lived in a graveyard, who often broke out of his shackles, and who repeatedly cut himself with stones. Jesus diagnosed possession by a multiple unclean spirit called Legion and performed an exorcism. Legion then entered a herd of swine, which promptly ran into the sea to drown themselves.

through the muscles; sometimes friends aided by pulling the participants until the flesh gave way. The pure in heart who endured the pain were rewarded by a vision that made clear the meaning and course of their lives. The entire tribe cooperated in the ritual because everyone was thought to benefit from the suffering and the visions.

Body Piercing and Tattooing. Body piercing and tattooing have been part of cultural rituals and practices around the world for millennia. At the Hindu festival of Thaipusum, for example, devotees, while in a trance, pierce their bodies to make themselves more pleasing to the god Murugan. The origins of the current, widespread American interest in these activities can be traced to the early 1970s, when a small group of aficionados regularly met in Los Angeles for tattooing and piercing parties. From this group emerged the journal *Piercing Fans International Quarterly*. One member, Jim Ward, opened Gauntlet, a store for the sale of specialized piercing jewelry. Another member assumed the name Fakir Musafar and coined the term "modern primitive" to describe a nontribal person who practices body modification in response to primal urges. Through his lectures, live and cinematic demonstrations of rituals and practices (he performed a ritual Sun Dance in his 1985 film *Dances Sacred and Profane*), books and journals (*Body Play* and *Modern Primitives Quarterly*), and the opening of a state-licensed school for body piercing and branding in California, Fakir has been a spokesman for body modification as a potentially spiritual and healing behavior. Although popular piercings are done mostly for fun, as a way to rebel, and to enhance sexual stimulation and enticement, they also may be done to memorialize a significant event, mark a life transition, and promote healing (e.g., reclamation of one's body following rape).

Deviant Self-Mutilation

The earliest reference to self-mutilation as a product of mental illness occurs in Book Six of Herodotus's *History* (fifth century B.C.E.), which describes a deranged Spartan leader who sliced his flesh into strips from his shins to his belly. The Gospel of Mark 5:5 describes a repetitive self-mutilator, a man who "night and day would cry aloud among the tombs and on the hillsides and cut himself with stones." Published medical reports began in the nineteenth century and mainly focused on dramatic cases of self-castration and eye enucleation. In the twentieth century self-mutilation was often misidentified as a suicide attempt, trivialized as wrist-cutting, and regarded solely as a symptom of mental illness. Not until the late twentieth century has the behavior been considered as meaningful unto itself and a clinically useful classification been developed based on the degree of tissue destruction and the rate and pattern of behavior (Favazza 1996). The importance of a classification system is that it links types of self-mutilation with specific mental disorders.

Major self-mutilation is rare and consists of acts such as limb amputation, castration, self-blinding, and eye enucleation. With the exception of transsexual self-castration, these acts tend to be violent and bloody. They most often occur as associated features of psychosis (acute psychotic episodes, schizophrenia, mania, depression) and intoxications. Some patients manifest indifference to their behavior and cannot explain it, whereas others offer idiosyncratic explanations that often defy understanding. Frequently, however, reasons are provided that have religious or sexual themes such as atonement, spiritual purification, identification with the suffering Christ, adherence to biblical texts about such acts as tearing out an offending eye or cutting off an offending hand or becoming a eunuch, demonic influences, response to heavenly commands and visions, desire to be a female, fear of homosexuality, control of hypersexuality, and repudiation of troublesome genitals (genitals that don't function well, are perceived as ugly, etc.) Many persons often exhibit a calmness after their self-mutilation, suggesting that the behavior may resolve or, more likely, temporarily pacify unconscious conflicts. A person who has committed an act of major self-mutilation is at high risk of committing a second act in the future and may be involuntarily confined in a jail or mental hospital. Treatment of major self-mutilation is directed at the underlying psychosis or intoxication. Prevention is difficult unless patients clearly state an intention to harm themselves.

Stereotypic self-mutilation refers to monotonously repetitive and occasionally rhythmic acts such as head banging and hitting, orifice digging, arm hitting, throat and eye gouging, tooth extraction, and joint dislocation. Head banging, the most common behavior, may occur at a rate of hundreds, even thousands, of times an hour and may cause self-induced seizures, vomiting, and retinal detachment. The behaviors appear to be devoid of symbolism and the determination of any thought content; even affect is often impossible. Stereotypic self-mutilators do not attempt to conceal their acts of self-harm. The behavior may be expressive of frustration, a turning inward of anger and aggression, a way to get attention, or an autoerotic response to understimulation.

Institutionalized mentally retarded persons have about a 13 percent prevalence of stereotypic self-mutilation. The behavior is also found in autism, de Lange syndrome, neurocanthosis, Tourette's syndrome, and Rett's disorder. In Lesch-Nyhan syndrome, a rare inborn error of purine metabolism that affects males, children bite off lip tissue as well as parts of their fingers and tongue. Treatment of stereotypic self-mutilation involves behavioral techniques such as withholding attention after a harmful act, isolation to exclude reinforcement, shaping, counterconditioning, and desensitization. Multiple medications are also usually prescribed since no single medication has proven to be effective regularly.

Compulsive self-mutilation of the superficial to moderate type includes behaviors that occur many times daily, such as hair pulling (trichotillomania), nail biting, and skin picking and scratching. Persons with delusions of parasite infestation injure their skin by attempting to dig out the imaginary organisms and to destroy them with toxic substances such as lye. Trichotillomania, a disorder of impulse control, typically begins at age thirteen, is ten times more common in females, and may become chronic with related behaviors of nail biting, skin scratching, and depressive and anxiety disorders. Treatment approaches include medications, psychotherapy, behavioral therapy, and hypnotherapy.

Episodic superficial or moderate self-mutilation refers to behaviors such as skin cutting, burning, and carving that occur every so often. They occur as symptoms or associated factors of anxiety, eating, dissociative, depressive, and personality disorders (especially borderline, antisocial, and histrionic types). More women than men injure themselves, especially between the ages of fifteen and twenty-five years. The highest rate occurs among prisoners, who may self-harm in order to relieve boredom, gain sympathetic attention, or manipulate officials.

Skin cutting, burning, and carving often provide rapid but temporary relief from a variety of troublesome feelings and thoughts. Patients with mounting anxiety claim that cutting themselves is like popping a balloon. Those in a depersonalized state say that self-mutilation makes them feel real again. Other claims for the behaviors are that they create euphoria, decrease unpleasant sexual feelings, help to establish control over racing thoughts and fluctuating emotions, and provide a sense of security, uniqueness, and relief from alienation.

In the *repetitive* type the behaviors may assume an autonomous course, and a specific impulse-dyscontrol syndrome of deliberate self-harm may develop. Persons with the syndrome are preoccupied with the behaviors, may adopt an identity as a "cutter" or "burner," and feel that they are addicted to their self-harm. The syndrome typically starts in late childhood or early adolescence and may rage for ten to fifteen years; isolated episodes of self-mutilative behavior may persist longer. In addition to skin cutting, burning, and carving, other symptoms such as anorexia, bulimia, episodic alcohol and substance abuse, and kleptomania may emerge. In some patients the behaviors are sequential, although in no particular order, whereas in others two, three, and even all four behaviors may be present simultaneously. Predisposing factors include a childhood history of sexual or physical abuse, childhood surgical procedures or illnesses, parental alcoholism or depression, perfectionistic tendencies, dissatisfaction with body shape, sexual conflicts, and difficulty regulating emotions. A possible biological basis for the syndrome is reduced brain levels of the neurotransmitter serotonin. Physical disfigurement from scarring and infections of wounds may result in isolation and social rejection. Although suicide attempts are not part of the syndrome, they are common, usually as overdoses, in persons who are demoralized over an inability to control their self-mutilation.

Even though repetitive self-mutilators gain brief relief from troublesome symptoms through their acts of self-harm, deep down they feel miserable about their behavior. Treatment of acute, uncon-

trolled episodes of cutting may be controlled by medications that raise serotonin levels. Long-term treatment is problematic and often includes multiple therapists over many years as well as various psychological approaches. Self-mutilators seem to threaten the mental integrity of persons, including therapists, who come into contact with them.

Self-mutilation that is the product of mental illness is a morbid form of self-help behavior; nevertheless, it clearly must be regarded as violent. It may be a symptom of specific mental disorders or, in the case of repetitive skin-cutting, may be a disorder in its own right. Simple body piercing for the insertion of jewelry is relatively nonviolent. Cultural rituals in which persons voluntarily participate or are coerced into participation in order to fulfill social expectations occupy an intermediate position in terms of violence. Even though significant damage may be done to body tissue the behaviors are rarely, if ever, fatal.

BIBLIOGRAPHY

Egan, Jennifer. "The Thin Red Line." *New York Times Magazine*, 27 July 1997.

Favazza, Armando. *Bodies Under Siege: Self-Mutilation and Body Modification in Culture and Society.* Baltimore: Johns Hopkins University Press, 1996.

Herpertz, Sabine, Hennig Sass, and Armando Favazza. "Impulsivity in Self-Mutilative Behavior: Psychometric and Biological Findings." *Journal of Psychiatric Research* 31 (1997).

O'Sullivan, Richard, et al. "Trichotillomania: Behavioral Symptom or Clinical Syndrome?" *American Journal of Psychiatry* 154 (1997).

Vale, V., and Andrea Juno. *Modern Primitives.* San Francisco: Re/Search Publications, 1989.

ARMANDO R. FAVAZZA

See also **Anorexia and Bulimia; Fashion; Performance Art; Sadism and Masochism; Self-Destructiveness.**

MY LAI MASSACRE

On the morning of 16 March 1968 members of Charlie Company, a unit of the U.S. Army Americal division, entered the hamlet of My Lai in South Vietnam and started shooting. After four hours of indiscriminate brutality and murder, 504 civilians lay dead or dying; the Vietcong, a guerrilla group of the Vietnamese communist movement whom the army was ostensibly attacking, were nowhere to be found.

The My Lai massacre occurred during the last stages of the North Vietnamese Tet offensive, a massive attack on major cities and strong points throughout South Vietnam that had been under way since late in January 1968. The My Lai massacre was essentially the culmination of fatigue, terror, and flawed U.S. military strategy, conditions that were not unusual during the Vietnam War. What distinguishes My Lai from other acts of technological overkill during the war was that it ultimately forced the United States, which had previously shown a degree of self-satisfaction regarding its role in Vietnam, to face the realities of its actions for Vietnamese civilians. The Vietnam War tested the United States' commitment to the Cold War simplicities that fueled its foreign policy, and My Lai provided an atrocious example of the failure of that policy.

My Lai lay in the Quang Ngai region, a stronghold of Vietcong activity and recruitment that had been declared a free-fire zone by the military: that is, the official U.S. policy for the region was to destroy all villages by any means possible, to cut off Vietcong support. My Lai, and other villages in the region, fell under this strategic policy and became the focus of an enormous military buildup. Although the plan seemed straightforward at the U.S. Army's divisional headquarters, the men on the ground were the ones who would test its efficacy. Charlie Company was on active service in the Quang Ngai region at this time, under the command of Captain Ernest "Mad Dog" Medina.

At 7:40 on the morning of 16 March 1968, Charlie Company landed on the outskirts of My Lai, where its assignment was to sweep through the village and eliminate all Vietcong resistance. While Medina believed his company was up to the task, he clearly ignored signs of severe strain and growing incidents of insubordination toward junior officers. The company was frustrated and angry. It had suffered losses through booby traps, mines, and snipers, and its demoralization began to show up in increasingly brutal behavior while on routine missions.

The First Platoon, led by Lieutenant William L. Calley, began moving through the village to flush out the enemy. They were operating under the faulty intelligence that all villagers would be at market at this time and that anyone they found would by default be Vietcong. As the platoon pushed on, Calley's men began a rampage of indiscriminate killing. The troops shot mothers and their babies, they shot the elderly, and they raped girls and young women before killing them. Terrified and panicked, many villagers tried to flee but were summarily rounded up into holding groups and shot at point-blank range.

While the command helicopters saw only the unfolding of a successful operation, other pilots grasped the enormity and savagery of the situation. Against orders, the helicopter pilot Hugh Thompson set down and attempted to rescue some of the villagers. Telling his gunner to keep the U.S. troops at bay, Thompson managed to lift a small group of civilians to safety. He subsequently returned to base and recounted the incident, a report that was quietly buried.

The massacre of civilians at My Lai generally drew little attention at task force headquarters. Murmurs of disapproval were quickly squashed in a cover-up that reached high up the chain of command. The actions of Charlie Company finally came to light a year later, in April 1969, after a Vietnam serviceman named Ronald Ridenhour, who had recently returned from a tour of duty, wrote letters of moral outrage to top government officials, describing corroborated rumors and eyewitness accounts he had heard about the My Lai attack.

In response to Ridenhour's allegations, and sensitive to the possible damage such an incident could do to the U.S. armed forces, General William Westmoreland, the army chief of staff, created a special panel to investigate U.S. military excesses in Vietnam. Lieutenant General William Peers was appointed on 24 November 1969 to head the panel. The Peers investigation discovered that the My Lai massacre involved 224 separate violations of military-conduct code, and it triggered war-crimes charges against a string of generals, colonels, captains, and lieutenants. But there were no concrete results, mainly because many of those charged were out of the service and much of the evidence was lost or forgotten.

On 13 November 1969, however, the incident moved out of military jurisdiction and into the public realm: the journalist Seymour Hersh broke the story in newspapers around the country. On 5 December, *Life* magazine printed a grisly series of photographs taken during the massacre by Ron Haeberle, who was on active service with Charlie Company as an army photographer.

The My Lai exposé triggered outrage across the country. Those in favor of the war saw the story as another attempt to tear the United States down, while those opposed to the war claimed it was

Victims at My Lai, 1968. RON HAEBERLE/TIME INC.

added proof that the military was morally bankrupt and the war was moving into a genocidal phase. Either way, the story contributed to growing domestic tensions and the grave apprehension among the public that the war no longer had a political purpose. The photographs and the story of the military cover-up made it clear that blind self-assurance in the U.S. cause was tragically flawed and politically irresponsible.

Public anger and dissatisfaction with the U.S. armed forces were further heightened by the proceedings following the Peers commission. While the Justice Department was reluctant to prosecute issues of military jurisdiction, the military tribunals refused to convict officers despite the evidence, and disciplinary actions were few and minor. Only Lieutenant Calley was singled out and found guilty (of the premeditated murder of twenty-two Vietnamese civilians), on 29 March 1971, three years after the incident. Calley's life sentence was considered a selfish internal sacrifice and elicited a great deal of public sympathy, especially among veterans' groups and conservative political organizations. Yet whether Calley was a scapegoat or not, President Richard Nixon removed him from the federal penitentiary at Leavenworth, Kansas, after he had served only four and a half years of his sentence.

Despite military assurances that the My Lai massacre was an isolated incident, a bond of trust had been broken. The recalcitrance of the armed forces confirmed their image as a powerful, careless, and incompetent war machine whose aims were essentially unclear to themselves and the American people. As Haeberle's stark photographs from My Lai made clear, no one in command tried to stop the massacre, and the effective closing of ranks against the investigation raised the question of whether My Lai was an aberration or simply a routine operation within Vietnam.

BIBLIOGRAPHY

Anderson, David, ed. *Facing My Lai: Moving Beyond the Massacre.* Lawrence: Kansas University Press, 1998.

Kolko, Gabriel. *Anatomy of a War: Vietnam, the United States, and the Modern Historical Experience.* New York: Pantheon, 1986.

Lamb, David. "A Day of Darkness." *Los Angeles Times,* 12 March 1998.

Olson, James S., and Randy Roberts, eds. *My Lai: A Brief History with Documents.* Boston: Bedford, 1998.

PAUL HANSOM

See also **Mass Murder: Collective Murder; Vietnam War; War Crimes.**

N

NAGASAKI. *See* Hiroshima and Nagasaki.

NARCO-TERROISM. *See* Drugs: Drug Trade.

NATIONAL ASSOCIATION FOR THE ADVANCEMENT OF COLORED PEOPLE

The National Association for the Advancement of Colored People (NAACP) was founded in 1909 by an interracial group of intellectuals, reformers, and socialists dedicated to achieving fully the civil and political rights of African Americans as guaranteed by the Fourteenth and Fifteenth Amendments. Although largely financed and controlled in the early years by sympathetic whites of the stripe of Oswald Garrison Villard, grandson of the abolitionist William Lloyd Garrison, and Mary White Ovington, the socialist settlement-house activist, it was W. E. B. Du Bois, founder of the Niagara Movement, a short-lived black protest organization, who shaped the public image of the NAACP as a militant association.

As director of publications and research and the sole black executive staff member, Du Bois edited the association's official publication, the *Crisis,* during a period in American history replete with grotesque torture, mutilation, castration, and rampant homicide committed by whites upon blacks. No fewer than 3,438 men and women were lynched between 1882 and 1951. White suprema-cists from janitors to judges justified mob violence as necessary in order to punish alleged black murderers and rapists lest they be acquitted by jury trial. More generally, such violence was deemed justifiable as a sine qua non to white domination.

As black outmigration from the South increased during the first decade of the century, the August 1908 riot in Springfield, Illinois (burial place of Abraham Lincoln), signaled that the race problem had become a national crisis. Two weeks after some two thousand terrorized African Americans had fled Springfield, the socialist writer William English Walling wrote an article admonishing would-be reformers to look to their consciences. Ovington's response and Villard's financial support led to the founding of the NAACP, an organization birthed by violence. Shortly after its founding, two lynchings occurred in the summer of 1911: one in the upper South, and the other in the North.

After a black man was charged with murdering a white man in Livermore, Kentucky, tickets were sold at a local theater to witness and participate in his lynching. The audience in the orchestra could fire unlimited shots into Will Porter's lifeless body, while those in the gallery were limited to only one. No lynchers were ever convicted. In Coatesville, Pennsylvania, following a gun duel with a factory guard, a wounded Zachariah Walker confessed to killing a popular local white man in self-defense. Hours later, lynchers stormed the hospital, ripped Walker's bed from the floor, and delivered him to a mob of four thousand men, women, and children. Walker was burned alive, his hospital bed serving as a pyre, and his remains were distributed as souvenirs.

Such terror spurred the NAACP to action. Du Bois's editorial in the *Crisis* grimly predicted that "nothing [would] be done," and implored black men, next time, "to perish like men and not like bales of hay." The association investigated the scene of the crime, hired private detectives to obtain evidence against the lynchers, entreated the U.S. attorney general to take action, and organized protest meetings to raise money for antilynching efforts. The process initiated with the Coatesville lynching resulted in the NAACP's most effective strategy against racial violence. Antilynching, in particular, and violence against blacks, in general, became the NAACP's primary focus during its first thirty years. The association published its first pamphlet, *Notes on Lynching in the United States,* in 1912, only months after Coatesville; the NAACP report *Thirty Years of Lynching in the United States, 1889–1919,* was released in 1919.

Publicizing racial violence also came in the form of parades, conferences, and journalistic exposés. Newly hired field secretary James Weldon Johnson organized the "Negro Silent Protest Parade" on 28 July 1917. Held in New York City, the parade brought national attention to the bloody East St. Louis Riot, which claimed the lives of thirty-nine blacks and eight whites. During the "Red Summer" of 1919, in which race riots erupted in twenty-six northern and southern cities, the association faced one of its pivotal challenges with the massacre in Elaine, Arkansas. When members of the all-black Farmers Progressive Household Union of America held a mass meeting in a local church, a deputy sheriff was killed in a shoot-out triggered by a white mob's attack on the assembly. In retaliation, hundreds of deputies and federal troops were called to the scene, resulting in the murder of twenty blacks, allegedly for resisting arrest.

In a trial that lasted all of one hour and five minutes, twelve black men were condemned to death, and sixty-seven were coerced, by threat of lynching, to plea-bargain in exchange for long prison sentences. The NAACP's new assistant executive secretary, Walter White, light-skinned and blond, posed as a reporter for the Chicago *Daily News* in order to investigate the Elaine riot and broadcast its details nationwide. The association eventually won a reversal of all convictions on appeal to the U.S. Supreme Court in 1923 (*Moore v. Dempsey*). This ruling was a powerful strike against the southern tradition of mob-led court proceedings and was one of the NAACP's most significant early legal successes.

The NAACP waged legal battles over other crucial issues: due process in jury trials, restrictive covenants, disfranchisement laws, equalization of teachers' salaries, and segregation of public schools, although antiviolence proved to be its most widely supported strategy before the 1940s. Even so, failure to secure congressional enactment of its federal antilynching bill was to be one of the association's biggest disappointments. Despite repeated pleas by NAACP officials to U.S. attorneys general, members of Congress, and five presidents (from William H. Taft to Franklin D. Roosevelt), innumerable demonstrations, and congressional hearings, lynching was never made a federal crime. In 1922, 1937, and 1940, federal antilynching legislation was passed in the House but died on the Senate floor.

Despite such legislative defeats, the NAACP's lobbying efforts, publicity, and legal victories helped to slow the pace of mob violence across the nation after the 1930s, until its resurgence in the 1950s with the Civil Rights movement. Throughout its history, the NAACP paid a high price for its assault on white supremacy. The beating in 1919 of John R. Shillady, NAACP secretary, by an Austin, Texas, mob and the near abduction of Thurgood Marshall, head of the NAACP Legal Defense Fund, by Columbus, Tennessee, police officers in 1946 were frightening omens of what was to befall Harry T. Moore and Medgar Evers. Moore, the NAACP state coordinator for Florida, was murdered along with his wife when their Miami home was bombed in 1951. Mississippi field secretary Medgar Evers died in the arms of his wife and children from an assassin's bullet in 1963.

In the wake of *Brown v. Board of Education,* racial violence became virtually state-sponsored in the South. The 1955 Interstate Commerce Commission's order banning segregated interstate travel was flouted, public school integration in Virginia, Georgia, Alabama, South Carolina, Louisiana, and Mississippi was completely stymied, and black voter registration in eight southern states slowed to a glacial pace. Although more than five hundred cases of reprisals against African Americans were recorded between 1955 and 1958, the NAACP was one of the primary targets in this official campaign to resist integration. Texas and Alabama hamstrung the local branches with injunctions. Georgia revoked the organization's tax-exempt status. Virginia passed sedition laws, and South Carolina banned public employment of association members.

Intimidation and personal threats had always been part of the job descriptions of NAACP officials, and continued to be so during the 1960s as the nation lurched toward greater fulfillment of the promises of the Fourteenth and Fifteenth Amendments.

BIBLIOGRAPHY

Berry, Mary Frances. *Black Resistance, White Law: A History of Constitutional Racism in America.* New York: Penguin, 1994.

Kellogg, Charles Flint. *NAACP: A History of the National Association for the Advancement of Colored People.* Vol. 1, *1909–1920.* Baltimore: Johns Hopkins Press, 1967.

Kluger, Richard. *Simple Justice: The History of* Brown v. Board of Education *and Black America's Struggle for Equality.* New York: Knopf, 1976.

Lewis, David Levering. *W. E. B. Du Bois: Biography of a Race, 1868–1919.* New York: Henry Holt, 1993.

Zangrando, Robert. *The NAACP Crusade Against Lynching, 1909–1950.* Philadelphia: Temple University Press, 1980.

DAVID LEVERING LEWIS
KHALIL GIBRAN MUHAMMAD

See also **African Americans; Civil Rights Movements; Hate Crimes; Lynching; Race and Ethnicity.**

NATIONAL CRIME VICTIMIZATION SURVEY

Using survey methodology, the National Crime Victimization Survey (NCVS) has collected data on the victims of crime since 1972. In the late 1990s, U.S. Census Bureau personnel conducted these interviews with probability samples of approximately one hundred thousand U.S. residents. Interviewers ask respondents about victimization involving rape or sexual assaults, robberies, aggravated and simple assaults, burglaries, personal thefts, and motor-vehicle thefts.

These surveys involve the victims of crime and thus provide information about crime victims unavailable in either the Uniform Crime Reports (UCR), which contain criminal statistics based on law-enforcement agency data, or self-report studies, based on data from interviews with offenders. The NCVS includes data on injuries received; the age, race, and family income of victims; the sex and

marital status of victims; the amount of economic loss; self-protective measures employed by victims; and whether victims reported the incident to the police. *Criminal Victimization in the United States* publishes annual summaries of these results, and researchers can obtain NCVS data in a format that links data for each type of incident, including sex and age of victim, location of incident, perceived race of the offender, and so on.

Historically, the NCVS produced two separate major programs. City-level surveys collected data from twenty-six cities between 1972 and 1975 (thirteen cities were surveyed twice). Each survey collected data from approximately twenty-two thousand individuals. This program provided city-level data that could be compared to data from the UCR for the same cities and made it possible for researchers to examine the relationships between the structural characteristics of cities and victimization rates. The city-level surveys were discontinued because of the cost. The second program is the national-level survey that began in July 1972 and is ongoing. Originally, this program surveyed both a sample of households and a sample of businesses, but the business part of the survey was discontinued in 1976.

In line with the criminologist Thorsten Sellin's dictum "The value of a crime for index purposes decreases as the distance from the crime itself in terms of procedure increases" (Sellin 1931, p. 346), the NCVS, which interviews victims, was expected to provide a more accurate picture of crime than that available from the UCR. This is likely the case for crime trends. The NCVS, however, is not error free. The NCVS measures relatively infrequent events, so that even with large-size samples there can be substantial sampling errors. For this reason, reliable geographical analyses at even the state level are not possible. Respondents tend to telescope criminal incidents into and out of the reference period (for the NCVS, six months preceding the survey). Respondents forget incidents with the passage of time (memory decay). There exists much empirical evidence documenting these flaws.

In 1993 the NCVS was modified to include new questions designed to jog respondents' memories and thus elicit more reports of criminal incidents. For this reason, crime rates based on the NCVS prior to 1993 are not comparable to those from 1993 onward. Other new questions provide more information on sexual assaults, unwanted sexual contact, and domestic violence.

The NCVS provides a detailed and comprehensive data source on the victims of crimes. These surveys, along with the UCR, furnish the most comprehensive data on street crimes in the United States.

BIBLIOGRAPHY

O'Brien, Robert M. "Police Productivity and Crime Rates: 1973–1992." *Criminology* 34, no. 2 (1996).
———. "Rare Events, Sample Size, and Statistical Problems in the Analysis of the NCS (National Crime Surveys) City Surveys." *Journal of Criminal Justice* 14, no. 5 (1991).
Sellin, Thorsten. "The Bias of a Crime Index." *Journal of the Institute of Criminal Law and Criminology* 22, no. 2 (1931).

ROBERT M. O'BRIEN

See also **Incidence of Violence; Methodologies of Violence Research; Statistics and Epidemiology; Uniform Crime Reports; Victims of Violence.**

NATIONAL RIFLE ASSOCIATION

The National Rifle Association of America (NRA) has five stated objectives: to protect the U.S. Constitution, especially as regards the Second Amendment right to keep and bear arms; to promote public safety and national defense; to train members of law enforcement, the military, the militia, and people of good repute in marksmanship and safety; to promote the shooting sports, including amateur competitions from the local to international levels; and to promote hunting and conservation.

The NRA was founded in 1871 by prominent community leaders in New York. Major General Ambrose Burnside, the NRA's first president, spoke of the need for such an organization by recalling the Union soldiers he led in the Civil War and that "not one man in one hundred could hit the broadside of a barn." The NRA sought to encourage rifle practice and to sponsor competitions.

The NRA's cofounder, General George W. Wingate, in *Why School Boys Should Be Taught to Shoot?* (1907), included the congratulations of President Theodore Roosevelt (himself an NRA life member) to the pupil who won the high school rifle competition in New York City that year. Roosevelt admonished that "it is a prime necessity that the volunteer should already know how to shoot if he is to be of value as a soldier." In 1914 the Boy Scouts agreed that the NRA should supervise rifle prac-

---

Purposes of National Rifle Association

Article II of the Bylaws of the National Rifle Association of America provides:

The purposes and objectives of the Association are:

1. To protect and defend the Constitution of the United States, especially with reference to the inalienable right of the individual American citizen guaranteed by such Constitution to acquire, possess, collect, exhibit, transport, carry, transfer ownership of, and enjoy the right to use arms, in order that the people may always be in a position to exercise their legitimate individual rights of self-preservation and defense of family, person, and property, as well as to serve effectively in the appropriate militia for the common defense of the Republic and the individual liberty of its citizens;
2. To promote the public safety, law and order and the national defense;
3. To train members of law enforcement agencies, the armed forces, the militia, and people of good repute in marksmanship and in the safe handling and efficient use of small arms;
4. To foster and to promote the shooting sports, including the advancement of amateur competitions in marksmanship at the local, state, regional, national and international levels;
5. To promote hunter safety, and to promote and to defend hunting as a shooting sport and as a viable and necessary method of fostering the propagation, growth, conservation, and wise use of our renewable wildlife resources.

The Association may take all actions necessary and proper in the furtherance of these purposes and objectives.

---

tice, which remains in the scouting merit badge program.

At the turn of the nineteenth century, Congress repealed the dormant 1792 Militia Act, which required every man to keep a firearm. To promote voluntary training, Congress established the National Board for the Promotion of Rifle Practice, which distributed military rifles to rifle clubs. Ever since, the NRA has conducted the annual national matches on behalf of the board.

NRA programs helped train Americans who found themselves overseas in World War I. Revulsion against the slaughter of that war led to opposition to militarism. However, even the anti-militarists in Congress voted for the 1924 militia bill, which provided for the sale of surplus military rifles to members of the NRA. Modeled after the example of neutral Switzerland, the program promoted the concept of citizen-soldiers, not a standing army.

The gun violence spawned by Prohibition, which also led to organized crime, and by Depression gangsterism prompted passage of the National Firearms Act of 1934, which required registration of machine guns and short-barreled shotguns. As originally proposed, the bill would have virtually banned pistols and revolvers. By informing its members and by testifying in congressional hearings, the NRA succeeded in killing that proposal. The NRA had entered politics.

With the outbreak of World War II and the beginning of the Battle of Britain, the NRA magazine ran ads pleading for the contributions of guns to "defend a British home." Fearing a Bolshevik-style revolution, the English government had restricted firearm possession after World War I, but the threat of a Nazi invasion changed everything. When the U.S. attorney general proposed that firearms should be registered to curtail subversion, the NRA protested to Congress. Citing how Adolf Hitler and Joseph Stalin disarmed their citizens to maintain their totalitarian dictatorships, members of Congress passed the Property Requisition Act of 1941, which declared that the individual right to keep and bear arms would not be infringed by registration or confiscation measures.

After the attack on Pearl Harbor in 1941, gun control proposals became irrelevant. The NRA's role was to train soldiers in marksmanship. Some 1.75 million men went through the NRA's preinduction rifle training program. After the war President Harry Truman praised the NRA for having "materially aided our war effort."

By the 1960s American gun manufacturers were complaining about the competition from the importation of military surplus bolt-action rifles, and Senator Thomas J. Dodd of Connecticut proposed protectionist measures. These proposals failed until given a new impetus by the assassinations of President John F. Kennedy—an NRA member—and of Martin Luther King, Jr. The result was the Gun Control Act of 1968, which strictly regulated commerce in firearms and banned trading a gun with a person from another state. At least two provisions were supported by all sides in the debate: a ban on possession of a firearm by a felon and enhanced penalties for use of a firearm in a federal crime of violence. The NRA had no full-time lobbying force, but sympathetic members of Congress and grassroots pressure defeated proposals to register all handguns.

The real purpose of the Gun Control Act, wrote liberal author Robert Sherrill, was to control blacks in the wake of ghetto unrest. Indeed, Robert F. Williams, in *Negroes with Guns* (1962), described how blacks in North Carolina formed an NRA club and acquired rifles to defend themselves against Ku Klux Klan violence. It is noteworthy that in the 1970s the NRA refused Federal Bureau of Investigation demands for membership information on NRA clubs organized by blacks.

In 1975 the NRA Institute for Legislative Action was created to lobby against antigun and antihunting laws. It was headed by Harlon Carter, retired director of the U.S. Border Patrol who became the NRA's executive vice president.

Perceived abuses and harassment of law-abiding gun owners by the Bureau of Alcohol, Tobacco, and Firearms led the NRA to promote enactment of the Firearms Owners' Protection Act of 1986, which President Ronald Reagan—an NRA life member—signed. In 1988 the NRA started its Eddie Eagle gun safety program, which by 1999 had reached seven million children.

In 1993 Congress passed the Brady Handgun Violence Prevention Act, the interim provisions of which required a five-day waiting period (with exceptions) and background checks for handgun purchasers. The part of the act that ordered the background checks to be conducted by local law enforcement officers was declared unconstitutional by the Supreme Court in *Sheriff Jay Prinz v. United States* (1997). In 1998 the interim provision of the act expired and the permanent provisions became effective. These provisions, backed by the NRA, provide for an instant background check on firearm purchasers.

The NRA has borne its share of criticism. Herblock, a political cartoonist for the *Washington Post*, depicted the NRA as pushing guns and dope on children. Former president George Bush resigned his membership in 1995 after the NRA ran an ad (later retracted) attacking certain federal police agencies as akin to storm troopers who trampled civil liberties. Whenever gun control measures are debated in the federal and state legislatures, major newspapers attack the NRA for what they perceive as its intractable opposition. The Fraternal Order of Police and several other police organizations accuse the NRA of endangering law enforcement. But the NRA supports harsh punishment for gun violence, has many police members, and has trained countless cops.

In 1994 Congress banned the making of new *assault weapons*, a term that originally meant military machine guns but was later applied to semiautomatic rifles with a military appearance. The 1994 elections resulted in the Republicans gaining a majority in the House of Representatives, which President Clinton attributed in part to the NRA. The NRA retained sufficient clout to keep in existence a revamped Civilian Marksmanship Program, which sells surplus military rifles to citizens.

The NRA elected its first female president, Marion Hammer, in 1996. At the end of the twentieth century, it appeared that the NRA would continue to be a viable, albeit controversial, political force because of its grassroots component. The lawful gun culture includes collectors, competitors, hunters, and persons who seek to defend themselves. America's sixty-five million gun owners do not see themselves as criminals and often vote against politicians who do. In 1999 NRA membership was more than three million.

Unfortunately, there are subcultures in the United States that use firearms for violent purposes. The NRA points to long periods of incarceration or the death penalty as the solution for the misuse of firearms by murderers, drug traffickers, and armed predators. Handgun Control, Inc., and other critics of the NRA maintain that the availability of firearms must be curtailed in order to keep them out of the hands of criminals. At bottom, these conflicting views reflect differing political values and contrasting perceptions about the efficacy of criminal law to ameliorate social ills.

BIBLIOGRAPHY

Bijlefeld, Marjolijn. *People for and Against Gun Control*. Westport, Conn.: Greenwood, 1999.

Davidson, Osha Gray. *Under Fire: The NRA and the Battle for Gun Control*. New York: Holt, 1993.

Kennett, Lee, and James Anderson. *The Gun in America: The Origins of a National Dilemma*. Westport, Conn.: Greenwood, 1975.

LaPierre, Wayne R. *Guns, Crime, and Freedom*. Washington, D.C.: Regnery, 1994.

Leddy, Edward F. *Magnum Force Lobby: The National Rifle Association Fights Gun Control*. Lanham, Md.: University Press of America, 1987.

"NRA: Celebrating 125 Years of Service to America." *American Rifleman* 40 (January 1996).

Sherrill, Robert. *The Saturday Night Special, and Other Guns . . .* New York: Charterhouse, 1973.

Tartaro, Joseph P. "Marksmanship and Citizen Soldiers Were Primary Interest of Early NRA." *Gun News Digest* 27 (fall 1997).

Williams, Robert F. *Negroes with Guns*. New York: Marzani and Munsell, 1962. Rev. ed., Detroit: Wayne State University Press, 1998.

Wingate, George W. *Why School Boys Should Be Taught to Shoot?* Boston: Sub-Target Gun Company, 1907.

STEPHEN P. HALBROOK

See also **Gun Control; Gun Violence; Militarism; Militias; Right to Bear Arms; Weapons.**

NATIVE AMERICANS. *See* American Indians.

NATIVISM

Although many think of the United States as a nation of immigrants, nativism—the hatred, fear, and resentment of immigrants and foreigners—has been a persistent part of American history. Nativism and nativist violence in the United States seem to become particularly widespread during periods when certain Americans believe that immigrants are posing a threat to some defining feature of American life. In the early and mid-nineteenth century, Protestant Americans feared that Catholic immigration would change America for the worse. In the second half of the nineteenth century, many white Americans reacted violently to the immigration of Asians. By the turn of the twentieth century, immigrants from southern and eastern Europe had become the focus of nativist violence. At the end of the century, some Americans see Latinos and Asians as taking away their jobs and increasing their tax burdens.

The Origins of American Nativism

In the first decades after the United States won its independence, anti-immigrant sentiment was a relatively unknown phenomenon. In fact, one of the complaints Thomas Jefferson enumerated against King George III in the Declaration of Independence was that the king had prevented people from emigrating to America. Americans believed that until their vast territory was more fully populated, and thus less easily occupied or invaded, their nation's independence could never be assured. Consequently, Americans did everything they could to encourage immigration—specifically by Protestant Europeans—in the fifty or so years after the end of the Revolutionary War. American attitudes began to change, however, when the composition of European emigration to America shifted. In the 1830s, as had been true one hundred and even two hundred years earlier, most immigrants to America came from Great Britain. By the 1830s the Irish outnumbered immigrants from other parts of Britain, and as a result Catholic immigrants began to outnumber Protestant immigrants. Americans therefore began to reassess their views on immigration: although they had always welcomed it, disdain for Catholicism was an equally strong tradition.

The Puritans who settled New England, for example, had harbored great animosity toward Catholicism. Even their name comes from their desire to "purify" the Anglican church of its Catholic vestiges. Puritans and their descendants had converted England's Guy Fawkes Day into Pope Day (5 November), which became one of the most important holidays in the North American colonies. Towns across North America held parades on this occasion, the highlight of which was the burning of a papal effigy. In addition, all colonies except Rhode Island established laws banning Catholics from holding office, voting, or even owning land.

Because there were few Catholics in the colonies outside of Maryland, there is little record of such resentments spilling over into violence. Instead, resentment of immigrants usually manifested itself in rhetorical or legal forms. Ben Franklin in 1751 asked, "why should Pennsylvania, founded by the English, become a colony of *aliens*, who will shortly be so numerous as to Germanize us instead of our Anglifying them, and will never adopt our language or customs, any more than they can acquire our complexion?" The fear of foreigners in other colonies (such as South Carolina, Georgia, and Virginia) is reflected in their enactment of a "head tax," a duty levied upon each immigrant, to discourage the Irish or Scotch from settling in them. Although the egalitarian ideology of the American Revolution resulted in the repeal of most of these restrictions in the 1770s, anti-Catholicism remained a part of the American psyche.

The Anti-Catholic Revival

The person who was perhaps most important in changing American attitudes toward immigration in the post-Revolutionary period was Samuel F. B. Morse. Morse, famous as the inventor of the telegraph and a painter, played a pivotal role in the development of American nativism. In a series of newspaper articles published in 1834, he linked the increase in Catholic immigration to a conspiracy by the Catholic monarchs of Europe to populate the western United States with Catholics so they could overthrow American democracy. Indeed, Americans were convinced that European monarchs wanted the American republic destroyed so that their subjects could not look to the United States as proof that alternatives to monarchy existed. Morse helped spawn an anti-immigration movement that would persist for generations, and he was recognized by contemporaries as the "founding father" of American nativism.

The revived anti-Catholicism reflected in Morse's writings manifested itself in violence. In New York's Five Points slum, where most of the city's Irish-Catholic population was concentrated, native-born citizens vowing to "keep those damned Irishmen in order!" attacked the neighborhood's Irish immigrants in a three-day riot in April 1834. A few months later a mob in Charlestown, Massachusetts, burned the Ursuline convent there after a rumor spread that priests were confining a nun against her will. Early nativists failed, however, to transform their crusade into a political movement. When Morse ran for mayor of New York in 1836, he captured only 6 percent of the vote.

Educational Disputes

Nativism revived a decade later when a number of educational questions dividing Protestants and Catholics became political issues, reawakening and exacerbating American anti-Catholicism. In most American schools, students began their day by singing Protestant hymns and reciting Protestant prayers. Teachers used the Protestant King James Bible to teach reading, and textbooks routinely made Catholics the villains in most of their history lessons. Catholic students and parents resented these practices, and as the Catholic population increased, their community leaders began to demand that the Bible no longer be read in the schools and that the hymns and prayers be eliminated. Other Catholics were willing to accept the Protestant influence in the public schools if the state would also finance Catholic parochial schools. Most Protestants condemned Catholics for meddling with the schools and refused either to change the existing schools or to finance Catholic ones. In 1842 in New York City these tensions between Protestants and Catholics erupted into election-day riots.

Nativists again tried to parlay American anti-Catholicism into political clout, and their organization, the American-Republican Party, managed to elect the mayors of New York, Boston, and Philadelphia. But violence fomented by some of the party's members, including the burning of churches and riots, embarrassed many of the party's initial supporters and convinced most Americans to abandon the American-Republican Party. By 1846 it had virtually disappeared.

The Know-Nothings

Nativists kept their movement alive by forming fraternal organizations. Rather than addressing Americans' fears, these groups appealed to their patriotism, as is reflected in the groups' names: Order of United Americans, Order of the Star Spangled Banner, and Order of the Sons of 1776. Some of these groups practiced ritualized secrecy. The Order of the Star Spangled Banner became known as the Know-Nothings, for example, because when asked about the organization its members were required to respond "I know nothing."

These fraternal groups would have labored in relative historical anonymity had not a number of factors combined in the early 1850s to swell the ranks of the organized nativist movement. First, the potato famine in Ireland and overpopulation of agricultural regions in the German states led to a remarkable increase in immigration, peaking at nearly a half million in 1854. Three million people immigrated to the United States in the decade ending in that year. By 1860 immigrants made up a greater proportion of the nation's population than at any time up to the end of the twentieth century. Second, in the early 1850s Catholics began to revive their demands for state financing of their parochial schools and the end of public-school Bible reading, efforts that revived anti-Catholic sentiment. Others were drawn to the nativist movement by the belief that immigrant political clout was blocking the enactment of liquor prohibition laws. Finally, the passage of the Kansas-Nebraska Act in 1854, which made it possible to introduce slavery in territory where it had previously been banned, attracted to the Know-Nothing movement many who saw it as an alternative to the old political parties responsible for the law or who believed that Irish Americans were especially pro-slavery.

Promising to reduce the political power of immigrants, the Know-Nothings burst on the American political scene in 1854–1855, electing the governors of eight states, a majority of the members of the Thirty-Fourth Congress, the mayors of Boston, Philadelphia, Baltimore, Chicago, and San Francisco, and thousands of local officials. They were especially popular in the North and Northeast. Of the 410 members of the Massachusetts legislature in 1855, for example, 407 were Know-Nothings. The Know-Nothings were not an especially violent organization. One of their chief grievances against Irish immigrants was that the newcomers used violence to keep peaceful citizens away from the polls, a charge that was not without foundation. In some places, however, Know-Nothings and Catholics engaged in election-day clashes and bloody riots, each group bearing part of the blame.

The Know-Nothings disappeared from the American political scene quickly because Americans became convinced that slavery was a more pressing issue. With southerners attacking antislavery settlers in Kansas and even antislavery Congressmen on the floor of Congress in 1856, voters in the North (where most immigrants and thus most nativists were located) felt they could wait to address the problems caused by immigrants until after the slavery issue was settled.

Anti-Chinese Violence

After the Civil War, the focus of American nativism shifted from Irish and Catholic immigrants to Chinese immigrants in the West. Chinese immigration had become significant after the discovery of gold in California in 1848. Poor Chinese crossed the Pacific dreaming of striking it rich in the mines. Californians, wanting to keep gold for themselves, soon passed laws imposing heavy taxes on "foreign" mine workers, though they were not enforced on Irish immigrants. Somewhere between 25 and 50 percent of all California state revenue from 1852 to 1870 (when the law was declared unconstitutional) was derived from this tax aimed at Chinese miners. Violent intimidation also drove many Chinese miners into other occupations.

As a result, many of the Chinese began working at railroad construction, and Chinese immigrants provided most of the manual labor for the building of the western portion of the first transcontinental railroad. Irish immigrants had done the work until about 1865, but when railroad owners found the

Chinese willing to work more cheaply, a switch was quickly made. After the railroads were completed, Chinese sought other work and soon found employment in California's burgeoning industries, primarily shoe, cigar, and textile manufacturing. Chinese immigrants were paid less than their white counterparts, a situation that persisted even after it became clear that Chinese workers often produced more shoes, cigars, and clothing than white workers.

Thus, the stage was set for an outcry against Chinese immigrants. Those with anti-Chinese sentiment usually voiced three concerns. First, nativists argued that the Chinese should not be allowed to continue emigrating to the United States because as nonwhites Asians were incapable of becoming "true" Americans. A second "threat" posed by Chinese immigration was the possibility that Asians might intermarry with whites. A California politician warned in 1878 that "were the Chinese to amalgamate at all with our people, it would be the lowest, most vile and degraded of our race, and the result of that amalgamation would be a hybrid of the most despicable, a mongrel of the most detestable that has ever afflicted the earth." A third reason American nativists opposed Chinese immigration was the fear that the Chinese would lower American living standards because they were willing to work hard for low wages. If Chinese were allowed to immigrate to the United States, American employers would soon expect whites to work harder for less money, thus making it impossible for whites to earn a decent living or to work at a reasonable pace. One meeting of workers held to protest Chinese employment in shoe factories complained that if hiring them continued, "American labor" would be reduced to "the Chinese standard of rice and rats," which was what Americans believed that the Chinese laborers lived on because of the low wages they accepted.

When Congress failed to redress the nativists' fears, Americans took matters into their own hands. Anti-Chinese riots, many incited by workers who feared that Chinese immigrants might take their jobs, occurred throughout the West (including Colorado, Wyoming, Idaho, Nevada, California, and Washington) in the late 1870s and 1880s. Ironically, those who incited these riots were often immigrants themselves, especially the Irish but also Italian and Slavic immigrants. In 1885, for example, the European-immigrant community of Rock Springs, Wyoming, rampaged through the town's Chinese immigrant enclave, killing fifty-one and permanently driving the rest out of town. In some cases these incidents could be characterized as pogroms rather than riots because they occurred with the tacit or even explicit support of government officials. This was the case in 1885 in Tacoma, Washington, where with the blessing of the mayor rioters drove the seven hundred Chinese inhabitants out of town and burned "Chinatown" to prevent them from returning. Even American Indians found the Asians a threat: in 1866 Paiute Indians attacked and killed fifty Chinese miners in southern Idaho.

Although anti-Chinese sentiment pervaded the West, it was particularly virulent in California, where the majority of the first generation of Chinese immigrants resided. A movement to ban Chinese immigration developed there in the 1870s, spearheaded by the Workingmen's Party of California (WPC). Led by the Irish immigrant Denis Kearney, a fiery orator who attracted a cross-section of working-class Californians to the organization, the WPC grew into a powerful force in California politics in the late 1870s. Through both the violence they fomented and their electoral clout, Kearney and the WPC forced Congress to consider legislation restricting Chinese immigration.

One might have expected the Chinese Exclusion Act of 1882, which suspended the immigration of Chinese laborers, to mitigate American anti-Asian sentiment. Yet the Rock Springs and Tacoma riots both took place *after* Congress had suspended Chinese immigration. In the end, however, the Chinese Exclusion Act did calm nativist fears, and although anti-Asian sentiment did not die (it soon focused on Japanese immigrants instead), the focus of nativists shifted back to European immigration.

Fear of Southern and Eastern Europeans

Fear of European immigrants revived in the 1880s and 1890s, a period when the majority of immigrants to the United States were coming from southern and eastern Europe (Italy, Greece, Russia, and the Austro-Hungarian Empire) rather than from northern and western Europe. Nativists argued that this new immigration threatened the American race, a term that by this point was understood to mean white, Anglo-Saxon, and Protestant. The southern and eastern European immigrants, in contrast, were primarily Catholic and Jewish. As a result, nativists for the first time began demanding numerical quotas on European immigration. One nativist organization promoting these views was the American Protective Association (APA), founded in Iowa in 1887. The APA stressed that Catholic immigrants posed a threat to American public schools and American politics. APA membership peaked in the early 1890s at about five hundred thousand.

A second facet of nativism in this period, and one that by the 1890s had begun to overshadow anti-Catholicism, was antiradicalism. Many Americans believed that immigrants brought European radicalism with them to America, and they especially blamed the newcomers for fomenting the labor unrest that characterized much of this period. The prominent role immigrants often played in the communist, socialist, and anarchist movements also helped convince many Americans that unless the country restricted immigration, radicals from abroad might soon dominate America. The association of immigrants with radicalism became especially pronounced in 1886. When labor unions in Chicago striking for an eight-hour workday were violently suppressed by the police, a group of German immigrant anarchists organized a protest meeting to be held at the Haymarket Square. Police tried to break up the meeting, and someone threw a bomb into the police lines, killing eight. Four of the Germans were convicted of murder and hanged, and the Haymarket incident convinced many Americans that immigrant radicalism posed a serious threat to the nation.

Southern methods of mob violence that had once been reserved for black victims were by this point used by nativist mobs as well. When the police chief of New Orleans was murdered in 1891, many in the city suspected that Italian immigrants and their recently publicized Mafia criminal organizations were responsible. The police arrested a number of Italians for questioning in the case, but before any charges could be filed, a mob pulled eleven of the Italians from the city jail and lynched them. Similar methods were used in the case of Leo Frank, a Jewish pencil factory owner accused of rape and murder in Atlanta in 1913. Although the evidence seemed to implicate another man, during the trial mobs gathered outside the courtroom aiming guns at the jury through the courtroom windows and shouting "Hang the Jew." Frank was convicted and sentenced to death, but when it appeared that his appeals might succeed, a mob kidnapped him from prison on 16 August 1915 and lynched him.

The Decline of Nativism

During and after World War I, nativists continued to pressure Congress to restrict European immigration (most Asian immigration had already been banned). Violence was one of the many factors that eventually led Congress to act. The Ku Klux Klan had been revived by this point, and its new agenda, which added anti-Catholicism, anti-Semitism, and antiforeignism to its traditional hatred of blacks, attracted five million members. The Klan's disdain of immigrants, demonstrated through its many acts of violence against Catholics and Jews (many of whom were immigrants), was part of the backlash against immigrants after World War I that drove Congress to pass the National Origins Act of 1924. This act reflected prevailing prejudices by setting immigration quotas that blatantly discriminated against southern and eastern Europeans and Asians. For example, the 1924 law (as eventually amended) permitted 65,721 immigrants from Great Britain annually, but only 5,802 from Italy and 2,712 from the Soviet Union. Asians were completely excluded.

With immigration reduced so dramatically, nativist violence began to decline as well. In addition, more and more Americans began to perceive the United States as a "nation of immigrants," and this also helped curb nativist violence. Changes in the immigration laws in the 1960s brought about immigration levels not seen since the eve of World War I. The new laws rescinded the tiny quotas originated in 1924 and replaced them with hemispheric limits. The unexpectedly large increase in immigration after 1965 resulted to a great extent from provisions exempting from quotas most immigrants joining family members already in the United States. Illegal immigration also increased dramatically after the 1970s. As a result, at the close of the twentieth century the immigrant population made up approximately one-third of New York City's total population and virtually one-half of that of Los Angeles.

Many journalists and pundits discerned an increase in American nativism in the 1980s and 1990s. For example, Chinese American Vincent Chin of Detroit was murdered in the early 1980s by two unemployed autoworkers who believed Chin to be Japanese. Yet the sheer number of new immigrants arriving in the United States could not alone account for the resurgence of nativism. The impression that the U.S. economy could no longer sustain the growth rate as it had with previous generations also played a role. In the past the American economy seemed so robust that there was room for all, but Americans in the 1980s saw the country as having finite economic resources that it could not afford to share with new immigrants. These fears were reflected in the violence directed at Korean-American shopkeepers during the Los Angeles riots of 1992.

Nonetheless, organized nativism and nativist violence were a far less significant factor in late-twentieth-century America than they had been in the period from 1850 to 1925. Americans generally no longer create movements or ideologies focused on the reduction of immigration or the maintenance of the country's ethnic status quo. Most Americans have learned to accept the United States as a multiethnic nation. This reflects a fundamental change in American thinking from that of the heyday of nativist violence.

BIBLIOGRAPHY

Anbinder, Tyler. *Nativism and Slavery: The Know Nothing Party and the Politics of the 1850s.* New York: Oxford University Press, 1992.

Bennett, David H. *The Party of Fear: The American Far Right from Nativism to the Militia Movement.* Rev. ed. New York: Vintage, 1995.

Billington, Ray A. *The Protestant Crusade, 1800–1860: A Study of the Origins of American Nativism.* Chicago: Quadrangle, 1938.

Feldberg, Michael. *The Philadelphia Riots of 1844: A Study in Ethnic Conflict.* Westport, Conn.: Greenwood, 1975.

Gorn, Eliot J. "'Good-Bye Boys, I Die a True American': Homicide, Nativism, and Working-Class Culture in Antebellum New York City." *Journal of American History* 74 (Sept. 1987).

Higham, John. *Strangers in the Land: Patterns of American Nativism, 1860–1925.* 2d ed. New York: Atheneum, 1963.

Ray, Sister Mary Augustina. *American Opinion of Roman Catholicism in the Eighteenth Century.* New York: Columbia University Press, 1936.

Reimers, David M. *Still the Golden Door: The Third World Comes to America.* 2d ed. New York: Columbia University Press, 1992.

Saxton, Alexander. *Indispensable Enemy: Labor and the Anti-Chinese Movement in California.* Berkeley: University of California Press, 1995.

Storti, Craig. *Incident at Bitter Creek: The Story of the Rock Springs Chinese Massacre.* Ames: Iowa State University Press, 1991.

Takaki, Ronald. *Strangers from a Different Shore: A History of Asian Americans.* New York: Penguin, 1989.

Wunder, John R. "Anti-Chinese Violence in the American West, 1850–1910." In *Law for the Elephant, Law for the Beaver: Essays in the Legal History of the North American West,* edited by John McLaren et al. Pasadena, Calif.: Ninth Judicial Circuit Historical Society, 1992.

TYLER ANBINDER

See also **Extremism; Foreign Intervention, Fear of; Hate Crimes; Immigration; Race and Ethnicity.**

NATURE VS. NURTURE

Freud and Darwin were both aware of aggression as a basic instinct. In *The Expression of Emotions in Man and Animals* (1873), Darwin described anger as one of the basic emotions, apparent in animals, infants, and people across many cultures. Although anger is not identical with aggression, it is the emotion that promotes fight rather than flight. Freud named aggression as one of the instinctive urges of the mind, placing it in the id, the mental center of all instinctive drives. According to his theory, people have a drive to destroy, to injure others, that must be repressed by the superego, the mental center for conscience. Parents have the burdensome task of socializing their children to curb their violent impulses and live by the many restrictions of society. For each individual, the task of repressing instinctive desires is a constant one, requiring mental energy. Like water under pressure in a pipe, the instincts are always striving for release and can burst forth when the superego's attention wanders.

Prior to World War II, ethology became established as a field by Konrad Lorenz and N. Tinbergen. Ethologists dealt with the behavior of animals in the wild and made observational studies of them. Observations included experimental interventions, but in settings more natural than behaviorism's lab-reared rats and pigeons. Ethology identified specific instincts, called fixed-action patterns, that comprised a species' behavioral repertoire. In his *On Aggression* (1966), Lorenz, winner of the Nobel Prize for his work on imprinting in graylag geese, popularized his ethological theory of aggression: Aggression is an instinct in most animals. Fighting for dominance within a species is natural and inevitable. As with other instincts, if no opportunity arises for the release of aggressive energy, aggression can be spontaneous and unprovoked. Thus, the metaphor of water under pressure applies to Lorenz's theory as well as Freud's. Lorenz, however, believed that animals have other instincts that curbed the extent of damage resulting from the aggressive instinct. Animals have instinctive signals for surrender, such as a wolf's upturning of its neck to a dominant animal, and combat can end before a serious injury or death is inflicted. Humans' lack of biologically based weapons, like canine teeth and claws, also means that they have failed to evolve the restraining instincts of the "lower" animals. Hence, expression of the aggressive instincts is especially hazardous for *Homo sapiens.*

Evolutionary Theory Applied to Aggression

After World War II a greater appreciation of the subtlety of evolutionary theory developed. Darwin's "struggle for existence" did not mandate aggression, because in some species cooperation and nonaggression are equally effective in securing resources and in within-species competition. For example, when male ground squirrels find a female with a suitor already present, rather than fighting for that mate they run and search for an unaccompanied female. In the ethological tradition, detailed observations were made of many animal species in the wild, and the outcome was disconcerting for the nonaggressive view of many species. Contrary to Lorenz's idea of self-limiting aggression, male lions fought to the death and male chimpanzees actually engaged in raids into other troops' territories, where they seemingly purposely sought out and attacked isolated males. There was a disturbing echo in their behavior of border raids of human warfare. Furthermore, when male lions won control of a pride, and male monkeys wrested control of a troop, the new dominant animal sometimes killed the offspring of the resident mothers, ensuring that they raised no biological offspring other than its own. The pessimistic view of Tennyson's "nature, red in tooth and claw" seemed closer to the truth, at least in some species, than Lorenz's faint hope that aggression was self-limited and regulated.

The water-under-pressure metaphor also fell out of favor; it was replaced by a strategic view of animal behavior. According to a strategic model, instincts do not build over time only to be needlessly and inappropriately released. Rather, animals make cost-benefit analyses of their behavioral choices and unconsciously pick the one with the least cost and greatest payoff. Ideas from an abstract mathematical subfield, game theory, were widely applied across biology, explaining everything from why a red-back spider would let its mate devour it to why elephant seals fight to the death to control a harem of females. The new evolutionary biology had several names. E. O. Wilson coined the word *sociobiology* to identify the fledgling discipline that sought to understand social behavior using the principles of evolutionary biology. Wilson's assertion that sociobiology might engulf many social sciences less grounded in biology raised the hackles of social scientists in a variety of fields, and led many to shy away from his term. Another field with related goals, called *evolutionary psychology*, has grown in influence since Wilson proposed sociobiology. Evolutionary psychology emphasizes "mental modules," mental processes localized to specific neural networks that are the adaptive legacy of natural selection. Evolutionary models of behavior also flourished in ethology and Darwinian anthropology.

All evolution-based theories of behavior made a precise distinction between ultimate and proximate causation. Proximate causation is the immediate mechanism of behavior, for example, the pleasure derived from eating a candy bar. Ultimate causation relates to the evolutionary history of a behavior, and tells how evolutionary pressures of various kinds—the natural environment, competition from members of the same species, threats from microorganisms—shaped the biology of an organism so that it responds in an adaptive way to particular circumstances. Preference for sweet and fatty foods presumably evolved because those individuals who lacked such preferences left fewer offspring than those who had such preferences, and because to some extent these differences in taste preference were heritable. Thus, people prefer fats and sweets because evolution created taste receptors for them and allied with the peripheral receptors a psychological reward in the brain.

Proximate vs. Ultimate Explanation

Ultimate explanations of behavior are discovered in part by tracing the phylogeny (i.e., evolutionary history) of behavior. Molecular genetic and fossil evidence suggests that the great apes, including gorillas, orangutans, and chimpanzees, are humans' closest living relatives. An aggressive instinct present in the common ancestors of all the living apes (humans now included) might be revealed in the aggression of mankind's nonhuman kin. The distribution of aggression among these species, however, is not a simple one. Orangutans appear to commit a behavior in the wild analogous to human rape. As noted by Jane Goodall, the common chimpanzee (*Pan troglodytes*) is an aggressive animal, with violence extending to border skirmishes. Figure 1 shows territorial aggression where male chimpanzees attack a lone male from another group.

Complexity enters when another chimpanzee species is included, the bonobo (pigmy chimp, *Pan paniscus*) chimpanzee. Bonobos are unaggressive, live in a common troop in relative harmony, and cement their social alliances with mutual sexual stimulation; in a phrase from the 1960s, they make love, not war. Similarly, gorilla males are not nearly as aggressive as the common chimpanzee.

These evolutionary differences must be based in different selective pressures. In the case of the two chimpanzee species, the bonobo have no competition from gorillas, which do not live in their region in Africa, and so have access to a wider variety of foods. More accessible food may have supported larger and more cooperative troops of males and females and thus the evolution of behavior away from male aggressiveness. Regardless of whether this explanation of the bonobo's evolution is correct, the lesson of these species' dissimilarities is that any biological basis to human aggression must be sought in a reconstruction of the particular circumstances of human evolution from the common ancestor shared by all apes, probably no more than five million years ago. In short, environmental factors interact with genetic predispositions in many and unpredictable ways.

Sexual Selection Theory

Evolutionary theory offers sexual selection as a broad explanation for human sex differences in aggression. Sexual selection, as applied to many species, focuses on a biological asymmetry in parental investment in offspring. In mammals, females have the larger sex cell (egg) than males (sperm), carry a fetus through its development, and nurse the neonate after birth. Males must provide sperm, but beyond that the extent of paternal investment in offspring is highly variable. In general, the sex that invests less in offspring gains more from mating opportunities than the sex that invests more; in most mammals, the less-investing sex is the male, and this certainly applies to humans, although less dramatically. With an evolutionary "score" kept by the number of surviving offspring, aggression and risk taking will gain more for males than females, because these behaviors can secure additional matings. In this theory evolution has left human males with a biologically based psychology more prone to aggression, and other risky tactics, that might win mates. The effective polygyny of the majority of human societies also may sexually select greater aggressiveness in males. Further, xenophobia and prejudice may be biologically evolved traits that fuel aggressive conflicts between human groups under circumstances of competition and threat. Humans, especially males, may have evolved instincts that predispose toward aggression.

This evolutionary biological view of aggression is not without its critics. A 1987 scientific conference in Spain led to the Seville Statement on Violence, which repudiated any biological basis to warfare in *Homo sapiens;* rather, it attributed warfare and aggression mainly to the effects of culture.

FIGURE 1. Primates fighting in group. Photo courtesy of the Jane Goodall Institute

445

A strong critic of the biological view was the Harvard geneticist Richard Lewontin, who in 1984 published a general criticism of biological views of behavior entitled *Not in Our Genes*. Lewontin and his coauthors accused evolutionary scholars of practicing "adaptive story telling," creating analogues of Kipling's *Just So* stories in which intellectual speculation ran rampant in the absence of sufficient empirical proof. In 1979 Stephen Jay Gould and Lewontin had proposed that a trait can be complex and appear adaptive, but instead is incidental to some other adaptation and so may have no particular adaptive purpose in itself. Their analogy was to the triangular space between the curve of an arch and the right angle that encloses it, called a spandrel. The spandrel itself has no function, whereas the arch, which lends the spandrel its form, supports a cathedral's ceiling. The large human brain, according to Gould, might be such an incidental feature, promoting a range of human behaviors not biologically but culturally. Gould argued that behavioral traits are highly flexible and "may never have been subject to direct natural selection."

Developmental Psychology Applied to Aggression

Work in other fields emphasized the proximal determinants of aggression rather than any evolutionary roots. In psychology the main explanation for aggression was social learning theory. In the 1960s Albert Bandura conducted experiments showing that young children will imitate an adult's aggressive actions directed toward a large, inflatable toy. Given further encouragement, even children who do not initially display aggression, when left alone with the clown toy, did so. Bandura argued that models—salient people who display aggression and receive reward for it—encouraged children's aggressiveness. These rewards could be "vicarious," that is, received by a model (e.g., a character in a TV program) instead of by a child directly. Considerable research has been done on TV programming and the media as a cause of aggression, which has been unexpectedly inconclusive because causality may also flow in the other direction, with tough and aggressive children preferring to watch programming containing aggression.

The Psychology of Sex Differences, by Eleanor Maccoby and Carol Jacklin (1974), did much to stimulate research on sex differences in aggression. Their book was a narrative summary of the many studies that compared behavioral and psychological traits in boys and girls. Aggression emerged as one of the largest, and most consistent, sex differences. Not only did boys display more aggression in rough-and-tumble play than did girls, but these different play styles also led to a strong sex segregation of play groups in childhood. Maccoby and Jacklin emphasized the role of peers in reinforcing aggression and in differentiating the aggressive tendencies of boys and girls. Developmental psychologists also found that an aggressive trait was highly stable from childhood to adulthood.

Hormonal Influences on Aggression

In contrast to this environmentally oriented tradition, the biological theory of aggression focused on hormones, in part because they were the logical place to find a biological basis for the well-established sex difference. Examinations of testosterone and androgens from the adrenal glands (on the kidneys) have revealed that the level of testosterone circulating in blood has a relationship to aggression (most studies have been of males). The relationship is not a strong one, however, possibly because the hormone has adequate physiological effects in a wide range of blood levels, and because it has a stronger effect on antisocial outcomes among lower-class than middle-class individuals. Hormones, however, also shape the development of the brain prenatally. Thus, theories of hormonal effects distinguish these prenatal, sensitizing effects from postnatal, activating effects; in some nonhuman animals, the sensitizing effects may extend into the early postnatal period. Some behavioral sex reversals have been documented in association with altered prenatal exposure to androgens. In particular, girls prenatally exposed to adrenal androgens chose to play with male-stereotyped toys at about the rate of boys, and much more than their unaffected sisters and female cousins. This hormone research presents some of the most compelling evidence for a biological influence on male-typed traits linked to aggression.

Behavioral Genetics Applied to Aggression

Another tradition of biological explanation of aggression focused on individual differences within human populations, with a particular focus on the antecedents of crime. In the latter part of the nineteenth century, Cesare Lombroso (*L'homme criminel*, 1887) proposed that criminals carried physical stigmata that separated them from law-abiding people—for example, a sloped forehead, a brow ridge over the eyes. Criminals were atavistic throwbacks to an earlier stage of human evolution. Lombroso's views, however, lost support when data collected on criminals largely disconfirmed them. Although criminals are typically more mesomorphic (muscular) than noncriminals, they do not appear to possess any distinctive facial features. The idea that criminals are evolutionary throwbacks also clashed with evolutionary theory, because the entire *Homo sapiens* species had diverged from its common ancestral relationship with the great apes.

The discipline of behavioral genetics took up the search for a genetic basis to individual differences in the predisposition toward criminality. Unlike Lombroso's efforts, the search was not for manifest, physical traits associated with crime but instead for evidence of genetic influences on crime. Both evolutionary explanations and behavioral genetic ones are interested in genetic effects, but they are dissimilar in emphasis. The former looks for genetic influences on behavior that are typical across a whole species, or those behaviors typical of men and women within *Homo sapiens*. Behavioral geneticists seek the genetic influences on individual differences in aggression—why one man is many times more aggressive than another man who lives in the same neighborhood and grows up under similar circumstances. Intellectually, the evolutionary explanations are heirs to Darwin's theory of evolution; behavioral genetic explanations are heirs to Sir Francis Galton's work on individual differences (*Hereditary Genius: An Inquiry into Its Laws and Consequences*, 1869, 1962). It was Galton, a polymath who investigated the resemblance of biological relatives for eminence in the sciences and humanities, who first proposed using twins to study genetic influences on behavior.

A number of twins studies of crime were conducted prior to World War II. With the caution that the number of twin pairs in each was relatively small, these early studies suggested a genetic influence on crime because monozygotic (MZ; one egg) twin pairs were more concordant for criminal behavior than dizygotic (DZ; two egg) twin pairs. The studies were limited to twins who could be located, in prisons and reform schools; criminals who escaped arrest were missed. Done when the political zeitgeist favored genetic explanations of crime, the studies were also perhaps prejudiced.

In the post–World War II period, there has been a tremendous increase in behavioral twins studies

of crime and aggression using the twin and adoption methods. In Denmark, Sarnoff Mednick and colleagues conducted a study of criminal behavior using national records on adoptions. They found support for genetic influences on property crime, but not on violent crime, when violent crime was analyzed separately. (The rate of violent crime was extremely low.) In the same country the national records were used to locate all the country's twin pairs born in the same years. A search of the twins' criminal records revealed greater concordance of criminal behavior in MZ than DZ twin pairs. These pioneering studies have stimulated a large number of studies on aggression and personality traits related to aggression. In a review of twenty-four genetically informative studies of aggression, mainly based on parental or self-reports of aggression, it was estimated that 50 percent of the individual differences in aggressive behavior were due to genetic differences (heritability, $h^2 = .50$). The estimates of shared family environmental effect was near zero, but the authors, Miles and Carey, cautioned that adoption studies rarely included abusive families in their samples. At least among a fair number of scientists, the consensus is that criminal behavior and aggression are heritable traits.

Molecular Genetics Applied to Aggression

Recent advances in molecular genetics are beginning to inform studies of the biological basis of aggression. One use of molecular genetics is in determining evolutionary phylogeny among humans and apes. The more closely related are two species, the more any sections of their DNA molecules—which carry the genetic information of heredity—are identical. Based on identity of DNA, humans appear most closely related to chimpanzees, and less so to the gorilla and orangutan. New data, however, may lead to reappraisals of the human evolutionary tree.

The other use of molecular genetics is to locate specific genes associated with aggression. In the first report of a specific genetic influence on aggression, a whole chromosome was implicated. Men with an extra copy of the Y chromosome, XYY males, were reported to be more aggressive than other men. Further evaluation of these cases, however, suggested that there was no effect specific to aggression; rather, the general mental retardation of these men brought them into greater contact with the criminal justice system.

With the advent of genome-wide sets of genetic markers, as well as greater knowledge about the molecular genetics of specific genes expressed in the brain, a search is under way for genes related to aggression and associated psychiatric disorders (e.g., a diagnosis of antisocial personality disorder or attention deficit hyperactivity disorder). One study, by Brunner and his colleagues, looked at a Dutch family in which some men were impulsive and aggressive, especially toward women. These affected men were also mentally retarded. A genetic cause was discovered in the DNA molecule: a mutation in the monoamine oxidase A (MAOA) gene on the X chromosome that rendered the enzyme produced by this gene inactive. Although this MAOA mutation explains a particular kind of aggression found in this family, it is extremely rare and cannot explain the more common forms of aggression and psychiatric disorders. Using the techniques of genetic linkage and association analysis, many genome regions and candidate genes are being screened for their association with psychiatric disorders. A replicated relationship has been found between a variant of the dopamine transporter gene and attention deficit hyperactivity disorder, a diagnosis that often co-occurs with a diagnosis of conduct disorder and that is also predictive of aggression. Another replicated relationship exists between a variant of the aldehyde dehydrogenase gene and alcohol consumption. In about half the Japanese population, this variant is protective against alcoholism because the defective gene allows a toxic by-product of alcohol metabolism (i.e., acetaldehyde) to accumulate in the body. Because alcohol is implicated in many crimes of violence, this gene would be indirectly protective against violence. Additional genetic markers will undoubtedly emerge as knowledge of the molecular genetics of behavior expands.

Critics of a biological basis of behavior, including aggression, have also attacked the findings from behavioral genetic studies. Their criticisms point to potential flaws in the methodology of twins and adoption studies. For example, MZ twins look alike in their physical appearance, and they also may be treated more alike, than DZ twins. Behavior geneticists have responded to these criticisms of the twins method by examining the relationship of physical appearance to traits; usually, it is not strong enough to explain twins' behavioral similarity. Further, if the more equal treatment of MZ twins is evoked by the twins themselves, then this is not a limitation of the twins study. The critics also complain that, in studies of rare pairs of MZ twins separated and raised apart, the twins were usually not raised in completely dissimilar circumstances. Adoption studies are criticized for their incomplete assessment of the whole environmental range. Although these critics have made methodological points that stimulated responses from behavioral geneticists, few scientists would concur with their strongest views, namely, that the heritability of behavioral traits is zero. Insofar as the majority of personality and intellectual traits are heritable, it is unlikely that aggressive traits will prove to be exceptional.

Cross-Cultural Studies of Aggression

Cross-cultural work also bears on the biological basis of aggression. In all societies, men are more aggressive than women, and men are more responsible for the execution of intertribal raids and warfare. Margaret Mead's description of societies without the usual sex roles (*Coming of Age in Samoa*, 1928) has been largely discredited (Derek Freeman, *Margaret Mead and Samoa*, 1983). In criminology, data from around the world have been used to examine the age-crime curve. Most common forms of crime peak in prevalence in late adolescence to young adulthood, and this is a universal. Although universality of a behavior is not automatic proof of a genetic basis (e.g., the universality of *Homo sapiens'* use of fire), it does eliminate many explanations based on a specific culture. For instance, greater male aggression cannot be attrib-

TABLE 1. Same-Sex Homicides in Various Societies

Location	Proportion of Total Same-Sex Killings Where Males Killed Males
Canada	94%
Miami	96%
Chicago	96%
Detroit	96%
Tzeltal Mayans (Mexico)	100%
Belo Horizonte (Brazil)	97%
New South Wales (Australia)	94%
Oxford (England, 1296–1298)	99%
Iceland	100%
Munda (India)	100%
!Kung San (Botswana)	100%
Tiv (Nigeria)	97%
BaSonga (Uganda)	98%
LaLuyia (Kenya)	95%

NOTE: Copyright Guilford Press, 1994. Reprinted with permission from Rowe 1994. For additional examples, see the original source, Daly and Wilson 1988.

uted to exposure to violent television programming, because this difference existed in cultures that largely lacked TV and, indeed, historically before the invention of TV. Martin Daly and Margo Wilson discovered that cross-cultural sex differences in homicide varied by their type. The greatest sex difference occurred for same-sex homicides among adults. As shown in table 1, almost all these same-sex murders were committed by men, and this pattern held across all the cultures investigated. Daly and Wilson regard this pattern in homicide statistics as confirmation of sexual selection theory, because homicide, a most severe form of resolving conflict, is more frequent among men than among women.

The nature vs. nurture debate over aggression is not closed and will undoubtedly continue. The position of the Seville Statement, that humans have no biological dispositions toward aggression, seems increasingly untenable in light of the accumulation of evidence, from both evolutionary theory and behavioral genetics, for some genetic influence on aggression. Admitting some genetic influence, and allowing for some environmental influence, however, will not resolve the nature vs. nurture debate, because questions will remain as to how much of each influence there is, under what circumstances each operates, and with what degree of malleability. Instead of one nature vs. nurture debate, there will be many smaller debates relevant to the many different ways in which aggression can be conceptualized: for instance, one focused on sex differences, another on the psychiatric diagnosis of conduct disorder, another on the propensity to organize for war, and another on genocide. The nature vs. nurture debate will yield no single answer, but many; it is to be hoped that a greater depth of understanding will result from scientists' efforts to answer the perennial question about aggression, that of the causative roles of nature and nurture.

BIBLIOGRAPHY

Bandura, Albert. *Aggression: A Social Learning Analysis*. Englewood Cliffs, N.J.: Prentice-Hall, 1973.

Berenbaum, Sheri A., and M. Hines. "Early Androgens are Related to Childhood Sex-Typed Toy Preferences." *Psychological Science* 3 (1992).

Brunner, H. G., et al. "Abnormal Behavior Associated with a Point Mutation in the Structural Gene for Monoamine Oxidase A." *Science* 262 (1993).

Christiansen, Karl O. "Crime in a Danish Twin Population." *Acta Geneticae Medicae et Gemellologicae: Twin Research* 19 (1970).

Cook, E. H., et al. "Association of Attention-Deficit Disorder and the Dopamine Transporter Gene." *American Journal of Human Genetics* 56 (1995).

Dabbs, James M., and Robin Morris. "Testosterone, Social Class, and Antisocial Behavior in a Sample of 4,462 Men." *Psychological Science* 1, no. 3 (1990).

Daly, Martin, and Margo Wilson. *Homicide*. New York: Aldine de Gruyter, 1988.

Freud, Sigmund. *Beyond the Pleasure Principle* [1920]. In Standard Edition, Vol. 18. London: Hogarth Press, 1955.

Goodall, Jane. *The Chimpanzees of Gombe: Patterns of Behavior*. Cambridge, Mass.: Harvard University Press, 1986.

Gould, Stephen Jay. *The Mismeasure of Man*. New York: Norton, 1981.

Gould, Stephen Jay, and Richard C. Lewontin. "The Spandrels of San Marco and the Panglossian Paradigm: A Critique of the Adaptationist Program." *Proceedings of the Royal Society of London B* 205 (1979).

Kamin, Leon. *The Science and Politics of IQ*. Potomac, Md.: Erlbaum, 1974.

Lewontin, Richard C., Steven Rose, and Leon J. Kamin. *Not in Our Genes*. New York: Pantheon, 1984.

Maccoby, Eleanor E., and Carol N. Jacklin. *The Psychology of Sex Differences*. Stanford, Calif.: Stanford University Press, 1974.

Mednick, Sarnoff A., et al. "Genetic Influences on Criminal Convictions: Evidence from an Adoption Cohort." *Science* 224 (1984).

Miles, Donna R., and Gregory Carey. "Genetic and Environmental Architecture of Human Aggression." *Journal of Personality and Social Psychology* 73, no. 1 (1997).

Rowe, David C. *The Limits of Family Influence: Genes, Experience, and Behavior*. New York: Guilford, 1994.

Tinbergin, N. *The Study of Instinct*. Oxford: Clarendon Press, 1951.

Tu, G. C., and Y. Israel. "Alcohol Consumption by Orientals in North America is Predicted Largely by a Single Gene." *Behavior Genetics* 25 (1995).

Waal, Frans B. de. *Bonobo: The Forgotten Ape*. Berkeley: University of California Press, 1997.

Wilson, E. O. *Sociobiology*. Cambridge, Mass.: Harvard University Press, 1975.

Wrangham, Richard, and Dale Peterson. *Demonic Males: Apes and the Origins of Human Violence*. Boston: Houghton Mifflin, 1996.

DAVID C. ROWE

See also **Developmental Factors; Sociobiology; Theories of Violence.**

NAVY. *See* Military.

NELSON, GEORGE "BABY FACE" (1908–1934)

In the 1920s and 1930s, a time filled with the most famous American mobsters, George Nelson was

George "Baby Face" Nelson, as shown on a 1934 police poster. CORBIS/BETTMANN

obsessed with attaining the reputation as the most dangerous and vicious of them all. Reaching only five feet four inches, Nelson (born Lester Gillis) was resentful of his diminutive stature. Born in Chicago in 1908, he was raised in the street gangs of the area. Wishing to be called "Big George" Nelson, he instead gained infamy as "Baby Face" Nelson. He became well known for his quick trigger finger and his excessively violent nature.

Nelson's early criminal career began with petty thievery, moving on to extortion of brothels and bookie joints, before he finally reached Al Capone's empire of organized crime in Chicago in 1929. Responsible for extorting money from labor unions, he was known to be ruthless in his beatings of union leaders who attempted to resist paying. After some of these beatings proved fatal, Nelson was dropped from Capone's payroll.

Imprisoned in Joliet, Illinois, in 1931 for a jewelry store robbery, Nelson managed to escape on 17 February 1932, and soon found work as a hired gunman. By 1933 Nelson had formed his own gang, and he began robbing banks in the Midwest.

Ever concerned with his reputation, Nelson was furious when these robberies were attributed to John Dillinger or "Pretty Boy" Floyd. Nelson's modus operandi was quite different from that of Floyd or Dillinger. While both of the better-known criminals were reputed to be levelheaded thinkers, killing only when it was necessary to escape, Nelson stormed into banks with guns blazing, unconcerned with the number of lives lost. In 1934 Dillinger broke out of jail, and he and Nelson joined forces. Members of their gang noted that Dillinger was astonished at Nelson's hotheaded nature. After a traffic accident, Nelson shot and killed the driver of the other car, claiming that the driver had recognized Dillinger sitting on the passenger side of Nelson's vehicle. In a later bank robbery, Dillinger had to convince Nelson to spare the life of the bank's vice president. It was later rumored that Nelson, Dillinger, and Floyd worked together in June 1934, in the robbery of a bank in South Bend, Indiana. Nelson never lost his insane desire to be the most feared and sought-after criminal. Within five months of the robbery in South Bend, all three gangsters ended their careers. The federal Division of Investigation (the predecessor to the Federal Bureau of Investigation) purportedly killed Dillinger on 22 July 1934 (although some claim it was another man who died, and Dillinger managed to escape), and Floyd was shot and killed on 22 October. On 27 November, cornered by two agents near Fox River Grove, Illinois, Nelson left the cover of a ditch and, in full view of several onlookers, walked toward the agents. Nelson, hit a total of seventeen times, advanced and killed both agents. He died of his wounds in a final moment of dramatic brutality. Nelson's death signaled an end to the era of the famous mobsters of the 1920s and 1930s. For a man obsessed with reputation and fame, this would perhaps be little consolation for the fact that even in death, Nelson has never been able to reach the infamy gained by Dillinger.

BIBLIOGRAPHY

King, Jeffery S. *The Life and Death of Pretty Boy Floyd.* Kent, Ohio: Kent Library State University Press, 1998.
Toland, John. *The Dillinger Days.* New York: Da Capo, 1995.

TRACY W. PETERS

See also **Capone, Al; Dillinger, John; Floyd, Charles Arthur "Pretty Boy"; Organized Crime.**

NEONATICIDE. *See* Infanticide.

NEO-NAZIS

Identifying neo-Nazi groups is difficult. Some experts consider all groups with a racist or anti-Semitic agenda as neo-Nazis, while others only label a group neo-Nazi if it adopts Nazi symbolism, avowedly admires Adolf Hitler, and uses some variation of the term *National Socialist* in its title. Though the first definition is too broad, the second omits many groups whose philosophies echo National Socialism's major themes, even if their demeanor and actions do not.

Organizations that mimic Nazi agendas have never achieved solid success in the United States. After World War II America reviled Nazism. Even anti-Semites or racists were leery of associating with groups that glorified gas chambers, death camps, and unprecedented oppression.

However, Nazi ideology manifests itself in other ways on the American political landscape. In the 1990s increasing numbers of extremist groups adopted core elements of Nazi ideology without openly glorifying the Third Reich. For example, just like Nazi ideologues, who charged in the 1930s that German Jews were not "Aryans" (a racially meaningless term) and threatened Germany because they controlled its political, cultural, and economic life, extremists in the 1990s contend that America is controlled by the Zionist Occupation Government, which favors Jews and other non-whites and threatens the existence of white Christian society. Such conspiracy theories are designed to arouse hatred of minorities and to sow distrust of the federal government. The views espoused by Germany's Third Reich and its American successors are partially rooted in the *Protocols of the Elders of Zion*, a fraudulent tract promoted by the Russian czarist police in the early 1900s that purports to be the secret plans of Jewish elders to control the world.

Other themes are common to both groups. Hitler declared that Jews were *untermenschen*, subhumans, who had to be "exterminated." Similarly, late-twentieth-century extremist groups such as the Aryan Nations, Ku Klux Klan, and Christian Patriot groups espoused Christian Identity theology, which holds that white northern Europeans are God's chosen people, Jews are Satan's descendants, and people of color are "mud people." America, a biblical promised land, they argue, must be cleansed of Jews, racial minorities, and homosexuals.

Nazis and neo-Nazis divide the world into "us" and "them." Just as the Nazis had to awaken Germans to the threat posed by the Jew, neo-Nazis contend they must awaken the white Christian world to the danger posed by non-Caucasians and non-Christians.

Racism, anti-Semitism, xenophobia, and homophobia constitute the ideological glue binding neo-Nazi groups together. The distinctly American nuance of this fascism melds conspiratorial anti-government attitudes with isolationist arguments and frontier myths. Since the end of the Cold War this animus, which used to be directed at communism and the Soviets, is directed at the federal government.

Neo-Nazism in U.S. History

Among the best-known American neo-Nazi groups were the American Nazi Party, founded by George Lincoln Rockwell in 1959, and its successor, the National Socialist White People's Party. Other neo-Nazi parties formed during the 1970s included the National Socialist Party of America (NSPA), the White Party of America, and the National White Peoples Party. Most lasted only a few years and were oddities more than substantial threats. NSPA gained notoriety when it scheduled a march in Skokie, Illinois, in 1977. Skokie, home

George Lincoln Rockwell and followers of his American Nazi Party pose next to their Volkswagen bus in Seven Corners, Virginia, May 1961. CORBIS/BETTMANN

to many Holocaust survivors, tried to prevent the march with a city council ordinance, but the Illinois Supreme Court ruled that the NSPA could hold its march, which it did in downtown Chicago in 1978. Thousands of counterdemonstrators confronted the handful of NSPA marchers.

Hate-group opponents have different strategies. Some opponents turn out in force to shout down rallies and speeches. Adherents of "no fireworks, no media" believe the best defense is to ignore them, minimizing confrontation and thereby media interest. Other organizations have attempted to bankrupt neo-Nazis with court action. An approach that emerged in the late 1990s was to have opponents pledge charitable contributions based on the length of neo-Nazi rallies—the longer the rally, the greater the contributions to fight the group that organizes the rally.

During the 1980s the more dangerous neo-Nazi groups included the Posse Comitatus, White Aryan Resistance, Aryan Nations, and the Order. Some of them, such as the Order, were responsible for robberies, counterfeiting, and murder. These neo-Nazi ideologues increasingly practice "leaderless resistance," a tactic associated with followers of the Aryan Nations leader, Richard Butler. They form small cells with no leaders or overarching organization to direct their terrorist activities. This, apparently, was the modus operandi of those convicted for the 1995 bombing of the Alfred P. Murrah Federal Building in Oklahoma City and those charged with or suspected in the 1999 synagogue arson in Sacramento, California; shotgun killings of a gay couple in Redding, California; shootings and murders of minorities in Illinois and Indiana; and the attack on a Jewish community center in Granada Hills, California, and the murder of a postal carrier in Chatsworth, California.

These neo-Nazi groups can cause great tragedy. A more subtle danger arises when those with neo-Nazi views adopt an overtly mainstream modus operandi. This tactic is best exemplified by David Duke, a former Ku Klux Klan leader, who eschewed his Klan membership upon being elected in 1989 to the Louisiana House of Representatives. In 1990 he ran for the U.S. Senate and won 45 percent of the vote overall and 65 percent of the white vote. In 1999 as an elected Republican Party official in Louisiana and chair of the executive committee of the party in Saint Tammany Parish, Duke no longer spoke of creating specific U.S. regions where Jews and racial minorities would be forced to live, but his views reflected similar strands of racism, and he remained connected with the neo-Nazi National Alliance, using political campaigns to promote his views.

Holocaust deniers, in presenting themselves to the world as academics interested in exposing "mistakes" in history, also use a mainstream modus operandi to achieve their goals. In fact, they mistranslate, falsify, and create phony documents to try to "prove" that six million Jews were never killed. Their agenda is avowedly pro-Nazi and anti-Semitic.

The threat to America from those with neo-Nazi views comes, therefore, from two sources: those who murder, maim, and break the law as well as those who break no laws but repackage their conspiratorial hate-filled views in a way that causes some Americans to pay them heed. One attacks people and property; the other truth and memory.

BIBLIOGRAPHY

Flynn, Kevin, and Gary Gerhardt. *Silent Brotherhood.* New York: Signet, 1995.

Laqueur, Walter. *Fascism: Past, Present, Future.* New York: Oxford University Press, 1996.

Sargent, Lyman Tower, ed. *Extremism in America: A Reader.* New York: New York University Press, 1995.

Stern, Kenneth S. *A Force upon the Plain: The American Militia Movement and the Politics of Hate.* New York: Simon and Schuster, 1996.

DEBORAH E. LIPSTADT

See also **Extremism; Hate Crimes; Ku Klux Klan; Race and Ethnicity; Skinheads; Terrorism.**

NESS, ELIOT
(1903–1957)

If his biographers and the media are to be believed, Eliot Ness and his squad of nine officers singlehandedly destroyed the empire of Al Capone, the Chicago-based Mafia leader labeled Public Enemy Number One during the Prohibition era. Although such claims are historically inaccurate, Ness's hard-hitting tactical operations did cause financial losses and serious disruptions to the Capone organization.

A graduate of the University of Chicago, Ness was twenty-six years old in 1929 when he was appointed to head a special unit of the Justice Department charged with attacking violations of the Eighteenth Amendment, which banned alcohol. The interdiction efforts of the Prohibition Unit were based on the Volstead Act, which had been passed in 1919 to provide a means of enforcing the

Eliot Ness in a photo from 1936. CORBIS/BETTMANN

Eighteenth Amendment. The bootlegging and violent gangsterism of Al Capone's organization, the Outfit, was the unit's chief target.

Ness used the somewhat novel device of notifying the press before a planned raid, and the resulting newspaper coverage was a masterpiece of showmanship: Ness stage-directed high-speed chases, the smashing of stills and beer barrels with sledgehammers, and face-to-face gun battles, to create media images that, in terms of public consumption, were perhaps even more eagerly sought after than booze. In most situations he and his squad of investigators came out winners, and a picture emerged of the mob being destroyed. Ness's tactical and investigative techniques so distracted Capone and his minions that other Justice Department personnel were able to infiltrate the organization and discover sufficient evidence to put Capone behind bars on charges that stemmed, ironically, not from murder or racketeering but from tax evasion.

After Capone's demise, Ness was appointed chief investigator of Prohibition violations and turned his attention to the territories in Kentucky, Ohio, and Tennessee where moonshine (illegally distilled corn whiskey) was being made. His pen-

chant for publicity garnered him a national reputation as a crime fighter, and in 1935 he was solicited by a reform administration in Cleveland, Ohio, to help clean up crime and corruption in that city. At the time Cleveland was as plagued by crime as Chicago. Its police force was openly on the take, a street gang known as the Mayfields controlled prostitution, gambling, and bootlegging, and the construction trade unions were effectively in the hands of the mob.

For the next six years Ness was shot at, physically assaulted, and continually faced with other threats against his life. He persevered, however, and was able to create a new environment in Cleveland, mainly by shaking up the police force. Bribery was not tolerated, and ranking officers were fired outright for being "on the pad" themselves or for allowing corruption in their commands. Ness's anticorruption policy, which had been so effective in going after Capone and had earned his former squad the moniker "the Untouchables," put the Cleveland police force beyond the reach of mob bribe money and enabled it to do what police are supposed to do—arrest criminals. During his tenure, the city was turned from crime capital of the state to one of the safest cities in the United States.

Most of Ness's career was spent in some type of law enforcement. During World War II he was a member of the Division of Social Protection in the Defense Department. Following the war Ness left law enforcement for the relative peace and quiet of the private sector.

BIBLIOGRAPHY

Abadinsky, Howard. *Organized Crime.* 5th ed. Chicago: Nelson Hall, 1997.

Messick, Hank. *The Silent Syndicate.* New York: Macmillan, 1967.

Sifakis, Carl. *The Encyclopedia of American Crime.* New York: Smithmark, 1982.

PATRICK J. RYAN

See also **Capone, Al; Organized Crime.**

NEUROPSYCHOLOGY

*How the physiology of the nervous system, including the brain, affects violence is studied in four subentries: **Brain Function, Brain Imaging, Head Injury,** and **Hemispheric Laterality.***

BRAIN FUNCTION

The belief that the roots of violent behavior can be found in the brain has a lengthy historical tradition. In 1812 the physician Benjamin Rush (cited in Elliott 1978, p. 147) speculated that anti-social behavior is associated with a "defective organization in those parts of the body which are occupied by the moral faculties of the mind." Research has since confirmed that "defective organization" in the brain is in fact related to aggression. This essay will describe evidence linking certain brain structures to violent behavior and discuss theoretical models constructed to account for such relations. The brain structures described here include subcortical structures, such as the amygdala and hypothalamus, and cortical structures, particularly the left hemisphere and the frontal lobes. These structures are intricately connected, with the cortical regions exerting important regulatory influences on impulses originating in the subcortical regions.

Subcortical Contributions to Aggression

The limbic system is a relatively "old" region of the brain and includes the hippocampus, amygdala, and septum. Other subcortical structures, such as the hypothalamus, are closely linked to the limbic structures. These subcortical structures play a crucial role in emotion, motivation, and learning.

Most evidence indicating that limbic structures contribute to aggression is drawn from research on nonhuman mammals. In the 1930s the work of Kluver and Bucy revealed that damage to the amygdala produced dramatic changes in emotional and social behaviors in monkeys. Specifically, monkeys that were previously highly aggressive became very passive following damage to the amygdala. Further, electrical stimulation of particular regions of both the amygdala and the hypothalamus has been shown to have an excitatory influence on aggressive behavior in cats. There appears to be little doubt that these structures are intimately involved in the control of both affective (defensive) and predatory aggression.

On the basis of studies of these animal models, scientists have speculated that abnormalities in the amygdala and hypothalamus may be responsible for serious violent behavior in humans. For example, Charles Whitman, who shot and killed sixteen people from a clock tower on the University of Texas campus in 1966, was later found to have been suffering from an amygdaloid tumor. However, it is not clear what, if any, effect the tumor had on his behavior.

Some theorists have suggested that there is a relation between epilepsy and violence. For example, it has been suggested that epileptic seizures originating in the temporal lobe (a region encompassing the amygdala) can heighten the sensitivity of the limbic system, thus increasing the likelihood that aggressive behavior will be exhibited. Vernon H. Mark and Frank R. Ervin (1970) have described a syndrome that they call episodic dyscontrol, which is characterized by periods of uncontrollable rage and violence. Electroencephalograph (EEG) studies suggest that this syndrome is associated with abnormal electrical activity in the temporal lobe, again raising the possibility of limbic involvement.

On the basis of such evidence, doctors have attempted to treat violent offenders surgically, usually by destroying the implicated limbic structures. It is difficult to assess the overall success of such efforts. In some cases, the violent behaviors seen prior to the surgery disappear; in some cases, the improvement is only temporary; and in some cases, no change is seen at all. In addition, because the limbic structures damaged in the surgery are central to a number of important functions, reductions in violent behavior are often accompanied by a range of undesirable side effects, such as disruptions in eating or sexual behavior.

While most theorists agree that limbic structures are important substrates of violent impulses, many have chosen to focus on cortical regions (with which these subcortical structures are connected) that are involved in the regulation of such impulses. This research has highlighted two broad neuropsychological deficits associated with antisocial behavior: verbal (associated with the left-hemisphere function) and executive (associated with the frontal-lobe function).

Empirical Evidence for Left-Hemisphere Deficit

One of the most robust correlates of severe antisocial behavior is impaired verbal ability. Verbal deficits have been found in children with conduct disorders, seriously delinquent adolescents, and adult criminals. These deficits have been shown to precede the onset of serious antisocial behavior and to remain even after the effects of potential confounds, such as race, socioeconomic status, academic attainment, test motivation, and the differential detection of low-IQ delinquents, have been allowed for. Because language functions are subserved by the left cerebral hemisphere in most individuals, these findings have been interpreted as evidence for dysfunction of the left hemisphere in antisocial individuals.

Some of the most convincing evidence of the relation between language deficits and antisocial behavior comes from the Dunedin Multidisciplinary Health and Development Study conducted in New Zealand. This study consists of a birth cohort of more than one thousand New Zealanders who have been observed from birth to age twenty-one through comprehensive, biennial assessments. In this study, boys with severe conduct problems, particularly those with co-morbid attention deficit–hyperactivity disorder (ADHD), are the most neuropsychologically impaired, and this impairment occurs primarily in the verbal domain. When T. E. Moffitt (1990) examined the developmental trajectories of these boys from age three to age fifteen, he found the co-morbid cases to have histories of extreme antisocial behavior that remained stable across this period. Their neuropsychological problems were as long-standing as their antisocial behavior. At ages three and five, these boys had scored more than a standard deviation below their age norm on the Bayley and McCarthy tests of motor coordination; at each of several ages (five, seven, nine, eleven, and thirteen), these boys scored more than three-fourths of a standard deviation below their age norm on verbal IQ. In addition, neuropsychological impairment at age thirteen has been shown to predict delinquent involvement at age eighteen.

A relation between poor verbal ability and the persistence of antisocial behavior has also been found among children with conduct disorders. B. B. Lahey and colleagues (1995) found that low verbal IQ was related to the persistence of conduct disorder (CD) over time, particularly when verbal IQ was considered in conjunction with a parental history of antisocial personality disorder (APD); only boys with above-average verbal IQ and without a parental history of APD improved across time.

Empirical Evidence for Frontal-Lobe Deficit

Antisocial behavior has also been found to be associated with deficiencies in the brain's self-control or executive functions. These functions are thought to be mediated by the frontal lobes and include operations such as sustaining attention and concentration, abstract reasoning and concept formation, anticipating and planning, and inhibiting unsuccessful, inappropriate, or impulsive behaviors. Evidence of the relation between executive deficits and conduct problems has been found among incarcerated subjects, among non-conduct-disordered subjects in laboratory situations, and among general-population samples. This relationship holds when controlling for IQ and appears to be especially strong for a subgroup of offenders characterized by both antisocial behavior and symptoms of ADHD.

In the 1990s several investigators used sophisticated measures, such as the self-ordered pointing (SOP) task and the conditional association task (CAT), to investigate the relation between aggression and frontal-lobe functions. Positron-emission tomography (PET) studies found that the SOP is specifically related to the mid-dorsolateral frontal region, whereas the CAT is specifically associated with the posterior dorsolateral frontal regions.

M. A. Lau, R. O. Pihl, and J. B. Peterson (1995) found that poor performance on these two measures was associated with stability of aggression among children between the ages of six and twelve. However, P. R. Giancola and A. Zeichner (1994) reported that only performance on the CAT was associated with intensity of shocks administered to a fictitious opponent in a laboratory setting. This suggests that only deficits in the posterior dorsolateral region are associated with aggression.

As was the case for verbal deficits, the evidence suggests that poor executive functioning may be especially characteristic of the most serious offenders. In the New Zealand study, adolescent boys who exhibited symptoms of both conduct disorder and ADHD scored more poorly on neuropsychological tests of executive functions than their peers who had either CD or ADHD alone.

In addition to these documented cross-sectional relations, longitudinal studies (involving the repeated observation of a set of subjects over time with respect to one or more study variables) have demonstrated that executive-function deficits are associated with the stability and continuity of conduct problems. Seguin and colleagues (1995) found that boys who exhibited a stable pattern of aggression between the ages of six and twelve performed significantly more poorly on measures of executive functions than did unstable aggressive or nonaggressive boys.

Neuropsychological Dysfunction and Antisocial Behavior

Several theories have been advanced to account for the relation between poor verbal ability and antisocial behavior. For example, James Q. Wilson and Richard J. Herrnstein (1985) suggest that low verbal intelligence contributes to a present-oriented cognitive style that in turn fosters irresponsible and exploitative behavior. They argue that because humans use language as a medium for abstract reasoning, humans can keep things that are out of sight from becoming out of mind by mentally representing them with words. Normal language development is thus essential in pro-social processes such as delaying gratification, anticipating consequences, and linking belated punishments with earlier transgressions.

Some theorists have speculated that a deficit in verbal skills may preclude children's ability to label their perceptions of the emotions expressed by others (victims or adversaries). Such deficiencies might also limit children's response options in threatening or ambiguous social situations, predisposing them to quick physical reactions rather than to more laborious verbal ones.

Many theorists have also speculated on the processes by which executive deficits contribute to antisocial behavior. Several researchers have developed theories based on the observed similarity between the behavior of antisocial individuals and "pseudopsychopathic" patients with frontal-lobe injuries. J. P. Newman and J. F. Wallace (1993) argued that "disinhibitory psychopathology" results from deficiencies in "response modulation" and "self regulation." Response modulation is the suspension of an ongoing behavioral response in order to assimilate feedback. This response modulation is hypothesized to be an automatic process. In contrast, self-regulation is the "controlled examination of one's behavior." Both response modulation and self-regulation are thought to depend on frontal-lobe functions. In sum, Newman and Wallace suggest that deficiencies in response modulation curtail an individual's capacity to pause in response to cues for punishment and thus make self-regulation impossible.

Lau, Pihl, and Peterson argue that frontal-lobe deficits may interfere with the linkage between specific stimulus characteristics and preestablished rules for responding. In the absence of this linkage, the individual is unable to bring these response rules to bear on the regulation of behavior. Instead, behavior is governed by the immediate stimulus. Thus, the rules that would normally act to inhibit aggressive responding are ineffective, and an impulsive-aggressive response will emerge.

Finally, Moffitt (1993) has differentiated between adolescent-limited offenders, whose antisocial behavior sets in relatively late and who are likely to desist offending upon entering adulthood, and life-course persistent offenders, whose antisocial tendencies become apparent early in childhood and who are likely to continue offending throughout adulthood. Life-course persistent offenders are thought to be characterized by early-emerging neuropsychological deficits that set in motion a series of social and academic failures. The cumulative effect of the neuropsychological deficits and the consequent social and academic failures results in a pattern of undercontrolled, explosive behavior that persists across the life course.

Conclusion

It now appears likely that both subcortical and cortical brain regions are involved in generating and regulating violent behavior in humans. Strong evidence has been found linking language and executive deficits to serious antisocial behavior. Evidence of limbic abnormalities in association with violence in humans, while suggestive, is as yet inconclusive. However, the days in which researchers sought to localize particular functions to specific parts of the brain are past; today, researchers adopt a systems approach to understanding brain function. Increasing emphasis is being placed on the interconnections between brain structures and on the ways in which structures and regions influence one another. One important implication of this systems perspective, as it relates to violence, is that there may not be one single way in which brain dysfunction gives rise to violence. Rather, dysfunction at any point within the system could cause violent behavior to emerge. Further defining and understanding exactly how the system operates and how things can go wrong within that system are substantial tasks facing researchers in this field.

BIBLIOGRAPHY

Elliott, F. "Neurological Aspects of Antisocial Behavior." In *The Psychopath: A Comprehensive Study of Antisocial Disorders and Behaviors*, edited by William H. Reid. New York: Brunner/Mazel, 1978.

Giancola, P. R., and A. Zeichner. "Neuropsychological Performance on Tests of Frontal-Lobe Functioning and Aggressive Behavior in Men." *Journal of Abnormal Psychology* 103, no. 4 (1994): 832–835.

Lahey, B. B., R. Loeber, E. L. Hart, P. J. Frick, B. Applegate, Q. W. Zhang, S. M. Green, and M. F. Russo. "Four-Year Longitudinal Study of Conduct Disorder in Boys: Patterns and Predictors of Persistence." *Journal of Abnormal Psychology* 104, no. 1 (1995): 83–93.

Lau, M. A., R. O. Pihl, and J. B. Peterson. "Provocation, Acute Alcohol Intoxication, Cognitive Performance, and Aggression." *Journal of Abnormal Psychology* 104, no. 1 (1995): 150–155.

Mark, Vernon H., and Frank R. Ervin. *Violence and the Brain.* New York: Harper and Row, 1970.

Moffitt, T. E. "Adolescence-Limited and Life-Course Persistent Antisocial Behavior: A Developmental Taxonomy." *Psychological Review* 100 (1993): 674–701.

———. "Juvenile Delinquency and Attention Deficit Disorder: Boys' Developmental Trajectories from Age Three to Age Fifteen." *Child Development* 61, no. 3 (1990): 893–910.

Newman, J. P., and J. F. Wallace. "Diverse Pathways to Deficient Self-regulation: Implications for Disinhibitory Psychopathology in Children." *Clinical Psychology Review* 13, no. 8 (1993): 699–720.

Seguin, J., R. O. Pihl, P. W. Harden, R. E. Tremblay, and B. Boulerice. "Cognitive and Neuropsychological Characteristics of Physically Aggressive Boys." *Journal of Abnormal Psychology* 104, no. 4 (1995): 614–624.

Wilson, James Q., and Richard J. Herrnstein. *Crime and Human Nature.* New York: Simon and Schuster, 1985.

BILL C. HENRY

See also **Psychophysiology.**

BRAIN IMAGING

In the 1990s important technological advances were made in the field of brain imaging. These developments have permitted scientists to visualize both structural and functional properties of the brain. In addition to a wide range of medical applications, neuroimaging technology has begun to be applied to the field of crime and violence research. Given the vast amount of information brain imaging techniques are capable of providing, they hold the promise of adding exponentially to what is currently known about the biological underpinnings of aggressive and violent behavior.

The most common methods of obtaining structural information about the brain include Computerized Tomography (CT) and Magnetic Resonance Imaging (MRI) scanning. Numerous studies using these techniques have provided valuable evidence of structural abnormalities among various offender groups. Frontal and temporal lobe abnormalities, in particular, have been associated with violent behavior (Raine 1993). The frontal regions are implicated in higher cognitive functions, such as abstraction, planning, devising behavioral strategies, assessing progress made toward goals, and judgment. The temporal lobes are the portions of the cerebral cortex that lie below the frontal and parietal lobes. The temporal lobes are involved in affective regulation, sexual behavior, audition, and speech perception. Abnormalities within the anterior-inferior regions of the temporal lobes are associated with violence. The anterior-inferior portion of the temporal lobes includes aspects of the limbic system, which is a collection of many structures, including the amygdala, hippocampus, septum, and cingulate gyrus. Learning and memory, motivation, and emotion regulation are among the most important functions of the limbic system.

Whereas CT and MRI studies provide useful information about structural abnormalities associated with violence, neuroimaging techniques such as Positron Emission Tomography (PET), which measures whole brain and regional glucose uptake, reveal the functional properties of the brain. Using PET, Raine and colleagues (1994) found that a sample of murderers pleading not guilty by reason of insanity had reduced glucose metabolism in the prefrontal cortex compared with the control subjects (see figure 1). Similar deficits were also observed in several other regions of the brain, specifically the posterior parietal cortex (bilateral superior parietal gyrus and left angular gyrus) and the corpus callosum (Raine, Buchsbaum, and LaCasse 1997); abnormal asymmetries of function were found in the amygdala, the hippocampus, and the thalamus. Furthermore, reduced prefrontal glucose metabolism is particularly characteristic of murderers who experienced less psychosocial

FIGURE 1. **Glucose Activation, Indicated by Brighter Areas in PET Scans, Is Markedly Reduced in One Murderer (Right) Relative to a Normal Control Subject.**

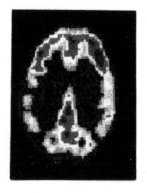 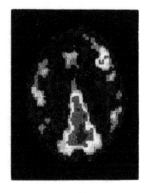

Normal   Murderer

deprivation in their early backgrounds than some other murderers, suggesting that biological predispositions to violent offending are more salient in murderers who lack social predispositions to engage in violence (Raine et al. 1998).

Functional deficits in these regions have important implications for violent behavior. Prefrontal deficits have been associated with behavioral disinhibition, increased risktaking, and impulsivity. The parietal region of the brain, which contains the somatosensory cortex, is involved in the integration of sensory input. Abnormalities in various regions of the parietal cortex, including the left angular gyrus, have been associated with cognitive dysfunction, including reduced verbal abilities. Finally, the corpus callosum is a large fiber bundle that interconnects the two hemispheres of the brain. Callosal dysfunction may result in less left-hemisphere regulation over emotions generated by the right hemisphere.

In addition to a study of murderers, evidence of reduced glucose metabolism was found in a sample of violent psychiatric patients. Volkow and colleagues (1995) demonstrated lower glucose metabolism in medial temporal and prefrontal cortices in violent psychiatric patients relative to normal control subjects. Goyer and Semple (1996) also demonstrated that inpatients with problems in controlling aggressive impulses who are also characterized by Axis-II personality disorders (disorders involving long-standing maladaptive behavioral patterns that interfere with personal and social functioning) demonstrate lower rates of glucose metabolism in orbital frontal, upper prefrontal, and left insular temporal-parietal regions. Taken together, these findings provide significant evidence for both structural and functional brain abnormalities in various groups of subjects including murderers, violent psychiatric patients, and aggressive personality-disordered inpatients.

Although it is clear that brain abnormalities often underlie violent behavior, the specific mechanisms of these relationships are not yet completely understood. On the basis of studies of the functions performed by various brain structures, scientists are able to speculate about how certain types of dysfunction may influence violent behavior. For example, cognitive dysfunction resulting from brain injury may lead to academic and occupational failure, which in turn predisposes certain individuals to delinquent lifestyles. Prefrontal deficits may lead to the inability to foresee the consequences of violent acts, while deficient auditory or speech perception may lead one to misperceive and misinterpret innocuous stimuli as threatening, thus eliciting a paranoid aggressive reaction. Although scenarios such as these are speculative, they help illustrate how brain abnormalities may render certain individuals more susceptible to engaging in violence and highlight the contribution of brain imaging to the study of violent behavior.

BIBLIOGRAPHY

Goyer, Peter F., and William E. Semple. "PET Studies of Aggression in Personality Disorder and Other Nonpsychotic Patients." In *Aggression and Violence: Genetic, Neurobiological, and Biosocial Perspectives,* edited by David M. Stoff and Robert B. Cairns. Mahwah, N.J.: Lawrence Erlbaum, 1996.

Raine, Adrian. *The Psychopathology of Crime: Criminal Behavior as a Clinical Disorder.* San Diego: Academic, 1993.

Raine, Adrian, and Monte S. Buchsbaum. "Violence, Brain Imaging, and Neuropsychology." In *Aggression and Violence: Genetic, Neurobiological, and Biosocial Perspectives,* edited by David M. Stoff and Robert B. Cairns. Mahwah, N.J.: Lawrence Erlbaum, 1996.

Raine, Adrian, Monte S. Buchsbaum, and Lori LaCasse. "Brain Abnormalities in Murderers Indicated by Positron Emission Tomography." *Biological Psychiatry* 42, no. 6 (1997): 495–508.

Raine, Adrian, et al. "Selective Reductions in Prefrontal Glucose Metabolism in Murderers." *Biological Psychiatry* 36 (1994): 365–373.

Raine, Adrian, et al. "Prefrontal Glucose Deficits in Murderers Lacking Psychosocial Deprivation." *Neuropsychiatry, Neuropsychology, and Behavioral Neurology* 11, no. 1 (1998): 1–7.

Volkow, Nora D., et al. "Brain Glucose Metabolism in Violent Psychiatric Patients: A Preliminary Study." *Psychiatry Research: Neuroimaging* 61 (1995).

PAULINE S. YARALIAN
ADRIAN RAINE

HEAD INJURY

If a laptop computer smashed on the pavement, would it be surprising to get an "error" message the next time it is used? Actually, it would be a surprise to get any message or other sign of life from it. Similarly, it is no surprise that traumatic injury to the brain can disrupt human cognitive processing and behavior. The brain and central nervous system control voluntary and involuntary muscular activity, thereby exerting a direct effect on all human activity. One cannot make a fist unless the brain directs the necessary muscular activity. The brain both initiates action and inhibits responding. The brain is the seat of perception, emotion, and cognition; it is the interface between the external world and the human organism. A complex interplay between these elements accounts for all behavior. Defects in any of these elements can disrupt or alter behavior. Aggression is one of the most common sequelae, or aftereffects, to a traumatic brain injury. It has been reported that as many as 70 percent of patients with brain injuries exhibit irritability and aggression.

Traumatic brain injury is one of the most serious and common health problems afflicting society today. The incidence rate for mild brain injury, which accounts for about 80 percent of all traumatic brain injuries, has been conservatively estimated at 130 per 100,000 population, or more than 325,000 occurrences per year in the United States. More than half of these mild brain injuries can be attributed to motor vehicle accidents (often alcohol related). It is most common in males between the ages of fifteen and twenty-four.

Head injuries may be open or closed. Open head injuries involve damage to the skull and exposure of brain tissue; they are serious, often fatal, and relatively uncommon. The majority of head injuries are closed head injuries, which may be mild, moderate, or severe. The classification is most often based on the length of the post-traumatic amnesia (PTA), which refers to the length of time—post-injury—for which the patient has no recollection. The convention is that an injury with a PTA of one hour or less is considered mild, one hour to twenty-four hours is moderate, and more than twenty four hours is severe. Head injuries may also be classified as blunt or penetrating. The penetrating injury involves an object, such as a bullet, penetrating the brain and is usually fatal. Blunt trauma involves the head either striking or being struck by an object and is the most common form of brain injury.

A host of psychological, cognitive, and behavioral sequelae have been attributed to traumatic brain injury. These include impulsivity (difficulty inhibiting or preventing a response), irritability, affective blunting (loss of animation), decrements in verbal and performance IQ, difficulties with word-finding, perseveration (continuing to dwell on something or persisting in an action that is ineffective), underarousal (failure to be stimulated by something that would ordinarily be interesting or exciting), and aggression. Moderate to severe head injuries will almost always have profound consequences and require lengthy rehabilitation, but even mild head injuries may produce serious and lasting effects.

The association between head injury and aggression in humans is correlational (that is, they are related, but the head injury does not necessarily cause the aggression). There are numerous anecdotal reports of post-head-injury aggressive behavior exhibited by individuals for whom the behavior would have been considered "out of character" prior to the injury. The relationship between head injury and aggression has been demonstrated in a number of research studies. On the basis of investigations of the incidence of prior head injury in both adults and adolescents convicted of murder and sentenced to death, Lewis and her colleagues at Columbia University (1986) reported a correlational association in more than 90 percent of the cases, far exceeding the base rate in the general population. Rosenbaum and colleagues at the University of Massachusetts (1994), in a controlled investigation with partner-abusive men, found that men who had sustained a prior head injury were almost six times more likely to be abusive toward their intimate partners than were their non-head-injured counterparts. Golden (1991) studied prison inmates and reported that 73 percent of their subjects in the brain-damaged group had committed violent crimes, compared with only 28 percent of those in the non-brain-damaged group. Raine and colleagues (1994) found that half of the twenty murderers in their sample had had a prior head injury, compared with none in the normal control group; they concluded, on the basis of nuclear imaging studies, that prefrontal dysfunction may predispose an individual to violence.

The nature of traumatic brain injury complicates attempts to associate behaviors, such as aggression, with damage to specific brain areas. This is because blunt trauma produces diffuse damage. In the most common method of injury, motor vehicle accident, the front of the head strikes either the windshield or steering wheel, which might be expected primarily to damage the fronto-temporal areas. However, when the head moving forward is stopped suddenly, the brain continues moving forward and compresses against the inside of the braincase (this is termed the *coup*). This may also produce shearing (damage that occurs when the fibers are stretched across the bony ridge that is part of the structure of the inside of the skull), which damages axons and fibers and can disrupt vascular flow. The brain then springs back and is compressed against the back of the skull, producing a *contracoup* injury. Since the head may

459

impact at any angle and with varying degrees of force, the location and degree of injury will also vary. Swelling, hematoma, and edema can result in increased intracranial pressure, producing further damage, possibly in areas distal to the original trauma. Atrophy and degeneration can occur post-injury and contribute to cognitive and emotional deficits.

There are several possible mechanisms for understanding how a traumatic brain injury may play an etiologic role in the occurrence of violent behavior. At least three levels of brain functioning directly influence aggressive expression. These are the hypothalamus and brain stem, the limbic system, and the neocortex. Intentionally created hypothalamic lesions in animals have been shown to elicit aggressive behaviors. Bard (1928) demonstrated displays of unprovoked aggression, which he labeled "sham rage," by sectioning a cat's brain rostral to the hypothalamus. Studies in which various anatomic sites are electrically stimulated have demonstrated that placement of the electrodes within a structure determines the effect on aggression and may act as a switch, turning it either on or off. For example, stimulation of the lateral hypothalamus apparently promotes aggression, whereas stimulation of the ventromedial hypothalamus evokes a defensive posture and inhibits aggressive responding. Destruction of the ventromedial hypothalamus has been shown to provoke attack in previously docile animals, and there is at least one reported incident of aggressive behavior by a woman whose ventromedial hypothalamus had been destroyed by a brain tumor. The limbic system, which subsumes the amygdala, controls the hypothalamus. Experimentation on animals has demonstrated that stimulation of the dorsomedial amygdala tends to inhibit attack behavior in cats, whereas stimulation of the ventromedial amygdala facilitates aggressive behavior.

The neocortex is the most evolved brain structure and is involved in those activities that are most uniquely human. Several theorists, notably Sigmund Freud and Konrad Lorenz, have posited the existence of aggressive instincts, drives, and urges. Frustration-aggression theorists believed that when individuals are frustrated in reaching their goals, they respond aggressively. Thus, humans often have the desire to act aggressively. Freud saw these aggressive id impulses as primitive and noted the need for higher-level psychic structures (e.g., the ego and superego) to inhibit aggressive responses. Physiologically, several areas of the brain have been identified as inhibitory centers, and damage to those areas has been associated with impulse-control disorders, including aggression.

The frontal (especially the prefrontal) and temporal lobes of the brain have been the focus of both research and theorizing regarding the production or inhibition of violent behavior. Although it is difficult to co-register precisely certain specific behaviors to anatomic locations, the frontal lobes have been associated with judgment, abstraction, planning, motivation, and impulse control, commonly referred to as "executive functions." Damage to the frontal lobes produces egocentricity, lack of empathy, difficulty regulating behavior, apathy, decreased cognitive flexibility, and irritability.

The temporal lobes are involved in regulating emotion and behavior. Episodic dyscontrol syndrome, which involves sudden, unprovoked displays of aggression, has been linked to traumatic brain injury, especially of the medial portion of the temporal lobes, which include limbic system structures. Elliott (1982) reported that episodic dyscontrol resulted from a traumatic brain injury in 36 percent of the cases he studied. He also was the first to suggest that episodic dyscontrol might be a significant contributor to relationship aggression.

Further complicating the picture are the interconnections and interdependencies of various brain structures in regulating behavior. The frontal and prefrontal areas, for example, have bidirectional interactions with the temporal, parietal, and occipital lobes as well as subcortical links to the limbic system. Complex behaviors, such as aggression, involve sensory, motor, memory, and cognitive elements requiring the coordination of functions from different brain areas. In the case of aggression, for example, the individual must first perceive the need to respond aggressively (that is, become aware of a stimulus and interpret it as a threat or insult), and that perception has both sensory and cognitive elements. The cognitive component involves learning, memory, and intelligence. The aggressive response itself requires the coordination of numerous muscle groups. Finally, there may be verbal production and an emotional component (affective coloration). The brain centers controlling and coordinating these various components are scattered throughout the brain. Depending on the location and degree of damage, the effects on behavior may range from subtle to gross.

In addition to these direct influences on aggressive behavior, traumatic brain injury also produces cognitive and personality changes that may increase aggressive behavior by increasing interpersonal conflict. The wife of a brain-injured man, for example, will often report that following the injury, her husband is "not the man she married," although she may have difficulty articulating how he is different. An accompanying reduction in intimacy can contribute to an increase in frustration, arguments, and, consequently, aggression. Brain injury can decrease intellectual functioning and performance. Decrements in expressive abilities (e.g., word finding) and hand-eye coordination are not uncommon and may also increase frustration, irritability, and aggression.

Late-twentieth-century developments in nuclear imaging, especially in functional nuclear imaging, have enabled doctors to identify with great precision the specific anatomic areas of damage associated with traumatic brain injury. However, in many cases, especially when the injury is mild, personality and behavioral sequelae may occur in the absence of identifiable areas of damage and may persist after damaged areas of the brain have apparently healed. Functional mapping of the brain is in its infancy and, especially for behaviors determined by contributions from several brain areas, primitive. Thus, to a large extent, the brain remains a mysterious black box whose productions we can readily observe but whose mechanics we can only surmise. As functional mapping of the brain progresses, so too will our understanding of the relationship between head injury and violent behavior.

BIBLIOGRAPHY

Bard, P. "A Diencephalic Mechanism for the Expression of Rage with Special Reference to the Sympathetic Nervous System." *American Journal of Physiology* 84 (1928).

Elliott, F. A. "Neurologic Findings in Adult Minimal Brain Dysfunction and the Dyscontrol Syndrome." *Journal of Nervous and Mental Diseases* 170 (1982).

Golden, R. N., et al. "Serotonin, Suicide, and Aggression: Clinical Studies." *Journal of Clinical Psychiatry* 52 (1991): 61–69.

Lewis, D. O., et al. "Neuropsychiatric, Psychoeducational, and Family Characteristics of Fourteen Juveniles Condemned to Death in the United States." *American Journal of Psychiatry* 145 (1988): 584–589.

Lewis, D. O., et al. "Psychiatric, Neurological, and Psychoeducational Characteristics of Fifteen Death Row Inmates in the United States." *American Journal of Psychiatry* 143 (1986): 838–845.

McKinlay, W. W., et al. "The Short-Term Outcome of Severe Blunt Head Injury, as Reported by the Relatives of the Injured Persons." *Journal of Neurology, Neurosurgery, and Psychiatry* 44 (1981): 285–293.

Raine, Adrian, et al. "Selective Reductions in Prefrontal Glucose Metabolism in Murderers." *Biological Psychiatry* 36 (1994).

Rosenbaum, Alan, et al. "Head Injury in Partner Abusive Men." *Journal of Consulting and Clinical Psychology* 64, no. 6 (1994).

ALAN ROSENBAUM

HEMISPHERIC LATERALITY

Biologically determined, gender related, lateralized differential hemispheric vulnerability distinguishes the male brain from the female brain. In the female the dominant hemisphere is functionally more efficient than the nondominant hemisphere. In the male the converse is true: the organization of the nondominant hemisphere is relatively superior to that of the dominant hemisphere. The superiority of girls in language acquisition and skills and the superiority of boys in visuo-spatial abilities, in exploratory drive, and in aggressivity derive immediately from this differential cerebral organization. The excess of males exhibiting infantile autism (a cardinal feature of which is complete absence of language, or language retardation), developmental dyslexia (a defect in linguistic organization), and childhood epilepsies (because of overrepresentation of males with left mesial sclerosis in the wake of febrile seizures) can all be understood as varying manifestations of this dominant hemispheric vulnerability characteristic of the male gender. In the same manner, aggressive psychopathy associated with the male sex and with diminished verbal, as opposed to performance, IQ can be seen as a reflection of the same phenomenon, as is schizophrenia of early onset in the male characterized by chronicity and deficit symptomatology and dysfunction of the left hemisphere. The argument is that aggression in males is the reflection of a failure of left-brain regulation of neural systems modulating aggression that originates in the right hemisphere.

The association of aggression and lateralized brain mechanisms has a long evolutionary history. It exists in reptiles, amphibians, birds, and mammals, including *Homo sapiens*. Studies have shown that aggression, derivative of right-brain activation, is under inhibitory regulation originating in the left hemisphere in both birds and mammals. Numerous observations demonstrate that a similar principle of cerebral organization is present in humans.

In the lizard, retinal fibers project to the contralateral hemisphere, and left-eye use occurs during aggressive responses—that is, the left eye follows the antagonist and the right eye looks away. Left-eye preference with respect to aggressive movements is also found in the American green chameleon. When the left hemisphere of a two-day-old chick is disrupted by an injection of cycloheximide, attack behaviors are evoked; this does not happen with right-brain disruption. Similarly in the rat, murderous attacks are higher in the animal with a lesioned left and an intact right hemisphere than in rats with intact brains or intact left and lesioned right hemispheres. In the comparison of birds (chicks) and mammals (rats) with cortical lesions of the left and right brain, left-brain lesions were shown to be associated with aggression, sexual arousal, and emotionality, whereas animals with similar right-sided lesions were similar to healthy animals.

Left-Hemisphere Dysfunction and Aggression

E. A. Serafetinides (1965) reported that aggression caused by temporal-lobe epilepsy was associated with left-hemisphere lesions of very early onset (before age seven) in males. W. Alwyn Lishman (1968) observed in the study of the psychiatric sequelae of penetrating head injuries in English soldiers wounded in World War II that psychopathy was significantly related to left frontal injuries. This clinical evidence led to the formulation of a model of the psychiatric syndromes considered manifestations of lateralized temporal-limbic dysfunction in which the locus of dysfunction was the dominant temporal lobe (Flor-Henry 1973). Pierre Flor-Henry and Lorne T. Yeudall (1973) compared the neuropsychological characteristics of thirty-five depressed patients, twenty-eight aggressive criminal psychopaths, and seven depressed aggressive criminal psychopaths. A modified Halstead-Reitan test battery yielding twenty-five neuropsychological indicators and the Wechsler Adult Intelligence Scale (WAIS) were administered. The correlations of diagnosis by laterality of dysfunction were highly significant—left in the psychopaths, right in the depressives, but nonsignificant when the depressed group was compared with the depressed psychopaths. Yeudall studied ninety-three criminal psychopaths incarcerated for homicide, rape, and physical assault, all of whom satisfied Hervey Cleckley's criteria for primary psychopathy on a battery of thirty-two neuropsychological tests: 90 percent had an abnormal profile and 75 percent had bilateral frontal dysfunction (left > right) and left temporal dysfunction.

D. Wardell and Yeudall (1980) investigated 201 criminals from the forensic unit of Canada's Alberta Hospital, Edmonton, using an expanded Halstead-Reitan test battery and the Minnesota Multiphasic Personality Inventory (MMPI). Left-hemisphere dysfunction was characteristic of the group and, interestingly, primary psychopaths had the largest verbal-performance IQ discrepancy and were characterized on the MMPI by psychopathy and schizophrenia scale elevations. David Wechsler (1958) was the first to note the relative decrement of verbal to performance IQ in antisocial personalities. Many subsequent studies in male delinquents have confirmed this finding.

Sinistrality and Criminal Behavior

Wardell and Yeudall found an incidence of sinistrality, or left-handedness, of 14 percent in their group of violent criminals. Other evidence suggests that the cerebral implications of sinistrality are a factor in criminal behavior: William Gabrielli and Sarnoff Mednick (1980) found that recidivism is much more likely in left-handed than in right-handed criminals: over a six-year period 65 percent of sinistrals were arrested again, as opposed to 30 percent of dextrals. Thirty-three percent of criminals with multiple arrests were sinistral, and 11 percent of those with a single arrest were sinistral against a base line of 7 percent sinistrality in nonoffenders.

Victor Krynicki (1978) found that in repeatedly assaultive adolescent males, the severity of aggression was correlated with sinistrality and left-hemisphere (temporal) dysfunction. William Grace (1987) found a significant correlation of sinistrality with the degree of conduct disorder and past delinquency in 254 incarcerated male delinquents. Marc Hillbrand and colleagues (1994) measured the finger oscillation of the dominant and nondominant hand and found that psychiatric patients with abnormal lateralization engaged in more frequent and more severe acts of physical aggression than those with normal differences between the two hands.

Deficient Callosal Inhibition

O. Fedora and S. Fedora (1983), in the neuropsychological study of twenty-eight psychopaths, twenty-eight antisocial criminals, and thirty-one dextral healthy controls, reported frontal and left-hemisphere dysfunction in both psychopathic and antisocial criminals. From a sample of 499 college students, Matthew Stanford and colleagues (1997) selected the twelve (male and female) most impulsively aggressive students and the twelve least aggressive students (by self report). Deficits on Wisconsin Card Sorting test and Trail Making B were found in the aggressive group, independent of a history of prior head injury. Bryan Woods and Marla Eby (1982) observed that repetitive aggression in a child psychiatric unit was associated with excessive mirror movements, particularly in males. Neurophysiologically, this suggests a defect in inhibition of the corpus callosum. L. Miller (1987), in an integrative review of the neuropsychological evidence in aggressive psychopathy, concluded that the aggressive psychopath is characterized by frontal and left-hemisphere dysfunction. He adds that "given the diversity of the populations studied, of the diagnostic criteria employed and the choice of measures it may seem remarkable that any commonality of findings occurs at all, and this may argue for the veracity of the underlying phenomena manifesting itself in the findings across groups and procedures" (p. 130).

Deficits in Language Processing

Aleksandr Luria (1973) emphasized the importance of the verbal regulation of behavior, and in a similar representation Miller concluded that a maturational deficit in the cerebral systems governing language processing is responsible for the inability of inner speech to modulate behavior. In a neurological study of extremely violent delinquents (male and female), "soft" signs (subtle indications of necrosis or dysfunction, which do not localize but which may lateralize) were not related to the severity of the violent behavior, but neuropsychological attention and language deficits were. On the other hand D. J. Stein and colleagues (1993) found an excess of soft signs on the left side of the body in impulsive personality disorders but on the right side in patients with a history of aggression. In a study of U.S. veterans who suffered missile injuries to the brain in Vietnam, Jordan Grafman and colleagues (1986) found that pathological anger correlated with left dorsolateral frontal convexity lesions, whereas right orbital frontal lesions were associated with depression. Observations by D. C. Taylor (1969; 1972) and I. Sherwin (1977) confirmed the finding of Serafetinides relating paranoid, aggressive psychopathic personalities to left-hemisphere epilepsies.

In a study following one hundred subjects with pure limbic epilepsy from birth, of the eighty-seven who survived to the age of fifteen, twelve exhibited severe antisocial aggressive behaviors: in all twelve the focus was contralateral to the preferred hand, a very significant lateralization to the dominant hemisphere. Catastrophic rage reactions were significantly associated with onset of the epilepsy before the age of one and with a significant decrement of verbal IQ in both sexes, again demonstrating disorganization of dominant hemispheric systems.

Antonio Convit and colleagues (1991) found in the quantitative electroencephalogram (EEG) analysis of twenty-one consecutive psychiatric patients in a special unit for the management of violence that severity of violence was correlated with increased left delta power (EEG voltage in the frequency band 1–3 Hz) and concluded that "violence is very significantly related to the hemispheric asymmetry in the EEG." Robert Hare and Janice Frazelle found that psychopaths failed to show a right-visual-field superiority in complex semantic processing, and Hare and Leslie McPherson (1984) found that psychopaths had a smaller right-ear advantage in a verbal dichotic listening task. A left-hemisphere deficit is implied in both investigations.

Another observation of Hare's relates to the slower electrodermal recovery time for the left hand to tone signals of high intensity. Malcolm Weller (1986) found electrodermal amplitude asymmetry (left < right) in seven of eight psychopathic patients. Earlier, John Gruzelier and Peter Venables (1974) had described a similar asymmetry. Jeffrey W. Jutai and colleagues (1987) found asymmetric-evoked responses in a phonemic discrimination task. Hare and Jutai (1988), using a divided-visual-field procedure to investigate the cerebral organization of language processes in psychopathy, found that normal controls or subjects with low psychopathy showed the expected right-visual-field superiority (left hemisphere projection), while the more strongly psychopathic subjects had a left-visual-field advantage (right hemisphere projection), again suggesting a subtle left-hemisphere dysfunction in psychopathy. Thomas Galski and colleagues (1990) reported that violent sexual criminals were characterized by left-hemisphere neuropsychological deficits. This was not the case for the nonviolent sex offenders.

Evidence from Brain Scanning

Cerebral circulation and neurometabolic studies also implicate the left hemisphere in violence.

Daniel Amen and colleagues (1996) compared the SPECT imaging results of violent and nonviolent psychiatric patients. The violent group was defined by reduced blood flow in the prefrontal cortex and increased flow in the frontal lobes (L > R), in the left basal ganglia, left limbic regions, and especially in the left temporal lobe. Using positron emission tomography (PET) scanning, Nora Volkow and colleagues (1987) found hypometabolism of the left temporal lobe in four extremely violent psychiatric patients. Similarly, Adrian Raine and colleagues (1994), subjecting twenty-two murderers to PET scanning, reported reduced metabolism in the lateral and medial prefrontal cortex during a continuous performance task. The murderers had a significant reduction of metabolic activity on the left lateral prefrontal cortex, but not on the right.

Conclusion

The evidence indicates that subtle dysfunction of the left hemisphere in the frontal and temporal regions exists in male aggressive and violent personalities. Physical—but not verbal—aggression is a male characteristic, whereas aggression in women is verbal rather than physical. In a discussion of developmental and gender effects and their etiological contributions to psychopathology, Flor-Henry suggested that the differential incidence of the major syndromes of psychiatric disorder in men and women was the consequence of their differential hemispheric organization: relatively weaker in the dominant hemisphere and stronger in the nondominant in men and, conversely, relatively stronger in the dominant and weaker in the nondominant hemisphere in women. In a sense, the aggressive male can be viewed as a pathological variant of the male pattern of lateral cerebral organization, where a hypofunctional left hemisphere, through reduced callosal inhibition, evokes enhanced but dysregulated right-hemispheric functions.

BIBLIOGRAPHY

Amen, Daniel G., Matthew Stubblefield, B. Carmichael, and Ronald Thisted. "Brain SPECT Findings and Aggressiveness." *Annals of Clinical Psychiatry* 8, no. 3 (1996): 129–137.

Bisazza, Angelo, L. J. Rogers, Giorgio Vallortigara. "The Origins of Cerebral Asymmetry: A Review of Evidence of Behavioural and Brain Lateralization in Fishes, Reptiles, and Amphibians." *Neuroscience and Biobehavioural Reviews* 22, no. 3 (1998): 411–426.

Cleckley, Hervey M. *The Mask of Sanity: An Attempt to Clarify Some Issues About the So-called Psychopathic Personality.* Rev. ed. St. Louis: Mosby, 1982.

Convit, Antonio, Pal Czobor, and Jan Volavka. "Lateralized Abnormality in the EEG of Persistently Violent Psychiatric Inpatients." *Biological Psychiatry* 30 (1991): 363–370.

Deckel, A. Wallace. "Hemispheric Control of Territorial Aggression in Effects of Mild Stress." *Brain, Behavior, anolis carolinensis and Evolution* 51 (1998): 33–39.

Fedora, O., and S. Fedora. "Some Neuropsychological and Psychophysiological Aspects of Psychopathic and Nonpsychopathic Criminals." In *Laterality and Psychopathology,* edited by Pierre Flor-Henry and John Gruzelier. Amsterdam and New York: Elsevier, 1983.

Flor-Henry, Pierre. "Psychiatric Syndromes Considered as Manifestations of Lateralized Temporal-Limbic Dysfunction." In *Surgical Approaches in Psychiatry,* edited by Lauri V. Laitinen and Kenneth E. Livingston. Baltimore: University Park Press, 1973.

———. "Psychosis, Neurosis, and Epilepsy: Developmental and Gender Related Effects and Their Aetiological Contribution." *British Journal of Psychiatry* 124 (1974): 144–150.

Flor-Henry, Pierre, and Lorne T. Yeudall. "Lateralized Cerebral Dysfunction in Depression and in Aggressive Criminal Psychopathy: Further Observations." *International Research Communications System* 7 (July 1973): 31.

Gabrielli, William F., and Sarnoff A. Mednick. "Sinistrality and Delinquency." *Journal of Abnormal Psychology* 89, no. 5 (1980): 654–661.

Galski, Thomas, Kirtley E. Thornton, and David Shumsky. "Brain Dysfunction in Sex Offenders." *Journal of Offender Rehabilitation* 16, nos. 1–2 (1990): 65–80.

Grace, William C. "Strength of Handedness as an Indicant of Delinquents' Behaviour." *Journal of Clinical Psychology* 43, no. 1 (1987): 151–155.

Grafman, Jordan, Stephen C. Vance, Herbert Weingartner, Andres M. Salazar, and Devyani Amin. "The Effects of Lateralized Frontal Lesions on Mood Regulation." *Brain* 109 (1986): 1127–1148.

Gruzelier, John H., and Rahul Manchanda. "The Syndrome of Schizophrenia: Relations Between Electrodermal Response, Lateral Asymmetries, and Clinical Ratings." *British Journal of Psychiatry* 141 (1982): 488–495.

Gruzelier, John H., and Peter H. Venables. "Bimodality and Lateral Asymmetry of Skin Conductance Orienting Activity in Schizophrenics: Replication and Evidence of Lateral Asymmetry in Patients with Depression and Disorders of Personality." *Biological Psychiatry* 8 (1974): 55–73.

Hare, Robert D. "Electrodermal and Cardiovascular Correlates of Psychopathy." In *Psychopathic Behaviour: Approaches to Research,* edited by Robert D. Hare and Daisy Schalling. Chichester, U.K., and New York: Wiley, 1978.

Hare, Robert D., and Jeffrey W. Jutai. "Psychopathy and Cerebral Asymmetry in Semantic Processing." *Personality and Individual Differences* 9, no. 2 (1988): 329–337.

Hare, Robert D., and Leslie M. McPherson. "Psychopathy and Perceptual Asymmetry During Verbal Dichotic Listening." *Journal of Abnormal Psychology* 93, no. 2 (1984): 141–149.

Hillbrand, Marc, D. Langlan, C. W. Nelson, J. E. Clark, and S. M. Dion. "Cerebral Lateralization and Aggression." In *The Psychobiology of Aggression: Engines, Measurement, Control,* edited by Marc Hillbrand and Nathaniel J. Pallone. New York: Haworth, 1994.

Jutai, J. W., R. D. Hare, and J. F. Connolly. "Psychopathy and Event-Related Brain Potentials (ERPs) Associated with Attention to Speech Stimuli." *Personality and Individual Differences* 8, no. 2 (1987): 175–184.

Krynicki, Victor E. "Cerebral Dysfunction in Repetitively Assaultive Adolescents." *Journal of Nervous and Mental Diseases* 166, no. 1 (1978): 59–67.

Lishman, W. Alwyn. "Brain Damage in Relation to Psychiatric Disability After Head Injury." *British Journal of Psychiatry* 114 (1968): 373–410.

Luria, Aleksandr R. *The Working Brain: An Introduction to Neuropsychology.* New York: Basic, 1973.

Miller, L. "Neuropsychology of the Aggressive Psychopath: An Integrative Review." *Aggressive Behaviour* 13 (1987): 119–140.

Nachshon, I. "Hemisphere Dysfunction in Psychopathy and Behaviour Disorders." In *Hemisyndromes: Psychobiology, Neurology, and Psychiatry,* edited by M. Myslobodsky. New York: Academic, 1983.

Prentice, W., and F. J. Kelly. "Intelligence and Delinquency: A Reconsideration." *Journal of Social Psychology* 60 (1963): 327–337.

Raine, Adrian, Monte S. Buchsbaum, Jill Stanley, Steven Lottenberg, Larry Abel, and Jacqueline Stoddard. "Selective Reductions in Prefrontal Glucose Metabolism in Murderers." *Biological Psychiatry* 36 (1994): 365–373.

Serafetinides, E. A. "Aggressiveness in Temporal Lobe Epileptics and Its Relation to Cerebral Dysfunction and Environmental Factors." *Epilepsia* 6 (1965): 33–42.

Sherwin, I. "Clinical and EEG Aspects of Temporal Lobe Epilepsy with Behaviour Disorder: The Role of Cerebral Dominance." *McLean Hospital Journal* (June 1977): 40–50.

Stanford, Matthew S., Kevin W. Greve, and John E. Gerstle. "Neuropsychological Correlates of Self-Reported Impulsive Aggression in a College Sample." *Personality and Individual Differences* 23, no. 6 (1997): 961–965.

Stein, D. J., E. Hollander, L. Cohen, M. Frenkel, J. B. Saoud, C. DeCaria, B. Aronowitz, A. Levin, M. R. Liebowitz, and L. Cohen. "Neuropsychiatric Impairment in Impulsive Personality Disorders." *Psychiatry Research* 48 (1993): 257–266.

Taylor, D. C. "Aggression and Epilepsy." *Journal of Psychosomatic Research* 13 (1969): 229–236.

———. "Mental State and Temporal Lobe Epilepsy: A Correlative Account of One Hundred Patients Treated Surgically." *Epilepsia* 13 (1972): 727–765.

Volkow, Nora D., and Lawrence Tancredi. "Neuroal Substrates of Violent Behaviour: A Preliminary Study with Positron Emission Tomography." *British Journal of Psychiatry* 151 (1987): 668–673.

Wardell, D., and Lorne T. Yeudall. "A Multidimensional Approach to Criminal Disorders: The Assessment of Impulsivity and Its Relation to Crime." *Advanced Behavioral Research and Therapy* 2 (1980): 159–177.

Wechsler, David. "Sex Differences in Intelligence." In *The Measurement and Appraisal of Adult Intelligence.* 4th ed. Baltimore: Williams and Wilkins, 1958.

Weller, Malcolm P. I. "Medical Concepts in Psychopathy and Violence." *Medical Science and the Law* 26, no. 2 (1986): 131–143.

Woods, Bryan T., and Marla D. Eby. "Excessive Mirror Movements and Aggression." *Biological Psychiatry* 17, no 1 (1982): 23–32.

Yeudall, Lorne T. "Neuropsychological Assessment of Forensic Disorders." *Canada's Mental Health* 25, no. 2 (1977): 7–15.

Yeudall, Lorne T., O. Fedora, S. Fedora, and D. Wardell. "Neurosocial Perspective on the Assessment and Etiology of Persistent Criminality." *Journal of Australian Academy of Forensic Sciences* 13 and 14 (1981): 131–159; 20–44.

PIERRE FLOR-HENRY

See also **Psychophysiology: EEG; Sex Differences.**

NEUROTRANSMITTERS

Following the **Overview,** *three subentries examine how neurotransmitters—"signaling" substances that cross synapses between nerve cells—affect violence and agression:* **Dopamine, Norepinephrine, and Their Metabolic Enzyme, Monoamine Oxidase; GABA;** *and* **Serotonin.**

OVERVIEW

Nerve cells (neurons) are the connections between the nervous system and innervated tissues like muscles and glands that have demonstrated links to the conduct of violence. Neurotransmitters are chemical substances that are synthesized in a presynaptic neuron and then cross the synapse (or space) between that neuron and a neighboring nerve cell on the other side of the synapse. Because the brain, muscles, peripheral nerves, and glands, which are all involved in physical displays of aggression or violence, are all linked using neurotransmitters as part of the signaling process, relationships between neurotransmitters and violence are plausible. Serotonin, dopamine, norepinephrine, and GABA (gamma-aminobutyric acid) are neurotransmitters that have been linked to violence.

Our understanding of neurotransmitters historically has been limited to a role defined by temporally brief (milliseconds to a second) point-to-point transmission. Researchers' ability to identify simple relationships between neurotransmitters and a behavioral outcome, as exemplified by the role of the neurotransmitter acetylcholine and transmission at a neuromuscular junction, or by a deficiency of dopamine as in Parkinson's disease, encouraged the hope of identifying a straightforward link between neurotransmitters and violence. Increasingly, relationships are being found, but they are proving to be quite complicated.

Neuromodulators are chemicals that have longer-term (minutes or more) effects upon transmission from nerve to nerve; they do not have their own actions but act in conjunction with activity in the synapse. Neuromodulators are thought to mediate affective and arousal states of the brain. Some substances that act as neurotransmitters can also act in neuromodulatory roles. Serotonin, for example, plays a neurotransmitter role in the raphe nucleus (a part of the brain stem) as well as a modulating role at the facial motor nucleus. This dual role illustrates but one aspect of the potential complexity of relationships between neurotransmitters and behavior. The multiplicity of serotonin receptors (at least fifteen different types have been identified) amplifies the number of possibilities for relationships between the neurotransmitter serotonin and behavior.

Serotonin is presently the neurotransmitter best recognized for its relationship to violence. It has been found to both increase as well as decrease aggression. Serotonin is synthesized from a dietary amino acid, tryptophan. Later, upon release into the synapse, it will either be inactivated by reuptake into the presynaptic neuron or metabolized by an enzyme in the synaptic cleft. The major metabolite of serotonin, 5-hydroxyindoleacetic acid (5-HIAA), has been used in studies as an indirect measure of serotonin. Each metabolic step, each receptor, and their feedback loops and interactions add to the possible permutations. Some of serotonin's relationships to violent behavior have been identified. Historically, studies in humans have relied on measurements of neurotransmitters or their metabolites in body fluids: blood, urine, and cerebrospinal fluid (CSF). One such study of body fluid measurement relating serotonin to one form of human violence, suicide, has stood the test of time. In 1976 Marie Asberg and colleagues measured 5-HIAA concentrations in the spinal fluid of patients with depression. They observed that, instead of an even continuum of concentrations, there were two groups—those with high and those with low concentrations. Patients with low concentrations of the serotonin metabolite were more likely to make a violent suicide attempt and more likely to die by suicide. The relationship between violent suicide and low 5-HIAA concentrations in cerebrospinal fluid has been replicated many times across continents and cultures.

Subsequent studies found that low CSF 5-HIAA concentrations also relate to violence directed toward other humans. Certainly, however, not all homicides, arsons, or other acts of violence are associated with low concentrations of the serotonin metabolite. The violence associated with low 5-HIAA has an impulsive, affect-laden quality as opposed to a planned, predatory quality. The precise biological cause of low spinal fluid 5-HIAA concentrations is unknown.

The consistency of results relating low concentrations of this serotonin metabolite and certain types of violence raises questions. Is a state, trait, or scar relationship present? That is, does the relationship between the neurotransmitter metabolite and violence occur only under certain conditions, subject to short-term modulation (state)? Is it fixed, persistent (trait)? Or is it the irreversible result of some trauma (scar)? Some evidence exists for each type of relationship, and all may coexist within the same individual. For example, administration of tryptophan, the serotonin precursor, decreases aggression in some human studies. Parallels exist between seasonal fluctuations in plasma tryptophan and violent suicide. This also argues for a state relationship.

Genetic studies provide evidence for trait relationships. Studies of nonhuman primates indicate significant genetic heritability for CSF 5-HIAA concentrations. Alteration or absence of genes that code for serotonin metabolism can alter behavioral traits. Monoamine oxidase A (MAO-A) is an enzyme for the metabolism of monoamines, including serotonin. Mutation of the gene that codes for MAO-A was associated with impulsive aggressive behaviors, including rape, arson, and attempted murder, among fourteen affected males in a Dutch family. Independently, a strain of mice was produced that lacked a functional MAO-A gene. These mice displayed increased aggressive behavior analogous to the enhanced aggression in the men with MAO-A deficiency.

Animal studies provide a potential example of a scar relationship. Monkeys raised by peers, rather than by a mother, do not modulate aggression normally. They also do not show the same relationships between neurotransmitters and behavior that mother-reared animals do. This loss of expected trait relationships suggests a permanent change.

Interactions between environmental events and biology also illustrate the complex interrelationships between neurotransmitters and violence. Repeated experience of victory and defeat in daily agonistic encounters among mice has been associated with changes in the activity of tryptophan hydroxylase, which is the rate-limiting step in serotonin synthesis. However, the alteration in enzyme activity by experience is not uniform across all regions of the brain. Winners in social encounters had increases in the hypothalamus of the activity of the enzyme responsible for serotonin synthesis; in contrast, repeated losers of the social confrontation had decreases in the enzyme activity in the same brain region. Studies of crustaceans show that previous social experience also colors the response to an infusion of serotonin. Socially isolated crayfish show a persistent enhancement in a neuronal response to sensory stimulation. However, the response to serotonin infusion is reversibly inhibited in subordinate and reversibly enhanced in dominant crayfish. A drug acting at 5-HT1 receptors showed different responses in the three groups of crayfish, but a drug acting at another subclass of serotonin receptors, 5HT2, produced the same response in isolate-reared, subordinate, and dominant crayfish.

Although it has become clear through research that neurotransmitters affect violence, our understanding of the complex relationships is as yet quite limited.

BIBLIOGRAPHY

Amstislavskaya, Tamara, and Natalia Kudryavtseva. "Effect of Repeated Experience of Victory and Defeat in Daily Agonistic Confrontations on Brain Tryptophan Hydroxylase Activity." *Federation of European Biochemical Societies Letters* 406, nos. 1–2 (1997).

Asberg, Marie, et al. "5-HIAA in the Cerebrospinal Fluid: A Biochemical Suicide Predictor?" *Archives of General Psychiatry* 33, no. 10 (October 1976).

Brunner, H., et al. "Abnormal Behavior Associated with a Point Mutation in the Structural Gene for Monoamine Oxidase A." *Science* 262 (22 October 1993).

Case, O., et al. "Aggressive Behavior and Altered Amounts of Brain Serotonin and Norepinephrine in Mice Lacking MAOA." *Science* 268 (23 June 1995).

Coccaro, Emil F. "Neurotransmitter Correlates of Impulsive Aggression in Humans." *Annals of the New York Academy of Sciences* 794 (20 September 1996).

Cooper, Jack R., et al. *The Biochemical Basis of Neuropharmacology.* 7th ed. New York: Oxford University Press, 1996.

Hen, Rene. "Mean Genes." *Neuron* 16, no. 1 (1996).

Kramer, Gary W. "Social Attachment, Brain Function, Aggression, and Violence." In *Biosocial Bases of Violence,* edited by Adrian Raine et al. New York: Plenum, 1997.

Kruesi, Markus, and Teresa Jacobsen. "Serotonin and Human Violence: Do Environmental Mediators Exist?" In *Biosocial Bases of Violence,* edited by Adrian Raine et al. New York: Plenum, 1997.

Yeh, Shih-rung, et al. "The Effect of Social Experience on Serotonergic Modulation of the Escape Circuit of Crayfish." *Science* 271 (19 January 1996).

MARKUS J. P. KRUESI

DOPAMINE, NOREPINEPHRINE, AND THEIR METABOLIC ENZYME, MONOAMINE OXIDASE

Studies of biochemical mechanisms underlying violent behavior have focused on the role of central neurotransmitter systems in modulating impulse control and levels of arousal. The neurotransmitters dopamine and norepinephrine are significant modulators of aggressive behaviors, even in the absence of pathology. The dopamine system appears to mediate responses to cues previously paired with a reward or satiating object. When something potentially useful is nearby (e.g., food or a mate), dopamine activity sets into motion a physiological process to elicit an emotional response that activates behavior to explore the possibilities. Excitement, anxiety, curiosity, or pleasure provide an impetus for flight or fight, the exploration of something novel or the avoidance of something aversive. Thus, when this system is activated, novelty seeking and self-stimulation behaviors increase. When the system goes awry, however, behavior may be activated in the absence of a threat or other appropriate stimulus. In the words of Robert Pihl and Jordan Petersen (1995), this approach system can "produce intra- and inter-personally dangerous asocial and disruptive behavior" (p. 385).

The Dopamine System

The dopamine system has been implicated in displays of aggressive or violent behavior. Dopamine metabolism in laboratory animals has been shown to increase when the animals are provoked to behave aggressively. Among humans, the overproduction of dopamine has been associated with psychosis and has been linked to antisocial behavior and violence. Studies have shown that antipsychotic drugs that decrease dopamine levels tend to decrease fighting behaviors.

Molecular genetic studies provide further support for a link between abnormalities in dopamine activity and the tendency toward violence. Genetic defects affecting dopamine metabolism have been found in many forms of excessive and compulsive behaviors that often coincide with violence, including drug abuse, conduct disorder, Tourette's syndrome, obsessive-compulsive disorder, and post-traumatic stress disorder. A genetic defect affecting so-called "reward pathways" involving dopamine transmission (which is associated with pleasure) has been reported in research subjects exhibiting severe drug-abuse habits as well as a history of aggressive behavior and violent crime. Also, there is evidence that cocaine addicts with a high incidence of early deviant behaviors and conduct disorder may be genetically susceptible to both drug dependence and aggressiveness due to a defect in the metabolism of dopamine. Violence among cocaine users occurs more often in those with a history of the same behaviors; however, chronic use of cocaine increases the likelihood of violent acts irrespective of a predisposition resulting from dopamine-activity disruptions. Thus, each of the above-mentioned disorders may share a common variable—inheritance of a constellation of defective or irregular genes for neurotransmitter metabolism. Nevertheless, large-scale analyses of several studies of dopamine levels in antisocial populations show inconsistencies among studies and no main effects. Variations in populations studied and definitions of antisocial conduct employed may explain these discrepancies. Moreover, main effects have been examined to the neglect of interactions between neurotransmitter systems, which precludes identification of significant players in a total neurobiological environment.

Norepinephrine

Norepinephrine (NE) is a transmitter substance produced from dopamine; dopamine is converted to NE through the action of dopamine beta-hydroxylase. Excess NE is destroyed by monoamine oxidase, and MHPG (3-methoxy-4-hydroxyphenylglycol) is one of NE's principal metabolites. NE has been of particular interest due to its involvement in stress responses, emotions, attention, and arousal. It plays a primary role in the initiation of the so-called fight-or-flight response by eliciting the release of adrenal stress hormones and exciting the central and autonomic nervous systems. Function of brain structures (e.g., the frontal cortex, limbic system, and brain stem) responsible for executive cognitive functions, mood, impulse control, memory, and emotion are affected by NE's stimulatory effects.

Significant changes in NE have been documented during preparation for, execution of, and recovery from activities that involve high arousal states, including violent behavior, although the direction of these changes is variable from situation to situation and from brain site to brain site. While NE activity is related to states of arousal, affect, and behavioral activation, it is not predictive of particular behavioral outcomes; rather, it may characterize an orientation to environmental stimuli. For example, NE activation as a result of amphetamine use is strongly associated with agitation and aggression, but the actual behavioral outcome is contingent on circumstance, setting, and individual predisposition.

Several studies have established a link between changes in NE and violence, although discrepancies exist. Some researchers found that subjects with criminal convictions exclusively for violent crimes had higher levels of NE than those with convictions for both violence and property crimes. MHPG levels in cerebrospinal fluid (CSF) have been positively related to aggression in military personnel, and stress-related urinary NE values were reportedly higher in violent incarcerated males. Also, drugs that increase NE activity are known to exacerbate violence in patients who are already agitated. On the other hand, a 1987 study by Matti Virkkunen reported that CSF MHPG was positively correlated with the number of property crimes, not violent crimes, in a subgroup of arsonists. Both arsonists and violent offenders had lower levels of MHPG than controls. Various psychiatric populations with antisocial behavior have shown significantly lower NE levels than controls. Directionality is obviously an unresolved issue when relating NE levels to violence: some studies show elevated levels of NE, while others show reduced levels. The majority of studies indicate that higher levels of NE are associated with aggression and violence; however, because NE values are highly variable, the most promising approach for the use of NE levels as a marker for violence is under conditions of stress or provocation, rather than a resting state. Although the precise role NE plays in violent behavior is unknown, because NE activity levels are suppressed by beta blockers and reserpine, these medications have been used in the treatment of violence. Thus, there are clear indications that NE's role in violence is significant, but highly dependent on its interaction with other central neurotransmitters.

Monoamine Oxidase

Monoamine oxidase (MAO) is an enzyme responsible for the breakdown of several neurotransmitters, including dopamine and norepinephrine. MAO is involved in several aspects of brain function by helping to regulate neurotransmitter concentrations and activity levels. As an enzyme, MAO helps to flush used neurotransmitter molecules from the nervous system. There are two MAO subtypes, MAOA and MAOB, with an affinity for different receptor sites located in different regions throughout the brain. MAOA primarily acts on norepinephrine (and also serotonin) and MAOB exerts a more general action on many neurotransmitters, but largely targets dopamine (and also phenylethylamine). While there is a broad range of optimal MAO levels, unusually high or low levels are believed to adversely affect social behaviors. Low MAO activity is thought to result in excessive neurotransmitter accumulation in brain cells (within the axon terminals). Excessive levels of dopamine and norepinephrine, in particular, have been associated with aggression, loss of self-control, and motivations to behave inappropriately. Because MAO concentrations within the brain are particularly high within the brain stem, hypothalamus, and prefrontal cortex (regions that modulate emotion and cognition), the relationship between deviations in its activity and effects on social and emotional behaviors is understandable.

Since the early 1980s, deviations in MAO levels have been linked with certain forms of criminality, particularly those involving psychopathy, aggression, and violent behavior. Several studies have related variations in MAO activity to tendencies toward alcoholism, sensation-seeking behavior, and impulsivity. Low platelet MAO levels were found in male student volunteers with histories of psychosocial problems, including convictions for various offenses, and among relatives of low-MAO subjects. One study found that offenders categorized as psychopaths had lower MAO levels than controls. A review of a large Dutch kindred spanning four generations found fourteen males to be affected by a complex behavioral syndrome that includes borderline mental retardation and impulsive aggressive behavior. A genetic defect, isolated on the X chromosome, was discovered in affected males and found to be associated with abnormalities in MAOA metabolism. Because this defect is rare, it is impossible to extrapolate these findings to other families in which impulsive aggression appears prevalent. Nevertheless, it is possible that subtler forms of MAO deficiency may exist in a subgroup of the population that exhibits these behaviors.

Hans Brunner, a forerunner of this research, attests that the causal relationship between an MAO metabolic abnormality and behavioral disturbance is not a simple one. It is clear, however, that MAOA inhibition results in significant elevations in serotonin in the brain, which most likely explains why MAO inhibitors are used for treatment of depression. Because a chronically high concentration of serotonin can lead to a down-regulation in activity of its receptors and, subsequently, lowered serotonergic activity (which is strongly related to impulsivity, aggression, and violence), MAO inhibition may play a role in impulsive aggressiveness. Low MAO activity has also been associated with excessive alcohol use and is believed to be a biological marker for vulnerability to alcoholism, often associated with aggressiveness, impulsivity, and antisocial behavior.

BIBLIOGRAPHY

Brunner, Hans G. "MAOA Deficiency and Abnormal Behaviour: Perspectives on an Association." In Ciba Foundation Symposium, *Genetics of Criminal and Antisocial Behaviour*, edited by Gregory R. Bock and Jamie A. Goode. New York: Wiley, 1996.

Brunner, Hans G., et al. "X-linked Borderline Mental Retardation with Prominent Behavioral Disturbance: Phenotype, Genetic Localization, and Evidence for Disturbed Monoamine Metabolism." *American Journal of Human Genetics* 52 (1993): 1032–1039.

Brunner, Hans G., et al. "Abnormal Behavior Associated with a Point Mutation in the Structural Gene for Monoamine Oxidase A." *Science* 262 (1993): 578–580.

Coccaro, Emil, and Dennis L. Murphy, eds. *Serotonin in Major Psychiatric Disorders*. Washington, D.C.: American Psychiatric Press, 1991.

Comings, David E. "Genetic Mechanisms in Neuropsychiatric Disorders." In *Handbook of Psychoneurogenetics*, edited by K. Blum, E. P. Noble, R. S. Sparks, and P. J. Sheridan. Boca Raton, Fla.: CRC, 1996.

Miczek, Klaus A., et al. "An Overview of Biological Influences on Violent Behavior." In *Understanding and Preventing Violence*. Vol. 2, *Biobehavioral Influences*, edited by Albert Reiss, Klaus Miczek, and Jeffrey Roth. Washington, D.C.: National Research Council, 1994.

Pihl, Robert O., and Jordan B. Petersen. "Alcoholism: The Role of Different Motivational Systems." *Journal of Psychiatry and Neuroscience* 20 (1995): 372–396.

Raine, Adrian. *The Psychopathology of Crime: Criminal Behavior as a Clinical Disorder*. San Diego, Calif.: Academic, 1993.

Virkkunen, Matti, et al. "Cerebrospinal Fluid Monoamine Metabolite Levels in Male Arsonists." *Archives of General Psychiatry* 44 (1987): 241–247.

Volavka, Jan. *The Neurobiology of Violence.* Washington, D.C.: American Psychiatric Press, 1995.

DIANA H. FISHBEIN

See also **Endocrinology.**

GABA

Gamma-aminobutyric acid, commonly known as GABA, is an amino acid that acts as a neurotransmitter in the mammalian central nervous system. It is a component of the nervous system of very simple organisms and is thus thought to be among the first neurotransmitters to have evolved. Neurons form a heavily interconnected network, and when one neuron fires, it encourages all of the neurons attached to it to fire also. GABA is an inhibitory transmitter: it acts as a chemical message to suppress neural firing in the brain. Thus GABA serves the important purpose of mediating brain activity and preventing neural firing from cascading out of control. In humans, it is the product of the secretions of special neurons found throughout the brain and spinal cord.

The GABA molecules do not suppress neuron firing directly through a chemical reaction; instead, they act indirectly, binding to sections of certain neurons known as GABA receptors and triggering those receptors. Once activated, the receptors initiate the chemical processes that alter the electrical characteristics of the neuron. GABA plays an extremely important, but not completely understood, role in the human brain. The GABA receptors are known to govern the neuronal systems that regulate anxiety, cognition, motor coordination, and arousal. Researchers have confirmed that alcohol consumption augments the sensitivity of the GABA receptors. GABA receptor–manipulating drugs can be used to treat alcohol withdrawal. Further, the effect of alcohol on behavior can be suppressed, and in fact intoxication can be "cured," by treatment with a drug known as Ro15–4513, which blocks a specific part of the GABA receptor. Unfortunately, this substance is not suitable for widespread use: since Ro15–4513 does nothing to decrease the overall toxicity of alcohol, injudicious use of it could easily lead to a potentially fatal case of alcohol poisoning.

A number of other substances derive their effects from interacting with the GABA receptors, either by increasing or decreasing their sensitivity. These substances include anticonvulsants, barbiturates, muscle relaxants, several anesthetics, and neurotoxins. Other drugs that operate by stimulating the GABA receptors include the class of tranquilizers known as denzodiazepines, examples of which include diazepam (commonly known as Valium) and chlordiazepoxide (Librium). Dysfunctions of the GABA receptors have been implicated in a number of adverse neurological conditions, such as epilepsy, Huntington's chorea, tardive dyskinesia, and Alzheimer's disease. Drugs affecting the GABA receptors can be useful in the treatment of maladies as diverse as asthma, panic attacks, intestinal disorders, and even intractable hiccups. Researchers suspect that a deficiency of GABA-secreting neurons in the temporal cortex may be an integral element of a biological basis for schizophrenia.

While science has clearly recognized GABA as playing a fundamental role in human neurobiology, our understanding of it is still incomplete. For example, the precise details about how alcohol acts on the GABA receptors to produce intoxication are still the subject of speculation and controversy. However, there is no doubt that the cycle of GABA production, transmission, and reception is responsible for a broad scope of human behaviors and emotions.

BIBLIOGRAPHY

Carlson, Neil R. *Physiology of Behavior.* Boston: Allyn and Bacon, 1991.

Den Boer, Johan A., Herman Gerrit Marinus Westenberg, and Herman M. van Praag, eds. *Advances in the Neurobiology of Schizophrenia.* Chichester, U.K., and New York: Wiley, 1995.

Enna, Salvatore J., and Norman G. Bowery, eds. *The GABA Receptors.* 2d ed. Totowa, N.J.: Humana, 1997.

NANCY GRIER HOGAN

SEROTONIN

Serotonin (5-HT) is an indoleamine-based neurotransmitter found in widespread distribution in the brain and in the body as a whole. As a neurotransmitter, 5-HT carries chemical messages from one nerve cell to the next. In the brain, 5-HT is thought to function primarily as a behavioral inhibitor. Accordingly, researchers believe that 5-HT may be involved in inhibiting aggressive impulses.

The notion that 5-HT plays a role in aggressive behavior first appeared in the late 1960s, when animal studies demonstrated that reducing brain 5-HT increased aggression and increasing brain 5-HT decreased aggression. This inverse relationship between 5-HT and aggression has been replicated in many, though not all, studies of lower mammals. In higher mammals, such as nonhuman primates, measures reflecting brain 5-HT function are inversely correlated with measures of aggression. In humans, numerous studies have demonstrated an inverse relationship between measures of aggressive behavior and measures putatively reflective of brain 5-HT. These studies have involved various measures of 5-HT, including cerebrospinal fluid concentrations of 5-HT metabolites (5-HT breakdown products), hormonal responses to brain stimulation with 5-HT drugs, and numbers of 5-HT receptors on blood platelets. In addition, they have been conducted using a wide variety of human subjects, including criminally violent offenders and psychiatric patients with personality disorders, alcoholism, and other drug-use disorders.

The most striking conclusion from this research is that impulsive aggression is the form of aggression most specifically related to brain 5-HT. Accordingly, measures of brain 5-HT function do not appear to be low in individuals who commit acts of *premeditated* aggression. This finding has potentially important implications regarding how we view the role of biology in criminal violence. For example, does criminality warrant medical treatment rather than punishment?

Not all studies demonstrate an inverse correlation between 5-HT and aggression. Most interesting, however, are the findings of a positive correlation between measures of brain 5-HT and aggression in some studies of prepubertal children and an absence of any correlation in older children and adolescents. This suggests the possibility that the relationship between brain 5-HT and aggression may change over development such that the relationship is positive in early childhood while transitioning in adolescence and becoming inverse by adulthood. This hypothesis awaits longitudinal study. Such studies may be difficult to conduct, however, given late-twentieth-century controversies concerning the use of children and adolescents as subjects in biological studies.

While the hypothesis that brain 5-HT is inversely related to impulsive aggression in humans received considerable support in the 1980s and 1990s, the nature of this relationship is still not fully understood. For example, is the "deficiency" in brain 5-HT function due to a problem in the amount of 5-HT available for neurotransmission or in the functional sensitivity of receptors that are stimulated by 5-HT? If the latter, which 5-HT receptor subtypes are affected, and if affected, what is the nature of a functional abnormality at these sites? While these questions remain open, there is emerging evidence of hypofunction at 5-HT-1a and 5-HT-2a/2c receptor subtypes. In addition, it is unclear where in the brain a reduction in 5-HT function, as related to impulsive aggression, might be located. Imaging studies suggest reduced perfusion of selected frontal areas of the brain in criminally violent offenders. Given the high level of 5-HT receptors in this area, it is tempting to speculate that the abnormal 5-HT function, previously suggested by other studies of such subjects, is localized to these areas of the brain.

The implications of an inverse relationship between brain 5-HT and impulsive aggression lead naturally to clinical strategies for individuals with problematic impulsive aggressive behavior. Since there is overlap in the results of biological testing of brain 5-HT systems between normal and aggressive individuals, biological testing in individuals is not practical for clinical purposes. However, clinical trial studies support the hypothesis that increasing brain 5-HT function with selective 5-HT uptake inhibitors (i.e., fluoxetine) will reduce impulsive aggressive behavior in humans. It should be noted that these studies have been conducted in individuals with moderate levels of aggression, whose behavior did not include many episodes of direct physical assault (mostly verbal and indirectly physical aggression). Accordingly, it is not known if severe forms of impulsive aggression can be affected by treatment with such agents. Even so, controversy regarding the criteria used to determine the best candidates for treatment with "antiaggressive agents" will be considerable. In 1999 research efforts were seeking to determine the optimal clinical definition of problematic impulsive aggressive behavior (in preparation for the fifth edition of the American Psychiatric Association's *Diagnostic and Statistical Manual of Mental Disorders,* or *DSM-V*) so that the gains that have been made in biological research could be translated into appropriate therapeutic interventions in the future.

BIBLIOGRAPHY

Brown, Gerald L., et al. "Aggression, Suicide, and Serotonin: Relationships to CSF Amine Metabolites." *American Journal of Psychiatry* 139 (June 1982): 741–746.

Coccaro, Emil F., and Richard J. Kavoussi. "Fluoxetine and Impulsive Aggressive Behavior in Personality Disordered Subjects." *Archives of General Psychiatry* 54 (December 1997): 1081–1088.

Coccaro, Emil F., et al. "Serotonergic Studies in Affective and Personality Disorder: Correlates with Suicidal and Impulsive Aggressive Behavior." *Archives of General Psychiatry* 46 (July 1989): 587–599.

Higley, J. Dee, et al. "Cerebrospinal Fluid Monoamine and Adrenal Correlates of Aggression in Free-ranging Rhesus Monkeys." *Archives of General Psychiatry* 49 (June 1992): 436–441.

Linnoila, Maruu, et al. "Low Cerebrospinal Fluid 5-Hydroxyindolacetic Acid Concentration Differentiates Impulsive from Nonimpulsive Violent Behavior." *Life Sciences* 33 (26 December 1983): 2609–2614.

Pine, Daniel S., et al. "Neuroendocrine Response to d,l-Fenfluramine Challenge in Boys: Associations with Aggressive Behavior and Adverse Rearing." *Archives of General Psychiatry* 54 (September 1997): 839–846.

EMIL F. COCCARO

NEW LEFT

The New Left was composed primarily of student activists who spent the 1960s fighting for civil rights, attempting to reform higher education, and opposing the Vietnam War. The initial idealism of the activists was born of faith in democratic values and peaceful change; but idealism became despair as the decade reached a climax with confrontation tactics and police coercion. The campus revolts against racism, bureaucracy, and war came to a violent end in 1970 when National Guardsmen killed four students at Kent State University in Ohio and police killed two students at Jackson State College (now Jackson State University) in Mississippi. The pathway from youthful optimism to national cynicism, polarization, and violence had a lasting impact on American politics and policing.

In 1960 the Civil Rights movement produced the Student Nonviolent Coordinating Committee (SNCC) to organize student sit-ins and protests across the South. White college students inspired by the Civil Rights movement and SNCC's opposition to violence formed the Students for a Democratic Society (SDS), which held its first convention in Port Huron, Michigan, in 1962. The convention issued the Port Huron Statement, a manifesto for a New Left student movement. SDS goals included striving for individual authenticity, empowering the poor, and promoting participatory democracy in the workplace and in government. SDS strategy centered on "peaceful dissent." Leaders such as Tom Hayden argued that the university was "an overlooked seat of influence," and that students could use it as an agency for peaceful social change.

SDS became one of several student groups that focused their energies on reforming higher education. Activists challenged the university's posture as a substitute parent, demanded new "relevant" curricula, and criticized the university's contribution to American materialism and bureaucracy. Campus protest escalated in 1964 when the University of California at Berkeley prohibited passing out leaflets on the Bancroft Strip, a twenty-six-foot-long strip at the entrance to the campus. Critics claimed that the prohibition denied students the right to free speech. Students protested, picketed, and held a sit-in; eight were suspended. When a former student was arrested for passing out leaflets, activists surrounded the police car holding the former student and held it captive. The police sent in six hundred officers, who forcibly retrieved their vehicle and the prisoner. This small confrontation grew into the highly publicized Free Speech Movement, which pitted students against university policy and police coercion. A recurring pattern was set: students protested, protest escalated into confrontation, police employed coercion, and charges of police brutality generated more student protest.

By 1966 student opposition to racism, university policies, and police brutality became intertwined with opposition to the Vietnam War. General Louis Hershey announced that the Selective Service System would begin to draft students with poor grades into the military, and he directed campuses to report the class ranking of all male students. Student leaders condemned the new policy and condensed the links between the university, the police, and the Selective Service System, as well as between government, bureaucracy, and capitalism, into the evocative phrase "the Establishment." In October 1967 students at the University of Wisconsin at Madison took on the Establishment. They staged a sit-in at a campus building to prevent the Dow Chemical Company from conducting job interviews. The activists were protesting the university's complicity with Dow, which manufactured war materials (including the notorious napalm gel) for use in Vietnam. Protesters were brutally ejected and visibly bloodied when the Madison riot squad used fists and clubs to end the sit-in. Widespread sympathy for the wounded victims generated a mass rally that evening as well as a broader-based student movement in the months ahead.

The original SDS commitment to "peaceful dissent" became increasingly tentative and finally came apart in 1968. Campus confrontations, the assassinations of Martin Luther King, Jr., and Robert Kennedy, highly publicized "police riots" at Columbia University and the Democratic National Convention in Chicago, and an escalation of violence in Vietnam persuaded many students that uplifting speeches and peaceful protests had little impact. White student radicals began to look favorably on armed black militants and Third-World revolutionaries. A 1969 struggle for control of SDS resulted in the emergence of the Weathermen faction, which advocated militant confrontation. The Weathermen graduated from the vandalism of their Days of Rage rampage in Chicago to clandestine armed struggle. They were not alone. New Left violence proliferated in 1970. Some five hundred incidents of bombing and arson occurred on campuses. Even a protest at the laid-back University of California at Santa Barbara resulted in the burning of a nearby Bank of America building.

Polarization between student activists and public authorities was a recipe for death. When President Richard Nixon expanded the Vietnam War into Cambodia, even peaceful campus protests were perceived by authorities as forerunners to student violence. That was part of the reason why quick trigger fingers prevailed at Kent State and Jackson State. The atmosphere of campus violence was so thick in the spring of 1970 that administrators closed down approximately 450 colleges and pleaded with students to go home for the summer. Many students were ready to go. As their optimism soured, they "dropped out" of politics and "tuned in" to a counterculture of sex, drugs, and rock and roll.

The New Left produced two enduring legacies. First, its initial idealism did not die. Many veterans believe that their activism changed campus life, hastened an end to the war, and launched the grassroots politics of feminism and environmentalism. Second, widespread campus violence prompted reforms in law enforcement. Congress created the Law Enforcement Assistance Administration to upgrade police technology and promote community policing. Henceforth the "iron fist" of violence that fueled New Left protests was to be held in abeyance while the "velvet glove" of civic cooperation was to stroke students into compliance. After the 1960s many New Left veterans were able to promote progressive change without encountering renewed police violence.

BIBLIOGRAPHY

Morgan, Edward P. *The 60s Experience: Hard Lessons About Modern America.* Philadelphia: Temple University Press, 1991.

Sale, Kirkpatrick. *SDS.* New York: Random House, 1973.

Whalen, Jack, and Richard Flacks. *Beyond the Barricades: The Sixties Generation Grows Up.* Philadelphia: Temple University Press, 1989.

MARK E. KANN

See also **Antiwar Protests; Kent State; Weatherman and Weather Underground.**

NEW ORLEANS

Founded by France in 1718, ceded to Spain in 1762, and purchased by the United States in 1803 following a retrocession, New Orleans became a multiracial, multiethnic immigrant port noted for its cosmopolitanism. The Crescent City, a largely Roman Catholic settlement that was absorbed by the Protestant United States, exhibited early and deep cultural divisions that sorely tested the ability of local authorities to establish, let alone maintain, order. Still, the South's largest city and a center for the burgeoning slave trade prior to the Civil War, New Orleans became a booming international marketplace. Grave institutional weaknesses, persistent political disarray, and contested racial issues, however, made collective violence a regular feature in the city's life, one that reached truly alarming proportions in the second half of the nineteenth century.

The Americans' attempt to control the metropolitan region was tested early in the Deslondes slave revolt of 1811 and the War of 1812. In the Deslondes revolt, the largest slave uprising in the United States, hundreds of insurrectionists marched on the city, burning plantations and sending refugees fleeing before them. Authorities marshaled regular troops and local militias, defeated the slaves in a pitched battle, and executed their leaders in a brutal public display. A militia consisting of free people of color, a legacy of New Orleans's unique colonial past, supported the government at the time of the revolt and successfully defended the city when the British invaded four years later as well. The product of an unusual three-tiered racial hierarchy (of white, black, and mixed origin), the free colored militia emerged during the era of Spanish domination as a stabilizing force for the regime and an institutional expression of New Orleans's unique social order. The Americans' initial weakness allowed the militia to retain its status, at least temporarily, until all external threats had been suppressed.

A weak constabulary found it difficult to maintain order as New Orleans grew from a town of 17,240 in 1810 to a city of 168,675 in 1860. Brawls involving sailors passing through the port seemed a nightly occurrence in the notorious "back swamp" area. Kaintocks, American riverboat men and traders from the western territories, left a similarly violent train through town, and both Creoles (native Lousianians of largely Roman Catholic and non-English-speaking origins) and Americans employed the *code duello* with some regularity— swords as well as firearms were the weapons of choice in New Orleans. The religious, cultural, political, and language differences separating an uptown "American" sector from the downtown "Creole" faubourgs, or suburbs, ultimately produced a division of the city into three semiautonomous municipalities between 1836 and 1852. In 1851 a riotous mob burned the Spanish consulate and a number of other buildings following Cuba's suppression of a New Orleans–based invasion and highlighted the divided city's institutional weakness. Reconsolidated under American control after a wave of largely Irish and German immigration undermined Creole dominance, the city endured a wave of political and election day disorders in the mid- to late 1850s. A nativist Know-Nothing movement hostile to the political influence of recent immigrants violently contended for control of the streets and the democratic process; even the newly formed Committee of Vigilance (modeled on San Francisco's) could not prevent the system from dissolving into chaos before the Civil War.

The federal occupation of the city in 1862 set the stage for Reconstruction and a new wave of intense, racially motivated violence. On 30 July 1866 Republicans tried to reconvene a constitutional convention at the Mechanics' Institute with the intention of extending the franchise to African Americans. Democratic mayor John Monroe called out a local police force that consisted largely of Confederate veterans to suppress the gathering. In what General Philip Sheridan called an "absolute massacre," Monroe's police opened fire on the convention's delegates and supporters; at least 34 blacks and 3 whites perished in the assault, and another 150 lay wounded.

Ushered in with such bloodshed, Reconstruction in New Orleans ended, for all practical purposes, with the Battle of Liberty Place on 14 September 1874. Determined to prevent the recently established White League from receiving a shipment of arms, a combined force of Republican militia and metropolitan police (under the command of the former Confederate general James Longstreet) confronted the white supremacist group in a skirmish that brought thousands of combatants to the foot of Canal Street. Federal troops later wrested the streets from the victorious White Leaguers, but the battle, in which twenty-one of the White Leaguers died (along with eleven metropolitan police), effectively demonstrated the fatal weakness of the local Republican government.

Political, ethnic, labor, and racial unrest plagued New Orleans in the last quarter of the nineteenth century. Elections continued to be marred by fraud and violence, including the murder of public officials. The assassination of police chief David Hennessy in 1890 led to the lynching of eleven Italians early the next year in an incident that had international repercussions. Enraged by the acquittal of those charged in Hennessy's death, a mob that included well-known representatives of the city's social and economic elite gathered at Henry Clay's statue on Canal Street, marched to the parish prison, and cold-bloodedly murdered their ethnically identifiable prey. The inclusion of three Italian citizens among the slain prompted a formal protest from the Italian government and, in some quarters, calls for war. Tensions cooled only after President Benjamin Harrison denounced the incident as "an offense against law and humanity" and offered monetary compensation. Shortly thereafter, shippers' efforts to exploit a deepening economic depression and play the races off each other pushed black-white tensions past the breaking point; in 1894 and 1895 white laborers drove blacks from the docks in a series of violent confrontations. The most serious incident, the Robert Charles riot of July 1900, symbolized the deterioration of race relations. A migrant from rural Mississippi, Charles resisted an aggressive police interrogation, triggering days of mayhem and rioting. Before being gunned down, Charles shot and killed seven whites (including four police officers) and wounded twenty others (including three policemen); gangs of young, working-class white males roamed the streets in the interim, kill-

In Canal Street, New Orleans, strike sympathizers burn a trolley car, probably in 1929.
CORBIS/UNDERWOOD & UNDERWOOD

ing at least three blacks and injuring dozens more in retaliation.

In the twentieth century, race remained the most likely source of disorder. Major labor conflicts disappeared with the 1920s, as did serious ethnic disputes. Governor Huey Long's use of the state militia to confront New Orleans's police over control of voter-registration lists roiled the political scene in the 1930s, but such episodes passed with Long's 1935 assassination in Baton Rouge. Still, a series of bombings that targeted black-owned homes punctuated legislative efforts to desegregate neighborhoods in the 1920s, and more notable racial demonstrations surrounded efforts at school desegregation a generation later. White mobs roamed the streets in 1960–1961, trying to enforce a boycott of experimentally integrated schools and harassing their opponents; their actions attracted national attention to the city's troubles. While city leaders proudly boasted that New Orleans suffered no massive rioting during the long, hot summers of the mid-1960s, they were caught short by two events—a 1970 shoot-out that engaged one hundred police and a group of Black Panthers (an organization of militant American blacks) and the

Mark Essex incident of January 1973. An embittered black migrant to the city like Robert Charles, Essex climbed atop the Howard Johnson hotel near the civic-center complex and rained gunfire on those below, killing nine (including five police officers) before he was slain. Confrontations between police and African Americans continued to generate conflict into the 1970s and 1980s. Numerous shootings, including that of a black Vietnam War veteran, produced a wave of lawsuits that eventually cost the city millions of dollars. The most notable episode of police violence was the Algiers incident of November 1980. Following the murder of an officer, police swept through a West Bank public housing project and employed excessive force in the course of their investigation. Mounting two raids based on information extracted from beaten witnesses, an all-white squad proceeded to shoot and kill two male "suspects" and a female companion. By the mid-1990s black officers were being convicted of murder in connection with their own criminal activity and, in one case, of ordering a "hit" on a black citizen who dared register a formal complaint of brutality. Shortly thereafter, a new police superintendent brought in from

Washington, D.C., Richard Pennington, made significant strides in professionalizing what had been a notoriously violent institution.

BIBLIOGRAPHY

Arnesen, Eric. *Waterfront Workers of New Orleans: Race, Class, and Politics, 1863–1923.* New York: Oxford University Press, 1991.

Hair, William Ivy. *Carnival of Fury: Robert Charles and the New Orleans Race Riot of 1900.* Baton Rouge: Louisiana State University Press, 1976.

Rousey, Dennis C. *Policing the Southern City: New Orleans, 1805–1889.* Baton Rouge: Louisiana State University Press, 1997.

ARNOLD R. HIRSCH

See also **Long, Huey; Riots; Urban Violence.**

NEWTON, HUEY
(1942–1989)

Huey Newton paid a high price for his lifetime of political activism. From the late 1960s until his death, he was shot, ambushed, harassed, and subjected to verbal and physical threats and abuse. His residence was repeatedly burglarized and wiretapped by the Federal Bureau of Investigation and the police, he spent three years in prison, he had countless arrests, and he was dragged into court more than two dozen times over a decade and a half. His wife and family were attacked, threatened, and placed under constant surveillance, and many of his friends were killed.

Despite the harassment that he and his associates suffered, Newton saw himself not as a victim but as a revolutionary. His unique brand of militant black nationalism was a blend of American patriotism and Marxist rhetoric. He viewed America's founding fathers as noble men who fought a war for the right to control their own destiny, men who took up arms to combat tyranny. He identified with Fidel Castro of Cuba and Che Guevara of Argentina because they led revolutions to empower downtrodden people. Newton believed that black Americans were prisoners of war, hostages in their own land who were oppressed by a white racist police force that threatened to undermine their very humanity.

Huey Percy Newton was born in Monroe, Louisiana, on 17 February 1942. At a young age he became aware that African Americans were not included in the great mass of Americans for whom "life, liberty, and the pursuit of happiness" were considered "inalienable rights." He learned that blacks lacked the educational opportunities that whites enjoyed. Like many black children, he was a victim of social promotion, passing from one grade to the next without receiving even a basic education. He was still illiterate when he graduated from high school. Motivated to improve his lot in life, Newton taught himself to read, and he was accepted to Merritt College in Oakland, California. He later went on to study law in San Francisco and in 1980 he received a Ph.D. in sociology from the University of California at Santa Cruz.

The most significant events in Newton's life revolved around his involvement with the Black Panther Party. In October 1966 at the age of twenty-four, Newton cofounded the Black Panther Party for Self Defense with Bobby Seale, one of his classmates at Merritt College. Newton and Seale were outraged by the violent tactics employed by white Bay Area policemen against blacks, and they decided that the best defense against oppressive force was the application of force. They armed themselves and fellow party members in an attempt to counteract the violence by police officers. They did not see themselves as the instigators of violence. They saw themselves as Americans committed to the idea of self-defense.

In 1967 Newton was arrested and charged with voluntary manslaughter for the killing of an Oakland police officer, John Frey. The shooting took place after Newton, who was driving in a car with a friend in the early morning hours of 28 October, was pulled over by Frey. As Frey led Newton to the patrol car, Newton managed to get Frey's gun away from him in a scuffle and fatally shoot him, A backup officer, Herbert Heanes, who had been called to the scene by Frey, then shot Newton in the stomach, Newton shot Heanes, and Newton and his friend fled the scene. In court Newton denied shooting the officer, though he later admitted, in private, to shooting him as well as the other officer; he testified that Frey had used a racial epithet while arresting him. The public outcry over Newton's arrest—at the time his claim of innocence was believed—marked the high point of the Black Panther Party's influence in the United States. Footage of a wounded Newton handcuffed to his hospital bed and flanked by an armed guard had aroused sympathy for Newton. Perhaps the public outcry was enhanced because antiwar and antidraft protesters were looking for a clear symbol of police brutality; they had been roughly treated by Oakland police during the Stop the Draft week protests during the week of 16 October, just a few days before the Newton incident. In those clashes between police and protesters, police had used billy clubs and mace. In a jailhouse interview Newton insisted that urban black neighborhoods were like occupied territories patrolled by an army of white police officers. He compared black Americans to Vietnamese citizens who were suffering foreign occupation during the Vietnam War.

Twenty-two months after he was incarcerated, his conviction was overturned and Newton was released. In 1971 he initiated a sea change in the Black Panther Party's ideology when he called for an end to the party's use of violent tactics. This shift away from violence—even in the name of self-defense—was intended to rekindle national enthusiasm for the party, which had fallen out of favor among white radicals and urban blacks, who had begun to view the Black Panthers as thugs and gangsters. (The Panthers ran a small-scale protection racket among drug traffickers and pimps, and they also forced local business owners to pay them protection money.) In the 1970s the Panthers instituted a number of community service programs such as breakfasts for schoolchildren and transportation for the elderly. Newton's efforts to

strengthen the political wing of the party were hampered by continuing interference from the FBI and other government agencies.

After his release from prison in 1970, Newton had begun to experiment with cocaine. He soon became an addict, and his behavior became erratic and often senselessly savage. In one incident in 1974, he attacked a seventeen-year-old prostitute, Kathleen Smith, and shot her; the bullet struck her spinal column and put her in a coma for three months before she died. A few days later, when his tailor, Preston Callins, came up to his penthouse to measure him for a suit, he used his pistol on the tailor's skull. Newton was arrested first for beating Callins, for which he posted $42,000 bail, then he was arrested for shooting Kathleen Smith and released again after posting $80,000 bail. His friends decided his next move; they arranged for him to jump bail and flee the country. When he returned in 1977, he paid Callins off to drop the charges, and he was twice put on trial for the murder of Smith, but both trials resulted in hung juries. These events further sullied the Panthers' reputation as well as his own. Throughout the 1970s the FBI frequently tapped his phones, opened his mail, and sent forged letters to Newton and members of the Black Panthers attempting to undermine the group. Newton's doctoral dissertation, entitled

Huey Newton talks to reporters on 27 September 1979 in Alameda County courtroom after the state of California abandoned a five-year effort to send him to prison for the slaying of Kathleen Smith. CORBIS/BETTMANN

477

War Against the Panthers: A Study of Repression in America, documents this government campaign.

The Black Panthers were increasingly facing internal and external pressures. For years they had suffered from infighting, which included political assassinations of party members and ex-party members; they had been abandoned by disillusioned blacks and white liberal supporters; and their protection racquet had led to increasing criminality among their members. With Newton's increasingly out-of-control behavior and the popularity of guerrilla politics declining in the 1970s, the party disbanded in 1982. In March 1989 Newton was arrested and sentenced to a six-month jail term for misappropriating funds intended for a Panther-founded school. On 22 August of that year he was shot and killed; Felix Mitchell, a drug kingpin who had become upset with Newton for driving some of his dealers out of East Oakland and for extorting drugs and money from others, had him killed.

BIBLIOGRAPHY

Anthony, Earl. *Picking Up the Gun: A Report on the Black Panthers.* New York: Dial, 1970.
Black Panthers: Huey! International Historic Films, 1995.
Hilliard, David, and Lewis Cole. *This Side of Glory: The Autobiography of David Hilliard and the Story of the Black Panther Party.* Boston: Little, Brown, 1993.
Newton, Huey P. *Revolutionary Suicide.* New York: Writers and Readers, 1995.
———. *War Against the Panthers: A Study of Repression in America.* New York and London: Harlem River Press, 1996.
Pearson, Hugh. *The Shadow of the Panthers: Huey Newton and the Price of Black Power in America.* Reading, Mass.: Addison-Wesley, 1994.

ADAM MAX COHEN

See also **Black Panthers; Cleaver, Eldredge.**

NEW YORK

Individual and collective acts of violence have played a central role in the growth and transformation of New York City over the last four hundred years. Riots, labor violence, terrorism, increased crime, and high-profile acts of individual violence all mark important stages in the development of the city and its central role in American urbanism.

Collective Violence

New York City's history has been permeated by a variety of forms of collective violence over its four-hundred-year history. Ethnic and racial conflict and labor and political strife have claimed the lives of hundreds of people. The intensity of collective violence in New York matches its position as the country's leading city of immigration, organized labor, and racial, ethnic, and political conflict.

Some of the earliest riots in New York were slave rebellions. In 1712 slaves burned several buildings and took up arms, resulting in the deaths of several whites and numerous blacks, who retreated into wooded areas north of the city. In 1741 a series of suspicious fires created a general panic that was unleashed on the black population, resulting in several weeks of public executions.

In colonial New York a number of demonstrations and riots erupted in protest of royal British policies. The most extensive began on 1 November 1765, when public protests and massive boycotts of British goods brought commerce to a standstill until the Stamp Act was repealed the next spring.

The first half of the nineteenth century saw numerous disturbances, as the city dealt with the conflicts emerging from industrial growth, including poverty, ethnic and class conflict, and the growing war of sentiment over slavery in the South. Labor violence between strikers, scabs, and police occurred in 1825 (stevedores), 1828 (weavers and stevedores), and 1829 (stonecutters). Riots aimed at stopping abolition activities flared up in 1834 and 1835.

The city's most serious election violence occurred during the municipal elections of 1834, when nativist Whig party members fought with supporters of the immigrant-dominated Democratic machine over access to polls. For three days the city was brought to a standstill by frequent street brawls involving thousands, until the city militia was called in and election returns were announced to a crowd of over ten thousand standing vigil on Wall Street.

In the 1837 Flour Riot, people stormed warehouses and distributed goods to the population after reports that grain was being withheld by speculators to drive up prices. Similar events during the depression of 1857 resulted in some of the city's first public works projects for the poor.

British-American antipathy was the source of the deadly Astor Place Riot of 1849, in which supporters of the American actor Edwin Forrest attacked the Astor Place Opera House during a performance by the English actor William Macready, who in a highly publicized feud with Forrest had been openly critical of the United States. The city militia killed between twenty-two and thirty-one people in an effort to disperse the angry crowd.

The struggle for political power between established Protestant immigrants and later-arriving Catholic immigrants was the source of frequent bloody confrontations in New York during the nineteenth century. Conflict between the politically connected rival street gangs the Bowery Boys (Protestant) and the Dead Rabbits (Catholic) culminated in the Dead Rabbits Riot of 1857, in which eight people were killed when the police and army attempted to quell street battles in the Bowery. Numerous but less serious street battles between rival volunteer fire companies were also endemic during this period. These companies were important sources of political power—seven of their members were elected as mayors—and became the battle forces for numerous ethnic, class, and religious divisions prior to the establishment of the relatively stable Tammany Hall machine after the Civil War.

By far the greatest civil unrest in the city's—and nation's—history occurred during the Civil War, with the Draft Riots of 13–16 July 1863. Among the mostly Irish poor there was widespread resentment of the Union's conscription plans, which favored the wealthy and rural over the poor and urban and magnified fear of increased competition with blacks for low-wage work following emancipation. The outbreak of disturbances began in the form of a general strike in which businesses were forcibly closed as workers paraded, breaking into shops and destroying telegraph lines and railways as they went. After gathering in Central Park, the crowd descended on the Ninth District provost marshal's office, where the draft was being held. Soon after, a fire company, whose members were enraged by the loss of their historic exemption, set fire to the building, beginning a reign of terror throughout the city. Assaults against government buildings were augmented by attacks against Republican officials and businesses that failed to close in support of the general strike. By the end of the first day of rioting, police and blacks were also targeted. Over the course of the riot, the Colored Orphans Asylum and other black institutions and tenements were burned, many blacks were beaten, and at least eleven were brutally murdered. Over the next two days there were pitched

battles between roving bands of rioters and police, militia, and artillery-wielding federal troops that were eventually called in from Gettysburg. Between 100 and 150 people were killed.

The economic downturn following the Civil War heightened ethnic and labor tensions. Catholic-Protestant hostilities were inflamed by the Orange Riot in July 1870, in which troops called in by the Protestant governor to protect a march commemorating the victory of William of Orange over the Catholic forces of France and Ireland opened fire on Catholic protesters; sixty-four protesters and three militiamen were killed. Further labor strife surfaced in the Tompkins Square Riot of 13 January 1874, in which sixteen hundred police attacked and beat seven thousand men and women gathered for a labor rally. Violent strikes also occurred in 1886 (sugar refiners, streetcar workers) and 1895 (streetcar workers).

The northern migration of unskilled black laborers to New York during the twentieth century created increased racial tensions, as these laborers remained segregated and faced discrimination. For the first time since the Civil War, racial tensions increased, and blacks frequently came into conflict with the police, who were viewed as an institution of segregation and unequal treatment. In 1935 three people were killed during rioting in the segregated slums of Harlem. In 1943 six were killed in a similar outbreak. Riots in Harlem and Bedford Stuyvesant in 1964 and 1965 were precursors to waves of more serious black rioting throughout the country in 1967–1968, which did not affect New York, in large part due to the conciliatory efforts of Mayor John Lindsay. During the 1950s and 1960s city streets and parks became the battleground for neighborhood turf wars that often erupted along racial and ethnic lines.

Crime and Individual Violence

In the late 1960s and the 1970s New York saw fewer riots than many other U.S. cities but a dramatic increase in violent crime and muggings, contributing to increased racial tensions and so-called white flight from the city. The city became obsessed with random violent crime from July 1976 to July 1977 when "Son of Sam" killer David Berkowitz murdered six people sitting in their cars or on their stoops and contributed to media hysteria through the release of letters to newspapers after each killing. The sense of crisis was heightened by the looting and rioting that broke out during the 1977 heat wave and electrical blackout. In the late

A black youth is taken into custody by two policemen in Harlem, New York City, during the fourth night of rioting in July 1964. CORBIS/BETTMANN

1980s and early 1990s the city also witnessed a dramatic increase in violent crime that was closely associated with the growth of the crack cocaine trade. By the late 1990s, however, shifting drug markets and changing police strategies had reduced violent crime rates to the levels of the mid-1960s.

In the 1980s and 1990s, several localized incidents of violence served as lightning rods for conflicting public sentiment about race. In 1984 a white subway rider, Bernhard Goetz, shot four black teenagers for allegedly threateningly asking him for money. In 1989 a crowd of white teenagers in Bensonhurst chased a young black man, Yusuf Hawkins, and beat him to death, resulting in a series of Civil Rights–style marches confronted by angry local crowds. In the Crown Heights section of Brooklyn in 1991, a Jewish man was killed during several days of rioting between mostly West Indian blacks and Hasidic Jews.

Terrorism

By European standards, major acts of political terrorism in New York have been limited. In 1920, during a period of national anarchist activism, a bomb was detonated next to the J. P. Morgan Company on Wall Street, killing thirty-three people and injuring four hundred. No one was arrested or claimed responsibility for the bombing.

In 1993 the most significant act of international terrorism in the United States took place in New York with the bombing of the World Trade Center. A group of Muslim fundamentalists drove a truck bomb into a garage underneath one of the towers. The blast killed five people, injured thousands of others, and tested the city's emergency response capabilities. Four suspects were arrested and convicted for the bombing. Since then, threats of terrorism linked to U.S. activities in the Middle East have caused the city to adopt stringent new security measures in and around government buildings and foreign consulates.

Violence has played a significant role in the political, social, and cultural life of New York City. The explosive processes of urbanism, industrialism, immigration, and migration have strained the government's ability to provide for the basic needs of the society. When such needs are not met, violence emerges in the form of race riots, political violence, labor unrest, and increased crime. As New York continues to play a central role in the global economy, the risks of domestic and international terrorism also increase.

BIBLIOGRAPHY

Bernstein, Iver. *The New York City Draft Riots: Their Significance for American Society and Politics in the Age of the Civil War.* New York: Oxford University Press, 1990.

Capeci, Dominic. *The Harlem Riot of 1943.* Philadelphia: Temple University Press, 1977.

Cook, Adrian. *The Armies of the Streets: The New York City Draft Riots of 1863.* Lexington: University Press of Kentucky, 1974.

Headley, Joel Tyler. *The Great Riots of New York: 1712–1873.* Indianapolis: Bobbs-Merrill, 1970.

ALEX S. VITALE

See also **Berkowitz, David "Son of Sam"; Crown Heights Riot; Draft Riots; Folk Narratives: New**

York City Crime-Victim Stories; Genovese, Kitty, Murder of; Goetz, Bernhard H.; Riots; Urban Violence; Wall Street, Bombing of; World Trade Center Bombing.

NO DUTY TO RETREAT

A vital legal transformation that has played a significant role in the history of the United States, the most homicide-prone nation among economically advanced democracies, was the replacement in most states of the traditional English common-law requirement of the "duty to retreat" in a potentially murderous situation by the newer American common-law doctrine of standing one's ground against a dangerous opponent—that is, no duty to retreat. The English doctrine stipulated that one must flee from the scene in a personal dispute that threatens to become violent. If, however, flight was blocked, English common law required that one retreat as far as possible—"to the wall" was the legal phrase—before injuring or killing an antagonist in an act of lawful self-defense.

During the nineteenth century in America the supreme courts of most states west of the Appalachians repudiated the English duty to retreat in favor of the American doctrine of standing one's ground. In upholding the no-duty-to-retreat doctrine these state courts resorted to tropes of honor and shame that spoke to a strong concern for the values of masculine bravery in a frontier nation. For example, the Ohio Supreme Court held in 1876 that a "true man" had no duty to retreat, while the supreme court in neighboring Indiana opined the following year that the duty to retreat was, in effect, a legal rationale for cowardice and that cowardice was simply un-American. In an earlier proceeding focusing on the issue of retreat a Tennessee supreme court judge contemptuously referred to a hunter who was a principal in the episode as a "timid, cowardly man," and after that the resulting legal outcome that significantly widened the right of violent self-defense was known as the "timid hunter" case.

Upheld by the U.S. Supreme Court in 1921 in an incisive decision written by Associate Justice Oliver Wendell Holmes, Jr., the concept of no-duty-to-retreat was both a symptom and cause of American violence. In contrast, England, with its deeply embedded doctrine of the duty to retreat, has long had a homicide rate that is nine to ten times lower than that of the United States. Unsurpassed among the other states in its allegiance to no-duty-to-retreat was Texas, and the result has been baleful. The anthropologist Henry P. Lundsgaarde's study of homicide in violence-prone Houston in 1969 concluded that a duty-to-retreat requirement would have significantly reduced the 268 killings that occurred there in that year because, wrote Lundsgaarde, in numerous instances "both killers and victims could easily have de-escalated the seriousness of the situation by retreat." In the 1980s and 1990s judges and legal scholars increasingly looked askance at no-duty-to-retreat as an obsolete encouragement to violence, but the influential Model Penal Code of 1985 did not require retreat and most western states still shunned the duty-to-retreat. At the grassroots level the mood in favor of violent self-defense in a crime-plagued nation was never stronger. Some tribunals reflected the public mood, such as the Florida Supreme Court, which in 1999 absolved wives from the rule that they must attempt flight before using deadly force against an abusive and extremely dangerous husband.

BIBLIOGRAPHY

Brown, Richard Maxwell. *No Duty to Retreat: Violence and Values in American History and Society.* New York: Oxford University Press, 1991.
Epps, Garrett. "Any Which Way but Loose: Interpretive Strategies and Attitudes Toward Violence in the Evolution of the Anglo-American 'Retreat Rule.'" *Law and Contemporary Problems* 55 (winter 1992).
Lundsgaarde, Henry P. *Murder in Space City: A Cultural Analysis of Houston Homicide Patterns.* New York: Oxford University Press, 1977.

RICHARD MAXWELL BROWN

See also **Fight-or-Flight Syndrome; Self-Defense and Security.**

NONVIOLENCE

Nonviolence can mean anything from disciplined action toward peace and reconciliation, in the spirit of Mohandas K. Gandhi and Martin Luther King, Jr., to simple avoidance of the use of physical force, in the spirit of autocrats who dominate by threat and intimidation. The different senses of nonviolence reflect the different conceptions of violence: the narrow and demanding sense of Gandhi and King reflects a broad conception of violence, including social oppression, incarceration, and verbal and physical abuse; the looser sense of nonviolence goes hand in hand with a narrow conception of violence that is limited to such acts as war, murder, rape, assault, and torture. This article discusses nonviolence mostly as a positive and active means to address conflicts and injustices through persistent and principled negotiation and other methods that rely on moral suasion rather than physical force.

Origins

Although never dominant, nonviolence has been part of the American tradition since colonial times, largely because of Roger Williams in Rhode Island and Quaker settlements under the aegis of William Penn in New Jersey and Pennsylvania. In both cases the philosophy of nonviolence consisted in part of replacing religious persecution with tolerance and replacing land seizure with accommodation through purchase or treaty. Williams was Penn's senior by forty years and must be considered the pioneer in these efforts, but Penn's vision was broader: to establish and preserve a society based on Christian principles without reliance on firearms. In settlement of debts owed to his father, an admiral who served both Cromwell and the Crown, Penn became proprietor of Pennsylvania and part of New Jersey. Penn joined the Society of Friends as a young man and became an intimate of George Fox, founder and leader of the Quakers. Although Penn himself spent little time in America, he dedicated the land to those who wished to establish a "peaceable kingdom,"and he drew up a constitution (called Concessions) that combined Quaker principles with democratic government.

Quakers avoid reliance on weapons, and a chief aim of the colony was to live in peace with Native Americans. To this end Penn signed a treaty with the Indians, as Williams had with the Narragansett in Rhode Island, and Quakers made continuing efforts at understanding as well as tolerance; there is a particularly moving account in the Quaker John Woolman's *Journal* (1774) of his visit to the Indians at Wyalusing on the Susquehanna River in northern Pennsylvania in 1763. Unlike in the Massachusetts Bay Colony, from which Williams was expelled and where Quakers and others were banned or even hanged, tolerance was extended to other colonists. Because prosperity accompanied peace, the colony attracted many non-Quakers, including Benjamin Franklin, an immigrant from Boston, under whose influence the democratic as-

sembly, needing to defend westerly settlements, established a militia about 1750. With this development Quakers largely withdrew from government, Quaker nonviolence took other forms, and Penn's experiment came to an end. Ultimately, the experiment cannot be counted definitively as a success or a failure. It did not endure, but it established nonviolence as a legacy that has reappeared in other peaceable communities, such as Oneida in the nineteenth century in upstate New York and the Life Center in the mid-twentieth century in central Philadelphia, as well as in alternative forms of nonviolence, such as the service and development work of the American Friends Service Committee (AFSC) and the lobbying of the Friends Committee on National Legislation.

The nonviolent practice of acquiring territory by purchase and treaty rather than by conquest was continued by the United States government in the nineteenth century with the Louisiana Purchase in 1803 and the purchase of Alaska in 1867.

Nonviolence in Wartime

War is an obvious challenge to nonviolence. The result has sometimes been confrontation, sometimes compromise, and sometimes capitulation. During the French and Indian War (1754–1763), John Woolman was clear that he would not fight but confused about how to respond when his house was requisitioned to quarter soldiers heading toward battle. He decided that it would be inhumane not to give the young men a bed and a meal but that he could not in conscience accept payment from the army. The Revolutionary War led to a split in the Society of Friends, with the "Free Quakers" renouncing nonviolence and joining the fight. The Civil War, however, did not involve confrontation between pacifists and government, because men could buy their way out of military service if they could find someone to serve in their stead.

World War I led to two dramatic developments pertaining to nonviolence in the United States: the imprisonment of pacifists and the establishment of the aforementioned American Friends Service Committee and the Fellowship of Reconciliation. Imprisonment was a sharp test for conscientious objectors, and those who chose to endure it provided strong leadership for the pacifist movement in the 1930s and 1940s. These acts of disobedience significantly advanced the cause of confrontational nonviolence. The AFSC is an example of constructive nonviolence. Influenced by the example of

Woolman, the AFSC originally sought to respond positively and constructively to humanitarian needs (but not military requirements) created by war and oppression. Initially, the AFSC, working with its British counterpart during World War I, concentrated on relief and ambulance work, as well as feeding destitute civilians (especially in Germany) after the war. In the late 1930s the AFSC helped many Jews to leave Germany. In 1947 the AFSC and its British counterpart shared the honor of accepting the Nobel Peace Prize on behalf of the Quakers, and its program of constructive nonviolence has continued to expand and to draw substantial support from both inside and outside the Society of Friends.

There were also other developments of both confrontational and constructive nonviolence during World War II. The Selective Service Act of 1940, unlike the draft of 1917, included a provision for conscientious religious objectors. The provision required conscientious objectors to do alternative service of national importance, and this requirement had implications for both confrontational and constructive nonviolence. On the constructive side, churches were asked to organize work camps for their objectors; a Catholic camp, Camp Simon, as well as camps for Mennonites, Quakers, and other peaceful churches were established. Many of the camps were modeled on the Civilian Conservation Corps camps of the 1930s and became in turn models for the youth work camps that were organized by David Ritchie for the AFSC in the decades following the war, which in turn were a model for the Peace Corps. Work in mental hospitals and in medical experiments was generally satisfying to both parties, but because of military-like rules and the dubious importance of the projects undertaken, there was much disappointment at many of the camps. Some of the organizers (AFSC in particular) came to regard the effort as too compromising because of its close connection with the war effort.

The requirement of alternative service led to a strengthening of confrontational nonviolence in the form of conscientious objection to cooperating with the selective service system. There were more objectors imprisoned during World War II than during World War I, and they came to play more significant roles in subsequent developments of nonviolence in the United States. The first of the militant conscientious objectors were eight divinity students from Union Seminary, among whom were George Houser (a leading figure in the Fel-

lowship of Reconciliation, the Congress of Racial Equality, and the American Committee on Africa) and David Dellinger (a leading figure in nonviolent direct action against the Vietnam War). These men were initially sent to the federal prison in Danbury, Connecticut. Other pacifists were placed in federal prisons in Ashland, Kentucky, and Lewisburg, Pennsylvania. They included Bronson Clark and Steven G. Cary, both of whom subsequently chaired the AFSC, Larry Gara, James Peck, and Bayard Rustin, the brilliant black Quaker who became a leading nonviolent strategist of the Civil Rights movement and a consultant both to Martin Luther King and to the AFSC.

Prison experience played a large role in strengthening and tempering the leadership of nonviolence in the United States in the postwar period, which witnessed not only the strengthening of traditional service and educational organizations but also the establishment of nonviolent lobbying groups, such as the Friends Committee on National Legislation (1943) and the Council for a Livable World (1962). More recently these lobbying efforts have included human rights organizations and have been expanded to include lobbying at the United Nations. These attempts to influence public life without taking part in either political parties or government itself have become one method of choice for persons committed to nonviolence.

Opposition to the Vietnam War was widespread, but because the war was politically unpopular, it had less effect on nonviolence as such. The important point to be kept in mind is that opposition to a particular war—for instance Henry David Thoreau's opposition to the Mexican War (1846) or Benjamin Spock's opposition to the Vietnam War (1967 to 1972)—may be based on political disagreement rather than on a commitment to nonviolence. The political principles expressed may be admired by pacifists, but they should not be confused with nonviolence. This unpopular war did, however, vastly increase the number of persons and organizations dedicated to seeking alternative solutions to conflict.

Sheltered Communities

Sheltered communities seek to set themselves apart from the mainstream of American life to cultivate alternative ideals and disciplines. Some of these communities are offshoots of historic peace churches. Both the Society of Brethren and the Amish, for example, derive from Mennonites and have strong principles of nonviolence. Others are secular or nonsectarian. An example is the Oneida community in upstate New York, founded in 1847 and whose manufacture of flatware has been a successful contribution to mainstream America. The Shakers established their own communities on principles that avoided not only violence but also sex. Their work, especially furniture manufacture, is much admired and is often of museum quality, but their admirers have chosen not to join such strict communities, and the movement has almost died out. The Life Center was established in central Philadelphia about the time of the Vietnam War; its members normally had jobs outside the community, the community efforts being directed less at daily chores than at the spirit of nonviolence and imaginative (and often ambitious) projects for promoting nonviolence.

Civil Disobedience

Civil disobedience is the open nonviolent refusal to obey a valid governmental order, be it legislative, administrative, or judicial. Tax refusal is perhaps the paradigm in the United States, since in the eighteenth century it led to the American Revolution and in the nineteenth to the imprisonment of Thoreau and the publication of his classic essay "Civil Disobedience" (1846). Other examples of civil disobedience are draft refusal (as opposed to draft evasion), lunch-counter sit-ins, and Martin Luther King's defiance of a court injunction against a civil rights march in Birmingham in 1963. Draft evasion, like the Underground Railroad, a network of antislavery people who helped slaves escape to free territory, is a modified form of civil disobedience because it is surreptitious rather than open. Civil disobedience is a tool suitable for use against claims of governmental injustice or oppression. There is much room for analysis and argument about the conditions under which this approach can be successful, but it demonstrates that practitioners of nonviolence need not be passive but can be active and courageous.

The illegality of civil disobedience raises problems, as does its interference with normal life. In recent German law blocking of driveways and roadways by sitting down has been deemed violent (*gewaltig*) because of its willful interference with ordinary work. Illegality raises moral problems, too, because law is normally an alternative to violence. There is, however, a difference between just and unjust legal systems. The philosopher John Rawls has argued very forcefully that

civil disobedience cannot be morally justified in a democracy with a just and accessible legal system. The dilemmas and paradoxes resulting from the illegality of civil disobedience can lead nonviolent activists to cynicism about law and about the good order of society. Both law and good order sometimes do mask oppression and injustice, and in these cases civil disobedience can be justified. Nonetheless, as the legacy of King shows, in the long run the U.S. Constitution is on the side of civil rights, and it stands to reason that civil rights are not likely to be advanced if law and order are overturned. Civil disobedience is a fine-tuned instrument for opposing legislative and judicial injustice and inequity without threatening the legal system itself.

Industrial and Labor Relations

Strikes, lockouts, and boycotts are instruments of nonviolent action, at least in the weak sense. From 1870 to 1950 labor's dramatic strides in organizational strength led to corresponding improvements in wages and working conditions. Much of this increase in the power of labor came through strikes and the threat of strikes, and none of it through the systematic use or espousal of armed force. Few labor organizers have openly espoused nonviolence (César Chavez, Mexican-born leader and organizer of Chicano farm workers in California is a notable exception) and the history of labor organization is replete with acts of violence by both labor and management. Furthermore, the bitterness and enmity has often been so sharp that the labor movement can certainly not be said to have been nonviolent in the strict sense. Nonetheless, in the period of labor organization from 1870 to 1950 overall, power was achieved primarily through strikes and boycotts on the one hand and legislation on the other, with violence constantly muddying the picture but of little lasting significance. On balance, labor organization is clearly part of the tradition of nonviolence in the United States.

Since 1950 labor relations have increasingly been a matter of negotiation and cooperation rather than confrontation. The prevalence of negotiation, which presupposes an equality of negotiating status if not of power, is itself a testimony to the prior achievements of labor action and labor legislation. Negotiation, unlike confrontation, both signifies and reinforces a partnership—of diverse interests, to be sure, but a partnership nonetheless—that allows both labor and management to reach a win-win solution to their conflict.

Business and Government

Business depends quite as much on cooperation as on competition: both are necessary for its vitality. Without competition, cooperative arrangements can turn into trusts and monopolies. Without cooperation, it would be difficult for businesses to forge long-term relationships with their customers and clients. Negotiation and win-win solutions to problems created by divergent interests have many applications in business in addition to those noted above about labor relations.

The Harvard Negotiation Project was founded as a joint effort of the Harvard Law School and the Harvard Business School, under the direction of Roger Fisher. Together with William Ury, Fisher wrote *Getting to Yes* (1991), a persuasive discussion of what the authors call "principled" negotiation, which they contrast with positional negotiation, in which the parties stake out their position and then bargain or manipulate for as much as they can get. The aim of principled negotiation being durable agreement, the negotiator wants the other side to be satisfied enough to have a stake in maintaining the agreement. Fisher and Ury urge a negotiator always to give in to good reasons but never to threats. They distinguish between positions and interests, and urge negotiators, when initial positions clash, to seek alternative positions that will serve the same interests.

While politics and law enforcement are the aspects of government that make the most news, the bulk of governance depends on compliance that is voluntary, democratic, and nonviolent. Negotiation plays an important role in this process, at various levels of governmental activity. Negotiation takes place within Congress and state legislatures among the various interests represented there; negotiation also takes place between the president and Congress (and likewise between governors and state legislatures) over details of legislation. In the last two decades of the twentieth century, negotiation became more commonplace between regulatory agencies or administrative departments and the regulated parties (often large corporations) about the wording of regulations that are to be adopted and promulgated to implement either acts of Congress or judicial decisions. Although it rarely makes the evening news, negotiation plays a critical role in furthering the tradition of nonviolence in the United States.

Race Relations

Slavery is inherently violent, and so were the urban race riots of the 1960s, the beating of the black man Rodney King by Los Angeles police in 1992, and the uprising that followed the acquittal of the police officers who beat King. Race and violence are so often and so closely connected in the history of the United States that nonviolence almost drops out of sight. But two different forms of nonviolence have been advocated and successfully practiced as tactics for overcoming racial oppression. One, associated especially with Tuskegee Institute educator and agriculturalist George Washington Carver, is education and disciplined work. This path requires little or no radical social change and has been followed by large numbers of descendants of slaves into the middle class. The other path is that of Martin Luther King. The nonviolence of King was a way of life as well as a tactic. He genuinely believed in loving those who hated him and in always responding to violence with nonviolence. One of his biographers tells of a time when a man jumped onto the stage where he was speaking and hit him hard in the face—and King looked at him with his arms at his side. He knew well that his confrontational nonviolent activism engendered anger and hate and endangered his life, but he stuck to it in practice as well as in theory.

King, taking inspiration from Gandhi and tactical advice from Bayard Rustin, demonstrated the potential effectiveness of civil disobedience and nonviolent direct action for confronting racial oppression. Civil disobedience is dated by some from the Boston Tea Party (1773); in matters of race relations a weak form of nonviolent civil disobedience was practiced by participants in the Underground Railroad. All civil disobedience involves deliberate (and usually open but peaceful) violation of a law that is seen as radically unjust. It is obviously an alternative to the use of armed force for the same purpose. Nevertheless, it remains controversial because it violates the law. The nature of the controversy can be seen in the stern rebuke of King by eight of his fellow clergymen from Alabama when he was arrested in Birmingham in 1963 and in King's response, "Letter from a Birmingham Jail," probably the most eloquent defense of civil disobedience as a tactic of nonviolence in the struggle for racial justice.

The civil disobedience practiced in the two decades following World War II, unlike that of the Underground Railroad, was open rather than secretive, and it aimed to correct injustice not by rescuing individuals (i.e., slaves) but by changing laws. Where civil disobedience is open, activists are likely to be arrested, as was the case with Gandhi in India and countless civil rights activists during the protests against segregation in the South during the 1950s and 1960s.

With the passage of the Civil Rights Act of 1964 and the Voting Rights Act of 1965, together with various Supreme Court decisions such as *Morgan v. Virginia* in 1946 and *Brown v. Board of Education* in 1954, racial justice in the United States has come to focus more on issues of economic equity and opportunity than on contesting unjust laws; therefore, civil disobedience in the late twentieth century and beyond lacks one compelling ground it had in the immediate postwar period.

Women's Rights

Deep-rooted nonviolence shaped the lives of suffragists such as Susan B. Anthony and Lucretia Mott, and the feminist activism of the nineteenth and twentieth centuries that led to the expanded role of women in public life was essentially nonviolent, although the women were militant in insisting on rights and powers. The achievement of women in securing a place in public life strengthened the tradition of nonviolent protest in the United States.

At the end of the twentieth century, violence against women was still a major problem around the world. While women face violence in every society, their plight is especially poignant in societies that are undemocratic and militaristic. Efforts to improve the status of women are therefore generally efforts that strengthen nonviolence. While these efforts are mostly coordinated through the United Nations, American women play a disproportionately large role, inspired no doubt by the success of such tactics in advancing the cause of women's rights in the United States.

Religion

All major religions contain a powerful element of nonviolence, but some also contain seeds of violence in the form of intolerance and what the legal theorist and political philosopher Carl Schmitt has called "political theology." The element of violence in religions stems from a fusion of religion and politics, that is, from attempts to dominate and control worldly affairs in the name of a god. The ideology, or political theology, that results from such attempts involves political intransigence and a refusal to compromise that often characterize those who believe themselves to be God's specially chosen emissaries on earth.

The element of nonviolence in religion stems from belief in a universal god. The god may be all-powerful, so that whatever happens is an expression of divine will and is therefore not subject to forceful opposition by humans. The god may be present in every human being, so that using force or coercion on another human suppresses something divine. Both of these conceptions are nonpolitical, abjuring manipulation and domination of worldly affairs. Religions that renounce violence can come into conflict with politics by attempting to set limits on what is legitimate in the sphere of politics, such as claiming that war is an illegitimate instrument of government.

It is important to recognize the distinction between limiting and dominating. The principal thrust of religious nonviolence is to limit the domain of politics, not to achieve a dominant role within it. When pacifists attempt to pass legislation or win elections, such pacifism is directly political and not an instance of religious nonviolence. Even the nonviolence of Gandhi and King was primarily a matter of limiting rather than dominating: neither formed nor joined a political party. The religious and moral claim is that there are worldly considerations that supersede those of politics and that are rightly invoked to limit the domain of politics. Politicians are understandably frustrated by such claims, but the refusal to acknowledge areas of human activity falling outside politics, however well-intentioned, opens the door to totalitarianism. The separation of church and state therefore acts as a buffer and as a protection for religious nonviolence in the United States.

Among the smaller religious sects in the United States—Quakers, Mennonites, Brethren, and Jehovah's Witnesses—there are peace churches. Among the mainstream denominations there are generally peace fellowships or subsidiary communities committed to nonviolence. While Roman Catholics in the twentieth century, for example, were not necessarily nonviolent, the Trappist monk Thomas Merton (influenced by Buddhism as well as Christianity) was deeply committed to nonviolence. Gordon Zahn and other Catholics were conscientious objectors during World War II, and the Catholic Worker movement, led by Dorothy Day and Ammon Hennacy, was one of the most noteworthy pacifist groups in the second half of the twentieth century.

Law and Justice

Common law is inherently nonviolent in the weak sense, because litigation provides an alternative to physical violence for resolving claims and counterclaims. The strength and independence of the judiciary in the United States is therefore an important source of nonviolence. Even though law involves coercion, only religious purists (e.g., some Quakers and Mennonites, as well as some existentialists and postmodernists) refuse to distinguish between this coercion and violence, as long as the process is fair and justice is served.

Law, however, is not necessarily nonviolent in the strong sense. On the one hand, laws may institutionalize and legitimize violence, as in the case of slavery, internment of aliens, and war; civil disobedience is sometimes a nonviolent response to this sort of legal violence. On the other hand, the legal process itself can be as intimidating and crippling as an attack by thugs in the street, and litigation can be so contentious that decisions are postponed for years, truth becomes secondary to victory, and victory depends on how much money is spent. A well-established alternative to the procedural contentiousness is alternative dispute resolution, a process of mediation rather than litigation that strives to reach mutually agreeable accommodation rather than victory. Alternative dispute resolution, now an adjunct to the court system in every state, reduces the caseload and backlog of the courts and saves money. Because it funnels contentious energies into a process of systematic compromise, it, too, promotes a spirit of nonviolence in the United States.

Injustice tends to generate rancor and violence, so nonviolent activists often advocate justice. The relation of peace and justice is, however, problematic. Justice requires enforcement, which entails some sort of coercion. It is not clear that there can be any nonviolent form of coercion. Perhaps, however, legal coercion is less violent, or less blatantly violent, than other forms. The law provides for coercion aimed at justice, but it is an imperfect system. Some nonviolent activists therefore advocate justice but oppose the judicial system.

Nonviolence in the 1990s

By the end of the twentieth century nonviolence had become integrated into both professional and academic life. Mediation and arbitration became the province of highly trained professionals whose skills provided alternatives to violence and litigation for resolving conflicts. Nonviolence was fostered in academic life through peace studies programs in the curriculum and through peace research. Peace studies were encouraged by the Consortium on Peace Research and Education, by the International Peace Research Association (which publishes a journal), and the U.S. Institute for Peace. In public education peer mediation training was incorporated into the curriculum of many middle schools and high schools. Nonviolence remained strong and deeply rooted, therefore, although rarely newsworthy and not ideologically dominant in the United States.

BIBLIOGRAPHY

Anderson, Jervis. *Bayard Rustin: Troubles I've Seen: A Biography.* New York: HarperCollins, 1997.

Axelrod, Robert. *Evolution of Cooperation.* New York: Basic, 1984.

Barbour, Hugh, et al., eds. *Quaker Crosscurrents: Three Hundred Years of Friends in New York Yearly Meetings.* Syracuse, N.Y.: Syracuse University Press, 1995.

Bedau, Hugo Adam, ed. *Civil Disobedience: Theory and Practice.* New York: Pegasus, 1969.

Brock, Peter. *Pacifism in the United States from the Colonial Era to the First World War.* Princeton, N.J.: Princeton University Press, 1968.

Buckmaster, Henrietta. *Let My People Go: The Story of the Underground Railroad and the Growth of the Abolition Movement.* Boston: Beacon Press, 1959.

Fisher, Roger, et al. *Beyond Machiavelli: Tools for Coping with Conflict.* Cambridge, Mass.: Harvard University Press, 1994.

Fisher, Roger, and William Ury. *Getting to Yes: Negotiating Agreement Without Giving In.* 2d ed. Edited by Bruce Patton. Boston: Houghton Mifflin, 1991.

Garver, Newton, and Eric Reitan. *Nonviolence and Community: Reflections on the Alternatives to Violence Project.* Wallingford, Pa.: Pendle Hill, 1995.

Gluck, Shema. *From Parlor to Prison: Five American Suffragettes Talk About Their Lives.* New York: Vintage, 1976.

Hentoff, Nat. *Peace Agitator: The Story of A. J. Muste.* New York: Macmillan, 1963.

Holmes, Robert L. *Nonviolence in Theory and Practice.* Belmont, Mass.: Wadsworth, 1990.

Jonas, Gerald. *On Doing Good.* New York: Scribner, 1971.

Kesten, Seymour. *Utopian Episodes: Daily Life in Experimental Colonies Dedicated to Changing the World.* Syracuse, N.Y.: Syracuse University Press, 1993.

Lynd, Staughton, and Alice Lynd. *Nonviolence in America: A Documentary History.* Maryknoll, N.Y.: Orbis, 1995.

Pruitt, Dean. *Negotiation Behavior.* New York: Academic Press, 1981.

Taylor, Ronald. *Chavez and the Farm Workers.* Boston: Beacon, 1975.

Woolman, John. *John Woolman's Journal and Major Essays.* Edited by Phillips P. Moulton. New York: Oxford University Press, 1971.

Zahn, Gordon. *Another Part of the War: The Camp Simon Story.* Amherst: University of Massachusetts Press, 1979.

Newton Garver

See also **Antiwar Protests; Capital Punishment; Civil Disobedience; Conflict Resolution; Disarmament and Arms Control; Peacemaking; Prevention: Violent-Crime Prevention; Quakers; Religion.**

NO-RULES FIGHTING. *See* Ultimate Fighting.

NUCLEAR WAR FICTION. *See* Literature: Nuclear War Fiction.

NUCLEAR WEAPONS. *See* Weapons: Nuclear.

NUREMBERG TRIALS. *See* War Crimes.

O

O. K. CORRAL GUNFIGHT

On 26 October 1881 the most famous gunfight in the history and mythology of the American West occurred in Tombstone, Arizona. Later misnamed the "gunfight at the O. K. Corral," it not only attracted national attention when it happened but also became the enduring symbol of the struggle between law and outlaw in the legend of the Old West. From the beginning, there were two versions of what happened that day: one depicted the fight as the triumph of law over outlaw in the heroic struggle to bring justice to the frontier, and the other saw it as the cold-blooded murder of innocent cowboys by outlaw marshals.

The fight was as compelling and confusing as the myth and antimyth it spawned. It had its origins in the growing tensions between the Earp brothers—Virgil, Wyatt, and Morgan, who represented not only the law in Tombstone but the power structure as well—and a loosely connected collection of cowboys, rustlers, and stage robbers who operated in the brush of southern Arizona and across the line in Mexico. The immediate cause of the shoot-out was the erratic behavior of Joseph Isaac "Ike" Clanton, one of the cowboys.

Clanton had entered into a clandestine deal with Wyatt Earp to accept a reward in exchange for information that would lead to the capture of certain fugitives. The secret arrangement would have proved embarrassing and dangerous to Clanton if it had ever leaked out. Clanton worried that the Earps' friend John Henry "Doc" Holliday

knew about the deal. On the night of 25 October, Clanton confronted Holliday in a saloon, but Morgan Earp intervened. Clanton did not drop the matter and kept drinking. Warned that Clanton was making threats, City Marshal Virgil Earp tracked Clanton down, knocked him to the ground, and hauled him into court. Outside the courtroom Wyatt Earp punched Tom McLaury, a friend of Clanton's, to the ground after a brief exchange of words.

These encounters should have ended the matter, but Clanton did not let up. When his younger brother Billy and friend Frank McLaury showed up, the situation grew more ominous. Frank McLaury apparently wanted to leave town, but Ike was still angry, and they were all of a type not to run from a fight. Over the next couple of hours, several citizens informed Virgil Earp that the cowboys were still threatening the Earps. Sheriff John Behan promised to defuse the situation and hurried off to find the cowboys, but shortly after two o'clock in the afternoon, with still more reports of cowboy defiance, Virgil determined to arrest the Clanton crowd.

With his brothers Wyatt and Morgan and joined by Wyatt's friend Doc Holliday, Virgil Earp moved up Fremont Street toward a vacant lot after meeting Sheriff Behan next to C. S. Fly's photographic studio, where the cowboys had stopped. Near the lot Behan told Virgil that the cowboys were leaving town. The Earps relaxed but never broke stride. When the officers approached the lot, they discovered that the Clantons and McLaurys had been joined by two more men, Billy Claibourne and Wes Fuller. Virgil ordered the cowboys to throw up their hands. The cowboys hesitated. Then Frank McLaury went for his gun as Virgil yelled, "No, I don't want that."

Wyatt Earp and Billy Clanton fired the first shots. Virgil, who had handed his shotgun to Doc Holliday to hide under his overcoat, fumbled for his pistol. Billy's bullet missed; Wyatt's hit McLaury's abdomen. By then Claibourne and Fuller had fled. Ike ran to Wyatt and grabbed his arm. Wyatt shoved him away, and Ike ran for his life. In that instant Morgan shot Billy Clanton in the chest. Almost simultaneously, the badly wounded Frank McLaury hit Virgil Earp in the leg.

By then everything was confusion, with Tom and Frank McLaury's horses plunging about in panic. Ike Clanton ran away. Morgan Earp was struck across his back, apparently by Billy Clanton, and fell down. In the meantime, Holliday, armed with Virgil Earp's shotgun, was waiting, and when Tom McLaury frantically leaped for the rifle on his horse, a load of buckshot tore into his side. He staggered toward the street and fell dead near the corner of Third Street. Back on their feet, Morgan and Virgil Earp fired simultaneously at Billy Clanton. Virgil's shot struck Billy in the right side, and Morgan's hit him in the wrist. Billy fell but shifted his pistol and gamely continued to fight.

The seriously wounded Frank McLaury moved into Fremont Street, seemingly focused on Doc Holliday. The two exchanged words as Frank fired a shot that struck Holliday's pistol pocket. Morgan Earp tripped over a water pipe and fell. From his prone position he fired at Frank McLaury just as Holliday squeezed off a shot as well. Morgan's shot struck McLaury just under the ear, while Holliday's tore across his chest. The cowboy went down dead. Meanwhile, Billy Clanton was still trying to fire his pistol when C. S. Fly, the photographer, took his gun away from him. He was carried across the street and died a short time later.

The street fight was not the end of the Earp-Clanton troubles. It fouled the political climate, threatened the position of the Earps in Tombstone, and led to a serious breakdown of order in Cochise County. Two attempts to have the Earps prosecuted failed. The cowboys then sought their revenge. On the night of 28 December 1881, Virgil Earp was ambushed and seriously wounded, and on 18 March 1882 Morgan Earp was killed as he shot pool in a local billiards parlor. After Morgan's

death Wyatt Earp, by then an acting deputy U.S. marshal, took matters into his own hands. Over the weeks that followed, he and his followers killed four of the cowboys before leaving the territory with murder warrants from Cochise and Pima Counties issued for them. Wyatt Earp never faced the charges, but the vendetta in Cochise County caused President Chester Arthur to threaten martial law in Arizona, spread the fame of Tombstone across the nation, and made Wyatt Earp a legend.

Walter Noble Burns resurrected the story of Wyatt Earp in his book *Tombstone: An Iliad of the Southwest* in 1927, and Stuart N. Lake immortalized the street fight as the "gunfight at O. K. Corral" four years later in *Wyatt Earp: Frontier Marshal*. The year after Lake's book appeared, Hollywood produced *Law and Order*, the first movie that promoted the gunfight as the climax of the troubles in Tombstone. *My Darling Clementine* (1946), *The Gunfight at the O. K. Corral* (1957), *Tombstone* (1993), and *Wyatt Earp* (1994) are only the most notable of two dozen films that have highlighted thirty seconds of gunfire on the way to making the O. K. Corral fight the emblem of the struggle between law and outlaw. Even the debunkers of the 1960s merely provided variations on the theme. At the turn of the twenty-first century the imagery of the O. K. Corral is as much a component of the language of politicians and social critics as it is a part of the fiction and history of the violent West.

BIBLIOGRAPHY

Tefertiller, Casey. *Wyatt Earp: The Life Behind the Legend.* New York: Wiley, 1997.

Turner, Alford, ed. *The O. K. Corral Inquest.* College Station, Tex.: Creative Publishing, 1981.

GARY L. ROBERTS

See also **Clanton Gang; Earp Brothers; Frontier; Gunfighters and Outlaws, Western; Holliday, John Henry "Doc"; Masterson, William "Bat"; Walkdown.**

OKLAHOMA CITY BOMBING

On 19 April 1995 the Alfred P. Murrah Federal Building in the state capital of Oklahoma was destroyed by a massive explosion. One hundred sixty-eight men, women, and children died; hundreds were injured, many of them maimed for life. It was soon evident that the blast was an attack, not an accident. A huge truck bomb designed to maximize damage had been set off close to the front of the building.

The Bombers

Many Americans were quick to suspect foreign enemies, notably "Islamic fundamentalists." This was not an entirely unreasonable speculation, given that two years earlier Islamic militants had bombed New York City's World Trade Center, killing six people. Speculation for many in 1995 became fact in the minds of some, resulting in assaults, threats, and insults directed at Arabs and Muslims across the United States. An alternate view blamed the bombing on Latin American drug cartels retaliating against the Drug Enforcement Agency, which had offices in the Murrah building. But the investigation eventually led to American antigovernment white supremacists.

Just over one hour after the bombing, an Oklahoma highway patrolman arrested Timothy James McVeigh for driving without a license plate and carrying a concealed weapon. His arraignment was postponed, and McVeigh was about to be released on bail when he was identified two days later as one of the suspected bombers and taken into federal custody. Following a successful defense motion for change of venue, he was tried on federal capital murder charges in Denver, Colorado. After a nine-week jury trial, McVeigh was convicted on 2 June 1997; eleven days later he was sentenced to die by lethal injection.

Throughout the trial Stephen Jones, McVeigh's defense attorney, argued that his client was the "patsy" of an international conspiracy—a theme he has since elaborated (Jones and Israel 1998). Jones's conspiracy scenario has some truth in the sense that McVeigh did not act alone or without significant encouragement and support from radical right militants. On 4 June 1998, Terry Nichols was given a sentence of life without parole for collaborating with McVeigh in planning and executing the attack, including buying the ammonium nitrate, helping to construct the bomb, and hiding McVeigh's getaway car. The week before, Michael Fortier—whose testimony helped convict McVeigh and Nichols—was sentenced to twelve years in prison for failing to warn authorities of the bombing plot and lying to Federal Bureau of Investigation agents, as well as transporting and conspiring to sell stolen weapons. Although no other persons were charged in connection with the bombing, McVeigh, Nichols, and Fortier were participants in a growing social movement that encouraged often violent challenges to the American legal order.

Explaining the Bombing and the Bombers

McVeigh, Nichols, and Fortier do not readily fit psychopathological, rational-choice, or socialization theories of criminal motivation. Questions regarding their competency to stand trial never arose. But given the horrific number of casualties

The north side of the Alfred P. Murrah Federal Building in Oklahoma City after the bomb explosion on 19 April 1995. AGENCE FRANCE PRESSE/ CORBIS-BETTMANN

resulting from the actions of McVeigh and Nichols and the inaction of Fortier, few would argue that their decisions and acts were entirely normal. A search for answers in their early socialization produced images of essentially average young men growing up in reasonably comfortable circumstances. Of course each experienced difficulties and disappointments—McVeigh's parents divorced when he was a teenager; Nichols had to drop out of college to help on the family farm; and Fortier preferred partying to working and gave up the idea of going to a community college—but no one anticipated they would eventually get into serious trouble.

The three men met in the army. Fortier at nineteen followed in his older brothers' footsteps. McVeigh at twenty set out to become a super soldier and so fixated on weapons and all things military that his fellow recruits cordially disliked him. His only friend at first was Fortier, who got along with everyone. With worsening financial and marital troubles, Nichols at age thirty-three decided to try the military. He and McVeigh developed a friendship based largely on their antigovernment attitudes: McVeigh's general resentments were complemented by Nichols's more articulate political views.

McVeigh was the warrior, an avid gun collector and survivalist who earned a Bronze Star in the Gulf War. Fortier did his hitch, then returned to an aimless civilian life. Nichols was discharged after a year and continued his history of financial and marital difficulties.

They had in common a growing hostility toward the federal government. After a failed attempt to become a Green Beret, McVeigh became increasingly disillusioned, finally resigning from the army in disgust over the downsizing of the military and the passage of gun control legislation. Nichols joined his brother James and others in the radical right's antigovernment campaign of harassment and disruption. Fortier was caught up in the Arizona militia movement's rhetoric, which pictured the federal government trampling individual freedoms and constitutional rights. By 1995 the three were outraged by the Ruby Ridge and Waco "atrocities" and the "martyrdom" of Richard Snell, as depicted by radical right ideologists. (Snell was an icon of the radical right who, having previously targeted the Murrah building for attack, was executed on 19 April 1995 for killing a black police officer in Arkansas.) McVeigh, Nichols, and Fortier agreed with many that the government had begun a war on the American people and that it was time to fight back.

For those who do not share the worldview of the radical militants, their violence is evidence of ignorance combined with paranoia. Even when clinical paranoia is not found in individuals, the concept of a "paranoid style" (Robins and Post 1997) may be invoked in an attempt to explain why large numbers of people share the belief that their kind and their way of life are threatened by a hostile conspiracy in which their government is implicated. Such an account makes it easy to dismiss the radical viewpoint without considering why such a large and increasing number of Americans held to or sympathized with at least some of its tenets and observations. In general, the political bases of rightist extremism have not been seriously considered, and such terrorists as the Oklahoma City bombers are typically prosecuted and punished (albeit more severely on average) as if they were legally indistinguishable from nonpolitical murderers. This approach encourages the widespread view that terrorism is primarily an international or leftist threat, against the reality that radical rightists account for an increasing majority of terrorist attacks in America.

BIBLIOGRAPHY

Hamm, Mark S. *Apocalypse in Oklahoma: Waco and Ruby Ridge Revenged.* Boston: Northeastern University Press, 1997.

Jones, Stephen, and Peter Israel. *Others Unknown: The Oklahoma City Bombing Case and Conspiracy.* New York: Public Affairs, 1998.

Robins, Robert S., and Jerrold M. Post. *Political Paranoia: The Psychopolitics of Hatred.* New Haven, Conn.: Yale University Press, 1997.

Serrano, Richard A. *One of Ours: Timothy McVeigh and the Oklahoma City Bombing.* New York: Norton, 1998.

Smith, Brent L. *Terrorism in America: Pipe Bombs and Pipe Dreams.* Albany: State University of New York Press, 1994.

AUSTIN T. TURK

See also **Extremism; McVeigh, Timothy; Mass Murder; Ruby Ridge; Terrorism; Waco.**

ORGANIZED CRIME

Modern organized crime—sustained systematic illicit activities in which violence or the threat of violence is utilized to initiate, preserve, and protect the activities—in the United States emerged from and along with the evolving structures of local politics characteristic of post–Civil War American cities. The key role of urban politics in the formation of criminal syndicates came about when "new style" working-class ward politicians, who because of the end of deferential voting patterns in American cities needed a far larger voter turnout than pre–Civil War politicians, began to utilize gangsters to discourage voters from voting for their opponents at election time. In return, the politicians, who controlled police hiring and advancement, made sure there was no interference with the illicit activities of their gangster allies. Some politicians actually were partners in criminal enterprises, while some policemen ran their own extortion rings, permitting vice operations to exist for a share of the proceeds.

One of the most important and subtle ways in which urban politics and policing were joined was exemplified by New York City's election process in the last decades of the nineteenth century. The thousands of poll clerks and election inspectors needed to supervise elections were chosen from lists provided by the political parties to both Democrat and Republican police commissioners. The city paid the tab (which came to several hundreds of thousands of dollars by the late 1880s) for the work of registering voters and the recording and counting of votes. The lucrative jobs of printing and distributing ballots were controlled by district leaders. It was a system designed for energizing patron-client networks binding the police, politicians, and thousands of political workers.

While these relationships were being forged, American city administrations were almost completely disorganized. By the early 1900s city administrations were "so chaotic that change in the direction of government was all but impossible. . . . 'Budget,' for example, was only a dictionary word; in turn-of-the-century America, not a single city possessed one" (Caro 1975, p. 61). There were no scientific accounting procedures and thus no rational system for the allocation of funds. It was completely haphazard.

Vice Enterprises

Given this situation, it is not surprising that political corruption was at the core of modern organized crime and that politicians and police were protectors of vice enterprises such as brothel prostitution and gambling, the most significant organized criminal activities operating in American cities over the last third of the nineteenth century, a

period in which both enterprises sustained extraordinary growth. By the first decade of the twentieth century the division of labor in sexual commerce included prostitutes, pimps, madams, collectors (who paid off the police), doctors, and bondsmen. Prostitution in cities with burgeoning immigrant populations such as New York, Boston, Philadelphia, and Chicago was a business managed by immigrants who were connected to urban machines and the police. Although the extent of brothel prostitution diminished during the twentieth century, its modes and methodologies remained fairly constant over time. Indeed, in the 1970s brothel prostitution in Manhattan's Times Square area was directed primarily by two second-generation American lawyers—Herbert Kassner and Seymour Detsky—who paid off corrupt cops and judges (Klausner 1987).

Certain forms of gambling underwent a similar process. Boxing, baseball, and horse racing were not only gamblers' delights but were often "fixed" by gambling combines that controlled or owned fighters, teams, horses, and racetracks. Numbers gambling (also called policy), which evolved from legal lotteries, was probably the most structured and labor-intensive gambling enterprise of all. The only racketeer who tried to tinker with the structure of numbers gambling was "Dutch" Schultz, the notorious bootlegger who also dabbled in the New York numbers racket. Around 1934 he tried to change the traditional economic relationships in policy by cutting back 5 percent of the customary sum given to policy workers in order to increase his take. Policy workers went on strike and he was forced to back down.

Organized Crime Innovators

In 1939 the Federal Bureau of Investigation issued a report on a group of New York–based gangsters labeled the "Broadway Mob," a multiethnic criminal affiliation of national significance. Several of its constituents did not last very long: Charles "Lucky" Luciano was sentenced to prison in 1936 and deported to Italy ten years later; Louis "Lepke" Buchalter was sentenced to prison in 1939 on federal narcotics charges and executed in 1944 for murder; and Benjamin "Bugsy" Seigel was murdered in 1947. Other early members of the Broadway Mob included Lepke's partner, Jacob Shapiro; Siegel's partner, Meyer Lansky; Abner "Longy" Zwillman, who ran the most important crime syndicate in Newark, New Jersey; and Frank Costello. The mob expanded to include the

Louis "Lepke" Buchalter (center, facing front), arriving in July 1943 in Albany, New York, to hear his sentence for murder. CORBIS/BETTMANN

nation's premier bookmaker, Frank Erickson from New York; Brooklyn's leading racketeer, Joe Adonis; Morris Dalitz and Morris Kleinman from Cleveland; and the mysterious Louis Shoenberg, described by the Internal Revenue Service in 1947 as the "boss of the underworld throughout the United States."

The mob held sway, its influence reaching at one time or another from Cuba to Los Angeles and Las Vegas; from Houston and Dallas to Hot Springs, Arkansas; and from south Florida to Philadelphia, Greater New York, and on to Montreal, Canada. As a loose and flexible affiliation, the racketeers did not all work together on shared projects although there was much commonality in their enterprises and interactions. Among their mutual interests were a variety of legal as well as illegal gambling projects and resort, hotel, and restaurant projects. Some of them joined in whiskey-distribution companies and vending-machine firms, while others invested their money in movie companies, oil wells, and real estate. They each also had several coteries of other racketeers and gangsters: some of the Italian Americans were leaders of so-called mafia syndicates (later called La Cosa Nostra families), and some of the Jewish American leaders had mobs consisting primarily of Jewish Americans—numerous bent lawyers, crooked accountants, and criminally inclined bank officials with whom they worked on various enterprises. They moved back and forth from their original stomping grounds in the United States to new ones such as Switzerland, where Lansky secretly established a private bank in the 1950s; Panama; the Bahamas, where racketeers incorporated companies and banks; and later to such European cities as Amsterdam and Hamburg, where they established casinos in the red-light districts.

The Business of Leisure and Pleasure. The most capable racketeers were those able to take quick advantage of what the economist and historian David Landes describes as the effects of the general rise in the standards of living created by mass production, urbanization, and higher productivity, which "created new wants and made possible new satisfactions, which led to a spectacular flowering of those businesses that cater to human pleasure and leisure: entertainment, travel, hotels, restaurants, and so on" (*The Unbound Prometheus: Technological Change and Industrial Development in Western Europe from 1750 to the Present*, 1969, p. 9). These were the urban organized criminals who had, as relatively young men, infiltrated segments of licit pleasure businesses while also controlling illicit ones. The variety of criminal conspiracies spawned in these new enterprises included narcotics, bootlegging, gambling, and prostitution syndicates that often metamorphosed into travel businesses, pornography film companies, whiskey firms, bars, restaurants, sports teams, and legal casinos.

Pleasure and leisure businesses represented some of the most significant arenas for organized criminal expansion: perhaps the apotheosis of this development was revealed in the early 1970s when a conglomerate called Sportservice Corporation came under the scrutiny of New York State legislators. Testimony before the state senate revealed that the company had a greater hold on American professional sports than any other entity and was also joined to organized crime in a variety of ways. In 1970 the company controlled or owned more than 450 separate corporate entities in at least twenty-three U.S. states, the District of Columbia, Canada, Puerto Rico, and England. The business had developed from a concessionaire for the Detroit Tigers in 1927 to a structure in 1970 that held concession rights for seven major league baseball clubs, eight professional football teams, four hockey teams, and fifty horse and dog tracks in the United States. It also operated as the concessionaire at approximately three hundred theaters and at bowling alleys, drive-in theaters, airport restaurants, and air-catering services. It owned outright a professional basketball team and had an interest in a National Hockey League club. The attorney general from Nevada reported to the New York investigators that the company was a financial "laundromat" for organized crime, providing phony loans to racketeers to help them wash their criminal money. The investigators uncovered loans and other business arrangements between the firm and organized crime figures from Detroit, Cleveland, St. Louis, Chicago, Wheeling (West Virginia), Las Vegas, Los Angeles, and New York.

Ethnicity and Urban Organized Crime

Organized crime has been one method of integrating segments of the urban poor into the political economy of urban capitalism. Naturally, the modes and timing of integration differ according to the population size and ethnicity of the urban poor, the structure of law enforcement, and the political economy of cities. Concerning ethnicity, the most important changes during the latter part of the nineteenth century and the first couple of decades of the twentieth century were the presence of several million Mezzogiorno Italians and Eastern European Jews. Out of those great migrations there were some who were criminally inclined and some whose children sought criminal careers in the booming underworlds of urban America. Beginning around the 1890s ethnically oriented organized criminal syndicates moved into tertiary industries and the control of significant labor unions. In addition, organized criminals, who for decades worked closely with political officials, also overwhelmed the government functions associated with the regulation of unions and the construction and waste-management industries.

Italian Americans. The power of urban ethnic criminal organizations has always rested upon a large population base whose patterns of social and geographic mobility reflect a strong adherence to working-class life and petit bourgeois forms of capitalism. This accounts for the longevity of Italian American criminal organizations as opposed to those of Jewish Americans. Italian Americans in New York predominated in the construction trades, worked on the waterfront and as garbage collectors, and came to control the unions representing these trades. Given that these unions were devoid of any transforming ideology and that violence is a mainstay of working-class culture, it was not too difficult for ambitious criminals to zip to the top of these organizations and to stay there for what was an inordinately long time. The longevity of Italian Americans as union racketeers was related to the length of time Italian Americans stayed in place both in terms of social class and geography—a far longer period of time than other European immigrant groups that came to the United States around the same time—from the 1880s to World War I. Italian Americans had a zeal for security that was reflected through the prism of past experience in which family and place took center stage and was combined with a generalized suspicion of the outside and outsiders.

Italian American neighborhoods in New York City, as elsewhere, substantially declined as suburbanization and other forms of mobility took root. Thus it was inevitable that the criminals who controlled some of New York's streets and political capital would represent other ethnic and racial populations.

One illustration of this transformation became evident in the 1970s. For many years the most dynamic center of New York's heroin trade was in northeast Manhattan, running on an east-west axis along 116th Street and a north-south axis along Pleasant Avenue. Few without criminal business chose to linger around that intersection. The neighborhood that sat at the epicenter of heroin importation and wholesaling was known as East Harlem or Italian Harlem. In 1939 it housed the largest Italian American population in New York City—about 150,000 persons in this one-square-mile area—also making it the most densely populated section of Manhattan and the largest concentration of Italian Americans in the United States.

East Harlem drug traffickers were well known by the 1940s, and the local leaders in organized crime then, and for many years to come, were Michael Coppola, Salvatore Santoro, Frank Livorsi, Joseph Gagliano, Joseph Vento, John Schillaci, John Ormento, and Dominick Petrelli. They and their associates managed a number of organized-crime enterprises such as policy gambling, extortion, and loan sharking in addition to the traffic in heroin. For decades organized crime and heroin trafficking continued in basically the same hands and out of the same locations. It was passed down from father to son and from uncle to nephew. The neighborhood was reminiscent of Chicago's infamous First Ward, whose organized crime activity went back to the 1890s.

Although the rhythm of life had seemed immutable, by the mid-1960s East Harlem began to experience accelerating and dramatic population changes. In little more than a decade Italian East Harlem had just about disappeared. The resident population became almost completely African American and Hispanic. The few remaining Italian American residents stayed either because they could not afford to move or out of loyalty to their church parishes.

Newcomers. Part of this transition from Italian American domination of organized crime can be explained by the passage of the 1965 Immigration and Naturalization Act, which dismantled the systems of quotas for immigrants based on national origin and replaced them with a preference system based primarily on family unification and occupational skills. Those who took advantage of this law were immigrants from Asia and Latin America.

Chinese organized-crime activity in the United States began around 1980, when Chinese criminal organizations were transferred to the United States. The Chinese began to displace traditional organized crime on the East Coast and established control of criminal activities on the West Coast. The criminological transformation was driven by large-scale Chinese immigration.

Similarly, in the New York metropolitan area of the 1990s there were approximately one million immigrants from the Dominican Republic, representing around 12.5 percent of their home country's population. In the 1980s a small proportion of Dominicans found economic and social mobility in the narcotics trade, when Colombian drug bosses in South America hired the Dominicans in New York as couriers, street sellers, and hit men. With their retail business expanding, the Dominicans slowly began to move into wholesaling. During the 1990s, as relations between Colombian syndicates and those in Mexico soured, the Dominicans were well placed to offer Colombians an alternative, less expensive route into the United States. By 1999 the U.S. Drug Enforcement Agency (DEA) estimated that Dominican drug traffickers transported as much as one-third of the approximately three hundred metric tons of cocaine that entered the United States each year. The DEA administrator testified before Congress that the leadership of these surging drug syndicates, both men and women, commanded the predominant forces at the wholesale level of narcotics operations on the East Coast.

Organized crime, like any other economic activity, responds to changes in the patterns of social and economic life in the United States. A century and a half had passed since the rise of criminal syndicates as a driving force in urban politics and economics, and there is still no other way to interpret the phenomena of sustained and systematic criminal activities than through an understanding of political economy.

BIBLIOGRAPHY

Caro, Robert A. *The Power Broker: Robert Moses and the Fall of New York.* New York: Vintage, 1975.

Czitrom, Daniel. "Underworlds and Underdogs: Big-Time Sullivan and the Politics of Vice in New York, 1886–1913." Paper presented to the American Studies Association meeting, New Orleans, 1990.

Hobson, Barbara Meil. *Uneasy Virtue: The Politics of Prostitution and the American Reform Tradition.* New York: Basic, 1987.

Jonnes, Jill. *Hep-Cats, Narcs, and Pipe Dreams: A History of America's Romance with Illegal Drugs.* New York: Scribners, 1996.

Klausner, Patricia Robin. "The Politics of Massage-Parlor Prostitution: The International Traffic in Women for

Prostitution into New York City." Ph.D. diss., University of Delaware, 1987.

Naylor, R. T. *Patriots and Profiteers: On Economic Warfare, Embargo Busting, and State-Sponsored Crime.* Toronto: McClelland and Stewart, 1999.

New York State Organized Crime Task Force. *Corruption and Racketeering in the New York City Construction Industry.* New York: New York University Press, 1990.

Nicholl, Bruce J. "Integration of International Organized Crime Activity." Paper presented at the National Strategy Information Center conference, The Gray-Area Phenomenon and Transnational Criminal Activity. Washington, D.C., 4 December 1992.

Pozo, Susan, ed. *Exploring the Underground Economy: Studies of Illegal and Unreported Activity.* Kalamazoo, Mich.: W. E. Upjohn Institute for Employment Research, 1996.

Stille, Alexander. *Excellent Cadavers: The Mafia and the Death of the First Italian Republic.* New York: Pantheon, 1995.

ALAN A. BLOCK

See also **Black Hand; Chicago; Federal Bureau of Investigation; Gambling; Mafia; Prohibition and Temperance;** *and individual biographies.*

OSWALD, LEE HARVEY
(1939–1963)

Lee Harvey Oswald was arrested for assassinating President John F. Kennedy on 22 November 1963, and Oswald's death at the hands of Jack Ruby while in custody two days later begot an obsessive interrogation of the "actual" history of this violent event. Questions about the scope of the Kennedy assassination did not dissipate with the findings of a U.S. government investigative committee. Although the Warren Commission concluded that Oswald had acted alone, theories continued to posit a conspiracy, with Oswald as pawn or unwitting patsy. How could such an insignificant man topple Kennedy? To confirm Oswald's culpability, historians and biographers have analyzed the psychological makeup of the assassin. Whatever prompted him to prop his mail-order rifle on the sill of a sixth-floor window of the Texas School Book Depository may, like so much of Oswald's "politics," have had more to do with personal self-image than profound conviction.

Born 18 October 1939 in New Orleans shortly after his father's death, Oswald spent most of his childhood alone but for his eccentric and self-absorbed mother, Marguerite; his two brothers were put in a home while Lee and his mother traveled in search of work. All of Marguerite's skewed energies got turned on Oswald. Caught between his mother's smothering attentions and his own solitude, Oswald became alternately withdrawn and abusive; on occasion he slapped his mother, and once he allegedly pulled a knife on his sister-in-law, Marge.

Psychological reports from school counselors indicate Oswald's strong fantasy of himself as the powerful outsider. He envisioned a life of dramatic significance distinguished from the masses. As a teen, Oswald at times fancied himself a criminal and a communist, but his plans were rarely backed up by action. When dreams faded (or failed), he would craft a new story, a new role to play.

At seventeen Oswald joined the U.S. Marines. The quiet teen, who was initially known as Ozzie Rabbit, affected a macho swagger. He was twice court-martialed, once for "trash-talking" his technical sergeant and once for accidentally shooting himself with an illegal firearm. His Young Turk act failed to inspire respect, and Oswald returned to his ongoing flirtation with grander schemes. Reading Marx and learning Russian, Ozzie was rechristened Oswaldkovich.

In 1959 Oswald wangled a personal hardship discharge but went home only briefly before heading to Moscow. Intent on a historic defection but dismissed by Soviet officials, Lee attempted suicide. Whether he meant to kill himself or only to make a dramatic statement, Oswald was finally allowed to stay in the USSR, although without Soviet citizenship. His time in Russia has prompted significant speculation, unsupported by any evidence released since, that Oswald was an operative of either American or Soviet intelligence.

Oswald seems to have been treated less as an asset than as a liability or embarrassment to the Soviets. He was relocated to backwater Minsk, where for a time his status as an American exile earned him a certain novelty among the locals. This soon wore off, however, and Oswald began to have second thoughts and contemplated returning home. His marriage to Marina Prusakova after a string of failed romances strengthened that resolve; despite some newlywed tension, Oswald had seemingly found someone with whom he could share—and who was able to moderate—his extravagant fantasies.

Oswald conceived of his return to the United States with his Russian bride in 1962 as "heroic," even dangerous. He hid what he referred to as his "Historic Diary," fearing searches. He warned his brother Robert to keep his arrival from the press for fear of "retaliations." But the empty tarmac

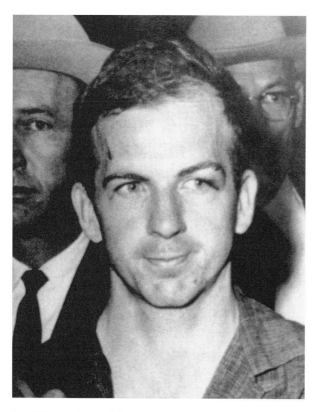

Lee Harvey Oswarld. CORBIS

moving her and their daughter into the home of friends, Lee left for Dallas in October 1963.

His first assassination attempt, against the right-wing politico General Edwin Walker, was painstakingly planned. Oswald took photos and left a "historical rationale" to be discovered among his possessions upon his capture. But he missed the shot and was never suspected of the crime. Some have suggested that the Walker shooting convinced Oswald that he was invincible, but it is more likely that he experienced profound frustration and a renewed sense of failure. It is also likely that Oswald's compulsion to realize his own fantasies of self-importance, rather than his political beliefs, incited his next assassination attempt. Despite a heated anti-Kennedy atmosphere in Dallas, Oswald himself professed to Marina and their Russian émigré friends nothing but admiration for the president and his family.

During the frantic manhunt following Kennedy's assassination, Oswald killed a Dallas police officer, which led directly to his arrest. He made portentous but enigmatic claims about his innocence before being shot by Ruby two days later. The debate about his guilt and about the circumstances surrounding Kennedy's death hinges on these statements and on the events of Oswald's life, leading some to see hidden plots and careful planning. However, it is Oswald's history of persistent failures and fantasies, rather than any actual conspiracy or conviction, that have fueled this perception. Ironically, Oswald has attained his place in the American imagination, but his many roles—wretch, loner, patsy—do not reflect the historic importance he so desired.

greeting them in Dallas prompted Lee to ask, "No reporters?" At twenty-two years old, Oswald sank once again into a sea of American faces.

His wife has said that the return to the United States exacerbated Oswald's dissatisfactions and desires. Jumping from job to job in Fort Worth and then New Orleans, he spent most of his time organizing an illegitimate offshoot of a pro-Cuba organization. He spent one night in jail for disturbing the peace, after an angry group of anticommunist Cubans attacked him. The incident led to a radio interview and a later debate with the leader of his Cuban opposition, Carlos Bringuier, and with the anticommunist activist Edward Scannell, but his surface-level political acumen fell apart under attack. His cumulative failures prompted depression. Some nights he would sit on the porch, dry-firing his rifle. His relationship with his wife grew tense—she often pointedly dismissed his plans (and his sexuality), and he became physically abusive on several occasions. They split up, then reconciled. New dreams of defection captured his interest. Oswald talked about hijacking a plane and flying to Cuba, but Marina scoffed. After

BIBLIOGRAPHY

Mailer, Norman. *Oswald's Tale: An American Mystery.* New York: Random House, 1995.

Oswald, Robert L., with Myrick Land and Barbara Land. *Lee: A Portrait of Lee Harvey Oswald by His Brother.* New York: Coward-McCann, 1967.

United States. Warren Commission. *Report of the President's Commission on the Assassination of President John F. Kennedy.* With additional material prepared by the *New York Times.* New York: McGraw-Hill, 1964.

MIKE REYNOLDS

See also **Assassinations; Kennedy, John F.**

OUTLAWS. *See* Gangs; Gunfighters and Outlaws, Western; Women: Outlaws.

P

PACIFISM. *See* Nonviolence.

PAINTING

From the colonial period through the twentieth century, violence has been a constant subject in American paintings. Benjamin West (1738–1820), considered the patriarch of eighteenth-century American history painting, often chose subject matter that showed either the aftermath of violence (as in *The Death of General Wolfe*, 1770) or the inevitability of violence (*Willian Penn's Treaty with the Indians*, 1771). Artists who trained with West often used history paintings to render images of the American Revolution; among them, John Trumbull in *The Death of General Warren at the Battle of Bunker Hill, 17 June 1775* (1786) and Charles Wilson Peale in *George Washington at the Battle of Princeton* (1780–1781) chose to paint Revolutionary War battles and war heroes.

Throughout the nineteenth century, violence remained an important component of the American artist's representational vocabulary. American expansion westward opened vast tracts of land, and nineteenth-century Americans took advantage of these new resources while concomitantly decimating the Native American population. Some artists, however, did not paint the horrors that accompanied the movement westward; instead, they created elaborate representations of the conquered landscape: for example, Albert Bierstadt's *Rocky Mountains* and *Lander's Peak*, which were painted in 1863. The painter and illustrator Winslow Homer in *Prisoners from the Front* (1866) also chose to portray a nonviolent, strangely quiet, aspect of a very violent period of American history, the Civil War. Homer's many images of the war appeared in national magazines. Frederic Remington, also an illustrator, in *The Charge of the Rough Riders at San Juan Hill* (1898) and other depictions, painted the more active circumstances of battle in the Spanish-American War of 1898. Like Homer, Remington's works infiltrated American culture, persuading many to accept the perils of violent combat.

In the twentieth century violence remained a significant theme in American art. For example, Jacob Lawrence represented the violent racism that African Americans faced while moving to urban centers in the North in his series *The Migration of the Negro* (1940–1941). Other artists from the first half of the twentieth century, such as Philip Evergood (*American Tragedy*, 1937) and Ben Shan (*Miners' Wives*, 1948) became interested in showing how violence affected the American workplace. The emergence of abstraction in the 1940s thwarted the emphasis on figurative violence, but the splattered paint in the work of Jackson Pollock and the splashed brushstrokes in the work of Franz Kline (*Mahoning*, 1956) represented a new type of implied violence, rendering the emotional turmoil that often accompanies the process of artistic production. War, labor disputes, and other forms of violence had left the canvas, but abstract expressionism revealed painting as an activity filled with violent brushwork and a metaphorically aggressive technique.

Four Examples

This article will examine four canvases, each from a different moment in American history. John Singleton Copley's *Watson and the Shark* (1778), Thomas Eakins's *The Gross Clinic* (1875), George Bellows's *Stag at Sharkey's* (1909), and Jackson Pollock's *Autumn Rhythm: No. 30, 1950*. Each work addresses violence in a distinctive way: as a narrative device that accentuates political tensions from American colonial history (Copley), as a painter's strategy that intensifies a surgical procedure (Eakins), as an emblem of hypermasculinity (Bellows), and as a metaphoric presence within the visual field of abstraction (Pollock).

Watson and the Shark. The inevitability of violence appears overtly in John Singleton Copley's 1778 painting *Watson and the Shark*. Copley (1738–1815) grew up in Boston and learned how to paint by watching his stepfather, Peter Pelham, work on engravings. On this large canvas, of which there are two copies, Copley depicts nine men on a boat in Havana Harbor trying to rescue a naked figure

who is about to be bitten by a large shark; the shark's mouth appears to break the picture plane in the right foreground. Copley poses several of the figures on the boat in a state of panic as their hands reach over the side with the hope of pulling the water-bound figure back to safety. Others are either viewing the scene with horror, trying to harpoon the vicious-looking shark, attempting to rescue the figure with a rope, or maneuvering the vessel to facilitate the rescue. The individual in the water is Brook Watson, the politically active Tory who commissioned Copley to paint this picture. The image commemorates an event that transpired in 1749, when, while taking a swim in Havana Harbor, Watson lost a leg to an attacking shark (Stein 1976). Instead of depicting the bloody violence of the actual shark attack, Copley presents the viewer with the dramatic moment a few seconds before Watson loses his leg.

Beyond this depiction of imminent violence, Copley also encodes his canvas with a signifier of slavery. At the top of the pyramid of men who make up the rescue team in the rowboat is a black figure. He is not relegated to a more obscure space on the small vessel; he stands proudly as he holds a rope overboard to the conspicuously white figure

Watson and the Shark, **a 1778 painting by John Singleton Copley.** CORBIS/BETTMANN

of Watson. Some critics have speculated that this black figure communicates Copley's and Watson's ambiguous sentiments toward slavery. One art historian has pointed out that although the black man is present during the rescue, the artist depicts him as an inactive and passive figure "whose capacity to act in the real world is blocked." Others have claimed that this figure is the "democratic equal of the whites" because Copley paints the black figure in elegant dress and he stands at the same level as the white individuals on the boat (Stein 1976). Copley's canvas resists easy definition, but the representation of the black figure is striking. Here, amid a narrative of impending bloody violence, is a figure from North American history whose very appearance within this painting raises the issue of slavery, an institution itself predicated on violence.

The Gross Clinic. Although there is no overt gore in Copley's canvas, other painters provided Americans with a theater of visual violence, including blood. The presence of blood in these works would capture the viewer's attention and highlight the element of violence taking place within the pictorial field. Thomas Eakins (1844–1916) lived most of his life in Philadelphia, where he studied at the famous Pennsylvania Academy. In 1875 Eakins completed his dramatic portrait of Dr. Samuel David Gross, which still hangs at the Jefferson Medical College, where Gross taught surgery. *The Gross Clinic* depicts the doctor presiding over four other physicians in various stages of their careers as a young boy's leg is being salvaged by removing necrotic bone (Johns 1983). Eakins does not shy away from representing the horrors of the operating room. He accentuates the flesh of the boy's leg by including the child's socks in the image, and he positions the body on an operating table that he dramatically foreshortens to enhance the visual drama. Gross looks out in a moment of repose, and in the background we see a number of seated students who are intently watching the master surgeon perform his craft.

Beyond Eakins's desire to visually narrate the intent ambience of a surgery class, there is also the unmistakable presence of violence, which charges the visual field with an aura of horror. To Gross's right, a woman (the child's mother) recoils from the boy's bloody leg, which has been opened to start the procedure. To make sure that the viewer comprehends how ubiquitous blood is during an operation, Eakins shows us Dr. Gross holding a scalpel, the surgeon's most important tool, which,

like his hand, is covered in blood. The connotation of the scalpel as an icon of a larger psychodrama within Eakins's biography has been explored (Michael Fried claims that Eakins was working through issues of castration, and his relationship to his father is suggested in this canvas), but what continues to strike viewers who are not aware of Eakins's familial history is the red paint that suffuses the middle ground of this canvas.

Stag at Sharkey's. George Bellows (1882–1925) captures blood for the sake of sport in his 1909 painting *Stag at Sharkey's.* Bellows is identified with a style of early-twentieth-century American artists referred to as the Ashcan School. These artists dedicated much of their production to the depiction of life in the expanding American city. In *Stag at Sharkey's,* Bellows renders the arena of the prizefight (or men). In Bellows's time, the sport of boxing took place not only in legally sanctioned rings but also in illegal venues referred to as "prizefights," where there were fewer rules and more brutality. Bellows captures the extreme violence of a prizefight battle between two muscular men, their bodies contorted as they physically punish each other. Bellows's use of very loose brushstrokes adds a sense of implied movement to this work and accentuates the physicality of these two men.

The violence in *Stag at Sharkey's* is similar to Bellows's work of two years later titled *Both Members of This Club,* which also depicts a prizefight. Although Bellows is fulfilling the realist's desire to capture the inner drama of urban life, in both paintings he also renders the peculiarity of the audience's sadistic pleasure in viewing this violence. In these canvases the audience indulges in pure spectacle, with no overlay of the redeeming pedagogical purpose that Eakins captured in *The Gross Clinic.* Violence is being paid for and consumed by a group of New Yorkers who are escaping the reality of everyday life through the vicarious thrill of watching two men pummel each other's athletic bodies (Doezema 1992).

Bellows's painting of raw violence is also a product of a turn-of-the-century culture obsessed with masculinity. By 1907 America had become an empire, Teddy Roosevelt was defining the national agenda by pushing for "the strenuous life," and there was a larger cultural anxiety that fostered a premium on hypermasculinity that is starkly evoked in *Stag at Sharkey's,* in which the artist overtly stages the cultural imperatives of conquest,

Stag at Sharkey's, **a 1909 painting by George Bellows.** THE CLEVELAND MUSEUM OF ART, HINMAN B. HURLBUT COLLECTION

strength, and muscularity, virtues that defined masculinity in the violent atmosphere of turn-of-the-century America.

Autumn Rhythm: No. 30. Copley, Eakins, and Bellows use a figurative painting technique to create visual constructions that overtly and mimetically represent violence, but in the expressionist work of Jackson Pollock (1912–1956) violence is an implied presence, represented in the abstract. In Pollock's work titled *Autumn Rhythm: No. 30, 1950,* the artist has dripped paint onto the surface of his canvas, rhythmically covering the entire picture plane with abstract splashes, splatters, and drips that alternate in color, length, and width. This technique, in which the canvas is spread out on the floor and the artist walks around it, allowing his brush and other implements to dip into a can and drop paint onto the canvas, brings a form of violence to the production of art. Pollock attacked the canvas with a type of bravado that left the marks of his aggressive performance.

A famous short film of Pollock working, *Jackson Pollock 1951,* by Hans Nemuth and Paul Falkenberg, highlights this painterly violence. Pollock's active technique is captured in the film by a camera placed below a piece of glass that has replaced the artist's usual canvas. Pollock assures us that this is the first time he has used this medium, a medium devised to enhance our viewing pleasure. As the viewer looks up through the glass, Pollock's strangely syncopated voice overlays his sinewy image as he swaggers confidently around the pane of glass, a cigarette dangling from his lips. He attacks his work with a masculine aggressiveness, dripping paint onto the transparent surface—essentially into the face of the viewer. The activity of Pollock's technique, coupled with the metaphorical splashes of violence that litter the pane of glass, impose an aggressive encounter with abstraction.

Pollock's overtly masculinized biography is one of the most enduring myths of American art history. In his time, his work was a lightning rod for diverse interests outside the art world. During the Cold War, curators, popular media writers, art critics, and even the U.S. government lauded Pollock's abstract expressionism as an affirmation of American freedom; the artistic liberty represented by Pollock's work, and its commercial success, was posited as a triumph of capitalism, one that stood in sharp contrast to the propagandistic rigidities of Soviet socialist realism.

Autumn Rhythm: No. 30, **a 1950 painting by Jackson Pollock.** THE METROPOLITAN MUSEUM OF ART, GEORGE A. HEARN FUND, 1957. (57.92)

At the End of the Twentieth Century

Were these eighteenth-, nineteenth-, and mid-twentieth-century painters aware that they were taking part in a larger cultural dialogue about the representation of violence? Could Copley have known that late-twentieth-century students would gasp at his *Watson and the Shark*? Was Eakins cognizant of the violence implicitly conveyed in the bloody mess that covers the surgeon's field in *The Gross Clinic*? Could Bellows have known that, decades later, his work would still strike viewers as frighteningly real in its depiction of violent fighting? Moreover, how would Pollock, whose own biography has become tainted with the trope of violence, respond to contemporary interpretation?

In the late twentieth century, a number of artists were working with a clear sense of how their work could and would be read as violent. For example, in the 1980s artists including Jenny Holzer, Barbara Kruger, Martha Rosler, Krzysztof Wodcizco, and an anonymous group of art-world agitators calling themselves the Guerrilla Girls began to play with the placement of their art in public venues. According to Hal Foster, "each treats the public space, social representation or artistic language in which he or she intervenes as both a target and a weapon. This shift in practice entails a shift in position: the artist becomes a manipulator of signs more than a producer of art objects" (1985, p. 100). These late-twentieth-century artists manipulated these spaces with a clear intent to violate the viewer's preconceived notions about space, gender, and representation. For example, the Guerrilla Girls disguised their identities by wearing gorilla costumes and went through the streets of New York pasting up posters that interrogate the patriarchy of the art world.

Although the blood and gore of earlier American canvases may be absent in many of these provocative works, which are almost corporate in their clean lines of presentation, these artists raised important questions by violently entering our public spaces in unconventional ways that forced us to examine our perceptions of and preconceptions about art and society.

BIBLIOGRAPHY

Boime, Albert. *The Art of Exclusion: Representing Blacks in the Nineteenth Century.* Washington: Smithsonian, 1990.

Doezema, Marianne. *George Bellows and Urban America.* New Haven, Conn.: Yale University Press, 1992.

Foster, Hal. *Recodings: Art, Spectacle, Cultural Politics.* Seattle: Bay Press, 1985.

Fried, Michael. *Realism, Writing, Disfiguration: On Thomas Eakins and Stephen Crane.* Chicago: University of Chicago Press, 1987.

Gibson, Ann. *Abstract Expressionism: Other Politics.* New Haven, Conn.: Yale University Press, 1997.

Guilbaut, Serge. *How New York Stole the Idea of Modern Art: Abstract Expressionism, Freedom, and the Cold War.* Chicago: University of Chicago Press, 1983.

Haywood, Robert E. "George Bellows's *Stag at Sharkey's:* Boxing, Violence, and Male Identity." In *Critical Issues in American Art: A Book of Readings,* edited by Mary Ann Calo. Boulder, Colo.: Westview, 1998.

Johns, Elizabeth. *Thomas Eakins: The Heroism of Modern Life.* Princeton, N.J.: Princeton University Press, 1983.

Stein, Roger. "Copley's *Watson and the Shark* and Aesthetics in the 1770s." In *Discoveries and Considerations: Essays on Early American Literature and Aesthetics Presented to Harold Jantz,* edited by Calvin Israel. Albany: State University of New York, 1976.

DAVID BRODY

See also **Fine Arts; Sculpture.**

PANZRAM, CARL
(1891–1930)

Consumed by an overt, undiluted rage, Carl Panzram never sought mercy or reprieve. His fervent last wish was that he should die by violence, like his many victims did before him.

Panzram, born into a family of Prussian-immigrant farmers outside of Warren, Minnesota, was criminally precocious as a child. In 1899, when he was eight, local Minnesota police arrested him on a charge of drunk and disorderly behavior. Soon he began engaging in burglary and arson (churches were among his incendiary targets), and he landed in his first penal institution, a reform school, by the age of eleven. At the age of sixteen, he graduated from reform school to the military prison at Leavenworth, Kansas. His later memoirs, as well as a book about him by Thomas Gaddis and James Long, attributed much of Panzram's ferocity to his brutal treatment at the hands of prison authorities. Although there is little reason to doubt that the young Panzram was brutalized, this treatment might have been a reaction to Panzram's aggressive behavior, which was already beginning to spin out of control.

Whatever the prime cause of his behavior, the nineteen-year-old Panzram emerged from Leavenworth as "the spirit of meanness personified," as he later put it. His principal vocation was still burglary, but he also became a merchant seaman. His "avocation," while traveling around the world, was rape and murder. In his own estimation, he committed one thousand acts of sodomy. Once, while passing through Kingston, New York, he strangled a woman, later claiming he did it "for the fun it gave me." In all, he confessed to killing twenty-one people. In one case, according to his own account, he lured ten sailors onto a yacht and proceeded to drug them, rape them, and kill them. In another instance, while in Portuguese West Africa, he hired eight Africans for a crocodile-hunting expedition; once in the jungle, he supposedly killed them all, sodomized the corpses, and fed the bodies to the crocodiles.

Panzram's final incarceration in 1928 resulted from his arrest for much more mundane crimes: a series of burglaries in the Washington, D.C., area. When sentenced to the federal penitentiary in Leavenworth, he vowed, "I'll kill the first man who bothers me." Panzram proved to be a man of his word. On 20 June 1929, he attacked Leavenworth's laundry foreman and beat him to death with an iron bar.

Panzram's conviction for this murder led to a death sentence. When the Society for the Abolition of Capital Punishment tried to intervene on his behalf, Panzram wrote to his unsolicited champions, "I wish you all had one neck and I had my hands on it." He finally got the sentence he desired on 5 September 1930. While standing on the gallows in Leavenworth, he snapped at the hangman, "Hurry up, you Hoosier bastard. I could hang a dozen men while you're fooling around."

BIBLIOGRAPHY

Gaddis, Thomas E., and James O. Long. *Killer: A Journal of Murder.* New York: Macmillan, 1970.

Nash, Jay Robert. *Bloodletters and Badmen.* New York: M. Evans, 1973.

Newton, Michael. *Hunting Humans.* Port Townsend, Wash.: Loompanics, 1990.

DAVID EVERITT

See also **Serial Killers.**

PARRICIDE

Fascination with Lizzie Borden, accused in 1892 of brutally hacking her father and stepmother to death with an ax, has never ceased. Indeed, a perusal of the classics, with such figures as Oedipus, Orestes, Alcmaeon, and King Arthur, reveals that the slaying of mothers and fathers has captured public attention since antiquity.

The term *parricide*, though technically referring to the killing of a close relative, has increasingly become identified in the public mind with the murder of an individual's father (patricide) or mother (matricide). Beginning in the 1980s a series of journalistic and literary accounts of youths killing their parents generated enormous public interest. Analyses of anthropological, legal, and psychological factors in cases where children have killed their parents have appeared in the 1990s.

In the 1980s and 1990s in the United States, on the average, four to six biological parents have been killed weekly by their children. Despite interest in this phenomenon, only one comprehensive study of parricides across the United States has yet been done. An analysis of Federal Bureau of Investigation Supplementary Homicide Report data, which consisted of all homicides between 1977 and 1986, indicated that typically the slain parent or stepparent was white and non-Hispanic. The typical father killed was in his early fifties; the mother, in her late fifties; the stepfather, in his mid forties; and the stepmother, in her late forties or early fifties.

The Parricide Offender

The typical killer of a parent or stepparent was white and non-Hispanic. In contrast to media depictions and public impressions, murders involving parents were overwhelmingly committed by adult offenders. The percentage of mothers and fathers slain by children under eighteen in single-victim/single-offender circumstances, however, was not insignificant: 15 percent of mothers and 25 percent of fathers were killed by juvenile offspring. The percentage of stepparents slain by youths under eighteen was even higher: 30 percent of stepmothers and 34 percent of stepfathers were killed by children under eighteen. When considered in relation to the proportion of total homicide arrests that involved juveniles during this period, juvenile involvement in these types of parricides was actually quite high. From 1977 to 1986 fewer than 10 percent of those arrested for homicide in the United States were under eighteen.

Parents and stepparents slain were overwhelmingly killed by sons. Of homicides involving fathers, mothers, stepfathers, and stepmothers as victims, 85 to 87 percent were perpetrated by sons. These percentages remained constant when these relationships were examined by offender age (juvenile and adult status). The proportion of males who committed these types of parricides was approximately equal to their 87 percent representation among homicide offenders in general during this decade.

Several important findings have related to weapons. First, a difference in weapon selection was discernible with respect to the gender of the victim. Offenders who killed fathers were significantly more likely than those who killed mothers to use firearms of some type—handguns, rifles, shotguns. Offenders who killed mothers were significantly more likely than those who killed fathers to use knives or cutting instruments, blunt objects, and personal weapons (hands, fists, and feet). Offenders who killed stepfathers were significantly more likely than those who killed stepmothers to use rifles and shotguns.

Second, differences also emerged between offender age groups in weapons used in the killings of fathers, mothers, and stepfathers. Juvenile offenders were significantly more likely than adult offenders to use rifles and shotguns in homicides involving biological parents and stepfathers. Juveniles were significantly less likely than adult offenders to use knives, blunt objects, and personal weapons to kill their fathers, mothers, and stepfathers.

A Typology of Parricide Offenders

Perusal of the professional literature reveals that three types of individuals typically kill their parents: the severely abused child, the severely mentally ill child, and the dangerously antisocial child. The severely abused child is the most frequently encountered type among adolescent parricide offenders. According to child development experts, adolescence begins with puberty, which typically commences by age twelve or thirteen, but may start earlier. Adolescence extends to young adulthood (approximately age twenty).

The Severely Abused Child. In-depth portraits of youths who have slain parents have frequently suggested that these youths were severely abused and that they killed their parents because they could no longer tolerate conditions in the home environment. These children, typically adolescents, were psychologically abused by one or both parents and often witnessed and suffered physical, sexual, and verbal abuse. They did not typically have histories of severe mental illness or of serious and extensive delinquent behavior. For them, the killings represented an act of desperation—the only way out of familial situations that they could no longer endure.

In some of these cases, the legal elements of self-defense were clearly present. The youths had reason to believe that their parents were threatening them with imminent death or serious injury and that deadly physical force was necessary to prevent the infliction of such harm. In many other cases, the physical danger from the parents did not appear to be immediate. Believing that they were unable to engage in physical battle as equals with

The Menendez Brothers

Whether Lyle and Erik Menendez were severely abused youths or sociopaths who killed their parents, Jose and Kitty Menendez, is a question that polarized the nation for several years in the 1990s. Jurors were hopelessly deadlocked in the 1993 trial, resulting in mistrials for Lyle and Erik. Jurors in the 1996 retrial found both brothers guilty of first-degree (premeditated) murder and recommended life in prison, thus sparing the lives of the two young men, who could have been legally sentenced to death (Lyle was twenty-one and Erik eighteen at the time of the murders). The defense at both trials argued that "the boys" were abused by both parents and that the brothers killed their mother and father because they feared that their parents were going to kill them for threatening to reveal the sexual abuse within the family. The prosecution argued that the abuse was a fiction. The state maintained that the "young men" plotted to kill to inherit their parents' estate—worth $14 million—because they feared that they were going to be disinherited.

Evidence was presented at the Menendez trials that, if true, would indicate that Lyle and Erik Menendez were victims of several types of abuse and neglect. However, even verification of child maltreatment would not necessarily uncover the underlying motivation for the double homicides. The Menendez brothers could have been both battered children and sociopathic. The two categories are not, as the opposing lawyers in the Menendez case seemed to argue, mutually exclusive. Some children raised in abusive homes become conduct disordered. In fact, the development of antisocial personality disorder is typically rooted in early and pervasive childhood maltreatment. Put another way, the Menendez brothers could have been abused and still have killed their parents for the money.

As in any parricide, the critical question in the Menendez case is, what propelled the homicides? Individuals who are severely abused often have mixed feelings about their abusive parents. These feelings may include fear, anger, hatred, hurt, and a desire for revenge, as well as love. If Lyle and Erik Menendez killed Jose and Kitty Menendez out of hatred and rage stemming from years of severe abuse, that motivation is clinically significant; but it is not the same as self-defense.

the abusive parents, the youths aggressed against their tormentors when they perceived that they had an advantage over their abusive parents and could prevail. In some cases, youths whose physical survival was not threatened felt that their psychological survival compelled them to kill their abusive parents.

Youths who fit this pattern are typically diagnosed after the homicide as suffering from posttraumatic stress disorder (PTSD) or depression. However, both diagnoses typically predate the killings. PTSD is a disorder that affects some individuals who have been subjected to events that severely threatened their lives or those of others.

The Severely Mentally Ill Child. On occasion, children who kill parents are recognized as severely mentally disturbed or psychotic. Psychotic individuals have lost contact with reality. Their personalities are typically severely disorganized, their perceptions are distorted, and their communications are often disjointed. Their behavior may be inappropriate to the setting and characterized by repetitive actions that appear without purpose. Although they may show excessive levels of motor activity, they also may be markedly inactive. They may experience hallucinations and bizarre delusions. Individuals with psychotic disorders often do not understand that they are mentally ill and frequently require hospitalization, at least until their mental disorder has been stabilized. Severely mentally ill individuals who kill their parents may believe that their parent is in league with the devil and that God is commanding them to kill that parent. In some parricide cases involving psychotic individuals, the illness is so visible and well-established that criminal prosecution is not completed or is halted for a period of time. In other cases, mental illness presents no bar to prosecution.

The Dangerously Antisocial Child. Dangerously antisocial children are individuals whom professionals in the late nineteenth and early twentieth centuries called *psychopathic* or *sociopathic* personalities. The two terms, which have become essentially synonymous in the public mind, have been replaced in the professional literature with two more-precise terms—respectively, *conduct disorder* or *antisocial personality disorder*—depending on the age of the individual and the presence of specific criteria. Individuals who are diagnosed as having conduct disorders or antisocial personalities, unlike those who are psychotic, are oriented in time and space and are free of delusions and hallucinations. Individuals who kill their parents to serve some instrumental, selfish end would fall into this category.

When Adults Kill Parents. Empirical studies and clinical case reports indicate that adults who kill their parents often have documented histories of psychopathology. Although abuse might have existed in the home as the adult child was growing up, it is not typically the driving force behind the parricide. Adults typically have more choices and resources and are more mature than juveniles. If the home situation is intolerable, a healthy adult can leave. When an adult resorts to murdering a parent, he or she is likely to be severely mentally ill or psychopathic.

When Adolescents Kill Parents. In contrast, when adolescents kill their mothers and fathers, severe mental illness is typically ruled out. Rather, the question most frequently asked is whether the adolescent is a severely abused or dangerously antisocial child. Twelve characteristics are commonly found in situations in which severely abused youths kill their parents, particularly fathers (Heide 1992):

- Pattern of family violence
- Adolescent's attempts to get help from others fail
- Adolescent's attempts to escape the family situation fail
- Adolescent is isolated from others and has few outlets
- Family situation becomes increasingly intolerable
- Adolescent feels increasingly helpless and trapped
- Adolescent's inability to cope leads to a loss of control
- Adolescent has little or no prior criminal record
- Ready availability of a gun
- Parental chemical dependency
- Evidence to suggest dissociative state (alteration in consciousness) in some cases
- Victim's death perceived as a relief

It is impossible to predict which youths will kill their parents, given the difficulties in predicting violent behavior in general and the relative infrequency of this phenomenon in particular. Estimates suggest that over the ten-year period examined, the number of biological fathers and mothers murdered by offspring under eighteen years, for example, averaged sixty-five per year. Some youths, however, are at a higher risk of slaying a parent. Five factors help target such youths (Heide 1992):

- The youth is raised in a chemically dependent or other dysfunctional family.
- An ongoing pattern of family violence exists in the home.
- Conditions in the home worsen, and violence escalates.
- The youth becomes increasingly vulnerable to stressors in the home environment.
- A firearm is readily available in the home.

Of the five factors, two are most important: the chemically dependent or other dysfunctional family, and the availability of a firearm. The likelihood that violence will be present, that conditions will worsen, and that youths will become increasingly vulnerable to stressors in the home environment is higher in alcoholic, drug-addicted, and other dysfunctional families than in healthy families. When firearms are readily accessible, the probability that an abusive parent will be killed by a youth pushed beyond his or her limits who sees no other way out is much higher than when guns are not available.

Treatment and Prevention

Adolescent parricide offenders typically represent a low risk to society. Most can be reintegrated into society if given effective treatment by mental health professionals trained to work with survivors of severe trauma.

The real killer in these types of cases is child maltreatment. Research and clinical observations strongly suggest that many, if not most, cases of adolescents killing parents could be prevented through education and dissemination of knowledge. Information about child development and parenting skills can be taught to parents and incorporated into high school curricula. Students at elementary and high school levels need to be informed about various types of child abuse and encouraged to take appropriate action if victimized. Children who are being raised in chemically dependent families must be educated about the risks they face and protected from harm by addicted parents. A supportive network available in the schools can guide children through the process of getting help. The media should be encouraged to continue to educate the public about different types of child abuse and sources of help.

Implementation of these recommendations would decrease the probability that youths will come to see murder as the only way to end parental abuse. In addition, incorporation of these strategies is certain to reduce the conditions that cause thousands of children in the United States today to experience unnecessary physical and emotional harm.

BIBLIOGRAPHY

American Psychiatric Association. *Diagnostic and Statistical Manual of Mental Disorders.* 4th ed. Washington, D.C.: American Psychiatric Association, 1994.
Ewing, Charles P. *Fatal Families: The Dynamics of Intrafamilial Homicide.* Thousand Oaks, Calif.: Sage, 1997.
Heide, Kathleen M. "Dangerously Antisocial Kids Who Kill Their Parents: Toward a Better Understanding of the Phenomenon." In *The Nature of Homicide: Trends and Changes: Proceedings of the 1996 Meeting of the Homicide Research Working Group, Santa Monica, Calif., June 1996,* edited by Pamela Lattimore. Washington, D.C.: National Institute of Justice, 1997.
———. "Evidence of Child Maltreatment Among Adolescent Parricide Offenders." *International Journal of Offender Therapy and Comparative Criminology* 38, no. 2 (1994).
———. "Parents Who Get Killed and the Children Who Kill Them." *Journal of Interpersonal Violence* 8, no. 4 (1993).
———. "Weapons Used by Juveniles and Adults to Kill Parents." *Behavioral Sciences and the Law* 11, no. 4 (1994).
———. *Why Kids Kill Parents: Child Abuse and Adolescent Homicide.* Columbus: Ohio State University Press, 1992.
Weisman, Adam M., and Kaushal K. Sharma. "Parricide and Attempted Parricide: Forensic Data and Psychological Results." In *The Nature of Homicide: Trends and Changes: Proceedings of the 1996 Meeting of the Homicide Research Working Group, Santa Monica, Calif., June 1996,* edited by Pamela Lattimore. Washington, D.C.: National Institute of Justice, 1997.

KATHLEEN M. HEIDE

See also **Borden, Lizzie; Child Abuse; Domestic Violence; Menendez, Erik and Lyle; Teenagers.**

PEACEKEEPING MISSIONS. *See* Military Interventions: Peacekeeping Missions.

PEACEMAKING

The origins of hostility, antagonism, and violence between societies or groups within a society are many and varied. Finding the best approaches to peacemaking depends on the origins and nature of the aggression.

The origins of hostility and aggression may reside in real conflict, in which essential material interests are at stake. Real conflict might concern territory required as living space, as in the case of the Palestinian-Israeli conflict; or it might arise between a dominant and a subordinate group over rights and resources, as between the elites and the general population of El Salvador and between Hutus and Tutsis in Rwanda and Burundi. Real conflict centers on survival and material well-being, and in turn greatly affects psychological well-being. The more real the conflict, the more it requires practical measures for peacemaking, like the division of territory or redistribution of rights.

Real conflict usually has psychological components, and psychologically based hostility often has roots in real conflict. Psychologically based antagonism may also arise from difficult living conditions stemming from severe economic problems, political disorder, or great and rapid social change. The frustration of basic human needs can lead to scapegoating or the creation or adoption of ideologies, like nationalism, communism, or Nazism, that identify some group as the enemy. Psychologically motivated aggression can also arise from a history of past antagonisms and violence between groups or of one group's victimization at the hands of another. As opposed to real needs, greed and the desire for conquest can also prompt aggression. As in the case of the Mundurucú headhunters in Brazil, who trained their youth to attack enemy villages, hostility and violence may become part of a group's culture: the word for "non-Mundurucú" is also the word for "enemy."

Peace can be characterized as "cold" or "negative," that is, restricted in nature. The peace between Israel and Egypt, resulting from the 1979 Camp David agreement, is such a cold peace; the peace between the United States and the former Soviet Union could also be so described. By contrast, peace can be based on harmonious relations, shared goals, and structures that promote a positive relationship between former enemies, making renewed violence less likely. Such a peace can evolve over a longer historical period, as between Great Britain and the United States following the American Revolution, or over a relatively short period, as between France and Germany, two historical enemies until after World War II.

Creating and maintaining peace can be achieved through several means. Limited contact between two parties in a cold peace can help prevent aggression. A nation's policy of maintaining its own strength, and hence power, can act as a deterrent to would-be aggressors; two or more nations so engaged employ a balance-of-power strategy. Nations that act as bystanders, or witnesses, to events and that are in a position to take action have great potential influence in both maintaining and creating peace—a potential often not exercised in the international community. In many instances a determined international community could have inhibited aggression: preceding Germany's 1939 invasion of Poland in World War II, Iraq's invasion of Kuwait in 1990, the violent conflict in Bosnia in the 1990s, and the genocide in Rwanda in 1994, bystanders remained passive, or in direct or indirect ways supported perpetrators. International bodies and agencies that have the means and the will to take effective early action could make force less necessary in the creation or maintenance of peace.

The resolution of conflict before it turns into violence, and efforts to halt renewed violence, have traditionally been the domain of diplomacy, usually with each party acting in its own behalf. In the 1980s and 1990s, new conflict-resolution strategies, including mediation, problem-solving workshops, and dialogue groups, have been developed and found useful. These strategies have had beneficial effects in conflicts as varied as those in Northern Ireland, in Israel between Israelis and Palestinians, and in Estonia. The United Nations has used these practices and should continue to do so; neutral third parties, like nongovernmental organizations, have also used them to bring about peace. The Carter Center, the Institute for Multi-Track Diplomacy, and applied projects initiated by academics are among these neutral third parties.

Outside specialists, usually in small groups, can help members of hostile parties engage each other peacefully. Participants usually must deal first with the legacy of past antagonism and violence between their groups; they may be guided to describe the suffering of their group, to empathize with each other, and assume responsibility for the harm done by their group. This process can pave the way for addressing current conflicts and issues. Healing of wounds from the past and reconciliation are especially important to peacemaking in cases of genocidal and ethnic violence; witness the activities of the Truth and Reconciliation Commission in South Africa, for example. Healing can be furthered by empathy and support from outside groups and memorials and rituals within a group.

Real engagement—identifying, creating, and pursuing shared goals—can help opposing groups overcome mutual stereotypes, prejudice, and hostility and promote reconciliation and positive relations. This is true both of ethnic and racial groups, such as African Americans and whites in the United States, and of nations, such as France and Germany, whose leaders after World War II fostered engagement between the two countries that helped overcome a history of antagonism.

Whatever the conditions that ignite the potential for violence among members of a group, the role of leaders is important. Leaders can instigate violent actions among followers or offer visions and practices that help people join together to deal with problems in peaceful ways. President Franklin D. Roosevelt's leadership during the Great Depression, a time when living conditions in the United States were trying, is an example of the latter. Bystander countries and the international community can influence leaders, as well as their followers, by using positive engagement, aiding development, and, when necessary, employing threats, sanctions, and boycotts. The earlier the international community approaches leaders who instigate or practice antagonism—before they commit themselves publicly to violence—the more effective such influence can be.

Leaders and citizens within a country, together with bystanders, can promote cultural changes that make violence less likely. Building democracies that are genuinely pluralistic and creating just social arrangements make both violence between subgroups of a society and the initiation of war unlikely. Violence is also less likely where groups can be counseled against devaluation and stereotyping of other groups and where the tendency for undue obedience to authorities can be curbed.

Communities in which children are harshly and punitively treated are more likely to be violent. Research in the last three decades of the twentieth century has provided substantial knowledge about ways to raise compassionate children. Nurturance, affection, and attention to children's needs, along with guidance and discipline that is not severe or punitive, are essential. Allowing children to participate in rule making and encouraging them to have a voice in community life, whether in the classroom, the home, or another group, can foster moral courage. This development, in turn, enables children to speak out against hostility and violence, first in their peer group and later as members of their society. Putting into practice research findings and theories about raising compassionate children requires substantial will on the part of society. Changing culture and society and raising caring children will inhibit violence on all levels and promote peace among individuals.

BIBLIOGRAPHY

Gregor, Thomas, ed. *A Natural History of Peace.* Nashville, Tenn.: Vanderbilt University Press, 1996.

Rothman, Jay. *From Confrontation to Cooperation: Resolving Ethnic and Regional Conflict.* Newbury Park, Calif.: Sage, 1992.

Rubin, Jeffrey Z., Dean G. Pruitt, and Sung Hee Kim. *Social Conflict: Escalation, Stalemate, and Settlement.* New York: McGraw-Hill, 1994.

Staub, Ervin. "Preventing Genocide: Activating Bystanders, Helping Victims and the Creation of Caring." *Peace and Conflict: Journal of Peace Psychology* 2 (1996).

———. *The Roots of Evil: The Origins of Genocide and Other Group Violence.* New York: Cambridge University Press, 1989.

ERVIN STAUB

See also **Conflict Resolution, International and Institutional; Nonviolence.**

PEARL HARBOR

At 7:55 A.M. on 7 December 1941, a strike force of several hundred Japanese warplanes screamed down on the unprepared U.S. naval base at Pearl Harbor, on the Hawaiian Island of Oahu. By the time a second wave of Japanese aircraft left an hour later, the Pacific fleet was in ruins. Eight battleships, three destroyers, and three cruisers were put out of action, and two battleships, *Oklahoma* and *Arizona*, were sunk in the harbor. Two U.S. aircraft carriers, however, *Lexington* and *Enterprise*, were at sea during the duration of the attack and remained undamaged. These carriers would later play key roles in the Midway victory in June 1942. A total of 188 American aircraft were destroyed, most of them on the ground. More devastating, a total of 2,323 U.S. servicemen were killed. The next day, before a joint session of Congress, President Franklin D. Roosevelt proclaimed 7 December 1941 a "date which will live in infamy." With only one dissenting vote, from the pacifist congresswoman from Montana, Jeanette Rankin, Congress granted Roosevelt's request to recognize the state of war that existed between the United States and Japan, and the United States entered World War II.

Although the Japanese attack on Pearl Harbor was a surprise and a humiliation for the U.S. military, it was also the climax of a decade of rising tensions between Japan and the United States. Throughout the 1930s the United States had watched as Japan steadily encroached on Chinese territory. On 27 September 1940, Japan joined the Axis powers with Italy and Germany and began to expand into northern Indochina. In October 1941 General Hideki Tojo, leader of the Japanese prowar party, became premier. Negotiations for a peaceful settlement continued in Washington in the fall of 1941, but both sides appeared resigned to war. On 25 November the Japanese dispatched a fleet of aircraft carriers toward Hawaii and began to amass troops on the Malayan border. Expecting a Japanese attack on Malaya or the Philippine Islands, Admiral Husband E. Kimmel and General Walter C. Short, the military commanders on Oahu at the time, took few precautions.

In retrospect, the Japanese raid on Pearl Harbor was tactically brilliant but strategically disastrous. Commanded by Admirals Chuichi Nagumo and Isoroku Yamamoto, the surprise attack provoked a strong response of anti-Japanese fervor among Americans that helped awaken "the sleeping giant," a term often used to describe the United States in the years before the attack. Throughout the war commentators often observed that in the Anglo-American camp, the Japanese were more despised than the Germans. The reason for this, according to those involved, was the perception

An explosion at the U.S. naval base during the Pearl Harbor attack, 7 December 1941.
HULTON GETTY/LIAISON AGENCY

that the Japanese were uncommonly treacherous and savage—a perception attributed to their attack on Pearl Harbor as well as to reported Japanese atrocities and the extraordinary fierceness of the fighting in the Pacific theater. The U.S. Marines, for example, adopted a well-known motto: "Remember Pearl Harbor—keep 'em dying." This rhetoric reflected more than just rage at being attacked; it clearly drew from an old strain of highly racial anti-Asian sentiment that viewed the "yellow race" as an inherently inferior one. For the duration of the war, and even beyond, the surprise attack on the Pacific fleet remained for many Americans the preeminent symbol of the inherent treachery of the Japanese.

BIBLIOGRAPHY

Dower, John. *War Without Mercy: Race and Power in the Pacific War.* New York: Pantheon, 1986.
Prange, Gordon W. *December 7, 1941: The Day the Japanese Attacked Pearl Harbor.* New York: McGraw-Hill, 1988.
Slackman, Michael. *Target: Pearl Harbor.* Honolulu: University of Hawaii Press, 1990.
Toland, John. *Infamy: Pearl Harbor and Its Aftermath.* Garden City, N.Y.: Doubleday, 1982.

NANCY A. BANKS

See also **Japanese Americans; World War II.**

PERFORMANCE ART

Historical Origins

The term *performance art* was coined in the early 1970s to describe a kind of live art activity that can be best understood by describing what it is not: not art, not theater, not literature, not music, and not dance. Performance art is whatever else remains, or whatever exceeds the boundaries of traditional media. The origins of performance art, with its tendency to define itself against the prevailing institutions, can be found in the Dada art movement of the early twentieth century, which also took an "anti-art" attitude. In its desire to exceed the limitations of any given form and to be inclusive rather than exclusive as a medium, it also encompasses the aesthetics of collage—just as the painters Pablo Picasso and Georges Braque would paste pieces of the daily newspaper into the space of a painting.

The three most immediate modern ancestors of performance art, however, were the Happenings, lifelike (as opposed to artlike) events organized by Allan Kaprow beginning in the late 1950s, first in New York and then around the United States; the Fluxus events, which George Brecht inaugurated in New York in 1960 and 1961; and the experiments at Judson Memorial Church in New York, from 1962 to 1964. Kaprow identified the Happenings as a variety of theater: "These events are essentially theater pieces, however unconventional. That they are still largely rejected by devotees of the theater may be due to their uncommon power and primitive energy" (*Essays on the Blurring of Art and Life*, Berkeley: University of California Press, 1993, p. 17). Brecht saw his pieces as a kind of music, what Dick Higgins, a friend and fellow Fluxus artist, called "concerts of everyday living." To most audiences, Brecht's work, which might consist, for instance, of water being poured or dripped, was more "noise" than "music." Judson Church was primarily a dance venue, although the activity engaged in by the dancers who worked there, including Trisha Brown, Yvonne Rainer, and Lucinda Childs, was to many hardly recognizable as dance. As Rainer described their work at the time, "The display of technical virtuosity and the display of the dancer's specialized body no longer make any sense. . . . The alternatives . . . are now obvious: stand, walk, run, eat, carry bricks, show movies, or move or be moved by some *thing* rather than oneself" (*Work: 1961–1973*, Halifax: Press of the Nova Scotia College of Art and Design, 1974, pp. 63–69).

Performance in the Early 1970s

The Happening, Fluxus, and Judson dance events all shared a common sense of transgression and were received by the art world in general as a kind of neo-Dada violence against art. By the early 1970s it seemed to many that some art was worth doing violence against. Painting, above all, seemed exhausted as a medium. Its gestures seemed mechanical, its audacities conventional and predictable, and its raison d'être simply the production of commodities designed to decorate the walls and lobbies of the affluent. The "event" works of the early 1960s offered a model that avoided the fate of most artwork in the contemporary marketplace at the time—particularly commodification. Such events happened only once or twice, they were not collectible, and they were immediate. They were thus capable of responding to the particular environment in which they were created—not only to the exigencies of time and place but also to their historical, social, and political moment as well. In the larger context of the Vietnam War and the growing women's movement, this last point was particularly important. To many artists, the prospect of making art to hang on walls seemed tantamount to complicity with the enemy, which was increasingly defined as the white, male, military-industrial complex. Probably no factor contributed more to the arrival of performance art as a medium than the desire to confront the status quo and to make art that was socially and politically efficacious.

There were, initially, two centers of performance art, one in New York and the other in Los Angeles. In New York, artists organized as early as 1967 to demonstrate against the war in Vietnam; the Angry Arts Festival in February 1967, for example, featured self-proclaimed "pinko beatnik poets" haranguing the public. Many of the strategies of the street demonstration soon blossomed into a confrontational brand of protoperformance, the master strategists of which were the political activists Jerry Rubin and Abbie Hoffman of the Chicago Seven. Their confrontational performance strategies were designed to elicit and expose the innate violence of their opposition to the establishment, and, as their presence at the riots at the Democratic National Convention in Chicago in the summer of 1968 demonstrated, their strategy could be almost horrifically successful.

As artists protested the war in New York, the city's museums were a particular target. "Do you realize," the art critic Gregory Battcock asked the newly formed Art Workers' Coalition in early 1969, "that it is those art-loving, culturally committed trustees of the Metropolitan and Modern museums who are waging the war in Vietnam?" (*Idea Art*, New York: Dutton, 1973, p. 111). These same museums, artists were beginning to realize, were also in the habit of systematically excluding women artists from their shows. Since inclusion in museum collections seemed to most women a virtual impossibility, performance art quickly became an especially attractive medium for them. At Womanhouse—a derelict mansion near downtown Los Angeles that Judy Chicago, Miriam Shapiro, and twenty-one California Institute of the Arts students, including Suzanne Lacy, transformed into a woman's art space—performance art soon dominated the scene. In performance art, Chicago felt, women were suddenly able to release "a debilitating, unexpressed anger." "Because performance can be so direct," she goes on to say, "because we were developing our performances from a primitive, gut level, we articulated feelings that had simply never been so openly expressed in artmaking" (1977, pp. 126, 128).

The Voice and the Body

Performance art allowed two new elements to enter into the world of art making: the voice and the body. Women, who felt their voices had been silenced and their bodies ravaged, seized on them as art-making tools. The collaborative performance piece *In Mourning and in Rage*, created by Suzanne Lacy and Leslie Labowitz, is an example. Performed in December 1977 outside the Los Angeles County City Hall to protest violence against women in U.S. cities, it was timed to coincide with a Los Angeles city council meeting, thus assuring media coverage of the performance. Ten women stepped from a hearse wearing veils draped over headdresslike structures that made each figure seven feet tall. They represented the ten victims of the Hillside Strangler, the serial killer then attacking women in the city. The strangler's crimes were explicitly linked to the national climate of violence against women and the sensationalized media coverage that supports this violence. The success of the performance could be measured by the number of talk-show appearances it generated for the performers themselves—guaranteeing that their voices would be heard.

C. Carr, since 1985 the performance critic for the *Village Voice*, explains the power of the voice in this way: "Here at the end of the twentieth century, few things are truly subversive, truly unprocessed and unlabeled, or more than just fashionably shocking. But what can still push an audience to either catharsis or panic is graphic, angry, impolite talk from the Other" (1993, p. xviii). A performance artist like Karen Finley, one of the four artists who in the summer of 1989 saw their grants rescinded by the National Endowment for the Arts due to political pressure from Congress, takes the power of voice to an extreme. Looking as if she is the victim of Tourette's syndrome and dressed innocently in a 1950s cocktail party dress, Finley stands on stage and, in one of her most compelling performance strategies, used throughout the 1970s and 1980s, suddenly spews forth verbal filth of an almost unimaginable kind. Part of the shock value of this performance is that one cannot believe she has, in fact, even imagined what she is saying. But her monologues are also a form of direct verbal assault that go back to the stand-up routines of Lenny Bruce, who received a one-year prison sentence in 1964 for saying "fuck" on stage at the Cafe Au Go Go in New York City. Finley goes much, much further.

She involves her body in the argument as well. The body is perhaps the chief marker of performance art's authenticity, and its celebration or mortification of the flesh represents an authentic gesture of the kind that was once embodied in, for instance, a seemingly heartfelt brushstroke on an abstract expressionist canvas. Finley strips as she performs and then notoriously smears her body with what appears to be excrement but turns out to be chocolate. "Then I stick little candy hearts (symbolizing 'love') all over my body—because after we've been treated like shit then we're loved. ... Then I add the alfalfa sprouts (symbolizing sperm) because ... we're just something to jerk off onto. ... Finally, I put tinsel on my body, because after going through all that, a woman still gets dressed up for dinner" (Juno and Vale 1991, p. 49).

Authenticity and Violence

When people manipulate their own body, they announce their possession of themselves, that their body is at their disposal. In other words, in performance the body becomes a vehicle for self-possession. The desire to assert control over one's own body informs, of course, the counterculture practice of body piercing. A mark of defiance, the pierced body announces its independence from the body politic. It insists on the materiality and individuality of the flesh as opposed to the anonymity and homogeneity of social life. It discovers, in its pain, a heightened awareness, the unification of mind and body.

It can be argued that performance art, marginalized and antitraditional in its own right, introduced body piercing to late-twentieth-century American culture. At the Museum of Conceptual Art in San Francisco in the fall of 1971, Chris Burden appeared as a Secret Hippie—though he wore "straight" attire, he had hammered studs in the shape of a star into his chest. In 1978, at the Center for Music Experiment at the University of California, San Diego, in a piece entitled *Mitchell's Death*, Linda Montano pierced her face with acupuncture pins as she recounted her former husband's death. On 21 July 1984, Stelarc suspended himself from meat hooks inserted into his skin and attached to cables and pulleys two stories above the street outside of the Mo David Gallery in New York. At the end of the 1980s, David Wojnarowicz sewed up his mouth in the film *Silence = Death*, protesting the nation's apathy about the AIDS crisis.

The ultimate mortification of the flesh, of course, is death. Death is the body's inevitable

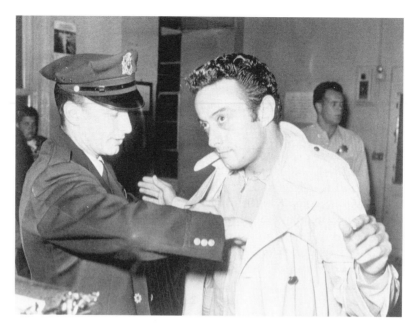

A policeman searches comedian Lenny Bruce after Bruce was arrested for allegedly using obscene language during his act in a North Beach nightclub in San Francisco on 4 October 1961. CORBIS/BETTMANN

finale, the most "authentic" fact, the moment of moments. In one of his earliest works Chris Burden took performance art to the edge of death. In his 1971 piece, *Shoot*, he had himself shot in the arm before a small audience in the gallery F-Space in Santa Ana, California. That same year he strapped himself to the floor of the gallery with copper bands. Nearby were two buckets of water, each wired with 110 volts of electricity. The audience was invited to kick over the buckets and electrocute him. On 23 April 1974 in Los Angeles, in a piece called *Trans-Fixed*, he nailed himself to his Volkswagen:

> Inside a small garage on Speedway Avenue, I stood on the rear bumper of a Volkswagen. I lay on my back over the rear section of the car, stretching my arms onto the roof. Nails were driven through my palms into the roof of the car. The garage door was opened and the car was pushed half-way out into Speedway. Screaming for me, the engine was run at full speed for two minutes. After two minutes, the engine was turned off and the car pushed back into the garage. The door was closed (*Chris Burden*, pp. 74–77, privately published by the artist, Los Angeles, 1978).

Looking at the photographic documentation, a simple question arises: If this is what he did, where is the blood? But that is not even the important question. The important question is, why is Bur-

den's explanation not considered as much a part of the event as the event itself? Perhaps one should approach the performance, not in terms of its authenticity (asking questions like, "What could possibly motivate such personal angst in such a nice young man?") but rather in terms of its reception —that is, in terms of our willingness as a culture to believe such stories and treat them as objects of fascination. In fact, the question is, what does our belief and adulation tell us about ourselves?

The best performance art has always been fully aware of this question and has self-consciously negotiated the border between the authenticities of self-expression and the inauthenticities of the staged, the posed, the organized, the manipulated, and the controlled. Such self-consciousness asks the audience to consider not merely the ostensible violence of the performance, but the ways in which one is implicated in that violence and perpetuates it.

BIBLIOGRAPHY

Carr, C. *On Edge: Performance at the End of the Twentieth Century*. Hanover, N.H.: Wesleyan University Press, 1993.

Chicago, Judy. *Through the Flower: My Struggle as a Woman Artist*. New York: Anchor, 1977.

Jones, Amelia. *Body Art: Performing the Subject*. Minneapolis: University of Minnesota Press, 1998.

Juno, Andrea, and V. Vale, eds. *Angry Women. RE/Search* 13 (1991).

O'Dell, Kathy. *Contact with the Skin: Masochism, Performance Art, and the 1970s.* Minneapolis: University of Minnesota Press, 1998.

Cleveland Center for Contemporary Art. *Outside the Frame: Performance and the Object: A Survey History of Performance Art in the USA Since 1950.* Cleveland: Cleveland Center for Contemporary Art, 1994.

Sayre, Henry M. *The Object of Performance: The American Avant-Garde Since 1970.* Chicago: University of Chicago Press, 1989.

Schimmel, Peter. *Out of Actions: Between Performance and the Object, 1949–1979.* Los Angeles: Museum of Contemporary Art, 1998.

HENRY M. SAYRE

See also **Dance; Theater.**

PHILADELPHIA

Philadelphia's history has been marked by sporadic outbursts of public disorder, often by a mob, vigilante group, gang, or assembled throng attempting to define the social order amid a period of rapid economic change and spatial conflict. The high tolerance for violence against particular groups or as a remedy for political impotence and social isolation has also characterized Philadelphia's experience. The Philadelphia story also suggests how improved, or at least expanded, government and the discipline of work and city life muted public violence or drove it underground, resulting in a tendency toward personal violent acts rather than collective acts intended to remake society.

Violence was spasmodic but frequent during the colonial era. Seamen and others who lived by day work, for example, organized as mobs to drive away impressment gangs, and in 1764 backcountry protesters known as the Paxton Boys marched to Philadelphia and threatened to overthrow the government unless it supported the farmers' war against the Indians. The religious revivals of the 1740s accentuated cultural differences and incited verbal and physical attacks on churches and government.

The American Revolution heated up religious, ethnic, and class rhetoric, and "out of doors" protests against British policies in several instances ended in assaults and property damage. When war came, order dissolved. Inflation, food shortages, British occupation, a new emphasis on private interest over public good, and the unraveling of political authority and rise of "popular politics"

swelled public unrest. Mobs threatened merchants who withheld goods and artisans who jacked up prices. The crisis exploded in 1778–1779 as "patriot" militia rounded up Quakers and suspected Tories and attempted to force merchants to lower prices. In October 1779 the Revolutionary Pennsylvania government sent cavalry and a brigade of foot soldiers to disperse the mob. The Revolution wrought a change that would affect definitions of violent behavior thereafter. Through mobs and militia, the artisans, small merchants, and others had reordered local authority, and by invoking the memory of the "citizen-soldier" of the Revolution, they and their ideological descendants ensured a democratic thrust in politics and the resort to direct action to defend their "American" interests.

From the Revolution to the Civil War, Philadelphia grew into a more economically complex, socially diverse city. Workingmen's parties, fire companies, gangs, fraternal orders, lodges, and parish and other associations often formed along ethnic or craft "tribal" lines. Race became an increasing factor in social and political organization. Blacks left white churches to form their own congregations and founded their own schools, clubs, and newspapers; the perceived threat to whites grew as the black community gained in numbers, education, and self-confidence. The streets and the public square behind Independence Hall became scenes of several violent clashes between whites and blacks competing for access to public places.

The changing nature of work compounded the problem of building social harmony. Factory work shunted increasing numbers of would-be artisans into wage labor with its accompanying loss of control over the workplace, and poverty gripped many unskilled workers. Merchants and mill owners hitched to the emerging national market promoted railroads and other improvements, some of which cut into workers' neighborhoods, endangering lives and reminding workers of their lost autonomy and power. A rash of riots broke out in the 1830s and 1840s to protest railroad construction, and strikes, such as the Ten-Hour Movement of 1835–1836, further disrupted public order. Election-day riots pitting rival fire companies and political clubs against one another also became a regular feature of city life.

Industrialization, immigration, democratic politics, race, and constricting settlement patterns made the period 1834 to 1849 the most violent in Philadelphia's history. Organized attacks on blacks and abolitionists, on nonstriking workers and scabs, and on Irish Catholics marked the patterns of shifting authority and concern in the city. Anti-bank, antirailroad, and labor riots took their toll. So, too, in the perceived absence of effective civil authority, did vigilante movements against prostitution and gambling and other "sins." The religious revivals and reform spirit of the age led to calls for strenuous purging of societal evils.

The most violent riots involved race and religion. The rising antislavery presence in Philadelphia, including an assertive black abolitionist witness, and the continued physical expansion of the black community sparked a riot in 1834, which began in the Moyamensing section bordering the city on the south, where blacks and whites had long vied for space and political power. In May 1837 a mob of three thousand burned Pennsylvania Hall, a new building erected by abolitionists. Such violence continued into the 1840s, in part due to the quiet support of the city's white leadership, which was tied to the South by commerce and family. The worst antiblack riot occurred in 1842. Outraged that a black temperance club had paraded across their south Philadelphia "turf," Irish gangs assailed black residences and institutions; they burned a church, drove many blacks from the area, and even chased a sheriff's posse away.

Irish Catholics also felt the brunt of violence. Uncertain economic conditions and a growing Irish Catholic population aroused Protestant workers during a time of widespread anti-Catholicism and nativism. Protestants attacked Catholics who wanted to have their children read the Catholic rather than the Protestant Bible in public school. Religious differences mixed with economic rivalry to fuel the weavers' riots of 1842–1843, in which striking weavers in the Kensington district, many of them Irish Protestants, stormed the homes of newly arrived Irish scabs, smashing their looms and furniture, and then took on the sheriff and 150 deputies at the Nanny Goat Market rather than disperse. In May 1844 the worst anti-Catholic riot in American history erupted in Philadelphia, spurred by the local Native American Club, eager to exploit anti-Catholicism for political advantage. The death of an American nativist by an Irish sniper provided a martyr for the nativists, who came from all over the city to march on the Nanny Goat Market area, the center of the Irish Catholic Third World. Nativists and Irish Catholics traded gunfire before nativists set fire to Irish houses and property. The nativist rampage lasted two days and ended with the burning of two Catholic churches and a new riot, in the Southwark district, in July. For the first time guns had been widely used in an American riot.

The riots of the 1840s sobered many merchants and others worried about attacks on property. In 1854 the consolidation of Philadelphia County into the city of Philadelphia and the establishment of a uniformed police force made a more regulated society possible and made it more difficult for criminals to "escape" the law across city boundaries. A new leadership of ethnic politicians also arose to harness hatreds into voting blocs rather than mobs, and the replacement of volunteer fire companies with professionals removed a principal source and staging area for ethnic and racial vigilantism. Intermittent political violence continued, reaching its apogee in the election-day riot of 1871, when Irish Democrats in the Moyamensing area attacked newly refranchised blacks, murdering their Republican leader, Octavius Catto. But the mob violence of the antebellum period abated by the mid-1870s, as industrial discipline, unified city government, and organized party politics spread over the city and displaced or disbanded armed mobs and vigilantism.

However corrupt the city governments were, they at least kept public order. Philadelphia remained relatively quiet into the early twentieth century. Murder rates went down as the regimentation of modern city life at work and at play, in part affected by the regular timetables of public transportation, smoothed some of the rough edges of urban jostling. The fact that Philadelphia remained a relatively "American" city amid the new immigration of the late nineteenth and early twentieth century, with no more than 25 percent of its population foreign-born or the children of foreign-born, likely contributed to the public accommodation and the decline of nativist violence.

Regarding personal violence, only those left out of the industrial workforce and competing for so-called pick-and-shovel work experienced rising rates of homicide during the late nineteenth century and into the mid-twentieth century. Blacks coming from the rural South were particularly affected. As the city became racially segregated in residence and work, personal violence remained geographically confined and relatively "unimportant" to party bosses and city fathers. Progressive reformers through the 1920s tried to improve slum conditions as a way to end child abuse, violence at home, and other social ills, with some success, and the New Deal programs of the 1930s also provided relief and even hope that kept large-scale public disorder down. To be sure, Philadelphia had numerous fascist, nativist, and other extremist organizations holed up in ethnic enclaves, but they generally did not seek to engage in organized violence.

In the post–World War II era, with suburbanization drawing wealth, jobs, and population away from Philadelphia and deindustrialization causing a breakdown not only of the economic order but of the discipline of the workplace, crime rates steadily climbed. Poverty swamped inner-city neighborhoods, affecting isolated blacks in particular. A riot in August 1964 grew out of (1) the Black Power push of the Civil Rights movement and a series of boycotts and protests against schools, supermarkets, and other institutions denying access or jobs to blacks, and (2) blacks' deep-seated distrust of city authorities, especially the police. The riot, which started when a white police officer stopped a black motorist for a traffic violation, rapidly escalated into what became the Watts-style "burn baby burn" attack on local stores, police and fire officials, and anything that smacked of the "establishment." The once vibrant Columbia Avenue, or "Jump Street," of North Philadelphia never recovered. The burned-out buildings stood as a mute testimony to the failure of such acts of civil disorder and rallied local black leaders to seek ways to defuse anger by mobilizing poor people. As a result, blacks began a significant move into local politics.

One irony of that outcome was that the city's first black mayor, W. Wilson Goode, was charged with ordering the firebombing of a row house and the destruction of a black neighborhood in 1985 in an effort to evict a radical conflict-driven group called MOVE, which had engaged in a shoot-out with police in 1978. A special commission and grand jury concluded that the mayor, police chief, and fire chief were guilty of bad judgment but not criminal behavior, and the mayor was reelected in 1987. The MOVE incident, along with charges of police corruption that persisted into the 1990s, led to investigations of city government and police, a new emphasis on community policing, and, in the late 1990s, a no-tolerance policy regarding crime. A lowering violent-crime rate, as reported to the Federal Bureau of Investigation, seemed to suggest that personal violence also was slowing at least. So, too, the breakup of organized-crime families in Philadelphia in the 1980s and 1990s promised to reduce other patterns of violence. As in the nineteenth century, violence begot efforts at better city government and more police protection in the City of Brotherly Love, and led to a more inclusive political process.

Police remove a rioter from a building in Philadelphia on 28 August 1964. CORBIS/BETTMANN

BIBLIOGRAPHY

Adams, Carolyn, et al. *Philadelphia: Neighborhoods, Division, and Conflict in a Post Industrial City.* Philadelphia: Temple University Press, 1991.

Feldberg, Michael. *The Turbulent Era: Riot and Disorder in Jacksonian America.* New York: Oxford University Press, 1980.

Lane, Roger. *Violent Death in the City: Suicide, Accident, and Murder in Nineteenth-Century Philadelphia.* Cambridge, Mass.: Harvard University Press, 1979.

———. *William Dorsey's Philadelphia and Ours: On the Past and Future of the Black City in America.* New York: Oxford University Press, 1991.

Warner, Sam Bass. *The Private City: Philadelphia in Three Periods of Its Growth.* 2d ed. Philadelphia: University of Pennsylvania Press, 1987.

RANDALL M. MILLER

See also **MOVE Bombing; Riots; Urban Violence.**

PHOENIX

Situated along the Salt River in central Arizona, the settlement that eventually became Phoenix was established in 1867 to meet the agricultural needs of military and civilian populations in the region. Its economy was based primarily on agriculture until 1940. World War II and the boom years that followed provided opportunities in the high-technology and service industries, and helped increase Phoenix's population more than tenfold during the next fifty years. By 1999 it had become the seventh largest city in the United States.

Phoenix possesses many of the social conditions that can lead to violence, yet despite rapid population growth, racism, high levels of poverty, and a reputation for being "the most crime-ridden city in the United States," the city has avoided serious and chronic outbreaks of violence. Violence has been primarily episodic or minor in nature, and most outbreaks were quickly contained before escalating into more serious problems.

Frontier Phoenix

From the 1850s until the 1880s the United States was at war with various Indian groups in the Arizona Territory, most notably the Chiricahua Apaches. Phoenix was located near settlements of Pima and Maricopa Indians, who were frequently at war with various Apache groups and thus provided protection to settlers along the Salt River. Thus Phoenix never experienced firsthand the brutal raids and reprisals that were characteristic of Indian-Anglo and Indian-Mexican warfare in Arizona. In addition the Phoenix economy basically revolved around farming. Phoenix and Maricopa County attracted a higher proportion of families than the mining areas in northern and southern Arizona, which tended to attract young, single men. The resulting population was far more stable and less prone to personal violence than that of stereotypic western mining communities.

Prior to 1880 Phoenix residents took the law into their own hands on at least four separate occasions. The last and most notorious incident took place during a particularly violent week in August 1879. In separate incidents two area residents had been murdered. Fueled by a grudge, John Keller shot and killed his former employer, a Salt River Valley farmer named Luke Monihon. Although a competent justice system was in operation, outraged Phoenix residents planned to lynch Keller anyway. The night before the extralegal hanging was to take place, William McClosky was jailed for killing a Phoenix resident, John LeBarr, during a barroom altercation. On the morning of 26 August, the heinousness of these crimes and a collective fear that justice would not be served prompted nearly two hundred men to march on the Maricopa County jail in Phoenix, overwhelm the jailer, and demand custody of the two alleged murderers. Soon after, they tied ropes around the two prisoners' necks and led them to the town plaza where they were hanged.

Vigilantism, a violent phenomenon associated with frontier settlement, is often a result of chronic crime and ineffective law enforcement. But court records and Phoenix newspapers reveal that crime, particularly violent crime, was neither a problem nor a major concern in frontier Phoenix.

From Statehood to World War II

Phoenix's population continued to grow after Arizona's statehood (1912), particularly after the outbreak of World War I created a cotton boom. Large numbers of Mexicans and African Americans migrated to the Phoenix area to meet the resulting labor demands. In addition, refugees from the Mexican Revolution continued to enter Arizona, sometimes settling in the Phoenix area. As the town became more racially diverse, violent incidents were often prompted by racial tensions.

In 1912 a minor riot broke out during a Mexican Independence Day celebration. In the melee three police officers and an Anglo resident were shot and stabbed by unidentified Mexicans. Order, however, was soon restored. In 1914 additional fears of violence were fueled by rumors that Mexican leftists were organizing hundreds of local Pima Indians to attack Phoenix. Still another rumor charged that a band of Mexicans was going to blow up nearby Roosevelt Dam. Nothing came of either alleged plot, but reactions to them and others revealed some of the fears that Anglos had of racial violence.

In 1916 a so-called Home Guard was organized with the purpose of stopping the apparent increase in random violence. In 1922 the Ku Klux Klan appeared in Phoenix and began a brief reign of terror that, under the guise of law enforcement, resulted in a number of beatings of black residents.

During the 1930s, the worsening economy played a role in a number of violent incidents. On 6 September 1934 striking federal relief workers battled police in the streets. The violence was quickly put down, and the next day twenty-six people were arrested and the National Guard was put on alert. That same year, some Phoenix residents took out their economic frustrations on Japanese immigrant farmers. From September through October numerous Japanese-operated farms were bombed, burned, or flooded. But as was usual in Phoenix, the outbreak of violence was short-lived.

Throughout the 1920s and 1930s, gambling, bootlegging, and prostitution were rampant in Phoenix. In addition, by 1920 there was also a lively traffic in opiates, morphine, and cocaine. Owing in part to Phoenix's close proximity to Mexico, drugs, and alcohol during Prohibition, were readily available. In addition, the Phoenix police department rarely enforced vice laws. Although widespread vice led to occasional brawls, shootings, and stabbings, violent incidents were still not chronic problems.

Phoenix Since World War II

The influx of civilian workers and military personnel to Arizona during World War II dramatically transformed and expanded Phoenix's economy. An outbreak of violence on 26 November 1942 threatened this new prosperity and led to a crackdown on Phoenix's heretofore loose attitude toward vice. Black soldiers stationed at Papago Park often frequented the Phoenix "colored" neighborhood; that November day during an argument a black soldier hit a black woman over the head with a bottle. When a black military policeman attempted to arrest the soldier, he resisted with a knife and was shot and wounded by the policeman. Black servicemen, many of whom had been drinking and were out of control, protested the shooting. Black military policeman soon assembled about 150 of the soldiers, but before they could be transported back to camp, they broke ranks when a jeep of armed blacks appeared. A shot of unknown origin then rang out and ignited a riot. By the time it was over, 180 black soldiers had been arrested, three black soldiers were killed, and eleven people were wounded (three black soldiers, two black military policemen, one black female civilian, one black city policeman,

three white soldiers, and one white policeman). The riot was primarily the result of a lone incident gone out of control, and—as the attempts of black military and civilian policemen to control the situation suggest—had little to do with racial tensions. Although the riot hurt relations between the community and the military, more damaging to those relations was the high rate of venereal disease among the servicemen stationed near Phoenix. Three days after the incident, military commanders began declaring the city off limits to all military personnel until city leaders cracked down on vice.

Despite racial discrimination and poverty in Hispanic and black neighborhoods, Phoenix avoided the violence experienced by other cities during the Civil Rights movement upheavals of the 1960s. The only significant outburst occurred on 25 July 1967, when fire bombs were thrown and guns fired at a police wagon. Apparently no one was injured, and the perpetrators remained unknown to the authorities. The Phoenix mayor soon imposed a curfew and ordered 380 police officers to patrol the troubled area, resulting in about 280 people, including 28 juveniles, being taken into custody. Shortly after the incident, city officials promised to provide jobs and job training for blacks. Most blacks had deplored the violence and criticized the young participants. These factors and the prompt response of policing authorities helped Phoenix avoid any major riots.

By the 1970s Phoenix continued to boom and attracted numerous honest and ambitious newcomers in search of opportunity. The favorable economic conditions also drew unsavory criminal elements. Political corruption, land fraud, and the influence of organized crime spilled out into the open when the Phoenix journalist and investigative reporter Don Bolles was murdered by a car bomb in 1976. Although three men eventually served time for the killing, no one knows who ordered Bolles's killing or why.

The sensationalism of the Bolles incident, which became national news, coupled with continued political corruption and shady land dealings throughout the 1980s, contributed to Phoenix's reputation as a crime ridden, lawless, and violent city. In addition most Americans associate the West with violence. Perhaps it is this perception that has contributed to Phoenix's violent reputation. Moreover, throughout the 1980s and 1990s, increased population, suburban sprawl, and reliance on automobiles have led to an increase in various types of violence in Phoenix. The rate of violent crime has increased, particularly in the communities surrounding Phoenix. The fact that most people in the Phoenix area are from somewhere else often leads to social isolation and other stresses, which has influenced the area's above-average suicide rate. But despite the aforementioned factors and despite its reputation, Phoenix remains a relatively violence-free city. In 1995 its violent crime rate was ranked sixty-first out of 121 cities with 150,000 or more people. Overall, violence in Phoenix continues to be an episodic, not a chronic, problem.

BIBLIOGRAPHY

Buchanan, James E., ed. *Phoenix: A Chronological and Documentary History, 1865–1976.* Dobbs Ferry, N.Y.: Oceana, 1978.

Luckingham, Bradford. *Minorities in Phoenix: A Profile of Mexican American, Chinese American, and African American Communities, 1860–1992.* Tuscon: University of Arizona Press, 1994.

———. *Phoenix: The History of a Southwestern Metropolis.* Tucson: University of Arizona Press, 1989.

———. "Trouble in a Sunbelt City." *Journal of the Southwest* 33, no. 1 (1991): 52–67.

Sheridan, Thomas E. *Arizona: A History.* Tucson: University of Arizona Press, 1995.

Zarbin, Earl. "The Whole Thing Was Done So Quietly: The Phoenix Lynchings of 1879." *Journal of Arizona History* 21, no. 4 (1980): 353–362.

PAUL T. HIETTER

See also **Urban Violence.**

PHOTOGRAPHY

Within two decades of its invention in 1839, photography was commonly employed to record scenes associated with war, rebellion, civil disorder, colonial conquest, and execution. Early instances of such documentation in Europe include the 1848 revolutions, British campaigns of expansion in India and Burma during the 1850s, and the Crimean War (1853–1856). Views of U.S. troops mobilized in the war against Mexico (1846–1848) were registered on daguerreotype, the first popular form of photography. Technical limitations within the medium prevented early photographers from depicting the violent action itself and from unposed close perspectives, but they were able to portray related activities and sights, such as street barricades, infantry encampments, and after-battle scenes.

Civil War to World War II

The American Civil War (1861–1865) was photographed extensively as a result of the initiative of Mathew Brady, who documented the First Battle of Bull Run in July 1861 and soon managed a civilian corps of camera operators attached to battalions of the Union Army. Brady published war images without giving individuals credit for their work at the front, and this action led some of these cameramen, including Alexander Gardner and Timothy O'Sullivan, to form a rival syndicate within two years. Among hundreds of evocative images from this period are panoramas of battlefield dead that convey a paradoxical effect of repose and disarray, as photographed at Antietam (1862) and Gettysburg (1863), and scenes of the haunted ruins of a defeated South in 1865, particularly Atlanta, Charleston, and Richmond, the former Confederate capital. These grim perspectives helped to dispel some of the romantic and heroic illusions about battle that had persisted in the civilian mind. Other photographic images of the era document slavery, whose institutional violence is pictured in slave enclosures, with their prisonlike living conditions. Photographed body portraits showed slaves as victims of repeated maltreat-

Charleston, South Carolina, after Union troops entered in 1865. The Mills House stands in the background.
CORBIS/BETTMANN

ment. The practice of lynching, which continued well into the twentieth century, is widely documented in photographs. These images are appalling not only in their physical brutality but also in the casual, satisfied countenances of white citizens shown gathered around a victim's corpse.

By the time of the Spanish-American War (1898), advances in camera and film technologies and competition among the new illustrated weeklies and Sunday newspaper supplements served to draw photographers closer to the immediacy of combat action. While artist-illustrators still provided most of the picture images from battlefronts, the American Jimmy Hare started his career at this time as a war photo-correspondent, perhaps the first professional of this kind, and he covered world conflicts for the next two decades. When the United States entered World War I (1914–1918) in 1917, however, government censorship prevented the general American public from seeing all but a few photographs from the front, and most of these were bland, patriotic images. Hare, sent by *Collier's Weekly* to France at the outset of hostilities, found it impossible to photograph independently outside official military channels. The U.S. Army Signal Corps and the Air Service maintained their own photography departments for the purposes of public information, military training, historical documentation, and strategy (including aerial reconnaissance).

In the 1920s further advancements in camera design—most notably the introduction of the Leica, with its 35mm roll film, fast lens, and rapid frame advance—made practicable the instantaneous depiction of events in conditions as uncertain and dangerous as those of ground warfare. The spreading tide of war in Europe, North Africa, and Asia over the next decade received significant coverage in the pages of American weekly photonews magazines such as *Life*, inaugurated in 1936, and *Look*, started one year later. Close proximity to battle action and its dynamic portrayal, qualities that define modern combat photography, were now possible. They are embodied in the famous "Death of a Loyalist Soldier" (1936), an image of the instant of fatality from the Spanish Civil War (1936–1939) taken by Robert Capa. Killed while covering the French colonial war in Indochina (1946–1954), Capa once remarked mordantly that his ambition was to remain unemployed as a combat photographer even while he maintained the professional ethic that the honesty and emotional power of battle pictures depended upon the cameraperson's contact with the action.

World War II

With entry by the United States into World War II (1939–1945), civilian photojournalists and military photographers pursued the coverage of battle in all areas and phases and on an unprecedented scale. Pictures of the Japanese attack on Pearl Harbor on 7 December 1941 received wide domestic distribution in newspapers and magazines and served to raise patriotic passions in support of an American declaration of war. For the duration of hostilities, every personal, press, and military photograph was submitted for approval through censorship boards. During the first two years, government policy strictly forbade publication of any depiction of American combat dead. No such restrictions were applied to enemy casualties, whose bloodied, burned, or decomposed remains were regularly shown in American news journals.

By 1943, however, in a move by President Roosevelt and the military to reinvigorate home-front support, the policy changed to permit the depiction of dead American soldiers, but only in photographs that preserved their dignity and their anonymity. The generic visual treatment of their identity served ultimately to enhance the symbolism of collective American loss. In the American print media, the reality of war horrors and massive losses was to be seen in photographs of enemy forces and, on occasion, of our Soviet ally, but U.S. soldiers were generally depicted through a visual rhetoric of epic endeavor and individual sacrifice. *Life* magazine, whose staff photographers included Robert Capa, Carl Mydans, W. Eugene Smith, and George Strock, instilled these patriotic, monumental images and values in the public mind.

The most painful images of the period appeared when Allied forces liberated eastern Europe from German occupation and photojournalists such as Margaret Bourke-White documented the Nazi death-camp system. The cultural critic Susan Sontag dates from that point, in 1945, the inception of a contemporary photographic inventory of suffering and injustice, whose uncertain ethical legacy she examines in *On Photography* (1977).

Korea, Vietnam, and the Persian Gulf

Within the first month of the Korean War (1950–1953), American news magazines featured the photograph of a U.S. soldier captured, bound, and executed. In the case of this undeclared war, engaged in by American forces under authority of the United Nations, the editorial intention to ignite patriotic passions with such imagery is obvious. David Douglas Duncan, a Marine veteran and *Life* correspondent, published the photo-narrative *This Is War!* (1951) based on his Korea assignment. The aspiration of his book is to convey an essential truth about men in battle that is both immediate and timeless, much in the spirit of Stephen Crane's novel *The Red Badge of Courage* (1895).

The Vietnam conflict (1961–1975), America's next major undeclared war, received press attention singular in its freedom of travel and access and its independence from government sanction. Historians of American journalism generally view the Vietnam War as a uniquely "uncensored war." Nonetheless, the military Press Information Office and editorial management in the media establishment were largely successful in guiding mainstream news in sanctioned directions for the first several years. By the time of the Tet Offensive in early 1968, however, experienced photojournalists like Larry Burrows, Horst Faas, Philip Jones Griffiths, Catherine Leroy, Donald McCullin, and Tim Page had begun to have an impact on American opinion with their unvarnished images of combat brutality and carnage. Two photographs—"Street Execution of a Vietcong Prisoner, Saigon" (1968), taken by Eddie Adams, and "Girl Accidentally Napalmed by South Vietnamese Planes" (1972), taken by Huynh Cong "Nick" Ut—became immediate icons of the war's vortex of senseless slaughter.

War-crime evidence of U.S. Army atrocities committed against Vietnamese villagers in the area of My Lai in March 1968 was recorded on film by Ronald Haeberle, an army staff photographer on assignment who had also brought along personal cameras. These unrestricted photographs, published in the 5 December 1969 issue of *Life*, show slain bodies, mostly of women, children, and infants, strewn along country lanes. By that time American public opinion had already shifted against the commitment of U. S. troops, influenced measurably by the searing photographic record of horrors in Vietnam. Since that decade American fiction and movies have often portrayed the war photojournalist as a culture hero, a hard-boiled yet principled freelance defender of truth against the allied forces of military barbarity, government cover-ups, and corporate media falsifications.

The 1991 Persian Gulf War marks the shift into a new era of warfare, into a realm that Paul Virilio characterizes as the "derealization of military en-gagement." With tactical innovations such as satellite targeting, smart bombs, and laser systems, the battlefield has become electronic. For a technologically superior military power like the United States, the enterprise of waging war, even at the level of ground battle, has become in significant measure a matter of distant or remote targeting and engagement. Where the challenge for previous combat photography was to capture sudden events and instantly changeable situations and to portray the immediate human experiences of war, in the case of an electronic battlefield still images often derive from second-order information and graphic data, such as an image recorded from transmitters on a "smart bomb." The picture of war is no longer based in the drama of eyewitness events that are potentially fatal to soldier and photographer alike; it comes instead from a command center that monitors the telemetry guiding long-range weapons and records visual display information on the destruction they cause.

Crime and Disaster

From its early decades to the present, American photography has compiled a portrait gallery of the nation's notorious rebels and criminals. In 1865 Alexander Gardner composed a picture story on the detention and execution of conspirators in the assassination of President Lincoln in a remarkable, unprecedented photographic series left unpublished in the popular press of the day because the necessary print technology was not yet available. After 1900, with the broad implementation of affordable and reliable halftone printing processes, photographs for news items on murderers and murders became a staple of American journalism. These dispatches have included photographs of John Dillinger, displayed on a morgue slab after being gunned down in a 1934 police ambush, and of the mobster Ben "Bugsy" Siegel, himself the victim of a gangland hit (1947). To their audience, such images seem to offer the psychological satisfaction of simple, summary poetic justice, the melodramatic conclusion to a criminal yet seductive existence that the public celebrates, with guilty pleasure, up to the point of sacrificial death. In the popular imagination the photograph of a slaughtered criminal functions as a memento mori in a performance of the final rites of notoriety in American culture, rites that are restorative of good conscience for the law-abiding.

Arthur Fellig, whose professional name, Weegee, is an apt indication of his uncanny skills in the

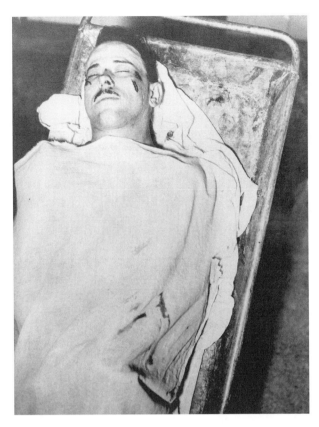

Morgue photograph of John Dillinger, 1934. CORBIS/ UNDERWOOD & UNDERWOOD

genres of street-scene and police-gazette photography, gathered together a decade of his images in the volume *Naked City* (1945). The book's impressionistic, sometimes screaming, prose and its grainy, candid, and often lurid photographs are characteristic of the tabloid news publications that first became popular during the 1920s in the United States. In a contemporary vein of dark, cynical urban realism, Luc Sante's *Evidence* (1992) reproduces from New York City police files the photographs of crime scenes in the 1910s. Visual sensationalism is now commonplace, and it finds its way frequently onto the pages of the traditional press. Photographs of accidental death became so routine in local newspapers by the 1960s as to require the victim to be a celebrity to gain national attention, as in the case of Jayne Mansfield in 1967.

Natural disaster has afforded the press rich picture opportunities at least from the time of the Johnstown flood (1889) and the Louisville cyclone (1890), which each killed over one hundred people. Urban catastrophes have received much photographic coverage, starting with the Chicago fire of 1871, whose devastation is recorded in a panoramic photograph in four panels. In 1906 Arnold Genthe photographed the San Francisco earthquake and fire. The best-known crash photographs of the first half-century bear the dateline 6 May 1937, Lakehurst, New Jersey, where twenty-two press photographers had gathered for routine shots of the arrival of the dirigible *Hindenburg*. But the airship suddenly ignited and fell to the ground, consumed in flames; the entire incident took place in less than one minute. The following day many major newspapers reported the event largely through photo spreads compiled from these camera-witness images. Since that time, photographs of transportation crash sites have become increasingly familiar.

Shifting Images

Boxing, the most intentionally violent of America's sanctioned sports, has supplied many gruesome images for the photo press. The first known photograph of a prizefight, albeit a blurry and retouched image, dates from 1882 and a match that featured John L. Sullivan. A clearer photograph exists of the Sullivan bout with Jake Kilrain in Mississippi on 8 July 1889, which continued for seventy-five rounds and was the last major bareknuckle championship match in the United States. Among many bloody contests photographed in close detail during the modern era, the 1962 welterweight championship bout was especially fierce. After eleven punishing rounds, Emile Griffith defeated by a knockout Benny Paret, who sustained fatal injuries in the ring that night.

Over the twentieth century, photography has made especially prominent in the public imagination moments of assault on public figures. Among the earliest instances is an assassination attempt against Mayor William Gaynor of New York City in 1910, an event photographed immediately after the mayor was wounded and staggered by two bullets at close range. In the twentieth century, the most famous of such assassination images registered the moments of impact of rifle bullets in the 1963 death of President John F. Kennedy. These instantaneous images are stills extracted and enlarged from original amateur movie footage, and their remote, grainy quality—accentuated through the reprocessing necessary before they could be printed as photographs—has contributed greatly to the aura of conspiratorial mystery that surrounds Kennedy's death. In the case of the

The *Hindenburg* disaster of May 1937 in Lakehurst, New Jersey. HULTON GETTY/LIAISON AGENCY

attempt made against the life of President Ronald Reagan in 1981, still images were made from videotape, which retains even less optical resolution and clarity.

Very familiar by now, both in the press and on television news broadcasts, are stills taken from photographic and video security cameras of crimes in progress. A majority of these felonies are robberies at automatic teller machines, convenience stores, and banks, and they frequently involve armed assault. One sequence of surveillance images recorded a 1974 California bank robbery committed by the self-proclaimed Symbionese Liberation Army accompanied by the kidnapped heiress Patty Hearst, who carried a carbine and adopted for the occasion the nom de guerre "Tania." Amateur videotape was the source of still images documenting the 1991 police beating of Rodney King, while traffic helicopter video transmissions were the origin for stills of the related Los Angeles riot in 1992. With the proliferation of such relayed images, the cumulative cultural effect has been to make any such real event simultaneously a media event, subject to any number of spatial and temporal permutations through media outlets. The Rodney King images, in particular, became a visual mantra of the time, in print and on the airwaves.

Social Reform

The camera has operated as an activist on behalf of various American social-reform movements in campaigns against dangers to the health and lives of children, workers, minorities, immigrants, and the poor. Photography was first put into such service in the late 1880s when newspaperman Jacob Riis documented living conditions in the tenement districts of New York City. These images, several taken with the aid of magnesium flash illumination to penetrate the darkness of slum quarters, were first shown to the public by Riis as lantern slide projections to accompany his lectures on the need for the regulation of urban housing and sanitation. The next influential reform photographer was Lewis Hine, who worked in the first two decades of the twentieth century to document the hazards of working conditions for child laborers in American mines and factories, as in his poster "Making Human Junk" (c. 1915), a photo assemblage that plots the debasement of healthy children into drudges. President Franklin D. Roosevelt's New Deal sponsored a corps of photographers, based within the Farm Security Administration from 1935 until 1942, to record, personalize, and publicize the ravages brought on, particularly in the South and the West, by drought, soil depletion, economic depression, and dislocation. Included

A photograph from 1890 by Jacob Riis shows impoverished immigrant families in New York City. HULTON GETTY/LIAISON AGENCY

within this group at one stage or another were the American masters of documentary photographic style Walker Evans, Dorothea Lange, Russell Lee, and Ben Shahn. Theirs was not a clinical exposure of systemic deprivation or private misery, but rather a complex dramatic testament to human suffering, anxieties, and perseverance.

While critics like Maren Stange and John Tagg fault social-reform discourse and its expression through photographs for patronizing, often prejudiced, and ultimately conservative attitudes, reform photography demonstrably assisted in the processes of social change that brought measurable material improvement in the circumstances of people's lives. Since the 1950s, camera advocacy has been a factor in civil-rights campaigns, from the struggles of African Americans to the women's liberation movement and gay-rights activism. The camera has also witnessed an often brutal public and police reaction that has confronted these campaigns.

Modern Approaches

With the massive American disillusionment that followed the Vietnam War and the assassina-

tion of national leaders in the 1960s, new sensibilities emerged in the photographic coverage of the nation's social ills. The photo-essays *Tulsa* (1971) by Larry Clark and *Cocaine True, Cocaine Blue* (1994) by Eugene Richards, for example, present noncommittal, deadpan eyewitness reportage on hard-drug use and the often arbitrary, senseless brutality that accompanies it. The experience of prison inmates, many of them violent offenders, receives respectful and at times admiring treatment by Danny Lyon in *Conversations with the Dead* (1971). Dramatic sympathy in Eugene Richards's *The Knife and Gun Club: Scenes from an Emergency Room* (1989) is directed more to an overworked medical staff than to victims of the city's mean streets. An older sense of advocacy photojournalism is regained in the story on spousal abuse and women's shelters documented by Donna Ferrato in *Living with the Enemy* (1991).

Commercial photography in the fashion and entertainment businesses since the period of the Vietnam War has adopted the iconographies of guerrilla warfare, terrorism, and urban crime many times. With the easing of censorship over depictions of adult sexuality after the 1960s, moreover, ritual violence and its simulation, formerly included among the underground practices of sadomasochism, entered the mainstream through advertising and the popular-culture media. With fine-art quality photographs of the transgressed, eroticized human body as both fetish and commodity, Robert Mapplethorpe in the *X Portfolio* (1979) tested the boundaries of aesthetic taste and public scandal. Mapplethorpe exhibitions in 1989 reignited political attempts to censor such visual materials.

Despite censorship efforts, aesthetic interest in the violated body has become even more prominent in gallery and museum photography. Andres Serrano's exhibition *The Morgue* (1992) portrays corpses of individuals who died as the result of crime, accident, disease, or suicide. Serrano's images fuse a highly stylized visual treatment—with close, fragmentary framing and sharp, limited focus—to a format of glossy color processing typical of evidence photographs and of medical textbook illustrations. Photographer and printmaker Joel-Peter Witkin has explored extensively forensic and postmortem applications of photography in fashioning an art genre. His photo-prints display an openly avowed fascination with mutations of animal and human flesh worked by congenital conditions, injury, disease, or mortality.

After the 1960s photographed violence and bodily injury became fully familiar to the American public through the mass media. Photographic images that once had been left largely to lurid tabloids became the stock-in-trade of print and television journalism. Such imagery was, in other contexts, stylized and merchandized through the fashion and entertainment industries or abstracted and aestheticized in the art world. Photography, a medium once held to promise greater human compassion and social understanding through the direct documentation of subjects like violence and suffering, had become by the late twentieth century—particularly as digital-image processes replaced the original plate and negative technologies—fully susceptible to postmodern conditions of impersonality and derealization.

BIBLIOGRAPHY

Capa, Robert. *Slightly Out of Focus*. New York: Holt, 1947.
Heller, Jonathan, ed. *War and Conflict: Selected Images from the National Archives, 1765–1970*. Washington, D.C.: National Archives and Records Administration, 1990.
Lewinski, Jorge. *The Camera at War: A History of War Photography from 1848 to the Present Day*. London: W. H. Allen, 1978.
Moeller, Susan D. *Shooting War: Photography and the American Experience of Combat*. New York: Basic Books, 1989.
Newhall, Beaumont. *The History of Photography*. Rev. ed. New York: Museum of Modern Art, 1982.
Rosenblum, Naomi. *A World History of Photography*. Rev. ed. New York: Abbeville, 1989.
Sontag, Susan. *On Photography*. New York: Farrar, Straus, and Giroux, 1977.
Stange, Maren. *Symbols of Ideal Life: Social Documentary Photography in America, 1890–1950*. New York: Cambridge University Press, 1989.
Tagg, John. *The Burden of Representation: Essays on Photographies and Histories*. Minneapolis: University of Minnesota Press, 1993.
Virilio, Paul. *War and Cinema: The Logistics of Perception*. 1984. Translated by Patrick Camiller. New York: Verso, 1989.

JAMES GOODWIN

See also **Fine Arts; Journalism; Weegee.**

PHYSIOLOGY OF VIOLENCE. *See* Endocrinology; Health and Medical Factors; Neuropsychology; Psychophysiology

PINKERTONS. *See* Private Security: Private Police.

PIRACY

Piracy has existed almost from the time men first took to the sea. Through the ages, almost every coastal nation or large expanse of water has suffered attacks by gangs of seagoing brigands. The Vikings were the first to engage in large-scale maritime plundering along the edges of the Atlantic. They sailed from bases in the Scandinavian fjords and terrorized northern Europe from the eighth to the eleventh centuries. It was not until five hundred years later, however, that European piracy came to the Western Hemisphere. During the reign of Elizabeth I (1558–1603), English marauders wreaked havoc on Spanish New World settlements and shippers. The more famous of these sixteenth-century adventurers, men such as Sir Francis Drake and Sir John Hawkins, became legendary figures in their own time and have remained national heroes.

Despite the renown attained by English sea raiders, the Elizabethan era was not to become the historical period most closely associated with pirates. Piracy enjoyed its heyday from the mid-seventeenth century through 1725 or 1730. During this span of less than one hundred years the men whose names are most often associated with ocean marauding—including Henry Morgan, Bartholomew Roberts, Long Ben Avery, Captain William Kidd, and Blackbeard—plied their trade in the Caribbean, on the Spanish Main, northward to the Bahamas, and along the shores of the English colonies from the Carolinas to Nova Scotia.

Pirates rarely left diaries, letters, memoirs, or other materials that could provide insight into their hearts or minds. Most of what we know of them comes from documentary evidence produced by their enemies—the public officials and naval officers determined to eradicate them—or the men and women who suffered economic loss and physical abuse at their hands. Members of pirate crews were usually men in their twenties who first went to sea as merchant sailors. There were a number of reasons why they turned from honest maritime employment to piracy. Some claimed they were forced into "going on the account," as it was called. When their ships were captured, the merchant sailors were given the choice of either signing on with their buccaneer captors or being murdered. This explanation was almost always true for men who could play musical instruments or who were trained in navigation. It was also true of many ordinary seafarers who were pressed into service by renegade captains in need of additional men. Although no accurate estimate can be made of the proportion of volunteers to forced recruits, claims of being pressured into careers as pirates are most often found in records of captured men who were on trial, pleading their innocence. Not all of those in the dock chose this exculpatory tactic. Many confessed that they willingly joined buccaneer crews to obtain freedom from a world of regulation and oppression. They proclaimed defiantly to those sitting in judgment that they turned to a life of piracy to obtain liberation from the constraints of society, adding that they often found on board pirate ships a measure of equality and a sense of brotherhood that were entirely lacking in merchant service, the Royal Navy, or elsewhere.

The two characteristics most closely associated with buccaneering are violence and pervasive cruelty. The very nature of plundering at sea requires a certain level of violence, but the ferociousness of the enterprise has been exaggerated. Scenes of cutlass-wielding raiders savaging their foes on decks awash with blood are the standard fare of film and fiction, but in fact, buccaneer commanders often went to great lengths to ensure that the ships they attacked could be taken with a minimum amount of fighting. They achieved this end by selecting as their prey vessels that were more lightly manned and carried fewer cannons than their own. Captains whose ships came under attack by pirates usually realized that they and their crew were likely to be killed if they offered resistance, and they frequently surrendered without a struggle.

While pirates tried to avoid pitched battles whenever possible, they did not hesitate to subject their captives to torture. Ample records have survived detailing the frequency of these acts and the viciousness of their methods. In addition to beating prisoners with clubs, bars, fists, sabers, and any other suitable instruments, they also devised an extensive catalog of other torments. Testimony from witnesses as well as victims includes accounts of branding, roasting, mutilation, dismemberment, and woolding—a torture unique to life on the sea (see sidebar).

At least a few pirates are recognizable as genuinely psychotic by the pleasure they obtained from inflicting pain. One of the most notable of these was Captain Jean-David Nau, known as L'Olonnais after his birthplace in western France, Les Sables-d'Olonne. The pirate historian A. O. Exquemelin chronicled some of the cruelties the captain committed on a series of expeditions in the late 1660s. According to Exquemelin, L'Olonnais hacked uncooperative captives to death, then licked their blood from his sword. Describing one incident Exquemelin wrote, "L'Olonnais, being possessed of a devil's fury, ripped open one of the prisoners with his cutlass, tore the living heart out of his body, gnawed at it, and then hurled it in the

---

Woolding

In the age of sail, coils of rope, known as woolding, were wound tightly around the lower segments of masts to strengthen them. The process of wrapping a length of rope around a captive's head and then twisting it with a stick in the manner of a tourniquet was also called woolding. As the rope was drawn tighter about the skull of the unfortunate victim, the pressure caused excruciating pain and, eventually, the victim's eyes would pop out of his or her sockets.

face of one of the others." Despite the well-known actions of a few mentally unstable individuals, torture was rarely employed by pirates solely for entertainment. In almost every documented instance, when pain was deliberately inflicted, it was done for the purpose of extracting information, usually about the location of valuables. In these cases the procedures were not conducted in the midst of drunken revels; they were carried out routinely, systematically, and in a manner that could best be described as purposeful and businesslike. When the desired information was obtained, the victim was usually released from his ordeal.

There are many reasons why piracy flourished in the Caribbean and along the North American coast in the decades from 1650 to 1725. Religious and national rivalries played a part. This was an age when leading European powers, both Protestant and Catholic, vied with one another to gain hegemony on the Continent and to build empires around the world. The War of the League of Augsburg (1688) and the War of Spanish Succession (1701–1714) were two of the most destructive manifestations of these rivalries, but since the Western Hemisphere was only a secondary theater in the conflicts, the preponderance of the warring nations' military efforts were concentrated in Europe and the Mediterranean or in African and eastern waters. Operations in the Americas were left to small contingents of regular forces, pirates, and officially sanctioned privateers. When prizes were taken by pirates, the booty was distributed with at least a nod toward equality. Captains, masters, and others with special skills received two or three times more than ordinary crewmen, although there is evidence to indicate that leaders often cheated the men of their portions. Among privateers, investors and ship owners had to be compensated along with officers and men. The methods for apportioning profits among each of these categories was fixed by law, although the amounts could vary owing to a number of circumstances. There is no way to estimate the amount of wealth plundered by seaborne marauders in the Americas during the seventeenth and eighteenth centuries, but it is certain that Spain's imperial ventures in the Western Hemisphere were hobbled economically and politically by their depredations.

The English government in Jamaica was openly hospitable to buccaneer fleets. Their visits to Port Royal to dispose of loot were a boon to the economy, and island leaders believed the presence of a large number of marauders reduced the possibility

Henry Morgan (1635–1688), who as a pirate and buccaneer terrorized the Spanish Empire. HULTON GETTY/LIAISON AGENCY

of attack from England's enemies. Policies of unofficial support for piracy were adopted by national as well as colonial governments. Leaders in England, France, and the Netherlands realized such measures provided defense for their West Indian holdings without cost to their exchequers, since pirates were compensated for their efforts from the purses of the hapless Spaniards they victimized. Henry Morgan, who terrorized the Spanish Empire during the 1660s and 1670s, was once summoned to London from his lair in Jamaica to answer for plundering without official sanction. He arrived in England in 1672, where he was lionized rather than punished. Two years later he returned to Jamaica with a knighthood and an appointment as lieutenant governor of the colony. Captain William Kidd, the most famous of pirates, had a legion of influential friends in both London and New York. Unfortunately, Captain Kidd's powerful associates were unwilling to come to his aid in 1701, when he was convicted of piracy by an admiralty court at Old Bailey and hanged. Edward Teach, the notorious Blackbeard, was widely known to have been under the protection of North Carolina's governor Charles Eden. Significantly, it was not a local force that brought Blackbeard's violent career to an end. An expedition sent to North

Carolina from the neighboring colony of Virginia captured his ship and killed him at Ocracoke Inlet, off the coast of North Carolina, in 1718.

During the 1720s international pressures, domestic politics, and the decline of religious rivalries moved the British to take decisive action to suppress American buccaneers. Naval patrols were augmented in the Caribbean, substantial rewards were offered for the capture of pirates, pardons were given to those who surrendered, privately owned vessels were licensed to pursue buccaneers, and London made it clear that colonial assistance to seagoing marauders would no longer be tolerated. The combined effect of these measures swiftly eliminated piracy as a serious problem in the West Indies and North America.

Although there are hundreds, perhaps even thousands, of books and articles on New World piracy, all information comes largely from two sources: A. O. Exquemelin's *The Buccaneers of America* (1678) and Captain Charles Johnson's *A General History of the Robberies and Murders of the Most Notorious Pyrates* (1724). Exquemelin sailed as a barber and surgeon on several seventeenth-century buccaneering expeditions and returned to Europe sometime after 1674. The account of his adventures was published in Dutch four years later and was quickly translated into Spanish and French. An English version appeared in 1684, and over the next three centuries publishers have issued at least forty-five more editions. Captain Charles Johnson's *General History* is a lengthy and detailed multivolume compendium of the lives of almost three dozen notorious pirates. Virtually nothing is known of Johnson, and although there has been speculation that Daniel Defoe actually wrote the book, there is no direct evidence of his authorship. Much of the information in the *General History* is accurate, although portions of it are undoubtedly fictional. Still, it is the basic source for a substantial amount of the surviving information on piracy, and like Exquemelin's work, it has gone through scores of editions since its original publication in 1724.

BIBLIOGRAPHY

Exquemelin, A. O. *The Buccaneers of America.* With an introduction by Jack Beeching. Translation by Alexis Brown. Baltimore: Penguin , 1969. Original edition, Amsterdam, 1678.

Johnson, Captain Charles. *A General History of the Robberies and Murders of the Most Notorious Pyrates.* Edited by Man-uel Schonhorn. Columbia: University of South Carolina Press, 1972. Original edition, London, 1724.

Rediker, Marcus. *Between the Devil and the Deep Blue Sea: Merchant Seamen, Pirates, and the Anglo-American Maritime World, 1700–1750.* Cambridge, U.K.: Cambridge University Press, 1987.

Ritchie, Robert C. *Captain Kidd and the War Against the Pirates.* Cambridge, Mass.: Harvard University Press, 1986.

Rogozinski, Jan. *Pirates: Brigands, Buccaneers, and Privateers in Fact, Fiction, and Legend.* New York: Facts on File, 1995.

B. R. BURG

See also **Blackbeard; Filibustering Expeditions; Hijacking; Kidd, Captain William; Privateers.**

PLEA BARGAINING

Plea bargaining, also referred to as plea negotiation, is one of the most commonly accepted practices in American criminal justice processing, and its history dates back to almost the very beginnings of American jurisprudence. In fact, it is generally believed that more than 90 percent of criminal convictions result from negotiated pleas of guilty.

Plea bargaining takes place between the prosecutor and the defense counsel or the accused, and it involves discussions that aim toward an agreement under which the defendant will enter a plea of guilty in exchange for some prosecutorial or judicial concession. These concessions are of four possible types:

1. The initial charges may be reduced to some lesser offense, thus ensuring a reduction in the sentence imposed.
2. In instances of multiple criminal charges, the number of counts may be reduced.
3. A recommendation for leniency may be made by the prosecutor, thus reducing the potential sentence from incarceration to probation.
4. In instances where the charges involve a negative label, such as child molesting, the complaint may be altered to a less repugnant one, such as assault.

The principal players in the plea bargaining process include the prosecutor, defense counsel, accused, and judge. The prosecutor plays the major role in plea negotiation. On a case-by-case basis, the prosecutor determines the concessions to be offered. Some jurisdictions have guidelines to provide consistency in plea bargaining cases, but in most there are no procedures to control the discretion of the prosecutor. Thus, such competing alternatives and factors as the seriousness of the crime, the attitude of the victim, the content of the police report, the applicable sentencing provisions, the strength of the state's case, the presiding judge's attitude toward plea bargaining, the court caseload, and the pressures exerted by the police and the community all may contribute to the prosecutor's decision.

The defense, whether a private attorney, assigned counsel, or public defender, has a very explicit role in the plea bargaining process. First, the counsel for the defense interacts directly with the prosecutor in the negotiation of the plea. Second, once a plea has been initially "bargained," there are well-established guidelines—from both the U.S. Supreme Court and the American Bar Association—that govern the defense attorney's actions. It is the responsibility of the defense to make certain that his or her client understands both the bargaining process and the plea. That is, the attorney must explain to the accused the facts of the various charges, the sentencing provisions of the alternative charges, and the rights waived by a guilty plea. Thus, the defense acts in an advisory role and is required to inform the client of all discussions and negotiations throughout the bargaining process.

Although it is the accused whose future is at stake, he or she has only a small role in the plea bargaining process. The accused rarely takes part in direct negotiations, with the exception of defendants who offer the prosecutor information about other cases in return for further concessions. In general, however, the accused's role is limited to an acceptance or a rejection of the prosecutor's offer.

Judicial participation by federal judges in plea negotiations is prohibited by the federal rules of criminal procedure. At the state level, some jurisdictions formally prohibit the practice while others encourage it. Some argue that judicial participation in plea negotiations would regulate the practice, ensure greater fairness, and make sentencing more uniform. However, opponents claim that such participation lessens the objectivity of the judge in determining the voluntariness of the plea and is inconsistent with the purposes of the presentence investigation report (a document, usually prepared by a probation officer, that provides the court with information concerning the background and character of the defendant, in order to assist in the determination of the most appropriate sen-

tence). Some argue that such judicial participation may suggest to the defendant that he or she may not receive a fair trial.

While debates continue over the appropriateness, fairness, and efficacy of plea bargaining, the practice persists. Furthermore, since most negotiations take place in judges' chambers, prosecutors' offices, courtroom hallways, restrooms, and even barrooms adjacent to the courthouse, it remains difficult either to assess fully the roles played by all participants or to regulate effectively the levels of their conduct and involvement.

The widespread use of negotiated pleas of guilt comes about as a result of overcrowded caseloads in U.S. criminal courts. Proponents of the plea bargaining process maintain that it is beneficial to both the accused and the state. For the accused, plea bargaining has three advantages:

1. It reduces the possibility of detention during extensive pretrial and trial processing.
2. It extends the potential for a reduced sentence.
3. It reduces the financial costs of legal representation.

For the state, plea bargaining has its own advantages:

1. It reduces the overall financial costs of criminal prosecution.
2. It improves the administrative efficiency of the courts by reducing the number of cases that go to a full (and time-consuming) trial.
3. It enables the prosecution to devote more time and resources to cases of greatest importance and seriousness.

While plea negotiation is common, it is also highly controversial. First, it encourages an accused to waive the constitutional right to trial. Second, it enables the defendant to receive a sentence generally less severe than he or she might otherwise have received. In the eyes of the public, the criminal has "beaten the system" and the judicial process has been compromised. Third, it sacrifices the legislative policies reflected in the criminal law for the sake of tactical accommodations between the prosecution and defense. Fourth, it ignores the correctional needs of the bulk of offenders, for in many instances the accused may ultimately plead guilty to a charge far removed from that of the original crime. Fifth, it raises the risk that an innocent person, fearing a determination of guilt and a harsh sentence if the case goes to trial, will accept responsibility for a crime if persuaded that a guilty plea will result in lighter treatment.

BIBLIOGRAPHY

Fleming, Roy B., Peter F. Nardulli, and James Eisenstein. *The Craft of Justice*. Philadelphia: University of Pennsylvania Press, 1992.

Katz, Burton S. *Justice Overruled: Unmasking the Criminal Justice System*. New York: Time Warner, 1997.

Rosett, Arthur, and Donald R. Cressey. *Justice by Consent: Plea Bargains in the American Courthouse*. Philadelphia: Lippincott, 1976.

Sanborn, Joseph B. "A Historical Sketch of Plea Bargaining." *Justice Quarterly* 3 (June 1986).

JAMES A. INCIARDI

See also **Crime, Legal Definitions of; Sentencing.**

POETRY. *See* Literature: Poetry

POLICE

Following the **Overview** *are four subentries:* **Community Policing, Police Brutality, Police Use of Force,** *and* **Police Violence.**

OVERVIEW

Policing is not only the only nonmilitary profession authorized to use lethal force, but it also requires intervention in nonviolent disputes, a function that often places police in the role of social, political, and economic arbiters. Moreover, contemporary policing involves an ever-increasing range of responsibilities and activities at several levels of government (municipal, county, state, and federal). In light of these critical social functions, a survey of the history of policing in the United States can be viewed as a struggle for control over two key issues: first, the definition of police work, or what police should do; and second, how best to oversee its operations.

In Search of a Definition of Policing

Most discussions of the history of police proceed chronologically, outlining the development of modern-day policing, and concluding with a definition of the role of police in a democratic society. This descriptive method has persisted in law enforcement and political circles, and it has been used to emphasize police reform over the years. In these studies the following questions recur: Should the police have a chiefly preventive role, helping communities take measures to prevent crime and reduce violence? Or should the police focus more on the deterrence of crime and the apprehension of criminals? The interplay of these often competing role definitions continues to shape the structure and function of the American police. Concepts of community policing and problem solving have blurred the boundary between crime fighting and social work. Under such efforts the police seek to be closer to the community, while at the same time addressing persistent crime and disorder problems. Such reshaping of the definition of police work has occupied much of this debate, and the results are likely to shape the future direction of police work, crime fighting, and the concept of community.

One of the biggest problems of policing in the United States is the fragmented and overlapping nature of police jurisdictions and responsibilities. Two different bases for organizing American policing—by level of government (federal, state, county, and local) and by specialized function (customs police, federal park police, university police, public housing police, transit police, and so on)—have resulted in a proliferation of police agencies with overlapping jurisdictions and functions. Often small, contiguous political jurisdictions maintain separate police departments to maintain local control over the police as well as to establish political power and status for the local police agency. In 1999 there were an estimated seventeen thousand police departments in the United States, not including specialized agencies such as university and transit police. Such fragmentation in police authority often causes concern that the police have too broad a mission and that their actions are ungovernable and, therefore, uncontrolled. As a result of the fragmentation, one agency may favor one style or form of policing while another agency, in close proximity, could encourage and emphasize a totally different perspective. Such variations in police styles can result in the abuse of police authority and distrust of the police.

The Emergence of Organized Policing

Social control in medieval European communities was largely organized around a system of self-policing. Under this system, men committed their time to the defense of the collective group by apprehending offenders. This system was rooted in a social hierarchy in which serfs owed specific obligations to the nobles on whose land they lived. By the early thirteenth century, self-policing had

531

begun to yield to a constable-based system, where "watches and wards" were organized for general police patrols and public safety. Watches and wards were typically composed of volunteers who patrolled during the nighttime hours and apprehended offenders. These offenders were then brought before the constable, a person seen as the chief representative of the lord of the manor and the legal system. Generally, these systems were loosely constructed and only marginally tied to both the legal system and to the community at large. Even though these policing systems did not clearly define the role of the police and featured little civic oversight of the police, they represented the emergence of organized and more formalized social control. These police were often seen as mercenaries who worked for the wealthy to control the working class and to maintain traditional hierarchical authority. Modern policing in the United States took its historical cues from Europe, especially England. In the wake of the Industrial Revolution and significant increases in urban violence, especially in London, society was in critical need of an organized system of policing. In 1829 a new system of policing was approved for the City of London with the Metropolitan Police Act, which laid the legal foundation for organized policing. The Metropolitan Police was a paid police force, organized along military lines, uniformed, and given the central mission to prevent crime and preserve social order. Sir Robert Peel, the architect of the "New Police," saw the police as drawing their authority not only from the law but also from the body politic. The legitimacy of their control had to come from the citizens' belief in and commitment to the constitutional authority and in the even-handedness of the administration of justice. A uniformed police force patrolling fixed areas and in constant contact with the public was the central element of this newly emerging system of policing in England.

In its early years the London Metropolitan Police had significant problems to overcome. First, there was a widespread suspicion of government authority and the fear that the police would become agents of the government and spy on the innocent. It was to address this concern that the police of London were uniformed; they were visible to the public as well as to would-be criminals. Second, given the ranks from which the police were to be drawn, chiefly from the lower and working classes, there was concern that these individuals could be corrupted, misuse their authority, or

otherwise violate their duties. Unfortunately, such was the case in the formative years of the London Metropolitan Police.

To prevent such problems, the Metropolitan Police was organized along strict military lines, with a concomitant emphasis on the impartial administration of justice and the law. These ideals notwithstanding, the legitimacy of the police was continually challenged by the suspicious lower and working classes. During its first eight years, the entire Metropolitan Police Force completely changed its ranks three times. Police officers were fired or forced to resign for drunkenness, corruption, excessive brutality, and other administrative violations. Persistence in the management of the force paid off, however, and ultimately the Metropolitan Police became a model police agency that was emulated throughout Europe and America. London's "bobbies" (named after Sir Robert Peel) continue to personify the image of civil and courteous police officers.

The Transplanted System: Policing and American Politics

In the early nineteenth century, while continental Europe continued to refine policing, many American cities began to develop their own police systems. Boston, New York, and Philadelphia, for example, established police departments in the middle to late nineteenth century, yet the character and quality of these organizations generally escaped the ideals set for them, often with disappointing results. Whereas the English police system enjoyed widespread public support and was seen as closely tied to constitutional principles as well as apolitical and impartial in the administration of the law, U.S. police departments of this era had no such presumptions. All too often the American police, particularly those in big cities, were seen as an affiliate of the political machines that controlled the cities. Police, therefore, were a political but not a legal force in these communities. Policemen were often poorly paid individuals without uniforms, and they lacked public support. Too often, they failed miserably in their attempts to emulate the professional and military crispness associated with their English counterparts. These police forces were largely corrupt and brutal and were held in rather low regard by the public. As the historian Mark H. Haller (1976) suggests about the Chicago and other American police forces, "In order to understand patterns of police behavior in American cities at the turn of the century, it is im-

Two Pittsburgh police officers, about 1952. CORBIS/
CHARLES HARRIS; PITTSBURGH COURIER

portant to grasp a critical fact: the police, although they were formally engaged in law enforcement, were little oriented toward legal norms" (p. 303).

In cities such as Boston and New York, local political bosses (such as Boss Tweed in New York) effectively ran the police. Throughout the late nineteenth century and into the twentieth century, police departments were the objects of ridicule and disdain. These departments were also under attack from social and political reformers who converged in the late nineteenth and early twentieth centuries under the Progressive movement. Progressives sought to instill "good government" values into the political and administrative process. They abhorred the political machines that had taken root in major cities, often in the major ethnic enclaves. Moreover, progressives sought to establish a "legitimate" basis for the provision of government services, rejecting the partisan political systems that were typical of the era. Progressives also saw the political exchange systems of large cities as amoral, likely to perpetuate the brutalizing of the local population by the politically powerful.

Scandal and Reform: A Legacy of the American Experience

The history of American policing has seen a recurring cycle of scandal and reform. Invariably associated with the allocation of values in society, the police often find their integrity most sharply questioned in the areas of sharpest social controversy: disputes between the haves and have-nots, decisions about the appropriate use of force, and the treatment of marginalized segments of the population. Such issues place police forces in a harsh spotlight of public concern that has revealed their failings over many years and in many places.

Early reform efforts were almost entirely focused on "taking the politics" out of policing by removing the police structure and function from the political apparatus within cities. During the early part of the twentieth century, under the auspices of the Progressive movement, police departments across America were exposed for political and financial graft and corruption. Police departments became powerful tools to be used for political ends; they represented jobs and income for those whose political allegiance was evident. Police officers earned more than the average nonskilled worker, and they enjoyed authority as well as a relative lack of supervision. Political machines appointed police chiefs as well, and police supervisors deferred to ward leaders on matters of hiring, deployment, supervision, and the promotion of officers. In the late 1890s in New York, the Lexow Committee received testimony that the going rate for promotion to sergeant was $1,600; for captains the rate was as high as $15,000.

Initial attempts to reform the lawless police of the late nineteenth and early twentieth centuries focused on increasing government (as opposed to political) oversight of the police. In general this trend meant that police departments became more centralized, thereby reducing their allegiance to local politicians. Reformers attempted to make policing more systematic through increased entrance, training, and promotion standards; they also sought to reduce the scope and breadth of police authority, thereby creating clearer criteria for the assessment of police behavior. By the 1920s the Progressives had succeeded in establishing the civil service as a means of depoliticizing government employment, including police appointments, and had increased legislative and civic oversight of the police. At the same time, progressive chiefs of police began to emphasize professional values for the management of police agencies.

August Vollmer, chief of police in Berkeley, California, was perhaps the most influential of America's reform chiefs at that time. Vollmer called for the creation of "professional police officers," persons trained in universities and systematically screened for advanced qualifications. A protégé of Vollmer's, O. W. Wilson, the police chief of Wichita, Kansas, and later Chicago, Illinois, continued to stress police reform through the development of professionalism and improvements in administration and operating policies.

Between 1920 and the early 1960s, police reform focused on the improvement of the organization and management of police departments, almost to the exclusion of other equally important concerns. Reformers like Wilson in Chicago sought to refine police organizations to better control police discretion. In 1950 in Los Angeles Chief William Parker inherited a police department riddled with scandal, but he modernized the management as well as the symbolism of the Los Angeles Police Department (LAPD). As a result of his efforts, the LAPD became known as America's most "professional" police department. But the scrutiny that ensued from the 1991 beating of Rodney King by Los Angeles police officers undermined the professional image of the LAPD.

The legacy of early reform efforts was primarily to focus attention on the means of policing rather than its ends. For practical purposes, this meant that there was great attention paid to how to oversee the police and perhaps to limit their discretion, while there was little agreement as to what the police should do.

The 1960s and Police Reform

Like the rest of American society during the 1960s, policing was fraught with turbulence and conflict. A revolution in U.S. civil rights law led the Supreme Court to rule consistently against long-standing police customs and practices, including in-custody investigations, searches and seizures, and a wide range of other procedures, which were challenged for abuse and violations of the Bill of Rights. At the same time, the police in the United States were confronted with large-scale civil disobedience. The convergence of the Civil Rights movement, the Vietnam War, and the onset of the hippie lifestyle resulted in a vociferous display of public protest. Such public events often pitted the demonstrators, who were focused on changing the status quo, against the police, who were sworn to protect the status quo.

Nightly news programs showed police using fire hoses and dogs to control civil rights protesters. Such media images were quite disturbing to the general public, which had observed racial tensions since the 1940s, commencing with the Zoot-Suit Riot in Los Angeles and disturbances in other cities. In the summer of 1968 in Chicago, however, the American public witnessed what was later referred to as a "police riot." White middle-class students and other antiwar protesters were beaten by Chicago police, and this action put police reform once again center stage in American political circles.

Community and Problem-Oriented Policing: A New Set of Police Roles?

Since the 1980s the language and symbolism of community and problem-oriented policing have captured the imagination of policy makers, chiefs of police, and the public at large. On the one hand, community policing attempts to link the police to communities and to mobilize local citizens to participate in crime-prevention activities. On the other hand, problem-oriented policing seeks to address patterns of community crime and disorder rather than focusing on individual incidents. The differences between these innovations and traditional policing have created a dilemma for the police. Most officers are resistant to change and want to perform traditional policing tasks, such as crime fighting and the delivery of emergency services. Progressive administrators who allow the label of "social work" to attach to community-oriented policing are likely to have their efforts thwarted. They must pay attention to the desires of police personnel who may be content with the status quo because it provides them with predictable rules and expectations. The changes required by community-oriented policing include time-consuming efforts to build relationships with other government and private agencies and to acquire and use a broad range of resources to identify and solve community problems. These community-oriented roles have given the police a new approach to their jobs. To properly implement community policing, many officers will be forced to change their style and behavior. For some, this will not come easily.

The Importance of Police Culture and Its Resistance to Change

One of the most persistent problems in reforming the police is the internal organizational and workforce cultures that typically pervade police

Police try to control the crowds at a John F. Kennedy campaign rally in Michigan, 26 October 1960. CORBIS

agencies; these cultures have consistently rejected the idea that the police should be more directly accountable to those outside the police agency. The police culture, as it has developed over the years, convinces officers of the importance of the status quo. Such a culture emphasizes the comfort level of the present conditions and introduces fear of the unknown or resistance to change. As in many other occupations, workers become complacent with their duties and obligations. Introducing changes often meets with opposition unless the changes quickly and clearly benefit the officers.

A major force in the development of police culture is the group of established officers who can influence young recruits by setting examples and shaping opinions. Young officers turn to these established officers for advice, support, and recognition. These latter are also most likely to resist change, since they have the most invested in the status quo.

Other groups that have an important influence on police culture include unions and benevolent associations. Officers representing these groups wield a great deal of power and influence. After all, they speak for a large number of officers. As the power and influence of these organized groups increase, their ideas and beliefs concerning the police structure and function can create a powerful force in the department. The procedures of established individuals and the persuasion of powerful groups can create a culture that can influence new recruits to appreciate the status quo. This process can be a strong impediment to change.

The move to community policing requires many changes, including the assignment of officers to specific areas for a period of time so they can get to know the people, places, and distinct aspects of the areas. Along with the long-term assignments goes the possibility of corruption and the need to monitor and oversee officers' actions.

Legislating Police Oversight: Scandal and Reform

Perhaps the most persistent issue confronting policing in a democratic society is "Who is guarding the guardians?" Given the awesome powers of the police—their ability both to restrict individual freedom by taking people into custody and to use deadly force—society has been rightfully concerned with creating mechanisms for overseeing police activities and functions. In addition, the emphasis on community policing and long-term assignments requires oversight. Typically, such oversight has started with the formation of a police commission that is politically appointed to oversee and review the performance of police agencies and individual officers. Sometimes a commission assists in the selection of a police chief, who is

535

typically appointed by a mayor or city manager. This concept is driven by the theory that elected officials responsible for local governance should oversee police functions. This chain of authority makes the police at least indirectly accountable to the political process and to the body politic.

The supervision of some police agencies has been mandated by city, state, or federal governments that believed that the police could not effectively manage themselves. Perhaps internal police cultural influences were too strong or the agency leaders too weak to create the needed change from within. In any case, legislated police oversight was considered scandalous by many officers, while the public and members of the department who recognized the need for change considered the mandated supervision as a reform movement.

Fortunately, other agencies have established procedures to police themselves. Procedures have been established that enable citizens to lodge complaints against police officers, and systems have been put into place that have created mechanisms to initiate internal investigations. These two steps have significantly increased officer accountability. By making it easy for civilians to complain about the actions of specific officers, supervisors have been given another method to evaluate their officers. This supervision is supported by the strict chain-of-command structure utilized in police agencies.

The Military Model of Controlling Police Discretion

Controlling police officer discretion has always been a concern for management. The structure of the police organization has provided a way to observe and regulate officers' actions. The command structure known as the military model has a distinct chain of command that filters information up and down a well-defined succession of supervisors and officers. In this structure, first-line supervisors, usually sergeants, are responsible for the behavior of a number of officers who provide services directly to the public. These front-line officers have the majority of contacts with the public, receive the largest number of complaints and commendations, and must make the greatest number of decisions. In this military model, their decisions are controlled first by policies and training and second by supervision and accountability systems. As in any organization, the responsibility lies with the chief officer but is administered by his or her agents: the captains, lieutenants, sergeants, and so on. Because the police have the ability to use force, management must implement all available means to control its use.

Controlling Police Violence

Concern about the use of excessive force has haunted policing since its earliest days. While steps have been taken to prevent police violence, it is a recurring problem that requires constant attention. Because police must interact with potentially violent citizens, they must be trained to handle all types of encounters with sufficient but not excessive force. Fortunately, the use of force is relatively rare, but when it occurs, it can create major problems for all concerned. One of the first steps a police department can take to get a handle on their potential problems with the use of force is to require officers and supervisors to document its use. By requiring reports on how officers control suspects, management can determine which situations, officers, and suspects create potential problems. Once the information is available, management can isolate the factors that may lead to a large number of force situations.

Knowledge about the use of force enables management to modify policies, strengthen supervision, and design a progressive disciplinary system. In fact, citizen complaints and certain types of officer behavior can serve as an early-warning system that can identify officers who receive a specified number of complaints, routinely use force to control suspects, or fire a weapon more than once in a six-month period. Certainly, none of these thresholds by itself indicates a problem, but each does raise a "flag." Officers who are identified can have the incidents investigated and their performance evaluated to determine if they are experiencing any particular problems or stress-related concerns. Training, counseling, or other remedial efforts could be suggested by the officer's supervisor, if needed.

Issues Confronting the American Police

American police faced a variety of major issues at the end of the 1990s. Such issues included public perception, acceptance, and involvement with police, the definition of police work, and the design of appropriate methods to control the police. Public perception of the police was influenced by media portrayals. Unfortunately, these images may not have been accurate or complete portrayals of what it was like to be a police officer or of the practices and challenges of a police department. It must be remembered that the ratings-driven media often dwell myopically on the more sensational aspects of policing rather than providing a wide-angle view. However, public opinion polls provided us with a sense of Americans' attitudes toward the police and the jobs they were performing.

Police commanders, like politicians, should take the results of these polls seriously. They define the areas of success and failure of the officers' and agencies' efforts. It is far easier to change or modify an opinion if the basis of that opinion is known and if the subgroups holding the strongest attitudes are identified. Whether a decision is made to change enforcement strategies, directed services (services targeted to a specific location, such as victim or child services or social service referrals), or tactical approaches, those who are most directly affected by police actions will hold the strongest opinions. Educating community members on the reasons for certain crime-fighting strategies, whether conducted in secret or community-based, will help sway public opinion and public acceptance of the police role. Any growth in public acceptance and approval of the police will help define police work more positively and will encourage community members to become part of the efforts rather than observers or impediments. As of 1999, police departments were systematically surveying community residents and businesspersons to better understand their concerns with crime and disorder as well as their assessment of the police. This information regularly shaped police policy and deployment in major cities like Chicago and Philadelphia. If agency managers are going to take seriously the consumers' perspective, then they will need to develop and administer methods to effectively supervise the officers. The supervision effort must come from within the agency and must serve to control the police officers. If this effort fails, history has demonstrated that the control of the police will come from outside the department and could come from political or community forces. It is far better to develop mechanisms that satisfy the needs of all parties rather than wait until some outside force dictates a form of oversight. Early identification of potentially problem officers, a strong review of reports, and a fair system of rewards and progressive discipline can encourage appropriate behavior and control the unwanted and unnecessary actions of police officers. Similarly, routine inspections and analysis of policy compliance can guide the direction of the agency. One way to strengthen the efforts of the agency and to foster public support is to assure that hiring and promoting of officers results in a force that represents the community.

Representing the Community in Police Employment

The racial, ethnic, and gender makeup of the agency helps define the quality of police work. Certainly, an important consideration in the recruitment, selection, and promotion of officers is the changing composition and role of the community. Officers who can relate to the citizens help form a necessary foundation for the department. As citizens play more important roles in community policing and problem-solving, they often look to an officer whom they know or to whom they can relate. It is certainly in the best interest of the department to have police officers reflect the ethnicity, gender, and philosophy of the community members they serve. In turn, although agencies can no longer discriminate against a member of any cognizable group, including women and minorities, it is also important to search out candidates who will best represent the police department. A balanced police force helps foster a broader definition of police work. By the late 1990s, most major police departments actively recruited persons from the community to the police occupation. Recruiting efforts by the police focused on increasing the number of racial minorities and women in policing. The active campaign for such recruitment suggests that many agencies recognized the need to have the department reflect the social and demographic composition of the community.

Zero Tolerance in the Face of Rising Crime

The notion of zero-tolerance, aggressive policing arose from police managers and politicians who thought that individuals who committed lower-level offenses were also responsible for more serious criminal activity; they assumed that targeting and detaining offenders of minor crimes can prevent more serious crimes. Patrick Colquhoun, who was responsible for helping Robert Peel create an organized police force in London in 1829, originally applied this idea in the 1790s, when he advocated the targeting of such crimes as public intoxication, gambling, and other minor offenses to deter serious criminal behavior. The "Bow Street Runners," a group of semi-organized police that emerged in the dock districts of London prior to Peel's creation of the New Police, operated under such principles. The theme of aggressive order maintenance as a police function has remained with the police throughout their history.

In some areas, including New York City, a zero-tolerance approach was undertaken in the mid-1990s to target low-level crimes, including panhandling, car window washing, public intoxication, excessive noise, and jaywalking. Along with zero tolerance, agencies held their managers responsible for the development of other crime-specific strategies. Perhaps the best-known project, COMPSTAT, relied on gathering timely, accurate crime information that was in turn used by the command staff to understand the areas' crime problems and to design strategies to attack specific problems. This outcome-based policing model went beyond community policing and was adopted by many agencies. However, any strains that may exist between communities and problem-oriented policing on the one hand, and zero-tolerance policing on the other, have yet to be resolved. Clearly, these styles of policing may be important for both defining what the police should do and how the community and government can oversee police practices.

The Police and Private Security—Beyond Public Policing

Policing in the twenty-first century will take many forms and cover a far wider range of actors than in earlier decades. Policing is thought to occupy the attention of those public officials charged with the imposition of the law, but in reality there are several other occupations that are charged with "policing" in the broadest sense of the term. Private policing has been available to those who could afford it since watchmen were hired in the early nineteenth century by businesses, shipping docks, and railroads to protect their goods. The demand for private policing has increased dramatically over the years, and in the twenty-first century there will probably be more than four times as many private police as public police.

The duties of the private police include many that are similar to those of the public police, but they have limited authority to use force. The most common image of the private police is the security guard. Most private police do fall into this category, guarding buildings, businesses, and homes. Many of these individuals are not well trained yet still serve as the eyes and ears of the public police. Some of those who work as private police may be off-duty police officers. While these people are trained officers, the distinction between public and private may become blurred. The private police also work in other capacities, including risk managers, bodyguards, and neighborhood-watch specialists. Many of these positions require sophisticated training and problem-solving skills. Private police also serve as security forces for our nuclear facilities. These private police forces contract with the Department of Energy and are trained to stop domestic terrorism on the sites. They are some of the best trained police in the country.

BIBLIOGRAPHY

Bayley, David. *Police for the Future*. New York: Oxford University Press, 1994.

Bittner, Egon. *The Functions of Police in Modern Society*. Chevy Chase, Md.: National Institute of Mental Health, 1970.

———. "Legality and Workmanship." In *Control in the Police Organization*, edited by M. Punch. Cambridge, Mass.: MIT Press, 1983.

Buerger, Michael. "The Challenge of Reinventing Police and Community." In *Police Innovation and Control of the Police*, edited by David Weisburd and Craig Uchida. New York: Springer-Verlag, 1993.

Carte, G. E., and Elaine H. Carte. *Police Reform in the United States*. Berkeley: University of California Press, 1975.

Critchley, Thomas A. *A History of the Police in England and Wales, 1000–1966*. London: Constable, 1967.

Cunningham, William C., and Todd H. Taylor. *The Hallcrest Report: Private Security and Police in America*. Portland, Oreg.: Chancellor, 1985.

Fogelson, R. *Big City Police*. Cambridge, Mass.: Harvard University Press, 1977.

Goldstein, Herman. *Problem-Oriented Policing*. New York: Free Press, 1990.

Greene, Jack R., Geoffrey P. Alpert, and P. Sykes. "Values and Culture in Two American Police Departments." *Contemporary Criminal Justice* 8, no. 3 (August 1992): 183–207.

Haller, Mark H. "Historical Roots of Police Behavior: Chicago, 1890–1925." *Law and Society Review* 10, no. 2 (winter 1976): 303–323.

Kappeler, Victor, Richard Sluder, and Geoffrey P. Alpert. *Forces of Deviance: The Dark Side of Policing*. Prospect Heights, Ill.: Waveland Press, 1998.

Kelling, George, and Catherine Coles. *Fixing Broken Windows*. New York: Free Press, 1996.

Lane, Roger. "Urban Police and Crime in Nineteenth Century America." In *Crime and Justice*, edited by Norval Morris and Michael Tonry. Chicago: University of Chicago Press, 1980.

Miller, Wilbur R. "Police Authority in London and New York City, 1830–1870." *Journal of Social History* 2 (winter 1975): 81–101.

Reiner, Robert. *The Politics of the Police*. Brighton, Sussex, England: Wheatsheaf Books, 1985.

Shearing, Clifford D. "The Relationship Between Public and Private Policing." In *Modern Policing*, edited by Michael

Tonry and Norval Morris. Chicago: University of Chicago Press, 1992.

Skolnick, Jerome H. *Justice Without Trial.* 2d ed. New York: Wiley, 1975.

Skolnick, Jerome H., and James J. Fyfe. *Above the Law: Police and the Excessive Use of Force.* New York: Free Press, 1993.

Stark, Rodney. *Police Riots.* Belmont, Calif.: Focus, 1972.

Terrill, Richard J. "Civilian Oversight of the Police Complaints Process in the United States: Concerns, Developments and More Concerns." In *Complaints Against the Police,* edited by Andrew J. Goldsmith. Oxford, England: Clarendon, 1991.

Walker, Samuel, and Betsy Wright. *Citizen Review of the Police, 1994: A National Survey.* Washington, D.C.: Police Executive Research Forum, 1994.

Wilson, James Q. *Varieties of Police Behavior.* Cambridge, Mass.: Harvard University Press, 1968.

JACK R. GREENE
GEOFFREY P. ALPERT

See also **Crime and Punishment in American History; Criminal Justice System; Crime, Legal Definitions of; Prisons; Private Security; Radio: Military and Police Uses; Texas Rangers; Urban Violence; Weapons.**

COMMUNITY POLICING

Community policing has attained popularity more rapidly and more completely than any other concept in the history of criminal justice. On the eve of the millennium the U.S. government had established a bureaucracy, the Office of Community Oriented Policing Services, and declared that it would be a national priority to put one hundred thousand new community police officers on the street. Sensitive to both the public pressure to "do something" about crime and the rhetorical attractiveness of community policing, virtually every police agency in the United States now claims to be engaged in some form of community policing.

In some police departments the transition to community policing has occurred almost instantaneously. At the typical celebratory press conference, the transition is symbolized by the opening of a "ministation" in a troubled neighborhood (complete with an appearance by the politician in whose district it is located) or, at minimum, the display of a matched pair of physically fit bicycle patrol officers. In other police departments, the conversion to community policing reflects genuine changes not only in agency philosophy, training, and practice but in the very structure of the agency as well. A close look at police departments across the United States (and many others in Canada, England, and eastern and western Europe) reveals that, though many claim to be doing community policing, both what they do and how they do it vary tremendously.

The ability of community policing to encompass so many diverse forms in its realization is the direct product of profound ambiguities in its definition. Scholars who have taken the problem of defining community policing seriously have variously argued that we should understand community policing as a philosophy, ideology, strategy, program, evolutionary process, and ongoing project. Understood in one or more of these ways, the concept, scholars then go on to argue, may then be seen to embody three, four, seven, ten, or as many as a dozen elements, principles, meanings, or dimensions.

Incident-Driven Policing

Although this definitional anarchy makes it possible for virtually any police agency to declare that it is doing community policing, the practices that have become most prominently associated with it gain unity only when they are understood in contrast to what has come to be called 911 or incident-driven policing. This type of policing, made possible by the technologies of the automobile, the telephone, and the wireless radio, is marked by a police force trained, managed, and organized to respond rapidly to citizen calls for help.

Occasionally described unkindly as "dial-a-cop" policing, it has placed police at the direct call of individual citizens. Indeed, the enormous clientele for this form of policing has caused police to develop increasingly sophisticated systems to receive citizens' calls for service, locate calls geographically, and deploy officers promptly to respond to citizen requests for service.

Although it is hard to imagine a more democratic or egalitarian form of policing than one that is ordered and dominated by direct citizen requests, the criticisms of this approach to policing have accumulated over time. Chief among them is that, although incident-driven policing, as it grew, became both more sophisticated and efficient, crime seemed to be unaffected by it. Beginning in the early 1970s research in Kansas City and elsewhere showed that neither increasing the number of officers on random motor patrol nor the speed of their response had much effect on reducing crime. Subsequent research by the RAND Corporation showed that detectives, who, like patrol officers, merely responded to crime "reactively," were by and large unlikely to solve a crime unless a witness at the scene told them "whodunit." To this mix of devastating criticism was added the charge that police officers who spend their working life responding to calls for service in a community were nevertheless isolated from it by being encapsulated in their patrol cars. It was alleged that, because they responded to neighborhood incidents through centralized dispatch and were governed by uniform agency policies created by a centralized administration, police officers not only failed to understand the context of the problems they confronted but also lacked the interest or ability to deal with their root causes.

The New Model

As a result of these criticisms, advocates of community policing put forth a vision of policing that can best be described as everything that 911, incident-driven, dial-a-cop policing was not. The community police officer would not be isolated from the community, but would be out of his or her patrol car, on the street, and in the homes and workplaces. Residents of the community would work in partnership with them. Where the incident-driven police officer reacted to crime by attempting to apprehend criminals, the community police officer would work to prevent crime by eliminating the problems that caused it. Where the 911 responder was directed to respond to complaints forwarded by central dispatch and handle them according to uniform agency policy and priority, the community police officer was not only required to discern the real needs of the community but was, in terms commonly used by advocates of the practice, empowered to engage "proactively" in innovative and nontraditional approaches suited to the special needs of individual communities. As scholars, practitioners, and advocates and critics alike have amply noted, this understanding of community policing, and its envisioned changes in police practice, relies on substantial doses of faith, philosophy, and ideology along with its envisioned changes in police practice.

Does Community Policing Work?

Because community policing is usually described as in the process of evolving and is typically implemented in addition to rather than as a replacement for incident-driven policing, it is not possible to establish either that it does or does not work. There have been numerous studies of particular community policing programs. However,

to further complicate the evaluation problem, community policing programs of different types advance different standards by which they should be judged. In addition to reducing crime and apprehending criminals, community policing programs often claim that their objective is to prevent crime, reduce citizens' fear of crime, reduce calls for service, improve relations between community and police, and improve police officer morale.

Those programs that have targeted street disorder have shown that police can reduce disorder and create street environments in which pedestrians feel safer. There is also evidence that community policing programs can improve community attitudes toward police and reduce citizens' fear of crime. There is some evidence that officers assigned to community policing tasks have higher morale than those who are not, but it is unclear whether this increase in morale will outlive the novelty of the nontraditional programs. However, the evidence that community policing actually reduces crime is, at most, minimal and subject to severe research design limitations.

However community policing evolves and whatever we come to learn about the effectiveness of its programs and tactics, there is no question that it has stimulated a great variety of experimentation with alternatives to incident-driven policing. It is nevertheless likely that, for the foreseeable future, incident-driven policing—dispatching police officers to respond directly to citizen calls for help—will remain the major way of getting police work done. It is equally likely that the community policing movement's philosophies, strategies, and tactics will ultimately complement those of incident-driven policing.

Three themes hold the most promise. The first is the philosophical conviction that policing can be improved by collaborative and cooperative partnerships, either with the community or with interest groups within it. The second is the strategic approach of problem solving as opposed to law enforcement. Problem solving urges police to understand the sources of the problems that citizens ask them to deal with and experiment with methods other than arrest or rapid patrol response. The third is the tactic of giving great attention through foot patrol and other mechanisms to minor crimes, incivilities, and disorder, which threaten the quality of life in public areas. Whether these three elements or still other strategies will ultimately survive the evolution of community policing remains to be seen.

BIBLIOGRAPHY

Goldstein, Herman. *Problem-Oriented Policing.* Philadelphia: Temple University Press, 1990.

Greene, Jack R., and Stephen Mastrofski, eds. *Community Policing: Rhetoric or Reality?* New York: Praeger, 1988.

Greenwood. Peter W., and Joan Petersillia. *The Criminal Investigation Process.* Vol. 1, *Summary and Implications.* Santa Monica, Calif.: RAND, 1975.

Kelling, George L., et al. *The Kansas City Preventive Patrol Experiment: A Summary Report.* Washington, D.C.: Police Foundation, 1974.

Rosenbaum, Dennis P., ed. *The Challenge of Community Policing: Testing the Promises.* Thousand Oaks, Calif.: Sage, 1994.

U.S. Bureau of Justice Assistance. *Understanding Community Policing: A Framework for Action.* Washington, D.C.: U.S. Bureau of Justice Assistance, 1994.

CARL B. KLOCKARS

See also **Private Security; Suburban Violence; Urban Violence; Vigilantism.**

POLICE BRUTALITY

Police brutality is the deliberate use by police of more force than is necessary to accomplish the legitimate police missions of subduing violent persons, apprehending criminal suspects, or protecting life and public order.

Charges of police brutality have been a constant in American society, but it has never been possible to determine with precision how often or where it occurs. It is likely, however, that police brutality today happens with less frequency than has been true in the past, when, in some places, it was openly a feature of police policy. In the Reconstruction South local police and sheriffs often were active participants in lynchings and other acts of racial violence. In the late nineteenth century one of New York's most celebrated police officials was Alexander "Clubber" Williams, who was nicknamed for the policing technique he most favored and with which he accumulated 358 brutality complaints, 244 of which resulted in fines against him. Far from affecting his career negatively, however, Williams's brutality helped him rise to the rank of inspector and to gain command of the police precinct in what is now Times Square in New York City. In the early twentieth century, the Los Angeles Police Department (LAPD) created a Strong-Arm Squad and a Red Squad, which dealt brutally with labor demonstrators and communists. Later, LAPD officers were dispatched hundreds of miles to California's borders to beat back Depression-era migrants to the Golden State. In the 1960s the nation was shocked by the fire hoses, clubs, and po-

lice dogs deployed against peaceful civil rights activists by Chief "Bull" Conner of the Birmingham (Alabama) Police Department and other southern police officials and by Chicago mayor Richard Daley's defense of the police beatings of demonstrators at the 1968 Chicago Democratic National Convention. In the 1970s the U.S. Justice Department sued Philadelphia mayor Frank Rizzo for encouraging an official policy of police brutality. In short, officially approved brutality has been a historical feature of U.S. policing.

Brutality still occurs, but it typically involves no complicity by police administrators, who punish it harshly when they discover it. The notorious beating and forcible sodomizing of Abner Louima in a police station in Brooklyn, New York, in 1997, for example, resulted in the arrests of four officers, severe discipline for many others suspected of doing nothing to prevent it or failing to provide information about it, and the disgraced removal of all the command and supervisory staffs, ranging from sergeants up through an assistant chief.

Brutality may be distinguished from other unnecessary force, which typically occurs when officers' incompetence, insensitivity, or haste in dealing with volatile situations helps to create real violence where there previously had existed only the potential for violence. Two representative illustrations help to clarify the distinctions between these two types of force.

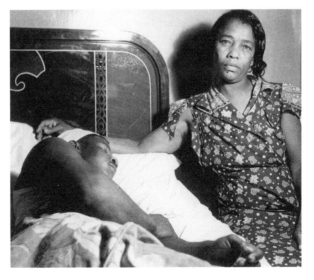

A woman stands next to the bed of an African American man injured by police brutality in the Bedford-Stuyvesant section of Brooklyn, New York City, in the 1940s. CORBIS/JOSEPH SCHWARTZ COLLECTION

An Example of Brutality

A police officer attempts to stop a traffic violator. Upon seeing the officer's red lights in his rearview mirror, the motorist accelerates and flees at high speed. Surprised and angered at this assault on his authority, the officer calls for assistance and gives chase. The chase ends when the motorist loses control of his car and strikes a retaining wall. The motorist flees on foot, but the original officer and two colleagues apprehend him. After he is handcuffed, the motorist curses the officers. En route to the police station, the officers stop their cars in a dark place and beat up the motorist to teach him the costs of fleeing from and resisting the police. They then explain away the injuries they have inflicted on the motorist by suggesting in their reports that the injuries must have occurred in the accident that ended the chase. Their assault on this individual is a case of brutality: it was deliberate, served no legitimate purpose, and was covered up by false reports.

An Example of Unnecessary Force

Several officers respond to a report that an apparently deranged man is waving a knife and shouting epithets at pedestrians on a busy street. When the officers arrive, they discover that, although the man has not actually attacked anybody, he has been loudly demanding that people stay away from him and warning of God's imminent revenge against sinners. The recommended procedure in such cases requires officers to clear the immediate area of bystanders, to remain at a safe distance, and to designate one officer to attempt, in a conciliatory and nonconfrontational way, to "talk the man down" and to take as much time as necessary in doing so. Assume that the officers in this example have received no such training and, instead, attempt to intimidate the man into submission, as police are trained to do with rational offenders. They draw and point their guns and approach the man, shouting at him to drop his knife. The man backs away, waving the knife as he does. Soon, he finds himself against a wall surrounded by several officers, who are shouting at him, and a barking police dog. One officer decides to reach in and grab the man's knife, but the man sees this and attempts to run. The remaining officers see him coming toward them with knife in hand, and they respond by firing. The man falls, shot eighteen times by four officers. The police chief defends the officers' actions by pointing out that the officers

fired only when they saw that their lives were endangered. Advocates for the mentally ill might point out, in this case, that the man had hurt nobody and argue that the officers themselves created this dangerous "final frame" (a phrase coined by Arnold Binder and Peter Scharf) by failing to adhere to widely accepted standards for dealing with the mentally and emotionally disturbed.

This shooting is a case of unnecessary force because, despite their presumably good intentions, these officers forced a confrontation in a way that violated police industry standards and that greatly increased the probability of bloodshed.

Distinctions Between Brutality and Unnecessary Force

For both theoretical and practical reasons, it is critical to understand the differences between brutality and unnecessary force that these two examples help to illustrate. The accompanying table summarizes these differences and indicates that brutality and unnecessary force may be differentiated along the dimensions of purpose, the settings in which the incidents typically occur, the mental state of the officers involved, and the typical causes of each incident.

Purpose. The example of brutality illustrates two purposes typically served by police brutality: retribution and deterrence. The beating that these officers gave the motorist was their way of getting even for what they saw as a challenge to their authority. The beating also served a purpose as a deterrent: the officers were teaching this person that the penalties for challenging police authority were high and would begin immediately on apprehension, rather than after adjudication in a courtroom. As John Van Maanen notes, brutality is often precipitated when officers who are abusive perceive conscious affronts to their authority. In such circumstances officers may use force to rapidly clarify the protocol for citizens' interactions with the police. From the perspective of some officers, the deterrent effect of harsh reactions to the behavior of such individuals should be permanent, as well as immediate. "Any cop who takes guff from anybody on the street gives them a license to abuse other cops. The best favor you can do for the people you work with is to let the mutts know that there's a price to pay for giving the police a bad time," were the words used by a police veteran when questioned about the use of force. At the same time, Van Maanen asserts, such officers un-

Key Differences Between Police Brutality and Unnecessary Force

Variable Factor	Brutality	Unnecessary Force
Purpose	Retribution; deterrence; substitute for or supplement to official punishment; evidence collection	Used to overcome resistance or resolve police emergency
Typical Setting	Private, without witnesses	Public places, usually with witnesses
Officers' Mental State	Angry or deliberate	Desperation
Causes	Pressure to "produce"; encouragement or tolerance by government and public; absence of accountability; individual malice	Poor supervision; poor training; insensitivity; absence of accountability

derstand that some affronts to their authority are not real choices because they emanate from persons whose behavior is attributable to madness, drunkenness, or other mitigating circumstances. In such cases there is no lesson to be taught, so that even abusive officers are not likely to respond with violence.

Jerome H. Skolnick and James J. Fyfe have suggested that police administrators and political leaders may encourage or tolerate brutality as a general deterrent, as well as an immediate deterrent to incurring disrespect from the offender. The logic is that if the criminal element knows that apprehension by the police is likely to result in summary punishment—or even death—they will choose another jurisdiction as their base of operations. While serving as Philadelphia's mayor from 1972 to 1979, Frank Rizzo repeatedly urged his police officers to be aggressive, sometimes even indirectly through his statements to reporters. He made statements such as "I'm going to make Attila the Hun look like a faggot" and "The way to treat criminals is *spacco il capa*" (to bust their heads), in an attempt to suggest that brutality was an effective crime-fighting technique. However much we may deplore such messages, the fact that brutality usually affects only the most unsympathetic people sometimes means that there is a tendency to overlook specific charges of brutality on grounds that the people making them got what they deserved.

In other cases brutality may serve as a substitute for or supplement to official punishment. When, as is sometimes the case, police officers perceive the court system as an obstacle to achieving justice, some officers may be tempted to extract "street justice" by brutalizing those arrested or, alternatively, by brutalizing the offenders rather than arresting them.

An additional purpose of brutality is to collect police evidence, albeit improperly. Referring to the familiar movie character played by Clint Eastwood in a number of films, Carl Klockars describes the "Dirty Harry problem," which involves officers who use "dirty" means to achieve good ends. In this scenario officers brutalize suspects or others to obtain information that might help to save lives or solve crimes. This motive for giving the third degree led the U.S. Supreme Court to limit police interrogation tactics. In 1936 in *Brown v. Mississippi*, the Court ruled that confessions obtained from defendants by torture would not be admissible in criminal proceedings.

Unnecessary force, by contrast, typically is employed simply to get officers out of trouble that they did not anticipate before attempting to overcome resistance or to resolve a police emergency. This usually occurs in scenarios such as those described in the example and may have its roots in a phenomenon Fyfe calls "the split-second syndrome." This syndrome is a self-perpetuating fallacy of logic held by many police officers and administrators and is based on the assumptions that (1) no two police-citizen encounters are the same, (2) any after-the-fact criticism of an officer's behavior in such situations is unfair "Monday morning quarterbacking" of decisions made in great haste under great pressure, and (3) as long as the citizen escalates the encounter, the police are justified in responding with subduing force. Thus, for example, it would be argued that, since the shooting (in the example of unnecessary force) occurred in a situation that was not precisely the same as any other, it would be unfair to use any a priori standard to hold the officers accountable. Instead, it would be asserted, these officers had to make split-second decisions under the most dire circumstances because of the irrationality and actions of the person they shot. Further, it would be suggested that any criticism whatever of decisions such as these puts officers' lives at risk by discouraging them from proper decisiveness in the future. While these arguments are intuitively appealing, they overlook the fact that even though no two situations in any line of endeavor are identical, many occupations and professions—the military, airlines, emergency medicine, firefighting—have developed general principles that may be applied to a wide variety of circumstances. Such principles also have been developed in policing, perhaps most notably in the hostage and barricade protocols that have been used so successfully in the late twentieth century, such as the recently developed procedures for dealing with mentally and emotionally disturbed persons that stress negotiation and deescalation rather than confrontation.

Typical Setting. Police brutality usually takes place in the privacy of police facilities or in dark streets and alleys. Except in cases when officers are captured unaware on videotape, the brutality is not documented and cannot easily be proven. Thus, the officers who engage in such brutality can conceal it either by failing to report it or by categorizing it as "necessary force used in the face of vigorous resistance." Police brutality usually takes place in private, victimizes people who have provoked the police in some way or whose credibility is otherwise questionable, and usually produces injuries that may be ascribed to a legitimate use of force. Consequently it is hard to convince most people that brutality has occurred or that it was not somehow deserved. It was for this reason that the videotaped 1991 beating of Rodney King and

the publicized 1997 forced sodomizing of Abner Louima came as such a shock to most Americans. In the few seconds of the King videotape and in the unambiguously brutal injuries sustained by Louima—a ruptured colon and a ruptured bladder—there appeared some substantiation of allegations that had long been discredited by most white Americans. Whether the brutal treatment of King and Louima was typical of U.S. police practices is another question; since officers who engage in brutality do their best to keep it a secret, there is no reliable method of determining how often or where it occurs.

Since unnecessary force typically is the unintended consequence of sloppy police interventions into public emergencies, it often occurs in full view of witnesses, at the very least those who have called the police for assistance. Hence, it probably is more likely to be a matter of public concern and debate than unsubstantiated claims of brutality and to bring criticism of the police, who have been guilty not of malice, but rather of a lack of sophistication and sensitivity.

Officers' Mental State. Some police brutality is expressive and consists largely of a demonstration of outrage at the arrogance of the offender or the heinous nature of the offenses he or she is believed to have committed. This apparently was the case in New Orleans in 1990 when a group of police officers captured Adolph Archie, a man who had shot and killed a well-liked police officer who was attempting to arrest him for robbery. Instead of bringing Archie to the normal booking facility, four officers took him to a quiet police station. When they left forty-five minutes later, Archie had

> two skull fractures, a broken larynx, and fractures of the cheekbones. He had bleeding testicles, and his teeth had been kicked in. The injuries to Archie's face varied in size and were . . . "characteristic of those made with a shod foot." His entire body had been . . . "exposed to blunt trauma." Archie died twelve hours later.
>
> (Skolnick and Fyfe 1993, p. 34)

Certainly, Archie's death carried a strong deterrent message, but it is doubtful that violence like this was motivated entirely by such deliberate thinking. As one examines incidents of police brutality, however, it becomes clear that many officers have acted coldly and deliberately and have engaged not in expressive violence but in purely instrumental violence that is impersonal and carefully designed to achieve some other goal. Somewhere in the middle of the continuum between the two extremes of fury and calculated deliberation, for example, is the beating of Rodney King. This incident apparently involved police anger at King's impertinence, but it is reasonable to conclude that it also involved what Van Maanen would regard as "remedial learning": the message is that running from the police carries a price. Further, it is likely that the instrumental actions of the officers (and the citizens who participated with them) in *Brown v. Mississippi* in 1936 involved virtually no anger. In that case three black men (Ellington, Brown, and Shields) were convicted of murder after a one-day trial. The only evidence against them was their own confessions, which, according to the U.S. Supreme Court decision, were obtained under the following circumstances:

> Upon [Ellington's] denial, [several white men] seized him, and with the participation of the deputy they hanged him by a rope to the limb of a tree, and, having let him down, they hung him again, and when he was let down the second time, and he still protested his innocence, he was tied to a tree and whipped, and still declining to accede to the demands that he confess, he was finally released, and he returned with some difficulty to his home, suffering intense pain and agony. The record of the testimony shows that the signs of the rope on his neck were plainly visible during the so-called trial. A day or two thereafter the said deputy, accompanied by another, returned to the home of the said defendant and arrested him, and departed with the prisoners to the jail in an adjoining county, but went by a route which led into the state of Alabama; and while on the way, in that state, the deputy stopped and again severely whipped the defendant, declaring that he would continue the whipping until he confessed, and the defendant then agreed to confess to such a statement as the deputy would dictate, and he did so, after which he was delivered to jail.
>
> ... [Brown and Shields] were made to strip and they were laid over chairs and their backs were cut to pieces with a leather strap with buckles on it ... and in this manner the defendants confessed the crime, and, as the whippings progressed and were repeated, they changed or adjusted their confession in all particulars of detail so as to conform to the demands of their torturers.
>
> ... [W]ith reference to the whipping of defendant Ellington, and in response to the inquiry as to how severely he was whipped, the deputy stated, "Not too much for a negro; not as much as I would have done if it were left to me". ... The facts are not only undisputed, they are admitted, and admitted to have been done by officers of the state, in conjunction with other participants.

The overwhelming issues in the *Brown* case are racial, and the facts speak of the great hatred underlying it. But it is far more than that; it is perhaps the worst example in U.S. history of the use of deliberate and methodical brutality to achieve the goal of rendering what the police and their cohorts saw as quick and deserved justice.

These considerations usually are not at play when officers use unnecessary force. Instead, such officers' minds usually are occupied with questions about how to resolve situations for which they have received no training or other preparation. Desperation commonly is a more accurate description of their mental states than deliberation.

Causes. The most important variable related to brutality and excessive force is cause. Once we know what causes a problem, we can begin to solve it. One reason that brutality exists is that the public, elected officials, and police leaders often are extremely ambivalent about the messages they send to officers in the field. On the one hand, we want the police to follow the law and to treat citizens with respect and dignity; on the other, we demand that they do everything possible to rid our neighborhoods of crime and disorder and to bring guilty parties to justice.

An anecdote recounted long ago by professor Lloyd George Sealy at John Jay College of Criminal Justice is illustrative. Shortly after the 1964 civil disorders in New York City, Sealy, then a distinguished New York City police captain, was assigned to be the first African American commander of central Harlem's Twenty-eighth Precinct. Within a few weeks at his new assignment, Sealy received a very serious and well documented brutality complaint against two officers whose careers had been marked by a long succession of unsubstantiated allegations of abusive conduct. Sealy immediately filed departmental charges against the two officers and took them off the busy foot beat they had patrolled together. Within a few days a group of community representatives—including ministers, merchants, and residents—came to the police station to meet Sealy and presented him with petitions (signed by several thousand citizens) demanding the officers be reassigned to their beat. "I don't understand," a surprised Sealy protested. "All I ever hear about these two officers is that they have beaten somebody up." That might be true, he was told, but these officers knew *who* to beat up and were the best in the precinct at keeping the streets safe at all hours.

This story illustrates that police are under great pressure to produce peace on the streets and that, whether in response to open encouragement like Mayor Rizzo's call to bust heads or the silent blessing of leaders like those who surprised Captain Sealy, they may be tempted to bend the law. But such officers can do so successfully only if they are not called to task for their misconduct. Where there is an absence of accountability, officers inclined to abuse have a license to do as they please.

Proper mechanisms for police accountability define appropriate guidelines for police interaction with citizens and handling emergencies, encourage citizens to complain when they believe that they have been wronged by police, and provide for objective investigation and review of complaints and use of force by officers. When accompanied by personnel practices that work to bar candidates of questionable character from policing, these procedures and practices are likely to reduce brutality to a minimum. Even then there is no way to absolutely control officers' behavior or to eliminate malice.

While poor supervision and training—the absence of adequate policies and instruction for field officers—often are at least part of the reason some police departments have reputations for brutality, these administrative inadequacies are much more clearly connected to the unnecessary use of force by police. This type of force consists of mistakes, incompetence, or insensitivity to cultural norms or ethnic differences, often by officers who have the best intentions but who simply do not know how to identify and employ the best methods to resolve the potentially violent situations that are part of police work. Once such mistakes are made, they often are perpetuated by the police commanders and managers who write off as unavoidable the bloodshed they cause. Hence, the best way to reduce unnecessary force is to provide officers with state-of-the-art information for dealing with sensitive and potentially violent situations.

BIBLIOGRAPHY

Astor, Gerald. *The New York Cops: An Informal History.* New York: Scribners, 1971.

Binder, Arnold, and Peter Scharf. "The Violent Police-Citizen Encounter." *Annals of the American Academy of Political and Social Science* 452 (November 1980).

Cipriano, Ralph, and Tom Infeld. "It Was a Long and Colorful Career." *Philadelphia Inquirer,* 17 July 1991.

Davis, Chief. "A Dissenting Opinion on 'Third Degree.'" *Proceedings of the International Association of Chiefs of Police, Seventeenth Annual Convention, 10–13 May 1910.* P. 96. Reprinted in *The Blue and the Brass,* edited by Donald C. Dilworth. Gaithersburg, Md.: International Association of Chiefs of Police, 1976.

Domanick, Joe. *To Protect and Serve: The LAPD's Century of War in the City of Dreams.* New York: Pocket, 1994.

Fyfe, James J. "The Split-Second Syndrome and Other Determinants of Police Violence." In *Violent Transactions: The Limits of Personality,* edited by Anne T. Campbell and John J. Gibbs. New York: Basil Blackwell, 1986.

Klockars, Carl. "The Dirty Harry Problem." *Annals of the American Academy of Political and Social Science* 452 (November 1980).

Murphy, Gerard R. *Special Care: Improving the Police Response to the Mentally Disabled.* Washington, D.C.: Police Executive Research Forum, 1986.

Paolantonio, S. A. *Frank Rizzo: The Last Big Man in the Big City of America.* Philadelphia: Camino, 1998.

Richardson, James F. *The New York Police: Colonial Times to 1901.* New York: Oxford University Press, 1970.

Skolnick, Jerome H., and James J. Fyfe. *Above the Law: Police and the Excessive Use of Force.* New York: Free Press, 1993.

Van Maanen, John. "The Asshole." In *Policing: A View from the Street,* edited by Peter K. Manning and John Van Maanen. New York: Random House, 1978.

JAMES J. FYFE
ROBERT KANE

See also **Government Violence Against Citizens; Los Angeles Riots of 1992; Weapons: Stun or Shock Devices.**

POLICE USE OF FORCE

In 1970 the sociologist Egon Bittner noted that the core of police work is coercion and that the police are distinguished by their monopoly on the legitimate use of force to do this work. Bittner makes the point that all the service functions of the police—such as directing traffic, aiding the sick and injured, and finding lost children—could easily be handled by other authorities. These duties, he suggested, are not the real work of the police; they are the province of the police only because nobody else is readily available seven days a week, twenty-four hours a day, to perform them. The real work of the police consists of using force or the threat of force to convince people to behave in ways that are consistent with the law and with public order. The police alone are empowered to use force to put an end to behavior that is violent, criminal, or disorderly. This task and the force used to accomplish it guarantee that police work will always be controversial and will always represent an ironic dilemma: the public authorizes and pays for a group of professionals whose job it is to regulate the conduct of the public, using force to do so whenever necessary. The public, at the same time, is very ambivalent about this authorization and historically has been skeptical about whether force is always used judiciously.

Legal Controls

Police authorization to use force does not come without limits. Police typically are expected to use the minimal amount of force necessary and, whenever possible, to avoid the use of force altogether. Indeed, William K. Muir has likened the police to politicians and has suggested that, like politicians, the most successful police officers are those who are able to coerce people to behave in acceptable ways without resorting to the use of force.

In the United States police use of force traditionally has been guided by criminal statutes. These laws define only the outer limits of acceptable force and are extremely vague and difficult to enforce. These laws are replete with words such as "reasonable" and "necessary" and are better described as homilies than as guides to action on the street in emergencies. Further, since these laws draw the distinction between criminal conduct and noncriminal behavior, they are enforceable only in the criminal courts, where evidentiary standards are stringent and where prosecutors and juries often find it difficult to apply the same rules to police behavior that are designed for criminal behavior. Relying on criminal courts to adjudicate the reasonableness of police use of force is further complicated by the lay juror's lack of expertise on professional police behavior.

All of this ambiguity is understandable. Most criminal trials involve relatively simple questions requiring simple "yes" or "no" answers: "Did the defendant steal the victim's car?" or "Did the defendant sell drugs to the undercover officer?" Since police officers are entitled to use some degree of force, in a trial in which police officers are the accused, a question of degree arises: "The defendants were allowed to use force, but did they use too much or just enough?" This typically is difficult to answer, but questions of whether professionals have exceeded the limits of their authority are not unique to the police. Whenever questions of professional misconduct are at issue, jurors must decide difficult questions of degree: Did a lawyer suborn perjury, or did he or she merely coach the client well? Was the accountant cheating, or did he or she merely take advantage of every legal loophole? In short, and regardless of whether the police are involved, the criminal law is neither an adequate guide to professional discretion nor a check on it.

Professional Standards

These shortcomings of criminal law became evident in the 1960s, when several riots in the United States followed controversial incidents involving use of force by police officers: in New York in 1964, riots followed the fatal shooting of a fifteen-year-old black boy by an off-duty police lieutenant; in 1965 a police attempt to subdue and arrest a black drunk-driving suspect led to the Watts riot in Los Angeles; in 1966 riots followed police shootings of young blacks in San Francisco and St. Louis; and in 1967 police shootings of young blacks precipitated riots in Jackson, Mississippi, and Tampa, Florida. President Lyndon Johnson appointed several blue-ribbon commissions to study the riots and related social upheaval. These investigators were surprised to find that there were, in essence, no professional guidelines for police use of force. By the late twentieth century, the police had become much more sophisticated in defining a continuum of use-of-force tactics appropriate for responding to different situations. Most police agencies in the United States train officers to employ no more force than is necessary by referring to scales of escalating force such as the following table shows.

Some observations may be made about this scale. First, it serves as a good illustration of why policing is controversial. The unpleasantness described in the table is at the core of the police role; thus police work may be seen as hurting people. Second, it is not always possible for officers to begin their encounters with citizens by engaging in the lowest degrees of force; persuasion typically is not appropriate when officers confront armed robbers. Third, since officers represent the state and the law, they have an obligation not to lose their encounters with those who resist. As the table indicates, when citizens resist by punching officers, officers are entitled to use clubs in response; when citizens attack officers with knives or clubs, officers are under no obligation to meet them with equal force but are entitled to shoot them. Fourth, the scale changes with technology and practice. Most people would not consider the use of a police dog to be a form of force, for example, but for several years the canine unit of the Los Angeles Police Department inflicted more hospitalizing injuries than the rest of the police department combined. Finally, this scale does not give the police carte

547

Scale of Escalating Force Used by Police

Provocation by Citizen	Appropriate Police Responses
Minor Public Order Offenses Includes disorderly conduct, public drinking or gambling, loitering, street prostitution, and so on.	**Mere Presence** Simply by their uniformed appearance, police may discourage or terminate such offenses as traffic violations, public drinking, and disorderly conduct. If the mere presence of the police fails to obtain the desired results, officers typically resort to persuasion. **Persuasion** Verbal requests to end improper behavior or (in the case of traffic violations) to produce vehicle identification and driver's license (e.g., "Why don't you fellows break it up and go home?" "Good afternoon, ma'am. I'm afraid you were speeding. May I have your license and registration, please?"). If this fails, police typically resort to voice commands. **Voice Commands** Firmly stated directions rather than polite requests (e.g., "I asked you guys once to get off the corner. Now I'm telling you. If you don't leave right now, you will all be arrested." "Ma'am, this is not the place to argue. Give me your license and registration now, or I will have to arrest you, and you can give it to me in the police station.").
Minor Physical Resistance Failure or inability to move or to cease wrongful actions.	**Firm Grips** Use of hands, typically on forearms or shoulders, that do not cause injury or pain and that are designed to direct the movements of intoxicated people or spectators or to separate disputants.
Nonassaultive Resistance Resistance to officers through active but nonviolent means, such as wriggling.	**Pain Compliance** Typically, grips on arms, wrists, or other body parts designed to cause pain that ends when subjects comply and which cause no lasting injury.
Nonlethal Physical Force Assaults with fists or feet.	**Impact Weapons** Includes use of nightsticks, batons, billy clubs, and such nonlethal devices as chemical sprays and electronic dart guns.
Deadly Force Attacks on officers or others with force capable of killing or likely to kill (includes use of guns, knives, and other cutting instruments).	**Deadly Force** Police officers typically respond with firearms.

blanche. The primary obligation of police officers to protect life places upon them the obligation to avoid forcing confrontations that can be resolved only through the use of force and to approach potentially violent situations in ways that minimize the possibility that they will have to use force.

Technology

Considerable efforts have been made to develop new police technologies for restraining citizens in the most bloodless manners possible. Probably the most widely used of these are chemical sprays that temporarily cause the eyes and mucous membranes to burn and tear. Other less widely used devices include electronic guns that fire shocking darts that are attached to wires; electronic stun guns that, like cattle prods, are hand-held and cause shocks on contact; and a variety of alternatives to traditional police bullets (gun-fired "bean-bags," for example, are small sacks filled with pellets that are designed to knock down, rather than penetrate, their targets). All of these devices suffer from several problems:

They are not perfect. Deaths have occurred following use of sprays and shocking devices by the police. Although it is not clear whether these devices caused the deaths, their use has engendered considerable criticism and resistance.

They are of limited use as alternatives to the most deadly forms of police force. Since they must be used at close range and are not always effective, officers typically can use them in safety only when other officers are on the scene who can quickly resort to firearms in the event the lesser devices fail to stop the assailants.

Although they are intended as a less drastic alternative to severe forms of force, there is evidence that some officers have used them as an easy way out of situations that could have been resolved by even less intrusive means.

Police and an injured rioter in Newark, New Jersey, after a 1967 race riot. HULTON GETTY/LIAISON AGENCY

How Frequently Do the Police Use Force?

There is no accurate answer to the question of how often police use force. As part of its Uniform Crime Reporting System, the Federal Bureau of Investigation collects data on justifiable homicide by police, but it does not publish them, probably because the statistics have proven to be inaccurate. Some individual jurisdictions, however, have maintained detailed statistics on use of force, at least in its most extreme form—shootings by police. Figure 1 shows the number of persons shot and killed or wounded by New York City police between 1971 and 1997; the figures indicate that New York police became increasingly restrained in their use of weapons over this period. In 1971 New York City's 31,671 officers shot 314 persons— nearly one a day—of whom 93 died. In 1997, by contrast, the 38,328 officers shot 50 people—less than one a week— killing 20, less than one-fourth the total 1971 fatalities. Figures derived from these

data show that the annual rate at which New York City police officers shot people fell from 9.9 per 1,000 officers in 1971 to 1.3 per 1,000 officers in 1997.

Information that occasionally becomes available suggests that New York City's downward trend may be unusual. Figure 2 summarizes in three-year periods data from five large cities, including New York, studied by William A. Geller and Michael S. Scott. These calculations indicate that the rate of shootings per 1,000 officers decreased in Chicago and Houston from 1980 to 1991 but increased in Los Angeles during that same time period. The data from Philadelphia (available only for the years 1984 to 1991) show the shootings per 1,000 officers increased as well. Figure 2 also shows that shooting rates per 1,000 officers have varied dramatically across these cities, ranging from 1.9 per 1,000 (New York, 1995–1997) to 10.6 (Houston, 1980–1982).

FIGURE 1.   Persons Shot by New York City Police, 1971–1997

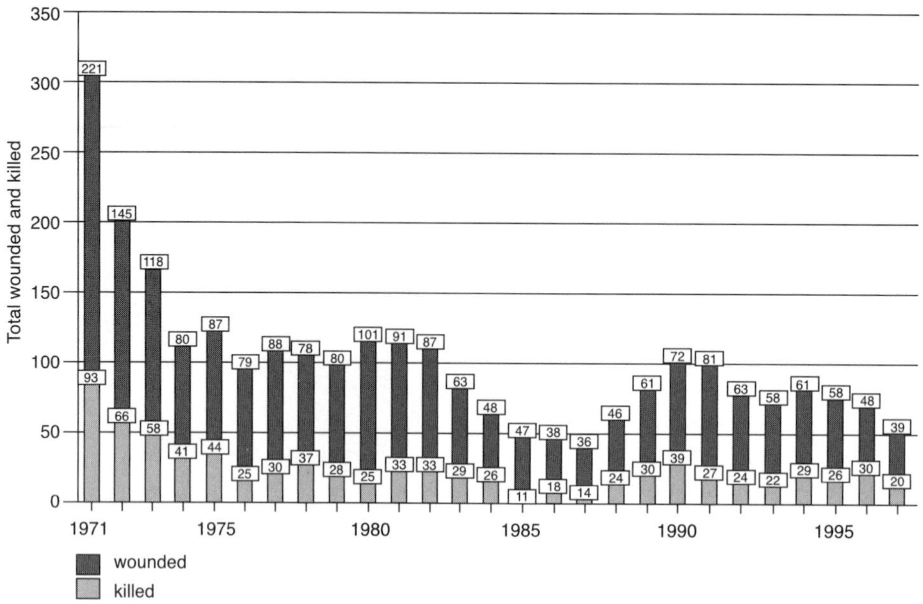

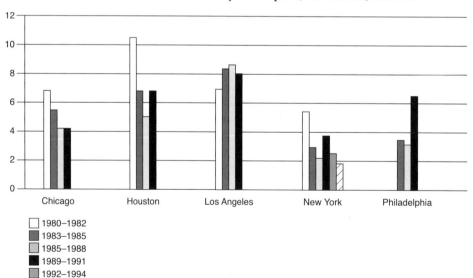

wounded
killed

SOURCE: New York City Police Department

There is no system for collecting data on lesser degrees of force, although a 1997 Justice Department study, by Lawrence A. Greenfeld and his colleagues, has provided some information. This report, based on interviews of 6,412 scientifically sampled Americans over the age of twelve, found that during 1996:

44,600,000 Americans had face-to-face contact with the police;

800,000 Americans were handcuffed but were subjected to no other types of force;

500,000 Americans "were hit, held, pushed, choked, threatened with a flashlight, restrained by a police dog, threatened or

FIGURE 2.   Annual Rate of Persons Shot by Police per 1,000 Officers, 1980–1997

1980–1982
1983–1985
1985–1988
1989–1991
1992–1994
1995–1997

SOURCE: Geller and Scott 1992; New York City Police Department

actually sprayed with chemical or pepper spray, threatened with a gun, or had some other form of force directed against them"; Males, minorities, and those under thirty were disproportionately represented, accounting, respectively, for 73 percent, 36 percent, and 57 percent of those handcuffed by the police (Greenfeld et al. 1997, pp. 12–13).

These findings are based upon surveys of U.S. households and do not include such high-risk groups as the homeless and persons incarcerated as a result of their contacts with police. Hence, they considerably understate the actual frequency of police-citizen contact and police use of force.

BIBLIOGRAPHY

Binder, Arnold, and Peter Scharf. "The Violent Police-Citizen Encounter." *Annals of the American Academy of Political and Social Science* 111 (November 1980).

Bittner, Egon. *The Functions of the Police in Modern Society.* Rockville, Md.: National Institute of Mental Health, 1970.

Fyfe, James J. "Police Use of Deadly Force: Research and Reform." *Justice Quarterly* 165 (June 1988).

———. "Shots Fired: An Analysis of New York City Police Firearms Discharges." Ph.D. diss., State University of New York at Albany. Ann Arbor, Mich.: University Microfilms, 1978.

———. "Training to Reduce Police-Civilian Violence." In *Police Violence,* edited by William Geller and Hans Toch. New Haven, Conn.: Yale University Press, 1996.

Geller, William A., and Michael S. Scott. *Deadly Force: What We Know.* Washington, D.C.: Police Executive Research Forum, 1992.

Greenfeld, Lawrence A., et al. *Police Use of Force: Collection of National Data.* Washington D.C.: U.S. Department of Justice, Bureau of Justice Statistics, 1997.

Muir, William K. *Police: Streetcorner Politicians.* Chicago: University of Chicago Press, 1977.

National Advisory Commission on Civil Disorders. *Report of the National Advisory Commission on Civil Disorders.* New York: Dutton, 1968.

President's Commission on Law Enforcement and Administration of Justice. *Task Force Report: The Police.* Washington D.C.: U.S. Government Printing Office, 1967.

Skolnick, Jerome H., and James J. Fyfe. *Above the Law: Police and the Excessive Use of Force.* New York: Free Press, 1993.

JAMES J. FYFE
ROBERT KANE

See also **Watts Riot; Weapons: Stun or Shock Devices.**

POLICE VIOLENCE

Police violence may be distinguished from police brutality in that police violence is officially sanctioned and authorized. From the victim's viewpoint, the distinction may seem semantic and irrelevant, since the victim suffers harm in either case. But from a social viewpoint, police violence indicates an even more serious problem than does police brutality. Because police violence is officially (although not always formally) approved, the likelihood of repetition is especially high. The legitimation of the violence by the government also adds a profound insult to the physical injury. Lastly, because the police (unlike, for example, motor vehicle clerks) are expected to act as moral exemplars, police violence sends a particularly disturbing message.

Historical Background

The founders of the American republic did not see law-enforcement violence as a distinct analytic category. To the founders, a tyrant who used soldiers or police to rob and murder citizens was very similar to a lone criminal, except that the tyrant had more resources. Violent abuses by British colonial law enforcement, such as the confiscation of property at gunpoint (including the attempted confiscation of firearms at Lexington and Concord) by Redcoats played a major role in precipitating the American Revolution. The U.S. Constitution includes many provisions designed to prevent law-enforcement violence—such as the controls on standing armies, the Second Amendment (preventing law enforcement from having a monopoly of force), and the Fifth Amendment's due process clause (implicitly prohibiting use of torture as an interrogation technique).

Victims

Historically, American law-enforcement violence has been directed most often against persons or groups perceived as deviant, and the violence has often been applauded as reinforcing social norms, especially in times of social stress and change. Particular targets of law-enforcement violence have included runaway or curfew-breaking slaves (the focus of the antebellum "slave patrols"), immigrants, strikers and other labor agitators (particularly in the late nineteenth and early twentieth centuries), antiwar activists (most notably during the Civil War, World War I, and the Vietnam War), other political dissidents, "hippies," racial minorities, sexual minorities, and religious minorities (such as Mormons in the nineteenth century and the Branch Davidians at Waco, Texas, in the late twentieth century).

A man being beaten by a policeman with a broken rifle in Lakewood, Colorado, July 1953. As the picture was taken the man fired a pistol bullet into the officer; immediately the other two officers opened fire on the man. Photographed by David Mathias and published on the front page of the *Denver Post*, 25 July 1953. LIBRARY OF CONGRESS

Protest marches or other large congregations of dissidents have often attracted police violence. Victims have included labor demonstrators (for example, at the Ford Motor Plant in Dearborn, Michigan, in 1937); civil rights demonstrators (for example, at Birmingham, Alabama, in 1963, where cattle prods and attack dogs were used), and abortion clinic protestors (in San Diego and Los Angeles, California, in 1989).

Types of Police Violence

Tacit Support for Third-Party Violence. In some cases, police or sheriff's departments may not formally participate in violence, but instead turn a deliberately blind eye so as to allow violence by mobs or organized groups such as the Ku Klux Klan or the Pinkerton Detectives. White-on-black race riots in the late nineteenth and early twentieth centuries often fit this pattern (for example, New York in 1900 and Detroit in 1943), as did the tolerance of Klan terror against critics of segregation up to and including the 1960s. Lynch mobs, which were common during the Jim Crow era, often included police officers and almost always enjoyed the tacit approval of the local police. More recently, the New York City Police Department failed to act to restrain black rioters carrying out a pogrom against the Hasidic Jewish community in the Crown Heights section of Brooklyn in 1991.

Police Riot. On rarer occasions, a "police riot" may take place, in which a large mass of police run wild and perpetrate indiscriminate assaults. The 1968 Democratic Convention in Chicago (in which both violent provocateurs and innocent bystanders were aggressively attacked) is one of the most famous police riots.

Police Gangsterism. At times, an entire police force may become so pervasively corrupted and violent that it often resembles a criminal gang, as was the case in New Orleans in the 1980s and early 1990s.

High-Speed Chases. While high-speed vehicular chases were unquestioned before the 1980s, they now generate great controversy because of the risks to innocent persons, as well as the triviality of the offenses that often precipitate the chase. Research by Geoffrey Alpert and his colleagues suggests that high-speed chases trigger an adrenaline rush and are frequently followed by unjustifiably severe use of force against suspects once the chase has ended. The Rodney King beating in Los Angeles in 1992 is a prominent, but by no means isolated, example.

A number of police departments have banned high-speed chases or authorized them only for certain offenses. Opponents of restrictions on high-speed pursuits argue that controls will increase the number of drivers who flee the police.

Interrogation Violence. One of the most pervasive forms of police violence in the nineteenth century, and much of the twentieth, was "the third degree"—the use of physical torture and other violence to extract "confessions" from suspects in custody. Starting in 1936 with the Scottsboro case (*Brown v. Mississippi*, 297 U.S. 278), the Supreme Court and the rest of the judiciary (particularly the New York Court of Appeals) began devoting increasing institutional energy to preventing suspects from being physically coerced into confession. As a result, while deceit and psychological coercion are commonly used to produce confessions, use of violence to produce confessions has become rare. (Violence upon apprehension, however—such as the use of "carotid control holds" (chokeholds) to restrain suspects, which has led to dozens of deaths from asphyxia, disproportionately of minorities—is still relatively common.)

Dynamic Entries. An increasingly common type of police violence is the "dynamic entry"—a violent break-in to a home or other building, typically to serve a search warrant. Dynamic entries are typically perpetrated by "SWAT teams" (see below), often result in the occupants of the home being held at gunpoint, and often are accompanied by extremely destructive searches. Dynamic entries to capture violent felons are the exceptions, while entries for the purpose of gathering evidence (usually searching for drugs or guns) are the norm. Dynamic entries are used much more often than in the relatively rare situations in which there is particular information suggesting that nonviolent service of a search warrant ("knock and announce") would endanger officer safety.

Police Militarization

A history of American police militarization that did not mention Los Angeles police chief Daryl Gates would be as incomplete as a history of communism that omitted Lenin. The first "Special Weapons Attack Team" was created by Gates in 1967, although the name was changed to "Special Weapons and Tactics" (SWAT) to make it more palatable to the public. More generally, Gates (following the path of his predecessor William Parker) emphasized a "war on crime" approach to policing, in which police officers were encouraged to act like an occupying army and in which great

---

The Donald Scott Case

On 12 October 1992 a combined force representing state and federal agencies (including the National Park Service, the Forest Service, the Drug Enforcement Administration, and the National Guard) broke into the home of southern California millionaire Donald Scott. The no-knock, late-night raid was designed supposedly to serve Scott with a search warrant so the officials could look for marijuana plants growing on his estate. Scott, meanwhile, could not possibly have had time to destroy the marijuana plants (alleged to be hidden in trees far from his home) even if the police had not broken in but merely demanded entry at the door. Scott, who, upon hearing the noise of the break-in, ran to the living room with his legally owned .38 revolver, was shot dead. The search yielded no evidence of drugs or illegal activity.

An investigation by the Ventura County, California, district attorney Michael Bradbury found that the basis of the warrant—a drug agent's claim that while in a surveillance plane one thousand feet above the ground, he saw individual marijuana plants concealed in leafy trees—had been fabricated. The district attorney also noted that the sheriff's department that participated in the raid had conducted an appraisal of the $5 million Scott ranch before the raid, apparently with the expectation that the ranch would be forfeited to the government.

The Scott case is a graphic, but not isolated, example of how changes in one part of the law-enforcement system (in this case the ability of law-enforcement agencies to generate major revenues through property forfeiture, an innovation resulting from the drug war in the 1980s) can have unintended consequences in promoting police violence.

---

emphasis was placed on the use of battering rams, helicopters, and other military weapons. Many civil libertarians argue that the concept of "policing as war" is antithetical to the system of peace officers maintaining order under a constitution.

At the close of the twentieth century, militarized law enforcement had become standard. Every one of the Federal Bureau of Investigation's fifty-six field offices had its own SWAT team, as did many other federal offices. Even the Department of Health and Human Services had a SWAT team, which carried out gunpoint raids on stores selling vitamins with improper labels. Paramilitary police units are nearly universal for large- and medium-sized city police departments, as well as the large majority of small-town (25,000 to 50,000 population) departments.

The U.S. military, particularly the National Guard, is pervasively involved in law enforcement, frequently participating in "dynamic entry" raids allegedly involving drugs. National Guard raids on public housing projects in Puerto Rico are routine, while militaristic assaults on public housing projects in the rest of the United States are increasingly common. Congressional creation of drug loopholes to the Posse Comitatus Act (*U.S. Code*, vol. 18, sec. 1835) have blurred the once-clear distinction between police and the military, and have been a major cause of the militarization of law enforcement. Another trend which began in Los Angeles and has proliferated nationally is that military equipment such as automatic rifles, machine pistols (particularly the Heckler and Koch MP-5), battering rams, and armored personnel carriers is now viewed as normal law-enforcement equipment.

The tendency to see law-enforcement problems through a military lens has resulted in numerous incidents of police violence. In Philadelphia in 1985, the police terminated a siege involving a group of criminals called MOVE by using a helicopter to drop a satchel bomb on the building where MOVE was encamped. The bomb killed seven adults and four children and also burned down sixty-one buildings, rendering homeless 236 residents of the low-income neighborhood, the same poor people who had long been terrorized by MOVE. In Ruby Ridge, Idaho, in 1992, a U.S. marshal killed a thirteen-year-old boy with machine-gun shot in the back, and an FBI sniper later killed the boy's mother while she stood in a doorway holding a baby. In Waco, Texas, in 1993, the Bureau of Alcohol, Tobacco, and Firearms il-legally procured the assistance of the Texas and Alabama National Guards to stage a military-style raid on a religious group known as the Branch Davidians, based on the failure of the cult's leader to comply with weapons registration laws. After the raid failed, a military-style siege ensued, until ultimately the FBI, implementing a plan created by the U.S. Army's Delta Force, assaulted the group with tanks and the chemical warfare agent CS.

Although American police are generally less violent than the police in most nondemocratic nations, police terrorism is a significant American export. As part of the "war on drugs," the United States continues a long-standing practice of providing substantial equipment, funding, and training to various Latin American paramilitary police units renowned for their ruthless violence and disregard for human rights.

Causes

Police violence is frequently justified on the grounds that contemporary criminals are much more violent and dangerous than in the past, and therefore scrupulous adherence to constitutional guarantees is a luxury that society can no longer afford. The justification was used in 1931, when the National Commission on Law Observance and Enforcement (the Wickersham Commission) condemned the widespread use of the third degree, and in the 1980s and 1990s, in response to criticisms of violence resulting from the war on drugs.

Police violence is facilitated by a code of silence, which encourages law-enforcement officers never to tell outsiders about misconduct, and by the practice of "testilying," through which law-enforcement officers perjure themselves to minimize assertions of police violence and shift blame to the allegedly aggressive victim. More generally, the foundation for law-enforcement violence is laid by public education programs, ranging from FBI press briefings to the DARE program (Drug Abuse Resistance Education, a program for schoolchildren invented by Daryl Gates), which aim to create a crisis atmosphere surrounding crime and to promote fear and loathing of those who are the targets of law-enforcement violence.

Citizen complicity is a sine qua non of police violence. The complicity is sometimes overt—as when southern juries in the 1960s refused to indict or convict police officers who had murdered civil rights workers. But complicity is more often implicit, as in citizen tolerance for police violence based on the assumption that the violence only threatens social outcasts or other persons who "deserve it."

Controls

As demonstrated by the judiciary's mostly successful campaign to end police torture of suspects in custody, judicial oversight can be a powerful control over police violence. In the 1985 case of *Tennessee v. Garner* (471 U.S. 1), the Supreme Court held that police could use deadly force to stop a fleeing suspect only if the suspect used a weapon to threaten someone or if the suspect allegedly had committed a crime threatening or inflicting serious bodily harm. Further, held the Court majority, a warning was required before shooting, if feasible. (At common law, deadly force had been allowed against any fleeing felon, but that rule dated from an era when felonies consisted almost exclusively of very serious violent crimes and the death penalty for felonies was standard.) *Garner* appears to have worked; one study, by Abraham Tannenbaum, suggests that the case cut the number of fatal shootings by police by sixty per year.

More recently, the Supreme Court has begun to enforce some limits on dynamic entries. In *Wilson v. Arkansas,* the unanimous Court held that the Fourth Amendment ban on unreasonable search and seizure includes the common-law "knock and announce" rule for service of search warrants. Consistent with the common-law standard, the Court also affirmed that there are exceptions to "knock and announce," but did not delineate the boundaries of the exceptions.

Police chief leadership often plays a decisive role in discouraging or encouraging police violence, such as when progressive chiefs encourage a high level of officer training that emphasizes resolving situations with the lowest degree of force necessary. Conversely, police executives can encourage police violence, as did Philadelphia police chief (and later mayor) Frank Rizzo in the 1970s and 1980s. Elected executive officials can also have a great impact, such as when Texas governor Miriam "Ma" Ferguson (1925–1927) fired the entire Texas Rangers force, notorious for anti-Hispanic violence, and rebuilt it from the ground up.

The most significant congressional effort to control violence came after the Civil War, when Congress enacted several civil rights statutes designed to address local government violence against freedmen (*U.S. Code*, vol. 42, secs. 1981, 1983, and 1985, and vol. 18, sec. 242). These statutes provide criminal and civil liability for civil rights violations, as do similar provisions in some state codes.

Civilian review commissions have been implemented in many jurisdictions, especially large cities, to control police violence, although clear proof of their effectiveness has yet to be demonstrated.

Long-Term Effects

Although police violence is seen by its practitioners as a means of enforcing social control, its long-term effect is destabilizing and is an important cause of riots and other civil unrest. As the Harlem Riot Commission wrote in 1935, "The insecurity of the individual . . . against police aggression is one of the most potent causes of existing hostility to authority."

BIBLIOGRAPHY

Alpert, Geoffrey P., Dennis Jay Kenney, and Roger Dunham. "Police Pursuits and the Use of Force: Recognizing and Managing 'the Pucker Factor': A Research Note." *Justice Quarterly* 14, no. 2 (June 1997).

Geller, William A., and Hans Toch, eds. *Police Violence: Understanding and Controlling Police Abuse of Force.* New Haven, Conn.: Yale University Press, 1996.

Kopel, David B., and Paul H. Blackman. *No More Wacos: What's Wrong with Federal Law Enforcement and How to Fix It.* Amherst, N.Y.: Prometheus, 1997. On-line at http://i2i.org/Waco.htm.

Kraska, Peter, and Louis J. Cubellis. "Militarizing Mayberry and Beyond: Making Sense of American Paramilitary Policing." *Justice Quarterly* 14, no. 4 (December 1997).

Skolnick, Jerome H., and James J. Fyfe. *Above the Law: Police and the Excessive Use of Force.* New York: Free Press, 1993.

Tannenbaum, Abraham. "The Influence of the Garner Decision on Police Use of Deadly Force." *Journal of Criminal Law and Criminology* 85, no. 1 (1994).

DAVID B. KOPEL

See also **Bureau of Alcohol, Tobacco, and Firearms; Crown Heights; Federal Bureau of Investigation; Government Violence Against Citizens; MOVE Bombing; Ruby Ridge; Scottsboro Case; Social Control; Waco.**

POLISH AMERICANS

The Polish presence in America dates from at least 1608, when several Polish artisans arrived in the Jamestown colony to found a glassblowing business. Over the next two and a half centuries, migration from Poland to America was primarily a movement of individuals or small groups (six people or fewer) whose motivation was primarily political. The most notable of these were Tadeusz Kosciuszko and Kazimierz Pulaski, who came to North America to serve with distinction in the American Revolution. Largely because of their efforts, American public opinion was quite favorable toward Poles during the decades immediately following the revolution, and thus treatment of Poles in general was quite good.

Beginning in the 1830s, groups of political exiles numbering several hundred arrived in America, with the first large group of economic immigrants settling in Panna Maria, Texas, in 1854. The economic exodus increased greatly beginning in the 1870s, with an average of more than 100,000 Poles arriving in the United States every year between 1870 and the beginning of World War I. Because of the large influx of immigrants from southern and eastern Europe during the same period (more than one million people per year), concerns began to be voiced by organized labor, urban politicians, educators, and others that the new immigrants could not readily be assimilated. The result was that immigrants often became caught between the excesses of big business on the one hand and the antipathy of organized labor on the other. Increasingly after 1870 Poles thus became the object of violence both because of their association with the larger wave of immigration and because, as Poles, they constituted the second largest nationality group of the new immigration after Italians, and were thus viewed as a threat to "the American way of life."

For the purpose of understanding the forms of violence directed at the Polish ethnic group in the United States it is helpful think in terms of a continuum, in which violence is defined as including acts ranging broadly from verbal abuse to aggravated murder. In its least overtly physical form, violence against Polish Americans manifests in the dehumanizing use of ethnic epithets such as "dumb Polak" by neighbors and employers and in the demeaning portrayal of Polish characters in jokes as well as in movies, in literature, and on television. Occasionally, this verbal abuse was accompanied by low-level forms of physical aggression. Examples of this include the subject of one interview who recalled as a child being bullied, spat at, and called "Polak" on the way to school, while another dreaded walking to school in the winter because other children would throw snowballs at the Poles.

This level of violence was carried over into the factories and mines where most Poles were employed. There, foremen often acted as arbitrary

---

Painted with a Red Brush

As a result of the fatalities in Milwaukee, the Haymarket Square riot, and other tragedies, the leftist newsweekly the *Nation* led the American press in characterizing Poles as anarchists, calling them bomb-throwing radicals "roving around with red flags." It further opined that

> the riots in Cleveland, Chicago, and Milwaukee are producing a rapid change of sentiment in regard to the partition of Poland. It has hitherto been considered by the bulk of American people as a monstrous crime on the part of the three powers which took part in it. But the events of the last few weeks are leading many to condemn the powers for not having partitioned the individual Poles as well as Poland. (Pienkos 1978, p. 143)

Characterizations such as these led public opinion to sanction increasingly more violent methods for dealing with Slavic labor activism.

---

lords of the realm, every bit as powerful over the life of the worker as the landlords the Poles left behind in the Old Country. Foremen routinely insulted and intimidated Polish workers, shoved them around, shorted their wages, or demanded payment for special favors. If a worker complained, the foreman had the authority to fire the person on the spot. One Pole described working at the A. D. Julliard Textile Mills in the 1920s, where workers were "physically pushed around and of course everything was 'Polak.' They were treated with contempt and as inferiors. . . . I used to see once in a while when they'd [the bosses] pass by a Pole standing by his machine they would spit on him" (Pula and Dziedzic 1990, p. 44).

Another level of violence against Poles in America can be seen in the neglect and abuse prevalent in the "company towns" and industries where many newly arrived Poles and other eastern Europeans went to work beginning in the late 1800s. In western New York, the Lackawanna Steel Company built a new factory complex at the turn of the century that was touted as a model town. The company constructed a number of impressive structures for the Anglo-Saxon company officials and management personnel, but the sections built for the workers were spartan and unsanitary. According to one observer, "Open sewers emptied into the low swampy land and the houses were often surrounded by fetid water. Elevated boards served as walks and the streets were usually quagmires of mud" (Sorrell 1969). Poles and other workers had little choice but to tolerate life in the company housing, which was crowded, congested, and plagued with disease; local physicians estimated in 1909 that "60 percent of the immigrants had some stage of tuberculosis."

Along with illness, immigrant workers at the Lackawanna Steel Company faced high accident rates and unnecessary industrial deaths. Safety signs were printed only in English, with the result that accidents among Polish and other non-English-speaking workers were twice as high as for English-speaking employees. None of the foremen spoke any foreign languages, but they frequently engaged in discrimination and ethnic slurs. Conditions were essentially the same in western Pennsylvania's Allegheny County where the steel industry flourished in the city of Pittsburgh. Between 1906 to 1910 the accident rate for non-English-speaking immigrants at Pittsburgh's South Works was twice the average of the rest of the labor force. In a single year 127 East Europeans died in industrial accidents in Allegheny County: indeed, nearly 25 percent of recent immigrants, of whom Poles were a heavy proportion, were killed or injured working in the steel mills each year.

Direct, physical acts of violence against Polish Americans were also generally related to the workplace and usually involved struggles between labor and employers, the latter being backed by the local police, military force, or company-hired thugs masquerading as "detectives." While the murder of Polish labor organizers such as John Kulski and Jock Yablonski appear to have been largely because of their leadership positions rather than their ethnicity, other such atrocities took place at least partially because of the low status in which the ethnicity of the labor activists was held. In 1886 a labor dispute in Milwaukee resulted in a "riot" in which five people were killed—all Poles.

The tendency of both company officials and government agencies to advocate overt physical violence against Slavic workers was a recurring theme in U.S. labor history beginning during the period of labor organization in the 1880s and lasting through World War II. For example, during a labor strike over poor working conditions and ill-treatment by the Standard Oil Company in Bayonne, New Jersey, in 1915, one oil company executive commanded, "Get me two hundred and fifty husky men who can swing clubs. If they're not enough, get a thousand or two thousand. I want them to march up East Twenty-second Street through the guts of Polacks" (Pienkos 1978, p. 143). The result is best described by historian John J.

Striking workers of the Standard Oil Company in Bayonne, New Jersey, surround an ambulance in which a wounded deputy is being taken to a hospital on 22 July 1915. CORBIS/BETTMANN

Bukowczyk: "For the next four days . . . [the] private army of so-called 'nobles' terrorized the strikers by sniping at pickets and launching armed sorties into the assembled crowds. No fewer than five strikers died and several more sustained gunshot wounds before the corporate reign of terror at the hands of . . . 'armed thugs' finally subsided" (1984, pp. 66–67). Ultimately, the Hudson County sheriff broke up the strikers' organization and dispersed the private company forces. He beat up the strikers' young socialist leader, arrested the union representative of the Industrial Workers of the World (IWW, or Wobblies) who had organized the strike, and banned sales of the radical prolabor newspaper the *New York Call*.

A similar strike occurred in Little Falls, New York, when more than thirteen hundred workers, most of whom were Polish and Slovak, struck the Phoenix and Gilbert Knitting Mills in the winter of 1912–1913. Backed by the local law-enforcement officials, the company was able to prevent labor activists, and even the socialist mayor of Schenectady, from addressing the workers in a mass meeting. The country sheriff explained that "socialist speeches at this time would tend to 'rioting' among the strikers, a thing we intend to prevent if we have to call out every regiment of the National Guard in the state." The city police chief commented further, "We have a strike on our hands and a foreign element to deal with. We have in the past kept them in subjugation and we mean to continue to hold them where they belong" (Snyder 1979, p. 29).

When picketers failed to move quickly enough in clearing a path for scabs to enter the mills, mounted police attacked the strikers with clubs, beating some into unconsciousness. When the strikers fled, police pursued them across the Mohawk River into the immigrant section of town where the officers assaulted the strike headquarters. The police threw women bodily from the steps, broke down the doors, smashed the framed union charter, and arrested the entire strike committee and other supporters.

Probably the most notorious case of brutality against Poles and other Slavic workers occurred in 1897 during a strike by Polish, Hungarian, and Italian coal miners in northeastern Pennsylvania. On 10 September of that year a peaceful march by four hundred miners in Lattimer encountered the county sheriff and eighty-six deputies who halted the marchers and commanded them to disperse. While the sheriff confronted the march leaders, some of his deputies, without any physical provocation or warning, fired into the crowd—killing nineteen and wounding thirty-eight. The "Lattimer massacre" has been characterized as "the most serious act of labor violence in Pennsylvania's history and nationally one of the most devastating, in which public authorities were responsible for attacking, wounding, and killing American laborers" (Turner 1983, pp. 147–148).

While the level and persistence of violence against Polish-Americans never reached the proportions of that directed at African Americans, the demeaning epithets, verbal assaults, and physical violence were sufficient to erect a formidable barrier to equal participation in the socioeconomic promise that initially lured many Poles to America.

BIBLIOGRAPHY

Bicha, Karel D. "Hunkics: Stereotyping the Slavic Immigrants, 1890–1920." *Journal of American Ethnic History* 2 (1982): 16–38.

Bukowczyk, John J. "The Transformation of Working Class Ethnicity: Corporate Control, Americanization, and the Polish Middle Class in Bayonne, New Jersey, 1915–1925." *Labor History* 25, no. 1 (1984): 53–82.

Greene, Victor R. "The Polish American Worker to 1930: The 'Hunky' Image in Transition." *The Polish Review* 21, no. 3 (1976): 63–78.

———. *The Slavic Community on Strike: Immigrant Labor in Pennsylvania Anthracite*. Notre Dame, Ind.: University of Notre Dame Press, 1968.

Leonard, Henry B. "Ethnic Cleavage and Industrial Conflict in Late Nineteenth Century America: The Cleveland Rolling Mill Company Strikes of 1882 and 1885." *Labor History* 20 (1979): 524–548.

Pienkos, Donald E. "Politics, Religion, and Change in Polish Milwaukee, 1900–1930." *Wisconsin Magazine of History* (spring 1978): 143.

Pula, James S., and Eugene E. Dziedzic. *United We Stand: The Role of Polish Workers in the New York Mills Textile Strikes of 1912 and 1916*. New York: Columbia University Press, 1990.

Sorrell, Richard S. "Life, Work, and Acculturation Patterns of Eastern European Immigrants in Lackawanna, New York, 1900–1922." *The Polish Review*, 14, no. 4 (1969): 68–72.

Snyder, Robert E. "Women, Wobblies, and Workers' Rights: The 1912 Textile Strike in Little Falls, New York." *New York History* (January 1979): 29–57.

Turner, George A. "Ethnic Responses to the Lattimer Massacre." In *Hard Coal, Hard Times: Ethnicity and Labor in the Anthracite Region*, edited by David L. Salay. Scranton, Penn.: Anthracite Museum Press, 1983.

JAMES S. PULA

See also **Immigration; Race and Ethnicity.**

POLITICS

*This entry is divided into two parts: **Government** and **Political Campaigns.***

GOVERNMENT

Governments are sometimes defined as institutions having a monopoly on legitimate violence, so it should be no surprise that much of the violence in U.S. history has been perpetuated by the government at local, state, and especially federal levels. As Richard Hofstadter has written, "The greatest and most calculating of killers is the national state, and this is true not only in international wars, but in domestic conflicts" (p. 6). Of course, many citizens and political theorists feel that governmental violence is a necessary or inevitable part of the effective functioning of the government.

In his book *A Country Made by War* (1989), Geoffrey Perret traces the important role successful war making has played in the history of the United States. Starting with the Indian wars (which lasted hundreds of years), through the Revolution and various wars of defense (War of 1812), identity (the Civil War), and expansion (Mexican- and Spanish-American Wars) and into the twentieth century (World War I, World War II, and the Cold War era, which includes the Vietnam conflict), the United States has been involved in wars almost continuously. These wars have not only directly shaped the destiny of the United States, but they have also indirectly molded the economy and the politics of the country. During many periods in U.S. history, military conflict has been a dominant political issue.

Consider how many U.S. presidents either had been prominent military figures—perhaps even heroes—before their election (George Washington, Andrew Jackson, William Henry Harrison, Zachary Taylor, Ulysses S. Grant, Theodore Roosevelt, Dwight D. Eisenhower, John F. Kennedy, and George Bush) or became distinguished for their wartime leadership (James Monroe, Abraham Lincoln, Franklin D. Roosevelt, and Harry S. Truman).

This long and important military history has produced what many scholars call the American way of war—technological and bloody. This style of war originated with the policy of genocide against most Native American tribes, which, according to James Reston, Jr., led to the total-war practices of William Tecumseh Sherman in his march to the sea (1864) and to Ulysses S. Grant's strategy of attrition. In fact, with its technological basis, the Civil War has been called, by Bruce Catton, among others, the first modern war. In World War I and World War II this way of war became a potent form of industrial war, with the creation and production of ever-more powerful war machines and war systems. Michael Sherry, in his history of strategic bombing, a method of bombing that the United States perfected, has labeled this way of war "technological fanaticism." The development of U.S. nuclear strategy, described so well by Gregg Herken and Fred Kaplan, paralleled the massive political effort behind the Cold War, which resulted in the buildup of an arsenal of superweapons (mainly nuclear but including chemical and biological capabilities) that could destroy human civilization many times over. The kind of industrial-technological war waged in both Vietnam and Iraq not only resulted in massive civilian deaths in the targeted countries but also had a profound impact on the economy and politics of its practitioner—in these cases, the United States.

Economically, war has significantly shaped the United States. At first this war policy was tied to a commitment to infrastructure development (the building of transportation, power, and communication systems such as ports, roads, bridges, rail lines, dams, canals, and telegraphs) as exemplified by the Army Corp of Engineers, westward expansion, and free trade; the Civil War and World War I then played a major role in the development of industrialization and mass production; and the middle to late twentieth century saw the creation of a permanent war economy and the military-industrial-scientific complex. In the history of international and interstate commerce (shipping, canals, railroads, and highways), of automation, and of computer and nuclear technology, the central role of military production and priorities stands out.

The threat of outside aggression, organized internal dissent, and an increase in crime rates (we talk of a "war on crime" and the "drug war") has been cited again and again to justify the acquisition of more police powers by the government at all levels. This has led to the creation of a massive national security apparatus second to none in the world in size and technological sophistication, as well as a criminal justice system with one of the highest per capita rates of incarceration and capital punishment. With the most powerful military in history, and world dominance in terms of military and economic might, with which it intervenes around the globe, the United States makes for a unique empire, with various motivations for its involvement in foreign wars and with an extraordinary amount of freedom and dissent existing domestically in continual tension with powerful policing agencies that thrive on the federal, state, and local levels.

Abuses of the government's policing powers are well documented: the Alien and Sedition Acts (1798) and other policies of the young republic; the suspension of habeas corpus by President Lincoln during the Civil War, which led directly to the Red Scare and the Palmer raids (raids organized by Attorney General Alexander Mitchell Palmer to eliminate socialists, anarchists, and other radicals) following World War I and to the internment of Japanese Americans during World War II; illegal operations in the twentieth century like the Federal Bureau of Investigation's provocations against those on the left of the political spectrum and Central Intelligence Agency and U.S. military interference in domestic affairs, such as the illegal surveillance and provocateur operations against Martin Luther King, the Black Panther Party, and antiwar activists in the 1960s and 1970s.

Many groups at various times and during various wars have been the victims of violence supported in some measure by the government. Especially on the local level, such support has often been crucial in facilitating extralegal violence against Native Americans, Loyalists during the Revolutionary War, abolitionists before the Civil War and freed slaves afterward, Irish immigrants, Mexican Americans, imported Chinese workers, labor organizers and so-called radicals, German Americans, Italian Americans, and Japanese Americans. Political adversaries, whether nonviolent protesters or violent dissenters, have also been victims of governmental violence, which the government (and segments of the public) often blames on the police or on the protesters themselves.

Other government policies, on the federal, state, and local levels, have often produced what observers as diverse as the academic pacifist John Stuart Mill, the pacifist A. J. Muste, the feminist Barbara Deming, and the activist and politician Tom Hayden have called institutional violence. Those who posit institutional violence cite such examples as proslavery legislation before emancipation and segregation laws afterward, antilabor statutes in general and ineffectual health and safety standards in particular, Bureau of Indian Affairs policies and practices leading to the decimation of Native American tribal cultures, dis-

criminatory immigration policies, laws limiting the rights of women, ineffective or nonexistent welfare and education legislation, and in general policies that favor one segment of the population or economy unfairly over others. For those who believe that abortion is murder or that animals and nature deserve legal protection, many medical, scientific, and environmental practices supported and legalized by the government are seen as inherently violent as well.

Elected officials, and those trying to get elected, have often mobilized political support around violence, whether it was in support of wars or of more domestic issues, such as anti-Chinese politicians in California in the mid-1800s and the Ku Klux Klan–supported officials in the South from the 1860s to the 1970s. Among the issues that have woven violence into politics are religious strife in the early colonies, treatment of Native Americans, the American Revolution, the long struggle over slavery, the continual outbursts of racism and jingoism that have met each new wave of immigrants, antiradical and anticommunist hysterias, relations with China and the former Soviet Union, and crime. The United States in the late nineteen nineties was among the most violent nations in the world in terms of domestic murder, governmental punishments, and international affairs. The reasons for this are complicated and little understood. What is clear is that this predilection for violence has been shared by the government.

BIBLIOGRAPHY

Herken, Gregg. *Counsels of War.* New York: Knopf, 1985.
Hofstadter, Richard, and Michael Wallace, eds. *American Violence: A Documentary History.* New York: Knopf, 1970.
Kaplan, Fred. *Wizards of Armageddon.* New York: Touchstone, 1983.
Perret, Geoffrey. *A Country Made by War: The Story of America's Rise to Power.* New York: Random House, 1989.
Reston, James R., Jr. *Sherman's March and Vietnam.* New York: Macmillan, 1984.
Sherry, Michael. *The Rise of American Air Power: The Creation of Armageddon.* New Haven, Conn.: Yale University Press, 1987.

CHRIS HABLES GRAY

See also **Alien and Sedition Acts; Central Intelligence Agency; Federal Bureau of Investigation; Government Commissions.**

POLITICAL CAMPAIGNS

Although violence associated with political activities, movements, and struggles has been common in the history of the United States, political violence directly associated with electoral campaigns has been relatively rare. The first major recorded incident was in 1742 when the two main factions of the Pennsylvania Colony fought over control of the polls at the Philadelphia Court House, resulting in bloody riots in Philadelphia. The Quakers, generally easterners, opposed the use of force against Indian tribes, whereas the Proprietary Party wanted a more aggressive policy. Such tensions continued into the late 1800s, but violence between these factions was uncommon after the eighteenth century.

Physical intimidation and attacks on a small scale have been reported in numerous elections in the United States, especially in elections involving candidates from the political machines that dominated much of urban politics from the early 1800s until the mid-twentieth century. But there have only been two major episodes of widespread electoral violence.

The first was the election riots in the 1830s–1850s, including the Philadelphia riot of 1834 and the Baltimore riot of 1856. During this era many political groups, local and national, were involved in violence related to elections; it was generally accompanied by fraudulent counts and open bribery. This period is well chronicled in Michael Feldberg's *The Turbulent Era: Riot and Disorder in Jacksonian America* (1980).

The second episode of widespread electoral violence took place in the South during Reconstruction; it consisted overwhelmingly of violence by southern whites directed at the former slaves and whites who were their allies in the Republican Party. This violence played an important role in the defeat of the Reconstruction policies of President Ulysses S. Grant's administration (1869–1877), as George C. Rable documents in *But There Was No Peace: The Role of Violence in the Politics of Reconstruction* (1984). The Ku Klux Klan was responsible for some but not all of this violence. In 1875 the coalition-devised "Mississippi Plan" of intimidation backed by threats of violence was used so successfully that the "Redshirts" of South Carolina adapted it to their own purposes and, along with outright violence, used it to administer a stunning defeat to the Republican Party in the 1876 election. This pattern of electoral violence was institutionalized in the southern Jim Crow laws that preserved the basically white-only electoral system until the middle of the twentieth century.

A number of political assassinations that directly impacted elections also can be considered electoral violence. Two were very much linked to the electoral violence around Reconstruction. In

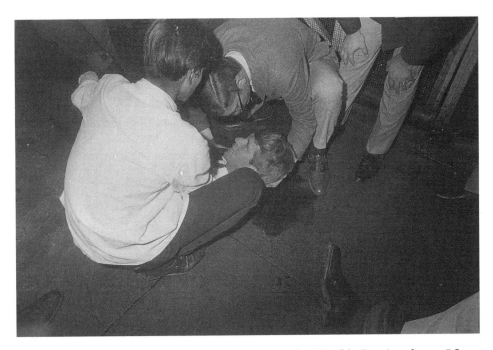

Robert F. Kennedy, after being shot at the Ambassador Hotel in Los Angeles on 5 June 1968. CORBIS/BETTMANN

1868 a Republican member of the U.S. House of Representatives, James Hinds, was killed in Arkansas. Twenty years later, also in Arkansas, John Clayton, a leading Republican, was favored to win election to the U.S. House of Representatives. Violence was precipitated when a faction of Democrats threw out the ballot box for a heavily black district whose votes would have won the election for Clayton. Instead, Clayton was defeated. When he went to Plumerville, Arkansas, in January 1889 to investigate the Democrats, he was assassinated.

There have been numerous assassinations and attempts, usually targeting sitting judges and officeholders, throughout U.S. history. But in the twentieth century there were several incidents that directly involved election campaigns. In 1900 the governor-elect of Kentucky, William Goebel, was assassinated during an infusion of violence-prone Republicans from eastern Kentucky into the state capital. Many Republicans disputed the election of the antirailroad Goebel, and some, the evidence indicates, were angry enough to kill him.

The most notable election-linked assassination was the shooting of Robert F. Kennedy in the final drive of his campaign to win the presidential nomination of the Democratic Party in 1968. While official inquiries and much of the evidence point to the guilt of a lone assassin, Sirhan Sirhan, there is little doubt that Kennedy's death fundamentally changed the course of the 1968 election. The attempted assassination of George Wallace, the leading third-party candidate in the 1972 election, may also have had a major electoral impact.

The United States has been spared the extreme levels of violence around elections that some countries have experienced, but it is clear that electoral violence was important on a number of crucial occasions.

BIBLIOGRAPHY

Barnes, Kenneth C. *Who Killed John Clayton? Political Violence and the Emergence of the New South, 1861–1893.* Durham, N.C.: Duke University Press, 1998.

Feldberg, Michael. *The Turbulent Era: Riot and Disorder in Jacksonian America.* New York: Oxford University Press, 1980.

Hofstadter, Richard, and Michael Wallace, eds. *American Violence: A Documentary History.* New York: Knopf, 1970.

Klotter, James C. *William Goebel: The Politics of Wrath.* Lexington: University Press of Kentucky, 1977.

Rabel, George C. *But There Was No Peace: The Role of Violence in the Politics of Reconstruction.* Athens: University of Georgia Press, 1984.

CHRIS HABLES GRAY

See also **Advertising; Assassinations; Kennedy, Robert F.; Sirhan Sirhan.**

POPULAR CULTURE

The appearance of industrially produced culture in the eighteenth century and the spectacular growth of a global entertainment-industrial complex since that time have begged a number of fundamental questions about the nature of aesthetic experience, questions that have continually perplexed both lovers of art and those who fear its power. It is not unusual for enthusiasts of the Shakespearean tragedies or the films of the Japanese director Akira Kurosawa to condemn popular television programs and Hollywood action movies for excesses of violence. To further complicate the paradox, such judgments are typically born of pessimistic estimations of the capabilities of other classes, a point often at odds with the political self-images of those who espouse them. As with the portrayal of sex in the popular arts, meaningful argument muddles somewhere between the rhetorical poles of "redeeming social value" and "gratuitous sensationalism." Among culture marketers, however, it is accepted wisdom that audiences numbering in the many millions are attracted to the enjoyment of portrayals of violence.

Although it has become unfashionable to make sharp distinctions between so-called "high" and "low" culture, any attempt to grasp the vital role of violence in popular culture depends on a clear understanding of the specific phenomenon referred to by these terms. The essayist and critic Dwight Macdonald is helpful in this regard. In "A Theory of Mass Culture" (1957) he describes the historical circumstances that produced what has come to be known as popular culture in the Western countries.

Medieval Models

Feudal European civilization had been the sum of two complementary cultural components: a court culture based on literate documentation and a folk culture based on oral communication. In the former, art, religion, mathematics, witnessed events, critical commentary, and other ingredients in the production of consciousness were set into print impressions and stored in libraries for generational continuity. Access was limited to a tiny group of clerics and clerically trained aristocrats. The clergy claimed strict right of regulation over content, which it could enforce by virtue of its gatekeeping monopoly over libraries and educational institutions. In the case of the vast nonliterate majority, stories, beliefs, skills, and styles were passed on by word of mouth and by personal example in a system of integral kinship relationships.

According to Macdonald, these two class-defined subcultures, court and folk, coexisted in parallel balance, divided physically by the castle moat and aesthetically by the cultural gap of literacy. A blood-soaked murder might be presented in a drama at court; a gruesome fairy tale might be told among the folk. There was one key area, however, where the court insisted on full cultural control. Religion was dictated by the court at the threat of torture and death. This was particularly important because religious belief was—and some argue still is—a basic source for all cultural expression.

The medieval cathedral, according to Walter Ong, S. J., as well as other cultural commentators, functioned as a model that presaged the structure, if not the content, of postindustrial popular culture. The building was an important cultural bridge between the elite and the populace, acting as a communication medium for the translation of the Bible and other religious messages into nonliterate forms such as sculpture, painting, and stained glass windows. Unlike laterally bartered folk art, the cathedral was a vertical medium of communication, transmitting cultural messages downstream from a centralized, highly literate gatekeeping class to a broad mass of consumers. The power of the portrayal of physical and psychic violence was already evident.

Cathedral architecture told as many types of stories as could be found in the Bible or as could be attributed to Christian etiology. These, of course, included many grotesque violent narratives, from the fratricide of Abel and the plagues of Egypt to the Crucifixion and the martyring of saints. The vivid portrayal of an afterlife in hell, whether metaphorized in the brutal pain of an eternal inferno or an unbearable frozen darkness, was a culturally delivered threat of violence that demanded obedience from an audience that feared such a fate. The violent divine retributions of the Old Testament could only be avoided by following the instructions of the interpreters of the New Testament.

Capitalism and Democracy

With the advent of industrialization, the bilaterality of nonreligious medieval folk culture disintegrated. The vertical model of the church, with its divine mandate for cultural conquest, was imitated by the new secular cultural elites of capitalism. Private enterprise usurped clerical function, taking control of production and distribution of a wide variety of cultural products to the nascent urban peasantry. A class of educated cultural professionals developed a secular analog to the clergy. It was their task to create culture—at first mostly in print but later by any medium that research and development could yield—to be sold at market to the newly semiliterate. Popularity, measured by quantity of units sold, became the objective of what the poet and critic Hans Magnus Enzensberger would later term the "consciousness industry" in his 1974 book of the same title.

It became apparent by the mid–eighteenth century that culture-for-profit would reshape and redefine artistic expression rather than simply distribute it more widely. A new industry of inexpensive periodicals and novels grew up around the printing firms located on London's Grub Street, which can be seen as a prototype for twentieth-century Hollywood. Targeting an audience immunized by ignorance from the traditional tastes and standards created by formal criticism, the "Scribblers," as Alexander Pope mockingly called the authors of these works, used the visceral more freely than the spiritual as selling points for cultural goods. Lurid murders that did not necessarily say much new or noteworthy about the human condition did well at the market stalls.

While the emerging pop culture industries of Britain and other European societies were somewhat fettered by the cultural policing of surviving state churches and lingering church influence, the United States proved to be an ideal incubator for the new system of marketed culture. Massive multinational immigration of barely literate and subliterate classes, as well as the lack of a specific politically empowered state religion, created a mythological vacuum that allowed the producers of popular culture a remarkable degree of freedom from any known moral standard for the arts. Immigrants of course could choose to cling to the traditions of their native cultures, but they did so at the risk of exclusion from American life. The acceptance of the language, styles, and values of American popular culture went hand in hand with a vision of personal assimilation.

This phenomenon can be traced back to colonial times. Thomas Paine's *Common Sense* (1776), a treasonous call for popular violence against the legally constituted authority of the crown, was published by a Scottish loyalist in Pennsylvania who took the job for profit. The pamphlet gingerly explained God's preference for democracy over monarchy to an audience ill-prepared in theological education to dispute that dubious, even heretical, reading. In a sense democracy became the religion of the new nation, and a willingness to kill and die for it in the Revolutionary War and in the frontier wars with Mexico and the Indian nations became the test of a crusader's zeal.

The Western

The Western novel, an American national etiology, emerged to fill the vacuum left by the immigrant's estrangement from his or her native culture. It became the most popular prose genre of the nineteenth century. The justification of violence was among its chief features. As described by John Cawelti in *The Six-Gun Mystique* (1984), the genre was constructed of three primary elements brought to resolution by a heroic act of violence. The first element was the pioneer settlers. Farmers, artisans, and urban professionals came to the frontier full of optimism and energy, ready to prove their worthiness through personal achievement of prosperity and collective accomplishment of manifest national destiny. Their morally admirable nonviolent values, however, seem to have been their undoing at the hands of the second element, the savages. Richard Slotkin's *Regeneration Through Violence: The Mythology of the American Frontier, 1600–1860* (1973) offers a capacious look at the consequences of this dilemma.

Here the Western splits into two distinct subgenres based on the personification of violent savagery: the outlaws are white racial fellows who, in order to feed insatiable, antisocial hedonistic desires for drink, money, and sex, chose to maliciously wrest these things from the good townspeople; or the "wild Indians," whose motives for inflicting violence upon the townspeople are only rarely glossed as anything more than an unfortunate failure to understand the needs and superiority of civilization, Eurostyle.

Whichever type of opponent the good settlers face, it is their very virtue that makes them incapable of coping with the threat of violence. While they can farm, hunt, read, work hard, or pray, they have neither the skill nor the stomach to take a human life with a six-gun on Main Street at twenty paces. However, just as it looks as if civilization has been stopped in its tracks in a lawless wilderness, along comes the third element of the genre, a heroic character usually referred to by critics as the "Violent Redeemer." Here is a man, and he is most certainly a man, who synthesizes the values of the townspeople with the violent capabilities of the criminals and savages. He can shoot a man at twenty paces, but, of equal importance, he cannot meet a lady without tipping his hat. He is the chosen one who can gun down the bad man on Main Street or lead the cavalry to a slaughter of the wild Indians. It is upon the foundation of his acts of righteous violence that the peaceful structures of civilization—courthouses, schools, churches, and general stores—are built. As was the case with the American Revolution, the freedom, prosperity, and peace of the populace are conditions built upon a foundation of justifiable violence.

The American Western can be seen as the first truly successful genre of industrialized culture, a prototype for the boom in popular genre construction that took place throughout the twentieth century. The Western's etiological mandate for the explanation of a national origin constituted a carte blanche for portrayals of degrees of violent behavior that by feudal standards would have been suppressed as gratuitous if not heretical. The evil depravities of the opponents of American society were clearly delineated in wanton acts of murder, rape, torture, theft, and destruction of private property. The hero's response had to be equal to the task of defeating this vividly drawn violence with a measured dose of the same.

It is worth noting that the happy ending for the frontier community—the defeat of chaotic violence by divinely sanctioned violence—is not necessarily a happy ending for the Violent Redeemer. As a man capable of beating violence on its own terms, the only role for the righteous vigilante in the newly stabilized community might be as a lawman. If, however, he wants to remain in free contact with nature, the ultimate source of his heroic capacity for violence, he must ride off into the sunset with the knowledge that the civilization he has enabled with his six-gun will continue to chase him as an obstacle in the path of its continental conquest.

As a literary form, the Western spanned a fairly wide spectrum of readers. The Deadwood Dick novels, written by Edward L. Wheeler in the 1880s, recount the exploits of a security guard for a gold-mining company in South Dakota and were among the most popular novels of the late nineteenth century, although they are rarely mentioned by critics or read in schools. The violent, psychologically unexplained acts of the bad guy, as well as his violent death at the hands of Deadwood Dick, constitute the structural basis for each narrative in the series.

By contrast, Owen Wister's *The Virginian* (1902), although also a paean to frontier violence, is a far more thoughtful treatment. The hero, as the leader of a vigilante posse, is forced to hang his best friend for cattle rustling, without benefit of a formal trial. His fiancée, a recently transplanted New England schoolteacher, is appalled that she has fallen in love with a man capable of what she believes to be savage violence. Furthermore, she must suffer a sundown gunfight between her betrothed and the outlaw responsible for the corruption of the friend he has executed. In the end, the teacher accepts the lesson of the Western: a peaceful society rests upon a bedrock of violence.

The Western novel's endurance through technological innovation is another marker of its postindustrial cultural character. Its adaptations to silent film, sound film, comic books, and radio and television shows were all hugely successful. As late as the early 1960s, Westerns were among the most highly rated series on American television. With shoot-outs, massacres, hangings, scalpings, and other acts of human abuse, the genre offered more than its share of violence to movie and television audiences. Much of this violence, however, was presented in an idealized form that brought little actual blood into view of the camera lens. Shot by a bullet or an arrow, a character might exclaim "Ooh, they got me" and then slump to the ground to convulse and die. But blood, guts, or real expressions of human suffering were rarely displayed to the audience.

In the 1960s, as changing racial and sexual attitudes sent the genre into decay, several film directors reexamined the premises of decades of stylized violence by forcing their audience to take a more realistic look at its bloody consequences. John Ford began this process with *The Man Who Shot Liberty Valance* (1962), a bold meditation on the interdependent relationship of civic law and personal violence. Further generic introspection led to spectacular hyperboles of violence, such as Sam Peckinpah's *The Wild Bunch* (1969) and Sergio Leone's *The Good, The Bad, and the Ugly* (1966). While the frontier American West would remain a setting for popular drama, the formula Western that audiences had supported through media adaptations for well over a century has virtually disappeared.

Some critics believe that the space epic replaced or displaced the Western by offering the excitement of violent heroic action in a new context free of the racism and sexism that underpinned the Western formula. The television series *Star Trek*, which premiered in 1966, is often cited in this regard. Beginning with the elliptical statement, "Space, the final frontier," each episode is a reiteration of the necessity of violence as a precondition for the peaceful development of society. Captain Kirk emerges as an intergalactic Violent Redeemer. He is reluctant to use violence but capable and proficient at it and ready to use it for the right cause. The genre came into its own with the *Star Wars* movie trilogy.

Detective, Gangster, and Crime Dramas

The other seminal generic source of violence in American popular culture has been the urban crime saga, realized since the nineteenth century principally in detective fiction, gangster films, and in radio and television crime series. Here, too, acts of violence are central to the story, but they do not carry the divine sanction of Western vigilantism. This is further complicated by the introduction of an intraracial ethnic element missing from the Western: the portrayal of immigrants, especially Italian Americans, as violent menaces to the urban civilization that has been built by northern Europeans. Life proved cheap in such films as *Little Caesar* (1930), *The Public Enemy* (1931), and *Scarface: Shame of the Nation* (1931). The gangster film's supposition that a poor, uneducated man of immigrant stock could use brutal personal violence to rise to the top of society had, not surprisingly, great appeal for a national audience plunged into economic depression.

The box-office success of the gangster film alarmed many civic and religious leaders who felt that, lacking the Christian purpose of the Western, the gangster genre served to glorify and glamorize violence for its audience. Although the Motion Picture Association of America's Production Code could be carried out to the letter by the gangster's death, the code's intention was too often trumped in the eyes of socially conservative cultural gatekeepers. The 1930 Production Code states that immoral and illegal acts must be balanced by "compensation . . . punishment or retribution." As Robert Warshow points out in his essay "The

Gangster as Tragic Hero," the violent demise of the urban gangster from the high position of wealth and power he attains, far from gaining audience support for just retribution, tends to exalt and create empathy for the figure, much as was the case in classic Greek drama.

Gangster violence would remain controversial for the balance of the twentieth century, finding its way into television as the crime series and into popular music as gangster rap. It is worth noting that the shift of the popular cultural center from the movie theater to the living room in the 1950s changed the terms of the debate over popular culture violence. The serial nature of television drama debunked the "tragic hero" argument. Given its structural feature of preserving the lives of principal characters, the television series tended to invest audience identification almost exclusively with defenders of the law. Criminals, who appeared and perished in less than an hour, were little more than cardboard figures of evil or derangement whose violent deaths made for quick episodic conclusions.

The Effects of Violence As Entertainment

At the same time, however, television brought the portrayal of graphic violence right into the home, making it a familiar feature of domestic life and, perhaps most controversially, easily accessible to children. Shelves of academic studies and several congressional hearings have condemned television violence as a factor in creating similar behavior in the population at large, either through copycat acts or by numbing viewers to the real consequences of violent acts. The latter is an argument often extended to violent children's cartoons, ranging from intergalactic space wars to the Roadrunner cartoons. In a single American children's cartoon, a character may be blown up with a bomb, shot with a gun, thrown off a high place, and set on fire. One critic sees the numbing of children's emotions to the natural empathy that ought to be felt in witnessing these things; another sees a sublimation in the play world of tendencies the human race has always exhibited.

The Untouchables, perhaps the most violent television series that had yet appeared, was the direct cause of a congressional investigation in 1959. Almost four decades later, a widely debated rating system was adopted by many television services to indicate violent programming. Generally speaking, however, the dual forces of commerce and First Amendment protections have thwarted any effective attempts to regulate television violence.

Many other violent genres can be cited in American popular culture. The horror stories of Edgar

Eli Wallach left, and Clint Eastwood in a scene from *The Good, the Bad, and the Ugly* (1966). CORBIS/BETTMANN

Allan Poe provided a cultural heritage for the emergence of the American horror film, although these films, including *Frankenstein, Count Dracula, The Werewolf,* and *The Mummy* are not set in America. The kind of irrational violence endemic to the genre would finally land on native shores during the 1970s and 1980s with the emergence of the slasher movie, which usually features the dismemberment of young lovers at the hands of a grotesque.

The popularity of violence as cultural entertainment is also demonstrated in the success of physical-contact spectator sports, such as boxing, American football, and ice hockey. To cite one example of the attractiveness of violence in sports culture, there is a lively black market in videotapes of professional hockey brawls; those in which blood is spilled bring premium prices. Professional wrestling, which has experienced an enormous boom in the cable television age, is an extraordinary exemplar of violence at the center stage of popular culture. In a grotesque parody of legitimate sports, wrestlers choke one another, slam their opponents over the head with chairs, and set each other on fire. Nowhere is there greater evidence in popular culture of the enduring power of the willing suspension of disbelief.

As popular cultural properties become sources for multimedia sales campaigns, every new action-hero film or children's cartoon is the potential center of a subculture of toys, games, software, recorded music, theme parks, and so on. However, the basic discussion about violence in popular culture has remained remarkably constant. Do the popular arts offer their audiences opportunities for the reconsideration of the violence that has, over the millennia, proved itself an essential characteristic of the human condition? Or do the popular arts, by means of their immediacy to all elements of society, open the Pandora's box of legitimization through example of the most hideous and repulsive forms of violent behavior that otherwise might remain repressed? The one thing that is certain is that portrayals of violent acts, in varying degrees of graphic excess, are consumed in great numbers by audiences seeking the satisfactions of aesthetic experience. Those who believe that visceral responses to gratuitous violence do not qualify as aesthetic experiences may reject this premise.

BIBLIOGRAPHY

Baker, Robert K. *Mass Media and Violence: A Report to the National Commission on the Causes and Prevention of Violence.* Washington, D.C.: U.S. Government Printing Office, 1969.

Barthes, Roland. "The World of Wrestling." In *A Barthes Reader,* edited by Susan Sontag. New York: Hill and Wang, 1982.

Brode, Douglas. *Money, Women, and Guns: Crime Movies from Bonnie and Clyde to the Present.* Secaucus, N.J.: Carol Publishing Group, 1995.

Brown, Bill, ed. *Reading the West: An Anthology of Dime Westerns.* Boston: Bedford, 1998.

Cawelti, John. *The Six-Gun Mystique.* 2d ed. Bowling Green, Ohio: University Popular Press, 1984.

Gedin, Per. *Literature in the Marketplace.* Translated by George Bisset. Woodstock, N.Y.: Overlook, 1977.

Gerbner, George, and Nancy Signorielli. *Violence and Terror in the Mass Media: An Annotated Bibliography.* New York: Greenwood, 1988.

Macdonald, Dwight. "A Theory of Mass Culture." In *Mass Culture: The Popular Arts in America,* edited by Bernard Rosenberg and David Manning White. Glencoe, Ill.: Free Press, 1957.

Slotkin, Richard. *Regeneration Through Violence: The Mythology of the American Frontier, 1600–1860.* Middletown, Conn.: Wesleyan University Press, 1973.

Warshow, Robert. *The Immediate Experience.* Garden City, N.Y.: Doubleday, 1962.

DAVID MARC

See also **Comics; Dance; Film: Overview; Internet; Literature: Popular Fiction; Music: Popular; Posters; Radio: Popular; Representation of Violence; Television: Historical Overview; Toys and Games; Video Games.**

POPULAR FICTION. *See* Literature: Popular Fiction.

PORNOGRAPHY

People throughout history have represented sexuality in various ways in literature and art, but in the 1950s a mass commercial pornography industry emerged in the United States that would have a dramatic effect on society. Eventually breaking into mainstream distribution outlets, by the 1990s pornography was a $10-billion-a-year industry in the United States. Legal, political, and social conflicts have arisen around the growth of the industry and the increasing levels of sexual explicitness combined with portrayals of violence. These conflicts, along with the emergence of a feminist antipornography critique in the late 1970s, focused attention on pornography's connection to sexual violence and the oppression of women in general.

U.S. law has traditionally used the term *obscenity*, not *pornography*, to describe proscribed sexual material. Obscenity prosecutions in the United States were relatively infrequent and largely uncontroversial in the eighteenth and early nineteenth centuries. After the Civil War obscenity became a more public issue, largely because of the work of Anthony Comstock and other moral crusaders. (Comstock obtained passage of the federal Comstock law in 1873 banning pornographic literature from the mail; he was the founder and secretary of the Society for the Suppression of Vice in New York City [1873–1915] and raided publishers and booksellers to root out obscene literature.) The obscenity question became increasingly politicized in the twentieth century, as the law was used to keep works such as James Joyce's *Ulysses* (1922) out of the country.

In 1957, in *Roth v. United States*, the U.S. Supreme Court first stated clearly that obscenity was outside the protection of the First Amendment. The decision kicked off a string of cases in which the Court wrestled with how to define and regulate obscenity. In its 1973 *Miller v. California* decision, the Supreme Court established a three-part test for identifying obscenity (material that appeals to the prurient interest; portrays sexual conduct in a patently offensive way; and does not have serious literary, artistic, political, or scientific value) and identified contemporary community standards as the measure of evaluation. That definition was modified slightly in *Pope v. Illinois* in 1987, when the Court ruled that community standards should be the test for patently offensive and prurient interest, but that serious value should be judged by the standards of a "reasonable person." In decisions after *Miller*, the Supreme Court upheld the constitutionality of zoning ordinances that restrict adult theaters, endorsed laws that ban child pornography, and upheld the use, within limits, of racketeering statutes against businesses that sell obscene materials.

Obscenity laws guided by these principles remain on the books across the United States but tend to be enforced only where there is strong political support for prosecutions. Such prosecutorial discretion means that material openly for sale in one jurisdiction may not be available in another, even though the laws may be the same. However, mail-order and computer pornography make graphic, sexually explicit material easily obtainable anywhere in the United States. As legal prohibitions have lessened, a once-underground industry with significant ties to organized crime has become a more routine business.

Venues and Content

The venues for contemporary commercial pornography include every type of communications media: printing, photographs, film, telephones, video, and computers. *Playboy* magazine, which debuted in December 1953, was the first sex magazine to break into mainstream distribution channels and take pornography more public. Competing magazines followed, and in the 1960s and 1970s pornographic films began to move out of underground showings into public theaters. In the 1980s videos began to swamp other forms of pornography, as the number of pornographic video titles steadily increased (almost nine thousand new graphic, sexually explicit titles were released in 1998, up from fifteen hundred in 1986) and the circulation of magazines decreased (*Playboy* dropped from a high of 7.2 million in 1972 to about 3.2 million in 1997). Computer pornography—both on the Internet and through CD-ROMs—emerged in the 1990s, although videos remain the market leader. The Supreme Court threw out much of the Communications Decency Act, a controversial part of the 1996 telecommunications law that prohibited not only obscene but also indecent material that could be viewed by children; the future of on-line pornography is unclear. (Indecency, a concept from the law governing radio and broadcast television, encompasses a kind of sexual material that is less graphic and explicit than obscenity. Indecency has been defined by the courts as "nonconformance with accepted standards of morality" and may involve patently offensive depictions of sexual or excretory activities.)

Contemporary pornography includes a wide range of materials, in terms of both production quality and content. Videos range from spliced-together collections of homemade footage, to the cheaply made movies that make up the bulk of the market, to the occasional big-budget effort that approaches Hollywood production values. Most videos are collections of sex scenes strung together with a minimally coherent plot. Oral, vaginal, and anal sex, penetration of women by more than one man at a time, and ejaculations onto women's bodies are standard in contemporary pornography. In pornography marketed to heterosexual men, videos include scenes of heterosexual and female-female sexual activity.

Although accurate statistics are difficult to find, it is clear that heterosexual pornography makes up the bulk of the commercial market (and is therefore the focus here). A significant amount of homosexual-male pornography is also available, with a much smaller amount of commercially produced pornography for lesbians. In addition to those general categories, there are many subgenres of pornography. Some focus on one type of sex (such as anal sex), ejaculations onto women (called "cum shots"), various fetishes, women with unusually large breasts, women dressed to look like children, transvestites and transsexuals, and orgy scenes. There are pornographic videos that highlight various configurations of interracial sex, usually drawing on overtly racist stereotypes. Other tapes specialize in pornography using pregnant women or women who are depicted as being under the age of consent. The level of violence in contemporary mass-marketed pornography has been the subject of much debate. Although there are subgenres of sadomasochist, bondage, and explicitly violent pornography, most of the market does not depict extreme violence, such as beatings or the use of weapons. However, various levels of less brutal violence (hair pulling, slapping, rough treatment) and coercion (physical and verbal) are present in much of the pornography that is typically labeled nonviolent.

The only type of pornography that is publicly unavailable throughout the United States is that using children. Laws against child pornography, which were upheld by the Supreme Court in the 1982 case *New York v. Ferber,* are strictly enforced, although there is considerable underground trade in such material and computers have facilitated the ability of networks of pedophiles (those who prefer children as sexual objects) to produce and exchange it.

Political and Social Debates

As pornography has changed, so have the debates over it. Until the 1970s political and social battles over pornography typically were struggles between liberal advocates of sexual freedom and individual rights and conservative opponents who viewed pornography as an attack on the traditional roles of sexuality within family structures. That opposition to pornography—which most often came from churches or religiously based movements, particularly Roman Catholic and evangelical Protestant denominations—endured into the 1990s. However, the bipolar structure of the debate

changed with the feminist critique of pornography, which emerged out of the larger grassroots struggle against patriarchal sexual violence during the second wave of the women's movement in the 1960s. Central to that struggle was the understanding of rape, battering, and child sexual assault not as random acts of deviant men but as predictable expressions of the culture's misogyny. In that sense, sexual violence was conceptualized as one "normal" expression of patriarchy's view of sex as a site of aggression, conquest, and control. Counteracting this kind of violence had to stem not simply from the individual and the psychological but from the collective and the political.

A similar ideological and structural analysis of pornography also emerged. Radical feminists identified pornography as a kind of sexist hate literature, the expression of a male sexuality rooted in the subordination of women that endorses the sexual objectification of, and sexual violence against, women. As the feminist author Andrea Dworkin wrote in *Letters from a War Zone* (1988), "In the subordination of women, inequality itself is sexualized: made into the experience of sexual pleasure, essential to sexual desire. Pornography is the material means of sexualizing inequality." Feminist critics argued that discussions of the issue should focus not on questions of sexual mores but on the harm done to women—those used in pornography and those against whom pornography is used, as well as to all women.

In the mid- and late 1970s, feminists formed groups to fight pornography, including Women Against Violence in Pornography and the Media (in San Francisco), Women Against Pornography (in New York), and Women Against Violence Against Women (with local chapters throughout the country). These groups engaged in public education, protests, and direct action against pornography. Feminist antipornography efforts moved into the legislative arena when Dworkin and the law professor Catharine MacKinnon drafted a civil-rights ordinance for the Minneapolis, Minnesota, City Council in 1983 that rejected the concept of obscenity and instead framed pornography as a systematic practice of exploitation and subordination based on sex.

The ordinance defines pornography as the "graphic sexually explicit subordination of women through pictures and/or words" that include one of eight types of images: women presented (1) dehumanized as sexual objects; (2) as sexual objects who enjoy humiliation or pain; (3) experiencing

Antipornography protesters near Times Square in New York City in 1978. Corbis/Leif Skoogfors

pleasure in sexual assault; (4) as sexual objects tied up or physically hurt; (5) in postures of sexual submission; (6) as body parts; (7) as being penetrated by objects or animals; and (8) in scenarios of degradation, humiliation, injury, torture, shown as filthy or inferior, bleeding, bruised, or hurt in a context that makes these conditions sexual.

Under the ordinance, people could bring suits under five causes of action that are defined as acts of sex discrimination:

1. Coerced into pornography: The ordinance would allow a person who had been coerced, intimidated, or fraudulently induced into making pornography to sue the maker, seller, exhibitor, and/or distributor for damages and for an injunction to remove the pornography from public view. Such a suit can be brought even if the person signed a contract or in some other way consented to perform.

2. Forced to view pornography: This clause would allow people who had pornography forced on them at a job, school, or home or in public to sue the individual or institution responsible.

3. Victimized by assaults caused by pornography: Complaints could be brought against the perpetrator of an assault directly caused by specific pornography and against those involved in the production and distribution of the specific pornography.

4. Defamed through pornography: Both public and private figures defamed through the unauthorized use of their name or likeness in pornography could bring suit. Authorization once given for the use can be revoked at any time prior to publication.

5. Subordinated through the trafficking of women in pornography: This clause defines as sex discrimination the production, sale, exhibition, or distribution of pornography. A trafficking complaint could result in the removal of the material as an action against the subordination of women.

The ordinance was passed by the city council but vetoed by the Minneapolis mayor in 1984. Later that year in Indianapolis the ordinance was passed and signed into law; but eventually it was ruled unconstitutional on First Amendment grounds by federal district and appeals courts in 1985, and that judgment was affirmed by the Supreme Court in *Hudnut v. American Booksellers Association* (1986). Several other efforts at writing all or part of the civil-rights ordinance into law at the federal, state, and local levels have either failed to win passage or been thrown out by a judge after becoming law.

Opposition to such legislation has come not only from pornographers but also from the wider publishing industry and from feminists who believe that restrictions on sexual material do not serve women's interests. Those forces—called, depending on one's politics, propornography or anticensorship, sex liberals or sexual libertarians—argue that such restrictions would limit women's ability to explore their sexuality, reinforce rather than undercut sexist stereotypes, and result in the suppression of feminist images and literature about sexuality. The disagreements around pornography first surfaced publicly at the annual Barnard Conference on Sexuality in 1982, and in 1985 the Feminist Anti-Censorship Task Force submitted a brief in the Indianapolis case arguing that the civil-rights ordinance was unconstitutional. Tensions continue within the feminist movement between opponents and supporters of the radical critique and the ordinance.

Effects

Much of the debate about pornography centers on the question of effects. Does pornography, particularly the material that explicitly eroticizes sexual violence, result in sexual violence against women, children, and other vulnerable people? Pornography's supporters and some researchers argue that there is no conclusive evidence for such a claim. Others contend that the evidence establishes a causal connection only in short-term effects involving overtly violent pornography, while still others find evidence for more long-term effects for a wider range of material.

No one argues that pornography is a sole causal factor in rape, in the sense that consuming pornography is both a necessary and a sufficient condition for rape; sexual assault obviously occurs in many cases without pornography use. The question is whether, in the complex realm of human behavior, the use of pornography can be said to be a sufficient condition for triggering a sexual assault. In her review of laboratory studies and the testimony of women and men, Diana Russell argued that pornography is a causal factor in that it can: (1) predispose some males to desire rape or intensify this desire; (2) undermine some males' internal inhibitions against acting out rape desires; (3) undermine some males' social inhibitions

against acting out rape desires; and (4) undermine some potential victims' abilities to avoid or resist rape.

One underlying question is what level of certainty is needed to establish a causal link before society can or should act. The limitations of social science and laboratory research suggest that definitive proof of a causal relationship between pornography and violence—at least at the level that seems necessary to satisfy most social scientists and policy makers—is beyond the capabilities of the methods; isolating with scientific precision the effect of one particular manifestation of misogyny in a culture that is generally misogynist is a difficult task. Many feminists have argued that attention to the lived experience of men and women—both those who use pornography and those who are forced to view pornography or who are victimized by assaults as a result of pornography—makes the connection clear and provides the evidence necessary for collective action. Such accounts of people's experiences supply specific examples of how pornography can (1) be an important factor in shaping a male-dominant view of sexuality; (2) contribute to a user's difficulty in separating sexual fantasy and reality; (3) be used to initiate victims and break down resistance to sexual activity; and (4) provide a training manual for abuse.

Out of discussions of that lived experience the feminist antipornography movement emerged. Although a small number of academics have played important roles in it, the movement has always been grassroots and activist in character, rooted in feminist communities, not the academy. Antipornography groups have kept the focus on harm to women and children, in part by providing a vehicle for women to tell their stories and be heard. Although often dismissed as anecdotal, those stories and analyses have fundamentally changed the nature of the debate; the feminist critique has become central to discussions of the issue. Although they reject the underlying critique of patriarchy, conservative antipornography groups have largely adopted the feminist language of harm, often downplaying the moralistic and religious rhetoric in the public sphere. Liberal defenders of pornography, often sympathetic to feminist goals in general, have had to respond to the feminist critique in their defenses of pornography on grounds of free speech or sexual liberation. Using the controversy over pornography as an opening, radical feminists have expanded the discussion to include the harms to women in prostitution, other parts of the commercial sex industry, and the international trafficking in women.

BIBLIOGRAPHY

Assiter, Alison, and Avedon Carol, eds. *Bad Girls and Dirty Pictures: The Challenge to Reclaim Feminism.* London: Pluto, 1993.

Attorney General's Commission on Pornography. *Final Report.* Washington, D.C.: U.S. Department of Justice, 1986.

Burstyn, Varda, ed. *Women Against Censorship.* Vancouver, Canada: Douglas and McIntyre, 1985.

Dines, Gail, Robert Jensen, and Ann Russo. *Pornography: The Production and Consumption of Inequality.* New York: Routledge, 1998.

Donnerstein, Edward, Daniel Linz, and Steven Penrod. *The Question of Pornography: Research Findings and Policy Implications.* New York: Free Press, 1987.

Dworkin, Andrea. *Pornography: Men Possessing Women.* New York: Plume, 1989.

Dworkin, Andrea, and Catharine A. MacKinnon. *Pornography and Civil Rights: A New Day for Women's Equality.* Minneapolis: Organizing Against Pornography, 1988. Also available at *www.igc.apc.org/nemesis/ACLU/Porn/newday/TOC.htm* (June 1999).

Itzin, Catherine, ed. *Pornography: Women, Violence, and Civil Liberties.* Oxford, U.K.: Oxford University Press, 1992.

Kimmel, Michael, ed. *Men Confront Pornography.* New York: Crown, 1990.

MacKinnon, Catharine A. *Feminism Unmodified: Discourses on Life and Law.* Cambridge, Mass.: Harvard University Press, 1987.

MacKinnon, Catharine A., and Andrea Dworkin, eds. *In Harm's Way: The Pornography Civil Rights Hearings.* Cambridge, Mass.: Harvard University Press, 1997.

Russell, Diana E. H. *Dangerous Relationships: Pornography, Misogyny, and Rape.* Thousand Oaks, Calif.: Sage, 1998.

Segal, Lynne, and Mary McIntosh, eds. *Sex Exposed: Sexuality and the Pornography Debate.* New Brunswick, N.J.: Rutgers University Press, 1993.

Strossen, Nadine. *Defending Pornography: Free Speech, Sex, and the Fight for Women's Rights.* New York: Scribner, 1995.

Williams, Linda. *Hard Core: Power, Pleasure, and the "Frenzy of the Visible."* Berkeley: University of California Press, 1989.

Zillmann, Dolf, and Jennings Bryant, eds. *Pornography: Research Advances and Policy Considerations.* Hillsdale, N.J.: Erlbaum, 1989.

ROBERT JENSEN

See also **Civil Liberties; Internet; Popular Culture; Sex Offenders; Women.**

POSSE. *See* Lynching.

POSTERS

The intensely visual culture of the United States now consists of digital imaging, television, movies, and innumerable slick magazines. But for much of the twentieth century it was the poster that made images an integral part of U.S. culture, transforming current events into the visual experience of everyday life, whether promoting war or protesting against it. Before the widespread use of radio, newsreels, and television, posters served as an efficient medium of mass communication, their graphic boldness and semiotic simplicity enabling them to reach more people more quickly than the newspaper. Though the poster is generally understood as one genre of lithography, any posted image (a woodcut from the seventeenth century, a billboard from the 1960s, a bumper sticker) can partake of that genre's fundamental function: to incite action. The visual and verbal rhetoric of posters commands an attention that is meant to prompt immediate decision: to purchase a ticket, to enlist in the navy, to join tomorrow's protest march.

Although the invention of lithography at the close of the eighteenth century made the mass production of images genuinely practicable, it was not until the close of the nineteenth century that increased urbanization and new advertising strategies combined to make the poster seem an inevitable means of establishing contact with a mass public. Both proslavery and antislavery campaigners had made use of the broadside, which was usually distributed by hand in the street, along with being posted, and which was generally more textually detailed and more pictorially allegorical than subsequent posters. Only in the 1890s, with the impact of European art nouveau and the invention of the halftone reproduction process, did American poster production enjoy a recognizable revolution. By the time World War I broke out, national agencies throughout Europe and in the United States recognized how powerful poster propaganda could be. Eight days after the United States declared war in 1917, New York City witnessed the appearance of twenty thousand recruiting posters. Between two and three thousand different posters supporting the war effort were produced in the United States, a few in runs exceeding one hundred thousand.

The history of visual culture and the history of violence in the United States thus converge under the auspices of the military. Still, this history does not preclude the recognition that a kind of violence lies at the heart of the poster medium as such, meant as it is to forcefully interrupt our everyday lives, to intrude into the psyche, to linger in the subconscious. In an article entitled "Mobilizing the Billboards" (1917), Lee Simonson went so far as to define the poster as "a mural decoration that successfully harangues the crowd. Its beauty is a sudden and unexpected simplicity, a violent juxtaposition of silhouettes, vivid patterns of light and shade that hold the eye spellbound." Posters, he concluded, should be "militant symbols." Probably the most famous poster in U.S. history—James Montgomery Flagg's image of a stern Uncle Sam, pointing his finger to say "I Want *You*"—was meant to isolate the viewer, to subject him to the feeling of ubiquitous scrutiny, and to compel him to recognize the authority of the nation and the state. The rhetoric of atrocity posters was no less forceful: a poster declaring that the viewer should "Remember Belgium" and depicting a German soldier who drags a young girl with him in front of a burning landscape was meant to provoke the fear of rape and pillage and to arouse the sort of ethnic hatred that helped sustain U.S. patriotism just as it provoked a new and dangerous nativism.

Charles Dana Gibson organized a group of fellow artists on behalf of the Division of Pictorial Publicity (formed in 1917 at the initiative of George Creel, head of the Committee on Public Information). The group volunteered its service to the U.S. government, and posters emerged as the essential means by which the government communicated with the governed—recruiting soldiers and promoting war bonds, demanding the conservation of fuel and soliciting the contribution of canned fruit, records, and books. If the poster exemplifies the official deployment of a mass-cultural phenomenon, this is precisely because military success depended on unifying the masses. As another one of Flagg's posters put it in 1917, "Wake Up, America! Civilization Calls Every Man Woman and Child." The modernity of this war is attributable not least to the centrally organized mobilization of entire civilian populations; and the unanticipated duration of the war made it necessary to effect that mobilization—above all, to instill patriotic fervor —over and over again.

Subsequent events in Europe—the Spanish Civil War and the rise of Nazi power in Germany —seemed to confirm the potency of poster propaganda, and during World War II the U.S. government continued to deploy the medium, along with

U.S. Army recruiting poster. Corbis

radio and film. The Office of War Information, created by President Franklin D. Roosevelt in 1942, became the central authority through which the American public was informed of war policy and progress. Businesses offered themselves as sites of display for posters, artists again volunteered their time and talent, and the information office published the *Poster Handbook: A Plan for Displaying Official War Posters* (1943), which urged all citizens to help their local communities by posting the monthly issue. Existing groups, from Boys' Clubs to church organizations, often served as the basis of local poster committees, whose members completed a "poster pledge." Such militaristic rationalization of civilian life was part of the totally organized information network. "Post promptly," the handbook insisted, "so you won't miss the tie-up with press, radio, and movies." Posters organized the nation's emotional response to news.

They were meant to stir nationalist passions: soldiers and civilians were told to "Remember

December 7th," a message inscribed above a burning U.S. flag or burning ships. And they were meant to stir fear and hatred: the photograph of an open-mouthed Hitler was accompanied by his chilling insistence that "We shall soon have our Storm Troopers in America!" Posters asked civilians to "Vacation at Home," to "Save Waste Fats for Explosives," to "Grow Your Own and Can Your Own" vegetables, to buy more and more war bonds, and to be a productive part of the nation's workforce: "If *you* worked as hard and as fast as a *Jap*, we'd smash Tokio a lot quicker." They made a novel appeal to women (to join the workforce if not the military), and they became part of a new emphasis on national security. Women patriots were depicted in posters as feminine, soft, and stereotypically attractive, yet aggressive, stout-hearted, and proud. In train stations and bus stations, outside grocery stores and banks, the population was reminded to "Keep the Enemy in the dark! Be careful what you say . . . or write." The image of dying or dead soldiers was coupled with accusations ("Someone Talked!") to underscore the message that "Silence Means Security." Beneath the words "Loose Lips Sink Ships" a viewer witnessed the lurid drowning of an American naval officer.

During the Vietnam era it was the public that deployed posters as a way of wresting control back from the government, as a way to express resistance, both radicalized and generalized. In a mass-media culture, posters were a residual, populist mode of organizing the counterculture. Recruitment posters were still part of military business as usual, but posters protesting the war soon became more ubiquitous. Organizations such as the Peace Brigade Committee and the Student Mobilization Committee produced posters that attacked administration policy, celebrated resistant solidarity, and proclaimed the existence of a counterpublic: in 1967, the "Year of the People—March for Peace"; in 1969, the "May 5 National Moratorium," organizing high schools and colleges to demand the "Total, Immediate Withdrawal from Southeast Asia." Such publicity and the demonstrations that ensued made President Richard Nixon, like Lyndon Johnson before him, consider his administration "under siege." The atrocity poster, reproduced by the latest photolithographic techniques, had come to expose the horrors not of the foreign enemy but of the domestic establishment. One poster called on its viewers to "AVENGE" the students lying dead on the campus at Kent State; another

showed hundreds of tombstones and a caption reading: "We Are The Unwilling . . . Led By The Unqualified . . . To Do The Unnecessary . . . For The Ungrateful." In this era of the poster's greatest commercialization, when its function became private as well as public, college dorm rooms were decorated with images of rock stars and images of protest, sometimes calling for violent protest against the violent crimes of the government. Though the Internet may have made the poster obsolete as a mode of countercultural communication, the poster remains a powerful means by which subcultures assert themselves and seek to subvert authority before the general public.

BIBLIOGRAPHY

Bogart, Michele H. *Artists, Advertising, and the Borders of Art.* Chicago: University of Chicago Press, 1995.

Chenault, Libby. *Battlelines: World War I Posters from the Bowman Gray Collection.* Chapel Hill: Rare Book Collection, University of North Carolina, 1988.

Crawford, Anthony R., ed. *Posters of World War I and World War II in the George C. Marshall Research Foundation.* Charlottesville: University Press of Virginia, 1979.

Darracott, Joseph, ed. *The First World War in Posters.* New York: Dover, 1974.

Eichenberg, Fritz. *The Art of the Print: Masterpieces, History, Techniques.* New York: Harry N. Abrams, 1976.

Gallo, Max. *The Poster in History.* New York: American Heritage, 1974.

Hutchison, Harold. *The Poster: An Illustrated History.* New York: Viking, 1968.

Judd, Denis. *Posters of World War Two.* New York: St. Martin's, 1973.

Paret, Peter, Beth Irwin Lewis, and Paul Paret. *Persuasive Images: Posters of War and Revolution from the Hoover Institution Archives.* Princeton, N.J.: Princeton University Press, 1992.

Rickards, Maurice. *Posters of Protest and Revolution.* New York: Walker, 1970.

U.S. War Information Office. *Poster Handbook: A Plan for Displaying Official War Posters.* Washington, D.C.: U.S. Government Printing Office, 1943.

BILL BROWN

See also **Popular Culture; Representation of Violence.**

POST-TRAUMATIC STRESS DISORDER

Post-traumatic stress disorder (PTSD) is a psychiatric diagnosis formulated in the 1980s to describe a group of psychophysiological phenomena that emerge in some people following exposure to trauma. It is important to note, however, that most people do not develop psychiatric disorders following trauma. Moreover, PTSD is not the only psychiatric diagnosis encountered in the traumatized: major depression, generalized anxiety disorder, substance abuse disorder, and adjustment disorders are also well-documented outcomes. Community-based studies have reported the incidence of PTSD in the general population ranging from 1 to 4 percent.

Diagnosis

The diagnosis *post-traumatic stress disorder* first appeared in psychiatric nomenclature in the 1980 publication of the third edition of the *Diagnostic and Statistical Manual of Mental Disorders (DSM-III)* by the American Psychiatric Association (APA). Prior to the incorporation of PTSD into psychiatric nomenclature, similar symptoms and responses following a variety of traumas had been described under a variety of names such as *DaCosta syndrome*, *shellshock*, *war neurosis*, and *railway spine*. In the years following its inclusion in the DSM, PTSD's diagnostic criteria changed to reflect increased understanding. For example, in early definitions traumatic events were viewed as rare events, usually at the borders of the range of human experience. Epidemiological studies have shown, however, that trauma is encountered more frequently than originally thought. It has been estimated that each year 6 to 7 percent of the U.S. population is exposed to a traumatic event (Ursano, McCaughey, and Fullerton 1994). Over the course of their lifetimes, 40 to 70 percent of Americans will be subjected to a traumatic event. Revisions of the *DSM* diagnostic criteria incorporated data such as these to refine the definition.

In the 1994 edition of the APA manual, *DSM-IV*, diagnosis of PTSD began with determining whether an individual was exposed to a traumatic event in which he or she experienced (or witnessed) bodily threat and responded with feelings of intense fear, horror, or helplessness. Following the event, the individual must experience difficulties in three major realms for at least one month in order to meet the diagnostic threshold for PTSD:

- persistent reexperiencing of the event
- avoidance of reminders of the event accompanied by emotional numbing
- persistent symptoms of increased autonomic arousal (e.g., an exaggerated startle response, irritability or angry outbursts)

Additionally, these symptoms must cause significant distress or impairment in functioning in order to warrant a diagnosis of PTSD.

Another trauma-related diagnosis, acute stress disorder (ASD), was introduced in *DSM-IV*. Acute stress disorder is very similar to post-traumatic stress disorder. The main distinctions are (1) ASD is manifested earlier and for a briefer time (symptoms occurring within four weeks of the trauma and lasting a minimum of two days and a maximum of four weeks) and (2) ASD has the diagnostic requirement that the individual experience three or more dissociative symptoms (e.g., "being in a daze," or experiencing amnesia for important aspects of the trauma).

Factors Influencing Vulnerability

Following exposure to a traumatic event, people commonly experience symptoms resembling PTSD. It is difficult to predict who will actually develop PTSD based on their responses in the immediate aftermath of the trauma. Research suggests that people who respond to the trauma by dissociating (becoming psychologically detached from their surroundings such as "being in a fog" or feeling "numb") may be more vulnerable to developing PTSD. The typical pattern for most survivors of traumas is for gradual resolution of post-trauma symptoms over time—only a minority of traumatized individuals develop PTSD or other psychiatric disorders. PTSD symptoms will resolve in approximately two-thirds of those given the diagnosis.

There are three key determinants of an individual's outcome following a trauma: the nature of the traumatic event, individual characteristics of the affected individual, and the individual's recovery environment. The magnitude of the traumatic event or stressor appears to be the most important factor in predicting an individual's outcome. Rape, for example, is a traumatic stressor that is highly associated with PTSD, with up to two-thirds of rape victims meeting diagnostic criteria for the disorder. Violence constitutes a traumatic stressor for most recipients and many witnesses; ironically, it can also be a traumatic stressor for the perpetrator.

Pre-trauma factors that have been reported to increase vulnerability to PTSD include the presence of a psychiatric disorder (e.g., depression), family history of a psychiatric disorder, past history of trauma, and an introverted, neurotic personality style. Research in the 1990s was also exploring the possibility of neuroendocrine vulnerabilities in individuals. For reasons that are not understood, women are twice as likely as men to develop PTSD. This finding holds true even when differences in the type of trauma to which men (e.g., war) and women (e.g., rape) are exposed are taken into account.

The trauma survivor's recovery environment plays a major role in assisting the individual in drawing meaning from the traumatic event as well as healing a shattered sense of safety and predictability. Circumstances in which traumatized individuals are scapegoated or blamed make a healthy assimilation of the trauma more difficult. In contrast, the mobilization of social supports enhances the individual's coping skills.

Prevention and Treatment

The APA's diagnostic recognition of PTSD generated increased attention to providing early psychological intervention following disaster in hopes of preventing psychiatric morbidity. While techniques such as debriefing, which involves a group meeting with trauma victims in which they are encouraged to describe and share their experience of a disaster or trauma, were widely employed beginning in the 1980s, research at the end of the 1990s was still insufficient to demonstrate whether or not such interventions are efficacious.

In treating persons who have developed PTSD, it is important to recognize that in cases where an individual begins to reexperience traumatic memories after a period of quiescence, the past trauma often serves as a metaphor to describe a difficult circumstance in the present. In such instances, careful exploration of current situations that may be causing the individual to feel threatened will generally be more fruitful than an exploration of the original trauma. Psychosocial treatments for chronic PTSD include hypnotherapy, psychodynamic psychotherapy, cognitive-behavioral therapies, and anxiety-management programs. Medications are sometimes used to treat the disabling symptoms (such as withdrawal and hyperarousal) of PTSD. All classes of antidepressant medications (tricyclics; serotonin reuptake inhibitors, or SSRIs; and monoamine oxidase inhibitors, or MAOIs) appear somewhat effective in treating PTSD. As of the late 1990s, there was little evidence to support the efficacy of antianxiety agents for the treatment of PTSD. The efficacy of anticonvulsant medications (mood stabilizers) for treating PTSD was being explored.

BIBLIOGRAPHY

Fullerton, Carol S., and Robert J. Ursano. *Posttraumatic Stress Disorder: Acute and Long-Term Responses to Trauma and Disaster.* Washington, D.C.: American Psychiatric Press, 1997.

Ursano, Robert J., Brian G. McCaughey, and Carol S. Fullerton, eds. *Individual and Community Responses to Trauma and Disaster: The Structure of Human Chaos.* Cambridge, U.K.: Cambridge University Press, 1994.

Van der Kolk, Bessel A., Alexander C. McFarlane, and Lars Weisaeth, eds. *Traumatic Stress: The Effects of Overwhelming Experience on Mind, Body, and Society.* New York: Guilford, 1996.

ROBERT J. URSANO
ANN E. NORWOOD

See also **Victims of Violence; Prisoners of War; War: Aftermath of, Psychoanalytic Aspects.**

POVERTY

In the late twentieth century the poverty rate in the United States for families with children exploded, rising from 7.7 percent in 1977 to 11.4 percent in 1993. In the 1990s the poverty rate for children was more than double what it was for adults, and two out of every five poor Americans were children (Bronfenbrenner et al. 1996). The increased poverty rate among children and youth was attributable largely to two phenomena.

First, in the wake of the computer-oriented technology revolution, there was a decline in the number of full-time jobs that paid a living wage available to semiskilled and unskilled workers. Modern computer systems were performing jobs that once provided working-class families with steady sources of family income. Telephone operators, bank tellers, and gas-station attendants had been replaced by automated answering systems, Internet banking, and pay-at-the-pump technology.

Second, American society was experiencing unprecedented levels of single motherhood, which is, in and of itself, a strong predictor of poverty. In late 1950s, 95 percent of children were raised in two-parent families. By the mid-1990s, the number had dropped to less than 60 percent (Bronfenbrenner et al. 1996). The inability to find affordable child care and gainful educational and occupational opportunities made some combination of public assistance and poverty an undeniable reality for many young mothers. In 1991, the probability of living below the poverty line was 40 percent for white single mothers and an astounding

60 percent for minority single mothers (Huston, McLoyd, and Garcia-Coll 1994). The implications of these numbers for children and youth were frighteningly clear.

As American children became poorer and poorer, the United States witnessed a major change in the way young people experienced childhood and adolescence. They became increasingly troubled, hostile, and violent—violent not only toward society, but also toward each other. Unfortunately, American citizens have only an incomplete understanding of the true magnitude and pervasiveness of youth violence. Although politicians and government officials would like to perpetuate the illusion that crime is on the decline and that they have regained control of America's streets, this take on youth violence is terribly misleading.

The overall crime rate *has* stabilized in some respects; it has even dropped in others. However, the single biggest change in the way violence plays itself out in America is the ever-growing youthfulness of modern-day victims and perpetrators of violent crime (Garbarino 1999). This is evident in two well-established and closely related facts. First, the average age of perpetrators of homicide

Children living in squalor. CORBIS/HULTON-DEUTSCH COLLECTION

decreased from thirty-three to twenty-seven between 1965 and 1993 (Bronfenbrenner et al. 1996). Killers are getting younger. Second, while the overall homicide rate in the United States has remained relatively constant from the 1960s through the 1990s, the youth homicide rate more than tripled between 1965 and 1990 (Bronfenbrenner et al. 1996). The youngest killers in the United States are growing in both raw numbers and proportional representation.

Mohandas K. Gandhi said, "Poverty is the ultimate form of violence." Gandhi understood that inequality is a central defining factor in the human experience, even though its physical concomitants are variable across cultures and societies. In some societies, for example, poverty may mean shortened life expectancy and institutionalized violence. In others it means a sense of relative deprivation that varies as a function of the gap between the "rich" and "poor," however they are defined. Regardless of the context: as a psychological assault against self-esteem and identity, poverty is an act of violence.

Effects of Poverty on Child Development

Poverty and Social Toxicity. The union of the key words *children* and *poverty* in a simple bibliographic query of relevant on-line resources (in this case, *Psychological Abstracts* and *Sociological Abstracts*) yields more than fifteen hundred articles—research reports, literature reviews, intervention-oriented program-evaluation studies—in the ten years between 1989 and 1999. There is no shortage of research on the topic of children and poverty. But what does being poor mean to a child?

From many points of view, being poor means being at statistical risk for a number of physical, social, and psychological pathologies. Poor children tend to live in environments filled with threats such as violence, racism, unstable care arrangements, economic deprivation, and community insecurity. These multiple threats to child development have been described by the term *social toxicity* (Garbarino 1995). Academic failure, child maltreatment, and learning disabilities increase in the face of potent social toxins, and poverty is both a cause and effect of such toxicity.

The enormous body of evidence linking child poverty to negative outcomes has been amply reviewed: for instance, advocacy organizations such as the Children's Defense Fund and the National Center for Children in Poverty have devoted their resources to chronicling the association between child poverty and negative child outcomes. Perhaps the best single compendium is the 1996 volume *The State of Americans* (Bronfenbrenner et al.), which offers data from a team of psychologists, economists, and sociologists that are used as the primary source throughout this article.

Put most simply, all this research validates Sophie Tucker's famous insight: "I've been rich and I've been poor and rich is better." Research documents the correlation between child poverty and nearly every aspect of child development: from mental and physical health to moral development, from child maltreatment to play. The consistent pattern is that poor children experience and manifest less of whatever is commonly understood to be positive and desirable, and more of whatever is thought to be negative or undesirable. Violence is no exception. This reality partly explains Gandhi's assertion that poverty *is* violence. But there is more to it than this. Being poor means that the odds are stacked against you through an accumulation of risk, a most important feature of the child-poverty equation.

Accumulation of Risk. It is no coincidence that the negative trajectories of poverty and youth violence exploded almost simultaneously in the late twentieth century, and the phenomenon has a number of empirically validated explanations. The relationship between poverty and violence is nonetheless indirect: poverty alone does not cause youth violence, any more than youth violence alone causes poverty. Just as there are large numbers of poor children and teens in the United States who are neither violent nor aggressive, so there are large numbers of violent and highly aggressive children and teens who will mature into productive and economically successful adults. Both poverty and youth violence have complex etiologies consisting of multiple risk factors. This idea follows what researchers and theorists call the accumulation-of-risk model (Sameroff et al. 1987).

The accumulation-of-risk model asserts that most children are capable of coping with low levels of risk until the accumulation exceeds a developmentally determined threshold. Once cumulative risk moves beyond this threshold, systems of strong compensatory forces (or opportunity factors) are needed to prevent the precipitation of physical and psychological harm. To identify this threshold, Arnold Sameroff and his colleagues

(1987) explored the impact of accumulated risk on the intellectual development of preschool children. Using a pool of eight risk factors that included assessments of maternal dysfunction (such as mental illness, low educational attainment, and substance abuse), family structure (for example, absent father and large number of siblings), and sociodemographics (for instance, poverty), Sameroff found that the presence of one or two major risk factors was associated with virtually no developmental damage. That is, intelligence quotients remained within the average-to-above-average range as children moved from zero to one and then two risk factors (mean IQ 119 with no risks, 116 with one risk, and 113 with two risks). However, as risk continued to accumulate, IQ scores soon began to plummet. As third and fourth major risk factors were added, average IQ scores decreased to about 93, well below the national average. The third and fourth risk factors exceeded the adaptive coping capacity of the children, and children began to exhibit signs of maladaptive functioning.

Extending Sameroff's approach, Carl Dunst and Carol Trivette (1992) included in the developmental equation the counterpart opportunity measure for each of the original risk factors (e.g., a present and highly supportive father as the opportunity counterpart to an absent father). This simultaneous assessment of both risk and opportunity is crucial to an understanding of the long-term effects of early developmental experiences because it more accurately captures the reality of how children develop. No child's social map consists of exclusively risk or exclusively opportunity—in the real world, risk and opportunity converge and interact. Dunst and Trivette's reconceptualization has important implications for research, policy, and practice because the authors document the validity of an "accumulation of *opportunity*" model. Such a model suggests that risk factors may be neutralized or at least partially offset by introducing opportunity factors into other realms of the child's life, even when patterns of risk are thought to be impervious to intervention. Additional evidence supporting this idea of opportunity-counteracting risk is embedded in the finding that maltreated children who have regular contact with a highly involved nonparental adult figure show psychological and behavioral trajectories similar to those of their nonmaltreated counterparts (Cicchetti and Rizley 1981).

This line of research suggests that poverty by itself is not associated with significant developmental harm. Even if coupled with one other risk factor, poverty is still not associated with significant dysfunction. It is only when poverty is part of a larger pattern of risk that it is associated with notably impaired functioning. Conventional single-variable studies are inadequate as a way of understanding the stress of being a poor child in the United States. Answering the question "What does it mean to be a poor child in America?" requires examining the complex contextual meaning of poverty in the lives of children.

Compounding Risk Factors. Poverty is increasingly part of an ecological conspiracy in which elements of social toxicity are compounded (Garbarino 1995). There is a general pathologizing of poverty in the sense that it has become increasingly associated with other developmental risks. For example, in the 1950s and 1960s there was significant poverty among two-parent families. By the 1990s, poverty was confined mainly to single-parent households. In fact, national survey data suggest that the rate of poverty among two-parent families is negligible relative to the corresponding rate for one-parent families (Bronfenbrenner et al. 1996). A major reason for this shift is the increasing tendency for both parents to be in the labor force, a factor that means that even a parent who is working at minimum wage will likely not be raising children in a "poor" family *if* that parent is teamed with a second wage earner. Accordingly, in modern America being poor statistically correlates to a likelihood of growing up under the supervision of only one parent, which in turn correlates to an increased the risk for developmental harm and dysfunction.

A study conducted in Chicago by Patrick Tolan (1995) offers insight into what happens when poverty begins to converge with other salient developmental risk factors. Tolan asked, What proportion of kids living in the most fractured families in the most stressful neighborhoods can be said to be "resilient," when resilience is defined as a fifteen-year-old being neither more than one year behind in school nor in the clinical range of the Achenbach Child Behavior Checklist (i.e., having an externalizing and internalizing behavior score that exceeds the point at which clinical consensus has determined that there is little or no doubt that professional mental-health services are required to restore "normal" functioning). Tolan's answer? Zero percent. Not a single child in the study met these generous criteria for resilience, highlighting the

potential for dysfunction when poverty is experienced within the context of a fractured family.

The Link Between the Effects of Poverty and Economic Inequality

An objective definition of poverty exists for purposes of official government policy. It is based upon the income needed to meet an agreed-upon minimal standard of living—a standard that was originally determined by the U.S. Agriculture Department on the basis of what it would take to purchase sufficient food to maintain a minimally healthy diet (Bronfenbrenner et al. 1996). Thus, the poverty line at a given place and time is defined as X dollars for a family of Y persons. But like most objective classifications of complex human phenomena, this simple definition misses a host of subtleties and complexities of what poverty really means for children and child development.

Steven F. Messner (1988) stresses the role played by economic inequality in the dynamics of aggression. The daughter of a colleague once wrote in a composition for school that she was the "poorest kid on her block" because she lived in the smallest house. She *did* live in the smallest house on the block, but it was a seven-bedroom house on a block of even larger mansions. What does it mean for a child to be poor if she uses such relative standards—where being poor means having less than others, no matter how much they have?

When most of the people of the world live on incomes of hundreds of dollars per year, what does it mean when we in the United States define the poverty level at $14,000 per year? India defines poverty as having access to less than 2,100 calories per day (Blanc 1994) in one's diet, and using that yardstick suggests that 20 percent of the population is poor in what North Americans would consider a predominantly poor society. Interestingly, this 20 percent figure is roughly the same as the North American poverty rate, but if poor children in other nations of the world are shoeless, how do we make sense of the fact that American "poor kids" often wear $150 running shoes? Analyzing the links between poverty and violence in the lives of children is a daunting task because poverty is defined contextually rather than absolutely. It surely is not a matter of simple accounting.

The point is that the child's subjective sense of deprivation is an important factor in understanding and interpreting the developmental significance of socioeconomic status. However, in addition to this subjective sense, there must be some degree of social validation before a child can be labeled appropriately as being poor. Relative deprivation is a crucial component of poverty, a necessary but not sufficient condition for making the "diagnosis." The truth of this assertion can be seen most clearly when one takes a historical perspective. For example, many items considered luxuries in the 1940s and 1950s (e.g., televisions and telephones) were by the 1970s considered a basic necessity. Poverty is a relative assessment.

Poverty is an assessment of one's position in a social order, and the underlying psychological meaning of poverty lies in *relative deprivation*. Poverty is not so much a matter of what a child or family has as it is what that child or family *does not* have in relation to other children and families. This relative deprivation is related to important issues of self-esteem and shame, issues that are central to understanding violence.

Shame and the Ensuing Rage

Being poor is about being left out of what society tells people they can expect if they are included. This is a social proposition at its root, and thus one that plays an important role in generating stress. A child once asked James Garbarino, "Dr. G., when you were growing up, were you poor or regular?" The young boy's question captures perfectly the psychological implications of living in poverty—being poor means being something other than regular; it means being inadequate, unworthy, not meeting the fundamental standards set by the larger society. It is not a matter of what you have, but what you do not have. The message is one of difference, one of inferiority and lowliness.

The United States suffers from many forms of injustice that spawn shame and, ultimately, social toxicity and violence. Racism is certainly at the top of the list. Racism creates a dynamic of humiliation and power imbalance that is likely to be perceived as threatening. Working with murderers in the Massachusetts state prison system, James Gilligan (1996) found shame and humiliation to be potent precursors of violence by creating situations in which individuals—and often groups—feel threatened by psychic annihilation. So threatened, these individuals and groups respond with violence at even the slightest provocation. Violence gives them a sense of having what they often lack amid the exploitation and humiliation of their daily lives—power and control. As one convicted killer put it, "I'd rather be wanted for murder than not be wanted at all."

These issues have significant implications for the wave of dramatic lethal youth violence that began shocking American society in the late 1990s. In these cases the core issue is not economic poverty, since these boys often come from middle-class families, but emotional and psychological poverty. The lethality of the rage and shame of these socially marginalized boys reminds us of the need to deal with spiritual and psychological poverty as well. These "lost boys" suffer an impoverishment of spirit that no material bounty can fill. Often these are the friendless and self-loathing boys discarded by teenage (and in many cases adult) society.

The Socioeconomics and Demographics of Violence

Homicide rates provide only an imprecise indicator of the overall problem of violence in the lives of American children and youth, for behind each murder stand many nonlethal assaults. This ratio between assault and death varies as a function of both medical-trauma technology (which can prevent an assault from becoming a homicide) and weapons technology (which can affect the lethality of an assault). An example from Chicago illustrates this point with striking clarity. The city's homicide rate in 1993 was approximately the same as it had been twenty years earlier. However, the rate of serious assault increased approximately 400 percent during that same period. Thus, the ratio of assaults to homicides increased substantially—from 100:1 in 1973 to 400:1 in 1993 (Garbarino et al. 1992). Despite a stable homicide rate, the streets of Chicago were becoming consistently and reliably more dangerous.

Data from Chicago's Cook County Hospital provide another perspective on the changing nature of violence facing children in America. In 1982 the hospital responded to approximately five hundred gunshot cases. In 1992 the number was approximately one thousand. However, in 1982 these cases overwhelmingly involved single-bullet injuries, whereas in 1992 more than 25 percent involved multiple-bullet injuries. Rates of permanent disability have increased substantially, while the homicide rate has remained about the same largely because of the compensatory improvements in medical-trauma services.

Class, race, and gender exert important influences on exposure to community violence. The odds of being a homicide victim range from 21:1 for young black males to 369:1 for young white females (Bell and Jenkins 1991). Being an American itself is a risk factor. The United States far exceeds all other modern industrialized nations in its homicide rate, not just for African Americans dealing with racism and deprivation, but also for whites, for whom the rate of 11.2 per 100,000 far exceeds that of the second-place country, Scotland, with 5 per 100,000 (Richters and Martinez 1993).

Whatever the exact constellation of causes, children growing up in the United States have particularly high levels of exposure to community violence, especially if they live in neighborhoods that simulate "urban war zones." A 1993 survey of sixth through tenth graders in New Haven, Connecticut, revealed that 40 percent had witnessed at least one incident of violent crime within the previous twelve months (Marans and Cohen 1993). In another study conducted throughout three high-risk neighborhoods in Chicago, 17 percent of the elementary school–age children had witnessed domestic violence, 31 percent had seen someone shot, and 84 percent had seen someone "beat up" (Bell and Jenkins 1991).

Some 30 percent of the kids living in poor high-crime neighborhoods of major metropolitan areas of Chicago have witnessed a homicide by the time they are fifteen years old, and more than 70 percent have witnessed a serious assault (Bell and Jenkins 1991). John Richters and Pedro Martinez (1993) have amplified these results. In one of their studies, 43 percent of fifth and sixth graders had witnessed a mugging in a *moderately* violent" neighborhood in Washington, D.C.—moderately as measured against the range of all neighborhoods in the city. However, this must be considered in the context of the fact that all the neighborhoods with violence above community levels are also low-income areas (Garbarino et al. 1992). These figures indicate that the extent of violence witnessed by children in low-income urban neighborhoods in the United States is much more like the experience of children in actual war zones in other countries (Garbarino et al. 1992) than it is the experience we should expect for American children, living in a nation of "peace." Indeed, it is intellectually useful to speak of the "urban war zones" as a basis for understanding the long-term effects of community violence on children and youth.

The Urban Gun Culture

Guns are one of the recurrent themes in the American war zone and account for much of the increasing seriousness of adolescent conflict. Being a child becomes more and more dangerous as chronic violence becomes a fact of life for more and more Americans. Drugs, guns, and gangs conspire to create dangerous environments for children and youth in urban neighborhoods—and, increasingly, elsewhere in U.S. society. These violent external threats often are added to the risk of violence inside the family and the broader range of risk factors that affect American children (e.g., poverty, parental substance abuse, absent fathers, and maternal incapacity), risk factors that produce the social environment for children that was described above as "toxic" in the sense of being socially poisonous and putting a child at risk for impaired development (Garbarino 1995).

A study conducted in 1987, when homicide rates were skyrocketing in major U.S. cities, showed that nearly all the children living in a Chicago public housing project had firsthand experiences with shooting by the time they were five years old (Dubrow and Garbarino 1989). Interviews with school-age children and youth confirm that the "gun culture" is a potent factor in the life of children in diverse settings in the United States (Garbarino 1995). Of homicides committed by teens, the percentage involving guns rose from 64 percent in 1987 to 78 percent in 1991. During the same period teen arrests for crimes involving weapons increased by 62 percent (Fox 1996). The spread of the gun culture into the lives of schoolchildren and youth since 1980 represents a clear and present danger to their mental health, social behavior, and educational success.

Interviews of high-risk children and other youth incarcerated for murder illuminate the effects of this gun culture on the experience of childhood. In Detroit a young boy whose idolized teenage brother was killed in a gang-related attack was asked, "If you could have anything in the whole world, what would it be?" His answer: "A gun, so I could blow away the person that killed my brother" (Marin 1989). In California, when a nine-year-old boy living in a neighborhood characterized by declining security was asked, "What would it take to make you feel safer here?" he replied bluntly after a moment of deliberation, "A gun of my own" (Garbarino 1995). In a middle-class suburb of Chicago, a classroom of eight-year-olds was asked, "If you needed a gun, could you get one?" More than a third of these children were able to describe *in detail* how they would go about obtaining a firearm.

But what predicts gun ownership? Studying a sample of 1,619 children who ranged in age from eight to eighteen years, investigators in Cleveland identified four motivation factors that predicted reliably whether a child or adolescent would own a handgun (Shapiro et al. 1997). The first factor, an aggressive response to shame, refers to the code of honor that legitimizes violence as an appropriate means of preserving self-esteem. The second factor is comfort with aggression, meaning that the child is not upset about being around guns and has comfortably accepted violence as part of his or her social world. The third factor, gun excitement, refers to the belief that guns are intrinsically exciting, stimulating, and fun in and of themselves. The fourth factor is safety and power, meaning that the child associates feelings of dominance and security with carrying a gun and being with other people who carry guns. Less than 1 percent of children and youth who had none of these motives possessed a gun, but more than one-third of the gun owners in the sample evidenced all four motives.

Understanding the urban war zone requires understanding the gun culture infusing the minds and hearts of American children and youth (and adults as well, for about one half of U.S. households contain at least one gun). Of course, most children and youth who are drawn to guns, who know how to get guns, and who say that having a gun would make them feel safer will not actually end up using a gun—a generalization about gun use that parallels adult gun ownership. (Even most armed police are likely to go through an entire career without actually firing their weapon in the line of duty.) Whether or not a child's integration into the gun culture results in his or her actually shooting someone depends upon the particular circumstances of that child, most especially whether he or she experiences an accumulation of biosocial and psychological risk factors in the absence of compensatory opportunity factors.

Drugs and Violence: Facts and Fiction

Drugs are repeatedly cited as causal agents, precipitating large amounts of violence in America. However, little evidence exists supporting a psychopharmacological explanation of the relationship. In fact, Delbert Elliott (1994) reports findings that suggest that marijuana and opiate drugs actually decrease violent tendencies.

Another widely held misconception is that drug addicts often commit violent crimes to support their drug habits. This, however, is a rather rare phenomenon (Elliott 1994). The strongest connection between drugs and violence concerns the structure and nature of their distribution. It is dealing drugs, not using them, that leads to violence.

Economically impoverished children and youth often turn to drug dealing as a way to make money—lots of money. Adolescent males living in the poorest neighborhoods of New York City report that a teenager selling drugs can bring in from $200 to $800 per day. This income potential has two important implications for the poverty-violence equation. First, it is common for these teen entrepreneurs to use their street money to supplement their family's income. It is not uncommon for parents in poor communities to be unable to meet the day-to-day physical needs of their families, and, in many cases, drug-dealing sons or close relatives help offset the cost of necessities like food, shelter, and clothing. Second, money gives someone who lives in a world suffused with poverty the feeling of power and adequacy, even if only on a superficial level. Hustling, as drug dealing is often called, for just a few hours a day can make "haves" out of "have-nots" as no other profession or pseudoprofession can. The "senseless" violence and killing we read and hear about in the urban war zone is often the result of drug-turf disputes. Street money plays such an immediate and meaningful salutary role in the lives of those who would otherwise be economically impoverished that they are willing to go as far as to kill another human being who threatens its source.

BIBLIOGRAPHY

Bell, Carl C., and Esther J. Jenkins. "Traumatic Stress and Children." *Journal of Health Care for the Poor and Underserved* 2, no. 1 (1991).

Blanc, Szanton, ed. *Urban Children in Distress*. New York: Gordon and Breach, 1994.

Bronfenbrenner, Urie. "Ecology of the Family as a Context for Human Development: Research Perspectives." *Developmental Psychology* 22, no. 6 (1986).

Bronfenbrenner, Urie, et al. *The State of Americans*. New York: Free Press, 1996.

Cicchetti, Dante, and Ross Rizley. "Developmental Perspectives on the Etiology, Intergenerational Transmission, and Sequelae of Child Maltreatment." *New Directions for Child Development* 11 (1981).

Coulton, Claudia, and Shanta Pandey. "Geographic Concentration of Poverty and Risk to Children in Urban Neighborhoods." *American Behavioral Scientist* 35, no. 3 (1992).

Crane, Jonathan. "The Epidemic Theory of Ghettos and Neighborhood Effects on Dropping Out and Teenage Childbearing." *American Journal of Sociology* 96, no. 5 (1991).

Dubrow, Nancy, and James Garbarino. "Living in the War Zone: Mothers and Young Children in a Public Housing Development." *Child Welfare* 68, no. 1 (1989).

Dunst, Carl, and Carol Trivette. "Risk and Opportunity Factors Influence Parent and Child Functioning." Paper presented at the Ninth Annual Smoky Mountain Winter Institute, Ashville, N.C., 1992.

Elliott, Delbert. *Youth Violence: An Overview.* Boulder: University of Colorado, Center for the Study and Prevention of Violence, 1994.

Fox, James. *Trends in Juvenile Violence.* Washington, D.C.: U.S. Department of Justice, Bureau of Justice Statistics, 1996.

Garbarino, James. *Lost Boys: Why Our Sons Turn Violent and How We Can Save Them.* New York: Free Press, 1999.

———. *Raising Children in a Socially Toxic Environment.* San Francisco: Jossey-Bass, 1995.

———. *Toward a Sustainable Society.* Chicago: Noble, 1992.

Garbarino, James, et al. *Children in Danger: Coping with the Consequences of Community Violence.* San Francisco: Jossey-Bass, 1992.

Gelles, Richard, and Murray Straus. *Intimate Violence.* New York: Simon and Schuster, 1988.

Gilligan, James. *Violence: Our Deadly Epidemic and Its Causes.* New York: Putnam, 1996.

Hewlett, Sylvia Ann. *The Cruel Dilemmas of Development: Twentieth-Century Brazil.* New York: Basic, 1980.

Hunt, Joseph McVicker. *The Challenge of Incompetence and Poverty.* Urbana: University of Illinois Press, 1969.

———. *Intelligence and Experience.* New York: Ronald, 1961.

Huston, Aletha, Vonnie C. McLoyd, and Cynthia Garcia-Coll, eds. *Child Development.* Special issue, "Children and Poverty" (1994).

Losel, Friedrich, and T. Bliesner. "Resilience in Adolescence: A Study on the Generalizability of Protective Factors." In *Health Hazards in Adolescence,* edited by Klaus Hurrelmann and Friedrich Losel. Berlin: Walter de Gruyter, 1990.

McClelland, David C. "Testing for Competence Rather than for Intelligence." *American Psychologist* 28, no. 1 (1973).

Marans, Steven, and Donald J. Cohen. "Children and Inner-City Violence: Strategies for Intervention." In *The Psychological Effects of War and Violence on Children,* edited by Lewis A. Leavitt and Nathan A. Fox. Hillsdale, N.J.: Erlbaum, 1993.

Marin, C. *Grief's Children.* Television documentary, WMAQ, Chicago, 21 June 1989.

Melton, Gary, and Frank Barry. *Protecting Children from Abuse and Neglect.* New York: Guilford, 1994.

Messner, Steven F. "Research on Cultural and Socioeconomic Factors in Criminal Violence." *Psychiatric Clinics of North America* 11, no. 4 (1988).

Miringhoff, Marc. "A Very Different Country." *Fordham Institute for Innovation in Social Policy Social Report* (May 1996).

Rainwater, Lee, and Timothy Smeeding. "U.S. Doing Poorly—Compared to Others." *National Center for Children in Poverty News and Issues* 5, no. 3 (fall–winter 1995).

Richters, John, and Pedro Martinez. "The NIMH Community Violence Project: I. Children as Victims of and Witnesses to Violence." *Psychiatry: Interpersonal and Biological Processes* 56, no. 1 (1993).

Sameroff, Arnold, et al. "Intelligence Quotient Scores of Four-Year-Old Children: Socio-environmental Risk Factors." *Pediatrics* 79, no. 1 (1987).

Shapiro, Jeremy P., et al. "Development and Factor Analysis of a Measure of Youth Attitudes Toward Guns and Violence." *Journal of Clinical Child Psychology* 26, no. 3 (1997).

Stack. Carol. *All Our Kin: Strategies for Survival in a Black Community.* New York: Harper and Row, 1974.

Tolan, Patrick. "The Limits of Resilience." Presentation to the American Psychological Association, New York, August 1995.

Wilson, William J. *The Truly Disadvantaged: The Inner City, the Underclass, and Public Policy.* Chicago: University of Chicago Press, 1987.

JOSEPH A. VORRASI
JAMES GARBARINO

See also **Capitalism; Class; Race and Ethnicity; Shame; Structural Violence; Urban Violence.**

PREVENTION

This entry is divided into two parts: **Early Health Preventions** *and* **Violent-Crime Prevention.**

EARLY HEALTH PREVENTIONS

The mortality and morbidity caused by violence is increasingly viewed as a major public-health problem in the United States. Thus, prevention of violence has become one of the most pressing issues facing society.

Although there have been numerous intervention programs aiming to stop aggression once it has started, only since the 1990s have early-prevention programs (which aim to stop aggression and violence before they start) been recognized as a key strategy against violence. Three things make early prevention particularly important. First, biosocial research has illustrated that biological and social risk factors for violence occur very early in life. Second, many studies have demonstrated that serious, chronic violent behavior is predictable from early antisocial behavior and has distinct developmental pathways. Third, risk is cumulative, and early exposure to risk factors increases the chance of being exposed to more risk factors later. Thus, the earlier the intervention, the more effective it should be in changing the long-term developmental trajectory toward violence.

Three Types of Early Prevention

Three stages in the life of the newborn or child fall within the scope of "early" prevention for violence: prenatal (before birth), perinatal (immediately around the time of birth), and postnatal (from infancy to age five). During these three stages, three types of health interventions can be implemented. Primary prevention focuses on good prenatal care for the whole population in order to increase protective factors, such as good nutrition, and decrease risk factors, such as birth complications. Secondary prevention targets high-risk pregnant women and their infants and tackles specific risk factors for later violence, such as drug use during pregnancy. Tertiary prevention provides individualized and therapeutic treatment to those young children who already manifest behavioral problems, such as conduct disorder, so as to prevent them from becoming delinquent in adolescence and violent in adulthood. Although most studies have consisted of tertiary interventions, primary and secondary interventions may ultimately prove to be more effective in preventing violence.

Effects of Home Visits by Nurses

Studies indicate that prenatal and early-childhood home visitations by nurses have been particularly successful in reducing the likelihood that a child will grow up to become antisocial and criminal. David Olds and his colleagues focused on four hundred pregnant women who experienced social adversity (low socioeconomic status, unmarried, teenage pregnancy). These women during pregnancy received an average of nine home visitations by nurses and twenty-three home visits from birth through the child's second birthday. The nurse visits focused on promoting three aspects of maternal function that are considered protective factors against violence: (1) positive health-related behaviors during pregnancy and the early years of a child's life, (2) competent care of one's children, and (3) maternal personal development. Nurses instructed mothers in prenatal and postnatal care of their child, the nature of infant growth and development, the importance of proper nutrition, and the benefits of avoiding smoking and drinking during pregnancy. They also gave advice to mothers about family planning, educational achievement, and participation in the workforce. This program reduced three risk factors for the development of violent behaviors: (1) maternal substance abuse during pregnancy, (2) child maltreatment, and (3) family size. Significantly, a fifteen-year follow-up of the children demonstrated that the nurse-visit program led to a reduction in arrests, convictions, and parole violations, as well as reductions in alcohol consumption and cigarette smoking. (A control group was used, and the allocation to experimental and control group was randomized.)

In other studies showing positive effects of home visits before and after birth, visits were made by health-care providers including nurses, psychologists, and social workers. These providers taught child-care skills, provided information on child development and nutritional advice, and fostered good parent-infant bonding. The frequency of visits varied from twice a month to once a month from pregnancy to ages two to three. Compared with the control group, the prevention groups showed the following significant beneficial effects: (1) fewer physical injuries in childhood, (2) higher intelligence and fewer behavior problems at ages two and three, (3) better school attendance and performance during later childhood, (4) reduced aggression as rated by their teachers at age eleven, and (5) fewer referrals to juvenile courts for delinquent offenses.

A Plan for Prevention

Early health preventions for violence show effective and promising results when they target the development of risk factors and promote protective factors. Decades of research have documented risk factors related to behavioral problems in children and violence in adults. Future studies on early health measures to prevent violence should build on this research and focus on health factors that may increase the risk of antisocial and violent behavior and that are amenable to treatment.

Primary prevention programs during the prenatal and perinatal periods could be aimed at preventing birth complications, stopping smoking and alcohol use, and avoiding teratogens (agents that cause developmental malformations), such as the influenza virus, during the first and second trimesters. Good nutrition during pregnancy could be promoted, including increasing the intake of folic acid, deficits of which have been related to childhood neurological problems. Furthermore, stress management during pregnancy could reduce pregnancy-induced hypertension and hypoxia (oxygen deprivation) to the fetus. During the postnatal period, attempts could be made to increase parent-infant bonding, promote breast-feeding (which some studies suggest may benefit health and mental development as compared with formula-feeding), and teach parenting skills, including knowledge of child growth and development.

Secondary prevention could focus on early identification of risk factors, especially in vulnerable populations such as pregnant teenagers and substance abusers. Such programs could address

584

the psychological problems of having an unwanted pregnancy and related neglect of infants. Early identification and treatment of high-risk factors in pregnancy, such as toxemia and diabetes, could help prevent injury to the fetal brain. For those babies suffering from birth complications or poor prenatal care, early health measures to prevent later tendencies to violence could include fostering good parenting and bonding and the identification and remediation of neurological and motor deficits. Tertiary preventions for those children already showing conduct disorders and hyperactivity (a risk factor) could include treatments such as medication, cognitive-behavior therapy, and education remediation programs.

BIBLIOGRAPHY

Farrington, David P. "Early Developmental Prevention of Juvenile Delinquency." *Criminal Behaviour and Mental Health* 4 (1994): 209–227.

Olds, David, et al. "Long-Term Effects of Nurse Home Visitation on Children's Criminal and Antisocial Behavior." *Journal of the American Medical Association* 280, no. 14 (1998): 1238–1248.

Raine, Adrian, Patricia Brennan, and Sarnoff A. Mednick. "Birth Complications Combined with Maternal Rejection at Age One Year Predispose to Violent Crime at Age Eighteen Years." *Archives of General Psychiatry* 51 (December 1994): 984–988.

Raine, Adrian, and Jiang-hong Liu. "Biological Predispositions to Violence and Their Implications for Biosocial Treatment and Prevention." *Psychology, Crime, and Law* 4 (December 1998): 107–125.

Raine, Adrian, et al., eds. *Biosocial Bases of Violence.* New York: Plenum, 1997.

Reid, John, and Mark Eddy. "The Prevention of Antisocial Behavior: Some Considerations in the Search for Effective Interventions." In *Handbook of Antisocial Behavior,* edited by David Stoff et al. New York: Wiley, 1997.

Southam-Geron, Michael A., and Philip C. Kendall. "Parent-Focused and Cognitive-Behavioral Treatments of Antisocial Youth." In *Handbook of Antisocial Behavior,* edited by David Stoff, et al. New York: Wiley, 1997.

Wasserman, Gail A., and Laurie S. Miller. "The Prevention of Serious and Violent Juvenile Offending." In *Serious and Violent Juvenile Offenders: Risk Factors and Successful Interventions,* edited by Rolf Loeber and David Farrington. Thousand Oaks, Calif.: Sage, 1998.

ADRIAN RAINE
JIANG-HONG LIU

See also **Developmental Factors; Maternal Prenatal Violence.**

VIOLENT-CRIME PREVENTION

Thousands of violence-prevention initiatives have been implemented in communities throughout the United States. Those programs reflect various diagnoses regarding the roots of violent crime, and most are directed toward the individual, the community, or the social and economic structure.

Individual-Level Interventions

Schools, churches, health-care agencies, social service organizations, prisons, and social clubs have all implemented programs aimed at reducing individual-level factors that cause violent crime and at preventing children's violence, sexual violence, family violence, and hate violence.

Children's Violence. In the United States at the end of the twentieth century, there was a resurgence of programs whose efforts are rooted in biocriminology. From this perspective, for example, prenatal, perinatal, and postnatal health-care programs that attempt to prevent or address low birth weight and premature births of infants will purportedly also reduce violence, because these problems have been implicated in the development of violent behavior. Prevention of substance abuse in pregnant and nursing mothers has also been advocated to reduce violence. Other biochemical models suggest that treating neurological abnormalities, hypoglycemia, and hyperactivity may reduce children's proclivity to violence. These strategies are generally implemented by public health agencies, such as community clinics, and by physicians and psychiatrists who treat children.

In contrast to these biological interventions, social-learning-based approaches aim to reduce violence in children by discouraging aggression and by teaching conflict resolution and social skills. Many of these programs begin by teaching children how to manage anger. Schools have been at the forefront of violence prevention among children, with curricular interventions taking place all over the United States. For example, at Roth Middle School in Dayton, Ohio, hundreds of students participate in Positive Adolescents Choices Training (PACT), which uses role playing to illustrate the kinds of real-life conflicts children experience that can escalate into violence. The students practice clear verbal communication, negotiation, and compromise, making them less likely to be suspended from school for fighting and more likely to resolve conflicts nonviolently.

Social-learning approaches also emphasize the negative effects that the mass media and popular culture—especially television viewing—have on children. Some programs educate parents about the influence of television and encourage them to limit their children's viewing time or the number of violent shows they can watch. These programs may also teach parents how to watch television with their children and provide alternative perspectives on the shows. Others focus on producing and promoting alternative programming so children may learn to model nonviolent behavior. Programs may focus on other types of media, including films, video and computer games, music, and music videos. For example, the Dorcester Youth Collaborative in Boston produced antidrug, antiviolence break-dancing videos. Other strategies, such as the national No More War Toys, aim to substitute nonviolent toys for the toy weapons and violent games that entertain many American children.

Some programs try to change youth behavior or values to make gang involvement less likely. These approaches include participation in religious activities, role model and mentoring programs, alternative youth clubs, diversion programs such as midnight basketball, and counseling for gang members. Because violence has been linked to substance abuse, many youth programs implement drug and alcohol prevention and treatment along with the other components of violence prevention.

Recognizing that interventions must be culturally specific to serve the needs of each community, many programs serve particular racial and ethnic groups. Although biased law-enforcement policies exaggerate the proportion of violence committed by people of color, these programs nevertheless recognize that poor and minority males are more susceptible to being both the perpetrators and victims of violent street crime. For example, the Paramount Plan, begun in 1982 in Paramount, California, in working with Hispanic youths and their parents to prevent youths from joining gangs, developed a culturally appropriate bilingual written curriculum, in which Hispanic families were used as examples, and similarly appropriate media materials.

Family Violence. Many social-learning-based programs also incorporate strategies to improve youths' self-esteem and offer counseling for children with violent families. Counseling for children who have experienced violence in their homes can be critical in breaking the cycle of violence passed from generation to generation.

Consistent with the classical law-and-order view of criminology, law-enforcement programs emphasize punishing or separating child abusers,

with no proven deterrent effect. Other approaches target parenting as the problem. These programs conduct family therapy, teach anger management, and promote positive, nonviolent parenting. For example, the Healthy Start program, begun in 1985 and expanded in 1987, in Hawaii identifies parents at risk of abusing their children before they leave the hospital after a baby's birth. Caseworkers conduct home visits in which they help parents learn to care for their babies and develop parenting skills. The program reported a reduction in cases of abuse and neglect among high-risk families from 20 percent to none in the first three years of the program. Since studies of juvenile offenders show that they are very likely to have been abused in childhood, endeavors such as Healthy Start arguably prevent not only violent crime in families but also violent crime that would be committed by those children later in life.

In the 1970s the battered-women's movement developed shelters for women and their children to escape violent homes, while male-centered programs attempt to teach men alternative nonviolent behaviors. For example, EMERGE, which was founded in 1977 in Boston, conducts group meetings for heterosexual, gay, and bisexual men who commit violence against their partners, their children, or both.

Sexual Violence. Programs addressing sexual violence also tend either to provide support services for predominantly female victims or to punish or reform male offenders. Although it is now recognized that males also may be victims of sexual violence, many more females report victimization than males. Girls are three times more likely than boys to be sexually abused. Males are most likely to perpetrate sexual violence against both female and male victims, as evidenced by the fact that women annually account for only 1 percent of those arrested for forcible rape.

Programs for women such as rape-crisis centers provide counseling and medical and legal assistance. They may also train women and girls to identify the risks of sexual violence and means of self-protection, including self-defense classes designed specifically for women.

While law-enforcement strategies tend to emphasize incarcerating sex offenders, they nonetheless penalize sex offenses less consistently than other crimes. More promising are preventive strategies that attempt to teach men and boys egalitarian social roles and attitudes, so that females are not regarded as male sexual property.

Hate Violence. Members of immigrant groups, racial and ethnic minorities, women, and gays and lesbians are particularly vulnerable to hate violence. In response, in the 1970s schools and community groups implemented programs directed at making individuals less likely to commit hate violence. Those programs include school curricula that teach students about racism, sexism, and homophobia. For example, the Teaching Tolerance program, begun in 1971 at the Southern Poverty Law Center in Birmingham, Alabama, provides curriculum and videos on the history of intolerance and how to stop it. Other community-based groups, such as Communities United Against Violence, which appeared in 1979 in San Francisco, provide assistance to victims of hate violence and public education and outreach.

Community-Level Interventions

Not only have antiviolence programs targeted individual behaviors, but they have also been organized to change community dynamics, structures, and opportunities to reduce violence. Consistent with macrosociological perspectives, such as those stemming from the work of the French sociologist Émile Durkheim, they link violence with other social problems. Violence in communities is linked to concentrated poverty, income inequality, community disorganization, poor educational and job opportunities, illegal markets for drugs and firearms, and negative relations with law-enforcement officials.

High rates of population turnover, community transition, and family disruption—indicated by high housing density, high residential mobility, and high percentages of single-parent families—have led some communities to reorganize to create a social environment less conducive to violence. Some have instituted communitywide support systems for parents and families. Other methods include tenant empowerment and resident management, community cleanup, neighborhood watches, and other crime-control strategies. For example, the Fairview Homes public-housing crime-prevention program in Charlotte, North Carolina, reduced crime by increasing tenants' control over their communities and by employing high-risk youth.

In many communities, schools are breeding grounds for violence and fail to prepare children for meaningful jobs. This failure, combined with few legitimate employment opportunities, leads many kids to drop out of school and turn to crime. In turn, illegal markets for firearms and drugs develop and create even more violence as turf wars between gangs break out and firearms proliferate. Community programs that address these problems in tandem include City Lights in Washington, D.C., and the Phoenix Program in Akron, Ohio, which improved school attendance and reduced criminal recidivism among high school students; the Eugene Lang I Have a Dream program, which reduced New York City high school dropout rates and increased college attendance among Harlem youths; and the Argus Community in New York's South Bronx, which reduced drug use, crime, and welfare dependency in the community. Religious and community leaders have organized truces between rival gangs.

The focus on the city as the locus of violent crime has created stereotypes of cities as violent and rural and suburban areas as safe havens. In addition, institutions tend to focus almost exclusively on street violence, ignoring violence committed in the household or by corporations or the state. Although poor and minority communities may be more vulnerable to street crime, law-enforcement officials arrest poor and minority offenders in disproportionate numbers and often ignore crimes committed by white middle-class youths. In response, watchdog groups emerged in some areas to monitor police violence against residents. For example, Cop Watch, which was instituted in March 1990 in Berkeley, California, observes police behavior and files reports to try to deter inappropriate (including violent) police behavior.

Community policing promotes a different relationship between the community and law enforcement. This approach emphasizes the police officer as a part of the community by assigning officers to particular neighborhoods, encouraging them to participate in community activities, to become acquainted with the residents, and to "walk the beat." It also promotes a more interactive relationship with community groups that seek to reduce crime and violence. Groups have organized to promote these efforts statewide: for example, the Institute for Community Oriented Policing in Washington State and KY COPS in Kentucky serve to develop and implement community policing statewide.

Interventions Aimed at the Social and Economic Structure

While community-based strategies have shown promising results, some programs seek to resolve problems on a national level. They promote national efforts to improve housing, education, job training, and urban revitalization. Such organizations include the National Council on Crime and Delinquency, the National Crime Prevention Council, the National Coalition on Domestic Violence, the Vera Institute of Justice in New York, the Violence Policy Center in Washington, D.C., and many others.

Some organizations, including the Drug Policy Institute in Washington D.C., call for major changes in national drug policies, claiming that they are a major cause of violence in the United States. Both the Center to Prevent Handgun Violence and Handgun Control, Inc., call for a comprehensive national gun control strategy, contending that the link between the widespread availability and use of firearms and the rates and lethality of violence in the United States cannot be ignored.

Humanistic criminologists suggest that nothing less than a fundamental redistribution of wealth will address our nation's epidemic of violence. Only by restructuring political and economic power will people have more equitable access to a decent education, health care, housing, and jobs—all related to violence. And some programs look beyond street crime, recognizing that corporate and state violence are directed against certain communities. For example, Corporate Watch, in Washington, D.C., identifies corporations that operate under unsafe conditions that result in harm and death to many workers. Other companies dump toxic wastes, particularly in poor and minority communities, causing violence to many through their "cost-saving" practices.

Finally, in addition to addressing the economic dimensions of violence, some groups recognize cultural problems in the United States that require change. For example, New Humanists, a group working via the Internet, recognizes that often violence is committed because of racism and hate. This group aims to reduce discrimination and violence by changing the social system. Groups working to end violence against women and children, such as the National Organization for Women and the National Council on Family Violence, demonstrate that these forms of violence transcend class and racial-ethnic boundaries.

These groups contend that the structural and cultural features of racism and patriarchy built into American society must be addressed to eliminate these forms of violence.

BIBLIOGRAPHY

Biskup, Michael D., and Charles P. Cozic, eds. *Youth Violence*. San Diego, Calif.: Greenhaven, 1992.

Neft, Naomi, and Ann D. Levine. *Where Women Stand: An International Report on the Status of Women in Over 140 Countries*. New York: Random House, 1997.

Pepinsky, Harold, and Richard Quinney, eds. *Criminology as Peacemaking*. Bloomington: Indiana University Press, 1991.

Prothrow-Stith, Deborah, with Michaele Weissman. *Deadly Consequences*. New York: HarperPerennial, 1993.

Reiss, Albert J., Jr., and Jeffrey Roth, eds. *Understanding and Preventing Violence*. Washington, D.C.: National Academy Press, 1993.

Turpin, Jennifer, and Lester R. Kurtz, eds. *The Web of Violence: From Interpersonal to Global*. Urbana: University of Illinois Press, 1997.

JENNIFER TURPIN

See also **Conflict Resolution; Drugs: Drug Prevention and Treatment; Nonviolence; Theories of Violence;** *and the list of organizations in the* **Appendix.**

PRISONERS OF WAR

Prisoners of war (POWs) are members of an active military service captured during or after battle and then incarcerated by a warring power. They lack any real legal protection other than that which their captors grant. The United States has had members of its armed services captured as POWs in every war from the American Revolution to the conflict in Kosovo in the late 1990s. Over the centuries the United States has designed or signed a variety of national and international conventions regarding the treatment of POWs. Prisoners go unprotected, however, if the capturing side refuses to recognize any rules, and violence is often the result.

Changes in the Nature of the POW Experience

Brutality toward POWs has increased over the years. While those of all periods share common concerns about food, shelter, medical treatment, possible execution, and exchange, only in the twentieth century have POWs from the United States been subjected to official policies of starvation, exposure, ideological conversion, and routinely applied torture. Although prisoners in the War of 1812 suffered beatings for breaking rules or crossing a guard, these seem to have been individual instances and did not involve the official use of pain for military or propaganda goals.

The treatment of prisoners during the Revolutionary War illustrates this. While American captives had some trouble establishing themselves as POWs (rather than as traitors to the crown), those captives who were recognized as POWs were incarcerated in prison ships, or hulks, primarily off the American coastline. Faced with filthy quarters, bad water, few rations, fever, and an indefinite stay ahead of them, many died. The living had to fight constantly just to hold on to personal clothing, blankets, and shoes. Though the British issued blankets sporadically, along with two-thirds the British soldier's already inadequate daily ration, a man usually died without outside assistance. Death resulted not because of an official British policy but because of an incompetent supply system and poor planning.

For many scholars the treatment of prisoners by the North and the South during the Civil War marks a turning point in the history of POWs in the United States. Though deaths in camps held by the Confederacy were more numerous, suffering in camps on both sides resulted from the fact that murderous conditions went uncorrected rather than from deliberate policy. In Elmira Prison in New York, where 385 deaths occurred in September 1864, and in the notorious Andersonville Prison in Camp Sumter, Georgia, where 2,677 deaths occurred in the same period, punitive neglect and poor planning were the order of the day. In both the North and the South, feces, foreign matter, or minerals usually contaminated the water and presented the greatest danger to health, although inadequate shelter (tents, dugouts, shacks), especially in the North, encouraged pneumonia, tuberculosis, and freezing. The paucity of rations, which were cut on occasion for camp punishment, fouled by poor storage or extorted by renegade prisoners, led to starvation, while deadlines (lines drawn within or around a prison that a prisoner passed at the risk of being shot), stocks, and shackles increased the suffering.

Union victors eventually convicted the Andersonville Prison commandant, Captain Henry Wirz, of murder; he was tried and then hanged in 1865, becoming the first person to be tried and executed in the United States for the mistreatment and murder of POWs, thereby setting a precedent for holding commandants responsible for deaths in their camps. Historians at the end of the twentieth century continued to argue about the availability of food in Andersonville as well as the policy of command responsibility for all actions of subordinates.

In contrast, POWs held by the Japanese during World War II faced torture, deliberate starvation, refusal of medical services, slave labor, and physically violent treatment daily. Additionally, many held in Manchuria served as involuntary test subjects for biological warfare and medical experiments. The death figures, when compared with those of POWs held in Germany (which followed the Geneva Convention of 1929 with its U.S. and British military prisoners), are startling: Allied prisoners in Europe had a death rate in captivity of 4 percent, while in the Pacific theaters of war under the Japanese the death rate was 27 percent. Some historians suggest that lack of food, medicine, and clothing were the result of poor Japanese logistics and that the depredations were caused by U.S. submarine warfare, not by policy. This idea was still hotly debated at the end of the twentieth century.

Rape became a unique and probable form of POW torture from the Gulf War on with the advent of women in combat units (as opposed to nursing units) of the armed forces. During the Gulf War women officially became prisoners of war—as women. During the Civil War one POW in

TABLE 1.   American Prisoners of War

War	Number of Captured Prisoners*
American Revolution	4,500
War of 1812	5,450
Mexican War	insignificant
Civil War	
Union POWs	211,400
Confederate POWs	220,000
Spanish-American War	insignificant
World War I	4,120
World War II	130,201
Korean War	7,140
Vietnam War	766
Gulf War	23
Kosovo	3

*All figures represent captured, not returned, prisoners.

SOURCE: Lary G. Bowman, *Captive Americans: Prisoners During the American Revolution* (Athens: Ohio University Press, 1976), p. 31; Robert C. Doyle, *Voices from Captivity* (Lawrence: University Press of Kansas, 1994), pp. 16–17, 22–23, 308.

Andersonville was a woman, but she had been dressed as a man—a fact discovered by the burial team. There were probably undiscovered others on both sides. Though army and navy nurses captured and taken prisoner in the Philippines during World War II were obviously members of the armed forces, the Japanese did not recognize them as such and interned them with captured female civilians at Santo Tomas Internment Camp in Manila. While the two female POWs from the Gulf War, one officer and one enlistee, both recognized as military POWs, had admitted to congressional committees that they had been molested or raped, this does not seem to have been the case with any of the army and navy nurses taken prisoner in the Philippines, or, obviously, of those women who had disguised themselves as men.

Ideological Conversion and Confession

POWs in Korea and Vietnam experienced mental and spiritual violence. The North Koreans, for example, introduced "reeducation" of "war-criminal soldiers." Prisoners were repeatedly tortured, starved, or put in solitary confinement in order to make them admit fraudulent war crimes, give names of other prisoners, or denounce their country, usually by signing a document. Most resisted fiercely, but twenty-one ultimately refused repatriation, staying with their captors. By the time the Korean War ended, 2,701 POWs from the United States had died because of their treatment. The attempt to discover why twenty-one stayed resulted ultimately in the 1955 Code of Conduct—which clearly defined how a POW should behave under pressure.

The Code of Conduct played a major part in the nature and demands of POWs during the Vietnam War, especially for the officers in the best-known prison, the Hanoi Hilton. The code demanded that all POWs constantly resist, refuse to give information or make propaganda statements (despite torture), and continue to attempt escape. Prisoners soon found the demands dangerously unrealistic—especially for a prisoner held by a country not observing any international conventions. Refusal to give information beyond name, rank, serial number, and date of birth (allowed under the code) usually resulted in being beaten, put into the ropes (or *strappado,* a technique that involves tying the prisoner's hands and arms behind his back, attaching a rope to the bound hands, then hoisting him into the air and letting him hang there until he confesses), sentenced to weeks in leg irons and sol-

A model of a prison cell built by North Vietnamese during the Vietnam War. LIBRARY OF CONGRESS

itary confinement, or starved. Escape proved unfeasible and deadly in light of the prisoners' state of malnutrition, their Caucasian features, and their height (Americans were noticeably taller than their captors). POW senior officers gradually modified the code. Prisoners under torture were told to hold out as well as they could until they felt death was imminent; then they could "confess." Eventually 766 POWs returned home (114 died in camps); 2,453 members of the armed services who were missing in action continued to haunt the United States at the end of the twentieth century, though many more were unaccounted for in World War II and the Korean War.

U.S. Treatment of POWs

The United States has generally maintained a clear record of compliance with existing international agreements regarding prisoners over the years and even helped to define the first of these agreements during the Revolutionary War. There have, however, been blots on the record. American treatment of "traitorous" Tory prisoners during the Revolutionary War, for example, was often ferocious enough that veterans and prisoners of war alike did their best to relocate in Canada after the war. As noted earlier, in both the North and the South, "enemy" prisoners were often treated in callous ways, although not as part of official policy.

Some significant (and better-documented) deviations from decent treatment appeared with

World War II. The journalist and author James Bacque shook the United States with the charge that General Dwight Eisenhower had deliberately starved German POWs to death in the Rhine Meadow Camps in April and May 1945. According to Bacque, there were at least one million prisoners missing of the approximately five million captured by the Allies by the end of the war. Bacque claims these lost million were hidden in the official record under the catch-all category "other losses" and that Eisenhower had starved and worked them to death. Later scholars show that the missing had simply been transferred to other commands or paroled. Ultimately, approximately fifty-six thousand German POWs died in Allied hands—about one percent of the total number. The Bacque charges brought one complicated fact to light. Eisenhower and the British High Command had changed the designation of the prisoners from prisoners of war (POWs) to disarmed enemy forces (DEFs) in order to get around the Geneva Convention agreement to feed prisoners the same nature and quantity of food as the holding power did its own personnel. Given the chaos in Germany, Austria, and the Low Countries, and the mass surrender that continued up to the end of the war, it rapidly became impossible for the Allies to live up to all of the Geneva Agreement. The answer was to change the designation and follow the rest of the Geneva provisions as well as they could.

The mass surrender of German army units to American and British forces was spurred by both the Allied propaganda of the "good life" in America and the fear of capture by the Red Army. Eisenhower had to feed, house, organize, and register all displaced persons returning from eastern Europe, former concentration camp victims, the Allies' own personnel, Red Cross and medical contingents, as well as the POWs. The German POWs, regarded by Washington, D.C., as those who had supported the Nazis, if not as Nazis themselves, were last on the priority list. In the spring of the last year of the European war, food stores were inadequate, shelter was frequently nonexistent, clothes and blankets were in tatters or unavailable, and men had to dig in the mud to construct shelters against the elements. More than one hundred thousand prisoners occupied camps marked off by barbed wire; many starved and died during the two months when logistics were still nightmarish because of the damage that had resulted from Allied bombing of infrastructure.

In the Pacific theater frontline treatment of Japanese POWs was also problematic after the fall of Bataan and Corregidor, especially during the Guadalcanal campaign. Allied personnel had

U.S. Air Force Colonel J. L. Hughes is paraded through the steets of Hanoi after capture by the Viet Cong in June 1969. National Archives

591

learned an unpleasant truth: Japanese soldiers surrendering often carried grenades or hidden pistols in order to take as many of the enemy with them as possible. The ferocity of the Guadalcanal deadlock began an increase in brutality, with frequent shootings of Japanese prisoners and occasionally mutilation of their bodies.

The record in POW camps in the United States was much better. Despite an occasional incident, such as the one in a Utah POW camp, for example, when a watchtower gunner sprayed the tents of the prisoners below, killing nine and injuring twenty, inspection by the Swiss and the International Red Cross, as well as the American Friends, ensured that the camps were under scrutiny. The Japanese POWs (eventually a total of 5,080) were sent to camps in the United States. They tended to be strictly segregated from the American population, more so than the Germans. They were an insignificant, even invisible, presence in the United States; most Japanese, the U.S. Army discovered, refused to surrender.

In Korea, which was a UN action, the treatment of enemy POWs was complicated by handing prisoners over to allies such as the South Koreans, who treated the North Koreans in a particularly brutal manner. In Vietnam, U.S. forces were responsible for some horrific civilian "collateral damage" during raids on suspected Vietcong-friendly villages, and late in the war frequently shot prisoners during firefights. The worst prisoner treatment flourished under American allies, the South Vietnamese authorities, to whom the American army was, upon occasion, required to turn over its prisoners (North Vietnamese army regulars and Vietcong). The U.S. treatment of enemy prisoners, however, became increasingly brutal on the front lines as those same frontline soldiers experienced atrocities or found their own men mutilated.

In the Gulf War few U.S. soldiers became POWs under the Iraqis, although thousands of Iraqis ended up in the hands of the Allies (primarily Americans). In this case the waiting American hospital tents and huge triage facilities were used primarily to house and treat the staggering wave of Iraqi troops who often surrendered en masse during that brief war.

Reintegration of Prisoners of War After Hostilities

The reintegration of POWs into American society has consistently proved more difficult than reintegration of other veterans of similar age and length of active duty who were not captured. As John Russell pointed out, POWs over the decades and the different wars have all exhibited strikingly similar symptoms and behavior. This may be due to a condition that Russell identifies as post-traumatic stress disorder (PTSD); symptoms include the presence of long-lasting and severe depression, memory lapses, decreased ability to concentrate, interrupted sleep cycles, and problems with both employment and marriage. In most PTSD cases mistreatment, torture, starvation, and camp parasites and illnesses also leave a lasting imprint on the physical well-being of the POWs after they return, from the debilitating recurrence of diseases like malaria to lifelong eye and teeth problems as a result of having experienced malnutrition.

Despite the apparent group solidarity and psychological esprit de corps among the Vietnam POWs when they returned from captivity, they experienced PTSD symptoms and a high rate of divorce: within one year 30 percent divorced and after ten years the rate was 90 percent. POWs from World War II (especially from Japanese camps), from the Korean War, and from the Vietnam War all displayed a noticeably higher incidence of suicide and violent death (such as from car accidents) when compared with other groups of combat veterans. One medical examiner at March Air Force Base, examining fifty-one returning POWs, noted in his records "only six" were in good health and he expected "some of the men might require psychiatric care for the rest of their lives." Contrary to the stereotype of the psychotic Vietnam War veteran, the POWs from Vietnam did not exhibit any greater homicidal impulses than other war veterans; in fact their violent behavior was more often directed toward themselves than to others. The explanation may be that the majority of these POWs were career service pilots with college (even advanced) degrees, and they were imprisoned in urban rather than jungle camps.

POWs from earlier wars are more difficult to analyze. Fewer figures and statistics are available about prisoners of the Mexican War and the Spanish-American War, for example, possibly because of the short duration of these wars. The Revolutionary War (a civil war of a sort) and the Civil War form a special category. These wars produced the greatest bitterness among combatants and the worst treatment of the enemy. Photographs of prisoners from both the Southern and Northern prisons (especially Andersonville) show the severe malnutrition and illness of the majority of the captives. It is within this particular psychological and physical health context that we must judge the poor transition of POWs into peacetime. Additionally, the POWs from both North and South were in such a physically weakened state that many soon died after their release.

In 1970 the site of the infamous prison camp for Union soldiers in Andersonville, Georgia, was made into a National Historical Site, and almost thirty years later, in 1998, a National Prisoner of War Museum on the site was dedicated to all former prisoners of war (and civilian internees).

BIBLIOGRAPHY

Bischof, Günter, and Stephen E. Ambrose. "Introduction and Preface." *Eisenhower and the German POWs: Facts Against Falsehood*, edited by Günter Bischof and Stephen E. Ambrose. Baton Rouge: Louisiana State University Press, 1992.

Bowman, Larry G. *Captive Americans: Prisoners During the American Revolution*. Athens: Ohio University Press, 1976.

Dower, John W. *War Without Mercy: Race and Power in the Pacific War*. New York: Pantheon, 1986.

Doyle, Robert C. *Voices from Captivity: Interpreting the American POW Narrative*. Lawrence: University Press of Kansas, 1994.

Hesseltine, William B. *Civil War Prisons: A Study in War Psychology*. Columbus: Ohio University Press, 1930.

Howes, Craig. *Voices of the Vietnam POWs: Witnesses to Their Fight*. New York: Oxford University Press, 1993.

Koop, Allen V. *Stark Decency: German Prisoners of War in a New England Village*. Hanover, N.H.: University Press of New England, 1988.

Krammer, Arnold. *Nazi Prisoners of War in America*. New York: Stein and Day, 1979.

Linderman, Gerald F. *The World Within War: America's Combat in World War II*. New York: Free Press, 1994.

Marvel, William. *Andersonville: The Last Depot*. Chapel Hill: University of North Carolina Press, 1994.

Russell, Edward Frederick Langley. *The Knights of Bushido: A Short History of Japanese War Crimes*. London: Cassell, 1958.

Russell, John F. "The Captivity Experience and Its Psychological Consequences." *Psychiatric Annals* 14, no. 4 (1984): 250–254.

Villa, Brian L. "The Diplomatic and Political Context of the POW Camps Tragedy." In *Eisenhower and the German POW: Facts Against Falsehood*, edited by Günter Bischof and Stephen E. Ambrose. Baton Rouge: Louisiana State University Press, 1992.

FRANCES B. COGAN

See also **Post-Traumatic Stress Disorder; War: Aftermath of.**

PRISONS

*Following the **Overview** are four subentries: **Prison Conditions, Prison Violence, Riots,** and **Women Prisoners**.*

OVERVIEW

Reformative incarceration emerged almost simultaneously with the birth of the American Republic. The state's use of penal incarceration, initially designed to exemplify an enlightened and rationalized rule of law, ultimately spawned a prison system unprecedented in the history of republican societies. Put into practice by citizens hoping to overcome the irrationalities and excesses of the ancien régime, prisons have come to anchor a system of punishment that—in the United States at least—reproduces a world of violence that the ancien régime could only imagine. Violence, both seen and unseen, permeates the history of the prison.

Despite the long-term secular expansion of imprisonment, however, there is no single history of the prison in the United States. Unlike European practice, punishment in the United States has remained primarily a state rather than a national responsibility. Although the federal government opened a national prison system at the end of the nineteenth century, most prisoners then, as now, were held in state prisons and jails. As a result, prison sizes, incarceration levels, funding, and degree of outside oversight have varied, and continue to vary, from state to state and region to region. The multiplicity of levels of prisons (from local jails, to minimum- and maximum-security state prisons, to federal prisons of different levels of severity), combined with the disparity of state histories, means that only a part of the story of the prison can be told here—namely, the history of leading models and defining developments.

Marginality in the Colonial Era

Colonial jails were marginal to the exercise of criminal punishment. Small in structure, located near courthouses, often overseen by an individual for profit and with minimal accommodations for prisoners, jails performed a variety of functions, but they were secondary to the process of punishment. For the most part, jails held prisoners awaiting trial or punishment, witnesses to a crime, and debtors. The penalty of imprisonment was included as a criminal punishment only on rare occasions. Community or government oversight of jails appears to have been infrequent.

Criminal justice in the colonial period thus was not centered on the long-term seizure of the convict's body. Although terms of indentured labor could be imposed in different colonies, for the most part colonial courts sentenced free men and women to corporal, financial, or capital punishments. Whipping, pillorying, and other punishments designed to inflict shame and pain were common. Fines and bonds were imposed on those convicted of minor offenses, and restitution was often included in penalties for crimes, especially against property. In Pennsylvania, for example, fines were most often imposed for minor crimes against the person, whereas whipping and restitution were imposed for theft. More serious crimes in the colonies were punished with a series of corporal penalties, the most severe of which was death. Hangings, although few compared with the number in England, were regular occurrences in the colonial world. Open violence (punishments inflicted in public) was an important coin of the penal realm.

For slaves in the colonial world, the corporal nature of punishment was even more pronounced. Most slave punishment took place within plantations and inflicted violence to the body. But colonial governments also inflicted violence—in the public forms of whipping, maiming, and hanging. In the North, slaves were sometimes sold out of the colony as penalty for legal infractions. Even more so than with free people, punishments of slaves did not usually involve imprisonment in jails. Instead, slaves were punished brutally and corporally.

The Penitentiary and Reformative Theories

Between the American Revolution and the Civil War, state governments dramatically expanded their prison systems and their reliance on reformative incarceration—especially in the North. Penitentiaries also appeared in southern states, but their role in the criminal-justice landscape was limited. Two periods were crucial to the emergence of the penitentiary in the United States. During the first, in the 1780s and 1790s, older prisons were reformed in states such as Pennsylvania and New York, and new ones were constructed in other states, including Virginia and New Jersey. During the second period, in the 1820s and 1830s, new, massive prisons were constructed, most important among them the Eastern State Penitentiary in Pennsylvania and the Auburn and Sing Sing penitentiaries in New York. During these two periods, prison reformers and state officials fundamentally altered the nature and assumptions of criminal punishments.

Philosophically, late-eighteenth-century proponents of reformative incarceration aimed to join utility to a larger vision of a republican penality. Penal reformers argued that older forms of corporal and capital punishments were not effective deterrents for crime. Although definitive figures for post-Revolutionary crime rates do not exist, it is clear that in places like Boston, New York, and Philadelphia many became convinced that criminality rose in the aftermath of the Revolution. Critics of traditional penalties argued that corporal punishments were too brief to affect a criminal's character and that capital punishments did little, if anything, to diminish crime. Activists like Benjamin Rush even argued that corporal and capital penalties spread violence through society. In addition, proponents of reformative incarceration believed that capital and corporal punishments were inappropriate for a new republican society, insisting that they smacked of monarchical government. Influenced by English arguments in favor of penitentiaries, American reformers focused their penal ideas on labor, order, and religious instruction in regularized and supervised institutions.

This new philosophy altered the economy of violence within punishment as well as the relationship of penal practices to the wider public. Early national reformers aimed to contain penal violence while concealing the everyday reality of punishment. Concerned with the communal effects of crime and punishment, penal reformers not only reordered penal priorities but interposed their authority between the public and those punished in its name. If the colonial penal world had been structured by the visible display of the force of the state, Revolutionary-era reformers hoped that the force of the state could be a negligible, if unavoidable, part of reformative incarceration.

The character and contradictions of the theory and practice of early national reformative incarceration can be seen in the history of Philadelphia's Walnut Street Jail—undoubtedly, the most important of the post-Revolutionary experiments. Built in 1773, the jail held military and political prisoners during the war for national independence. But during the 1780s and 1790s its place in the criminal-justice system began to change. Pennsylvania experimented with new penal systems, first one based on public, penal labor and then one based on incarceration within a prison. In both, the importance of the jail increased. Since proponents of these new systems aimed to reform the prisoners and not simply punish them, the time spent in the prison assumed increased importance. Consequently, in 1788 and 1789 movements were begun to instill new disciplinary forms within the prison: to separate types of prisoners (felons from debtors, vagrants, witnesses, those awaiting trial, and so on); to regulate the movement of goods and people in and out of the institution; to separate the sexes; to limit access to liquor (a staple of the old prison); to expand external oversight; and to organize labor better. The first steps toward a new vision of incarceration were being taken.

But the significant reorganization of the Walnut Street Jail took place during the 1790s. Pennsylvania further isolated prisoners by ending all labor in public. Officials intensified prison discipline. They made greater efforts to enforce cleanliness and sobriety, to improve classification and separation of prisoners, and to enjoin inmate silence. Crucially, they linked labor and labor discipline to the process of reformation. Punishments ranged from a reduction of privileges to an early form of solitary confinement. In many respects, the practices at Walnut Street Jail during the 1790s established the parameters of penal philosophy for the next two hundred years.

Initially, the proponents of reformative incarceration declared the reform of Walnut Street Jail a success. Crime rates appeared to decline in Pennsylvania. Officials imposed discipline on the prison, and the state regularized the structure of prison authority. Some semblance of labor and reformation was achieved and the conditions of prisoners improved. Walnut Street itself became a model for penal reformers elsewhere—its practices praised on both sides of the Atlantic.

But these successes, such as they were, were short-lived. By the end of the eighteenth century, Walnut Street entered into a period of irreversible decline. The prison became overpopulated, the labor system dissolved, prisoners' health declined (judging by statistics on death and disease), escapes and violence increased, and recidivism seems to have expanded. No matter what the basis for judgment—claims for crime control, for reformation, or for more humane treatment of inmates —Walnut Street had failed by the 1820s. A major prison riot in 1820 marked the system's death knell.

The Walnut Street Jail was not alone in facing these problems. Throughout the northern states, prison systems were in a crisis by the 1820s. Newgate Prison in New York exploded in riot in 1818; inmates at Charlestown Prison in Massachusetts burned their workshops in 1813 and rioted in 1816. Legislators began to question the wisdom of reformative incarceration. Increasingly, calls for a return to corporal punishments or for new systems for transporting convicts out of the United States could be heard.

Intensification and Debate

Ultimately, the crisis of reformative incarceration produced not retreat but intensification. The prison had achieved too much ideological power to be simply dismantled. In this intensification the states of Pennsylvania and New York led the way. During the 1820s penal reformers and state officials developed two distinct models for prison organization—the separate system (pioneered in Philadelphia's Eastern State Penitentiary) and the silent system (pioneered in New York's Auburn and Sing Sing prisons). Pennsylvania sought to impose a system of constant solitary confinement in cells; New York aimed to combine solitary confinement at night with collective labor during the day. Solitude and labor were central to both systems. The classic penitentiary of the nineteenth century had been created.

Heated debate followed. Proponents of each model propagandized in newspapers and reports. Leading figures from both the United States and Europe visited the pioneer institutions and passed judgment on the two prison forms. The debates turned on a series of issues: Was corporal punishment necessary to control inmates? Did solitary confinement drive inmates insane? Could you truly reform criminals or only discipline them? The separate system, in theory, eliminated the need for corporal punishment within the prison (the practice was somewhat different), whereas whipping remained an open tool of discipline in the silent systems of New York. Most important was the issue of economics. The silent system promised a greater economic return to states for their huge fiscal investments. Proponents of New York's system argued that the silent system enabled prisoners to labor productively for the state, whereas in Philadelphia only limited handicraft production could take place. Most likely, this last consideration proved decisive. In the antebellum United States (Europe favored the separate system), most new penitentiaries were constructed in accord with the models at Auburn and Sing Sing prisons.

But the disagreement over the labor system turned on more than economics. Both the silent and the separate system promised to overcome a crisis of authority that the failures of reformative incarceration had made clear. The collapse of the first generation of prisons was one instance of the dashing of Revolutionary-era hopes for a unified, rationalized society. Growing conflicts in politics and society, expanding instability in the economy, and the increasingly contested and complex nature of public life in northern cities made the apparent rise of recidivism and the turmoil in prisons symbols of wider social problems.

Although both systems offered greater promise than earlier models of reforming inmates and controlling crime, they did so through different models of society and authority. The Eastern State Penitentiary drew on a combination of monastic and artisanal models. Architecturally designed to resemble a medieval fortress, it projected the image of a Gothic retreat while deploying highly sophisticated modern techniques for controlling and observing space. Immuring convicts within solitary cells, the separate system aimed to produce true penitents. The silent system, on the other hand, looked more toward military and factory models and, with its collective labor practices, stimulated new techniques for the control of laborers and groups. Most famous was the lockstep, whereby lines of prisoners were compelled to move together, looking downward and outward in order to avoid communication. Military models offered strategies for disciplined, hierarchical behavior. Prison officials modeled themselves on military officers as they sought to command their charges through the use of force. Both of the New York penitentiaries implemented highly graduated scales of punishments for infractions of the rules of silence (it was here that the whip often made its entrance into prison life). Both the lockstep and the complexity of internal punishments would come to be marks of the nineteenth-century penitentiary. Auburn and Sing Sing, then, pointed more toward the emerging industrial world than did the utopian schema at the Eastern State Penitentiary.

Whatever the prison form, prison populations in the early-nineteenth-century North shared certain characteristics. Overwhelmingly, inmates were sentenced for property crimes. Relatively few were sentenced for crimes against persons or against morals; this is partly attributable to the fact that minor personal offenses were punished either by fines or by only brief incarceration. Most inmates were native-born white males, but African Americans and immigrants (especially the Irish) were overrepresented in many prison populations.

Most southern states (with the exception of the Carolinas and Florida) built prisons in the period between the Revolution and the Civil War. Southern proponents of the penitentiary articulated the Revolutionary and Enlightenment ideologies that were used to justify the penitentiary in the North. And in their architectural and internal forms, southern prisons were (perhaps more brutal) counterparts to their northern cousins.

But the penitentiary in the South looked out on a different situation and did not assume the same social or symbolic function as it did in the North. Southern penitentiaries were not linked, as in the North, to the dominant economic and social tendencies of the region. Slavery remained the main mechanism of social discipline in the South. Slaves were not sent to the penitentiary; as in the colonial period, they continued to be punished primarily by their masters. Prison populations reflected this different function. Most of the inmates in southern penitentiaries were either poor white (both native and immigrant) or free black males. In the lower South (which had few free blacks) the penitentiaries held white inmates almost exclusively, whereas in the upper South the racial balance more closely approximated that in the North—with African Americans seriously overrepresented. In many southern states the percentage of those committed for crimes of violence was much higher than in the North. Just as the southern economy and society did not revolve around wage labor, so penitentiaries took a backseat to the coercive power of slavery.

Consolidation and Degradation

In the aftermath of the Civil War, the prison system simultaneously expanded and degenerated. As imprisonment became increasingly central to penal practice in the South, the westward movement of the United States spread prisons throughout the continent. Prisons for women and reformatories for young offenders were established, especially in the North and Midwest. Within prisons, however, the story was different. Overcrowding became rampant, and the effort at reformation declined. Observers complained that contraband flowed into the prison freely while labor—a linchpin of the nineteenth-century penitentiary—became increasingly irregular. Prison officials in the

Sing Sing Prison, New York, 1840. LIBRARY OF CONGRESS

North, South, and West increasingly relied on the imposition of severe corporal sanctions.

The deterioration of prison conditions was not surprising. For one thing, the ethnic and racial makeup of the country's prisons underwent telling transformations. In particular, the number of immigrants in northern prison populations and of African Americans in southern prison populations increased dramatically. Immigrants and blacks had always been overrepresented in northern prisons, but in the late nineteenth century states incarcerated them on a new scale. In Illinois in 1890, for example, 60 percent of the prison population were either first- or second-generation immigrants, while in California during the early 1880s, 45 percent of the prison population were immigrants (Rothman 1980). Few inmates had received much formal education, and most were men who had been unskilled or semiskilled laborers. Changes in the South were even more striking. Before emancipation the (often overwhelming) majority of southern inmates were white. But in the late nineteenth century the vast majority (sometimes up to 90 percent) of southern inmates were black, often convicted of offenses against the racial codes of the New South. Growing brutality accompanied the increasing social, racial, and ethnic distance between inmates and the dominant classes and cultures of the North, South, and West.

The changing nature of imprisonment was starkest in the South. Following emancipation, southern officials of whatever political party moved to expand the region's use of incarceration. Initially, efforts were made to expand and improve southern penitentiaries—institutions, already inhumane and inefficient during the antebellum period, that had decayed during the Civil War. But rapidly southern states moved beyond the prison to the convict lease system. Taking the notion that prisoners should labor even more than their northern counterparts, they began leasing their inmates—primarily black males—to private contractors to perform dangerous and difficult work. Leased convicts became a central workforce in the mines and on roads and railroads. Conditions in the mines and camps were even more degraded than in northern prisons and the levels of violence at least equivalent. Forced to labor where others would not, convicts became one of the bases of the industrialization of the New South.

The convict lease system marked an unprecedented deployment of penal labor by business and the state. From their beginnings, penitentiaries had aimed to integrate themselves into local labor markets. Nineteenth-century penitentiaries had connected themselves to the wider economy by contracting with private manufacturers to employ convicts within prison walls or by organizing production themselves with the intent to sell finished products on the market. But this production was always limited in output and consistently under attack. Prisoners resisted discipline and limited production. Labor organizations struggled to limit prison production to the state's use or to activities that did not compete with local producers. More fundamental than productivity, however, was the fact of labor. Officials designed prison labor to inculcate habits of (mostly unskilled) labor among prisoners, to inure inmates to the petty degradations that accompanied being part of the labor market, and to indicate the undesirable alternatives to honest toil. The classic connection between

597

the prison and the economy derived from the former's ideological function. With convict leasing, the penal system assumed a much more direct economic importance. It would be difficult to argue that northern penitentiaries were crucial participants in nineteenth-century economic development. But the convict lease system allowed the forced mobilization of labor that was central to the economic plans of the dominant groups of the New South. In a manner unique in U.S. history, convict leasing directly fused state violence (that is, government violence), prison labor, and economic development.

To be sure, southern inmates resisted this regime much as their northern counterparts resisted theirs. And both were able to disrupt and diminish the consistency and productivity of labor within incarceration. Each, however, thereby provoked increased levels of punishment and official violence. Whipping was only the most conventional of these punishments. Wardens used various forms of gags, water punishments, confinement, and other deprivations of privileges to control inmates. Prisoners formed communities, but only under conditions of extreme duress.

Although clearest in the South, a general decline in rehabilitationist ambitions marked the penal world after the Civil War. To be sure, there were the beginnings of new strategies to transform character and reintegrate inmates into society: parole, the indeterminate sentence, efforts further to separate inmates within and between institutions. For the most part, however, late-nineteenth-century incarceration maintained the physical and disciplinary shell—but lacked the hope—of its early national progenitors.

Individualization, Industrialization, and Rehabilitation

During the Progressive Era, a new generation of private reformers and public officials invested new hopes in incarceration and articulated new theories of reformation. Progressive penology aimed to reverse some of the fundamental tenets of nineteenth-century penal thought and practice. In particular, penologists placed renewed emphasis on individualized punishment. Only now, they suggested, individualization would be founded on integration with, rather than separation from, the wider community.

Consequently, the early twentieth century witnessed greater emphasis on the individual case. To some extent, this emphasis simply extended the earlier development of parole and the indeterminate sentence. Both parole and the indeterminate sentence had shifted attention from the specific crime committed to investigation of the criminal's character while strengthening oversight of the convict. But the Progressive investment in individualization went significantly further. Drawing on the growing authority of the social sciences, Progressive penal reformers aimed to integrate psychology, sociology, and the case study into punishment itself. Drawing as well on growing middle-class concern with the "culture" of immigrant and laboring populations and notions of inherited degeneracy and eugenics, penologists sought to make the individual convict, not the criminal act, the focus of the penal process.

In practice the effects of Progressive reforms were limited. The number of psychologists, social workers, parole officers, and so on was never sufficient to fulfill the aims of reformers. Prison officials and caseworkers frequently were in conflict. Nor was the basis for Progressive reforms ever clear. Progressives believed that they could obtain scientific knowledge of the sources and treatments of criminality. But often their claims and prescriptions were simply common observation cast in the rhetoric of medicine. The tensions between the custodial and the reformative elements of the Progressive program were never resolved. Even prisons designed explicitly to bring to bear the new social scientific approaches—like the Norfolk Penal Colony in Massachusetts—rapidly devolved into custodial institutions. At Norfolk, despite initial intentions to rehabilitate instead of coerce, it was only a few years before prisoners were punished with solitary confinement in windowless cells where they were fed only bread and water. Specific cases of Progressive reforms did occur, of course. Some nineteenth-century inheritances, like the lockstep and the striped uniform, were eliminated; communication between prisoners and the outside world was improved; and at Sing Sing experiments were made in inmate self-government. But for the most part, the immediate effects of Progressive individualization were minimal.

The 1920s, 1930s, and 1940s were the era of the big house. New prisons at Jackson, Michigan; San Quentin, California; Stateville, Illinois; and elsewhere were huge complexes of incarceration. The size and diversity of the population within these complexes, which could hold thousands of inmates, led to complicated social divisions among inmates and systematic, if hidden, compromise and negotiation between inmates and prison authorities. The big houses also aimed to integrate mass production into the practice of incarceration. At Jackson, Michigan, for example, the new prison built in the 1920s drew on the example of the state's automobile industry. This effort, however, did not survive the coming of the Great Depression. Prisoners increasingly spent their time either idle or in make-work activities. Boredom and a numbing dullness seem to have become dominant aspects of inmate life.

Violence haunted the big house. Observers believed that the peace of the big house was extremely tense and unstable. Violence, among inmates and between guards and inmates, occurred daily; sexual violence was an ever-present possibility; and prison officials formally employed punishments ranging in severity up to extended imprisonment in unlit isolation cells. Indeed the era of the big house was bracketed by prison riots in the 1920s and the 1950s.

State-run big houses, of course, did not reflect the entire prison system. As always, local jails were both common and commonly removed from these reform efforts. The first half of the twentieth century witnessed the expansion of the federal prison system, which, although it remained considerably smaller than the state systems, was characterized by greater professionalism; the existence of federal maximum-security prisons like Alcatraz—with their greater discipline—were sharply differentiated from most state-run prisons. Large southern prison camps, like the infamous Parchman Farm, continued to be run in extremely brutal fashion. In fact, big houses tended to be concentrated in the Northeast, Midwest, and California. During the late nineteenth and early twentieth centuries the South became the region with the largest number of prisoners and the highest incarceration rate; thus caution is in order as to the reach and influence of Progressive and big-house reforms.

Nonetheless, the era of the big house and of Progressive individualization left important legacies for prisons and prisoners. The desire to deploy new techniques in the name of rehabilitation as well as the push for more professionalization of prisons, though limited before World War II, would be taken up anew in the 1950s and 1960s. In those decades a combination of forces—including a growing willingness on the part of the state to commit fiscal resources, the rising importance of humanitarian rhetoric and human-rights language following the Holocaust, a relatively low

A prison uniform and head cage from around 1915, as worn by Thomas Mott Osborne, a prison reformer.
LIBRARY OF CONGRESS

crime rate during the 1950s, and the prestige of the social sciences—led to expanded efforts to achieve rehabilitation within prisons. Some prisons increased their use of therapeutic programs and allowed inmates greater access to libraries and education. New prisons, most notably Soledad in California, were designed to minimize the appearance of incarceration—fences and gun towers replaced concrete walls, and the internal space was designed to place emphasis less on cells and more on collective living areas. Prisoners began to assert their rights in court and sought, sometimes successfully, to improve their living conditions through writs of habeas corpus and judicial intervention. Courts displayed a growing willingness to insist on prisoners' rights—a willingness that challenged the older informal and personalist structures of the big house. In prisons like Stateville, in Illinois, a more legalistic and bureaucratic prison regime emerged. And the overall reliance on incarceration in state prisons declined. In the early 1970s the rate of incarceration in state and federal prisons was lower than at any time since the late 1920s.

Expansion and the New Punitiveness

Like that of the Progressives' efforts, the reach of these new developments was limited. Their overall effects, however, are difficult to gauge because the strategy of rehabilitation unraveled so quickly. During the 1960s and 1970s punishment became deeply politicized, and the rehabilitationist regime collapsed. Prison populations became more racially diverse, with minorities systematically overrepresented. Owing to the growing importance, first, of Black Muslims and, later, of more explicitly political militants, black and then Latino inmates grew more direct and open in their challenge to prison authorities. If the 1960s witnessed the expansion of political militancy, the 1970s and 1980s saw the growth of prison gangs organized along racial lines. Racial tensions within the prison, and in debates concerning prisons, increased. Caught up in the turmoil of the 1960s, prisoners—especially minority prisoners—were transformed into symbols of conflicts within the politics of the nation as a whole. Riots at Attica and Soledad, among others, revealed that conflicts within prisons had reached the point of explosion.

As a result, the rehabilitationist regime came under attack from all sides. Radical and liberal critics argued that rehabilitation had merely legitimated greater psychological coercion within prisons while ignoring—because of its emphasis on individual treatment—the social roots of crime. Conservative critics and politicians pointed to increases in violent crime and violence within prisons during the late 1960s and the 1970s; drawing on the growing popular identification of criminality with young minority males, they were able to link renewed reliance on rigorous punishment to an imagined restoration of the social order disrupted during the 1960s. Arguing that rehabilitation simply coddled inmates while denigrating individual responsibility, the conservatives recast public debate on crime and punishment. The United States entered a new era in penal practice and policy.

Mobilizing popular fear about violent crime, the prison apparatus expanded dramatically. Between 1980 and 1994 the number of inmates in state or federal prisons increased from an estimated 319,518 to 991,612, while the rate of prisoners sentenced to terms of more than one year increased from 139 per every 100,000 individuals to 389 per

100,000 (Maguire and Pastore 1996). By the end of the century the numbers in state and federal jails totaled around 1,200,000. If the population of local jails was included, the inmate population rose to roughly 1,800,000 (Schlosser 1998). The United States had altered course, making imprisonment an increasingly central aspect of the social order.

This growth was not uniform. Incarceration rates were heaviest in the South and West and lowest in the Northeast. In the last quarter of the twentieth century, California, for example, built over twenty new prisons and increased its inmate population at least eight times over. Nationally, the expansion fell most heavily on minority males. Beyond the increase in violent crime, much of this expansion (especially in the federal system, where drug offenders made up the majority of inmates) can be traced to the administrations of Presidents Ronald Reagan and George Bush and their War on Drugs—a policy that focused primarily on minorities. In the 1980s and 1990s the racial composition of prisons also changed. African Americans had, with the exception of the slave South, always been overrepresented in prison populations; but in the mid-1990s they and Latinos became the majority of prison inmates. Finally, not only were more men and women being sentenced to prison, but sentencing became increasingly severe.

The effects of this population explosion within prisons were enormous. Growing numbers of prisons and prison systems faced overcrowding; violence (by both guards and inmates) intensified; and racial gangs were increasingly important players within prisons. Legislators sought to strip away inmate privileges and diminish their material conditions. If the big house maintained peace through compromise and negotiation and the rehabilitationist prison aimed to re-create the prison environment along therapeutic lines, later prisons increasingly resembled the English philosopher Thomas Hobbes's imagined state of nature—filled with violence and isolation. Benjamin Rush's eighteenth-century fear that punishment was producing more violence was, perhaps, even more apposite at the end of the twentieth century.

One of the starkest examples of the growing violence of the late-twentieth-century prison was the spread of super-max facilities. At places like Pelican Bay and Corcoran in California, new institutions were constructed that superficially resembled the solitary-confinement penitentiaries of the nineteenth century. Peopled by inmates who were serious offenders or had been dispatched from other prisons, the super-max facilities were designed to isolate inmates and increase state control over the prison. At Pelican Bay's Security Housing Unit, inmates were kept in their cells for nearly twenty-three hours a day and watched electronically so that there was little contact even between them and their keepers. In the super-max prisons the intensification of punishment and the deterioration of prison conditions reached their apex.

The super-max prisons, however, were only one point on a continuum. The 1990s also saw growing efforts to try juveniles as adults, the popularity of "boot camps" (where juveniles were subject to military-style discipline), a willingness to privatize prisons, the continued expansion of the death penalty, and the return of the chain gang. The penal apparatus not only displayed a greater acceptance of violence but continued to retreat from public oversight.

In this context a comparison with the late eighteenth and early nineteenth centuries is important, for if the return of solitary confinement resembles the move to the penitentiary, it is a resemblance that obscures more than it clarifies. The penitentiary emerged as part of a wider effort to contain state violence and to diminish the death penalty. Its proponents hoped that, through the call of conscience, inmates could be reconciled to the community. Punishment was not seen as the front line of social order. The penal world at the end of the twentieth century operated in a system of growing violence, was increasingly designed to warehouse rather than reform, and served to separate rather than integrate. In the history of prisons and prisoners in the United States, such a penal world—in both its size and its aims—was unprecedented. The technology of the penitentiary may have lingered, but the vision did not.

BIBLIOGRAPHY

THE EMERGENCE OF THE PENITENTIARY

Hirsch, Adam J. *The Rise of the Penitentiary: Prisons and Punishment in Early America.* New Haven, Conn.: Yale University Press, 1992.

Masur, Louis P. *Rites of Execution: Capital Punishment and the Transformation of American Culture, 1776–1865.* New York: Oxford University Press, 1989.

Meranze, Michael. *Laboratories of Virtue: Punishment, Revolution, and Authority in Philadelphia, 1760–1835.* Chapel Hill: University of North Carolina Press, 1996.

Rothman, David J. *The Discovery of the Asylum: Social Order and Disorder in the New Republic.* Boston: Little, Brown, 1971.

THE SOUTHERN EXPERIENCE

Ayers, Edward L. *Vengeance and Justice: Crime and Punishment in the Nineteenth-Century American South.* New York: Oxford University Press, 1984.

Lichtenstein, Alex. *Twice the Work of Free Labor: The Political Economy of Convict Labor in the New South.* New York: Verso, 1996.

Oshinsky, David M. *Worse Than Slavery: Parchman Farm and the Ordeal of Jim Crow Justice.* New York: Free Press, 1996.

PRISON REFORMERS AND REFORM

Rothman, David J. *Conscience and Convenience: The Asylum and Its Alternatives in Progressive America.* Boston: Little, Brown, 1980.

Rotman, Edgardo. "The Failure of Reform: United States, 1865–1965." In *The Oxford History of the Prison: The Practice of Punishment in Western Society,* edited by Norval Morris and David J. Rothman. New York: Oxford University Press, 1995.

Simon, Jonathan. *Poor Discipline: Parole and the Social Control of the Underclass, 1890–1990.* Chicago: University of Chicago Press, 1993.

PRISONS IN THE TWENTIETH CENTURY

Bright, Charles. *The Powers That Punish: Prison and Politics in the Era of the "Big House," 1920–1955.* Ann Arbor: University of Michigan Press, 1996.

Clemmer, Donald. *The Prison Community.* Boston: Christopher, 1940.

Jacobs, James B. *Stateville: The Penitentiary in Mass Society.* Chicago: University of Chicago Press, 1977.

Keve, Paul W. *Prisons and the American Conscience: A History of U.S. Federal Corrections.* Carbondale: Southern Illinois University Press, 1991.

Sykes, Gresham M. *The Society of Captives: A Study of a Maximum Security Prison.* Princeton, N.J.: Princeton University Press, 1958.

TOWARD THE CONTEMPORARY PRISON

Cahalan, Margaret Werner. *Historical Correction Statistics in the United States, 1850–1984.* U.S. Department of Justice, Bureau of Justice Statistics. Washington, D.C.: Government Printing Office, 1986.

Cummins, Eric. *The Rise and Fall of California's Radical Prison Movement.* Palo Alto, Calif.: Stanford University Press, 1994.

Maguire, Kathleen, and Ann L. Pastore, eds. *Sourcebook of Criminal Justice Statistics, 1995.* U.S. Department of Justice, Bureau of Justice Statistics. Washington, D.C.: Government Printing Office, 1996.

Morris, Norval. "The Contemporary Prison: 1965–Present." In *The Oxford History of the Prison: The Practice of Punishment in Western Society,* edited by Norval Morris and David J. Rothman. New York: Oxford University Press, 1995.

Schlosser, Eric. "The Prison-Industrial Complex." *Atlantic Monthly,* December 1998.

U.S. Department of Justice, Bureau of Justice Statistics. *Correctional Populations in the United States, 1994.* Washington, D.C.: Government Printing Office, 1996.

MICHAEL MERANZE

See also **Corporal Punishment; Crime and Punishment in American History; Criminal Justice Systems; Death Row; Sentencing; Weapons: Stun or Shock Devices.**

PRISON CONDITIONS

The word *prison* derives from the Latin verb *prehendere,* to capture or seize, and prisons are monuments to the goal of captivity. The architects who designed early prisons—such as William Blackburn in the 1780s—thought of stone and mortar as means of social engineering, especially as ways of separating malefactors from law-abiding citizens and from one another. This emphasis was partly due to the fact that earlier forms of confinement consisted of chaotic cohabitation of persons of all ages and sexes, which offended the sensibilities of puritanical reformers, who were concerned about the potential for unrestrained licentiousness.

By the turn of the nineteenth century sequestration of inmates had taken the form of complete physical and social isolation, which was achieved via long rows of individual cells. In the postcolonial United States the obsession with isolating prisoners from one another resulted in an impassioned rivalry between two extreme prescriptions for personal insulation: the so-called Pennsylvania system, which involved unmitigated solitude, and the congregate system, which permitted prisoners to eat, exercise, and work in proximity to one another but enforced silence at all times and rigid regimentation. Some prisons hooded inmates whenever they left their cells, assuring maximal sensory deprivation when prisoners were at large.

The most minute deviations from the regimes that kept prisoners from contact with one another (and their keepers) earned severe punishment. Prisons exercised considerable ingenuity in inventing painful restraints, shackles, whipping devices, and dungeons for nonconforming inmates. Despite these efforts at enforced conformity, prisoners resisted in ways that reveal a persistent convict subculture. Based on his research of eighteenth- and nineteenth-century prison memoirs, Randall McGowen has described tortuous but effective ways that evolved among English prisoners to circumvent the rigors of their confinement:

Only the new convicts challenged the regime head-on, and a beating or a week of reduced diet demonstrated the folly of such attempts. The old hands avoided direct confrontations; they were the model prisoners whom many commentators suspected of hypocrisy but against whom nothing could be proved. They taught new prisoners methods for communicating with each other, shortcuts in finishing work, and the names of guards who could be played upon. Convicts shared food and warned of the approach of guards. They developed a form of ventriloquism, the art of talking without moving one's lips. The prison at night was filled with the sound of tapping as pipes became the medium for telegraphic communication. Some prisoners created chat holes through which they could speak to each other. They relayed information on where to find nails that would make oakum picking, the separation of strands of old rope, easier. They told how to step on the treadwheel so as to make that ordeal less exhausting. Some engaged in an illegal trade with guards and among themselves for tobacco and other small luxuries. Witnesses before parliamentary committees testified to the intransigence of prison culture and the solidarities formed among prisoners. (p. 97)

Though the specific details of prisoners' practices changed over two hundred years, the phenomenon McGowen described still existed at the end of the twentieth century. Prison conditions continued to impose regimentation and strictures. These strictures circumscribed autonomy and assaulted the self-respect of prisoners. In coping with these challenges, prisoners tried to salvage a vestige of autonomy and a modicum of self-esteem. Each prisoner had to make his own effort to this end, but norms evolved among inmates that facilitated the process.

Most of the methods devised by prisoners were designed to ameliorate the pains of imprisonment without causing harm to others or seriously violating the rules. No one was harmed, for instance, when the inmates communicated between cells by tapping water pipes or disseminated tips for easing onerous tasks. In fact, the prisoners' sanity was endangered by the practices of prison administrators of the nineteenth century—extended solitary confinement, for instance, occasioned suicides and insanity in Pennsylvania—and coping strategies helped the inmates to survive. Among the threats to the prisoners' sanity was the prison's concern for keeping them occupied to the extent of having them perform useless labor, for instance on the treadmills, which had no function other than to exact pain and discomfort (guards were called screws because they could adjust the tension of the treadmills).

Different types of activities have shaped the criminal underworld of prisons, including drug trading, gambling, gang rivalry, and extortion.

Prisoners in lockstep at Auburn Prison, New York, around 1910. COURTESY OF THE CAYUGA MUSEUM

Prison administrators disapprove of transgressions in prison that are crimes in the outside world and punish them severely. The concern of prisons with controlling in-house crimes shapes features of institutional regimes that circumscribe the lives of non-offending inmates, as well as offenders. The regime also produces escalating contests of will— chains of transgression and repression—involving the most serious offenders. When these escalations culminate, the prisoners come to be seen as uncontrollable and typically find themselves isolated in the equivalent of eighteenth-century conditions.

The most dramatic of retrograde conditions exist in super-maximum and maxi-maxi prisons, where technology has made it possible to re-create the punitive environments of the past. In these institutions, which are designed to serve the most recalcitrant offenders, the prisoners live in segregation, are moved in shackles, are surveyed by cameras, and have no contact with staff (other than as distorted and disembodied loudspeaker voices). The courts have scrutinized such settings and have suggested the need for mental-health assistance for prisoners living under such stressful conditions.

The maxi-maxi prison was one of several developments in twentieth-century prison construction. Other trends were driven by the need to build institutions quickly and cheaply, as prison populations exceeded prison capacity. Small to medium-sized facilities that house several hundred residents in dormitories were also constructed. Such settings tended to be used for a prisoner who was serving a two- or three-year sentence for a drug-related offense or a property crime.

A third trend has been the "unitizing" of prisons and municipal detention facilities. A unit is a part of a prison that can be operated independently of other parts, so that a group of staff can work continuously with the same prisoners. With detention facilities, this arrangement is referred to as the "new generation jail" (Zupan), and it is considered a safer, more humane form of short-term confinement. In prisons, units can facilitate different activities for groups of inmates in different parts of the institution and the matching of the skills of staff with the needs of prisoners.

Among programs offered in prisons, the most enduring is work. During the nineteenth century the hope was that prisons could be self-sustaining by becoming factories. The gigantic size of some U.S. prisons was inspired by the desire to accommodate shops and industrial plants of the kind that prevailed outside prisons in the 1920s and 1930s. Because of the sturdiness and fortresslike character of prison construction, many plants constructed early in the century with such considerations in mind have survived. As a consequence many American maximum-security prisons

A typical prison cell in Alcatraz Prison, San Francisco, 1956. CORBIS/BETTMANN

conform to the familiar stereotype: they are depressing and ungainly facilities that house two thousand or so prisoners and are located far from the metropolitan areas where prisoners originate, because the physical plant originally served a quarry or an iron mine or was located at a rail terminal. Prisons are also frequently built in remote rural locations to provide employment to workers in economically depressed communities.

Among the reasons for the demise of the industrial prison was pressure from businesses and unions to eliminate products of cheap prison labor. The usual compromise resolution was to allow inmates to manufacture commodities, such as Formica furniture, for the use of government agencies. Prisoners also stamp license plates and print government documents. In more advanced vocational programs, a few prisoners provide computer services, answer telephones, and make optical lenses for Medicaid recipients; others tame wild horses or train guide dogs for the blind. But such ventures occupy only a small fraction of the aggregate time available to U.S. prisoners, who mostly face endless days of relative inactivity.

Education is a standard program option in prisons and ranges from remedial instruction to preparation for high school certification. College course work is rarely offered because legislators have been reluctant to provide perquisites to convicts. The same sentiment has caused politically oriented officials to dispose of other prison amenities, such as gymnasium equipment and television sets. This, however, is the sort of gambit that prison professionals (such as the American Corrections Association) view as counterproductive. The informed opinion of correctional administrators is that when prisoners face enforced idleness they become more likely to commit infractions and engage in conflicts. Programming and custody are defined as inextricably linked, and a paucity of programming is seen as an invitation to disorder and violence.

These problems feared by administrators range from individual predatory behavior to the collective violence of gang wars and riots. Such events occur less frequently than the public suspects, but vulnerable inmates are occasionally assaulted or raped in prisons. Gangs that maintain contact with affiliates in the community are also occasional sources of problems, in that they may import and distribute drugs or engage in rivalries and vendettas.

While program participation by inmates is correlated with reduced recidivism rates, it is not clear whether this correlation can be attributed to the high level of motivation of participants or the rehabilitative effect of work and education. The evidence suggests that both factors are at play and that sustained participation in prison programs both reflects and cements motivation. The same point holds for rehabilitative enterprises such as substance-abuse treatment, in which prisoners who drop out tend to have high recidivism rates, while those who stay in do better than inmates who are not assigned to treatment.

Prison violence is also a product of person and setting. While some personal attributes—age, for instance—are related to involvement in incidents, violence in the outside community does not predict violence in prisons. Most prison violence results from private disputes and group rivalries, but the institutional environment exacerbates such conflicts in that it enforces cohabitation, forecloses escape or avoidance, and creates stress. The prisoner subculture also contributes to violence because it stigmatizes inmates who show fear and disapproves of efforts by those who invoke staff assistance when they feel endangered. Prison staff are responsible for the safety of their charges and are obligated to protect prospective victims by segregating them. Paradoxically, the segregated settings are invariably more confining than the prison at large and offer fewer amenities, which add disincentives to invoking protection.

A final problem related to prison violence is the inflexibility of disciplinary procedures. Persons who are emotionally disturbed are less able to cope with the prison environment; they are thus disproportionately involved in infractions. When such inmates are punished, however, their problems are frequently aggravated rather than ameliorated. Being locked up for attempting suicide, for instance, is bound to increase a prisoner's despondency.

In the late twentieth century most prisons were congested. Tension increases under such circumstances because inmates under stress are more likely to engage in conflicts or to manifest displeasure with staff. Crowded prisons are also more difficult to manage because there is less space to separate would-be predators from victims or to group the inmates in sensible ways.

In general, most prison staff do not see their goal as punishment; being sentenced to imprisonment is punitive, but prisons are not in the pain-inflicting business. Guards are presumed to supervise their charges courteously, to monitor their movements, and to provide basic services that prisoners need for day-to-day existence. (In this connection officers speak of themselves as babysitters.) Prisoner-to-officer relationships can and do develop, despite norms that discourage such friendships. And though prisons vary in quality (those in southern states have sometimes been slower to advance), prison conditions have arguably improved over time. This is especially important in the United States, which confines a far larger proportion of its citizenry than other industrial nations.

BIBLIOGRAPHY

McGowen, Randall. "The Well-Ordered Prison: England, 1780–1865." In *The Oxford History of the Prison: The Practice of Punishment in Western Society*, edited by Norval Morris and David J. Rothman. New York: Oxford, 1995.

Sykes, Gresham M. *The Society of Captives: A Study of a Maximum Security Prison.* New York: Atheneum, 1965.

Zupan, Linda L. *Jails: Reform and the New Generation Philosophy.* Cincinnati: Anderson, 1991.

HANS TOCH

See also **Crime and Punishment in American History; Death Row.**

PRISON VIOLENCE

The perception exists that violent criminals are incapacitated when they are incarcerated. Since imprisonment blocks these individuals from committing crimes on the streets, it is assumed that they desist their violent behavior. Prison research and observation lead to quite a different conclusion. Incarceration of violent offenders does not necessarily diminish violent behavior, although that might be the result of intensive supervision and solitary confinement. For most prisoners, violent behavior during incarceration is quantitatively similar to that exhibited previous to incarceration. Confinement of violent offenders therefore creates a displacement effect whereby violence increases in prisons as it decreases on the streets.

When individuals are grouped together, their interaction pyramids into a common culture that has emergent properties. Although these properties would likely be prosocial in a therapeutic community, in a prison that houses more than a few violent individuals, the antisocial properties emerge. It is possible that antisocial cultural properties not only allow some prisoners to maintain the same frequency of violent behavior that they demonstrated while free, but encourage and allow other prisoners to be more violent while incarcerated than they ever were on the streets. Prisons are not only graduate schools for criminals, they frequently function as training grounds for the criminally violent.

Disciplinary records do not provide an accurate picture of the volume of prison violence, because few acts of violence (perhaps one incident in four) are reported to prison authorities. The convict code forbids prisoners—even those who are victims of violence—from "snitching," on pain of death. Moreover, because correctional officers are accountable for the management of their areas of supervision, there is typically little motivation to bring disciplinary problems to the attention of superiors.

The major forms of violence in correctional institutions are homicide, rape, assault, and threats of any of these. Threats of violence are inextricably linked to the potential for future violence. When the linkage between the threat and the violent act is broken, it is more likely that the threatened prisoner gave in to the aggressor's demands than that the aggressor was bluffing or that correctional officers intervened. Threats of violence as well as acts of violence produce domination of the strong over the weak, the violent over the nonviolent, and gangs over isolated individuals. Threats often are sufficient to subdue victims of economic crime and rape, or to discriminate against certain types of prisoners (such as child molesters, or white men in institutions dominated by Latino and African American gangs).

Evolution of Prison Subcultures

American prison subcultures were once developed from interactions among white prisoners of high status. People of color were consigned to the periphery and suffered high levels of violent victimization. As the United States urbanized and people of color came to be increasingly centralized in large metropolitan areas, the proportions of white, Latino, and African American prisoners began to shift. White criminals continued to enter the prison as isolated individuals or, rarely, as members of organized crime families, but the numbers of Latino and African American prisoners increased much more rapidly than did white prisoners. More important, many of the latter were members of street gangs, and they imported their gang structures into the prisons. These gangs changed the balance of power in prison subcultures, increasing the victimization of non-gang members (particularly white prisoners) and protecting gang members from violence and threats of violence from non-gang members.

Another change in the prison subculture was caused by the so-called War on Drugs, which brought tens of thousands of drug users and sellers into prisons over a relatively short period of time. This new breed of inmate was not a career criminal in the usual sense and did not subscribe to the convict code or any other shared normative system that would bring order into the prison subculture and could reduce the frequency of violence and threats of violence among prisoners. These prisoners also produced a strong and steady demand for illegal drugs, which were much easier to smuggle into prisons than alcohol or food. Once behind the walls, drugs spread beyond the original user groups to other prisoners. The drug trade and consequent drug use by prisoners increased levels of violence over that ascribed to the traditional black-market manufacture of alcoholic beverages, resulting in fights among drug sellers over territory, fights between sellers and users over prices and delivery, and the enhancement of violent tendencies caused by the abuse of stimulants such as amphetamines.

Creation of Prisoner Hierarchies

Prisoner societies are hierarchical, and status depends on individuals' potential for violence more than anything else. Status in prison is expressed in terms of reputation. The potential for violence in prison is a constituent part of the social fabric, along with criminal history, gender, and race, and functions to sort prisoners into positions arranged from low to high status. To the extent that the resulting status hierarchy is accepted as legitimate by prisoners, incidents of violence for the prisoner population as a whole might decrease. Acceptance of the existing status hierarchy was standard in traditional white-dominated prison subcultures but became uncertain as racial polarization, gang organization, and drug use in prisons increased.

Because material goods are hard to come by in prisons, they are highly valued by inmates. A heating coil that can be plugged into a cell outlet and used to heat water for coffee, tea, and soup, for example, can make life a great deal more pleasant for a prisoner and can earn him money or favors if he heats water for other prisoners who lack coils. Prisoners earn scrip or prison currency by working in prison industries or in prison maintenance. Together with money placed on their books by friends and family outside the prison and then translated into scrip, wages are used to purchase essentials and luxury items at the prison store. Prisoners who rank low in violence potential may be victimized for scrip on the way to the store and victimized for store-bought goods while returning to their cells. Prisoners who give up their goods too easily will be accosted again and again, having identified themselves as easy prey. Violent threats power other forms of economic victimization, such as payments from the weaker party's friends and relatives outside the prison to a receiving party designated by the aggressor.

Prison violence is, for the most part, rational and instrumental in achieving psychological, economic, and sexual goals for its participants. In men's prisons, low-status prisoners are as much in danger of losing their virginity as being robbed of their commissary items. Homosexual rape is a constant threat to low-status prisoners. The raped man is perceived as a newly created woman, having undergone an instantaneous transgender experience, and is targeted by other rapists thereafter. Worse, he may be assaulted by groups of individuals who take pleasure in torturing him. One alternative for the rape victim is to make an agreement with a high-status prisoner, wherein the victim pledges unlimited sexual access in return for protection from sexual assault. Relationships that develop between prisoners, whether consensual or based on threats of violence, often end in violence, such as when a lovers' triangle ends in violent assault or homicide. Violence in women's prisons is less frequent in occurrence than in men's prisons. Verbal aggression, which is almost continuous but nonviolent in men's prisons, is more important as a status sorter in women's prisons, where sexual victimization is rather unusual, and theft by manipulation or burglary is more common than theft through physical attacks and threats.

Prisoner violence toward correctional officers is statistically relatively rare (accounting for about 0.1 percent of prisoner aggression). Despite this, it is a major source of fear for those who work behind the walls. Officers are in continual danger of being assaulted by a mentally unstable prisoner, and they are subject to financial and emotional manipulation by prisoners seeking preferential treatment. The officers' fear of victimization by prisoners lives on in the stories of correctional officers who were taken hostage by prisoners in prison riots and assaulted, raped, disfigured, tortured, and even killed.

Combating Prison Violence

Prison violence can be reduced by strategies such as architectural modifications, increased electronic monitoring, a lower prisoner-staff ratio, permanent segregation of predatory prisoners, and a decrease in the imprisonment of nonviolent criminals. With the exception of the last two strategies, each alternative carries a high price tag.

The best way to implement a comprehensive program of correctional violence reduction is to cease building new prisons and to allocate future budget increases toward improving existing prisons. Alternatively, gang conflicts, race wars, and drug-related individual violence will continue to plague correctional institutions and can be expected to rise throughout the foreseeable future.

BIBLIOGRAPHY

Bowker, Lee H. *Prison Victimization*. New York: Elsevier, 1980.

Owen, Barbara. *"In the Mix": Struggle and Survival in a Women's Prison*. Albany: State University of New York Press, 1998.

Stevens, Dennis J. "The Depth of Imprisonment and Prisonization: Levels of Security and Prisoners' Anticipation of Future Violence." *Howard Journal of Criminal Justice* 33 (1994).

Toch, Hans, Kenneth Adams, and Douglas J. Grant. *Coping: Maladaptation in Prisons*. New Brunswick, N.J.: Transaction, 1989.

LEE H. BOWKER

RIOTS

While the primary objective of penal institutions is a matter of some debate, few would disagree that prisons should at least control and contain the inmates in an efficient, safe, and just manner. Prisons are generally successful in this endeavor. There are times, however, when inmates challenge the institution's authority through riots, which are "the most striking of all unexpected events, for they represent a complete and public denial of one of the most fundamental premises on which the prison is built, namely, that the officials, the surrogates of the free community, stand in unquestioned power over the inmates" (Sykes 1958, p. 109). The first recorded prison riot in colonial America occurred in 1774 at an institution built over an abandoned mine shaft in Simsbury, Connecticut. Since that time, there have been hundreds of riots in American prisons. The actual number of American prison riots is unknown, partly because corrections officials have an incentive to keep altercations quiet and partly because most prison disturbances receive little publicity. Yet when a disturbance becomes so serious that it draws the attention of the media, it is typically described as a riot and joins the long list of notorious examples of prison officials' loss of control.

Another reason that riots are not always documented is that there is no clear definition of what constitutes a prison riot. Disturbances in prisons are as diverse as the inmates in them. Prison riots vary dramatically in terms of the level of violence, the objectives of the instigators, and the duration of the disturbance. Some riots are racial brawls between inmates, while others involve elected leaders with organized agendas and specific goals. A general definition of a riot is offered by Bert Useem and Peter Kimball (1989): "a prison riot occurs when the authorities lose control of a significant number of prisoners, in a significant area of the prison, for a significant amount of time" (p. 4).

Categories of Prison Protests and Riots

Many prison riots are essentially protests against what inmates feel is unjust or unacceptable treatment. These protests take several forms and vary in terms of the level of aggression employed by the rioters. Sometimes a riot is simply a passive demonstration, such as a hunger strike or a labor strike. Another form of protest is self-mutilation, a tactic often employed in order to call attention to oppressive conditions. For example, in 1951 inmates at the Buford Prison in Georgia cut their heel tendons to protest their isolation from one another. Protests can also involve escape efforts that are either peaceful and secretive or aggressive and overt.

The most serious forms of protest involve an overt and violent challenge to correctional authority. These instances are primarily what the term *riot* is used to describe, and they pose the greatest threat to the penal system. Prison riots can be grouped into four general categories. First, inmates may riot to protest the institutional conditions. Such disturbances are usually aimed at substandard facilities, a lack of rehabilitative programming, and overcrowded conditions. Second, inmates may also direct their dissent toward elements in the inmate population itself, such as racial makeup, gang affiliations, antisocial or mentally ill inmates, or radical groups. Third, inmates may challenge certain institutional practices such as staff turnover, civil rights violations, and security breaches. Finally, inmates may oppose external policies such as inadequate funding, sentencing that is too harsh, public apathy, or discriminatory sentencing.

Causes and Consequences of Riots

Several models of the prison riot have been advanced. The first emerged from a study conducted by Vernon Fox in 1971. Fox believed prison riots to be spontaneous outbursts with several distinct stages. The first stage is an episode of undirected, random violence. The second stage sees the emergence of inmate leaders, who organize and control the disturbance. The third stage occurs when the inmates interact with the correctional authorities and discuss alternatives available to avoid any further rioting. The fourth stage is the surrender of the inmates, either by force or by negotiation. The fifth and final stage of a riot consists of institutional reorganization, where the prison officials, by making necessary institutional changes, attempt to reestablish order and efficiency, and thus restore confidence.

A different model is based on conflict theory. This approach asserts that prison disturbances result from unresolved conflicts between two or more parties—between individual inmates, between several inmate groups, or between inmates and correctional staff. Smith found that there are four possible reactions to conflict: the participants may bargain with each other, one participant may withdraw from the conflict, the participants may engage in physical combat, or a third party may be called in to mediate the conflict.

A third model of riots is based on theories of collective behavior. Six conditions make it probable that a riot will occur: structural conduciveness, in which structural conditions facilitate inmate protest; strain or tension between inmates or between inmates and correctional staff; spread of a generalized belief among inmates about the unacceptable conditions of prison life; factors that precipitate protest, such as the denial of privileges, unfair treatment, and brutality; ability to mobilize and organize for action, which involves inmates constructing and adopting a protest plan; and ability of inmates to gain control over parts of the institution, fellow inmates, and the correctional staff.

Four general sociological theories have been used to help explain why prison riots occur in the first place. *Deprivation theory* asserts that riots and protest are a natural reaction to oppressive and poor conditions. *Resource-mobilization theory* contends that inmates will always be opposed to prison authorities and that they resort to rioting only when they have access to material and organizational resources. *Breakdown theory* suggests that when access to institutions that direct individuals toward "proper behavior" (for example, religion, family, and education) is impeded, in the case of prison inmates, rioting is often the result. *Collective-behavior theory* asserts that when the familiar routines of a group get disturbed, members compensate for the change. In prisons the disruptions might mean televisions, books, or gym equipment were taken away or some unwelcome dietary change or change in the institutional schedule occurred, in which cases inmates often compensate by rioting.

Most prison riots seem to have common components. While the term *riot* suggests a certain degree of chaos, most inmate disturbances are not riots and are actually comparatively orderly and end very quickly. By contrast, a full-fledged prison riot is a dynamic occurrence that has several stages. In the pre-riot stage prisoners collect necessary materials and pool their cognitive resources (e.g., knowledge of the guard schedule or layout of the facility) to carry out their intentions. During

The gutted remains after one of two Auburn, New York, prison riots in 1929. Prisoners rioted and set fires after the removal of significant reform measures. COURTESY OF THE CAYUGA MUSEUM

the initiation stage the inmates engage in a first act of rebellion and the prison officials react. If this stage is not stifled, the expansion stage begins, in which inmates attempt to seize and control as many resources as possible: human (additional inmates to participate in the riot or hostages), material (weapons or other objects), and spatial (strategic areas of the prison). The fourth stage is the siege, in which inmates have captured some resources and the authorities have organized their forces to regain control of the institution. Termination is the final stage of a prison riot, when control of the institution is regained by the correctional management.

It is estimated that the financial cost of a single riot can exceed one hundred million dollars. Immediate financial costs include paying additional personnel to settle the disturbance, repairing the institutional damage from the riot, and providing medical care for injured inmates and staff. Long-term financial costs include providing counseling for the parties involved, mapping out new prevention techniques to avoid future incidents, correction of the grievances of the inmates, and raising staff salaries to appease the workers.

Several measures have been shown to reduce the likelihood of prison riots and the costs associated with them. Preventive strategies include in-mate grievance mechanisms, which allow inmates to voice their complaints; inmate councils, which allow inmates better communication with prison officials; and attitudinal survey instruments, which assess the prisoners' views. By refining the training of staff members, inmate dissatisfaction can be recognized early and dealt with appropriately.

Once a prison riot begins, it can be handled in a number of ways. Prison officials can select a "tactical solution" and forcibly retake the prison, they can negotiate to end the riot by meeting the needs and demands of the protestors, or prison officials can select a "waiting solution" and simply let the riot subside. Several of these tactics are often used in conjunction with each other, as one approach may bolster the prospects for the success of another. There is no proven strategy to contain a riot. Tactical responses to a riot must be chosen in an unpredictable and high-pressure environment, with profound social and political implications.

History of Prison Riots

The history of prison riots in America appears to follow a cyclical pattern. Gresham Sykes (1958) points out that prisons are constantly shifting from states of order into states of disorder. These fluctuations occur over time; riots ensue when the

609

Attica Prison Riot

In 1971 the inmates at the state prison in Attica, New York, seized thirty-nine hostages and a quarter of the grounds. The prisoners were protesting abominable conditions, racism, and inhumane treatment. The riot came to an end four days later when Nelson Rockefeller, the state's governor, refused to negotiate and ordered the police and the National Guard to retake the prison. In doing so, thirty-two inmates and eleven guards were killed. Some of the inmates who survived were tortured and punished. Many considered the Attica experience to be the worst prison riot in American history.

In the aftermath of this disaster, prison officials across the country took steps to ensure that similar riots would not occur in the future. Unfortunately, many of the conditions that facilitated the riot at Attica were still in existence at the end of the twentieth century. Many concluded that while prisons had been changed, the conditions had not improved.

The inmates filed a $2.8 billion civil liability suit against the State of New York in 1974. In 1996 a federal court in Buffalo, New York, awarded $4 million to an Attica inmate for the torture he endured following the riot. This was the first of 1,281 inmates to win damages in the long-running case.

---

state of disorder becomes too great for inmates. This cyclical pattern is indicated by several major waves of riots in the twentieth century. This first wave of riots took place about the time of World War I. While the available information on these early incidents is limited, it is clear that this first surge in prison protests led to many institutional changes, including the introduction of counseling services and educational programs and a reduction in regimentation and harsh discipline. This initial wave of riots ended at the Kansas State Penitentiary in 1915.

The second wave of riots started in 1929 and lasted about two years. This phase coincided with the introduction of the rehabilitative model, which emphasized individual case management, counseling, indeterminate sentencing, and parole. This second wave of protest led to a series of penal reforms, including increased visitation and personal property privileges.

The third wave of prison riots, which began in 1951 and lasted until 1954, eventually included more than forty-five riots in twenty-one states. Two major issues were raised by inmates involved in this series of riots: the coercive methods used in the rehabilitation programming and the problems faced by Black Muslims. While the riots did not lead to a diminished emphasis on rehabilitation—most of the rioters were seen as irrational thugs making ridiculous requests—there was a negative

response to the Black Muslim issue: the American Correctional Association passed a resolution denouncing the Muslims as a "race hatred" group. Subsequently, Black Muslims were denied Islamic reading materials, visits from ministers, and dietary alternatives.

Four riots stand out since the 1960s. The first occurred at the Oregon Penitentiary in 1968, where twenty-two hostages were taken, five inmates killed, sixty-one persons wounded, seven buildings destroyed, and more than one million dollars in property damaged.

In perhaps the most famous prison riot in the second half of the twentieth century, the state prison in Attica, New York, experienced an inmate takeover in 1971 in which thirty-two inmates and eleven guards were killed. The negotiations between inmates and correctional officials were televised, and consequently the entire nation began to doubt the purpose and effectiveness of incarceration and the rehabilitative ideal.

A third riot occurred in 1975 in Joliet Prison just outside Chicago, Illinois. The prison, built in 1860, housed a population that was 75 percent black, 10 percent Hispanic, and 15 percent white. Over half of the inmates belonged to one of four gangs, and tensions between the gangs and the correctional staff remained high. The riot started when the warden, Fred Finkbeiner, in a crackdown on inmate gangs ordered an audit of records of business transactions by the Jaycees, an inmate group.

The final riot of this period and the most brutal, occurred at the New Mexico State Penitentiary in 1980, during which thirty-three inmates were slain and hundreds were injured. In this riot shifts in management policies to increase inmate control created a hostile environment that was ripe for protest and violence.

BIBLIOGRAPHY

Barak-Glantz, Israel. "The Anatomy of Another Prison Riot." In *Prison Violence in America*, edited by Michael Braswell, Steven Dillingham, and Reid Montgomery, Jr. Cincinnati: Anderson, 1985.

Braswell, Michael, Steven Dillingham, and Reid Montgomery, Jr., eds. *Prison Violence in America*. Cincinnati: Anderson, 1985.

Colvin, Mark. *The Penitentiary in Crisis: From Accomodation to Riot in New Mexico*. Albany: State University of New York Press, 1992.

Dillingham, Steven D., and Reid H. Montgomery, Jr. "Prison Riots: A Corrections' Nightmare Since 1774." In *Prison Violence in America*, edited by Michael Braswell, Steven Dillingham, and Reid Montgomery, Jr. Cincinnati: Anderson, 1985.

Fox, Vernon. *Violence Behind Bars*. New York: Vantage, 1956.

Sykes, Gresham. *The Society of Captives: A Study of Maximum Security Prison*. Princeton, N.J.: Princeton University Press, 1958.

Useem, Bert, Camille Graham Camp, and George M. Camp. *Resolution of Prison Riots*. New York: Oxford University Press, 1996.

Useem, Bert, and Peter Kimball. *States of Siege: U.S. Prison Riots, 1971–1986*. New York: Oxford University Press, 1989.

TODD R. CLEAR
CHRISTOPHER P. KREBS

See also **Riots.**

WOMEN PRISONERS

All prisons, from colonial through modern times, have a violent heritage, but the experiences of women prisoners add a unique component to America's penal history. Extracting personal accounts from historical documents often proves difficult because so few penal institutions have kept complete records on women prisoners.

Reports from as early as 1788 indicated that the Philadelphia prison not only allowed men and women to roam about the yard together, but permitted the sale of liquor at a bar inside the walls. Conditions such as these gave rise early to unfavorable prison circumstances for women.

The rapid expansion of prison construction from 1825 to 1835, as the United States increasingly turned to long-term incarceration for criminals, accounted for the continuing problems that developed for women criminals. More prisons quickly led to more prisoners, as officials appeared reluctant to allow cells to remain empty; overcrowding emerged as a characteristic of the U.S. prison, despite the appearance of many new facilities. Few states or territories were prepared for the housing shortage that emerged as inmate populations increased, leading to even more indiscriminate mixing of various categories of criminals. As prisoner numbers increased, so did the size of the female inmate population. To respond to the sexual abuses and misconduct that resulted when male and female prisoners lived in common, New York, Maryland, Connecticut, and the District of Columbia by 1835 established separate quarters for women inside their male penitentiaries. By 1873 Indiana had constructed the first totally separate facility for women prisoners. The impetus in the late nineteenth century toward reformatory penology, distinct from penitentiary incarceration, bypassed female inmates, whose slight numbers deterred tightfisted legislatures from releasing construction funds for new institutions for women. In general, states built women's prisons only gradually, usually after a scandal. Into the mid–twentieth century, female inmates continued to be incarcerated in facilities built for and managed by men.

Numbers of women prisoners steadily multiplied throughout the nineteenth century, but they remained a minority population within individual prisons and jails. This immediately placed the women at a disadvantage when they entered a facility, where male guards processed them as new inmates. The intake procedures reinforced female vulnerability, as guards and male trustees examined and measured the naked women prisoners. Although the men tried to show some courtesy to middle-class white women, few amenities were extended to prostitutes and women of color. When faced with the arrival of women prisoners, wardens sometimes relied on makeshift arrangements, housing them in abandoned prison rooms, dilapidated cells, or portable shacks. Few facilities employed matrons for female prisoners, and when women secured jobs, they rarely had sufficient power or inclination to offset the corrupt practices that ranged from malfeasance to physical torture. Further, work programs were unevenly distributed to prisoners, so jail or penitentiary time was often served in idleness.

611

Female workshop, Sing Sing Prison, New York, 1854. LIBRARY OF CONGRESS

The demands of prison work also brought physical torment to women inmates. In 1917, in the Missouri penitentiary, the political activist Kate Richard O'Hare found that an unrelieved nine hours daily spent over a sewing machine destroyed her health. Within three months, O'Hare suffered from swollen feet, cramped muscles, and varicose veins. The intense summer heat, freezing winter cold, and inferior diet added to her ill health. Other women, especially women of color, performed heavy field labor barefoot and with rags for clothing.

Male and female prisoners alike suffered physical punishment, climate extremes, poor water, and bad food, but women of the nineteenth century faced yet another set of difficulties. These difficulties rested on social perceptions promoted by nineteenth-century criminologists such as Cesare Lombroso and R. F. Quinton, who believed that criminality stripped women of their womanhood. When a woman committed a crime, she placed herself not only in legal jeopardy, but also in peril of reaping society's moral outrage. The extreme penalties imposed for trivial infractions—such as five years at hard labor for stealing a pair of drapes, the sentence received by a former female slave in Texas in the 1860s—suggest that society cared more about its covenants concerning gender roles than about the crimes themselves. Since female criminals no longer enjoyed the protection of their womanly identities, and since prisons proved to be centers of corruption, women prisoners became targets for a range of violent practices. Poor women and women of color confronted the most extreme prison punishments. With few advocates to intervene on their behalf, these women faced longer sentences, served more time, and endured greater physical and sexual torment while incarcerated.

Lacking secure housing inside jail or prison, women were easy targets. Male prisoners often had sexual access to the women; guards and wardens always had access. Rape was common, although women prisoners sometimes participated willingly in liaisons with officials to curry favor and with prisoners to defy regulations.

Women who became pregnant while in prison faced punishment and separation from the baby. A male prisoner might have been disciplined if identified as the father, but parenting by guards was usually ignored. In Texas in the 1870s, a pregnant woman prisoner's head was shaved and she was placed in the hole (a totally dark underground cell) on limited rations. In 1914 a pregnant twenty-three-year-old African American, in the New Mexico penitentiary since the age of sixteen, was placed on bread and water and sequestered for weeks in a dark cell. Infants born under these circumstances typically were put up for adoption, although many did not survive the first days of penitentiary life.

Any rule infraction or rejection of sexual advances earned women a myriad of punishments. In Kansas women's arms were twisted above their heads and chained to a cell wall as late as 1914. In Texas, African American women inmates reported receiving whippings as late as the 1920s.

Women also did violence to themselves to escape the harsh conditions of prison. Some women may have tried to become pregnant, hoping their medical condition would lead to early release. In Nebraska in 1888, a woman prisoner slit her throat rather than serve her twenty-five-year sentence. In New Mexico, a woman prisoner used a rag to cut off the circulation in her leg until it swelled and turned blue; rather than winning release, however, she was placed on the discipline roster.

For women, prison violence proves constant, but society largely overlooks conditions inside the walls. Women continue to be separated from their children and denied access to medical and educational support. Pregnant inmates often lack appropriate prenatal care and a well-balanced diet. Among the many changes needed for women inmates, protection from sexual assault remains a primary concern of prison advocacy groups. Limited budgets, poor staffing, and inadequate housing serve as barriers to effective and widespread change in women's prisons. Despite the efforts of those committed to reform, American prisons remain institutions where administrators and legislators tolerate multifaceted and ongoing violence against women inmates.

BIBLIOGRAPHY

Butler, Anne M. *Gendered Justice in the American West: Women Prisoners in Men's Penitentiaries.* Urbana: University of Illinois Press, 1997.

Freedman, Estelle B. *Their Sisters' Keepers: Women's Prison Reform in America, 1830–1930.* Ann Arbor: University of Michigan Press, 1981.

Lombroso, Cesare, and William Ferrero. *The Female Offender.* New York: D. Appleton, 1900.

McKelvey, Blake. *American Prisons: A Study in American Social History Prior to 1915.* Reprint. Montclair, N.J.: Patterson Smith, 1968.

Rafter, Nicole. *Partial Justice: Women in State Prisons, 1800–1935.* Boston: Northeastern University Press, 1985.

ANNE M. BUTLER

See also **Rape; Women; Women Outlaws.**

PRIVATEERS

Privateers were privately owned armed vessels commissioned by a government to plunder enemy ships or to wage war at sea. In theory, after privateers captured enemy ships and cargoes, a court oversaw distribution of the proceeds from their sale. Successful privateering voyages returned profits to sailors and investors. Privateers also provided military capability for coastal nations without formidable navies, such as the United States during the War of 1812.

In raiding commerce for private profit and national goals, privateersmen relied on violence or threats of violence. They often attacked noncombatants, and they were known to murder and torture for sport. Captain Thomas Cavendish, an Elizabethan contemporary of Sir Francis Drake, plundered a Manila galleon off Mexico in 1587 and executed one of its passengers, a Spanish friar, simply because he was Catholic. Cavendish's crew also reportedly tormented prisoners with thumbscrews.

Privateering waned during the seventeenth century. But in 1708 a new prize act signed by Queen Anne not only guaranteed English privateers all of the value of their prizes but bounties as well. During and after the American Revolution, the United States maintained similar policies. Thus, from 1708 until 1815 privateering was common throughout the Atlantic. Baltimore, New York, Newport, Salem, and other ports sponsored thousands of privateering voyages. Respectable and affluent men financed privateers, and sailors in search of money and reputation manned them.

Gratuitous violence, although never the norm, persisted. After Rhode Island privateersmen aboard the schooner *Revenge* captured a Spanish ship's captain off St. Augustine in 1742, they "Gave him 200 lashes," rubbed salt in his wounds, and, according to the log keeper, "made the Doctor Come with Instruments Seemingly to Castrate him."

The heyday of American privateering came during the War of 1812. American privateers audaciously attacked British shipping and captured more than 1,345 prizes. Their feats, aided by radical advances in American naval architecture, allowed the new United States to gain great respect in a war with the strongest naval power in the world.

During that war, notions of gallantry and patriotism inspired more bloodshed than did sadism or the lure of wealth. Most cargo vessels, outgunned and outmanned by privateers, surrendered peacefully to avoid bloodshed. American privateers, however, occasionally sought battle with British warships (which carried no valuables), primarily for honor. Cannon fire at close quarters, boarding parties, and desperate hand-to-hand combat created dreadful carnage, as when the American privateer *Decatur* fought the British schooner *Dominica* in 1813. Twenty-three were killed and fifty-seven wounded. All were young, many still boys. "To see this youthful crew . . . in their mangled condition was enough to freeze the blood with horror," wrote an observer in Charleston. Yet, expressing the patriotic values of his era, the same onlooker later watched "the departure of the brave [privateer] in pursuit of fresh laurels, and in sincerity wished him a successful cruise."

Most European and American nations abolished privateering in 1856, with the Declaration of Paris. Only Spain, Mexico, and the United States refused to sign, although all finally agreed to abolish privateering by 1908. Privateering was outlawed not because of its violent nature, which seems not to have concerned diplomats discussing war, but chiefly to protect neutral goods and neutral ships.

BIBLIOGRAPHY

Coggleshall, George. *History of the American Privateers and Letters of Marque, During Our War with England in the Years 1812, '13, and '14.* New York: privately printed, 1856.

Hickey, Donald. *The War of 1812: A Forgotten Conflict.* Urbana: University of Illinois Press, 1989.

Jameson, J. Franklin, ed. *Privateering and Piracy in the Colonial Period: Illustrative Documents.* New York: Macmillan, 1923. Reprint. New York: A. M. Kelley, 1970.

Lane, Kris E. *Pillaging the Empire: Piracy in the Americas, 1500–1750.* Armonk, N.Y.: M. E. Sharpe, 1998.

Stark, Francis R. *The Abolition of Privateering and the Declaration of Paris.* New York: Columbia University, 1897.

Swanson, Carl E. *Predators and Prizes: American Privateering and Imperial Warfare, 1739–1848.* Columbia: University of South Carolina Press, 1991.

W. Jeffrey Bolster

See also **Filibustering Expeditions; Hijacking; Piracy.**

PRIVATE SECURITY

*This entry is divided into two parts: **Gated Communities** and **Private Police** (such as the Pinkertons).*

GATED COMMUNITIES

In 1996 an estimated nine million American domiciles had active security mechanisms, installed to prevent unwanted or criminal intrusion. Efforts to ensure personal and economic security now extend from the front door of apartments and houses to the perimeter of communities and neighborhoods. Americans are responding to the threat of external violence—both real and perceived—by forting up, moving back to the moats, walls, and drawbridges of another time. Such efforts have profound implications for the country as a collective democracy, raising the specter of a separate threat to American society: invalidation of the social contract.

Gated communities are residential areas with restricted access, effecting the privatization of what would otherwise be public space. The gating of residential developments has a profound impact both on the privatized neighborhood and surrounding communities. The locking in of position and equity makes sense, perhaps, for those behind the gate, but may negatively impact the quality of life of those outside it. It is common sense that excluding crime from one area will merely displace it to another. Gating may also affect traffic patterns, reducing volume in the gated neighborhood while diverting cars to public streets. In addition, the uses that neighborhood streets traditionally afford citizens, from parking to afternoon walks to Sunday drives, are denied, with respect to gated communities, to all but those who own property behind the gates.

California leads the nation in gated developments, but they are found across the country and are common in Florida, Arizona, Texas, and New York. In 1994 the planner and consultant Oscar Newman estimated that some thirty thousand gated communities existed nationwide, and indications are that this number is on the rise.

Evolution of Secure Communities

The earliest gated communities were ancient fortified cities. The first walled cities in the New World were Spanish fort towns built on islands in the Caribbean. In the United States, residential areas featuring gates and private streets were first constructed in St. Louis at the turn of the twentieth century.

Gated compounds were built for the East Coast and Hollywood aristocracy in the early decades of the twentieth century. Such communities were rather rare in the United States, however, until the 1960s and 1970s, with the advent of retirement developments. Communities like Leisure World, in Arizona, were self-contained cities surrounded by walls, accommodating older middle-class Americans. In the 1980s upscale real estate speculation and the trend toward conspicuous consumption saw the proliferation of gated communities built around golf courses and designed for exclusivity, prestige, and leisure. The decade also marked the emergence of gated communities built primarily out of fear, as the public became increasingly preoccupied with violent crime. Gates began to be found in a range of developments from suburban single-family tracts to high-density apartment complexes. Since the late 1980s, gates have become ubiquitous in many areas of the country; gated developments now routinely encompass entire villages, and even incorporated cities might feature guarded entrances.

Insulation of Homes and Neighborhoods

In the late 1990s, almost 65 percent of Americans lived in suburbs. Along with the trend toward gating in new residential developments, existing neighborhoods are installing barricades and gates with increasing frequency to seal themselves off. Since the 1950s, there has been a continual move away from the traditional city grid pattern to suburban cul-de-sacs and nonconnecting streets (Southworth and Ben-Joseph 1993). Streets laid out in the traditional grid pattern are frequently adapted by means of street barricades and rerouting to restrict access and limit the ability of outsiders to penetrate. Such restructuring accomplishes results similar to those produced by gated communities, deterring both casual visitors and criminals. Further, such adaptations achieve a physical design that insulates neighborhoods, since the people one sees are usually persons who live within one's own subdivision.

Security mechanisms for suburban fortified developments range from elaborate manned guardhouses to roll-back iron gates to simple electronic arms. Guardhouses are usually built with one lane for visitors and a second lane for residents, who may gain access with an electronic card or remote control device, or by punching in a keypad code. Some gates with round-the-clock security require that residents' cars have identification stickers. Unmanned entrances might have intercom systems with video monitors.

Older, originally ungated communities seeking privacy are installing gates on their own initiative and at their own expense; one community in southern California, Hidden Valley, went so far as to spend $50,000 on an electronic antiterrorist bollard of the type used to protect embassies and the vice president's mansion. The device has impaled several cars that tried to enter without authorization. Gated residential developments are now available to the middle class in typical suburban tract homes, as well. New executive residences are on the rise. These exuburbs (i.e., the area beyond the suburbs that is not truly rural and is usually composed of hobby farms with large lots) usually offer as their major amenities a gated entry, perimeter fence, and a pool and golf course or tennis courts. Some have electronic gates, and others have guardhouses at the main entrance. The cost to employ guards, however, can be prohibitive, in which case the gatehouse serves strictly as a psychological deterrent to outsiders.

Individual home security systems are also common. The more sophisticated include video monitors that allow residents to view motorists requesting admittance at the main gate or even to observe the comings and goings of their neighbors by means of cameras placed throughout the development. Homes may now be built with safe rooms featuring steel walls and doors, or underground bunkers equipped with special phone systems to alert police or private security. Home security has become especially popular among the high-tech communities of Silicon Valley and the exclusive neighborhoods of Long Island to thwart a wave of home burglaries that occurred in the 1990s.

Inner City: Fearspace

The fastest-growing type of gated community is the security zone, characterized by the closed streets and gated complexes of the low income, working class, and middle class perches. Poor inner-city neighborhoods and public housing projects are using security guards, gates, and fences to keep out drug dealing, prostitution, and drive-by shootings. Other neighborhoods, frightened by spillover crime from nearby areas, are obtaining city permission to take their streets out of public use, limiting access to residents. In the inner suburbs, in areas both near to and far from high-crime areas, new subdivision tracts and townhouse developments are built within walls, and existing communities tax themselves to install security gates. Whether violence from crime is acute or infrequent, the threat actual or only perceived, the fear is very real.

At public housing projects throughout the country, housing authorities are installing fences and using guardhouses to restrict access to residents and their guests. Inner-city communities are now doing the same, blocking streets to create mazes that deter drive-by crime and quick getaways, and gating apartment complexes and even entire neighborhoods. These gates and walls are more often paid for by the city government or local housing authority than by the residents. In this case, walls differ from those discussed previously in that they were essentially forced on the people living inside them as an exigency, rather than chosen by them as an amenity.

The installing of gates, security cameras, and guards at low-income housing projects has angered some residents to the point that on one occasion in Washington, D.C., firefighters arriving to put out protest fires were stoned by a crowd. Comparisons were made to jails and zoos, with residents telling reporters, "It's disrespectful. We aren't animals. We don't need to be caged" (quoted in Escobar and Gaines-Carter 1992). The new security measures did dramatically reduce drug dealing and vandalism, however, and the majority of tenants came to support the measures within a few months.

While it makes surface sense that the poor should have access to the same security amenities as the rich, some question the wisdom of fencing off public housing projects and poor neighborhoods. As stated by Professor Mark Baldassare of the University of California, Irvine, gated communities discourage residents from interacting with the outside world. "The wealthy want that, but the poor don't. The poor need to link up with the community outside their walls because they need the jobs, the contacts, the resources. . . . Putting a housing project in a fortress-like setting further stigmatizes the residents" (quoted in O'Donnell 1992).

A Threat to the Social Contract

In the United States, gating is most common in areas with high levels of demographic change, especially large amounts of foreign immigration; areas with high median income levels; regions with extreme residential segregation patterns or without a clearly dominant white majority; and areas with high crime rates and high levels of fear of personal violence. Developers of gated communities do not, however, prominently advertise the security or safety of such properties, because they do not want to assume liability for such claims. Even the most high-tech security systems cannot guarantee a crime- or violence-free environment. According to a report by David Guterson, in 1993 gated communities in southern California had to deal with a serial rapist, robberies, domestic murder, drugs in the schools, and a toxic cloud of chlorine gas released from a nearby chemical plant (Guterson 1993, p. 62). Data collected for a study of gated communities in Fort Lauderdale, Florida, in 1988 and 1989 show that while barriers and gates initially retard crime, crime levels return to area levels within a year or two.

The gating of residential developments has a profound impact on property values, both in the privatized neighborhood and in surrounding communities. Despite a common perception, however, gating does not always necessarily result in raised property values for the gated community. Opponents of gated communities claim that gated areas decrease property values in adjacent neighborhoods. Street barriers have similar impacts, and it is not feasible to restrict auto access to all streets. In some cities, barrier location was one of the most divisive political issues in the 1990s.

Disposable income and the desire for physical security drive the proliferation of private gated communities. But the violence outside the gates is not reduced or thwarted when residences secede from the larger community. Gates do not ensure a violence-free environment, and typically only effect a migration of crime from the restricted-access community to other areas of the city or suburb. Americans can run but we cannot hide from the shared dimensions of citizenship. It is difficult to imagine a social contract among citizens who seek to reduce or eliminate opportunities for ordinary social contact. Our mutual contract must be to reduce violence in American society, not to ghettoize it or immure ourselves from it. Gates may serve to move and remove violence but not to address its causes or heal the communities most affected by it.

BIBLIOGRAPHY

Blakely, Edward J., and Mary Gail Snyder. *Fortress America: Gated Communities in the United States.* Washington, D.C.: Brookings Institution, 1997.

Escobar, Gabriel, and Patrice Gaines-Carter. "A Housing Complex Divided: Anti-Crime Fencing Angers Some Potomac Gardens Residents." *Washington Post,* 4 June 1992, A-1.

Guterson, David. "Home Safe Home." *Utne Reader* 21 (March-April 1993): 44–52.

Kershner, Richard. "Food-Drive Planner Hopes Numbers Add Up." *Los Angeles Times,* 31 October 1991.

O'Donnell, Santiago. "More Than a Fence: Eight-Foot Barrier Helped Cut Crime, Instill Hope at Potomac Gardens." *Washington Post,* 10 December 1992.

Pertman, Adam. "Closed Communities Grow." *Boston Globe,* 14 March 1994.

Southworth, Michael, and Eran Ben-Joseph. "Regulated Streets: The Evolution of Standards for Suburban Residential Streets." Working Paper 593. Institute of Urban and Regional Development, University of California, Berkeley, 1993.

EDWARD J. BLAKELY

See also **Weapons: Conventional** *and* **Handguns.**

PRIVATE POLICE

The early history of private police in the United States is closely tied to the Pinkerton National Detective Agency, commonly known simply as the Pinkertons. The agency's founder, Allan Pinkerton, was a Scotsman who left his native land in 1842. Ironically, his arrival in the United States in that year may have been at least partially the result of his outspoken views on freedom of speech and representative government. One account of his life claims that he was heavily involved in the abortive Chartist movement in the United Kingdom, which sought to achieve greater representation for the "common man" by presenting Parliament with a massive, popularly subscribed petition. When that movement failed and a warrant was issued for his arrest, Pinkerton emigrated to America, settling north of Chicago, Illinois.

A legend, generated in large part by Pinkerton himself, developed around the origins and later exploits of the Pinkerton security company. One story related how Allan Pinkerton, who had started a barrel-making business after his move to the United States, joined local law enforcement after foiling a group of counterfeiters; he was subsequently invited by the Chicago Municipal Police to become their first detective. Little of this story has been confirmed by any source other than the Pinkerton company. It is clear that in 1850 Pinkerton founded his own agency and within a few short years secured the contracts with U.S. railroads that would make the Pinkertons famous.

In the middle of the nineteenth century, rail travel became increasingly important to both commerce and the population at large. Railways were the first large national corporations in the United States, stretching across several states and in some cases entire regions. Security proved a weak point for the companies. Although laws against robbery and violence existed in all jurisdictions through which trains passed, there was no agency with interstate police abilities. Police forces existed at the local level and were authorized to act only within their jurisdictions. Thus, a crime that occurred on a moving or temporarily stopped train could slip through the cracks of the system. Moreover, trains were vulnerable to ambush, since they were not guarded across their entire routes. An ambush could take place in a remote area with the local sheriff a hundred miles away. The Pinkerton National Detective Agency was among the first to step in and assume the role of a quasi-national law-enforcement agency. Although initially employing only five detectives, contacts made by Allan Pinkerton in the years leading up to the Civil War proved significant. Among those with whom he associated were the chief engineer of the Illinois Central railroad, West Point graduate and future commander of the Army of the Potomac George McClellan, and a lawyer named Abraham Lincoln.

Pinkerton came to national prominence during Lincoln's inaugural procession to Washington, D.C., following the 1860 election. At the time, secessionist sentiment ran high in Baltimore, Maryland. Pinkerton and his agents heard of a plot to assassinate Lincoln as he moved by rail through the city. Intercepting Lincoln, Pinkerton warned him of the danger and persuaded him to change his itinerary so as to travel secretly at night. When the incident was made public, there were claims that the threat was grossly exaggerated and that the plot was a hoax. Lincoln's political opponents used the event to ridicule the new president, and in the process sullied the Pinkerton reputation. This did not, as might be expected, slow the growth of the Pinkerton agency.

During the Civil War the Pinkertons were employed by the Union Army in an information-gathering role. Since there was no established agency within the government dedicated to spying, there was no precedent for the Pinkertons. Their success was somewhat mixed. Although the agency's counterespionage record was fairly respectable, the Pinkertons are held partially responsible for at least one Union military debacle. This came in the fall of 1862, while advising General George McClellan in his role as commander of the Union Army of the Potomac. Pinkerton's estimate of the size of Confederate general Robert E. Lee's Army of Northern Virginia was too high by as much as 200 percent. Subsequently, the already cautious McClellan failed to press home his own attacks before, during, or immediately after the Battle of Antietam (Sharpsburg, Maryland) in September of that year.

Wartime spying, although profitable, was not the basis for the Pinkertons' later success. After the war Pinkerton returned to his base in Chicago. There, contacts that he had made in the capital during the course of the war proved lucrative. Although initially based in Chicago, the Pinkertons' network had spread with the railways across the nation by the late 1800s. Two of the most famous criminals pursued by the Pinkertons were George

Parker (born Robert Leroy Parker) and Harry Longabaugh, better known today as Butch Cassidy and the Sundance Kid.

Among other innovations, the Pinkerton agency created a national criminal database for use by its agents. The company claims that by the 1870s it had amassed the single most extensive collection of criminal portrait photos, or mug shots, in the world. Not limited to local jurisdictions, the Pinkertons became the premier private security and detective corporation in the country. Employed almost exclusively by corporations, the agency's transition to the role of strikebreaker was perhaps inevitable.

During the recurrent periods of boom and bust experienced by the U.S. economy in the late nineteenth century, the debate over the role and rights of the industrial worker attained higher and higher levels of attention. Simultaneously, the increasing momentum of liberal and progressive ideals found expression among the workers of the United States in the advances of organized labor. Whichever side was in the right, big business or labor, it was the owners of the corporations who could afford to hire the Pinkertons to help them suppress labor unrest and protect their facilities. This brought the Pinkertons into conflict with labor, in often violent confrontations.

The most famous of these occurred at the Carnegie Steelworks in Homestead, Pennsylvania, in the summer of 1892. Although the Pinkerton company had previously been involved in between fifty and seventy labor disputes, the Homestead Strike was its most intense. When negotiations between labor and the Carnegie company broke down in late June 1892, the company hired the Pinkertons to secure its factory facilities against possible occupation and destruction in the event of a strike. Pinkerton supplied and armed three hundred men who, after talks between labor and management broke down on 1 July, boarded barges in Pittsburgh for the trip up the Monongahela River. (Land routes to the factory were controlled at the time by prolabor elements.) Accounts of what happened upon their arrival at the Homestead docks differ. There were between three thousand and ten thousand workers waiting for the three hundred Pinkerton agents when their barge drew close. It is disputed which side opened fire first, but in the ensuing exchange of gunfire at least eight men were killed. Most accounts place the casualties at three Pinkertons and five strikers dead, with perhaps three times that number wounded, but sources vary on this point as well. In the end

the Pinkertons' barge was captured, and without any means of escape the agents were forced to surrender. The factory itself was occupied some days later by troops of the Pennsylvania National Guard. Following this incident, the Pinkerton company changed its policy with respect to labor disputes. The Pinkertons would defend facilities against offensive actions by a striking labor group, but they would not take aggressive action to break up a strike.

Private companies fulfilled the obvious security needs created when miners discovered gold in California in 1848. Whereas the Pinkerton National Detective Agency sought criminals operating against the railroads and their interests, guarding specified cargo was not initially among their services. The gold rush changed that. During transshipment between the mines and the cities and further eastward from the West Coast, gold was particularly vulnerable to robbery. In the Far West the Adams company, and in the east the American Express company, stepped in to provide security details and escorts for valuable shipments. American Express, under president Henry Wells and company secretary William Fargo, eventually formed a corporation operating exclusively in the West, Wells, Fargo, to provide secure transportation for merchandise. It was from this tradition that present-day security companies such as Brink's arose, offering specialized protection to high-value items in transit.

Private Prisons

Despite the adverse attention that some privately run prisons attracted in the late 1990s, the phenomenon of a private prison industry is not new. Confinement facilities at the federal, state, and local level were run as private businesses or on contract long before the prison "boom" of the 1980s and 1990s. Among the first major prisons run in whole or in part by private enterprise were New York State's Ossining and Auburn facilities, which were originally run under contract. Since 1980 security companies such as the Wackenhut Corporation, based in Coral Gables, Florida; Pricor, based in Texas and Louisiana; and the Corrections Corporation of America have greatly expanded their operations to fill the burgeoning gap created by tougher sentencing laws without commensurate public confinement facility construction or funding.

In 1980 U.S. local, state, and federal institutions contained 315,974 prisoners. By 1990 that number more than doubled to 738,894. In 1997 the total U.S. prisoner population stood at 1,197,590. Overall the average rate of expansion in the 1990s was around 7 percent per year. Leading the way in that expansion were West Virginia, Wisconsin, and Texas. These states increased their prisoner populations between 75 percent (Texas) to 89.5 percent (West Virginia) between the years 1992 and 1997. Prison space supplied by government facilities could not keep up with the explosion in the prisoner populations at any level. Accordingly, privately run for-profit facilities now account for more than 117,000 beds in the U.S. criminal justice system. Regardless of the debate over whether or not privatization of the prison system is ethically or morally defensible, it appears that economics will rule the day. Almost all studies of the ability of the private prison industry to operate more economically and efficiently suggest that they do. Though the estimates range between 7 and 45 percent, depending upon the region, the type of facility, and the existence or lack of local support, it appears that private prisons are generally as safe and secure as their publicly funded counterparts and provide the same levels of support or better.

BIBLIOGRAPHY

Bolton, Jill K. *Confronting Corrections: The Option of Privatization.* Albany, N.Y.: Albany Law School, 1995.

Bowman, Gary, Simon Hakim, and Paul Sedenstat, eds. *Privatizing the United States Justice System: Police, Adjudication, and Corrections Services from the Private Sector.* Jefferson, N.C.: McFarland, 1992.

Horan, James D. *The Pinkertons: The Detective Dynasty That Made History.* New York: Crown, 1968.

Irwin, John. *It's About Time: America's Imprisonment Binge.* Belmont, Calif.: Wadsworth, 1994.

Lipson, Milton. *On Guard: The Business of Private Security.* New York: Quadrangle, 1975.

Logan, Charles H. *Private Prisons: Cons and Pros.* New York: Oxford University Press, 1990.

Martin, John Bartlow. *Break Down the Walls: America's Prisons, Present, Past, and Future.* New York: Ballantine, 1954.

Murphy, John W., and Jack E. Dison, eds. *Are Prisons Any Better? Twenty Years of Correctional Reform.* Newbury Park, Calif.: Sage, 1990.

ROBERT L. BATEMAN III

See also **Federal Bureau of Investigation; Kidnapping; Militias, Authorized; Police; Prisons; Self-Defense and Security; Stalking.**

PRIZEFIGHTING. *See* Boxing.

PROHIBITION AND TEMPERANCE

While the gangster with a tommy gun has become an enduring symbol of the Prohibition era, few scholars have paid much attention to the violence associated with the temperance movement in the United States, from its emergence in the early nineteenth century to the adoption of national prohibition in 1920. Temperance advocates and prohibitionists were social reform agitators who sought, either through moral suasion or legal coercion, to curtail the consumption of alcohol. Their agitation sought to change a deeply entrenched social practice and engendered much opposition. Their activities spawned violence on both sides: violence inflicted upon "drys" by their opponents, and violence by some prohibitionists to achieve their ends. The most dramatic and drastic forms of violence—killing, attempted killing, and crowd violence (the forms most likely to be recorded in the historical record)—help to reveal some of the relationships between violence and social reform in the American past.

Violence associated with reform falls into two main categories: violence used by opponents to block reform, and violence used by reformers to achieve their ends—in their view, a righteous violence. Both forms are associated with the temperance and prohibition movements, but in different ways. For a brief period around the turn of the twentieth century, some drys resorted to violence in agitating for prohibition. On the other hand, throughout the nineteenth and early twentieth centuries, resistance to temperance and prohibition was often expressed in violence.

Violence Against Prohibitionists

Opposition to temperance and prohibition was widespread, ranging from voting against anti-liquor measures to violating prohibition laws. Because the prohibitionists sought to change the deep-seated and widely practiced social activity of drinking alcohol, it is no surprise that some of their opponents would greet their efforts with violence. Most violence was probably minor (hitting agitators who picketed a saloon or pelting temperance speakers with garbage) and is lost to the historical record; but its extent can be hinted at by looking at serious violence directed at prohibitionists: killings, attempted killings, and mob actions.

The drys themselves recorded instances of deadly violence against temperance agitators. At its peak during the first three decades of the twentieth century, the temperance movement sought to encourage the faithful and to preserve the records of its achievements and struggles by publishing reference books; two such books, *The Pocket Cyclopedia of Temperance* (1916) and *Standard Encyclopedia of the Alcohol Problem* (1925–1930), included information on violence against prohibitionists in articles on so-called temperance martyrs.

Combining the information in the *Standard Encyclopedia* and *The Pocket Cyclopedia* produces fairly accurate figures of the serious violence directed against prohibitionists. Between 1874 and 1908 six drys were killed over advocacy of their cause. At least another nineteen drys were mobbed, beaten, shot at, or had their homes (or businesses) dynamited for their support of temperance. These numbers exclude prohibitionists who suffered violence as a result of official or unofficial law enforcement or (from the sources available) who suffered violence in uncertain circumstances. Including such figures would roughly double the number of serious, life-threatening assaults and triple the number of the killings. Although the violence occurred in all areas of the nation, the South and West were disproportionately represented, reflecting those regions' reputations for being more violent than other parts of the United States. The deadly violence against prohibition occurred from the decade after the Civil War through the second decade of the twentieth century. The earlier period of temperance agitation was free of such violence, probably because guns were far less prevalent in the prewar period.

The violence was directed mostly against prohibitionists of some social standing, reflecting the basic constituency of the temperance movements. Editors and ministers predominated as victims of individual or mob assaults, including movement luminaries such as Albert Banks, clergyman, dry editor, and propagandist who was shot and wounded in 1881 in Vancouver, Washington, and Samuel W. ("Sam") Small, journalist, dry, and evangelist, who was mobbed and beaten in Atlanta, Georgia, in 1891 and shot in the leg in Hazelton, Indiana, in 1892. Among the prohibitionists killed were a doctor, a judge, a minister, four editors of reform or other newspapers (including the minister), and a former U.S. senator, Edward Carmack of Tennessee.

By the first decade of the twentieth century, prohibition had become a bitter and dividing issue among Tennessee Democrats. In 1905, then Senator Edward Carmack, who had entered politics through his career as newspaper editor, be-

came a champion of temperance legislation. When he lost the primary battle for renomination as senator, he remained active in politics, focusing on the evils of liquor in political life. In 1908, Carmack ran (and lost) in the Democratic primary for governor and sought to have the state party platform adopt a prohibition plank. Carmack used his editorship of the *Tennessean* to attack antiprohibition Democrats, including Duncan Cooper. In response to his strong prohibition agitation and personal attacks, on 9 November 1908, Cooper and his son engaged in a gun battle with Carmack on the streets of Nashville and killed him. Although the killers were convicted of murder, Governor Malcolm Patterson, who had defeated Carmack in the Democratic primary of 1908 and who was a steadfast opponent of prohibition, pardoned them.

There are certain patterns to the violence. First, as the Carmack example shows, violence was most likely to occur when prohibition became a political controversy. Second, no woman was killed or seriously harmed by the opponents of temperance, a singular fact because women constituted so much of the temperance movement from the 1870s through the 1920s. The lack of women victims probably points to the gender conventions of American society at that time.

Violence by Prohibitionists

On the other hand, the temperance advocates did not engage in deadly violence against their enemies. No prohibitionist engaged in violence to the point of killing to bring about the goal of a dry nation. Some prohibitionists did engage in direct action against liquor sellers, destroying their places of business and their stock. Assaults on people sometimes resulted from such attacks, but the prohibitionists seldom engaged in life-threatening violence. There was no prohibitionist equivalent to the abolitionist John Brown or the antiabortionists Michael F. Griffin and John Salvi. The closest approximation to such figures among prohibitionists was Carry Nation. A look at Nation and her movement in the context of the righteous violence of other movements illuminates the relationship between some of the basic contours of violence associated with social reform movements.

When social reform advocates resort to violence, two things stand out. First, they believe that their violence is morally justified, and that violence is an acceptable means of bringing about the changes they want. Second, they act violently because they perceive that their movement is losing ground. Hence, John Brown's moral certainty of the evil of slavery and his belief that sin could only be expiated by the spilling of blood convinced him that violence was acceptable. He, in turn, convinced others to fight and kill with him in Kansas and Virginia, because the abolitionists thought that their enemies had gained the upper hand after the Compromise of 1850 (with its Fugitive Slave Law) and the Kansas-Nebraska Act (which repealed the Missouri Compromise). Similarly, the advocates of violence in the antiabortion movement seek moral grounding in theories of justifiable homicide. Significantly, the first killing by antiabortionists came after it became clear that the Supreme Court was not going to overturn *Roe v. Wade,* which made abortion legal, and the second after a pro-choice candidate, Bill Clinton, was elected president.

This embrace of violence through moral rationalization and tactical fear of failure is evident in the career of Carry Nation, who captured the national imagination in 1900 when she began single-handedly destroying saloons in Kansas. Nation was motivated, like many drys, by a personal religious belief that liquor selling was sinful. In her autobiography she recounts receiving visions from God showing her the evils of liquor. She adopted violence only after she had tried other means. Kansas, where Nation lived, was a state that had a two-decades-old policy of prohibition. In her hometown of Medicine Lodge, working with the Woman's Christian Temperance Union, she closed the town's seven bars through tried and true techniques: picketing with song and prayer and issuing moral appeals to the sellers and purchasers. But if such methods were fine in the battle against legal saloons, they struck Nation as ineffectual against the illegal bars of Kansas, where for more than a decade the prohibition law had been widely and openly flouted, often with the connivance of the state's political leaders. And at the national level the temperance movement was stalled. In the last decade of the nineteenth century, Congress passed no law that advanced the cause of prohibition. Also, between 1889 and 1907, no state adopted prohibition. The Woman's Christian Temperance Union lost its driving force with the death of Frances Willard in 1898, and the Prohibition Party, organized in 1869, splintered into two warring camps. The leading temperance organizations seemed unable to advance the cause or indeed to stop the rollback movements in states with prohibition. Hence, with conviction, and at a time when

The prohibition champion Carry Nation, holding a hatchet and a Bible, in the early twentieth century.
CORBIS/BETTMANN

the movement was faltering, Nation turned away from moral suasion and turned to violence.

Her violence struck a chord among some temperance advocates. While some debated the value or morality of violence, others joined Nation. Wielding a hatchet, Nation led her group on raids of about a dozen illegal saloons. In a short period in late 1900 and early 1901, Nation and her group and others who emulated them engaged in vigilante raids against bars in Kansas's major cities, Topeka and Wichita. Saloonkeepers and patrons attempted to resist these raids with force. The violence escalated; temperance agitators were beaten, shots were fired in anger by saloon defenders, and riots erupted in the wake of attempted temperance smashings. In response the local authorities closed down the saloons, removing the target of the drys' violence. Nation then departed the state for a national tour, ending the episode. Yet, the response of some Kansas prohibitionists to Nation's actions shows that the potential for righteous violence existed within the temperance crusade.

This response raises a new question: Why was there only one Carry Nation? Part of the answer lies in the changing circumstances of the prohibition movement. Soon after Nation's actions in Kansas, the Anti-Saloon League emerged as the dominant organization in the temperance movement. And the league's nonviolent techniques—political lobbying, official law enforcement, and garnering public support—boosted the fortunes of the crusade. Between 1902 and 1919, for example, the league's Washington office pressured the U.S. Congress to enact laws that prohibited the sale of liquor in federal buildings, banned the transport of liquor through the mails, ended liquor sales in national soldiers' homes, retained a law excluding all alcoholic beverages from army posts, created Oklahoma as a dry state, and limited and then prohibited the transportation of liquor into dry states. A similar record of success can be found in the prohibitionists' campaigns in the states in the same period. The very success of the drys in gaining what they wanted through the political process made righteous violence superfluous.

The history of the prohibition movement tells us something about how reform movements prompt or retard violence. While much more study still needs to be done on the relationship of violence to the temperance movement, some suggestive outlines have emerged. The paucity of righteous violence in the prohibition crusade underscores that violence in social movements is just one of the many tools that reformers can use to achieve their ends. When other techniques are working, violence may not be necessary. The deadly violence used against prohibitionist agitators, with its gender, temporal, and regional variations, hints at an overlooked form of resistance to temperance. In short, studying prohibition and violence tells us something of how reform movements prompted or retarded violence, raising questions about the relationship of violence to other reform movements.

BIBLIOGRAPHY

Bader, Robert. *Prohibition in Kansas: A History.* Lawrence: University Press of Kansas, 1986.

Blocker, Jack S., Jr. *American Temperance Movements: Cycles of Reform.* Boston: Twayne, 1989.

Cherrington, Ernest, ed. *Standard Encyclopedia of the Alcohol Problem.* 6 vols. Westerville, Ohio: American Issue Publishing, 1924–1930.

Dannenbaum, Jed. *Drink and Disorder: Temperance Reform in Cincinnati from the Washington Revival to the WCTU.* Urbana and Chicago: University of Illinois Press, 1984.

Hamm, Richard F. *Shaping the Eighteenth Amendment: Temperance, Reform, Legal Culture, and the Polity.* Chapel Hill: University of North Carolina Press, 1995.

Isaac, Paul E. *Prohibition and Politics: Turbulent Decades in Tennessee, 1885–1920.* Knoxville: University of Tennessee Press, 1965.

Pegram, Thomas. *Battling Demon Rum: The Struggle for a Dry America.* Chicago: Ivan R. Dee, 1998.

Wilson, Clarence T., Deets Picket, and Harry G. McCain, eds. *The Pocket Cyclopedia of Temperance.* Rev. ed. Topeka, Kans.: Temperance Society of Methodist Episcopal Church, 1916.

RICHARD F. HAMM

See also **Alcohol and Alcoholism; Bureau of Alcohol, Tobacco, and Firearms; Organized Crime.**

PROSTITUTION

Prostitution is commonly viewed as the exchange of sexual services for money, drugs, or some other form of compensation. It is frequently referred to as "the world's oldest profession." Many people consider prostitution to be immoral and a social problem because it violates a primary sociocultural value, monogamy. In the United States, since prostitution is illegal in every state but Nevada (where it is legal in certain counties), a discussion of prostitution must also include its treatment by the criminal justice system. According to estimates from the Federal Bureau of Investigation's Uniform Crime Reports, between 1975 and 1989 there were an average of 88,819 arrests for prostitution annually. Of this number, 61,564 arrests were of female prostitutes.

Estimates based on police arrest data indicate that between 1 million and 1.5 million prostitutes were working in the United States during 1995. However, the actual number may be three or four times this figure, or somewhere between 3 million and 6 million, because many prostitutes are never arrested, or are arrested for a separate crime (such as possession of a controlled substance). In addition, some prostitutes work on a part-time basis (e.g., once a week), as a supplement to a "legitimate" career; thus they are not visible to law-enforcement authorities or social-science researchers.

Historical Perspective

Studies suggest that prostitution was a much more common occupation in the 1800s and early 1900s than it is at present. A 1992 study of prostitution in New York City by Timothy J. Gilfoyle indicated that 10 to 15 percent of all young women living in New York City during the eighteenth century were temporary or long-term prostitutes. In the nineteenth century prostitution was the second most profitable business after tailoring. Gilfoyle reported that prostitution yielded about four times the annual income per employee as the brewery industry. During the mid-1800s in New York City, married men commonly viewed houses of prostitution as social gathering places, and as a result, sex with prostitutes became the norm.

During the 1930s and 1940s, the incidence of male sexual activity with prostitutes was reported to have declined. According to a national study of sexual behavior conducted by A. C. Kinsey and associates published in 1948, while 69 percent of the white male population in the United States had had some form of sexual encounter with a prostitute, many of the male respondents reported having had just one or two such experiences. Kinsey also noted that most of the men who engaged in sexual relations with prostitutes were unmarried, and either bachelors or divorcés. The most significant change was that the middle-aged fathers in the sample were much more likely than their sons to have visited a prostitute when they were in their twenties.

Prostitution and Economic Status

Prostitution occurs at all socioeconomic levels. In the lower income groups, the term *streetwalker* is typically used to identify women who dress provocatively and solicit on the streets of inner-city neighborhoods; weekly illegitimate income for these women ranges from $200 to $5,000. The prostitutes in most danger of violent assaults by both johns (clients) and pimps (men who solicit clients for prostitutes) are these street hustlers. A major factor in how much prostitutes earn each week is the number of hours they work. According to a 1998 study by C. Coston and L. E. Ross, the average workweek for a prostitute is thirty hours, with a range of two hours to seventy hours. Women of color are overly represented among the low-paid streetwalkers, while white and Asian women are more likely to choose to work for higher-paying "escort services."

The term *call girl* and *high-class prostitute* are often used to describe women who work for an escort service. These women generally work by appointment, are taken to expensive, first-class restaurants and hotels, and charge a high rate for their services. Escort and call-girl services usually employ younger, more attractive, and better-educated women than the topless bars and street pimps. Such services charge each customer $1,000 to $3,000 for a few hours of work. Some call girls are independent businesswomen, while others run or are employed by a high-priced brothel or service. For example, in the 1980s, a former debutante, Sydney Biddle Barrows, whose ancestors include original *Mayflower* settlers, operated an exclusive Manhattan brothel until the vice squad of the New York Police Department closed it down in 1984.

Laws Related to Prostitution

The criminal statutes in almost all states (the exception is Nevada) prohibit prostitution. The trend during the 1980s and 1990s was to sanction pimping (the pimps) and solicitation to a greater degree than prostitution itself.

The Model Penal Code provides the rationale for the continuing criminalization of prostitution. The reasons generally given for viewing prostitution as a crime are as follows: preventing sexually transmitted diseases, including AIDS; maintaining the authority of law enforcement to arrest organized crime figures, who typically become involved in prostitution and related activities; protecting prostitutes from becoming crime victims; protecting children and young adolescents who are forced into prostitution; and strengthening the integrity of the family.

The criminal statutes on prostitution vary greatly from state to state. For example, in the state of Arizona it is a misdemeanor to work at a brothel or house of prostitution. However, it is a felony to compel, induce, encourage, or hire an individual to live and work in a house of prostitution. In some states, patronizing a prostitute is considered a trivial offense put into the state criminal code in order to allow the police discretion in making arrests during raids on brothels or houses of prostitution. However, in other states, prostitution and engaging (hiring) a prostitute are viewed as equally serious crimes.

The goal of legislation in a number of states is to halt the spread of AIDS on the part of prostitutes who are intravenous (IV) drug users. For example, in Florida, women convicted of prostitution are required by law to receive screenings for sexually transmitted diseases, including AIDS. The

Prostitutes in the Times Square area, New York City, July 1971. CORBIS/BETTMANN

California law mandates HIV testing for those convicted of prostitution and other sex offenses; a prostitute who tests positive for HIV and who is subsequently rearrested for prostitution is charged with a felony (rather than a misdemeanor).

Efforts to Decriminalize Prostitution

While there have been efforts to liberalize the criminal codes in California, Louisiana, and Nevada, in most states the criminal justice system punishes prostitutes, driving them further into dependency upon pimps and johns. Criminalization has served to control and harass poor, primarily African American and Hispanic women who work as prostitutes.

There is a movement among feminists to draw attention to the plight of streetwalkers—those prostitutes who are the most vulnerable to exploitation, who earn a low income, and who live in high-crime urban areas. Kathleen Barry, a leading feminist in this field, defines involuntary prostitution as a circumstance in which females are forced to work as prostitutes because of financial necessity, exploitation, or the threat of violence. Barry is one of many advocates for the decriminalization of prostitution. Proponents of decriminalization contend that legalization and state regulation of prostitution would eliminate most health and security risks.

Because of the criminalization of prostitution, many women prostitutes—particularly the streetwalkers of the inner cities—have arrest records. Women who may want to quit prostitution and enter a legitimate line of work find it difficult to do so because of their criminal histories. In applying for a training program or job, these women are usually obligated to divulge their criminal record —or risk being fired if they lie on an application and the employer later learns the truth. Thus, the criminalization of prostitution compels these women, who may want to have the opportunity to make a fresh start, to continue working as prostitutes for reasons of economic necessity.

A resolution was passed by the United Nations in 1949 calling for the decriminalization of prostitution. Although fifty countries have ratified this resolution, the United States has not agreed to it. While there does not appear to be a single definition of decriminalization, the term usually refers to the repeal of laws against both commercial and noncommercial sex between consenting adults.

One of the arguments in favor of decriminalizing prostitution is the huge expense of continuing to fund police sweeps and prosecution for this activity. The cost of viewing prostitution as a criminal activity in just one city—San Francisco—is estimated at more than $7.6 million per year. There are two points of view among those who are in favor of

PROSTITUTION

removing the criminal statutes that surround prostitution. One view is that prostitution should be legalized and that both prostitutes and houses of prostitution should be licensed and legally regulated. From a public health perspective, the women would be required to have monthly gynecologic exams and periodic blood tests to identify those who are HIV positive or who have other sexually transmitted diseases (STDs). A woman testing positive for HIV or other STDs would not be able to work as a prostitute. In addition, zoning ordinances would ensure that houses of prostitution are located in business districts rather than in residential areas. These procedures are similar to those followed by the counties in Nevada where prostitution was legalized. In the Nevada statutes, prostitution is expressly prohibited except in a licensed house of prostitution.

The alternative view is that women should be able to engage in prostitution with no supervision, no regulations, and no health requirements. This view ignores the public health concerns about the spread of AIDS and related diseases.

Prostitutes as Crime Victims

Streetwalkers and other prostitutes are often at risk of criminal victimization because they work in an unsupervised and unregulated profession and they engage in sexual activities with strangers who may have a criminal background. Coston and Ross's 1998 study of the extent and frequency of criminal victimization against fifty-nine streetwalkers found that thirty-seven had been robbed or raped within a twelve-month period. In addition, seven of the prostitutes had been assaulted. As a result, for self-protection, fifteen of them carried a knife, twelve carried scissors, eight underwent training in self-defense, and two carried lye in their purse. In 1993 M. H. Silbert and A. Pines conducted a study of two hundred prostitutes and found a strong association between violent pornography and sexual abuse. Nearly three-quarters of the women interviewed reported being raped one or more times, and 60 percent reported that they were sexually abused as minors. In 19 percent of the case of rape, when the victims told the assailant that they were prostitutes, the assailant became more violent. The women suffered excessive bodily injuries, including broken bones.

Prostitution and Health Risks

When compared with the general population of young women, prostitutes—particularly those who are IV drug users—are more likely to contract sexually transmitted diseases. Several studies have indicated that street prostitutes frequently visit hospitals to be treated for physical assaults, sexually transmitted diseases, pneumonia, and chemical dependency. The research that has been done is limited, usually based, again, on prostitutes who have been arrested. Nevertheless, several authorities have found a high correlation between IV drug use and HIV infection in prostitutes.

According to the Centers for Disease Control and Prevention (1993), the cities with the highest AIDS death rate among female IV drug users (many of whom were also prostitutes) were Newark and Jersey City, New Jersey, New York City, San Francisco, Miami, and Los Angeles. As a result, several states have instituted legislation specifically aimed at reducing the number of prostitutes who are transmitting the AIDS virus.

James A. Inciardi conducted the first study of adolescent delinquents, prostitutes, and drug users on the streets and in crack houses in Miami. Inciardi, Ruth Horowitz, and Anne E. Pottieger, in a 1993 study of 611 delinquents, found that because of prostitution, IV drug use, sex-for-crack exchanges, and failure to use condoms, many of the study subjects were at high risk of HIV infection and AIDS. The risk was highest for the females. With regard to the 511 male delinquents, 20, or 4.9 percent, reported one or more acts of prostitution. In sharp contrast to the males, 87 of the 100 females interviewed had been involved in prostitution. During the twelve-month period prior to the interviews, the mean number of acts of prostitution for each of the 87 female adolescent prostitutes was 431. Forty-two percent of the female adolescent prostitutes used crack or cocaine and marijuana daily, pills a few times a week, and heroin on occasion. Twenty-seven of the adolescent females interviewed estimated that they had engaged in a total of over nineteen thousand acts of prostitution, including the trading of sex for crack, during the twelve-month period prior to the interviews.

Professor Inciardi's ethnographic study in Miami demonstrated the high potential risk of HIV infection by these young women living in crack houses. In the words of one fourteen-year-old house-girl who was asked about safe-sex practices in 1990: "Condoms, in here? I never see no rubbers, no condoms. If a man givin' you crack for brains [oral sex] an' you say rubber, he laugh, or he beat you, you know, slap you around a little, or he call the rat (crack-house proprietor) who then slap you around too" (1993, p. 188).

625

The legal and public health policies in parts of Nevada are much more likely to curtail the spread of AIDS than the policies and practices of Miami. In the Nevada counties that have legalized prostitution, there is a strong emphasis on preventing sexually transmitted diseases. All customers must wear condoms, and the prostitutes receive health benefits such as monthly gynecologic exams and periodic blood tests for HIV infection and other sexually transmitted diseases. Any woman in Nevada who continues to work as a prostitute after she receives notification that she is HIV positive is arrested and charged with a felony.

BIBLIOGRAPHY

Barry, Kathleen. *Female Sexual Slavery.* Englewood Cliffs, N.J.: Prentice-Hall, 1979.

Centers for Disease Control. "Human Immunodeficiency Virus Infection in the United States." *Morbidity and Mortality Weekly Report* 42 (14 December 1993).

Coston, C., and L. E. Ross. "Criminal Victimization of Prostitutes: Empirical Support for the Lifestyle/Exposure Model." *Journal of Crime and Justice* 21 (January 1998): 53–70.

Federal Bureau of Investigation. *FBI Uniform Crime Reports.* Washington, D.C.: U. S. Government Printing Office, 1990.

Gilfoyle, Timothy J. *The City of Eros: New York City, Prostitution, and the Commercialization of Sex, 1790–1920.* New York: Norton, 1992.

Giobbe, E. "Surviving Commercial Sexual Exploitation." In *Making Violence Sexy: Feminist Views on Pornography,* edited by Diana E. H. Russell. New York: Teachers College Press, 1993.

Inciardi, James A., Ruth Horowitz, and Anne E. Pottieger. *Street Kids, Street Drugs, Street Crime: An Examination of Drug Use and Serious Delinquency in Miami.* Belmont, Calif.: Wadsworth, 1993.

Kinsey, Alfred C., Wardell B. Pomeroy, and Clyde E. Martin. *Sexual Behavior in the Human Male.* Philadelphia: Saunders, 1948.

Luxemburg, Joan, and Thomas Guild. "Women, AIDS, and the Criminal Justice System." In *It's A Crime: Women and Justice,* edited by Roslyn Muraskin and Ted Alleman. Englewood Cliffs, N.J.: Regents/Prentice-Hall, 1993.

Posner, Richard A., and Katharine B. Silbaugh. *A Guide to America's Sex Laws.* Chicago: University of Chicago Press, 1996.

San Francisco Task Force on Prostitution. *Final Report.* Submitted to the Board of Supervisors of the City and County of San Francisco. San Francsico: San Francisco Task Force on Prostitution, 1996.

Shedlin, M. G. "An Ethnographic Approach to Understanding HIV High-Risk Behaviors: Prostitution and Drug Abuse." *NIDA Research Monograph* 93 (1990).

Silbert, M. H., and A. Pines. "Pornography and Sexual Abuse of Women." In *Making Violence Sexy: Feminist Views on Pornography,* edited by Diana E. H. Russell. New York: Teachers College Press, 1993.

Weiner, A. "Prostitution." *Encyclopedia of Social Work Supplement.* Washington, D.C.: National Association of Social Workers, 1997.

BEVERLY J. ROBERTS

See also **White Slavery; Women: Overview.**

PROTESTS. *See* Antiwar Protests; Civil Disobedience; Civil Disorder.

PSYCHOLOGICAL VIOLENCE

The term *psychological violence* refers to the infliction of psychological (mental and emotional) injury on a person by psychological means that do not require physically touching or injuring the victim. The injury may be inflicted in a way that is relatively simple and immediate, as with words or gestures (such as laughter) or in a way that is more complex and longer-term, as with relationships (where injury may take the form of rejection or infidelity). Psychological injury can also be caused by three other forms of violence: (1) *physical violence* (the infliction of physical injury by means of direct physical assault); (2) *sexual violence* (the infliction of psychological injury by means of coerced but not physically injurious sexual activity); and (3) *structural violence* (violence in the form of increased rates of preventable deaths and disabilities that are inflicted on the poor by social and economic structures—that is, the division of society into rich and poor).

While these different forms of violence can be differentiated from each other in this way for analytical purposes, in reality they coexist, overlap, and reinforce each other in many ways. For example, psychological injury can precipitate or exacerbate physical illness and even death (asthma, heart attacks, high blood pressure) as a psychophysiological response to emotional stress, and in that sense it functions as a form of physical violence as well. And psychological violence (insulting, slighting, disrespecting, rejecting, ridiculing, or any other means of shaming and humiliating) has long been viewed as the ultimate cause of physical violence, a view that is described in the writings of the ancient philosopher Aristotle (in *The Rhetoric,* written about 330 B.C.) and the medieval theologian Saint Thomas Aquinas (in the first part of the second part, question 47, of his thirteenth-century treatise *Summa Theologica*) and that has found continued acceptance in the twentieth-century work of psychologists including Heinz Kohut (1977) and James Gilligan (1996). Physical and sexual violence can also cause psychological injury (as in post-traumatic stress disorder, and the "soul murder" or "death of the self" discussed below). Structural violence is the deadliest form of violence, in part because it leads to increased rates of all the other forms of violence. Despite these interrelationships, the point of this essay will be to clarify the characteristics of psychological violence that differentiate it from the other types and to examine its nature in isolation from the other types.

The Death of the Self

One paradox at the heart of the concept of psychological violence is that words are the only alternative to actions and are thus essential to the *prevention* of physical violence. In this light, there are understandable and legitimate reasons not only to resist censorship but even to attempt to expand further, to the greatest degree possible, peoples' legal freedom to say and write anything they want to—for it is when people stop talking that they start fighting (Kors and Silverglate 1998). Yet words themselves can be among the main *causes* of physical violence—a psychological fact that was recognized by the U.S. legal system in the concept of "fighting words" (insults that provoke otherwise law-abiding people to violence). In addition, words alone, in some circumstances, can cause measurable and severe degrees of psychological damage and disability, and even physical illness and death, so that far from preventing violence, they can be another form of it.

One essential prerequisite for preventing all violence is to teach people to recognize that psychological violence *causes all* forms of violence, but that that does not mean that it *justifies any* form of violence. In other words, teaching children not to provoke violence by insulting or ridiculing people can help to reduce the amount of violence in the world. But helping them to acquire sources of self-esteem that are stable, internalized, and nonviolent—so that they (1) can tolerate and even learn from the criticisms and other blows to their self-esteem that they receive from other people and (2) can respond to them by means of constructive rather than destructive or violent behavior—is also a means of preventing violence.

At its most extreme, physical violence causes physical death. The most extreme degree of psychological violence causes the death of the psyche (the soul, the self, the personality). This phenomenon has been observed and described by many people, and has been given terms like "soul murder" and the "death of the self." Many of the most physically violent prison inmates, for example, report having felt as if they themselves had died before they began killing other people, meaning that their personality had died, that they felt dead inside—numb and empty, or filled with lifeless matter, like straw (Gilligan 1996). They use words to describe themselves that refer to the living dead, such as "zombie," "vampire," or "robot." They report themselves as having lost the capacity for feelings, meaning not only emotions but also physical sensations. This feeling of inner deadness and numbness is more intolerable even than pain would be, so they mutilate themselves and mutilate and kill other people, without either emotions or physical sensations, in order to see if they can have feelings, even pain, and often find that they still do not.

What causes the "death of the self"? These prison inmates' souls did not just die—their souls were murdered, often by the most extreme degrees

---

The Power of Words

The incongruity represented within the concept of psychological violence, and the distinction between it and physical violence, can be illustrated most clearly by noting two contradictory proverbs, each of which expresses a vital truth.

Members of Western culture are all familiar with the proverb "Sticks and stones may break my bones, but words will never hurt me." Indeed, parents and teachers often quote that proverb in the course of teaching children not to respond to insults or criticisms with their fists and to measure their self-worth by internal standards of their own rather than by other peoples' estimates. But many may not be as familiar with a Maori proverb that is equally true: "Broken bones heal quickly, but the wounds caused by words can last a lifetime."

Or as Avishai Margalit (1996, p. 87) put it, "The psychological scars left by humiliation heal with greater difficulty than the physical scars of someone who has suffered only physical pain."

of violent child abuse and physical neglect to which it is possible to subject a child without killing his body as well. Those forms of child abuse not only injure the body, but they can also kill the soul. But the most violent prison inmates also were subjected to the most extreme degrees of two other forms of abuse that can also destroy the self, even though they do not directly, in and of themselves, injure the body—sexual abuse and psychological abuse. One study of thirty-one serial and multiple murderers, for example (Frazier et al. 1974), found that even those who had not been subjected to the other forms of child abuse (physical injury, physical neglect, or sexual abuse) had all been subjected to overwhelming emotional abuse. They differed from their nonviolent siblings in having been singled out in their families for exposure to shame and humiliation like emotional scapegoats, the "whipping boys," so to speak, on whom the parents' needs to taunt and tease and ridicule was discharged. As the authors of this report put it, "The recurrence of a pattern of verbal shaming and humiliation by parents before . . . friends and other family members was recounted frequently and corroborated by family members."

As that example illustrates, *the essence or emotional content of psychological violence,* the factor that most powerfully kills the self of those who are exposed to it (and in turn leads many of them to kill other people's bodies and souls*), is the infliction of shame and humiliation on the victim.* This psychological truth is revealed by the etymology of the word that means both "overwhelming shame and embarrassment" and "making dead"—namely, *mortification.* Shame and humiliation are the essence of psychological violence—that is, they are the means by which psychological injury is inflicted on a person. The larger ramifications of this idea have been explored by Avishai Margalit:

> Cruelty is the ultimate evil. Preventing cruelty is the supreme moral commandment. Humiliation is the extension of cruelty from the physical to the psychological realm of suffering. Humiliation is mental cruelty. A decent society must be committed not only to the eradication of physical cruelty in its institutions but also to the elimination of mental cruelty caused by those institutions.
>
> (1996, p. 85)

What is the psychological mechanism by which shame and humiliation bring about the death of the self? Considered as an emotional state, shame means the absence of self-love; it is the opposite of

pride, which means self-love. What we call the self is a fragile and vulnerable psychological construct that cannot survive without love, any more than the body can survive without oxygen. There are only two possible sources of love for the self—from others, in the form of affection, honor, respect, esteem, or admiration; and from the self, in the form of self-respect, self-esteem, pride in one's self, or the sense of self-worth. To feel overwhelmingly shamed (rejected, insulted, ridiculed) by others—or ashamed, oneself, of one's own inadequacies, failures, or "unlovability"—is to experience a deficiency of love for the self. What psychological violence has in common with the other forms of violence is that all violence expresses contempt and lack of love, but psychological violence does so directly (in the form of insults, ridicule, taunting, disrespect, rejection, slights, accusations of inferiority, and so on), whereas the others do so indirectly, through the medium of physical assault, sexual violation, or the infliction of social and economic inferiority.

History of the Concept

Some of the deepest insights into psychological violence and its relationship to shame, other forms of violence, and the death of the self can be found in the Jewish rabbinical tradition, especially the Talmud, which instructs that "a man can die of shame sooner than of starvation"; "humiliation is worse than physical pain"; and "shaming another in public is like shedding blood."

These same relationships are revealed by the words used for violence in ancient Roman law (e.g., in the sixth-century *Digest* commissioned by the emperor Justinian). *Injury* comes from the Latin *iniuria,* which means "insult" (and "injustice" and "rape") as well as "injury." One does not need to add insult to injury; it is already there, in the word (and the act) itself. That is why violence to the body (as in violent or sexual child abuse, or the battering or rape of an adult) can kill the soul even when it does not kill or even injure the body. Conversely, to be subjected to psychological violence—to be insulted, shamed, and unloved—is to the psyche what being assaulted, injured, and raped is to the body. In fact, our word *assault* comes from the same Latin root as *insult,* and their meanings even in English overlap: *insult* means "assault" (as when surgeons refer to the wound or trauma created by an incision as the surgical "insult"). Insults are assaults (psychologically), just as physical assaults are experienced, emotionally, as insults.

The term *soul murder* has been used to refer to the most extreme forms of psychological violence at least since 1832, when the German jurist Anselm von Feuerbach wrote of the bizarre case of Caspar Hauser, a man who had been imprisoned in a dark cellar throughout his childhood, separated from all human contact except for an occasional glimpse of his jailer, until the age of seventeen, when he was found wandering in the streets of Nuremberg, appearing like "a child scarcely two or three years old, with the body of a young man." He had not been physically killed or assaulted, but as von Feuerbach noted, his childhood "existence was . . . similar to that of a person really dead; . . . he may be said to have been the subject of a partial *soul-murder*." (Werner Herzog dramatized the story of Hauser's life and psychological death in the powerful 1974 film *Every Man for Himself and God Against All*.)

The Swedish dramatist August Strindberg, in an 1887 review of a play by his Norwegian colleague Henrik Ibsen, used the term *soul murder* to refer to taking away a person's reason for living, and said such psychic murder was on the increase even as instances of actual murder were becoming rarer—a concept that he simultaneously illustrated with great power in his own play *The Father*, describing a man whose wife tormented him into a state of psychotic jealousy by her manipulation of the biological fact that the paternity of a child is always uncertain. Ibsen himself used the term *soul murder* (and illustrated the concept) repeatedly. In his play *John Gabriel Borkman* (1896), the character Ella Rentheim accuses the title character of being "guilty of a double murder—the murder of your own soul, and mine." The play speaks of soul murder as a "mysterious sin" mentioned in the Bible "for which there is no forgiveness," and as "killing the instinct for love," "killing the love-life in a human soul," and murdering "love in a human being."

One of the best-known uses of the phrase is in the autobiography of Daniel Paul Schreber, the German judge whose description of his descent into incurable madness became the subject of Sigmund Freud's theory of the psychology of paranoia. Schreber's father, a famous pediatrician who strongly influenced German parenting practices during the half century before the rise of Nazism, has subsequently been discovered to have subjected his son to child-rearing methods that,

Paul Scofield and Vanessa Redgrave in Henrik Ibsen's *John Gabriel Borkman* **(1896), performed in 1996 at the National Theatre in London, England.** CORBIS/ROBBIE JACK

though they did not involve physical injury, appear to have been tyrannical, cruel, bizarre, and utterly lacking in human empathy, treating him more as an object without feelings than as a person (Schatzman 1973). Schreber *père* is transmuted in Schreber's delusions into God (the Father), whom he describes as one who "dealt only with corpses" and who constantly attempted to "unman" him, transform him into a woman for his own sexual pleasure, and commit "soul murder" on him.

Leonard Shengold makes the important point that "soul-murder victims are afraid of feeling emotion, because emotion is the beginning of feeling more than is bearable" (1989, p. 311). But what is it that is unbearable? It is the awareness that, to the person who inflicted this form of violence on you, you do not exist—that is, that you are not a real, live, separate human being, with a mind, will, feelings, and identity of your own; that you are not recognized as existing in your own right; that you therefore cannot be loved or empathized with (since you do not exist), nor can your own feelings and wishes be taken into account; and that to your soul murderer you are only a lifeless object—a slave, automaton, or robot that exists for the satisfaction of his or her own wishes and desires. You are treated as if you were dead, and so you begin to feel dead.

Contemporary Patterns of Psychological Violence

Harassing or insulting adults on the basis of their sex or sexual orientation, race, age, social class, or any other group or personal characteristic constitutes a form of psychological violence from which, increasingly, there is legal protection (Matsuda et al. 1993). However, children are probably the most frequent victims of soul murder because they are the most vulnerable, by virtue of not having had time to develop the internalized sources of self-esteem that reduce one's vulnerability to psychological assaults from others. And psychological injury is inflicted whenever any of the other forms of child abuse are, for the emotional attitudes of hate and contempt (lack of love) that cause all forms of abuse are communicated by all the other forms just as powerfully as they are by purely psychological violence.

In a book-length study published in 1986, James Garbarino, Edna Guttmann, and Janis Wilson Seeley analyze the psychological maltreatment of children, which they refer to as "an assault on the psyche, an attack on the self" (p. 232), into five categories: *rejecting* (and humiliating); *ignoring* (mentally neglecting and abandoning); *isolating* (socially, as in the example of Caspar Hauser, above); *corrupting* (morally and legally); *and terrorizing* (as by verbal threats).

Emotional and social maltreatment, deprivation, and neglect not only deform and even kill the soul; they can have the same effect on the body as well. Rene Spitz (1945) documented an infant mortality rate of over 33 percent in a sample of ninety-one orphans "in spite of good food and meticulous medical care," which could only be attributed to the massive social and emotional deprivation suffered in an environment devoid of anything remotely resembling normal relationships with a parent or family. Similar syndromes of "nonorganic failure to thrive," growth retardation (dwarf-

ism) "simulating idiopathic hypopituitarism," and failures of emotional as well as physical development have been traced to emotional and psychosocial deprivation by many medical investigators —see, for example, the landmark study by G. F. Powell and colleagues that appeared in the *New England Journal of Medicine* in 1967. In other words, psychological violence damages the body severely enough to emphasize the artificiality of attempting to separate psychological from physical violence. Even the seventeenth-century French philosopher René Descartes, who is often misquoted and misunderstood on this point, recognized that there are two-way causal relations and interactions between the mind and the body. In that sense the body cannot actually be separated from the soul. Violence toward either one ultimately constitutes violence toward the other.

BIBLIOGRAPHY

Brassard, Marla, Robert Germain, and Stuart Hart, eds. *The Psychological Maltreatment of Children and Youth.* Elmsford, N.Y.: Pergamon, 1986.

Feuerbach, Anselm von. *Caspar Hauser: An Account of an Individual Kept in a Dungeon, Separated from All Communication with the World, from Early Childhood to About the Age of Seventeen.* Translated by H. Linberg. London: Simpkin and Marshall, 1833.

Frazier, Shervert H., et al. "A Clinical Study of Serial and Multiple Murder." In *Aggression*, edited by Shervert H. Frazier. Research Publications of the Association for Research in Nervous and Mental Disease, vol. 52. Baltimore: Williams and Wilkins, 1974.

Garbarino, James, Edna Guttmann, and Janis Wilson Seeley. *The Psychologically Battered Child.* San Francisco: Jossey-Bass, 1986.

Gilligan, James. *Violence: Our Deadly Epidemic and Its Causes.* New York: Grosset/Putnam, 1996.

Kohut, Heinz. *The Restoration of the Self.* New York: International Universities Press, 1977.

Kors, Alan Charles, and Harvey A. Silverglate. *The Shadow University: The Betrayal of Liberty on America's Campuses.* New York: Free Press, 1998.

Margalit, Avishai. *The Decent Society*, translated by Naomi Goldblum. Cambridge, Mass.: Harvard University Press, 1996.

Matsuda, Mari, Richard Delgado, and Charles R. Lawrence III. *Words That Wound.* Boulder, Colo.: Westview, 1993.

Powell, G. F., J. A. Brasel, and Robert M. Blizzard. "Emotional Deprivation and Growth Retardation Simulating Idiopathic Hypopituitarism." *New England Journal of Medicine* 276, no. 23 (1967).

Schatzman, Morton. *Soul Murder: Persecution in the Family.* New York: Random House, 1973.

Shengold, Leonard. *Soul Murder: The Effects of Childhood Abuse and Deprivation.* New Haven, Conn.: Yale University Press, 1989.

Spitz, Rene. "Hospitalism: An Inquiry into the Genesis of Psychiatric Conditions in Early Childhood." *Psychoanalytic Study of Child* 1 (1945).

Strindberg, August. "Soul Murder." *Drama Review* 13 (1968). Reprint of Strindberg's 1887 review of *Rosmersholm,* by Henrik Ibsen.

JAMES GILLIGAN

See also **Emotion; Shame; Temperament; Theories of Violence: Psychology.**

PSYCHOPATHY, BIOLOGY OF

Psychopathy is distinguishable from antisocial deviance or persistent criminality. Psychopaths exhibit a distinctive emotional style and manner of human interaction, marked by callous exploitation of others (guiltlessness) and an absence of close personal attachments (lovelessness). Unbounded by moral imperatives, abiding loyalties, or genuine intimacies, the psychopath operates as a social strategist or predator, fulfilling immediate selfish aims without regard for broader consequences. The term *primary* (or *true*) *psychopath* has sometimes been used to refer to individuals of this type.

Hervey Cleckley formulated the classic clinical description of the psychopathic personality based on his years of experience with psychiatric inpatients.

> In the psychopath . . . the observer is confronted with a convincing mask of sanity. . . . Let us say that, despite his otherwise perfect functioning, the major emotional accompaniments are absent or so attenuated as to account for little. . . . If we grant the existence of a far-reaching and persistent blocking, absence, deficit, or dissociation of this sort, we have all

that is needed, at the present level of our inquiry, to account for the psychopath.

(Cleckley 1976, pp. 368, 371)

His criteria for psychopathy included irresponsibility and antisocial acting out (that is, expressing one's impulses in overt behavior without regard to social norms), but he considered these behaviors by-products of a core affective (emotional) deficit that was manifested by traits of superficial charm, egocentricity, deceitfulness, absence of nervousness, lack of remorse or shame, incapacity for loyalty or love, poverty in major emotional reactions, and limited self-insight. The most well-researched instrument for assessing the disorder is Robert Hare's *Psychopathy Checklist* (*PCL*; see table 1). Developed to identify Cleckley-type psychopaths in prison populations, the *PCL* defines psychopathy in terms of twenty specific criteria that coalesce around two broad tendencies as revealed by factor analysis (a statistical technique for identifying common measurement dimensions among dependent variables): emotional detachment and antisocial behavior. The *PCL*-defined criminal psychopath exemplifies both tendencies.

According to the *Diagnostic and Statistical Manual of Mental Disorders-IV* (*DSM-IV*, American Psychiatric Association, 1994), antisocial personality disorder (APD) is closely related to the behavioral but not the emotional factor of the *PCL*. This is because the criteria for APD consist primarily of behavioral signs and symptoms (e.g., rule breaking, recklessness, and aggression in childhood and in adulthood). In prison settings, the prevalence of APD (70–80 percent) is much higher than *PCL*-defined psychopathy (25–30 percent), which requires the presence of emotional detachment as

Table 1. The Hare *Psychopathy Checklist—Revised:* Items and Factor Representations

Emotional Detachment Factor	Antisocial Behavior Factor
1. Glibness/superficial charm	3. Proneness to boredom
2. Grandiose sense of self-worth	9. Parasitic lifestyle
4. Pathological lying	10. Poor behavior controls
5. Conning/manipulative	12. Early behavior problems
6. Lack of remorse or guilt	13. Lack of realistic, long-term goals
7. Shallow affect	14. Impulsivity
8. Callous/lack of empathy	15. Irresponsibility
16. Failure to accept responsibility	18. Juvenile delinquency
19. Revocation of conditional release	

Note: The remaining three *PCL* items do not relate strongly to either factor: (11) promiscuous sexual behavior; (17) many short-term marital relationships; (20) criminal versatility.

well. Individuals who display persistent antisocial behavior in the absence of the core emotional symptoms of psychopathy are sometimes referred to as secondary psychopaths. A variety of risk factors, including neonatal insult, intellectual weakness, parental absence, environmental impoverishment, physical or sexual abuse, and deviant peer modeling, have been implicated in the development of chronic antisocial deviance.

Biological Factors in Psychopathy

It is generally acknowledged that hereditary influences and social-environmental factors interact to shape most forms of behaviors through their combined influence on brain structure and function. From this perspective, biology plays a role in all behavior disorders. However, to understand any psychopathological syndrome, it is fruitful to ask at what level biological factors come into play, the degree to which innate and experiential factors are involved, and how psychological and behavioral deviations accrue.

A prominent theoretical viewpoint is that psychopathy is an extreme variant of normal temperament. *Temperament* refers to affect-related dispositions, such as anxiousness, dominance, aggressiveness, and sociability, that show evidence of inheritance and that tend to be manifested early in life. From a sociobiological perspective, traits such as these vary within the normal population because successful adaptive strategies differ across times and settings. The psychologist David Lykken has argued that primary psychopaths are constitutionally fearless and well adapted to survival in hostile, competitive environments. Such individuals tend not to be responsive to disapproval or punishment and—in the absence of intellectual, temperamental, or psychosocial factors that can facilitate socialization (e.g., expert parenting, an enriched home or school environment, or positive peer influence)—are likely to gravitate toward deviant or illicit activities that promise instant gratification. Alternative theories posit that psychopaths are temperamentally low in arousability or hyperresponsive to reward cues. Cognitive models of psychopathic behavior, with an emphasis on deviations in thinking, attention, and memory, have also been proposed.

Behavioral and psychophysiological studies using Cleckley's criteria for psychopathy and Hare's *PCL* have provided compelling support for Lykken's low-fear hypothesis. Psychopaths perform poorly in passive-avoidance learning situations where a dominant response must be inhibited in order to avoid punishment. In contrast to non-psychopathic individuals, psychopaths choose delayed over immediate punishment when a noxious stimulus is unavoidable. In procedures involving delayed anticipation of a noxious stimulus, such as a shock or loud noise, psychopathic criminals show weaker electrodermal (palmar sweating) activation during the warning interval. Although this finding could also be explained by a low-arousal hypothesis, other research has demonstrated that psychopaths do not show a normal increase in the startle response to sudden noise when anticipating a noxious stimulus or when viewing graphically aversive pictures (e.g., mutilated corpses, weapons, or scenes of violent attacks). In the light of evidence that the increase in the startle reflex under unpleasant circumstances is mediated by subcortical fear systems in the brain, these findings imply a heightened threshold for fear activation in psychopaths. Furthermore, this deviation is closely linked to the classic emotional-detachment features of psychopathy.

Behavior-genetic studies have also been conducted to examine the transmission of psychopathy within families. One weakness of many such studies is that diagnostic criteria have been limited to criminal offenses and behaviors. However, most of the evidence indicates that there is a substantial inherited component to psychopathy, with familial patterns indicating that multiple genes contribute to the disorder. Personality questionnaire studies also reveal links between psychopathy and heritable temperament traits. High overall scores on Hare's *PCL* are related to high dominance, aggressiveness, and sensation seeking and low empathy; high scores on the emotional-detachment factor in particular are related to low anxiousness and high social dominance. All of these traits show substantial inheritance and stability across time. Relatedly, research conducted in the 1990s established the validity of Hare's two-factor model of psychopathy in juvenile offenders and in young children with conduct problems.

No consistent evidence has emerged for gross brain abnormalities in primary psychopaths, and psychopathic criminals do not show reliable performance differences on neuropsychological tests. But structural brain abnormalities and neuropsychological deficits have been found among antisocial criminals, particularly those who are impulsively violent. Research conducted in the 1990s also showed that psychopathy, and in particular

Two Faces of Criminal Psychopathy

The following cases, taken from the author's empirical research with incarcerated offenders, illustrate nonviolent and violent manifestations of criminal psychopathy. Summaries are distilled from information obtained from a structured clinical interview and from official prison records. At the end of each case, scores on Hare's *Psychopathy Checklist* are presented: Total score (out of a maximum of 40), Emotional Detachment score (out of a maximum of 16), and Antisocial Behavior score (out of a maximum of 18).

"Raymond"

This inmate presented himself as the consummate con artist. His exact age was not possible to determine because a different birth date was listed on each official document, but in the interview he stated that he was forty-one years old. His criminal record listed thirteen aliases and included three full pages of offenses, such as forgeries, frauds, thefts, possession of stolen property, drug crimes, and prison escapes. The interviewer's comments included the following: "Supremely confident, articulate, often using illustrations and images to make his points. . . . He looks with absolute disdain on those who are not as intelligent or as ambitious as himself. . . . There was never the slightest suggestion [during the interview] of him being attached to anyone in the course of his life, and he showed no remorse for anything he had done." In the interview, he described outrageous scams, such as masquerading as a police officer to pass phony checks at the bank and bribing the prosecutor in one of his trials with the aid of a prostitute. His institutional files included entries such as "He is suspected of smuggling pills into the prison and selling them to other inmates," and "It is known that this prisoner is packing money into the institution under his false teeth. . . . All staff are to keep a watchful eye on him."

Psychopathy Checklist scores: Total—34/40; Emotional Detachment—15/16; Antisocial Behavior—13/18.

"Eric"

At the time of the assessment, this inmate was twenty-four years old. His official criminal record revealed a history of convictions dating back to age fourteen for crimes including thefts, breaking and entering, false pretenses, prison escapes, drug offenses, possession and use of weapons, and, as a juvenile, "willfully killing a dog." At one point during his late teens, he escaped to California from a Canadian federal prison but was extradited from the United States after being charged with attempted murder. At age seventeen, he was convicted of negligent homicide following an incident that began with the theft of a car and ended with the death of a police officer. According to prison records, "It has been noted [that] the subject feels no remorse for this incident." Other file comments included the following: "Antisocial behavior dating from age nine. . . . In interview situations, he tends to distort the truth and exaggerate, making it difficult to separate fact from fantasy. . . . Indicates he feels no compunction about hurting people and does so with little emotional reaction, and without any specific provocation necessary. . . . He is obviously a severely personality-disordered individual whom I would consider entirely capable of seriously injuring or killing others."

Psychopathy Checklist scores: Total—34/40; Emotional Detachment—13/16; Antisocial Behavior—17/18.

---

the antisocial behavior factor of Hare's *PCL*, is associated with reduced levels of the brain neurotransmitter serotonin. Other research has demonstrated a link between low brain serotonin and impulsive aggressiveness.

Psychopathy and Violence

In a public mind fueled by lurid press reports and popular fiction and film, the term *psychopath* conjures up images of sadistic brutality and serial murder. While it is true that some of society's most notorious killers are prototypic psychopaths, many psychopaths are nonviolent, and most are not murderers (see sidebar, p. 633). Cleckley characterized psychopaths as devoid of strong emotion (including violent rage), and his criteria included no specific reference to aggressivity. Indeed, he noted that psychopaths typically do not commit major crimes of violence, and he concluded that "such tendencies should be regarded as the exception rather than the rule, perhaps, as a pathologic trait independent, to a considerable degree, of the other manifestations which we regard as fundamental" (p. 262).

In contrast to Cleckley's characterization, empirical research has revealed a robust link between psychopathy and violent behavior in male criminal offenders. The primary research strategy has been to examine directly the relation between psychopathy and the incidence of violent crime by comparing psychopathy scores or diagnoses with violence measures (e.g., number of violent convictions, violent recidivism, and convictions for specific subcategories of violent crime). In these studies, psychopathy diagnoses have been based on Hare's *PCL* or global ratings of Cleckley's prototype.

In general, higher clinical ratings of psychopathy are associated with a heightened incidence and frequency of violent crime and aggressive behavior, although not all studies have reported this relation. Group differences tend to vary with crime type. Nonpsychopaths are more likely than psychopaths to be imprisoned for murder, which is characteristically a crime of passion committed against a known victim; psychopaths are more likely than nonpsychopaths to victimize strangers in a nonlethal fashion.

Psychopaths are also more likely to engage in aggressive and disruptive behavior in prison as a means of controlling others. Outside prison, their violent crimes more frequently involve coercion, threats, and weapons. Psychopaths are more likely than nonpsychopaths to victimize strangers for purposes of material gain, and they are more likely to commit violent offenses within a shorter span of time after being released from prison than nonpsychopaths. As further evidence of the coercive, manipulative quality of psychopathic aggression, therapy-outcome research indicates that treatment techniques designed to enhance one's sensitivity in human interactions may increase the risk of relapse into violent behavior among psychopaths.

A number of significant limitations are evident in this research on the connection between psy-

chopathy and violence. One is the possibility that relations between psychopathy and violence might arise in part because clinical ratings of psychopathy are based on case facts that include documented episodes of violence. A second limitation is that these studies rely on official crime records, which characteristically underestimate true incidence. Furthermore, not all studies distinguished among different types of violent offenses committed, and those that did used a crude classification based on official crime codes. Consequently, virtually no hard data exist concerning the underlying motives for violent crime among psychopaths.

On balance, the empirical data indicate that psychopathic individuals are more likely than non-psychopaths to commit violent crimes of a coercive nature in order to achieve immediate goals. The behavior of serial murderers like Ted Bundy, John Wayne Gacy, and Kenneth Bianchi is a rare manifestation of this basic predatory style, actuated by a peculiar blend of experience and extreme temperament traits. Angry, assaultive aggression is more the province of the extreme antisocial offender than of the true psychopath. In this regard, it is important to bear in mind that all of the empirical research on psychopathy and violence has been conducted with incarcerated male offenders. Criminal psychopaths may be a breed apart from the charming ne'er-do-wells encountered by Cleckley on the psychiatric inpatient ward, and psychopathic traits may be expressed differently by individuals from advantaged, noncriminal backgrounds and by women as compared to men.

BIBLIOGRAPHY

Cleckley, Hervey. *The Mask of Sanity: An Attempt to Clarify Some Issues About the So-called Psychopathic Personality.* 5th ed. St. Louis, Mo.: Mosby, 1976.

Hare, Robert D. *The Hare Psychopathy Checklist—Revised: Manual.* Toronto: Multi-Health Systems, 1991.

Lykken, David T. *The Antisocial Personalities.* Hillsdale, N.J.: Lawrence Erlbaum Associates, 1995.

Patrick, Christopher J., and Kristen A. Zempolich. "Emotion and Aggression in the Psychopathic Personality." *Aggression and Violent Behavior* 3, no. 4 (1998): 303–338.

Patterson, C. Mark, and Joseph P. Newman. "Reflectivity and Learning from Aversive Events: Toward a Psychological Mechanism for the Syndromes of Disinhibition." *Psychological Review* 100, no. 4 (1993): 716–736.

Raine, Adrian. *The Psychopathology of Crime: Criminal Behavior as a Clinical Disorder.* San Diego, Calif.: Academic Press, 1993.

Christopher J. Patrick

See also **Bundy, Ted; Forensic Psychiatry.**

PSYCHOPHYSIOLOGY

The effects of physiological processes on violent behavior are summarized in four subentries: Autonomic Activity, EEG, Heart Rate, and Vagal Tone.

AUTONOMIC ACTIVITY

The 1990s saw a substantial increase in biological research in the area of criminality and antisocial behavior. Psychophysiology is the biological paradigm most frequently employed in the study of antisocial populations. Collectively, psychophysiological studies have demonstrated associations between antisocial behavior and problems and deficiencies in arousal and orienting (explained below). Throughout this article the terms *antisocial* and *criminal* will be used to describe both violent and nonviolent behaviors. Although not all psychophysiological studies have addressed violent behavior per se, criminal and antisocial behaviors are risk factors for violence.

Introduction to Psychophysiology

Among the most frequently recorded psychophysiological measures are skin conductance activity (SC), heart rate (HR), electroencephalography (EEG), and event-related potentials (ERP). This article will focus on SC and HR activity.

Skin conductance activity is measured by electrodes placed on the fingers or palm of the hand. SC activity fluctuates in response to changes in the electrical activity of the skin; increased sweating leads to increased SC activity. These changes are recorded using a polygraph. Resting skin conductance levels (SCLs) and spontaneous SC responses that are not elicited by external stimuli (nonspecific fluctuations, NSFs) provide indices of electrodermal arousal. Responses that occur following the presentation of an external stimulus are termed *orienting responses*.

Heart-rate measures are generally divided into tonic (resting) levels and phasic activity (reactivity to external stimuli). The resting HR level has been assessed frequently in offender and antisocial groups because of the relative ease with which it can be recorded (e.g., using portable equipment or taking a pulse). In contrast, fewer studies have reported on phasic HR changes occurring in response to external stimuli.

Psychophysiological Underarousal

Although most early studies, from the 1960s and 1970s, assessed SC levels and psychopathic behavior in criminal populations, investigations in the 1990s focused on community samples. These studies show that antisocial individuals are characterized by low SC activity and HR levels during resting situations. Four of ten studies of arousal conducted after 1978 found statistically significant differences between antisocials and normals when measured for arousal levels during rest periods. Though only one of these studies found significant effects for SCLs, three found significantly fewer NSFs in antisocial individuals. However, Marcus J. Kruesi and colleagues (1992) have shown that low SCLs measured at age eleven predict institutionalization two years later in a sample of children with behavioral disorders. Thus, although not all studies reveal underarousal in antisocial individuals, there is some evidence that general antisocial behavior is associated with fewer NSFs and lower SCLs.

Consistent relations between lower resting HR and antisocial behavior have been demonstrated among noninstitutionalized antisocial individuals. Among all psychophysiological studies of antisocial behavior, the best replicated finding appears to be that of lower resting heart rate in noninstitutionalized antisocial populations.

Fearlessness and Stimulation Seeking

Theories of fearlessness and stimulation seeking have been put forth to explain how underarousal may translate into antisocial behavior. SC and HR measures provide indices of anxiety and fearfulness, with lower HR levels indicative of fearlessness. This interpretation is consistent with theories suggesting that reduced fear predisposes an individual to antisocial behavior: fearlessness is a prerequisite for engaging in certain behavior, such as fighting, because fearless individuals are less concerned about negative consequences (injury) from their actions. Consistent with this theory are findings of low heart-rate levels in bomb-disposal experts. It has been suggested (Mednick 1977, pp. 1–8), fearlessness in children would also reduce the effectiveness of punishment, thus impeding socialization.

The theory of stimulation seeking proposes that when antisocial individuals seek out stimulation, they bring their arousal levels to a normal range. According to this theory, there is an optimal level of arousal that organisms seek to attain and maintain. Autonomic underarousal in antisocial individuals leads these individuals to engage in pathological stimulation-seeking behaviors, such as assault and robbery.

Orienting Deficits Theory

The presentation of novel stimuli in one's environment is normally followed by an orienting response, or what may be termed a "what is it" response. This orienting response is accompanied by increased autonomic activity and, thus, changes in SC levels. Studies by Michael E. Dawson and colleagues in 1984 and 1989 showed that the skin conductance orienting response (SCOR) is a measure of information processing in that it reflects how an individual attends to and processes novel stimuli. Thus, the size of the SCOR provides information about the functioning of the central nervous system by assessing the amount of attention allocated to the processing of external stimuli.

Several studies provide evidence of orienting deficits in antisocial populations, as evidenced by reduced frequency of SCORs. Reduced orienting is particularly characteristic of psychopathic, antisocial, and criminal subjects who also exhibit schizotypal features, such as paranoia, reduced emotionality, and inability to make close friends. This finding—that schizophrenics are more violent than normals—is consistent with the notion that reduced SC orienting is associated with schizotypal personality disorder (some of the symptoms of which resemble those of psychopathy) and with schizophrenia.

Few studies have assessed phasic heart-rate activity in relation to antisocial behavior; one longitudinal study found that reduced heart-rate orienting at age fifteen predicted criminal behavior at age twenty-four (Raine, Venables, and Williams 1990b).

Classical Conditioning

Hans Jurgen Eysenck proposed poor classical conditioning as an important factor in the genesis of antisocial behavior. Classical conditioning is the process by which a conditioned stimulus (CS) takes on the properties of an unconditioned stimulus (UCS) and comes to elicit a conditioned response (CR) as a result of repeated pairings of the conditioned stimulus with the unconditioned stimulus. For example, punishment (UCS) naturally elicits distress (an unconditioned response, UCR) in children. According to conditioning theory, fighting will become a CS if it is repeatedly paired with punishment. Eventually, the thought of fighting will come to elicit distress because of its association with punishment. Thus, fighting becomes the CS that will elicit the same response as the UCS, distress and fear. In most cases, this distress and fear will deter the child from fighting. However, if a child showed deficient conditioning, the thought of fighting would fail to become associated with being punished and fighting would not be inhibited.

Several studies indicate that antisocial individuals show poor classical conditioning. Despite the various paradigms used and the different subtypes of antisocial populations assessed, all of these studies obtained significant results. Thus, poor conditioning may play an important role in the development of general antisocial behavior.

At least two studies of antisocial individuals also reveal a biosocial interaction, such that poorer conditioning and orienting are most characteristic of antisocial individuals from better social backgrounds. If an individual lacks the "social push" for antisocial behavior (by virtue of a benign home background), yet still becomes antisocial, then the causes of the antisocial behvior are more likely to be biological than social.

Protective Factors

Whereas the majority of studies of antisocial behavior have focused on psychophysiological correlates as *risk factors,* two studies (Raine, Venables, and Williams 1995, 1996) report on psychophysiological correlates that serve a *protective* role. In one prospective longitudinal study, it was found that fifteen-year-old antisocial adolescents who did not go on to become criminals by age twenty-nine had higher heart-rate levels, higher SC arousal activity, and better SC conditioning when compared with their antisocial counterparts who became adult criminals. The authors of another study, which replicated these findings, suggest that higher HR levels indicate fearfulness, better orienting indicates superior attentional abilities, and better conditioning indicates the ability to learn the association between crime and punishment—all factors that operate to reduce the tendency to engage in crime (Brennan et al. 1997).

Violent Offenders

Little research has been done on autonomic activity in violent offenders versus antisocial but nonviolent populations. Although studies have found that heart rate is particularly low in violent offenders relative to nonviolent offenders (Farrington 1987; Wadsworth 1976), and in aggressive versus nonaggressive children (Raine, Venables, and Mednick 1997), specificity for violence has not yet been shown for SC measures. In addition, a reanalysis of data from a previous study (Raine, Venables, and Williams 1990a) revealed that when offenders were subdivided into violent and nonviolent groups, the violent group had the lowest heart rates of all. These conclusions are limited, however, by small (five violent offenders and twelve nonviolent offenders) sample sizes (Raine 1996). Additional research, with large sample sizes, is needed to establish whether psychophysiological correlates differ among violent and nonviolent offenders.

Summary

Antisocial individuals show tendencies toward low electrodermal arousal as indicated by a reduced frequency of NSFs. Orienting deficits have also been shown, particularly in antisocial individuals with concomitant schizotypal features. Although few studies have assessed phasic HR activity, lower resting HR levels have repeatedly been shown in antisocial individuals. These biological risk factors interact with environmental variables to place certain individuals at increased risk for developing antisocial lifestyles. Researchers have begun to examine psychophysiological protective factors that defend against adult criminal lifestyles. These factors will undoubtedly play a leading role in prevention and intervention strategies aimed at reducing antisocial behaviors.

BIBLIOGRAPHY

Brennan, Patricia A., et al. "Psychophysiological Protective Factors for Male Subjects at High Risk for Criminal Behavior." *American Journal of Psychiatry* 154, no. 6 (1997).

Dawson, Michael E., and Keith H. Nuechterlein. "Psychophysiological Dysfunction in the Developmental Course of Schizophrenic Disorders." *Schizophrenia Bulletin* 10, no. 2 (1984).

Dawson, Michael E., et al. "Is Elicitation of the Autonomic Orienting Response Associated with the Allocation of Processing Resources?" *Psychophysiology* 26, no. 5 (1989).

Eysenck, Hans Jurgen. *Crime and Personality.* 3d ed. St. Albans, U.K.: Paladin, 1977.

Farrington, David P. "Implications of Biological Findings for Criminological Research." In *The Causes of Crime: New Biological Approaches,* edited by Sarnoff A. Mednick et al. New York: Cambridge University Press, 1987.

Kruesi, Marcus J., et al. "A Two-Year Prospective Follow-up Study of Children and Adolescents with Disruptive Behavior Disorders: Prediction by Cerebrospinal Fluid 5-Hydroxyindoleacetic Acid, Homovanillic Acid, and Autonomic Measures?" *Archives of General Psychiatry* 49 (1992).

Mednick, Sarnoff, and Karl O. Christiansen, eds. *Biosocial Bases of Criminal Behavior.* New York: Gardner, 1977.

Raine, Adrian. "Autonomic Nervous System Activity and Violence." In *The Neurobiology of Clinical Aggression,* edited by David M. Stoff and R. F. Cairns. Hillsdale, N.J.: Erlbaum, 1996.

———. *The Psychopathology of Crime: Criminal Behavior as a Clinical Disorder.* San Diego: Academic, 1993.

Raine, Adrian, Peter H. Venables, and Sarnoff A. Mednick. "Low Resting Heart Rate at Age Three Years Predisposes to Aggression at Age Eleven Years: Evidence from the Mauritius Child Health Project." *Journal of the American Academy of Child and Adolescent Psychiatry* 36, no. 10 (1997).

Raine, Adrian, Peter H. Venables, and Mark Williams. "Autonomic Orienting Responses in Fifteen-Year-Old Male Subjects and Criminal Behavior at Age Twenty-four." *American Journal of Psychiatry* 147, no. 7 (1990a).

———. "Better Autonomic Conditioning and Faster Electrodermal Half-Recovery Time at Age Fifteen Years as Possible Protective Factors Against Crime at Age Twenty-nine Years." *Developmental Psychology* 32, no. 4 (1996).

———. "High Autonomic Arousal and Electrodermal Orienting at Age Fifteen Years as Protective Factors Against Criminal Behavior at Age Twenty-nine years." *American Journal of Psychiatry* 152, no. 11 (1995).

———. "Relationships Between Central and Autonomic Measures of Arousal at Age Fifteen Years and Criminality at Age Twenty-four Years." *Archives of General Psychiatry* 47 (1990b).

Raine, Adrian, et al. *Biosocial Bases of Violence.* New York: Plenum, 1997.

Wadsworth, M. E. J. "Delinquency, Pulse Rate, and Early Emotional Deprivation." *British Journal of Criminology* 16 (1976).

PAULINE S. YARALIAN
ADRIAN RAINE

See also **Aggression; Temperament.**

EEG

Developed in the early 1930s, electroencephalography (EEG) was the first procedure that allowed scientists to observe the functioning of the human brain. Through electrodes placed on the surface of the scalp, EEG measures the electrical activity of the cells in the underlying cortex of the brain. The electrical activity is commonly broken down into four waves, or frequencies: alpha and beta waves are generally associated with wakefulness and activity, while theta and delta waves are associated with drowsiness and sleep. All frequencies are present in all individuals but vary in relative strength. EEG is generally taken while subjects relax with their eyes closed, although conditions may vary. The electrical leads are positioned to correspond to the locations of the brain lobes (frontal, parietal, temporal, occipital), but no more detail than the general location can be extrapolated; structures deeper in the brain cannot be accurately assessed. (See Ray 1990 for a detailed review of EEG.)

The ability to study the human brain through EEG quickly came into wide use among psychologists and neurologists. It was not long before this technology was applied to the study of the criminal mind. Violent behavior was thought to be associated with brain abnormality, but this general theory has taken different forms throughout the years.

One theory of the origin of violent behavior related it to episodes of epileptic fits, particularly in individuals whose epilepsy originated in the temporal lobes. Studies of epileptic patients in general tend not to reveal increased violent behavior during epileptic fits; however, prisoners tend to show an incidence of epilepsy higher than that of the general population. Research in this field has often been criticized for poor methodology and inadequate controls, which make it difficult to interpret the findings (Volavka 1995).

Other researchers examining criminals through EEG have reported a general increase in "abnormal" EEG ratings. Typically these studies are conducted by a physician or psychologist who visually examines the EEG readout and judges whether the subject has a normal or abnormal EEG. Abnormalities may consist of many different phenomena and are not consistently defined across all studies. These studies have reported the incidence of abnormal EEGs in violent or aggressive subjects to be as high as 70 percent (Surwillo 1980). Most studies of violent subjects show more EEG abnormality than that found in the nonviolent population. These findings appear to be affected by such variables as the nature of the violent offense (Hill and Pond 1952).

Another theory that emerged from EEG research is that violent subjects show an "immature" EEG pattern; that is, adult offenders have EEGs more typical of children. These results led researchers to speculate that the development of the brain in criminals is somehow inhibited (Hare 1970).

In line with the evidence that autonomic functioning (skin conductance and heart rate) is reduced in violent offenders, EEGs have shown an overall reduction in brain arousal of such subjects. One researcher even found EEG to be predictive of future criminality. In a sample of unselected fifteen-year-old schoolboys, reduced cortical activity, as evidenced by increases in theta and delta, or slow, waves, increased the chances of a child becoming a criminal by age twenty-four (Raine et al. 1990).

Some researchers have examined the possibility that certain regions of the brain are dysfunctional, rather than the brain as a whole, as had been previously theorized. Results from these types of studies can be difficult to interpret but tend to show an increase in abnormality specific to the frontal and temporal regions (Volavka 1990). Sometimes these findings are lateralized to the left hemisphere.

Research utilizing EEG has been plagued with problems. Early on, EEG records were analyzed visually, which added a measure of subjectivity to the data. Eventually computers were used, creating more quantitative data and increasing the scope of questions that could be explored with this technology. However, these technological advances were unable to overcome the problems posed by distortion from the skull and a lack of regional detail, imperfections that make EEG unappealing to many researchers. With the advent of newer techniques, such as magnetic resonance imaging (MRI) and positron-emission tomography (PET), interest in EEG declined in the last decade of the twentieth century, but it continued to hold a place in psychological research. Clinically, EEG may be used in forensic settings as one part of a comprehensive neuropsychological evaluation of a defendant either during trial when an insanity plea is proposed or during sentencing. In research settings EEG is used less often in favor of the newer imaging techniques. However, EEG is far less expensive than these other methods and is more portable, allowing researchers to assess prisoners without having to transport them to nearby hospitals. Therefore, at the end of the twentieth century researchers were still using EEG to evaluate violent offenders.

BIBLIOGRAPHY

Hare, Robert D. *Psychopathy: Theory and Research.* New York: Wiley, 1970.

Hill, Denis, and D. Pond. "Reflections on One Hundred Capital Cases Submitted to Electroencephalography." *Journal of Mental Science* 98 (1952): 23–43.

Raine, Adrian, Peter H. Venables, and Mark Williams. "Relationships Between Central and Autonomic Measures of Arousal at Age Fifteen Years and Criminality at Age Twenty-four Years." *Psychophysiology* 27, no. 5 (1990): 567–575.

Ray, William J. "The Electrocortical System." In *Principles of Psychophysiology: Physical, Social, and Inferential Elements,* edited by John T. Cacioppo and Louis G. Tassinary. New York: Cambridge University Press, 1990.

Surwillo, Walter W. "The Electroencephalogram and Childhood Aggression." *Aggressive Behavior* 6, no. 1 (1980): 9–18.

Volavka, Jan. "Aggression, Electroencephalography, and Evoked Potentials: A Critical Review." *Neuropsychiatry, Neuropsychology, and Behavioral Neurology* 3, no. 4 (1990): 249–259.

———. *Neurobiology of Violence.* Washington, D.C.: American Psychiatric Press, 1995.

LISA M. GATZKE

See also **Neuropsychology: Brain Function** *and* **Hemispheric Laterality.**

HEART RATE

According to Adrian Raine, Peter H. Venables, and Sarnoff A. Mednick, "low resting heart rate is the best-replicated biological marker of antisocial and aggressive behavior in childhood and adolescent community samples." While heart rate variability and reactivity have been compared with diverse indicators of antisocial behavior, it is only resting heart rate that has been specifically related to patterns of aggression and violence.

Resting heart rate is easy to measure in large community samples. Using the pulse rate, the heart rate can be measured using no equipment, although the use of some kind of pulse meter under controlled conditions is usually more accurate. Resting heart rate is a peripheral measure that reflects both sympathetic and parasympathetic nervous system activity.

There are two main theories concerning resting heart rate in relation to aggression and violence. The first suggests that high heart rate indicates fearfulness and an inhibited temperament (at least in children), whereas low heart rate indicates fearlessness and an uninhibited temperament. According to this theory, less inhibited people are more likely to be aggressive, because they are less concerned about the consequences of their actions. Also, a lack of fear militates against passive avoidance conditioning (the association of anxiety with disapproved behavior as a result of punishment by parents and other socializing agents). Thus, lack of fear leads to a weak conscience. The second theory suggests that low heart rate is an indicator of low cortical arousal (i.e., low brain activity); this in turn leads to risk-taking and sensation-seeking behavior to increase arousal, and hence to an uninhibited temperament and aggression.

The first important study that related resting heart rate to violence was carried out by Michael E. J. Wadsworth (1976) as part of the National Survey of Health and Development; it was a large prospective longitudinal survey, or follow-up study, of children born in Great Britain in March 1946 who have been tracked to the present day. When the children were eleven years old, their pulse rates were measured while they were waiting to have a medical examination. Wadsworth considered that this was a measure of autonomic functioning under stress, but it is perhaps more plausible to regard this as a measure of resting heart rate. Conviction records were obtained for 1,813 boys up to age twenty-one. Eighty-one percent of the boys convicted of violence had below-average

heart rates at age eleven compared with 54 percent of the unconvicted boys. Interestingly, experiencing a broken home before age five predicted both low heart rate and convictions for violence. Low heart rate predicted violent behavior among boys from unbroken homes but not among boys from broken homes, suggesting perhaps that the effect of this biological risk factor is only apparent in the absence of this major social risk factor (coming from a broken home).

In the Cambridge Study in Delinquent Development, which is a prospective longitudinal survey of 411 London boys, resting heart rate was measured at age eighteen (Farrington 1997). Low heart rate was significantly related to convictions for violence, self-reported violence at age eighteen, and teacher-rated aggression at age fourteen. For example, 25 percent of the boys with below-average heart rates were convicted of violence up to age forty, compared with 11 percent of those with above-average heart rates. These relationships held up independently of numerous other predictors of violence: personality traits (daring, impulsiveness, extraversion, poor concentration ability), ability and achievement personal accomplishments (low verbal and nonverbal IQ, poor performance in school), family situations (poor supervision, separation from a parent, convicted parent), and socioeconomic conditions (low income, poor housing, large family size). Indeed, only low heart rate and poor concentration or restlessness were related to aggression or violence in all analyses independent of all other variables. Low heart rate was related to violence especially among boys from large families and boys in conflict with their parents, suggesting that the effect of this biological risk factor was most apparent in the presence of major social risk factors. Low heart rate was not related to measurements of nervousness or risk-taking behavior, casting doubt on explanations of the link based on fearlessness or low arousal.

Adrian Raine et al. reported results obtained in a prospective longitudinal survey of 1,795 Mauritius children. Heart rate at age three was related to aggression at age eleven (based on parent ratings). The researchers compared low- and high-heart-rate groups and low- and high-aggression groups, identified according to having scores more than one standard deviation from the mean. For example, 66 percent of low-heart-rate children were identified as aggressive, compared with 35 percent of high-heart-rate children; average-heart-rate children were excluded from this analysis. Low heart rate predicted aggression independent of other factors: gender, ethnicity, a disinhibited temperament, having divorced or separated parents, socioeconomic deprivation, body size, physical health, and motor activity—all measured at age three. By measuring heart rate at age three, this study eliminated later environmental influences on heart rate such as cigarette smoking, alcohol use, drug use, exercise, and puberty.

In addition to these three major studies of heart rate in relation to aggression and violence, there are a few smaller-scale studies. For example, Daniel J. Kindlon et al. in Montreal reported a link between low heart rate at ages eleven through twelve and teacher-rated fighting, kicking, and bullying at the same age. There are also heart-rate studies investigating general delinquency and general antisocial behavior rather than aggression and violence; all studies in which heart rate was measured between ages three and eighteen yield consistent findings.

Despite the remarkably replicable results, a number of uncertainties remain. Since most results are based on the study of males, it is unclear how far results are replicable for females. It is also unclear how far results are replicable if the heart rate is measured after age eighteen. More research is needed on interactions between heart rate and other biological, psychological, and social risk factors. Most important, the causal chain linking low heart rate to aggression and violence remains to be elucidated, as do relationships between aggression, violence, and heart-rate variability and reactivity. In order to resolve these and other issues, a new generation of longitudinal studies should include frequent, repeated measures of heart rate, aggression, violence, and other important biological, psychological, and social variables.

BIBLIOGRAPHY

Farrington, David P. "The Relationship Between Low Resting Heart Rate and Violence." In *Biosocial Bases of Violence,* edited by Adrian Raine et al. New York: Plenum, 1997.

Kindlon, Daniel J., et al. "Longitudinal Patterns of Heart Rate and Fighting Behavior in Nine- Through Twelve-Year-Old Boys." *Journal of the American Academy of Child and Adolescent Psychiatry* 34 (1995): 371–377.

Raine, Adrian. *The Psychopathology of Crime.* San Diego: Academic, 1993.

Raine, Adrian, Peter H. Venables, and Sarnoff A. Mednick. "Low Resting Heart Rate at Age Three Predisposes to Aggression at Age Eleven Years: Evidence from the Mauritius Child Health Project." *Journal of the American Academy of Child and Adolescent Psychiatry* 36 (1997): 1457–1464.

Wadsworth, Michael E. J. "Delinquency, Pulse Rates, and Early Emotional Deprivation." *British Journal of Criminology* 16 (1976): 245–256.

DAVID P. FARRINGTON

See also **Temperament.**

VAGAL TONE

Vagal tone is one of many psychophysiological measures of autonomic nervous system functioning. Specifically, it is a measure of the regulation of the heart. Whereas heart rate (or pulse) reflects the state of arousal at a given moment, vagal tone reflects how well the organism is able to speed up or slow down heart functioning, particularly in response to stimulation. (See Porges et al. 1994 for a detailed explanation of vagal tone and how it is measured.)

The autonomic nervous system is divided into two branches, the parasympathetic and the sympathetic. These generally work in opposition to each other in regulating the function of organs, including the heart. When a person is in a relaxed, nonstressful physical and mental state, the parasympathetic system works to slow heart rate, lower blood pressure, and increase digestive and eliminative processes. The sympathetic system takes over when an individual is under mental or physical stress, working to increase respiration, increase heart rate, increase blood pressure, stop digestive and eliminative processes, and cause the release of hormones into the bloodstream.

While both the parasympathetic and sympathetic nervous systems influence heart rate, vagal tone is more strictly under parasympathetic control. That is, vagal tone indicates the ability of the organism to maintain a slow heart rate, even under stress. Individual differences in vagal tone are thought to be related to one's competency to react physiologically to external stimuli, and the ability to suppress vagal tone in response to stressful situations is considered indicative of the ability to regulate one's emotions (Porges et al. 1994).

The many studies of the relationship between cardiac functioning and antisocial behavior, including violence, have primarily considered measures of heart rate. Comparatively few studies have been made of the relationship between vagal tone and antisocial behavior. In children a relationship has been established between vagal tone and emotional reactivity, such as crying and irritability, to stressful stimuli (see Porges et al. 1994). Adults' ability to cope with moderately to highly stressful situations appears related to vagal tone (Fabes and Eisenberg 1997). A study of impulsive criminal offenders suggested significantly elevated vagal tone in subjects with intermittent explosive disorder (characterized by discrete episodes of failure to resist aggressive impulses, often resulting in serous assaults or destruction of property), indicating high autonomic and emotional reactivity (Virkkunen et al. 1995). Although this appears an area of potential importance to the understanding of emotional reactivity and regulation, considerable research is still required to establish how aggression and violence may be related to vagal tone and one's ability to suppress or regulate it.

BIBLIOGRAPHY

Fabes, Richard A., and Nancy Eisenberg. "Regulatory Control and Adults' Stress-Related Responses to Daily Life Events." *Journal of Personality & Social Psychology* 73, no. 5 (1997): 1107–1117.

Porges, Stephen W., Jane A. Doussard-Roosevelt, and Ajit K. Maiti. "Vagal Tone and the Physiological Regulation of Emotion." In *Monographs of the Society for Research in Child Development* 59, no. 2–3 (1994): 167–186.

Virkkunen, Matti, David Goldman, David A. Nielsen, and Markku Linnoila. "Low Brain Serotonin Turnover Rate (Low CSF 5-HIAA) and Impulsive Violence." *Journal of Psychiatry and Neuroscience* 20, no. 4 (1995): 271–275.

LAURA A. BAKER

PUERTO RICANS

The relationship between Puerto Rico and the United States was spawned in violence when the island was invaded by U.S. forces in 1898. Not as bloody as the Cuba and Philippine campaigns, the Puerto Rico war is largely overlooked; postwar resistance to U.S. occupation and civic repression go equally unacknowledged, contributing to a general notion that Puerto Ricans are complacent about their colonial past and ambiguous relationship with the United States.

Claims that all violence relating to Puerto Ricans originates in the U.S.–Puerto Rican relationship are overstatements, but it nevertheless informs many dimensions of their history and culture. The ambiguity of the relationship causes trenchant resentment and sometimes violent debate among political factions espousing various forms of relationship to the United States—statehood, independence, or the status quo of "association" with a restrained degree of self-government. Dissent against U.S. colonialism and the local government has provoked repressive state actions by U.S. and Puerto Rican officials, who often cast separatism as a form of subversion, criminalizing it despite its consonance with democratic principles of self-determination.

Physically or ideologically violent policies and practices have often been rationalized as objective measures of social engineering needed to cope with dire economic conditions. Prime examples are the widespread campaign for female sterilization and the testing of oral contraceptives on Puerto Rican women. Because of its potential for controversy in a predominantly Catholic society, the campaign for sterilization of women was somewhat subtle, almost covert. It was mobilized through the expansion of public-health services, beginning in the late 1940s. By the late 1960s the availability of alternative contraceptive methods, the liberalization of attitudes toward contraception, feminist consciousness, and awareness of the government's role in pushing sterilization as well as the risks involved made sterilization less attractive. These officially sanctioned measures had been devised to address presumed overpopulation, as was a vigorous labor emigration policy, which supplied the United States with cheap, unskilled labor.

Because labor emigration has been intensively promoted by the United States since 1899, Puerto Ricans are divided between island and diasporic communities across the United States. Circular migration inextricably connects both communities. As a racialized immigrant group, Puerto Ricans tend to share a subordinate position in the United States with other racialized groups as well as prevalent conditions of poverty and societal distress. Urban Puerto Rican communities in the United States are daily confronted with a high incidence of criminality, leading to elevated prosecution and incarceration rates within the criminal justice system. Persistent racism has made Puerto Ricans the target of prejudice, de facto discrimination, police brutality, and hate crimes.

The issue of violence, then, encompasses communities on the island and in the United States; its manifestations range from the everyday brutality of life in urban ghettos to ideological repression. It is the latter that is most dramatic and paradoxical.

The Violence of Repression

Resistance to U.S. occupation, especially after it failed to restore the autonomy that Spain had granted Puerto Rico in 1897, led to the suppression of newspapers and the incarceration of journalists. Dissonance between the democratic principles that the United States represented and colonial realities was a prime factor in the emergence of separatism.

Separatism became particularly strong during the 1930s, exacerbated by the persistence of the island's colonial status, impoverished economic conditions, and U.S. policies aimed at cultural assimilation (e.g., the instituting of public education in English). Salient incidents in that period generally involved the Nationalist Party. In 1935 five nationalists were murdered during a university strike; two party members responded by assassinating the chief of police and were then beaten and killed while in police custody. After their leader, Pedro Albizu Campos, was successfully tried and sentenced for sedition by federal prosecutors in 1937, a nationalist demonstration in Ponce ended with violence and twenty-one deaths (including men, women, and children) and between 150 and 200 wounded. Sources differ as to how many of the dead were nationalists and how many were bystanders. The Ponce Massacre, as it came to be known, has remained a significant Puerto Rican historical landmark.

After World War II, the U.S.–Puerto Rican colonial relationship became an issue in the ideological struggle of the Cold War. Attempts at reformulating the relationship produced the Estado Libre Asociado in 1952. (Estado Libre Asociado is literally translated as Free Associated State but usually rendered in English as "commonwealth," a translation that is widely contested by Puerto Ricans, who question its implication of autonomy.) The change ostensibly increased Puerto Rico's self-governance but did not substantially alter the degree of power held by the United States.

Though the number of nationalists was greatly diminished after a brutally aborted islandwide rebellion in 1950, separatism flourished, later splintering into factions. To address its persistence, particularly in the context of the Cold War, in 1960 the Federal Bureau of Investigation employed COINTELPRO, its counterintelligence program directed at repressing domestic unrest, especially among minority civil rights movements.

COINTELPRO targeted radical and moderate Puerto Rican separatists on the island and in the United States, subjecting them to "dirty tricks": disinformation campaigns, surveillance, and undercover infiltration. The FBI trained the Puerto Rican police in counterintelligence strategies; it has

also been charged with manipulating legal processes and with murder. Separatists' exercise of freedom of speech, right to assembly, and other such constitutional rights to dissent were curtailed through official repression.

COINTELPRO continued to operate in Puerto Rico into the 1970s, even after public outcry ostensibly led to its dismantling. The Puerto Rican police became a major official instrument for "managing" separatism. In 1978 in Cerro Maravilla, an undercover agent entrapped two pro-independence university students into attempted sabotage. The two students were ambushed and executed by police. Ensuing legal and congressional processes led to the trial and sentencing of these officers. Still at issue is the alleged cover-up of high-level participation by Puerto Rican and U.S. government officials.

The 1960s saw the emergence of diverse separatist movements in Puerto Rico and in the United States—among others, the Young Lords Party, the Puerto Rican Socialist Party, the Movement for National Liberation, the Armed Forces of National Liberation, the Puerto Rican Independence Party, and Los Macheteros—representing the ideological gamut from electoral participation to guerrilla warfare. The more radical movements have claimed responsibility for sabotage activities in the United States and Puerto Rico, such as the 1975 bombing of the Fraunces Tavern, near Wall Street in New York City, which targeted corporate executives. A series of business and government locations in New York, Chicago, and Washington, D.C., were also bombed that year, including Citibank and Chase Manhattan Bank facilities, the State Department, the Bureau of Indian Affairs, and the U.S. Mission to the United Nations. In 1983 Los Macheteros struck a Wells Fargo depot in Hartford, Connecticut, reaping $7 million for financing further revolutionary activities. In Puerto Rico guerrilla activity included the 1979 armed attack on a busload of U.S. Navy sailors on their way to a U.S. communication base in San Juan, which resulted in the death of two of its occupants, and the 1981 operation in the Muñoz Air National Guard Base in Carolina, Puerto Rico, in which $50 million worth of damage was reported on U.S. Air Force aircraft and other military equipment.

Criminal prosecutions under federal law produced a post-1960s generation of Puerto Rican political prisoners who claimed the status of freedom fighters; they argued that their activities (which peaked in the mid-1980s) should be recognized as a war for independence and national sovereignty. In August 1999 President Bill Clinton offered executive clemency to fifteen Puerto Rican political prisoners. At the time it was a conditioned offer and the provisions seemed unlikely to be accepted. The prisoners were being asked to admit the criminal nature of their acts, subject themselves to regular parole conditions, and desist from associating with each other, all of which would have undermined the proindependence and anti–United States message that underpinned their ideological structure.

Though radical activism appeared diminished in the 1980s and 1990s, evidence of official action against political dissent resurfaced in the revelation that the police had surveilled and maintained secret dossiers on many Puerto Ricans, including political and civic leaders who were not separatists. Akin to President Richard Nixon's enemies lists of the 1970s, this residue of the more active COINTELPRO era underscored how pervasive state-sanctioned practices have been throughout Puerto Rico's history and how subtle the uses of ideological violence have been.

BIBLIOGRAPHY

Churchill, Ward, and Jim Vander Wall. *The COINTELPRO Papers: Documents from the FBI's Secret Wars Against Domestic Dissent.* Boston: South End Press, 1990.

Fernández, Ronald. *Los Macheteros: The Wells Fargo Robbery and the Violent Struggle for Puerto Rican Independence.* New York: Prentice Hall, 1987.

History Task Force (Centro de Estudios Puertorriqueños, Hunter College). *Labor Migration Under Capitalism: The Puerto Rican Experience.* New York: Monthly Review Press, 1979.

Torres, Andrés, and José E. Velázquez, eds. *The Puerto Rican Movement: Voices from the Diaspora.* Philadelphia: Temple University Press, 1998.

VILMA SANTIAGO-IRIZARRY

See also **Immigration; Race and Ethnicity; Spanish-American War.**

PULLMAN STRIKE

On 11 May 1894 workers at George Pullman's Illinois railway car factory declared a local strike that escalated, after the American Railway Union (ARU) voted its support on 21 June, into "a struggle between the greatest and the most powerful railroad labor organization and the entire railroad capital" (*New York Times*, 27 June 1894). The strike halted production in Pullman, Illinois, a model town south of Chicago owned and operated by the company. Popular magazines had praised the town since its founding in 1880 for establishing co-operative relations between labor and capital, yet critics argued that Pullman's "paternalist" idea of social unity contradicted such American values as individualism and self-determination. Dissatisfaction grew during the nationwide recession of 1893 when Pullman substantially cut wages and laid off workers (the number of employees fell from 4,500 in July to 1,100 in November) but refused to lower rents. On 10 May 1894 workers presented a list of grievances to Pullman's vice-president, Thomas Wickes, who promised them immunity from retaliation. The next day, the company triggered the strike when it summarily fired three of the petitioners.

After mediation attempts failed, the strikers asked the ARU for support. Although he informally supported the Pullman workers, the ARU's president, Eugene V. Debs, did not want to pit his fledgling union (founded in 1893) against the powerful General Managers' Association (GMA), an alliance of twenty-four railroad companies that shared 220,000 employees and a total capitalization of $2,108,552,617. Against Debs's advice, the ARU delegates voted for a boycott: on 26 June 1894 union members refused to operate all trains to which Pullman cars were attached.

The strike kindled a conflict over the future of organized labor in the United States as a whole. The GMA involved the federal government by claiming that the boycott violated the Sherman Anti-Trust Act of 1890, a law that prohibited the disruption of mail-service and interstate commerce. After President Grover Cleveland sent federal troops to Chicago on 3 July 1894, riots broke out, resulting in the destruction of railway property (seven hundred freight cars were burned in a Chicago stockyard on 6 July alone), over five hundred arrests, and the loss of twelve lives. Appalled at these unwanted outbreaks and pressured by waning funds, Debs offered to end the strike under the condition that the affected companies would rehire all workers. On 10 July, when he called for a general labor strike to support his demands, Debs was arrested and charged under the Sherman Anti-Trust Act with conspiracy to obstruct interstate commerce and mail service.

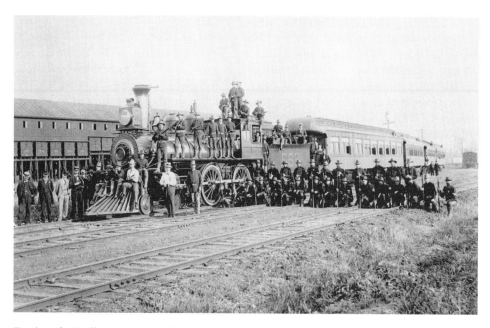

During the Pullman Strike of 1894, the 15th U.S. Infantry Company C poses beside a special Rock Island Railroad patrol train in Blue Island, Illinois. CORBIS/BETTMANN

Without gaining any concessions from Pullman or the GMA, the unions ended the strike on 25 July 1894. A governmental Strike Commission convened in August and heard 109 testimonies to assess the causes of a strike that cost both sides an estimated $7 million and that resulted in the wide-scale criminalization of labor, with hundreds arrested and indicted. Even more pervasive than this statutory criminalization was the practice of black-listing. Most workers resigned their union membership in hopes of being rehired. Unionism had suffered a sharp defeat and did not gain legal protection until the Clayton Anti-Trust Act was adopted in 1914 to exempt unions from indictment under the Sherman Anti-Trust Act.

BIBLIOGRAPHY

Lindsey, Almont. *The Pullman Strike: The Story of a Unique Experiment and of a Great Labor Upheaval.* Chicago: University of Chicago Press, 1942.

Report on the Chicago Strike of June-July 1894, by the United States Strike Commission. Washington, D.C.: Government Printing Office, 1895.

Smith, Carl. *Urban Disorder and the Shape of Belief: The Great Chicago Fire, the Haymarket Bomb, and the Model Town of Pullman.* Chicago and London: University of Chicago Press, 1995.

COLLEEN GLENNEY BOGGS

See also **Chicago; Labor and Unions; Strikes.**

PULP FICTION. *See* Literature: Pulp Fiction.

Q

QUAKERS

That members of the Religious Society of Friends, or Quakers, known for their powerful stance of nonviolence, have been the catalysts and recipients of so much violence in American history might appear incongruous. However, one could say that, in their powerful and relentless mission to "bear witness" on many controversial issues—the right to freedom of worship, the abolition of slavery, justice for Native Americans, equality for women, and birth control—many Quakers have been "pacifist aggressive" and have positioned themselves at the centers of social storms.

Indeed, the relationship between Quakers and American violence begins early, with what historians Hugh Barbour and J. William Frost (1988) term the "Quaker invasion of Puritan Boston" (p. 53). Because Puritan Boston was founded on an English tradition of hierarchy, which placed men in authority over women, the Quaker notion of equality of women, as manifested in Quaker acknowledgment of women ministers, constituted a challenge and a threat to both civil and religious authority. When Mary Fisher and Ann Austin arrived in Boston in 1656, preaching Quaker theology, their Quaker pamphlets were burned, and they were imprisoned and then run out of town. That some three dozen Quakers met with similar treatment over the next three years—including brandings, whippings, and ear-croppings—did not deter Marmaduke Stephenson, William Robinson, and Mary Dyer, who arrived in the late 1650s. After repeatedly being banished (with the threat of the gallows) and repeatedly returning to Boston—each time winning converts by their persistence—the three were finally hanged in Boston Common in 1660. Hence, though Quakers themselves eschewed violent means to their religious ends, their confrontational strategies—challenging authority in public—often provoked violence against them.

The hangings did not deter Quaker missionaries, indicating some measure of the internal logic of Quaker belief structures: persecution and martyrdom had come to be an important part of early Quakers' understanding of how one draws closer to a state of divinity. The renowned Quaker philosopher William Penn even titled one of his many treatises *No Cross, No Crown*, referring to the Quaker belief that suffering (that is, the crucifixion) was a necessary prerequisite for salvation (the crown). The American Revolution brought one of the most powerful tests of what Friends called their "testimony" of nonviolence. Often the refusal to bear arms was interpreted as sympathy with the enemy. As a result, many Quakers were ostracized, and in an egregious infringement of due process, a group of Philadelphians were interned in western Virginia for the duration of the war.

An important tenet of Quaker faith and practice is active service on behalf of society's disfranchised. Hence, when the eighteenth century brought increased tolerance for diversity of worship, Quakers turned their efforts to the controversial

Mary Dyer, a Quaker martyr, being led to execution in 1660.
CORBIS/BETTMANN

issues of the antebellum era: the abolition of slavery, justice for African Americans, women's rights, and the rights of Native Americans and prisoners. They again ran afoul of their neighbors who had conflicting ideas of social justice. African American Quaker Paul Cuffe's 1759 protest against taxation of freed blacks who did not have full citizen's rights brought out the wrath of his Massachusetts community. Benjamin Lundy (the editor of the first Quaker antislavery newspaper), the poet and essayist John Greenleaf Whittier (who organized and lectured on behalf of slaves), and Prudence Crandall (who opened a Connecticut school for young black women) all suffered personal threats and destruction of property as a result of their abolitionist activity. So, too, did Samuel Janney for his advocacy on behalf of both African Americans and Native Americans. This commitment to social justice was stereotyped in nineteenth-century American literature in the use of Quakers as paragons of virtue (e.g., Captains Bildad and Peleg in Herman Melville's 1851 novel, *Moby-Dick*; the kindly Halliday abolitionists in Harriet Beecher Stowe's 1852 novel, *Uncle Tom's Cabin*; and the Quaker "Gentle Boy" in Nathaniel Hawthorne's 1937 collection, *Twice-Told Tales*).

The dawn of the twentieth century brought American Friends a new set of challenges, as the United States became an international leader and American life became ever more complex. Added to their concerns about race relations and women's rights were concerns about rights of privacy and the right to take a social stand on religious beliefs. The work of Mary Calderone centered on privacy rights, in her advocacy for Planned Parenthood and for sex education and abortion rights; her founding in 1964 of the Sex Information and Education Council of the United States led to a barrage of hate mail and verbal attacks from conservative religious groups and local school boards.

Taking a social stand for religious belief is perhaps best exemplified by the Quakers' leadership in providing counseling for draft resisters, beginning with World War I and continuing through the Vietnam War. Draft counselors were labeled traitors and cowards, and some draft resisters chose to be imprisoned rather than compromise their nonviolent convictions. Given that Quakerism is a mystical religion that continues to encourage its community to listen to what Quaker founder George Fox called the "still, small Inward voice" of the divine and then to seek out opportunities to take principled stands that challenge social injustice, a continued tension between "pacifist" Friends and the larger American society may be inevitable.

BIBLIOGRAPHY

Barbour, Hugh, and J. William Frost. *The Quakers.* New York: Greenwood, 1988.

Kenworthy, Leonard, ed. *Living in the Light: Some Quaker Pioneers of the Twentieth Century.* Kennett Square, Penn.: Friends General Conference and Quaker Publications, 1984.

Kraditor, Aileen S. *Means and Ends in American Abolitionism: Garrison and His Critics on Strategy and Tactics, 1834–1850.* New York: Pantheon, 1969.

EMMA J. LAPSANSKY

See also **Nonviolence; Religion.**

QUANTRILL'S RAID

On 21 August 1863, in one of his bloodiest battles during the Civil War, Confederate guerrilla William Clarke Quantrill and his raiders sacked Lawrence, Kansas, a prosperous town with three thousand inhabitants that was considered the seat of abolitionism.

Quantrill (1837–1865), who had lived in Lawrence under the name of Charley Hart, had been driven out as an undesirable. He became a career criminal and used his Civil War commission as a captain (1862) as an opportunity for theft, destruction, and murder. Quantrill rampaged freely as a Confederate military hero, although he probably had no personal conviction in the cause of the Confederacy. His guerrilla raids on towns sympathetic with the Union were led on horseback, his reins in his teeth, a Colt revolver in each hand. He was an excellent horseman and crack shot. His band grew to several hundred men and included at times Frank and Jesse James and Cole and Jim Younger. (Only Frank James and Cole Younger took part in the Lawrence raid.) Soon after the Civil War, the James and Younger brothers founded their own famous outlaw gangs that applied guerrilla tactics to the art of civilian bank and train robbery.

On the morning of 18 August 1863 Quantrill and about three hundred guerrillas set out from their Blue Springs, Missouri, camp. On their way to Lawrence, they picked up another 150 men and eluded Union patrols by camping during the day and riding at night. They crossed into Kansas around 6 P.M. on 20 August. Although a federal scout spotted the raiders, only the border posts were warned, and the towns were not alerted. The raiders entered Lawrence around dawn on 21 Au-

---

Reprisal: General Order No. 11

In an attempt to eliminate the support given to Quantrill and his raiders by family and friends in the Missouri counties bordering Kansas, three days before Quantrill's raid on Lawrence, Brigadier General Thomas Ewing, commander of the District of the Border in Kansas, issued General Order No. 10 on 18 August 1863, ordering all men and women who were determined to be aiding and abetting the bushwackers to leave Missouri. Following Quantrill's raid, however, Senator Jim Lane, furious about the murder of the town's men and the property damage, including the burning of his own house, pressed Ewing for a harsher measure. Ewing thus issued General Order No. 11 on 25 August, which ordered that by 9 September all persons in the Missouri counties of Jackson, Cass, and Bates were to remove themselves to the nearest military post to establish their loyalty to the Union. Thousands of Missourians, primarily women and children and the elderly (able-bodied men were off fighting the war), began moving, carrying only clothing and some household goods and abandoning their homes and much of their livestock. As the refugees moved north and south in Missouri, they suffered from the cold and deprivation, most walking on foot and many without shoes. Their abandoned homes were looted and burned by marauding Union troops. More than two-thirds of the population of the Missouri counties made the 9 September deadline, which left vast stretches of Missouri uninhabited. In the spring of 1864, the order was relaxed and many refugees were allowed to return home. The historian Albert Castel called General Order No. 11 "the harshest military measure directed against civilians during the Civil War."

---

gust, first trampling the tents of recruits of the Fourteenth Kansas Regiment, killing seventeen. The first civilian killed was Reverend S. S. Snyder, who was shot as he sat on a stool milking his cow. Quantrill's screaming horde charged up Massachusetts Street, taking the town by surprise. Mayor George Collamore had been warned earlier of a possible raid by Quantrill, but the town's citizens scoffed at the possibility. Quantrill led the way to the Eldridge House hotel, dispatching patrols to side streets. The raiders agreed to spare the hotel's guests if they dressed quickly and came out. The guests were searched, robbed of money and valuables, and sent to the Whitney House Hotel, where Quantrill set up his headquarters and demanded breakfast. The raiders then burned the Eldridge and proceeded to kill, burn, and plunder indiscriminately. Quantrill had issued an order to kill every man and burn every building in Lawrence.

Patrols robbed every house, first knocking on a door, then shooting any man who answered or ordering women to bring out all money and jewelry. Each house was then burned, and any men seen fleeing from the smoke and flames were shot. No women were killed during the raid. All the stores and banks were looted and burned. Store owners were first roused from their homes to open their safes and then were shot. After his shop had been looted and set on fire, D. W. Palmer and another man, whose hands had been tied, were thrown bodily into the burning building. Men survived by hiding in cellars, attics, and cornfields and under sidewalks, and sometimes under their wives' petticoats or within carpets and draperies the women were allowed to salvage from the burning homes. Mayor Collamore was found dead in his well, where he smothered while hiding from the raiders.

After four hours, when a lookout spotted the dust of a patrol of approaching federal troops, Quantrill decided to leave. He selected one prisoner being held at the livery stable to drive two of his wounded men, then ordered the rest of the prisoners shot. Most of his men had acquired fresh horses. All of the nearly two hundred business buildings were burned, and half the town's dwellings were totally or partially destroyed. The raiders left behind more than $1 million in property damage and 183 dead men and boys. One drunken straggler, Larkin Skaggs, continued to shoot people, but after he realized the other raiders had left, he tried to flee; a mob pursued him, cornering and killing him. He was the only raider killed in Lawrence.

Although old bitterness remained between proslavery and abolitionist forces because of the sectional disputes from 1854 to 1861 and Quantrill was angry about his earlier treatment by residents of Lawrence, the primary reason for the massacre was reprisal for a raid on Osceola, Missouri, by Senator James Henry Lane, Quantrill's Union counterpart, earlier in the year. Lane lost his Lawrence home in the raid but escaped capture and death. Quantrill, eventually dubbed the "bloodiest man in American history," was fatally wounded during a raid into Kentucky in May 1865.

BIBLIOGRAPHY

Castel, Albert E. *William Clarke Quantrill: His Life and Times.* New York: Frederick Fell, 1962.
Fellman, Michael. *Inside War: The Guerrilla Conflict in Missouri During the American Civil War.* New York: Oxford University Press, 1989.
Goodrich, Thomas. *Bloody Dawn: The Story of the Lawrence Massacre.* Kent, Ohio: Kent State University Press, 1991.
Leslie, Edward E. *The Devil Knows How to Ride: The True Story of William Clarke Quantrill and His Confederate Raiders.* New York: Random House, 1996.
Schultz, Duane. *Quantrill's War: The Life and Times of William Clarke Quantrill, 1837–1865.* New York: St. Martin's Press, 1997.

LOUISE B. KETZ

See also **Civil War; Guerrilla Warfare; James, Jesse.**